Blood and Ruins

RICHARD OVERY

Blood and Ruins

The Great Imperial War, 1931–1945

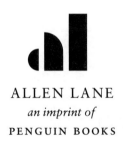

ALLEN LANE
an imprint of
PENGUIN BOOKS

ALLEN LANE

UK | USA | Canada | Ireland | Australia
India | New Zealand | South Africa

Allen Lane is part of the Penguin Random House group of companies
whose addresses can be found at global.penguinrandomhouse.com

First published 2021

002

Copyright © Richard Overy, 2021

Set in 10.2/13.5 pt Sabon LT Std
Typeset by Jouve (UK), Milton Keynes
Printed and bound in Great Britain by Clays Ltd, Elcograf S.p.A.

The authorized representative in the EEA is Penguin Random House Ireland,
Morrison Chambers, 32 Nassau Street, Dublin D02 YH68

A CIP catalogue record for this book is available from the British Library

ISBN: 978-0-713-99562-6

We have entered the classical age of war on the largest scale, the age of scientific war with popular support – there will be wars such as have never yet been on Earth.

Friedrich Nietzsche, 1881

Contents

Preface

In December 1945 the former American secretary of state, Cordell Hull, was awarded the Nobel Prize for peace. Too ill to attend, he wrote a short message endorsing the search for peace after 'the staggering ordeal of the most widespread and cruel war of all the ages'.[1] Hull was well known for his overblown rhetoric, but on this occasion the note he struck seems as pertinent today as it did seventy-five years ago. The era that Hull experienced saw global war on a hitherto unimaginable scale; the many conflicts that are now subsumed under the umbrella title of 'world war' generated suffering, deprivation and death of almost limitless dimensions. There has been no war like it either before or since, not even the Great War. There may be more world wars in the future, capable, as Hull pointed out in 1945, of 'wiping out our civilization', but they have not happened yet.

A war so widespread and cruel challenges the historian in many ways. With the passage of time since the 1940s it has become progressively more difficult to imagine a world in which more than 100 million men (and a much smaller number of women) donned uniform and went off to fight using weapons whose destructive capability had been honed in the First World War and developed dramatically in the years that followed. It is just as difficult to imagine major states being able to persuade their populations to accept that up to two-thirds of the national product should be devoted to the purposes of war, that hundreds of millions should accept war-induced poverty and hunger, or that peacetime wealth and savings should be taken over and blown away by the insatiable demands of conflict. How hard it is, too, to comprehend the massive scale of deprivation, dispossession and loss suffered through bombing, deportation, requisitioning and theft. Above all, the war challenges our modern sensibilities in trying to grasp how widespread acts of atrocity, terrorism and crime could be committed by hundreds of thousands of people who were in most cases what the historian Christopher Browning has memorably described as 'ordinary men', neither sadists nor psychopaths.[2] Common though acts of atrocity are every day in the civil wars and insurgencies of the present, the era of the Second World War witnessed a tidal wave of violent coercion, imprisonment, torture, deportation and mass, genocidal killing, carried out by uniformed servicemen, or security and police forces, or partisans and civilian irregulars, both men and women.

Once it was enough to explain the war as a military reaction by peace-loving nations to the imperial ambitions of Hitler and Mussolini in Europe and the Japanese military in East Asia. The standard Western accounts, together with the Soviet official histories of the war, have focused on the narrative of the military conflict between the Allied and Axis states. The history of the military conflict is now thoroughly understood and documented in many excellent accounts and for that reason will not be repeated here in full.[3] The focus on the military outcome, important though it is, begs too many questions about the broader crisis that brought about war, about the differing nature of the many wartime conflicts, about the political, economic, social and cultural context of war, and finally about the unstable violence that continued long after the formal end to hostilities in 1945. Above all, the conventional view of the war understands Hitler, Mussolini and the Japanese military as causes of crisis rather than its effects, which is what they were. Proper sense cannot be made of the origins of the war and its course and consequences without understanding the broader historical forces that generated years of social, political and international instability worldwide from the opening decades of the twentieth century, and which eventually prompted the Axis states to undertake reactionary programmes of imperial territorial conquest. The defeat of these ambitions in turn slowly paved the way to a relative global stabilization and the final crisis years of territorial empire.

This new history of the Second World War is based on four main assumptions. First, that the conventional chronology of the war is no longer useful. Fighting began in the early 1930s in China and ended in China, South East Asia, Eastern Europe and the Middle East only in the decade after 1945. The warfare between 1939 and 1945 may provide the heart of the narrative, but the history of the conflict goes back at least to the Japanese occupation of Manchuria in 1931 and forward to the final insurgencies and civil wars prompted by the war, but unresolved in 1945. Moreover, the First World War, and the violence that preceded and followed it, profoundly influenced the world of the 1920s and 1930s, supporting the contention that little is to be gained by separating the two giant conflicts. Both can be seen as stages of a second Thirty Years War about the reordering of the world system in a final stage of imperial crisis. The structure of the book reflects these less-conventional temporal perspectives. There is much on the 1920s and 1930s, without which the nature of the global war and the way it was fought and understood at the time cannot be properly explained.

Secondly, that the war should be understood as a global event, rather than one confined to the defeat of the European Axis states with the Pacific War as an appendix. The unstable regional zones in Central Europe, the

Mediterranean and Middle East, and in East Asia, all fed into the wider crisis of global stability and explain why warfare reached not just the major states but areas as remote as the Aleutian Islands in the northern Pacific, Madagascar in the southern Indian Ocean, or the island bases of the Caribbean. The Asian war and its consequences were as important to the creation of the post-war world as the defeat of Germany in Europe, arguably more so. Here the creation of modern China and the unravelling of the colonial empires went hand-in-hand across the era of world wars.

Thirdly, that the conflict needs to be redefined as a number of different kinds of war. The principal form is the familiar war between states, either wars of aggression or wars of defence, because only states could mobilize sufficient resources and sustain armed conflict on a large scale. But there were also civil wars fought alongside the major military conflict – in China, in Ukraine, in Italy, in Greece – and 'civilian wars', fought either as wars of liberation against an occupying power (including the Allies) or as wars of civilian self-defence, principally to cope with the impact of bombing. Sometimes these different forms overlapped or converged with the war waged between states – partisans in Russia or Resistance fighters in France – but the partisan wars, civil wars and insurgencies constitute small parallel wars, fought in the main by civilians, intent on securing their protection or liberation. Civilian mobilization helped to give the Second World War its 'total' character and it plays an important part in what follows.

Finally, that all three of these factors – chronology, area and definition – derive from the argument presented here: that the long Second World War was the last imperial war. Most general histories of the war focus on 'great power' conflict and the role of ideology but miss out or gloss over the significance of territorial empire in defining the nature of the long period of war from 1931 to the messy aftermath of 1945. This is not to see the war through a narrow Leninist lens, but simply to acknowledge that what links all the differing areas and forms of conflict together is the existence of a global imperial order, dominated principally by the British and French, which shaped and stimulated the fantastic ambitions in Japan, Italy and Germany, the so-called 'have not' nations, to secure their national survival and express their national identity by conquering additional imperial zones of their own. Only recently have historians come to argue that the Axis empires created their own global 'nexus' to imitate the older empires they wanted to supplant.[4] Imperial designs and imperial crises from the Great War onwards, or even earlier, frame the origins and course of the second conflict, just as the eventual outcome of the war brought to an end half a millennium of colonialism and supported the consolidation of the nation state.[5] The centuries of remorseless European expansion gave way to the contraction of Europe. What was left of traditional colonial rule collapsed rapidly in the decades after 1945 as the two superpowers, the United States and the Soviet Union, dominated the creation of a new global order.

The content of what follows is dictated by these four avenues of approach. There are five broadly narrative chapters (Prologue, 1–3 and 11) and seven thematic chapters (4–10). The first chapters explore the long-term factors that shaped the crisis of the 1930s and the coming of war, rooted in the imperial and national competition of the late nineteenth century and the period of the First World War. A second war was not inevitable, but the fracturing of the global system of trade and finance in the 1920s, coinciding with the growing insecurity of the global imperial systems and the rise of popular nationalism, created tensions and generated ambitions difficult to resolve through co-operation. A mix of ultra-nationalist ideology, economic crisis and sudden opportunity encouraged Japan, Italy and Germany to pursue 'New Order' imperialism and provoked a major disaster for the established empires – British, French, Dutch, even Belgian – in the wake of an unexpected series of defeats between 1940 and 1942. Although the 'New Order' states would have preferred to construct their regional empires without confronting the Soviet Union and the United States immediately, they found that their ambitions could not be secured in the end without defeating or neutralizing those powers: hence the 'Barbarossa' campaign and the Pacific War; hence, too, the special case of the genocidal war against the Jews, who were blamed by the Hitler regime for orchestrating global conflict and frustrating German national self-assertion. This section describes a world of international and political uncertainty, in which the new empires seemed poised for possible triumph before the potential strength of the United States and the Soviet Union could be mobilized.

The next chapters describe a worldwide war in which the territorial ambitions of the new empires were overturned and the conditions created for a different and more stable world order, based on the principle of nationality at the expense of empire and on the restoration of a global system of trade and finance that had collapsed in the 1930s. Soviet and American economic and military power explain this transition. Significantly, both were hostile on grounds of ideology, communist or liberal, to the survival of traditional colonial empires – as indeed was China, the other major ally – and they helped to shape in the later 1940s and 1950s a world of national states, in many cases dominated by the Cold War superpowers but not ruled as territorial empires. Germany and Japan fought to the bitter end from fear of national extinction, but they too were allowed a renewed national existence once the domestic forces pursuing empire were defeated. In this section the defeat of the New Order states was explicit, though not entirely pre-ordained. The greatest sacrifices of personnel and resources for all sides were made in the last two years of war, before either victory or defeat seemed inevitable. And violence, though on a greatly reduced scale, persisted in the years after 1945 as the residual political and ideological conflicts of the wartime years were resolved, though not in all cases, under the fading star of empire and superpower ambition. This forms the subject matter of the final chapter, when traditional empires were finally unravelled to create today's world of nation states.

The outline of the last imperial war provides the framework for the thematic chapters in which key questions are explored about the wider experience of conflict, both for the millions of servicemen engaged in fighting and for the civilian societies that sustained the commitment to total war.[6] How did states mobilize the colossal manpower and material resources they needed, and with what results? How did the armed forces involved organize and use these resources, and with what effect? How did states, parties or individuals justify the wars they were fighting and sustain popular engagement in costly, often barbarous campaigns, even in the face of defeat? Why did parallel civil or civilian wars develop, and with what social or political consequences? Finally, there are chapters on the damage that the war did to all the populations that experienced it. What is called here the 'emotional geography of war' is an attempt at mapping what the war did emotionally and psychologically to all those sucked into its orbit, and in particular to the more than 100 million men and women mobilized to fight it. Behaviour and expectations were changed by war, driven by a wide range of human feelings: on the one hand fear, hatred, resentment or anger, and on the other courage, self-sacrifice, anxiety and compassion. This is an element of wartime experience difficult to describe historically and yet central to any explanation of what the war did to individuals who found themselves under the constant pressure of exceptional wartime circumstances, both on and off the battlefield. The final theme explores the excessive violence and criminality provoked by the war which resulted in widespread atrocities and tens of millions of deaths, the larger part civilians. It asks two central questions: why was the death toll so high among both servicemen and civilians – around five times the level of deaths in the First World War – and why were perpetrators willing and able to indulge in cruel levels of violence of all kinds across all theatres of war? These two questions are clearly related but are not the same; death came in many guises and for many reasons, a remorseless companion of the conflict.

The sources for any new history of the Second World War are now too plentiful to do justice to them all. Forty years ago, when I first started writing on the war, it was possible to read most of what had been written about the conflict that had something useful to say. The last four decades have witnessed a worldwide explosion of historical writing on all aspects of the Second World War and the years that surround it. This has made it impossible to embrace more than a fraction of the existing literature, and I have focused here on the historical material that supports the central arguments of the book rather than pretend an encyclopaedic comprehensiveness. There can no longer be a definitive history of the war in one volume, or indeed in many. The recent publication of the *Cambridge History of the Second World War* needed three large volumes, yet even then could not include everything. I have followed the rough rule of using material published in the past few years, since this in many cases incorporates the body of knowledge already available in particular fields, though there are many essential studies that go back a long time and I have tried not to neglect them. I have been fortunate in particular to benefit from a wealth of new studies on issues of empire and on the wartime history of Asia, both long-neglected aspects of the historiography. Where I have supporting archives in areas I have researched closely, I have used them. Historians now enjoy a rich feast of personal recollections available in book form or oral archives to illuminate, or occasionally to contradict, what historians have had to say about wartime experience, and I have also drawn from this menu, though more sparingly than many of the recent narrative histories of the conflict. There is inevitably a good deal left out or treated too summarily, as readers will discover; they will also find that some familiar topics are broken down to fit the differing perspectives in the thematic chapters – bombing, the Holocaust, fighting power are obvious examples – but I hope that the core of what the war means historically is clear enough. This is intended as a history that asks large questions about the war years in the hope that individual experiences will make greater sense once the framework in which people were compelled to operate is better understood. It is also a history of death, terror, destruction and impoverishment, of Cordell Hull's 'staggering ordeal'. Blood and ruins were its bitter cost.

Richard Overy
November 2020

Acknowledgements

A great many colleagues, fellow scholars and students have in one way or another contributed to the outcome of this book over years of discussion and advice. I would like to thank individually a fraction of them, but to the rest I give a grateful acknowledgement for engaging with the work I have done on the war in useful, critical ways. Thanks are due in particular to my colleague at Exeter Martin Thomas, who has encouraged me more than anyone to persevere with the imperial approach to the history of the war. The department at Exeter has been a fortunate home for anyone hoping to link the history of the war and its excessive violence with the history of imperialism.

I am grateful to the following for assistance, advice and conversation during the writing of this book: Evan Mawdsley, Matthew Heaslip, Laura Rowe, Richard Toye, Roy Irons, Richard Hammond, Olivier Wieviorka, the late Sir Michael Howard, Hans van de Ven, Rana Mitter, Paul Clemence, Lucy Noakes, Zoe Waxman, Andrew Buchanan, Stephen Lee, Joe Maiolo, Klaus Schmider, Sönke Neitzel and Robert Gerwarth. To all those authors whose invaluable work has contributed to what I write, I should like to give generous thanks. I have tried to ensure throughout that their contribution is recognized in the footnotes. I owe a very considerable debt as ever to my wonderful editor at Penguin, Simon Winder, who has patiently waited for this book longer than any publisher ought to have, and read with critical engagement everything I have written. I am very grateful to my agents Gill Coleridge, and now Cara Jones, for their unstinting support throughout this history's lengthy gestation. And a final thanks to the team who worked on producing the book: Richard Duguid, Eva Hodgkin, Charlotte Ridings, Jeff Edwards, Sandra Fuller and Matthew Hutchinson.

A Note on Usage in the Text

Throughout the text I have used the terms 'Allies' and 'Axis' because they are in such common usage that it is difficult to avoid them without complication. Nevertheless, it is worth pointing out that the three main Allies were not allied in any formal sense, except for an alliance signed between Britain and the Soviet Union in 1942. Nor were the Axis states actually a coherent alliance. The term was originally applied to German–Italian relations and was coined by Mussolini. Japan became allied to both in the Three Power Pact of September 1940, as did a number of other European states who joined the war against the Soviet Union, except for Finland, which was a co-belligerent. But until September 1940 Japan was not in any formal sense linked to the European Axis. After that date, world opinion almost unanimously talked about the 'Axis states', including Japan, and the name has stuck in almost all modern history writing and I have used it here as contemporaries used it, while conscious of its faults.

It is also important to highlight problems with the great many statistics and numbers that appear in the book. The inexact nature in many major and minor battles of the number of participants and their supporting weapons is notorious; so, too, the problem of calculating casualties to manpower and machines, which can depend on how the length or area of a battle is defined in different national narratives. I have tried to use what seem the most up-to-date and reliable statistics, but I am conscious that there are in many cases estimates that diverge from these figures. With other measurements, I have been less precise. When using the term 'ton' as it applies to statistics of shipping, or bombs dropped, or resources produced I have not differentiated between a British ton, a metric tonne and an American ton. They are all different weights, but it is tiresome to have to explain that each time, and the difference is not so large as to render the use of 'ton' unacceptable. The American short ton is equal to 2,000 pounds, the British long ton to 2,240 pounds and the metric ton (1,000 kilos) is equivalent to 2,204 pounds. I have generally used kilometres rather than miles as they are used worldwide. One mile equals 1.6 kilometres.

On the question of transliteration of Chinese, Arabic and Indian personal and place names, I have generally tried to use the current practice, except in cases where the name is still commonly understood in its traditional form (e.g. Calcutta not Kolkata or Chiang Kai-shek rather than Jiang Jieshi). Chinese place names are particularly difficult where current transliteration bears little resemblance to popular Western usage (Guangzhou for Canton, for example), and I have tried to put in parenthesis the original name when first used, though in the case of Beijing I have avoided either Peking or Beiping, the names used at the time. Names transcribed from Arabic can take a number of forms, and again I have chosen what now seems to be accepted academic usage.

List of Illustrations

Front endpaper: A drawing of the Italian army arriving at the port of Benghazi in the Ottoman Empire's province of Cyrenaica during the Italian–Turkish war of 1911. The war ended with Italy in control of the provinces of Cyrenaica and Tripolitania, renamed Libya by the Italian conquerors. Italy was one of eleven European empires. *D and S Photography Archives/Alamy*

Back endpaper: The United Nations General Assembly in New York in 1971, where delegates representing 132 states stand for a minute's prayer to mark the opening of the assembly session on 21 September. *Granger Historical Picture Archive/Alamy*

Frontispiece: German foreign minister Joachim von Ribbentrop reads out his statement at the signing of the Three Power Pact between Germany, Italy and Japan in the Reich Chancellery on 27 September 1940. The Pact confirmed the imperial ambitions of the three states in Europe, Africa and Asia, where they intended to found a new geopolitical order. *INTERFOTO/Alamy*

Prologue: French artillery firing during the Rif War against the Berber insurgency in Morocco, 1925. In one of the major colonial wars of the twentieth century, the tribesmen fought against Spanish and French forces from 1921 to 1927 to retain their independence. *Photo 12 Collection/Alamy*

Chapter 1: Japanese soldiers shelter behind sandbags in the battle for Shanghai beneath publicity for Coca-Cola. The city was the most cosmopolitan of China's leading ports and a major target for the Japanese invaders. It was captured after heavy fighting against Chinese Nationalist troops in November 1937. *CPA Media Pte Ltd/Alamy*

Chapter 2: A troop of tired German soldiers rest on the wayside somewhere in Soviet Ukraine following the opening of Operation 'Barbarossa' on 22 June 1941. Most German soldiers went on foot or bicycle across the Soviet countryside. *World of Triss/Alamy*

Chapter 3: The Allied supreme commander in the West, General Dwight D. Eisenhower, walks past an overturned German Panzer VI 'Tiger' tank after the battle at Mortain during the advance across France, August 1944. *Pictorial Press Ltd/Alamy*

List of Tables

Abbreviations

AI	Air interception radar
AM	Amplitude Modulation
ASV	Air-to-surface-vessel radar
AWPD	Air War Plans Division
BBC	British Broadcasting Corporation
BEF	British Expeditionary Force
BIA	Burma Independence Army
BMW	Bayerische Motoren Werke
CLN	Comitato della Liberazione Nazionale/Committee of National Liberation
CLNAI	Comitato della Liberazione Nazionale Alta Italia/Committee of National Liberation of Upper Italy
DCR	Division Cuirassée de Réserve/Reserve Armoured Division (France)
DKG	Deutsche Kolonialgesellschaft/German Colonial Society
DLM	Division légère mécanique/Light mechanized division (France)
DP	Displaced Person
ELAS	Greek National Liberation Army
FFI	Forces françaises de l'intérieur/French forces of the interior
FLN	Front de Liberation Nationale (Algeria)
FM	Frequency Modulation
FUSAG	First United States Army Group
GCCS	Government Code and Cipher School (UK)
GKO	State Defence Committee (USSR)
HF/DF	High Frequency/Direction Finding
HMS	His Majesty's Ship
IFF	Identification, Friend or Foe
IMT	International Military Tribunal
INA	Indian National Army
JSC	Joint Security Control
LCVP	Landing Craft, Vehicle, Personnel
LMF	Lack of Moral Fibre
LST	Landing Ship, Tank
LVT	Landing Vehicle, Tracked

MIT	Massachusetts Institute of Technology
MPVO	Main Directorate of Local Air Defence (USSR)
NAACP	National Association for the Advancement of Colored People
NCO	Non-commissioned officer
NKVD	People's Commissariat of Internal Affairs (USSR)
NSDAP	National-sozialistische Deutsche Arbeiterpartei/National Socialist German Workers' Party
OKW	Oberkommando der Wehrmacht/Supreme Command of the Armed Forces
OSS	Office of Strategic Services (USA)
OUN	Organization of Ukrainian Nationalists
PKW	Panzerkraftwagen/armoured fighting vehicle
POW	Prisoner of war
PPU	Peace Pledge Union
PWE	Political Warfare Executive
RAF	Royal Air Force
RKFDV	Reichskommissar für die Festigung deutschen Volkstums/Reich Commissar for the Strengthening of Germandom
RSHA	Reichssicherheitshauptamt/Reich Security Main Office
RuSHA	Rasse- und Siedlungshauptamt/Race and Resettlement Main Office
SA	Sturmabteilung/Storm Detachment
SCR	Signal Corps Radio
SD	Sicherheitsdienst/Security Service
SHAEF	Supreme Headquarters, Allied Expeditionary Force
SIGINT	Signals Intelligence
SO	Special Operations (USA)
SOE	Special Operations Executive (UK)
SS	Schutzstaffel (originally protection squad, under Himmler elite NSDAP security)
Stavka	Soviet Supreme Command of the Armed Forces
UN	United Nations
UNRRA	United Nations Relief and Rehabilitation Administration
USMC	United States Marine Corps
USS	United States Ship
USSR	Union of Soviet Socialist Republics
VHF	Very High Frequency
V-Weapons	Vergeltungswaffen/Vengeance weapons
Waffen-SS	Military units of the SS
WASP	Women Airforce Service Pilots (USA)
WAVES	Women Accepted for Volunteer Emergency Service (USA)

WVHA	Wirtschafts- und Verwaltungshauptamt/Economic and Administrative Main Office
ZOB	Jewish Fighting Organization (Poland)
Z-Plan	Ziel-Plan/Target Plan (Germany navy)
ZZW	Jewish Military Union (Poland)

Maps

(pp. xxvi–xxxix)

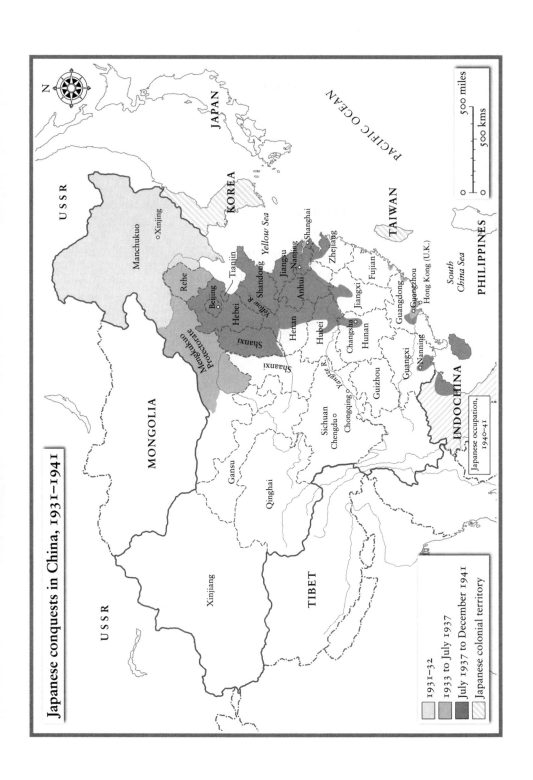

Japanese conquests in China, 1931–1941

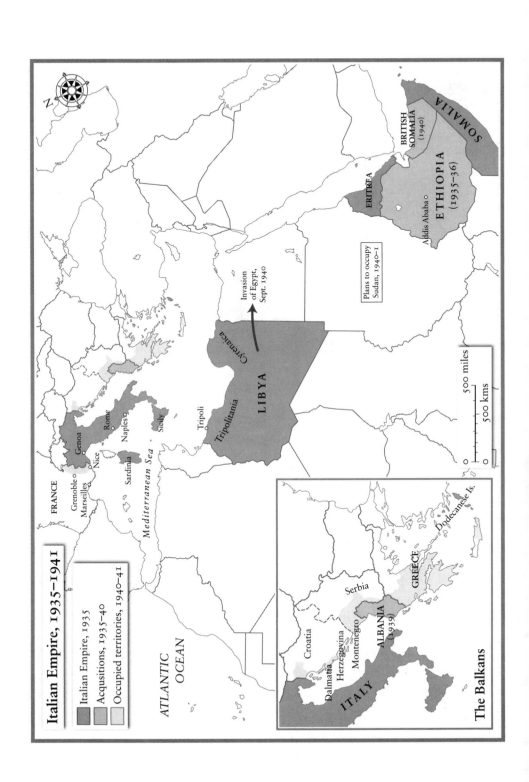

Italian Empire, 1935–1941

- Italian Empire, 1935
- Acquisitions, 1935–40
- Occupied territories, 1940–41

FRANCE

Grenoble
Marseilles
Nice
Genoa
Rome
Sardinia
Naples
Sicily

Mediterranean Sea

ATLANTIC OCEAN

Tripoli
Tripolitania
LIBYA
Cyrenaica

Invasion of Egypt, Sept. 1940

Plans to occupy Sudan, 1940–1

ERITREA
Addis Ababa
ETHIOPIA (1935–36)
BRITISH SOMALIA (1940)
SOMALIA

500 miles
500 kms

The Balkans

ITALY
Croatia
Dalmatia
Herzegovina
Montenegro
ALBANIA (1939)
Serbia
GREECE
Dodecanese Is.

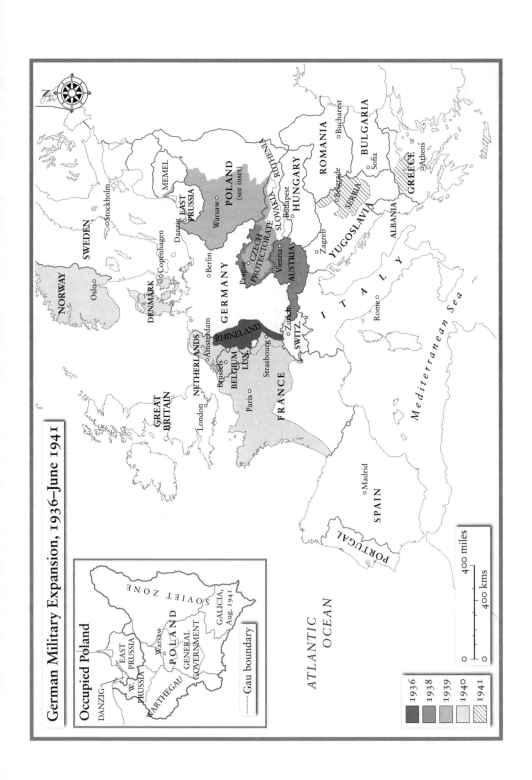

German Military Expansion, 1936–June 1941

Occupied Poland

--- Gau boundary

400 miles
400 kms

1936
1938
1939
1940
1941

NORWAY
Oslo

SWEDEN
Stockholm

DENMARK
Copenhagen

GREAT BRITAIN
London

NETHERLANDS
Amsterdam

BELGIUM
Brussels

LUX.

FRANCE
Paris

RHINELAND
Strasbourg

GERMANY
Berlin

MEMEL

EAST PRUSSIA
Danzig

POLAND
(see inset)
Warsaw

CZECH PROTECTORATE
Prague

AUSTRIA
Vienna

SWITZ.
Zurich

RUTHENIA

SLOVAKIA

HUNGARY
Budapest

ITALY
Rome

ROMANIA
Bucharest

BULGARIA
Sofia

YUGOSLAVIA
Zagreb
Belgrade

SERBIA

ALBANIA

GREECE
Athens

SPAIN
Madrid

PORTUGAL

ATLANTIC OCEAN

Mediterranean Sea

Occupied Poland

DANZIG

EAST PRUSSIA

W. PRUSSIA

WARTHEGAU

POLAND
Warsaw

GENERAL GOVERNMENT

GALICIA, Aug. 1941

SOVIET ZONE

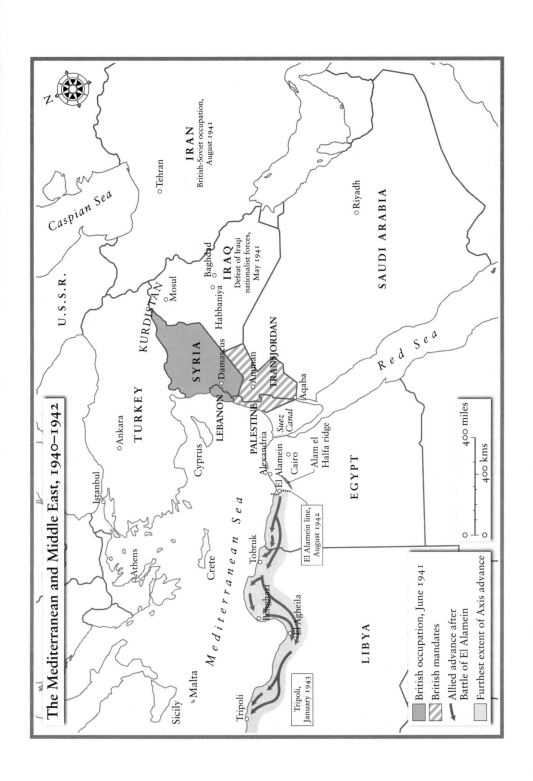

The Mediterranean and Middle East, 1940–1942

U.S.S.R.

Caspian Sea

IRAN
British-Soviet occupation, August 1941

Tehran

Ankara

TURKEY

Riyadh

SAUDI ARABIA

KURDISTAN

Mosul

Baghdad

IRAQ
Defeat of Iraqi nationalist forces, May 1941

Habbaniya

SYRIA

Damascus

Amman

TRANJORDAN

Aqaba

LEBANON

PALESTINE

Suez Canal

Alexandria

El Alamein

Cairo

Alam el Halfa ridge

El Alamein line, August 1942

Istanbul

Athens

Cyprus

Crete

Malta

Sicily

Mediterranean Sea

Tobruk

Benghazi

El Agheila

Tripoli

Tripoli, January 1943

LIBYA

EGYPT

Red Sea

400 miles

400 kms

British occupation, June 1941

British mandates

Allied advance after Battle of El Alamein

Furthest extent of Axis advance

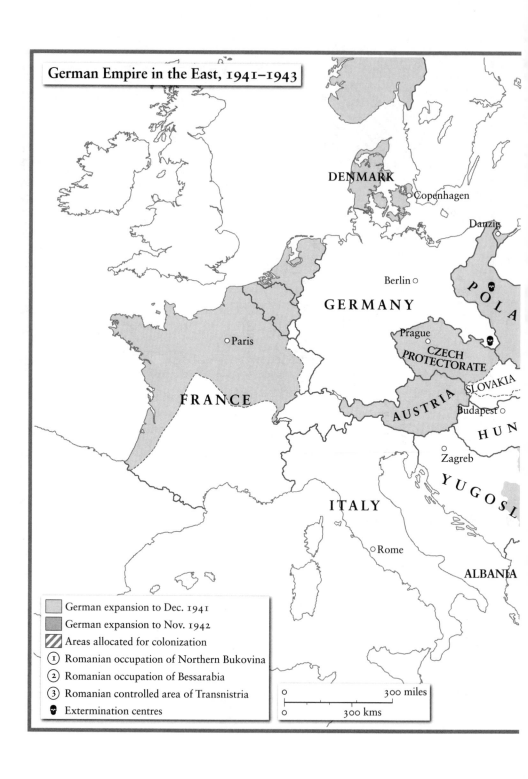

German Empire in the East, 1941–1943

DENMARK
○ Copenhagen
Danzig ○
Berlin ○
P O L A
GERMANY
Prague ○
○ Paris
CZECH
PROTECTORATE
SLOVAKIA
FRANCE
AUSTRIA
Budapest ○
H U N
○ Zagreb
Y U G O S L
ITALY
○ Rome
ALBANIA

German expansion to Dec. 1941
German expansion to Nov. 1942
Areas allocated for colonization
① Romanian occupation of Northern Bukovina
② Romanian occupation of Bessarabia
③ Romanian controlled area of Transnistria
☠ Extermination centres

300 miles
300 kms

Siege of Leningrad,
Dec. 1941–43

Battle of Moscow,
Dec. 1941

✕ ○ Moscow

U S S R

Tallin

ESTONIA

Riga ○ LATVIA

LITHUANIA

REICH
COMMISSARIAT
OSTLAND ○ ○
Minsk

EAST
PRUSSIA

BELORUSSIA

○ Warsaw

N D

GENERAL
GOVERNMENT

REICH
COMMISSARIAT
UKRAINE

○ Kiev ✕

Battle of Kiev,
Sept. 1941

UNDER
MILITARY
ADMINISTRATION

Khar'kov ✕ ○

Battle of Khar'kov,
March 1942

✕ ○ Stalingrad

Battle of Stalingrad,
Aug. 1942–Feb. 1943

RUTHENIA

GARY

① ② ③

Donets
Basin

UKRAINE

○ Rostov

CRIMEA

○ Maikop

ROMANIA

Belgrade ○

Bucharest ○

SERBIA

AVIA

Black Sea

BULGARIA

○ Sofia

○ Istanbul

TURKEY

○ Athens

GREECE

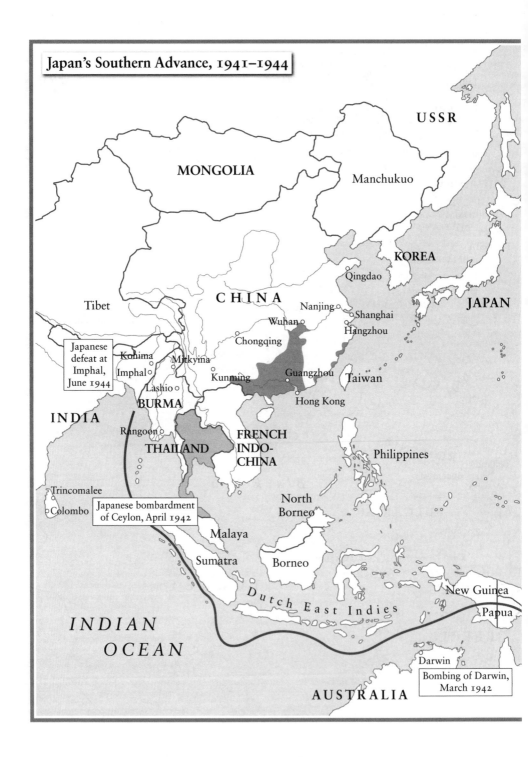

Japan's Southern Advance, 1941–1944

USSR

MONGOLIA

Manchukuo

KOREA

Qingdao

JAPAN

CHINA

Nanjing

Shanghai

Tibet

Wuhan

Hangzhou

Chongqing

Japanese
defeat at
Imphal,
June 1944

Kohima

Mitkyina

Imphal

Kunming

Guangzhou

Taiwan

Lashio

BURMA

Hong Kong

INDIA

Rangoon

THAILAND

FRENCH
INDO-
CHINA

Philippines

Trincomalee

Colombo

Japanese bombardment
of Ceylon, April 1942

North
Borneo

Malaya

Sumatra

Borneo

New Guinea

INDIAN
OCEAN

Dutch East Indies

Papua

Darwin

Bombing of Darwin,
March 1942

AUSTRALIA

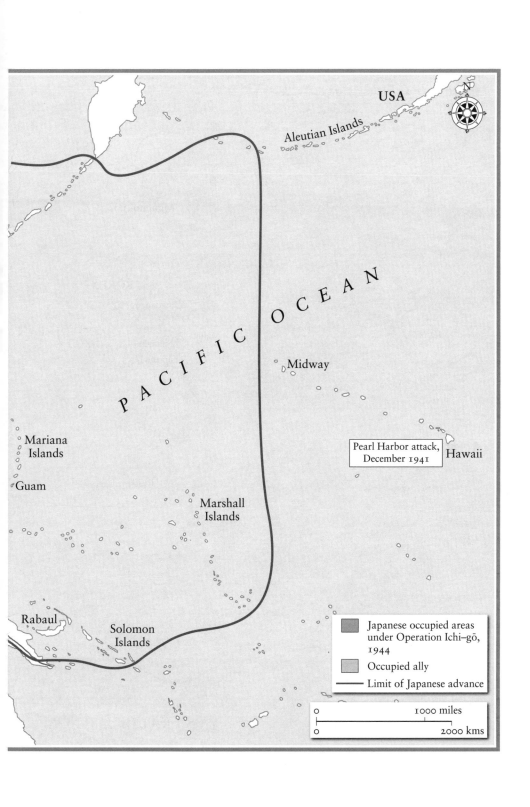

USA

Aleutian Islands

N

P A C I F I C   O C E A N

Midway

Mariana
Islands

Guam

Marshall
Islands

Pearl Harbor attack,
December 1941

Hawaii

Rabaul

Solomon
Islands

Japanese occupied areas
under Operation Ichi–gō,
1944

Occupied ally

Limit of Japanese advance

0   1000 miles

0   2000 kms

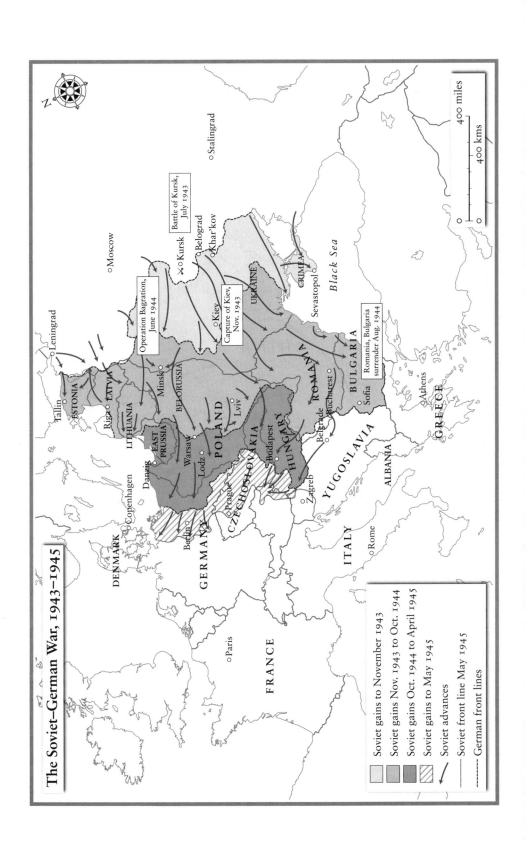

The Soviet–German War, 1943–1945

Battle of Kursk, July 1943

Operation Bagration, June 1944

Capture of Kiev, Nov. 1943

Romania, Bulgaria surrender Aug. 1944

Leningrad

Moscow

Stalingrad

Kursk

Belograd

Khar'kov

Kiev

UKRAINE

CRIMEA

Sevastopol

Black Sea

Tallin

ESTONIA

Riga

LATVIA

LITHUANIA

Minsk

BELORUSSIA

EAST
PRUSSIA

Danzig

Warsaw

Lodz

POLAND

Lviv

ROMANIA

Bucharest

BULGARIA

Sofia

Belgrade

YUGOSLAVIA

ALBANIA

GREECE

Athens

Copenhagen

DENMARK

Berlin

GERMANY

Prague

CZECHOSLOVAKIA

Budapest

HUNGARY

Zagreb

ITALY

Rome

FRANCE

Paris

400 miles

400 kms

Soviet gains to November 1943

Soviet gains Nov. 1943 to Oct. 1944

Soviet gains Oct. 1944 to April 1945

Soviet gains to May 1945

Soviet advances

Soviet front line May 1945

German front lines

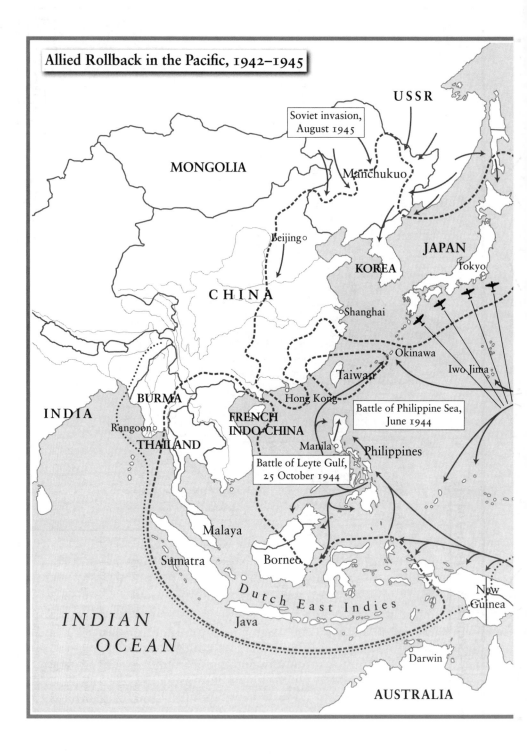

Allied Rollback in the Pacific, 1942–1945

USSR

Soviet invasion,
August 1945

MONGOLIA

Manchukuo

Beijing

CHINA

KOREA

JAPAN

Tokyo

Shanghai

Okinawa

Taiwan

Iwo Jima

Battle of Philippine Sea,
June 1944

BURMA

Hong Kong

INDIA

Rangoon

FRENCH
INDO-CHINA

THAILAND

Manila

Philippines

Battle of Leyte Gulf,
25 October 1944

Malaya

Sumatra

Borneo

Dutch East Indies

New
Guinea

INDIAN
OCEAN

Java

Darwin

AUSTRALIA

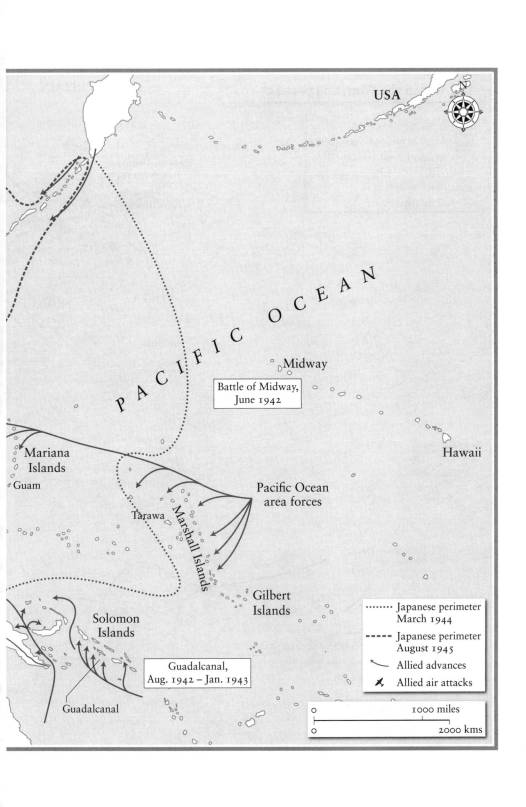

USA

N

PACIFIC OCEAN

Midway

Battle of Midway,
June 1942

Mariana
Islands

Guam

Pacific Ocean
area forces

Tarawa

Marshall Islands

Hawaii

Gilbert
Islands

Solomon
Islands

Guadalcanal,
Aug. 1942 – Jan. 1943

Guadalcanal

.... Japanese perimeter
March 1944

- - - - Japanese perimeter
August 1945

Allied advances

Allied air attacks

0   1000 miles

0   2000 kms

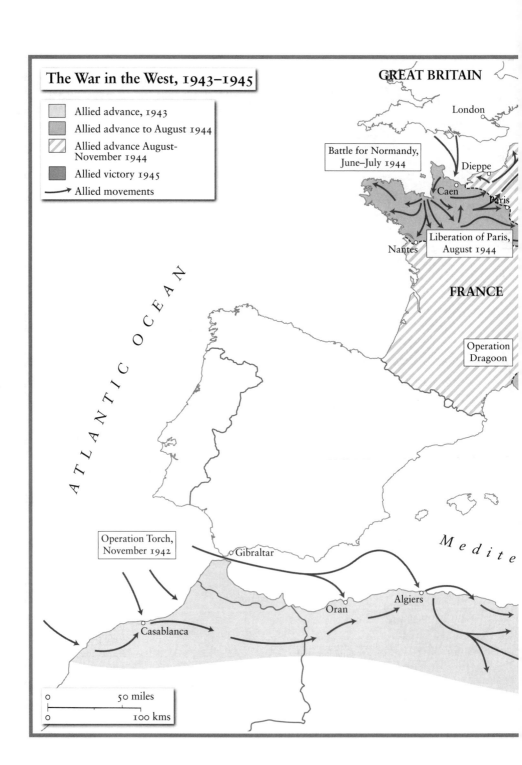

The War in the West, 1943–1945

- Allied advance, 1943
- Allied advance to August 1944
- Allied advance August–November 1944
- Allied victory 1945
- Allied movements

GREAT BRITAIN

London

Battle for Normandy, June–July 1944

Dieppe

Caen

Paris

Liberation of Paris, August 1944

Nantes

FRANCE

Operation Dragoon

ATLANTIC OCEAN

Operation Torch, November 1942

Gibraltar

Medite

Oran

Algiers

Casablanca

50 miles

100 kms

NETHERLANDS
Rotterdam

Hamburg

Berlin

Warsaw

Brussels
Essen
Dortmund

BELGIUM
Cologne
Leipzig
Dresden

GERMANY

Mannheim

Prague

Strasbourg

Dijon
Augsburg
Munich
Vienna

Lyon
AUSTRIA
Budapest

Marseilles

Pisa

ITALY

Battle of Cassino,
May 1944

Rome
Anzio
Cassino

Salerno

rranean Sea

Palermo
Messina

Invasion of Sicily,
July 1943

Bizerte
Tunis

Axis defeat in Tunisia,
May 1943

Prologue
'Blood and Ruins': The Age
of Imperial War

'Imperialism, as it was known in the nineteenth century, is no longer possible, and the only question is whether it will be buried peacefully or in blood and ruins.'

Leonard Woolf, 1928[1]

The quotation that has given the title to this history of the Second World War comes from *Imperialism and Civilization*, written by the political economist Leonard Woolf to demonstrate the significance of modern imperialism for defining modern civilization in the early twentieth century. The Western world moved through an extraordinary revolution, claimed Woolf, over the course of the hundred years to the 1920s, as industry, mass politics and the decline of aristocracy transformed society. It was a transformation that gave rise to the modern concept of the nation state, but it was accompanied by the onset of a remarkable wave of imperial conquests down to the time when he was writing. The new civilization he regarded as 'a belligerent, crusading, conquering, exploiting, proselytizing civilization', and much of the recent historical writing on empire has reinforced this judgement. Domination of the globe by a handful of colonizing nations represented a moment unique in world history.[2] For Woolf, imperial expansion was a dangerous, explosive force and it was likely, if it collapsed, to do so violently. This was the context that witnessed the Great War and twenty years later gave rise to a war even more global and more destructive.

Woolf was certainly right to argue that the long roots of the global violence, which ended in the 1940s and 1950s with the collapse of territorial empire, were to be found in the last decades of the nineteenth century, when the pace of economic and political modernization quickened across the developing world. Large-scale industrialization and urbanization in Europe, North America and Japan coincided with and helped to promote an enhanced sense of nationhood. Two of the modernizing powers, Italy and

Germany, were new nations; the first founded only in 1861, the second a decade later. Japan, the only state in Asia to begin modernizing in European terms, was in a real sense a 'new' nation too, refounded with the 'Meiji Restoration' of 1868, which overthrew the traditional Tokugawa Shogunate in favour of a new elite of economic and military reformers under the Meiji emperor. Economic modernization, together with increased education, rapid social mobility, and the evolution of a centralizing state apparatus, were means to bind the nation together. These processes also created, even in nations with a much older pedigree, a new sense of national identity and a more genuinely national politics. Social change brought mass political organization and demands for liberal reforms and greater popular representation. With the exception of the Russian Empire, all the modernizing states by 1900 had parliaments (with limited franchises) and observed the rule of law for those defined as citizens. For the established political and economic elites these changes undermined the traditional distribution of social power and political authority. It was in this environment of rapid and unpredictable change that the developing, industrial powers embarked on a fresh wave of territorial imperialism to divide up or to dominate those parts of the globe still outside the web of existing colonial empires, and it is through the prism of this final dynamic drive to empire that the long-term origins of the Second World War can best be understood.

What Woolf viewed as the 'new imperialism' of the forty years before the outbreak of war in 1914 was in many ways an extension of existing imperial structures. Britain, France, Spain, Portugal and the Netherlands had a hodge-podge of territories worldwide – colonies, protectorates, spheres of influence, entrepôts, areas of privileged treaty rights – long before the 'new' imperialism. Yet this new wave of empire was different. It derived from a growing sense of competition between the modernizing nations, partly because they were searching for new sources of materials and food and for new markets, partly because 'empire' came to be seen as a way of defining the identity of the late-century nation state as a progressive 'civilizing' agent for the rest of the world, and partly as a symbol of national prestige. This last was especially the case for the new nations, whose identity was fragile, divided by regional loyalties and social conflicts. In December 1894 the German chancellor, Prince Chlodwig zu Hohenlohe-Schillingsfürst, announced that the 'maintenance of our colonial possessions is a demand of national honour and an indication of our national reputation.'[3] In Italy in 1885, the Foreign Ministry claimed that in the 'veritable steeplechase for colonial acquisitions in all parts of the world', Italy had to find 'its destiny as a great power' by acquiring colonies of its own.[4] For the Japanese reformers running the new Meiji state, some form of imperialism was regarded as an essential demonstration of the new 'national way' (*kokutai*), and the occupation of the Kurile, Ryūkyū and Bonin islands in the 1870s was the first step in building what was now called the Great Empire of Japan (*Dai Nippon Teikoku*).[5] Over the half century that followed, these were the three states whose wish to create major empires would result in world war in the 1940s.

The link between forging a modern national identity and the acquisition or extension of empire became a commonplace in the years before 1914, even for the traditional dynastic empires in Eastern Europe, Romanov and Habsburg, whose imperial aspirations in the Balkans would eventually result in war. For those nations intent on consolidating or building an overseas empire, the relationship between nation-building and imperialism was explicit. The term 'nation-empire', rather than simply nation, defines those states that took part in the scramble for territory. What has been described as the 'nationalization of imperialism' remained of central importance down to the 1930s and the onset of a final wave of violent territorial acquisition.[6] Empire played a role in defining the metropolitan power more clearly by highlighting the alleged contrasts between citizen and subject, civilized and primitive, modern and archaic – polarities that defined the way imperial states saw the peoples and territories that they came to control, and continued to do so down to the 1940s. This world view was shared by all the imperial powers and it was based on an almost complete disregard for existing cultures and values in the occupied territories. In most cases hopes for what empire might provide, from new consumers to religious converts, were exaggerated. What Birthe Kundrus has called 'imperial fantasies' played an important role in stimulating the competition between states, even where it was evident that the costs of empire might well outweigh the often-limited advantages of possessing it.[7] These were powerful fantasies about the settlement of wild frontiers, or the prospect of an Eldorado of riches, or an exalted 'civilizing mission', or the fulfilment of a manifest destiny that would reinvigorate the nation. They shaped the way 'empire' came to be regarded in the fifty years that followed.

The fantasies that sustained the wave of new imperialism were not generated in a vacuum. They drew upon and, in turn, stimulated a body of intellectual and scientific engagement with empire that was shared among the many imperial states. The notion of national competition owed much to the application of a Darwinian paradigm about the survival of the fittest and the natural character of the contest between modern states. This was a widely debated argument in the years before 1914, but there was a prominent line of thinking, associated with some of Darwin's most distinguished successors, that 'healthy' nations were destined by nature to subject lesser peoples to their rule. The British statistician Karl Pearson, in a lecture in 1900 on 'National Life from the Standpoint of Science', told his audience that the nation had to be kept up to a high standard of efficiency 'chiefly by war with inferior races, and with equal races by the struggle for trade routes and for the sources of raw materials and of food supply. This is the natural history view of mankind.'[8] The German General Friedrich von Bernhardi, in *Germany and the Next War*, published in 1912 and widely translated, explained national competition in terms that many must have regarded as a given: 'Those forms survive which are able to procure themselves the most favourable conditions of life, and to assert themselves in the universal economy of nature. The weaker succumb.'[9] A key element in the application of Darwinian theory was the struggle for resources, for which it was widely assumed more imperial territory would in the end be needed. In 1897 the German geographer Friedrich Ratzel coined the now notorious term 'living space' (*Lebensraum*), when he argued that modern superior cultures needed to expand territorially to provide food and material resources for a growing population, and that this would only be done at the expense of 'inferior' cultures. The conclusions from Ratzel's *Political Geography*, written when the young Adolf Hitler was a schoolboy in Austria, were discussed by the future dictator in the 1920s with his close companion Rudolf Hess.[10]

The sense of cultural superiority that informed European imperialism also drew from contemporary scientific theory that suggested a natural hierarchy of the races, one that relied, so it was argued, on genetic difference. Although there was little convincing scientific evidence, the state of primitive backwardness or overt barbarism in which the colonized world was alleged to subsist meant that material resources and land would merely be wasted if they were not taken over by more advanced nations, whose part it was to bring the fruits of civilization to exotic and decadent peoples. This contrast was taken for granted and was used to justify strategies for racial discrimination and a permanent state of subjection. In 1900, Lord Curzon, the British viceroy of India, could argue that 'all the millions I have to manage are less than schoolchildren'. In Germany this view was even extended to the empire's European neighbours in the east, which could be regarded, as the *Leipziger Volkszeitung* put it in 1914, as 'the seat of barbarism'.[11] More dangerously, assumptions of superiority, whether biological or ethical, were used to justify the level of extreme violence that actually underlay the wave of new imperialism.

In almost all cases where territory was expropriated from established polities, it was done so with a greater or lesser degree of brutality or threat. The fate of the Native American population, or the Australian Aborigines, was understood even before 1914 to have been a regrettable yet unavoidable consequence of the spread of white conquest. The mass violence that accompanied expansion into Africa and Asia from the 1870s was regarded in the same way, as a necessary violence if civilization were to be exported for the benefit of those who suffered it, and one that did not raise contemporary moral qualms. In 1904 in German South West Africa, a doctor could write that 'The final solution [*Endlösung*] to the native question can only be to break the power of the natives totally and for all time.' Final solution, like living space, was not an invention of National Socialism, however suspicious historians might be of any probable causal link between the two eras.[12] Nor was such language distinctively German in the years before 1914. The twin concepts of 'race and space' that would come to dominate the imperialism of the 1930s and 1940s were laid down in a fertile period of reflection on the function and imperatives of empire before the First World War.[13] At the same time, contrasting moral universes were constructed for the treatment of the home population, as privileged agents of empire, and of the subject peoples, who could be treated with a level of coercion and arbitrary justice quite distinct from that of the metropolitan centre.

This 'mental map' of the relationship between the modern nation and its territorial empire nevertheless scarcely matched the historical reality of the years of new empire-building. Indeed, for the whole period down to the unravelling of territorial empire after 1945 there existed a gulf between empire as an 'imagined community' and the actual costs and risks to the national communities that were supposed to find their modern identity through the nation-empire. This was true even for the two major imperial powers, Britain and France, both of which had to devote resources to conquering and defending ever larger territories. Britain dominated an imperial area in 1911 of 31 million square kilometres, with 400 million people; France controlled an area of 12.5 million square kilometres and 100 million people, an area twenty times larger than the motherland.[14] In the new nations setting out for the first time on the path of empire it proved harder to create popular enthusiasm for overseas colonies that were smaller and less well-endowed than those of the older empires and which attracted few emigrants and little investment. The failed Italian invasion of Abyssinia in 1895 left Italy with nothing but parts of Somalia and Eritrea as its new empire, and domestic hostility to further imperial adventures. There were only a few thousand Italians in the tiny empire, but 16 million emigrated to other destinations. Before Italy went to war against the Ottoman Empire in 1911 to seize control of Tripolitania and Cyrenaica (modern Libya), a young radical journalist, Benito Mussolini, warned that any government demand for blood and money to fuel the conquest would be met by a general strike. 'War between nations will therefore become war between classes,' he claimed, a view that informed his own later imperialism when he distinguished between 'proletarian' nations like Italy and the rich plutocratic powers.[15] In Germany attitudes to overseas empire were similarly ambivalent before 1914. There was enthusiasm for overseas colonies among predominantly bourgeois circles of businessmen, churchmen and educators, and by 1914 the German Colonial Society (DKG) had an estimated 40,000 members – but this was double the number of Germans settled in the overseas territories.[16] Popular education and culture before 1914 helped to create an interest in the exotic and romantic aspects of overseas colonization but there was much more interest in an imagined continental empire in the 'east'. This was to prove an enduring leitmotiv in German attitudes to territory down to the active pursuit of European empire in the 1930s and 1940s, and it is worth exploring in some detail.

The creation of Germany in 1871 had included areas of eastern Prussia with large Polish populations, the result of the earlier eighteenth-century partition of Poland with Russia and Austria. The area came to be regarded as a vital breakwater against the menacing ocean of Slavs to the east and in 1886 the German chancellor, Otto von Bismarck, inaugurated the 'Royal Prussian Settlement Commission' whose purpose was to shift the Polish population, if possible, back across the frontier into Russian Poland, and to populate the territory with German settlers who would eradicate what were regarded as primitive forms of agriculture (the derogatory 'Polish economy') and provide a stable frontier force against any further threat. This 'inner colonization', as it came to be called, was widely publicized. In 1894, an organization for the east, the *Ostmarkverein*, was set up to encourage the colonization process. Ideas about 'race and space' were easily applied to the east, and well before 1914 fantasies evolved about spreading German imperialism further eastwards into land regarded as ripe for colonization, where modern civilization would bring order and culture to a land currently 'sunken into deepest barbarism and poverty'.[17] A frontier literature of so-called 'novels of the east' (*Ostromanen*) developed, allowing Germans to elide overseas imperialism with the colonization of the eastern frontier. The Pole in these novels was presented misleadingly as 'dark' – dark skin, dark eyes, dark hair – to enhance the colonial aspect by defining the Pole as 'the other', in contrast to the cultured German. In one of the most famous of the eastern novels, Clara Viebig's *The Sleeping Army* (1904), a copper-coloured Polish peasant deplores the 'white invaders with yellow hair'.[18] Just before the outbreak of war in 1914, a society for 'inner colonization' was set up whose journal compared African empire with the Polish east and argued the case for expanding in both directions into the space needed by the healthy German race.[19]

One major factor that characterized the development of the 'new imperialism' was its inherent instability and widespread violence, characteristics that marked imperial expansion from the 1870s down to the 1940s. Much of the argument for empire in the later part of the nineteenth century and the decade before the First World War was based on strategic necessity in what was widely regarded as a natural and unstable contest between the many nation-empires; but it was also based on the need for security in zones of influence or economic interest where imperial pressure had provoked a violent response from local communities. The idea of the pre-war period in Europe as a belle époque is a Eurocentric construction. Violence during the pre-war age was exported from Europe across the globe. The ascendancy of the modernizing states was the result of a sudden acceleration in the development of transport links and modern weaponry, which, together with money and training, usually gave military advantage to the imperial power. Japan quickly imitated European organization of modern military services after 1868 and adopted the most advanced technology, but it was the only Asian or African state to do so effectively. The conquest of traditional societies was complete, whether in southern Africa against the Zulus or Matabele, or in the Dutch East Indies with the violent conquest of the sultanate of Aceh, or in modern-day Vietnam, where the French conquered Annam and Tonkin. Violence was an explicit characteristic in all imperial relations, even through to the final eclipse of empire after 1945.

More significant for the later history of the world wars were the conflicts over empire between more equal adversaries and more developed states. The focus on 1914 as the end of peace is entirely misleading. The increasingly globalized world that emerged before the war was regularly destabilized by large-scale conflicts (and moments of acute crisis) which profoundly affected relations between the major powers of Europe and the future of Asia. The most significant were those waged by Japan, first against China in 1894 as Japan began to encroach on the Chinese tributary state in Korea. This was a large-scale conflict, won by Japan's newly forged army and navy; Korea became a protectorate and the large island of Formosa (present-day Taiwan) became a colony, turning the Japanese Empire overnight into a major player in the colonial game. The second war was waged against the Russian Empire, whose rulers had prevented Japan annexing part of the northern Chinese province of Manchuria after its defeat of China and had pushed on to establish Russian interests in the region. In 1904–5 a large Russian army and almost the entire Russian fleet, sent on a fool's errand of a 30,000-kilometre voyage from the Baltic to the Sea of Japan, were comprehensively defeated and Japan acquired the extensive Russian economic interests in Manchuria. Japan lost 81,500 dead and 381,000 wounded in the war, out of around 2 million mobilized, marking this as the largest external conflict that Japan had ever waged and transforming Japan's role in the region.[20]

The war between Spain and the United States in 1898–99 was not intended as a war for empire, but Spanish defeat left America in temporary possession of the Philippines, Puerto Rico, Guam and a number of small islands in the Pacific. The idea of creating a 'Greater America' flourished briefly, but when the Supreme Court ruled that the new territories were not part of the United States, interest waned in the idea of any American 'empire'. Pacific bases were strategically useful, but the territories taken from Spain existed in a kind of limbo, not part of any formal empire but dependent on the American occupiers.[21] In addition in 1899, a major war broke out between Britain and the two independent Boer southern African republics of Transvaal and Orange Free State. The South African War between 1899 and 1902 was Britain's largest conflict for half a century. Some 750,000 were mobilized and 22,000 were casualties; Britain, in this case fighting fellow white European settlers, was widely condemned by other Europeans for doing so, but eventually won a war that added substantial territory and resources to its African empire, reinforcing the neo-Darwinian view that more imperial territory could only be won by fighting for it.[22]

Colonial issues were a vital catalyst for what proved to be the key decisions that shaped the coming of war in 1914. The alliance blocs that formed from the 1880s were fed chiefly by strategic anxiety about the growing power and military capability of rapidly modernizing and politically unstable states, but these anxieties were also fed by imperial rivalry. Russian humiliation by Japan pushed Russian interests back to south-east Europe and relations with the Ottoman Empire; conflict over imperial issues between France and Britain led to the Anglo-French entente in 1904, and similar uncertainties prompted the addition of a Russian–British entente three years later, a collaboration that shaped the eventual European war. The protection of global interests, rather than merely European, also fuelled growing competition to expand military strength; the naval race between Britain and Germany in particular made no sense separated from the wider globalization of their interests. Indeed, the nature of German imperial ambition, stemming from the belief that a new nation needed an empire as a symbol of its position as a world power, accounted for the contribution Germany made to the more serious international incidents before 1914, and, especially, the Moroccan crises of 1905 and 1908 in which Germany tried to contest agreements reached between Britain, France and Spain over the allocation of protectorate rights.

As important as Morocco, however, was the decision taken in 1911 by Giovanni Giolitti's Italian government, under pressure from internal nationalist opinion, to declare war on Turkey and occupy what was left of the Ottoman Empire in North Africa. Nationalist and colonial lobbies argued that following the humiliation in Abyssinia, the solidification of the new Italian nation needed imperial expansion to justify a great power status. One of their leading spokesmen, Enrico Corradini, defined Italy without its share of empire as merely a 'proletarian nation', precisely the term later used by Mussolini to justify the new Italian imperialism in the 1930s.[23] The main object of the war was prestige as much as trade or territory, for the war coincided with the fiftieth anniversary of the creation of the new Italian nation. Anxious, as Germany had been over Morocco, that France and Britain might block any further attempt at Italian empire-building in Africa, the Italian government ran a considerable risk, though in the end the two major imperial powers did not hold Italy back. The result was not the short colonial war Italian leaders wanted, but, like the Russians in 1904, the Italians found themselves fighting another major power.[24] The war lasted a year, from October 1911 to October 1912, and Tripolitania and Cyrenaica were only ceded by the Turks because the North African war had prompted the independent Balkan states to take advantage of Turkish distraction to launch an attack on Turkey's remaining European territory. The Italians called the new colony 'Libya', in homage to the name the region had enjoyed under the Roman Empire, and began to formulate fresh demands to pressure the British and French for concessions in East Africa.[25] In the Aegean, Italy occupied the Turkish Dodecanese islands as forfeit, and now assumed a semi-colonial responsibility for European subjects. The conquest of Libya, like the Japanese defeat of China and Russia, coloured for a generation the view that territorial empire for imperial newcomers could only be secured by waging war, even against a major adversary.

There is a good case, and one not usually argued, for saying that Italian hubris in North Africa was more properly the trigger that unleashed the Great War. Subsequent Balkan victories expelled Turkey from most of its European territory and opened up for Serbia the prospect of becoming a major player in the region. Neither of the interested dynastic empires, Russia and Austria-Hungary, both facing growing domestic political crises, was prepared to abandon their strategic interests in the region. Since

1882 Italy had been an ally of Germany and Austria, so that the Italian occupation of the Dodecanese islands in 1912 also opened the prospect that Russia might face further obstacles in trying to create effective warm-water access to the Mediterranean, which an active Balkan intervention might secure. Though the general European war that broke out in late July and early August 1914 is usually attributed to great power rivalry endorsed by powerful national sentiments and a mix of hubris and in-security among the principal actors, the role of empire-building, and the definition of modern states as nation-empires, mattered a great deal in explaining why states with much to lose saw a European war as unavoid-able. Yet, if Serbia had accepted the Austrian ultimatum in July 1914, historians would now be writing about another brief imperial crisis to add to the long list since the 1890s.[26]

In a very obvious sense the Great War *was* an imperial war – all the states that joined it in 1914–15 were empires, either traditional dynastic empires or nations with overseas imperial territories. As the war became a prolonged attritional conflict, the stakes were raised so that the very sur-vival of the nation-empire defined the nature of the struggle. Historical focus on the long and sanguinary stalemate on the Western Front has ren-dered the conflict in narrowly nationalist terms, but the war was fought worldwide and with clear imperial ambitions.[27] Russia hoped to extend its influence into the Eastern Mediterranean and Middle East at the expense of the Ottoman Empire; in turn the Ottoman Empire, in the throes of a nationalist revolution, declared war on the Allied powers – the British, French and Russian empires – in October 1914 in the hope of reversing the erosion of the Turkish Empire in the Middle East and North Africa. Italy, although formally allied to the so-called Central Powers – the German and Austro-Hungarian empires – by the Triple Alliance of 1882, opted not to join the war in 1914. Instead, after negotiating a vaguely worded agree-ment in London in the spring of 1915, which suggested that Italy would be compensated with imperial territory in the Balkans and the Mediterranean basin, the Italian government joined the Allied side. Though the principal hope was that the Austrian Empire would be defeated so that the land claimed as Italian in the north-east of the peninsula could finally be liber-ated, Italian ambitions were also imperial. In Libya, Italian forces faced a widespread rebellion from 1912 onwards, encouraged by Turkey. While Italy was arguing about intervening in the war, two major defeats in Libya left 3,000 Italian dead. Some 40,000 troops were kept in the colony to defend it against a *jihad* declared from Constantinople in November 1914. By 1918 Italy had managed to cling on to the Libyan littoral, but Tripoli, the capital, was under virtual siege.[28]

The British and French war efforts were also global in scale. Immediately on the onset of European fighting, the Allied empires attacked and occupied German colonial territories in Africa and the Pacific. Togo fell in August 1914, South West Africa in May 1915 and Cameroon by February 1916; German East Africa, though never completely conquered, fell largely under Allied control by 1916. In the Pacific, Britain called on Japan, with whom the country had negotiated a treaty in 1902, to occupy the northern Pacific islands (known as *Nan'yō* by the Japanese) which Germany had purchased from Spain thirty years before, and to seize the Shandong peninsula in China belonging to the German overseas empire. Japan declared war on Germany and captured the colonies by the end of 1914, extending Japanese imperial influence even further in China and opening for the first time a wide Pacific frontier.[29] In 1915 the Japanese government presented China with the '21 Demands', exacting concessions in Mongolia, Fujian province and Manchuria along the lines of the unequal treaties extracted by the imperial powers before 1914.[30] Japan recognized that there was little the other warring powers could do about the extension of Japanese influence while they were bogged down with war in Europe. The '21 Demands' included a requirement that China agree not to grant any further ports or islands to the European imperial powers, setting a pattern for further Japanese imperial penetration in China in the decades that followed.

By far the most significant of the imperial struggles outside Europe was the situation across the Middle East. Using Egypt as the base (occupied by the British since 1884 and declared a protectorate in 1914) a long and complex war was fought against the Ottoman Empire for control of the region from the Eastern Mediterranean to Persia (modern Iran). British imperial strategy became focused on the dangers to its global empire if any other power were to dominate this region, and during the course of the war Britain was determined to find a way to control, in one mode or another, the whole of the arc of southern Asia and the Arab world, from Palestine to Afghanistan.[31] The initial plan, formalized in the Sykes–Picot agreement of January 1915, was to divide the Ottoman Empire into spheres of influence: to tsarist Russia was allocated influence at Constantinople and in Anatolia, the Turkish heartland; for France, a sphere based on a loosely defined greater Syria; and for Britain, influence across the area from Palestine to Persia. Before any of this could be realized, Ottoman attacks against the Suez Canal, regarded as the key artery of the British Empire, had to be repelled. By the time British Empire forces had rolled the Turks back into Syria and northern Iraq, Russia had left the war following the Bolshevik Revolution, leaving Britain and France as the sole imperial legatees of the whole of the Middle East. Turkey's German ally had supported Turkish imperial efforts not only with equipment and officer-advisers, but also by stirring up religious or nationalist rebellion against Britain and France across their empire areas and spheres of influence, particularly in India, Afghanistan, North Africa and Iran.[32] All these efforts failed, and by 1918 it was clear that the whole of the Middle East would be dominated by, and probably divided between, Britain and France, securing a further key region for extending and consolidating their imperial hegemony.[33]

For Germany, the loss of all its colonies and the Allied sea blockade of the homeland compelled German imperialists by default to embrace instead the idea of a larger European empire, and in particular, a wide sphere of German domination in the east. This was by no means another imperial fantasy. German forces by 1915 were deep in Russian Poland and had occupied the Russian Baltic states. They pushed back the frontier with 'Slavdom' that had coloured pre-war views about the necessity for a form of eastern colonialism. In the regions under German military occupation in the east there were patterns of control that echoed colonial practices in Europe's overseas territories, and especially the distinction between citizen and subject. Occupied populations were governed by different legal regimes, were forced to salute and bow when German officials passed by, and provided a coerced labour force.[34] After the founding of the German Fatherland Party in 1917, ideas about creating a wide area of settler colonies in the east assumed growing popularity. 'I see my fatherland at the height of its power as the Empire of Europe,' claimed the hero of a patriotic story for German youth.[35] The presence of German soldiers on Russian imperial territory reinforced the popular prejudices about Russia as a primitive polity, ripe for colonization, while the language used by the occupiers echoed the colonial vocabulary of the overseas empires. There were no words, came a report from the Eastern Front in 1914, to describe the 'vulgarity and bestiality' of the population on the Russian side of the frontier.[36]

The apogee of German imperial ambitions during the war came with the Treaty of Brest-Litovsk, signed under compulsion by the revolutionary Bolshevik government in March 1918, which opened up an area of German occupation that embraced the whole of the western Russian empire, including Belarus, the Baltic states, Russian Poland, Ukraine and the Caucasus coast of the Black Sea, further indeed than Hitler's army was to get twenty-five years later. The prospect that this opened for the British was an imperial nightmare: a solid German-Ottoman-Habsburg bloc dominating the Eurasian heartland and the Middle East. The situation worsened with the launch of Germany's last military fling in March 1918 on the

Western Front, which pushed the Allied armies back and threatened catastrophic defeat. 'We are near a crash,' warned Sir Henry Wilson, military
adviser to the government. Lord Milner, one of Britain's so-called pro-
consuls of empire, told the British prime minister, David Lloyd George,
that it seemed likely that the Central Powers would now 'be master of all
Europe and Northern and Central Asia'. Popular British fears imagined,
too, a German Africa from the Atlantic to the Indian Ocean, with German
annexation of the Belgian Congo.[37] This crisis illustrates acutely the imperial and global dimensions of a war that came to be fought over the future
of empire as much as the survival of nation.

Britain's imperial nightmare never materialized. Germany's weaker
allies crumbled during 1918, while the March Offensive failed. Supported
by American troops, following the United States' declaration of war on
the Central Powers a year earlier in April 1917, the Western Allies finally
succeeded in driving German armies back towards the German frontier.
On 11 November the European war came to an end, bringing the collapse
of three major empires, the German, Austro-Hungarian and Ottoman, to
add to the collapse of the Russian dynastic empire in 1917. Both Britain
and France saw their victory as an imperial one. The British Empire had
contributed a remarkable quantity of manpower, alongside the money
and resources needed by the mother country across a global battlefield.
The white settler colonies contributed 1.3 million men, while from India
1.2 million were mobilized; African colonies supplied hundreds of thousands of labourers, of whom an estimated 200,000 died.[38] The French
Empire supplied 500,000 soldiers (most from French West and North
Africa) and over 200,000 conscripted labourers, alongside 1.6 billion
francs in contributions and 5.5 million tons of supplies.[39] The solidarity
of the empire became a central motif in wartime propaganda and both
major empires expected that the war to make the world safe for democracy would, paradoxically, secure the survival of undemocratic empire as
well. This paradox is central to understanding the dilemmas that all the
empires faced after 1918; it also helps to explain the role of imperialism
in generating a second major conflict twenty years later.

The key problem for the surviving empires after the war lay in the difficulty of reconciling the principle of nationality with the idea of empire,
a challenge conventionally associated with the American Democrat president, Woodrow Wilson, whose address to the US Congress on 18 January
1918 set out what came to be known as the 'Fourteen Points' for the
framing of a new internationalist world order. The speech became famous
overnight worldwide because Wilson's Point XIV invoked the right to
'political independence and territorial integrity to great and small states

alike'; at the end of the speech, he reiterated his view that all peoples and nationalities had the 'right to live on equal terms of liberty and safety with one another'. Although he never used the term 'self-determination', the ambiguities in his speech allowed that interpretation and Wilson was inundated thereafter with petitions, lobbies and deputations from colonial inhabitants who mistakenly understood his statement as an opportunity to seek their own emancipation.[40] In truth the idea of 'self-determination' that was fashioned out of Wilson's statement originated with the revolutionaries in Russia in 1917, following the overthrow of the tsarist regime in March. Still willing to fight the war, the revolutionary Provisional Government announced on 9 April 1917 that its chief war aim was 'the establishment of permanent peace on the basis of the self-determination of peoples'. A year later, after the seizure of power in November 1917 by the Bolsheviks, the radical communist wing of the Russian socialist movement, Lenin, chairman of the new government, called for 'the liberation of all the colonies; the liberation of all dependent, oppressed and non-sovereign peoples'.[41] The appeal from Russian Communism, which was soon institutionalized with the creation of the Communist International (Comintern) in 1919, so alarmed the imperial powers that they sent armies of intervention in 1918–19 to support the anti-Bolshevik 'White' Russian armies. Japan, with its recent history of conflict with Russia, sent 70,000 soldiers to Siberia in 1918, and briefly explored the idea of creating a dependent Siberian province, backed by 250,000 troops to extend Japan's empire northwards. Bolshevik military successes and Japanese domestic instability finally provoked Japan's withdrawal in 1920.[42]

The first signs of an impending crisis of empire provoked by the idea of self-determination appeared with the coming of peace, when a number of subject peoples expected their contribution to the Allied victory to be matched by political concessions from the metropolitan powers whose war effort they had assisted, while others expected that Wilsonian rhetoric would help undo unwelcome, and in some cases very recent, imperial shackles. In the spring of 1919, Wilson and his entourage at the Paris Peace Conference were bombarded by petitioners or petitions asking for full sovereignty and an end to the imperial presumption that subject peoples were not capable of self-rule. The petitioners included Persia, Yemen, Lebanon, Syria, Tunisia, French Indochina (now Vietnam, Laos and Cambodia), Egypt and Korea. The Indian nationalist Lala Lajpat Rai, co-founder of the India Home Rule League of America, sent a telegram to Wilson thanking him for conferring a new charter for freedom 'for all small and subject and oppressed nationalities in the world'. American intervention, Rai insisted,

had placed 'the Imperial Powers of Europe in the shade'.[43] In no case were
the petitions satisfied, and in the year after the end of the war there were
widespread, often violent, protests against imperial rule. In Korea, demonstrations in March 1919 were ruthlessly suppressed; in India, riots in the
city of Amritsar were met by a hail of bullets, leaving 379 dead; in Egypt,
nationalist leaders were exiled and 800 killed in anti-British riots. 'Is this
not the ugliest of treacheries?', wrote one of the Egyptian delegates to
Paris. 'Is it not the most profound repudiation of principles?'[44] Only in
Ireland did nationalists succeed in defying the 110,000 British troops
deployed there and achieve a form of independence in 1922 as the Irish
Free State.

In the end the priority for the peace conference was to create sovereign
states in Eastern and Central Europe to replace the collapsed dynastic
empires: Poland, Yugoslavia, Czechoslovakia, Finland, Estonia, Latvia, Lithuania and a rump Austria were the result. The principle of self-determination
was extended nowhere else. The British and French delegations were able to
persuade Wilson to take out the term 'self-determination' from the draft
Covenant of the League of Nations organization, which was to be the
principal agent of the internationalized order, and substitute instead a commitment to the territorial integrity and political independence of existing
states.[45] This was the start of a political process in 1919 in which Anglo-
French pressure succeeded in limiting substantially the liberal ambitions of
both Wilson and their own critics of empire. Under the terms of the Treaty
of Versailles the defeated German Empire was treated punitively, losing all
its overseas territories, Alsace-Lorraine, a Polish 'corridor' through East
Prussia and part of Silesia, and small parcels of land to Belgium and Denmark, then compelled to disarm almost completely and to accept a bill for
reparations worth 132 billion gold marks as the price for allegedly launching the war in the first place. The accusation of war guilt played a critical
part in alienating German society across the political spectrum from the
peace settlement, but so too did the terms of the decision to strip Germany
of its colonies on the ground that German colonialism in particular was too
brutal and exploitative to justify allowing Germans to share in the 'civilizing
mission', a claim that seemed to German minds mere hypocrisy.

Unsurprisingly, the beneficiaries were chiefly the major imperial states.
One of the first acts agreed when the Allies met in Paris, in January 1919,
was to confirm the British and French occupations of German and Ottoman imperial territories. Rather than annex them outright, they agreed to a
mandate system, making them trustees for peoples 'not yet able to stand by
themselves' in the 'strenuous conditions of the modern world'. The mandate system was formalized in the creation of the League of Nations

Permanent Mandates Commission in 1921, whose personnel, led by the Swiss academic William Rappard, were supposed to oversee the activity of the mandate powers to ensure that they were indeed preparing the populations of the mandated territories for eventual self-rule, but in effect the mandated powers treated the new acquisitions as additions to their imperial map or, as the British Conservative politician Neville Chamberlain later put it, empire in a 'colloquial sense'. The mandates in the Middle East were the result of sharp negotiation between Britain and France, but they took over the entire area – Lebanon and Syria for France, Transjordan, Iraq and Palestine for Britain – regardless of former promises to Arab leaders who had supported the campaign against the Turks. The mandates for former German colonies in Africa were divided up again between the British and French empires, with the concession for the Belgians that Rwanda and Burundi, in the eastern Congo basin, would be allocated to them.[46] Japan won the mandate over the German North Pacific islands; Australia and New Zealand over German New Guinea and Western Samoa. The populations objected to their treatment. 'The French Government,' wrote Joseph Bell from former German Cameroon in October 1919, 'is forcing us to live under his Government Administration but our country don't want French Government.' Petitions proliferated once again at Geneva, where the Mandates Commission operated, but the new mandate powers, who dominated the League, disregarded them. Of the nine members of the Commission, most were diplomats or colonial officials, eight of them representing imperial states, including four from the mandated powers themselves.[47]

Empire eventually survived both internationalist and nationalist pressures in the years immediately after the Great War because of a willingness to confront threats with violence. Indeed, for all the imperial powers, facing an unstable and politically dangerous world, empire became more important rather than less, helping to define and strengthen the nation-empire while suppressing the right to full national independence across Africa, the Middle East and Asia. Woodrow Wilson, for all his brief worldwide popularity, had never intended his principles to undo the world of empires. In his view, the imperial powers should act in a position of trusteeship, bringing the benefits of civilization to peoples too primitive for full statehood, as the United States was doing with the Philippines and the other territories acquired from Spain. His behaviour at Paris in 1919, when he reacted negatively to non-European petitioning, confirmed this preference, but much of the United States public interpreted the failure to curb European and Japanese imperialism as simple hypocrisy, and in 1919 the American Senate rejected the settlement arrived at in Paris and the League of Nations as the agent for sustaining it.[48] This decision did not disengage the United States from world affairs entirely, as is sometimes suggested, but it left the League firmly in the hands of those major powers with a vested interest in sustaining empire.

The most significant of the surviving empires were those of Britain and France. After the war, the French Empire came to play a more important part in metropolitan culture and to provide a greater degree of economic advantage. With the addition of the mandated territories, the French Empire reached its greatest geographical extent, Greater France as it came to be called (*la plus grande France*). The contribution made during the war encouraged the idea, associated chiefly with the minister of colonies, Albert Sarraut, that the empire needed to be centralized and consolidated to extract the most from it. In 1923 his popular book *La mise en valeur des colonies françaises* ('The development of the French colonies') laid out the wider purpose of empire: 'the increased strength and wealth of the ensemble of overseas Frances' would guarantee 'the future power and prosperity of the mother country'. With an empire, observed one businessman, France was 'a world-important nation'.[49] Successive French governments created an empire linked more closely with the metropolitan economy, protected to some extent after 1928 by a new set of regulations, the Kircher tariffs, and based on a common currency bloc. By 1939 the empire absorbed 40 per cent of French exports and supplied 37 per cent of imports; by the same year over 40 per cent of French overseas investment was in the empire.[50]

The reality, of course, was not entirely consistent with the popular image, since the history of French imperialism was punctuated during the 1920s and 1930s by violent conflicts. Among the most violent were the Rif war in Morocco and the suppression of a Syrian revolt, both in 1925–26, and the savage response to a communist insurgency in Indochina in 1930–31. In this last case, contemporary estimates claimed that around 1,000 demonstrators were shot or bombed, 1,300 villages destroyed, and 6,000 imprisoned, tortured or executed. Workers on the plantations, who joined the insurgents, laboured for fifteen to sixteen hours a day, overseen by armed guards and confined to their villages.[51] Here, as throughout the empire, the French government and colonial authorities were less willing to make superficial political concessions to colonial nationalism than the British. But at home, the empire attracted a great deal of popular engagement. By the late 1920s there were over seventy journals and papers devoted to colonial issues. In 1931, at the height of the world recession, a major colonial exposition was held at Vincennes in Paris, in a vast purpose-built colonial palace decorated with exotic murals and symbols of the scattered territories. In five months some 35.5 million tickets were sold. The exhibition, while playing on the idea of a unitary empire, presented the colonial world as the 'other', reinforcing the hierarchies that operated in reality in the empire.[52]

The British Empire remained the world's largest by a considerable margin. There was no question that the empire contributed to Britain's position as a global economic power. As other markets shrank or were closed off, British exports to the empire rose from one-third to almost half of all trade between 1910 and 1938, by which date empire areas supplied 42 per cent of imports; by 1930 almost 60 per cent of overseas investment went to empire areas. The empire was not yet a closed trading bloc, but imperial preferences were practised. As in the French case, the relative decline of sectors of British industry was masked by the ability to export over-priced products to empire areas, while British investment in overseas supplies of tin, rubber, oil, copper and a range of other primary materials gave British trading houses and industries a major presence in the world market. Empire became embedded in British popular culture, even though for many Britons it remained a remote reality, an imagined community rooted in a propaganda of unity and paternalism that, like the French, did not account for the almost permanent state of emergency and coercive action played out somewhere in the empire year on year. The key date in the imperial calendar was Empire Day, founded in 1903 on the date of Queen Victoria's birthday and by the 1920s celebrated by almost all the country's schools. In 1924–5 a major Empire Exhibition was mounted at Wembley in London, attracting 27 million visitors to a 216-acre site, where 'races in residence' were housed in the exhibition grounds to be stared at like animals in a zoo.[53]

These economic advantages were not shared by the three newcomers to the imperial scramble in the late nineteenth century – Italy, Japan and Germany. It is no accident that in the 1930s, when the global economy collapsed and internationalism with it, these were the three powers that launched a new wave of violent territorial imperialism, building on pre-war notions of 'nation-empire'. Their view of the world order after 1919 was, for different reasons, coloured by profound resentment at the outcome of the conflict and at the dominant position assumed by the major Western powers when it came to shaping the post-war settlement and the subsequent international political arena. This was true even for the Allied powers Italy and Japan, both of whom were victors in 1919 and, unlike Germany, still possessed colonial empires after the war. Nationalist circles in all three countries understood that the Great War had made the major global empires, British and French, achieve a territorial peak. Their global power, backed by the League of Nations and the rhetoric of internationalism, was used to restrain other states from further imperialism, while at the same time it allowed both states to exploit their status as 'nation-empires' to the full. Indeed, the more vigorously the British and French propagated the fantasy of a united empire as the source of national strength and prosperity, the more the disadvantaged states imagined that gaining more territory was the only avenue to enhancing their status and protecting their populations from economic risks. It was taken for granted that further territorial acquisition was only possible through war. Very recent history confirmed this: the Spanish–American war of 1898, the South African War, the Russo-Japanese War, the twenty-year conquest of Libya and, in the 1920s, major imperial conflicts in Morocco, Syria and Iraq demonstrated this evident truth. Resentment at what was regarded as a lack of autonomy in deciding national futures fed into a growing rejection of 'Western' or 'liberal' values based on peaceful collaboration and democratic politics. It is not difficult to understand why nationalist sentiment in these three states came to favour territorial solutions that might end what they viewed as their permanent subordination to the large territorial- and resource-rich British and French empires, and to the United States.

Japanese resentment was rooted in the history of Japanese expansion, which had catapulted the country into the position of a major player in the regional power politics of East Asia and the Pacific by the end of the Great War – a status that had not yet been fully acknowledged by the Allies. Although Japan was invited to the Paris Peace Conference as one of the Council of Ten, composed of representatives of the major Allied states, the key decisions were negotiated by the major Western powers. Japanese demands that a 'racial equality' clause should be included in the Covenant of the League was rejected by great powers who were not prepared to advance the principle themselves. The League remained, in the Japanese view, a Western construction, inadequate for 'national self-rescue measures'; in the mid-1920s the idea was unsuccessfully mooted that Japan set up an Asian section of the League to better represent Japanese interests. The hoped-for gains from the war – 'a prominent position in the Orient', as Foreign Minister Motono Ichirō put it – were gradually eroded.[54] The Western powers recaptured market share in China. Japan had to agree to return the German Shandong concession, captured in 1914 with great nationalist fanfare, to Chinese sovereignty; the American recognition of Japan's special interests in China in the 1917 Lansing–Ishii agreement was repudiated in 1922; the Anglo-Japanese alliance signed in 1902 was abrogated in 1923. 'Everywhere in the world,' observed Japan's delegate at the peace conference, 'the so-called Americanism is advanced ...'[55] At the Washington Disarmament Conference in 1922–3,

Japan had to accept a ratio of naval strength of 5:5:3 in favour of Britain and the United States, and to do so again at the London Naval Conference in 1930.[56] Above all, Western support for a new nationalist China, emerging slowly from the warlord conflicts that followed the fall of the Empire in 1912, alienated Japan, which saw its position in China as essential to its future national-imperial interests. The Nine-Power Treaty negotiated at Washington in 1922, which Japan also signed, insisted on an open-door policy in trade with China and implicitly repudiated the idea that Japan might have a privileged position in Asia. Japanese critics of the international system talked about a new order in Asia based around 'Oriental thought', rejecting Western models of peacemaking, capitalism and liberal democracy as inherently incompatible with Japan's strategic and political interests.[57]

A central question for Japanese nationalists – what had been the point of the 'blood sacrifices' made in the wars with China and Russia? – was also a central question for Italy. Nationalist propaganda in the early 1920s played on the theme of building a new Italy 'in the name of the dead', whose sacrifice, so it was argued, had been a mockery in the light of the peace settlement in 1919. Although Italy suffered 1,900,000 dead and wounded during the war, the Italian delegation was treated throughout the peace conference as an ally whose contribution did not entitle it to equal consideration. During the war, nationalists hoped for post-war Italian annexations in Dalmatia, even Turkey; at the Colonial Ministry Italian officials talked of creating an Italian Africa from Libya to the Gulf of Guinea.[58] In January 1919, at a congress summoned by the Italian Colonial Institute to consider the peace settlement, one delegate insisted that Italy 'must attain territorial equality overseas' with the British and French.[59] At the very least the Italian government expected that Britain and France would honour the secret territorial commitments in the Treaty of London, signed in 1915 to persuade Italy to enter the war. These included the promise of territory in Dalmatia, control over Albania, recognition of Italian interests in the Mediterranean, and the possibility that Italy would share in the spoils of the German and Ottoman empires as 'just compensation'.[60]

Unfortunately for the Italian delegation, Wilson was hostile to the treaty and refused to be bound by it, while Britain and France used his intransigence to mask their own desire not to make concessions to Italy. Political divisions in Italy over what constituted a just peace made it difficult to co-ordinate a programme to demand fulfilment of the London treaty.[61] In April the Italian premier, Vittorio Orlando, flounced out of the Paris conference, but on his return in May it was clearer than ever that

Italy would not be granted additional territorial concessions beyond former Austrian territory in the north-east of the Italian peninsula, or even be allowed to manage a mandated territory. The outcome created the myth of the 'mutilated victory' (*la vittoria mutilata*). In his memoirs Orlando argued that 'never has a peace left behind it such a wake of resentment and hatred, not only of the defeated toward the victorious but of the victorious toward their victorious allies'.[62] It was that legacy of resentment that characterized the ambitions of the radical nationalist government appointed in October 1922 under the leadership of Benito Mussolini and his recently founded Italian Fascist Party. Though animated by a profound hostility to what he called 'the plutocratic and bourgeois alliance' of Britain, France and the United States, there were limits to what even a Fascist regime could achieve in circumstances where Italy was heavily reliant on foreign credits and struggling to control the few colonies it did possess, in Libya and East Africa. For most of the 1920s Italy, like Japan, lacked international autonomy, chafing at the bit to be allowed to pursue a more forward policy in the Balkans, the Mediterranean basin and Africa but hesitant about the risks involved in building on the legacy of imperial fantasies frustrated at Versailles.[63]

The German case differed from both the Italian and the Japanese. Germany was a defeated empire, stripped of its overseas colonies and its internally colonized Polish territories. Here the resentments fuelled by that defeat enjoyed a much broader social base than in Italy or Japan, and a more dangerous political and cultural articulation. The early experience of the post-war years of widespread hunger, unemployment, hyperinflation and political violence (including the violent frontier in the east with Poland) scarred an entire generation and imposed on Germany hardships and humiliations that none of the imperial powers suffered in the 1920s to the same degree. The national sacrifices made in the war created an unmediated sense of shared victimhood.[64] The blame for this existential crisis was directed chiefly at the victorious Western powers that imposed the peace settlement. Across the political spectrum there was resentment at the accusation that Germany alone bore guilt for the war, that Germany should be territorially restricted and disarmed, and that the German people were not humane and efficient colonizers. This last assertion from the Paris conference, termed in the 1920s the 'Colonial Lie' (*Koloniallüge*), was a calculated insult, used to justify the takeover of German colonies and to restrict Germany in the future to a subordinate position in Europe. When the Allied treaty terms were discussed by the Weimar National Assembly in March 1919, the delegates, predominantly socialists and liberals, rejected the colonial proposals by 414 votes to 7 and called for 'the reestablishment of Germany's colonial rights'.[65] Ten years later, Adolf Hitler, now the leader of a rapidly growing National Socialist Party, used an election statement to reject 'as an impertinent attack on our national honour the lying and monstrous assertion that the German people lack the ability to administer colonies'. The nationalist right in the 1920s interpreted the restrictions imposed on Germany as a form of reverse colonialism in which Germany's future was held hostage to the economic and political interests of the imperial powers, a 'tributary exploitation colony', as Hitler put it.[66] Unable to challenge the Western monopoly of power, radical nationalists turned their resentment inward, against German Jews and Marxists who had, it was alleged, 'stabbed Germany in the back' in 1918, opening the way for Western colonization of the German heartland.

The right to be considered what was called a 'Culture Nation' (*Kulturnation*), capable of sharing with other empires the civilizing and modernizing mission, was a recurrent theme in the 1920s. In 1926 the German Foreign Ministry sponsored an information film titled 'World History as Colonial History', which illustrated not only the economic help that colonies might bring but challenged the claim that Germany was incapable of ruling subject peoples.[67] Though it was now a 'post-colonial' state, the links with Germany's colonial past were kept alive through organizations and propaganda directed at re-establishing Germany at some point as an overseas empire. The German Colonial Society acted as an umbrella for a host of small associations set up to campaign for colonial rights; it numbered 30,000 members with 260 local branches and supported a wide range of colonial journals. News of the former colonies and of the other major empires was widely disseminated. Subsidies and investment for German companies working in former colonies saw their number actually increase, from seventy-three in 1914 to eighty-five by 1933. The pre-war Colonial School continued to function, and in 1926 a Colonial School for Women was set up, both designed to train administrators and experts for a putative future empire. In 1925, a Colonial Exhibition was hosted, incongruously, in Berlin. The foreign minister, Gustav Stresemann, used the occasion to highlight the contrast between all the other European empires, including those of Spain, Portugal and Denmark, and the Germans who were, uniquely, a European 'people without space' (*Raum*).[68]

The most prominent source of resentment after 1919, as Stresemann understood, was the idea that the Germans, as a vigorous, progressive and cultured people, lacked sufficient territory to be able to display those qualities and to nourish a growing population. Among nationalist circles in Germany, and indeed beyond them, the idea that territorial expansion

somehow defined a modern nation and permitted it to exercise rule over
a hierarchy of subject peoples became a standard trope in reflecting on
Germany's imperial past and possible imperial future. The key element
was 'space'. In the 1920s the ideas pioneered by Ratzel on the natural
necessity for *Lebensraum* became widespread in Germany, not least
because of the restricted territory allotted under the Paris peace treaty –
the 'unjustified, unfounded and senseless mutilation of our own living
space', as one German geographer put it in 1931.[69] The popularity of the
new science of geopolitics in Germany in the 1920s, pioneered, among
others, by Karl Haushofer, derived not so much from the science itself,
which was too abstruse for many, but from the vocabulary of living space
and its implications for the German situation. The popularity of a novel
by the former colonist Hans Grimm, *Volk ohne Raum* (*A People without
Space*), which sold 315,000 copies after its publication in 1926, relied on
the title itself, chosen by the publisher as a rallying cry for German
claims. The concept of *Raum* was more than the English word 'space' suggests; it denoted an area where the *Volk* or people (again rendered poorly
in the English version) would plant their special cultural qualities and
biological–racial attributes at the expense of subject or alien peoples, and
in particular, according to the radical nationalist wing, of the Jews as the
archetype of the cosmopolitan 'anti-nation'.[70]

   The idea of securing additional territory to rule or dominate by a
people defined in terms of its racial homogeneity and cultural superiority
was deemed to be compensation, as Haushofer put it, for the 'heavy and
bloody sacrifices' of the war.[71] But these aspirations, widely shared in
German society, begged the question of where compensation for Germany's alleged mistreatment would come from. The colonial lobby,
though large and well-organized, understood that securing overseas colonies under the circumstances of the 1920s was a chimera, though it was
hoped that the Western powers might allow Germany a collaborative
colonial project at some future date. Most of those nationalist circles that
addressed the question of 'race and space' focused on the pre-war strand
of imperial thinking, reinforced by the brief empire established in 1918
in the Ukraine, that only eastward expansion promised *Raum* in an
authentic and plausible sense. Here it might be possible, as the German
legal philosopher Carl Schmitt suggested later in the 1930s, to build a
German-dominated 'Greater Area' (*Grossraum*) in Central and Eastern
Europe and to keep other powers at arm's length. The 'east', though
never very clearly defined, featured regularly in discussions about 'space'.
Geopoliticians in particular emphasized that well beyond Germany's
now limited borders were areas of historic German influence – whether

language, or farm practices, or legal traditions, even forms of house construction – that justified seeing the east as 'German space'. This concept of German 'racial and cultural territory' was captured in numerous maps used in school textbooks or political propaganda. A map produced by Albrecht Penck and Hans Fischer in 1925 of this German cultural and racial region – widely imitated and disseminated – showed German space stretching far into Ukraine and Russia, from Lake Ladoga in the north to Kherson in the far south of Ukraine, and into the territory of the so-called 'Volga Germans', eighteenth-century migrants whose descendants were now living under Soviet rule.[72] A young Heinrich Himmler, later head of the SS and the man responsible for Germany's ferocious imperialism in Poland and the Soviet Union, noted in his diary in 1921, after attending a lecture on Germany's future territorial objectives, 'The East is what is most important for us. The West dies easily. We must fight and settle in the East.'[73] There was in the 1920s nothing specifically National Socialist about these views.

German dreams of reversing the verdict of the Great War and the peace settlement, like Italian fantasies about a Mediterranean empire, or Japanese ambitions for exclusive domination of Asia, remained aspirations in the 1920s but they sustained national ambitions that stretched back to the decades before the Great War. They did not make a second global war inevitable. In reality, the resentments that fuelled these fantasies were not universal in any of the three states, and as the world order stabilized in the mid-1920s around an American-led economic revival and the suppression of non-European nationalisms, so it proved possible for all three states to find ways to work, however reluctantly, within the prevailing structures of international political and economic collaboration. In Germany and Japan, the hunt for further territory was not such a significant concern for much of the population as it was for nationalist circles. In Italy, where democracy collapsed in the wake of bitter conflict between radical nationalism and the centre and left, Mussolini's first political priorities were to stabilize his rule and supervise Italian economic revival. All three states were dependent in the 1920s on the Western powers' contribution to the slow recovery of the world trading and investment economy, and all three paid lip-service to the internationalist spirit embodied in the League of Nations. In 1925 victors and vanquished signed the Locarno Pact, guaranteeing the frontiers in Western Europe laid down at Versailles. Germany was permitted to join the League in 1926. In 1927 Germany was even invited, against strong French and Belgian opposition, to join the Permanent Mandates Commission, responsible for supervising her former colonies, recommending as commissioner the director of the Federation of German Industry, Ludwig Kastl, rather than a leader of the noisy colonial lobby. Germany insisted that the mandate terms be respected, including the commitment to prepare the former colonies for eventual independence, and it was a German who first coined, in 1932, the term 'decolonization' (*Dekolonisierung*) to describe a process that already seemed under way.[74]

This was, in the end, a tentative accommodation set against a postwar world where stability was viewed as probably temporary and certainly unpredictable. Gustav Stresemann masterminded a German foreign policy of 'fulfilment' in the hope that evidence of German good faith might be a better path to undoing elements of the peace settlement, but he did not rule out the possibility of more fundamental change. In Japan the liberal Minseitō party, in power for much of the late 1920s, campaigned for disarmament and co-operation with the West as the more sensible path to achieving Japanese goals and encouraging economic development.[75] The mid-1920s saw a period when Japan even practised a strategy of friendship towards China to replace a decade of confrontation. Even in Italy, where Mussolini self-consciously summoned the idea of a 'new Italy' to challenge the values and interests of the West, it proved necessary to speak at least 'verbal pacifism', as he put it, rather than run the risk of conflict. A solution to Italy's new ambitions for empire would have to wait, so he thought, for 'chaos in Europe'.[76] There were, anyway, enough problems in Italy's existing colonies. Somalia and Eritrea had to be pacified; the garrisons were raised from 2,500 to 12,000 men, but it took ten years before regional insurgencies had been suppressed. In Libya the cost was even greater. Starting in 1922, before Mussolini came to power, a major war was fought against Arab tribesmen for control of most of the country's desert hinterland, which only ended in 1931 following years of savage repression. There were too many risks involved in pursuing new territory before the existing empire was secure, but the campaign kept to the fore the idea that imperial territory could only be acquired by conquest.[77]

This period of accommodation ended abruptly with the onset of a global economic recession in 1928–9 that was to have catastrophic consequences for the decade that followed. Historians are generally agreed that the economic crisis played the major part in destroying the efforts to reconstruct a global order after 1919 and sustain any useful commitment to internationalism. In many respects, the collapse of the world economy was a more decisive turning point than 1914 or 1919 in shaping the crisis that resulted in a global war in the 1940s.[78] The story of the crisis is now well-known, but it is worth remembering the scale of the disaster, which

hit a world economy that had displayed continued weaknesses throughout the 1920s despite the brief trading and investment boom in the middle
of the decade. By 1932 there were more than 40 million registered unemployed in the industrial economies, and tens of millions more on short
time or who were laid off as a result of a precipitous fall in prices and
output. Across the recession from 1929 to 1932 world trade fell by an
extraordinary two-thirds. Poorer areas of the world reliant on one or two
export products were plunged into desperate poverty. The closing of
credit lines led to widespread bankruptcies, and almost produced national
bankruptcy in Germany in 1932. There was a widespread panic that the
crisis spelt nothing less than the end of capitalism, as communists had
been gleefully predicting. Nationalists in Germany, with equal satisfaction, saw the slump as the 'twilight of the world economy' and the
hated Western system that had sustained it.[79]

The sense that the Western model of economic collaboration and internationalism was doomed drew on a decade of writing by latter-day
Cassandras, including, most famously, Oswald Spengler's *Decline of the
West* (*Der Untergang des Abendlandes*). The president of the League of
Nations Assembly exhorted member states in the summer of 1932 to collaborate or prepare for the worst: 'The entire world is suffering from a
terrible crisis and lack of confidence. The last hopes of the world are now
in our hands.'[80] But the League, despite its efforts to define what was
needed to alleviate the crisis, was powerless to stop the rush towards economic nationalism. As the crisis deepened, co-operation seemed far riskier
than protecting the home economy. In June 1930, the United States introduced the Hawley–Smoot Tariff, cutting off the American market from
foreign imports; in November 1931, after a long political debate, Britain
abandoned liberal trade and imposed a range of tariffs, followed in August
1932 by an Imperial Preference system to give privileged access to empire
imports; in France the Kircher tariffs reduced duty on colonial products
at the expense of the wider world.[81] The crisis provoked the creation of
special trading and currency blocs, for the dollar, for sterling and for the
franc. The world's strongest economies might have played a role in protecting the system they had long profited from, but they chose not to, at
the expense of the rest.

The political consequences were profound for states that found themselves penalized by the new programmes of economic nationalism. In
Japan the recession was a calamity: exports, particularly of raw silk, fell
by 53 per cent, imports by 55 per cent; the large Japanese agricultural
sector, stagnant for much of the 1920s, experienced further disastrous
decline with a halving of farm incomes, leaving millions of peasants in

crippling poverty.[82] The effort to work within the Western system was exposed as fruitless and a wave of anti-Western sentiment led to the collapse of the moderate Minseitō government. The rising tide of nationalist revolt against the global system brought the military into a more dominant position in Japanese government and an end to the democratic experiments of the 1920s.[83] In Italy, hit less severely than other economies during the recession, the crisis was interpreted by the regime as an opportunity to reignite the Fascist revolution at home by embarking on a more active imperial policy abroad, as each of the major states withdrew into a protective carapace. In Germany the recession was interpreted by much of the population as further punishment by the victorious powers. When a tariff agreement was sought with Austria in 1931, the French vetoed it. Throughout the recession, which left two out of every five Germans unemployed, brought a 40 per cent reduction in industrial production and a fall of more than half in German exports, Germany was still expected to repay war reparations and service the large international debt acquired in the 1920s. The lament that Germany was little more than a colony itself began to make greater sense during the slump. In 1930, Hitler's National Socialists, the most radical nationalist party, deeply hostile to the globalized economy and Western tutelage, became a serious political force; by 1932 it was the largest party, and in January 1933 the government party when Hitler was offered the chancellorship. Here, as in Italy and Japan, the nationalists who had traded on established imperial fantasies of 'race and space' in the 1920s could argue that they had been proved right. The world tipped dangerously in their favour.

This was the context in which first Japan, then Italy, and finally Hitler's Germany redeemed their festering resentments by embarking on a renewed wave of territorial imperialism in the 1930s. Prompted by the economic crisis, the view hardened that a revised global economic and political order was needed, one that would no longer be based on the defunct internationalism of the previous decades but instead would be based on closed imperial-economic blocs, dominated – as were the British and French imperial zones – by a strong metropolitan power.[84] More than ever, imperial power was seen as indispensable to national survival, reviving the imperial paradigm established in the late nineteenth century. This option, as the Japanese foreign minister Arita Hachirō put it, was unavoidable: 'small countries have no other choice left but to strive as best they can to form their own economic *blocs* or to found powerful states, lest their very existence be jeopardized.'[85] The struggle for additional territory and secure resources, if necessary through war, turned the clock back to an earlier imperial age. Joseph Stalin, the Soviet dictator, observing the crisis of capitalism from the one state where economic development had been little affected by the worldwide recession, understood that trade war, currency war, 'the intensified struggle for markets' and extreme economic nationalism 'have put war on the order of the day as a means for a new redivision of the world and of spheres of influence'. For once, Stalin's judgement, not always well regarded by historians, was borne out by events.[86]

I

Nation-Empires and Global Crisis, 1931–40

'... in an act of outrageous violence, Chinese soldiers blew up a section of the Mantetsu track located to the northwest of Beitaying [military base] and attacked our railway guards. Our guards immediately returned fire and mobilized artillery to shell Beitaying. Our forces now occupy a section of the base ...'

Asahi, Osaka, 19 September 1931[1]

This front-page article in the popular daily newspaper *Asahi* presented the Japanese public with an account of Chinese perfidy that became embedded in Japanese popular perception of who was to blame for the onset of the subsequent Japanese invasion and occupation of the whole northern Chinese province of Manchuria. It was a travesty of the truth. A group of Japanese engineers from the Kwantung Army, stationed in Manchuria to protect the empire's economic interests in the region, planted the explosives early on the morning of 18 September 1931 as a flimsy excuse to begin a programme of military expansion into China that was not to end until 1945. It was a small incident in global terms, but its ramifications were much larger. It was the point in the depths of the world economic crisis when the first step was taken to create a new imperial and economic order by violence. The shots at the Beitaying base signalled the onset of what was to become in the 1930s a new imperial age.

The circumstances of what the Japanese government came to term the 'Manchurian Incident' were shaped by the wider global crisis and the desperate efforts in Japan to find some solution to mounting poverty and economic isolation. The Kwantung Army, which took its name from the Japanese concession area on the Chinese Manchurian coast, known as the Kwantung Leased Territory, had been plotting for some years to extend the Japanese Empire into mainland China. Provoked by the scale of the economic crisis, and mindful of the persistent threat of Chinese nationalism, the army commanders finally decided to act independently of Tokyo. After Japanese soldiers had themselves blown up the short section of the Japanese-owned South Manchurian Railway (*Mantetsu*), they stormed the local Chinese garrison in the port of Mukden. They captured the rest of the town and, in a carefully planned assault, fanned out from the Leased Territory, first seizing the areas around the main rail network, then driving the 330,000 ill-equipped forces of the local Chinese warlord, Zhang Xueliang, out of the southern and central regions of Manchuria, completing the occupation of the province by early 1932. The army deployed 150,000 men, and for the loss of around 3,000 dead conquered an area almost the size of Europe. Despite the flagrant breach of discipline, the Japanese Showā emperor, Hirohito, approved the action two days later. Almost overnight the Japanese Empire was transformed in size and wealth.[2]

The 'Manchurian Incident' did not directly cause the world war that broke out eight years later, but it did inaugurate a decade of renewed imperial expansion to follow on from the 'new imperialism' of the pre-1914 world and the imperial settlement at the end of the Great War. None of the three states that eventually defined the new imperialism – Italy, Germany and Japan – began with a definite plan or blueprint for expansion, but each acted opportunistically in established spheres of interest. Nor did they concert their imperialism, though they observed each other's achievements closely and drew courage from each other's successes. Even though leaders in all three states hoped that a more general war might be avoided for the moment while their imperial projects were completed, the instabilities provoked by these three separate programmes fuelled the drive to the global war that opened up between 1939 and 1941.

A NEW IMPERIAL AGE

The critical factor for Japan, Italy and Germany was territory. Control over territory, exercised in a variety of formal and informal ways, lay at the heart of empire. The model for this principle of 'territoriality' was the forty years of violent territorial expansion and pacification that preceded the 1930s and was, in some cases, still going on. Indeed, it is only in this longer context that the decisions taken in Tokyo, or Rome, or Berlin to wage their local wars of aggression make historical sense. The discourses of 'race and space' that had supported empire since the late nineteenth century had lost none of their explanatory force for the generation that came to power in the 1930s. Though this form of imperialism appears in retrospect anachronistic, even delusional, the paradigm of empire at the time seemed familiar and near. The results of the redistribution of territory in 1919–23, or the consequences of the economic catastrophe after 1929, only served to strengthen rather than weaken the belief that seizure of more territory and resources was an indispensable means to save the nation, build a stronger economy and satisfy the needs of a superior culture.

Japanese, Italian and German leaders were by no means the only ones to believe that the era of empire was not yet over, despite all the evidence that nationalist ambitions, rising economic costs and persistent insecurity marked the gradual decay of the global imperial project. Rather than drawing the obvious lesson that traditional imperialism was a fading enterprise, they argued that what they needed was more of it, marked with their own particular character. The other factors usually emphasized in analysing the origins of the Second World War – the arms race, diplomatic crises, ideological conflict – were effects of the new wave of empire-building, not causes. The major states in the League of Nations might, perhaps with reluctance, have lived with ideological difference or increases in military spending if that was all that divided them; the factor that the major imperial states could not accept was that the new wave of empire-building, in its raw territorial sense, was now incompatible with their own view of empire and the new language of internationalism they had woven around it.

The central question to ask is why, given all the evident drawbacks to possessing empire, the substantial security risks involved and the growing strength of nationalist sentiment, did these three states decide on 'territoriality' as the principle underlying their challenge to the existing order in the 1930s? These decisions seem all the more remarkable because, unlike the wars before 1914 in which territory could be conquered through large-scale conflict without outside intervention – the South African War or the Italian–Turkish War are good examples – the objects of imperial aggression in the 1930s were all sovereign states and members of the League of Nations, protected, at least on paper, by the principle of collective security. There is no simple answer to this question, and the exact circumstances differed between the three regional zones, but there are nonetheless striking similarities in the justifications and explanations given for control over further territory. It might be added that the generation that grew to political and military leadership in the 1930s was a generation that grew up with the world of imperial fantasies, surrounded by a culture that played up the superiority of modernizing and 'advanced' states as leaders in the march of civilization against the less developed or primitive peoples they conquered, a generation that was profoundly affected by the experience of wars and the violent assertion of modern nationhood. Empire, claimed the Italian Fascist leader Giuseppe Bottai, briefly governor in 1936 of the Ethiopian capital Addis Ababa, had 'worked this desire in me to live war in the depth of my consciousness ... Twenty years or more of my life *inside* war.'[3]

The starting point in explaining the pursuit of territorial empire is, paradoxically, the nation. In all three states the pursuit of empire was bound up with the aim of achieving national autonomy, which meant in effect releasing the nation from a situation in which its development seemed limited or framed by the existing international order – 'Great power intervention and oppression' as one Japanese pamphlet put it.[4] Japanese nationalists, a *Mantetsu* official explained, saw Manchuria as 'a lifeline ... from which it is impossible to retreat if the nation expects to exist'.[5] These forms of what has been called 'catastrophic nationalism' anticipated the possible extinction of national self-expression, and called for the urgent reassertion of the national mission.[6] Mussolini regularly invoked the idea that Italy's development was strangled by the string of British possessions in the Mediterranean that allowed Britain 'to encircle, to imprison Italy'.[7] Asserting national interest was regarded as a necessity to protect the home population by guaranteeing its economic future and its demographic development, as well as supplying a more secure sense of national identity as one of the major nation-empires, rather than a subordinate power. 'We want an *empire*,' Hermann Göring told an English acquaintance in 1937 during a discussion about what was inhibiting Germany's national future.[8]

In each case, nationalist discourse described the nation as special, destined to dominate and lead the region around it. 'One nation in Europe must assert its authority over the others,' wrote the German political commentator Wilhelm Stapel. 'Only the German nation can be the agent of that new imperialism.'[9] In turn, the national population was supposed to prove itself worthy to take part in the regeneration of the nation. 'We are becoming and we will become,' declared Mussolini in 1933, 'ever more a military nation.'[10] In Germany, the 'national reawakening' in 1933, with the National Socialist revolution, was bound up with the idea that the national body could now assert its true strength, uncorrupted by the alleged internationalist and cosmopolitan threats from Jews, Marxists and liberals, which might have turned Germany, so Hitler had feared, into a 'second Switzerland'.[11] In Japan, where the military leadership came to dominate national politics from 1931 onwards, a widespread campaign to raise national awareness and enthusiasm for territorial expansion was inaugurated – the 'national defence' campaign – which played on the themes of national honour and sacrifice for the nation. Criticism of the new direction was stifled, as it was in Italy and Germany, by the secret police and the censor. Here, as in Europe, the pursuit of national autonomy justified the new imperialism, and in turn created a bond between state and people in constructing a new order.[12] Empire was seen as an essential signal of national virility and racial value, and an arena in which conventional moral norms could be set aside, as they had been in the nineteenth century.

The second factor was more practical. The new imperialism was bound up with broader economic ambitions. Empire-building was designed to transcend the limitations imposed by the existing global economic and territorial structures by acquiring additional 'living space' to cope with population pressure and land shortages, securing access to resources of raw materials and food, and establishing an economic bloc where trade and investment would be controlled by the imperial centre rather than the business community. The three states shared a growing commitment to state planning, and a hostility to the Western model of liberal capitalism and the Western values that sustained it. Capitalism, Hitler told an early party rally, 'has to become the servant of the state and not its master'; a 'people's economy' served the community rather than international business interests.[13] Economic imperialism had also to serve the needs of the people. The lure of economic advantage was evident in all three cases. For Italy, the conquest of Libya and Ethiopia was supposed to create fresh agricultural land for anywhere between 1.5 and 6.5 million Italian peasants, who could settle in the empire rather than migrate to the New World. Albania, annexed in 1939, was allegedly so underpopulated that it could absorb 2 million Italians.[14] Here was *lo spazio vitale* (living space), a term as common in Italy as in Germany. Ethiopia was presented as a land of golden opportunity, an Eldorado teeming with untapped mineral resources. Reports on Albania suggested as yet undiscovered sources of oil.[15] Japanese aspirations to control Manchuria were rooted in the hope that at least 5 million poverty-stricken Japanese peasants could be settled there by the 1950s, while Manchuria's rich industrial and raw material resources, already heavily developed with the help of Japanese investment well before the invasion, were regarded as essential to Japan's future in a world where the development of trade and access to raw materials seemed dangerously insecure. Between 1926 and 1931 some 90 per cent of Japanese overseas investment went into Manchurian projects. Without secure control of these assets, so it was argued, Japan could not continue to modernize economically, or to develop the forces necessary to defend the Empire.[16]

The German case was no different. Here ideas about securing further *Lebensraum*, central to Hitler's own view of German development, had wide currency once Germany's economic setbacks in the 1920s and 1930s were blamed on an absence of adequate resources and secure access to markets. Popular propaganda about other European empires highlighted the huge disparities between the size of the motherland and the overall area of the empire – France enlarged by a factor of 22, the Netherlands by a factor of 60, Belgium by a factor of 80. The territory of the British Empire was calculated to be 105 times larger than the home islands. Germany, on the other hand, after the loss of national and colonial territory in 1919, was smaller than it had once been.[17] To create and dominate a Central and Eastern European economic bloc, with controlled trade and self-sufficiency in key resources and food, became a central plank of the Hitler regime's economic policy, but was a view widely shared in Germany. 'Economic space [*Raum*],' Göring claimed in the same 1937 conversation, 'must simultaneously be our political space.'[18] Hitler himself had a crudely economic view of empire. Reflecting on British imperialism in 1928 in his (unpublished) second book, he concluded that for all the rhetoric of exporting culture and civilization, 'England needed markets and sources of raw materials for its goods. And it secured these markets through power-political means.' In the end, national prosperity meant conquest, securing 'the bread of freedom from the hardship of war'.[19]

The third factor was opportunity. The hesitations and frustrations of the 1920s gave way to a new sense that the crisis of the post-war order in the 1930s might make it possible to act autonomously in building a new order, with only limited risk of provoking a greater crisis. These calculations were critical in explaining the timing of the new wave of imperialism. The failure of the international community to cope with the effects of the global recession accelerated the drift towards national solutions to the crisis and a breakdown of collaboration, expressed most clearly in the failed World Economic Conference in London in June 1933.[20] A consequence of the global crisis was the unwillingness of the major League states to run risks at a time when they could ill afford the cost of international policing. The failure of the League to do more than censure Japan for its occupation of Manchuria was interpreted as a clear message that the system of collective security did not work when dealing with major League members. Japanese leaders later boasted that Japan had been 'the herald of the downfall of the League of Nations', without whose initiative at exposing the 'incapacity and worthlessness' of the League, Germany and Italy might not have had the opportunity to pursue their own aggressive policies.[21] It was true that the invasion of Ethiopia, which followed four years later, was also not opposed forcefully, nor was Germany's violation of the Versailles settlement when rearmament was publicly announced in 1935, or in March 1936 when the Rhineland frontier zone was remilitarized. Each successful step invited the belief that Britain and France, as the major empires and League states, would not obstruct the path to further empire-building. 'We think that Geneva's just a collection of old women,' an Italian journalist told a British colleague in Addis Ababa in 1936; 'we all think so, and we have always thought so.'[22] All three states left the League: Japan in March 1933, Germany in September 1933, and Italy in December 1937.

The further failure of Britain and France to prevent German and Italian armed support for General Francisco Franco's nationalist revolt in Spain between 1936 and 1939, or to oppose the German occupation of Austria in 1938, or Germany's break up of Czechoslovakia in the same year, strengthened this conviction, and, above all, persuaded Hitler that Britain and France would make 'extremely theatrical gestures' about a German invasion of Poland, but would once again not intervene militarily.[23] For all three states, however, the critical thing was to act before either the Soviet Union or the United States were able or willing to play a larger part in world affairs. Japan and Germany were well aware that the Soviet Union, building up a major industrial and military presence in the 1930s under the Five-Year Plans, was a potential danger to any future imperialism. One of the factors governing the occupation of Manchuria, despite the long common frontier with the Soviet Union that resulted, was the need to provide a solid defence against any risk of a Soviet move against the Japanese Empire and to safeguard its strategic resources.[24] Hitler, in the one major strategic document that he penned during his dictatorship, the so-called Four-Year Plan memorandum, drafted in August 1936, highlighted the threat the Red Army would pose in fifteen years' time, and the need for Germany to solve the problems of living space well before that.[25] The United States was something of an unknown quantity. Forced back into relative isolation by the catastrophic effects of the economic depression, and reliant chiefly on its navy for hemisphere defence, it was clear that it posed only a future threat – but a threat nonetheless. Throughout, the United States maintained a critical stance towards imperialism of all kinds, even if the American public was not yet willing to embrace the idea of armed intervention to prevent it.[26] For the imperial world, both old and new, the shadows of Lenin and Wilson stalked their ambitions: empire had to be built sooner rather than later.

The sense that building a new order around a renewed wave of territorial imperialism was really possible did not make the decisions to do so easy. The background to the seizure of Manchuria, or the invasion of Ethiopia, or the invasions of Czechoslovakia and Poland, reveals a good deal of hesitation and circumspection on the part of the political leadership in all three countries, despite the later post-war view that they formed part of a grand plan to dominate the globe. Whether they liked it or not, there was still an element of 'permission' needed from the major League powers. Mussolini finally overcame the anxieties of his military commanders and some of his Fascist colleagues about invading Ethiopia by arguing that he had secured, wrongly as it turned out, a verbal agreement from France and Britain that they would not obstruct him. Before the occupation of Albania he dithered over what the other powers might do (though in this case the League simply registered Albanian protest for the record and did nothing at all).[27] The German occupation of the German-speaking areas of Czechoslovakia after the Munich Agreement of 30 September 1938 is usually seen as a triumph for Hitler's bullying diplomacy, but it left the German dictator fuming that he had been denied his short war against the Czechs on the insistence of the Western powers. Before the war against Poland a year later, he insisted to his entourage that there would be no second Munich.[28]

One of the reasons for caution was the much higher visibility of imperial conflicts by the 1930s, including those in the established empires. This was thanks principally to the development of modern media – worldwide newspaper reporting, popular newsreels and radio – but also to the work of the League of Nations, which, for all its alleged timidity, gave a public platform to debate violations of national sovereignty, including very public discussion of Japan's illegitimate seizure of Manchuria and Mussolini's attack on Ethiopia.[29] International debate forced the aggressors to justify their actions in all three cases by claiming speciously that invasion was carried out to protect their interests against failed states. In the League debate over Manchuria, the Japanese delegation insisted that as a 'single organized state', China was a 'fiction'. They also indicated that Manchuria was not a colony in any formal sense but had been set up as an 'independent' state of Manchukuo, under the deposed Manchu Emperor Puyi.[30] Mussolini justified the assault on Ethiopia on the grounds that the country was nothing more than 'a conglomeration of barbarous tribes', a 'non-state'.[31] Hitler justified extending a German protectorate over the Czech lands of Bohemia and Moravia on the grounds that the national state had ceased to function effectively, even though Czechoslovakia was in every sense a modern European nation rather than a potential colony. In this case, too, the 'protectorate', a term long associated with European imperialism as a way to disguise actual control, was presented as if it enjoyed some political autonomy.[32] War against Poland was announced by Hitler on the morning of 1 September 1939 with the assertion that the Poles, too, were not a state-building people, and that without German rule 'the worst barbarism would prevail', unconsciously echoing Mussolini's condemnation of the Ethiopians in 1935.[33]

Caution was dictated not only by international circumstances but also by the problems of developing any consensus among the political and military elites at home about the course of future policy. This was clearly the case in Japan, where domestic politics was shaped by conflict between civilian political parties and the military, between the army and the navy, and between factions within the army itself. When army commanders in the Kwantung peninsula launched the invasion in September 1931 they did so in defiance of the civilian government. The subsequent stand-off between the army and the politicians brought the resignation of the Minseitō cabinet and a virtual end to civilian supervision of the army's imperialism, but army factionalism persisted until the mid-1930s.[34] Arguments between the navy and the army hinged around the competing claims of the northern or southern advance: the navy wanted to prioritize defence in the Pacific and a possible seizure of the resource-rich European colonies in South East Asia, which was to prove a disastrous choice; the army looked north to the Soviet threat and wanted to consolidate its continental strategy in northern China first, by building a strong, self-sufficient industrial and trading bloc to make possible the further expansion of Japanese military power and to defend the empire. These arguments were suspended rather than resolved with the publication on 7 August 1936 of the 'Fundamentals of National Policy' that endorsed both a strong empire-defence on the Asian continent and naval preparation for extending the empire southwards.[35]

Whatever the arguments for strategic caution, Japanese expansion into mainland China continued remorselessly throughout the 1930s. The Manchurian invasion proved impossible to reverse and, indeed, became the springboard for further Japanese territorial aggression, partly to stabilize the frontier with Nationalist China, partly to secure further resources and communication hubs, and partly because the Japanese army and its political supporters in Tokyo developed an unanticipated appetite for further empire. The spread of Japanese territorial control never attracted the same international attention in the 1930s as Manchuria had done (or the attention of many modern-day historians). On 17 February 1933, 20,000 troops invaded and occupied Rehe province, south of Manchuria and a part of Inner Mongolia. The invasion brought the Kwantung Army within striking distance of the Chinese capital, Beijing. From March to May 1933 the army fought what was called the 'Great Wall' campaign, seizing more territory south as far as the Great Wall and occupying the Chinese city of Tanggu, which subsequently became a major Japanese-controlled port, the largest in China. In 1935 Japanese forces moved on into other Inner Mongolian provinces, and in June forced an agreement on the local

Chinese commander to vacate Hebei province, the area surrounding Bei-jing. Occupation of more of Inner Mongolia allowed the Japanese to sponsor a second 'independent' state of Mengkukuo, a Mongol homeland ruled nominally by Prince Demchugdongrub but dominated, like Man-chukuo, by the Japanese army. In January 1936 the Tokyo government finally approved a strategy to establish control over the rest of northern China, where the army could cut Chinese nationalist forces off entirely from the richest regions of China and the major source of Chinese rev-enues. Within four years of the seizure of Manchuria, Japanese expansion had extended over a vast area of mainland Asia, transforming in the pro-cess the nature of Japan's imperial economy.[36]

The acquisition of Manchuria and other regions of northern China made it possible for Japan at last to challenge the existing economic order in Asia with some prospect of success. The object was to reduce the contrib-ution of the other major trading powers to the whole region and to redirect resources to support Japanese industry. The key was the economic development of resources in Manchukuo and north China. Manchuria had been the industrial heart of China, supplying 90 per cent of China's oil, 70 per cent of its iron, 55 per cent of its gold supplies, and so on.[37] Between 1932 and 1938 Japan invested 1.9 billion yen in the region. The army and government insisted on state economic planning and direction to ensure that its goals were met. The Manchukuo Economic Construction Plan was published in March 1933, and eventually twenty-six corpor-ations were set up for individual products. Chinese banks were taken over or co-ordinated with Japanese banks, a yen currency bloc was established, and the railway network doubled in length. In 1937 a North China Devel-opment Company was set up to ensure that the region would serve planned Japanese interests. North China too was incorporated into the yen bloc.[38] With the resources now available from the new territory, Japanese steel output rose from 2 million tons in 1930 to 5.6 million tons in 1938; coal increased over the same period from 31 million to 49 million tons. The economic expansion was swallowed up by military demands. The army raised its sights, in the Outline Plan of 1937, to a 55-division army by the early 1940s; defence spending was 14 per cent of state spending in 1934, but 41 per cent by 1938. The new economic bloc was declared in 1934 a zone of special interest only to Japan – the so-called Amau doctrine – and in 1938 the prime minister, Prince Konoe Fumimaro, issued a warning that a new economic order had been born in East Asia from which third parties were excluded. The industrial boom, according to the army's Outline Plan, was to supply all the necessary resources for the empire's defence by 1941 and 'strengthen our ability to lead East Asia'.[39]

Japanese military strategy in China was nevertheless ill-defined. The restless border with Chiang Kai-shek's Nationalist China and his warlord partners in the north invited further military encroachment, yet more territory would be difficult to control with relatively limited forces, and it would not solve the problem of establishing a stable context for the exploitation of the territory already acquired. The priority was to control north China politically and militarily rather than embark on a major war against the Nationalist south, and no plans were made for the Sino-Japanese war that finally erupted in July and August 1937. The initiative was for once taken by the Chinese. Chiang's strategy to establish national unity first before confronting Japanese encroachment – which meant in effect destroying Chinese communism – faced growing opposition by late 1936. On a visit to the city of Xi'an in the northern province of Shaanxi, Chiang was kidnapped by General Zhang Xueliang, the erstwhile local warlord, who wanted him to lead a national campaign against the Japanese in co-operation with the communists. After widespread national and international pressure for his release, most significantly from Stalin, Chiang returned to his capital, Nanjing, where he claimed to have had a vision during his brief captivity that it was his destiny to save China from Japan.[40]

The opportunity to adopt a new course came unexpectedly with a trivial incident near Beijing between Japanese and Chinese soldiers, one of many such frictions but one that was taken by Chiang as the moment to finally confront Japan's continued violation of Chinese sovereignty. The so-called 'Marco Polo Bridge' incident (the English name for Lugouqiao, an ancient bridge on the outskirts of Beijing) began on the night of 7 July 1937 when a company of the Japanese China Garrison Army undertook night exercises near the bridge. They came briefly under fire, lost contact with one soldier from the unit and demanded the right to search the small fortress city of Wanping to find him. When access was refused, Japanese troops stormed the city, killing 200 Chinese soldiers in the process. Local commanders on both sides quickly searched for a ceasefire in an incident that scarcely qualified as a *casus belli*.[41] The crisis nevertheless swiftly escalated, reflecting the more profound issues at stake between China and Japan in the 1930s. In Tokyo, the army minister Sugiyama Hajime overrode the more cautious attitude of Konoe's cabinet to order the transfer of three divisions to seize complete control of the region. On 16 July Beijing itself was surrounded; Japanese army operations began on 26 July and within two days the former capital was captured. The nearby port city of Tianjin fell on 30 July. Japanese plans now broadened out to a final settlement of the 'North China Incident' with the destruction of Chiang's main armies and, if possible, the overthrow of his regime. This did not yet mean a major war, but Chiang chose to 'nationalize' the Marco Polo Bridge incident as a threat to the very survival of the Chinese nation. In his diary shortly after 7 July he wrote: 'This is the time for the determination to fight,' and a few days later added that the crisis was 'the turning point for existence or obliteration'.[42] Following the fall of Beijing, he summoned on 7 August a 'Joint National Defence Meeting' of all the leading political and military figures in Nationalist China to ask their support in a major war against the Japanese enemy. The meeting reacted with unanimity. Chiang broadcast the news of war – 'Japan's limitless expansion impels China, gives it no choice, but to act in self-defence' – and his best army units were sent to Shanghai, where Chiang judged that the first critical confrontation should take place.[43]

The Japanese armed forces expected a lightning campaign, 'a quick victory after a short war', first with the destruction of Chiang's main military resources then Japanese occupation of China as far south as the lower Yangtze River. Army leaders hoped to secure Japanese aims within a month; others predicted three months at most. The plans have much in common with the later German Operation 'Barbarossa', where military hubris once again prevailed against military and geographical reality. The Japanese army was numerically inferior but much better armed, better trained and more mobile than its Chinese adversary, yet the plans for military advance took little account of the enormous space and varied geography of the regions now targeted. The advance soon slowed down; Japanese forces were unable to inflict decisive victory against an enemy that could retreat and regroup in the vast Chinese hinterland. From a few divisions in summer 1937, the Japanese army had to expand to twenty-one divisions by the end of the year, thirty-four divisions a year later, and fifty-one divisions by 1941.[44] The further Japanese forces were drawn into central China, the more difficult became logistical supply; the greater the territory to control, the more fragmented the Japanese army became. Chiang's stature grew with what he called the 'war of resistance'. The atrocious nature of much Japanese war-making in China, including the use of poison gas and germ warfare (anthrax, plague, cholera), only inflamed Chinese hatred of the invader and consolidated a sense of national unity that Chiang had tried in vain to create earlier in the 1930s. Chiang's resolve also hardened, in contrast to Japanese expectations that, faced with military reality, he would give up. In 1938 alone, eleven efforts were made to get him to accept peace terms, and all were rejected.

Chinese resistance nevertheless proved fragile wherever it was tested. The Japanese armed forces, renamed the North China Area Army in August 1937, fanned out from the conquest of Beijing west and south

along the main rail routes, whose capture was essential to maintain mobility and supply. Together with a section of the Kwantung Army in
Manchuria, Japanese forces advanced towards Chahar and Shanxi provinces to the west, and soon captured the vital railroad hub at Nankou
from nationalist forces under General Tang Enbo, sent there by Chiang
early in August.[45] Because the Nationalist regime depended on local warlord allies on the northern front line, including Song Zheyuan, whose
forces at Tianjin and Beijing had soon abandoned the battle in July,
Chiang decided that it would be better strategy to attack the Japanese in
a more vulnerable area closer to his own armed forces, the Guomindang
Central Army. His choice of Shanghai as the main battleground would
eliminate the Japanese threat to a major source of revenue and deliver an
adequate response to the seizure of Beijing; it might even involve outside
powers in support, but his principal aim, he told army leaders, was to
conduct a long war of attrition, the opposite of Japan's intention. As
Chiang's forces converged on Shanghai, the Japanese army and navy expanded their strength to five divisions and stationed thirty-two naval vessels in
the port. On 14 August, the small Chinese air force began the campaign
with a disastrous air raid aimed at the Japanese flagship, which instead
destroyed local hotels and a gaming room, killing and injuring more than
1,300 civilians. The large Chinese ground force initially pressed the Japanese back towards the seafront, but the assault stalled. Japan poured in
additional troops, the Japanese navy blockaded the China coast, and the
Japanese naval air force began on 15 August what was to become a prolonged bombing offensive against Chinese bases, ports and cities.

In the last week of August, the Japanese undertook an ambitious
amphibious operation to land divisions near Shanghai, strongly supported
by naval gunfire. By 13 September, Japanese forces were ready for a
counter-offensive across difficult terrain, criss-crossed with water obstacles and improvised Chinese lines of defence. It took until 12 November
to achieve victory, with high casualties on both sides: 40,300 Japanese,
187,000 Chinese (including three-quarters of Chiang's young officer
corps).[46] Japan's imperial headquarters wanted the whole area captured,
now including Chiang's capital at Nanjing, in the hope that this would
bring a decisive end to the war. The victors at Shanghai scrambled along
the route to the capital in pursuit of a demoralized and disorganized
enemy, burning villages and slaughtering their inhabitants. Chiang had
already ordered the government to retreat to Chongqing, far to the west,
while he transferred his military headquarters to Wuhan, further to the
south. A token force was left to defend Nanjing, but it was swept aside
by a wave of Japanese violence against soldiers and civilians alike. The

capital fell on 13 December to the forces of General Matsui Iwane and his
deputy, Prince Asaka, and Japanese troops embarked on days of pillage,
rape and murder.[47] By the end of 1937, the Japanese occupiers had secured
a large area of central and eastern China at great cost but were still far
from securing the quick victory anticipated in July. On 16 January 1938,
Prince Konoe announced that Japan would no longer have any contact
with Chiang's regime – in effect a formal, if belated, state of war.

Despite exceptional military losses and a severe shortage of adequate
armament, Chiang and his generals, now supported by forces loyal to the
independent Guangxi Clique from the far south of the country, prepared
for further major campaigns. The first, and one of the largest of the war,
took place around the major rail junction at Xuzhou to the north of Nanjing involving more than 600,000 troops. Japanese forces approached in a
pincer movement from the north and south. The victorious armies at Shanghai were now organized into the Central China Expeditionary Force and,
together with the North China Area Army, they captured Xuzhou in May
1938 but failed to spring the trap on forty Chinese divisions, whose soldiers
retreated in small groups under cover of a dust storm and fog. In early April
during the approach to Xuzhou, Chinese armies had inflicted one of the few
tactical defeats on the Japanese when an outnumbered force at the town of
Taierzhuang north of Xuzhou was driven out by troops under the command of the Guangxi leaders, generals Li Zongren and Bai Chongxi, but it
was not enough to halt the tide. The fall of Xuzhou was a major defeat, and
it opened the way to Wuhan and control of the whole central Chinese plain
along the Yangtze River. Japanese planners hoped that the seizure of Wuhan
and consolidation of Japanese control over north-central China would
'bring the war to an end', produce a new pro-Japanese government and
make it possible for Japan 'to control China'. Victory would also free Japan
to face what was regarded as the more serious threat in the far north from
the Soviet Union, now supplying Chiang's armies and air force with their
only modern weapons.[48] Chiang reacted to the threat by an act of extraordinary callousness. He ordered the dykes of the Yellow River to be opened
to create a vast flooded area to keep the Japanese away from Wuhan and
the south. His motives were crudely strategic, 'to use water as a substitute
for soldiers', but the cost to the local Chinese population was disastrous, as
was the general Nationalist scorched-earth policy to deny the Japanese
resources. No warning was given and 54,000 square kilometres of low-
lying farmland were inundated; post-war estimates claimed 800–900,000
died (recent research suggests the figure was closer to half a million). More
than 4 million became refugees from the flooded plain.[49]

The Yellow River inundation certainly prevented the rapid seizure of

Wuhan, but in full spate the river could be used by the Japanese navy to move men to the interior and to provide covering fire. In August, the Japanese Eleventh Army was ordered to advance on Wuhan, and through excessive heat, plagued with malaria and dysentery and short of food and supplies, the Japanese infantry trudged or sailed towards the city. The battle involved almost 2 million men and ended with Japanese occupation on 21 October 1938; Chiang moved the centre of power permanently to Chongqing, shielded by mountains from the areas now under Japanese control. Further south, a successful amphibious landing saw Japanese forces capture the major port of Guangzhou (Canton) on 26 October, while the Japanese navy seized the southern island of Hainan in February 1939, thus dominating the Gulf of Tonkin and the French colony of Indochina. The wave of occupations in 1938 completed the acquisition of the richest industrial areas of China – Manchuria, Beijing, Shanghai, Wuhan and Guangzhou – and denied Chiang an estimated 87 per cent of the nation's productive capacity.[50] Japan now occupied a vast area of central and eastern China and the pace of advance inevitably slowed. During 1939 pressure was exerted on the new frontier provinces of Hubei and Hunan, but after two years of major warfare, the capture of China's productive area and the destruction of one Chinese army after another, Japan was little closer to completing the China Incident and consolidating its imperial presence on the mainland.

The Sino-Japanese war had the unusual character that neither side was in a position to win, and the longer the war went on, the less the likelihood of outright victory. Chiang's decision to wage a war that would wear the enemy down by regular attrition made sense only if the Japanese military and government decided that their Chinese empire would have to be given up, and of this there was no prospect. Chinese forces fought with major disadvantages: short of modern weapons, with poor training facilities, a lack of experienced frontline officers, a residual air force entirely dependent on foreign aid, and almost no navy. Although Japan had a modern army by the standards of the 1930s, a substantial army and navy air force, one of the world's largest navies, a significant base of military production at home, and an officer corps with solid battlefield experience, it proved difficult to bring these strengths to bear to win more than local victories. The sheer scale and diverse geography of the regions Japanese forces occupied made victory elusive; rural areas that were temporarily secured were lost once Japanese troops moved on. Because of the fundamental problem of logistics, Japanese forces were expected to live off the land, but villagers soon became adept at concealing their grain in underground stores, making food supply a battle in itself. If there was enough warning of the approaching Japanese, an entire village would decamp to woods or nearby mountains with their food supply: 'cleared the walls and emptied the fields', as Japanese reports put it.[51] The problem of policing rear areas provided wide opportunities for insurgents to establish base areas from which to harass the Japanese enemy, both communists in the north-west and guerrilla fighters sent in by Chiang across the porous frontline between the two sides. In 1939 much of Japan's military effort was devoted to fighting insurgencies rather than pushing on to defeat the regular Chinese armies, while across the summer months troops were needed in Manchuria for a major frontier battle with Soviet forces on the heights of Nomonhan, which ended with an armistice agreed in September. In December 1939, Chiang gathered seventy understrength divisions to launch an unexpected counter-offensive in the north, in the Yangtze valley and around Guangzhou, but the fighting was inconclusive once again. By 1940 both sides faced stalemate. To create the fiction that Chiang really could be replaced, the Japanese in March 1940 established a puppet 'National Government of the Chinese Republic' in Nanjing under the Nationalist renegade Wang Jingwei, who favoured agreement with Japan rather than sustaining the war, but he was in no position to deliver the settlement that the Japanese wanted except to confirm what they had already got.[52] The Japanese government had not expected or wanted a protracted war, with its exceptional economic and human costs, but the dynamic nature of the conflict for a new order in Asia made it impossible to admit that the strategy had failed. By 1941 the war in China had cost 180,000 Japanese dead and 324,000 wounded. Figures for Chinese losses, which were much higher, have proved difficult to calculate with any precision.

Italian imperial ambitions under Mussolini were more modest than those of Japan, but here too territorial conquest was the key component. Mussolini as early as 1919 had declared that imperialism was 'an eternal and immutable law of life' and throughout his dictatorship he never deviated from the desire to make the new Italian nation the core of a Mediterranean and African empire, a modern version of Ancient Rome.[53] His initial hopes were to expand Italian territory in Europe, to acquire the areas in what was now Yugoslavia promised in the 1915 Treaty of London and denied to Italy at the Paris peace conference, but the military leadership, backed by King Vittorio Emanuele III, reined Mussolini back because of the serious risks of major war. As the international order plunged into crisis in the early 1930s, Mussolini and the Fascist Party radicals decided to pursue a course of active imperialism regardless of the opposition. The obvious area for expansion was in East Africa, where for years Italy had tried to extend its influence from the Italian colonies of Eritrea and Somalia into the still independent state of Ethiopia (Abyssinia) – although Mussolini toyed briefly with the dangerous idea of taking Corsica from the French. Conflict against Ethiopia was difficult to reconcile with the caution displayed by some prominent Fascist Party leaders, by the army and by the royal household, or with his own anxiety about not risking his political position. Mussolini finally overrode all objections to the risks involved and, mindful of the success of Japan in defying the League over Manchuria, he ordered plans to be drawn up for the conquest of Ethiopia in the autumn of 1935. Extensive preparations went ahead as Eritrea and Somalia were filled with troops and supplies; the flow was carefully watched by the British as Italian ships, crowded with troops and vehicles, plied their way through the Suez Canal.[54] For Mussolini, Ethiopia would be just the beginning. In 1934 he argued privately that Italy must conquer Egypt, currently under British domination ('we shall only be great if we can get Egypt'), then in March 1935 he added the future conquest of Sudan to the list; he ordered two radio stations, Radio Bari and Radio Roma, to start broadcasting anti-British propaganda across the Arab world, and exploited a ten-year Treaty of Commerce and Friendship signed with the Yemen to embarrass the British in their neighbouring protectorate of Aden.[55] In Malta, local Italian Fascists clamoured for recognition that Malta was really an Italian island under the heel of British colonialists and should return at some point to the Italian motherland, while the Italian navy drew up contingency plans to seize the island.[56] Mussolini's imperial vision saw the Eastern Mediterranean and north-east Africa as stepping stones to a new Roman Empire.

The invasion of Ethiopia was prepared as a short military campaign, an Italian blitzkrieg, but few plans were made for the period after the conquest and little effort made to understand the nature of the people Mussolini wanted to subject to Italian rule. At the same time, he came under pressure from the British and the French, who proposed various schemes to give Italy a greater say in Ethiopian affairs, even a limited League mandate over part of Ethiopian territory, to make war unnecessary. However, Mussolini had embarked on his empire-building precisely to escape the situation in which Italy could be compensated only at the behest of the League powers, and on 22 September 1935, despite the reservations of the king and the Italian Colonial Ministry, he rejected the League proposals. By then it was too late to opt for a limited solution because there were 560,000 men and 3 million tons of supplies packed into Italy's cramped colonial territory in the Horn of Africa.[57] On 3 October, citing Ethiopian provocation, the Italian army and air force, under the overall command of General Emilio De Bono, moved forward on the northern and southern fronts. The Ethiopian emperor, Haile Selassie, ordered the traditional war drum of the empire to be pounded in front of his palace in the capital Addis Ababa summoning his people to combat. It was an asymmetric conflict, which Mussolini wanted to finish swiftly to avoid further international complications or League interference, but it soon stagnated. Haile Selassie, aware of the uneven balance of forces, ordered his armies to fight a guerrilla war to take advantage of the topography and Italian disorientation: 'Hide, strike suddenly, fight the nomad war, steal, snipe and murder singly.'[58]

This was the largest colonial war since the South African War thirty-five years before. The outcome was predictable, but under De Bono the Italians made slow progress. By December, Mussolini was forced to consider the possibility of settling for limited territorial gains. British and French politicians were pressing him to accept this outcome at the expense of Ethiopian sovereignty, until the so-called Hoare–Laval Pact (named after the two ministers who devised the offer) became public and, in the resulting outcry, had to be disavowed. De Bono was replaced by General Pietro Badoglio in November; in December, General Rodolfo Graziani, attacking northwards from Somalia, won a battle at Dolo, using poison gas for the first time on Mussolini's direct orders. Heedless of their emperor's advice, Ethiopian commanders opted for open battle. After two engagements at Tembien and the defeat of 50,000 Ethiopians at Amba Aradam, Ethiopian military resistance was destroyed by a combination of anti-personnel bombs and poison gas (both mustard gas and phosgene), which undermined the coherence of army units and provoked widespread demoralization.[59] Mussolini still considered the possibility of imposing a protectorate, or a puppet state under Haile Selassie like the puppet state of Manchukuo, but with the fall of the Ethiopian capital in May 1936, he decided on outright annexation. On 9 May he announced to an ecstatic crowd in the Piazza Venezia in Rome, 'Italy finally has its empire.'[60]

The claim proved premature. The whole of Ethiopia was not yet conquered and a vicious pacification war was fought over the following year. The cost for the Italian forces was high: 15,000 dead and 200,000 wounded. More than 800,000 Italian soldiers and airmen served in the war to create what was now called Italian East Africa (*Africa orientale italiana*). From Ethiopia's scattered forces and civilians caught in the crossfire an estimated 275,000 died.[61] More deaths followed the Italian victory. Mussolini ordered the execution of any Ethiopian nobles who refused to acknowledge and collaborate with the new Italian administration, as well as the elimination of religious leaders, alleged sorcerers and witches, and local 'minstrels' who traditionally travelled through Ethiopian society bringing news and rumours. In February 1937, following a failed assassination attempt on the Italian governor, Graziani, an orgy of reprisal took place in Addis Ababa that left at least 3,000 Ethiopians dead, women raped and houses looted.[62] The new regime soon institutionalized racial difference. Ethiopians could not become citizens but remained subjects; marriage was banned between Italians and Ethiopians in December 1937; cinemas, shops and public transport were segregated. In 1939 a decree was introduced imposing penalties for anyone violating the principle of racial difference under the title 'Sanctions for the Defence of Racial Prestige against Natives of Italian Africa'.[63]

What Mussolini had hoped would be a swift victory turned into a long, draining conflict. A large garrison had to be maintained and paid for: in 1939 there were still 280,000 troops in East Africa. Casualties mounted as local Ethiopian resistance challenged Italian suzerainty; the harsh three-year pacification campaign resulted in 9,555 Italian dead, 140,000 sick and wounded, and unnumbered thousands of Ethiopian victims.[64] Defence spending in Italy had been 5 billion lire in 1932–3 (22 per cent of government expenditure), but by 1936–7 it totalled 13.1 billion (33 per cent) and in 1939–40 reached 24.7 billion (45 per cent). The war in Ethiopia cost an estimated 57 billion lire, paid for by loans and taxes; later intervention in Spain cost a further 8 billion.[65] The effort to construct 2,000 kilometres of modern roads to make it easier to police the new colony almost bankrupted the colonial budget.[66]

The rising levels of military expenditure could not be compensated by any economic advantages brought about by extending the empire. Unlike the Japanese experience in Manchuria, trade with Ethiopia remained one-sided. Exports to the empire rose from 248 million lire in 1931 to 2.5 billion in 1937, but chiefly to meet the extensive military demands. The idea that Ethiopia would supply the food to feed Italians in the empire and export a surplus to Italy proved a chimera: in 1939 100,000 tons of wheat had to be imported into Ethiopia as crop yields declined, and in 1940 only 35 per cent of the region's needs could be produced locally. Although it was intended to modernize Ethiopian agriculture by bringing in millions of Italian migrants, only 400 peasants had arrived by 1940, 150 of them bold enough to bring their families with them.[67] There were more workers than farmers, but the 4,000 Italian firms that operated in East Africa largely serviced the huge military presence, or looked for quick, short-term profits rather than undertaking the economic transformation of the new African empire. There was some effort made to search for oil and minerals, but without success. The Italian governor of Harrar province in Ethiopia deplored the corruption and self-seeking brought on by 'gold fever', but in truth there were few riches for Italians to enjoy in the heart of the new empire.[68] The search for additional foodstuffs for Italy's population, which the conquest failed to solve, had in the end to be remedied by a strict policy of domestic self-sufficiency or 'autarky'. Wheat imports fell by two-thirds between 1930 and 1940 while domestic wheat production expanded by almost one-third. Investment in industry to sustain the new commitment to empire and its defence expanded substantially, but it all had to be found from domestic resources and required, as in Japan, increased intervention by the state in planning industrial development.[69]

In the end the new empire brought a brief wave of enthusiastic nationalist support but little else. This did not stop Mussolini from capitalizing on what he regarded as his new-found status as leader of an autonomous nation-empire. In defiance of the Western powers, he committed air and land forces to support Franco's nationalist rebellion through almost three years of combat in the Spanish Civil War. The Italian *Corpo truppe volontarie* in Spain numbered 30,000 by August 1937, and eventually over 76,000 Italian soldiers, airmen and Fascist militia served on the Nationalist side, fighting in some cases against Italian anti-Fascist exiles supporting the Spanish Republic. A further 3,266 Italians died during the campaign, raising the total dead from the wars of the 1930s to more than 25,000.[70] Collaboration with German 'volunteers' in Spain moved Mussolini closer than ever to Hitler's Germany, though Italian leaders were keen to ensure that Italy's expanding vision of empire was independent of anything Germany might do. Mussolini, in particular, soon speculated on the possibility of new imperial targets. In a private conversation in 1938 he sketched out aspirations to dominate the southern Balkans as far as Istanbul, to seize Tunisia and Corsica from France, and to annex the British and French Somali colonies in the Horn of Africa; in February 1939 he imagined expelling the British Empire from the Mediterranean basin by taking the Suez Canal, Gibraltar, Malta and Cyprus.[71] Fantastic as these remaining ambitions now seem, the relative success in Ethiopia, and Mussolini's growing confidence that he could replace the 'age-weakened forces' of the old empires, made them seem less fantastic at the time. The Fascist phase, as the Italian anti-Semite Telesio Interlandi put it in 1938, was defined by 'a will to Empire'.[72]

This will found expression again in the Italian takeover of Albania. Like Ethiopia, Albania was widely regarded as a natural object for annexation. A brief protectorate exercised by Italy between 1917 and 1920 had to be given up under international pressure and Albania became a member of the League of Nations. A 1926 defensive alliance gave Italy virtual responsibility for the defence of Albania, while close economic ties were forced on the Albanian ruler Ahmet Zogu (better known as King Zog).

Nevertheless, Zog and his political allies wanted to retain independence and, despite Italian hopes that some kind of protectorate might be re-established in the 1930s, no further gains could be made.[73] By the late 1930s, with Italy's new imperialism well established, Mussolini and his foreign minister (and son-in-law) Galeazzo Ciano, moved to convert informal influence into direct rule. There were strategic benefits, since control of Albania meant domination of both sides of the Adriatic Sea. It was also a potential foothold for the construction of a European dimension to Italy's empire, which Mussolini had hoped for since the 1920s. Italy still ruled the distant Dodecanese islands, taken from Turkey in 1912 and confirmed as an Italian possession in the 1923 Treaty of Lausanne. Reinforced with an army garrison and airfields within striking distance of the Suez Canal, ruled by a governor general with plenary powers, the islands were Italy's first small step to a larger empire in Europe and the Levant and a model for the takeover of Albania.[74]

Acquisition of Albania as part of Italy's empire presented the inviting prospect of eventually linking the territory from the Adriatic to the Aegean under Italian rule. Plans were initiated in May 1938 to annex Albania, supported by spurious claims that the country was rich in oil and chrome to feed Italy's war economy, and by early 1939 they were ready. After the German occupation of Prague in March 1939, which provoked no Western intervention, Ciano favoured immediate action. Mussolini hesitated once again; both the king and the army were unimpressed by the plan and anxious that Italy lacked the military capability, bogged down in Ethiopia and Spain, to take on more commitments. The end of the Spanish Civil War in March 1939, when the Italian Littorio Division captured the last Republican outpost in Alicante, freed up resources. An ultimatum was presented to King Zog on 5 April to turn Albania into an Italian protectorate, and, following the expected refusal, 22,000 Italian troops, supported by 400 aircraft and 300 small tanks, invaded early in the morning of 7 April. The operation was hastily put together and poorly organized. Soldiers who did not know how to drive were given motorcycles; staff who knew no Morse code were recruited to signals units; infantry could be seen in photographs of the invasion beaches cycling into battle, a striking contrast with the images of German troops marching through Prague.[75]

The deficiencies were masked by Italian propaganda which hailed the invasion as a triumph of modern arms, but it succeeded only because there was almost no armed opposition. Italian casualty figures remain contested. The official loss was reported as 12, but Albanian estimates suggest anywhere between 200 and 700 Italian deaths. Zog fled from his capital and on 13 April the Italian monarch was declared king of Albania.

Although, like Manchukuo, Albania was not formally a colony but a puppet state, the country was exploited along colonial lines. A lieutenant general was appointed, and the Albanian administration dominated by Italian advisers; the economy was controlled or taken over by Italian interests; Albanians became subjects of the Italian king; the Albanian language was forced to take second place to Italian in public life; resistance was crushed by a tough police presence. Even Ciano, who benefitted extensively and corruptly from his role in Albania, complained that the new Italian administrators 'treat the natives badly' and 'have a colonial mentality', but this was an inevitable consequence in an authoritarian state committed to crude methods of territorial expansion.[76]

The imperialism embarked upon by Japan and Italy meant in the end a commitment to large-scale military mobilization and war-making across most of the 1930s. In both cases hundreds of thousands of young Japanese and Italian men experienced warfare for years on end long before the coming of global conflict: the Japanese armed forces from 1931 onwards, the Italian army and air force almost continuously from the pacification of Libya in 1930–31 to the Albanian invasion in 1939. By contrast, Hitler's Germany began its programme of expansion later and, for most of the decade, acquired further territory through a series of bloodless coups. Only in 1939 with the invasion of Poland did German soldiers fight a war for empire on the scale of China or East Africa. The assertion of national autonomy meant something very different for Germany as a disarmed and impoverished power. The first years of Hitler's government were spent in rejecting the strategy of 'fulfilment' of Versailles briefly pursued in the 1920s. In October 1933 the German delegation walked out of the Disarmament Conference at Geneva in protest at the failure of other states to disarm. In the same year, the regime defaulted on Germany's major international debts and formally repudiated reparations. In 1936 the Rhineland was remilitarized, tearing up the 1925 Locarno agreement. But despite the publicity surrounding the challenge to Versailles and Locarno, German leaders pursued a cautious strategy while Germany was still weakly armed. When the Rhineland was reoccupied on 7 March 1936, Hitler was observed to be in a state of high anxiety lest he had pushed his early ambitions too far. The young architect Albert Speer found himself on Hitler's train that day on its way to Munich, and later recalled 'the tense atmosphere that emanated from the Führer's section'. Hitler, he claimed, always looked back at the remilitarization as 'the most daring' of his undertakings.[77]

There were two major priorities for Hitler before there could be any thought of constructing imperial living space: economic recovery from the

disastrous situation brought on by the economic crisis, and the remilitarization of Germany to a level that would restore Germany's great power
status and provide the room for manoeuvre in whatever direction the
regime chose to move. Rearmament began in 1933, expanded with a five-
year programme in 1934, and was publicly declared, in defiance of the
peace settlement, in March 1935. Expenditure rose from 1.2 billion
Reichsmarks in 1933/4 to 10.2 billion in 1936/7, by which time much of
the military infrastructure had been restored. The production of weapons
and training of conscripts was a long-term programme. High levels of
defence spending, as in Japan and Italy, required close supervision by the
state of the rest of the economy to avoid an economic crisis and to control
consumer spending by a population that had experienced years of poverty
and unemployment and now wanted to spend again. Plans were put in
place to make Germany more self-sufficient in food and raw materials
and less reliant on a potentially hostile world market, while at the same
time creating a German-dominated trading bloc in central and south-
eastern Europe as a safety net in case of an international crisis. Between
1934 and 1939 trade deals with Romania, Yugoslavia and Hungary
shifted the balance of Eastern European trade strongly in Germany's
favour. The purchase of oil and food raised exports from Romania to
Germany between 1933 and 1938 from 18 per cent of Romanian trade to
37 per cent.[78] When the Spanish Civil War broke out, Germany used aid
to Franco as a lever to secure advantageous trade deals in yet a further
extension of a German 'informal' economic empire. As a share of Spanish
exports, German trade rose from 11 per cent at the end of 1936 to almost
40 per cent two years later, providing much needed metals for German
military industry.[79] Hitler was obsessed with the role blockade had played
in the Great War and anxious that in any future conflict, Germany would
control enough resources in the European trading bloc, like the Japanese
yen bloc, to shield Germany from external economic pressure.

By 1936 the strains imposed by high defence spending and the slow
revival of international trade brought a crisis. The military leadership and
the economics minister, Hjalmar Schacht, who had masterminded much
of the recovery, wanted to restrain further military spending and encourage trade. Hitler was hostile to the idea of limiting the growth of German
military power at just the point when he felt confident at last about pursuing a more active policy of imperial expansion, and in August 1936 he set
down in a strategic memorandum his views on the economic and military
future. In recognition of the growing Soviet threat, Hitler wanted German
military preparations to be on as large a scale as possible, together with
an accelerated programme of self-sufficiency. The failure to defeat the

Bolshevik threat would lead, Hitler argued, to the 'final destruction, even extermination of the German people'. To find the resources necessary to feed the population and supply the necessary raw materials for the struggle ahead could only be solved, he concluded, by 'expanding the living space, and in particular the raw material and food basis, of the German people'.[80] The direct result of the memorandum was the public declaration of a Second Four-Year Plan in October 1936 (the First had been a re-employment plan), with the party leader and commander-in-chief of the German air force, Göring, as its director. The plan marked a sharp break in German policy. The state now controlled prices, wage levels, the import-export trade, foreign currency transactions and investment. The so-called 'managed economy' (gelenkte Wirtschaft), like Japanese and Italian state economic planning, was essential in order to balance the demands of accelerated rearmament with domestic economic stability.[81] Under the plan, a large-scale investment programme was established for synthetic substitute materials (oil, textiles, chemicals, rubber) to provide the economic foundation for large-scale military production. By 1939 two-thirds of all industrial investment was going into strategic materials, while military spending absorbed 17 per cent of the national product (compared with 3 per cent in 1914) and 50 per cent of government expenditure.[82] Beyond this, additional resources were to be provided by extending German 'living space' into a new European empire.

There is nevertheless much less certainty about exactly what Hitler planned to do to establish the 'living space in the East and its ruthless Germanization' that he had first suggested as a long-term goal to army leaders in February 1933.[83] Despite the efforts of historians to unearth his intentions from the scattered remarks Hitler made from the writing of Mein Kampf onwards, there is little evidence of programmatic planning on Hitler's part, beyond the desire to expand future German living space in Eurasia. Hitler himself was clearly influenced by the discourses he discovered in the early 1920s about 'race and space', which framed much of his subsequent thinking. The idea of conquest in a metaphorical 'east' was borrowed by Hitler from German imperial thinking that stretched back forty years, but aside from Hitler's strong anti-communism and regular assertions that the future of the German people lay 'in the east', there is frustratingly little from the 1930s to suggest what Hitler's precise aims were or how he defined the east in his own mind. The idea that he sought ultimate 'world dominion' remains a speculation, though he clearly wanted German expansion to provide the foundation for an empire that would match the global power of Britain or France, or even of the United States.[84] For Hitler the view of what was possible in practice was reactive rather than programmatic, his strategy opportunistic and short-term, even if his obsession to secure living space was invariable.

By the mid-1930s it was easier to understand who Hitler's friends were than to anticipate his enemies – except for the Jews, who remained consistently in Hitler's vision the principal enemy of the German people in its struggle for national assertion. In the course of 1936 the imperial aggressors, Japan and Italy, drew closer to Germany. In November 1936, Japan and Germany signed the Anti-Comintern Pact to co-ordinate their resistance to international communism (joined a year later by Italy). By 1938 both Germany and Italy had recognized the Japanese puppet state of Manchukuo. In October 1936 Italy and Germany reached an informal agreement, later nicknamed the Axis pact following Mussolini's claim that Europe would now have to revolve around the 'axis' of Rome and Berlin. In the discussions, Hitler confirmed that in his view the Mediterranean was 'an Italian sea', while he assured the Italian leadership that German ambitions now lay 'towards the east and towards the Baltic'.[85] The Italian conquest of Ethiopia, carried out in defiance of the League powers, impressed the German public. In 1937 as many books were published in Germany approving Italian colonization in Libya and Ethiopia as there were critical accounts of the British Empire – 'a pirate state', 'robbing half the world'. In a book on *Colonies and the Third Reich* by Hans Bauer, Italy's conquest of Ethiopia was applauded as a model for Germany to emulate in tearing up the Paris peace settlement and acquiring its own colonial living space.[86]

Speculation in Germany about the direction of Hitler's strategy was reflected in the renewed popularity of the lobby for overseas colonies. As Versailles was rapidly undone, the vociferous minority of colonial enthusiasts in the 1920s hoped that Hitler might find the means to restore the lost African and Pacific territories, or to find new ones. In 1934 the National Socialist Party established a Colonial Political Office under the former colonial administrator (and party leader) General Franz Ritter von Epp, and then in 1936 'co-ordinated' the existing colonial organizations into a new Reich Colonial League (*Reichskolonialbund*) with von Epp as its leader. In 1933 there had been only 30,000 supporters of the colonial lobby, but by 1938 the new League had a million members, by 1943 over 2 million.[87] Propaganda literature on the colonies proliferated, from no more than a handful of publications in the early 1930s to between forty-five and fifty each year later in the decade. Young Germans were targeted with heroic colonial adventure stories and films; a 'Handbook for Schooling Hitler Youth in the Colonies' was produced to prepare them for a colonial future.[88] There was widespread discussion, fuelled by Schacht, that African territories would somehow alleviate the shortages of scarce metals or more exotic foodstuffs. 'It is clearer than ever,' announced the economics minister in a speech in Leipzig, 'that for an industrial state the possession of colonial areas for raw materials to expand the home economy is indispensable.'[89] Yet in the end, the popular clamour for overseas colonies, though manipulated by the Hitler regime in 1936–7 to try to drive a wedge between Britain and France, held little appeal for the new German leadership, whose territorial appetites were continental rather than conventionally colonial. 'We want a free hand in Eastern Europe,' Göring told his British contact in February 1937, and in return Germany would respect Britain's imperial interests.[90] The idea of an African empire resurfaced only later, when the old empires had been defeated in the summer of 1940.

The first time that Hitler indicated a definite programme for expansion was in a meeting held at the Reich Chancellery on 5 November 1937, subsequently made notorious by the notes taken by his army adjutant, Fritz Hossbach. He called together the commanders-in-chief of the armed forces and the foreign minister, Count Konstantin von Neurath, to explain to them the strategy he had now arrived at to solve the German problem of 'space' and the future of the racial community. The size and racial solidity of the German people gave them 'the right to a greater living space'. The future of the nation was 'wholly conditional upon the solving of the need for space'. Overseas colonies were, he considered, an insufficient solution: 'areas producing raw materials can be more usefully sought in Europe, in immediate proximity to the Reich.' The British Empire was weakened and unlikely to intervene, and without Britain, France too would abstain. Hitler told his listeners that Austria and Czechoslovakia, which, he claimed, could feed 5 or 6 million Germans between them, would provide that space and, if international circumstances permitted, sooner rather than later, at some point in 1938. The army and the Foreign Ministry were unenthusiastic, anxious about risking the fruits of economic and military revival.[91] The lukewarm response from the army commanders and von Neurath provoked a significant political revolution. By February 1938 the army leadership had been replaced and the War Ministry scrapped. Hitler assumed the role of supreme commander of the armed forces and created a special institution, the *Oberkommando der Wehrmacht* (OKW) to cement his new position. Foreign Minister von Neurath was sacked in favour of the party foreign affairs spokesman, Joachim von Ribbentrop. Schacht, still critical of the risks of further rearmament and unwilling to relinquish his campaign for gains in Africa, was replaced by the party press officer, Walter Funk, a bibulous and ineffectual personality, dominated now by Göring.[92]

Even this new strategic trajectory was hedged around with uncertainties. Hitler was aware that the timing of the start of German expansion depended on the attitude of the other major powers and the extent to which they might be distracted by anxieties over the Japanese and Italian threat, or the opaque menace of growing Soviet power. But in the end, the possible date of 1938 became the firm date. A month after the 'Hossbach' meeting, the army was told to prepare contingency plans for the occupation of Austria and Czechoslovakia. By March 1938 Hitler judged that circumstances were favourable enough to take the first step. The consequences were not predictable, and Hitler hesitated as he had done with the Rhineland. In the end Göring took the lead in forcing Austrian submission and permitting the entry of German troops on 12 March. The absence of serious international protest paved the way to the next decision. On 28 May Hitler called a meeting of the military leadership, confirming that the provisional plans for 'Case Green', the invasion and conquest of Czechoslovakia, would go ahead. The army chief of staff, General Ludwig Beck, noted Hitler's assessment of the opportunity: 'Russia: will not take part, not geared up for war of aggression. Poland and Romania: Fear of Russian aid, will not act against Germany. East Asia: Reason for England's caution.' Hitler concluded that the time had come to act: 'favourable moment must be seized ... Lightning march into Czechoslovakia.' Decisive, coercive action in Central Europe, like the Italian invasion of Ethiopia, was also a signal that Germany now disregarded the old international order and wished unilaterally to construct a new one.

The subsequent story of British and French intervention and the agreement at Munich on 30 September to allow Germany to occupy the majority German areas of Czechoslovakia is well known. Though Hitler wanted a short, imperial war – not least to match the action already taken by Japan and Italy – a European crisis provoked much more international concern than distant Manchuria and Ethiopia. On 28 September, following meetings the day before with a British envoy, Sir Horace Wilson, sent by Neville Chamberlain to explain that an invasion of Czechoslovakia would result in war, Hitler was reluctantly persuaded by Göring and von Neurath that he should take the Czechs by stages. So anxious were a number of senior commanders about the risks Hitler ran that they began to consider a coup against the dictator in the autumn of 1938, though it was to be another six years and after several major defeats before a coup materialized. In the end, Hitler backed down from his small war and accepted a compromise that gave Germany almost immediate access to the Sudeten German areas of the Czech state, occupied on 1 October. The Czechs had to accept virtual autonomy for the Slovak half of the state, and to reach unfavourable economic agreements with Germany. Six months later, on 15 March 1939, after the Czech president, Emil Hácha, had been summoned to Berlin and subjected to heavy, irresistible pressure by Germany's leaders, German forces marched into Prague. The following day, Hitler declared a protectorate over the provinces of Bohemia and Moravia. Slovakia was established as a puppet regime.

The imperial character of these annexations is evident, though it was a different kind of imperialism from the imperialism of the traditional dynastic empires that had ruled the region only twenty years before and more akin to the pattern of empire practised outside Europe. Even the case of Austria, which was incorporated into a Greater Germany with the backing of an almost unanimous plebiscite, was part of this process. Austrians found themselves subject to a legal system they had not instigated, while the name chosen for the region, the Ostmark, echoed the term coined for the area of internal colonization before 1914. The Austrian past was extinguished in favour of a German present. The Sudeten areas acquired as a result of the Munich Agreement were similarly incorporated into Greater Germany, overturning the ambitions of local German-speaking nationalists for an autonomous Sudetenland. In the Czech lands the protectorate resembled the system imposed in Manchukuo: the Reich protector acted as a viceroy in the region, responsible for external affairs and defence, while a system of local governors (*Oberlandräte*) oversaw the police, the local administration, and the enforcement of laws and ordinances that derived ultimately from the government in Berlin. A Czech administration was kept in place under Hácha for organizing the day-to-day running of the protectorate, but according to the 16 March decree its activities had to be carried out 'in harmony with the political, military and economic needs of the Reich'. Some 10,000 German officials supervised the work of 400,000 Czechs.[93] The armed forces exercised a separate military layer of supervision over key strategic resources, civil defence, the press and propaganda, and the conscription of Czech Germans. In all the annexed areas and the protectorate, citizenship became a defining factor in separating citizens from subjects on the basis of race, as it was in Ethiopia. In Austria and the Sudetenland citizenship was reserved for those classified as ethnic Germans, while Jews and non-Germans became subjects; in the protectorate, Czech Germans could apply for Reich citizenship (though many did not), but Czechs remained subjects of the Reich protector, while Jews lost even this limited privilege. Germans who married Czechs lost their right to citizenship, encouraging a racial apartheid in the protectorate. Citizens and subjects were treated by two different legal regimes: citizens subject to Reich laws, Czechs to the ordinances and decrees enforced by the viceroy. Czech resistance was crushed savagely with the same lack of restraint practised by Italy in Ethiopia or Japan in China.[94]

Throughout Austria, the Sudetenland and the protectorate, key economic resources were taken over by German state corporations or German banks, while gold and foreign currency resources, either belonging to the state or privately owned by local Jewish populations, were seized by force and allocated to the German central bank.[95] The key institution was the Reichswerke 'Hermann Göring', a state-backed corporation established in June 1937 to acquire state control of German iron-ore supplies. The Reichswerke quickly acquired a controlling interest in the major Austrian iron-ore and machine-engineering sectors by compelling private interests to sell their capital stakes to the state. In the Sudetenland, where the Four-Year Plan organization had already identified a range of important mineral resources well before its annexation, the Reichswerke moved at once to take control of the supplies of lignite (brown coal), which was then used to develop local synthetic oil production at Brüx.[96] The protectorate provided not only additional mineral resources, and extensive iron and steel works, but also the major European arms producers Škoda and the Czech Armaments Works. By the end of 1939 the Reichswerke organization had a controlling shareholding in all these companies. Firms owned or part-owned by Austrian or Czech Jews were expropriated under legislation to 'Aryanize' Jewish commercial interests, a process that had begun in Germany at the start of the dictatorship. Louis Rothschild was held as a hostage by the German occupiers until he had signed over to the Reich the extensive Rothschild holdings in the protectorate. The capital assets of the Reichswerke eventually reached over 5 billion Reichsmarks, five times larger than the nearest German corporation, the chemical giant I. G. Farben. The resources available for the Reich, like the state-controlled Manchurian resources for Japan, helped to sustain high levels of military production and to do so within a closed economic bloc, controlled entirely from Berlin, which provided the capital needed for colonial exploitation.[97]

This was not fully 'living space' in the sense in which Hitler appears to have understood it. Though he spoke at the Hossbach meeting about expelling a million people from Austria and 2 million from Czechoslovakia, the population transfers which took place largely involved the emigration of around half a million German, Austrian and Czech Jews, who sought refuge abroad from the racial remodelling explicit in German plans for the captured territories. There was much discussion among German officials responsible for the new territories about whether future policy should be based on racial assimilation or racial separation. Only later in the war did the regime explore the prospect of expelling all Czechs who could not be 'Germanized' – an estimated half of the population – and treating the protectorate as an area for German settlement.[98] A programme to dispossess Czech farmers and to settle their lands with Germans began on a small scale, growing in scope only later: by 1945 16,000 farms occupying 550,000 hectares had been confiscated.[99]

It is not clear when Hitler decided that living space in the east could be found more usefully in Poland. Until the end of 1938, the Poles were regarded as potential allies in a German-dominated anti-Soviet bloc, who would hand back the German lands they were granted at Versailles and voluntarily become a German satellite. Only when the Polish government repeatedly refused the German request for an extra-territorial rail and road link across the Polish Corridor and the incorporation of the League-run Free City of Danzig back into Germany did Hitler decide to launch against the Poles the small war he had been denied in 1938, and to take Polish resources by force. Poland now contained the extensive former German coal and steel region in Silesia, but also promised wide areas for German settlement and the production of an agricultural surplus to feed the German population. At the meeting on 23 May 1939 when Hitler presented to the military leadership his intentions against Poland, he claimed that 'Danzig is not the object in this case. For us it involves rounding off our living space in the East and securing our food supplies.' Food supply could only come from the East because it was sparsely populated, continued Hitler. German agricultural proficiency would raise the productivity of the region many times over.[100]

An imperial war against Poland nevertheless ran the same risks of intervention from the other European powers as the Czech crisis the year before. Hitler might well have accepted a second protectorate solution if the Poles had simply acquiesced to German threats, but at the end of March 1939, against Hitler's expectations, Britain and then France publicly guaranteed Polish sovereignty. While over the summer months the German military campaign was carefully prepared, German diplomacy sought to separate the Poles from their guarantors, and the two guarantors from each other, though without success. Propaganda was used to whip up domestic support for a war to protect the Germans living in Poland from alleged Polish atrocities and to supply a pretence for invasion. Since Britain and France would not be moved from their support of Poland, Hitler sought an agreement with the Soviet Union to guarantee that a combined Soviet-British-French bloc would not obstruct his small war. The Non-Aggression Pact, signed on 23 August 1939, was used by Hitler to justify to all around him that the Western states would now no longer dare to intervene. Though it has often been argued that Hitler sought a general war in 1939 because the costs of rearmament to a brittle and overstretched economy forced his hand to wage a war against the West before it was too late, almost all the evidence demonstrates that Hitler wanted a localized war to support the expansion of living space in the East, rather than a major conflict with the British and French empires – an end to a decade of empire-building rather than a prologue to world war.[101] There were certainly economic motives for seizing more land and resources but not for waging world war, for which these additional resources would eventually be needed when, or if, it happened. Hitler's view was that major war should be prepared for only by 1942–43, when the armament programmes were completed.[102] On 21 August, Hitler authorized the introduction only of limited economic mobilization, designed for a local and temporary state of conflict; the order to initiate the full mobilization of the economy was given only after Britain and France had declared war.[103]

The risks multiplied, however, the closer drew the planned date for invasion. Hitler hesitated once again. Invasion was scheduled for 26 August, then postponed when news arrived of an Anglo-Polish Alliance, together with the information that Italy would not honour the Pact of Steel, signed in May, to join Germany's side in a more general war. Intelligence from London suggested that this time Britain was not bluffing.[104] Hitler overcame his doubts and issued the order to march on 28 August, for a campaign to begin on the morning of 1 September. His long-held view that the French and British empires were in terminal decline, hedged about with fears of Italian ambitions in the Mediterranean and Japanese ambitions in East Asia, fed a fixation that the West would find some way to let Poland down once it was clear that the Poles were militarily beyond help. One of his military adjutants noted that Hitler made it clear he wanted war with the Poles but 'with the others he wanted no war at all'. Göring later insisted to his post-war interrogators that Hitler was sure he would reach an agreement with the West over Poland as he had over Czechoslovakia. 'As we saw it,' claimed Göring, 'he held much too rigidly to this.'[105] Hitler rejected all advice to the contrary because he did not want to be cheated of his first imperial war by a show of inconsistent leadership and misplaced anxiety. 'I have at last decided,' he told his foreign minister, von Ribbentrop, 'to do without the opinions of people who have misinformed me on a dozen occasions, and I shall rely on my own judgment, which has in all these cases [from the Rhineland to Prague] given me better counsel than the competent experts.'[106]

The sudden, bold decision, which this time remained unwavering, had much in common with Mussolini's rejection of the timid advice in 1935 not to risk war over his projected invasion of Ethiopia. Like the African adventure, the build-up of forces before the war made it difficult to contemplate abandoning the campaign. For many German military commanders, the war with Poland was a welcome renewal of the drive to the East in the Great War, in which many of them had fought, and of the post-war conflicts along the new German–Polish frontier in 1919–20, when demobilized soldiers joined the volunteer *Freikorps* to fight the Poles. Poland was regarded as a mere 'seasonal state' (*Saisonstaat*), the illegitimate offspring of the peace treaty, and an area ripe for future German settlement.[107] The army chief of staff, General Franz Halder, expressed in spring 1939 a 'sense of relief' to an audience at the Armed Forces Academy that war with Poland was now on the agenda: 'Poland,' he continued, 'must not only be struck down, but liquidated as quickly as possible.'[108] Soldiers were told in the summer of 1939 that the enemy they faced was 'cruel and sly'; an armed forces' report on the Poles claimed that the peasant population was marked by 'cruelty, brutality, treachery, and lies'. Halder considered Polish soldiers to be the 'stupidest in Europe'. German officers easily imbibed the anti-Polish prejudice and the sense that Poland deserved its fate in blocking German expansion into 'ancient German land', as the commander of an infantry division told his men on the eve of the invasion. 'This,' he continued, 'is the living space of the German people.'[109] Hitler did not consider the coming war to be a conventional great power conflict but a war against a barbarous and threatening enemy in which no pity should be shown, one to be waged, he told his commanders on 22 August, with 'the greatest brutality and without mercy'. Later that same day, Hitler spoke about the physical elimination of the Polish people from a land that was to be 'depopulated and settled by Germans'.[110]

At 4 p.m. on 31 August Hitler ordered the invasion to begin the following morning. He assured Halder that 'France and England will not march'. Joseph Goebbels, Hitler's propaganda minister, noted in his diary that 'Führer does not believe England will intervene'.[111] During the night, under the codename 'Himmler', an operation was mounted to simulate a Polish attack on German frontier posts: SS men left six dead concentration camp prisoners dressed in Polish uniforms at Hochlinden border station, while at the Gleiwitz radio transmitter a crude message in Polish was broadcast, while a dead Polish prisoner was left on the floor as evidence of Polish territorial violation and a justification for war. This was a device as crude as the sabotage of the Manchurian railway by the Japanese army in 1931. Shortly before 5 a.m. on 1 September, the first German aircraft attacked the small Polish town of Wieluń while the German training ship *Schleswig Holstein*, on a tour of duty in Danzig, opened up its guns on the Polish fort in the harbour. The campaign that followed was designed to be so swift that the Western powers would be presented with a fait accompli. 'Case White' had been worked on since April, and by 1 September there were 1.5 million German soldiers stationed in East Prussia, eastern Germany and Slovakia, supported by 1,929 aircraft and 3,600 armoured vehicles, most of them grouped into 10 motorized divisions and 5 newly created 'Panzer' divisions. These were highly mobile combined arms units with large numbers of tanks, supported by waves of bombers and dive-bombers roaming deep into Polish territory, designed to provide the spearhead for a more conventional army based on foot and horse that followed on to exploit the damage done by the armoured fist.

The Polish army was fully mobilized only late in the day, to avoid antagonizing the Germans. It was, on paper, not much smaller than the German, with 1.3 million men under arms, but it was supported by 900 mainly obsolescent aircraft and only 750 armoured vehicles.[112] Polish preparations were based on more traditional operational experience. The hope was that the Polish armies could hold the attack near the borders while mobilization was completed, and then would retreat in good order to stand their ground around established strongpoints. The air force was soon outmatched; half was destroyed in the first week of combat and a hundred of the remainder were ordered to fly to bases in neighbouring Romania to avoid complete annihilation.[113] German forces rolled forward against stiff local resistance, but after a week they were only 65 kilometres from Warsaw. It was not an entirely asymmetrical battle, as it is often presented; between 13 and 16 September a bitter battle raged along the Bzura River in front of the Polish capital. German losses of armour and aircraft rose steadily. Then, on 17 September, at German prompting, 1 million Soviet forces invaded from the east to occupy a zone of Poland assigned to Soviet interest under the terms of the secret protocol to the Non-Aggression Pact. Battling now on two fronts against high odds, Polish defeat was only a matter of time. Refusal to make Warsaw an open city resulted in heavy destruction by artillery and aerial bombardment from 22 September. Warsaw capitulated five days later, and Modlin, the final Polish redoubt, on the 29th. Limited fighting continued into early October. Some 694,000 Polish military went into German captivity, 230,000 into Soviet, though an estimated 85,000–100,000 escaped into Romania and Hungary. Polish military dead totalled 66,300 with 133,700 wounded; German losses were 13,981 dead and missing with 30,322 wounded, almost the same as Italian losses in Ethiopia, while the Soviet Red Army, facing a thin and demoralized Polish defence, ended up with 996 dead and 2,000 injured.[114] Despite the wide divide in numbers and quality, German aircraft losses were substantial: 285 destroyed and 279 damaged, some 29 per cent of the aircraft committed.[115] On 28 September Soviet and German representatives met to sign a second agreement, a Treaty of Friendship, to draw up the demarcation of their spheres of influence. Within four weeks Poland had ceased to exist as a modern state.

The short campaign was little affected by the news on 3 September that Britain and France would honour their pledge to Poland by declaring war, though the evidence on German streets that day showed alarm and despondency rather than the outburst of national zeal evident in 1914. Hitler remained confident for weeks that their declaration of war was merely pro forma and that they would seek ways of extricating themselves from the commitment once Poland was divided between the two dictatorships. Almost no military or material help was granted to the Poles by the Western powers, who had privately written off Poland as a territory to be restored only later, when the war was won.

In the shadow of a larger war that Hitler had not wanted, the imperial project already begun in the Czech lands was applied more ruthlessly to Poland, where a past language of colonization, commonly used before 1914, was revived to define and justify the subjection of the captive population. Despite the changed character of the conflict after the Western declaration of war, German planners, security forces and economic officials set about establishing a long-term imperial settlement of the region, alongside the demands of wartime improvisation. The object, as one German planner in East Prussia put it on the day of the invasion, was 'an act of total colonization'.[116] Hans Frank, head of the National Socialist Lawyers Association, and governor of the rump Polish area known as the General Government, saw his fiefdom as a 'laboratory for colonial administration', and although the regime in Berlin preferred not to call them colonies, Frank's economics minister, Walter Emmerich, thought German rule really was a 'special European variant of colonial policy'.[117]

The final constitutional arrangement of the captured areas was the subject of much debate. The German conquests were provisionally divided up into a number of distinct units: the province of Posen, taken over by the Polish state under the peace settlement in 1919, was transformed into a new German district, the Wartheland; the former Prussian region further north on the Baltic Sea became the Reichsgau Danzig-West Prussia; the remainder of the territory, including Warsaw, became the General Government, with its capital at Cracow. Upper Silesia, lost to Germany in a plebiscite in 1920, was reincorporated into the Reich. Its industrial resources were taken under German trusteeship and many were assigned to the supervision of the Reichswerke 'Hermann Göring'. A total of 206,000 Polish industrial and commercial businesses were taken over and distributed to German owners or state corporations.[118] The Wartheland and Gau Danzig were known as the 'annexed eastern territories', and a special police frontier separated them off from the rest of Germany to prevent the easy movement of Poles into the Reich. In the case of the Wartheland, the overwhelming majority of the population, 85 per cent, was Polish. Only 6.6 per cent were German and in the city of Posen, its new capital, only 2 per cent.[119] However, the new ruling class throughout the different regions was German. Ethnic Germans were directed to wear a distinguishing badge (since skin colour was no indication of ethnicity). Poles were treated as a colonized people, who were supposed to raise their hats and make way on pavements and footpaths for any German who passed and were banned from theatres and public buildings designated for Germans only. A number of German women who had been trained at the Colonial School for Women in the north German town of Rendsburg for a role in a future overseas empire were now redirected to work in the East (*Osteinsatz*), to practise skills once intended for Africans.[120] Poles were subjects, not citizens. They were ruled by local governors, who were responsible for regional administration and who acted as the link between local government and the ministries in Berlin, and with the security apparatus run by Heinrich Himmler.

The first object of German imperial policy was to destroy any surviving vestiges of Polish national and cultural life and to racially restructure the entire area. Before the invasion, five special action units (*Einsatzgruppen*) were set up by Himmler's second-in-command, Reinhard Heydrich. Composed of approximately 4,250 police and security men, their task was not only to police the rear areas behind the front, but to capture and execute the Polish political, cultural and nationalist elite, as the Italian army and police had done in Ethiopia.[121] The purpose was to decapitate the Polish elite, in order to reduce Polish society to a level that matched the colonial imagination of the 'East', consistent with Hitler's injunction to army leaders in August that he wanted 'the destruction of Poland'.[122] The exact number of men and women murdered during what was known as Operation 'Tannenberg' will never be known with certainty, but they numbered tens of thousands, perhaps as many as 60,000. Some of those murdered were Jews, but the policy was directed principally at the Polish elite. Franz Halder noted after a conference with Heydrich: 'Spatial cleansing: Jews, intelligentsia, clergy, nobility.'[123] Jews were nevertheless victimized in other ways, beaten or humiliated or occasionally murdered, their property seized by German officials or looted by German soldiers. By October many were herded into the first major ghettoes or deported from the annexed territories to the General Government, but they were not yet systematically murdered.[124]

The imperial ideal was eventually to 'cleanse' the whole colonial area of Jews and of Poles who could not be 'Germanized' and to replace them with German settlers, but in the meantime racial segregation and racial subjection was imposed by the new imperial masters as self-defined 'bearers of culture'.[125] On 7 October 1939, Himmler was appointed by Hitler as Reich Commissar for the Strengthening of Germandom, with instructions to organize the 'new territories of colonization by means of population displacements'.[126] Himmler had long been a supporter of the idea of an eastern empire settled by German colonists. He chose the title of his new office himself and began at once a planned programme to settle Germans and to expel Poles from eastern farmlands. A racial register was implemented to identify Poles whose physical features suggested some German blood. Himmler declared in December 1939 that he wanted 'a blond-haired country' in which the 'development of Mongolian types in the newly colonialized East' would be forcibly prevented.[127] The imperial antonyms – civilized/ barbarous, familiar/exotic, cultured/uncultured – were exploited to emphasize the role of difference or 'otherness', as they had been before 1914.

The war against Poland can better be understood as the final stage in a largely uncoordinated movement to found new territorial empires in the 1930s, rather than the conventional view that sees it as the opening conflict of the Second World War. Looked at from this longer perspective, the effort to found new imperial orders linked the fate of Japan, Italy and Germany in the regions in which they had chosen to build them. In all three nations a nationalist consensus emerged in favour of empire after years of popular resentment and national frustration, a view represented by the national leadership, though not entirely caused by it. Through narrowing down strategic options and silencing, often forcibly, those domestic elements that were hostile to or critical of the new imperialism, the three new empire states took risks to achieve what they wanted, yet the more they achieved, the more possible seemed the attainment of the longer-term goal of fragmenting the global order – a new Roman Empire, leadership of Asia, a Germanized Empire in Eastern Europe. But the result was a strategic deadend. The irony is that imperial projects that were supposed to enhance security, to protect the national interest and, in the end, to enrich the metropolitan populations, created instead growing insecurity and high costs, as most imperialism did. The risks were regarded as worth taking because the old international order seemed to be in the throes of collapse, and it is probably the case that if the other major powers had had to deal only with the seizure of Manchuria, Ethiopia and the Czech lands, they would in the end have lived with that changed reality.

The problem was the dynamic nature of all imperial expansion. The new conquests proved to be irreversible improvisations, like much of the empire-building before 1914, and they opened the way to further conflict. The Japanese seizure of Manchuria sucked Japan into a defence of strategic interests in northern China, and eventually into a major war with Chiang Kai-shek's Nationalist regime; Italian occupation of Ethiopia whetted Mussolini's appetite for more, if a major colony could be gained at relatively little cost; Hitler's search for living space proved to be an elastic concept, stretching further as opportunities arose, but it ended with a major international war over Poland that he had not wanted. Both Japan and Germany, despite anxiety about the future menace of the Soviet Union, found themselves against expectations with a long common frontier with it. For Japan the result was two major border conflicts with the Red Army, in 1938 and again in summer 1939. Although the Japanese army was defeated in 1939, a ceasefire was signed on 15 September because neither side wanted to risk an all-out war while the European situation was so uncertain.[128] Hitler postponed potential conflict with the Soviet Union by the Non-Aggression Pact, but he well understood that the new common frontier in occupied Poland was not likely to be permanent. In the background was the unpredictable attitude of the United States as it watched the new empires expand. The common bond for Italy, Germany and Japan was the determination not to let go what had been gained; in all three cases these were territorial acquisitions made through conquest, with a 'blood sacrifice' that was not to be abandoned, as it had allegedly been abandoned after the Great War. There was no way, except large-scale war, for the other powers to expel the new imperialists from their new-won territory. The issue of territoriality cut both ways.

THE WINDING ROAD TO WORLD WAR

The Second World War was a result of decisions taken in London and Paris, not in Berlin. Hitler would have preferred to consolidate his conquest of Poland and complete the German domination of Central and Eastern Europe without a major war against the two Western empires. That this did not happen was largely due to growing confidence in 1939 that Franco-British military and economic strength would be equal to the task of defeating Germany in the long run, and to a growing resolution on the part of both the French and British publics that the threat of a major international crisis, which they had lived with for almost a decade, could only be resolved by picking up the threads of 1918 and fighting Germany once again. For Britain and France, declaring war was a much larger issue than the smaller wars fought by the three aggressor states because they understood that their war would be a global war, involving their imperial interests across every continent, and facing threats in not one theatre, but three. The choice to face Germany first was dictated partly by the accidental circumstances of the Polish crisis, but largely because the two victors in the Great War had come to assume that the unresolved outcomes of the settlement of 1919 made a second round of European warfare unavoidable, after which they hoped to found a more resilient international order in which the peace of Europe and the peaceful pursuit of empire might both be permanently secured.

This was a decision taken after years of instability, but it was a fateful and difficult decision to take after the shattering experience of the Great War. Though the German, Italian and Japanese leadership all imagined that at some point they might face a major conflict with states challenging their new regional empires, they did not want or expect it in the 1930s. For British and French statesmen, on the other hand, it appeared axiomatic that a new war, if it came, would be a renewed 'total war', more deadly and costly because of new weapons, and a profound threat to economic stability. Acceptance of war was only justified if the menace to imperial security and national survival were deemed to be sufficiently dangerous and irreversible. Both states assumed that the growing bellicosity and military strength of the three Axis regimes were directed principally at them, a continuation of the struggle for great power hegemony begun in 1914, rather than the more functional view taken by German, Italian and Japanese leaders that war was the necessary means to secure regional domination of an imperial area. Of the three states, Germany was the one most feared not only because of Germany's potential military and economic strength, but also because Hitler seemed to personify hostility to the Western view of civilization and its values. Throughout the 1930s, the major Western democracies hoped that they had judged the crisis wrongly and that the new generation of authoritarian statesmen they opposed would share their revulsion at the prospect of a renewal of the terrible bloodletting of the Great War and not engage in what British politicians liked to describe as a 'mad dog act'.[129] These were major concerns and they explain the caution with which both states approached the international crises of the 1930s, as well as the eventual decision taken in 1939 that the cataclysm would finally have to be faced, come what may.

The reluctance of the British or French governments to contemplate a second major war in a generation was echoed by the wider public. In both countries during the inter-war years there existed a forceful element in

public opinion hostile to the idea of war as a solution to any future crisis
and fearful about what war might mean. The spectrum of popular anxiety
stretched from former soldiers who had experienced the trenches and
wanted no more war to young socialists and communists in the 1930s for
whom peace was a political commitment. If absolute pacifism (or 'integral'
pacifism as it was called in France) was confined to a minority of the anti-
war movement, hostility to the idea of a new war reached a wide circle.
The major anti-war movement, the British League of Nations Union, had
a nominal membership of 1 million, and campaigned nationwide for the
virtues of peace against the menace of war. In 1936, a large pacifist congress in Brussels established the International Peace Campaign to unite the
anti-war and pacifist lobbies across Western Europe; the British branch
was chaired by Lord Cecil, head of the League of Nations Union and a
major establishment figure.[130] Right up to 1939, the anti-war lobby campaigned for peaceful solutions. The British National Peace Council
organized a petition in late 1938 for a 'New Peace Conference' and had
collected over a million signatures by the time it was presented to the prime
minister just days before Chamberlain gave his historic guarantee to
Poland.[131] The movement against war was reinforced by the widespread
belief that any future conflict would be bound to involve attacks on the
civilian population using a mix of weapons of mass destruction – bombs,
gas or even germ warfare. So embedded did fear of bombing become that
politicians in both Britain and France persuaded themselves that every
effort should be made to avoid general war, particularly against Germany,
if the consequence would be immediate and annihilating air attack against
vulnerable cities.[132] The French prime minister from April 1938, Édouard
Daladier, regarded bombing as 'an attack on civilization itself', while his
pacifist foreign minister, Georges Bonnet, just before the Munich conference in 1938, thought 'war with *bombs*' would result in revolution.[133] On
the eve of the Czech crisis Chamberlain told the Cabinet how he had flown
back from Germany over London and imagined the hail of German high
explosive and gas over the capital: 'We must not lose sight of the fact that
war today is a direct threat to every home in this country.'[134]

There were also profound issues of security in the British and French
global empires which made the prospect of a renewed war, with all its
extravagant costs and dangers, difficult to embrace. It is important to
remember that Britain and France, though leaders of the League system
and, until the mid-1930s, the most heavily armed of the major powers,
were not like the United States in the 1990s: they were relatively declining
powers, with large obligations worldwide, critical electorates unwilling to
endorse war easily, and economies recovering from the effects of the

depression in which the decision to divert resources to large-scale military spending had to be balanced against the social needs and economic expectations of democratic populations. Under these circumstances, commitment to the integrity of the existing international order and the security of the empire, while avoiding major war, involved a complex balancing act. Unlike the aggressor states, Britain and France derived many advantages from the world as it was, and it would indeed have been surprising if the two powers had engaged sooner in warfare against the new wave of imperialism, however much critics then and now might wish they had. For the two global empires there was too much at stake in a rapidly changing world to abandon peace for war. 'We have got most of the world already, or the best parts of it,' claimed Britain's first sea lord in 1934, 'and we only want to keep what we have got and prevent others from taking it away from us.'[135] When the idea of handing back the Tanganyika mandate to Germany was raised in Parliament in 1936, Anthony Eden, then secretary for the colonies, objected that there were 'grave moral and legal obstacles to any transfer of territory'.[136] In opinion polls taken in 1938 to test British and French views on conceding any overseas territory, there were substantial majorities against. Some 78 per cent of British respondents preferred war to abandoning any former German colonies held as British mandates. In response to Italian claims on Tunisia and Corsica, Daladier publicly announced in November 1938 that France would not relinquish 'a centimetre of territory'.[137] Not until May 1940 did the two empires consider giving territory away, in a desperate effort to buy Italian neutrality during the Battle of France. But when the British War Cabinet debated handing over Malta to Mussolini, the majority still demurred, though by just one vote.[138]

Despite efforts in Britain and France to emphasize in the 1930s the importance of imperial unity and the advantages they enjoyed from empire in all its many forms, overseas territory remained a source of persistent insecurity, both internal and external. Arab protest continued in the Middle East mandates and French North Africa. Britain conceded self-government to the Iraq mandate in 1932 (though British informal control continued), conceded an Anglo-Egyptian treaty in 1936 that confirmed virtual independence and joint control of the Suez Canal, and maintained two divisions in Palestine to cope with Arab insurgency and violence between Arab and Jewish populations. The conflict in Palestine was the largest military undertaking by British forces between the wars, and the tough repression of the insurgency resulted in at least 5,700 Arab dead and 21,700 seriously injured, imprisonment without trial and a blind eye to torture by the security forces.[139] In India, following a wave of riots and assassinations, the British used 'civil martial law' to allow them to imprison nationalist and communist opponents during periods of heightened tension – a total of 80,000 political prisoners between 1930 and 1934. Strikes and protests were met with volleys of shots. At Cawnpore in March 1931, 141 were killed; in Karachi in March 1935, 47 more.[140] India was eventually granted a limited measure of self-government in 1935, which enfranchised only 15 per cent of the population and failed to satisfy the majority Congress Party's demand for full independence. There was widespread strike activity and labour protests in African and Caribbean colonies badly affected by the economic slump, in Tanganyika, Northern Rhodesia, Gold Coast and Trinidad; in the African copper belt, workers were shot and killed in a wave of strikes in the middle of the decade, while in Barbados popular protest against economic hardship in 1937 left fourteen dead from gunshots and bayonets.[141]

Much of the protest from poor workers and farmers was blamed on local communist movements, which all imperial powers fought against with harsh programmes of exile, imprisonment and police repression, but there were also political movements representing the nationalist aspirations that had emerged in 1919, some of which were appeased with limited sovereignty – as in Iraq or Egypt – and some challenged with summary arrest, the suppression of anti-imperial organizations and publications and, in the French case, a state of siege declared throughout the empire in 1939.[142] Communism as an international movement was ideologically committed to campaigns to end colonial empire, which explains British and French anxiety. When the British Air Ministry began to plan the 'Ideal' long-range bomber in the mid-1930s, its range was not based on the threat from Germany, but on a possible war with the Soviet Union, whose cities and industries could be hit from empire air bases. Long range would also contribute to what was called 'Empire reinforcement' against a Soviet threat.[143] Fear of communism also explains the ambivalent attitude taken towards the Spanish Civil War, when Britain and France pursued a formal policy of non-intervention rather than supporting the democratic republican government. Given the widespread popular fear of a general war and the manifold problems of holding together global empires that were difficult to defend adequately against external threats and internal political protest, the reduction of risk became a central component of both British and French strategy in the 1930s.

This avoidance of risk is usually defined by the term 'appeasement', but it is an unfortunate term, as one of its proponents, the British prime minister Neville Chamberlain, later remarked. Appeasement has become the lightning conductor for a long line of critical and hostile analysis of Western behaviour in the face of dictatorship, and a watchword for any current failure to act with firmness against any threat to Western security.[144] Yet as a description of British and French strategy in the 1930s it is highly misleading. In the first place the term implies a commonality of interest between both states, and between the officials, politicians and soldiers responsible for making strategic judgements. In reality, policy was never monolithic but reflected a variety of assumptions, hopes and expectations which changed in reaction to circumstances, while policymakers employed a wide range of possible options in order to preserve the key elements of Anglo-French strategy: imperial security, economic strength, and domestic peace. It is more useful in many respects to describe this strategy in the terms made more familiar in the age of the Cold War twenty years later – containment and deterrence.[145] The record of both states in their approach to international problems in the 1930s was never simply a spineless abdication of responsibility, but a prolonged, if sometimes incoherent, effort to square the circle of growing international instability and their own desire to protect the imperial status quo.

Containment as a form of what is now called 'soft power' took many forms, from French efforts to maintain a system of alliances in Eastern Europe to the Anglo-German Naval Agreement of 1935, which placed agreed limits on what naval rearmament Germany could undertake. Economic concessions or agreements were also an important part of the strategy, and it was widely assumed that trade agreements or loans might assuage the belligerent posture of potential enemies or win over new friends. In Britain in particular the idea that a general settlement – a 'Grand Settlement' Chamberlain called it – might be achieved by getting the major powers to sit down together to revise Versailles and its aftermath, though never seriously tested, indicated a willingness to engage flexibly with the post-war order, as long as it could be based on negotiated, mutually acceptable grounds. In the United States, President Roosevelt echoed the idea in a 'New Deal for the World', to be brokered by peaceful means once the aggressor states were put into quarantine. The ambition to contain the crisis in the 1930s proved in the end illusory, but the resentment felt by Japan, Germany and Italy at the continued effort made by the Western powers to limit the damage they might do is an indication that 'appeasement' scarcely describes the reality of deteriorating relations between the states involved.[146]

Under Roosevelt, the American government also favoured strategies that would contain the new imperialists, but the priority was to limit any threat to the Western hemisphere. Roosevelt took more seriously than he should the idea that the Japanese or Germans would find subversive ways to threaten the United States from Central and South America.

Hemisphere defence became the favoured strategic profile since it involved
no commitment to active war abroad and satisfied isolationist opinion.
The Neutrality Laws pushed through Congress by isolationist politicians
in 1935 and again in 1937 limited what the president could do, but did
not prevent efforts to contain any hemisphere threat by expanding the
United States navy under the 1938 Vinson Act, up to the limits set in the
1930 London naval treaty.[147] Fear that the Panama Canal might be
bombed by German aircraft from South America or seized by the Japanese led to efforts to expand United States bases there, which eventually
numbered 134 army, navy and air force installations.[148] Efforts were made
to counter Japanese and German propaganda and economic interests in
the wider hemisphere by funding pro-American newspapers and undertaking pre-emptive purchase of scarce raw materials the aggressor states
needed. In Brazil, where wild rumours suggested a possible German
Anschluss (annexation) of the German communities living in the country,
the Washington government brokered an arms deal, followed in 1941 by
a guarantee to defend Brazil against any foreign threat.[149] None of this
amounted to intervention in the wider world conflicts, for which Roosevelt
had no mandate. One of the first experimental opinion polls, taken in
1936, found that 95 per cent of respondents wanted the United States to
keep out of all wars; in September 1939 only 5 per cent of those asked
favoured helping the British and French.[150]

The other side of the coin of containment was deterrence. This was a
word widely used in the 1930s well before the nuclear stand-off. Its purpose can be summed up by a comment made by Chamberlain to his sister
in 1939 on the eve of the final Polish crisis: 'You don't need offensive forces
sufficient to win a smashing victory. What you want are defensive forces
sufficiently strong to make it impossible for the other side to win except at
such a cost as to make it not worthwhile.'[151] Over the course of the 1930s,
both Britain and France chose to move from a position of limited military
spending to large-scale and expensive military preparation. Rearmament
was not a sudden reaction to German moves against Czechoslovakia and
Poland, but a policy that had been pursued, often with considerable domestic protest, since at least 1934, but with accelerated tempo from 1936
onwards. In Britain, the government had recognized by the mid-1930s that
the manifold potential threats compelled a large programme of remilitarization. The Defence Requirements Committee, set up late in 1933,
recommended in 1936 a substantial increase in military spending for imperial defence, with priority given to the Royal Navy and the build-up of a
strong defensive and offensive air force. A rough four-year plan was drawn
up which saw expenditure rise from £185 million in 1936 to £719 million

in 1939. British intelligence estimates suggested that a possible war with Germany would not come until at least the end of the decade so that British and German spending followed much the same trajectory, except that in 1934 Britain was already armed while Germany was not.[152]

The defence of the home islands was complemented by defensive preparations overseas. British forces were stationed throughout the Middle East, in Iraq, Jordan, Egypt, Cyprus and Palestine. Egypt was regarded as particularly important and the Suez Canal as 'the centre of the Empire', because of the vital maritime link between Europe and the Asian territories. The treaty with Egypt in 1936 allowed Britain to station a garrison of 10,000 men at the canal, while Alexandria remained a vital naval base. To defend the British Empire east of Suez – some five-sevenths of British imperial territory – a major naval base at Singapore was approved in 1933, and completed five years later at a cost of £60 million.[153] The situation in China with growing Japanese encroachment was more challenging, and the defence of Hong Kong against a determined Japanese assault was regarded as unfeasible, but instead British loans and material for Chinese forces allowed the British to fight what has been called a 'proxy war' to defend both British and Chinese interests.[154] This did little to assuage anxieties in Australia and New Zealand that they were now very isolated in the face of a Japanese threat, but Britain had little choice, given the range of commitments, but to spread its growing defence effort ever more thinly across the empire.

France too began from an established base in the 1930s, with an army very much larger than the British army and a substantial navy. Economic crisis in the mid-1930s held down the level of military expenditure, but in 1936, prompted by German moves in remilitarizing the Rhineland, the newly elected Popular Front government, combining left and centre-left parties, embarked on a large programme of rearmament that, like the British and German plans, was designed to reach a peak by 1940. Spending rose from 15.1 million francs in 1936 to 93.6 million in 1939. For France, the priority was to build the Maginot Line defences and to arm and equip them: a necessity, so it was believed, because of the demographic gap between the French and German populations. For that part of the army not at the frontier defences, the French high command developed a doctrine based on the successful campaign that defeated the Germans in 1918. The doctrine was built around massive firepower as the means to support an attack or neutralize an oncoming enemy, allowing the infantry, still regarded as the 'queen of battle', to occupy ground step-by-step, though with limited mobility. The exploitation of firepower required a highly centralized and managed 'methodical battle', in which auxiliary arms such as tanks and aircraft would play a supporting role, rather than prepare the way for a war of manoeuvre. Artillery and machine guns were key, and infantry would move only at the pace of the supporting 'curtain of fire'.[155] The emphasis given to a prepared battlefield in metropolitan France meant that French planners paid less attention to the empire. Colonies were made to pay for their own defence expenditure: Algerians had to find the 289 million francs needed to modernize the French naval base at Mers el-Kébir; no major naval base was constructed in Indochina after plans for a submarine unit at Cam Ranh Bay were vetoed by the French navy commander-in-chief, Admiral Darlan, who made it clear that the French Asian empire simply could not be protected if war came.[156]

The framework for a policy of deterrence was much more in evidence by the time of the Munich crisis in September 1938, and even more so a year later. The twin approaches of containment and deterrence supported strategies that were designed to help Britain and France avoid war while remaining credible powers capable of protecting their global economic and territorial interests. Yet it is important to recall that even before the outbreak of war in September 1939, one or other of the major democracies had come close to open conflict with the new imperial states. In south China, a state of flimsy armed truce existed between Japanese forces and the British, which constantly threatened to spill over into open war. Conflict with Italy was certainly prepared for in 1935–6 during the Ethiopian crisis, as a way to limit the threat to British imperial interests in the Middle East and Africa. In August 1935, twenty-eight warships and the carrier HMS *Courageous* were sent to Alexandria as a warning to the Italians; the RAF units in the Middle East were strengthened and army reinforcements sent out. The local naval commander-in-chief was keen for a pre-emptive strike, but the British Chiefs of Staff and the French government both wanted to avoid a war which might in practice unravel imperial interests throughout the region.[157] In 1938–9 it was the turn of the French navy to chafe at the bit for the opportunity to inflict a sudden defeat on the Italian fleet, restrained this time by British hopes that Mussolini could still be divided from Hitler by cautious diplomacy.

The clearest example of 'brinkmanship' came with the crisis over Czechoslovakia in 1938. The story of German threats and British and French betrayal at the Munich Conference, when the Czech government was compelled to allow German occupation of the German-speaking areas of the Sudetenland, usually presents this as the high point of deluded and feeble appeasement. Yet, in reality, Munich was a moment when Hitler was compelled to abandon the war that he craved for German living space because the risk of confronting Britain and France in a major conflict was considered at that stage too risky. From the perspective of the time, it did seem that Hitler had been forced to accept the territorial change that the British and French were prepared to allow, a result of containment, even if one that served the Czechs ill. In the week before the Munich Conference both the British and French armed forces were placed on alert. The Royal Navy received mobilization orders; trenches were hastily dug in public parks in London as improvised air-raid shelters. French mobilization orders were sent out on 24 September and a million men were under arms, even though both the French and British Chiefs of Staff had little confidence that they could restrain Germany by war since the programmes of rearmament were still in mid-stream and the Maginot Line not yet completed.[158]

Mobilization had nevertheless been the trigger that had plunged Europe into war in 1914. Hitler had not anticipated this and up until a few days before the planned invasion of Czechoslovakia he still insisted to his anxious military commanders that Britain and France would not intervene. Despite British and French fears that they might end up waging a war they could not win, neither government was prepared in the end to allow Germany a free hand to invade and conquer the Czechs. By 25 September 1938, the view in Berlin saw Hitler 'backing away from Chamberlain's determined stance', a very different perspective on the British leader.[159] Two days later, when Hitler had hoped to order mobilization, Sir Horace Wilson, a personal emissary from Chamberlain, delivered a message – repeated twice for the interpreter to be sure that Hitler understood – that if Germany attacked Czechoslovakia, France was bound by treaty to fight Germany. In this event, Wilson continued, 'England would feel honour bound, to offer France assistance.'[160] Hitler responded angrily that if this were the case, European war would break out in a week, but the meeting unnerved him. The following morning the French ambassador confirmed French intentions to oppose a German invasion. When a delegation led by Hermann Göring arrived soon after, Hitler was asked if he wanted general war in all cases, to which he replied: 'What do you mean? Whatever the case? Obviously not!'[161] In ill temper he agreed to Mussolini's suggestion, prompted by the British, for a conference. His army adjutant noted in his diary: 'F. [ührer] wants no war' and 'F. [ührer] above all things does not think of war with England'. The climbdown was obvious in Berlin. 'Führer has given in, and thoroughly', noted another diarist on 27 September; and two days later, 'Strong concessions from the Führer.'[162]

A European war was averted in 1938 not simply because the British and French governments feared it, but because Hitler was deterred from stepping across that threshold. Significantly, when Chamberlain drove through the streets of Munich after the conference, he was cheered by German crowds, genuinely relieved that war was avoided. The response in Britain and France was one of spontaneous relief that peace had been saved. French women knitted gloves to send to Chamberlain in case he was cold in the aircraft that conveyed him back and forth to Germany; a street in Paris was hastily renamed 'rue de Trente Septembre'; a new dance, 'Le Chamberlain', was invented, though its intention may well have been ironic.[163] *Le Temps* concluded the day after Munich that France, with its global imperial responsibilities, had a 'profound and absolute' need for peace.[164] Whether both states would actually have fought in 1938 remains a speculation, but in the end neither had to because this time Hitler judged the risk too great. A year later, with the crisis over the German threat to Polish sovereignty, both states did accept the probability of war, though they hoped that Hitler might again be deterred. They assumed up to the last moment before the German invasion of Poland on 1 September that, if they made unambiguously clear their intention to fight, he would once again not run the risk.

Many factors changed between September 1938 and September 1939 to make the British and French governments more confident about pursuing a firm line over the German threat to Poland. Despite the relief that the Czech crisis had not resulted in war, both Chamberlain and Daladier had few illusions that if Hitler continued to expand into Eastern Europe, they would have to use violence to restrain him. This did not exclude the possibility that diplomatic solutions or economic agreements might render further German expansion unlikely, and both were pursued in 1939. But once German forces occupied the Czech state and established the protectorate on 15 March 1939, it was evident to the democracies that the next move meant war. Informed by the intelligence services shortly afterwards that Germany would imminently attack Poland, Chamberlain gave a spontaneous guarantee of Polish sovereignty in the House of Commons on 30 March. A few days later France echoed the guarantee, but also added Romania and Greece. Poland was not itself of much importance to either Britain or France, but it became, almost by chance, the occasion rather than the cause of the final showdown between the two sides. Unknown to the Western powers, Poland's refusal in the early months of 1939 to make any concessions to Germany on the status of the Free City of Danzig, or the Polish 'corridor' through former Prussian territory, prompted Hitler to order preparations in April 1939 for a campaign to destroy Poland in late August of that year. Britain and France were now locked into an inevitable conflict if the German menace to Poland materialized. In the year that separated the Czech and Polish crises, the two states finally agreed to concert their actions. France had been inhibited throughout the 1930s by the uncertainty of whether Britain would support French forces militarily in the event of a European conflict. In February 1939 staff talks were agreed, and the following month a 'War Plan' was drawn up that reprised the strategy that had brought victory in 1918: a three-year campaign in which Germany would be bottled up by French fortifications, economic blockade and air action until Hitler either capitulated or lacked the means to resist an Anglo-French invasion. 'Once we had been able,' the plan concluded, 'to develop the full fighting strength of the British and French Empires, we should regard the outcome of the war with confidence.'[165]

Both states made it a priority to ensure that their empires would indeed rally to the cause in 1939 if it came to war. For Britain this had been far from certain, following the decision of the major Dominions not to support the idea of war over the Czech crisis. But in the spring of 1939 Canada's premier, Mackenzie King, won domestic support for joining Britain in any possible European war, and the governments of Australia and New Zealand followed suit, helped by the completion of the Singapore naval base in 1938 and sustained by the idea of a 'one voice' Commonwealth. In South Africa, strong hostility from the Afrikaner community to the idea of waging war divided the white population right up to the outbreak of war itself, when the new prime minister, Jan Smuts, persuaded parliament that declaring war was to protect South Africa's own interests against a threat of German neo-colonialism. When war came, the British viceroy in India, Lord Linlithgow, simply announced that India would follow suit, regardless of Indian opinion.[166] For France, anxious to underpin its continental strategy, the empire was even more important in preparing for European war in 1939. Partly this reflected the official propaganda of *le salut par l'empire* ('salvation through the empire'), which was evident throughout the months leading to war. While Daladier ordered tightened repression of political opponents throughout the colonial empire, the public face was to play up the idea that '100 million strong, we cannot be defeated'. Plans were made to conscript substantial numbers of colonial soldiers to serve in France or to release French soldiers from overseas duty, including five West African divisions, a division from Indochina, and half-a-dozen divisions from North Africa, a total of 520,000 soldiers by 1939.[167] Efforts to rally the imperial economy to produce more war materiel largely failed, but the supply of raw materials and food for the French war effort did expand. For better or worse, reliance on empire was seen as a positive advantage in the confrontation with an enemy whose access to overseas supplies could be severed at will by the British and French navies.

The change in popular mood after the wave of relief following the Munich agreement complemented the changing military and strategic picture. Opinion polling found that large majorities favoured no further concessions to Germany when ink on the agreement was scarcely dry. A poll in France in October 1938 found 70 per cent against giving anything more away; polls in 1939 showed that 76 per cent of respondents in France and 75 per cent in Britain supported the use of force to preserve the status of Danzig.[168] More significant was the seismic shift in the attitude of the anti-war lobby in both countries. The popular response to the European crisis was distinct from the nationalist enthusiasms of 1914. It was rooted more in the belief that the collapse of the internationalist project and the rise of militaristic dictatorship presented a profound challenge to Western civilization that could no longer be ignored. The mood was one of resignation, since war was certainly not widely welcomed, but it was nourished by a growing sense of responsibility for democratic values and a rejection of what many writers now viewed dramatically as a looming Dark Age. In 1939, Leonard Woolf wrote *Barbarians at the Gate* as a warning to his fellow countrymen of the fragility of the modern world they took for granted.[169]

The transformations in 1939 did not make war inevitable, but it made it difficult to avoid once Poland became the object of German aggression. The French government would have preferred a situation in which some agreement might be reached with the Soviet Union to encircle Germany, and more assistance extracted from the United States, where large orders were placed in 1938 and 1939 for aircraft and aero-engines. In spite of a deep well of conservative distrust of Soviet motives, a military agreement was explored in the late summer of 1939, but it stumbled on the impossibility of getting the Polish government and high command to allow Soviet forces on Polish soil. Neither British nor French senior commanders rated the Red Army as a useful military ally and they all exaggerated the potential strength of the Polish army, a misperception encouraged by Poland's earlier victory over the Red Army in 1920. When the German–Soviet Pact was announced on 24 August Chamberlain blustered about 'Russian treachery', but he had never been an enthusiast for military collaboration, and for neither government did the pact make any difference to their commitment to honour the pledge to Poland if Germany invaded.[170] Whether or not Stalin would have entered an alliance in good faith still remains an issue of conjecture rather than fact. A German Pact suited Stalin and Soviet interests far more, and fitted with the ideological preference for a war between capitalist-imperialist states from which Soviet Communism would eventually pick up the ruined pieces of Europe.

The calculation that Hitler would be deterred by the sight of the rapidly rearming British and French empires, or by the wave of anti-fascist sentiment washing across the democracies, was not entirely misplaced. A weaker hand had forced Hitler to climb down from war in 1938. Intelligence sources suggested serious economic crisis in Germany, even the possibility of an anti-Hitler coup. Even after the German invasion of Poland on 1 September, Chamberlain gave him the opportunity to withdraw his forces rather than face a world war. The idea of a conference was briefly mooted by the Italian leadership on 2 September, echoing Mussolini's intervention in September 1938, but the British condition, the foreign secretary Lord Halifax told his Italian counterpart Ciano, was 'the withdrawal of German troops from Polish soil', which ended any prospect of peace.[171] Historians have searched for convincing evidence that Chamberlain wanted to wriggle out of his commitment even at this late stage, but there is none. Only a complete German capitulation to British and French demands for an end to the violence would have averted world war, and by 1 September that was the least likely outcome. Neither containment nor deterrence had in this case worked. Chamberlain announced a state of war on the radio at 11.15 on the morning of 3 September; Daladier announced a state of war at 5 p.m. that afternoon. A temporary alliance of imperial elites and democratic anti-fascists had made possible a new world war. 'We can't lose,' observed the British army chief of staff in his diary.[172]

A BATTLE OF EMPIRES: THE WAR IN THE WEST

The declaration of war in September 1939 utterly altered the nature of the confrontations of the 1930s. Hitler saw his war with Poland as a limited war for German living space justified, in his eyes, by the prior existence of large European empires that had been won not very long before at the point of the sword. When he made a 'peace offer' to the democracies on 6 October, a week after the Polish surrender, he jibed at states that accused him of wanting world power for taking a few hundred thousand square kilometres of land when they themselves ruled 40 million worldwide.[173] Britain and France, on the other hand, saw the conflict as a struggle against the new wave of violent empire-building, and even though they were not yet at war with Italy and Japan, their view of the crisis was genuinely global. They had to hope that war with Germany would not encourage either of the other two states to take advantage of their distraction in Europe, just as they had to hope that the Soviet Union would not take advantage of its Pact with Germany to exert its own pressure on their overstretched empires. At the same time, they looked for moral support from the United States, and the active provision of men, money and supplies from their empires. The future shape of the Second World War was determined not by German ambition in Eastern Europe, which had triggered the conflict, but by the Anglo-French declaration on 3 September. From the German perspective, war had been forced on Germany by external forces. In a broadcast to the German people the following day, Hitler blamed not the democracies for the state of war that Germany now faced, but the 'Jewish-democratic international enemy' who had harried them into fighting.[174] For Hitler the war was now to be two wars: one against the imperial enemies of the Reich, one against the Jews.

What followed the British and French declarations of war was entirely different from 1914, when millions of men were in action, with high numbers of casualties, from the opening days of the conflict. Britain and France knew that Germany was too embroiled in the Polish campaign to launch an attack in the West, but neither state had any interest in actively supporting Polish resistance. The two allies had already privately agreed that Poland could not be saved; the French commander-in-chief, General Maurice Gamelin, had made a limited promise to the Poles that France would attack fifteen days after mobilization. On 10 September Gamelin told the Polish military attaché that half his armies were in action against the German Saarland, but it was not true. A handful of French units had moved forward 8 kilometres, killed 196 Germans, and then retreated back.[175] Gamelin told the writer André Maurois, that he would 'not begin the war by a Battle of Verdun', flinging infantry at German fortifications. He planned what he called a 'scientific war', consistent with French army doctrine.[176] The almost complete inactivity in the West (the first British soldier was killed in action on 9 December after treading on a French landmine) fuelled Hitler's pre-war hope that the Allied declaration of war was 'merely a sham' and that the West really was, as Albert Speer recalled in his memoirs, 'too feeble, too worn out, and too decadent' for a fight.[177] In the first weeks of the Polish war, he ordered extreme restraint on the Western front in the belief that he could finish in Poland quickly and present Britain and France with a fait accompli.

Hitler was nevertheless anxious that German forces should not simply sit on the defensive once victory over Poland had been achieved. On 8 September he mooted for the first time the idea of an autumn offensive in the West. On the eve of the Polish capitulation, on 26 September, he hosted a meeting of army and air force commanders at which he stressed that time was on the Allies' side to build up their forces in France by the summer of 1940, and that an early strike at France through the Low Countries would unhinge the ill-prepared enemy, secure air and naval bases to strike at Britain, and protect the vulnerable Ruhr industrial region from Allied incursions and bombing. The plan was issued on 9 October as War Directive no. 6 for '*Fall Gelb*' ('Case Yellow'), but in the interim Hitler made the first of a number of attempts to get the Allies to accept Poland's hopeless position, divided between the German and Soviet dictatorships.[178] His speech on 6 October had a mixed reception in the West, where there was still a lobby in favour of realistic compromise. Daladier told Chamberlain to ignore it – 'pass over Herr Hitler in silence' – but the British spent days working out a response. Winston Churchill, now first lord of the admiralty, wanted a draft that left the door open to 'any genuine offer', and the final version, while rejecting any idea that aggression could be condoned, did give Hitler the improbable option of abandoning his conquests without penalty.[179] The effect of the rebuttal was to transform Britain in the eyes of the German leadership into the principal enemy bent, as Hitler informed the naval commander-in-chief, 'on the extermination of Germany'. Goebbels ordered the German press to cease their portrayal of Chamberlain as a helpless and risible figure, and to present him instead as a 'vicious old man'.[180]

Once Hitler had decided that a quick offensive in the West was the safest option, army leaders tried their hardest to dissuade him. The Polish campaign showed that more training, enhanced equipment and serious thinking about battlefield tactics were necessary before risking a confrontation with the French army, aside from the need to rest and regroup. A study by the army chief of operations, Carl-Heinrich von Stülpnagel, suggested postponing a major campaign until 1942.[181] Hitler remained obdurate and set the date for an offensive between 20 and 25 October. The weather played into the army leaders' hands. The winter of 1939–40 was to be the worst of the century. The invasion date was postponed to 12 November, postponed again to 12 December, and once more to 1 January 1940, then finally to an unspecified date in the spring. In the meantime, the plan changed its shape. In October Hitler had second thoughts about a direct assault across the flat north European plain; he wondered instead about concentrating the armoured divisions for a strike from further south, but no new plan was settled, reflecting Hitler's own uncertainty. The chief of staff of Army Group A, Colonel Erich von Manstein, also believed that a decisive blow could be struck by concentrating German armour further south so that it could break through to encircle enemy forces as they advanced into Belgium – the so-called 'sickle-cut plan'. His ideas were disregarded by his seniors, and von Manstein himself was

redeployed to the East as a commander of an army corps still in the process of formation in order to keep him quiet. When secret details of the
original 'Case Yellow' plan fell into Allied hands following the forced
landing of a German courier plane in Belgium on 10 January, Hitler and
the army high command faced further uncertainty about the direction of
attack. By chance, von Manstein's views were relayed to Hitler by his
military adjutant, and on 17 February the colonel was invited to present
his plan in person in Berlin. Hitler was captivated by it and ordered a new
directive; by the time the campaign was ready in May 1940, the 'sickle-
cut' was in place.[182]

On the Allied side the only certainty was that war had been declared.
Every other calculation was edged with uncertainty. Hopes for Polish resistance for months rather than weeks evaporated, but since Anglo-French
planning was based on a long war, in which Germany would eventually be
brought to defeat – as in 1918 – by economic shortages, popular disaffection, and a final military confrontation, there was less evident need for
urgent action, even with the German army now free to turn West. Allied
intelligence and common sense together suggested that Germany would not
be ready to mount an offensive until 1940 at the earliest, if not later,
although there were regular scares in the late autumn. The French high
command viewed such an offensive very much on the lines of the original
German plan. The Maginot Line would force the enemy to invade on a narrow and defensible front somewhere in Belgium, where his forces would be
either defeated or bottled up. The Allies believed that time was on their side
as they slowly built up the military forces and economic resources necessary.[183] A Supreme War Council, composed of military and civilian leaders,
was established in early September 1939 to formalize Franco-British collaboration, as it had been in 1918. The experience of the Great War clearly
coloured Allied thinking about how best to wage a new one. In November,
'making full use of the experience gained in the years 1914–1918', the Allies
announced that they would co-ordinate communications, munitions, oil
supply, food, shipping and economic warfare against Germany.[184]

Military collaboration proved a more vexed question, but after several
months of uncertainty, Gamelin insisted that British units in France would
be under command of General Alphonse Georges, commander-in-chief of
the north-east front in France. In November, Gamelin drew up the Allied
operational plan, which consisted of an advance into Belgium to defend a
line along either the Escaut River or the Dyle. Gamelin finally opted for
the Dyle Plan because it promised to protect the major French industrial
region in the north-east, despite the risk that it would take eight days to
reach the river before a solid defensive line could be constructed. The

small British Expeditionary Force would be among the armies moving into Belgium. The stumbling block was Belgian neutrality, for in 1936 the Belgian government had abrogated a Franco-Belgian defence treaty, and stubbornly refused, right through to the moment when German soldiers crossed the frontier, to hold joint staff talks or to allow the Allies to enter Belgian soil to avoid any danger that their neutrality might be compromised.[185] As a result, the Dyle Plan would have to be activated hurriedly, if at all. Gamelin stuck to it nonetheless, convinced that a methodical offensive/defensive strategic line in neutral Belgium remained the best French option. The German plans that fell into Allied hands in January 1940 did not suggest a rethink, but instead reinforced the view that creating a Belgian front had been the right choice.[186]

The long period of relative inactivity, now known as the Phoney War, was certainly not free of problems. Popular opinion needed evidence of military success to sustain what had been a temporary domestic alliance in favour of a firm declaration of war. Instead, complained the French journal *Revue des Deux Mondes*, 'Paix-Guerre' had simply been replaced by 'Guerre-Paix'; the *New York Times* carried the headline in October 1939 '38 WAR REPORTERS SEARCH FOR A WAR'.[187] The defeat of Poland and the Hitler peace offer in October had strengthened those circles, chiefly on the philo-fascist right or the pacifist left, that favoured a compromise peace, but there was evidence of more widespread disillusionment with war. British Gallup Polls in October 1939 and February 1940 found a rising proportion of respondents in favour of peace talks: 29 per cent against the earlier 17 per cent.[188] The large Allied forces mobilized in the winter of 1939–40 to sit on the French frontier in freezing temperatures also found it hard to maintain any enthusiasm for a war that seemed remote from their bleak and demoralizing daily routine. The French philosopher and front-line soldier, Jean-Paul Sartre, lamented that all he and his companions did was eat, sleep and avoid the cold: 'that's it . . . one is exactly like the animals'. A British conscript marooned in a frozen billet felt as though 'drama had given way to farce'.[189]

Despite the efforts to pick up the threads of collaboration from the previous conflict, there remained a residue of mistrust between the two sides, not least because the French government and high command wondered whether Britain was sufficiently committed to a land war for the defence of France. The British decision to keep forces and equipment in key empire areas ran against the French intention of recruiting substantial numbers of colonial troops for service in France. It became clear from the start of Anglo-French discussions that the rate at which the British Expeditionary Force could be built up was too slow to meet a German assault

some time in 1940. French mobilized forces amounted to eighty-four divisions, with twenty-three fortress divisions to man the Maginot Line. Since
French intelligence calculated (wrongly) that the Germans could field 175
divisions, there was a wide gap to make good.[190] The British contribution
was distorted by the priority given to the air force and navy during the
1930s and the relative neglect of the army. The British army had sent only
five divisions to France after almost four months of war; a further eight
underequipped Territorial Army divisions arrived by the time of the German invasion. The first, and only, British armoured division joined the
battle after it had already begun. The most that the British Chiefs of Staff
would offer was a 32-division army by the end of 1941, at the earliest.[191]
Air support for the campaign in France was also very limited. The build-
up of fighter and bomber aircraft in the late 1930s had been designed to
defend the British Isles and to create a bomber force to retaliate against
German attacks. The RAF was reluctant to abandon this strategic profile,
with the result that the great majority of British aircraft remained in Britain. By May 1940 there were around 250 operational RAF aircraft in
France, little more than the 184 aircraft in the Belgian air force.[192]

Though the preparations for actual combat presupposed that at some
point Germany would be the principal enemy, there was no certainty
about what would happen in the wider world now that a state of war
existed. The position of Italy was difficult to judge once it was clear that
Mussolini's declaration of 'non-belligerence' in September 1939 (a term
chosen because it seemed less demeaning to the Axis alliance than 'neutrality') was serious. The French navy had begun the war by imposing a
blockade on Italian trade, but on 15 September it was lifted in return for
economic agreements that saw Italian aircraft, aero-engines and Fiat
trucks supplied to the French armed forces in return for foreign exchange
and raw materials (though Mussolini refused to supply aircraft for Britain). Count Ciano told the French ambassador, 'Win some victories and
we shall be on your side.'[193] The British did reinforce the Suez garrison
and build up stocks for a possible second theatre of war. The Allies treated
Mussolini as an opportunist for whom the opportunity was not yet sufficiently inviting.[194] The position of Japan was also inconclusive. Japanese
forces in southern China put increasing pressure on the French and British
empires during the summer of 1939 to close all trade with southern China,
and after the outbreak of the European war the noose tightened. French
and British forces were withdrawn from the enclave at Tianjin and the
Royal Navy China Squadron moved to Singapore. Hong Kong was sealed
off by the Japanese, and Chinese vessels trying to ply from the colony
were periodically shelled and sunk by the Japanese navy. The British had

no desire for all-out war with Japan, but Allied interests in China survived in the winter of 1939–40 only because of continued Chinese resistance.[195]

The most dangerous uncertainty was the attitude of the Soviet Union. From the moment of the German–Soviet Pact in August 1939 the two Allied powers began to treat the Soviet Union as a potential enemy and the pact as a virtual alliance. Stalin, it is now known, did hope that the pact would create a new 'equilibrium' in Europe around a Soviet–German axis. 'This collaboration,' he told Ribbentrop, 'represents a power that all other combinations must give way to.'[196] The Allies assumed the worst following the Soviet invasion and occupation of eastern Poland and subsequent pressure on the Baltic States to allow Soviet forces on their territory for protection. Chamberlain and Daladier were both deeply hostile to communism and anxious lest the war against Germany might tempt the Soviet Union to move towards the Middle East or the Asian empires. In October the British embassy in Moscow sent a long report analysing the possibility of war with the Soviet Union, and though the British Chiefs of Staff remained opposed to risking any broader conflict, it remained within the realm of Allied contingencies.[197] When on 30 November the Soviet Union attacked Finland, after the Finnish government had rejected requests to cede bases to Soviet military forces, there was a wave of indignant protest across Britain and France. Their ambassadors were withdrawn from Moscow and on 14 December the two states took the lead in expelling the Soviet Union from the League of Nations. In London, blasted by a ferocious anti-Soviet press campaign, the Soviet ambassador, Ivan Maisky, asked himself the question 'who is the No. 1 enemy? Germany or the USSR?'[198]

The Soviet–Finnish war brought Scandinavia unexpectedly into the Second World War. It alerted the Allies to the strategic importance of the region, if either the Soviet Union or Germany came to dominate or occupy it. Scandinavia was the source of important strategic raw materials – high-grade iron ore in particular – while the Norwegian littoral provided potential air and naval bases for attacks on Britain. Limited military aid was sent to the Finns (some 175 British and French aircraft, 500 artillery pieces), while British planners came up with two possible operations, codenamed 'Avonmouth' and 'Stratford', both approved by the Supreme War Council in February 1940. The first involved sending a small Anglo-French force to the Norwegian port of Narvik that would enter Swedish territory and secure control of the iron-ore mines; the second plan was to send an additional force of three divisions to establish a defensive line in southern Sweden. Neither Norway nor Sweden would agree, and in March the British War Cabinet vetoed the whole idea despite strong French pressure for military engagement.[199] The Finns finally sued for an armistice on 13 March before any Allied plan could be put into effect, but the defeat provoked the first of two major political crises for the Allies over the issue of Scandinavia. Political hostility to Daladier had been growing during the spring as anti-communists blamed him for not being more active against the Soviet Union, while the centre and left disliked the failure to get to grips with Germany. His reputation was for irresolution. On 20 March Daladier was forced from office, though he remained minister of defence. He was replaced by his finance minister, Paul Reynaud, whose reputation was starkly opposite – impulsive, active, belligerent. He wrote almost at once to Chamberlain that what was now needed to counteract the psychological and moral impact of the Finnish defeat were 'bold and prompt' actions.[200]

Reynaud's preference nevertheless was for action away from the front-line facing Germany, along lines already suggested under Daladier. He wanted the British to take the lead in Scandinavia by mining the routes used to supply Germany with iron ore, and he wanted a combined Anglo-French air force posted to Iraq and Syria to bomb the Soviet oilfields in the Caucasus to cut off some of Germany's oil supply. The Caucasus plan was given more serious attention than it deserved. A British report suggested that three bomber squadrons could knock out the oilfields and 'paralyse the Soviet war machine', a claim for which there was not a shred of evidence. Only the opposition of the British War Cabinet to the inevitable risk of all-out war with the Soviet Union prevented the operation from going ahead.[201] On Norway Reynaud was more insistent, but the British wanted to focus on the threat in the West by laying mines along the Rhine to slow down German deployment. The French Cabinet in turn rejected the British proposal from fear that French rivers might be mined in retaliation. The deadlock was finally ended when the British agreed to mine Norwegian waters if the French undertook to accept the Rhine mining later in the year. The date for the mining operation off the Norwegian coast, Operation 'Wilfred', was fixed for 8 April 1940.[202]

The Norwegian operation ended a month later with Chamberlain's resignation, a victim, like Daladier, of the incompetence of Allied strategy in Scandinavia. Both British and French intelligence failed to provide any serious advance warning of the German invasion of Denmark and Norway, which began on the morning of 9 April. News that a German fleet was heading across the North Sea arrived on the evening of 8 April from the Reuters press agency. German planning for a possible operation in Scandinavia went back many months. A study was ordered on 12 December to see if it was possible, given Germany's limited naval resources, to occupy Norway and safeguard the flow of iron ore. Hitler was anxious that Norway should not be occupied by the British, but there were also concerns that the Soviet Union might use its aggressive presence in the region to occupy northern Norway. In January General Nikolaus von Falkenhorst was appointed overall commander of a combined naval, air and army operation given the codename '*Weserübung*' ('Weser Exercise').[203] The German leadership hoped that a political upheaval in Norway prompted by the Norwegian national socialist Vidkun Quisling might make military action unnecessary, but Quisling's influence was greatly exaggerated. As Allied interest in Scandinavia mounted, Hitler issued the directive for '*Weserübung*' on 1 March.[204] It was a complicated and risky operation at a time when the main axis of German military preparation was in the West, but Hitler gauged the risks of an Allied flank in the north as too great.

On 2 April Hitler ordered the operation to start a week later, and by 8 April, as the first mines were being laid by the British, German submarines, transport vessels and warships were at sea to support landings at Trondheim and Narvik, while German paratroopers prepared the first operation of its kind against the Norwegian capital, Oslo. On the morning of 9 April German forces crossed the Danish frontier and after a brief exchange of fire, leaving sixteen Danish soldiers dead, the Danish government capitulated. German paratroopers and airborne infantry seized the main airfields in southern Norway, while transport vessels landed troops and supplies along the southern Norwegian coast. Supply by air and sea over the next two months brought 107,000 troops, 20,339 vehicles and 101,000 tons of supplies to support the invasion. By early May more than 700 aircraft were supporting German operations.[205] The German forces soon controlled most of southern and central Norway despite heavier Norwegian resistance than had been expected. Between 15 and 19 April a combined British, French and Polish force was landed at three points along the coast, and briefly took control of Narvik, where the German units were outnumbered. Although German naval casualties were proportionately high (3 cruisers, 10 destroyers, 4 submarines and 18 transport vessels), the campaign showed the evident strengths of the German armed forces in what turned out to be their only major combined arms operation. Close air support, effective use of artillery and infantry working together, and effective communications, magnified the fighting power of the German forces and demoralized Allied soldiers, most of whom had never seen rugged mountain terrain, let alone fought in it. On 26 April the British abandoned Trondheim; Allied soldiers held on to Narvik until 8 June when the remaining 24,500 were evacuated back to Britain, but German victory in Norway had been assured by the beginning of May at a total cost of 3,692 dead and missing, against Allied fatal losses of 3,761.[206]

The failure in Norway infuriated Reynaud, who had staked his new premiership on the promise of success. The British, he complained in late April, were 'old men who do not know how to take a risk'. Popular opinion in Britain swung against Chamberlain as news of the debacle filtered through. Although much of the blame for the poor preparation and execution of the Allied intervention was Churchill's, as first lord of the admiralty, the press campaign in early May was directed at the prime minister. The political crisis reached a peak on 8 May when the House of Commons debated on Norway. Chamberlain looked, according to one eyewitness, 'heart-broken and shrivelled' as he defended his record through angry exchanges, but a large number of his own supporters voted against him when a division was called by the Labour opposition and the following day he decided to resign.[207] The only Conservative politician with whom the opposition parties would agree to work was Winston Churchill and on 10 May he became head of a new government. Within six weeks both the democracies had experienced a major political crisis over Scandinavia. It is all the more remarkable that the one common belief that still united the two allies was the expectation that the war would end with Anglo-French victory and that, serious though the failures in Scandinavia had been, the strategy for containing Germany militarily was still expected to work. There is little evidence that either government anticipated the upheaval which materialized over the two months that followed.

The same morning on which Churchill was appointed prime minister, German forces began the campaign in the West. Allied intelligence was more prepared for this eventuality than for the Norwegian campaign, since Allied strategy was based on resisting a German assault rather than starting their own offensive, but the intelligence services failed entirely to anticipate the shape of the German campaign, which quickly unhinged all Allied preparations. Its remarkable success surprised German commanders no less. Many of them, like their Allied counterparts, imagined in the end something like a repeat of the Western Front of the Great War if the operation failed. Instead, for the loss of 27,000 men, the whole of the Netherlands, Belgium and France fell under German control. Nothing could have been more different from the war experienced by the commanders of both sides twenty-five years before. Both during the war and for long after it, the defeated Allies tried to explain their humiliation in terms of overwhelming German strength, fuelled by years of frenetic rearmament, a grim contrast with the tardy and uncoordinated efforts in the West. Historians have now dispelled this image by demonstrating that the total resources available to both sides actually favoured the Allies, in some cases by a generous margin.

French, Belgian, Dutch and British army divisions for the north-eastern front in France numbered 151, German army divisions 135, including 42 in reserve; Allied artillery pieces amounted to 14,000 against 7,378 German; Allied tanks, many of them superior in firepower and armour to their German counterparts, amounted to 3,874 in contrast to 2,439 German. Even in the air, where Germany was always assumed to be far in the lead by the end of the 1930s, the balance favoured the Allies; estimates range between 4,400 and 5,400 aircraft (which included substantial numbers held in reserve) in contrast to the 3,578 operational aircraft available on 10 May for the German air force in Air Fleets 2 and 3.[208]

Although these figures are not wrong, they are misleading in several important respects. The army and air force numbers include Belgian and Dutch forces, but neither of the two small armies had concerted plans with the French, while the two small air forces had no co-ordinated defence plan with the French and British and were all but wiped out in attacks on their air bases in the first day of the campaign. Air parity for Britain and France was also a statistical illusion. The French high command had by 10 May only 879 serviceable aircraft on the front facing the Germans, while the British contingent of 416 was a fraction of the 1,702 front-line aircraft available to the RAF, kept in Britain for defence of the island. The remaining French aircraft, a good number of them obsolescent by 1940, were in depots or at bases in the rest of metropolitan France, while 465 were in North Africa in case of an Italian offensive. Those that were available at the vital front were assigned to individual armies rather than concentrated together, making the disparity with the centrally controlled and concentrated German air force even more marked. In reality, the two Western Allies had only around 1,300 aircraft facing the 3,578 German.

In artillery the gap was also less significant than the raw numbers suggest. The French relied a great deal on 1918 artillery pieces, while too few of the modern 47mm anti-tank guns were available by May 1940 with crews trained in their use, leaving many divisions using the 37mm gun from the First World War, which was ineffective against modern tanks. Anti-aircraft guns were also in short supply: 3,800 compared with 9,300 German.[209] Though the best French and British tanks had larger calibre guns and thicker armour than the best German tanks, they were a small part of the overall tank force, while French tanks were slow and greedy for fuel. More important was the way the tanks were organized. German forces put all the tanks into ten combined-arms Panzer divisions and six motorized divisions, a concentrated force designed as the spearhead of a largely infantry and horse-drawn army, in order to punch through and disorganize the enemy line; French tanks, even those in the three light mechanized divisions (DLM) or the three Reserve Armoured Divisions (DCR), were designed to work in the context of the infantry battle, helping to prevent an enemy breakthrough, rather than as independent offensive units. Of the 2,900 tanks committed by France, only 960 were in these mechanized units; the rest were scattered among the regular divisions. None, of course, had yet seen or experienced modern tank fighting, unlike the German army.[210] The important conclusion about the balance of forces is that the German side enjoyed local superiority at precisely the points that mattered.

These differences were magnified by the strategy chosen by the two sides. Since the defeat of France was the critical turning point of the war, the conflict is worth examining in some detail. The German arguments about the shape of 'Case Yellow' were fully resolved by March. The German armed forces were organized in three army groups: Army Group B, with three Panzer divisions, was to punch through the Netherlands and Belgium towards France in order to lure the bulk of the French and British forces into a counter-offensive in Belgium; Army Group C sat behind the German Westwall defences to pin down the thirty-six French divisions manning the Maginot Line; the key was Army Group A under General Gerd von Rundstedt, with seven armoured divisions facing the south Belgian Ardennes forest and Luxembourg. Moving rapidly through the forest, it was to cross the Meuse River by day three of the campaign and then strike north-east towards the Channel coast, keeping a defensive shield along the exposed left flank while encircling the Allied forces and annihilating their resistance. The success of the plan depended on the French army swallowing the bait of the offensive through northern Belgium, and an elaborate deception plan was carried out to make it appear that this really was the principal axis of German attack.

The ruse was not in the end necessary because Gamelin and the French high command had long since decided on the advance into Belgium. In March Gamelin chose to extend the Allied risk even further by the so-called 'Breda variant', which involved a rapid deployment across Belgium by the French elite Seventh Army (previously a reserve formation), supported by the British Expeditionary Force, to meet up with the Dutch army in order to create a continuous defensive front. Breda was even further from the French frontier than the Dyle River, but Gamelin gambled that thirty Allied divisions could make it to the Dutch front in time to prevent a German breakthrough. The overall balance in the north was to be sixty Allied divisions against twenty-nine German; on the southern sector of the front the balance was reversed, eighteen against forty-five. The French had for years assumed that the Ardennes forest was virtually impassable for modern armies and it was guarded by a light Belgian covering force and seven under-equipped reserve divisions.[211] The risks were exceptional for both sides, but each was locked in a different way into the legacy of 1918: Gamelin, supported by British commanders, wanted to restore the continuous line and the methodical battle that had eventually worn the Germans down and was confident that this would be the outcome once again; German commanders worried that this would indeed be the result, so gambled everything on a rapid breakthrough and encirclement that had eluded them in 1914.

When the German armed forces began the assault in the West by launching devastating raids on enemy airfields and seizing the key Belgian fort of Eben-Emael in a daring paratroop strike, Gamelin reported that this was 'just the opportunity he was awaiting'.[212] The French First and Seventh armies, together with the BEF, were at last allowed on to Belgian soil to push towards the Dyle line and on to Breda. The French Ninth and Second armies were north and south of Sedan and the only obstacle to a German thrust from the south if it came. In the event almost nothing worked according to plan. Allied forces drove towards Breda only to discover that the Dutch army had abandoned the area and moved further north. On 14 May Rotterdam was bombed in support of a German army advance into the city; the following day the Dutch commander-in-chief announced that 'this unequal struggle must cease' and promptly surrendered. Belgian defence along the Albert Canal in the east soon collapsed under the weight of the German assault and Belgian units retreated back into the path of the advancing French. A front of sorts was established along the Dyle River against the outnumbered German divisions, but there was no fully prepared defensive line, while Allied deployment was hampered by the flood of refugees (eventually estimated at between 8 and 10 million French and Belgian civilians) that clogged vital highways for advancing and retreating forces.[213] On 16 May the defenders of the Dyle line were told by General Georges, the overall commander, to retreat as quickly as possible back to the French frontier because further south, through the allegedly impassable Ardennes, the whole French line had been unhinged.

The German operational plan had been met just as German commanders had hoped with the Allied advance into the Belgian trap. Hitler set up his headquarters at Münstereifel in a converted anti-aircraft bunker. He thought France would be defeated in six weeks, opening the way to a settlement with Britain, whose leaders would not want to 'risk losing the empire'.[214] It was here that news began to arrive about the assault of Army Group A through Luxembourg and the Ardennes on 10 May. The Panzer units were organized on three axes, one under Lieutenant General Heinz Guderian, Germany's leading exponent of armoured warfare, towards

Sedan, the second under command of Lieutenant General Hans Reinhardt towards Monthermé, north of Sedan, and a third under General Hermann Hoth towards the Belgian town of Dinant, designed to provide flanking defence to the other two thrusts. The move forward soon stumbled as armoured divisions competed with infantry divisions for space on the narrow roads. The 41,140 vehicles and 140,000 men created a 250-kilometre traffic jam which the commanders struggled to overcome. The crisis was mediated to some extent by careful logistical planning. Fuel dumps had been set up along the way, while three truck transport battalions provided fuel, ammunition and supplies for the armoured divisions as they moved forward. Once movement was finally achieved, this logistical commitment was critical in allowing rapid mobility. Petrol cans were handed out to tanks on the move, like water for thirsty marathon runners.[215]

The most critical moment of the campaign came between 11 and 13 May with the armoured thrust brought to a virtual standstill, a sitting target for Allied air power. There were few Allied aircraft over this vulnerable sector because the German air force kept a protective umbrella over the advance, while the bulk of the Allied air force was contesting the advance further north, but the small number of French pilots who did report the endless streams of vehicles and tanks were simply not believed. As the German columns pushed through Luxembourg and the southern Ardennes, they battled with Belgian frontier forces and French cavalry, but no reports reached Georges or Gamelin that this might represent the major German thrust because the French plan was predicated on the idea of a main battle on the Flanders plain further north. On 13 May, despite the deployment nightmare through the Ardennes, all three German Panzer thrusts had reached the river Meuse. The crossing of the river was a moment of high drama. The bridges had been destroyed and the French were dug in along the far bank. The bulk of the German air force was now ordered to pound the enemy positions, and 850 bombers and dive-bombers spread a carpet of smoke and debris across the riverbank. The French Fifty-Fifth Division, opposite Guderian at Sedan, had only one anti-aircraft gun. Although damage was found later to have been much less than expected, the psychological impact of persistent bombardment left French defenders fearful and demoralized.[216] Guderian's three divisions battled their way across against heavy artillery and machine-gun fire but by 11 o'clock in the evening enough had been achieved to allow the first bridge to be constructed and the first tanks crossed. Further north, General Erwin Rommel led his Seventh Panzer Division in person across the river at Houx, near Dinant, and against fierce French resistance had carved out a bridgehead of 3 kilometres by evening; Reinhardt's two

Panzer divisions at Monthermé met stiffer resistance because of the difficult topography, and it took two days to overcome the defenders and break out of the pocket carved out on the western bank of the Meuse. Nevertheless, the Meuse crossings created panic among the weaker reserve divisions and at last alerted the French high command to the seriousness of a situation they had pretended could not happen.

In the middle of the night of 13/14 May at the headquarters of General Georges the news was finally presented in detail. Georges famously collapsed in tears: 'Our front has been broken at Sedan! There has been a collapse.'[217] What followed was the very reverse of the methodical battle Gamelin had planned. Reserve divisions in General Charles Huntziger's Second Army melted away; to the north General André Corap's Ninth Army was facing a similar crisis. Efforts at counter-attacks broke down because the French high command had not expected a mobile battle of manoeuvre. Communications were poor and fuel supplies for French tanks and trucks difficult to organize, so that hundreds of French vehicles found themselves immobilized in the path of the advancing German Panzer divisions. Units forced to march long distances at speed arrived exhausted or without equipment. In Belgium the advance became a defensive retreat, leaving valuable supplies and fuel dumps behind. It was not, as is sometimes suggested, a walkover, since there was local and often fierce resistance, but the response was disorganized and improvised, the reverse of French planning. On 16 May Churchill in London claimed that it was 'ridiculous to think that France could be conquered by 160 tanks', but when he flew to Paris the following day to meet Gamelin at the French Foreign Office, he found staff already burning papers. When he asked Gamelin where was the French reserve, he received the laconic reply '*il n'y en a pas*' – there is none.[218]

The scale of the crisis only slowly unfolded as French commanders and politicians came to understand what had happened, and the uncertainty and poor communication accelerated the rout. Although the breakthrough on the Meuse was supposed to be slowed down and consolidated in case of a French counter-attack, the French response was so disorganized and piecemeal that all three Panzer corps now turned and raced towards the Channel ports of Calais, Boulogne and Dunkirk, as the Manstein plan required. This provoked a temporary panic at German headquarters. After a week of remarkable success, Hitler now worried that the long, exposed flanks of the advancing Panzer divisions were bound to invite a powerful French response. On 17 May he argued with his commanders about whether the whole move should slow down. 'The Führer is terribly nervous,' observed Franz Halder. 'He is frightened by his own success and does not want to risk anything, and therefore would rather stop us.'[219] Army Group C was unleashed against the Maginot Line on 18 May to ensure that the thirty-six French frontier divisions remained where they were. Two brief counter-attacks, one from the north by the tanks of the BEF at Arras on 18 May, one by the recently formed French Fourth Armoured Division at Moncornet on the 17th, led by Colonel Charles de Gaulle, created more anxieties for Hitler. The reality was different. The shock of the German advance and the complete incoherence of the Allied response played exactly to the strengths of German mobile warfare. Although the Panzer divisions were delayed twice by Hitler's panicked interventions, once after Moncornet, once after Arras, they had covered a remarkable amount of ground in just a week and the Panzer corps commanders were keen to press on to the coast and encircle the entire body of the French Seventh and First armies, the BEF and the Belgian army, trapped in the Flanders pocket. The decisive blow was stayed not by a Hitler 'halt order', as is often suggested, but by the nervous commander of Army Group A, von Rundstedt, who ordered the Panzer divisions to form up together, refit and rest, some to move south to undertake the second part of the operation, 'Case Red', to defeat French forces in the rest of the country, some to drive to Dunkirk. Hitler approved von Rundstedt's orders and gave him the responsibility for deciding when the advance should be recommenced. On 28 May, the twenty-one trapped Belgian divisions were taken out of the equation when the Belgian king surrendered. Two days earlier the German army had finally been given permission to complete the annihilation of the twenty-five French and ten British divisions that remained in the pocket behind a thin defensive line.

The temporary loss of nerve at Hitler's headquarters was nothing to the crisis that overwhelmed the Allies. As news filtered in, the French government faced a reality they regarded as incredible. At 7.30 on the morning of the 15 May, Reynaud telephoned Churchill with the grim conclusion that 'We are beaten, we have lost the battle.'[220] On the 20th Gamelin, whose relationship with Reynaud had never been good, was relieved of his post and replaced by the French commander in Syria, General Maxime Weygand, a veteran general of the Great War and a Reynaud ally. Marshal Philippe Pétain, who had triumphed at Verdun in 1916, was recalled from his post as ambassador in Madrid and appointed vice-premier to try to stiffen the fragile morale of the French people. Their appointments prompted a brief rallying of confidence in London and Paris: Weygand drew up (or rather inherited from Gamelin) a plan to attack the long German flanks from north and south, but it bore no relation to the reality on the ground; more realistically he prepared for a retreat to the line of the

Somme and Aisne rivers, calling for the battered forces to display a 'constant aggressiveness' as they did so.[221] But the scale of the calamity could not be concealed. There remained only forty French divisions along the new front line, with three motorized reserve groups to try to plug any gaps opened up by the Germans. The British War Cabinet and chiefs of staff drew the obvious conclusion. On 25 May a Commission set up under the former Cabinet secretary Maurice Hankey reported on 'British Strategy in a Certain Eventuality'. He concluded that a global war would not be decided by events in France, but with American and empire aid and the protection of the air force and navy, Britain could continue alone.[222]

The British and French began to think about an evacuation on 18 May, just over a week after the start of the campaign. Given a brief respite by the German halt, which allowed the BEF commander, Major General John Gort, to establish a perimeter north and south of the pocket, defended in the main by remnants of the French Seventh and First armies, Operation 'Dynamo' began from Calais and Boulogne on 26 May. The embattled soldiers were at last given more air protection from RAF Spitfires and Hurricanes flying from bases in southern England. While the battle to eliminate the pocket raged all around them, 338,682 soldiers were embarked at Dunkirk on a motley 861 ships, 247,000 of them British, 123,000 French. There was also a French evacuation, largely ignored in British histories of Dunkirk. The French admiralty moved 45,000 soldiers to Britain, 4,000 to Le Havre, then a further 100,000 to the north French ports of Cherbourg and Brest, where they were supposed to rejoin the fighting along the Somme.[223] The British operation was terminated on 4 June with the loss of 272 vessels, including 13 destroyers, and the abandonment of all the heavy equipment – 63,000 vehicles, 20,000 motorcycles, 475 tanks and armoured vehicles, and 2,400 guns.[224] The soldiers left behind them, as one later wrote, 'an infinity of destruction . . . a scene of utter military shambles.' The British army did not surrender in June 1940, but the battle in Belgium and France must be understood to be a major defeat, not a heroic evacuation. The army left to defend Britain had in June 1940 just 54 anti-tank guns and 583 artillery pieces. The regular army had been for the moment emasculated as a fighting force.[225]

While the collapse of resistance on the north-east front continued in late May, both the major Allies began to consider the awful scenario of capitulation, unthinkable two weeks before. Weygand, despite his apparent resilience and energy, told the French Cabinet on 25 May to think about abandoning the fight, and Reynaud was the first to pronounce the word 'armistice', though it was an ambiguous term, as the Germans had discovered in November 1918. This had to be agreed with the British according to a commitment, made on 25 March 1940, that neither ally would make a separate peace. On 26 May Reynaud flew to London to explain to Churchill that France might have to consider giving up. Unknown to him, the British War Cabinet had begun that morning to discuss a proposal from the foreign secretary, Halifax, presented to him by the Italian ambassador, for a possible conference convened by Mussolini. Italian motives remain unclear, since by now Mussolini was also preparing to declare war to profit from what seemed to the Italian leadership a ripe opportunity for exploiting the imminent conquest of France. After three days of debate the British decided against any initiative. Though often seen as a turning point at which the appeasers might nearly have triumphed, some discussion of the consequences of a comprehensive defeat were inevitable, and not even Halifax had favoured any settlement that compromised Britain's primary interests. Eventually winning support from Chamberlain, who kept a seat in the War Cabinet, Churchill carried the debate in favour of rejecting any approach to Mussolini. British leaders were already contemplating a war without France. 'If France could not defend herself,' Churchill told his colleagues, 'it was better that she should get out of the war.'[226]

France continued to fight for three more weeks in rapidly deteriorating circumstances. The option of an armistice remained the most likely outcome, but other alternatives were explored. The idea of a 'Breton redoubt' was raised in late May, where French forces, perhaps reinforced by a new British contingent, could hold a defensive line around Brittany and the port of Cherbourg, and a study was commissioned to test its feasibility.[227] More hope was placed in the idea that France could continue to resist from its North African empire, where large forces had already been based to safeguard against the possibility of an Italian pre-emptive strike from Libya, and whither thousands of French soldiers could be transported from the mainland. Reynaud set in train in early June plans to evacuate 80,000 men to French Morocco; de Gaulle, now a junior minister of war after his success at Moncornet, asked the French Admiralty on 12 June to move 870,000 men to Africa in three weeks. Only the British navy had this kind of capacity and the British effort was devoted to moving all the remaining British forces in western France (and 19,000 Polish soldiers) to add to those rescued at Dunkirk. Operation 'Aerial', the abandonment of France, was ordered on 14 June and completed ten days later. A further 185,000 men got back to England, with the loss this time of just 6 destroyers and 3 per cent of the transport shipping.[228] On 22 June Weygand asked the French commander-in-chief in North Africa, General Charles Noguès, what the prospects were for resistance from North Africa with the forces to hand. By that stage much of the French fleet and approximately 850 aircraft were now stationed in the African empire, but only 169 modern tanks and 7 divisions were ready for combat from the 14 available. Though Noguès possessed a force sufficient to keep an invasion at bay, Weygand did not consider it realistic to pursue the imperial option, any more than a redoubt in France. On 26 June, Noguès accepted, with 'the death of the soul' that empire resistance was over.[229]

Long before that, France's fate had been sealed by a comprehensive German victory. On 5 June the German armed forces were ready for the second stage of the campaign, 'Case Red', defeating what remained of French forces and forcing surrender. The French line hastily formed along the Somme, Aisne and Oise rivers fielded only 40 divisions against the 118 available to the Germans. By this stage the large infantry tail had caught up with the German spearhead, providing the new German front line with relatively fresh forces. General Georges told Weygand that they were fighting only for honour since there was little else left: 'no reserves, no relief forces, no reinforcements . . . without cavalry, without tanks. Tragic situation . . . struggle without hope, a situation without escape.'[230] Despite the great disparity in strength, the French units showed better organization and determination than had been possible in the first weeks of collapse, but the outcome was inevitable. On 9 June German Army Group A had reached Rouen, and by the 12th German armies were close to Paris, pressing back French forces to north and south. On 10 June Weygand told Reynaud that a 'definitive rupture' of the front was imminent.

The French government abandoned the capital and made first for the Loire valley, then eventually to Bordeaux. Paris, where air bases had been bombed on 3 June, was declared an open city and on the 14th the German army entered in triumph. At a meeting of ministers on 12 June, Weygand told his listeners that the time for an armistice had arrived; Reynaud remained undecided, but when Georges held a meeting with French commanders on the 15th, they all agreed that the battle had to be stopped.[231] Reynaud, exhausted and frustrated, bowed to reality and resigned the next day, to be succeeded by the chief spokesman for an armistice, Marshal Pétain. Even now the issue was not settled for Weygand had imagined an armistice as 'a suspension of the fighting', which might allow French forces to regroup. Pétain, on the other hand, in announcing the decision on the radio at midday on 17 June told the French people that 'we must cease combat'. Weygand told Georges to announce that he had only decided to 'attempt to end the combat' and to order all commanders to continue fighting.[232] The Battle of France ended not with Pétain's announcement, but eight days later. Although the fight was clearly over, and thousands of soldiers now abandoned their units to return home, those forces still intact in western and central France continued fighting, though they were exhausted and short of equipment. The 120,000 men of General Frère's Seventh Army straddled the Loire valley and tried to block each step of the river system as the Germans approached. They ceased fighting only on 25 June.[233]

The agreement to ask for an armistice was complicated by the decision taken in May 1940 by the Italian dictator to intervene on Hitler's side against the democracies. Mussolini had disliked the state of 'non-belligerence' he had been forced to declare in September 1939 because Italy was prepared neither economically nor militarily, after a decade of combat, for a confrontation with Britain and France. In December he gave an ambiguous promise to Hitler that he would eventually honour his commitment to the Axis. In March 1940 he had written that Italy could not remain neutral for the whole war without becoming 'a Switzerland multiplied by ten'.[234] But Mussolini remained constrained by the opposition of the monarchy and the military leadership to risking a conflict for which Italy was manifestly not ready. The Italian commander-in-chief, Marshal Badoglio, told Mussolini that preparations would not be complete until 1942 at the earliest, which was at best an optimistic assessment. It is difficult to judge the extent to which Mussolini respected this advice because he was trapped in his own rhetorical vision of Italy's military potential, but he was also uncertain whether Germany would actually attack in the West, and, even if it happened, how quickly the campaign would be decided.[235] When Hitler asked if Italy could supply twenty to thirty divisions to fight alongside German forces in the Rhône Valley, the Italian army command rejected the idea out of hand. What Mussolini and his circle wanted was what they called a 'parallel' war, 'not "for" or "with" Germany,' as the deputy war minister, Ubaldo Soddu, put it, 'but one for ourselves'.[236] However, once news of German victories began to roll in, Mussolini decided that Italy could stand by no longer. On 13 May he announced that he would declare war within a month. On 28 May, after hearing of the Belgian surrender, he fixed the date for 5 June, in case he missed the bus and could claim 'no title to participate in the succession'. The declaration was delayed until 10 June when Mussolini announced war from the balcony of the Palazzo Venezia in Rome to a crowd whose enthusiasm was observed to be muted.[237]

The declaration did not mean that Italy was ready to participate, but it prompted immediate retaliation from British and French bombers which raided Turin and Genoa two days later. Mussolini was only stirred into action by the news that Pétain had called for an armistice. He ordered the Italian army on the western frontier to begin an offensive against France three days later. Then he hurried to Munich to meet Hitler in order to discuss possible armistice terms; on the train to Germany, he talked of asking for the maximum – occupation of all of France, seizure of the French fleet, occupation of Tunisia, French Somaliland and Corsica – but when he arrived he felt at once, he told Ciano, that 'his role was second-class'.[238] Hitler wanted a more modest armistice so that German hands would not be tied in any future peace settlement and to prevent driving the French back into the arms of Britain. The armistice also provided the opportunity, according to von Ribbentrop, to expel Europe's Jews to the French colony of Madagascar now that France was defeated.[239] Hitler refused to permit a common armistice agreement. On 19 June the French high command was informed through the German embassy in Spain that Hitler was ready to consider the conditions for an armistice, and the following day the French delegation drove through the front line to arrive at Compiègne, where the Germans had been forced to sign the armistice twenty-three years before. A brief ceremony in the same railway carriage as 1918 confirmed the armistice on 22 June, but it could only come into effect when Italy had agreed to cease hostilities.[240]

Since Italian forces had only begun to fight on the 20th, Mussolini was compelled to wait a few days so that there was something definite that could be ended. Some twenty-two understrength and poorly equipped divisions attacked the French south-east frontier and made almost no progress against well-dug-in and determined French opposition. The town of Menton was occupied, but otherwise the Italian side had only 1,258 dead and 2,151 frostbite cases to show for three days of ineffectual combat.[241] An armistice was nonetheless reluctantly agreed and on 23 June a French delegation arrived to sign an agreement at the Villa Incisa in Rome. Although the French delegation understood that they had little choice, they could not accept that the armistice represented military defeat at the hands of the Italians. Mussolini kept his promise to Hitler and the terms were far more modest than the extreme ambitions he had harboured, but in both the German and the Italian case, the terms were not all that different from the Versailles settlement imposed on Germany – and in some sense worse. French sovereignty was effectively lost by the occupation of northern and western France; the French armed forces were to be reduced to a rump 100,000, though limited colonial forces could be kept to ensure that Britain could not easily occupy French imperial territory; naval bases and fortifications were to be demilitarized, weapons surrendered and the fleet to be immobilized. Italian negotiators also insisted that the Italian Armistice Commission would have jurisdiction in Corsica, French North Africa, French Somaliland and Syria.[242] Pétain's France, its centre now at the spa town of Vichy, ruled with limited independence over a stretch of unoccupied territory in the centre and south of the country.

The defeat of the Allies in 1940 transformed the nature of the war. It encouraged Italian and Japanese aggression to take advantage of a widening window of opportunity by threatening the European empires with a terminal crisis. The defeat shocked Stalin, who had expected a much longer campaign, but, as he told the British ambassador Stafford Cripps, in July 1940, the outcome meant that there was no going back now to 'the old equilibrium'.[243] To underline his argument, the Soviet Union began to encroach on Eastern European territory, annexing the Baltic States and the Romanian provinces of Northern Bukovina and Moldova. The Allied defeat accelerated the United States rearmament programme and alerted American opinion fully to the threat posed by the Axis states. But the greatest consequence for Hitler was the realization that the European axis could now create a 'New Order' in the whole of Europe, just as Japanese leaders now prepared to grasp the opportunity suddenly handed to them in Asia by the defeat of the European Allies. This had not been a plan in the 1930s; it was an unanticipated consequence of the decision by Britain and France to declare war, but it presented the Axis leadership with an exceptional strategic opportunity. The principal barrier to the security of any 'New Order' remained British resistance. At the meeting with Mussolini in Munich on 18 June Hitler had insisted that he had no desire to destroy the British Empire, which he still considered 'a great factor in the equilibrium of the world', but if there were no peace settlement with the West in 1940, war would be waged that was 'total, absolute and pitiless'.[244]

'A CATARACT OF DISASTER'

When Churchill rose in the House of Commons to deliver his speech on 20 August 1940, famously remembered for his brief remarks about 'the Few' of RAF Fighter Command, he spent most of a slow-moving account summarizing the catastrophe that had overtaken the Western powers in the summer of 1940. 'What a cataract of disaster,' he told fellow MPs. 'The trustful Dutch overwhelmed . . . Belgium invaded and beaten down; our own fine Expeditionary Force cut off and almost captured . . . our Ally, France, out; Italy in against us . . .' Such a prospect only three months before would, Churchill concluded, 'have seemed incredible'.[245] Though his speech also contained an ebullient declaration of continued resistance, it was not greeted with much warmth by the chamber. Churchill's secretary, Jock Colville, listening in the gallery of the Commons, found the session languid. He could not even recall later hearing the memorable sentence about the 'Few'.[246] The Soviet ambassador in London, Ivan Maisky, was in the gallery too. Though he thought the speech oratorically limited – 'not at his best today' – he found the parliamentary lobbies full of a 'new-found confidence' despite the cataract of disasters.[247] A few weeks before, Churchill's son, Randolph, had explained to Maisky that British belligerency after the collapse of France was essential to preserve the empire: 'if we lose our empire, we shall become not a second-rank, but a tenth-rank power. We have nothing. We will all die of hunger. So, there is nothing for it but to fight to the end.' Like father, like son, Maisky might have thought.[248]

The list of disasters was, as Churchill insisted, not what had been expected from the declaration of war on Germany. Churchill's military secretary, Hastings Ismay, later wrote that if the British Chiefs of Staff had remotely imagined in August 1939 that this would be the outcome, 'they would have unhesitatingly warned the Cabinet that to go to war would be to invite overwhelming disaster.' Instead, he concluded, they would have recommended 'humiliating concessions'.[249] Now the British Empire faced the prospect of world war alone. In the wake of the French defeat and the expulsion of the British forces fighting on the European Continent, the future of the British Empire suddenly became open to international speculation. This was scarcely surprising given the scale of the defeat and the self-evident difficulty Britain now faced in defending outposts of empire while the home islands were themselves under threat. 'What can the future hold for us, personally, now?' wrote the British MP Henry 'Chips' Channon in his diary in July 1940. 'What a mess . . . Our reign is slowly ending; I shall regret its close.'[250] In India, the news was met, according to reports on Indian opinion, with 'bewilderment' and 'depression', though anti-imperialists saw it as the writing on the wall for the whole institution. 'It will go to pieces,' wrote the Congress Party leader Jawaharlal Nehru, 'and not all the king's horses and all the king's men will be able to put it together again.'[251] Outside the empire, a probable British collapse was now taken for granted. Soviet commentators assumed that Germany would invade and occupy Britain with relative ease, while American opinion, even when sympathetic, was suddenly uncertain about British survival. Even Britain's recent French ally experienced a wave of Anglophobia directed at the limp contribution Britain had made to the campaign and the bankruptcy of the British world order. Among the new French government ministers gathered at Vichy were hostile critics, including the new prime minister, Pierre Laval, and his successor, Admiral Darlan, who both thought Britain's empire claims were hollow echoes of a lost age.

'England's day has passed,' wrote Laval in July 1940. 'No matter what happens now, she will lose her Empire.'[252]

The frailty of the British position was not lost on Churchill's new government. While Churchill hoped to inspire the British people to fight on for the sake of the empire and the ideals it stood for, he privately deplored 'our weakness, slowness, lack of grip and drive'.[253] Nevertheless, the defeat of France was swiftly turned into a more positive outcome for the empire than the facts merited. Chamberlain considered that the French had been 'nothing but a liability' and that Britain was better off alone, a view that Churchill had already privately expressed when in charge of the Admiralty.[254] When public opinion was tested about the prospect of waging the war alone, polls showed that three-quarters of those asked expected to continue the war, while a more modest 50 per cent were confident of the eventual outcome.[255] The idea of fighting 'alone' was a rallying cry for a country that now saw itself as a latter-day David fighting a fascist Goliath, but for Churchill and his political supporters the concept 'alone' embraced not only the home islands but the entire British Empire. Churchill was sentimental about the empire, and stocked his Cabinet, as the historian Lewis Namier observed at the time, with a line of 'Kipling imperialists' who shared that sentimental attachment.[256] For Churchill, survival of the empire was a central priority: 'My ideal,' he claimed in 1938, 'is narrow and limited. I want to see the British Empire preserved for a few more generations in its strength and splendour.'[257]

Nonetheless, Britain's strategic options remained narrow after the defeat of France. The priority was survival, and that meant avoiding destruction or defeat at the hands of a German enemy whose forces now ranged from northern Norway to the Atlantic coast of France. In the summer of 1940 one option was still to pursue a compromise peace with the enemy, acknowledging that there was no effective way to defeat the Axis. This was the view of a minority, and how large it was is difficult to guess, but the minority had political representation. The most prominent spokesman for a negotiated settlement was the former First World War prime minister David Lloyd George. Though he continued to argue that the country should wage war more effectively than it had done under Chamberlain, his preference, which he made clear in the press and parliament, was for some kind of settlement with Germany. Chamberlain thought Lloyd George was a potential Marshal Pétain, waiting in the wings to replace a bankrupt government, and Churchill later repeated this jibe in his parliamentary riposte to a speech by Lloyd George in May 1941, the last major speech he was to make.[258] Lloyd George was stung by the comparison, but it is not unlikely that, like Pétain, he felt crushed by the terrible cost of the previous conflict and hopeful that peace would allow Britain to shed the pre-war years of drift in favour of a reinvigorated national identity under Germany's watchful eye. For this there was no mandate in 1940. Churchill was determined that he should not have taken the premiership in May only to end the war ignominiously weeks later, but it was the much-maligned Chamberlain who, at the end of June, gave a worldwide broadcast in which he insisted that Britain 'would rather go down in ruin than admit the domination of the Nazis'.[259]

Britain was not defenceless in the summer of 1940, though after Dunkirk the entire British army was temporarily reduced to the rank of a minor state. The Royal Navy was still the world's largest, even if its resources now had to be spread between four theatres: home waters, the Atlantic, the Mediterranean and the Asian empire. The RAF was growing in defensive strength, both in terms of numbers and in terms of the integrated system of control and communication that was designed to ensure that fighters were used sparingly and effectively against any incoming enemy aircraft. Britain's global trading and financial economy and large merchant fleet meant that distant resources could be brought in to feed a war economy that was already overtaking German production in a range of weapons. Large orders placed in the United States committed American industry by August 1940, despite the Neutrality Laws passed in the 1930s, to supply 20,000 American aircraft and 42,000 aero-engines, in addition to a regular supply of 100-octane fuel, which allowed British fighter aircraft enhanced performance over their German rivals.[260] In July, it was agreed that Britain should pursue a three-pronged strategy for prosecuting the war against Germany and Italy that reflected current capabilities. The first was blockade and economic warfare, a key element in the Anglo-French planning for war in 1939; the second was political warfare against Axis-occupied Europe, to be carried out through a mix of political propaganda and sabotage ('set Europe ablaze' was Churchill's description); the third was long-range 'strategic' bombing of Germany and Italy, directed primarily against centres of industry within bombing range.

None of these campaigns could be conducted with any real hope of success. Blockade was frustrated by the unexpected fact that Germany and Italy now dominated most of continental Europe with access to a rich range of raw material and food resources, which German businesses and the German armed forces began almost immediately to co-ordinate for the German war effort. Political warfare and sabotage were at best a speculation. Radio and leaflet propaganda was difficult to co-ordinate between a number of rival organizations, each with its own agenda. Though intelligence sources suggested that in occupied Europe there was a receptive audience, the prospect of fomenting widespread resistance or local rebellion was almost non-existent, while the teams organized under the Special Operations Executive (SOE), placed incongruously under the minister of economic warfare, Hugh Dalton, took time to train before even a limited infiltration was possible. Most hope in the summer of 1940 was placed in the bombing of Germany. In a well-known letter in July to Lord Beaverbrook, minister of aircraft production, Churchill concluded that only 'an absolutely devastating, exterminating attack by very heavy bombers' would bring down the Hitler regime. Bombing had begun on the night of 11/12 May 1940 against targets in the Ruhr–Rhineland industrial region and continued almost every night when conditions permitted for the rest of the year. The impact on Germany was negligible, though the raids compelled thousands of Germans to sit in air-raid shelters over the summer nights and provoked widespread popular demands for the German air force to retaliate. Intelligence information had at first painted an optimistic account of the damage to industrial plant and popular morale, but the picture soon became bleaker once it was clear that only a small fraction of aircraft found the target area, and an even smaller fraction of bombs actually hit it.[261] Though later accounts have emphasized the psychological boost bombing gave to British morale, the early raids attracted very modest attention.

Beyond these efforts, Britain's leaders looked for support overseas. In the United States, opinion was divided not only over the prospects for British survival, but over the issue of American intervention in any more active way in the European war. Wooing the United States was a central ambition for Churchill, but he was wary of giving too much away. When there was talk in the summer of the British fleet sailing for the New World in the event of an invasion crisis, he told the British ambassador, Lord Lothian, to 'discourage any complacent assumption on United States' part that they will pick up the *débris* of the British Empire . . .'[262] For their part, American politicians could be put off by constant reiteration of the theme of empire, for which there was little support across America's political divides. 'We should all get on much better,' Senator Arthur Vandenberg told Lord Halifax, 'if you British would stop talking about the British Empire.'[263] Empire aid, on the other hand, could be taken for granted, although the role of the empire in the summer of 1940 was also more ambiguous after the Allied defeat than the heady rhetoric in London suggested. It was to take time before the manpower and industrial resources of the empire could be fully mobilized, and many of those resources were to be used for local defence rather than sent to Britain. In the first fifteen months of the conflict, Britain supplied 90 per cent of the empire's military needs.[264]

Mobilization of empire manpower varied widely. The instinct of the white Dominions was at first to reject the idea of sending forces overseas again, as they had done in the First World War, and to use their armies for home defence. The Australian government eventually reluctantly agreed to send forces to the Middle East; Canadian mobilization was made possible only because Francophone Canadians were promised no conscription and no oversea posting. In South Africa, where similar tensions existed between British and Afrikaner communities, South African volunteers who were prepared to fight outside the country wore a distinctive orange tab, itself a reminder of the dominant Dutch presence. Dominion support for the war continued in the summer of 1940, but the Australian premier, Robert Menzies, was attracted by the idea of a negotiated peace (though he later recanted), while in Canada there were bitter arguments about the terms for setting up RAF training facilities in the Dominion, and strong complaints about the conditions the first Canadian troops were forced to accept in camps in Britain.[265] In Éire, which was still a Dominion (though since 1937 an independent state), Prime Minister Éamon de Valera refused to abandon Irish neutrality even when offered the possibility of a united Ireland, which he had fought for two decades before. 'We, of all people,' he told the Irish parliament on 2 September 1939, 'know what force used by a stronger nation against a weaker one means.' Churchill grumbled about the Irish being 'at war but skulking', but the Irish government remained unmoved throughout the conflict.[266]

In the rest of the empire there was a mixed reaction. The situation in India was particularly delicate because there was an implicit assumption among Indian politicians from a variety of very different political backgrounds that support for the war would be recompensed with immediate promises of political reform or even independence. Indian troops were sent to support the Asian rim of the empire, in Iraq, Kenya, Aden, Egypt and Singapore, while substantial internal funds were raised to support the defence of India. But even though the main Indian parties were opposed to fascism, they wanted the British to concede an acceptable political price for fighting against it. On 29 June 1940 Gandhi called for full independence. Churchill's government was unwilling to make any major concessions beyond allowing a War Advisory Council to be established in Delhi, composed of Indians, together with an expanded Executive Committee, but with the key portfolios of defence, finance and home affairs firmly in British hands. The Congress Party began a campaign of civil disobedience in October, and 700 Congress leaders were immediately added to the 500 Indian Communist Party leaders already in prison. A Revolutionary Movement Ordinance was prepared in order to allow the government in India to outlaw the Congress Party and crush its organization, but the Cabinet in

London hesitated to use it. Nevertheless, by spring 1941 7,000 Congress members had been convicted and 4,400 incarcerated. Even for those Indians who supported participation in the war, Britain was only able to supply very limited resources because of the demands of home defence. India eventually contributed over 2 million volunteer troops, but the military condition of the Indian forces in the first years of the conflict was rudimentary. When war broke out the whole of the Indian subcontinent had no modern fighter aircraft and only one anti-aircraft gun; almost two years later, on the eve of the Japanese invasion of South East Asia, forces in India still possessed no modern fighter aircraft, tanks or armoured cars, and only twenty anti-aircraft and twenty anti-tank guns.[267] When Indian troops moved to other theatres, they had to be supplied almost entirely from British sources. So weak was the British position that when the Japanese insisted in early July 1940 that Britain close the 'Burma Road' supply line to Chiang Kai-shek's Nationalist forces in China, Churchill was forced to comply, unable to risk 'all the inconveniences of a war with Japan'.[268]

The other serious problem was Egypt. Although the country was nominally independent under the 1936 treaty, the British maintained a major political and military presence and enjoyed special privileges for the defence of the Suez Canal lifeline to the Asian empire. In May and June 1940, as British forces faced defeat in Europe, the Egyptian government of Ali Maher not only refused to be drawn into the war but actively sought to end the British presence. There was thought of imposing once again the protectorate that had been established in the First World War, or of declaring martial law, but in the end heavy-handed threats were enough for King Farouk to sack Maher and replace him with an Anglophile politician, Hassan Sabry. Though more accommodating to British demands, he too refused to commit Egypt to war; the Egyptian government only declared war on what was left of the Axis on 25 February 1945, to ensure a seat in the new United Nations organization. The British regarded their presence in Egypt as a vital component of their global strategy. The ports at either end of the canal were reinforced and heavy guns installed, in violation of the 1888 Canal Treaty.[269] German and Italian shipping was denied entry during the war but securing the defence of the canal against a determined enemy was difficult to reconcile with British priorities in Europe, and the threat to Suez remained a real one for the next two years. East of Suez, the promise that empire unity would mean British protection was impossible to redeem as long as the major threat remained that of German invasion. German intelligence passed on to the Japanese in November 1940 a secret document captured from a vessel sunk in the Indian Ocean which showed clearly the current British view that little could be done to save the imperial position in South East Asia if the worst happened. The empire was still a limited resource for Britain in 1940, but Britain was also now a limited resource for the empire and its many outposts.

These awkward issues were thrown into sharp relief by the reality now facing the three Allied empires – Dutch, Belgian and French – after German conquest. The Belgian and Dutch empires were cut off entirely from their mother countries. The armistice agreement with France allowed the Vichy authorities to retain what control they could over the French Empire, but the course of the war undermined the French imperial project almost entirely, leaving the empire in the hands of others. In 1942 the Vichy minister of colonies, Jules Brérié, finally resigned: 'my role is terminated, because we no longer have an Empire.'[270] For all three imperial states there were many imponderables to consider. The Axis plans for a New Order in Europe were uncertain and the fate of the overseas territories unknown. In mid-June 1940 at the meeting between Mussolini and Hitler, their foreign ministers, Ciano and von Ribbentrop, could be seen poring over a map of Africa in which they divided the wreckage of empire between them: North and West Africa for Italy, sub-Saharan Africa for the Germans. All such grandiose plans waited on the defeat of Britain, but in summer 1940 the idea of a German African empire re-emerged as a possibility and was enthusiastically pursued by the colonial lobby in the Foreign Office and the German navy, and by the Colonial League, whose leader, Ritter von Epp, was made provisional minister of colonies in June.[271] The first speculative planning suggested a German imperial bloc of former French colonies, the Belgian Congo, Nigeria, even South Africa and the Rhodesias, and included the use of the French island of Madagascar as a semi-autonomous home for Europe's Jewish population.[272] The German decision to allow France to retain the empire was not a permanent one, but merely reflected the desire to win France over from any possible rapprochement with Britain, though in the end Britain made sure that would not happen by treating Vichy France as a virtual enemy.

None of the three former imperial powers could be certain that Britain would not take advantage of their defeat to extend British influence into their imperial spheres, either from short-term strategic necessity, or with some longer-term plan in mind. In May 1940 Britain had occupied the Danish dominion of Iceland to forestall the Germans, and immediately began to treat the islanders in a familiar colonial fashion, arresting and deporting the island's small number of communists and controlling the country's trade.[273] Neither was the position of the United States encouraging. The American anti-colonial lobby actively promoted the idea that in future colonial empires should be held on trust from an international

body, like the mandates in 1919; more radical anti-imperialists saw the
European war as an opportunity to extend independence to all the former
dependencies. When Britain faced growing opposition to its rule in Iceland, United States forces took over in June 1941, and two years later the
island was declared an independent republic. In 1942 the American secretary of state, Cordell Hull, called for an international charter guaranteeing
eventual independence after the war to colonial peoples under a system of
international trusteeship.[274] The defeat of the metropolitan states bankrupted their claims to maintain imperial rule. The year 1940 was indeed a
critical turning point in the final crisis of the global imperial project.

   For Belgium and the Netherlands, the outcome of the military campaign
in 1940 produced a complex political situation. Both were now cut off from
their own empires and found themselves in the unfamiliar position of being
occupied themselves, subjects rather than rulers. The decision of the Belgian
king to stay in Brussels undermined the claims of those Belgian ministers
who had fled abroad to represent a Belgium in exile and placed the Belgian
Congo in a constitutional limbo. Because of the Congo's rich mineral
resources, including the world's largest uranium deposits, all the major powers were interested in its fate. There was talk of a possible Franco-German
arrangement to take the colony over; in Brussels the German authorities
hoped to press German claims on Belgium's colonial mining corporations; in
May 1940 the British government refused to recognize the Congo's neutrality because they hoped to use the Congo's rich resources for the Allied war
effort. In an attempt to ensure the survival of Belgian sovereignty, the king
decreed that the minister of colonies in exile, Albert De Vleeschauwer, should
have executive authority for the Congo and Rwanda-Burundi in order to
maintain their neutrality, but after pressure from the British, De Vleeschauwer agreed in July 1940 that the Congo's resources should be used for the
Allied war effort. A year later the Congo's currency and trade were integrated into the British economic zone.[275] The United States was also
interested in the Congo and by August 1941 had stationed 1,200 troops
there, including black troops who were removed at the insistence of the Belgian government-in-exile, to avoid encouraging the population of the colony
to see black Americans as a symbol for their own eventual liberation. De
Vleeschauwer struggled to maintain Belgian sovereignty in the face of British
and American intervention, but by 1943 there was now every indication that
after the war the United States would insist on the internationalization of the
former colonies as a prelude to independence.[276]

   The Netherlands faced a similarly bleak situation. The Dutch queen,
Wilhelmina, had sought refuge in London with a government-in-exile, but
there was little the exiled Dutch could do to hold the empire together. The

Caribbean colonies of Curaçao and Surinam were taken under British and American trusteeship, which left open their future fate.[277] German designs on the colonial economy were frustrated by the British naval blockade and the hostility of the Dutch colonial administration. The Dutch government in the Indies interned 2,800 Germans and 500 members of the Dutch National Socialist Party living in the colony, and in retaliation the German authorities in the Netherlands arrested 500 prominent Dutch citizens and sent them to Buchenwald concentration camp. Growing popular interest in the future of the colonies as a key element of Dutch national identity was interpreted by the Germans as a political threat, and the main political movement, Nederlandse Unie, was eventually banned.[278] The Dutch East Indies were immediately subject to pressure from the Japanese government to guarantee substantial increases in the supply of oil, rubber, tin and other raw materials essential for the Japanese war effort. The Indies were threatened with military intervention if they allowed other powers to undermine Japan's commercial interests, and although the government in Batavia (present-day Jakarta) successfully stalled the discussions with Japanese emissaries well into 1941, the Japanese had already assumed that the Indies were now part of their new economic order in Asia and seized the entire colony early in 1942, bringing the Dutch empire to a provisional end.[279]

The French Empire was an entirely different case, though its eventual fate during the war brought it closer to the Dutch and Belgian experience. The attitude of the Germans to the new Vichy regime encouraged the hope that the empire could be salvaged from the wreckage of metropolitan France. German economic demands from the African empire had to be met as a priority, but they were generally less excessive than expected and French forces were allowed to remain in the empire to keep domestic peace.[280] Marshal Pétain saw the empire as an essential element in the creation of a new order in France. Vichy propaganda played on the idea of unity between the mother country and the colonies and presented Pétain as the 'saviour of the Empire'; the Maritime and Colonial League trebled its membership during the war to over 700,000; a grand ten-year plan was elaborated for the economic development of the empire, including a new Trans-Saharan railway, some of which was built using forced Jewish labour; constitutional plans suggested a possible imperial parliament and imperial citizenship. The empire became, in Charles-Robert Ageron's term, a 'compensating myth' for the humiliation of defeat.[281] Yet the imperial reality was less rosy. Italian demands for territory were kept at bay only with German assistance but it was clear that at some point Mussolini hoped to achieve major territorial concessions at French expense. In

Indochina, pressure from the Japanese army to be allowed to deploy troops and aircraft in northern Vietnam proved impossible to deflect and by September 1940 there were 6,000 Japanese soldiers and 5 air bases in place, the start of a steady encroachment.[282] However, the main threat to the integrity of the French Empire in 1940 came paradoxically not from the Axis states, but from the former British ally. While Axis claims were for the moment held on a leash, there was no way of restraining Britain.

British policy towards its recent ally was coloured by the hope in June 1940 that the French government might continue the fight alongside Britain with the aircraft, troops and ships available in the empire. The British colonial minister, Lord Lloyd, was sent to Bordeaux on 19 June to try to extract a promise that French resistance would continue from North Africa and that the French Mediterranean fleet would sail there in support. The promise was briefly given, but summarily reneged on.[283] When the armistice was signed, the empire abandoned the struggle as well. All that was left to the British were a small number of French forces that had been brought to England and the deputy war minister, Charles de Gaulle. On 18 June he was allowed to make a broadcast from London calling on Frenchmen to continue the fight, and ten days later he was recognized by the Churchill government as the leader of the 'Fighting French'. The fighters brought to Britain were not enthusiastic. Out of 11,000 sailors all but 1,500 opted to return to France; only 2,000 soldiers answered the call. But though his supporters were few, the British decision to pretend that there still was a French ally alienated the new regime at Vichy, which condemned de Gaulle to death *in absentia* as a traitor.[284]

The confrontation between the British authorities and the Vichy government now involved the fate of the French fleet. The British Chiefs of Staff did not want the fleet to fall into German hands because it would tilt the balance of naval power in the Mediterranean strongly against them. With some reluctance the War Cabinet decided that the fleet would have to be captured or destroyed pre-emptively. On 3 July the Royal Navy launched Operation 'Catapult' against the French navy. Some 200 ships were boarded and seized in British ports, the naval vessels in the Egyptian port of Alexandria were disarmed and a battlecruiser at the West African port of Dakar was torpedoed. At the main base at Mers-el-Kébir, near the Algerian city of Oran, a British squadron commanded by Admiral James Somerville blockaded the port and gave the French commander, Admiral Marcel-Bruno Gensoul, an ultimatum to either scuttle his ships, or sail to a British, American or Caribbean port, or accept the consequences of combat. Gensoul assumed it was a bluff and refused to comply. After eleven hours of waiting, the British ships finally opened fire, sinking the battleship

Bretagne and damaging two others. On 6 July, the battleship *Dunkerque* was hit by a torpedo and severely damaged. The French navy lost 1,297 killed, 351 wounded. A few days later Vichy broke all diplomatic relations and sent bombers to raid the British naval base at Gibraltar.[285]

The assault on the French fleet shocked French opinion but it was only one part of Britain's naval strategy directed at the French Empire. The blockade was now extended to France and the French African colonies, cutting North African trade and reducing key imports of food and oil into French colonies. Oil imports to Algeria dropped to just 5 per cent of the pre-war level. Vichy convoys were attacked by British vessels. The effects created local food crises and sustained the resentment of the Vichy regime and pro-Vichy colonists against British intervention.[286] After Mers-el-Kébir, Admiral Darlan had briefly explored the idea of a joint Italian–French naval attack against Alexandria until it was vetoed by Mussolini.[287] The British also put pressure on French colonies to side with de Gaulle. At first only the Pacific New Hebrides had done so, but they were followed later in 1940 by Gabon, Cameroon, Chad and Tahiti, dividing the empire into two armed camps.[288] In August, the British hoped to bring Senegal over to the Free French side and, with de Gaulle's co-operation, undertook a second operation, codenamed 'Menace', against the capital, Dakar, where the battleship *Richelieu* was berthed, and where both the Polish and Belgian national gold reserves had been stashed away for safety. The result this time was a fiasco, with heavy damage to the Royal Navy vessels involved and stiff resistance from the Vichy garrison. The operation was suspended, but it gave notice to every European empire that Britain was prepared ruthlessly to impose British wartime interests on the colonies of others. In the autumn, rumours abounded that France was about to conclude a separate peace, or to take the empire into a pan-European bloc directed at Britain. Churchill fulminated against the French and threatened to bomb Vichy if the regime joined the German war effort.[289] Watching from the Netherlands, the Dutch fascist leader, Anton Mussert, claimed that 300 years of British imperialism represented the real enemy of Europe, and called on the Dutch settlers in South Africa to restart the Boer War.[290]

For the European Axis states, the British Empire remained the one stumbling block to the political reordering of continental Europe and the Mediterranean basin, but little effort was made to co-ordinate their strategies for bringing Britain to defeat or capitulation. The sudden opportunity opened up by victory in France exposed just how little thinking there had been beforehand about future strategy, but in neither Rome nor Berlin was there much enthusiasm for working out this strategy together. Mussolini insisted that his was a 'parallel war', not one combined with Hitler's. He accepted the arguments about limiting territorial claims against France with an ill grace, and disapproved of the German decision to allow Vichy to keep defence forces in North Africa against the British because they could also be used against Italy.[291] The two regimes had different views of the coming New Order; for Mussolini it was imperative that Italy establish a European imperial presence, as Hitler had now done across the whole north of the Continent, and not be confined to an empire in Africa or the Middle East. Hitler in turn was happy enough for Mussolini to develop a Mediterranean sphere, but he instructed his armed forces to give no secrets away to the Italians. When, in late June, Mussolini offered to send an Italian expeditionary corps to take part in whatever campaign Hitler was planning against Britain, Hitler gave a polite but definite refusal. In turn, Mussolini refused Hitler's offer of German aircraft to carry out bombing of the Suez Canal. 'Evidently,' wrote Ciano in his diary, 'faith in us and in our possibilities is not excessive!'[292] The 'Pact of Steel' by which the Italian–German alliance was supposed to have been sealed in May 1939 remained little more than a gesture. Until the spring of 1941 the two allies went their separate ways.

The strategic options available for Hitler and his military leadership to end the war in the West in the summer of 1940 could be reduced to two: either to find a political solution that the British would accept, or to find a military means to end British resistance. Neither was straightforward, first because it was unclear whether the peace party in Britain really did have the political means to deliver a compromise agreement, secondly because it was not clear that any of the possible military options, from blockade to invasion, was sure to succeed. In the end he tried all the strategic options, in the hope that one would work. The political solution seemed less likely after Churchill's speech on 18 June pledging Britain to fight on alone, but Hitler privately could not understand why the British wanted to continue. Franz Halder, the army chief of staff, recorded a meeting with Hitler on 13 July: 'The Führer is fully occupied with the question, why England does not want to take the path to peace?'[293] Hitler's confusion lay in the mixed messages emanating from Britain about the possibility of reaching agreement. Behind the scenes, a string of go-betweens kept alive in 1940 the idea that there were influential circles in Britain capable of delivering a negotiated settlement. In Britain, noted Goebbels in his diary in late June, 'there are two parties: a powerful war and peace party'; a few days later he observed 'Rumours of peace from England thicken.'[294]

In early July Hitler decided that he would make one more public appeal to Britain to see sense. In the days leading up to the speech planned for the Reichstag on 19 July, Hitler explained to his staff that he did not want to be the instrument for destroying the British Empire because German blood would be spilt only for the benefit of the Americans and the Japanese.[295] Historians have been understandably sceptical about the claim, but Hitler shared with Churchill a sentimental admiration for what the British Empire had achieved. In the 1930s, and again during the war, Hitler came back to the theme that the British Empire was a model for Germany's own colonial plans – as it was for other German imperialists.[296] This schizophrenic view of the British enemy was reflected in the speech eventually delivered on 19 July. Hitler prefaced the offer by prophesying the destruction of an empire 'which it was never my intention to destroy or even to damage'; it was followed by a brief appeal to reason: 'I see no ground which could compel the struggle to continue.'[297] The appeal, he told Goebbels, was to be a 'short, brief offer' with nothing precise, but it was to be his 'very last word'.[298] Churchill refused to respond. When Robert Vansittart, the Cabinet's diplomatic adviser, asked him why he had not replied, Churchill told him he had nothing to say to Hitler, 'not being on speaking terms'.[299] Lord Halifax rejected the offer a few days later, and Hitler reluctantly accepted that this was 'the final refusal'.[300]

Hitler anticipated rejection, though there is little doubt that a British request for an armistice would have been his preferred option, despite the fact that the preservation of the British Empire ran against the interests of his Italian, Japanese and Soviet allies. But even before the speech was made, he had re-issued the November 1939 directive for an air–sea blockade of Britain and had authorized military planning for a possible invasion of southern England. The invasion directive for Operation 'Sea Lion' (Seelöwe) was issued on 16 July for a landing on the English south-east coast. The precondition for the invasion was the suppression of the RAF to a level where it would no longer have 'any worthwhile capacity to attack the German crossing'.[301] In the discussions with his staff a few days before, he had also suggested for the first time a more radical military solution to the problem of British resistance. Trying to grasp the grounds of British intransigence, he began to suspect that Britain counted on reaching an agreement with the Soviet Union. Two days after his peace offer, Hitler met his commanders-in-chief and elaborated his thinking into a possible campaign: 'Russia must be watched very closely,' recorded his air force adjutant. 'An attack on Russia had to be planned for, and in the greatest secrecy.' Hitler called for newsreels of the Soviet–Finnish war so he could understand his putative victim more closely.[302] On 31 July he finally explained his strategic conclusion to his military commanders. Since Britain would not give up, preparations should be undertaken for a possible pre-emptive strike against the Soviet Union to rule out any final hope that Britain might harbour for fomenting a two-front war. For the present this was a contingency only, not a firm directive for enlarging the war, but it framed Hitler's subsequent conviction that the solution to the defeat of the British Empire lay in the East.

This decision has commonly been seen as the root of the massive operation undertaken a year later against the Red Army and a clear indication that Hitler was no longer interested in invading or subjugating Britain. This is to distort the reality. The German high command favoured the idea that somehow, either through blockade or invasion or political initiatives, they might secure a British capitulation and Hitler, as he told his commanders on 21 July, did not want the British 'to take the initiative out of his hands'.[303] The suggestions about a Soviet alternative were initially a reaction against British intransigence rather than deliberate. Hitler's priority in the summer of 1940 was still to end British resistance, not yet to carve out an empire in Russia. The British and Soviet strategies were complementary, not stark alternatives. There were, nevertheless, solid grounds for Hitler's concern about Soviet ambitions. Stalin used the opportunity of Germany's war with the West to press Soviet claims agreed under the secret terms of the Pact in August 1939. Step by step, the Soviet Union was trespassing towards the new German imperial sphere in the East. When Churchill sent the radical socialist politician Sir Stafford Cripps to Moscow in June 1940 as ambassador ('a lunatic in a country of lunatics', Churchill later commented) it raised the distinct possibility in Berlin that a British–Soviet rapprochement might be the aim.[304] 'Unclear,' Hitler told his military staff on 21 July, 'what is happening in England'; a few days later Goebbels noted that a few heavy blows would be needed 'to bring [England] to its senses'.[305]

The German plans for military action against Britain were serious enough. For all the thoughts of the Soviet threat, German forces spent almost a year in constant combat with the British at sea, in the air and, in spring 1941, on land as well. None of this substantial effort made sense if Hitler's gaze was now fixed solely on the Soviet Union. The production of land armaments was scaled down in summer 1940 in favour of redirecting resources to aircraft and naval production, while the high command prepared the directives and material necessary to carry out the amphibious invasion. The planning was extensive and detailed, and again made little sense if the invasion scare was simply designed to put psychological pressure on the British leadership to abandon the fight. It was nevertheless an unanticipated campaign for the German armed forces which put the onus on the navy and the air force to create the appropriate conditions for a crossing. Neither service had been oriented before the war to the conduct of major amphibious operations or long-range air warfare. The navy had suffered severe losses during the Norwegian campaign and there were still too few submarines to pose a major threat to British naval intervention. Much more rested on the capacity of the German air force to protect the invasion sea lanes and suppress British air power. The problem was that German air fleets had been used to best effect so far in support of land offensives in Poland in 1939, and Scandinavia and Western Europe in 1940; the air force had little experience of long-range independent operations. The reorientation to a major overseas campaign and the building of suitable airfields took time. In the end, the German air force prepared for a larger version of what had been carried out in Poland and France, destroying enemy air power and softening up the enemy's military infrastructure prior to invasion, then building a protective umbrella over the invasion force against enemy naval power while offering tactical air support for ground operations.[306]

Both sides realized that air power was the critical factor in the summer of 1940. The British Chiefs of Staff observed in July that 'the crux of the matter is air superiority'.[307] What followed in the late summer months was the first major air-to-air conflict of the war. The two air forces were organized very differently, the German air force in large air fleets combining together bomber, fighter, dive-bomber and reconnaissance aircraft in each one, the RAF in separate commands defined by function – Fighter Command, Bomber Command, Coastal Command – but with no combined force for supporting army or navy operations. In France the German air force stationed Air Fleets 2 and 3 with the great bulk of its air strength, a total of seventy-seven combat squadrons; in Norway the much smaller Air Fleet 5 (six squadrons) was expected to attack targets on the east and north-east coasts. In early August, on the eve of the German air campaign, there were 878 serviceable Messerschmitt Me109 single-seat fighters, 310 Messerschmitt 110 twin-engine fighters, 949 serviceable bombers and 280 dive-bombers. The RAF had in early August 715 serviceable fighters (19 squadrons of the Supermarine Spitfire and 29 squadrons of Hawker Hurricanes) with a further 424 aircraft available at one day's notice. Bomber Command was much smaller than its German equivalent, with only 667 bomber aircraft in July 1940, and around 85 per cent of its sorties in the summer were directed at targets in Germany rather than against German air bases, stores and invasion shipping.[308] The RAF had a larger pool of fighter pilots than the German air force, and across the period of daytime air fighting British factories turned out 2,091 new fighter planes, German factories only 988. The critical element of the battle was fighter-to-fighter combat and it was this that was to decide the issue of the battle over southern England. The commander-in-chief of British home forces, General Alan Brooke, gave the RAF the simple order: 'to prevent the enemy establishing air superiority'.[309]

The Germans began the campaign to achieve air superiority with a whimper rather than a bang. Probing attacks – *Störangriffe* – were carried out with a handful of aircraft by day and night through late June and July to test the defences and to give aircrew the chance to orient themselves to conditions over British soil. The probing failed to detect the nature of Fighter Command organization, which depended on a complex network of communications to give warning of approaching raids and to co-ordinate the fighter response. The central element was the use of radar (radio direction finding) developed from the mid-1930s. A chain of thirty radar stations to detect high-flying aircraft, and thirty-one for low-flying aircraft, stretched from Cornwall in the far west to the north of Scotland; they were supported by a ground Observer Corps of 30,000 organized in 1,000 observation points. The radar and observation posts were linked by a web of telephone lines to Fighter Command headquarters and the numerous fighter stations so that warning could be given in a few minutes and fighter aircraft scrambled for action. Though the commander-in-chief of Fighter Command, Air Chief Marshal Hugh Dowding, later com-plained that the system had often supplied 'inaccurate and insufficient intelligence', enough was supplied to ensure that almost all enemy incur-sions were met with some measure of fighter resistance, and time was not wasted on standing patrols.[310] After more than a month of preparation and probing, Göring, commander-in-chief of the German air force, wanted to test RAF resistance with a flourish of attacks against Fighter Com-mand targets beginning with the code-named 'Eagle Day' and ending, so he hoped, four days later with British air defences crushed. On 1 August, Hitler's headquarters issued the order to begin the campaign for air supremacy and 'Eagle Day' was fixed for 5 August.[311] Poor weather condi-tions delayed the opening of the campaign for more than a week. 'Eagle Day' was then ordered for 13 August, but cloud forced a half-hearted opening and not a single Fighter Command station was attacked that day. German losses were forty-five aircraft, RAF losses just thirteen.

The messy opening to what came to be called the Battle of Britain was sustained over the course of the following weeks. The promise that the RAF would be crippled after just four days, based though it was on the suc-cesses enjoyed earlier in 1939 and 1940, proved impossible to realize. Over the three-week period of the opening phase of the battle fifty-three raids were made on RAF stations, with growing intensity in the last ten days of August as the weather improved. Of these, thirty-two raids were on fighter stations, all but two directed at 11 Group in south-east England, but only three stations were temporarily put out of action, all of them forward sta-tions near the coast. Satellite airfields allowed aircraft to be flown despite damage to the main station, while careful camouflage veiled the scattered aircraft. Radar stations had been briefly bombed earlier in August, but because the German side did not consider them important, the chain remained relatively unscathed. Though much has been made of the narrow margin between success and defeat, a view embroidered by Churchill's famous line about the 'few' of Fighter Command, at no point during the last weeks of August and early September was Fighter Command significantly reduced in size or its number of pilots insufficient. On 6 September Fighter Command had 738 serviceable aircraft while the German fighter force was down to an average of 500.[312] By this stage the Junkers Ju87 dive-bomber and the twin-engine Me110 had been more or less withdrawn as too vulnerable to be risked against high-performance single-engine fighters. Losses on both sides were high. It was a tough and dramatic confrontation, but that was what Britain's air defences were for.

The German enemy also considered the RAF to be the 'few'. By late August German intelligence suggested that 18 fighter stations had been knocked out and that Fighter Command was down to around 300 aircraft at most. German radio announced that 'domination of the air' had been achieved.[313] To pilots who reported back the sight of blazing buildings and pock-marked runways, and regularly exaggerated by a high margin the number of aircraft shot down, the claim initially tallied with their own experience. This explains the decision to switch by the end of August to a range of military and economic targets designed to weaken the British defence effort immediately prior to invasion. At Hitler's headquarters the news from the air front suggested that air supremacy was all but assured. 'English fighter defence strongly affected,' wrote the official OKW diarist on 3 September, 'the question is can England therefore continue the struggle.'[314] The final stage of the pre-invasion air plan was to attack London with a series of heavy blows to disorient the capital at the point of greatest threat. On 2 September the air force was directed to organize attacks on London and three days later Hitler ordered them to begin, still hoping that the news about air supremacy was right. On the night of 5/6 September bombs dropped on thirty London boroughs, from Croydon in the south to Enfield in the north, aiming at military, transport and utility targets.[315]

The myth has lingered on that Hitler shifted air attacks to London on 7 September as revenge for RAF raids on Berlin in late August and that this change in target saved Fighter Command. In reality the switch to London and to other military and industrial targets was consistent with the pre-invasion planning, and bombs had fallen on London areas for more than a week before, including the extensive raiding on the 5/6 September.[316] Hitler was able to use the switch as the opportunity to still criticism from the German communities in western Germany that had been subjected to

RAF bombing for four months. In a widely publicized speech on 4 September, he promised the German public that he would raze British cities to the ground, but the claim was rhetorical. The disabling attacks on London were supposed to be followed a week or so later by invasion. Hitler had fixed the date for 15 September, when the tides were favourable and fine weather not impossible. On the 3rd he altered the date to 20/21 September. Göring continued to insist that the RAF was on its last legs. The war against Britain, he told Goebbels, would all be over in three weeks.[317]

The British had been preparing for invasion for months, and indeed the political and military leadership had expected it to happen within a few weeks of the French defeat and to be a disaster. Brooke observed in July that the shortage of trained men and equipment was 'appalling'. At Dunkirk the army had lost 88 per cent of its artillery and 93 per cent of its vehicles.[318] Between June and August 1940, a further 324,000 men were called up, but it was too late to train and equip them. There were 300,000 First World War rifles available for the 22 army divisions, only half of which could be regarded as ready for the kind of mobile combat the Germans would wage.[319] So desperate did the situation seem that Cripps was instructed when he got to Moscow to try to buy Soviet aircraft and tanks, a request that was politely turned down.[320] There was no way of working out exactly when the invasion might come and though historians have generally been sceptical about German intentions, the British certainly thought it was going to happen. The population, according to Home Intelligence reports, remained expectant but less anxious than in the early summer, buoyed up by news from the air battles, which, like German reports, greatly exaggerated the losses inflicted on the enemy. In early September the Ministry of Information observed that the public mood seemed 'extraordinarily good', reflected not least in the fact that drunkenness seemed to have decreased.[321] In early September evidence from photo-reconnaissance and decrypts of German air force 'Enigma' messages, or 'Ultra' (first broken in May 1940) suggested an imminent invasion, and on 7 September the codeword 'Cromwell' was issued to put the whole military system on highest alert to expect invasion within twelve hours. Nothing happened, but the following weekend, 14–15 September, was widely regarded as 'invasion weekend' because of favourable tides and moon. Men were ordered to sleep in their uniforms to be ready to fight at a moment's notice when they heard the toll of local bells.[322]

By chance, 14 September was the date on which Hitler met with his commanders-in-chief to review the prospects for Operation 'Sea Lion'. Throughout September he had received mixed messages about the possibility of an invasion. His chief of operations, Alfred Jodl, favoured the more indirect route suggested in the summer to 'go round via Russia'.[323] The navy commander-in-chief, Grand Admiral Erich Raeder, had initially been in favour, but by September thought the risks too high. Göring continued to insist that his force had met the requirements and the timetable. Hitler understood that the invasion had to work at the first attempt because the political fall-out from failure would undermine the year's successes, but on 14 September, according to his air adjutant, he still considered 'a successful "Sea Lion" as the best solution for victory against England'.[324] The principal issue was the air war. The invasion plan had always been predicated on achieving air mastery. Despite Göring's assurances, OKW had come to realize by the middle of September that British air resistance had not been broken; the invasion depended critically on using the air force to shield the cross-Channel force from naval interception and to provide air support for the initial beachheads. Hitler decided to review the position on 17 September, by which time the German air force had been badly mauled in daylight raids on London two days before, losing almost one-quarter of the attacking force on what became for the British 'Battle of Britain Day'. 'Sea Lion' was postponed again and on 12 October abandoned for the year, to be revived if necessary the following spring.

The British Empire did not collapse or accept defeat in 1940, but the year was a turning point in the long history of European imperialism. Defeat and occupation in Europe undermined fatally the claims of the other metropolitan powers, France, Belgium and the Netherlands, to dominate distant territories. For the British Empire, the crisis raised awkward questions about the future. Nevertheless, the British government refused to confront the paradox of emphasizing the value of the empire to Britain's war effort, while at the same time using force to stifle demands for greater political autonomy in India and running Egypt under virtual martial law. The priority was the survival of the home islands. Neither side, German nor British, could find a strategy capable of undermining the other's war willingness, or of achieving a decisive military result, but it seems almost certain that with an army of 180 divisions and the spoils of much of continental Europe, Germany would have found a way in 1941 of bringing the war in the West to an end if Hitler had not turned to the East. Britain, by contrast, had no way of achieving victory over Germany. Expelled from Europe twice in Norway and France, facing crisis in Africa, economically weakened, desperately defending its access to the wider world economy, Britain faced strategic bankruptcy. The war Britain waged for a year after the fall of France was the one prepared for in the 1930s – air defence, a powerful navy, and lesser imperial conflicts. This was the war Chamberlain had prepared for, but Churchill was the one forced to wage it.

2

Imperial Fantasies, Imperial Realities, 1940–43

'The Governments of Germany, Italy and Japan consider it the prerequisite of a lasting peace that every nation in the world shall receive the space to which it is entitled . . . it is their prime purpose to establish and maintain a new order of things . . .'

Three Power Pact, September 1940[1]

At one o'clock in the afternoon of 27 September 1940, the foreign ministers of Germany and Italy, together with the Japanese ambassador in Berlin, sat down at a gilded table in the gala hall of the Reich Chancellery, surrounded by a sea of ornate uniforms, to sign formally the Three Power Pact between their three empires. Outside, crowds of schoolchildren waved Japanese and Italian flags, though, according to Count Ciano, the Italian foreign minister, 'without conviction'. Ciano found the atmosphere in the hall frostier than he had expected, but attributed the Berliners' ill temper and poor health to the long nights spent in air-raid shelters under British bombs.[2] After the signatures had been affixed to the document, which at Japanese request had been written in English to speed up the formalities, there were three loud knocks on the vast entrance door. As it swung open, Hitler entered with exaggerated theatricality, sat silently at the table, and waited for the three signatories to make their prepared speeches for the world's news. On the other side of the globe, in Tokyo, a less grandiloquent ceremony took place. The emperor had agreed the pact only a week before, which explains the hasty drafting in English to avoid any mistakes in translation. The Japanese foreign minister, Matsuoka Yōsuke, appended his name to an agreement that he later claimed was designed to inaugurate 'the construction, not the destruction, of world peace.'[3] The pact was intended to last for ten years. It committed the three states to give military assistance to each other in the event that any new power entered the war against them – a threat directed obtrusively at the

United States. But more than that, the pact divided the Old World up between the three imperial powers: Germany in continental Europe, Italy in the Mediterranean basin and Africa, Japan in East Asia. Here each was to solidify and extend a 'New Order'. The geopolitical agreement publicly signalled the moment when the three powers felt confident enough to declare that the old imperial order, dominated for centuries by the British and French empires, was finally at an end.

THE BRITISH PROBLEM

The grand declaration of a new political order still left suspended the question of what to do with a British Empire that had not admitted defeat. The 'British problem' cut both ways: Britain was a barrier, however fragile it looked, to consolidating the new orders; but for Britain, the issue was how to obstruct these ambitions without overstretching resources and risking further failures, even the loss of the empire.

The German postponement of Operation 'Sea Lion' exposed the uncertainties that still existed in German planning to bring the war with Britain to an end. Two avenues were advocated by Hitler's political and military circle: first, the creation of a 'continental bloc' to convince Britain that there was no political alternative to a compromise peace; second, a peripheral strategy aimed at eliminating Britain by military means from the Mediterranean, where British forces were weakened by the demands of home defence. The first was already under way following the defeat of France, once it was realized that the European economy could now be dominated from Berlin. German economists and officials began to talk of a 'greater economic area' that now embraced all of Europe and not just the East; plans were set in motion for integrated markets, a common currency bloc based on the Reichsmark, a common currency clearing scheme and German economic penetration of European industry and banking.[4] The reconstruction of the economy by turning Berlin into Europe's financial and commercial capital was designed to challenge the dominant position the City of London had previously enjoyed. It was a preliminary step to isolating Britain politically, and it reflected pre-war thinking about a new global order of economic zones, popular also among Japan's leaders. This idea of a 'continental bloc' required, if possible, the recruitment of Vichy France and Franco's Spain to the Axis camp, as well as the consolidation of the relationship with the Soviet Union founded on the German–Soviet Pact. By the autumn, with Britain undefeated, the idea of welding 'a powerful effective alliance against Britain' seems temporarily to have attracted Hitler too.[5]

In late October 1940 Hitler undertook what was for him an unusual itinerary. Against the standard practice of expecting European politicians to visit him in Berlin, he boarded the Führer train for a series of summit talks, first with General Franco, then Marshal Pétain, and finally his fellow dictator, Mussolini. The object was to test the idea of a continental bloc and a Mediterranean option against the British Empire. It is not clear that he expected much success from the tour, but the staff at OKW, supported by the commanders-in-chief of the air force and navy, had been arguing for some time that a better way to get at Britain was to occupy Gibraltar, threaten British shipping from air bases in Africa and capture the Suez Canal, not only cutting Britain off from the Asian empire, but opening the path to the oil of the Middle East. The military planners had produced a directive for Operation 'Felix', the capture of Gibraltar. Mussolini's forces were now on Egyptian territory with a large army, but the whole enterprise depended on political agreement with Spain, France and Italy to isolate Britain and to co-ordinate the campaign. The initiative was doomed to failure over the issue of empire. Franco's price for co-operation was a share of France's empire in Africa and extensive subsidies, but it was not clear even then that he would join the war effort. When they met at Hendaye on 23 October on the Franco-Spanish border, it soon became clear to Hitler that nothing was to be gained from the Generalissimo; concessions from the French African empire would alienate France and make the 'bloc' unattainable. At Montoire on the 24th, Pétain echoed Franco's reluctance, and worried about the Spanish and Italian threat to French possessions; Mussolini, met at Florence on the 28th, remained strongly opposed to any bloc that involved accepting the status quo of the French Empire or making concessions to Spain.[6] That same day he had ordered the invasion of Greece without telling Hitler in advance, a symbolic rejection of any idea of political co-ordination.

The remaining prospect for the idea of an anti-British bloc was the Soviet Union, which had already reached a separate rapprochement with Mussolini earlier in the summer.[7] On 10 November the Soviet foreign minister, Vyacheslav Molotov, arrived in Berlin to extend agreements arrived at in the division of Poland the year before. It was von Ribbentrop's hope that he could build on the success of his earlier negotiations by persuading the Soviet Union that its proper sphere of influence was towards the British Empire in Asia and the Middle East, which was now open to political pressure and might soon be cut off from the Suez lifeline. There was talk that Stalin could be persuaded to join the Three Power Pact directed at Britain, but when von Ribbentrop broached the idea, Molotov said it was possible only with major German concessions. Hitler, von Ribbentrop later recalled, was reticent about the idea and more inclined to see a 'monstrous danger' in appeasing Stalin further.[8] The political solution collapsed when it was clear that Molotov and Stalin were principally concerned to extend Soviet interests into south-eastern Europe and Turkey, areas of German and Italian interest. The net result was that none of the putative members of a pan-European alliance was interested in fighting the British Empire, except for Italy. Following the three days of meetings, Hitler's views on the relationship between the assault on the Soviet Union and the eventual defeat of Britain hardened, but it had already been reinforced by political failure in Spain and France. On the train from Montoire, Hitler had told his OKW staff that there was no real alternative to knocking out the Soviet Union in the summer of 1941 in order to be sure then of defeating Britain. Hitler was ill at ease with diplomacy, more confident about violence.[9]

By the autumn German strategy had reached something of an impasse. There remained in place the blockade directive, re-stated on 1 August 1940 before the onset of the air battles, and, by default, an air–sea blockade now became the principal means to put direct pressure on the enemy. The object was to impose a level of economic warfare against British food and raw material supplies sufficient to deplete the British war economy and undermine popular willingness to continue the war. On 16 September Göring directed the air force to switch to a pattern of night-bombing directed at port installations, food and oil stocks, warehousing and food processing targets, and key utilities; from November operations were authorized against the British aeronautical industry and, in particular, the aero-engine sector. The naval campaign against British shipping had been conducted since the start of the war, but Hitler now ordered its intensification. There was little co-ordination between the two services, due largely to Göring's unwillingness to release German aircraft for the war at sea, and the navy had to make do with a handful of aircraft to supplement what surface vessels and submarines could achieve. Aircraft dropped 5,704 mines around the British coastline between August 1940 and June 1941, while the handful of long-range Focke-Wulf 200 'Condor' aircraft contributed to sinking 119 merchant ships in the year from June 1940 with a total tonnage of 345,000. More success was hoped for from the naval blockade. The plan was to sink a monthly average of 750,000 tons of Britain's 22 million tons of merchant shipping, a rate of loss that was expected to force the British government to abandon the war.[10]

The sea blockade comprised much more than the submarine fleet that straddled the Atlantic approaches from the bases now available on the French Atlantic coast. Knowing its weaknesses in capital ships, the German

navy instead used hit-and-run tactics, operating a mix of converted merchant raiders ('ghost ships') and individual warships. These proved hard for
the Royal Navy to track across great expanses of ocean. The 'ghost ships'
accounted for half-a-million tons of shipping by the end of 1941; the *Scheer*,
Hipper, *Scharnhorst* and *Gneisenau* accounted between them for a further
265,000.[11] The new battleship *Bismarck*, launched in May 1941, destroyed
the British battlecruiser *Hood* on her maiden voyage, but was sunk a few
days later before she could inflict any further damage. The key instrument
of blockade, however, was the German submarine (*Unterseeboot* or U-
boat). The German commander Admiral Karl Dönitz had at his disposal
relatively few of them. Although by early 1941 there were almost two hundred U-boats, at any one time there was an average of only twenty-two at
sea, and in January 1941 only eight.[12] Nevertheless, they were able to exact
a growing toll once secure bases were available in western France. In the
autumn Dönitz ordered his vessels to operate in so-called 'wolf packs'
(*Rudeltaktik*). Because of the air threat to shipping around the southern
coasts, British trans-oceanic trade had been transferred to the west and
north-west coast. It was here in the northern approaches that the German
U-boats were concentrated. From September onwards German submariners enjoyed what they called 'happy times'. In October 1940 they
sank 350,000 tons, but by April 1941 reached a peak of 687,000 tons.[13]

   The British government had long anticipated a renewal of the submarine
war but had not expected the outcome faced from the summer of 1940, with
German control of most of the northern European littoral. Though shipping
was convoyed from the start of the war (for coastal shipping from 6 September 1939, for ocean-going shipping two days later) the invasion threat in
autumn 1940 tied up many smaller escort vessels to defend Britain's south-
east coast. From October, once the invasion threat was lifted, escorts could
be increased in number, sailors trained for convoy protection and anti-
submarine warfare, and more aircraft detailed to the campaign. Over the
winter the aircraft of Coastal Command, including the long-range Sunder-
land flying boats, forced the German submarines away from inland waters
and the northern approaches, further out into the Atlantic. New technology
helped to improve escort and aircraft performance: the use of high-powered
illumination, the introduction of metric wavelength radar (called ASV Mk I
and II for aircraft, type 286 for escort vessels) and improved depth-charges.[14]
From February 1941, the anti-submarine defences were reorganized with
the establishment of the Western Approaches Command in Liverpool,
responsible for the entire anti-submarine campaign with enhanced naval
escort and air strength, but the key element of strategy, with the help of
naval intelligence, was to try to avoid the submarines altogether. Over the

course of 1940 and 1941 losses from convoyed shipping remained low; out of 8,722 ship sailings on the main North Atlantic route in 1940–41, 256 were lost, some to submarines, some to conventional maritime causes. Ships sailing independently, or stragglers, were regular targets, but finding a convoy and breaking its formation was a formidable task.[15]

The cumulative losses across all seas did, nevertheless, constitute a substantial danger to the British war effort. The volume of imports fell sharply and was subject to stringent controls (in November 1940 the trade in bananas was suspended for the duration). In March 1941, Churchill dubbed the sea war the 'Battle of the Atlantic', which, like the Battle of Britain, has assumed an iconic status in the memory of Britain's war. He chaired the Battle of the Atlantic ad hoc committee, which authorized a faster turn-round time in port, swifter repair of merchant vessels and further restrictions on imports. Every effort was expended on producing more escort vessels. The overall effect by the early summer of 1941 was to limit the U-boat radius of action and impose rising losses. In March three U-boat 'aces' were killed attacking convoys with strong escorts; in May 1941 another 'ace', Otto Kretschmer, was captured together with his vessel's cypher tables for the German naval Enigma, enabling Bletchley Park to begin reading naval messages regularly from the summer onwards. Between January and May 1941 U-boats had made contact with 23 per cent of all convoys, from June to August 1941 only 4 per cent.[16] After a year of effort, the attrition of British shipping proved too little to affect Britain's capacity or willingness to wage war.

The same was true for the air war conducted chiefly against British ports and commerce from September 1940 to June 1941. Although the popular memory of what the British soon christened the 'Blitz' sees German bombing as indiscriminate terror-bombing, Hitler twice insisted when asked by his staff that he would not yet authorize terror, though he reserved the right to do so in retaliation for RAF bombing, whose sheer inaccuracy during the autumn and winter months was interpreted in Germany as deliberately indiscriminate.[17] The port cities, including London and the inland port of Manchester, were the principal targets over the course of the nine-month campaign. Out of 171 major raids, 141 were directed at ports and their storage and processing facilities, absorbing 86 per cent of all incendiaries dropped and 85 per cent of all high explosives.[18] German leaders were hopeful that the regular night-bombing would also act to demoralize the population and provoke social and political protest to supplement the official anxiety about food and trade. In November orders went out to attack the aircraft industry, a campaign that included the bombing of Coventry (Operation 'Moonlight Sonata') on the night of 14/15 November, during which much of the city centre was burnt down, though the bombers were supposed to be aiming for thirty aero-engine and component factories, some of which suffered severe damage. Attacks continued against Birmingham later in the month, but from December 1940 to June 1941 the priority remained port areas and trade targets, some of which, including Glasgow, Belfast and Bristol, also contained targets for the aero industry. On 6 February Hitler confirmed this priority, and once again emphasized the importance of attacking military-economic targets rather than residential areas.[19]

The nine-month blockade campaign was an anomaly among the many campaigns pursued by the German leadership during the war. It was a strategy based on an uncertain rate of attrition rather than a decisive battle. No serious evaluation was made of Britain's economic dependence on overseas supplies, and precise intelligence on the economic effects of the bombing was almost impossible to infer from damage reports. For aircrew and commanders, it was a long and increasingly demoralizing campaign as they suffered high losses for no obvious strategic advantage. As in the Battle of Britain, achievements were exaggerated to justify the campaign, but it brought capitulation no nearer. Hitler lost interest in the bombing as a war-winning weapon and by December 1940 doubted that much effect would be had on British industry; two months later he expressed the same view about British morale. On this occasion his judgement was sound. The bombing certainly created widespread and temporary crises among the bombed populations, but it did not force the government's hand. The blockade effects on British trade and output were modest in the extreme. German air intelligence guessed that British aircraft output in 1941 would be 7,200 after the damage apparently inflicted, but actual output was 20,094.[20] British calculations made later in 1941 showed that only around 5 per cent of a growing volume of output was lost on account of bombing.[21]

Indeed, much more damage to Britain's economic prospects was caused by the exhaustion of Britain's overseas financial resources because of the exceptional level of economic mobilization during 1939–40. By December 1940 more than half the pre-war reserves of gold and US dollars had been spent, and the remainder would be used up by March 1941, leaving Britain effectively bankrupt with a dollar zone that supplied essential imports. Large imbalances were built up with the sterling bloc too, which eventually amounted to £3,355 million by the end of the war, but they could be frozen for the duration.[22] Reliance on supplies from the New World was critical, and in December 1940 Churchill appealed personally to President Roosevelt to do something to prevent an economic catastrophe. Though American leaders remained sceptical that Britain really had exhausted its capacity to pay, Roosevelt committed his regime to become the 'arsenal of democracy' in a speech in late December, and the following month introduced into Congress what would become the Lend-Lease Act, promising shipment to the British Empire of goods without immediate payment. Before the Act became law on 11 March, the United States Reconstruction Finance Corporation lent an emergency $425 million to avoid a British default. 'Without this aid,' Churchill privately minuted, 'the defeat of Hitlerism could not be hoped for.'[23]

The German campaign against the British home islands was in the end sustained because it was difficult to abandon without admitting failure. Giving up the Blitz would have sent a hopeful message to the occupied areas, and to the United States, and would not have been understood by the German population in western Germany still subject to RAF raids on every night when the weather allowed. There were also positive advantages to even an unsuccessful offensive. Continued combat in the West was designed to allay any fears in Moscow that Hitler would risk a two-front war by attacking in the East, a view that Stalin clung to right through to the moment of German invasion in June 1941. In addition, the British armed forces were compelled to keep a large presence at home in case of a spring invasion, which the government widely expected. 'We are all saying and thinking,' wrote the MP Harold Nicolson in his diary in February, as he observed the evacuation of civilians from areas in Kent, 'that invasion of this country is inevitable.'[24] The immediate consequence for the British war effort was the impossibility of providing extensive reinforcement for the empire, a crisis that opened up for Hitler's Italian ally the prospect of a 'parallel war' in the Mediterranean and Africa against a weakened opponent.

Italian ambitions in the summer and autumn of 1940 had indeed been inflated by the prospect that German victory over Britain was likely and that the opportunity to take advantage of the conflict in northern Europe might not last that long. The Three Power Pact gave to Italian leaders a renewed sense that Italy now mattered as a great power, invited to join in the redivision of the world, but there had to be concrete evidence that this enhanced status could be justified. Mussolini, observed the Italian journalist Orio Vergani, 'wanted to arrive at the table of the putative peace with a victory that was entirely Italian'.[25] The aftermath of the defeat of France, in which exaggerated Italian claims on French territory, colonies and military resources had been rejected by the German leadership, encouraged a growing hostility towards the German ally and serious doubts about whether in any new European order Italy would be anything more than a 'lucky profiteer' or 'meek collaborator' in the wake of

German victory.[26] The paradoxical result was that Italy, the weakest of the three signatories of the pact in September 1940, was the first to embark on a further programme of empire-building.

There were a wide variety of largely unrealistic contingency plans already available – invasion of Malta, occupation of the French Empire, attacks against Aden, Egypt or Suez, an invasion of Switzerland, the French valley of the Rhône, Yugoslavia or, Case G, an invasion of Greece. The principal criterion of Italian policy, confessed General Quirino Armellini in his diary, was to act: 'to start with we'll go to war, then we'll see what happens.'[27] Mussolini was left with a difficult decision between continuing the war in Africa against the formal British enemy, or a war in southern Europe to forestall a potentially hostile German ally. Historians have rightly highlighted the idiosyncratic nature of Italian strategic planning and Mussolini's irrational, if hesitant, pursuit of military ambitions far beyond Italy's capability, but the Italian dictator was trapped in a situation of his own making, where inaction seemed as dangerous to Italy's new imperial ambitions as action. Mussolini could also claim that since the onset of his active imperial policy he had always turned out to be a victor – in the savage Libyan pacification, in Ethiopia, in Spain, in Albania, even in the brief and inglorious assault on France – proof enough, as one observer put it, 'of his infallibility'.[28] These were delusions of grandeur that none of his commanders found the courage to deflate.

For the first months of the Italian war effort against the British Empire, Mussolini's luck held. The British protectorate in Somaliland, bordering the new Italian African empire in Ethiopia, was relatively undefended. In August 1940, a mixed force of Italian soldiers and local *askari* troops attacked the British garrison and forced its evacuation to another British protectorate across the Red Sea at Aden (present-day Yemen). British Empire forces lost 206 men, the Italians 2,052. At sea both the Royal Navy and the Italian navy were keen to conserve naval forces whose primary objective was to protect convoy routes across the Mediterranean. The fleets clashed indecisively off the coast of Calabria at Punta Stilo on 9 July when British vessels were saved by poor Italian aerial reconnaissance, while Italian bombers arrived late and attacked their own ships. Though neither side received serious damage, Mussolini declared to the Italian public a few days later that 50 per cent of British naval strength in the Mediterranean had been annihilated.[29] In North Africa, Mussolini was impatient to begin an invasion of Egypt, with the ultimate aim of cutting the Suez Canal lifeline for the British Empire. The Italian commander, Marshal Rodolfo Graziani, was reluctant to risk an all-out assault faced with desert conditions, threatened supply lines and inadequate transport. Mussolini assured him that the advance into Egypt should begin the moment the first German soldier set foot on British soil, but with the long postponement of Operation 'Sea Lion', Mussolini became impatient for any advance that could be presented as a triumph. On 13 September Graziani finally succumbed to the pressure from Rome and moved seven divisions of infantry across the Libyan border to the small settlement of Sidi Barrani some 80 kilometres inside the western Egyptian desert, where he stopped and set up an elaborate network of camps. The British Empire forces withdrew to better defensive positions following a skirmish that left 120 Italians dead and 50 of the enemy. This time Mussolini announced to the Italian people the greatest triumph of arms for 300 years; a road – the 'Victory Way' – was immediately constructed across the sand dunes to Sidi Barrani.[30]

Mussolini sensed that colonial conflict would not be sufficient to win Italy an equal place alongside Germany in the settlement of Europe. An initiative in mainland Europe remained a surer path to reinforcing the idea of a 'parallel war'. During August and September, he moved closer to a possible war with Yugoslavia or with Greece, knowing full well that conflict with either had been vetoed by the German leadership when the two sides had met in mid-August. War with Yugoslavia was regarded rather as the German war with Poland – a rectification of the post-1918 settlement when Italy had been denied her territorial claims across the Adriatic. Plans were made for an invasion force of thirty-seven divisions to attack through Slovenia, but uncertainty about the German reaction prompted Mussolini to cancel the preparations in late September.[31] War against Greece was the only remaining option, a cynical calculation of Italy's potential power position in an Axis-dominated Europe, to be bought at the cost of Greek independence. The Italian commander in Albania, Sebastiano Visconti Prasca, thought Greece was ripe for conquest, a 'military walkover' that would elevate his own military reputation. Count Ciano saw an opportunity to expand his colonial satrapy in Albania into Greek territory; the governor of the Italian Aegean islands, Cesare De Vecchi, harboured the idea of a land bridge linking the empire in Albania with the empire in the eastern Aegean through the conquest of Greece. To prompt a breakdown in Italian–Greek relations, De Vecchi even sent an Italian submarine from Rhodes to torpedo the ageing Greek cruiser *Helli* on 15 August 1940. Despite every provocation, Greek military and political leaders made concerted efforts to conciliate their belligerent neighbour, and indeed there was as yet no certainty that Mussolini would approve a war.[32]

The turning point for a hesitant Mussolini seems to have come with news on 12 October that German forces had entered Romania to safeguard the Ploesti oilfield. The German encroachment on southern Europe, regarded by Italian leaders as Italy's 'political-economic sphere', called for a response. At a meeting on 15 October with Fascist leaders Mussolini announced that war would begin against Greece eleven days later. Poor weather postponed the start until 28 October. Mussolini warned Prasca that success depended above all on the speed of the operation. He had no intention of telling Hitler: 'he will learn from the newspapers that I have occupied Greece.'[33] The final decision, so late in the day, left Italian preparations in complete disarray, the victim, as one witness called it, of Mussolini's 'incurable improvisationism'.[34] A limited military build-up had already begun, but after cancellation of the Yugoslav plan, Mussolini had ordered the demobilization of half the 1.1 million troops in mainland Italy. The original planning for a Greek campaign had foreseen only eight divisions in a limited assault on Epirus and the Ionian islands; in mid-October, while half Italy's divisions were demobilizing, Mussolini decided to increase the assault force to twenty divisions, with a campaign to seize the whole of Greece, possibly with Bulgarian co-operation. Divisions arrived in Albania short of equipment, men and supplies; poor airfields meant that much of the Italian air force designated for the campaign had to operate from bases in southern Italy. Poor intelligence on Greek military potential and dispositions compounded the difficulties. The offensive was to begin with only 60,000 troops, 270 combat aircraft and 160 L/3 light tanks in wintry weather across the most hostile terrain for combat.[35]

The Greeks understood the threat they faced and activated mobilization plan 1B with units stationed on the Albanian frontier and in Thrace, in case Bulgaria had co-ordinated an attack with Italy. Intelligence evidence suggested by October that the main threat came from the Italian army in Albania, and an entrenched defensive front was established with artillery and machine-gun nests concealed in the mountainous region through which the Italian troops would have to fight. Without a declaration of war, the Italian assault opened on the morning of 28 October, in time for Mussolini to inform Hitler as he arrived for the summit meeting in Florence that Italian forces were again victoriously on the move. The war was a predictable disaster. The Greek forces had few modern armaments or aircraft and limited supplies, but they enjoyed the advantage of high morale in defence of their homeland and a close knowledge of the zone of combat. Italian units took heavy losses at once; radio and telephone communication was so poor the army had to rely on old-fashioned runners ('not a single effective telephone operator' complained the campaign commander in December); the army needed 10,000 tons of supplies a day but the small and congested port facilities in Albania meant that only 3,500 tons could be delivered.[36] Aircraft could only be used sparingly because of poor weather, while flights from southern Italy in support of ground forces took too long to be useful for any crisis on the ground. Within days the Greek army opened a wide hole in the Italian front line.

In mid-November, the Greek commander-in-chief, Alexandros Papagos, launched a counter-offensive that took the Greek army 80 kilometres into Albanian territory. On 22 November the Albanian town of Koritsa was taken. Bells pealed across Greece, the first Allied victory, observed an American journalist in Athens, since the start of the war. In the capital's streets jubilant Greeks chanted 'We want Tirana!'[37] Mussolini's 'lightning war' threatened to bring to an abrupt end Italy's European empire. Instead of the swift and triumphant progress to Athens, the Italian army was compelled to recall thousands of men to the colours simply to save Albania. A further twenty-one divisions were fed into the Greek war between November 1940 and April 1941, more than half a million men with 87,000 draft animals and 16,000 vehicles.[38] In March 1941, with both sides exhausted and the Italian commanders sacked and replaced, a major Italian offensive was launched, but within four days it too ground to a halt. In conditions ironically reminiscent of the harsh alpine front in which Mussolini had fought in the First World War, losses were exceptional. Total Italian casualties ran to 154,172 for the campaign (including 13,755 dead), around one-quarter of the poorly equipped soldiers forced to fight in sub-zero temperatures with poor food and medical supplies. The Greek army had casualties of approximately 60,000, 14,000 killed and thousands maimed by frostbite, their swollen blackened limbs amputated in primitive field hospitals high in the Greek mountains.[39]

The Greek fiasco had dangerous repercussions for the rest of Italy's overseas empire because the frantic efforts to reinforce Albania starved both Graziani in Egypt and the Italian forces in Ethiopia of any prospect of reinforcement and tied down the Italian navy to support the large-scale supply mission across the Adriatic Sea. The Royal Navy took immediate advantage of the new Italian priorities. On 12 November 1940, escorting a convoy from Malta to Alexandria, Admiral Cunningham's Eastern Mediterranean fleet, strengthened by the arrival through the Suez Canal of the aircraft carrier *Illustrious*, launched a devastating attack on the main Italian naval port at Taranto using Fairey 'Swordfish' biplanes that carried a mix of flares, bombs and torpedoes. The mission benefitted from the poor air-sea reconnaissance of the Italian air force, but chiefly from the tactical advantage of the new British aerial torpedoes which could travel beneath the harbour's protective netting (which in this case was incomplete) and, thanks to a new magnetic fuse, explode under the keel of unsuspecting warships. There was little effective anti-aircraft fire; illuminated by the flares from the lead aircraft, two waves of torpedo-bombers hit the port. The battleship *Conte de Cavour* was struck fatally, while two other battleships, *Caio Duilio* and *Littorio*, were seriously damaged, though reparable.[40] Although the destruction was not as extensive as the Royal Navy at first believed, the main Italian fleet retreated hastily to Naples, and a few months later, following a damaging assault off Cape Matapan in Greece on 28 March 1941, when the British Alexandria fleet sank three cruisers and two destroyers and damaged the battleship *Vittorio Veneto*, the Italian navy decided that no Italian battleship should sail further than the range of fighter protection, ending any threat that the main Italian battle fleet still represented.[41]

Italy's African empire, sealed only five years before by the conquest of Ethiopia, unravelled in just months following the Greek disaster. Though British forces across the Middle East and Africa were also weakened by the demands for manpower and military resources to defend the home islands, they were better organized and more technically advanced than Italian forces. Churchill, like Mussolini, was anxious for a victory somewhere and harried the British commander-in-chief in Cairo, General Archibald Wavell, to reply to Graziani's incursion into Egypt. Though greatly outnumbered in Africa (Italy had 298,500 Italian service personnel and 228,400 local troops in Libya and East Africa, against a total of 60,000 British Empire forces), Wavell prepared a counterstrike to take advantage of the Italian preoccupation with Greece. Operation 'Compass' was launched across the desert on 9 December with 30,000 soldiers from the Seventh Armoured Division, an Indian division and part of an Australian division in the slow process of formation. British Empire forces moved rapidly on two axes, infiltrating the static Italian line and attacking it from the rear. Surprise and panic overwhelmed the front line of General Italo Gariboldi's Tenth Italian Army. Short of equipment, with few anti-tank weapons, and little experience in armoured warfare, the Italian resistance disintegrated. By 4 January British Empire forces reached Bardia, where 45,000 Italians surrendered; on 23 January, Tobruk fell with a further 22,000 prisoners. The Seventh Armoured Division cut across the desert to block the retreating Italian units at Beda Fomm, and by 7 February 1941 the battle was over, with much of eastern Libya in British hands, along with 133,000 prisoners, 1,290 guns, 400 tanks and thousands of vehicles. Only 8,500 Italian soldiers battled their way to temporary safety in western Libya. British Empire dead numbered 500 for the whole two-month campaign. Wavell might have pushed on to Tripoli, the last North African port in Axis hands, ending any prospect of further Italian resistance in the desert, but he was under pressure from other theatre demands.[42] His next objective was Italian East Africa. Here the Italian governor, Amadeo of Savoy, duke of Aosta, faced an impossible task. Cut off from all supplies by the British naval blockade, facing widespread insurgency from the Ethiopian population, short of vehicles, fuel and munitions (most of which dated from 1918), all he could hope for was a holding operation. Only five British Empire divisions were needed to overturn the Italian empire, two Indian divisions attacking from Sudan, one South African and two British Empire African divisions from Kenya. Starting on 21 January, the campaign was effectively over by 6 April when Addis Ababa was captured. The Ethiopian emperor Haile Selassie was restored to the throne under British supervision in May 1941. In a matter of a few weeks almost the entire Italian empire in Africa was at an end.

The defeats in Africa and Greece did not eliminate Italy from the war, but they exposed the extent to which the Fascist regime had failed to develop a modern military machine and an apparatus of command and control capable of matching imperial ambition to the available resources. Though there has been much recent argument to suggest that the Italian military was more effective as a fighting force in the field than the popular post-war image has suggested, this remains a difficult case to make convincingly. There is less doubt that, sensibly led and properly resourced, Italian soldiers would have performed more effectively, and later in the war that proved to be the case as improvements were slowly made. Nor is there any doubt about the courage of men who faced grim conditions, with obsolete equipment, and fought as best they could. But the armed forces that were defeated in 1940–41 were neither well led nor effectively resourced and the effect on morale was correspondingly debilitating. The principal problem was the structure put in place to run the Italian war effort. Mussolini concentrated decision-making in his own hands, but his decisions were those of a military amateur who was prone to intervene arbitrarily and reluctant to take the advice of his commanders. Collaboration between the separate branches of the armed forces was poor.[43] At best, the Italian army in 1940 was equipped for a limited colonial war but was quite unprepared for modern mobile warfare: there were very few anti-tank guns; antiquated artillery (in the desert out of 7,970 field guns only 246 had been fabricated since 1930); and tanks were light, poorly armoured and underpowered.[44] Though Mussolini longed for armed forces capable of conducting *la guerra lampo*, lightning war, the Fascist state was a permanent barrier to military efficiency.

Facing defeat on all fronts, Mussolini was finally forced to ask Hitler for military assistance. A formal request was made on 17 December and Hitler hesitated before finally agreeing. By this stage, the effects of Mussolini's improvised assault on Greece threatened to destabilize the entire Balkan region, an area where Germany had important interests in the supply of raw materials and oil. The prospect of British intervention (on 2 November a Royal Navy mission arrived in Athens, and the first RAF units a few weeks later) suggested a replay of the earlier Scandinavian crisis, with a threat on the German wing as preparations were made for the main campaign against the Soviet Union.[45] Italian defeat, which seemed probable by December 1940, also had unfortunate repercussions for the reputation of the Axis, whose political claims had been publicly declared in the Three Power Pact only three months before. The German leadership agreed to help the Italians not from sympathy for their plight, but because it served German interests. The assistance, as one of the planning staff at OKW put it, was 'unwillingly given and unwillingly accepted'.[46] Unknown to Mussolini, Hitler had already directed his armed forces on 13 December to prepare for intervention in Greece under the codename Operation 'Marita'. With Bulgarian agreement, German forces were moved towards the Bulgarian–Greek frontier during the early part of 1941. The Twelfth Army under Field Marshal Wilhelm List, with five army corps and the support of the Eighth Air Corps, was in place by the end of March with plans to invade in early April. Little of this was co-ordinated with the Italians, who remained stuck on the Albanian front until the German attack.

While preparations for stabilizing the Balkans went ahead, Hitler authorized the transfer of air and armoured resources to assist the Italians in North Africa. Air Corps X, commanded by General Hans Geisler, an expert in anti-shipping operations, arrived in Sicily in December 1940 with 350 aircraft and began to set up bases from which to neutralize the British threat to Italian supply operations from airfields and submarines in Malta. On 16 January, the aircraft carrier *Illustrious*, responsible for the Taranto raids, was crippled by German aircraft. Though Malta was not completely neutralized, the repeated air attacks in the spring of 1941 suppressed British naval activity against Italian convoys to the North African theatre until the German aircraft were moved away in the summer. In January and February 1941, the Fifteenth Armoured Division and the Fifth Light Motorized Division, were moved to Libya under the command of General Erwin Rommel, one of the stars of the tank war in France. The German *Afrika Korps* provided a new spine for a demoralized Italian army. By February 1941 there were only six Italian divisions left in western Libya and a hundred aircraft. Graziani, the overall Italian commander in North Africa, succumbed to a nervous breakdown and was relieved by Italo Gariboldi. More Italian armour arrived alongside the German army corps and

Rommel immediately set out to test British Empire capability. Operation 'Sonnenblume' ('Sunflower') was designed by Hitler's headquarters to be a limited advance to a more defensible line east of Tripoli, but Rommel sensed that the enemy forces in front of him, exhausted by weeks of pursuit across the desert, were in no condition to obstruct him. British Empire forces were thinly spread and their tank numbers heavily reduced following 'Compass'. Rommel drove them back across the desert and efforts to rein him in by Hitler's high command and the Italian commander in Libya failed entirely. Though nominally Rommel's superior, Gariboldi was unable to insist that the German commander follow the Italian lead. Instead, Rommel pushed on towards Tobruk, which he besieged on 8 April 1941. Though Rommel was generally dismissive of his Italian allies – and shocked at the poor level of Italian equipment – the counter-offensive in the desert was a combined German–Italian effort and provided Italians for the first time with the prospect of a real victory.

The sharp reversal of fortunes in the desert was chiefly the result of a political decision reached in London that Britain should send an expeditionary force to help the Greeks against the Axis. Britain had guaranteed Greek independence in the spring of 1939 at the same time as Poland's. But intervention in Greece weakened an already fragile military presence in North Africa, leaving Egypt and the Suez Canal vulnerable but promising no real prospect that Greece could be saved once German forces were seriously committed to the fight. Churchill, like Mussolini, was also keen on a victory in Europe and, like Mussolini, unable to match political ambition to military reality. On 9 January, following arguments with the chiefs of staff and the War Cabinet, Churchill got his way. Wavell was instructed to divert forces from the African front to aid the Greeks, but he was strongly opposed to the idea. 'What you need out there,' replied an angry Churchill, 'is a court martial and a firing squad.'[47] Churchill persisted, but the Greek dictator, Ioannis Metaxas, was reluctant to accept aid for fear that it would prompt an immediate German invasion. However, following his death in January 1941, the new prime minister, Alexandros Koryzis, finally signed a formal military agreement with Britain on 2 March 1941 as the German threat loomed. The agreement was supposed to be part of a broad anti-Axis front that Churchill's foreign secretary, Antony Eden, was sent to the Mediterranean to negotiate. Arriving in Athens on 19 February, Eden undertook a futile tour of Turkey and Yugoslavia to persuade them to join with the Allied cause. Neither would be drawn into the net, since it was clear that Germany, for the moment, was the winning side – a fact even more evident as British Empire forces were simultaneously in full retreat back across Libya. Soldiers from New Zealand and Australia under the command of Major General Bernard Freyberg formed 'W Force' and landed in mainland Greece on 7 March. Like the intervention in Norway, which the campaign strongly resembled, British forces were expelled in six weeks of fruitless efforts to shore up a collapsing ally.

By the time German forces were unleashed against Greece on 6 April (an operation that British intelligence already knew about from Ultra intelligence intercepts), the political situation had changed again. The Yugoslav government, which had spurned Eden's efforts, joined the Three Power Pact on 25 March, but was immediately overthrown in an anti-German military coup. Eden was briefly hopeful that Belgrade would now join a Greek–British alliance but the new Yugoslav regime was equally wary of commitments that would provoke a German invasion. The coup enraged Hitler, however, and within days the campaign against Greece was broadened to include an operation to destroy Yugoslavia, to be inaugurated with a merciless bombing raid on Belgrade. Directive No. 25 now switched List's Twelfth Army to attack southern Yugoslavia as well, while new units were formed in Hungary and Austria to attack from the north. Some 900 aircraft were released from the war with Britain for the new campaign. In stark contrast to the hurried and improvised deployment of Italian forces in October 1940 against Greece, German planners achieved the seemingly impossible in a matter of two weeks. On 6 April 1941 the offensive opened with thirty-three divisions, eleven of them armoured. What followed was a model of 'lightning war'. In difficult mountainous terrain, in an unfamiliar landscape, Yugoslav and Greek forces were swept aside. By 17 April Yugoslavia surrendered; a Greek armistice followed on the 20th, signed with a local German commander. Unconditional Greek surrender to the Germans came a day later, while List's Twelfth Army held the Greek–Albanian border to prevent Italian forces from entering. Mussolini protested that this was properly an Italian victory, since it was his war. Hitler reluctantly agreed to allow Italians to be present at a second surrender ceremony in Salonika on 23 April where the Greek commander, General Georgios Tsolakoglou, was forced to acknowledge the Italian claim. The reality was not lost on the Italians. When the distribution of the spoils was discussed in Vienna later in April, it was evident that Italy's role was now that of German satellite. Mussolini's confused, belligerent and ill-organized strategy in 1940 led, six months later, to the final extinction of an independent Italian empire. 'The fate of we allies,' complained Ciano, 'can be tragic: the fate of a colony.'[48]

The outcome for the British Empire was almost as tragic. By 14 April it was clear that a Mediterranean Dunkirk was necessary. A few days later the embarkation began and 50,000 troops, both British Empire and

Greek, were shipped to the island of Crete or on to Egypt. Since a strong British Empire presence on Crete represented a continued threat to German security, a daring operation was planned using the elite paratroops of General Kurt Student. On 20 May the German paratroops landed and, despite exceptionally heavy losses, secured the main airbase at Maleme. Over the next ten days a bitter contest for the island continued, but the British Chiefs of Staff could see no reason for yet another comprehensive defeat and on 31 May the British Empire garrison began evacuation to Egypt for the loss of 3,700 men, 2,000 of them among the crews of Royal Navy warships which were harried and bombed by waves of German aircraft. The defeats in Greece and Crete confirmed that a British presence on mainland Europe was impossible, and in turn exposed the shrunken force in Egypt to an even more serious threat. The War Office drew up a contingency plan for a 'Worst Possible Case': abandoning Egypt, retiring to the Sudan, or even retreating as far as southern Africa. On 24 April, Wavell, who had opposed Britain's Greek fiasco, informed the War Office in London that he had not a single formation complete in organization and equipment. 'We are fighting, as we have done since the beginning of the war,' he continued, 'with improvisation and insufficiencies.'[49] At home in Britain the joke circulated that the acronym BEF now stood for 'Back Every Fortnight'. Home Intelligence reported the one question that most preoccupied the public: 'Are the Germans *always* going to beat us whenever we meet them on land?'[50]

While the crisis in Greece and Crete played out, British forces faced a further threat to their position in the Middle East when Iraqi nationalists launched a coup on 1 April to curtail British influence and to link hands with Axis forces. The crisis in Iraq had been brewing since 1940, when the radical nationalist Rashid Ali al-Kailani, a professor in the Baghdad school of law, became prime minister. He was supported by a cabal of Iraqi officers – known as the Golden Square – who wanted to use Allied defeat in Europe as the opportunity to rid Iraq of the residual imperial connection with Britain. He was ousted on 31 January 1941 after pressure from the British government, but he had already established contact with the Germans and Italians with a view to Axis assistance. In early April, his military coup forced the regent, Prince Abdulillah, to flee to the British Palestine mandate. Rashid formed a 'government of national defence' which was almost immediately recognized by Germany and the Soviet Union, the two powers that Britain feared most as a threat to the region.[51] It is not clear that Rashid really wanted an armed conflict with the weakened British forces still in Iraq, but fearful of a sudden German descent on Iraq after the push into the Balkans, the chiefs of staff approved

Operation 'Sabine' to move thousands of British and Indian troops to the southern Iraqi port of Basra to defend Britain's vital oil concessions and the overland route to the Mediterranean theatre. Rashid's government demanded that they be moved; the British not only refused, but brought in further forces, in violation of the Anglo-Iraqi defence agreement. The Iraqi army prepared for war. The pro-German grand mufti of Jerusalem, Amin al-Husayni, who was in Baghdad, exiled from Palestine by the British, declared a *jihad* against the imperial enemy, summoning Muslims to a holy fight.[52] On 25 April a treaty was concluded with Italy to supply arms, in return for a promise to give Italy access to oil and port facilities, and weapons began to reach Iraq via Vichy-controlled Syria. The British oil pipeline to Haifa, on the eastern Mediterranean coast, was cut off, and the Iraqi army prepared to surround and capture the main British air base at Habbaniya, 90 kilometres from Baghdad, on the banks of the Euphrates River. On 1 May, 9,000 Iraqi soldiers, supported by artillery and a number of light tanks, dug in on a low plateau overlooking the airfield and prepared for battle.

On paper, the forces were unevenly matched. There were only 1,400 air force and army personnel at Habbaniya, supported by 1,250 local troops from the Iraq Levies, raised by the British to assist their military presence in the region. The base was home to an RAF training unit with a motley assortment of obsolete trainer aircraft and nine Gloster Gladiator biplane fighters. The force concentrated at Basra was cut off from providing immediate aid by the Iraqi decision to flood the area leading to Baghdad. With great reluctance, given the weakness of the British position in Egypt, Wavell was forced to put together a scratch mobile relief column, 'Habforce', which set off from Palestine and Transjordan to save Iraq. Habbaniya in fact saved itself. A mix of instructors and student pilots flew the trainers, primed with bombs, all day long against the Iraqi positions. Demoralized, short of water and food, and relentlessly bombarded and strafed, the army disintegrated. On 6 May it was in full retreat on the road to Fallujah when it ran into Iraqi reserves coming the other way. In the ensuing chaos, the RAF inflicted a deadly barrage on the exposed men and vehicles. The army was pursued to Fallujah, where a fierce battle ensued until, by 20 May, the city was in British hands. The comprehensive destruction inflicted by artillery and bombs reminded one British soldier of the pictures he had seen 'of the battered towns of Flanders during the Great War'.[53] Over the following week, 1,400 soldiers of 'Habforce', strongly supported by aircraft flying from Habbaniya and Basra, converged on Baghdad and on 30 May Rashid, al-Husayni and officers of the Golden Square fled to Iran and Turkey, leaving the mayor of the city to negotiate an armistice. For modest losses, the

Iraqi army and air force had been routed and the uprising suppressed. The conflict was a familiar one for the British, using local levies and Indian troops to support a small British force, and assuming that the enemy, while numerous, was inadequate in military terms. 'For us,' wrote Somerset de Chair, an intelligence officer at Habbaniya, 'it was but another campaign along the eastern marches of our Empire.'[54]

What gave the Iraqi campaign added urgency was fear that the Axis states, now positioned in the Balkans and Aegean, might take the opportunity to support the revolt and unhinge Britain's already fragile position astride the Middle East. Rashid tried to use contacts with the Germans to get them to assist the Iraqi cause, but the crisis in the Balkans absorbed German efforts, while Hitler regarded the area as properly the sphere of Italy and Vichy France. Only once the revolt was under way did it seem possible to undermine the British, but German support was limited to small arms shipments, a military mission in Baghdad and two squadrons of aircraft, one of Messerschmitt Me110 heavy fighters, one of the obsolete Heinkel He111 bomber; the Italians sent a squadron of Fiat CR-42 biplanes. They were permitted to use an air base at Aleppo in Syria by the Vichy French authorities and later landed at Mosul, in northern Iraq. They engaged in sporadic raiding, but by the end of May had lost 95 per cent of the original force. Like the Italians, the Germans were most interested in the oil of Iraq. A German Petroleum Mission arrived in May 1941 to survey the industry and to see what prospect there was of taking it over once the British had been ejected, making it clear that Axis success would replace one imperial master with another.[55] The intervention came too late and in too limited strength to affect the outcome. Hitler's War Directive No. 30, published on 23 May, promised assistance to Rashid's revolt but by then the conflict was almost over; a second Directive, No. 32, published on 11 June, made it clear that the operation to clear the British from the Middle East would happen only after the end of the imminent campaign against the Soviet Union.[56] For Hitler, the Middle East was still a sideshow, beyond his strategic reach.

For the remainder of the war, the German effort to exploit Arab anti-British sentiment by provoking further armed uprisings was confined to political warfare. The propaganda campaign aimed at the Arab world was the largest political offensive launched by the Axis. An Arab-language radio station had been operated by the German Foreign Office from Zeesen, south of Berlin, since April 1939 and by 1941 was broadcasting round the clock the central message that British imperialism and the Jews were the primary enemies of the Arab world and of Islam, and that Muslims everywhere should rise up against them.[57] Broadcasts were supplemented by a constant stream of leaflets and pamphlets distributed by air across the Middle East, a total of 8 million by the spring of 1942. The Germans mobilized quotations from the Koran to support the cause of Arab liberation from Britain, 'the unjust, violent criminal'. Play was made with the idea of a world Jewish conspiracy to enslave the Arab peoples. The SS issued a million copies of a pamphlet claiming that the giant Jew-King Dajjal, foretold in the Koran, would be slain by God's servant, Hitler: 'He will kill the Dajjal, as it is written, destroy his palaces and cast his allies into hell.'[58] The campaign had little success; the Iraqi revolt was the only time Arab hostility to Britain's imperial ambitions resulted in violence. Radio propaganda was hampered by the shortage of radios – in Saudi Arabia there were only 26 in the whole country, and the 55,000 in Egypt were owned chiefly by Europeans resident there – while the exploitation of the Koran in support of a clear political motive was resented by Muslim clerics. The Iranian mullah Ruhullah Musavi, better known later as Ayatollah Khomeini, condemned National Socialist propaganda as 'the most poisonous and heinous product of the human mind.'[59] German and Italian claims that they were anti-imperialist were difficult to sustain after the brutal suppression of Libyan Arab and Berber populations; although supposed to respect the local Arab peoples, the German soldiers in North Africa, according to one report, treated them as racial inferiors, calling them 'coloured', 'nigger' and even, confusingly, 'Jew'.[60]

The British nevertheless remained pessimistic after the Iraqi revolt about the continued threat to the security of the region. The chief of the Imperial General Staff, General John Dill, told his chief of operations only two weeks after the surrender of Baghdad, 'I suppose you realise we shall lose the Middle East.'[61] The assistance given to Axis air units by the Vichy French authorities in Syria showed once again that Britain could expect no sympathy from the former French ally. There were substantial French forces in Syria and Lebanon, with at least 35,000 French and colonial troops and 90 tanks. Wavell was told to eliminate the threat, and on 8 June a mixed force of British, Australian, Indian and Free French troops moved west from Iraq towards Damascus and north from Palestine towards Beirut. After bitter fighting, the French commander, General Henri Dentz, sued for an armistice. Britain assumed military control of the French mandate, while the Free French tried to reassert, with mixed fortunes, French control of the civil government.[62] British forces and officials now occupied the entire Middle East from Egypt to the Iranian frontier, the greatest extent of British influence across the region. To mask the extent of British control, an effort was made to mount a campaign to advertise the virtues of British democracy. Like the Germans, the British publicity offices mobilized the Koran in support of their propaganda. One colourful poster distributed in Iraq proclaimed 'The religion of Islam is the spirit of democracy . . . Democracy is the essence of the Koran . . .'[63] The campaign suffered from Britain's evident willingness to use traditional imperial practices to retain control – press censorship, summary arrest, deportation, advisers embedded in central and local government – while preaching the virtues of liberal politics. The American Legation in Baghdad reported to Washington the sheer depth of British penetration of the governmental and economic apparatus, all designed 'to serve the well-being of the British Empire'.[64] The British priority remained the security of their communications and oil supplies, but by the end of June 1941 a new threat emerged with the German invasion of the Soviet Union. The possibility opened that German forces would push into the Middle East from the Caucasus together with an advance through Egypt; worse still was the geopolitical nightmare that Japan and Germany might join forces to drive the British and their allies entirely from Eurasia.

THE MACKINDER MOMENT

The English geographer Halford Mackinder is famous for promoting the idea that the Eurasian continental space, from Central Europe to the Pacific Ocean, was the geopolitical 'heartland' of the globe. Control of the resources of this vast land mass, the 'world island', would bring with it domination of the 'outer periphery' of the maritime states. 'Who rules the Heartland commands the World-Island,' he wrote in 1919. 'Who rules the World-Island commands the World.'[65] Mackinder first coined the idea in a 1904 article on 'The Geographical Pivot of History' to alert the British to the possibility that their global power might be overturned thanks to modern communications, which now made it possible to exploit the vast material resources of the Heartland. In 1919 he even suggested that Germany and Japan might be able to dominate Eurasia between them at the expense of Russia and China: Germany with its feet planted firmly across Central and Eastern Europe, Japan with the advantage of 'an oceanic frontage'.[66] The idea had little impact in Britain, and might have remained in obscurity had it not been for the German geographer Karl Haushofer, who read Mackinder's work and was already writing about the geographical 'pivot' in the immediate years after the Great War. It was Haushofer who popularized the term 'geopolitics' to describe the close relationship between geographical circumstances and national power. One of Haushofer's students at the institute in Munich where he worked was the young Rudolf Hess, Hitler's future deputy and an early member of the National Socialist Party. Hess introduced Hitler to Haushofer, who supplied the future dictator with texts on geopolitical subjects to read during his incarceration in Landsberg Prison after Hitler's failed coup in 1923.[67]

Although the precise link to Mackinder is hard to trace, it is not unlikely that Haushofer gave him a second-hand account of the geographical pivot. By the time Hitler was dictating *Mein Kampf* to his fellow-prisoner Hess, he had clearly imbibed the idea that German destiny would be found in the Heartland. 'Only an adequate large space on this earth,' wrote Hitler, 'assures a national freedom of existence,' and this was space to be found in an imagined 'East'.[68] Haushofer later praised Hitler's 'geopolitical mastery', which reflected his own ideas about what he called 'space-conquering powers' drawn from his travels around the British Empire, whose geopolitical mastery he also admired. Haushofer hoped that Germany would help to construct a Eurasian land power that would exclude and dominate the maritime Anglo-Saxons. His early work on Japanese colonization in Korea and Manchuria persuaded him that Japan too might take part in the project as the 'continent-minded partner of a continental politics of the world'.[69] In 1913, he published a major study of Japan's world position and geopolitical future as a 'greater Japan'. Geopolitics became popular in Japan in the 1930s because the science appeared to confirm the wisdom of Japanese territorial expansion as the means to overcome Western hegemony. In a 'Manifesto of Japanese Geopolitics' written in 1940, the scholar Tsunekichi Komaki made the case for Japanese primacy throughout Eastern Asia.[70] Mackinder's 'Heartland' began as an abstract speculation about the future power structure of the globe, but it ended up as a description of the way German and Japanese imperialists sought the Eldorado of Eurasian domination. The fantasy that the world geopolitical order could be turned on its head by large-scale territorial conquest was the most extreme of the expansionist ambitions pursued by Germany and Japan in the 1930s and 1940s. Yet the area they now sought to conquer was a vast geographical extent on top of what had already been acquired and it had to be captured at the expense of three of the world's most powerful states. The gap between geopolitical imagination and geopolitical reality could only be bridged by a mix of racial arrogance and wilful disregard for military and geographical realities. Mackinder had never expected the 'heartland' to be conquered entirely from without; throughout history no state external to Eurasia has ever established permanent suzerainty there.

Geopolitical fantasy was nevertheless not enough to explain the timing of the decisions for conquest, for in both cases there were compelling short-term economic, strategic and ideological factors at work which both supported and complemented the wider vision of Eurasian power. In Hitler's case, the decision to strike at the Soviet Union was developed incrementally, in response to a range of changing circumstances, through which fantastic imperial ambitions could be justified to himself, to his armed forces, and to the wider German public as both necessary and unavoidable. The decision was also Hitler's to make. As in 1939, with preparation for the war against Poland, Hitler did not want to be dissuaded once his mind was made up, although Göring and von Ribbentrop, among his close circle, both sought to persuade him for months that finishing off Britain first made greater strategic sense. It was a decision hedged about with uncertainties. In December 1940, the army commander-in-chief, Field Marshal Walther von Brauchitsch, asked Hitler's army adjutant whether the dictator was really only bluffing over plans to invade the Soviet Union, and was assured that Hitler was now determined to do so. A month later, OKW staff were still so unsure whether Hitler was 'firm in his intention' that they needed to be reassured again that the decision was now irreversible and should no longer be questioned.[71]

Until then, the planned campaign had developed in something of a vacuum. For Hitler there were mixed motives as he wrestled with the problem of defeating the British Empire, confronting the 'Jewish-Bolshevik' menace in the East, and fulfilling his desire to seize real 'living space' for the German people. The proximate cause was the refusal of Churchill's government to make peace. When at the end of July 1940 Hitler had summoned the heads of the armed forces to a meeting to discuss future strategy, he announced that he wanted to annihilate the Soviet state in one great military blow in the spring of 1941, but the purpose was to remove Britain's last prospect of a European alliance. The anti-British motive was repeated as a strategic mantra over the ten months between August 1940 and June 1941 and appeared again in his rambling address to the nation on the morning of 22 June 1941, announcing the onset of Operation 'Barbarossa': 'the hour has come, in which it is necessary to engage against the conspiracy of Jewish-Anglo-Saxon warmongers with the equally Jewish powers of the Bolshevik Moscow centre.'[72] Smashing the Soviet Union in order to force Britain to a settlement was regarded sceptically by army planners, and in particular by the chief of staff Franz Halder, who noted in January 1941 that the invasion 'does not affect England . . . We must not underestimate the risks we are running in the West.'[73] For Hitler, the British ploy masked a war of naked aggression as a pre-emptive strike dictated by the actions of others – a reversal of reality, like the earlier war against Poland.

In truth, the campaign against the Soviet Union was more than a round-about route to defeat Britain. It was an object for war in its own right not only to remove a major threat to German empire-building in Eastern Europe, but to form the future site of a Eurasian empire ruled from Berlin. The initial idea in 1940 for a campaign against the Red Army came from the German army leadership in early July, who were keen to deliver a punitive blow to keep the Soviet Union at arm's length and safeguard the eastern border. It was Hitler who turned this suggestion into a grander plan, announced on 31 July to military leaders, to annihilate the Soviet state before it was too late. The Soviet moves into the Baltic States and Romania were a clear threat. German intelligence could detect the Soviet moves to fortify and garrison the new western frontier with German-occupied Poland – the so-called 'Molotov Line' – while Soviet airbases moved closer to the border in range of Berlin. After Molotov's visit in November 1940, Hitler indicated that the Soviet Union should be destroyed as soon as possible since Stalin's appetite appeared unappeasable. The most dangerous scenario was a simultaneous assault from an Anglo-American alliance in the West and a Soviet strike from the East. 'The Führer's great anxiety,' recalled von Ribbentrop in his memoirs, was for Germany to be drawn into 'a gigantic two-front war, which would cause great destruction of life and property'.[74] The imponderable nature of the current strategic situation made a rapid defeat of the Soviet Union seem militarily rational. On 30 March 1941, in a speech lasting two and a half hours to all the commanders involved in the coming campaign, Hitler pronounced that the destruction of the Soviet state would rid Germany of the 'Russian-Asian threat for all time'.[75] This was a conflict with which German commanders were happy to identify, whatever misgivings they might have about its feasibility. 'Hitler's contention that the Russians would seize the first favourable moment to attack us,' recalled Albert Kesselring, commander of Air Fleet 2 for the invasion, 'seemed to me indisputably right.' It was of the greatest importance, he added, 'to keep communism away from Western Europe', an attitude that would not be out of place ten years later at the height of the Cold War.[76]

One question the German military commanders seem not to have considered seriously, even as they accepted the strategic necessity of a German–Soviet war, was what the conquest of the vast Eurasian territory was ultimately for. Underlying all Hitler's arguments that he was compelled by circumstances to wage war, was his understanding that conquest would produce the ultimate German empire, vast in scale and potentially unassailable by the maritime great powers. Hitler was more reticent in his reviews of strategy about the naked imperialism that the seizure of further

Lebensraum involved, but during a lengthy meeting on 9 January 1941 with his generals he reminded them of the 'immeasurable riches' in materials and land that would fall into German hands. Once the empire stretched far into Russia, he continued, Germany 'will have all means possible for waging wars against continents'.[77] Conquest of the area designated by Hitler in August the previous year, from Archangel in the north to Astrakhan in the far south, would give Germans the territory they deserved, to be carved out from Mackinder's 'World-Island'. 'This space in Russia,' Hitler told his circle a few months later, 'must always be dominated by Germans.'[78] This was the apotheosis of the decades-long German fantasy of the 'East' as imperial space.

Each of these motives reinforced the others, creating for Hitler a lethal cocktail of justifications for action, but the prize was a German Eurasian empire scarcely imaginable two years before. While his decision slowly solidified between July and December 1940, the armed forces undertook the detailed planning. The final document prepared for Hitler to approve or correct in mid-December was based on two major studies carried out by the army and by Hitler's headquarters. The first study, undertaken by Major General Erich Marcks, was completed by August. He suggested two axes of assault, one towards Leningrad, one to capture the industry of Ukraine, before swinging south and north to encircle Moscow. Marcks was privately pessimistic about a campaign whose terminal objectives stretched from Archangel to the Volga, and one that might provoke a larger war against the United States as well, but his doubts never reached Hitler.[79] The second study was prepared by Lieutenant Colonel Bernhard von Lossberg on instructions from Hitler's headquarters. Completed in mid-September, the Lossberg plan anticipated three separate thrusts: one to the north to capture the Baltic ports needed for supply; one in the centre, with the bulk of the armoured and motorized divisions, intended to capture Moscow; and one in the south fanning out to occupy Odessa and the Black Sea coast as well as the rich resources of Ukraine, all to be completed in one campaigning season.[80]

The final draft, drawing from both plans, was presented to Hitler on 5 December after he had used the Molotov visit as confirmation that destiny was calling him to eliminate Russia, 'which will always, whenever possible, stand in Germany's path'. The three-pronged attack was the preferred option, but Hitler wanted to concentrate on capturing Leningrad and the resources of Ukraine first before moving on Moscow. Jodl, his chief of operations, accordingly modified the draft directive, although Halder and the army leadership privately hoped to retain Moscow as the main axis. On 18 December, Hitler signed War Directive No. 21 for an operation that he had decided to title 'Barbarossa', after the red-bearded Holy Roman emperor who had led the twelfth-century Third Crusade to the Holy Land. The Directive was hugely ambitious and it largely ignored other evaluations that questioned whether the German armed forces could hope to conquer and occupy a territory on this scale. The army Military Geography branch of the General Staff presented a detailed report in August 1940 that highlighted the large Soviet industrial resources already established in Siberia, and the simple facts of topography and climate that severely limited what would be possible.[81] General Georg Thomas, head of the Armed Forces' Economic Office, tried unsuccessfully to demonstrate to Hitler right up to the moment of the invasion that oil supplies were simply inadequate. 'What one does not have, but needs,' Hitler is said to have replied in June 1941, 'one must conquer.'[82]

The months of discussion and planning rested on a number of assumptions that were never seriously questioned at the highest level. The ability of the German armed forces to defeat the Red Army was taken for granted. The Marcks plan anticipated a campaign of between eight and eleven weeks, a larger version of the defeat of France; von Lossberg thought the main stages necessary to reach the terminal line might take from nine to seventeen weeks. Existing convictions about the fragility of the Communist state and the incompetence and low morale of Red Army commanders and rank and file were reflected in regular judgements that were casual and ill-informed. 'The Russian colossus,' claimed Hitler's chief of operations, 'will be proved to be a pig's bladder; prick it and it will burst.'[83] The armed forces remained remarkably ill-informed about the state of Soviet industry and the Soviet military machine. A 'Handbook on the Military Forces of the USSR' distributed by army intelligence in January 1941 claimed on flimsy evidence that the Red Army was 'unsuited for modern warfare and incapable of decisive resistance'. German generals regularly described the enemy in derogatory racial terms as 'Mongols' or 'Asiatics', as 'hordes' rather than armies, redolent of colonial warfare. In May, General Günther Blumentritt imagined a campaign of eight to fourteen days against an army of 'ill-educated, half Asiatic' soldiers, led by incompetent officers. Brauchitsch imagined a campaign of up to four weeks, with heavy fighting near the German–Soviet frontier, and then a series of mopping-up operations.[84] Hitler warned his commanders that the Russians would prove to be a 'tenacious adversary', but they were a mass 'without leadership'. On the eve of 'Barbarossa', he predicted victory in four months, a more cautious estimate than the guesses of most of his commanders.[85]

The confident belief that German armed forces were vastly superior to the Soviet enemy underpinned the strategy of a swift victory, which was essential to free Germany from resource bottlenecks for the confrontation with Britain and the United States. Yet the planning took little account of the problem of supplying scattered forces across a wide geographical area where terrain and climate were utterly different from the earlier European operations. The German army's capacity to mount sustained mobile warfare in an area where only 5 per cent of the roads had hard paving was questionable from the outset. The refusal to take such constraints seriously is all the more remarkable given that many senior commanders, including Halder, had served on the Russian Front during the Great War. Yet it was Halder who assumed that 'Everything must be achieved with the motor. Increased motorization . . .'[86] By 'Barbarossa' the army had 600,000 vehicles, but many were captured trucks and vans which were difficult to maintain or to find spare parts for. The campaign began with more than 2,000 different vehicle types. The problem of finding additional motorized transport meant reliance on as many as 750,000 horses, many of which had to be led or ridden to the front because horses took up too much space as railway freight, while none of them was used to the extremes of heat in a Russian summer or cold in winter.[87] Railway supply, on which German forces had relied since 1939, was not guaranteed for the campaign in the Soviet Union because German locomotives and rolling stock could not use the wide gauge Soviet rails, which would have to be replaced by German engineers across European Russia. To ease the probable supply bottlenecks, improvisations were introduced. Tanks carried double the usual load of fuel and ammunition and pulled trailers with 200 litres of petrol to keep them mobile for longer.[88] The poor terrain, however, was bound to increase fuel consumption, exacerbating an already critical situation with the supply of oil. The assumption remained, however, that the campaign would be over so quickly that the potential logistical crisis could be set aside.[89]

From November 1940 to May 1941 preparations gathered pace. In mid-November, Hitler authorized Fritz Todt, general plenipotentiary for construction, to begin work on a new military headquarters in the east, on a 250-hectare area of woodland near the East Prussian town of Rastenburg. Under the pretence that this was a new chemical works, Askania Nord, a vast network of bunkers, blockhouses and offices was built, eventually surrounded by barbed wire, concrete bastions and minefields, from which Hitler would conduct his largest campaign. He named the site *Wolfsschanze* (Wolf's Lair). The Allies ran their war effort from their capital cities, but Hitler chose to run the campaign in isolation from the ministerial and military apparatus in Berlin, compelling visitors to travel by a shuttle train that went back and forth between the German capital and the new headquarters.[90] Detailed planning continued but absolute secrecy was required, to prevent Stalin and the Red Army from grasping what was about to engulf them. As soldiers and airmen were gradually moved eastwards, the pretence was maintained that they were resting and preparing for operations against Britain. So restricted was information that German servicemen themselves were only told about the operation they were about to embark on a few hours before it began. There was a widespread rumour that the Russians had given permission to advance to the Middle East across Soviet soil to envelop British Empire forces, a strategy that would indeed have had a profound effect on the future course of the war.[91] When 'Barbarossa' finally took place, it was a surprise to the troops of both sides.

The war for *Lebensraum*, like the war against Poland, required along-side the military preparations the means to turn Eurasia into colonial space. Hitler once again entrusted Himmler and the security apparatus with 'special tasks' to be carried out by four *Einsatzgruppen*, composed altogether of approximately 3,000 security police, SS and SD (security service) personnel. They were to follow the armies into the Soviet Union with orders to decapitate the Communist system by murdering Communist Party officials, intellectuals, military commissars and any Jews in state service. Hitler spent much of his long speech to the generals on 30 March explaining that they were taking part in a war of annihilation against the Bolshevik enemy, and would be permitted to use the most brutal methods, free from the requirements of the conventional laws of war. One of those present recalled that the 250 military officers who heard the incitement to act with irregular and illegal force did so without stirring or uttering a word. Not all of them shared a willingness to participate on the terms Hitler laid down, but many did. 'Barbarossa' was intended from the out-set to be a different kind of war. While Himmler organized the murder squads, he also inaugurated planning for the new colonial area on the pattern of ethnic cleansing already developed in Poland in his role as Reich Commissar for the Strengthening of Germandom (RKFDV). The initial 'General Plan for the East' (*Generalplan Ost*), produced in 1940 by Himmler's deputy Konrad Meyer-Heitling, extended only to the German–Soviet frontier in former Polish territory. A new plan was ordered on 21 June, on the eve of 'Barbarossa', and was ready after only three weeks, extending spatial planning into the vast regions of Eurasia where the Slav population and the Jews were to make way for long-term German settlement in 'zones of colonization' to be developed over thirty years.[92]

Preparations were also made to seize or exploit the economic resources of the region systematically as Hitler intended. In February and March an 'Economic Staff East' was activated under Hermann Göring's authority as head of the Four-Year Plan, and he finally approved the new organization on 19 March. The staff of more than 6,000 – twice the size of the *Einsatzgruppen* – were to be responsible for seizing material stocks, oil and foodstuffs, and for taking over the administration of Soviet industrial enterprises to serve the German war economy. The four planned Economic Inspectorates were to operate across the anticipated zone of conquest, from Archangel in the north, through the area surrounding Moscow, down to Baku and the Iranian frontier in the south.[93] On Göring's instructions, the planned exploitation of agriculture was undertaken by Herbert Backe, state secretary in the Ministry of Agriculture, who cynically calculated the extraordinary statistic that up to 30 million people would starve in the grain-deficit areas in the occupied territories, so that grain could flow to Germany and its armed forces. A secret decree in April 1941, signed by Paul Körner, Göring's deputy, gave Backe the authority to act ruthlessly. The announcement of what came to be called the 'Hunger Plan' was made at a meeting of state secretaries on 2 May, a month before the invasion, without any objection, moral or otherwise. 'Poverty, hunger, and frugality have been borne by the Russian individual for centuries,' claimed Backe. 'His stomach is elastic – therefore, no false pity.'[94]

By June 1941, the largest invasion force in history was in place. The army had over 3 million men, 3,600 tanks and 7,000 artillery pieces organized in three army groups, North, Centre and South, supported by 2,500 aircraft. The numbers of tanks and aircraft were not significantly different from a year before against France. There were, however, eighteen Panzer and thirteen motorized divisions, an increase over the previous campaign made possible only by allocating fewer tanks and vehicles for each division. Panzer divisions for the invasion of France had around 300 tanks each; for 'Barbarossa' the number was approximately 150, except for Army Group Centre which averaged 210. Of these, only 41 per cent were the better Mark IV and Mark III models, the rest were a mix of light tanks and captured Czech and French equipment.[95] The seventy-eight infantry divisions relied chiefly on horse and cart, and progress on foot over long stretches of bleak countryside. The German army, however, was not alone. The campaign was joined by forces from Finland, Romania and Slovakia, and soon by small contingents from Italy and Hungary, which brought the overall number of the invasion force to 3.7 million men, organized in 153 divisions.

Given that Hitler's priority was to serve German interests, the decision of other states to participate needs some explanation. In the case of Finland and Romania there was a desire to regain territory lost to the Soviet Union in 1940, and even the prospect of seizing more to create a 'Greater

Finland' and a 'Greater Romania'. The Finnish regime was cautious about the link with Hitler, but the temptation to reverse the outcome against the Soviet aggressor overcame any qualms. To resist Soviet power, claimed the speaker of the Finnish parliament, 'Finland would ally herself even with the devil'.[96] The campaign was presented as a crusade against godless communism and 480 Lutheran pastors were attached to the army to rein-force the Christian message of what came to be called the 'Continuation War', to emphasize the link with the war of 1939–40.[97] Finland was let into the secret of 'Barbarossa' because German forces were to be posted in the far north of the country to protect German mineral interests in Scandinavia. Even a small *Einsatzgruppe* was set up in Finland, eventually responsible for murdering around 1,000 Jews and communists. The Finn-ish government would nevertheless only go so far. Once the lost territories were regained, Finnish forces stopped short of joining the siege of Lenin-grad and would not help the German move towards Murmansk. From November 1941, in the words of the president, Risto Ryti, Finland was to fight a 'separate war'.[98]

Romania was the only other major ally for the start of the invasion. With the German military already committed to protect Romanian oil, the campaign against the Soviet Union could hardly be concealed. Hitler admired the Romanian dictator, Marshal Ion Antonescu, who had firmly established his rule as 'Leader' (*Conducător*) in spring 1941, though he had a poor opinion in general of Romanians and their armed forces. The Romanian regime was also cautious in joining the German invasion after Hitler had insisted that Romania hand part of Transylvania back to Hun-gary in the Second Vienna Award imposed in August 1940, but it was argued that only alongside Germany would it be possible to keep the Soviet Union from threatening what remained of the territorial integrity of the state, and perhaps to reverse the terms of the Award. Like the Finns, Romanians saw the war as a crusade, a 'great holy war' in the words of vice-president Mihai Antonescu.[99] The regime mobilized the Army Group Antonescu, made up of 325,685 men of the Third and Fourth Romanian armies. Although nominally commanded by Antonescu, the units were integrated with the German Army Group South for the advance towards Odessa. Although some Romanian politicians wanted to halt at the fron-tier of Bessarabia and Northern Bukovina once they had been recaptured, Antonescu recognized that, once committed, Romania would have to fight until the Soviet Union was defeated or suffer severe retribution.[100]

Slovakia and Hungary joined with less enthusiasm. The Slovak govern-ment was pressured to comply, since German forces would launch the southern branch of the invasion partly from Slovak soil, but it contributed two divisions for rear area security duty and a small mobile group attached to Army Group South, which was destroyed in a Soviet counter-attack later in July. The Hungarian government and the regent, Miklós Horthy, were not keen to join the campaign either, although some generals hoped they might restore the larger boundaries of 'historic Hungary' if they did so. Only when three bombers, alleged to be Soviet, attacked the town of Kassa on 26 June did Horthy and his Cabinet finally approve participation by a mobile corps of around 45,000 men, but they left, according to one Hungarian commander, with 'no great enthusiasm' for a war whose purpose they could not understand.[101] The idea of a European 'crusade' made little impact and was used by German propaganda only to provide a shallow moral justification for aggression. Alfred Rosenberg, the future minister for the Occupied Eastern Territories, observed to his staff two days before the onset of 'Barbarossa' that this was no crusade to slay Bolshevism, but 'to pursue German world policy and to safeguard the German empire'.[102]

This candid reality makes it difficult to explain why Mussolini, whose armed forces were already stretched to the limit in North Africa and the Mediterranean, volunteered to send an Italian contribution, the *Corpo d'Armata*, to join the invasion. Although Hitler wanted 'Barbarossa' kept entirely secret from his Italian ally, Italian intelligence sources supplied regular details of the coming campaign, and on 30 May, without telling Hitler, Mussolini ordered the preparation of three divisions – two infantry, one motorized – to be sent to the East once the campaign had begun.[103] Hitler was not happy with the offer when it was made two days before 'Barbarossa' began, but it was hard to refuse. Italians, he told his air adjutant, Nicolaus von Below, 'had no fighting strength worth speaking of'.[104] Mussolini's gesture reversed the humiliating request for German assistance he had been forced to make in late 1940, and, as with the French campaign, Italy would have a foot in the door of any subsequent European peace settlement, even if Italy was now the junior partner.[105] In August 1941, Mussolini went in person to the Eastern Front to review with Hitler the recently arrived Italian contingent in Ukraine. His German ally expanded on his great plans for spring 1942, going beyond the Urals and on to Persia and the Caspian Sea. 'What then?' replied Mussolini, irritated for once by his fellow dictator's geopolitical fantasies. 'Shall we weep for the moon like Alexander the Great?' Hitler remained, according to his interpreter's account, 'silent but furious'.[106]

On the other side of the German–Soviet frontier the evidence of German intentions was difficult to calculate. The Soviet leadership did not ignore the German threat and after the fall of France the commissar for defence, Marshal Semyon Timoshenko, announced that Germany was now 'the most important and strongest enemy'.[107] Stalin was aware that his initial hope for an exhausting war between the capitalist powers from which the Communist world would profit was undone by French defeat, but right down to the final day of invasion he wanted to avoid provoking Germany because Soviet forces were not yet ready for a major war. A new trade agreement was negotiated in January 1941 and Soviet trains, laden with resources, were still travelling to Germany on the weekend of the German assault. The plan, if war came, was for small frontier forces behind fixed defences to hold up any enemy attack long enough for full mobilization to bring the bulk of the Red Army to bear and drive the enemy back to their own territory. The preparations were not yet ready in summer 1941: new mechanized corps were still in the process of formation, the fortifications on the new frontier were still under construction and the mobilization plan was incomplete when war arrived. The army chief of staff, General Georgii Zhukov, in response to the clear evidence of a German build-up, ordered a creeping mobilization in late April, and on 13 May thirty-three divisions were ordered to the western Soviet Union, but only a handful were fully equipped by June, while the essential camouflaging of airbases was ordered only three days before German aircraft bombed and strafed the rows of unconcealed Soviet aircraft.[108] The stumbling block for further preparation was Stalin himself, who saw every piece of intelligence, particularly from Western sources, as deliberate provocation to ignite a German–Soviet war. Air reconnaissance indicated advanced German preparations, while 236 alleged German agents were caught along the frontier area. More than eighty intelligence warnings were received in Moscow, including the precise date of the German attack, but Stalin remained adamant.[109] By mid-May the army was suggesting a possible spoiling attack to disrupt German preparations, but nothing materialized. The claim that this formed part of a more general Soviet plan to invade Germany that summer remains unconvincing, not least from what is known of Stalin's own anxiety to avoid a conflict.[110] On 14 June Zhukov tried to get him to order mobilization, but Stalin replied: 'That's war,' and refused.[111] Only on the night of 21 June did Timoshenko and Zhukov finally manage to extract from Stalin an order for a higher state of alert, but too late for the bemused defenders; German bombs and shells began to fall on them in the early hours of the following morning as the warning telegrams were being decoded.[112]

Hitler waited for the final realization of his historic decision in a state of evident agitation. 'Nervous and troubled,' recalled his air adjutant. 'He was garrulous, walked up and down continuously, and seemed to be waiting anxiously for news of something.'[113] Nikita Khrushchev later wrote that Stalin, too, in the days before 22 June, seemed to be a man 'in a state of confusion, anxiety, demoralization, even paralysis'.[114] When Hitler wrote to Mussolini on the night of 21 June with news of the imminent invasion, he confessed to 'the months of anxious deliberation' over 'the hardest decision of my life', almost certainly this time the truth. At 3.30 the following morning, Axis forces attacked all along the front. Hitler dictated his proclamation to the German people while the first shots were being fired and, bleary-eyed after only three hours' sleep, he announced in the Reichstag a state of war with the Soviet Union. He then left for the Wolf's Lair. Hitler had never been to Russia and knew little about the people he set out to conquer. He was unsure, he told von Ribbentrop, 'what strength we shall find once we have really pushed open the door to the East'.[115] In Moscow, there was more uncertainty as Stalin gathered with the Politburo. He wanted to 'urgently contact Berlin' to be reassured that the attack had not been authorized by Hitler. Molotov was sent to see the German ambassador to ask what was going on, only to be told formally that the two countries were at war. 'What have we done to deserve this?' was Molotov's reply. Once the situation was clear, Stalin at 7.15 in the morning ordered Soviet forces to 'annihilate' the invader; in the evening he directed the Red Army to take the battle on to German soil.[116]

The reality at the front line was utterly different. The element of surprise and the muddled state of preparation on the Soviet side of the frontier flattered Axis forces as they moved remorselessly forward. The three main army groups operated at first in self-contained offensives, designed to trap and annihilate the bulk of the Red Army before it could retreat behind the Dvina and Dnieper rivers. Army Group North, tasked with seizing the Baltic states and Leningrad, crossed Lithuania by 26 June and pushed deep into Latvia, before waiting for the infantry divisions to catch up. Riga fell on 1 July, and the Germans plunged on by mid-July to a position only 96 kilometres from Leningrad. Army Group Centre, commanded by Field Marshal Fedor von Bock, which contained the bulk of German armour, moved rapidly into Belorussia, capturing Minsk in a pincer movement on 28 June and netting 324,000 prisoners. Bock then moved on to Smolensk, which fell on 16 July after bitter fighting along the extended flanks of the Panzer divisions, organized by Timoshenko in a desperate effort to stem the German flood. The hardest fighting took place in front of Army Group South, commanded by Field Marshal Gerd von Rundstedt, because German intelligence had failed to detect the Soviet decision to concentrate forces on the southern axis to protect the industrial resources of Ukraine. The Kiev Special Military District was reinforced with mechanized corps that possessed most of the modern tanks available. The border areas were fiercely defended, and a vast week-long tank battle developed in the approach to Dubno and Ostrog that denied the quick advance towards Kiev, though it destroyed most of the Soviet armour in the process. Lvov (now Lviv), in the path of von Rund-stedt's right flank, was finally captured on 30 June, and by 2 July the Soviet Fifth and Sixth armies were in full retreat.[117] Romanian and Ger-man forces to the south took until the end of July to occupy the 'lost territories' in Bukovina and Bessarabia, and began to cross the Dniester River in early August on the way to Odessa. Poor roads, heavy rainfall and stubborn resistance held up the plan to mount a pincer attack around Kiev in order to cut off Red Army forces west of the Dnieper, and the progress of Army Group South stalled short of the initial objectives. Only by mid-July did von Rundstedt's forward armoured units reach within striking distance of Kiev. He told Hitler's air adjutant that 'he has not come up against such a good opponent at any time in the war'.[118]

The rapid German advance in the north and centre of the front unhinged Soviet plans for a forward defence. There were substantial forces available along and behind the frontier in June 1941, on paper outnumbering the attacking force in military equipment: 186 divisions of 3 million men, 19,800 artillery pieces, 11,000 tanks and 9,500 combat aircraft.[119] Soviet air power was neutralized, however, within a few days by attacks on airbases, with the destruction of around 2,000 aircraft; by early July total losses were 3,990, but even the many damaged aircraft could not easily be repaired in what was now a fighting zone. Many Soviet aircraft were obsolescent, while they all lacked radios, making central control of the air forces all but impossible. The tank arm was composed chiefly of older models, which were poorly armed and armoured, princi-pally the T-26 light tank: the small number of the modern, better-armed T-34 medium and KV1 heavy tanks made up just 8 per cent of the tank arm and were distributed to only a few armoured units. Even though they could outfight all German tanks, they were too few to make a difference, and could be outmanoeuvred because, once again, they lacked radios.[120] Everywhere, the field army was short of ammunition and fuel in the chaos imposed by round-the-clock bombing; 200 out of 340 major military sup-ply dumps were overrun in the first weeks of combat, exacerbating the issue of supply. Communication was primitive and broke down rapidly with the German advance so that commanders could not manage the bat-tlefield, or even know what was happening to neighbouring divisions. Out of 319 military units – infantry, mechanized and cavalry – poured into the battles in the first month of 'Barbarossa', almost all were destroyed or badly mauled.[121] The massive losses of Soviet personnel owed much to the crude tactics inherited from the Great War when infantrymen were ordered forward in wave after wave against machine-gun fire. A German report of the front line in front of Kiev described the slaughter as infantry were pushed forward four times under withering fire until German machine guns became too hot to touch: 'The fury of the attacks,' the report continued, 'had exhausted and numbed us completely ... What we were now engaged in would be a long, bitter and hard-fought war.'[122] In places where an organized defence or counter-attack proved possible with better leadership and supply, Soviet forces showed that they could inflict heavy damage on the enemy, but the tide was almost always one-way. By the end of September 1941, Soviet irrecoverable losses of men (dead, missing or taken prisoner) amounted to an astonishing 2,067,301.[123]

The early successes brought a sense of elation to the German side and seemed to confirm the pre-war predictions of Soviet fragility. The expansive plans for the whole campaign at last seemed feasible. Halder famously recorded in his diary on 3 July the conclusion 'that the Russian campaign has been won in the space of two weeks'. The euphoria was widespread. 'The reason I'm not worrying about the struggle on the Eastern Front,' Hitler told dinner guests on 27 July, 'is that everything that happens there is developing in the way that I've always thought desirable ... I always thought that having the sun in the East was the essential thing for us.' Two weeks later he could claim of the territories of Russia, 'this ground is safely ours.'[124] On 23 July, Halder assumed that Moscow and Leningrad would fall within a month, that the army would reach the Volga by October, and finally arrive at the oil cities of Baku and Batum by December.[125] For months, German commanders assumed that there could be no significant reserves of Soviet manpower and equipment after destroying most of the airpower and armour available at the front and watching the reality of Soviet losses in prisoners and the piles of dead. They assumed that any state which suffered losses on this scale, much greater than those imposed on France in 1940, would sue for peace and bring 'Barbarossa' to a swift and victorious conclusion. Intelligence estimates in Britain and the United States shared the view that the Soviet Union would soon be beaten and German forces reach the Volga, confirming pessimistic pre-war assessments of Soviet staying power. Although both states moved to offer the Soviet Union a flow of military supplies, belief in imminent Soviet defeat meant initial caution, in case the goods fell into German hands.[126]

The belief that the Red Army was beaten was, in truth, an optical illusion. German forces had shown their professional skill in advancing fast against a disintegrating defence, but the campaign highlighted many of the drawbacks and deficiencies that the more pessimistic pre-war prognoses had suggested. The prediction that the Soviet soldier would prove a tough opponent was vindicated by the suicidal resistance shown by many units even when entirely cut off from any prospect of safety. Since many soldiers were bypassed by the German advance, they melted into the forests and swamps to ambush German soldiers, holding up German units as they scoured the countryside to root them out. The savage treatment of captured Germans set up a harsh cycle of retribution as the German army and security units murdered alleged partisans and irregulars and burnt down the villages that were thought to shelter them. Prisoners were routinely despatched by both sides. General Gotthard Heinrici described in a letter to his wife in early July the grim reality the men of his infantry division confronted:

> The Russian who was right in front of us, is now destroyed. The whole incident was incredibly bloody. In some cases we gave them no quarter at all. The Russian was like a beast towards our injured soldiers. In return, our men shot and beat to death everything in brown uniforms. The vast forests are still full of scattered soldiers and fugitives, some of them unarmed, some armed, and they are extremely dangerous. Even when we send divisions through these forests, tens of thousands of them manage to avoid capture in this impassable terrain.[127]

A few weeks later he told his wife 'We have all underestimated the Russian' and, two days later, 'Our swift advance has turned into a slow stumble.' Later the same month he risked the censor: 'the war here costs us. Was it really necessary?'[128]

The topography and climate contributed further difficulty. The infantry and vehicles kicked up a thick, choking dust on the dirt roads, but a sudden rainfall would turn the roads to rivers of mud. For all three army groups, zones of dense forest or swampland were difficult to negotiate, while the seemingly endless distances as the front broadened out presented problems quite different from those encountered in Poland or France. The infantry became exhausted by long forced marches, the threat of sudden ambush, and the heat. One soldier wrote home about the 'Infinite, the Never-able-to-reach-one's-goal' nature of the endless landscape, 'the same over and over again here'.[129] Another complained of 'The bloody Russian forests! One loses the overview of who is a friend and who is an enemy. So we are shooting at ourselves . . .'[130] The effect on the thousands of horses was if anything more severe, particularly on the heavy horses needed to pull artillery. Over long distances, on poor roads and in intense heat, the horses were worn out within days, but since the infantry divisions had to try to catch up with the armour far out in front, horses were pushed to the limit, on occasion dying in harness. The breakdown of thousands of vehicles made reliance on horses even more essential, but by November only 65 per cent of the horses were left, now facing the tough winter weather with insufficient fodder.[131] The predictions about supply difficulty were fulfilled almost at once. Only a few hundred kilometres of rail tracks were converted by mid-July, leaving heavy reliance on the horses and vehicles. Army Group Centre needed twenty-four trains of supplies a day but got only half. All along the front line, fuel was in critically short supply, the more so because the poor roads and dust slowed down the tanks and increased fuel consumption, while poorly constructed bridges over the network of Russian rivers were often too flimsy to support tanks and heavy vehicles, forcing detours that consumed even more fuel. The problem of lorries, already a logistic crisis with so many different models, was made worse by the sandy tracks which wore out the tyres, and the dust that clogged the engines. 'We are fighting in a solid mass of dirt,' observed one soldier in mid-July. The army lost one-quarter of its transport strength in the first four weeks; but following further months of transporting goods and men on inadequate tracks, in poor weather, the German armed forces would be left by November with just 15 per cent of their vehicles still roadworthy.[132]

The quick victory was a gamble based on a complete misreading of Soviet strengths and the nature of the zone of combat, just as the Japanese four years before had misjudged how difficult it would be to inflict a swift defeat on Chinese forces in the vast expanse of central China. German forces all along the line needed to rest and refit, while holding at bay persistent counter-offensive operations by an enemy clearly not willing to accept defeat, though too weakened for the moment to achieve anything decisive. The situation was made more difficult by the revival of arguments over strategic direction that had been suspended rather than resolved the previous December. On 19 July, Hitler sent out Directive No. 33, which effectively brought to a halt the advance of Army Group Centre towards Moscow. Some of its resources were diverted north, to help with the encirclement of Leningrad, and south to help von Rundstedt envelop large numbers of Soviet forces around Kiev, before driving towards the Donets Basin and the Caucasus oilfields beyond. The advance on Moscow was to be resumed only in early September when the supply crisis had been improved. Army leaders vigorously objected that defeat of the Red Army around Moscow would bring the final decisive result, and throughout late July and early August the strategic initiative was lost as arguments continued over priority. Hitler's view that the economic resources in Ukraine were critical made strategic sense only as long as the resources could be extracted and used quickly, of which there was no guarantee. Moscow was, in his view, an 'indifferent' target by comparison. 'My generals know nothing of the economic aspects of war,' he complained when on 24 August General Guderian, commander of Second Panzer Army, tried to insist that his forces drive to Moscow rather than move south to Ukraine.[133] Hitler, frustrated after a month of argument and inconclusive combat, got his way. Guderian led his forces south with less than half the necessary complement of tanks, and after bitter fighting in poor weather, finally met up with von Rundstedt's northern wing at the town of Lokhvitsa, east of Kiev, trapping five Soviet armies that Stalin had insisted should stay and fight for the Ukrainian capital. On 19 September the city fell, while the encircled Soviet armies fought on for another six days of savage combat before capitulating. The Kiev operation netted an exceptional 665,000 prisoners, a result that suggested final victory must be close at hand.

While Army Group South, much depleted in numbers and near exhaustion, moved on beyond Kiev into the Donets industrial region and the Crimea, the units of Army Group Centre that were sent northwards helped Field Marshal Ritter von Leeb's army group to cross Estonia by the end of August, and reach the outskirts of Leningrad by 8 September. With the capture of Shlisselburg (Schlüsselburg) Leningrad's last land link to the interior was severed. Bitter fighting along the crude defensive lines built by thousands of civilians continued until 25 September, when Hitler moved units back to Army Group Centre. The city was laid to siege, bombed and shelled every day, while Hitler hoped the inhabitants would starve to death rather than force the army to undertake a costly campaign of urban warfare. Hitler wanted the city to disappear: 'It was conceived by Asiatic Slavs as a gate of entry to Europe. This gate of entry must be closed.'[134] From October the city could only be supplied irregularly across Lake Ladoga where a precarious 'ice road' was built when the lake froze in mid-November. Priority was given to food for workers and soldiers, but by December even they got only 225 grammes of coarse bread a day, while the rest of the inhabitants got only 140. Over the winter months as many as 900,000 Leningraders died of starvation and disease in conditions of appalling hardship until the ice-road in January began to supply an average of 2,000 tons a day to enable the survivors to live out a siege that ended only in 1943.[135]

With hopes for success north and south, Hitler finally allowed Army Group Centre to rebuild its forces to destroy what he believed to be the last reserves of the Red Army before Moscow assembled on the Soviet Western and Reserve Fronts. Directive No. 35, issued on 6 September, focused principally on defeating the armies commanded by Timoshenko (and from mid-September by Colonel General Ivan Konev) to the west of Moscow, rather than seizing Moscow itself, which was to be encircled further to the east, although army commanders and rank and file saw the city itself as their goal after endless campaigns through the battered and abandoned countryside. The onset of the new campaign was delayed by weeks as desperate efforts were made to resupply depleted units. Army Group Centre was by September down to one-third of tank strength, while tanks for repair had to be shipped all the way back to Germany. Manpower proved to be a further bottleneck. Army Group Centre had lost 220,000 men by September, but obtained only 150,000 replacements, with little prospect of any more. The new operation, codenamed without irony 'Typhoon', could be supplied with fuel and food for the troops for only a few weeks by a completely overwhelmed supply system. Nevertheless, the drive on Moscow reignited German optimism. Even the quartermaster-general, Eduard Wagner, who knew just how precarious the supply position was for any major operation, wrote on 5 October that 'the last great collapse stands immediately before us ... Eastward of Moscow. Then I estimate the war will mostly be over.'[136] On 2 October, the date 'Typhoon' began, Hitler returned to Berlin to address the German people in the Berlin Sportpalast a day later. He had returned, he told his audience, from 'a struggle of truly world-decisive significance', a claim with much truth. Bolshevism, the 'ugly, bestial, animal-like enemy,' he continued, was slain and 'would never rise again' – a claim that turned out to have very little truth.[137]

Operation 'Typhoon', like earlier offensives, began well. The plan followed a familiar pattern: the cities of Vyazma and Briansk were to be enveloped by three Panzer armies and the net closed tightly by oncoming infantry in order to prevent escape, following which the road to Moscow and beyond would be all but defenceless. Soviet commanders failed to realize that a major operation was imminent, or that the weakened German army was capable of one, until an urgent warning came only two days before Guderian's Second Panzer Army broke through towards Orel and Briansk. On 2 October the northern wing of Army Group Centre drove at Vyazma against stiff resistance. Orel fell on the 3rd, and both Vyazma and Briansk were encircled four days later. Some Soviet forces were able to escape from Vyazma only because Third Panzer Group literally ran out of fuel and could not close the circle for a day, but the end result, like Kiev, was to net or kill 1 million Soviet soldiers, a success that seemed finally to open the way to Moscow once the encircled pockets had been eliminated. This proved a costly delay because closing the pockets meant days of draining and lethal close combat at just the point that the heavy autumn rains, the period of *rasputitsa*, set in. Moscow receded into the distance as German soldiers, horses and vehicles struggled with pockets of continuous Soviet resistance, declining supplies and quagmire roads that slowed progress to a crawl. Movement had already been hampered by a completely inadequate road system, with regular traffic jams on narrow tracks, demolished bridges, and Soviet delayed-action mines which blasted craters 30 metres wide on the few paved highways. On the road to Briansk used to supply Guderian's Second Panzer Army there were thirty-three Soviet demolitions, including eleven major bridges; detours took extra time and fuel, and led the vehicles into marshy terrain and dirt tracks.[138] The mud merely compounded an already precarious situation in which fuel and ammunition could not be supplied in anything like adequate quantities to sustain an offensive well before the rains set in. Third Panzer Group ran out of fuel only two days into the operation and had to be supplied by air; two weeks later, the group ran out of ammunition, which had to be shipped all the way from Warsaw.[139] Under these conditions the fighting power of Army Group Centre dwindled away. On 1 November, von Bock announced that 'further advances should be temporarily suspended'.[140]

Throughout the month from the start of 'Typhoon' Soviet resistance had been sufficient to slow down the momentum of attack, but when the ground froze in mid-November, the exhausted and depleted German units were asked to make one more effort to capture the Soviet capital. Hitler dithered between a belief that it was still possible to push on to the maximum target line beyond Moscow and acknowledgement that the decisive defeat of the Red Army would have to be postponed until 1942. On 19 November he even told Halder that a negotiated peace might be necessary after all, because 'the two opposing groups could not destroy each other'. The following day Fritz Todt, minister for munitions, told Hitler bluntly that 'This war can no longer be won by military means.'[141] The generals had already requested a controlled withdrawal to the October lines to prevent further losses, but Hitler decided the offensive should continue regardless. The fighting capability of the army groups, after more than four months of continuous, draining combat, had in reality come to an end. By 21 November the operation ground almost to a halt; a few units managed to push their way to within sight of the Soviet capital by early December, but these were acts of desperation. The troops struggled in the biting cold without adequate clothing, short of rations, with tanks and guns that could no longer function effectively in temperatures well below zero. 'We are all so tired of Russia, tired of the war,' wrote one soldier, reflecting evidence of widespread demoralization.[142] Army Group Centre was down to half its notional strength, having lost 350,000 casualties since the onset of the war, and facing a constant attrition of weapons that could not be resupplied as the transport system seized up almost entirely. When Guderian's Second Panzer Army was finally halted near Tula on the approach to Moscow, there were just forty tanks left.

The constant delays in pushing 'Typhoon' on to encircle Moscow gave the Soviet side the respite Stalin needed. In mid-October, a panic seized the capital and government offices were hastily evacuated further east to Kuibyshev. Stalin decided to stay in his threatened capital on 18 October and the population was mobilized to dig outer defensive lines amidst the rain and snow. Stalin appointed Zhukov commander of the Western Front defending Moscow. The 80–90,000 troops initially available were soon supplemented by scratch units, short of trained officers, men and equipment, concentrated along the 'Mozhaisk Line', but when the line crumbled Zhukov withdrew to a defensive belt 16 kilometres from Moscow's centre. On 19 November, as von Bock's exhausted men staggered forward once again, Stalin asked Zhukov, 'Are you certain we can hold Moscow? ... Speak the truth, like a Communist.' Zhukov had no certainty, but he told Stalin, 'We'll hold Moscow without a doubt.'[143] Over the last weeks of November, large reserves were formed and fed into the defence, many of them withdrawn from the Soviet Far East and Central Asia, once there was unambiguous intelligence that Japan was going to attack south, towards British, Dutch and American possessions. On 1 December, von Brauchitsch reported that there were 'no large reserve formations' left to the Red Army. In reality, Zhukov now commanded 33 infantry and 7 cavalry divisions, 30 infantry brigades and 2 armoured brigades, a total of 1 million men, 700 tanks and 1,100 aircraft.[144]

The Red Army planned a limited operation to drive back the approaching German pincers, and establish a firm defensive line well to the west of the capital. At three o'clock in the morning of 5 December, in deep snow, the Soviet army moved forward on two main axes, one north, one south of Moscow. German troops and commanders were taken by surprise and struggled to adopt defensive positions, for which the offensive posture of the operation had not prepared them. The northern city of Klin was recaptured on 15 December, while to the south, Guderian's force was pushed 130 kilometres back from Tula to Kaluga, where the two sides fought a ferocious house-by-house battle until the Germans were forced to withdraw. German commanders struggled to cope with unavoidable retreat and to prevent a complete breakdown of Army Group Centre as freezing, undernourished troops began to panic. In the far north the Red Army retook the city of Tikhvin, while in the south the capture of Rostov by Army Group South, fighting at the end of its tether, was reversed. For the first time, the German army was in retreat and would continue falling back until the

March rains brought the mutually exhausting counter-offensive to a halt. Some 80,000 Germans perished, but the Red Army, still in many cases tactically inept and led by inexperienced officers, lost 440,000 more soldiers.[145] To end what threatened to be a complete collapse, Hitler issued a 'stop order' (*Haltebefehl*) on 26 December to compel soldiers to stay where they were and defend the line; a week before, Hitler had dismissed von Brauchitsch and assumed direct command of the German army himself, so that he could control his commanders more closely and prevent their urge to withdraw.

The failure of Operation 'Barbarossa' became evident well before December. The gamble that the Soviet Union could be decisively defeated in four months, or even fewer, had been high risk from the start given the shortages of equipment and trained men, and the inadequate state of intelligence on Soviet capability. 'We have been punished,' wrote a general staff officer in December 1941, 'for overestimating our strength and for our hubris.'[146] There were also solid strategic explanations for failure. The principal object of the invasion was never clearly articulated, so that a tension existed between the army's desire to eliminate its Soviet counterpart, and Hitler's obsession with territory to exploit. This tension led first to the long delay to the invasion in July and August while priorities were argued over, then to continued intervention from Hitler as he divided German forces in pursuit of the maximum territory. The singular failure to take sufficient account of the logistical problems in operating in three main theatres at long distance over some of the most inhospitable terrain and underdeveloped infrastructure in Europe merely underlined a more general failure of imagination about what constituted the 'East'. For the German armed forces, the campaigns in Poland and France involved relatively short distances and could be served by the German rail network. In the Soviet area, the regular insistence that units move between army groups meant long and taxing journeys of 450–650 kilometres with little rail support, on poor roads and under constant harassment from the enemy. The question is usually asked about how the Soviet military machine managed to survive the German onslaught without collapsing. But viewing the many obstacles that German armed forces had to contend with, particularly in the final months of 1941, it might well be asked how the German military machine managed to occupy an area so large, and to hold on to most of it into 1942. There existed a permanent gulf between the expectations of Hitler and the army staff and the reality of conditions at the front, a gap that was bridged only by the exceptional endurance and professional competence of armed forces called upon to do more than was operationally feasible in deteriorating conditions. German soldiers fought on with a growing fatalism. On 2 January, facing encirclement at Yukhnov, General Heinrici wrote once again to his wife: 'It is so frustrating to know what is coming, what is inevitable, yet anything I say is like talking to a wall. Hence fate will take its course without mercy. It will be the same on a large scale. I no longer fool myself about the whole course of the war.'[147]

Against the background of the first German defeats in the East, the global war was transformed fundamentally. On the morning of 7 December 1941 (8 December in Japan), Japanese carrier aircraft bombed the American Pacific naval base at Pearl Harbor, while Japanese army units began offensives in South East Asia and the Philippines against the British, Dutch and American presence. The operation had been kept secret, even from Japan's ambassador in Berlin, General Ōshima Hiroshi, who since the summer of 1941 had been pressing Tokyo to join the war against the Soviet Union and 'destroy communism at its source'. This would have been the 'Mackinder moment' had it happened, with perhaps the whole of Eurasia coming under German–Japanese domination, but Japanese leaders were reluctant to take advantage of German successes even though, as the foreign minister Toyoda Teijiro wrote to Ōshima in late July, 'Barbarossa' gave the Japanese army 'an excellent opportunity to settle the northern question'.[148] On 25 July, the OKW chief of staff, Field Marshal Wilhelm Keitel, reported to von Bock that 'the Führer's hope that Japan sees with respect to Russia that its finest hour has arrived seems in vain.'[149]

Indeed, by July 1941 Japanese leaders had already decided that a southern advance to the oil and resources of South East Asia made greater strategic sense and stuck by the Neutrality Pact which had been agreed with the Soviet Union in April 1941 by Toyada's predecessor, Matsuoka Yōsuke. The Japanese preference was for a German–Soviet peace, so that Stalin could join the Three Power Pact in a Eurasian campaign against the maritime Western powers, an outcome that would have had more in common with Mackinder's geostrategic speculations. As a result Japanese leaders were lukewarm when German leaders pressed them to join in defeating the Soviet Union, and Japan gave no direct support to the German campaign.[150] Instead, Japanese leaders hoped that Germany might aid them in the event of war with the United States, even though Germany was not committed to do so under the terms of the Three Power Pact, because Japan was the aggressor. Hitler had wanted to avoid war with the United States, because his priority, laid out in a directive in March 1941 on 'Co-operation with Japan', was to defeat Britain, still seen as Germany's primary enemy, but when news of Pearl Harbor arrived, he assumed that Japan would now keep America away from Europe and distract the British.

In contrast to Japanese reluctance to help in the campaign against the Soviet Union, Hitler opted to join forces with Japan against the United States.[151]

In the four days following Pearl Harbor, the United States was not at war with the European Axis, but Chiang Kai-shek, delighted at America's enforced entry into the Asian conflict, declared war on the Axis at once. On 11 December, Hitler left the crisis in Russia to address the German parliament with a declaration of war on the United States, followed the same day by Mussolini. To show his solidarity, Hitler told von Ribbentrop to sign a German–Japanese Agreement on Combined War Strategy, which remained in practice a hollow declaration of intent, since Germany gave almost no strategic or military assistance to Japan's war in Asia. Nevertheless, in Germany and Japan the news of Pearl Harbor – and the subsequent string of Japanese victories in the southern advance – aroused immediate public enthusiasm, despite the evident risks. Crowds gathered outside the imperial palace in Tokyo to thank the emperor for his divine guidance.[152] German Secret Police reports showed that the German population accepted war with the United States – 'the only possible answer' – and assumed that Japanese victories would divert America to the Pacific, reduce Lend-Lease aid to Britain, weaken the British and Soviet war effort and shorten the war. As the victories mounted, in contrast to the dire news from Russia, Goebbels decided to introduce each radio announcement with a fanfare for Japan.[153] The German navy also welcomed the war against a state which would soon wield by far the largest navy in the world. In a meeting with Hitler the day after the declaration of war, Grand Admiral Raeder assured him that the British would be left stranded by the United States as it diverted all its effort to the Pacific war.[154]

There has never been much doubt that the declaration of war on the United States was a strategic misjudgement of fatal proportions. For all three states, already engaged in draining and costly campaigns against China, the Soviet Union and the British Empire, the addition of war with the world's largest economy was scarcely a rational choice, and indeed leaders in both Japan and Germany had hoped to avoid it. The decision was assisted by derogatory views of the capacity or willingness of the United States to wage a major war given its relative military unpreparedness and the long history of isolationism. On the day of the declaration Hitler told his lunch guests that American officers were merely 'businessmen in uniform' not real soldiers, and a few days later asserted that American industry was 'terribly overestimated'.[155] Yet a sleeping colossus is still a colossus. The declarations of war have to be understood in less than rational terms. For Japanese leaders the conflict was justified as an unavoidable war of self-defence against encircling Western powers and included war against Britain and the Netherlands as well. The West schemed, General Tōjō claimed, to turn the country into 'the "little Japan" of before', ending 2,600 years of imperial glory. Japanese leaders saw Japan's war as a sacred mission to eject the individualist and materialist culture of the West and build a family of Asian nations under the 'father-emperor', the traditional aim of *hakko ichiu* ('the eight corners of the world under one roof'). Against the rational calculation of odds was the belief that the spirits of dead emperors and fallen soldiers would safeguard an empire that had never suffered defeat. Early victories were attributed to Japan's 'spiritual power' and the protection of 'imperial ancestors', later defeats to a 'lack of true patriotism'. In these terms, the Japanese declaration of war was not just a product of risky geo-political calculation but reflected a cultural outlook profoundly different from that of the Western enemy.[156]

For Hitler, war with America made explicit what was in his view an undeclared war already pursued from Washington through Lend-Lease aid to Britain and the Soviet Union, assistance in the war at sea, and the freezing of all German economic assets. Hitler had anyway long expected that the new German Empire would one day find itself at war with the United States. A formal state of war greatly simplified the Atlantic battle once submarine captains no longer suffered, so he told the Japanese ambassador, the 'psychological fatigue of trying to distinguish between American and British shipping'.[157] In the weeks following the declaration German U-boats were sent west for Operation *'Paukenschlag'* ('Drumbeat') where they prowled along the American coastline sinking ships still not sailing in convoy or with air protection. In the first four months of 1942, 2.6 million tons of Allied shipping was sunk, more than in the whole of 1941.[158] But beneath the argument that a state of war merely gave formal status to a hitherto undeclared conflict there lay a more menacing conspiracy theory. In Hitler's distorted view of reality, American hostility to Germany was provoked by world Jewry. One of Hitler's interpreters noted down his views: 'America equals Jews everywhere, Jews in literature, Jews in politics, Jews in commerce and industry and a completely Jewified president at the top.'[159] In the National Socialist version of the world, Roosevelt was a Jewish lackey who drove on the Jews in London and Moscow to continue the war. On 12 December Hitler convened a secret meeting with Party leaders to explain that war with the United States had been engineered by the Jews and that the prophecy he had made in January 1939 to annihilate the Jews if Germany were ever dragged into global war would now be realized. Joseph Goebbels, who was present as gauleiter of Berlin, noted the following day in his diary: 'The World War is here, the extermination of the Jews must be the necessary consequence.'[160] Although historians have hesitated to see the meeting as the categorical starting point for the genocide (since hundreds of thousands had already been murdered in the conquered Eastern territories at the hands of security forces and the army), the link Hitler created between world war and Jewish complicity made the declaration of war a rational reckoning for him, rather than the irrational gamble it otherwise appears to be.

Japan's leaders understood that war with the United States was far from ideal, but it also ended another confusing stage of undeclared war in which the United States restricted Japanese access to key industrial resources, including oil, and supplied aid and finance to Japan's Chinese enemy. The decision had much in common with Hitler's claim that the British enemy could only be defeated by attacking a larger, and potentially more powerful opponent: fighting the United States (and the British Empire), it was argued, would help somehow to resolve the conflict in China. In both cases, it was evident that further warfare could not be conducted successfully without access to additional material resources, whether in Ukraine or South East Asia. After ten years of imperial expansion, Japan saw Eastern Asia in much the way the United States viewed the Western Hemisphere – as its natural area of domination which other powers ought to respect. Japanese leaders found it hard to understand why the current situation should not be accepted as an accomplished fact, and negotiations with the United States had begun from the basis that Japan had a legitimate claim to be the leader of a new Asian order, not from any sense that Japanese expansion was a violation of international norms. In January 1941 Foreign Minister Matsuoka Yōsuke publicly rebuked the United States for failing to make any effort to grasp the nature of Japan's role in Asia, which was to 'forestall the destruction of civilization' and establish a just peace.[161] American intransigence was interpreted as part of an international conspiracy to stifle and then extinguish Japan's national existence. Unsurprisingly, there was almost no common ground between the two sides when efforts were made by the Japanese in 1941 to find a *modus vivendi* with the United States that would allow them to resolve the China war on their terms and, at the same time, gain secure access to the strategic resources needed to sustain the empire.

Ironically enough, the concern of Roosevelt and his military leaders was focused much more on the European conflict than on the Pacific. In his speeches during 1941, the president referred to Hitler and Germany 152 times, but to Japan only 5.[162] It was assumed that Japan could be deterred by evidence of American naval power (in May 1940 Roosevelt ordered the Pacific Fleet to stay permanently at Pearl Harbor following ocean manoeuvres) and by economic pressure on a state heavily reliant on American supplies of metals and oil. As early as 1938, Roosevelt had called for a moral embargo of oil, steel, aircraft and finance for Japan, while money was made available for pre-emptive purchasing of materials needed by Japanese industry.[163] In January 1940, the 1911 Commercial Treaty with Japan was abrogated. Following Japanese entry into French northern Indochina in summer 1940, the Export Control Act introduced formal restrictions on a range of strategic materials for Japan, including aviation fuel, scrap iron and steel, iron ore, copper and oil-refining equipment. A year later, after southern Indochina was occupied, Japanese assets were frozen and on 1 August Roosevelt ordered that Japan would have to apply for federal licences for all oil products, although he did not want all applications rejected in case that pushed Japan too far. Japan was expected to be cowed by the pending economic crisis provoked by American firmness, though the American ambassador to Japan, Joseph Grew, warned Washington that to 'threaten the Japanese is merely to increase their own determination'.[164] The complete dislocation of Japan's economic situation indeed accelerated the shift to more radical solutions.

During 1941 the Japanese political and military leadership argued out the merits of trying to solve the China crisis by diplomacy or by further warfare against Britain and the United States, a situation that they had hoped to avoid. Like Hitler's decision to attack the Soviet Union, Japanese leaders arrived incrementally at the point where war seemed both necessary and unavoidable. American politicians failed to understand the impact the four years of the China war had had on Japan. Japanese society was now geared for total war, with shrinking supplies of goods and food for the civilian population, heavy financial obligations and a popular culture of sacrifice and austerity.[165] For the United States there was no sense of desperation in the face of impending disaster, but for Japanese leaders the failure in China and the strangling effects of embargo forced them to embrace solutions that they would rationally have avoided. The uncertain nature of the Japanese response to the crisis was personified in the summer and autumn of 1941 by Matsuoka's ejection from the Foreign Ministry and the collapse of Prince Konoe's government. The two principal architects of Japan's New Order were superseded by General Tōjō Hideki, a military bureaucrat who personified the ambivalence among Japan's elite over the country's options. As minister of war in July 1941, Tōjō hosted the first meeting at which it was agreed that the southward advance to eliminate aid for Chiang Kai-shek and seize the oil and raw materials of South East Asia would now have priority. The army and navy, hitherto divided over future strategy, temporarily pooled their planning. The German–Soviet war removed the Soviet threat to Manchuria, and although the army doubled the size of the Manchurian Kwantung garrison during the summer, in case the opportunity arose to profit quickly from imminent Soviet defeat, the southern advance to isolate China made more immediate strategic sense.[166] In late July the army occupied southern Indochina to cut off the principal supply route of aid to Chiang (estimated at 70 per cent of all supplies in 1940). The result accelerated the drift to war. On 9 August, following the American oil restrictions, which threatened to cut three-quarters of Japan's oil imports, army plans were approved for a war, starting in November. Navy preferences pushed the deadline forward to October. The campaign was approved at an imperial conference on 6 September, and justified in Konoe's words as a war of 'self-defence'.[167]

However, on 16 October Tōjō succeeded Konoe as prime minister and immediately promised that renewed efforts would be made to reach a diplomatic solution that would pave the way for Asian peace under Japanese guardianship, but not, as Konoe put it, 'plunge us immediately into war'. The deadline for deciding war or peace was shifted to late November. After days of Cabinet discussion, during which the prospects for both options were exhaustively examined, one more diplomatic effort was approved. At an imperial conference on 5 November the emperor was informed in the passive voice that war could not be avoided if the final gambit failed. The Cabinet and military staffs saw war as something forced on them, not something they had chosen. Tōjō authorized two plans to be presented to Washington: Plan A promised immediate withdrawal from Indochina, and from China (except Hainan, the northern territories and Manchukuo) within two years, but expected a range of concessions on restoring trade, closing off aid to China, and American agreement not to intervene in Japanese–Chinese relations; Plan B was a more modest proposal to promise no further aggression, if the United States promised to end the trade embargo and repudiate any role in China.[168] Both plans were presented to Washington by the ambassador, Nomura Kichisaburō and a veteran diplomat, Kurusu Saburo. The plans were little more than wishful thinking by November 1941, but the Japanese side took them seriously as a compromise offer. On 22 November, American radio interception of Japanese diplomatic traffic (codenamed 'Magic') read the message sent to the Japanese negotiators insisting that 29 November was the final deadline for a political agreement: 'This time we mean it, that the deadline absolutely cannot be changed. After that, things are automatically going to happen.'[169] The American military were on full alert from late November throughout the Pacific region, but where the Japanese strike would come remained unclear.

Roosevelt was not opposed to some form of compromise, if it kept the peace in the Pacific and met American interests, but his secretary of state,

Cordell Hull, who conducted the negotiations with Japan, was resolutely against any agreement that left any part of China in Japan's hands. Against the advice of the military leadership and the president's wishes, he delivered a note to the Japanese negotiators on 26 November, making clear that in the long run agreement could only be based on a restoration of the situation before the occupation of Manchuria, a demand that was clearly not remotely negotiable for Japanese leaders.[170] Regarding this as an ultimatum, the government discussed their choices on the 29th. Tōjō concluded that 'there was no hope for diplomatic dealings' and the war option prevailed. Few Japanese leaders seem to have actively favoured war with the United States and the British Empire. The decision was taken with a fatalistic acceptance that fighting was preferable to humiliation and dishonour. Tōjō had told the imperial conference on 5 November that Japan would become a third-class nation if it accepted America's terms: 'America may be enraged for a while, but later she will come to understand.'[171] Once Japan had seized control of the oil and resources it needed, it was hoped that the shock to American opinion would open the way to an agreement that met Japan's national objectives. There was still the option, revived in November, that Japan might broker a peace settlement between Germany and the Soviet Union, leaving the United States isolated, but neither belligerent was interested.[172]

The day the Hull Note was delivered to Ambassador Nomura, the Japanese navy's Mobile Striking Force under command of Admiral Nagumo Chūichi was sailing from its base in the Kurile Islands to attack, if ordered, the American Pacific fleet at Pearl Harbor. On 2 December he received the coded message 'Climb Mount Niitaka 0812' authorizing the attack to go ahead on 8 December, Japanese time. Troop convoys were also on the move south from China and Indochina towards the Philippines and Malaya. The latter was reported in Washington, where it was assumed that Japanese forces aimed to occupy Malaya and the Dutch East Indies, but Nagumo's fleet remained sealed in secrecy until the hour of the attack. The plan to launch a surprise raid on Pearl Harbor went back to the end of 1940, when navy leaders began serious preparation for a southward advance, but it had been a topic in Japanese naval circles since the 1920s.[173] The details were worked out by Kuroshima Kameto, the eccentric staff officer to the fleet commander, Admiral Yamamoto Isoroku, who would lock himself naked in a darkened room for days to think out planning solutions.[174] A seaborne air attack on this scale was a novelty. One model was the British attack at Taranto in November 1940; Japanese embassy officials turned up in Taranto the day after the raid to observe at close quarters its effect. They were also much influenced by the German success in Norway in using air power to neutralize Britain's much larger naval presence. In spring 1941 Japan's aircraft carriers were put under a single fleet commander, to maximize their striking power. Japanese aerial torpedoes were modified to enable them to operate in the relatively shallow water of the docks at Pearl Harbor without sinking into the seabed, and naval pilots were trained rigorously in low altitude torpedo and dive-bombing. Although Yamamoto was one among a number of senior Japanese officers anxious to avoid a clash with America, he understood that the Pearl Harbor attack was an essential first step to prevent the Pacific Fleet from posing any threat to the operations in South East Asia and the seizure of oil and resources, which was the priority in the southern advance. When the plan was presented to the naval staff, however, it was turned down because it concentrated too much of Japan's naval strength away from the Asian campaign and put the carrier force at risk. Only Yamamoto's threat to resign forced the navy's hand, and on 20 October the plan was reluctantly approved. Nagumo's First Air Fleet was tasked to destroy at least four of the American battleships at anchor, together with the port facilities and oil storage. The force consisted of 6 aircraft carriers with 432 aircraft, 2 battleships, 2 cruisers and 9 destroyers; the naval element was modest for such a risky operation, but for years Japanese naval strategists had seen air power as the critical element in naval warfare.

Surprise was complete on the morning of 7 December, although Nagumo had been instructed to attack even if his force was detected as it approached Oahu. The American failures are by now well known: aircraft were packed together on the ground because the local commander, Admiral Husband Kimmel, had been warned of possible sabotage; the limited radar system was closed down at seven o'clock in the morning (the one sighting that occurred was thought to be B-17s on exercise) and the Aircraft Information Center (modelled on the RAF system) was not yet operational; there were no anti-torpedo nets; a handful of Japanese midget submarines detailed to penetrate the harbour defences in the early hours of the morning before the air attack were spotted and one destroyed, but no general warning followed; above all, the American intelligence available prompted alert warnings that Japan was about to act but all reason dictated that this would be in South East Asia.[175] In truth, Yamamoto ran his luck to an exceptional degree in an operation which he judged had only a fifty–fifty chance of success.

In the early dawn, two waves of Mitsubishi 'Zero' fighters, B5B 'Kate' bombers and D3 'Val' dive-bombers were flown off the carriers, a total of 183 in the first wave, 167 in the second.[176] Despite the intensive training, the operation was fraught with difficulty. The most successful phase was the destruction of almost all the American aircraft on Hawaii – 180 completely destroyed, 129 damaged. The attack on the American capital ships met less success. Out of forty torpedo bombers, only thirteen hits were scored; the dive-bombers found it hard to distinguish targets and failed to do more than damage to two of the eight cruisers moored; the second wave found the targets now obscured by smoke. Not only was the hit ratio poor, but many Japanese bombs failed to explode. The spectacular explosion and sinking of the USS *Arizona*, an iconic image from the battle, was achieved by one lucky bomb that penetrated the forward magazine. The airmen returned to report devastating damage, but, like the British raid on Taranto, the result was less spectacular once the smoke had cleared. The American carriers were all at sea during the raid. Four battleships were sunk and one beached; minor damage was inflicted on three others; two cruisers and three destroyers were seriously damaged, and two auxiliaries sunk. The twenty-seven fleet submarines sent by the Japanese navy to intercept any breakout and then to blockade Hawaii managed to sink only one oiler and damage one warship in two months.[177] The attack achieved more than Yamamoto had hoped, but with more experience and better tactics, the raid could have achieved much more.

What the attack did do was kill or maim Americans: a total of 2,403 dead and 1,178 injured. Roosevelt was relieved of the problem of persuading a divided American public to join the war. Only a few days before Pearl Harbor, he told his confidant, Harry Hopkins, that he could not bring himself to declare war: 'We are a democracy and a peaceful people. But we have a good record.'[178] The Japanese attack galvanized American opinion and ended the years of debate between isolationists and interventionists. Defeating Japan at all costs united Americans of every opinion. For the British Empire, also now threatened by Japanese aggression, the American fury at Japan threatened to undermine any chance of a commitment to join the war in Europe, until German and Italian action relieved Roosevelt once again of the prospect of convincing the American public to fight the European Axis as well. To secure a common strategy, Churchill led a delegation to Washington on 22 December where, in three weeks of discussions codenamed 'Arcadia', the British delegates tried to secure American commitment to their view of the war. Tentative agreement had already been reached earlier in March 1941 in informal military staff talks that Europe was their joint priority. In the first meeting between Churchill and Roosevelt at Placentia Bay in Newfoundland in August 1941, the 'Atlantic Charter' was drafted in which defeat of 'Nazi Germany' was defined as the key to a new world order.

At the December summit, Churchill secured assurance from Roosevelt, despite the strong reservations of the American navy, that Europe remained the priority. The two sides also took the unusual, indeed unique, step in the war of pooling their strategic discussions in a common forum, the Combined Chiefs of Staff, together with combined boards for shipping, munitions output and intelligence.[179] There nevertheless remained significant divergences. Roosevelt and his military staffs were not attracted to the idea of simply following British plans for what the many Anglophobes around the president viewed as an 'empire war'. The initial priority was to prevent a Soviet defeat. 'Nothing could be worse than to have Russia collapse,' he told his treasury secretary. 'I would rather lose New Zealand, Australia, anything else than have Russia collapse', a view that sat uneasily with Britain's empire interests.[180] Roosevelt and his army commander-in-chief, General George Marshall, assumed that a frontal assault on Hitler's Europe would be necessary in 1942 to help the Soviet war effort, but the British were firmly opposed to the risk – an argument that was only resolved later in 1942 when the operation became manifestly unfeasible. To show that Roosevelt thought in terms of American global strategy, he used the 'Arcadia' conference to launch on 1 January 1942, only three weeks after the Pearl Harbor attack, a declaration on behalf of what he called the United Nations, composed of all those many states at war with the Axis. Like the Atlantic Charter, the declaration of key principles of self-determination and economic freedom marked the point at which the values of the older imperial order were superseded by the values of American internationalism, a shift that became explicit as the war continued.

There was a curious sense of unreality in the weeks of Anglo-American discussions. Across South East Asia and the Western Pacific, the Japanese army and navy moved rapidly and decisively to achieve the southward advance. The scale was quite different from 'Barbarossa'. Given commitments in China and the operation against Pearl Harbor, the Japanese military could only muster limited forces: 11 army divisions out of 51 available and 700 aircraft; the navy could supply around half of its 1,000 aircraft, and had 2 carriers, 10 battleships and 18 heavy cruisers to support the army's amphibious operations.[181] It was a campaign even riskier than Pearl Harbor because it involved spreading forces very thinly between four major operations: the capture of the Philippines, the occupation of Thailand, the capture of Malaya and the Singapore naval base, and the conquest of the Dutch East Indies. It was, nevertheless, an exceptional moment of triumph in the long war that Japan had waged since 1937. Western defences were weak, chiefly because the British could spare little from the war in Europe and the Middle East and American reinforcement had only just begun. Dutch forces consisted of local colonial troops after the German conquest of the Netherlands. Most British Empire forces in the region were inexperienced Indian divisions. Daily digests of disaster arrived in London and Washington, starting with the sinking of two British capital ships, sent originally at Churchill's insistence to deter the Japanese. The battleship *Prince of Wales* and the battlecruiser *Repulse*, confident as they sailed into the South China Sea that they were beyond the range of any known Japanese aircraft and poorly informed about Japanese capability, were sunk on 10 December by torpedo bombers sent from bases in Indochina. In a matter of a few hours, British naval power in the East was extinguished. Only the Japanese gave the contest a name, the 'Battle off the Malay Coast'.[182]

The two major campaigns against British Malaya and the American Philippines protectorate began on 8 December. Pilots with specialized training for long oversea flights attacked the Philippines, flying from Japanese Empire bases on Taiwan; as in Oahu, they found American aircraft lined up on the tarmac at Clark Field and destroyed half the B-17s and one-third of the fighters. Amphibious landings began on the 10th on the main island of Luzon and made rapid progress towards the capital, Manila, which surrendered on 3 January. The United States commander, General Douglas MacArthur, appointed earlier in the year, withdrew his mixed American–Filipino force south to the Bataan peninsula. With no air cover and only 1,000 tons of supplies shipped by American submarine, the force was doomed. MacArthur was evacuated to Australia on 12 March to fight another day. Bataan was surrendered on 9 April, and on 6 May, after a gruelling and determined defence of the island fortress of Corregidor, the surviving American commander, General Jonathan Wainwright, gave up the fight. The Japanese Fourteenth Army captured almost 70,000 soldiers, 10,000 of them American. They were marched along the Bataan Peninsula to an improvised camp; ill, exhausted and hungry, they suffered beatings, killings and humiliation from Japanese Empire forces who suffered themselves from a poverty of medical supplies and food and who had been taught to despise surrender.[183]

In northern Malaya, General Yamashita Tomoyuki's Twenty-Fifth Army began an amphibious assault on 8 December, fielding at first only a few thousand men because of difficulty in finding sufficient shipping. His army was met by a poorly organized defence which crumbled in days, withdrawing in confusion step by step down the peninsula, until Johore in the south was abandoned on 28 January on the orders of the British commander-in-chief in Malaya, Lieutenant General Arthur Percival, and the large empire force evacuated to Singapore Island. Yamashita eventually commanded around 30,000 men for the assault on the island, which was regarded by Japanese imperial headquarters as a critical objective for any further advance into the Dutch East Indies. Yamashita fielded far fewer than the estimated 85,000 British, Indian and Australian troops (as reinforcements arrived the total reached around 120,000) now crammed into an island base that had not been prepared for defence against a landward invasion.[184] On 8 February, Yamashita ordered two divisions and the Imperial Guards to begin a night-time assault. Churchill cabled that the defenders should fight and die to the last man, but this was the stuff of empire adventure stories. After weeks of demoralizing retreats against an enemy often invisible and evidently brutal, the defending forces panicked. As they fought to board the few remaining ships in Singapore Harbour, Percival agreed with Yamashita to surrender. The capture of 120,000 men was the largest and most humiliating defeat in British imperial history.[185] Other British outposts collapsed rapidly. On 25 December, Hong Kong surrendered to the Japanese Sixteenth Army after holding out for eighteen days against inevitable occupation; British Borneo, with its oilfield sabotaged by the retreating forces, surrendered on 19 January. Very soon British Burma too came under threat.

The campaign to capture Burma had not been the Japanese military's initial intention. The original invasion force was designed to eliminate the nearby British airfields that might have threatened the security of the Malayan campaign. But Japanese commanders were tempted by the evidence of just how weak British Empire forces proved to be, to move further and occupy Burma and threaten India as well. The Japanese army hoped that perhaps further expansion might even result in 'forcing Britain to submit and the United States to lose its will to fight'.[186] More prosaically, conquest would cut the supply lines from India to Chiang's armies in south-west China and allow the Japanese to occupy the rich rice-producing regions and the oilfield of Yenangyaung, which produced 4 million barrels a year. The British had a poorly armed, mixed force of around 10,000 British, Indian and Burmese troops, and 16 obsolete Brewster Buffalo fighter aircraft.[187] They retreated in disorder to Rangoon as the Japanese Fifteenth Army, under General Shōjirō Iida, inaugurated the main Burma operation on 22 January with four divisions of 35,000 men. Because the Burma supply route was essential for China, Chiang had offered the British in December the chance to deploy Chinese troops against a possible Japanese assault, but General Wavell, now commander-in-chief in India, not only brusquely refused the offer, but also sabotaged Chiang's effort to establish a Joint Military Council in Chongqing to oversee grand strategy for the war in Asia.[188] British unilateral seizure of supplies of Lend-Lease aid for China, stored in Rangoon, exacerbated the tension between the two allies, not least since the supplies made little difference. British Empire forces abandoned Rangoon on 7 March and retreated hastily northwards. Chiang deeply resented the patronizing attitude of the British, the 'superior race complex' as one American eyewitness described it.[189] 'You and your people have no idea how to fight the Japanese,' Chiang told Wavell in December, even before the fact was plainly evident. 'Resisting the Japanese is . . . not like colonial wars . . . For this kind of job you British are incompetent.'[190]

Chiang did not expect much more from the United States, now a wartime ally, but he wanted American assistance. Roosevelt agreed to send a chief-of-staff to Chiang and the choice fell on the former military attaché to China General Joseph 'Vinegar Joe' Stilwell, famous for his sour view of almost everyone except himself. Stilwell privately considered Chiang to be a 'stubborn, ignorant, prejudiced and conceited despot', but he arrived at Chongqing in early March 1942 to take up a post he accepted with reluctance.[191] His first initiative was to persuade Chiang to let him take command of two of the best remaining Chinese armies, the Fifth and Sixth, and use them to retake Rangoon and keep the Lend-Lease supply route open. Chiang warned him that most Chinese divisions were composed of little more than 3,000 riflemen with a few machine guns, a handful of trucks and no artillery.[192] Undeterred, Stilwell, with no combat experience and little or no intelligence on the enemy, moved to obstruct the Japanese in central Burma. The result was a predictable disaster. With almost no air cover and scant regard for the Chinese officers he was supposed to command, Stilwell was forced to retreat in the face of a competent Japanese campaign. Lashio in northern Burma was seized on 29 April and by May the Japanese army controlled almost all of Burma. On 5 May Stilwell fled westward with a small party, leaving thousands of Chinese soldiers to their fate. The Sixth Army was all but annihilated. Remnants of the Fifth struggled in appalling conditions to reach the Indian frontier town of Imphal later in the year, where Stilwell had already arrived on 20 May, blaming Chiang, the Chinese generals and the British for what went wrong.

The long British retreat back to India was hampered by a massive exodus of refugees, eventually estimated at around 600,000, most of them Indians and Anglo-Burmans. It was difficult to keep the scattered forces of Major General William Slim supplied or reinforced, and the ragged, exhausted remnant that arrived in India had lost almost all military equipment. 'They DO NOT know their job,' complained the overall British commander, General Harold Alexander, 'as well as the Jap, and there's an end of it.'[193] British Empire casualties numbered 10,036 out of the 25,000 who eventually fought in Burma, but at least 25,000 Chinese soldiers were

lost, while Japanese casualties amounted to only 4,500 for the whole campaign.[194] An unknown number of refugees died in appalling conditions as
they struggled to cross the only two available passes into Indian Assam.
Perhaps as many as 90,000 died of starvation, disease and the almost
unpassable monsoon mud that, ironically, saved India from Japanese invasion.[195] Stilwell returned to Chongqing as overall commander of American
military personnel in China, which were few, but Burma and the vital road
to supply the Chinese was lost, along with any confidence Chiang might
have had that China would be taken seriously as an allied power. That
Chiang accepted Stilwell back was due to his continued desire to win American support, though he now regarded the alliance 'as just empty words'.[196]

Further south, the conquest of the Dutch East Indies was a foregone
conclusion following the loss of Singapore and by 18 March the Allies surrendered the archipelago, leaving the rich resources of the region in
Japanese hands. To complete the whole campaign, a string of Pacific islands
was captured, from the American-held Wake and Guam in the north to the
British Gilbert and Ellice Islands in the far south. In just four months Japanese forces conquered almost the entire empire area of South East Asia and
the Pacific. The army captured 250,000 prisoners, sank or damaged 196
ships, destroyed almost every Allied aircraft in the region, and all for the
cost of 7,000 dead, 14,000 wounded, 562 aircraft and 27 small ships.[197]
This was a lightning war (*dengekisen*) of the kind Japanese military leaders had admired in the German campaigns of 1940 and hoped they might
achieve against the Anglo-Saxon powers.[198] Japan's *Blitzkrieg* was easily
won, but at just the point that the German version had failed. The reasons
for Japanese success are not hard to find. Unlike the logistical problems
that plagued the German campaign, Japan's dominant navy and large merchant marine were equal to the task of supplying men and equipment. The
doctrine and practice of amphibious warfare had been worked on for
years with obvious success. The Western states, on the other hand, had
woeful intelligence on the state of the Japanese armed forces, a result not
only of little effort to gather up-to-date information, but also a product of
complacent racism that dismissed Japanese military capability. The governor of Malaya memorably told Percival 'Well, I suppose you'll see the little
men off!'[199] Japanese intelligence on the other hand was thorough, gleaned
by agents who mingled with the large pool of Japanese living or working
in South East Asia and drew on Asian hostility to colonial rule. Japanese
forces were well aware of just how feeble the defence of empire was likely
to be; the army could field thoroughly trained troops and pilots, many of
whom had seen prolonged combat in the harsh conditions in China.[200] The
troops available throughout South East Asia to repel the Japanese invasion

had few if any among them who had seen action. Poorly armed, with often limited training, increasingly prey to the demoralizing fear that Japanese soldiers were unstoppable, they were generally little match for the enemy. The conquest of Hong Kong exemplified the problem. The financial and trading centre for the British Empire in China, the colony was defended by two aged destroyers, a few torpedo boats, five obsolete aircraft, and army units riddled with venereal and other diseases. A Volunteer Defence Unit of local expatriates was formed with men from fifty-five to seventy years of age. The Canadian brigades shipped in just before Hong Kong fell had had almost no battle training.[201] For years European imperial forces had been used to an easy domination. Now they faced a rival empire keen to sweep away white rule and equipped for the moment to do so.

The collapse of the British Empire in Asia and the Pacific was complete. Conquest stretched from the frontier of north-east India to the distant Gilbert and Ellice Islands in the South Pacific. The Japanese high command had no plan to invade India, and shelved the navy's proposal to invade the north and east coast of Australia because the army could not spare further manpower.[202] Nevertheless, on 19 February the Australian port of Darwin was bombed, while an effort to occupy Port Moresby in New Guinea, close to Australian targets, was only turned back when a Japanese carrier was sunk and another damaged by two American carriers in the Battle of the Coral Sea on 7–8 May. To rub salt in British wounds, Nagumo took his carrier force into the Indian Ocean in April to bombard the British naval bases at Colombo and Trincomalee in Ceylon (Sri Lanka), sinking three British warships and forcing what was left of the Royal Navy's Eastern Fleet to retreat to Bombay (Mumbai) to avoid further damage.[203] So anxious were the British Chiefs of Staff at Japanese threats to the Indian Ocean that they organized an invasion of the French colony of Madagascar on 5 May (Operation 'Ironclad') to pre-empt any Japanese landing, but it took six months of combat to force the surrender of the Vichy garrison.[204]

The geopolitical transformation of the region in only a matter of weeks produced a fundamental shift in the relationship between the United States and its imperial ally. The surrender of Singapore with a few days' fighting was contrasted unflatteringly with the courageous defence of the Bataan Peninsula. The rapid collapse of British Empire defence in Asia was added to the many failures of Britain's war effort and confirmed the American military, and much of the American public, in their desire not to be drawn into a strategy of rescuing an empire that had spent two years failing to save itself.[205] Roosevelt and his advisers moved swiftly to articulate a global strategy to compensate for Britain's debilitated world role, along lines already widely discussed in Washington. The Johns Hopkins geographer Isaiah Bowman, a key influence on Roosevelt's negative attitude to empire, assumed that the time had come when the United States had 'to make a sudden shift into a new world order' after years of being 'tentative, timid, doubtful'. In May 1942, Norman Davis, chair of the United States Council on Foreign Relations, concluded that 'The British Empire as it existed in the past will never reappear,' and added, 'the United States may have to take its place.'[206] The president's Advisory Committee on Problems of Foreign Relations, appointed in 1939, had already outlined commitment to colonial self-determination, freedom of trade and equal access to raw materials as hallmarks of the new order.[207]

Nothing divided American and British opinion so much as the growing political crisis in India. Roosevelt had raised the issue of Indian independence at the 'Arcadia' conference, to which Churchill, in his own words, responded 'so strongly and at such length' that Roosevelt preferred not to raise it in future discussions face to face (advice that he passed on to Stalin).[208] The president nevertheless saw the Indian issue as an important one, with Japan poised for a possible invasion, and in April 1942 sent a message to Churchill encouraging him to grant Indian self-government in return for Indian participation in the war. Harry Hopkins, who was present when the telegram arrived, was subjected to a night-long tirade from Churchill about the president's interference. A month earlier Churchill had sent Stafford Cripps, the former ambassador to Moscow, to offer the Indians a complex federal constitution in which Britain would keep responsibility for Indian defence, but the Congress Party rejected it as a half-measure, designed to 'Balkanize' India, and the Indian situation remained deadlocked. Nevertheless, for most British leaders the issue of the future of the British Empire was a matter for Britain to decide, not the United States.[209] Following Cripps's failure, American opinion hardened during 1942 against British imperialism. Gandhi wrote to Roosevelt in July urging the Allies to recognize that making the world 'safe for freedom' rang hollow in India and the empire. The Indian nationalist movement wanted the Atlantic Charter and the United Nations Declaration to fulfil the pledge that Woodrow Wilson's Fourteen Points had failed to honour at the end of the First World War. Roosevelt's personal representative in India, William Phillips, sent the president regular reports of the apathy and hostility of much of the Indian population ('frustration, discouragement and helplessness').[210]

It was an American journalist who coined the term 'Quit India' in the summer of 1942, but the term was soon taken up by the Congress Party when the leaders met in early August to frame a resolution asking for an immediate declaration that India would become independent. What followed was, as the viceroy Lord Linlithgow described it, 'by far the most serious rebellion since that of 1857'.[211] On 9 August all the Congress leaders were arrested, including Gandhi, and incarcerated for the rest of the war; by the end of 1942 there were 66,000 Indians held in detention; by the end of 1943, almost 92,000, many in insanitary and overcrowded prisons, shackled and fettered. The early arrests provoked widespread rioting and violence across central and north-west India. The authorities kept scrupulous account of the destruction or damage to 208 police stations, 332 railway stations, 749 government buildings, and 945 post offices. There were 664 bomb attacks by the angry, and mainly young, protesters.[212] The British, relying on Indian policemen and army units, lifted all restrictions on the use of force with the Armed Forces (Special Powers) Ordinance, allowing the police and army to use guns as well as sticks, and eventually the use of mortars, gas and strafing attacks by aircraft to disperse crowds. Police opened fire on at least 538 occasions, killing, according to official statistics, 1,060 Indians, but almost certainly the figure was higher. Permission was given for widespread flogging as a deterrent. One district officer, after ordering twenty-eight men to be flogged in public with a dog whip, wrote: 'Illegal without a doubt. Cruel? Perhaps. But there was no further trouble throughout the district.'[213] The India Office in London made great efforts to restrict news of flogging and police violence from reaching a wider public, but in Britain and the United States anti-imperialist lobbies highlighted the news. The deliberate exercise of imperial violence at its most ruthless was endorsed by Churchill, who loathed Gandhi, and feared that the crisis might undermine the Raj entirely. Order was restored, but the resentments that fuelled the rebellion would resurface after 1945 when the wartime emergency was over.

During the summer of 1942 Roosevelt developed his ideas about the future of the colonial empires without risking consultation with his British ally. In June the Soviet foreign minister, Molotov, visited Washington and Roosevelt chose the moment to test Soviet attitudes to the idea of trusteeship as the gateway to eventual independence. Molotov approved, since anti-colonialism was orthodox thinking in Moscow. Roosevelt concluded by explaining his view that 'the white nations ... could not hope to hold on to these areas as colonies'. These sentiments marked a fundamental difference between American and British approaches to the probable post-war order. In discussion with one of Roosevelt's close advisers on trusteeship in the Caribbean later in the year, Churchill explained that, as long as he was prime minister, Britain would cling to its empire: 'We will not let the Hottentots by popular vote throw the white people into the sea.'[214] Through most of the year following the Japanese southern advance, American strategic planning was soured by differences of opinion with the British. In May 1942, Brigadier Vivian Dykes, the British secretary to the Combined Chiefs, complained that the United States was set to put Britain in the 'position of a satellite to America'.[215] The tension was persistent over distinct views about the future of the British Empire and the post-war international order. Although this did not inhibit collaboration, the United States now joined with the Soviet Union and China in the struggle to eliminate imperialism old and new.

RACE AND SPACE: RULING WARTIME EMPIRES

The territorial empires created by the Axis states were unusual in a number of respects. Unlike the older empires, which grew haphazardly over many decades, they were created in less than ten years, in the German case in just three years, but were swiftly and completely destroyed by failure in war. Yet despite the commitment to waging war, which placed severe demands on the imperial centre, all three Axis states set about building the institutional, political and economic bases for the new empires even while the fighting was going on. The delusion that the empires were now permanent features, whatever the outcome of the wider conflict, now seems difficult to explain, even more so once the Soviet Union and the United States became the major Allied belligerents. But since the Axis wars were about building empires, their fragile and improvised character was deliberately ignored in favour of fantasies of a long imperial future.

The operation of the new empire areas had features in common. Leaders in all three shared a language of 'living space' and approved harsh measures to defend it once conquered. The empires constituted a mix of different administrative and political forms rather than a coherent whole and lacked common structures of control (like the older colonial empires). The final political shape of the new empire areas was held in abeyance until the end of hostilities, but in each case the dominant imperial power was not to be restrained by conventional notions of sovereignty and international law. While the war continued, large parts of the conquered territories were run by military government or administration; the material resources of the captured regions were intended to serve military needs as a first priority. Under both military and civilian administration, collaborators were sought to assist in running local services as well as the police and militia forces needed to help the army maintain local security. The

Japanese inherited the existing colonial system of governance left by the defeated empires; the Germans and Italians inherited state structures that could be exploited where necessary, even in the hated Soviet system, to ensure local stability. In none of the new empires were local national sentiments fostered if they threatened the unity of the new order or undermined the interests of the occupier. Any acts deemed to be hostile to those interests were effectively criminalized. To establish authority, extreme levels of terror were introduced that mimicked other colonial contexts, but which exceeded them in sheer scale and horror: deportation, detention without trial, routine torture, the razing of villages, mass executions and, in the case of Europe's Jews, extermination. Between them, the new empires cost the lives, both directly and indirectly, of more than 35 million people. If a fundamental difference existed between the Asian and European experience, it lay in the extent to which racial policy shaped the structure of empire. Although Japanese soldiers and officials certainly regarded the Japanese race as superior, and had a particular loathing for the Chinese, the ideology of empire was aimed at the idea of Asian 'brotherhood', with Japan very much the older brother. In Europe, and in Germany in particular, the structure of the new order was racially based, with 'Germans' or 'Italians' at the apex of a hierarchical empire that condemned millions of the new subject peoples to displacement, starvation and mass murder.

Japan's new territories of the 'Southern Region' (*Nampō*) were seen initially as an area where the mistakes made in trying to subdue and pacify a large part of China might be avoided. These were colonial areas where it was possible to pose as liberators of Asia from the Western yoke. The empire in China was imposed on a people who did not see the enemy as a liberator but as an occupying power whose remit rested in the end on the willingness to use the army and military police (*Kempeitai*) to enforce compliance. The Chinese territories occupied in the 1930s were nominally ruled by Chinese puppet regimes, one based in Manchukuo, one in inner Mongolia, a 'Reformed Government' in Beijing under Wang Kemin, the Shanghai Special Municipality in China's most important city, and a Provisional Government in the Nationalist capital, Nanjing, first under Liang Hongzhi, then from March 1940 under the former Chinese Nationalist Wang Jingwei. In December 1939, Wang signed a formal agreement that allowed Japan to station troops and embedded 'advisers' (whose advice was not to be ignored) throughout the area of central and southern China occupied since the start of the war in 1937.[216] In none of these areas was Chinese sovereignty a reality: north China was in effect run by the North China Political Affairs Commission; Manchukuo was a colony in all but name; Wang's regime, while it claimed to be the legitimate Nationalist government, was used instrumentally by the Japanese supreme command to pressure Chiang Kai-shek into agreeing a peace and, when that failed, Wang was used to help combat Communist resistance through the Rural Pacification Movement, mobilizing the limited military forces the Japanese allowed. Wang and his successor in 1944, Chen Gongbo, were watched throughout by the Advisory Group of Japan's China Expeditionary Force based in Nanjing.[217]

Throughout the area that became 'national' China under Wang, the Japanese had undertaken widescale 'pacification' programmes aimed at creating order at a local level congenial to Japanese interests. Special Service agents, civilians in distinctive white shirts emblazoned with the motto *senbu-xuanfu* ('announcing comfort'), were instructed in the March 1938 'Outline for Pacification Work' to 'get rid of the anti-Japanese thinking . . . and to make [the Chinese] aware that they should rely on Japan'. They were to be encouraged to observe 'the gracious benevolence of the Imperial army' – a difficulty following the massacres in and around Nanjing a few months before, and one of the many paradoxes confronted by the young idealists in the Special Service as they tried to reconcile Japanese violence with the rhetoric of peace and mutual co-operation they were told to broadcast.[218] At village level, so-called 'peace maintenance committees' composed of local Chinese were responsible for re-establishing order and educating the inhabitants into the habit of bowing to any Japanese soldier they passed (or run the risk of random violence). Following the pattern of the mass 'Concordia League' established in Manchukuo to bind the population to loyalty to the emperor and his representatives, Chinese neighbourhood associations were used to express pro-Japanese sentiment and to isolate for punishment those who refused to participate. Individuals who obeyed were rewarded with a 'Loyal Subject Certificate'.[219] For ordinary Chinese, accommodation was the route to survival, dissent a sure path to arrest, torture and death.

Many of the devices used to establish 'order' were transferred to the Southern Region in the wake of the rapid military occupation. Planning for a possible southern advance had begun in 1940 and in March 1941 the Japanese army produced a document outlining 'Principles for the Administration and Security of Occupied Southern Regions', reaffirmed at the Imperial Headquarters Liaison Conference in Tokyo in November, two weeks before Pearl Harbor.[220] There were three central policies, maintained in all the different areas taken under occupation: the establishment of peace and order; the acquisition of the resources needed by Japanese military and naval forces; and organizing as far as possible the self-sufficiency of the occupied territories. Beyond that, the occupied area was divided up like

China into a patchwork of different dependent and satellite units, where no decision was to be made about their eventual fate. The November meeting laid down that 'premature encouragement of native independence movements shall be avoided'. After the invasion, the captured areas were divided up for military government (*gunsei*) between the army and navy according to strategic priorities. The army administered Burma, Hong Kong, the Philippines, Malaya, British North Borneo, Sumatra and Java; the navy was responsible for Dutch Borneo, the Celebes (Sulawesi), the Moluccas islands, New Guinea, the Bismarck archipelago and Guam. Malaya and Sumatra were united in a single Special Defence Area as the core of the new southern zone; Singapore, renamed Syanan-to ('Light of the South'), was given a special status with its own military administration, and in April 1943 became the headquarters of the Southern Army when it moved from the Indochinese capital of Saigon.[221]

The anomalies were Thailand and French Indochina, both encroached on by the Japanese army, although not as enemy states. The Thais were induced to allow Japanese troops and aircraft access to the fronts in Malaya and Burma, but the end result was a form of occupation. The Thai government of Field Marshal Plaek Phibunsongkhram signed an alliance with Japan on 11 December 1941 and on 25 January, following bombing attacks by Allied aircraft, declared war on the Allies, assuming that they were joining the winning side. There was also the Japanese promise that territory in Malaya, regarded as part of historic Thailand, would be restored. On 18 October 1943, the northern Malayan provinces of Perlis, Kedah, Kelantan, and Trengannu were indeed transferred to Thai rule.[222] French Indochina, under a Vichy colonial regime, had been forced to accept Japanese troops in the north in summer 1940, and a full occupation in July 1941, when Saigon became the headquarters of the Southern Army. On 9 December 1941 a Franco-Japanese Defence Pact confirmed Japan's right to operate from French territory with French assistance and Field Marshal Yoshizawa Kenkichi was appointed Ambassador Plenipotentiary to oversee Japanese interests. The commander of the Southern Army, Field Marshal Terauchi Hisaichi, treated Indochina as if it were occupied territory.[223]

The acquisition of the Southern Region prompted the establishment in Japan of a structure to oversee the new imperial project in what was now called the Great East Asia War. In February 1942 a Council for Construction of Greater East Asia was set up, and on 1 November a formal Ministry for Greater East Asia was appointed, although its remit did not extend to the Malayan–Sumatran Special Defence Area, which, together with the rest of the Dutch East Indies, was declared in May 1943 'to belong to

Japan for all eternity' as integral elements of the Japanese colonial empire.[224] The south also now joined the Great East Asia Co-Prosperity Sphere, an amorphous concept of Asian collaboration under the leadership of the Japanese Imperial Way, first given the name by Matsuoka in a newspaper interview on 1 August 1940. The sphere was supposed to bind together the peoples of East Asia and the Pacific, once free from Western domination, so that they could march forward together to a peaceful and prosperous future. It quickly became the touchstone of planning in Tokyo for the occupied areas, embedded in political and media discourse as a means to legitimize Japanese occupation as something other than mere colonialism. The ideology of harmony and unity generated for the wider empire was matched by a political transformation in Japan itself, when in August 1940 the political parties dissolved themselves and formed an Association for the Promotion of a New Order, rejecting liberal parliamentarianism in favour of a common commitment under the emperor to promote the Imperial Way in Japan and its territorial conquests. The population was united in a single Imperial Way Assistance Association. Political harmony in Japan, according to the then prime minister, Prince Konoe, was the precondition for Japan to take the 'leading part in the establishment of a new world order'.[225] Nation and empire became culturally and politically inseparable.

The ideological underpinning of the Japanese New Order was essential to the self-understanding of the thousands of officials, propagandists and planners who radiated out from Japan to help run the new territories. They were animated by an idealistic view of what Japan could now achieve for the whole Asia-Pacific area and were welcomed initially by that fraction of the occupied population who hoped that the rhetoric of the Co-Prosperity Sphere meant what it said. The problem for the Japanese intellectuals and writers mobilized to promote the ideology was the tension between the claim that Japan was ending European and American colonialism and the need to position Japan clearly as the 'nucleus' or 'pivot' of the new order. In Java, the propaganda team that accompanied the military administration developed the idea that Japan was only regaining the central position that it had played thousands of years before as the cultural leader of an area from the Middle East to the American Pacific coast. 'In sum,' claimed the Japanese journal *Unabara* (*Great Ocean*), 'Japan is Asia's sun, its origin, its ultimate power.' The occupiers promoted a 'Three-A Movement' to get Indonesians to understand that their future lay with 'Asia's light, Japan; Asia's mother, Japan; Asia's leader, Japan'.[226] In the end the new sphere was designed to create a form of empire consistent with Japan's cultural heritage and distinct from that of the West. According to the Total War Institute in a publication in early 1942, all the peoples in the sphere would obtain their 'proper positions', the inhabitants would all share a 'unity of people's minds', but the sphere would have the empire of Japan at its centre.[227]

Among those who were initially enthusiastic about the idea of a different Asia, the reality of military government and Japanese intervention soon created disillusionment. The Indonesian journalist H. B. Jassin, writing in an arts magazine in April 1942, complained that the people had 'absorbed everything Western and denigrated everything Eastern', but by contrast he thought the 'Japanese are great because they could absorb the new while retaining what was theirs.' But in his post-war memoirs he recalled the bitter irony of enthusiasm for the rhetoric of co-operation and harmony 'which later turned out to be nothing more than beautiful balloons, each bigger and more brilliantly coloured than the last, but their contents only air'.[228] Even the head of the Japanese propaganda mission in Java, Machida Keiji, later acknowledged how futile the ideological effort was, given the reality of military rule and the hostility of much of the army leadership to ideas that would excite Indonesian ambitions: 'The great banner of the "Greater East Asia Co-Prosperity Sphere" in fact meant only a new Japanese colonial exploitation, a sign advertising beef that is really dog meat.'[229]

The military occupiers were in general more pragmatic and more self-centred than the civilian ideologues. The menace at the core of Japanese rule was made evident at once on the arrival of Japanese forces. In the East Indies, the military administration immediately banned Indonesian nationalist symbols, imposed censorship, prohibited all meetings, outlawed the possession of firearms, and imposed a curfew. Suspected looters were publicly beheaded or left bound hand and foot in the sun to die. Javanese had to bow low to all Japanese soldiers and, if they failed, would receive a slap across the head, or worse. So widespread was the abuse that local Chinese called the early occupation 'the period of people struck by moving hands'.[230] In Malaya a wave of executions and beatings followed victory, aimed at any who were thought to be anti-Japanese or to retain pro-British sentiments. The motive, according to the euphemistic language of the military administration, was 'to indicate the right way for the purpose of eliminating their possible mistakes'. Severed heads were left on poles in the street as a warning to others. In Singapore, the *Kempeitai*, housed in the Young Men's Christian Association building, undertook what was called 'purification by elimination' (*sook ching*), a term the German SS would have understood. The main target was the Chinese community (though not only the Chinese) and included teachers, lawyers, bureaucrats and young

Chinese men linked to political forces in Nationalist China. Estimates of the number executed vary widely, from 5,000 to 10,000. Purification in mainland Malaya may have accounted for 20,000 more.[231]

In all the occupied areas, the three policies agreed in November 1941 were applied with mixed results. The pursuit of order combined the threat or reality of draconian punishment with strategies for the same pacification and self-government committees at village level that had been practised in China. In Malaya, Peace Committees were set up to restore order, using a large number of the incumbent Malayan officials inherited from the British colonial administration. Complaints or bad work were judged to be anti-Japanese and risked severe punishment. In time, neighbourhood associations were introduced, like those in Japan and northern China, while local police and volunteers were enlisted in paramilitary militia and auxiliary police forces. Eventually in most territories local 'advisory councils' were inaugurated, but they had no authority and allowed the Japanese officials and military to gauge local opinion without conceding responsibility. Mass movements of solidarity, now modelled on the Imperial Way Assistance Association in Japan, were created to act as a form of social discipline. In the Philippines, political parties were dissolved and a single 'Association for Service to the New Philippines' established, superseded in January 1944 by a 'People's Loyalty Association'. Overseeing their conduct were the *Kempeitai*, attached to each army unit.[232] They dominated the policing of the territories, but they could do so only by recruiting large numbers of agents and spies willing to denounce their compatriots. The numbers of military police were small, spread across a vast territory. In Malaya at the peak of activity there were only 194 *Kempeitai* in service.[233] Their behaviour was entirely arbitrary, and they could also discipline Japanese forces, even senior officers, if they chose. Accounts show many cases where entirely groundless accusations were made: if the victims were fortunate, they would survive hideous tortures, until their innocence was demonstrated; if not, they confessed to improbable crimes and were executed.

The colonial character of Japanese rule on the ground certainly imposed a prudent accommodation on the occupied populations, but it also provoked armed and unarmed resistance, which was treated with an exceptional severity. Resistance was made possible by the sheer geographical extent of the Japanese-controlled territory, where thinly spread garrison and police forces were confined to the towns and the rail lines that linked them. Mountain terrain, forest and jungle gave guerrilla forces the opportunity to operate hidden and mobile campaigns. By the time the southern area was occupied, Japanese forces had had much experience with resistance in Manchukuo and China, led primarily by Chinese Communists. In Manchukuo, the Japanese army instituted a crude system of rural resettlement into 'collective hamlets' to cut guerrillas off from the isolated villages and farms that helped to supply them. By 1937 at least 5.5 million people had been displaced into some 10,000 hamlets. In 1939 and 1940, following a programme of roadbuilding to ease communications, a major operation was launched to rid Manchukuo of all armed resistance. Some 6–7,000 Japanese soldiers, 15–20,000 Manchurian auxiliaries and 1,000 police combat units were mobilized. Villages suspected of giving succour to the resistance were burnt down and their inhabitants, men, women and children, massacred. The security units adopted what the Japanese called the 'tick' strategy of sticking to an identified guerrilla group and following it relentlessly until it was cornered and destroyed. Thousands of guerrilla hideouts were discovered and eliminated, and by March 1941 resistance had all but come to an end.[234]

Much of the resistance in the Southern Region was also conducted by communists, who were regarded as a special menace by the Japanese authorities. Overseas Chinese played a major part, since they were linked with the wider war in China. By 1941 there were 702 'Salvation Movement' groups across South East Asia supplying aid and moral support to the Chinese war effort, both nationalist and communist.[235] In Malaya, communist resistance began almost at once with the founding of the Malayan People's Anti-Japanese Army, supported by a broader Malayan People's Anti-Japanese Union. By 1945, it was estimated that the army numbered between 6,500 and 10,000 fighters, organized in 8 provincial regiments, with assistance from perhaps as many as 100,000 organized in the Union.[236] By this stage, the resistance had the support of Allied infiltrators organized through the British Special Operations Executive. Between 1942 and the end of the war the resistance had mixed fortunes. Japanese counter-insurgency counted on the support of spies and agents, including none other than the general secretary of the Malayan Communist Party, Lai Tek, who in September 1942 betrayed a top-level guerrilla meeting in the Batu Caves in Selangor, allowing the Japanese to ambush and kill prominent Communist leaders. During 1943 major security operations devastated the guerrilla ranks, and for much of the time mere survival among the dense jungle and mountains was the priority. The movement engaged in isolated acts of sabotage, and assassination of those who worked for the Japanese authorities, but regular Japanese inducements to offer bribes or amnesty to the resisters depleted their number. Those in the Union suffered more, since they were not mobile like the guerrillas. Some resettlement schemes were operated to prevent remote villages from assisting the rebels, but on nothing like the scale in Manchukuo, or the later dislocation of millions during the British 1950s counter-insurgency. Whether the Anti-Japanese Army claim that 5,500 Japanese forces and 2,500 'traitors' were killed matched reality or not, resistance remained a constant irritant to the occupying power, and a reminder that 'peace' and 'harmony' in the new empire were merely relative.[237]

In the Philippines – outside Malaya the only other main site of sustained resistance – the overseas Chinese, both communist and nationalist, also played a part, although in this case the Chinese constituted only 1 per cent of the Philippines population, where they amounted to more than a third of the Malayan population. Since many of them were young male immigrants, they avoided Japanese 'cleansing' operations by joining small Chinese left-wing resistance movements set up in early 1942, the Philippine Chinese Anti-Japanese Guerrilla Force and the Philippine Chinese Anti-Japanese Volunteer Corps. In cities, resistance was led by the Philippine Chinese Anti-Japanese and Anti-Puppet League. Right-wing Chinese, linked to the mainland Nationalists, organized a further four small groups, fragmenting even further the Chinese effort.[238] The chief communist resistance group was Filipino, the People's Anti-Japanese Army (*Hukbalahap*), formed under the leadership of Luis Taruc in March 1942. The first battle they fought that month, against 500 Japanese troops, was commanded by the redoubtable Felipa Culala (known as Dayang-Dayang), one of many women who joined the armed resistance. By early 1943 there were an estimated 10,000 Huk fighters, but a force of 5,000 Japanese troops deployed in March that year on the main island of Luzon inflicted a severe defeat, compelling the Huk to focus on survival and recruitment, as in Malaya.[239] By 1944, the Huk again numbered perhaps 12,000 men and women, but they were now armed by the United States with weapons and an effective radio network, which proved invaluable, particularly on the smaller island of Mindanao.[240] They eventually linked up with American-led guerrillas to support the later United States invasion in autumn 1944.

The second strand of Japan's occupation policy, the supply of resources for the occupiers and the Japanese war effort, proved more complex than the planners in 1941 could have envisaged. Directives in each of the occupied territories made it clear that Japanese needs took priority. The intention was for Japanese forces to live off the land, since supplying them over such large distances was deemed impracticable. This meant imposing on the occupied populations 'pressure upon the people's livelihood ... to the limit of their endurance'.[241] This proved to be the case even in Indochina, which was still under limited French rule. The main rationale behind the southern advance had been to take control over key resources lacking elsewhere in the Greater East Asia Co-Prosperity Sphere, and that meant principally bauxite and iron ore from Malaya, and oil and bauxite from the Dutch East Indies. Although the Western Allies suffered from the collapse of rubber and tin supplies from Malaya and Thailand, neither was an urgent necessity for Japan. The supply of rice and other foodstuffs was needed for the local troops, but also for supply to the Japanese home islands. A wide range of other goods was requisitioned or purchased for the use of the occupier and could not be withheld. In August 1943, the military administration in Malaya published an ordinance 'for the Control of Important Things and Materials', giving the Japanese the right to commandeer whatever was needed. To cope with the difficulty of organizing a decentralized economy in Malaya, a Five-Year Production Plan was published in May 1943, followed a month later by a Five-Year Industrial Plan. To ensure supplies, monopoly associations were set up, together with central agencies for price control and licensed trade, but declining means of transport and widespread corruption made it difficult to turn plans into reality.[242]

In some cases, supply for the home island economy was successfully sustained, in others not, but the overall results scarcely matched the optimistic expectations of the supreme command. Bauxite exports from Malaya and the Indonesian island of Bintan to feed the aluminium industry reached 733,000 tons by 1943, but output of Malayan manganese ore, affected by British demolitions, sank from 90,780 tons in 1942 to just 10,450 tons in 1944. Iron-ore imports from the south had reached 3.2 million tons in 1940, but fell to 271,000 tons in 1943, 27,000 tons in 1945. Ironically, the high-quality iron ore of Malaya had been developed by Japanese firms in the 1930s, supplying 1.9 million tons in 1939 for Japan's economy, but only a tiny fraction of this figure during the war years. Supply was maintained only by expanding output in occupied North China.[243] The two main export industries of South East Asia, rubber and tin, were allowed to languish, creating widespread unemployment and poverty among the Malay workforce. Japan needed only around 80,000 tons of rubber a year (and seized stocks of 150,000 tons), so production fell to less than a quarter of pre-war output by 1943; 10–12,000 tons of tin was all that was needed, and as a result output fell from 83,000 tons in 1940 to just 9,400 tons in 1944.[244] The key resource was oil, which had triggered the decision to invade. The valuable oilfields of Borneo, Sumatra, Java and Burma produced annually more than enough oil to cover the needs of the Japanese armed forces. The attempt by the British and Dutch to render the oil wells inoperable largely failed. The Japanese forces had expected to take up to two years to get the flow of oil back to the pre-war level, but some installations were working again within days, most significantly the major field at Palembang on Sumatra, which produced almost two-thirds of the region's oil. To manage the exploitation, some 70 per cent of the oil industry personnel were sent from Japan, leaving the home industry short of skilled men. By 1943, southern oil was flowing at 136,000 barrels a day, but almost three-quarters of this was consumed in the southern war zone, leaving the home islands with little of the bonanza.[245] In 1944 Japan imported only one-seventh of the oil that had been available before the American embargo, 4.9 million barrels instead of 37 million, a situation that had worsened with an American air and sea blockade which Japanese military leaders had failed to anticipate.[246] Oil had made the war seem necessary, but war consumed the oil.

The final policy objective – to make the Southern Region self-sufficient and so reduce the need for trade or transfers from the Japanese home islands – succeeded only at the cost of widespread impoverishment and hunger for the indigenous populations. Self-sufficiency was difficult to impose at short notice on areas that were primarily export-based colonies serving the world market. Sales to the West had made it possible to import the food and consumer goods needed for the home population. With the collapse of multilateral trade, the occupied areas were forced to rely on what could be produced locally or bartered. The south was not integrated within the yen currency bloc operated in China, Manchukuo and Japan. The financial system broke down in most of the area following the collapse of the colonial banks, except in Indochina and Thailand; since there were no local bond markets, and taxation was undermined by the collapse of exports, the Japanese military administrations simply printed money as military scrip and declared it to be the legal tender.[247] Financial self-sufficiency was enforced by harsh punishment for anyone who refused to accept the crudely printed Japanese notes, or who retained stocks of old money. 'Tremble and obey this notice', ran the posters put up in Malaya to announce that only military scrip – nicknamed 'banana money' from the banana tree illustrated on the notes – was valid currency. Violations were met with torture and execution. Efforts to reduce the money supply to prevent hyperinflation included large-scale lottery sales and taxes on cafés, amusement parks, gambling and prostitution (so-called 'taxi hostesses').[248]

Inflation was, nevertheless, unavoidable as a result of competition for food and goods from the Japanese garrison forces, despite efforts to impose coercive price controls. The difficulty of controlling the economies of so large an area led to widespread corruption, hoarding and speculation, usually at the expense of the poorer urban population. Collapsing transport networks made it difficult to move rice from surplus to deficit areas, while damaged irrigation systems and the loss of draught animals to disease and requisitioning led to falling yields.[249] As Japanese demands rose, so the living standards of the bulk of the population deteriorated. In Malaya, unsuitable for large-scale rice production, the population consumed more root vegetables and bananas, but these provided an average of only 520 calories a day. Supplementing food by resort to the black market was unavailable for ordinary workers. In Singapore the cost-of-living index rocketed during the war from an index figure of 100 in December 1941, to 762 by December 1943 and 10,980 by May 1945. A sarong in the Malayan state of Kedah had cost $1.80 in 1940, but $1,000 in early 1945.[250] Malayans were observed to work barefoot and almost naked, with rags instead of clothes. In Java, rationing by 1944 only provided 100–250 grammes of rice a day, too little to sustain normal life. Estimates suggest that 3 million Javanese died of starvation under the occupation, even in an island initially self-sufficient in foodstuffs. Signs appeared in the streets of Batavia, 'The Japanese must die, we are hungry!'[251] In Indochina, the French agreement in 1944 to allow the Japanese to extract higher levies from the rice crop left the peasant farmers in Tonkin desperately short of food. Here, too, an estimated 2.5–3 million died of starvation over the winter of 1944–5.

In addition to the crisis in living standards, occupied populations had to cope with growing demands from the occupiers for compulsory labour service, which imposed a harsh regime on an already debilitated workforce. The model had been worked out in Manchukuo, where the Japanese authorities ordered that all men aged between sixteen and sixty had to do four months of forced labour (*rōmusha*) for the Japanese army every year; for families with three males or more, one was obliged to undertake one year of labour service. An estimated 5 million Manchurians worked for the Japanese, aided by 2.3 million labourers deported from the North China area between 1942 and 1945.[252] In the Southern Region, shortages of labour to construct roads, railways, airbases and fortifications led to the imposition of *rōmusha* labour battalions, most notoriously with the construction of the Burma railway linking Bangkok to Rangoon, on which an estimated 100,000 Malays, Indonesians, Tamil Indians and Burmese died of disease, exhaustion and malnutrition, a death rate of one-third of those recruited. On Java, village headmen were given the unappealing task of supplying labour quotas, effectively by coercion, to meet Japanese demands. By late 1944 there were 2.6 million *rōmusha* employed on defence work, but estimates suggest that most of the 12.5 million workforce that could be recruited served at some time as forced labour. Workers transferred to overseas projects, like the 12,000 Javanese taken to Borneo in late 1943, were ill-treated and starved.[253] Forced labour was regarded as expendable, and their treatment confirmed the wartime colonial status of the captured regions.

The language of liberation exploited by the Japanese to mark the end of the regime of European and American imperialism was nevertheless real enough. Japanese commentators contrasted the new conception of an Asian order with the 'egoism, injustice and unrighteousness' of Western, and particularly English, rule. Tōjō claimed that Japan's purpose was now 'to follow the path of justice, to deliver Greater East Asia from the fetters of America and Britain'.[254] But this was not intended as a 'Wilsonian moment' in which Japan would grant unconditional independence, because President Wilson's promises in 1918 were regarded among Japanese leaders as mere hypocrisy. As the Total War Institute put it in the same 1942 analysis, independence was not 'to be based on the idea of liberalism and self-determination', but was defined in terms of being a co-operative member of the Japanese sphere.[255] Nor was the vision of the sphere a product of Pan-Asianism, as many anti-colonial nationalists at first believed because of Japan's earlier flirtation with the concept, because Pan-Asianism assumed an equality between the peoples of Asia. A candid assessment by the Southern Area Army of independence for Burma made clear the relationship many of the conquerors had in mind. Any new regime 'shall have on the surface the appearance of independence, but in reality ... shall be induced to carry out Japanese policies'. In Japanese government and military circles, independence was usually, though not invariably, viewed as an opportunity to acquiesce in Japan's special status as the imperial centre. How this might have worked in the case of India as an Asian 'brother' of Japan was never put to the test, but it was something Japanese leaders thought about a good deal. Even before the southern advance, contact was made with the Bangkok-based Indian Independence League, led by Rash Behari Bose. Once installed in Malaya, with large numbers of captured Indian soldiers willing to abandon prisoner-of-war status, the Japanese set up an Indian National Army (INA) under the Sikh captain Mohar Singh, to co-operate with the League. Tensions led to the arrest of Singh and the near collapse of the INA, but in March 1943 it was reactivated under the former Congress politician Subhas Chandra Bose, who, with Tōjō's consent, declared on 21 October 1943 the Provisional Government of Free India (Azad Hind) with himself as head of state, prime minister, minister of war and minister of foreign affairs. A division of the INA fought in 1944 in the failed invasion of north-east India, with catastrophic casualties, and Free India under Japanese supervision never materialized.[256]

In January 1942, Tōjō announced to the Japanese Diet that Burma and the Philippines might both at some point win independence if they proved loyal to Japan and its interests. Before the invasion, Burmese and Filipino nationalists had visited Japan as a potential supporter of anti-colonial campaigns. The Japanese army agreed to establish a Burma Independence Army in December 1941, composed initially of a group of thirty 'Thakin' nationalists, including Aung San, the later nationalist leader. The army made no promises, and when the BIA swiftly grew to 200,000 strong, it was dissolved and a Japanese-led and trained Burma Defence Force established in its place. In 1943, Burma was finally promised independence and on 1 August the new state was declared, with the nationalist Ba Maw, freed from British exile in East Africa, as head of state. Although lip-service was paid to Burmese sovereignty, in reality the Japanese kept a close controlling hand. 'This independence we have,' complained Aung San in June 1944, 'is only a name. It is only the Japanese version of home rule.'[257] Much the same happened in the Philippines following Tōjō's promise. The military administration allowed a puppet regime to be installed in January 1942, led by the Filipino politician Jorge Vargas. Its role was advisory, and the provisional council of state made clear its willingness to support the military administration and to work for inclusion in the Greater East Asia Co-Prosperity Sphere. In summer 1943 a new constitution was introduced without political parties, or popular suffrage, and Salvador Laurel, rather than Vargas, was appointed head of state. Unlike Burma, the Filipino elite made their peace with the Japanese, and accepted that the new state had only limited sovereignty so long as the Japanese military presence remained.[258]

There was initially no intention of offering 'independence' to the rest of the captured region, which was to be integrated with Japan. When the Greater East Asia Ministry organized a Great East Asia Conference in Tokyo in November 1943, only Burma and the Philippines were invited from the southern sphere. Changing circumstances as defeat loomed opened up the possibility of further 'independence'. On 7 September 1944, Tōjō's successor, Koiso Kuniaki, announced that Indonesia might win independence 'at a later date' and allowed the nationalist flag to be displayed, as long as it flew next to a Japanese one.[259] Concessions were made to integrate Indonesians with the Japanese administration, though in a secondary role, but a notional independence was only offered in the last days before Japan's surrender. The only other case was in the anomalous French possession of Indochina. Growing Japanese irritation with the attitude of French officials and businessmen in 1944, following the liberation of France and the end of Vichy rule, resulted in a recommendation from the

Supreme War Leadership Conference in Tokyo on 1 February 1945 for the
military to take complete control of Indochina with a view to creating pro-
Japanese independent regimes. On 9 March, Japanese troops launched
Operation '*Meigo Sakusen*' ('bright moon action') when they began dis-
arming French colonial forces; desultory fighting continued until May.
Although Japan did not formally grant independence, the former emperor
of Cochinchina, Bao Dai, declared an independent Vietnam on 11 March.
Cambodia declared its independence two days later, and Luang Prabang
(Laos) on 8 April. Each state had a Japanese 'advisory board' and had to
collaborate with Japanese forces, and each had a Japanese governor general and general secretary, severely circumscribing any real idea of
independence.[260] The final concessions in the Southern Region owed something to the need to win a measure of popular support for imminent
military action against the invading Allies, but it seems likely that Japan
wanted to create aspirations for independence that would make it difficult
for the returning colonial powers to reassert their authority, as indeed
proved to be the case. How Japan's Greater East Asia would have evolved
if Japan had won the war or reached a compromise peace remains a speculation. The wartime Sphere was an imperial construct, built on warfare
and ruined by war.

The New Order constructed by the European Axis faced an entirely different geopolitical reality, though it too was built and ruined by war even
more completely than the empire of Japan. The countries invaded and
occupied in 1940 and 1941 were not colonies but independent sovereign
states with their own political, legal and economic structures. The principal
aggressor was Hitler's Germany, which had to rescue Mussolini's failing
imperialism in Europe and North Africa, and as a result the shape of the
New Order was determined largely from Berlin and in German interests.
The central concept of a German-dominated *Grossraum* (literally 'Great
Area') was not unlike the idea behind the Co-Prosperity Sphere, where
conventional Western notions of sovereignty were set aside in favour of an
array of states and territories acknowledging the unique role of the imperial centre as the directing hand of the whole. In 1939, the German legal
theorist Carl Schmitt published an influential study on *International Law
and the Grossraum* in which he defended the idea that in the future hegemonic states would expand into a defined 'great space' in which a hierarchy
would exist with the expanding state at the core and the other subjugated
states, even if nominally 'independent', gravitating around it. Conventional
international law on the absolute sovereignty of the modern nation-state
was, Schmitt argued, inappropriate for a new geopolitical era of 'great

areas'. The 'obsolete interstate international law', he continued, was largely a Jewish construction.[261] Schmitt was only one of many theorists who legitimized Hitler's aggression by viewing the creation of the *Grossraum* as the hallmark of a new age, in which, like Japan's dependencies, each component of the New Order would have its function and place according to German assessments of its merits.

Few Germans, Hitler included, could have imagined in 1939 that by late 1941 the German *Grossraum* would extend from the Spanish frontier to central Russia, from Greece to arctic Norway. The area was not treated uniformly, but consisted, like the Japanese Empire, of a mosaic of different forms of governance. Hitler throughout insisted that the final decisions on the geopolitical shape of the New Order were reserved for the period after the war was won, but there already existed in wartime a fundamental distinction between the occupied area of Western, Northern and South-eastern Europe and the German perception of the whole Eastern area. The East was destined to become the heart of the new territorial empire, with the destruction of existing states and the adoption of a colonial pattern of exploitation, a process already under way in the Czech lands and Poland before victory in the West. In the rest of Europe, functioning states were retained under German supervision, using the established institutional and administrative systems.

The first priority was to complete the building of what was called 'Greater Germany'. In addition to the lands annexed to Germany from Czechoslovakia and Poland, Alsace-Lorraine and Luxembourg were declared de facto German territory under a chief of civil administration, and the small territories lost to Denmark and Belgium in the post-1919 settlement were taken back. Outside Greater Germany, occupied territory deemed to be on the military front line – northern and western France and Belgium – came under military government, while a nominally independent administration continued to function alongside the military, one in the French spa city of Vichy, the other in Brussels. The Netherlands was run by a Reich commissioner, Arthur Seyss-Inquart, Norway by a Reich commissar, Josef Terboven, despite the presence of a collaborating 'government' under the Norwegian National Socialist Vidkun Quisling.[262] The situation in Denmark was unique to the occupied area. Because Danes had not resisted the occupation, the Germans operated *occupatio mixta*, a concept in international law used to define the situation when a neutral power is occupied by a belligerent power but is not subsequently at war with the occupier. The Danes were allowed to keep their political system intact and, until 1943, maintained jurisdiction. Danish international lawyers defined the status as 'peaceful occupation' in which Denmark supposedly

retained its sovereignty, while allowing the Germans to take over its execution. Only following the appointment in November 1942 of a senior
German representative, the SS leader Werner Best, did the relationship
deteriorate, and on 29 August 1943 the government and the king, Christian X, refused to continue to run the state. The Germans declared martial
law and ruled Denmark until 1945 through a council of permanent ministerial secretaries. Although legally dubious, the Allies announced in June
1944 that Denmark, thanks to the presence of resistance, could be counted
as one of the United Nations at war with Germany.[263]

The situation in South-eastern Europe, where Hitler had not expected
to intervene militarily, was far more complex. The area was regarded by
Italian leaders as part of the Italian 'sphere' agreed in the Three Power
Pact, which explained the decision to attack Greece, but the failure of Italian forces meant that Germany, assisted by its allies Bulgaria and Hungary,
defeated and occupied both Greece and Yugoslavia. By the time Greece
capitulated, Italy's African empire was already in tatters. Eritrea, Somalia
and Ethiopia were lost to British Empire forces and Libya had become a
battleground, where Italy's colonial presence was challenged not only by
Allied forces but by Libyan rebels, who were keen to use the war as the
opportunity to overthrow Italian rule. The British used 40,000 Libyan
auxiliaries for non-combat roles, and promised the exiled King Idris, resident in Cairo, home rule for Libya after Italian defeat. The Italian army,
military police and local settlers began a savage pacification campaign
against Arab and Berber villages, echoing the vicious counter-insurgency
conducted in the early 1930s. Each time the British Empire forces were
driven back towards Egypt, the violence escalated. Suspects were hanged
in public in grotesque ways, some with a meat hook jammed in the jaw, left
to bleed to death like animals in a slaughterhouse. The final spasm of colonial violence provided a squalid coda to Italy's African imperialism.[264]

The loss of Africa made the success of Italy's European empire all the
more important, but the reliance on German arms forced Italy to practise
what Davide Rodogno has called 'dependent imperialism', an oxymoron
that exposed Italy's subordinate position in the new Europe. In the event
of Axis victory, complained one of the Italian armistice commissioners in
July 1941, 'Europe will remain under German hegemony for some centuries.'[265] Italy had to share the spoils of South-east Europe with Germany
and Bulgaria, and as a consequence controlled a ragged set of territories
rather than a coherent sphere. From Yugoslavia Italy occupied southern
Slovenia, south-west Croatia, a short stretch of the Dalmatian coastline,
Montenegro, part of Kosovo, and western Macedonia. The rest of Croatia
and Slovenia was a German sphere, while a rump Serbian state was

established with a puppet government subservient to the German military. In Greece, Italy took the Ionian islands, most of the string of Aegean islands, and much of mainland Greece except eastern Macedonia and Thrace, which were annexed by Bulgaria, and Hellenic Macedonia taken over by Germany. Until 1943, an uneasy condominium existed between the Italian and German military administrations.

The territories were linked to Italy in a variety of different ways. Slovenia was annexed as the Italian province of Ljubljana; Montenegro was assigned as a protectorate, and was ruled by a high commissioner and a military governorate; the Dalmatian coast was annexed in June 1941 under an Italian governor; Greek territory was ruled as a virtual annexation, but German refusal to admit a final territorial settlement in the armistice signed with Greece meant that the annexation was only de facto, while German forces claimed control of important enclaves including the major port of Piraeus. The situation in Croatia remained ill-defined throughout the Italian occupation. Croatian nationalists hoped to create an independent Croat state, despite the presence of two occupying armies. Mussolini explored the idea of reconstructing the historic monarchy of Croatia, and a potential Italian candidate was found, to be named Tomislav II (after the Croatian tenth-century King Tomislav), but he refused what must have seemed a poisoned chalice.[266] Germany wanted a form of protectorate under the leader of the Croatian Peasant Party, Vladko Maček, but Mussolini pressed for a government under the Croatian Revolutionary Movement (*Ustaša*) leader, Ante Pavelić, a fellow fascist sheltered in Italy before the war. Although the Italian leadership explored the idea of annexing some or all of Croatia, the German presence was obtrusive. A German plenipotentiary-general, General Edmund Glaise von Horstenau, was based in Zagreb and German advisers embedded in the Croatian regime. In September 1943, following the Italian surrender, Germany took over responsibility for the whole of Croatia as a satellite state run by a puppet regime.[267]

Although none of the territories was formally a colony, Italy borrowed from colonial practice in Africa to organize control of the European empire. Decisions concerning the area were taken in Rome or by the appointed delegates (military governors, high commissioners, lieutenant governors, etc.) in each region. At local level collaborating officials (*podestà*) were appointed. There was no intention of allowing a degree of autonomy, or the development of popular nationalism. Where possible, local police or militia forces were used to establish order under Italian supervision. Those who directly threatened Italian civil or military rule became the victims of a widespread repression operated by the military police, often manifested in extreme violence like the repression in Libya and Ethiopia. Italian officials and forces were spread very thinly across the European empire and were generally poorly resourced (in Crete an estimated 40 per cent of soldiers had no boots and were forced to wear locally made clogs). Fear and frustration played a part for men supposed to represent an imperial race. Increasingly dilapidated and prone to chronic diseases, like the garrisons of the Japanese army, Italian forces took out their frustration on those who resisted. Concentration camps sprang up across the territories, where prisoners suffered in crude conditions from neglect, hunger and an absence of medical assistance. As in Ethiopia, an effort was made to decapitate the local elite of teachers, academics, doctors, lawyers and students who might challenge Italian rule. Other prisoners were captured resisters, or merely suspects; some the victims of ethnic cleansing in Slovenia and Dalmatia. The number of camps and of those incarcerated are not known with any certainty, but a report produced after the war by Yugoslavs investigating war crimes posited a precise figure of 149,488 civilian internees. Later research has suggested a figure of 109,000, but in either case the numbers victimized through the Italian imperial experience was high.[268] As the Italian war effort faced terminal crisis in 1943, Italian Foreign Ministry officials suddenly reproduced what they called the *Carta d'Europa* (European Map) for a summit meeting between Mussolini and Hitler in April 1943, which now suggested a post-war order that would allow the free development of nationality in the new Europe. Rather like the Japanese decision to foster liberation as the empire faced defeat, the Italian initiative came at the end of the Italian imperial experiment and was perhaps intended for Allied consumption.[269] The German negotiators insisted that no commitments should be made, and the Italian Empire in Europe remained provisional until it disappeared entirely later in the year with Italy's surrender.

The key factor for both Germany and Italy in the occupation of continental Europe was the acquisition of and access to material resources and foodstuffs that could support the occupation and boost the domestic war economy. In this the Italians were at a permanent disadvantage in the face of German competition. As one German general put it in March 1941, 'the Italians must gradually accustom themselves not to be treated as an equal in that relationship.'[270] The fate of Balkan resources clearly illustrated that state of inequality. Even though the region was nominally in the Italian sphere, Germany had penetrated the Balkan economy extensively before 1940, and dominated, in particular, access to Romanian oil, which was of critical importance for both states. Unlike Japan's seizure of the oil of the Dutch Indies, the Germans could not take over the oilfields of their Romanian ally, which used oil for its own industrial development and as a key export overseas. But from summer 1940 Germany was the main customer for Romanian oil, restricting Italian access. An entry into Romanian production was secured by seizing the oil assets of enemy states, particularly the large Dutch Shell 'Astra' company, and in March 1941 a single German holding company, Kontinental-Öl, was established to oversee German oil acquisitions.[271] In the second half of 1941 Germany took more than half of all Romanian production, but it was never enough. By 1943 Romanian exports reached their lowest level of the war. Germany's share dropped to 45 per cent, only 2.4 million tons from the 11.3 million tons of oil available to Germany, much of it now domestic synthetic production.[272]

Other resources in the Balkans fell under German control at Italy's expense because German authorities, particularly Göring's Four-Year Plan organization, were better prepared and more ruthless in securing German interests. In Croatia, German representatives signed agreements in May 1941, without informing the Italians, giving Germany preferences for the production of metal ores and for any new ore fields developed during the war. In April 1941, German negotiators secured privileged access to bauxite reserves in Herzegovina, even though it was in the Italian occupation zone, and insisted that the lead and zinc mines in Kosovo be linked to German-controlled Serbia rather than Italian Albania. Only in June 1941 did Italy establish an Italian–Croatian Economic Commission, but by then it was too late. Croat leaders were committed to supporting German penetration and rejected a larger Italian presence.[273] In Greece the same pattern emerged. Germany chose to occupy Macedonia, where the key minerals were to be found, and took some three-quarters of goods exported. In 1942, Germany absorbed 47 per cent of all Greek production, Italy only 6 per cent, despite occupying by far the larger portion of Greek territory. Poor transportation, shortages of fuel, and uncoordinated planning hampered Italian efforts to extract even a minimum from their own 'great area'.[274]

German interests prevailed completely in the rest of the western half of the *Grossraum*. In summer 1940 Göring, as plenipotertiary for the Four-Year Plan, announced that the economy of the new order had to be supervised and co-ordinated by the German state, because the priority was short-term support for the war effort rather than the construction of an integrated European economy. Private German firms were allowed to participate, but only on the basis of trusteeship rather than ownership. In Alsace-Lorraine the iron-ore mines were placed under a trustee appointed by the Reichswerke holding company, Karl Raabe, and they remained in German state hands until near the end of the war. The industrial cherries in Lorraine were also taken over by the Reichswerke, providing a steel-making capacity of 1.4 million tons. The remaining firms were distributed chiefly to smaller German iron and steel companies, whose ambitions could more easily be restricted.[275] In Belgium, there was less direct German participation in occupied industry, but the Belgian coal, iron and steel, and engineering industries were expected to support the German war effort. Little coal was exported, since Germany did not need more coal, but steel production was required for military needs in the Reich, and following a slowdown in output in the winter of 1941–2, the German steel magnate Hermann Röchling, head of the state-created Reich Iron Union, oversaw a rationalization of Belgian output that increased the proportion of steel for German use from 56 per cent in 1941–2 to 72 per cent by the early months of 1944.[276] Dutch and Norwegian resources were similarly aligned with the needs of the occupier for food, raw materials, engineering and repair facilities. Businessmen across the *Grossraum* collaborated from a mix of motives, but chiefly to keep their businesses intact and to prevent the forced transfer of their workers to Germany. Unlike the strategy of seizure and expropriation practised in occupied Central and Eastern Europe, private businesses generally survived as long as they were not Jewish-owned. Jewish businesses were subjected to the central German policy of 'Aryanization' through a variety of methods, from outright confiscation to compulsory purchase, although local regimes also initiated their own version of Jewish dispossession to forestall German efforts to acquire all Jewish assets.

The western *Grossraum*, though a sphere of German domination, like the Japanese sphere, was not imperial living-space. That was to be found in the East, first in the areas occupied in 1939–40 but, above all, in the fantastic vistas opened up by the invasion of the Soviet Union of a vast area for colonial settlement, ethnic cleansing and ruthless exploitation. The East was empire in its more literal and brutal sense, closer in reality to the Japanese experience than the domination of states further to the west. As in the Italian case, the formal term 'colony' was not generally approved, but the language used for the new Eurasian territories reflected, as in Poland, a colonial spatial imagination. Once the invasion was underway, Hitler himself borrowed liberally from the colonial model in describing the future of the eastern area. In his recorded conversations (the so-called 'Table Talk') in the weeks following the 'Barbarossa' invasion he returned regularly to the theme that Russia would provide the German equivalent of British India, where a vast population was managed by only 250,000 imperial officials and soldiers. 'What India was for England,' he claimed in August 1941, 'the spaces in the East will be for us.' For the task of running the new empire, Germany would produce 'a new type of man, natural rulers ... viceroys'. The German colonist 'ought to be housed in outstandingly beautiful settlements'. On 17 September, when complete victory still seemed in sight, he reflected that the 'Germans must acquire the feeling for the great, open spaces ... The German people will raise itself to the level of their empire.' A month later, when 'Barbarossa' was already stalemated, he reflected that the East 'seems to us like a desert ... There's only one duty: to Germanise this country by the immigration of Germans, and to look upon the natives as Redskins.'[277] The reference to the near genocide of the native Americans was an analogy that sat uneasily with the image of British rule in India, but both were historical comparisons exploited by Hitler to confirm the colonial paradigm. The object in the East, one way or another, as he told his close ally Martin Bormann on 16 July, was to 'dominate it, administer it, and exploit it'.[278]

The regular invocation of 'space' in describing the East, common to a whole generation of German academic experts who studied the region, was deliberate. It suggested that this was space that could be colonized, rather than space which was already occupied by a large urban and rural population, organized in a major state, with established social and administrative structures. Alfred Rosenberg, appointed minister for the Occupied Eastern Territories on 20 July 1941, reflected earlier in his diary his view of the Russian area: 'The East is fundamentally different from the West, with its cities, industries, discipline ... people will have to understand that the desolation is worse than can be imagined.'[279] As German forces, officials and policemen began to occupy the Soviet area, their impressions confirmed a predisposition to see this as colonial space. One army intelligence officer recorded the stark impression of the Russians he dealt with: 'The people here spit and blow their noses right on the floor. Human body odours are not regulated here, tooth cleaning is rare ... Sessions even with learned and high-placed bodies can become an ordeal for a Western European.'[280] For the ordinary soldiers, enduring the experience of Russia and the Russians was a persistent reminder of how different the war in the East was. When the soldiers of the Sixth Army under General von Reichenau complained of the climate and the lack of decent food, he told his officers that 'the soldier must put up with privations as in colonial warfare'.[281] The irregular fighting from Soviet soldiers, with ambushes, night attacks, the murder and mutilation of prisoners, seemed redolent of warfare against 'barbaric' indigenous resistance. 'The struggle we are waging against the partisans,' Hitler claimed, 'resembles very much the struggle in North America against the Red Indians.'[282] Germans posted to the East found the transition as uncongenial as a posting to a remote and inhospitable colony. Female guards at the Majdanek concentration camp

in Poland complained of the bitter cold in winter, excessive heat in a
mosquito-ridden summer, the grim barracks and unhygienic conditions,
prisoners whose language they could not remotely understand, and the
constant fear of attack. Compensation came, as it did in the colonies, with
the rigid practice of apartheid between Germans and Slavs, leaving the
best of everything to the colonizer and sustaining a secure sense of civilized superiority.[283]

As in conquered Poland, the population of the Soviet Union was treated
by the German occupiers as a colonial people, capable only of being subjects, not citizens. For many Soviet citizens this treatment proved a
disappointment. In the first weeks of occupation, many people assumed
that, with the end of the Stalinist regime, life would get better. 'You have
freed us from destitution and Communism,' ran one letter sent in July
1941; one family wanted to 'wish Mr. Adolf Hitler good luck in your
future work'. But within months the seizure of food and widespread killings suggested that Stalinism might be the lesser of two evils.[284] The
occupiers and occupied had a different legal regime. The Soviet population had to observe routine courtesies to any German they met, which
included removing their hat or cap, and failure to do so could lead to a
beating or worse. 'Germans only' signs kept occupier and occupied apart.
The general German view of the subject people was of simple-minded,
lazy, slovenly individuals, incapable of understanding very much, 'a child-
like incapacity to express themselves', and obedient only with the
whip – an instrument wielded by many of the German administrators
despite Rosenberg's efforts to get flogging banned.[285] To induce greater
co-operation, Hitler famously remarked, 'We'll supply the Ukrainians
with scarves, glass beads and everything that colonial peoples like.'[286]
Some effort was made to secure goodwill by gestures for the colonized
people, including organized carnival days, particularly 1 May or 22 June
(celebrated, ironically, as 'liberation day'). In Orel, on May Day 1943, the
population was assembled so that men could be presented with two packets of Russian tobacco each, and women with a total of 4,625 pieces of
jewellery; for selected workers there were extra bags of salt.[287] In general,
however, the pacification of the local population was harsh and extreme,
even in areas where there existed some popular desire to collaborate. The
German authorities established local police and auxiliary units, the
Schutzmannschaften, who were issued with clubs and whips, and occasionally firearms, and were used as the first line of discipline against any
infractions by the population. Like the Japanese in East Asia, the Germans
relied heavily on informers and agents, who carried on the inherited Soviet
practice of denunciation. The victims were in many cases partisan families

or Jews, whose fate is dealt with in later chapters, but there was regular and widespread killing of anyone, in Hitler's term, 'who even looks askance at us'. In the Poltava district of Ukraine, local paramilitary police units throughout 1942 shot on average anywhere between two and seven people every single day.[288] The routine executions characterized what was an extreme expression of colonial rule, if recognizable enough.

Little hard thought had been given to the way the new space was to be administered once the territory was occupied. Rosenberg assumed from his discussions with Hitler and other leaders before 'Barbarossa' that it was intended to set up a mix of small independent states, together with annexations and protectorates across the whole zone, from the Baltic to Baku. But by the time he was formally appointed minister for the Occupied Eastern Territories, Hitler had begun to change his mind about any firm commitments on the post-war organization of the new empire. He told Rosenberg that there were to be 'no final political decisions in advance'. When local nationalists declared a government in Lithuania, it was swiftly suppressed. Ukrainian supporters of Stepan Bandera's Organization of Ukrainian Nationalists announced a new Ukrainian regime in Lvov on 30 June 1941 with Bandera as *providayk* (Leader), to exercise 'sovereign Ukrainian authority', but on 5 July Bandera was detained and placed under house arrest in Berlin. The OUN had expected a 'Croatian' solution in Ukraine, but they were told that Ukrainians were not Germany's 'allies'.[289]

Rosenberg was not opposed to establishing some kind of Ukrainian entity on German terms, but his new ministry, like the Greater East Asia Ministry, was a largely toothless organization. 'I have not received *total* authority,' complained the new minister in his diary once it became clear that all responsibility for organizing the economy of the occupied regions rested with Göring and his Economics Staff East, while Himmler, as head of the SS and the German police, insisted that security, ethnic resettlement and the solution to the 'Jewish question' in the conquered area was the responsibility of his organizations, of which there were at least five distinct strands.[290] Because the East was still a fighting zone, the areas immediately behind the front line remained under military administration, run by a structure of field commanders, district commanders and smaller garrison commands. Like the Japanese military governments, the German structure was responsible for a wide range of tasks, including pacification and surveillance of the population, securing supplies for the war effort, policing the local area, mobilizing local labour, as well as a Jewish department, responsible for registering and marking Jews and disposing of Jewish property.[291] They relied on collaborators from among the local population, who were appointed as mayors and local rural officials, replicating the civilian administration. Even in areas that were civilian-run, the armed forces maintained an organizational presence and a sense of priority. So incoherent was the resulting structure for controlling the occupied area that Rosenberg's ministry won the nickname 'Cha-ostministerium', Ministry of Chaos.

As the front moved forward, civilian occupation areas were established: Reich Commissariats, each run by a commissar appointed by Hitler. There were two at first, Reich Commissariat Ostland, which incorporated the Baltic States and most of Belorussia under Party leader Hinrich Lohse, and Reich Commissariat Ukraine, which included part of Belorussia and much of Ukraine in 1941, and then more of Ukraine in 1942, controlled by the gauleiter of East Prussia, Erich Koch. Within these areas, Hitler and Himmler wanted the area of Ostland as far as Bialystok to be annexed to Germany, Galicia to be joined to the Polish General Government, the Crimea to be a German colony with the archaic name Gottengau, and an area of German settlement to be known as 'Ingermanland' stretching past Leningrad. Two more Reich Commissariats were planned, one around the Moscow area and one for Caucasia, once German forces had captured the southern region. Hitler conceded that the price for Romanian participation would be a strip of territory in south-west Ukraine, given the name Transnistria, which would be part of a 'Greater Romania'. Here Antonescu established thirteen military governors (*pretorii*) to administer a structure of counties, using local Ukrainian police and officials to keep order.[292]

The administration of the German commissariats was laid down in the *Braune Mappe* (Brown Folder) drawn up by Rosenberg's ministry. There were some 24 regional General Commissariats (of which the most important was Belorussia, with a capital at Minsk), and below them district and town commissars, 80 for urban areas, 900 for the countryside.[293] The German presence was spread very thinly. The general commissars had around a hundred staff, the town and rural commissariats little more than two or three, aided by the locally appointed police and militia. In the district of Glubokoye in Belorussia, only 79 German officials oversaw a population of 400,000. Throughout the entire area of occupation, with an estimated population of 55 million, there were only 30,000 German officials to cover everything from agronomy to mining.[294] Many rural inhabitants saw Germans rarely, unless on one of the numerous punitive raids searching for partisans and their accomplices. Here in the countryside the Soviet *raion* (district) was kept in place, run by a local mayor or village headman. Under the terms of a military decree issued in July 1941, the subject population was denied any right to exercise authority above

the level of the *raion*. Power rested entirely with the German ruling hierarchy, aided by an extensive range of collaborators, willing, resigned or
coerced. Alongside the civil organization, Himmler established a network
of higher SS and police leaders, usually attached loosely to a General
Commissariat, and SS and police leaders at district level. Although nominally under the authority of the commissars, Himmler allowed his men to
ignore what the civilians wanted – 'a bunch of overpaid bureaucrats' in
his view – and take orders directly from him.[295] Rosenberg deeply resented
Himmler's security apparatus, yet it was through this that the daily routine of 'colonial' policing was brutally exercised.

For almost all of the occupied population, the critical factor was not
how they were administered but how the local economy could supply
them with food and work now that the Soviet system had disappeared.
'Economic life,' noted one German official in summer 1941, 'has completely died out in the old Russia.' The systematic destruction by the Red
Army of anything useful for the invader left a scene in Ukraine, another
German observer claimed, of 'complete devastation and emptiness'.[296]
Not everything was destroyed in areas where the German armed forces
arrived swiftly enough, but thousands of factories and their workforce
had already been hastily transferred to the Russian interior, denuding the
conquered area of useful industrial capacity. German economic strategy,
set out in the so-called '*Grüne Mappe*' (Green Folder), closely matched
that of Japan: the armed forces were to live off the land; absolute priority
was given to the supply of materials and equipment for the war economy
and the armed forces; the local population was to be supplied only to the
extent that it met German interests to do so, the rest would suffer the fate
designed in the 'Hunger Plan'. On 28 June 1941, Hitler confirmed that
Göring would enjoy 'complete powers of decision' over all aspects of the
occupied economy, exercised through the Economic Staff East set up
before the invasion.[297] Material stocks and machinery were seized by
Booty Brigades and sent back to Germany. There were substantial stocks
of metals, raw materials, leather and furs, but transporting the loot proved
difficult and much was lost or damaged in transit. Out of 18 million tons
of raw materials seized (mostly iron and coal) only 5.5 million tons made
its way to the Reich.[298] Not until September, when German forces were
poised to occupy the industrial south of Ukraine, did Göring approve the
establishment of state monopoly companies to take over what remained
of Soviet industry and exploit it for the war effort. A textile monopoly, the
Ostfasergesellschaft, co-ordinated production for the armed forces; heavy
industry and mining was taken over entirely by a Reichswerke subsidiary,
the Berg und Hüttenwerkgesellschaft Ost (BHO); oil, which Göring

regarded as 'the chief economic aim of the invasion', would be run by the Continental Oil monopoly, once the Caucasus had been captured. The purpose, explained Paul Pleiger, Göring's deputy for heavy industry, was not for the moment 'economic, colonial exploitation' but the short-term requirements for winning the war.[299]

Restoring production was, as the Japanese found in South East Asia, far more difficult than pre-war planning had suggested. The only major success was the restoration of manganese ore production at Nikopol, which was an absolute priority for producing high-quality steel. After a slow start, Göring's state secretary at the Air Ministry, Erhard Milch, was given emergency responsibility for restarting output. By June 1942 the mines were again producing the pre-war total of 50,000 tons a month, surpassing Soviet production by September; before they were recaptured, 1.8 million tons were shipped west. Elsewhere the damage was difficult to undo in wartime conditions. In the main industrial region in the Donets Basin, only 2,550 industrial motors remained out of the 26,400 before the invasion; mines had been detonated, plant that could not be evacuated was sabotaged, and transport everywhere was slow and unreliable. The dam feeding the largest hydro-electric plant in the Soviet Union at Zaporizhzhia had been blown up, leaving the whole industrial zone short of power. Forced labourers rebuilt it by 1943, shortly before the Germans, when they retreated, blew it up again. The rich Donbas coal and ore mines could not be restored. German engineers and Soviet miners managed to extract 4 million tons of coal between 1941 and 1943, just 5 per cent of pre-war output; the 380,000 tons of iron ore and 750,000 tons of lignite ('brown coal') in two years was a drop in the ocean of German supply.[300] Efforts to revive iron and steel production proved limited, even when private Ruhr companies were invited to participate as 'godparents' – but not owners – of the damaged plants, an invitation accepted reluctantly by companies already facing pressure on production at home. Oil was the greatest disappointment. When the German army finally arrived in the Caucasus oil-producing city of Maikop in autumn 1942, the fifty drilling machines needed to start production again were still stuck in the Reich awaiting transport. Oil engineers and equipment had to be sent east from the small German natural oilfields, starving the home industry of expertise, but when the engineers arrived in Maikop they discovered the comprehensive Soviet destruction of the wells. From December 1942 until 17 January 1943, when the area was abandoned, the engineers extracted little more than 1,500 tons from a field that had provided 3.4 million tons in 1940.[301] For all the talk of relying on Soviet oil to fuel the war effort, restoring damaged facilities and finding a way to pipe the oil, or to transport oil products in Germany's small tanker fleet, would have required years more effort even if the Caucasus had been conquered. Nothing more clearly illustrated the element of unreality at the heart of Hitler's strategy.

As the war in the East turned into a battle of attrition, the armed forces wanted to make more of local production of armament and equipment to ease the pressure on the transport system, but only in 1942 was an effort made to revive ammunition production through what was called the 'Ivan Programme', a plan to produce over 1 million shells a month. After cannibalizing machinery and materials from damaged plant, and bringing in further resources from Germany, production finally began in May 1943 with only 880 of the 9,300 workers required. A few months later the programme was wound up as the Red Army approached. Overall employment at the revived factories in the region numbered only 86,000 by spring 1943; Soviet workers who escaped deployment as forced labour in Germany proved difficult to discipline and frustratingly itinerant.[302] The net result of the war for material resources was entirely negative. The great cost of the war effort in the East cancelled out the limited supplies of raw materials and finished goods supplied or seized. A survey carried out by the Research Office for War Economy in March 1944 calculated that the Occupied Eastern Territories had supplied only 4.5 billion marks' worth of goods to the German war effort from a total for the whole *Grossraum* of 77.7 billion, evidence of just how impoverished and damaged the former Soviet economy had become. The value of the booty seized in the whole of the occupied East was calculated at a mere 59 million marks; booty from the rest of Europe was worth 237 million. Even allowing for the very real difficulty of calculating the value of wartime supplies, the statistics show that the fantasy of Eastern riches was just that – a fantasy.[303]

Much the same story unfolded with the supply of food from an area eventually destined, in Hitler's view, to be the granary of Europe. Food produced in the occupied areas was to be consumed first by the armed forces, then any surplus was to be sent back to boost German domestic rations. Food for the Soviet population was not a priority under Backe's 'Hunger Plan', particularly in areas where little was expected in terms of economic resources. 'Large territories to be neglected (starvation),' noted General Thomas, head of the Armed Forces' War Economy Office, in July 1941. The *Grüne Mappe* spelt out that wooded and urban areas were not to be fed. Even in the surplus-producing area of Ukraine, the difficulty of finding food for the armed forces only a month into the campaign led to a directive to 'exert even stronger pressure on the population', seizing anything that could be consumed without regard for the survival of those who produced it. Kiev was supposed to starve and when German forces occupied it in September, an effort was made to ban all attempts by the peasant hinterland to bring goods into the city so that the pre-war plan to export food to Germany could be maintained.[304] The strategy broke down not only because an estimated 50 per cent of army food (including half the fodder for the hundreds of thousands of horses) had to be sent to the East, rather than food sent back, but also because a deliberate hunger policy would deny the armed forces the use of local labour, prejudice the following year's food supply and prompt hunger riots in rear areas.

Göring finally directed that whoever worked for the German occupiers 'should not starve *absolutely*', but families and those who did not work got little.[305] Rations were set at levels scarcely able to sustain active labour or community life: 1,200 calories a day for 'useful work', 850 calories for work of no direct benefit to the occupier, 420 calories for children under 14 and for Jews of all ages. Mass famine was avoided, but only because many urban families fled to the countryside where food was assumed to be more plentiful. But here, too, regular requisitioning of the harvest, high demands for taxation in kind, and enforced rationing left many villagers short of food. They compensated by growing vegetables on allotments, and by digging secret cellars where food could be hidden from the regular searches, but the diet was basic at best.[306] So comprehensive was German requisitioning that a 'dead zone' with no plant or animal products characterized the area 150 kilometres from the front-line units. In the Russian cities of Kursk and Kharkov right at the front line, rations were set at 100 grammes of bread a day.[307] Urban consumers survived where they could because of a large black market operated mainly through barter deals. Price inflation was impossible to regulate with the German presence so thinly spread. In one Belorussian field command, the official cost in summer 1942 of a kilogram of bread was 1.20 roubles, but the unofficial price was 150 roubles; a litre of sunflower oil traded officially at 14.5 roubles, but on the black market at 280 roubles.[308] Under these conditions, mass hunger was a daily reality, and resentment at German food policy a key element in alienating a population that had hoped for better. Nor did the 'granary of Europe' live up to German expectations. More food was obtained from the Soviet Union during the years of peace from 1939 to 1941 under the German–Soviet Pact than the wartime years. Most of the food extracted was consumed in the occupied area, not in Germany. Some 7 million tons of grain were taken each year by the German armed forces and civilian occupiers in the East, leaving only 2 million tons sent to Germany in 1941–2, 2.9 million tons in 1942–3 and 1.7 million tons in 1943–4. This represented 10 per cent of German grain consumption in the first and last years, and a more substantial 19 per cent in 1942–3, following insistence from Hitler and Göring that every last gramme of food should be squeezed out of the Soviet area whatever the cost to the local population.[309]

One of the main reasons why stable economic conditions were difficult to recreate in the East lay in the gigantic wartime programme of biopolitical restructuring undertaken even while the war was going on. Hitler had spelt out in a major speech on 6 October 1939, after the defeat of Poland, that he wanted a 'new ethnographic order' in the new German Empire. The war, Hitler told Himmler ten days later, was 'a racial war, with no legal limitations'.[310] Himmler and the bevy of academic experts assembled by the SS in the Reich Security Main Office (RSHA), the Office of the Reich Commissar for the Strengthening of Germandom (RKFDV) and the SS Race and Resettlement Main Office (RuSHA) embarked on a complex undertaking to Germanize selected regions of the occupied territories, to eliminate any surplus population from the rest of the colonized area, and to eradicate, in one way or another, the large Jewish population present across the whole region. The first short-term plans, *Nahpläne I–III*, had mixed results. By the end of 1940, only 249,000 Poles and Jews had been deported from the annexed Polish territories, instead of the 600,000 called for in the 'Planning Principles for the Occupied Eastern Territories' presented to Himmler by the RKFDV deputy, Konrad Meyer-Heitling, in January 1940, or the 800,000 called for in *Nahplan II* in April 1940. Many Poles evaded deportation, or returned covertly, while rail transport proved a persistent bottleneck. Large numbers of Polish workers were deported west instead of east, to overcome Germany's chronic labour shortages, but this was the opposite of ethnic cleansing. To make sure that Poles sent to Germany would not contaminate the German racial body, they were investigated by staff from the Race and Resettlement Main Office to screen out those deemed racially undesirable. Finally, Hans Frank, governor of the Polish General Government, refused to allow his fiefdom to become a dumping ground for Poles and Jews resettled from the annexed Polish territories. Jews were instead herded into ghettoes or forced to labour on the *Ostwall* fortifications along the frontier with the Soviet Union, soon to be redundant with the invasion. *Nahplan III*, drawn up in December 1940, called for the expulsion of 771,000 Poles and Jews not living in ghettoes, but this new wave of ethnic cleansing halted in March 1941 because of priority for military transport. For Himmler and the frustrated apparatus for racial resettlement, the war against the Soviet Union opened at last the possibility of breaking the logjam by expelling all those racially unacceptable into the distant wastes of Russia, where hunger and cold would finish millions of them off.

'Barbarossa' was nevertheless a threat as well as a promise of racial utopia. The occupied area contained millions of Slavs and Jews who might swamp the small German presence and defeat the object of seizing living space for the German race. One solution was elimination of a large part of the existing population, an outcome already anticipated in Backe's 'Hunger Plan' and now confirmed in General Plan East in July 1941. A second solution lay in positive efforts at Germanizing key areas in the East by bringing in German settlers and deporting non-Germans. These were long-term plans, but they were set in motion over the first years of occupation. The General Government, Estonia, Latvia, Galicia and the Crimea were to be thoroughly Germanized by settling Germans from the West as well as Germans already living in the East and elements of the Eastern population with evidence of German traits or German blood who were capable, in the bizarre language of racial planning, of *Wiedereindeutschung*, becoming German again. An estimated 4 million were screened by local SS and Resettlement staffs in Poland, Alsace-Lorraine and the occupied Soviet area, and placed in one of three main categories: Category O, suitable for settlement in the East; Category A, return to camps in the Reich to be re-educated into being German; Category S, racially unsuitable, to be returned to place of origin, or, in a few cases, sent to a labour camp.[311] Traces of a surviving German biological and cultural presence in the Soviet area were searched for in order to show that German colonists from the past had not been entirely swallowed up by their Slav environment. Rosenberg's ministry sent the ethnographer Karl Stumpp as head of 'Commando Stumpp' to make a census of Ukrainian villages that seemed residually 'German', though the SS race officials did not regard many of Stumpp's Germans as racially acceptable, while many of the villagers themselves resisted re-classification as potential members of the *Volk*.[312]

At the same time work began on the physical reconstruction of the region, to secure the long-term colonization of a space that might stretch as far as the Urals or beyond. The object was to create arteries of German blood running through the large Slav body by building 'settlement and security points' (*Siedlungs- und Stützpunkte*) every 100 kilometres or so with an SS garrison and a small settler population. These 'security points' would safeguard the local area of German settlement, and also make it possible to pacify and control the Slav hinterland. There would also be towns of no more than 20,000 inhabitants, surrounded by a necklace of villages peopled by sturdy German farmers, thus avoiding the social dangers of the large city while rooting the colonizers firmly in the soil of the new land. These colonies, Himmler remarked in a speech late in 1942, 'are like strings of pearls that we will extend to the Don and the Volga, hopefully to the Urals'.[313] Major cities were to be eradicated or German-ized on Hitler's insistence. Moscow and Leningrad were 'to be levelled', while Warsaw was to be reduced to a city of 40,000 Germans in order to remove a key element of Polish national identity.[314]

Responsibility for the building programme was given to the SS eco-nomic expert Hans Kammler, under the overall leadership of another of Himmler's administrative strands, the Economic and Administrative Main Office (WVHA). Kammler drew up a 'Provisional Peacetime Building Programme' which was inaugurated in February 1942, even though peace was still a remote prospect. The first series of *Stützpunkte* was begun even sooner, in July 1941, when Himmler gave Odilo Globocnik, head of SS and police security in the Lublin area, responsibility for the garrisons. Shortages of labour, particularly Jewish labour following mass killings, slowed up the programme and by the autumn of 1942 construction was all but abandoned.[315] Military tasks took priority, including the major highways needed across Poland and Ukraine to help ease the army's logistical problems. The Organisation Todt, responsible for military con-struction, worked on no fewer than 24,993 kilometres of roads and hundreds of damaged bridges. The 2,175-kilometre *Durchgangsstrasse IV* (Highway IV) was planned to reach the Crimea and the Caucasus and work began on the road in Galicia in 1941 in collaboration with the local SS leader Friedrich Katzmann. He spared Jews living on the corridor through which the road would run so that they could be worked to death building it. 'It is no concern,' Katzmann claimed, 'if on each kilometre one thousand or ten thousand Jews die.' The Jewish workers were given little food, were subject to arbitrary beatings and, if they slacked or collapsed, were shot out of hand, not by the SS but by the local construction guards working for the Organisation Todt. An estimated 25,000 died or were killed by the time the labour camps closed in 1943.[316]

The challenge was to find the settlers who would populate the new lands. Thousands of Germans from the Baltic States, Romania and the Soviet zone of occupation in Poland were eventually settled in the annexed and occupied territories, a total of 544,296 by the end of 1942 according to the official report of the RKFDV.[317] But for the colonies in the con-quered Soviet area, the prospect of finding Germans both willing to go and racially acceptable was more challenging. Erhard Wetzel, responsible in Rosenberg's ministry for resettlement, observed that the German popu-lation in the West 'refuses to be settled in the East . . . simply because it views the Eastern territories as too monotonous or depressing, or too cold and primitive.'[318] A model German settlement was established on Himmler's orders in and around the city of Zamość in the eastern General

Government, where more than 50,000 Poles from 300 villages were deported from their farms and homes in November 1942 to make room for Germans. But by the time the project was halted a few months later, there were only 10,000 Germans there instead of the 60,000 planned, most from Bessarabia and Romania, some resettled for a second time.[319] Both the SA and the SS tried to persuade members to volunteer for settlement in the East, but the SA by January 1943 had only 1,304 applications (instead of the 50,000 at first envisaged), of which a mere 422 had actually gone to the East, while the SS by June 1942 had just 4,500 applications despite Himmler's vaulting ambition to fill the colonies with his own men.[320] To help fill up the space, former settlers from German East Africa were found Polish farms so that in the reconstruction of the East, according to a newspaper report in autumn 1943, they 'could still perform truly pioneer work in every area'.[321] As early as June 1941, an appeal was made to the Dutch, as fellow 'Germanic people', to 'look to the East!', but instead of the thousands hoped for, only a few hundred volunteers out of the 6,000 who left to work for the Germans went to settle on the land. They were soon disillusioned by their patronizing treatment at the hands of the German authorities and the unfamiliar environment. Dutch hopes that they would be given permanent territory as a Dutch colony were rejected. German complaints that the Dutch were regularly drunk and ill-disciplined encouraged many to leave, but even the Dutch Commission for the Secondment of Farmers to Eastern Europe complained that most Dutch volunteers were a 'bunch of adventurers'.[322]

The utopian planning for settlement nevertheless continued despite the absence of a potential body of German colonists. At their most extreme, the plans envisaged the massive *Entvolkung*, depopulation, of the occupied East. A version of a General Plan East, drawn up by Wetzel, suggested a thirty-year programme of colonization in which 31 million people would have to be expelled, leaving 14 million to work for the imperial power. The final version of the General Plan East presented to Himmler on 23 December 1942, and the final General Settlement Plan, drawn up by Hans Ehlich in late 1942, both suggested fantastic projects at a time when the German war effort was already in deep crisis. Among the peoples of the occupied East, the plans calculated that 85 per cent of Poles, 50 per cent of Czechs, 50 per cent from the Baltic States, 75 per cent of Belorussians and 65 per cent of Ukrainians were 'expendable', a total of 47,925,000 racial aliens to be expelled or eliminated, not including the Jews, most of whom had already been murdered.[323] The fantasist-in-chief was Himmler himself who imagined, even as late as autumn 1942, a German imperial presence lasting for 400–500 years, and an empire peopled by 600 million Germans, carrying on, as he later claimed, the 'battle for life against Asia'.[324]

AN EMPIRE 'CLEANSED OF JEWS'

The organized mass expulsion or death of tens of millions did not happen on the lines suggested in the many versions of general planning for the East, though millions did die from the consequences of the war, while hundreds of thousands more were evicted or deported from their homes. The exception was the fate of the Jewish population across the region. It was the Jewish tragedy that the large majority of European Jews still inhabited what had once been the tsarist 'Pale of Settlement', where Jews from the Russian Empire were forced to live, from the Baltic States to south-western Ukraine; the tragedy was compounded with the reality that all Germany's most bitter anti-Semites were concentrated in the security apparatus that occupied these very same areas, which they hoped to turn into a Germanic paradise. Out of 11 million Jews in Europe, calculated by Adolf Eichmann's department for Jewish affairs in the Gestapo head office, 6.6 million lived in the occupied areas of the East, and a further 1.5 million in the rest of the Soviet Union.[325] As a result, the great majority of the Jews killed in the genocide that unfolded in 1941–3 were from the East, though by no means all. Their fate was entirely distinct from the fate of the millions of others left to starve or deported to make room for Germans or recruited for forced labour, because the Jews were singled out as the principal racial enemy of the German people, to be eliminated, one way or another, first from Germany, then from the conquered East and finally from the entire German *Grossraum*. These were to be areas 'cleansed of Jews' (*judenrein*) in the racial language of the regime. What has come to be known after 1945 as the Holocaust or Shoah involved Jews wherever they lived in occupied and Axis territory. The East mattered because that was the common destination of all the Jews in German hands, where they were murdered in ways that became, step by step, more systematic.

The war against the Jews was closely linked to the grandiose plans for ethnic restructuring, but this was only one strand in explaining the euphemistic 'final solution' to the Jewish question, a question only because Hitler and the National Socialist elite constructed the Jews as a problem in their own imagination. At root Hitler and the anti-Semites around him possessed a Manichaean view of the world in which the German people, representing a force for racial good, were pitted against the 'Jew' as the source of all the evil in the world. In Hitler's bizarre eschatology, the survival of the German people was conditional on the elimination of the Jews. Jews represented the 'anti-nation' bent on challenging the 'self-preservation of races'.[326] In 1936, in one of the few documents he wrote himself, shown to only a handful of his close colleagues, Hitler developed the idea that failure to destroy the Jewish threat would be 'the most gruesome racial catastrophe' since the collapse of the Roman Empire, resulting in 'the complete destruction' of the German *Volk*.[327] The terms of the contest that Hitler anticipated were stark: either German annihilation or Jewish annihilation. His first explicit public reference to annihilation came on 30 January 1939, in a speech to the German parliament, when he prophesied that 'annihilation' (*Vernichtung*) was the fate awaiting the Jews if they plunged Germany again into a worldwide war.

For Hitler, the war and the subsequent steps to Jewish annihilation were inseparable. Indeed, when he later referred to his prophecy, he dated it to 1 September 1939, the first day of the war. When Germany found itself finally facing global war in December 1941, the prophecy was summoned up at the fateful meeting on 12 December as justification for the uninhibited destruction of the Jews across the *Grossraum*. A few days later Himmler noted in his diary after a conference with Hitler: 'Jewish question: to be extirpated as partisans.'[328] On 30 January 1942, on the actual anniversary of his prophecy, Hitler announced that now 'the hour will strike when the most evil world enemy of all times will have ended his role for at least one thousand years.'[329] Two weeks later he told Goebbels that the Jews 'will also experience their own annihilation with the annihilation of our enemies', once again linking together both genocide and war. In a speech to the German parliament in late April 1942, Hitler finally spelt out the guilt of world Jewry for all the suffering and dangers Germany had faced, from the outbreak of the First World War onwards, to justify the decision for their extirpation:

> The hidden forces that already pushed England into the First World War in 1914 were Jews. The force that weakened us then and finally, under the rumour that Germany could no longer bear her banners victoriously home, compelled surrender, was Jewish. Jews fomented revolution in our people and robbed us of any further possibility for resistance. Jews since 1939 have further manoeuvred the British Empire into its most dangerous crisis. Jews were the bearers of that Bolshevik infection, which once threatened to destroy Europe. They were also at the same time the warmongers in the ranks of the plutocrats. A circle of Jews has even driven America against all that country's own interests into the war, simply and only from the Jewish-capitalist point of view.[330]

This toxic mix of delusional resentment and historical fabrication framed the Jew as the German nemesis to be fought to the death. For Hitler these views were not the fruit of reason, which would soon have exposed their fanciful nature, but of intense belief. Hitler never visited a camp or killed a Jew in person, but his metaphorical equation of Jew with historical evil governed the way the actual killing unfolded over the middle years of the war by creating a permissive narrative of vengeance.

The onset of the mass killing of Jews in 1941 was initially an uncoordinated and variable phenomenon, but it can only be understood against the background of a regime that had isolated and pilloried the Jews since 1933. Up until 1940 the intention was to dispossess Jewish wealth and compel Jews to emigrate, and hundreds of thousands did so. The discourse on the historic threat of Jews at home and abroad was widespread, but the core of Hitler's paranoid vision was embedded in the political education of a whole cohort of SS, police and security forces, and was also embraced by academic networks willing to find answers to Hitler's 'Jewish question'. These were the circles who ensured that Hitler's metaphorical view of the 'Jew' would be transmuted into the policies that persecuted and murdered real Jews. Conditions altered with the war once millions of Polish Jews came under German control. On 21 September 1939, Reinhard Heydrich, head of the RSHA, ordered all Jews to be concentrated in the General Government and placed in ghettoes or work camps.[331] Jews living in the annexed region of Warthegau were to be deported to the General Government, but moving the Jews proved difficult and major ghettoes had to be established on what was now German territory. In one case, in the town of Kalisch, a ghetto/work camp was established by autumn 1940, but all the Jews who were too weak, old or sick were taken to the nearby forest and shot – an early example of genocidal initiative at purely local level.[332]

In the General Government, where most Polish Jews were already concentrated, Hans Frank ordered compulsory labour for all Jewish men aged between eighteen and sixty and they laboured in harsh conditions on projects for the war effort. Odilo Globocnik in Lublin organized 76 work camps for around 50–70,000 Jewish men, building fortifications, roads or water courses, where they were made to labour knee-deep in water day after day. The forced labourers already experienced lethal violence: they could be shot or hanged for trying to evade work or for alleged slacking. The diet was so debilitating that workers died or were shot if they could work no longer. By 1941 many of the 700,000 Jewish workers were slaving in rags without footwear.[333] The rest of the Jewish population was forced into one of an estimated 400 ghettoes, both large and small. As the ghettoes filled up, the German authorities worried about the threat of disease or the cost to the Germans in feeding the Jews, while the slow pace of deportation led to regular arguments between the civilian authorities, the RSHA security apparatus, the police and the armed forces. Demands for labour for the war effort conflicted with the desire to isolate and impoverish Jewish communities, and soon conflicted with the ambitions of the Himmler security apparatus to clear areas of Jews altogether or to leave Jews to starve or die of disease. The defeat of France briefly opened up the idea of shipping all Jews to the French colony of Madagascar. Himmler suggested this to Hitler in May 1940 and found him 'very much in agreement'.[334] The island was to become a German protectorate, with a German governor overseeing an inhospitable colony where Jews would be the unfortunate colonized. The plan proved quite unrealistic with British control of the seas, and it was the British who seized the island later, in May 1942, to forestall a possible Japanese occupation. The approach of the 'Barbarossa' campaign encouraged the view that Jews might now be pushed far to the East, and this seems still in the summer of 1941 to have been Hitler's preferred solution. 'It does not matter,' he told Croatia's defence minister in July, 'whether the Jews are sent to Madagascar or Siberia.'[335] Yet the habit of mistreating, plundering or murdering Jews as racial enemies was already widespread enough to make the shift from 'evacuation' to mass killing in the summer of 1941 on former Soviet territory less difficult to explain.

The murder of Jews began almost at once after 22 June 1941 in what Wendy Lower has called a 'mosaic of local holocaust histories', each mass killing with its own story, but the many smaller pieces helping to build the image of a larger genocide.[336] Hitler had ordered the *Einsatzgruppen* to murder Jews in Soviet state service, and Jewish members of the Communist Party, or any Jews in official positions, but the terms of the conflict soon opened the floodgates of violence directed at Jews, partly because they were easily identifiable and concentrated in the villages and towns first overrun. The security units were aided by the armed forces, whose members were soon assisting the *Einsatzgruppen* in rounding up and guarding Jews, and occasionally murdering them as well. Troops were all issued with instructions down to company level on 21 June for ruthless and aggressive action against 'Bolshevik agitators, snipers, saboteurs and Jews'. By September, OKW issued a directive on 'Jews in the Newly Occupied Soviet Territories' which reinforced the need for 'indiscriminate and energetic' efforts 'especially against the Jews'.[337] The insinuation that Jews were behind every case of looting, or arson, or shooting as the troops moved in became embedded in official discourse in the first weeks of the conflict. It mattered little that most, if not all the allegations were fanciful because Jewish guilt was assumed as a given. The report from *Einsatzgruppe A* in December 1941 asserted that Jews 'were extremely active as saboteurs and fire-raisers'; by the end of October 30,000 had already been killed on this spurious claim.[338]

The reaction of military commanders was in many cases shaped by their own anti-Semitism and hatred of communism, and they readily acquiesced in the assumption that many of the alleged 'partisans' active on the German army flanks were Jews. They also included Soviet Roma communities as potential spies and saboteurs, and Roma were routinely killed alongside the main Jewish target. The SS military units needed little prompting. As early as July 1941 the SS Cavalry Brigade was instructed to kill all male Jews indiscriminately, followed shortly after by instructions to eliminate families too. In a two-week killing spree in early August, they murdered an estimated 25,000 Jews.[339] The ease with which 'partisan' and 'Jew' could be elided together allowed military and security units wide licence to murder at will, not least in the case of occupied Serbia, where the mass murder of Jewish men was an accomplished fact by November 1941 on the grounds that they were all potential partisans or saboteurs. Hundreds had already been murdered as hostages on instructions from OKW to kill 100 for every German soldier killed by the guerrillas. A further 8,000 were liquidated on orders from the military regime in Belgrade once it was clear there was no room to deport them to the East. Women, children and Roma followed a few months later when 7,500 were gassed over a two-month period, in which each day a set number of women and children were promised resettlement and taken off in a lorry, where they were locked in until the gas had killed them. Children were given sweets to reassure them that all was well. On 9 June 1942 the terse message was relayed to Berlin: 'Serbia is free of Jews.'[340]

The main instigators of mass murder were the *Einsatzgruppen A, B, C* and *D*, aided, once the scale of the murders became evident, by regular 'order' police recruited in the Reich and by local Ukrainian, Baltic and Belorussian auxiliaries. Between them they murdered an estimated 700,000 by December 1941, 509,000 of the victims across the civilian and military zones of Ukraine (including 96,000 killed by Romanian army and security units in Transnistria).[341] In some cases, local military commanders ordered ghettoes to be constructed, but they were often only temporary as SS and police units, spurred on by Himmler, arrived to liquidate them. In Belorussia, murders reached a climax by October, with massacres of 2,000 at Mogilev on 1–2 October, up to 8,000 in Vitebsk and 7–8,000 at Borisov ten days later. In Minsk a large ghetto was set up, but 10,000 were murdered in early November to make room for some of the first deportees from Germany. At Mogilev the army had hosted a top-level meeting of commanders from Army Group Centre in late September where Arthur Nebe, commander of *Einsatzgruppe B*, lectured on the Jewish question and anti-partisan warfare to encourage military co-operation. Army units fanned out into the countryside in October hunting 'bandits' but killing instead large numbers of Jews. The army commander-in-chief in Belorussia, General Gustav von Mauchenheim, directed that 'the Jews have to disappear from the countryside, and the gypsies [Roma] are to be annihilated too', and his 707th Infantry Division killed an estimated 10,000 Jews in the area around Minsk, in addition to those killed in the Minsk Ghetto.[342]

Treatment was not consistent, and some Jews survived either because they had skills the army needed, or because they evaded the early round-ups, or because they were herded into ghettoes where survival was a matter of chance. In Latvia and Lithuania, where popular pogroms in June following the German arrival abetted the work of the local SS, ghettoes were constructed only after the first wave of killing. In Riga, half the Jewish population was dead before the ghetto was instituted in October 1941, but in early December 27,000 of the ghetto population were murdered in the nearby forest of Rumbula to make way, once again, for German Jews. In Ukraine, on the other hand, the ghetto created in Zhytomyr was cleared of 3,145 Jews shortly after its construction; the ghetto in Yalta was established on 5 December, but twelve days later its inhabitants were murdered.[343] Ukraine was also the site of the genocide's largest single massacre, in the Babi Yar ravine outside Kiev, allegedly in retaliation for 'Jewish' terrorism in the city. On 29 September, a large part of the Jewish population was marched through the city, many hoping that they were to be deported, until they reached the site where, all day, groups were beaten, stripped and machine-gunned into the ravine, 33,771 in total over two days. In the whole Kiev province 137,000 were murdered in September even while the fighting was going on further east.[344] One eyewitness, Iryna Khoroshunova, expressed in her diary a sense that is now universal: 'I only know one thing: there is something terrible, horrible going on, something inconceivable, which cannot be understood, grasped or explained.'[345]

Historians are divided over the point at which Hitler might have ordered the extermination of the Jews, but this is to overlook the reality that genocide was practised from June 1941 onwards without any direct orders from the highest authority to exterminate the Jews. No one in Berlin would have disapproved the killings, least of all Hitler, who was shown the reports from the *Einsatzgruppen*, or Himmler, who over the summer months of 1941 pressed the security units to be more ruthless. Hitler's intervention was needed only at certain key junctures. The marking of

German Jews with a yellow star followed Hitler's direct instructions after the Atlantic Charter was published in August; on 18 September, Hitler finally ordered the deportation to ghettoes in the East of all German, Austrian and Czech Jews, which began in late October. By then, the RSHA was already talking of deporting to the East all Jews in the occupied *Grossraum* in line with Hitler's deportation orders for Central Europe. Hitler seems to have been particularly incensed at news that Stalin had ordered the deportation to Siberia of the 'Volga Germans', thousands of German speakers in southern Russia descended from eighteenth-century colonists, and he approved Rosenberg's statement that 'the Jews of central Europe' would suffer the same fate if the Soviet Germans were murdered.[346] Finally, in December 1941 and January 1942, those involved in Jewish policy took the lead from Hitler's statements about annihilation to assume that a more comprehensive, European-wide elimination of the Jews, either through deliberate killing or their being worked to death as labour, was now the approved course. Hans Frank, unable to move his large Jewish population but keen to Germanize the General Government, returned from the meeting on 12 December to report to his administrators that they could now move on by one means or another to liquidate more than a million Jews living there. There is no Hitler order for this radicalization of the genocide, but none of those involved was in any doubt that not only the Jews in the Soviet Union and eastern Poland, already murdered in vast numbers, but all Jews within Germany's grasp were to be shipped at some point to the killing fields in the East. This was the main conclusion of the notorious Wannsee conference convened on 20 January 1942 (postponed from December), in which Heydrich discussed the final solution to the Jewish question in Europe as evacuation to the East, once Hitler approved it. Heydrich, and Himmler too, still thought in terms of exploiting Jewish labour power as far as possible, as the deportees were worked to death further and further to the east, but those present at Wannsee assumed that those who could not labour would die. Evacuation in the end meant extermination, one way or another.[347]

There was no central plan for the treatment of the Jews developed at Wannsee. The waves of killings across the course of 1942 depended, as they had in 1941, on local initiatives by SS, military and civilian authorities and regular promptings from Himmler and, until his assassination in June 1942, Heydrich. The most significant of these initiatives involved the shift from face-to-face killing (responsible for around half of all the deaths in the Holocaust) to murder in gas facilities, either vans and lorries adapted to the role, or in fixed gas rooms or chambers. The use of gas facilities was developed first in October and November 1941 as a solution to the urgent need to find ghetto space for deported German and Czech Jews. Arthur Greiser, gauleiter of the Warthegau, wanted permission to murder up to 100,000 Jews still living there after the failed deportation plans. A small manor house was chosen near the village of Chelmno and gas vans were used to murder Jews from November onwards. At the same time, Odilo Globocnik proposed, and Heydrich accepted, a fixed gassing installation at the former labour camp at Belzec, near Lublin, where Jews incapable of work were to be killed.[348] The shift to gassing involved a method already familiar from the so-called T4 programme (from the Berlin address, Tiergarten 4) for gassing the mentally disabled in Germany and Austria, and later in occupied Poland. Globocnik had 120 of the T4 personnel transferred to Lublin, while more assisted in other killing sites.[349] Belzec began gassing Jews from March 1942, while two other facilities on Polish territory at Sobibór and Treblinka were under construction. Sobibór began gassing in May 1942, Treblinka in July. These camps became the site of what was called *Aktion Reinhard*, where Jews were shipped only for extermination. Those still deemed to be capable of work were kept back but in the first wave of killing in the General Government 160,000 were gassed. After Heydrich's assassination Himmler told senior SS officers, 'We will be done with the great migration of the Jews within a year; then, none will wander any more. A clean sweep has to be made.'[350]

The so-called 'second wave' of killings followed, launched from summer 1942. This was the most lethal period of the genocide. In the second half of 1942 some 1.2 million were murdered in the General Government. In Ukraine, where much of the killing was still done face to face, a further 773,000 were killed, emptying the Reich Commissariat almost completely of Jews. 'Jewry: the cleansing of the territory is in its final stages' ran a report on 31 December 1942. The few thousands left were finished off in the following months.[351] The remorseless killing masked continued argument and uncertainty surrounding the use of Jewish labour and the survival of pockets of Jews in ghettoes and work camps. In April 1942, under pressure from the armed forces and civilian employers in the East, Himmler ordered that men aged from sixteen to thirty-five should be kept for factory and construction labour. But from summer 1942 his attitude changed. Rather than accept the survival of what he regarded as islands of racial impurity in the areas to be colonized, he asked for all projects employing Jews to be closed and the Jews killed rather than employed for the war effort, but the armed forces and the civilian administrators continued to defy the orders. In early 1943 there were still 120,000 Jews in work camps in Poland, and only by summer 1943 was Himmler able to insist that they all close down so that their Jewish population could be murdered alongside all remaining Jews.[352] In Galicia, 140,000 Jews were murdered in the first six months of 1943, having evaded earlier waves of killing. In German-occupied Ukraine, 150,000 of the survivors were liquidated in 1943. A few camps survived for the building of *Durchgangsstrasse IV*, but the last was liquidated in December 1943 and any remaining Jews killed off. By this time two large camps for labour and extermination had been constructed at Auschwitz-Birkenau and Majdanek, where more than a million Jews from Central, Western and Southern Europe were gassed. These included the last remnant of Jewish workers in the General Government and the large Łódź ghetto, who were killed in August 1944 as the Red Army approached, and half the Jews of Hungary, deported only in the summer. At Auschwitz-Birkenau, 965,000 of the 1.1 million Jewish deportees were killed, including 216,000 children and adolescents.[353] By this time the dedicated extermination centres had been closed down, their work finished.

However poorly co-ordinated and prone to friction the killing process in the East was, the end result for the Jews was the same – to die swiftly or slowly, but to die. With the Jews of the wider *Grossraum* the situation was more complicated because deportations could not easily be carried out without the collaboration of the occupied or allied administrations. The German security apparatus lacked the manpower or the necessary local knowledge to be able to act independently even in occupied areas; in allied or satellite states, care had to be taken that German policy was not seen to ride roughshod over local interests and attitudes. Reliance on local police and officials coloured the success or otherwise of German plans. The assumption that German pressure and resources explained the extension of the genocide to the rest of Europe was for long after 1945 the accepted narrative, but it tells only half the story. The European-wide existence of anti-Semitism, in one form or another, played a critical role in decisions to promote deportation, and in most cases required little German pressure, although only in the case of Romania and Croatia did this lead to autonomous mass killing of Jews. The extension of Jewish persecution was from this perspective pan-European and not straightforwardly German. Hitler's Germany mattered because it provided the opportunity for other states to solve their 'Jewish question', if they chose to, by feeding their Jewish population into the German Moloch. To outline the opportunity, Eichmann's Jewish affairs department in the Gestapo, the German Foreign Ministry and the SS all sent delegates to the occupied and allied areas to conduct the diplomacy of genocide, though even their presence did not always guarantee compliance.

There was no standard pattern to the way Jews were targeted in the rest of Europe but once again a variety of responses, dependent on local circumstances, political calculation and social attitudes to the 'Jewish question'. Anti-Semitism also took different forms: in some cases it was based on racial prejudice, or on fear that Jews would undermine national identity; in other cases there existed a strong religious element where Christians blamed the Jews as 'Christ-killers'; in others a strong economic motive to dispossess Jewish wealth for national needs; or a combination of all of these, evident in the persecution and eventual expulsion of Jews from Slovakia, Hungary and Romania. These three Axis states did not need to borrow German anti-Semitism but developed an indigenous prejudice and discrimination, in the case of Hungary and Romania dating back decades. In the Western occupied states, the fiction that Jews were to be resettled was used to persuade Jewish communities to collaborate, but also to distance local collaborators from the reality of participation in genocide. Whatever the motives and circumstances in these different cases, many Europeans understood that there was a 'Jewish question' to which they too might give an answer.

In Romania, harsh anti-Semitic laws were passed by King Carol's dictatorship in early 1938, stripping 225,000 Jews of their citizenship, closing Jewish newspapers and sacking Jewish state employees. Legislation against Jews continued into 1943 under Marshal Antonescu. Random acts of violence and the destruction of Jewish property were regularly perpetrated by Romanian fascists, but the crisis for Romanian Jews arrived with the 'Barbarossa' campaign and the reconquest of Bukovina and Bessarabia, where there lived 800,000 Jews, many of them 'stateless' under Romanian residence rules.[354] Here the army, local Romanian peasants and resident ethnic Germans blamed the large Jewish communities for abetting the year-long Soviet occupation, and during July and August 1941 perpetrated a wave of massacres and pogroms killing perhaps as many as 60,000 Jews. The SS *Einsatzgruppe D* also provided some of the killers, but the main thrust was Romanian. Antonescu, in pursuit of a declared policy of ethnic cleansing (which included not only Jews, but Roma, Hungarians and Russians), ordered the deportation of the remaining Jews and around 147,000 were relocated to Transnistria, where they were housed in insanitary, makeshift camps, deprived of possessions, semi-starved and ill, and the butt of further murderous atrocities. Of those deported, more than 100,000 died or were killed. In addition, since Transnistria was to be the heart of 'Greater Romania', Soviet Jews were targeted too, either for murder or for a precarious life in the same makeshift camps. Of these an estimated 130–170,000 perished.[355] In the autumn of 1942, for reasons that remain unclear, Antonescu changed his mind about deportation and rejected

German requests that Jews from the rest of Romania be sent to the extermination camps in Poland. Deportation had in fact been planned after agreement with the SS representative Gustav Richter, but by late September the plans were shelved. Antonescu was subject to international pressure not to comply, but the best explanation was the challenge to Romanian sovereignty that compliance seemed to imply, 'a slap in the country's face' as the liberal party leader put it in a speech that same month. Jews already deported to Transnistria faced the death penalty if they tried to leave, but by March 1944, when most had already died, Antonescu handed over the area to German forces and repatriated 10,700 who remained. In this case, there existed clear limits to the German effort to kill all Jews, even if Romania's own actions caused the death by neglect, disease and murder of more than a quarter of a million.[356]

Slovakia proved far more compliant. Under informal Reich 'protection' since March 1939, the new state was animated by a radical anti-Semitism, even though only 4 per cent of the population was Jewish: there existed profound resentment at a Jewish minority that dominated business and banking, and whose separate identity was underlined by speaking German, Hungarian or Yiddish rather than Slovak. Consideration of the Slovak 'Jewish question' began in earnest in 1939 but the principal aim initially was Jewish dispossession. By September 1941, 85 per cent of Jewish businesses had been closed or taken over by non-Jews (including Germans). A year earlier, the Slovak parliament passed a decree that the Jewish question should be solved within a year. When the year was over, a Jewish Codex was introduced, severely restricting Jewish life. The government of Jozef Tiso then asked the SS representative, Dieter Wisliceny, if Germany would take the impoverished Jews and free Slovakia of the cost and responsibility. A Constitutional Law was passed on 15 May 1942 to legalize deportation, and, after agreement that Slovakia would pay 500 marks for each deportee to cover German 'security costs', 58,000 were deported in Slovak trains to detention camps, from where the SS took them to the extermination centres. Jews fit for labour, or with special exemption, remained in Slovakia, but when Germany occupied the satellite state in August 1944, a further 13,500 were deported to their deaths in Auschwitz-Birkenau, among the last to be murdered. The possessions of the deportees were taken over by the state and distributed to Slovak schools and other institutions. Some 9,000 Slovak Jews survived out of 89,000, hidden by friends, masquerading as ethnic Slovaks, or fleeing across the border to Hungary, where the Jews survived the first years of war despite a virulent Hungarian anti-Semitism.[357]

Hungarian society was if anything more anti-Semitic than that in

Slovakia and Romania, and certainly more so in much of the inter-war period than in Germany. Here economic resentment at Jewish roles in business and the professions played an important part. Efforts to restrict Jewish numbers in professions and business went back to the early 1920s. In 1938 and 1939, First and Second Jewish Laws were enacted, restricting Jewish access to the professions and removing the right to state employment. Regulations were introduced through 1940 to dispossess Jews and to use their wealth to fund land redistribution; thousands of Jews were denied the right to trade. The talk among anti-Semitic politicians and economists by the early 1940s focused on the need for the forced emigration of Hungary's 835,000 Jews. When the Hungarian premier, Pál Teleki, visited Hitler in 1940 he called for a European-wide solution to the 'Jewish question', which not even Hitler had yet considered possible. Around 14,000 stateless Jews and refugees were pushed across the border with German-occupied Galicia in July 1941, where German security forces, unwilling recipients, murdered almost all of them in the city of Kamianets-Podilsky, by far the largest mass murder in the early weeks of 'Barbarossa'.[358] Within Hungary, Jews were herded into ghettoes and able-bodied men into labour camps. Demands to send the Jews to the German camps in Poland were resisted by the regent, Admiral Horthy, and the conservative circles around him, until his rule was swept aside by German military occupation on 19 March 1944. No longer held back, Eichmann and the sixty or so German officials who accompanied him were astonished at the speed and comprehensiveness of Hungarian efforts to register, ghettoize and deport Hungarian Jews, which at times threatened to overwhelm the German murder apparatus. Deportations began on 15 May 1944, only two months after occupation, and within eight weeks 430,000 had been sent off, three-quarters of them to immediate death in Auschwitz. In all some half a million were deported, but efforts by the conservative elite to protect the Jews of Budapest, coupled with demands for Jewish labour from the Hungarian armed forces, prevented total annihilation and around 120,000 survived the threat of deportation.[359]

The exceptions among the Axis camp were Bulgaria and Italy (until German occupation of two-thirds of the peninsula in September 1943). Anti-Semitism was certainly present in both, but as with Horthy in Hungary, there were strong internal restraints against simply doing Germany's bidding. In Bulgaria major anti-Semitic legislation – the Law for the Defence of the Nation – was enacted in November 1940 only after a vigorous debate among Bulgaria's elite over its legitimacy. In 1941 measures to acquire a share of Jewish wealth came into force, and on 26 August 1942, after discussions with the RSHA in Berlin on securing a more radical

Jewish policy in Bulgaria, a Cabinet decree authorized the establishment of a Commissariat for Jewish Affairs, resettlement of Jews from the capital, Sofia, the confiscation of Jewish wealth, and a definition of 'Jew' more sweeping than the German counterpart. Preparations for the deportation of Bulgaria's Jews followed, but in March 1943 government members protested against the idea that Germany should determine the fate of Bulgaria's Jews, much as the Romanian regime had done. Beginning in March, Jews were deported from the areas Bulgaria occupied in 1941 – Thrace in Greece and eastern Macedonia from Yugoslavia – but Tsar Boris, hostile to accommodating German demands, approved the postponement in March of the deportation of Bulgarian Jews, and in May 1943, following pressure from abroad and at home, he approved the decision to end the deportation programme, which he had never favoured. Further south, the German military administration and the SS began deportations in March 1943 from Greece, where there was little opposition, and 60,000 were eventually sent to Auschwitz. But by autumn 1943, the RSHA abandoned further pressure on the Bulgarian government and the 51,000 Jews, despite the rigours of the discriminatory legislation, survived the war.[360]

The attitude of Italian empire-builders to the 'Jewish question' was similarly based on a strong current of domestic anti-Semitism among a Fascist minority, but also on resistance to the idea that Germany should dictate what Italy did with its Jews. Pressure from within the Fascist movement, rather than imitation of Germany, led in 1938 to the publication of a series of Jewish laws which followed the European pattern of eliminating Jews from state service, expelling many from the professions, and introducing a forced labour regime, but no concentration camps were created as Mussolini wanted. In 1942, Mussolini approved the establishment of 'Centres for the Study of the Jewish Problem' in six major Italian cities to spread propaganda about the urgent need to solve the 'Jewish question' in more radical ways, but it led to no major initiatives until the Italian surrender and the German occupation.[361] Even in the Italian occupied areas, local military commanders and officials in Rome resisted German efforts to get them to hand over Jews and Jewish refugees, 'for obvious reasons of political prestige and humanity', as one of them put it. The Jewish expert in the German Foreign Office regretted in October 1942 that on the final solution the Axis enjoyed 'no united policy in these matters'.[362] This changed dramatically in September 1943 when German forces occupied mainland Italy and its remaining empire. The German security police and Gestapo began rounding up Italian Jews in Rome in October 1943, and further north a month later – particularly recent immigrants who were, as in France, targeted first. The Italian interior minister in the puppet Salò government, Guido Guidi, on 30 November ordered the arrest and internment of all Jews by local Italian police, but the majority of arrests were carried out by the Germans, who set up camps at Fossoli and, later, at Bologna as holding centres for deportation. Only 6,806 Jews were eventually deported, out of the 32,802 registered by the Salò regime, while 322 died in Italy and 950 remained unaccounted for after the war.[363] For the German genocide apparatus this was a disappointing outcome, but consistent with their view of the Italians as unreliable allies. The detection and arrest of Jews depended on local initiatives rather than anything more systematic. Many Jews, perhaps as many as 6,000, fled to Switzerland, some made it to Allied lines, while thousands were hidden in Catholic institutions, or simply blended into a population in which they were not obviously Jewish. Those who were caught sheltering Jews might suffer a few days' incarceration, but were not routinely shot or hanged, as in the East.[364]

The fate of the Jews in the occupied territories in Western Europe and Scandinavia also varied from area to area, but the German authorities had more direct responsibility here to enforce Jewish policy than they had among Axis allies. Even then, the tasks of registering, identifying, and even arresting Jews for deportation depended heavily on non-German cooperation, which was never uniform. In Belgium, local police arrested only 17 per cent of the Jews taken by the German security services, in the Netherlands some 24 per cent, but in France local police forces made 61 per cent of the arrests of Jews for deportation, despite a decline in the willingness to comply as the prospect of liberation drew nearer.[365] If there was a common denominator in the occupied areas, it lay in the willingness to work with the German search for Jews in 1942, when the largest numbers were deported from the West, and a decline thereafter as Germany's fortunes of war were more obviously in crisis. In France, a 'Jewish question' had long existed, prompted by the politics of the nationalist right, and public anti-Semitism became more obtrusive as war approached. 'Peace! Peace! The French don't want to go to war for the Jews . . .' was one response to the Czech crisis in 1938. In 1939 measures were taken to limit the participation of Jewish refugees in the professions, while those defined as stateless (including the author Arthur Koestler) were rounded up and placed in one of the many concentration camps that sprang up in France in 1939 and 1940. These differed little from the German example thanks to the degree of neglect in providing food or adequate accommodation and the tough labour regime imposed on internees. In September 1940, the food ration was 350 grammes of bread a day, 125 grammes of meat. But in many cases the ration was not supplied. In the camp at Gurs, internees tried to survive on 800 calories a day. Deaths were common-place from disease and malnutrition. By spring 1940 there were 5,000 refugee Jews in the camps, but by the peak in February 1941 there were 40,000.[366] None of this programme was instigated by the Germans, and almost all the camps were run by the French authorities. The main camp at Drancy, outside Paris, was only taken over by the Germans for deporta-tions in June 1943.

A wave of anti-Semitic legislation followed the establishment of the Vichy regime in June 1940. The German ambassador reported back to Ber-lin in July 1940, after a talk with Prime Minister Pierre Laval, 'the anti-Semitic tendencies of the French people are so strong that they do not need any further support on our part whatsoever.'[367] On 5 October 1940 a comprehensive Jewish Statute was published, banning Jews from state ser-vice and other professions and defining 'Jew' as anyone with two Jewish grandparents, rather than three in the German case. Jewish immigrants who had been naturalized after 1927 had their status withdrawn, allowing them to be rounded up for the camps. When German plans for taking Jew-ish businesses into trusteeship were being prepared, Vichy swiftly published a pre-emptive French law to allow dispossession. By 1942 there were 42,227 French trustees of Jewish property, but only 45 German.[368] A census register of all Jews was ordered by the Vichy government, and the subse-quent lists helped the Gestapo to round up known Jews when the Vichy zone was occupied in November 1942. Some case has been made to argue that the Vichy regime tried to pre-empt the Germans in order to avoid something worse, but the evidence is slender. Many things the Germans did not demand, including the imposition of the yellow star for Jews in June 1942 and the word '*juif*' stamped on Jewish identity and ration cards, or the harsh regime of internment camps, where perhaps 3,000 died in French custody.[369] The first wave of German arrests in the occupied zone occurred in May 1941 when Jews were placed in four more camps, three run by the French, but the arrests and deportations to the camps in Poland only began in the summer of 1942 after Theodor Dannecker, Eichmann's deputy in France, insisted that, at the least, all Jewish refugees and Jews who had lost naturalization should be deported. Vichy co-operated to the extent of send-ing around 11,000 non-French Jews from the southern zone, including 4,500 from among the Jewish internees. In 1942 some 41,951 were deported, followed by 17,069 the following year, and 14,833 in 1944, well short of the 100,000 in 1942 that Eichmann and Dannecker had asked for. Of these, 68 per cent were foreign Jews, 32 per cent French.[370] Vichy did not endorse mass murder, but the conditions imposed on Jews and the hunt for them by French police and officials played into German hands.

The experience of Jewish communities in Belgium and the Netherlands varied widely. In Belgium 95 per cent of the Jewish population of around 75,000 were foreign nationals, not Belgian. Despite their obvious vulnerability, only 29,906 were deported, mainly in 1942, while thousands were sheltered by Belgian civilians, or evaded arrest. In the Netherlands, on the other hand, there was a large, historically rooted Jewish population numbering around 185,000, of whom more than 75 per cent – 140,000 – were deported to the camps and most murdered. Thousands were hidden by Dutch households, of whom at least 16,100 survived, but thousands more were detected or denounced to the Dutch and German police among a public some of whom did not disapprove of German efforts to solve the 'Jewish question'. In the Netherlands, the German authorities depended on the response of Dutch officials and the Jewish communities following Reich Commissioner Seyss-Inquart's order in January 1941 to register all Jews. There was almost no objection, although at that point few could have imagined what the registers would be used for. The Dutch police proved particularly collaborative, since the official line was not to antagonize the Germans unduly, though they would only apprehend Jews and deliver them to the German police, rather than formally arrest them. In small towns and villages, it was Dutch policemen who collected the Jews and delivered them for deportation in the peak year from July 1942 to July 1943. After that, as in France, the expectation of German defeat and eventual liberation led to a slow-down in collaboration, but by then most of the 140,000 were dead. In Belgium, the Jewish community was small and socially marginal, which may well explain why a much larger fraction survived. Anti-Semitism was not a key issue even among the parties of the extreme right, and certainly less so than in the Netherlands and France, and by October 1942, at the height of the deportations, some 20,000 Jews were sheltered by non-Jews. The Belgian bureaucratic regime for registering the Jews was less developed than the Dutch, while the largely immigrant Jewish population was already versed in the art of avoiding obedience. Nevertheless, in Belgium too bureaucrats and policemen collaborated as far as they could in tracking down Jews, while Belgians were no more diffident than the French or Dutch in taking over Jewish possessions, wealth and housing once the Germans had taken their share.

Only in two Scandinavian countries did it prove possible to save almost all the Jewish population. No pressure was put on the Danish government to deliver the small population of Danish Jews until the resignation of the government in August 1943 and the wave of strikes and protests that followed. Assuming that Jews played a part in the resistance movement, Hitler and von Ribbentrop in September 1943 urged the Reich plenipotentiary,

Werner Best, to deport all Danish Jews. Best seems to have regarded the deportations as a mistake in further alienating Danish society, and when a rescue operation to take Jews by boat across to Sweden began, Best and the German police made little effort to stop them.[371] In Finland, the small Jewish community of around 2,200 faced no threat of domestic anti-Semitism and no pressure was put on the Finnish government to deliver up the Jewish population, save for eight refugee Jews who were sent back to Germany. Only in 1944, when there were fears that Germany might occupy Finland to prevent withdrawal from the war, were plans made to send Finnish Jews to Sweden. A handful of children and mothers were sent in the summer months, but the Finnish government was reluctant to let the Jews leave in case the Allies assumed that Finland accepted participation in the wider genocide. In the end, German security and police forces were spread too thinly to intervene, and the Jews survived until Finnish forces surrendered to the Red Army, fortunate to have escaped the widening German net as it closed in on surviving Jews, even in the face of imminent defeat.[372] Consistent to the last, Hitler is alleged to have claimed in April 1945, shortly before his suicide, that 'National Socialism can justly claim the eternal gratitude of the people for having eliminated the Jew from Germany and Central Europe.'[373]

The bleak narrative of European collaboration in the German pursuit of a Europe 'cleansed of Jews' was related to the creation of the German Empire in the East only because Hitler, like Himmler or Eichmann, could not in the end envisage either a territorial empire in the East, nor a larger *Grossraum*, as an area inhabited by millions of Jews. They were defined as the world enemy of German efforts to construct a German-centred imperial order. All the ambitions to create such an order, blithely expressed in the Three Power Pact in September 1940, ended in utter failure, but not before the violent empire-building engulfed Eurasia and its fringes in programmes of deportation, dispossession and murder narrowly concentrated in time, in contrast to the history of earlier empire-building, even its genocidal aspects, which was spread over decades, or even longer. The new empires could certainly have been built at lower human cost, but the permanent tension between imperial fantasy and imperial reality prompted a spasm of unlimited violence that turned the empire from imagined utopia into a dystopian nightmare of frustration, punishment and destruction.

3

The Death of the Nation-Empire, 1942–45

'. . . if we win we must win in both the East and the West, and if we lose it must be the same.'

Ōshima Hiroshi, November 1942[1]

In late November 1942, the Japanese ambassador in Berlin called a conference of his fellow ambassadors in Europe to lecture them on the current outlook of the war. His talk coincided with three significant battles in each of the war's major theatres: at Stalingrad in southern Russia, where German and Soviet armies were locked in a titanic struggle for the city; on the island of Guadalcanal in the British Solomon Islands, where a more modest number of Japanese soldiers and American marines were fighting at the very furthest perimeter of the Japanese advance; and in northern Libya, where a British Empire army pursued a German–Italian force along the North African coast following their disordered retreat from the (second) battle of El Alamein. Ōshima told his colleagues that it was time for Japan, Italy and Germany to try to co-ordinate their strategic planning, and he hoped that would mean operations against India and a possible link-up with German forces in the Middle East. He had arrived at the conclusion months before that 'it will be practically impossible for Germany to overthrow the Stalin regime' and was one among a number of senior Japanese diplomats who still hoped that Germany would make peace with the Soviet Union, brokered perhaps by the Japanese, so that a larger 'Four Power Pact' could turn Eurasia against the Anglo-Saxon powers.

The idea that the wars of aggression could be ended by advantageous peace settlements was a persistent Japanese illusion. In spring 1943, a delegation arrived in Berlin from Japan to try to persuade Hitler to abandon the Soviet campaign in favour of a Mediterranean strategy to terminate the British and American presence there. A meeting of senior soldiers and politicians in Tokyo a few weeks later assumed that a

German–Soviet peace was the key to the whole war; the Western Allies would then have to reach agreement in Europe, fearful of Communist encroachment, following which Chiang would have no choice but to accept terms in China, opening the way to a comprehensive and favourable peace settlement with the Allies.[2] Hitler would have none of it (nor indeed would Stalin). To every suggestion, he insisted that defeating the Soviet Union took priority and he could never agree terms. In July 1943, with the Axis war effort now in crisis, Hitler assured Ōshima that, between them, the Germans and Japanese would overcome every obstacle.[3]

Only with hindsight perhaps is it possible to see just how deluded Axis leaders were by the turning point of the war in 1942–3. The battles being fought while Ōshima mused on a future Axis global strategy did not signify with certainty the eventual Allied victory, which was far away, but they did place a final limit on the territorial stretch of the Axis. Stalingrad, Guadalcanal and El Alamein were the furthest points of advance. After that followed the long and fiercely contested retreat across the newly acquired territories, except in the case of Mussolini's Italy, where the collapse of the war effort occurred much sooner. That it took so long to lever the remaining Axis forces out of their conquests reflected the rejection of a political solution in favour of military defiance, and the impossibility for those who hoped for a compromise peace short of defeat, like Ōshima, to deflect the leadership from the chosen course of confrontation rather than surrender. It also reflected a wilful disregard of the costs of continued warfare for the Axis home populations, who were expected to, and did, sustain the war effort right down to the moment of surrender. How and why populations continued the fight even in the face of imminent and total defeat still remains a difficult question to answer.

IMPERIAL DEAD ENDS: EL ALAMEIN, STALINGRAD, GUADALCANAL

For much of 1942, Axis leaders could still imagine a successful outcome. As late as November 1942, when Italy's military fortunes were already in terminal decline, Mussolini could boast that the 'so-called United Nations' had displayed 'nothing but failures and catastrophes'.[4] In summer 1942 the German army and its allies were still far inside Russia and Egypt, while Japanese forces sought to secure the outer perimeter of the vast land and ocean area captured earlier in the year and to consolidate Japan's grip on Chinese territory. These were all areas where Allied 'failures and catastrophes' had been much in evidence in the first half of the year.

For Japanese military leaders, the sudden success in seizing the vast Southern Region opened an intoxicating vision of further conquests. 'Where do we go from here?' wrote the Combined Fleet's chief of staff in his diary. 'Advance on Australia? On India? Invade Hawaii?' The naval planning staff drew up new proposals, among them Rear Admiral Yamaguchi Tamon's plan to conquer Australia and New Zealand prior to an invasion of the coast of California.[5] Before any decision could be made, a token raid on Tokyo by Lieutenant Colonel James Doolittle's small carrier-borne bomber force on 18 April 1942 forced a strategic re-appraisal. Instead of the Pacific, the Japanese army turned back to China. Doolittle's raid certainly boosted American morale but, as Chiang feared, it prompted the Japanese Expeditionary Army to order an operation to seize areas where the Chinese had airbases that could be used by the Americans. Two columns of 50,000 soldiers fanned out from Hangzhou (Hankow) and Nanchang into Zhejiang and Jiangxi provinces, opening a wide rail corridor and devastating the area around the bases. The rapid success was to be followed by a final knockout blow in September against Chiang's capital at Chongqing, employing sixteen Japanese divisions, but the campaign was abandoned because of the demand for manpower to protect the long ocean perimeter of its new territories – an early indicator of how difficult it would prove to be for Japan to fight two wars at the same time.[6] The Doolittle raid also prompted a Japanese navy plan to seize Midway Island in the central Pacific as a base to threaten further American sorties and to interrupt ocean communication from Hawaii to Australia. Admiral Yamamoto instituted a complex plan to lure the American carrier fleet, which by then was reduced to three vessels, USS *Enterprise*, *Hornet* and the recently repaired *Yorktown*, to defend Midway so that he could destroy them and secure Japanese domination of the mid-ocean. In addition to an invasion force and support group for Midway itself, a secondary task force was instructed to seize two of the far-north Aleutian Islands off Alaska, Attu and Kiska, as bases to protect the northern perimeter. The Japanese carrier force had four of Japan's six fleet carriers – *Kaga*, *Akagi*, *Hiryū* and *Sōryū* – under command of Vice Admiral Nagumo Chūichi, which were supposed to neutralize aircraft on Midway and engage the American carriers as they responded to the threat.

The subsequent battle pitted a small and vulnerable American carrier force against a large portion of the Japanese Combined Fleet. The American commanders, Admiral Chester Nimitz in Hawaii and Rear Admiral Raymond 'Electric Brain' Spruance in charge of the carriers, had one un-anticipated advantage. A few days before the Japanese task forces arrived off Midway on 3 June, the navy's intelligence unit in Hawaii, run by Captain

Joseph Rochefort, had broken Japanese naval codes sufficiently to be sure that Midway Island was the enemy's destination and that the Japanese carrier strike force was approaching the island from the north-west, unlike the smaller invasion force moving due east.[7] Spruance and his fellow task-force commander, Rear Admiral Frank Fletcher, positioned the three American carriers north of Nagumo's group, to be ready to attack. Aircraft were scrambled at seven o'clock on the morning of 4 June 1942 once the Japanese carriers were located, but attacks by torpedo bombers from the carriers and medium bombers from Midway achieved nothing by mid-morning, when, for the loss of almost all the ninety-four aircraft despatched, not a single bomb or torpedo had hit the Japanese carriers.

The last gamble for the American side was the squadrons of fifty-four Dauntless dive-bombers which, in the absence of radar on Japanese ships, were only spotted as they dived – a 'beautiful silver waterfall', one eyewitness recalled. A total of ten bombs hit three of the Japanese carriers. At this point they were particularly vulnerable as crew refuelled the aircraft, surrounded by ordnance waiting to be loaded. *Kaga* was a blazing wreck within minutes; Nagumo's flagship *Akagi* was hit by one bomb that detonated the bombers already packed with fuel and bombs and became another inferno; the *Sōryū* was hit a few minutes later with the same result. Although *Yorktown* was crippled, and later sunk by Japanese torpedoes, there were enough dive-bombers left to finish off the fourth Japanese carrier, *Hiryū*, in the late afternoon. One-third of the highly trained carrier pilots were lost in the melee.[8] The Battle of Midway (the Japanese navy declined to give the engagement a name) has always been seen as a key turning point, but for all the intense drama of the day and the severe Japanese losses, it was less than that. For the long war ahead, Japan still had a formidable surface and submarine fleet, while the United States had for the moment only two carriers left, and, after damage to *Saratoga* and *Enterprise* and the sinking of *Wasp* in September and of *Hornet* in October 1942, briefly none.[9] The failure to capture Midway, and the earlier abandonment of the operation to seize Port Moresby, was quickly compensated by the full occupation in May and June 1942 of the British Solomon Islands protectorate much further to the south of the perimeter, where it was intended to build an airfield on Guadalcanal, the southernmost island, so that aircraft from there could interrupt the supply lines between Australia, the western United States and Hawaii.

While Japan was seizing further territory in Asia and the Pacific, Axis forces in North Africa pushed on to cross the Egyptian frontier to a point only 96 kilometres from the major British naval base at Alexandria and the Suez Canal beyond. This was the third swing of the pendulum as

British Empire forces engaged the Italian army, supported by just three German divisions of the German *Afrika Korps*, in a campaign that moved backwards and forwards across Cyrenaica as one side or the other reached exhaustion point. For most of the conflict after their disastrous defeat in summer 1941, British Empire forces had outnumbered, often by a significant margin, the ground and air forces available to the Axis. In November 1941, Operation 'Crusader', launched to relieve the siege of Tobruk by Wavell's replacement, General Claude Auchinleck, resulted in a messy attrition battle, but the problem of supply faced by Rommel and his Italian allies forced them to disengage and retire to El Agheila, where Rommel had started from earlier in the year. A sudden improvement in the flow of equipment allowed Rommel to renew the offensive in January 1942 against a tired enemy, and now British Empire forces were driven back to a line at Ain el Gazala, just west of the recently relieved Tobruk. The Italian chief of staff, General Ugo Cavallero, planned Operation '*Venezia*' ('Venice') with Rommel and the overall German commander in the south, Field Marshal Albert Kesselring, to retake Tobruk and push on to the Egyptian frontier. On 26 May, Rommel, who treated his Italian colleagues as subordinates rather than allies, ordered the assault on the Gazala line. The Axis had 90,000 men organized in 3 German divisions, the 15th and 21st Panzer and the 90th Light Division – the only German units that fought for almost the whole North African campaign – and 6 under-strength Italian divisions, all supported by 600 aircraft and 520 tanks (220 the less effective Italian models).[10] The British Eighth Army, now commanded, after several replacements, by Lieutenant General Neil Ritchie, had 100,000 men, 849 tanks and 604 aircraft, including Wellington medium bombers flying out of bases in Egypt. Dug in behind the Gazala line, with wide minefields in front, including the southern redoubt of Bir Hacheim, manned by a Free French unit, Ritchie's position looked on paper too strong for Axis armies already tired by their earlier effort.[11]

The Axis offensive proved risky and costly, but the response of the British side highlighted the deficiencies already exposed before – sending in units piecemeal, leaving infantry undefended by armour, unable to co-ordinate a battle of manoeuvre effectively – and allowed Rommel to gain the initiative. Bir Hacheim fell on 10 June after a bitter contest, allowing Rommel to swing north and attack the strung-out British armour in a fierce tank battle that ended with the almost complete annihilation of the Allied force. The Eighth Army fed 1,142 tanks into the battle and lost 1,009. By 13 June, the substantial armoured forces were down to just seventy operational tanks.[12] The Eighth Army retreated in disorder to Mersa Matruh on the Egyptian border and this time Rommel stormed

Tobruk in a single day, 20/21 June, capturing not only essential supplies of oil and food, but 33,000 British, South African and Indian soldiers, including 6 generals. Although Rommel's tired army was also reduced by the end of June to a mere hundred tanks (forty of them Italian), he chased the Eighth Army deep into Egyptian territory, to a 65-kilometre line between the small railway halt of El Alamein and the impassable Qatarra Depression. Mussolini flew to Libya with a large entourage on 26 June, ready to enter Cairo in triumph in the very near future. The news of the fall of Tobruk reached Churchill as he sat in the White House in conference with Roosevelt. The shock was visible. Promises were made to supply tanks and aircraft, even to send at once the American Second Armoured Division (which Roosevelt vetoed) or to establish an American army covering the region from Egypt to Tehran (which Churchill vetoed, unwilling to bring in Americans to a key imperial zone). The American ambassador in Cairo, Alex Kirk, privately reported on 'British bungling' due to 'defective strategy and dilatory methods' but Auchinleck himself confessed in his report to London that 'we are still largely an amateur army fighting professionals'.[13] Churchill gloomily confided in Ivan Maisky on 3 July, after making clear that defeat would make slim the prospect of a 'Second Front' in Europe in 1942: 'The Germans wage war better than we do . . . Also we lack the "Russian spirit": die but don't surrender.'[14]

That Russian spirit was again in evidence in the German conquest of further extensive territory during the summer and autumn of 1942 following the harsh defensive battles of the winter of 1941. Hitler hoped to complete the annihilation of the Red Army denied him in 1941, but the same strategic arguments emerged that had undermined the campaign the previous year. The army high command still favoured the seizure of Moscow as the decisive operation; Hitler preferred to continue the interrupted campaign southwards to the Volga and the Caucasus, perhaps now with the real prospect of joining forces with Rommel's drive towards the Suez Canal and Middle East oil. Critics talked of 'utopian offensive plans', but Hitler made it clear that he would not be deviated again by experts and commanders who said 'that is not possible, that won't work'. Problems, he continued, 'must unconditionally be solved' by sound leadership.[15] Hitler was intellectually committed to the idea that blockade – in this case cutting the Red Army off entirely from the heavy industry and oil it needed – was a vital component of modern warfare. As if to confirm his judgement, intelligence sources greatly underestimated the Red Army's potential strength and the capacity of Soviet industry, while it disregarded the growing weakness of German forces. By March 1942 the German army had lost over 1 million casualties, not all of whom could be replaced, together with large quantities of equipment from aircraft to small arms, only a fraction of which the German war economy was currently capable of making good. Of 162 divisions on the Eastern Front, only 8 were classified as fully combat ready for the coming battles.

On 5 April, Hitler issued Directive No. 41, 'to wipe out the entire defence potential remaining to the Soviets', to cut the Red Army off from essential supplies, then to capture Leningrad. The German campaign was codenamed Operation 'Blue'. It was a complex plan with four stages, each stage intended to unfold in sequence. German armies were to approach from three axes: in the north from the Orel area towards Voronezh, from the area around Kharkov (now Kharkiv) further south, and finally from the Crimea towards Rostov. They would meet at the great bend of the river Don where Army Group South would split: Army Group B was to hold the area from Rostov to Stalingrad to protect Army Group A as it moved into the Caucasus to capture the oilfields. In the process it was assumed that, once again, short encirclements would be enough to ensnare large swathes of the Red Army and end its capacity to resist. At this point Stalingrad was not centre stage. Hitler hoped it would be neutralized rather than captured. Cutting the Volga supply route to central Russia was the key, but not the city itself.

Hitler in his directive had ordered Army Group Centre to stay on the defensive, but the opposite conclusion was taken by Stalin, who assumed that the front facing Moscow, as in late 1941, was the most threatening, and as a result left the south relatively weaker. Hitler was not the only one guilty of utopian offensive planning. Stalin hoped that he could build on the winter successes by launching a series of offensives against the long 1,600-kilometre line to drive the Germans out of Soviet territory entirely.[16] This was to begin with offensives in the south, which Soviet intelligence mistakenly assumed was the weakest part of the German defensive line, first to retake the city of Kharkov, a vital Ukrainian rail junction for the German armed forces, then to recapture the Crimea. Beginning on 12 May, Marshal Semyon Timoshenko pushed two major army groups into Kharkov and beyond as German defences temporarily wilted in the face of an enemy much more organized and heavily armed than in 1941, but it proved possible for German Army Group South to draw the Soviet forces into a trap as Timoshenko pushed the armour on too fast beyond the infantry. In a classic battle of encirclement, Operation 'Fredericus' cut the vulnerable rear lines of the Soviet armies, and after ten days the trap snapped shut. By 28 May 240,000 Red Army soldiers, 1,200 tanks and 2,600 guns were lost, a victory that seemed to underscore Hitler's optimism about 'Blue'.[17] A second Soviet offensive to retake the Crimea was repulsed and three further armies, the Forty-fourth, Forty-seventh and Fifty-first, annihilated with the loss of 170,000 prisoners. In June, von Manstein was given the task of capturing Sevastopol on the Black Sea, supported by von Richthofen's Fourth Air Fleet. The city surrendered after an unendurable bombardment only on 4 July, with 95,000 more prisoners, earning von Manstein a field marshal's baton, but holding up the start of the main operation.[18]

The new campaign opened on 28 June and within days the same pace of advance was achieved as the year before and with much the same level of surprise. Even after Churchill had warned Stalin via Ultra intercepts of German dispositions, and even after the discovery of the battle plan when a German aircraft crashed behind Soviet lines on 19 June, Stalin was as convinced of deliberate disinformation as he had been in June 1941.[19] Voronezh was taken on 9 July, but progress was held up by furious flank attacks which had to be staved off before the northern wing could swing south, pursuing what seemed a demoralized and disorganized enemy. On 25 July Rostov was seized and this time held against opposition that melted away across the plains leading to Stalingrad. After the great encirclements of 1941, Red Army soldiers had no desire to fall into any new German trap, but their caution left the German army unable to fulfil the aim to 'wipe out' the enemy's capacity for further warfare. 'The Army High Command,' complained von Bock, now commander of Army Group South, 'would like to encircle an enemy who is no longer there.'[20] German armour met up in the Don bend without trapping the numbers expected, and was now only 120 kilometres from Stalingrad. 'Blue' had not gone to schedule or achieved its maximum aims, but despite the growing pessimism of his commanders as they occupied large tracts of largely undefended Russian territory, Hitler believed 'the Russian is finished' and issued a fresh directive on 23 July for what was now called Operation '*Braunschweig*' ('Brunswick'). Under the code name 'Edelweiss', Army Group A, commanded by Field Marshal Wilhelm von List, was to clear the area south of the Don before moving into the Caucasus region where the army would divide, part to capture the Black Sea coast as far as Baku, part to seize the passes over the Caucasus, and part to occupy the oil city of Grozny; Army Group B, now commanded by Colonel General Maximilian von Weichs after Hitler had sacked von Bock a second time, was to cross the river Don to seize Stalingrad, secure control of the lower Volga and then move on to capture Astrakhan, under the codename 'Heron' ('*Fischreiher*').[21] The contradiction was clear to many of Hitler's commanders: more and more territory to be occupied by fewer and fewer troops.

Red Army forces displayed a mounting panic as the German advance rolled towards them, abandoning hastily constructed defensive lines, and their heavy weapons, ignoring the threats of their officers and the military commissars. On 28 July Stalin issued his own *Haltebefehl* to the troops. Order 227, *Ne Shagu Nazad* (Not a Step Back), insisted that 'each metre of Soviet territory must be stubbornly defended, to the last drop of blood'.[22] Security service 'blocking units', created for the panics of 1941, moved into place to catch all alleged cowards and slackers, who could either be shot or placed in penal battalions, although most were simply returned to their units. This did not prevent further authorized withdrawal, since Stalin too did not want a repeat of the prisoner losses of the previous summer, and he ordered commanders to avoid the German army's now notorious pincers.

Army Group B pushed towards the Don River, its long flanks protected by the Axis forces from Romania, Italy and Hungary, now expanded considerably under German pressure: five Romanian divisions, ten Hungarian and five Italian. German armour found the flat steppe ideal tank country, but there was little to fight. 'It was,' recorded one German soldier, 'easily the most desolate and mournful region of the East that came before my eyes. A barren, naked, lifeless steppe, without a bush, without a tree, for miles without a village.'[23] This was to be new German territory once Stalingrad, now the definite objective of General Friedrich Paulus's Sixth Army, had been captured in a swift *coup de main*. On the map the vast new territories looked impressive. Further south the oil city of Maikop was occupied by Army Group A in early August, and on 21 August German alpine troops raised the flag at the summit of Mount Elbrus, the highest peak in the Caucasus mountains (an achievement that sent Hitler into fury over time wasted mountaineering). This was the point when ultimate victory in all three Axis theatres seemed fleetingly possible.

The summer of 1942 was the low point in the war for the Allies, which were forced to fight three separate wars in Russia, North Africa and Asia, with little connection between them save the supply of Lend-Lease goods. Even this was limited in 1942 as the inter-Allied logistical structure was slowly put in place against the continued threat of submarine attack in the Atlantic (a campaign dealt with in Chapter 6). American belligerency at first made small difference to the overall Allied war effort, despite the enormous economic potential now at the Allies' disposal, and despite the brief triumph at Midway. Roosevelt made much of telling the American public, and his Axis enemies, about the sheer scale of American military production, but the public might well have asked what the 47,826 aircraft and 24,997 tanks produced in 1942 were doing. No American bomb dropped on German soil until January 1943; no American ground units were in action in mainland Europe until July 1943; the first land battle in the Pacific began in August 1942 with just one division. From anxiety before Pearl Harbor that the American public did not want war, Roosevelt now worried that there was not enough war to satisfy them.

For American planners, faced with the crisis of the British Empire and the Soviet Union, it was essential to frame American strategy in American terms. The collapse of the British position in South East Asia ended a brief period in which American, Australian, Dutch and British Empire forces were united under a British overall commander, General Wavell. In the Pacific theatre the United States military established two American commands: Pacific Ocean Command under Admiral Chester Nimitz, and the Southwest Pacific Command under General MacArthur. Australian forces were now integrated into the United States' command structure under MacArthur, a step that Australian leaders welcomed after the British failure to hold Asia and the sudden threat of a possible Japanese invasion, and, until late 1943, Australians constituted the majority of ground forces in the south-west Pacific.[24] The Pacific theatre was now an American affair until much later in the war, in 1945, when Britain was at last in a position to offer to participate. At the 'Arcadia' meeting in December 1941, it had been agreed that Europe was the priority, but Churchill and his chiefs of staff wanted to focus on the Mediterranean theatre first before trying to re-enter the European mainland. They developed, in agreement with Roosevelt, a plan codenamed 'Gymnast' for an operation against French North Africa as a way of relieving the pressure on Egypt, but American military leaders saw this as backdoor support for the British Empire, and preferred to relieve pressure on the Soviet Union by an early landing in northern Europe.[25] General Marshall's director of plans, Brigadier General Dwight D. Eisenhower, fulminated against 'amateur strategists', as indeed Churchill and Roosevelt were, and planned for an early operation in Europe, given the codename 'Sledgehammer', followed by a major assault with forty-eight divisions in 1943, codenamed 'Roundup'. This was a strategy more consistent with the American military doctrine of concentration of force, and a rejection of the peripheral strategy favoured in London. Roosevelt was told that 'Gymnast' was not possible, and the news was passed on to Churchill on 9 March.[26]

The direct approach to confronting Germany had a number of motives apart from the desire to avoid any impression that the United States was fighting Britain's war. In the aftermath of Pearl Harbor, American opinion was affected by a sense of powerlessness in the face of the Japanese assault and growing disillusionment with Roosevelt's leadership after the first wave of angry enthusiasm for war. Isolationist leaders abandoned their campaign, but rank-and-file isolationists preferred a Japan-first strategy and retained their distrust of involvement in a European war. Polls in the first months of 1942 consistently recorded large majorities in favour of concentrating on the Pacific.[27] Marshall's hope for an initial landing in German-occupied Europe later in 1942 was one way to still the criticism and to reignite commitment on the home front. In March, Roosevelt told Churchill that the United States wanted a campaign in Europe 'this summer'.[28] The other concern was the survival of the Soviet Union. Fear of a possible Soviet–German armistice explains Marshall's insistence that a front had to be established in Western Europe to siphon away German forces from the East. The fear also underlay Roosevelt's decision in March to back the idea of 'Sledgehammer'. In June 1942, during Molotov's visit to Washington, Roosevelt assured him that Stalin could 'expect the formation of a Second Front this year', a commitment that even Marshall considered to be premature.[29] For all Roosevelt's grasp of geopolitical realities, his strategic and operational understanding was limited. The promise to the British to support 'Gymnast', like his unconditional promise of a 'Second Front' to Molotov, were political calculations, designed to ensure continued British and Soviet belligerency, rather than sober military commitments.

Marshall's planning opened yet another serious breach in the Anglo-American alliance. The dismal failures in Libya only confirmed American prejudices against a North African adventure. Marshall was sent twice to London to argue his case, and although the British gave lip-service to the idea of 'Sledgehammer' and 'Roundup' because of fears that American leaders would otherwise turn away to fight Japan, the private view of Churchill and the British Chiefs of Staff was entirely negative.[30] Following Molotov's visit, Churchill and General Alan Brooke, chief of the Imperial General Staff, arrived in Washington to try to change Roosevelt's mind. The North African operation was, Churchill claimed, 'the true Second Front in Europe', though later in the year he tried to persuade Stalin that the bombing of Germany was now the 'Second Front'.[31] The president hedged by allowing planning to continue on both 'Sledgehammer' and 'Gymnast', but on 8 July, back in London, Churchill cabled to confirm that the British rejected entirely the idea of an invasion of mainland Europe in 1942. Fears that this would affect the Europe-first strategy were not misplaced. Marshall told Roosevelt two days later that if the British persisted, he would turn to the Pacific 'and drive for a decision against Japan'.[32] Churchill privately deplored Marshall's threat – 'Just because the Americans can't have a massacre in France this year, they want to sulk and battle in the Pacific' – but it was a serious one.[33] Marshall won the support of the other Joint Chiefs, as well as the secretary of war, Henry Stimson, and the secretary for the navy, Frank Knox, to lobby Roosevelt for a shift in priorities that properly reflected American interests. The revolt against British strategy was only ended when Roosevelt, for whom the Atlantic commitment had always been more important, finally ordered Marshall on 25 July to abandon an invasion of Europe and prepare for 'Gymnast' (now renamed 'Torch'), so that American forces would be in action before the end of the year – if possible, before the mid-term Congressional elections in November. July 1942 was the only time that Roosevelt invoked his formal role as commander-in-chief, signing under that title, in order to compel his military staff to obey him. Eisenhower, architect of the 'Sledgehammer' plan, thought the decision would be 'the blackest day in history'.[34] American military chiefs found themselves forced to prepare for an operation they did not want in a region where British interests were evidently at play.

The British view that 'Sledgehammer' would have been a disastrous failure was not wrong. The American plan, drawn up by Eisenhower and his team, to take between five and ten divisions across the Channel to occupy Cherbourg and the Cotentin Peninsula as a prelude to a fuller invasion the following spring, bore no relation to reality. When an Anglo-Canadian raid (Operation 'Jubilee') was mounted in force against Dieppe on 19 August to test the defences and offer some support to the Soviet Union, it was eliminated in a matter of hours by German defenders who puzzled over its purpose. The American preoccupation with 'Sledgehammer' stemmed as much from the desire to impose an American strategy on a recalcitrant ally, whose apparent obsession with the defence of Egypt seemed remote from the real war for Europe, as a desire to help the Red Army. Marshall's frustrated disappointment was shared by the Soviet leadership. Molotov took a promise to be a promise and Stalin took the assurance at face value. The Soviet military leadership shared the American strategic doctrine of the direct approach, and both suspected that British preferences betrayed a greater concern with long-term imperial interests than with the task of defeating Germany together.

'Nineteen forty-two was a year of extraordinary contrasts,' wrote Churchill's military chief of staff, Hastings Ismay, in his memoirs. 'It opened on a scene of hideous calamity,' but it ended with 'a complete reversal of fortune.'[35] While the Allies wrangled over priorities, the scene was set for the three battles that separately but simultaneously transformed the strategic outlook in the Pacific, Russia and North Africa and passed the initiative to the Allies. At Guadalcanal, El Alamein and Stalingrad a turning point was reached: all three are worth exploring in some detail. There were profound differences in scale and context between them. Guadalcanal involved a handful of divisions and a good many ships and naval aircraft fighting over control of an island airfield; El Alamein was also small in scale by comparison with war on the Eastern Front but was waged as a major air and tank battle over substantial distances, unlike Guadalcanal; the Stalingrad campaign was a titanic struggle spread over much of southern Russia, involving hundreds of thousands of men, entire air fleets and thousands of tanks. Nor could the three combat environments have been more different. Guadalcanal was a small island, 145 kilometres long and 40 kilometres wide, covered for the most part by a dense jungle where huge wasps, scorpions, snakes, giant crocodiles and leeches (which dropped on human flesh from the trees above) all added to the dangers posed by the enemy; malaria, dysentery, dengue and 'scrub typhus' were endemic.[36] Nearly all the soldiers of both sides who fought on Guadalcanal succumbed to one or other disease. El Alamein was fought in barren desert over distances hundreds of kilometres from supply bases (in Rommel's case by July 1942 over 1,450 kilometres from the main port of Tripoli), where soldiers coped with extreme heat, plagues of flies, sandstorms that could change local topography overnight, choking and blinding dust that made combat a military blind man's buff, and the regular threat of skin ulcers, dysentery and severe dehydration. Stalingrad was fought for the most critical weeks amidst the ruins of a large conurbation, some 65 kilometres wide, first in intense heat, later in bitter cold. Dysentery, typhoid fever and frostbite probably affected the attacker more, but the battleground was one of shared hardships on a major scale. One thing the three had in common: none was a decisive struggle of a few days, but each lasted for months before reaching a conclusion, when local victory was unequivocally clear.

The Solomon Islands were occupied in May 1942 when the capital Tulagi was seized from the retreating British. In June, Korean labourers and Japanese engineers, with a small garrison of around 1,700 troops, were sent to Guadalcanal, the largest island, to construct a strategic airbase, to be finished by mid-August. It was not only to be a threat to Allied shipping but would protect the Japanese navy's main base at Rabaul on New Britain, further to the north. The Japanese military did not anticipate Allied intervention until at least 1943, but the United States naval commander-in-chief, Admiral Ernest King, urged the Pacific Fleet to undertake a counter-offensive as soon as possible in the summer months. Knowledge of the potential danger from the airstrip on Guadalcanal made the island an obvious target but only in early July was Operation 'Watchtower' authorized by Nimitz, employing the navy's First Marine

Division.[37] The preparations were hurried and inadequate for a major amphibious operation in terrain about which so little was known that navy intelligence relied on old copies of *National Geographic* and a handful of interviews with missionaries to build a picture of the target island. Aerial photographs were taken but arrived for the invading marines only after they were already ashore.[38] Both MacArthur and the head of the navy's South Pacific Command, Vice Admiral Robert Ghormley, thought the risks too high and urged cancellation, but King was insistent that a blow had to be struck somewhere. Despite limited training and a shortage of supplies for a campaign of unpredictable length, Major General Alexander Vandegrift's First Marine Division was embarked from New Zealand on twenty-five transports commanded by Rear Admiral Richmond Turner, protected by a naval task force under Vice Admiral Frank Fletcher, including the only serviceable carriers.

The seventy-six ships arrived undetected off the northern shore of Guadalcanal on the night of 6/7 August 1942 and marines clambered into the landing craft, most of the 23,000 destined for the shore, with smaller detachments to capture Tulagi and two other small islands. They were fortunate that complete surprise was achieved, helped by heavy rain and mist as the convoy approached, but there was little the Japanese garrison could have done against overwhelming odds. The Korean labourers and soldiers fled into the surrounding jungle, leaving stores and equipment behind undamaged. At Tulagi and the smaller islands, resistance was stiffer, but over by 8 August. The marines got the first taste of Japanese battlefield behaviour in these early engagements, when soldiers refused to give up even when it was pointless to continue fighting. On the two smallest islands, 886 were killed and only 23 men captured, a ratio to be repeated across the Pacific.[39] The marines established a firm defensive perimeter around the airfield, which they named Henderson Field after a marine major killed at Midway. The airfield came under regular air attack from long-range bombers sent from Japanese bases further north, prompting Fletcher to withdraw his carriers after two days, and Turner to withdraw the vulnerable transports, some still unloaded, a few days later, leaving just four days' supply of ammunition. The few major surface vessels left were almost completely destroyed on the night of 8/9 August in a night-time attack by a Japanese task force in the channels around Savo Island to the north of the airfield. The marines were fortunate again that the Japanese military in Rabaul miscalculated the nature of the threat they faced, assuming that only 2,000 marines had landed instead of more than 20,000, an intelligence failure that persisted for weeks. On 18 August, a small relief force of 2,000 men led by Colonel Ichiki Kiyonao, the man whose soldiers had sparked the Marco Polo Bridge incident in 1937, was landed near the airbase with orders to take it back. Without waiting for the second half of his soldiers to disembark, he rushed to attack the marines' perimeter. His unit was annihilated almost to a man and Ichiki, badly wounded, committed ritual suicide before he could be caught.[40]

The failed attack coincided with the arrival of the first marine aircraft on the now-completed airstrip. From that point on, except for a few occasions when heavy naval gunfire temporarily rendered the runway unusable, or damaged the aircraft based there, regular reinforcement of what came to be called the 'Cactus Air Force' ('Cactus' was the codename for Guadalcanal) gave the American garrison an important force multiplier. Above all, aircraft could be used to attack the transport ships that moved backwards and forwards between Rabaul and Guadalcanal as the Japanese supreme command came to realize that the American bridgehead was a genuine threat, and a challenge to the prestige of the Japanese army after months of easy conquests. On 28 August, General Yamamoto ordered Operation 'Ka', a major troop convoy using the 5,600 soldiers who had been detailed to land on Midway, supported by a large naval force, including three of Nagumo's remaining carriers. A carrier-on-carrier engagement followed in the Battle of the Eastern Solomons, forcing Nagumo to disengage after losing thirty-three valuable carrier aircraft; left to fend for itself, the troop transport was attacked from the air and forced to turn back.[41] Over the following months, thousands of Japanese soldiers were fed in, unit by unit, at night – 20,000 by October, 43,000 by the end of the campaign. But their performance against embedded defences and a professional marine corps failed entirely to match the battle performance displayed in seizing the Southern Region. A second major assault planned for September under Major General Kawaguchi Kiyotake met the same fate as Ichiki's. The assault force was divided for attacks east, west and south of the airfield, but poor communication led to uncoordinated operations, spread over three days, lacking in tactical imagination. The main operation on 12 September against a low ridge to the south of the airbase – soon nicknamed 'Bloody Ridge' – consisted of repeated charges at the defensive line until Kawaguchi's force mainly lay in rapidly decomposing piles of those killed. Japanese soldiers named Guadalcanal the 'Island of Death'.

On 18 September, the Japanese Supreme Headquarters gave Guadalcanal priority over all other operations, bringing to a sudden end the plan to advance on Chongqing and undermining operations on Papua New Guinea. Lieutenant General Hyakutake Harukichi was ordered to use the Seventeenth Army to snuff out the American bridgehead, but while the Japanese navy continued to duel effectively with the weaker United States

navy task forces, and to bombard the airfield regularly, the army operations repeated the same pattern against an American force with extensive
heavy artillery and tanks concentrated in a small enclave. A three-day
assault between 23–25 October was beaten off once again with heavy
Japanese casualties. One more attempt was made to send a large amphibious force to arrive on 14 November, with 11 troop ships crammed with
30,000 men, escorted by a large task force based around the battleships
Hiei and *Kirishima*. A small American squadron under Rear Admiral
Daniel Callaghan was sent north after successfully protecting a troop
transport of 6,000 men to Henderson Field, and engaged in a head-on
collision with the battleship force under Vice Admiral Abe Hiroaki. Callaghan was killed, but Abe's flagship *Hiei* was badly damaged, and Abe
wounded. The Japanese battleship was sunk by air attack the following
day as it tried to limp away. Vice Admiral Kondō Nobutake was ordered
by Yamamoto to sail on in the damaged battleship *Kirishima* and bombard the airbase, so that the troop convoy could get through, but it was
met by two battleships deployed by Fletcher's replacement, Vice Admiral
William Halsey, one of which, the *Washington*, had a commander who
understood the recently introduced fire-directing radar. The Japanese battleship was wrecked in a first accurate salvo and sank on 15 November.[42]
The troop transport was stranded as it approached in daylight, expecting
that the enemy air force had been neutralized. Instead, it was met by a hail
of bombs that sank six transports at sea. Four more made it to the beach
but were destroyed by air and artillery bombardment.

The First Marine Division was relieved finally in November and
December and Vandegrift handed responsibility to the army commander
of the 50,000 men of XIV Corps, Major General Alexander Patch. By
then the conflict was almost over. The remaining Japanese garrison dug in,
but in Tokyo the decision was taken to abandon the struggle for an island
base that could no longer be supplied reliably and had cost many more
ships and pilots than Midway. On 31 December Emperor Hirohito
approved the withdrawal and on 20 January 1943 Operation 'Ke' was
begun to evacuate those soldiers still capable of walking.[43] In night-time
convoys, 10,642 men were lifted off Guadalcanal, leaving behind the
wounded and debilitated to mount a final feeble defence. With almost no
food or proper supplies, the evacuated soldiers were skeletal, almost all ill,
many of them incapable of ever returning to combat again. Over the five
months of the battle the Japanese army (and ground naval forces) had lost
32,000 men, the majority to starvation and disease as food supplies dwindled away; an estimated 12,000 Japanese seamen died, and over 2,000
aircrew, including hundreds of the most experienced pilots.[44] The First

Marine Division, which undertook the bulk of the campaign, lost 1,242 men killed, a fraction of the losses that would be sustained in later battles across the Pacific; the United States navy lost 4,911 crew, the air forces 420.[45] For the Japanese armed forces, Guadalcanal was a disaster, absorbing a large military effort with heavy losses of men, ships and aircraft for a single distant airbase. The disproportion revealed a paranoia about defence of the new perimeter, but the battle also came to symbolize, as did Stalingrad, a moment of truth for a regime whose armed forces had already reached the limit of what could be achieved.

The long struggle on the El Alamein line developed simultaneously with the unfolding battle on Guadalcanal. There was much more at stake in the desert battle than in the Pacific, for beyond the barren landscape where the battle was fought lay the fading possibility of Axis conquest of Egypt, seizure of the Suez Canal and acquisition of Middle East oil. Hitler was privately buoyant about the prospects when he discussed the Middle East with his armaments minister, Albert Speer, in August: 'The English will have to look on impotently as their colonial empire falls to pieces . . . by the end of 1943 we will pitch our tents in Tehran, in Baghdad, and on the Persian Gulf.'[46] Churchill called the coming conflict the 'Battle of Egypt' and asked Auchinleck to defend the territory as if he were resisting the invasion of Kent. He was pessimistic at the outcome: 'Nothing seems to help them,' he complained to the army chief of operations, 'I doubt that army's offensive spirit.' Roosevelt, too, doubted the outcome for an army whose commanders had made 'every mistake in the book'.[47] So real was the threat perceived to be that embassy staff in Cairo spent the first days of July 1942 burning secret papers, whose charred sheets wafted on the wind into the nearby streets, while in London the chiefs of staff drew up a 'Worst Possible Case' for evacuation to the Upper Nile in Sudan, and a final defensive line in Syria and Palestine.[48]

In truth, the Axis success at Gazala and Tobruk had weakened a force already strung out far from its supply bases. A successful offensive was fanciful with only 10,000 tired troops left. At the moment in late June when Rommel hoped his opponent was too battered and demoralized to resist a final thrust, the *Afrika Korps* was down to fifty-five operational tanks, the Italian armoured divisions down to fifteen. The *Ariete* Division had just eight tanks and forty guns, losing thirty-six of these on the opening day of the new offensive.[49] It was certainly the case that the Eighth Army rank and file were disillusioned by the months of defeats and retreats. Censors detected an increase in 'indiscreet and defeatist talk' in soldiers' letters.[50] On the El Alamein line there was a general expectation of further withdrawal to the Nile Delta. To stem the crisis, Auchinleck took the unusual step of abandoning his Middle East Command in Cairo to his deputy, to take direct command of Eighth Army, leaving a vacuum at the heart of the military machine in the Middle East. By dint of effort, he organized a series of defensive boxes, wide apart, which he hoped would have enough concentrated firepower to hold up the enemy attack. On 1 July began what historians usually call the First Battle of Alamein, the first stage of a contest that went on until early November. The first battle quickly devolved into a series of smaller engagements as Rommel tried to break down the boxes and swing once again into the enemy rear as he had done at Gazala. Conditions were poor as sand was whipped up along with the usual battle dust, while Rommel had scanty intelligence on the enemy, not least because German interception of secret information from the American military attaché in Cairo, on which the Axis had relied up to June, was finally discovered and eliminated. His armour was held up at once by fire from an undetected box at Deir el Shein and it took almost the whole day to defeat and drive off the Indian brigade which held it. When the Italians and the German Ninetieth Light Division tried to push through further north to the sea to encircle and cut off the main Eighth Army box, heavy concentrated artillery fire pinned down the advance and provoked a temporary panic, blocking further movement. The German and Italian divisions were bombarded relentlessly from the air by the Western Desert Air Force, which at one point was mounting the equivalent of an operational sortie every minute. On 2 and 3 July Rommel bullied his men to attack again, but the high casualties, shortages of fuel and vehicles, and sheer exhaustion, brought the abortive drive to the Delta and the Suez Canal to an end. Luck might have helped Rommel, but the operation was a gamble, given the state of the *Afrika Korps*. He ordered a halt and prepared to dig in opposite the Alamein defences.

With growing reinforcement, Auchinleck opted not to stay on the defensive but to try to defeat an enemy now considerably weakened. He launched four attacks during July, none of which succeeded in breaking the enemy line. Over the course of the month since Rommel's initial attack, the Eighth Army had suffered 13,000 casualties and had achieved almost nothing. In early August, Churchill and General Brooke arrived in Egypt on the way to meet Stalin. Churchill, infuriated by what he saw as Auchinleck's lack of drive, sacked him and appointed General Harold Alexander as head of Middle East Command in his place; one of the Eighth Army Corps commanders, Lieutenant General William Gott, was appointed to command the whole army on 6 August. He was killed in an air crash the following day, and Churchill was finally persuaded to appoint Lieutenant General Bernard Montgomery as his replacement. He arrived from England to

Eighth Army headquarters on 13 August. According to reputation, so friends told the New Zealand Second Division chief of staff, Montgomery was 'understood to be mad'. He was certainly regarded as an eccentric egotist, keen to stamp his mark on every command. The German file on Montgomery was closer to the truth, describing a 'hard man', quite ruthless in carrying through what he wanted.[51] To make clear that all talk of further retreat was to cease, he told the army on his arrival '*Here* we will stand and fight; there will be no further withdrawal ... If we can't stay here alive, then let us stay here dead.' He was soon faced with the prospect of a renewed Axis offensive thanks to Ultra intelligence, which left him little time to impose a fresh start. Yet his initial impact proved salutary in the extreme. Within a week, censor reports showed that 'a breath of fresh, invigorating air has swept through British troops in Egypt.'[52]

By the end of August, both sides had used the pause to rebuild their shattered forces. The flow of new troops to the Axis armies was impressive given the logistical problems, but the German and Italian divisions remained critically low on supplies of fuel and ammunition, which were intercepted and sunk by Allied submarines and aircraft. Between one-third and one-half of the oil and vehicles shipped to Libya were lost in September and October, a restraint on Axis strategy in the desert that could not be reversed given the commitment of German air power on the Russian front and the erosion of the Italian merchant fleet.[53] The transport bringing what fuel there was to a front hundreds of miles distant consumed up to three-quarters of the supply before it arrived. The capture of Tobruk had provided little relief because it could handle only 10,000 tons of cargo a month, even without regular bombardment, when the Axis armies needed 100,000.[54] Cavellero and Kesselring both promised Rommel that emergency measures would be taken to provide the fuel and ammunition needed, but by the time Rommel was ready to retake the offensive there was enough fuel for just eight days of campaigning. The balance of forces was less pessimistic: there were now 84,000 German and 44,000 Italian troops facing 135,000 Empire forces, and 234 German and 281 Italian tanks facing 693 of the enemy.[55] Air power was a critical difference because Rommel was now far away from the airbases that could support him, while the Western Desert Air Force was within easy flying distance of the front and the Axis supply lines.

Rommel planned what was by now a conventional German battle plan, to penetrate the Allied front through the southern minefields and then swing north-east to cut off the main forces on one of the flat ridges at Alam el Halfa, where Allied infantry was dug in with artillery and anti-tank guns. Montgomery's defence rested heavily on plans already drawn up by Auchinleck's staff, but it hinged on using air power to degrade Axis armour as it struggled through the minefields and to concentrate artillery in a defensive barrage along the ridge itself. New equipment promised to make a significant difference: Allied armoured forces now had growing numbers of American Grant and Sherman tanks, which had a major advantage over British tanks because they could fire both armour-piercing and high-explosive shells – the first to deal with enemy armour, the second to eliminate anti-tank and artillery batteries. Montgomery was also supplied with growing numbers of heavier anti-tank guns, which could at last cope with the existing German models. What Montgomery did add to the plan was to insist that he was fighting a largely static defensive battle, relying on artillery and air power, and to avoid a mobile war of manoeuvre, which the Eighth Army had failed entirely to master.

Of the two plans, only the British one worked. What might have been the Second Battle of Alamein was named instead after the Alam el Halfa Ridge, since the overall engagement was limited to the German failure to seize it. On the night of 30 August, the Panzer divisions began their move through the minefields so that they would arrive in open desert by morning. Instead, the cramped build-up of men and vehicles became exposed to relentless heavy bombing throughout the night as flares illuminated the target. The hold-up meant that fuel consumption was dangerously high and by the morning Rommel had to abandon the idea of a broad sickle-cut around the enemy army in favour of a more limited assault on the Alam el Halfa Ridge itself. Here his force was pinned down by a deadly artillery barrage and concealed anti-tank batteries. For two days Rommel's forces probed without success, almost devoid of fuel and facing a pounding from air and artillery that undermined German and Italian morale – a barrage 'such as I have never experienced', wrote one of the victims after seven hours of shelling.[56] By 2 September Rommel was forced to order a fighting withdrawal back to his starting lines but the Italian motorized divisions, with no fuel or transport, abandoned two-thirds of their men and one-third of their guns. This was the final fling of a limited, undersupplied force. It was not, however, decisive. Rommel and his fellow Italian commanders dug in behind a dense belt of 445,000 mines in the knowledge that the enemy would grow stronger by the day.[57] Alam el Halfa as much as the final battle, Second Alamein, put an end to the hope that British battlefield ineptitude would deliver the Middle East to the Axis.

For the final battle, Montgomery did have the opportunity to impose his mark on the army under his command. He opted for a set-piece battle – almost certainly the only option on a narrow front defended in depth – because he understood the limitations of the force under his command: 'I limit the scope of operations,' he claimed, 'to what is possible, and I use the force necessary to achieve success.'[58] Given the weaknesses already displayed, Montgomery's decision to draw up a clear and detailed plan for the coming operation faced up to reality, though he has often been blamed for his excessive caution. The outline for what was to be known as Operation 'Lightfoot' was drawn up on 6 October and then modified following discussion with his commanders four days later. Montgomery wanted the battle to be a team effort, even while he played the full part of team captain. The earlier defeats had highlighted the difficulties in organizing a multinational empire army under British commanders.[59] Montgomery spent time mending bridges. He also understood how important it was to integrate ground and air attack and developed a close relationship with Air Vice-Marshal Arthur Coningham's Western Desert Air Force. The tactical headquarters of air and ground were now to be close together. He also insisted on integrating armour and infantry through the simple method of getting the commanders to mix together and discuss how they might co-operate. The failure to provide proper cover for infantry had long been a bone of contention. Finally, artillery was to be concentrated to deliver a lethal barrage, reminiscent of 1918.

To ensure that the plan was understood, and the concept of combined arms properly adopted, Montgomery introduced a month of intensive training, including battle inoculation in exercises using live ammunition and mines.[60] Behind all the reforms lay a wealth of new equipment, much of it from the United States, which provided 21 per cent of the tank force and almost half the squadrons of the Western Desert Air Force. The American army air forces established the Tenth Air Force in Egypt, armed with B-24 and B-17 bombers, which pounded the Libyan ports supplying the Axis and the convoys plying the dangerous routes across the Mediterranean.[61] By mid-October the weight of men and equipment facing the Axis front was potentially overwhelming: 12 understrength Axis divisions of 80,000 men (4 German, 8 Italian) facing 10 Allied divisions with 230,000 men; 548 tanks (including 280 of the weaker Italian models and only 123 of the most effective German tanks) opposed to 1,060 for the Allied forces; 350 aircraft against 530, with many more Allied aircraft available from bases further east.[62] The difference in the numbers of artillery pieces and all-important anti-tank weapons was much narrower, but Italian divisions were seriously under strength and short of modern guns. The 'Folgore' parachute division, which distinguished itself in the final battle, nonetheless lacked almost all heavy equipment.[63]

The Allied plan for El Alamein was to attack with infantry to the north of the line against enemy infantry, principally Italian, and then follow up with armour to stave off the expected counter-attack. The Axis front was to be 'crumbled' by daily attrition. An elaborate deception plan, which Montgomery insisted on, seemed to show a mass of armour in the south, compelling Rommel to keep the Twenty-first Panzer and the Italian armoured *Ariete* Division opposite what was in effect a phantom threat.[64] The operation was scheduled for the night of 23 October, while Rommel was absent in Germany to recover his health. A massive artillery barrage prefaced the opening infantry assault, cutting German line communications. Rommel's replacement, General Georg Stumme, had little idea what was going on, so drove to the front, only to suffer a fatal heart attack when his car was strafed. By the time Rommel arrived on the evening of the 25th, the British Empire push in the north threatened a critical breakthrough, supported by relentless artillery and air attack. Montgomery's plan did not work perfectly, but the reforms paid dividends. Axis tank and anti-tank forces held off British armour for two days, but by 26 October Fifteenth Panzer had only 39 tanks left, while the Eighth Army still had 754.[65] The Axis forces 'crumbled' in an unwinnable war of attrition.

By then, Rommel realized he had been tricked in the south and moved the Twenty-first Panzer and half the *Ariete* Division north to stop the breakthrough. He warned the German OKW that this was a battle he could not win, and when Montgomery altered his plan to mount Operation 'Supercharge' on 1 November – a combined infantry/armour assault on the north of the line – the breakthrough could not be contained. Rommel informed Hitler and the Italian supreme command that he was withdrawing. On 3 November, Hitler issued yet another *Haltebefehl* – 'no other road but victory or death' – but the Axis front was indeed melting away. Rommel had just thirty-five tanks left by 2 November, and had lost half his infantry and artillery, including all his heavy 88mm anti-aircraft guns used for destroying enemy armour.[66] Hitler relented and permitted a limited retreat, but General Antonio Gandin at the Italian Supreme Headquarters continued to insist on holding the line. The result was that six Italian divisions were almost entirely destroyed, those in the south abandoned with little ammunition, food or water and no vehicles. The Allies captured 7,429 German prisoners and 21,521 Italians, to add to the 7,000 Axis dead and wounded; Eighth Army had 13,560 casualties, 2,350 of them dead.[67] Montgomery had developed only a limited plan for pursuit and while Allied forces chased Rommel along the Libyan coast, reaching Tripoli by January, they were unable to ensnare what remained of the battered Axis armies. The defeat was nevertheless comprehensive enough. The Italian war effort was virtually over, while the German armed forces wasted a large quantity of manpower and equipment for a campaign to secure the Middle East and its oil for which the resources were manifestly inadequate and the strategy unfocused. Hitler in the end had wasted valuable military assets fighting over long stretches of desert. Although the Second Battle of El Alamein is often presented as a matter of touch-and-go, Rommel was never sufficiently supported by Hitler to make victory possible. Rommel would fight another day as his forces retreated into French Tunisia, but on 8 November 65,000 American and British soldiers were landed in north-west Africa in Operation 'Torch' to crush Axis forces from west and east. Only then, on 15 November, did Churchill authorize the church bells to be rung across Britain for the first time in the war.[68]

The contests at Guadalcanal and El Alamein were important turning points in both theatres, but they were dwarfed by the gigantic conflict that emerged from the German effort to cut the Volga and to capture Soviet oil. The battles engulfed millions of soldiers and resulted in military casualties greater than those suffered by either Britain or the United States in the entire war. While 22 divisions battled in the desert, there were 310 German and Soviet divisions locked in combat in and around Stalingrad, a force of well over 2 million men.[69] Like El Alamein, the date of the start of the Stalingrad battle was unclear. Soviet history had the battle beginning on 17 July 1942 when the Sixty-second and Sixty-fourth Armies clashed with the German Sixth Army along the Chir River, only 96 kilometres from Stalingrad, but it was only later in July that Hitler finally decided he wanted to capture the city rather than lay siege to it. Army Group B was immobilized for some time in July and again in early August waiting for fuel and ammunition, and only when Paulus, Sixth Army commander, had succeeded in clearing the Don bend in weeks of stubborn fighting, eventually trapping 100,000 Red Army soldiers at Kalach by 10 August, was it possible to cross the river Don and begin the advance on Stalingrad in earnest. By then Paulus had lost half his armour, with just 200 tanks facing more than 1,200 Soviet, while German units suffered 200,000 casualties in August.[70] To speed up the seizure of Stalingrad, which had now taken on a symbolic significance for Hitler as 'Stalin's city', he transferred General Hermann Hoth's Fourth Panzer Army from Army Group A, where it was essential to the conquest of the Caucasus, to support the attack on Stalingrad. The change proved disastrous, weakening the drive for the oil but without giving Army Group B a decisive edge in the capture of the city. Hoth was forced to battle across the Kalmyk Steppe against stiff opposition, ending up 20 kilometres from the urban centre with only 150 tanks left.

The change in priority was Hitler's decision. As in 1941, the confused effort to achieve everything with declining forces on long and vulnerable lines of communication showed the obvious limitations of Hitler's military leadership. He became more intolerant of his commanders the more the crisis unfolded. In September he took over direct command of Army Group A for two months to ensure that the commanders did what he wanted. General Halder noted in his diary that Hitler's strategy was 'nonsense, and he knows it'.[71] On 24 September Hitler sacked his army chief of staff, after months of icy arguments, and replaced him with Lieutenant General Kurt Zeitzler, a younger, more pliant, but above all more enthusiastically National Socialist commander than any alternative candidate. The change marked the point when Hitler wanted a more ideologically committed leadership, which he assumed would follow his strategic impulses more willingly.[72] The Caucasus campaign that Hitler temporarily commanded was closely linked to Stalingrad, since the long flank exposed as the German armies forced a way across the Kuban plain and along the Black Sea coast was supposed to be protected by Army Group B. First Panzer Army, commanded by Field Marshal Ewald von Kleist, was now expected to carry out everything in the south with limited infantry support. With exhausted troops, uncertain supply and weak transport infrastructure, fighting through a mass of forest and gullies, armour was not the ideal weapon. Despite the inexperience of Soviet troops and commanders sent to the region – none were trained mountain units for the mountain battles for which they lacked skis, crampons, ropes and alpine boots – Kleist's forces failed to reach and capture either Grozny or Baku, and the key element of Operation 'Brunswick' ground to a halt in November against fierce opposition, at the same time as the effort further north to seize Stalingrad.[73]

Stalin's reaction to the German advance was equivocal, because he still considered the threat to Moscow a real one and insisted that the Soviet army continue counter-attacking the central front at Rzhev and Vyazma even as the crisis unfolded further south. German estimates of Soviet strength proved wildly inaccurate, however, for between July and September, as the threat to Stalingrad and the Soviet oilfields unfolded, Stavka, the Soviet high command, had enough reserves to direct fifty divisions and thirty-three brigade units to the southern fronts. In 1942, Soviet tank and aircraft production was far ahead of German output, while Russian factories turned out three times as many artillery pieces – a critical factor in improving Red Army performance. As the German armies edged ever closer to the Volga and to Stalingrad itself, Stalin became increasingly agitated at the prospect that the German campaign might actually work, and angered by what he saw as the duplicity of his Western allies in failing to divert German forces with a 'Second Front': 'from now on,' he told

Maisky in October, 'we will know what kind of allies we are dealing with.'[74] On 26 August, three days after the first of Paulus's armoured corps reached the Volga north of Stalingrad, Stalin appointed Zhukov to be his deputy supreme commander, an implicit recognition of his own limitations which had cost the Red Army endless casualties and produced strategic crisis.[75] Even more radical was the decision taken on 9 October to downgrade the role of the military commissars by removing their right to dual command and restoring absolute responsibility to military commanders, reducing the importance of the ideological dimension of war at just the point that Hitler was moving in the opposite direction. The changes did not reduce Stalin's regular and direct interference as head of the State Defence Committee, but it did at last allow commanders to command without worrying about the Party line, while German commanders were limited by Hitler's capricious intervention in everything they did.

The struggle for the city itself was only part of a much wider battlefield as German and Axis forces held off Soviet attacks around a large rural perimeter to the north and south. Many of the reinforcements from both sides sent to the front ended up fighting in the environs of Stalingrad, not in the urban area. The Soviet attacks did not succeed in breaking the perimeter – the major assault on 19 October by General Konstantin Rokossovskii's Don Front north of Stalingrad was a major costly failure – but they did tie down Axis forces and reduce their manpower and equipment steadily over the early course of the battle.[76] The wider battlefield meant that Paulus, whose Sixth Army finally met up with Hoth's Fourth Panzer on 3 September, could only commit a small proportion of his force to the task of taking Stalingrad – just eight out of twenty understrength divisions – while those outside the city were seldom any more combat-ready than the battered forces inside.[77] It is nevertheless the harsh contest for the city that has become the core of the story of Stalingrad. Paulus seems to have had little confidence that he could capture it but von Weichs, commander of Army Group B, promised Hitler on 11 September conquest in ten days.[78] Stalingrad was subjected to a pulverizing attack by Werner von Richthofen's Fourth Air Fleet on 24–25 August but it had little effect on the battle, except that the rubble was difficult for armour to penetrate and provided excellent cover for the defenders hidden amidst the twisted girders and crumbled walls. After seizing part of the old city and penetrating to the Volga in the south, a major offensive was planned for 13 September to seize the entire western bank of the river. Facing Paulus was a redoubtable opponent, General Vasily Chuikov, who was appointed commander of the 62nd Army on 12 September after his predecessor, General Aleksandr Lopatin, had tried to retreat across the Volga.

In three days of fierce fighting, block by block, the Germans pressed forward taking most of the central area of the city. By day, superior firepower and airpower allowed Paulus the initiative; by night, organized Red Army 'storm groups' using sub-machine guns, knives and bayonets, infiltrated the captured areas, terrifying the German soldiers enough to win back what had been lost.[79] 'Barbarians,' complained one German soldier in his diary, 'they use gangster methods, Stalingrad is hell.'[80]

The battle for the city was indeed an extraordinary endurance test for both armies, who fought with declining numbers, short of equipment and food, threatened on all sides by snipers and storm groups. Chuikov fought as close as he could to the front line to prevent German artillery from firing, but the Sixty-second Army was supported by heavy artillery fire directed from the far bank of the river, and numerous batteries of the feared Katyusha rockets, whose salvo weighed four tons and spread over an area of ten acres. The city defenders were also supported by more than 1,500 aircraft of the Soviet Eighth Air Force, instead of the 300 Chuikov had started with; improved Soviet tactics and radio communication meant that German air superiority, taken for granted by German troops since the onset of 'Barbarossa', could now be more effectively challenged. By October Paulus was left with the task of seizing the jetty areas, which were used to supply Chuikov from across the Volga, and the extensive industrial zone to the north. He could now call on only 66,569 effective combat troops out of the 334,000 under his command, and they fought in the desperate hope that one last push would finally leave Chuikov's forces no choice but to surrender. Impatient for success, Stalin spurred on the defenders. On 5 October, he told General Andrei Yeremenko, commander of the Stalingrad Front, 'I am not pleased with your work ... turn every street and every building in Stalingrad into a fortress', but in effect this was already the reality.[81] On 9 November, with seven battered divisions, Paulus undertook Operation 'Hubertus' to force a salient to the Volga 500 metres wide, but counter-attacks and heavy artillery fire brought the operation to a halt with the Sixty-second Army still clinging on to a few kilometres of riverbank. Zeitzler now tried to persuade Hitler to abandon the city and shorten the line, but Hitler retorted: 'I won't leave the Volga!'[82] By then Paulus's army was probably too weak to disengage without a major crisis. There were few working vehicles, while almost all the horses had been sent away by November to avoid further losses.[83] On 18 November, Chuikov received a cryptic message to expect a 'special order'. At midnight he was told that the German armies in and around the city were about to be encircled.

For all the focus on Stalingrad, the critical operation was 'Uranus', the Soviet plan to encircle and cut off the Germans in the Stalingrad area.

Although Zhukov claimed after the war that he had suggested the plan to Stalin in a dramatic meeting in the Kremlin in mid-September, there is no record of the meeting in Stalin's appointments diary. Discussion of a possible encirclement involved a wider circle of the General Staff, led by Colonel General Aleksandr Vassilevskii, who with Zhukov presented the plan for Operation 'Uranus' to Stalin on 13 October.[84] The plan was straightforward: large reserve forces were to be built up to the north and south-east of the long German salient leading to Stalingrad, which was defended by Germany's weaker Axis allies, Romanians, Hungarians and Italians, placed there to free up German divisions for the main assault. The corridor had to be wide enough – more than 150 kilometres – to make sure that Paulus could not break out and to prevent a counter-attack to reopen the salient. This was to be just part of the plan, for once again Stalin and his staff were keen to unhinge the whole German front. Operation 'Mars' was planned on a scale not very different from 'Uranus' to drive back Army Group Centre at the same time. After that, if success was achieved, larger planetary operations were advanced – 'Saturn' in the south, 'Jupiter' in the north – which would lead to the destruction of German Army Groups South and Centre.

For 'Uranus', the Red Army, under strict secrecy and elaborate deception operations, gathered a force of over 1 million men, 14,000 heavy guns, 979 tanks and 1,350 aircraft.[85] German intelligence almost entirely failed to detect the build-up, again because of a rash underestimation of Soviet strengths. On 19 November in the north, a day later in the south, 'Uranus' unfolded. As expected, the weak flank forces collapsed and by 23 November the two pincers met at the village of Sovetsky, a few miles south of Kalach, scene of the earlier disaster in August. The effort to flesh out the wide corridor with 60 divisions and 1,000 tanks was quickly completed, and as many as 330,000 men of the Sixth Army and Fourth Panzer Army (and a number of Romanian and Croatian units) were trapped. The remarkable success of the operation showed the extent to which the Red Army had learned from its many past mistakes, just as it highlighted the strategic incoherence of Hitler's military direction. Any thoughts Paulus might have had about fighting his way out of the trap were crushed when on 20 November Hitler ordered him to stand fast in the city. The promise of air supply proved impossible to fulfil because of poor winter weather and growing intervention from the revived Red Air Force; 488 transport aircraft and 1,000 crew were lost in the attempt.[86] When von Manstein, commander of the newly created Army Group Don, tried to break through in Operation 'Wintergewitter' ('Winter Storm'), his units were repulsed by Soviet armoured reserves. Paulus was left to fend for himself.

The campaign to reduce the Stalingrad pocket did not begin until 10 January, codenamed Operation 'Kolt'so', ('Ring'). In the meantime, Soviet forces had tried a second envelopment of von Manstein's Army Group Don, an operation now known as 'Little Saturn'. Italian covering forces were destroyed, but von Manstein evaded the noose. Army Group A, still struggling in the Caucasus, was ordered on 27 December to pull back quickly towards Rostov to avoid being cut off as well. Zeitzler managed to extract the retreat order from Hitler, and immediately phoned it through from the anteroom of Hitler's private headquarters, assuming, rightly, that Hitler would try to rescind the order.[87] Army Group A managed to squeeze through the narrowing gap, to re-form under von Manstein's command at more or less the same positions held before 'Blue' had begun. Operation 'Kolt'so' completed the rout. The Red Army assumed that around 80,000 had been trapped, but the total was more than 250,000. Some 280,000 soldiers, 250 tanks, 10,000 artillery pieces and 350 aircraft surrounded the pocket; Paulus could muster barely 25,000 men capable of fighting, 95 tanks and 310 anti-tank guns.[88] Food and ammunition were on the point of disappearing entirely. Resistance was nevertheless surprisingly stout for the first week. The outer, rural areas were reduced quickly, and by 17 January only half the pocket remained. On 22 January Soviet forces prepared for the final push and met up with Chuikov's veterans four days later. Paulus was told by Hitler not to seek terms, while his men starved around him, unable to fire their guns for want of any remaining supplies 'What orders should I give,' he radioed out of the pocket, 'to troops that have no more ammunition?'[89] One soldier writing on the 19th confessed 'my morale is again at zero ... Here only white expanses, bunkers, misery, no proper home. That must slowly but surely ruin the spirit.'[90] Soldiers began to surrender even before Paulus's headquarters in the Univermag department store was stormed on 31 January and his surrender taken. Resistance continued in the north of the city until 2 February. The whole campaign exacted an exceptional toll from both sides. Precise figures for Stalingrad remain unclear, but the German dead on the Eastern Front between July and December 1942 amounted to 280,000, the Italian dead and missing, 84,000; at Stalingrad 110,000 Axis prisoners were taken, most of whom died. Soviet irrecoverable losses (the dead and missing) in the campaigns in the south amounted to 612,000.[91]

The more ambitious plans embodied in 'Saturn' and 'Jupiter' failed to materialize. Operation 'Mars', designed to unhinge German Army Group Centre, directed personally by Zhukov and regarded by Stalin as more essential than 'Uranus', was a disastrous failure with little gained and the loss of almost 500,000 casualties and 1,700 tanks, but the failure was masked by success at Stalingrad.[92] Stalin and the Soviet high command were disappointed that more did not result from the rout in the south, but Stalingrad was nevertheless a remarkable victory, grandiose beside the more modest successes on Guadalcanal and at El Alamein. World opinion was riveted on the conflict. 'STALINGRAD', ran the headline in the French journal *La Semaine* on 4 February, 'THE GREATEST BATTLE OF ALL TIME'.[93] Among the German public, victory or defeat at Stalingrad seemed to deliver a more profound meaning than a simple battle. The defeat meant the end of the ambition to use Soviet resources to fight the battle with the West, and a possible fatal challenge to the whole imperial project. Strategically it delivered the Soviet Union from the endless crises faced for the first fifteen months of war, though it did not end the German threat entirely. All three battles demonstrated the perils of imperial overstretch, evident in so many examples of territorial empire-building, yet a temptation hard to resist when the security of the empire could be achieved only by further fighting. Nevertheless, all three battles had to be won by the Allies against enemies with a daunting reputation. They were not simply lost as a result of Japanese, German and Italian strategic and tactical failures or poorer resources, but because the Allies learned to fight more effectively. The result changed the course of the war.

'WAR IS A LOTTERY'

There is no historical consensus on just when Adolf Hitler realized that the war was lost for Germany and his imperial project overturned. When a visiting Turkish military delegation asked him in summer 1943 if he expected to win, he simply replied: 'War is a lottery.'[94] But there is no doubt that Hitler did not want to be the one to admit defeat. At the annual gathering in Munich in November 1942 to mark the anniversary of the Hitler Putsch of 1923, he was heard to say, 'I will never give back earth a German soldier has trodden on.' Less than three months later, Stalingrad and the Don steppe were already lost to German occupation. Hitler responded with angry dejection, but he persisted with orders that every metre of ground was to be held, even as the conquered territory in the East continued to be abandoned. After every briefing meeting with his generals, according to one post-war testimony, he would insist that the war 'will finally end in German victory'. He refused to countenance the idea of a compromise peace with one Allied side or the other, but counted on the break-up of the enemy alliance instead. Only in February 1944, discussing the long German retreat across Ukraine, was he heard to admit that there was irrefutably a moment when withdrawal would lead to catastrophe. Any further retreat 'ultimately meant defeat for Germany'. Commanders who gave up ground without orders were to be sacked or shot, though most were not.[95] For Hitler there was no question that the war should continue to the bitter end of what became, in effect, a long retreat.

Leaders in Japan and Italy also hovered between illusory optimism and realization of the grim truth that the war could not now be won, though a solution short of complete defeat might still be possible. Guadalcanal, El Alamein and Stalingrad were thousands of miles from the home country, and indeed it took almost three years for the Allies to impose comprehensive defeat on all their enemies from the victories in the winter of 1942-3. The turning point nevertheless brought to an end two years in which the new imperial order declared in the Three Power Pact in September 1940 was supposed to create closer strategic links between the new empires, building on military successes to establish a more genuinely global imperial reach that both imitated and replaced the now dislocated European colonial world. The degree of collaboration between the three Axis empires was in practice never very extensive, but an addition to the Pact, signed on 21 December 1940, did provide for three technical commissions to be established in each of the Axis capitals: one 'general commission', one 'economic commission' and one 'military commission'. They were composed of a mix of politicians, officials and military representatives, and were supposed to be a forum for interchange of information on strategy, military affairs, technology and intelligence. They began work only in the summer of 1941 and links between the three capitals proved to be exiguous at best. The Japanese soon lost interest in the Italian commission, because they regarded Italy as little more than a satellite of Germany, while Italian negotiators refused to allow details of military technology to be revealed to Japanese delegates. Intelligence co-operation was limited by the need to protect their own imperial interests. In spring 1942, the function of the military commissions was downgraded – to 'act at the margins' – because military strategy was determined outside the scope of the Pact.[96] More might have materialized if the German army had pushed down towards Iran and Iraq from the Caucasus and the Italians from Suez. Japanese leaders were not averse to an Indian Ocean link if Britain could be driven from the Middle East, and on 18 January 1942 had signed an agreement with Germany dividing spheres of imperial interest in the Indian Ocean on longitude 70 degrees east. The agreement led to regular squabbles over alleged infringement of the demarcation line, but by the end of 1942 a joint strategy in the Indian Ocean was no longer a possibility.[97] All that remained was limited collaboration against

British Empire shipping with a handful of German submarines operating from a Japanese-controlled base in Malaya – but this did little to help Japan. After Stalingrad, both Germany and Japan understood that they now fought separate wars to save their empires.[98]

Collaboration between the Allies was certainly closer than that with the Axis by this stage, but there were still major differences and arguments that soured the relationship. When Churchill and Roosevelt met at the Moroccan city of Casablanca in January 1943, recently captured from Vichy French forces in the first days of Operation 'Torch' the previous November, the central issue was how to bring about eventual Axis defeat. Indeed, Allied strategy from 1943 onwards was, in its simplest form, the expulsion of the Axis powers from their newly won empires, followed by invasion and occupation of the imperial centre if necessary. This was a more straightforward strategy for Stalin and Soviet armed forces because they faced only one major enemy in a clearly definable space, while the Western Allies faced three major enemies in distinct theatres of operation, where in 1943 a major amphibious assault was the only way to bring the enemy to battle. There was little agreement between them on the most effective way to pursue victory, and much argument over what was strategically possible or desirable. Stalin had declined the invitation to go to Casablanca because he was too closely involved in the last stages of the Stalingrad campaign (which was true), but his absence emphasized his displeasure over the failure of the Western Allies to provide either a 'Second Front' in 1942 or the promise of one early in 1943. His absence left Roosevelt, Churchill and their military staffs free to argue their own view of how the three Axis enemies were to be challenged, while constantly aware of the need to offer some relief to a Soviet ally still bearing the brunt of the fighting.

The meeting in Morocco, appropriately codenamed 'Symbol', underlined the extent to which Roosevelt and his staff had been led to support the British preference for action in Africa rather than Europe against the advice of all Roosevelt's senior commanders. Meeting at Casablanca was only possible because Roosevelt had insisted on an operation that saw American troops in action in 'Europe' (which it was not) rather than divert even more resources to the war against Japan, which had already absorbed nine out of the seventeen American divisions now overseas.[99] Operation 'Torch' had been difficult to mount because of the long ocean journeys from the American east coast and from Scotland for troops not yet fully prepared for amphibious assault against Vichy French forces whose willingness to resist was uncertain. The American supreme commander for 'Torch', General Eisenhower, rated the prospects of success at no more than 50 per cent. Two task forces, one American to Casablanca and Oran, one Anglo-American to capture Algiers, landed on 8 November 1942. Opposition was stronger in Morocco than Algeria, but within days all three ports were in Allied hands, and a ceasefire was negotiated on 13 November with Admiral Darlan, the former Vichy prime minister, who was by chance in Algeria to see his sick son. With Roosevelt's approval, he was soon installed by Eisenhower – against widespread protest in the American and British press – as an imperial high commissioner for French North and West Africa, approved by the French Imperial Council.[100] To counter objections, Eisenhower insisted that this was a temporary expedient, but how temporary was unclear. Churchill's confidant, Brendan Bracken, warned him that 'We must set a limit to the Quisling Sailor's role', but Eisenhower and Roosevelt preferred the stability Darlan seemed to offer for a military campaign already facing problems.[101]

The military plan was for Lieutenant General Kenneth Anderson, the British commander, to form First Army for a rapid move east to capture Tunis before the Germans and Italians could reinforce it, but the inexperienced troops became stalled in heavy rain on the approach and were subject to fierce counter-attacks by a German garrison that had been rapidly expanded on Hitler's orders. Eisenhower postponed the advance in December for two months to improve the supply lines and bring up heavy weapons. The first indication of how fraught Allied military relations would become was revealed in the judgement of General Brooke that Eisenhower 'as a general is hopeless'; Montgomery, who would fight under Eisenhower until the end of the war in Europe, thought 'his knowledge of how to make war, and how to fight battles, is definitely NIL.'[102] Eisenhower had no combat experience, unlike his British counterparts. His skills as they emerged were the skills of a military manager, a necessity in the circumstances of regular and major strategic and political disagreements over the two years that followed. Indeed, much of his first months in North Africa was spent trying to navigate the politics of the French Empire, which he rightly understood to be a 'dangerous political sea'.[103] The storm over the appointment of Darlan subsided when he was assassinated in Algiers on Christmas Eve by a young French monarchist, but his death still left unresolved how to administer French imperial territory and command French forces now, ipso facto, on the Allies' side. On 11 December, in response to 'Torch', German and Italian forces had occupied all of Vichy France, whose political authority in North Africa was now nullified. The Americans preferred General Henri Giraud, who had escaped from German prison, as Darlan's successor, but the British wanted some role for de Gaulle, whom Roosevelt loathed, because he enjoyed popular support both in France and in the Free French colonies. Eisenhower brokered a compromise only in June 1943 when a Committee of National Liberation was set up with Giraud and de Gaulle as co-presidents. There remained the paradox that Roosevelt, otherwise keen to display his democratic credentials at home with the Atlantic Charter, endorsed an imperial administration in North Africa with no popular mandate. The explanation given by Eisenhower was one of 'military necessity' to paper over the contradictions in American policy and the arguments with the British.[104]

The Casablanca Conference convened on 14 January and became an inter-Allied battleground over the future direction of Allied strategy. Roosevelt understood that his Joint Chiefs were themselves divided over priority for the European against the Pacific theatre, where American forces were fighting a real war against the Axis, day after day. Marshall and the American army leadership wanted to fight a similar real war against the Germans by invading France as soon as it was feasible, but they found the British unenthusiastic. The president's own motives for accepting 'Torch' and an inevitable involvement in the Mediterranean theatre were political as much as military. He and most of his advisers and commanders assumed that British concern for the region reflected their imperial interests. Eisenhower for one had no illusions that 'the Britishers instinctively approach any military problem from the viewpoint of the Empire'; for the British, explained an American foreign service official, 'reacquisition and perhaps expansion of the Empire is an essential undertaking'.[105] One of the reasons for Roosevelt's involvement in the region was to ensure that neither Britain nor France should re-establish a dominant imperial role in the Mediterranean and Middle East as they had in 1919. He was also aware of the need to protect American oil interests in the Middle East, which he was keen to expand. An American presence was intended to temper British ambitions and promote an American global strategy. British negotiators generally did not express their political motives openly, but with Churchill there was no doubt that maintaining Britain's role in the region was indeed part of Britain's grand imperial strategy. When Roosevelt discussed a scheme of colonial trusteeship with Stalin later in the year, Churchill muttered 'nothing would be taken away from the British Empire without a war'.[106]

At Casablanca the British delegates argued firmly against a major invasion of Europe in 1943 and refused to be drawn on a precise plan for a 'Second Front'. Instead, they wanted to exploit the imminent conquest of North Africa with further operations against Italy. There had been at least four earlier British plans drawn up between November 1940 and October 1941 for possible invasions of Sicily or Sardinia, and the belief that the

Italian dictatorship was too brittle to withstand any further military reverses continued to colour British thinking about the next stage after 'Torch'.[107] The British side, expecting the defeat of Axis forces in Tunisia in two months, wanted an American commitment to invade one of Italy's major islands, and, after much argument, Operation 'Husky' was agreed for the capture of Sicily, with the implication that this might open the way to an invasion of mainland Italy. The American team won assurance that at some point there would be an invasion of north-west Europe, supported by an agreement between the RAF and the US Army Air Forces that they would conduct a round-the-clock combined bomber offensive against Germany to prepare the way for the larger invasion. The campaign to keep open the Atlantic sea lanes was also regarded as an essential preliminary to invasion. The British accepted the American Pacific commitment, as long as it did not impinge on priority for Europe. On the last day of the conference, Roosevelt announced that the Allies would only accept the unconditional surrender of all Axis states.

The American side had arrived poorly prepared for the debates, while the British had a headquarters ship, HMS *Bulolo*, in Casablanca harbour, with a large support staff.[108] The American military chiefs left the conference convinced that Roosevelt had given too much away. When the Western Allies met again in Washington in May, for the 'Trident' Conference, the American side was better prepared, and the balance between the two Allies shifted in the United States' favour. The Pacific campaigns were to continue as an American priority. Marshall wanted the Mediterranean theatre wound up altogether, so that there would be forces enough for what was now to be called Operation 'Overlord' against the coast of northern France, a negotiating position that forced the British side to compromise. Limited operations against Italy were agreed, if they did not suck in too many Allied resources, while preparations were to go ahead for a landing in force on 1 May 1944 in Normandy or Brittany, a decision that shaped the strategy of the Western Allies for the remainder of the war.

The Mediterranean campaign did, as the American side feared, become larger and more costly than the Allies wanted. The campaign for Tunisia, supposed to be completed in less than two months, took seven. Italian and German forces further east abandoned Tripoli on 23 January 1943 and moved rapidly to defend the Mareth Line of fortifications, built by the French before the war in southern Tunisia to keep out the Italians. Here Montgomery's Eighth Army arrived to prepare to breach the line and join up with the Anglo-American force approaching from Algeria. The Tunisian fortress was now reinforced at Hitler's insistence, even though there was little chance of evacuation if Axis armies faced defeat. In the north Rommel

commanded German forces; further south the Italian First Army was commanded by General Giovanni Messe. They were considerably outnumbered
by Allied forces – for the battle on the Mareth Line in March, Messe had 94
tanks against 620 – but the mountainous terrain suited the defender.[109]
Rommel ordered spoiling attacks against the oncoming forces from Algeria
and, on 14 February at the Kasserine Pass, inflicted a major reverse on the
American II Corps until he was forced to pull back. General Alexander,
appointed as overall ground commander under Eisenhower, thought the
American troops 'soft, green and quite untrained', and this British prejudice
coloured the final plans for ending Axis resistance, which gave the American divisions a subsidiary role.[110] Cut off from adequate supplies by an
Allied air and sea blockade, the outcome was not in doubt even though the
improvised Axis defence lines proved difficult to penetrate. On 9 March,
Rommel, in poor health, was relieved of command and replaced by the
commander of German Fifth Panzer Army, Colonel General Hans-Jürgen
von Arnim. A week later the Mareth Line was overrun and Messe retreated
north. The two Allied armies joined forces and drove the enemy back to a
small enclave around Tunis and Bizerte. Tunis fell on 7 May to the British,
Bizerte to the Americans. By the time of surrender the once formidable
Afrika Korps was left with two tanks and no ammunition. Most German
troops had surrendered by 12 May, but Messe continued to fight a day
longer. A final net of around 275,000 prisoners were taken, on this occasion
the great majority German, a greater loss than at Stalingrad in February.
Allied casualties were heavy too, a reflection of a genuine inexperience.
Anderson's First Army suffered 27,742 casualties in what was supposed to
be a mopping-up campaign.[111]

By this time, planning for the invasion of Sicily was well-advanced.
Eisenhower took little part since Alexander remained overall ground commander, assisted by a team of British commanders – Montgomery, Admiral
Andrew Cunningham and Air Chief Marshal Arthur Tedder. The invasion
was to be the first real test of amphibious capability in Europe and it
required the assembly of a formidable 2,509 ships to transport 160,000
men of the American Seventh Army, the British Eighth Army and the First
Canadian Division, together with 14,000 vehicles and 600 tanks.[112] The
initial plan posited landings on the north-west coast by the Americans and
the south-east corner by the British, but it was clear that this would disperse
forces too widely – 'a dog's breakfast' was Montgomery's view of the plan –
and, following his vigorous intervention in early May, the eventual invasion
was concentrated in a triangle on the south and south-east coast of the
island.[113] The US Seventh Army under General George Patton was to land
on the south coast around Gela, Montgomery's Eighth Army around Avola

in the south-east and the Canadians in between, near Pancino. For the Italian high command, there was no certainty where the next blow would fall and what was left of Italian fighting power was thinly spread between Sicily, Sardinia, Corsica and the mainland. The overall commander on the island, General Alfredo Guzzoni, had six divisions, two German (including the Hermann Göring Panzer Division) and four Italian, of which only one was effectively ready for combat. Between them they could muster 249 tanks and a little over 1,000 aircraft against the 2,510 that the Allies had in the theatre. Shoreline defences were largely absent. A naval commander complained that 'everything was an absolute fiasco', but the Italian navy, with only three small battleships and ten destroyers still undamaged, refused to leave their base at La Spezia to contest the Allied landings.[114] The morale of the Italian forces was low as they faced the prospect of defending the homeland with inadequate weapons alongside a German ally that they distrusted, but Mussolini was optimistic, assuring Fascist leaders in June that the Allies were too slow and incompetent to secure a foothold on Italian territory. If there was any doubt about the Allied objective, it was removed by the remorseless bombardment by sea and air of the two islands of Pantelleria and Lampedusa, on the path to Sicily, which surrendered on 11 and 12 June respectively. Eisenhower set up his headquarters in an uncomfortable bombproof tunnel on Malta. '[M]y chief ambition in this war,' he wrote to Marshall a few weeks earlier, 'is finally to get to a place where the next operation does not have to be amphibious.'[115]

The Allied convoys arrived off the Sicilian coast on the morning of 11 July with little opposition on the beaches. The Axis air presence had been reduced through the bombing of airbases to only 298 German and 198 Italian aircraft, but after four more days of air combat there were just 161 Axis aircraft left. By the end of the month the Italian air force was reduced to just 41 modern fighters and 83 bombers.[116] The massive Allied air effort was complemented by the effective use of gunfire support from the naval task forces to reduce German and Italian counter-attacks against the small beachheads secured on the first day. The Hermann Göring Division attacked the American landing at Gela and reached within 3 kilometres of the beach before naval gunfire drove the tanks back; the Italian Livorno Division, one of the few still capable of effective combat, attacked the same day further west with a long column of tanks, but they were all but obliterated by more than a thousand rounds from the guns of two destroyers and two cruisers lying offshore.[117] Naval gunfire was to prove again and again an essential contribution to Allied landing operations. The two Allied armies then began the pursuit inland, but Montgomery was determined that his army would be the one to cut off the enemy and seize the north-east port of Messina while the Americans guarded his left flank. Patton already resented the British behaviour in Tunisia and shared the view that 'this war is being fought for the benefit of the British Empire'.[118] He ignored Montgomery and drove against almost undefended territory around the west coast to capture Palermo on 22 July and then raced on to Messina, determined to beat Montgomery to the city. The Eighth Army captured Catania without a fight on 14 July, and Agrigento two days later. Kesselring gave up on his Italian ally once it was clear that Italian soldiers were surrendering in their thousands, and assumed direct command of German forces. Montgomery was held up around Mount Etna by effective German defence, but by then a planned evacuation was being prepared. The Eighth Army reached Messina on 16 August, just behind Patton, but neither was able to cut off the enemy whose escape in daylight across the Straits of Messina failed to be anticipated. The Germans evacuated 39,569 men, 9,000 vehicles and 47 tanks; Italian forces managed 62,000 men, but only 227 vehicles and 12 mules. The Allies captured 122,204 prisoners, but the Axis armies lost 49,700 dead or missing against an Allied total of 4,299, a ratio more common in the battles of the Pacific.[119]

Mussolini's fantasy of resistance to save what was left of the shrunken empire illustrated the extent to which he had lost any sense of proportion by 1943. The Sicilian invasion brought his twenty-one years in power to an abrupt end. Conditions in Italy had already strained what support remained for the Fascist regime. Shortages of food and the onset of heavy bombing, including, after much debate on the Allied side, the bombing of targets in Rome on 19 July, confirmed the popular understanding that the war was lost, at least for Italy. Popular disillusionment undermined the grip of the dictatorship on its people, but it did not produce a popular revolution. Instead, Mussolini was unseated in a palace coup, prompted by his own commanders and Fascist Party colleagues, many of whom had never supported the unlimited war their leader had provoked or the evidently one-sided alliance with Germany. The Italian chief of the armed forces, General Vittorio Ambrosio, told the king in March that Mussolini would have to be replaced, perhaps by Marshal Badoglio, and by June he had plans prepared for Mussolini's arrest. When Mussolini met Hitler at Villa Gaggia in the foothills of the Dolomite Mountains on 19 July, the day Rome was bombed, his commanders asked him to discuss a way for Italy to leave the war, but he refused. On his return to Rome, with no guarantee of German assistance, he summoned the Fascist Grand Council, which had not met since 1940, in the hope that he could reassert his authority over a war effort in crisis.

It was an opportunity for his opponents in the Party, principally the former ambassador to London, Dino Grandi, to end the dictatorship. Grandi drafted a motion for the Council to reject personal rule, restore the prerogatives of the crown, and to establish a collegial government based on a cabinet and parliament. Grandi revealed his plans to the king, which included ending the Axis alliance and joining the Allied cause. The resolution was presented to the Grand Council on 24 July during a nine-hour meeting, which went on into the early hours of the 25th, when a vote was finally taken on Grandi's motion. Nineteen of those present voted in favour, seven against.[120] Mussolini left, unaware of what the decision meant. Later on the 25th he attended a regular briefing with the king, who told him that he was relieved as prime minister, to be replaced by Badoglio. As the dictator left the audience, he was arrested and taken to a police barracks. He had prepared nothing for his own security, assuming that he could simply defy the vote. He regarded the possibility of a royal coup, his wife told Hitler's interpreter, 'with incomprehensible apathy'.[121] The dictatorship that had led Italy to brief imperial triumph and ultimate disaster ended without a fight.

Unlike Mussolini, Hitler and the German leadership had already anticipated a possible crisis in Italy. News of Mussolini's fall flung Hitler into an immediate rage against 'the Jews and the rabble' in Rome.[122] His first instinct was to order German forces to arrest the king, Badoglio and the other conspirators and reinstate his fellow dictator but the impulse passed. The king and the new government both insisted that they intended to sustain the war effort side by side with Germany. Instead, OKW began the movement of substantial German forces into Italy, a redeployment already begun from the Eastern Front with news of the invasion of Sicily. Within two weeks, Operation 'Alarich' resulted in the transfer of eight divisions to northern Italy, and by early September there were nineteen German divisions in or en route to the peninsula. Operation 'Konstantin' was also set in motion to strengthen the Balkans, in the event that the Allies moved there next.[123] The object was only partially to halt the Allied advance; the wider purpose was to prepare for Italian 'treachery', as Hitler put it, if the Badoglio government sued for peace, which seemed likely. Badoglio's decision to seek an armistice, which took effect on 8 September, opened the way for a direct confrontation with German armed forces as they swiftly moved to turn Italy overnight from ally to occupied territory. Italian soldiers were disarmed and interned and most sent off to Germany as forced labour. On the Greek island of Kefalonia, the local Italian commanders resisted the demand to disarm and on 15 September fighting broke out with the German army garrison. Hitler ordered no prisoners to be taken and around 2,000 Italians died or were murdered in the brief conflict and its vengeful aftermath.[124]

Hitler was uncertain how to treat his former ally. Military leaders preferred the idea of direct occupation, but Hitler feared the effect on his other Axis allies. His instinct was to create a new Fascist government, with or without Mussolini, to give the impression that Italy was not just an occupied country, but on 12 September German paratroopers staged a daring raid on the hotel on the Gran Massif where Mussolini was imprisoned and spirited him to Munich, where the two dictators met two days later amidst extravagant gestures of friendship. Mussolini quickly discovered that his return to power would only be at the behest of his German ally, who would dominate the peninsula. A Reich plenipotentiary, Rudolf Rahn, was appointed at once; the German commanders insisted on establishing zones of operation in which they organized a military administration; the Italian prefects were kept in place to run day-to-day affairs, but they were shadowed by German 'advisers', and in effect were subject to constant German supervision, a situation rather like rule in Manchukuo.[125] Mussolini railed against the idea of running a 'ghost government', but he had little choice. Rome was ruled out as the seat of the new regime, but Mussolini's preference for Bolzano or Merano in the far north-east was rejected and the Germans installed him in the small town of Salò on Lake Garda, with the ministries of what was now called the *Repubblica Sociale Italiana* (Italian Social Republic) scattered across the cities of the Po Valley.[126] The Germans now viewed Italy as an 'occupied ally', an oxymoron that left no one in doubt that Italy was now a German dependency. Italians who had cheered the fall of Mussolini now found themselves subjected to a novel version of dictatorship.

For the Allies, the change in regime seemed to suggest that Churchill's desire to knock Italy out by sustaining the Mediterranean theatre had borne fruit. But at the 'Quadrant' meeting in Quebec in August, Churchill found the American side still determined to limit the campaign in the Mediterranean. Henry Stimson deplored what he called 'pinprick warfare', and the American delegation were all presented with a paper prepared by the War Department's operations division before the conference to illustrate that any additional commitment in the region was an 'uneconomical' use of resources whose result would be to allow Germany a 'strategic stalemate' in Europe – a view that would be justified by events.[127] Though Churchill now began to think of possible operations in the Eastern Mediterranean as well as the invasion of Italy, American pressure to commit to 'Overlord' scaled his ambitions down. All agreed that the priority was to seize Rome quickly (Eisenhower hoped by October) while Axis forces were disorganized, but the plan took no account of German preparations. Kesselring, as commander-in-chief in the south, persuaded Hitler that the Allies should be resisted well south of Rome, supported by the large forces in the north now under Rommel's command.

The choice of Italy as a major front line is, with hindsight, hard to understand. Nothing recommended it as a battlefield, and a simple glance at a map would have made clear that the mountain ranges and numerous river crossings made swift progress for a mobile army against a competent enemy quite implausible. Allied leaders underestimated the extent of the resistance they would meet, or just how quickly the German armed forces could turn Italy into a heavily fortified front. Nor were there obviously compelling strategic advantages in invading Italy, except to make sure that the armistice was genuinely observed. Montgomery was unhappy with an invasion 'without any clear idea – or plan – as to how they would develop operations ... There was no clear object laid down.'[128] Both Eighth Army and General Mark Clark's Fifth Army, designated for the Italian campaign, were exhausted by long combat and faced a daunting task in autumn weather and hostile topography to move anywhere near Rome. Moreover, the campaign was ordered on the understanding that at least seven divisions and a great many landing craft would soon be pulled back to prepare for 'Overlord', a decision that once again made little strategic sense if Italy were to be taken seriously as a theatre of operations.

In the event, the invasion of southern Italy opened up a strategic stalemate, as American analysts had predicted. On 3 September 1943, in Operation 'Baytown', Montgomery moved the Eighth Army into the toe of the Italian boot and moved through Calabria with only light resistance. The key operation was 'Avalanche', to be launched by Clark's Fifth Army in the Bay of Salerno below Naples. The plan was risky since it involved only three divisions landing across 50 kilometres of bay, divided by a river. Clark declined a pre-landing bombardment because intelligence indicated only weak German forces and the possibility of complete surprise. On 9 September, one British corps and one American landed on beaches far apart. The German Tenth Army was waiting for them. Kesselring activated Operation '*Achse*' ('Axis') to move reserves quickly to snuff out the beachhead and a fierce battle ensued in which it seemed likely that the landing would fail.[129] Clark was saved by heavy naval gunfire and the Allies' aerial superiority, and after more than a week in which Eisenhower warned the Combined Chiefs that the outcome was 'touch and go', Kesselring pulled his battered forces back to a series of formidable defence lines running coast to coast south of Rome, astride the Cassino massif, with sections codenamed the 'Gustav', 'Hitler' and 'Bernhardt' lines. The Allies entered

Naples on 1 October, following a popular rising against the German occupiers, while in the east the Foggia airfields were taken by the Eighth Army,
to be used as bases for the strategic bombing by the US Fifteenth Air Force
of the Romanian oilfield and targets in Austria and southern Germany. But
by the end of October, Eisenhower's desire for a quick capture of Rome
evaporated, and by November the Allies halted at the Gustav Line, engaged
in a costly war of attrition. General Alexander defended the campaign now
on the grounds that it tied down German forces, but Allied forces were tied
down too, to little purpose.

The other Allied front, in the Pacific, faced a similar problem in dislodging
a tough defender from island bases whose capture still seemed remote from
the wider issue of how to defeat Japan. Following victory on Guadalcanal,
MacArthur and Nimitz hosted a conference on 10 March 1943 to design
future strategy against Japan. Given the wide range and number of Japanese garrisons and airfields on the southern perimeter, there was no
alternative but to work forward slowly to eliminate them, building up
Allied – mostly American – naval and air power until, at a later date, it
would be possible to threaten Japan directly. The first stage was codenamed
Operation 'Cartwheel', under MacArthur's command but with the assistance of Halsey's Third Fleet of carriers and battleships, temporarily
assigned from Nimitz's Central Pacific Command. 'Cartwheel' involved a
series of thirteen amphibious operations through the Solomon Islands and
along the coast of New Guinea in order to isolate and neutralize the main
Japanese military and naval base at Rabaul, on New Britain, part of the
Australian New Guinea territory captured in February 1942.[130] The planning was carried out at MacArthur's headquarters on New Guinea by Rear
Admiral Daniel Barbey, in overall charge of the amphibious landings programme, and Rear Admiral Richmond Turner in command of the
amphibious force as he had been at Guadalcanal. Nimitz was given little
to do until fresh naval forces were available. The Joint Chiefs directed him
to invade the Gilbert and Ellice Islands (today two separate nations, Kiri-
bati and Tuvalu) in November 1943, but the Marshall Islands only in June
1944, still leaving the central Pacific campaign over 3,800 kilometres from
the Japanese home islands. By the time Nimitz organized the seizure of
Tarawa and Makin in the Gilberts in November, he had seventeen new
carriers and thirteen battleships, a formidable surface force that now
eclipsed entirely the Imperial Japanese Navy. In total, American shipyards
in 1943 provided 419 new warships, including 40 new carriers, to be
deployed worldwide.[131]

The Japanese navy, with chief responsibility for the defence of the circle of occupied islands, regarded retention of the outer ring, according to Navy Directive 213 issued on 25 March 1943, as 'a matter of vital importance to the national defence of our Imperial homeland'.[132] The 'New Operational Policy' was to hold every strongpoint to the last man in order to wear down the American war effort, in effect turning every island base into a fortress blocking Allied progress, under the ambitious slogan a 'Hundred Years' War'.[133] For much of 1943, the garrisons sat and waited, their supply lines increasingly threatened by the expansion of American army and navy air power. 'Cartwheel' began with the assault on the Solomons island chain in an operation led by Halsey's Third Fleet, under the odd codeword 'Toenails'. The assault was ordered on 3 June and began with preliminary raids two weeks later on New Georgia. The main aim was the island of Munda, secured by late July. Most Japanese troops were stationed on the larger islands of Kolombangara and Bougainville, but it was decided that garrisons could be bypassed, isolated and starved out, rather than confronted in costly landings – a strategy that was adopted throughout the 'island-hopping' campaigns in the last two years of war. A smaller island, Vella Lavella, was captured easily on 15 August as a stepping-stone to Bougainville, and the Japanese evacuated Kolombangara rather than risk its isolation. On Bougainville there were an estimated 35,000 Japanese troops defending the airfields and beaches, 65,000 in total in the Seventeenth Army, commanded by General Hyakutake, by far the largest challenge in clearing the Solomons. It was decided not to occupy the whole island, but an enclave on the west coast around Cape Torokina where airfields could be established, and a firm defensive line constructed against Japanese counter-attacks from the heavily garrisoned north and south.[134] Persistent air raids reduced Japanese air power on the island and at Rabaul, while prior to the main assault the Treasury Islands, some 120 kilometres from Bougainville, were seized almost unopposed on 27 October by American and New Zealand troops (the latter returned from the North African campaign), to be used as a staging post and advanced radar station for the main landing. The assault on Bougainville, Operation 'Dipper', began on 1 November; by mid-December there were 44,000 American troops ashore and the lodgement established. Fighting continued spasmodically until 18 December, when the enclave was secure. In March 1944, Hyakutake launched a series of frontal assaults with troops debilitated by disease and hunger, repeating the tactical errors he had made on Guadalcanal. In one night-time *banzai* charge, 3,000 Japanese dead were counted the following morning, lying in distorted piles where the artillery and machine-gun fire had left them. Hyakutake withdrew his forces into the jungle.[135] By August 1945, when the war ended, only one-third of his men were still alive. The Solomon Islands pincer for 'Cartwheel' was complete.

MacArthur began the second pincer, along the northern coast of New Guinea, in September 1943 after waiting on the success of 'Toenails'. On 4 September the Australian Ninth Infantry Division seized the harbour at Lae unopposed except for air attack, and on 22 September the port of Finschhafen, which was defended, though not heavily. A second Australian force secured the beachhead and then the port by 2 October. A Japanese landing two weeks later to win back the base was destroyed. The early successes were consolidated, but it was a further seven months before the drive resumed against the remaining Japanese garrisons along the northern coast. By this time, the naval base at Rabaul too was vulnerable to American naval and army aircraft thanks to 'Cartwheel' and in February 1944 the fleet moved to Truk, further north in the Caroline Islands, leaving the 95,000 troops still stationed at Rabaul isolated for the rest of the war. With the Solomon Islands close to neutralized, Nimitz began the central Pacific part of the plan agreed with MacArthur, drawing away naval support from the army campaign. He chose two islands to attack in the Gilbert and Ellice group: Betio Island in the Tarawa atoll, and Makin. The operations were to be directed by Admiral Spruance as commander of a new Fifth Fleet, with the commander from Guadalcanal Richmond Turner in charge of the Fifth Amphibious Force and Holland Smith commanding the Fifth Amphibious Corps of marines. Two of the Ellice islands, Funafuti and Nanumea, had been occupied by October and airfields constructed to support the later landings.[136] Makin was defended by only 300 Japanese troops supported by 271 Korean labourers. They were faced on 21 November by an assault force of 6,000 men, mostly from the untried Twenty-seventh Infantry Division. Despite the disparity in manpower, it took until the afternoon of the following day to declare the island secure, with 56 dead and 131 sick and wounded from the American side.[137]

This was nothing compared with the assault on Betio by Second Marine Division, which began the same day as the attack on Makin. Learning from previous experience, the Japanese Special Naval Force had created an island fortress that covered every line of advance with concealed gunfire from pillboxes and hidden bunkers. The small island had little shelter and was battered for days beforehand by heavy shelling and bombing, but the defenders were dug in effectively enough to avoid the worst of the bombardment, although it destroyed Japanese communications, hampering co-ordination of the defence. It took almost three days of the hardest fighting yet experienced to secure the island and its large airfield. True to the 'New Operational Policy', the strongpoint was defended to almost the last man. Some 4,000 Japanese died, leaving just 146 alive, mostly drafted Korean labourers. Marine losses were 984 dead and 2,072 wounded.[138] The Marine commander, Holland Smith, commented after an inspection of the ruined island: 'Look at this defence in depth. The bastards were masters ... You could take one redoubt, but every redoubt was covered by two others.'[139] News of the cost for taking one small island shocked American opinion, where the losses were at first exaggerated. A concerted effort was made by navy planners and the amphibious force to ensure that the entry to the Marshall Islands, originally scheduled for summer 1944 but now accelerated after the seizure of the Tarawa atoll, was more effectively handled and less costly in American lives, but it was a campaign that might well have been abandoned. Nimitz agreed with MacArthur in January 1944 to focus on the south-west Pacific and the path to the Philippines until Admiral King, in 'indignant dismay' at MacArthur's 'absurd' plan, got the Joint Chiefs to specify an assault on the Marshalls, codenamed Operation 'Flintlock'.[140] Nimitz determined to avoid the most heavily defended islands at the eastern end of the archipelago, Wotje and Maloelap, which secret intelligence indicated were being heavily reinforced, like Betio. Instead, he picked out two islands in the west, Kwajalein and Eniwetok, as the target, from where it would be possible to bomb the main Japanese naval base at Truk.

Kwajalein was invaded on 1 February 1944 after four small islands had been occupied to mount artillery fire against the defenders. Although it took four days for the Fourth Marine Division and Seventh Infantry Division to secure the island, the defence had been hastily constructed of trenches and foxholes rather than the deep shelters on Betio. Some 8,000 defenders were killed at a cost of 313 marines. Nimitz was pleased enough with the result to order a rapid invasion of Eniwetok, originally scheduled for 1 May. Here again a number of smaller islands were secured first, and Eniwetok then invaded four days later, on 21 February. The island was captured in two days despite stronger defences, with the loss of 348 dead against 4,500 Japanese and Koreans, fighting almost entirely to the death. The eastern islands remained in Japanese hands until surrender in 1945, cut off by sea and air from any hope of action.[141] The way was now open for Nimitz and Spruance to aim for the Mariana Islands, 2,150 kilometres closer to Japan.

The scale of combat in both the Pacific and the Mediterranean in 1943 was dwarfed by the Soviet–German war in the months after the German collapse at Stalingrad, where the Red Army still faced over 200 Axis divisions spread across a land front of more than 1,500 kilometres. Stalin and the Soviet leadership hoped that the Casablanca Conference would confirm the Anglo-American intention to invade France in 1943, now that North Africa was almost conquered. The failure to offer anything concrete at Casablanca other than a possible invasion of Sicily left Stalin, as Churchill had feared, 'disappointed and furious'. Stalin told Roosevelt that Sicily was no substitute for 'a Second Front in France'.[142] The alliance reached perhaps its lowest point when Stalin was told the results of the 'Trident' Conference in May, once it was clear that the Western Allies would not open the Second Front until spring 1944 but would continue to fight in the Mediterranean. Churchill added insult to injury by suggesting that his Mediterranean plans might have prevented a renewed German offensive against the Red Army, when Stalin knew full well that Operation *'Zitadelle'* ('Citadel'), the main German operation of 1943, was about to be launched in one of the largest battles of the entire war. Stalin sent a blistering reply on 24 June, reiterating all the promises and pledges made by the Western Allies over the previous year: 'here is not simply the question of disappointment . . . here is the question of [the Soviet Government's] confidence in the Allies which is severely tried . . .'[143] He refused to reply to further letters for six weeks, provoking anxiety in Washington and London that he might be about to negotiate a separate peace, an unfounded proposition embroidered by persistent rumours, and sustained in some post-war histories.[144] Stalin continued to define any Mediterranean plans as 'diversionary'. Even later in the year, when planning for 'Overlord' was well advanced, he remained sceptical of the alliance. On the way to Tehran and the first summit between the three Allied leaders, in late November, he was heard to remark that the 'main issue being decided now is whether or not they will help us'. By this stage Soviet victories in 1943 made the help seem less necessary to Stalin. 'We'll have enough power,' Zhukov recalled him saying, 'to finish off Hitler's Germany alone.'[145] The claim was never tested, but it remained true that the Soviet Union bore the brunt of fighting against the Axis for almost three years: 'colossal sacrifices', Stalin reminded Churchill, against Anglo-American losses that were 'modest'.[146]

    The course of the war on the Eastern Front by the end of 1943 encouraged Stalin's growing optimism after a year in which the balance finally swung heavily in favour of the Red Army. That the front still hung in the balance after Stalingrad was evident in the fate of the Ukrainian city of Kharkov, which changed hands twice within a month in February and March. Stalin had insisted after the operations to clear the Don steppe that the Red Army keep on the offensive across the vast front despite months of exhausting combat. In the far north, Operation 'Spark' began on 12 January and within a week opened up a narrow corridor to

Leningrad for a limited break in the long siege, but here a second operation to encircle German Army Group North had to be abandoned when the German commander, Field Marshal Georg von Küchler, shortened and strengthened the defensive line. Further plans to encircle and destroy German Army Group Centre by Rokossovskii's renamed Central Army Group came to nothing – 'Appetites,' complained Rokossovskii, 'prevailed over possibilities' – but further south Operation 'Star' in early February, aimed at Kursk and Kharkov, was more successful. Kursk was recaptured on 8 February, Belgorod on the same day, and on 16 February, when an SS Panzer Corps abandoned the city, Soviet forces reoccupied what was left of the city of Kharkov, punching a large salient into the German front line.[147] But the Stavka made the same mistake of a year before, pushing on tired troops to ever more ambitious projects, in this case trying to cut off German Army Group South while driving to occupy the industrial southern Ukraine. Von Manstein persuaded Hitler to allow him to mount a defensive counter-attack, and on 19 February his reinforced armies pushed west of Kharkov against an overstretched Red Army. As the Soviet advance rapidly disintegrated, von Manstein seized Kharkov on 15 March, and Belgorod a few days later, where he halted to create the southern balcony of a large salient still protruding into the German line around Kursk, 185 kilometres wide and 128 kilometres deep.

The Kursk salient became the site of one of the major set-piece battles of the war. For Hitler, the collapse after Stalingrad made him uncertain of how to respond to the new situation. Planners at OKW had suggested in December 1942 to try once again to capture the oil of the Caucasus and win back the strategic initiative, but Hitler recognized by February that this was a military fantasy.[148] On 18 February he made clear to his commanders that he would 'undertake no great operation this year …', but following von Manstein's success at Kharkov Hitler accepted his suggestion that Army Groups Centre and South pinch off the Kursk salient, in order to shorten the German line, inflict a damaging defeat on the encircled Red Army, and win back some of the lost prestige after Stalingrad.[149] This was not an offensive on the scale of 1941 or 1942, but one designed to block further Soviet offensives in 1943 by inflicting serious local damage. Other smaller operations were envisaged south of Kharkov – 'Habicht' and 'Panther' – to support Kursk, but in mid-April, with Operational Order 6, Hitler opted for 'Citadel', an assault on the neck of the Kursk bulge, north from the area around Orel and south from around the recently recaptured city of Belgorod.[150] By this time the Soviet high command had already decided that the Kursk salient would be the German object once the mud from the spring thaw had dissipated, a judgement soon confirmed by regular reconnaissance. On 12 April, Stalin met with Zhukov and Vasilevskii to agree on a response. Stalin was less than happy with the idea of a defensive battle, but he was persuaded that a solid field of defence around Kursk would blunt the German assault, and could then be followed at once by a strong counterstroke from reserve forces in the rear to drive the German front back towards the Dnieper River. Orders went out to the Central Army Group under Rokossovskii and the Voronezh Army Group, under General Nikolai Vatutin, to expect a German offensive from at least 10 May, and by the end of April both commanders confirmed that they were in position to conduct the defence.[151] By early May much of the necessary equipment and additional manpower was in place, while the mobilization of 300,000 civilians in the bulge helped to build 8 defensive rings, with 3,000 miles of trenches and anti-tank ditches, supported by thousands of earth-and-timber gun emplacements, surrounded by thick layers of barbed wire and 942,000 anti-tank and anti-personnel mines.[152]

The German plan of operation followed a predictable pattern, with a pincer movement aimed to cut off and encircle the large number of armies now visibly pouring in to strengthen the salient. Ninth Army to the north, commanded by Colonel General Walter Model, made one arm of the pincer, while to the south the Fourth Panzer Army under Hoth, supported by Army Detachment Kempf (named after the commander, General Werner Kempf), supplied the other. The problem for Hitler was to decide when to strike. Von Manstein and Field Marshal Günther von Kluge, commanders of Army Groups South and Centre, were keen to start as soon as possible, assuming that the Soviet side was unprepared, but Model insisted that after the tough fighting of the winter and spring, his forces needed time for reinforcement of infantry and armour. On 4 May, Hitler postponed 'Citadel' until 12 June, but active partisan activity in the area of Army Group Centre cut back reinforcement to such an extent that Model was forced to conduct a punitive operation, 'Gypsy Baron', to make his lines of supply more secure, still further delaying the start of the offensive to 19 June. By this time Hitler was anxious to ensure that, after Tunisia, Italy would stay in the war, but once it was clear that Mussolini would continue to fight, 'Citadel' seemed less risky. The outcome was nevertheless not certain, and both General Guderian, inspector general of armoured forces, and the head of German army intelligence in the East, Reinhard Gehlen, advised cancellation.[153] Hitler delayed again, only this time in order to allow more of the latest heavy tank models, the Panzer V 'Panther' and the Panzer VI 'Tiger', to reach front-line units, though by the time he finally ordered the operation to begin on the morning of 5 July, only 328 of them had arrived, of which 251 were with the attacking force. Most tanks were the weaker Panzer III (309) and the Panzer IV (245), while the average number of tanks for each armoured division was now just 73, half of the strength they should have possessed.[154]

For the Soviet side the coming operation was far from predictable. This was the first time that the Red Army had dug in for a defensive battle and defied Stalin's hope for a 'pre-emptive offensive'.[155] Deep defensive operations were not the natural preference for an army trained for the offensive, and the lack of familiarity with a new tactical field explains some of the problems encountered in the battle when it came. The long German delay was unexpected, and provoked uncertainty, although it provided the opportunity to reinforce the Soviet armies, which were almost up to full strength by June with 40 per cent of Red Army forces and 75 per cent of Soviet armour crammed into the defensive zones. Stalin was impatient and by June was thinking again about taking the offensive first, but Zhukov's view prevailed. Troops were put on alert regularly, only for no attack to materialize. By late June, radio intercepts and the interrogation of German soldiers snatched by Soviet patrols all pointed to an imminent attack, and from 2 July the Red Army was on full alert. On the 4th a captured soldier confirmed that 'Citadel' would begin the following morning. Zhukov ordered a counter-barrage after midnight by artillery, rockets and bomber aircraft that temporarily persuaded the surprised German commanders that they were the victims of a Soviet offensive that they had failed to detect.[156] Once it was clear that the barrage was a spoiling attack, German forces began their own offensive at 4.30 a.m. The battle pitted very large forces on both sides. The Soviet army and air force fielded 1,336,000 men (and some women), 3,444 tanks and self-propelled guns, 19,000 artillery pieces and mortars, and 2,650 aircraft (3,700 with the addition of the reserve long-range forces); behind the bulge was the Steppe Army Group commanded by General Ivan Konev with 573,000 men, 1,551 tanks and self-propelled guns, and 7,401 guns and mortars.[157] The German Army Groups mustered 900,000 men (though only 625,271 were combat troops), 2,699 armoured fighting vehicles, 9,467 artillery pieces and 1,372 aircraft.[158] The German side enjoyed an edge in the quality of tanks, self-propelled guns and bomber aircraft; the Soviet side a substantial advantage in numbers.

The subsequent battle, which lasted little more than ten days in the Kursk bulge itself, was a failure for the German army, a conclusion that is worth emphasizing. For all the tactical skill of German ground and air forces, 'Citadel' was not the 'lost victory' that von Manstein lamented in his post-war memoirs, but a vindication of Zhukov's original plan. In the north, Model's Ninth Army pushed forward 11 kilometres in the first two days to the small town of Ponyri, but they faced a ferocious barrage of fire which forced the German infantry to struggle for every defensive strongpoint. The attack stalled by 7 July opposite the heavily defended Olkhovatka ridge, where better co-ordinated Soviet ground attack aircraft supported the Soviet Thirteenth Army's defence. A further breakthrough eluded Model and by the 9th the assault ground to a halt. Zhukov signalled to Stalin that the time had come for the first counter-offensive blow, and on 12 July forces from the Western, Briansk and Central Army Groups launched Operation 'Kutuzov', which rapidly broke the German front and threatened with encirclement the Second Panzer Army, which despite its name possessed no tanks. Model pulled back Ninth Army across the battered countryside to try to seal the breach, but this part of the German offensive was over. In the south, German forces made greater progress, partly because Soviet intelligence had mistakenly assumed that the northern pincer was the stronger and had given Rokossovskii more resources. On the southern wing, Hoth could deploy nine armoured divisions, with two weaker divisions in the XXIV Panzer Corps in reserve. In two days of fighting, Vatutin's front caved in 30 kilometres towards the main Oboyan–Kursk highway, but by 7 July German armour ran up against the first of the main defensive lines, held by the First Tank Army. Grim fighting allowed the Panzer divisions to cross the Psel River, the last natural barrier before Kursk, but the bridgehead achieved by the SS 'Death's Head' Panzer Division was the furthest point of advance.[159] Hoth turned the Second SS Panzer Corps against a small rail junction at Prokhorovka.

For years the subsequent tank battle at Prokhorovka was portrayed as the greatest tank-on-tank battle of the war, which ended in a Soviet victory and hundreds of destroyed tanks. The truth has turned out to be more mundane. To stop the advance of two divisions of the SS Second Panzer Corps, one of the units in reserve, the Fifth Guards Tank Army commanded by General Pavel Rotmistrov, was ordered forward in great haste and sent into battle on 12 July with insufficient advance reconnaissance or planning. Rotmistrov seems to have mistakenly believed that he was part of the Belgorod counter-offensive, and moved his armour in mass towards two SS divisions, 'Leibstandarte' and 'Das Reich', around 500 tanks against 204 in the German units. His force ran into a concealed anti-tank ditch and was ground down by the superior firepower of the German tanks, mainly the Panzer IV with an improved gun. In two days the Fifth Guards lost 359 tanks and self-propelled guns (208 were a complete loss); the two SS Panzer divisions lost only 3 on 12 July.[160] This was a major tactical victory, but it did not bring 'Citadel' closer to success, as von Manstein hoped.

The Soviet southern front did not collapse but continued to fight back; by the 16th even the badly mauled Fifth Guards had 419 tanks and 25 self-propelled guns once more.[161] The onset of 'Kutuzov' forced von Manstein to send divisions and aircraft north to help von Kluge, though German air support in the south had already been eroded heavily by constant combat, while infantry losses made it difficult to hold terrain even when the armour was successful. Indeed, the overemphasis on Kursk as a tank battle misses the reality that this was a battle of infantry, artillery and aircraft, much like the final battles of the First World War. With declining confidence, Hoth mounted further attacks south of Prokhorovka to try to break Soviet resistance. Operation 'Roland' began on 14 July but with exhausted troops and no reserves could not pierce the Soviet line. 'I watched as shattered soldiers made all sorts of basic errors,' recorded one German soldier, 'because they could no longer keep their mind on the job.'[162] In the end the southern pincer had to be abandoned by 23 July because, further south, fresh Soviet offensives towards the Mius and Donets rivers forced von Manstein to detach more of his forces away from 'Citadel'.[163]

On 13 July, Hitler had already called von Kluge and von Manstein together to announce that the operation would have to be wound up – not, as is often suggested, because of the Allied landings in Sicily, though this was one consideration, but chiefly because of the sudden crisis prompted by the breakthrough on Model's front. Hitler's response to the crisis in Italy was slow in coming, and only one of the three divisions in the SS Second Panzer Corps, 'Leibstandarte', was actually sent to the Mediterranean on 17 July. 'Citadel' was ended because it had failed in its initial aims; the Soviet counter-offensive, unanticipated by the German side, then compounded the failure. In the attritional battles of July and August, the German side lost 203,000 casualties, almost one-third of the starting force, and 1,030 aircraft. Across the whole Eastern Front 1,331 tanks and self-propelled guns were lost. Soviet losses were much higher – at Kursk alone 70,000 dead or missing, 1,600 tanks and 400 aircraft – but by summer 1943 their material could be replaced more easily than German as Soviet factories focused on crude mass production.[164] The longer effort to contain the southern pincer meant that Operation 'Rumiantsev', the southern counter-offensive, could only begin on 3 August, when the reserve Steppe Army Group and Vatutin's Voronezh Army Group were released towards Belgorod. By this stage, after weeks of attrition, von Manstein's army group had only 237 armoured fighting vehicles and 175,000 men; by late August it was down to 133,000. Belgorod fell swiftly to the Red Army on 5 August and Stalin ordered the first celebration of the war in Moscow with an artillery salute by 120 guns and a sky full of fireworks. Despite a further attempt by von Manstein to block the onward rush, Kharkov was captured on 23 August, changing hands for the last time.

After Kursk the tide was all one way. The operations south of Kharkov in July to distract von Manstein from Kursk made slow progress, but in mid-August Stavka ordered the Southwestern and Southern Army Groups to recapture the western Donbass as a step towards retaking the industrial regions of Ukraine and breaching the Dnieper River further west. On 30 August Taganrog was taken; on 8 September Stalino (now Donetsk); and by 22 September the Red Army reached the Dnieper south of the city of Dnepropetrovsk. Consistent with Stalin's strategy of attack across the whole front, so as to give the German army no opportunity to pause, Western Army Group, commanded by General Vasily Sokolovskii, launched Operation 'Suvorov' on 7 August aimed towards Smolensk, scene of some of the heaviest fighting in 1941. It was recaptured on 25 September following a 240-kilometre stretch of bitter fighting. While the German front caved in, Hitler ordered the establishment of an *Ostwall* (Eastern Line) behind which the German armies could stand to hold back the tide. The southern part was codenamed 'Wotan', running from Melitopol on the Sea of Azov to Zaporozh'e, a line defending the raw materials and industry of Nikopol and Krivoi Rog which Hitler regarded (with exaggeration) as vital to the future prosecution of the war. The northern part of the *Ostwall*, the Panther Line, ran north along the Dnieper and Desna rivers to Narva on the Baltic Coast. The sheer length made an effective fortified line impossible, and troops found on arrival a line on a map rather than a firm defensive position. German forces succeeded in retreating without a rout, but by late September von Manstein had pulled Army Group South back across the Dnieper, with his 60 divisions down to an average of 1,000 men each, with only 300 tanks for the entire army group.[165] On the way the units were ordered to adopt a ruthless scorched-earth strategy, blowing up what they could, burning villages to the ground and compelling men and women to march with them as forced labour. In the far north, German Army Group North, denuded of men and equipment to help further south, faced a major Soviet drive with only 360,000 men and 7 tanks, but succeeded in holding a defensive perimeter that was pierced only in January 1944, when Model, sent to replace von Küchler, withdrew back to the Panther Line, leaving Leningrad at last free of its two-and-a-half-year siege.

The Red Army battled almost continuously across Ukraine and into eastern Belorussia from August 1943 to April 1944, although Hitler's insistence that Nikopol and Krivoi Rog hold out, despite their isolation as the Red Army swept past south and north, meant that until February

1944 some part of the Ukrainian industrial zone remained in German hands. With Soviet forces by late September along the Dnieper, Zhukov proposed an airborne assault to speed up the seizure of territory on the far riverbank. The result was a complete failure, as with a great many wartime airborne operations, but as many as forty small bridgeheads were made by troops who were told that the first ones across the river would be awarded the coveted title 'Hero of the Soviet Union'. No less than 2,438 awards were made, 47 of them to generals.[166] Army Group South proved just strong enough to hem in the bridgeheads south of Kiev during October. But Vatutin's Voronezh Army Group – now renamed First Ukrainian to take account of the changed geography of battle – had sent one division across the river north of Kiev, near the village of Liutezh, into an area of swamps and marsh which the Germans regarded as no danger. In complete secrecy, the Third Guards Tank Army was moved into the bridgehead; poor weather prevented German air reconnaissance while, south of Kiev, deception measures were designed to make von Manstein believe this was where an attack would come. On 3 November, the German defence was taken by complete surprise as two whole armies poured out of the swampy terrain.

Kiev was taken three days later, on the eve of the annual celebration of the Bolshevik Revolution on 7 November. In his commemoration speech Stalin proclaimed the 'year of the great turning point'; Molotov hosted a sumptuous celebration feast, so generous with alcohol that the British ambassador collapsed face down on the table.[167] Kiev was a symbolic victory, like Stalingrad, but it was only part of a great sweep across the rest of Ukraine. To the south, Konev's Steppe Army Group (now the Second Ukrainian), stormed across the Dnieper to threaten Nikopol, while in the far south the German Seventeenth Army was cut off in the Crimea beyond all prospect of rescue. After a draining five months of combat the Soviet offensive paused, the troops exhausted by the effort, short of supplies and even footwear. But in the early spring of 1944, the rest of southern Ukraine was finally reconquered; Nikopol fell on 8 February, Krivoi Rog two weeks later. Konev by mid-March had reached the Dniester River and the border of Moldova, and by 7 April he entered Romanian territory at Botoşani. To the north, Zhukov and Vatutin captured Rovno (the former capital of the Reich Commissariat Ukraine) and Lutsk, scene of the major tank battles of summer 1941, before swinging south to reach the edge of the Carpathian Mountains and the Jablonica Pass into Hungary. These were the first of what Stalin was to call the 'Ten Crushing Blows' of 1944.[168]

The Soviet offensive in 1943 was massive in scale, from the Leningrad front to the Sea of Azov in the south, and it was fought at a high cost in personnel and equipment. The 6 million troops of the Red Army fought almost continuously from July through to December. Since the opening of Soviet archives, much has been made of the deficiencies of the Soviet forces that drove the German army back: poor training at every level, inadequate staff work, poor intelligence-gathering, clumsy tactics, defective military production, and so on. From this perspective, it is difficult to understand how the Red Army, driven back relentlessly in 1941 and 1942, was capable of reversing its fortunes so dramatically. The conventional view today, as Boris Sokolov has put it, suggests that the German army was simply 'buried with corpses', overwhelmed by the sheer number of bodies the Red Army could throw at them.[169] This is a profound misunderstanding of the reality. By 1943 Red Army units, like German, were short of manpower after the colossal losses of 1941–2. The population pool available to the Soviet war effort after the loss of territory was little larger than the pool available to the Axis, around 120 million. German forces had to be spread widely in occupied Europe, but most of the best fighting units were on the Eastern Front, while the Red Army had to keep sizeable forces in the Far East against a possible Japanese threat. Soviet mobilization was more ruthless: younger and older men were recruited, and a substantial number of women; wounded soldiers were returned quickly to combat units, while the number of supporting service troops was smaller than for German forces. However, even greater numbers would not count, were it not for the continuous effort made from 1942 onwards to learn from mistakes, improve training and modify tactics to try to reduce losses. In November a formal 'Section for the Exploitation of War Experience' was established to process and disseminate all the lessons necessary to make Red Army and Air Force combat more effective.[170] At the same time, priority was given to the mass production of weapons so that the shortage of trained infantry could be mitigated by enhanced firepower, air support and mobility, using weapons that were now the equal of German ones, including the La-5, Yak-1b and Yak-7b fighter aircraft, and the massive ML-20 and SU-152 self-propelled guns. Lend-Lease supplies made this priority possible, though even by the time of Kursk the quantity of aid was still relatively modest. Despite the surviving deficiencies, incremental improvement was sufficient to turn Soviet forces from the clumsy and inept entity of 1941 into a formidable fighting machine, which the German armed forces, for all their obvious operational experience and tactical ingenuity, could not defeat.

In November 1943, Stalin finally acceded to his Allies' request for a summit meeting, which had been pursued by Churchill and Roosevelt since the summer. Stalin had insisted that he was too busy visiting the front line to meet them (in fact, he went only once during the whole war, on 1 August 1943, to the headquarters of Western Army Group), and he had no desire to meet at Scapa Flow as Churchill had suggested. Instead, the three leaders agreed on the Iranian capital, Tehran, in a country jointly occupied by British and Soviet troops in 1941. There was only one chief purpose to the summit, as both Stalin and Roosevelt understood: to cement a firm agreement that the Western Allies would at last mount a major campaign in France in 1944 to relieve the Soviet front. At a foreign ministers' meeting in Moscow in October, a prelude to Tehran, Cordell Hull had briefed Molotov on the details of 'Overlord' to reassure the Soviet side that their Allies would not let them down. To show good faith, the United States Military Mission in Moscow began from late October to provide the Soviet side with daily briefings on the preparation for invasion.[171] Although Churchill had been forced to confirm 'Overlord' when he met with Roosevelt again in Quebec in August, he still had deep doubts that simultaneous fronts in Italy and France would be 'strong enough for the tasks set them', while the British Chiefs of Staff remained wary of making 'Overlord' 'the pivot of our strategy on which all else turns'. Before he left for the November summit, Stimson warned the president that Churchill 'wanted to stick a knife in the back of "Overlord"'.[172] For Roosevelt and Hopkins, both in poor health, the journey to Tehran was a major physical challenge, but the choice of a sea journey in the battleship *Iowa* proved valuable as an opportunity for the Joint Chiefs, who accompanied the president, to reach an absolute agreement that 'Overlord' was the 'primary U.S.–British ground and air effort against Germany' in 1944, with the Italian campaign going no further than a line from Pisa to Rimini, after which resources could be released from the Italian theatre for a simultaneous invasion of southern France codenamed Operation 'Anvil'. A working paper urged that there should be no distractions in the Balkans or Aegean, argued for by Churchill. 'Amen!' wrote Roosevelt on the text.[173]

The two Western leaders met first at Cairo in the 'Sextant' meeting, where they invited Chiang Kai-shek to discuss the war in China. Chiang was flattered by the attention, even more so since at the October meeting in Moscow Soviet leaders had reluctantly been persuaded to include China as one of the signatories of a Four-Power Declaration on war aims, giving China at last equal status with much more powerful allies and opening the way to China's eventual membership of the United Nations Security Council.[174] Roosevelt was anxious to keep China in the war and he promised Chiang a campaign in Burma to open the supply route, if the British would undertake an amphibious operation in the Bay of Bengal, codenamed

'Buccaneer', to draw off Japanese forces. The two leaders discussed an end to colonialism and agreed that after the war the British Empire would have to be wound up.[175] Roosevelt refused a private meeting with Churchill from fear that Stalin would suspect the creation of an Anglo-American 'bloc' against him. The party then flew to Tehran on 27 November, where Stalin had arrived by air from Baku, despite his fear of flying. The following day he met Roosevelt alone, without Churchill, and was assured that an invasion on a large scale would happen in 1944; the conversation pre-empted any attempt that Churchill might make to unhinge the commitment. When on the 29th Stalin asked Churchill directly to his face if he wanted 'Overlord', the prime minister was forced to agree, aware now that he was outnumbered. Despite his misgivings, Churchill had little room for manoeuvre. The following day, Roosevelt announced that agreement had been reached on the principal issue of the Second Front. 'I am happy with this decision,' was Stalin's laconic observation.[176] Stalin also approved the American suggestion for a simultaneous invasion of southern France and dismissed British suggestions for further action in the Balkans and Eastern Mediterranean as 'indecisive', as indeed they were. On other issues, Roosevelt again got what he wanted from Stalin on the basis of the October meeting. A post-war international order, dominated by what Roosevelt called the 'Four Policemen' (the United States, the Soviet Union, Britain and China), was provisionally agreed, together with the joint occupation and dismemberment of a defeated Germany. Stalin gave the first intimation that he would join the war against Japan after Hitler was defeated. Once the decisions were made, a birthday celebration for Churchill at the British Embassy allowed expressions of amity. A tipsy Stalin toasted 'My fighting friend Roosevelt' and 'My fighting friend Churchill', while Churchill rejoined with 'Roosevelt, the President, my friend', but 'Stalin the mighty', a contrast that needed no interpretation.[177]

Amity was less in evidence when Roosevelt and Churchill returned to Cairo to continue discussions about China and the Mediterranean. The promise to help Chiang (who had returned from Cairo a few days before, to discover that a plot against him by the so-called 'Young Generals' had been thwarted) became for the British a major bone of contention. For almost a year there had been inter-Allied argument over an operation to open the Burma Road, codenamed 'Anakim', which the British had persistently rejected.[178] Roosevelt was determined to redeem the commitment to a Burma operation in order to keep China in the war, but after three days of argument with the British side, who did not want to carry out 'Buccaneer' any more than 'Anakim' without substantial American assistance, Roosevelt abandoned the idea. On 7 December, Chiang was informed that action in Burma was to be postponed until later in 1944, a decision that did not surprise him.[179] At the same time differences arose over a new obsession of Churchill's to seize the former Italian colony of Rhodes from the German occupiers ('Rhodes madness' wrote a critical Brooke in his diary in October), which he continued to urge at Cairo.[180] The American position was to avoid any further commitments in the Eastern Mediterranean. Churchill hoped to persuade the Turkish government to join the war, for which a successful Dodecanese operation might be adequate bait, but when the Turkish president, Ismet Inönü, arrived in Cairo to meet Allied leaders, he remained non-committal about any change in Turkey's neutral stance. Cairo, as much as Tehran, exposed the fractures in Anglo-American thinking about the future strategy of the alliance, but Churchill was unable to achieve any alteration in the firm commitment to the invasion of France. When Roosevelt returned to Washington, he told Stimson: 'I have brought home "Overlord" safe and sound.'[181]

Tehran and Cairo shaped the coming year of operations. Allied leaders understood that the successes of 1943, which had eliminated the Italian Empire as an enemy, made the defeat of the other Axis empires likely, even if there was no way of judging the time and expense of achieving it. The spring and summer of 1944 confirmed the Allied ability to undermine further Axis resistance in a series of large and complex battles and by the autumn there was no doubt about the certainty of victory, but the ultimate defeat of Germany and Japan proved frustratingly elusive. Although a defensive posture had been forced on the armed forces of both Axis powers, with available technology, and favourable topography, defence could do a great deal to hold up and damage an enemy with vastly greater material resources, particularly an active defence, when limited counter-attacks and spoiling actions could be used to augment the capability of the defenders. The advantages for the defender were many. It was possible to dig in and conceal artillery, even tanks if there was not enough fuel for mobile warfare. Hidden from sight, defensive guns were difficult to locate or to destroy. The creation of a full field of fire, with interlinked pillboxes or redoubts using machine-gun and mortar fire, like the defence of Betio, made advances by enemy infantry and tanks hazardous in the extreme. Mortar fire, using smokeless powder, was particularly difficult to locate (often coming from a reverse slope) and deadly. Modern mortars were light, easily carried by one man, and capable of delivering twenty-five to thirty bombs a minute with a high trajectory and short range, ideal for defence against an advancing enemy. So frustrated did the British army become with the remorseless mortar fire from German lines, that in August 1944 a Counter-Mortar Committee was set up to garner scientific advice on how to combat them. Narrow wave radar was explored, and sets designed to help locate mortar positions became available by the autumn, though not widely, but the mortar threat was never eliminated.[182]

Alongside the mortar were varieties of anti-tank weapon which could also be well concealed for ambush. The German hand-held one-shot *Panzerfaust* anti-tank weapon, which was easy to use and portable, imposed high losses on Allied armour. In addition, the mines and barbed wire familiar from the First World War were used extensively to provide extra protection. Just how difficult a competent modern defensive field could be can be illustrated from two examples. The small island of Peleliu in the Palau chain, assaulted in September 1944, was for the Japanese an underground battle waged from 500 caves and tunnels carved out of the coral, many with steel doors, roofed over with boulders and iron beams, almost all skilfully camouflaged. Caves blasted out of the coral were then sealed up with the artillery inside, firing through small slits. The guns and pill-boxes had been set up to give a total field of fire from every direction and all the advantages supplied by the nature of the terrain were exploited to the full. The tiny island took from 15 September to 25 November to subdue completely. The operation was so demanding that the First Marine Division could not see action again for six months.[183] A second example from the Italian campaign shows the same degree of defensive preparation. Before Operation 'Olive' mounted by the Eighth Army against the Adriatic end of the German Gothic Line, German engineers had created a formidable defensive position. There were 8,944 metres of tank ditches, 72,517 anti-tank mines, 23,172 anti-personnel mines, 117,370 metres of wire, 3,604 dugouts, 2,375 machine-gun posts and 479 anti-tank gun units.[184] The surprising thing is not how slow progress was in Italy, or in the Pacific, or in the Normandy countryside, but how defences of this depth and lethality could be overcome at all. During the campaigns of 1944, chiefly against a retreating and defensive enemy, Allied forces had to learn how to cope with what lay in front of them by developing tactics and technology designed to neutralize the advantages a defender enjoyed and to capitalize on their growing material ascendancy.

In the war in Asia, even the defensive posture was briefly abandoned as the Japanese army resumed the offensive in Burma and China to stave off strategic calamity. The idea of a renewed campaign in China, after a year in which the Japanese occupying armies had done little more than conduct punitive raids against Chinese guerrilla forces, was the brainchild of Colonel Hattori Takushirō in the Operations Section of the Japanese army. The 'Long-Range Strategic Plan' called for the conquest of a railway corridor linking Japan's occupied area in central China with Indochina to create a new supply line from the south-east Asian conquests back to the home islands, now that the sea route was subject to an intensified American blockade. Hattori hoped that this would stabilize the war and make possible renewed offensives in the Pacific area by 1946. The immediate aim was a campaign, beginning in summer 1944, to seize the main rail routes through Henan, Hebei and Hunan provinces and on to the Indochina border, given the codename '*Ichigō-sakusen*' ('Operation Number One'). Tōjō approved the plan in December but insisted that the ambitions be scaled down to capturing American airbases in the region – a defensive rather than an offensive strategy. Hattori and the local commanders in China wanted more than this, and in defiance of Tokyo began a two-stage campaign in mid-April 1944: '*Kogō*' marked the first stage of consolidating the Beijing–Hankou rail link; '*Shōkei*' was the second stage, driving south towards Changsha and Hengyang to link up with Japanese forces moving north from Indochina. The North China Area Army and the Chinese Expeditionary Army committed 500,000 from the 620,000 troops in China to the operations, the largest campaign in Japan's history.[185] Nationalist Chinese forces facing them were chronically short of supplies, trained men, medical facilities, even uniforms, and with little prospect of assistance from Chiang's other armies because of a renewed attempt by General Stilwell to open the supply route from India to China.

'*Ichigō*' was successful in all its phases against a weakened and demoralized enemy, despite the long logistical lines to Japanese front-line forces, and the poorer quality of infantry recruits following the transfer of experienced divisions to the Pacific war. After seizing complete control of the Beijing–Hankou railway, on 26 May 150,000 Japanese troops poured into Hunan province and, by 18 June, had captured the city of Changsha, which they had been unable to take earlier in the war. The Chinese commander, General Xue Yue, had only 10,000 men against a besieging force of 30,000. The next target, Hengyang, defended for forty-seven days by Xue and General Fang Xianjue, fell on 8 August. The American air commander in China, General Claire Chennault, was desperate to get the Chinese armies in Hengyang more supplies but was told by Stilwell 'let them stew'.[186] The length of the campaign and the crisis developing in Burma and the Pacific brought renewed attempts by the Japanese general staff to end the operation, but Hattori insisted it should continue even after the capture of six American airbases. Forces moving from the Japanese enclave at Guangzhou and from Indochina completed the capture of a continuous south–north rail route. The campaigns cost the Japanese army 23,000 casualties, but Chiang's depleted Chinese forces lost three-quarters of a million men.[187]

A similarly ambitious campaign against the Allies was planned in Burma by the Japanese Fifteenth Army under command of Lieutenant General Mutaguchi Renya who, like Hattori, saw Japanese occupation of north-east India not only as the means of eradicating the airbases in Assam currently supplying Lend-Lease goods over the mountains to China, but possibly provoking an anti-British revolt in India and encouraging the Allies to come to terms. In January 1944, Tōjō approved Operation 'Ugō', a more cautious operation to occupy a 'strategic zone in north-east India around Imphal', even as a British–Indian force was pushing further south into the Arakan region of Burma, where the Japanese garrison suffered a heavy defeat in late February. The attack on the towns of Imphal and Kohima was launched on 7/8 March by a force of 3 infantry divisions and 20,000 volunteers from the Indian National Army, whose commander, Subhas Chandra Bose, wanted his force to help 'liberate' his homeland. Lacking motor transport, the Japanese army brought with them 12,000 horses and mules, and more than 1,000 elephants. The British commander, Lieutenant General William Slim, was warned in advance of the operation and prepared a defence on the Imphal plain. The 155,000 defenders, supported by extensive air forces, outnumbered Mutaguchi's 85,000 men, who were short of supplies, had no tanks and enjoyed little air support. The fighting was savage on both sides. Slim later recalled 'quarter was neither asked, nor given'.[188] Although Kohima was surrounded and besieged, air supply kept the garrison fighting both here and at Imphal, until the Japanese army, debilitated by hunger, disease and months of attrition, retreated, losing some 70 per cent of the force as casualties. On 4 July 1944, Operation 'Ugō' was terminated on orders from imperial headquarters.[189]

Further north in Burma, Stilwell had persuaded Chiang, despite the conclusions from the Cairo summit, to let him once again try to open the Burma Road using Chinese troops from Force X, trained and armed in India, with support from Force Y based in Yunnan province. Chiang was reluctant to repeat the disaster of two years before, but Roosevelt sent a sharply worded message that if he did not 'the United States and China would have limited opportunity for further cooperation'. Chiang gloomily contemplated that China would now 'fight this war alone', but he gave in.[190] Stilwell reached the city of Myitkyina in mid-May, where he once again stalled against stubborn Japanese defence. By the time British, Indian and Chinese troops had forced the Japanese Thirty-third Army to retreat southwards in August, Stilwell's force had casualties of 80 per cent. Slim continued the pursuit of the retreating Japanese across the Irrawaddy plain; Mandalay was captured on 20 March 1945, and Rangoon, a city now in ruins following Allied bombing, was entered in late

April, by which time the Burmese National Army of Aung San had switched sides to the Allies. The remaining Japanese troops withdrew into Malaya. In the north the Chinese X and Y Forces finally reopened the Burma Road in February 1945 (now called, with little justice, the 'Stilwell Road') but the first supplies took months to reach China.[191] The defence of Burma for the Japanese was a deadly contest. Out of the 303,501 troops committed over three years, 185,149 died of combat, disease or hunger, a grim reminder of the failure of the Japanese army to provision the frontiers of their empire. British dead for the whole campaign amounted to 4,037; Indian and West African troops, who did much of the fighting, lost 6,599.[192]

Both '*Ichigō*' and '*Ugō*' were aimed in the first place against the American air effort, to prevent United States air forces from supporting Chiang and bombing the home islands. But for the Japanese war effort the much greater danger lay in the Pacific where Nimitz, following the successful seizure of bases in the Marshall Islands, moved on to target three islands in the Marianas – Saipan, Tinian and Guam – close enough to Japan to interrupt any remaining sea traffic and to bomb the Japanese home islands. Spruance's Fifth Fleet now had formidable naval resources available. Rear Admiral Marc Mitscher was given command of Task Force 58, which included fifteen carriers and seven new battleships to shield the invasion force for the islands. The Joint Chiefs' directive of 12 March 1944 ordered Nimitz to begin operations on 15 June, while General MacArthur in the south-west Pacific completed the capture of northern New Guinea as a stepping-stone to a possible invasion of the southern Philippines. To speed up this operation, MacArthur ordered his amphibious and air forces to leapfrog past Japanese garrisons, which could be neutralized or destroyed later. Shielded by Vice Admiral Thomas Kinkaid's Seventh Fleet, and with the combined Australian–American amphibious force under Rear Admiral Barbey, a series of five amphibious landings was launched, beginning with the seizure of the Admiralty Islands, where Seeadler Harbour was later used as a staging base for the Philippines. There followed operations 'Persecution' and 'Reckless' to seize beachheads surrounding the port of Hollandia on 22 April 1944. The three landings here were not seriously opposed, while interception of Japanese communications, which were decrypted at an Australian base set up in the Brisbane racetrack, gave MacArthur's forces the opportunity to anticipate Japanese attacks or their plans for reinforcement.[193] After consolidating at Hollandia, further operations captured Wakde Island, finally secure by 25 June after heavy fighting, and then Biak, which was invaded on 27 May. The strength of the garrison had been badly miscalculated, and only after a

month of bitter fighting were the airfields in Allied hands, but the island
was not finally pacified until August with the loss of one-fifth of the Allied
infantry committed and almost all the Japanese defenders. Western New
Guinea was cleared by Australian forces and airbases constructed for the
next move north, with the south-west perimeter of the Japanese Empire
now fully breached.[194]

The Japanese navy understood clearly that the Marianas would be the
next American target and began reinforcing the islands in June, shortly
before the planned invasion. Lieutenant General Saitō Yoshitsugu had
31,629 men on Saipan, a much larger garrison than the American intelligence estimate, which suggested only 11,000 combat troops. Defences
were not yet complete, but ready enough to inflict heavy damage. The
three marine and two army divisions assigned to Operation 'Forager'
came under the command once again of Richmond Turner and Holland
Smith, a total of 127,000 men brought to the islands by task forces which
numbered 535 ships, capable of transporting a colossal 320,000 tons of
supplies.[195] Saipan was to be invaded on 15 June, Guam, the former
American base, on the 18th, Tinian on 15 July, but the fierce resistance on
Saipan made the original schedule unworkable. The invasion force of Second and Fourth Marine Divisions landed on eight beaches on 15 June but
took heavy casualties from artillery firing from a range of hills overlooking the sea. The heavy naval gunfire support had done little to destroy
concealed artillery positions and the marines were raked by machine-gun,
mortar and heavy artillery fire. On 18 June, Mitscher moved Task Force
58 away from Saipan to protect the invasion from an oncoming Japanese
fleet, the Mobile Force under Vice Admiral Ozawa Jisaburō. Spruance
assumed that the enemy fleet wanted to destroy the landing ships and
disrupt the amphibious operation, but Ozawa saw this as an opportunity
for a major fleet engagement to destroy Task Force 58 'with one blow'.

The balance of forces greatly favoured Mitscher, even though Ozawa
brought with him nine carriers and five battleships, the heart of what
remained of the Japanese Combined Fleet. Mitscher's carriers were loaded
with 900 aircraft, made up of the most modern naval models, the Grumman 'Hellcat', the Curtiss 'Helldiver' and the Grumman 'Avenger'
torpedo-bomber, with crews better trained than their Japanese counterparts. These were double the number available to Ozawa, while the
prospect of reinforcement from Japanese land-based aircraft had been
eroded by almost a week of continuous bombing and strafing by American planes.[196] The outcome of what is known as the Battle of the Philippines
Sea was a disaster for the Mobile Force. On the morning of 19 June,
Ozawa sent off two waves of aircraft to attack Mitscher's fleet, which was

positioned to take maximum advantage of radar intelligence. Out of 197 aircraft despatched, only 58 returned. A third wave that morning saw twenty-seven out of forty-seven return, but the fourth and final wave of eighty-two aircraft failed to find the American fleet and flew on to Guam where thirty were shot down, while most of the rest crashed on the damaged runway, leaving just nine to return to the Japanese carriers. Although an exact figure has proved elusive, at least 330 Japanese carrier and ground-based aircraft were shot down in what American airmen nicknamed the 'Great Marianas Turkey Shoot'. The following day a further sixty-five Japanese carrier aircraft were lost, while the carriers *Shokaku* and *Taiho* were sunk by submarines. The fleet returned to Japan with only thirty-five operational carrier aircraft left.[197]

With almost no threat now from enemy sea or air power, the battle on Saipan became a case of daily attrition of Saitō's force as it moved back through defensive belts to the north of the island. By 30 June, short of food and water, and bottled up by remorseless naval gunfire, the defenders prepared for a last act. Saitō committed suicide, leaving behind more than 4,000 soldiers, liberally supplied with sake, to carry out a massed *banzai* charge carrying what weapons they could find or improvise. Behind the first wave came the wounded and sick, with bandages and crutches, who chose to die with their comrades. During the night of 7/8 July, they charged in a screaming mass. The first American unit overrun lost 918 men killed or wounded from a total of 1,107. After hours of combat, often hand-to-hand, there were 4,300 dead Japanese. Two days later the island was declared secure, but not before hundreds of civilians crowded to the cliffs on the north shore where they committed mass suicide, stabbing or strangling their children first before leaping from the clifftops themselves.[198] Almost all the Japanese defenders died, but there were 14,111 American casualties, one-fifth of the combat troops.[199]

The operation against Guam began on 21 July, after thirteen days of bombardment, the longest in the Pacific war. Against a more prepared defence, it took a week to establish a major beachhead, and the island was only declared secure on 11 August, after three weeks of harsh combat during which a further 1,744 Americans were killed. An estimated 3,000 Japanese soldiers fled into the jungle, where some remained until the end of the war. The third island, Tinian, was invaded on 24 July, but was secure by 1 August with few of the difficulties faced on Saipan or Guam. The fall of New Guinea and then the Marianas proved too much for Japan's senior statesmen to forgive, and Tōjō was forced to resign as premier on 18 July with his hope frustrated that victory in Burma, China and the Marianas would encourage the United States to negotiate a compromise peace.

By this stage, it was clear to the Japanese leadership that Germany's imperial adventure was doomed as well. Ambassador Ōshima warned the Tokyo Foreign Office in early June 1944 that 'it is going to be very hard for Germany to wage war from now on', a view that prompted growing anxiety that soon Japan would be the only Axis power still left fighting the Allies.[200] In the two weeks following Ōshima's message, major operations in Europe from both West and East proved to be decisive. The launch of 'Overlord' on the morning of 6 June 1944 finally redeemed Roosevelt's promise to Stalin confirmed at Tehran. Two weeks later, on 23 June, the Red Army launched Operation 'Bagration' to clear the German army from Belorussia. The subsequent battles did not end the war, but they sealed Germany's fate.

The invasion from the West seemed more certain after the Tehran Conference, but it remained a contested issue over the scale of risk, and Churchill's own lingering doubts about its feasibility. Planning for the assault had begun in April 1943, directed by the British Lieutenant General Frederick Morgan, but it led to further inter-Allied wrangling. Two possible sites were explored, one the Pas de Calais, across the narrowest part of the English Channel, the other from the mouth of the Seine River to the Cotentin Peninsula in Normandy; the American planners preferred Normandy, the British the Pas de Calais. After two days of argument at the headquarters of Lord Louis Mountbatten, chief of Combined Operations, the Normandy option prevailed. At Quebec ('Quadrant') in August 1943, Morgan presented a plan for a narrow assault with three divisions in May 1944.[201] Only after Tehran was serious planning undertaken, once Roosevelt had agreed on a supreme commander for the enterprise. George Marshall wanted the chance to command in the field, but Roosevelt hesitated to lose his regular counsel in Washington, and Eisenhower was preferred. He left the Mediterranean command to a British general, Henry Maitland Wilson, in January 1944, and took Montgomery with him, despite their prickly relationship, as overall ground commander of the Allied force, to be designated the Twenty-first Army Group. On 21 January the new command team met to inspect the plan. A three-division landing was regarded as too weak for any chance of success and the plan was changed to five, and later six. The port of Cherbourg was regarded as an essential target, as well as the city of Caen, around which Allied air forces could be based. It was planned to build up a force of thirty-seven divisions in the beachhead, before driving the German army across France. Two other factors appeared critical to success: first the Combined Bomber Offensive, agreed at Casablanca, had to weaken the German air force and

German war production sufficiently to reduce the risk for 'Overlord'; and second, the Italian front had to be stabilized so that troops and shipping could be moved to Britain for the invasion.

Not until the summer of 1943 did the Combined Chiefs insist that the bomber offensive focus on damage to Germany that would help 'Overlord'. American air force planners drew up a list of seventy-six key targets, with priority for the German aircraft industry, and this aim was incorporated in the 'Pointblank Directive' issued to Bomber Command and the US Eighth Air Force on 10 June 1943. The two air forces were asked to supply regular reports to the Combined Chiefs on the success of the bombing campaign to help judge the right moment for invasion. In September the Combined Chiefs made support for 'Overlord' the overriding priority for the bomber force.[202] The results were mixed. Air Marshal Arthur Harris, in charge of Bomber Command, insisted that he continue the strategy of night attacks on industrial cities as the best way to undermine the German war economy. With Operation 'Gomorrah' in late July and early August of 1943, he undertook a spectacular series of raids on Hamburg, resulting in the death of 34,000 civilians, but little affecting the industries needed for war. The Eighth Air Force, which only reached an effective strength by the end of 1943, targeted the German ball-bearing and aircraft industries, but with rates of loss so high that by November the daylight campaign had almost come to a halt, to be resumed deep into Germany only in February 1944. Harris followed Hamburg with a sustained bombardment of Berlin across the winter of 1943–4, but these raids also took high casualties without any clearly decisive effect on German air power. Harris had devoted an estimated 2 per cent of his bombing effort to fighter aircraft assembly plants and he was ordered to do more.[203] With the evidence that German fighter strength was growing steadily despite the bombing, General Ira Eaker, commander of the Eighth Air Force, and his successor in January 1944, Brigadier General James Doolittle, were told that 'Pointblank' 'must be pressed to the limit' if German air power were to be degraded sufficiently.[204] The same month, General Carl Spaatz was appointed overall commander of American strategic air forces in Europe, a commander committed to the idea that the German air force could be fatally undermined not only by the destruction of aircraft production but through the attrition of the German fighter force as it tried to stop the bomber streams.

The key to eliminating the German air force was the long-range fighter. Until the last months of 1943 no effort had gone into providing fighter escort for American bombers by day over German soil, but the realization that there was no other way to reverse the high loss rates prompted an urgent programme to fit extra fuel tanks to three aircraft, the P-38

Lockheed 'Lightning', the Republic P-47 'Thunderbolt' and the North American P-51 'Mustang'. Of the three, the 'Mustang' proved the most successful, capable of flights beyond Berlin or as far as Vienna. The United States Eighth Fighter Command, under Major General William Kepner, was keen to use the long-range aircraft to bring the fight to the German air force, and he allowed his large number of fighters, over 1,200 by early 1944, to fly 'freelance', pursuing enemy fighters as they assembled or climbed to intercept, chasing them back to bases where they were strafed on the ground.[205] The object was to give the enemy fighter arm no respite. Although Eighth Air Force bomber streams, now directed at the German aircraft industry as a priority, took their highest percentage losses in raids in spring 1944 against a reorganized Reich Air Fleet, commanded by Colonel General Hans-Jürgen Stumpff, the haemorrhage of the German fighter force proved irreversible. In February, one-third of German fighters were lost, by April 43 per cent. Since almost four-fifths of all fighters were now defending the Reich, the result was to starve the fighting fronts of replacement aircraft. Between January and June 1944, the German air force lost 6,259 aircraft in combat and 3,626 due to accidents, a reflection of the declining training regime for German pilots.[206] The air battles over Germany more than the bombing ensured that 'Overlord' when it happened would enjoy complete air supremacy. On 6 June, the opening day of the operation, German Air Fleet 3 in northern France had only 520 serviceable aircraft, and just 125 fighters; the Western Allies mustered 12,837 in total, including 5,400 fighter aircraft.[207] 'In the sky there are more American fighter-bombers and bombers than birds,' wrote one German soldier in the first days of the invasion, '. . . one never sees German aircraft.'[208]

The situation in Italy was less significant than the destruction of German air power, but the Combined Chiefs had made it an objective that the Italian campaign should reach the 'Pisa–Rimini' line north of Rome well before the onset of 'Overlord' to ensure that the Mediterranean theatre would not distract from the larger enterprise by tying down resources in manpower and shipping. The stalemate at the Gustav Line in late 1943 could have been accepted, since German forces were tied down regardless; Kesselring had thirteen divisions in the south of Italy, eight more in the north. It was Churchill who persisted after Tehran in viewing 'the stagnation in Italy' as somehow a blemish on the British record and urged once again a final effort to reach Rome by February, well before the invasion of France.[209] One solution, already suggested by General Clark, was an amphibious landing behind the Gustav Line to cut German communications and perhaps move through the Alban Hills to Rome as the Germans retreated. Eisenhower was against the idea, but Churchill prevailed, hoping for an even more ambitious landing at the mouth of the Tiber, in striking distance of the capital, though too far from the Gustav Line. Churchill had to persuade Roosevelt to allow enough landing craft to stay in the Mediterranean a few more weeks so that Operation 'Shingle' could take place, but Alexander and Clark insisted on a more modest landing of two divisions on the beaches at Anzio – near enough to the German line to offer a threat, but also close to the hills that led to Rome.[210] The operation was planned too rapidly, and little thought went into how it would develop after the landing. The chosen commander of the American VI Corps, Major General John Lucas, was visibly gloomy about its prospects, suspecting a second Gallipoli, with 'the same amateur ... still on the coach's bench'.[211] The rehearsal for the amphibious operation Lucas considered 'a fiasco', after losing forty-three amphibious vehicles and nineteen large artillery pieces into the sea. On 22 January the landing was made, in a sector where there were very few German soldiers. By day two the force had carved out a 40-kilometre front, at which point Lucas dug in rather than risk a more aggressive advance in the German rear. Kesselring issued the alarm code-word 'Richard' to indicate a coastal attack and summoned what few forces he could from Rome and three divisions from the north. By 2 February, with Lucas still inert, General Eberhard von Mackensen's Fourteenth Army had surrounded the beachhead, where it sat bottling up the Americans until May.[212] Lucas was replaced by one of his divisional commanders, Major General Lucian Truscott, but it made little difference to the blockade beyond raising morale.

The landing at Anzio was a strategic failure, raising further doubts among its critics that 'Overlord' could succeed. A simultaneous attempt to breach the Gustav Line, with the aim of meeting up with the forces from the beachhead, failed in abysmal weather to dislodge German defenders dug in to advantageous mountain terrain. The nodal point of the line was the town of Cassino and the high bluffs above, topped by the Benedictine abbey of Monte Cassino. The cost in reducing the town and storming the cliffs greatly outweighed the advantage of pushing further up the peninsula. In February and March, a New Zealand Corps, including the Fourth Indian Division, tried twice to storm the town without success, partly due to the obliteration bombing that preceded the attack which had blocked all the streets with rubble. On 15 February, the American Fifteenth Air Force bombers dropped 351 tons of bombs on the abbey on the mistaken assumption that the Germans were using it for defence, killing 230 Italian civilians who had taken refuge there.[213] The German First Parachute Division then occupied the ruins, which they held until May. Alexander was forced to rethink the campaign. Operation 'Diadem' brought the Eighth

Army over from the Adriatic coast to help break the deadlock: while the Cassino heights were stormed, Clark's Fifth Army was to push up the western coast and the Eighth Army would open up the Liri Valley and turn the German line to encircle Kesselring's forces. There were over 300,000 Allied troops, including a French expeditionary corps under General Alphonse Juin, and the Polish II Corps commanded by Lieutenant General Władysłav Anders. Victory here, it was thought, would prevent the German army from transferring divisions to oppose 'Overlord'.[214]

The operation was finally launched on 11 May, only three weeks before the invasion of France. Within a week the British XIII Corps had opened up the Liri Valley, west of Cassino, while Truscott was at last able to break out from the Anzio beachhead. Surprise had been complete against a German force worn down by months of tough mountain fighting; four of the leading German commanders were away from the battle, two in order to be decorated by Hitler in person. The hardest battle was for the heights overlooking the ruins of Cassino. Anders's corps forced a way up, battling almost suicidal German resistance and taking heavy casualties. By 17 May, Polish units were just below the abbey, but the depleted and exhausted German defenders began to withdraw. The following day Polish scouts found the abbey occupied only by the wounded. A Polish flag was unfurled over the battered building and a Polish bugler played the *Kraków Hejnal*, a Polish national hymn. It was the most symbolic moment in the Poles' long fight against the German enemy. A few hours later, British officers insisted on adding the Union Jack.[215] Kesselring understood that he could not withstand the sheer weight of the Allied operation and began to withdraw to avoid encirclement. Instead of closing the ring, Clark ordered Truscott, now pushing forward from Anzio, to move north to Rome to ensure that the capital fell to American forces. The German Tenth and Fourteenth Armies squeezed through the gap between the Allied forces, as the Germans had done at Messina, and moved north of Rome. Clark's forces entered Rome on 5 June, the day before the invasion of Normandy, to Churchill's irritation that a clear British victory had been forestalled.[216] The German army in Italy was not all but annihilated, as it could have been. The argument that the Italian front helped 'Overlord' is open to question. Alexander had more than 25 divisions in Italy, which suffered 42,000 casualties in the campaign to reach Rome. At least some of this force might have contributed to more rapid success in Normandy, and would almost certainly have suffered lower losses.

In London, the Italian campaign mattered only to the extent that it did not absorb more of the essential landing craft for 'Overlord'. In the end enough were released to satisfy Eisenhower. The enlarged landing agreed in

January meant further delays as resources and shipping were built up. A date of 31 May for the operation was agreed in February, but the ideal conditions of adequate moonlight and low tide, to facilitate the crossing and landing, came in the first week of June. In May, Eisenhower finally decreed that 5 June would be D-Day. To ensure success, it was necessary to find some way of protecting shipping as supplies were brought ashore, since the capture and repair of a major port would almost certainly take time. It was decided to build two artificial harbours, or 'Mulberries', built of concrete and metal, which would be constructed in the first days off the Normandy beaches; they were towed over in pieces on D-Day, to be assembled by a task force of 10,000 workers.[217] It was also essential to find a means to limit the German capacity for rapid reinforcement of the defending army in Normandy. In January, Eisenhower's British deputy, Air Chief Marshal Tedder, recruited the British government scientist Solly Zuckerman to plan the bombing of 100 nodal points in the French railway network to handicap German troop movements. The plan was approved by Eisenhower, but it provoked profound opposition. Churchill told the War Cabinet in April that bombing French targets and killing French civilians might create an 'unhealable breach' between France and the Western Allies. Both the strategic bomber commanders, Spaatz and Harris, claimed that bombing small rail targets with heavy bombers was an 'entirely ineffective' and 'uneconomical' use of their forces.[218] Their refusal to agree to the campaign infuriated Eisenhower, who threatened to resign rather than battle with the 'prima donnas'. They also refused to relinquish command to Eisenhower's tactical air force commander, Air Marshal Trafford Leigh-Mallory. In desperation, Eisenhower told Churchill he would 'go home' if he did not get his way.[219] A compromise was arrived at which placed the bomber forces under Eisenhower's direct command but permitted Spaatz to continue bombing German air and oil targets when he had the opportunity. Roosevelt intervened to insist that there should be no scruples about the bombing, and the five-week campaign, according to French officials, reduced rail traffic in the north and west of the country to 15 and 10 per cent of the January figure, but more than 25,000 French civilians were killed in the preparations for invasion.[220] In the end, the heavy bombers proved less useful than Leigh-Mallory's fighter bombers and light bombers, which in a few days before the invasion destroyed seventy-four bridges and tunnels with pinpoint attacks, successfully isolating north-western France.[221]

The third element for success was the extent to which the German side could be deceived about the direction and timing of the landing. This was a daunting prospect, given the sheer size of the force now gathering in southern England, which eventually reached almost 3 million men. A deception plan was approved in January under the codename 'Bodyguard' with the object of persuading the German side that the Pas de Calais was the real object of the invasion. The key was the creation of an entirely fictitious 'First Army Group' in south-east England, placed ostentatiously under General Patton, who had been temporarily sidelined for striking a psychiatric casualty. Dummy camps and equipment, fake radio stations and false information from double-agents all contributed to a picture of much greater strength concentrated opposite Calais. By June 1944, German military intelligence assumed there were eighty divisions waiting to invade, when the true figure was only thirty-eight.[222] The deception worked to the extent that it matched German assumptions. Hitler and the military leadership assumed that the quickest Channel route, closest to the vulnerable Rhine–Ruhr industrial region, was the obvious site for invasion. The man chosen to organize defence in France, Field Marshal Rommel, was convinced that the Pas de Calais was the primary goal, but evidence of a concentration of forces in south-west England led by the late spring to the view that there might well be a diversionary or secondary landing in Normandy to test German defences, while the larger assault on the Pas de Calais would follow later. The result was that German forces in France in Army Group B were divided between Fifteenth Army under Colonel General Hans von Salmuth, who had twenty divisions, including almost all the motorized and armoured units, to defend from the Seine to the Netherlands, and Seventh Army under Colonel General Friedrich Dollmann in Brittany and Normandy with fourteen divisions, but only a single Panzer division. So effective was the deception that not until August did Hitler authorize the transfer of Fifteenth Army to stem the Allied tide further west.

The invasion was long expected by Hitler, who believed that the defeat of the Western Allies was the 'decisive battle'. In Directive No. 51 on 3 November 1943, he claimed that invasion in the West was greater than the danger in the East and would have to be confronted decisively to end the Anglo-American threat once and for all. In March 1944, he addressed German commanders, according to Rommel, with 'wonderful clarity' about his strategy in the West:

> The whole of the enemy's landing operation must under no circumstances last longer than a few hours or at most a few days, for which the attempted landing at Dieppe can be regarded as an 'ideal case'. After a defeated landing the enemy will under no circumstances repeat it. Months would be needed . . . to prepare a renewed landing. But not only will this put off the Anglo-Americans from a fresh attempt, but also the demoralizing impression of a failed landing operation.

Defeat, Hitler continued, would mean that Roosevelt would not be re-elected, while Churchill was now too old, ill and powerless to revive the invasion.[223]

Rommel had to prepare the defensive field in the first months of 1944 in anticipation of an invasion whose date was far from certain. The Atlantic Wall already existed, but it was far from complete. Rommel was given 774,000 workers and 3,765 vehicles from the Organisation Todt construction empire; by 6 June they had constructed 12,247 out of a planned 15,000 defensive posts, placed half a million obstacles along the beaches, and laid 6.5 million mines, but defences on the north-east coast were much stronger than in Normandy. Along the eastern coast there were 132 coastal batteries, but along the western sector only 47.[224] The army units available were also weaker in reality than the number of divisions suggested. Many of the soldiers were older men, or men recovering from wounds, more suitable for static defence; the average age of the six divisions manning the Atlantic Wall fortifications was thirty-seven. Some twenty of the fifty-eight divisions in France were effectively garrison troops. They were also a mix of nationalities, including units recruited in the Russian steppe. In many cases the troops had been all but idle for long periods; they were less well-resourced with modern equipment, or even standard weaponry, and for the coastal divisions, very short of fuel.[225]

The problem faced in all amphibious warfare was to judge between smashing the landing on the beaches or waiting for the beachhead to solidify and then hitting it with mobile reserves to drive the enemy into the sea. Rommel favoured defeat on the coast, using the coastal defence divisions supported by reserves held a short distance behind to be deployed where they were needed. The supreme commander West, von Rundstedt, and the commander of Panzer forces in France, General Geyr von Schweppenburg, both preferred to hold back a large mobile reserve, to be directed at the main axis of attack – in this case the area around Calais, more suitable for armour. Hitler resolved the argument with an unfortunate compromise: Rommel was allowed to maintain the coastal defences in the expectation that the Allies might land in not one, but two or even three places, while von Schweppenburg controlled a central mobile reserve of four Panzer divisions for deployment where needed. As a result, the central reserve was not strong enough to be decisive, even if it could move under constant air attack and resistance sabotage, while the coastal defence was too limited to drive the invaders back from the beaches.[226] Timing was essential to success, but there was no way to know when the invasion would come. Troops were regularly placed on high alert only for the apparent danger to pass. Heavy bombing of the north-east and lighter bombing in Normandy, a deliberate part of the hoax, suggested invasion as expected along the Calais coastline. When fine weather in May brought no Allied action, Hitler's high command began to wonder whether invasion would even come before August. The sudden deterioration of the weather in early June brought a moment of relief. Rommel went to Germany to celebrate his wife's birthday, while many of the senior staff on the critical day of invasion were away conducting tabletop exercises.

In mid-May, Eisenhower and Montgomery addressed the commanders of the invasion on the precise plan. To the west, at the foot of the Cotentin Peninsula, General Bradley's First Army would invade across beaches 'Utah' and 'Omaha' with two divisions; further east towards Caen, General Miles Dempsey would lead the British Second Army with three divisions (including Canadian and Free French units) on beaches 'Gold', 'Juno' and 'Sword'. They would be supported on either flank by airborne operations, the British by 6th Airborne Division, the Americans by the 82nd and 101st Airborne Divisions. There were to be more than 12,000 aircraft in support and 1,200 naval vessels escorting more than 4,000 ships for the amphibious landings. Montgomery expected to seize Caen within days and then hold the eastern pivot against German counter-attack, while the American forces broke into Brittany and then wheeled round towards Paris and the Seine; he scheduled the invaders to reach Paris in ninety days. For the following three weeks there descended a complete information blackout to retain operational surprise. Troops were confined to camp, sailors locked in their ships and all diplomatic traffic, mail abroad and telegraph connections temporarily suspended. Eisenhower was observed to be edgy and taciturn in the final days – the 'D-Day jitters', his aide recorded – though in retrospect it is difficult to see why he feared a possible disaster given the vast forces at his disposal. Alan Brooke was even more pessimistic in his diary, reflecting that at its worst the operation 'may well be the most ghastly disaster of the whole war'.[227] The anxiety was compounded with the change in the weather that had persuaded Rommel to travel to Germany. In three days of tense meetings, Eisenhower interrogated the senior meteorologist, John Stagg, about the prospects. The original invasion date of 5 June had to be abandoned because of gale-force winds and rain, but on the evening of the 4th, Stagg announced an improvement in a day's time, enough to justify the risk. Eisenhower contemplated the decision and then famously called out, 'OK. We'll go.' The invasion fleets set sail the following day for invasion in the early hours of 6 June.[228]

The element of surprise was indeed almost complete. The idea of Normandy as a diversion made it difficult for the German commanders to grasp whether this was the full invasion or not. Hitler was told of the invasion only at midday and was evidently relieved that the tension of waiting was over. The landing, he told his staff, was 'right in the place where we expected them!'[229] Resistance was uneven, and dangerously intense only on 'Omaha' beach (the full details of the amphibious phase are discussed in Chapter 5), but by the end of the day 132,450 men were ashore, supported by heavy equipment and thousands of tons of supplies. Rommel counter-attacked with Twenty-first Panzer Division in the late afternoon, but von Schweppenburg's armoured reserve was held up by Allied air power, as Rommel had known it would be. On 7 June the beachheads linked up, and by the 11th the lodgement held 326,000 men, 54,000 vehicles and 104,000 tons of supplies.[230] Bayeux was captured within two days, but Montgomery's aim to capture Caen quickly was frustrated by an improvised defence. In Operation 'Perch', launched on the 13th, designed to capture the town of Villers-Bocage and push on to Caen, a thin German line inflicted a heavy defeat on the Seventh Armoured Division, and the front line solidified.

At OKW, Jodl had predicted shortly before the invasion that the fighting would show the difference in morale between 'the German soldier threatened with destruction of his homeland, or the Americans and English, who even now do not comprehend why they are fighting in Europe.' German soldiers did fight with unexpected vigour, but the contest was in the view of many a finite one. 'It was a struggle like the last century,' recalled one Panzergrenadier, 'as the white man fought against the Indians.'[231] The regular army units succeeded in establishing a weakly held defensive line, while Rommel was able to bring up divisions from reserve. The Allied armies struggled with the terrain, which favoured the defenders – woods, low hills, narrow lanes and high hedgerows, the *bocage* country. Ambushes were easy to mount, and snipers enjoyed generous cover. Even with dominant air power, which prevented German movement in daylight on all except the cloudiest days, German defensive tactics proved difficult to surmount. 'The real "Nazi" German,' wrote one Canadian trooper, 'fights to the very last and no fooling. They are young, and tough, and fanatical as hell.'[232]

Despite the many advantages enjoyed, progress was so slow that at Eisenhower's headquarters there was fear that the trench stalemate of the First World War might be repeated. The only initial success came when Bradley pushed into the Cotentin Peninsula in order to capture Cherbourg. The four divisions in the peninsula were cut off from the rest of the German line and defence crumbled. By 22 June, American forces on land, supported by a naval barrage, began the port siege. Hitler ordered the garrison commander, Lieutenant General Karl-Wilhelm von Schlieben, to hold at all costs, down to the last man, but on the 26th he surrendered, although some of the garrison held out for a further five days. Hitler fumed at the 'dishonourable swine' who gave up rather than die. He had now all but abandoned the idea of driving the invasion back into the sea and ordered Rommel on 29 June to hem in the enemy 'through small engagements'.[233] Dissatisfied with von Rundstedt's approach to the battle, he replaced him with the former commander of Army Group Centre, Field Marshal von Kluge.

Further east, Montgomery's armies were blocked north of Caen. In poor weather, Rommel was able to move up four Panzer divisions, brought in to strengthen the defence, and between 29 June and 1 July launched a counter-attack on the Caen front which was repulsed only by intense artillery fire. Eisenhower by early July was 'smouldering' when he visited the front, frustrated at what he saw as Montgomery's excessive caution, but after Cherbourg Bradley's army group found progress just as difficult through countryside quite unsuited to rapid, mobile warfare. On 8 July, Montgomery finally launched an all-out attack on the German positions, Operation 'Charnwood', but Rommel had already pulled back to a prepared defensive zone, 16 kilometres deep, south of Caen, dominated by the Bourguébus Ridge, where seventy-eight of the 88mm tank-busting anti-aircraft guns were set up. On 13 July, Montgomery planned a major thrust, Operation 'Goodwood', to tie down and destroy German armour to help Bradley break out further west: 'all the activities on the eastern flank,' ran a report for Brooke, 'are designed to help the forces in the west.'[234]

'Goodwood' lasted for three days of intense fighting during which British and Canadian troops battled through the first three lines of defence, to be held up by the ridge of anti-tank artillery. On 20 July a severe downpour turned the land to mud and Montgomery brought the operation to an end. The aim of wearing down the German defenders at considerable cost was nevertheless achieved. The day after the end of the battle, von Kluge told Hitler that 'the moment has drawn near when this front, already so heavily strained, will break'. By then, German units had lost 2,117 armoured vehicles and 113,000 men, including Rommel, injured in a strafing attack by Allied aircraft. Allied forces had lost heavily in tanks, but by late July still had 4,500, against a German total of 850. By this time more than 1.5 million men and 330,000 vehicles had been brought into the beachhead.[235] Eisenhower's frustration was understandable, but Montgomery achieved his purpose. By late July there were 6 Panzer divisions with 645 tanks on the eastern axis south of Caen, but opposite Bradley's renamed Twelfth Army Group there were only 2, with 110 serviceable tanks between them. It was here, on 25 July, that Bradley's fifteen divisions, now supported by an American Third Army commanded by Patton, began Operation 'Cobra', a breakout that finally destroyed the brittle shield holding the Allies at bay. By this stage the twenty-five divisions facing the Allies were worn down by weeks of attrition with little reinforcement. At least eleven of them were no longer considered capable of combat, while mobility was reduced largely to horses – facts that encouraged Hitler to order the line to stand fast, since a mobile retreat to a longer defensive line in eastern France appeared no longer possible.[236]

The German collapse on the western sector of the front was now swift and complete. After bombing by 1,500 heavy bombers on the first morning, the dazed defenders were overrun. American armoured columns, previously stuck in the *bocage*, now used bulldozers and Sherman tanks with steel 'teeth' (nicknamed 'Rhinoceros') to push through the hedgerows and orchards, while German forces confined to the roads were strafed and bombed by American fighter-bombers. The town of Coutances was captured in two days from half-a-dozen shattered infantry divisions, and Bradley then moved on to the Breton city of Avranches, covering 40 kilometres in 36 hours. Patton's army was now fully activated, and he drove at speed to capture the whole of Brittany, forcing the six German divisions still there to retreat to the ports of Brest, St Nazaire and Lorient, which Hitler had declared to be 'fortress cities'. Patton then wheeled east towards Paris and the Seine, with almost no German forces to obstruct the advance. The German commanders realized that the whole of Army Group B faced encirclement, but Hitler ordered von Kluge to organize a counterstrike against the breakout at Avranches. With five understrength Panzer divisions and 400 tanks, von Kluge had to organize an operation from the area around Mortain to cut the neck of Patton's advance. Warned in advance by Ultra intelligence, Bradley deployed an anti-tank defensive line.

The German operation began during the night of 7 August but was brought to a standstill by remorseless air attack and, within a day, was back to the starting lines, faced with threats on both flanks.[237] Around Caen, the movement of Panzer divisions to the Mortain attack fatally weakened the front. On 8 August, Montgomery switched to a general offensive and within two days approached the town of Falaise, behind the German front. To close the trap, Patton was ordered to send part of Third Army north and by the 11th he had arrived at Argentan, just 32 kilometres from the Canadians nearing Falaise, where he halted. As the pincers closed, Hitler sacked von Kluge and replaced him with Walter Model, summoned back from the East, but it was evident that disaster was unavoidable. Model ordered the remnants of Seventh Army to escape through the 'Falaise Gap', but twenty-one divisions were destroyed, including seven Panzer and two parachute divisions.[238] Thousands did escape, leaving much of the heavy equipment and thousands of vehicles behind; mingled with corpses and dead horses, the guns and trucks blocked the roads in tangled heaps. Eisenhower visited the chaos two days later: 'It was literally possible,' he later wrote, 'to walk for hundreds of yards at a time, stepping on nothing but dead and decaying flesh.'[239]

As German forces fled eastward to avoid capture, Patton pushed on across an almost undefended countryside to reach the Seine at Mantes-Gassicourt, north-west of Paris. A southern wing of his Third Army crossed the Seine south of Paris, and by 25 August had driven to a point only 100 kilometres from the German border. German soldiers in small detachments struggled to cross the river, using improvised rafts, or even swimming across. 'We are gaining ground rapidly,' wrote one soldier to his family, 'but in the wrong direction.'[240] On the far side of the Seine, Model could assemble only 4 weak divisions with 120 tanks against an onrush of 40 Allied divisions. By this point, a second landing operation had taken place on the French Mediterranean coast against Army Group G, commanded by Colonel General Johannes Blaskowitz. Operation 'Anvil', so named in the initial Allied planning as the counterpoint to the Normandy hammer, was supposed to take place simultaneously with 'Overlord', but the shortage of landing craft and the long struggle on the Gustav Line forced its postponement. Churchill was strongly opposed to its revival, since he hoped that the capture of Rome might allow Alexander to move rapidly towards north-east Italy, even to threaten a breakthrough to Vienna – a fantasy that Alexander came to share. Instead, forces were to be moved from Italy, including all four French divisions and 70 per cent of the tactical air forces, to support a renamed Operation 'Dragoon' for a landing on the coast of Provence to support the breakout in Normandy. Irritated by the decision, Churchill told the chiefs of staff that 'the Arnold, King, Marshall combination is one of the stupidest strategic teams ever seen', though a drive to Vienna, even with enhanced forces, was yet further evidence of how removed from strategic reality Churchill had become.[241] German forces in southern France were substantially weakened by the transfer of units to Normandy, and certainly represented an easier target than Kesselring's retreating armies north of Rome. As in the case of 'Overlord', a similar uncertainty existed about the site and timing of any Allied landing in the Mediterranean. Even when troop convoys were spotted passing west of Sardinia on 12 August, OKW believed the Gulf of Genoa was the most likely destination. Blaskowitz made limited preparations in case the enemy did land on the south French coast, but they were far from complete by mid-August.[242]

'Dragoon' was approved by the Combined Chiefs on 2 July, for an operation to begin on 15 August, the day the pincers were supposed to close at Falaise. The operation was entrusted to Lieutenant General Alexander Patch's American Seventh Army, spearheaded by the VI Corps under Truscott, a veteran of Anzio. The day after the landing, a Free French army corps under General Jean de Lattre de Tassigny, with seven divisions, was to capture the naval base at Toulon and the major port of Marseilles. The landing was made with massive naval support, including 5 battleships, 9 carriers and 24 cruisers, supported by more than 4,000 aircraft of the Mediterranean Air Force. Churchill even came on a destroyer to witness what he still regarded as a 'well-conducted but irrelevant and unrelated operation'.[243] The landings, including a paratroop operation, came on stretches of the Provençal coast between Toulon and Cannes which had not been anticipated, defended by only one Panzergrenadier regiment. At almost all the landing beaches there was only token resistance and the move inland was ordered to commence at once. Army Group G headquarters reacted slowly, since it was uncertain whether this was a major landing or merely a raid in strength. The Eleventh Panzer Division was stuck on the wrong side of the river Rhône, with all the bridges destroyed by air interdiction, and could not be deployed to contain the beachhead. By the end of the first day there were 60,150 troops and 6,737 vehicles ashore and the beachhead was rapidly enlarged.[244]

Hitler's headquarters finally reacted to the very real danger that the whole front in France would collapse by ordering Nineteenth Army, holding the southern coast, to withdraw, a striking contrast to Hitler's insistence that everything had to be held. Added to the order was a requirement to undertake a scorched-earth policy as the army retreated up the Rhône Valley, together with the seizure of all French men of military age as hostages, but this proved impossible to fulfil. Blaskowitz received Hitler's order only after two days because communications had all but broken down entirely; over the following weeks he skilfully withdrew his forces, under constant air attack, up the valley to a defensive position between the Swiss border and Alsace. French forces liberated Toulon and Marseilles, while the American divisions reached Grenoble on 23 August and then linked up with Patton's Third Army as the retitled Sixth Army Group, under Lieutenant General Jacob Devers. On 20 August, the Vichy government was hastily evacuated by German security forces to Sigmaringen, near Lake Constance in southern Germany, to avoid capture. Five days later, at de Gaulle's insistence, Paris was occupied by French forces under General Philippe Leclerc, although freeing the city had not been one of Eisenhower's intentions. The Committee of National Liberation, headed by de Gaulle, arrived to establish a new French regime in a country that in less than three months of conflict had been almost entirely cleared of the German enemy.[245]

The campaign in France was a disaster for German forces. Around 265,000 were killed or wounded, and an estimated 350,000 taken prisoner. Almost all equipment was lost in the hurried retreat. The success of the Allied invasion, which had so worried Eisenhower, Brooke and Churchill, is not difficult to explain. Overwhelming air power, dominant navies that allowed the Allies to mount complex amphibious operations, and ground forces generously supplied, except for brief moments of logistical crisis, all created a permissive environment for effective operations. The outcome was predictable, despite the tactical skill with which German soldiers continued to defend untenable positions. If Hitler had ordered an earlier withdrawal to a prepared defensive position on the German border the rout might have been avoided, although France would still have been lost. The cost to the Allies was nevertheless high. By the end of August, Allied casualties were 206,703, more than half of them American.[246] The Normandy operation and the destruction of Army Group B was the high point of Anglo-American achievement during the war. In Germany, public morale plummeted after the news from the fronts. 'Nobody believes any more in victory in the war,' ran one police report from Bavaria, 'since on every side in the theatres of war there is retreat. The morale of the population is for this reason as bad as can be thought.'[247]

While the Western Allies were still hemmed into the Normandy beachhead, the Red Army began one the largest and most decisive operations of the war. Operation 'Bagration', named by Stalin after a fellow-Georgian general, a hero of the war against Napoleon, was launched in full on 23 June, though attacks on the German rear areas in Belorussia began two days before. Although Stalin liked to pretend that the operation was timed to help his Allies, who seemed stuck in the *bocage* country, the operation against Field Marshal Ernst Busch's Army Group Centre, the last significant force on Soviet territory, had been planned months before as part of a rolling series of offensives along the whole vast front, starting with an offensive against the Finnish army in the Karelian Isthmus, which began on 10 June, down to major operations in the south into Romania and the Ploesti oilfield, which began on 20 August. This was a colossal undertaking, reflecting the growing confidence and material strength of the Red Army. For the German side, with an army split between fronts in the west, south and east, it was essential to guess correctly where the main weight of the Soviet summer offensive would come. Given the success the Red Army had enjoyed in southern Ukraine, it was assumed that the enemy would focus on the south and the Romanian axis. Gehlen, the head of army intelligence in the East, followed up his earlier intelligence failures by predicting that Army Group Centre could expect 'a calm summer' – one of the most egregious errors of the war.[248] German forces were stronger in the south, weaker in the centre, a position that exactly suited Soviet plans.

The German misjudgement was compounded with an elaborate deception plan to mask the intention to demolish Army Group Centre. Only five people knew of the whole operation – Zhukov, Vasilevskii, his deputy Alexei Antonov, and two operational planners – and they were forbidden to mention 'Bagration' either by telephone, letter or telegraph. No date was fixed until preparations were complete, but the whole front opposite Army Group Centre went ostentatiously on the defensive, digging trenches and bunkers, while further south a phantom army of dummy tanks, camps and gun parks was set up, defended by active anti-aircraft artillery and patrolled by fighter aircraft to give it greater realism. Reinforcement of the army groups to undertake the offensive, the First, Second, and Third Belorussian Army Groups, together with the First Baltic Army Group, was done in complete secrecy. By July there were a million tons of supplies and 300,000 tons of fuel in place, some of it the fruit of Lend-Lease supplies which reached a peak in 1944.[249] Deception was an important factor, but the remarkable success of 'Bagration', carried out across major river systems and through countryside far from ideal for rapid mobility, against a German Army Group that had defied repeated attacks from autumn 1943 onwards, owed most to the changed operational approach. The Red Army this time did what the Germans had done so successfully in 1941, pushing through heavy spearheads deep into the enemy front to encircle German forces and disorient the defenders. Busch had 51 understrength divisions numbering 480,000 men (though only 166,000 were regular combat troops) and had been ordered by Hitler to hold 'fortress cities' in Belorussia – Mogilev, Orsha, Vitebsk, Bobruisk – as elements of a static defensive line against which they expected the usual costly Soviet frontal assault. There were no Panzer divisions and only 570 armoured fighting vehicles, because an attack was expected in the south, where Model's Army Group North Ukraine had eight Panzer divisions. The front was supported by 650 aircraft, but only 61 fighters since fighter aircraft were now defending the Reich or fighting in France. So thin was the defensive force that each kilometre of front was held by an average of 100 men.[250] The four Soviet Army Groups were composed of 166 rifle, cavalry and armoured divisions, a total of 2.4 million men and women, 31,000 artillery pieces, 5,200 tanks and self-propelled guns and 5,300 aircraft, though by no means all were used in the initial assault.[251]

This vast force was unleashed on the morning of 23 June, beginning at the north of the salient and rolling slowly south over the next two days. Special plough tanks were sent through the minefields, followed in the early morning dark by infantry, tanks and artillery working together. Flares lit up the front, while searchlights dazzled the defenders; as the German defence crumbled, mechanized forces pushed through the gaps to exploit the ruptures and move on quickly, under orders this time to leave pockets of resistance to be cleared up by the advancing infantry. The advance belied all the German prejudices about the predictable and clumsy Red Army operations of the past. The 'fortress cities' were swiftly surrounded, their commanders denied the opportunity by the German high command to withdraw. Vitebsk fell on 26 June, Orsha a day later, Mogilev and Bobruisk on the two following days. Soviet armour moved at extraordinary speed, given the problems of terrain, and swung west behind Minsk, the Belorussian capital, which fell on 3 July, trapping the German Fourth Army in a great encirclement. On 29 June, Model, Hitler's military fireman, replaced Busch as commander of Army Group Centre, but he could see there was nothing to do but withdraw in as much order as was possible. In two weeks, a hole 400 kilometres wide and almost 160 kilometres deep had been carved out of the German front and more than 300,000 German prisoners taken. The Soviet press observed the slow Allied progress in the West in tones, according to a British journalist in Moscow, that were both 'carping and condescending'.[252] The contrast was evident as the Red Army pursued an enemy retreating in disorder away from the prospect of capture, as the German army was to do in France a month later. The Third Belorussian Army Group pushed into Lithuania, seizing Vilnius on 13 July and Kaunas on 1 August. Advanced units of the Baltic Army Group reached the Gulf of Riga in early August, temporarily cutting off Army Group North from what was left of Army Group Centre. The advance slowed down and halted by the end of August more than 480 kilometres from the starting line in June, the most successful of all the major Soviet operations.

There was more to come as the next offensives opened further south, once it was evident that 'Bagration' had been a success. On 8 July, Stalin and Zhukov planned two drives into Poland, a first offensive by the First Ukrainian Army Group (now commanded by Konev) towards Lvov and Brody, which was launched on 13 July, followed by a second operation by part of Rokossovskii's First Belorussian Front aimed at Brest and then the river Vistula, which flowed through the Polish capital, Warsaw. Konev made slow progress in atrocious weather towards Lvov, but on 16 July the German line was penetrated and General Pavel Rybalko pushed the Third Guards Tank Army through a narrow corridor, under heavy fire. The penetration worked as it had at Minsk, and eight German divisions were encircled around Łódź; Konev pushed on to take Lvov on 27 July, reaching the Vistula where a major bridgehead was secured at Sandomierz. Rokossovskii was equally successful, pushing against a disintegrating front as 'Bagration' drew German forces north. Lublin was seized on 24 July, Brest on the Soviet border four days later. The army group raced for the Vistula, which was reached by the 26th, and then turned north to occupy the eastern bank of the river opposite Warsaw. Further attempts to push across the Narew and Vistula rivers were repulsed by a German line that revived on a narrower and more easily defended front, thanks once again to Model, shortly before his transfer to France. There remained the final offensive towards the Balkans, which was launched against what was now a much-weakened German front following the transfer of twelve divisions (including six Panzer divisions) to help further north. Between 20 and 29 August, Army Group South Ukraine collapsed almost entirely, with the loss of around 150,000 soldiers and the destruction of Sixth Army, reconstituted after the disaster at Stalingrad and now once again the victim of encirclement.[253] On 23 August, the government of Marshal Antonescu was overthrown and the Romanian army sought an armistice. The Soviet successes from June to August now prompted Germany's Axis partners and co-belligerents to abandon a failing war effort while it was still possible.

In almost all cases, Germany's wartime partners had already anticipated German defeat and sought from at least 1943 onwards a way of disengaging from a commitment evidently to be punished by the Allies. The Finnish government was under pressure from the Allies to stop fighting, but there was a fear – real enough – that Finland, like Italy and Hungary, would then be occupied by German troops, 200,000 of whom were in the far Arctic north. With the success of 'Bagration' clear, the Finnish government finally decided to risk abandoning the war. Marshal Mannerheim assumed the role of head of state and on 5 September Finnish forces gave up fighting. The armistice with the Soviet Union (and Britain, which had declared war in December 1941) required the Finns to return all the territory annexed after the first Soviet–Finnish war in 1940, and to cede a military base near Helsinki, but Stalin did not want to occupy Finland and insisted that the Finns eject the Germans, which they did from October onwards, at first following their retreat at a distance, then, after witnessing the German scorched-earth policy in Lapland, with military violence.[254] Romanian leaders had also been in secret contact with the Western Allies, but it was the sudden impact of the Red Army invasion, which had demolished the Romanian defensive line in three days, that accelerated King Michael's decision to arrest Antonescu. By 31 August the Red Army was in Bucharest, a day after capturing the Ploesti oilfield. Despite Hitler's insistence that the oil was vital for Germany's war effort, little preparation had been made to protect it. There was still a substantial German presence in Romania, but the Romanian forces were now made to change sides and fight alongside the former Soviet enemy, clearing Romania of Axis forces by mid-September.

In Bulgaria, Hungary and Slovakia, there were very different circumstances. Slovakia had tried to reduce any military commitment to the German war effort after the disasters of 1942, but not until 1944, following 'Bagration', did the Slovak army commanders decide to reject the German alliance. On 29 August German troops entered Slovakia and fought against a popular uprising, which was finally crushed by October; Slovakia was only liberated by the Red Army in early April 1945. Bulgaria, although a signatory of the Three Power Pact and a co-belligerent against Britain and the United States, unlike Slovakia had not declared war on the Soviet Union. Stalin nevertheless wanted a Soviet presence in the country since concessions in Bulgaria had been part of the deal he had wanted to strike with Hitler in November 1941. On 5 September the Soviet Union declared war, and three days later forces from the army groups occupying Romania moved south. On 9 September, the communist 'Fatherland Front' seized power in Sofia and resistance ceased. Soviet troops and aircraft arrived in Sofia a week later, and the Bulgarian army was compelled, like the Finnish and Romanian, to fight against the Germans in Serbia and Hungary. By this time, Hungarian efforts to disengage from the war were well known to German counter-intelligence. Hungarian intermediaries had begun negotiations with British diplomats in Istanbul in September 1943 but were told that only unconditional surrender was acceptable and to wait to do so until the Allies arrived at the border. The same month Hitler ordered operational planning to begin for the occupation of his untrustworthy ally, whose raw material resources Hitler now regarded as vital. As Miklós Horthy's government continued to waver in early 1944, Operation 'Margarethe' was activated on 19 March with the almost unopposed entry of German forces. The government was placed under the pro-German General Döme Sztójny and a German plenipotentiary, Edmund Veesenmeyer, was installed. But in the autumn Horthy tried again to disengage Hungary from the war, by reaching agreement with Stalin.[255] A Hungarian delegation in Moscow negotiated a preliminary agreement on 11 October to abandon all territory gained since 1937 and to declare war on Germany. This time the German occupiers forced Horthy to stand down as regent and replaced the government with one drawn from the fascist Arrow Cross Party, under prime minister Ferenc Szálasi, who quickly made himself the Hungarian *Führer* by combining his office with head of state.[256] Hungary kept fighting until the end in April 1945, a reluctant Axis partner alongside Mussolini's rump Italian Social Republic.

DEFEAT AT ANY PRICE

In July 1944, while the battles still raged in France, Russia and China, two separate plots were hatched to assassinate the leaders of the German and Japanese war effort by military officers anxious to avert the worst as defeat loomed nearer. Following months of criticism of Tōjō's leadership among the military and political elite, a general staff officer, Major Tsunoda Tomoshige, planned to kill Tōjō with a bomb filled with potassium cyanide. He and his fellow conspirators were linked to retired Lieutenant General Ishiwara Kanji's radical East Asia League and they wanted Tōjō removed, a government under the emperor's uncle, Prince Higashikuni, and immediate peace talks with the Allies through Soviet mediation. Before the plot could be carried out, Tōjō resigned as prime minister. Tsunoda was denounced, arrested and imprisoned for two years. The other conspirators were, surprisingly, left free, including Ishiwara, who claimed without hindrance a few months later 'the people are disgusted with the military and with the government, and they do not care any more about the outcome of the war.'[257]

The plot to kill Hitler had little in common with Tsunoda's abortive coup except in the fact that it failed. The chief conspirators came from among German junior staff officers, who found it almost impossible to persuade senior generals, despite their evident frustration and disillusionment with Hitler's military leadership, to back the assassination of their supreme commander. The circle was small, based around staff officers from Army Group Centre, led by Colonel Henning von Tresckow, but by 1944 they had established contact with the civilian conservative resistance led by Carl Goerdeler and the former army chief of staff Ludwig Beck. The circle was joined in April 1943 by Lieutenant Colonel Claus Schenk von Stauffenberg, a former enthusiast for Hitler's national revolution, and a willing supporter of the military war effort, until he was repelled by the violence towards Jews and prisoners of war. Like his fellow resisters, he wanted to stop Hitler before Germany was destroyed with its national honour besmirched. But he hoped that with Hitler's death, the Western Allies would allow Germany to survive as a great power, run on authoritarian lines by true 'national-socialists'. The conservative resistance shared the hope that compromise agreement could be reached in the West, allowing German forces to concentrate on holding back the Soviet menace.[258] For more than a year the military plotters had sought the opportunity to assassinate Hitler, but the schemes had all misfired. By 1944, with Germany faced with invasion and destruction, the plotters wanted not just assassination but regime change. The conspirators agreed to kill Hitler and then at once to activate Operation 'Valkyrie', an existing contingency plan for the army to put down a possible coup or revolution at home. After the crisis in France and the Soviet advance through Belorussia in June, the conspirators prepared to act.

No one could be found who would actually do the deed, except for von Stauffenberg himself, who, despite the loss of his right hand, right eye and two fingers from his left hand in the battle for Tunisia, volunteered to carry a bomb to a staff meeting with Hitler and somehow trigger the detonator mechanism. Even this commitment almost came to naught. Von Stauffenberg carried the bomb into three separate meetings at Hitler's quarters in Obersalzberg and at the Wolf's Lair but decided not to use it unless Himmler and Göring were present. On 20 July 1944, von Stauffenberg finally decided there could be no further delays. The story of the assassination attempt is well known. The bomb that ought to have killed Hitler, as well as Keitel and Jodl, his closest military staff, lost its full effect because it was placed under a thick oak table in a wooden hut rather than an enclosed bunker. Von Stauffenberg returned to Berlin convinced that Hitler must be dead and Operation 'Valkyrie' was activated later in the day. By this time Hitler had already spoken to Goebbels in Berlin to say that he had survived, though the bomb severely affected his health for some time. A branch of the plot was also activated in Paris later that day, when army security units arrested all SS, SD and Gestapo personnel on orders from plotters on the army staff.[259] Within hours the plot fell apart as loyal troops realized Hitler was still alive. Von Stauffenberg and his chief accomplices were hastily executed in the War Ministry courtyard. In Paris, the prisoners were released. Over the following weeks, hundreds were arrested as the Gestapo and SS followed up leads forced by torture from the main conspirators. Himmler activated Operation 'Thunderstorm' in the autumn, dragging 5,000 social democrats and communists into the terror network in case they turned to plotting. Hitler gloated that the coup gave him 'proof that the whole General Staff is contaminated', making worse still the distrust he had for the professional commanders.[260] The evidence shows, however, that the armed forces remained overwhelmingly loyal to their supreme commander, while much of the wider public expressed a mix of dismay at the attempt on Hitler's life and relief that he had survived. 'The fact that the individual soldier on the front was being killed,' explained a captured German lieutenant to his father, a fellow prisoner of war, 'and that the officers at home were breaking their oath, infuriated the people.'[261] Letters and diaries show contemporary civilian fears that without Hitler, political and military chaos, even civil war, might follow; worse still, as one father wrote to his soldier son, 'a new stab-in-the-back myth'.[262] The bomb plot led to a temporary strengthening of belief in Hitler's essential leadership, and a determination to continue the war to atone for the treachery of the few.

In both Japan and Germany there were much wider circles pessimistic about the probability of defeat and the terrible costs of the war, though demoralized sentiment never amounted to any clear social or political threat to those who wished to fight on. The failure of the von Stauffenberg plot was blamed then and since on the inability of the conspirators to seek any mass base of support, but in the context of the Third Reich, creating a mass base demanding an end to the war and a new government was mere fantasy. In Japan, it proved possible for senior officials and intellectuals to criticize the way the war was run, even to canvass the idea of negotiating an end to the conflict, but only within the narrow circle of the elite. Prince Konoe was the most senior of the Council of Elders (jūshin) to express regular pessimism about the outcome of the war and to pressure the imperial court to get rid of Tōjō. The emperor's chief adviser, Kido Kōzichi, also believed the war irretrievably lost by early 1944, as did a number of senior naval and army commanders, but they were reluctant to act against the military leadership. Tōjō's successor as prime minister in July 1944, General Koiso Kuniaki, governor general of Korea, remained publicly committed to the war, yet privately favoured seeking peace, but there was no way in Japan's political order for the army and navy leadership to be overruled and they remained committed to a final great battle, the hondo kessen, to save the homeland.[263]

For ordinary Japanese civilians, on the other hand, evidence of defeatism and illegal resistance was stamped on firmly by the authorities. Evidence of anti-war sentiment had already emerged as early as 1942 expressed in casual but imprudent comments, or anonymous graffiti and letter-writing, or rumours of defeat. They were all investigated by the Special Higher Police (popularly known as the 'Thought Police'), who focused particularly on the possibility that anti-war feeling might lead to a revolutionary situation beneficial to communism. They even arrested members of the Central Planning Board because their views on state economic planning were deemed to be too Marxist.[264] Yet it proved difficult to track down the rumour-mongers and those responsible for 'public scribblings', and the number of incidents, though small, rose steadily throughout the war. The Home Ministry recorded an average of twenty-five anti-war and inflammatory cases each month from April 1942 to March 1943, but an average of fifty-one per month for the year April 1944 to March 1945.[265] Hostility to the emperor also increased during the war, expressed in a wave of graffiti-writing, but arrests and prosecutions were few. Those who were caught might expect to be taken by the military police, the *Kempeitai*, and subjected to torture in order to reveal a wider circle of defeatists. Control at local level depended on surveillance by the neighbourhood association, whose leaders reported any cases of dissent or defeatism among their community. Families suspected of anti-war sentiment were kept under watch by the military police throughout the war. The space for any organized protest was non-existent, and the costs of stepping out of line severe.[266]

The threat of terror also hung over every German head for any acts against the war effort from alleged sabotage to spontaneous expressions of defeatism. The regime was led by men obsessed with the fear that internal unrest might repeat the crisis of 1918 and every example, however trivial, was dealt with severely. Numbers were once again small in relation to the size of the population. Prosecutions before the People's Court, established in Berlin to hear cases of wartime treason, rose from 552 in 1940 to a peak of 2,003 in 1944, the year of the bomb plot. The total number sentenced in the final years of war, 1943–5, amounted to 8,386.[267] The risks in expressing anti-war or defeatist talk were substantial in a dictatorship where denunciation was routinely practised, and the risks multiplied during the last two years of war when the Gestapo and military police increasingly resorted to brief hearings in kangaroo courts to condemn to death anyone found guilty of weakening the war effort. The day following the bomb plot, Heinrich Himmler was appointed to command the Replacement Army (responsible for training and organizing new cohorts of recruits), whose staff had played a key part in the conspiracy. He warned the army commanders that no repeat of 1918 would be tolerated; any sign of defeatism among the army rank and file, he told his representative at OKW, would be stamped on brutally by officers recruited to shoot 'anyone opening his mouth'.[268] The terror worsened as the war situation deteriorated, directed at political prisoners, who were killed arbitrarily, at foreign labourers who absconded from work, and at ordinary Germans, both civilians and soldiers, who flouted the demand to support the final struggle against the enemy. By the early months of 1945, special police and military patrols, empowered to kill suspects at will, toured the bombed cities. In Düsseldorf, a young soldier serving ten years in prison for saying that the war seemed pointless, was taken out and shot; a seventeen-year-old was seized from his sickbed on grounds that he was malingering, taken away and murdered; an elderly man was accused of supplying deserters with food, tortured brutally and hanged in public with a sign round his neck proclaiming 'I am a traitor'.[269] In neighbouring Bochum, a man who commented to a squad clearing up bomb damage that 'the war is lost' was beaten to death by a fellow civilian who took popular justice into his own hands.[270]

The terror directed at the home populations as defeat loomed nearer was real enough and clearly inhibited any open expressions of protest against the war and its consequences, or any broader social and political movement to end the war. Both populations had been subject to close police scrutiny for a dozen years and understood the cost of dissent. Yet on its own terror does not adequately explain the willingness, often enthusiastic, to continue to fight and work for a failing war effort. In both cases, Japanese and German, there was a complex mix of factors at work – psychological and material – which affected individuals in a wide variety of ways. There was no standard model of commitment for either servicemen or civilians. The German security service reported in autumn 1944 that although people seemed resigned, fearful, hopeful for peace, even apathetic and indifferent, they remained willing 'to hold out unconditionally'.[271] One factor that transcended the growing evidence of demoralization was the belief that victory of a sort was still a possibility, confirmed for many Germans by Hitler's apparently providential survival in July. Leaders in both countries continued to talk of victory when its meaning was evidently hollow, but among the wider population there was a strong desire to clutch at any straw that might suggest a turn of the tide. In Germany, the regular propaganda about new secret 'wonder weapons', begun by Goebbels in 1943, was repeated regularly in diaries and letters, echoing a standard trope that Hitler had a surprise in store for the Allies, a hope that survived through to the last months of the conflict despite growing scepticism at the real value of the vengeance weapons, the V1 cruise missile and the V2 rocket, when they were released against Britain in the summer of 1944. When German forces were unleashed through the Ardennes against the American front in December 1944 in Operation 'Autumn Mist', there was evidence of an upsurge of popular optimism that another route to victory had opened up with an unexpected repeat of the campaign of 1940.[272] In Japan, the introduction of *kamikaze* suicide tactics in autumn 1944 provoked the same public enthusiasm that a means had at last been found, as one letter to the press put it, 'that will force the enemy to surrender'.[273]

More significant for understanding the fight to the bitter end was the belief among soldiers and airmen that even in defeat it was a duty to fight to the end in order somehow to preserve the nation, even when confidence in the national leadership had evaporated. This was a sentiment both destructive and self-destructive, fuelled by a growing fatalism or nihilism as the prospect of death became daily more real. Even though the possibility of victory was now remote and unrealistic, Japanese and German servicemen sought to exact a high cost from the enemy responsible for their defeat, killing them as an act of revenge against their own fate. The *kamikaze* Special Attack Force evidently fell into this category, and 4,600 sacrificed themselves in order to inflict damage on the ships and men of the enemy. The culture surrounding them emphasized how honour for the emperor and nation overrode all moral qualms at sending men off on suicide missions. The naval press release when suicide missions began in October 1944 spoke of the 'unswerving loyalty of divine eagles' and the groups were given honourable names – the 'Loyal Bravery Unit', the 'Sincerity Unit'.[274] They were expected to kill as many of the enemy as they could on their suicide missions, but the same held true for the ordinary soldier who was ordered in 1945 to prepare an envelope with a last testament and a lock of hair, to be left behind for his family after he had inevitably sacrificed himself in battle. Some soldiers saw their imminent death as a welcome price to pay, as long as Americans died too. 'Now we must learn the lessons of "Saipan" and "Guadalcanal",' wrote one Japanese officer. 'We must take those bastards and kill them like grinding them to pieces.' He experienced a kind of 'serenity' in contemplating his death in battle.[275] Civilians were expected to kill at least one of the invading enemies with whatever weapon they had to hand. One schoolgirl was given an awl and told to plunge it into an American abdomen.

German forces did not organize suicide units, but they fought to inflict damage wherever they could, even in hopeless situations. The catchphrase 'victory or annihilation' will certainly not have inspired every soldier, since the latter seemed most probable, but some kind of private vindication of the German cause through inflicting death on the enemy sustained soldiers for whom victory was now a chimera. The loss of comrades in huge numbers by 1944 – in that year, 1,802,000 were killed – summoned an urge to avenge those who died, to kill or be killed regardless, 'a heroic nihilism' as one soldier put it in his autobiography, though it was a heroism marred by harsh vengeance against occupied civilians as well as enemy soldiers.[276] One German veteran of the war in Italy explained that savage fighting reflected 'their rage over . . . the uselessness of the sacrifice they had willingly made year after year, and over the senselessness of the war.'[277] The stark reality was well understood, but many soldiers seem to have been willing to participate in what was a profoundly dramatic and emotional moment as the nation faced its nemesis. 'Your great hour has struck . . .' Field Marshal von Rundstedt told his troops before the onset of Germany's final counter-offensive in the West. 'I don't need to say any more. You all feel it: it's all or nothing.'[278] In the last six months of the conflict there were enough German soldiers who absorbed the morbid ethos of inevitable death to sustain almost suicidal resistance up to the very last days of the war.

Fear for the fate of the nation clearly lay behind not just public policy but also private reflection on the final months of fighting. Propaganda in both Japan and Germany had warned the population to expect the worst from defeat at the hands of enemies determined to eradicate the German and Japanese nations together with their populations. The main trope of German propaganda from at least 1943 onwards was the argument that the counterpoint to victory was the extermination of the German people by an unholy alliance in the pay of the Jews. A propaganda directive in February 1945 highlighted the fate awaiting a Germany delivered up to Soviet conquest: 'all the suffering and dangers of the war are minor when compared with the fate that the enemies plan for Germany in a "Bolshevik peace".' The menace of the Bolshevik 'bullet in the back of the head' for the German people could only be averted, it was claimed, by the most strenuous national resistance to the very last moment.[279] In Japan, public discourse played on the notion of Western barbarism, which would be unleashed without constraint on Japanese society unless popular resistance kept the barbarians at bay. The propaganda exploited the claim that all Japanese women would be raped, and all men castrated. The physical or sexual threat to women if they could not be defended was a widespread fear.[280] The extent to which fantastic fears were really shared by the wider public or the fighting forces is impossible to know, but the constant repetition of the idea that the nation was to be exterminated and the population violated, in a context where it was not clear exactly what the Allies might be driven to do in a spasm of revenge, made continued resistance seem less irrational than it does to a post-war audience.

In both cases, these fears were used to justify extreme levels of mobilization in the final year of war by a state and political apparatus that still retained its power to compel. In Japan, the population as a whole was mobilized for the final battle to drive the Americans back into the sea when they invaded. In March 1945, Public Law No. 30 mobilized all citizens in coastal areas for the work of defence, including school-age children, but a second decree that month called for the creation of a Patriotic Citizens' Fighting Corps to establish Volunteer Fighting Units for all men aged sixteen to sixty and women aged seventeen to forty.[281] They were voluntary in only a nominal sense, since few people could afford the risk of not participating; men and women engaged in training sessions with bamboo spears, and stone throwing to simulate grenade attack. The plan was to mobilize at least 10 million people for Japan's last stand. In Germany too, the aftermath of the July plot saw an effort by the regime to organize extreme effort on the part of the population, from which it was once again difficult to stand aside. On 21 July, the day after the assassination attempt, Goebbels was appointed plenipotentiary for total war, an appointment welcomed, according to secret intelligence reports, because it demonstrated a commitment to the fullest efforts to avert defeat and the fears that went with it. Reluctant though many older and younger Germans might have been to serve a last gasp mobilization, the appeal to join the final 'struggle for the homeland' (*Kampf der Heimat*) was difficult to avoid. On 29 September 1944, the Party began to organize a popular home militia – the *Volkssturm* – with the intention of building a force of 6 million men, not fit for normal military service, to defend the Reich in its final crisis. Hitler's decree setting up the militia pointed out that the enemy's 'final goal is to exterminate the German people'. When the age cohort of Hitler Youth born in 1928 was asked to volunteer for service early, a remarkable 70 per cent did so. Years later, one of the young volunteers recalled a simple motive: 'we wanted to save the Fatherland.'[282]

For the Allies, the absence of an obvious slogan to mobilize the final drive for victory brought its own difficulties. Although by autumn 1944 the Allies were clearly 'winning' the war, Allied populations, particularly in the West, were no less war-weary and uncertain than those of the Axis. Yet because they no longer faced the earlier menace of defeat, it proved more difficult to rouse the resolve necessary to finish the war once and for all, or to dissipate frustration that the knockout blow could not be inflicted as people had hoped after the victories in the summer, when Rome, Paris and Brussels returned to Allied hands. The psychological difference between the two sides was clear. For Germans and Japanese there was no tangible 'post-war', only victory or destruction; for Allied populations, ending the war rapidly with as small a cost as possible promised demobilization and a better future. The initial belief that victory was near, and the disappointment when it not only failed to materialize but seemed ever more distant, was shared by both servicemen and civilians. In the United States, Roosevelt on his return from the Tehran Conference in November 1943 deplored the popular view 'that the war is already won and we can begin to slacken off'.[283] A few weeks before, *Life* magazine was given permission to publish the first photograph of dead American servicemen in an effort to revive enthusiasm for the war effort. The home-front optimism that Germany was close to defeat persisted through the Normandy landings and the race across France. But the slow-down in the campaigns, as Henry Stimson observed, ended the 'easy-going confidence of a short and quick victory' and instead produced a realization that the Allies 'were in for a long war and a very hard fight'.[284] In Britain, the onset of the V-weapons campaign dampened the enthusiasm for the campaign in France, leaving a population in the threatened area, according to Home Intelligence reports, in a state of anxiety and 'incredible tiredness', but longing more than ever for an early end to the war. Montgomery hoped he could deliver what they wanted but by October it was plain that the struggle was far from over. 'We have in front of us some very hard fighting,' he wrote to Brooke. 'If we emerge successfully, I suppose we shall have about won the war. But if we are seen off the war is likely to drag on.' By February 1945, the British Chiefs of Staff were predicting an end to the fighting in Europe no earlier than the last week of June, but probably a war lasting until November.[285]

At the many front lines, the mood of men mired in constant bitter conflict reflected sentiments at home. After the initial success in France, the fighting grew tougher. More British soldiers were killed in September and October 1944 than during the Normandy campaign. 'The day of great achievements seemed to be over,' complained one British soldier. 'Every prospect ahead was uninviting.' Troops who had earlier taken bets when exactly in the autumn the war would be finished (October was the general prediction) found themselves mired in mud and rain on the Flanders plain, as their fathers had been, in constant danger and longing for the end. The slow pace and heavy casualties created a cynical view of victory that always slipped out of grasp. 'The war's over,' one American tankman told the reporter Martha Gellhorn in December 1944. 'Don't you know that? I heard it on the radio a week ago . . . Hell, it's all over. I ask myself what I'm doing here.'[286] A British officer in liberated Brussels was treated to the news from an NCO in early September that the radio had announced 'Germany's given up and Hitler's gone to Spain', but it was wishful thinking. 'If only that peace rumour had been true!' he recorded in his diary as he moved off a few days later to the next battle.[287] The closer peace

seemed, the less willing some soldiers were to take risks and be killed too
soon, unlike German and Japanese soldiers dug in for defence who knew
that the chance of survival was slight. The replacement system in the
American army, which by now was mobilizing boys of eighteen to meet
the urgent and unanticipated need for more soldiers, simply fed infantry
one at a time into a depleted unit, with no companions or effective preparation, and they took correspondingly high casualties alongside veterans
who were keen to survive at their expense.[288] The Red Army faced similar
problems as younger and older men, or men still recovering from wounds,
were recruited to replace the depleted ranks of more experienced troops.
Conditions for soldiers at the fighting front were abysmal – shortages of
food and footwear, limited medical supplies, widespread theft and violence. 'In the last while,' wrote one soldier to his family, 'I've been feeling
an acute tiredness from the war . . . But it's all useless of course. The war
isn't going to end this winter.' Spirits revived with the success of 'Bagration', but the evidence shows that many Soviet soldiers thought the enemy
was defeated and they could stop at the Soviet frontier, their job done.
Instead, they were faced with the prospect of driving on into Germany:
the physical and mental exhaustion of the army meant a long pause, so
that victory here also meant months of bitter fighting well into 1945.[289]

The problem posed by the tension between the desire for peace and the
reality of a deadly enemy still to be defeated was exacerbated for British
and American forces by the plans for demobilization and reconversion to
peacetime production, which began in 1943 even before victory was clearly
in view. In the United States, cuts in military production were followed by
plans to reopen factories producing some limited output of civilian goods,
while commercial advertising began to focus on the goods that would soon
be available once again with victory. Programmes for industrial reconversion were drawn up, provoking a year-long battle between the military,
who wanted more shells, bombs and tanks after the high losses sustained in
the invasion of France and Italy, and civilian officials who responded to
widespread public demands for an end to controls and rationing. As workers left for what they saw as safer jobs in civilian industry, the capacity of
military production contracted by a quarter.[290] Soldiers were already being
returned home under a demobilization scheme of Adjusted Service Rating,
which gave individual servicemen a points' score for the number of months
in combat, their age, family status, wounds and medals. A score of 85 points
meant release home and an end to the fighting for men who had been in
combat since 1942 or early 1943. Bomber crews were returned to the
United States after thirty operations, if they survived that long, nicknamed
the 'Happy Warriors'. Soldiers and airmen could work out their eligibility,

reducing the willingness to take risks the closer to the prospect of return they each arrived.[291] In Britain a similar problem emerged with the handbook on 'Release and Resettlement' published in September 1944, setting out eligibility for demobilization. That same month, when Hitler ordered the creation of the *Volkssturm*, the British volunteer militia, the Home Guard, was stood down, its service no longer needed. In the field, older men, and men abroad for a long time, were given favourable demobilization ratings, but all servicemen could work out their demobilization number. Ten per cent of servicemen classified as essential skilled labour for the reconstruction programme were to be freed from service first, which provoked a scramble to demonstrate 'skills' that men did not possess.[292] Although in neither case did the promise of release prevent continued combat, for both servicemen and civilians the focus on the post-war world made the current struggle less bearable. 'From all indications,' wrote the American army deputy chief of staff to Eisenhower in early 1945, 'it is going to be one hell of a job to keep the war in any priority.'[293]

In this sense, the hopes of German and Japanese leaders that their enemies might suffer from declining war-willingness the longer and more costly the conflict became were not entirely misplaced. Arguments over strategy continued to bedevil Anglo-American relations, while collaboration with the Soviet Union remained volatile as suspicion over Stalin's ambitions in Eastern Europe surfaced from the autumn of 1944. In both Europe and the Pacific, Allied progress slowed down with a long and complicated logistical trail to the new front lines and it became difficult to bring to bear the large material advantage enjoyed by the Allied side at the point it was most needed. German commanders scorned the slow response of the enemy to their moments of advantage, while German intelligence observed a declining capacity for rapid advance and tension between the Allies. 'History teaches us,' Hitler announced to his generals at the end of August, 'that all coalitions break up, but you must await the moment ... we shall carry on this struggle until, as Frederick the Great said, "one of our damned enemies gives up in despair".'[294] In Japan, the idea that at least one local victory might be enough to start talks with a war-weary enemy affected even Emperor Hirohito well into 1945.

Everywhere along the main fighting fronts in Europe and Asia a relative stalemate set in. The final Japanese counter-offensive in China left both sides exhausted. Although '*Ichigō*' lasted through to early 1945, more ambitious plans to move on once again to try to seize Chongqing were simply beyond Japanese capability. The rail route from Vietnam to Korea proved a hollow victory. General Chennault's Fourteenth Air Force in China continued to fly from new airfields, attacking the rail lines and traffic. Although the long 1944 campaign had almost fatally weakened Chiang's Nationalist regime, enough could be done to prevent any further Japanese encroachment, leaving the contest in a state of suspense. Marshall and Roosevelt had long decided that there was no point in a major campaign on mainland Asia, and Chinese armies were denied the supplies they needed. Most resources sent to China were to support the American air forces, including the new Boeing B-29 heavy bombers, which were seen as a more effective way to undermine Japanese resistance than a ground war in China.

Chiang gained one thing from the last months of the Japanese campaign: he insisted that the acerbic Stilwell should be removed, after he tried to get Roosevelt to insist that Chiang give him overall command of all Chinese forces, despite his failures in Burma. 'This is imperialism, fully exposed,' wrote Chiang in his diary when told the American demands.[295] Roosevelt reluctantly agreed and Stilwell was forced to leave China in late October after years of deliberate effort to poison relations between the two allies. He was replaced by General Albert Wedemeyer, deputy to Mountbatten, now British commander-in-chief in South East Asia, who considered Stilwell, with much justification, to be incapable of commanding even a regiment. Wedemeyer set out to reform Chiang's armies, building an initial force of thirty-six re-equipped divisions using American equipment. He planned Operation 'Carbonado' for a campaign in southern China to seize either Hong Kong or Guangzhou late in 1945 or 1946, but the Japanese surrendered before the operation could begin.[296] Without Stilwell, Chiang deferred to American leadership, though he kept secret a mission to Tokyo in March 1945 by Miao Pin to try to negotiate a complete Japanese withdrawal from China.[297] In the early summer of 1945, the Japanese Expeditionary Army tried to seize one of Chennault's new airfields at Zhijiang. It was the last gasp of Japanese aggression. Wedemeyer deployed 67 Chinese divisions, 600,000 men, against the 50,000 troops of the Japanese Twentieth Army. In the last major battle of the Sino-Japanese war, Nationalist armies finally defeated and drove back their faltering enemy.[298]

In South East Asia and the Pacific, Allied strategy was subject to persistent arguments that slowed down the progress of the Allied campaigns after the successes on Saipan and in Burma. From early in 1944, Churchill was obsessed with the idea of an amphibious landing on northern Sumatra as a prelude to retaking Singapore, given the codename Operation 'Culverin'. The motive was chiefly to reassert Britain's reputation in her Asian empire after the debacle of 1942 and to restore colonial rule; Churchill was convinced that Britain had to be seen as the liberating power, rather than the United States.[299] To American leaders, action in Sumatra would contribute little or nothing to the defeat of Japan, and clearly showed that imperial interests were paramount, but Churchill persisted with the idea long after his staff had tried to get him to focus on helping the United States in the Pacific. 'What a drag on the wheel of war this man is,' complained the Royal Navy chief of staff after yet another fruitless meeting to persuade Churchill to abandon his fixation.[300] 'We are definitely on the downward grade,' warned Britain's Information Service in the United States, 'in the opinion of the average American.' An opinion poll in December 1944 found that 58 per cent of Americans blamed Britain for declining Allied co-operation, but only 11 per cent blamed the Soviet Union.[301] The Sumatran plan was only finally abandoned when it became clear that the requirements for landing craft, amphibious equipment and fleet protection could simply not be met, but Churchill continued to advance further unrealizable plans for invading Malaya (Operation 'Zipper') and Singapore (Operation 'Mailfist'), all of which had to be abandoned.

The arguments with the British were complemented by an even more damaging confrontation between Nimitz and MacArthur over the direction that Pacific strategy should take into 1945. From early in 1944, the Joint Chiefs had assumed that the Philippines could be side-stepped so that the United States navy, assisted by MacArthur's forces, could take Taiwan and then the home islands. Admiral King thought the Philippines mattered little, although Japanese military leaders saw the loss of the islands as a potentially disastrous limitation of their field of operations. MacArthur argued that he had a moral obligation to liberate the island population he had abandoned two years before, but the Joint Chiefs were not impressed enough to give up the idea of using Taiwan as the most appropriate stepping-stone. Only when it became clear that Taiwan was too heavily defended, while the Philippines appeared vulnerable to assault, did King and Nimitz agree to an army invasion under MacArthur, but no joint command for the campaign was agreed. Although MacArthur glibly claimed that he would conquer the Philippines 'in thirty days', avoiding what he called the 'tragic and unnecessary massacre of American lives' in the island-hopping campaign, Marshall and others assumed the army would be bogged down in difficult terrain when the urgent priority was to get closer to Japan, while the navy worried that their timetable for invading Iwo Jima and Okinawa might well be postponed if the Philippine campaign dragged on.[302] MacArthur seemed oblivious to the reality of combat against Japanese dug in for defence, and to the obvious costs to the Filipino people if a protracted struggle developed. The Philippines could certainly have been bypassed and neutralized at a lower price. Not until September 1944 was the new strategic direction finally approved and the arguments ended, and a date of 20 October was agreed for the initial landing on the smaller Philippine island of Leyte. With the war in both Europe and China deadlocked by the late autumn, a further stalemate in the south Pacific now seemed possible.

Shielded by a large naval presence, 6 army divisions (2 in reserve) numbering 202,500 men landed on Leyte, defended by a single Japanese division of 20,000 troops. As Marshall had feared, the operation became literally bogged down almost at once. In two months, there were three typhoons and nearly 900mm of rain. Men struggled in monsoon mud to get stores unloaded and protected; constructing airfields that were essential to the enterprise was held up by the waterlogged conditions, and three operational fields were only completed by mid-December. Living in sodden clothing with soaking feet brought a rash of trench foot and sickness. The thinly defended island was only secured after more than two months of bitter fighting, on 31 December, but the elimination of Japanese units cut off in the hills and jungle lasted until May 1945. As the campaign stalled to MacArthur's frustration, Nimitz warned him to postpone the next steps. The main island of Luzon would now be invaded only on 9 January. Rather than a thirty-day walkover, conquest of the islands would happen only much later in 1945. In February at the Yalta Conference, the Combined Chiefs of Staff gloomily predicted a war against Japan lasting until 1947.

The only bright spot in the campaign was the naval victory secured between 24 and 25 October when the Japanese navy tried to do what it had failed to do at Guadalcanal and Saipan, to attack and destroy the landing craft and stores in Leyte Bay. Like most major Japanese naval operations, Operation 'Shō-Go' ('Victory') was over-elaborate. Four fleet forces were mustered separately, rather than concentrated for a single assault: a major fleet, based around two super-battleships with three old battleships and ten heavy cruisers, formed the western arm of a pincer movement; a second squadron formed the eastern pincer to enter Leyte Gulf with two battleships and one heavy cruiser, supported by a third reserve force; and further north, to tempt away Halsey's fleet carrier task force supporting the Leyte operation, a decoy fleet of four carriers with a few aircraft on board, and two ageing battleships. Halsey took the bait and headed north on the night of 24/25 October in order to intercept the carriers, but then received urgent warning to return as the two Japanese pincers closed in on Leyte. He detached half his force, leaving the other half to sink all four carriers, but the help at Leyte was not needed.[303] The aircraft, destroyer screen and guns at Leyte first destroyed the eastern pincer as it sailed through the Surigao Strait, and then turned back the main force under Admiral Kurita Takeo, which had fought its way through the western San Bernardino Strait, losing all but two of the heavy cruisers and the super-battleship *Musashi* on the way. Kurita was so shaken by the unexpected resistance that he retreated, ostensibly, as he later claimed, to chase a phantom American carrier force, though with no aircraft his ships would have been no match even had there been one. The Japanese navy lost three battleships, four carriers, six heavy cruisers and seventeen other warships.[304] The Battle of Leyte Gulf finally broke the back of what was left of the Japanese surface fleet; even had the Leyte beaches and landing craft been heavily damaged, the United States navy would almost certainly have restored the situation. Ominously, the first *kamikaze* attacks were launched on 25 October, hitting three jeep carriers, one critically, the start of a year-long suicide campaign.

In Europe, all three main fronts facing German forces, in France and Belgium, Italy and Poland, became stalled by the autumn, a combination of stiffening German resistance and the strain on Allied forces in combat continuously from the summer with supply bases far in the rear. The capacity for the German army to continue to frustrate the Allies was unexpected after the disordered retreats across Belorussia and France. On 4 September, as Montgomery's army group closed on Antwerp, Eisenhower told his commanders that the German enemy along the entire front was close to collapse: 'they are disorganized, in full retreat, and unlikely to offer any appreciable resistance.'[305] Although he rejected Montgomery's demand that his army group be allowed to cross the Rhine and drive for Berlin on a narrow front ('based merely on wishful thinking', he told Marshall a week later), Eisenhower did expect to seize the Ruhr and Saar industrial regions within the foreseeable future.[306] In Italy, as German forces fell back from Rome to the Gothic Line north of Florence, Alexander talked of a single thrust to clear northern Italy before driving towards Vienna against a crumbling enemy, many of whose divisions now numbered little more than 2,500 men, short of equipment and air support.[307] In both cases, the hope that German forces were close to collapse proved premature. In Italy, the transfer of army divisions to support the campaign in southern France left Alexander short of the striking power he needed, while the British Chiefs of Staff counselled caution in difficult terrain and approaching bad weather. Allied forces were now to advance on two separate axes: Clark's Fifth Army, now with only five divisions, was to force a path over the mountains towards Bologna, aided by the arrival of the newly formed Tenth Mountain Division; Lieutenant General Oliver Leese's Eighth Army was to undertake

Operation 'Olive', an advance up the coastal plain towards Rimini. Although the Gothic Line was successfully forced on the coast, the battle took a heavy toll of Allied forces, and beyond lay a series of river crossings now made into torrents by heavy autumn rains. Alexander faced stiffening German opposition, in terrain ideal for defensive fighting, with troops exhausted by the campaign, the mud and the demoralizing sense that the Italian front was regarded by the Allied leadership as a backwater. Clark later wrote that his advance 'merely ground to a halt because men could not fight any longer . . . our drive died out, slowly and painfully.'[308] By late November, Alexander had modified his aim to the seizure of Bologna and Ravenna in a December offensive, but this proved beyond exhausted troops and the line ground to a halt. On 30 December, Alexander postponed any further major offensive until the spring.

On the Western Front, the pace slowed in the first week of September after the initial hectic pursuit, while supplies and heavy artillery were moved forward. The supply situation, Eisenhower told the Combined Chiefs, was 'stretched to breaking point', since maintenance relied on ports that were now nearly 500 kilometres away in north-west France.[309] He nevertheless approved an ambitious plan proposed by Montgomery to use the First Airborne Army to seize crossings over the Rhine at Nijmegen and Arnhem, supported by XXX Army Corps under Lieutenant General Brian Horrocks, approaching along the salient created past Antwerp. It was an uncharacteristic operation for Montgomery: planned in haste, with air support poorly integrated, limited intelligence on German strengths, no set-piece artillery barrage, and with significant German forces on either flank. Eisenhower approved Operation 'Market-Garden' only because he believed that the enemy was still too disorganized to resist a bold strike and he wanted crossings over the lower Rhine, to complement the crossings he hoped that Bradley's Twelfth Army Group would make further south. Montgomery, on the other hand, regarded 'Market-Garden' as a means to secure his preferred strategy of punching rapidly into Germany and moving towards Berlin – an option that American commanders had no desire to encourage if it meant a British victory at their exclusion. The outcome is well known. The many potential pitfalls in the operation were realized once it opened on 17 September. Bridges were seized at Nijmegen, but at Arnhem the Germans counter-attacked with the forces of II SS Panzer Corps, which Montgomery had not anticipated; XXX Corps was stuck on a single narrow road, the infantry unable to move forward fast enough, and under regular attack. The lack of ground support at the critical moment brought disaster at Arnhem, where most of the airborne troops were killed or captured. The operation was called off on 26 September with 15,000 Allied casualties; 3,300 German soldiers were killed or wounded. The northern drive into Germany evaporated.

The Twenty-first Army Group now had to spend months clearing the area around the salient, in deteriorating weather, in a flat countryside of canals and shattered villages, 'the abomination of desolation', as one soldier described it.[310] Eisenhower insisted that Montgomery now devote full effort to opening the port of Antwerp, which was blocked as remnants of the German Fifteenth Army retreated, in unexpected good order, to the island of Walcheren at the mouth of the river Scheldt, from where it was possible to interdict Allied shipping. The First Canadian Army was tasked with clearing the area north of Antwerp but had been held up by the need to capture the ports at Le Havre, Boulogne, Calais and Dunkirk, all designated fortresses by Hitler, and not until October did it prove possible to clear the area further east. Walcheren was finally captured on 8 November, and Antwerp at last opened to Allied marine traffic. The first Liberty ships docked on 28 November, giving the Allies a much closer supply base that would permit longer operations into Germany. The front here stabilized in the poor weather, with mounting casualties. The draining effort of fighting for almost six months led to an average loss of 40 per cent of the strength of each infantry division in Montgomery's army group.[311] Neither the race to Berlin in 1944 nor the rush to Vienna was feasible under the prevailing conditions.

The drive to capture the Saarland and the Roer dams further south also ground to a halt in the late autumn as German forces withdrew into the *Westwall* fortifications and the defence of the Hürtgen Forest, a densely wooded battleground where the American army could not deploy the winning combination of air, armour and artillery. Some 29,000 casualties were suffered by General Courtney Hodges's First Army as infantry were forced to push back the enemy in the harshest conditions, for territory that was hardly essential for the campaign and with the dams at the end still in German hands.[312] The US Third Army under Patton crossed the Moselle River with four divisions, but the effort cost heavy consumption of fuel and supplies and again came to a halt short of Eisenhower's objectives. By the time the American offensive could be resumed in November, the weather had deteriorated sharply, and German forces in the West, which had numbered only thirteen infantry and three armoured divisions fit for combat in early September, now numbered seventy divisions, including fifteen armoured.[313] Bradley now echoed Montgomery's earlier overoptimism in hoping that the Twelfth Army Group, supported by the Sixth Army Group assembled from the forces that had driven up the Rhône Valley, would seize the Saar basin and move on the Ruhr. By December

American armies, against bitter opposition, had reached the German *Westwall* fortifications but had not yet crossed the Rhine. As in Italy, the major offensive here had to be postponed until the spring.

On the Eastern Front, German resistance also stiffened. The local population in the eastern provinces was mobilized to dig ditches and trenches for a new *Ostwall*, some 700,000 German men, women and teenagers, together with Polish labourers, all mobilized by compulsory order. In some areas, women and boys far outnumbered men, working twelve-hour shifts to complete hundreds of kilometres of improvised barrier in a matter of weeks. The Party and SS played the main part in mobilizing labour for defences that the armed forces regarded sceptically. The joke circulated that it would take one hour two minutes for the Red Army to force the new line – one hour to recover from laughing, two minutes to get across – but the object of the mobilization was to try to avert panic and flight and to strengthen resolve for the final battle for the homeland.[314] More significant was the order from the new army chief of staff, Guderian, appointed on 21 July following the assassination attempt, to construct a network of fortress cities, twenty-five in number, from Memel on the Baltic coast to Oppeln in Silesia, which were to be held according to Hitler's directive as strongpoints to slow down the Soviet advance when it came.[315] The expected blow across the Vistula, however, did not materialize. Soviet forces were exhausted by the long campaign through Belorussia and eastern Poland and needed to rest, regroup and await the establishment of more robust supply lines before the final charge into the Reich, which was postponed until January 1945.

The Soviet attempt further north to cut off German forces in Danzig and East Prussia was halted by strong German pressure and high Soviet casualties. Instead, Stalin focused on occupying the Baltic States in order to isolate German Army Group North, which Hitler refused to allow to retreat and escape encirclement. By 10 October, the Red Army reached the Baltic coast close to Memel, and 33 German divisions, numbering almost 250,000 men, were trapped further north on the Courland Peninsula in Latvia, where most remained on Hitler's orders until the final German defeat.[316] A second Soviet attempt to move into East Prussia, launched on 16 October, crossed the German border and almost reached the critical rail junction at Gumbinnen before being driven back, to the surprise of the Soviet forces, by a vigorous German response that resulted in another stalled Allied offensive. Stalin's other concern, both military and political, was to embed the Red Army rapidly in the Balkans and Central Europe to forestall any attempt by the West to intervene. After assisting the Yugoslav National Liberation Army to capture Belgrade in late October, the Soviet focus was on Hungary as the gateway to Vienna, but fierce German and Hungarian resistance slowed the advance, since Hitler wanted to protect the small oilfield south-west of Lake Balaton. Budapest became the main fortress in the south, held by a mix of German and Hungarian units. On 28 October, Stalin ordered General Malinovskii's Second Ukrainian Army Group to seize Budapest in a day, since the drive to Vienna was politically essential, but not until 26 December did it prove possible to encircle Buda, the western half of Budapest, and lay it to a costly siege.[317] The campaign only ended in February after most of the Hungarian capital had been destroyed by bombing and shelling and the garrison reduced to around 11,000 from the total of 79,000 in December. Around 100,000 Hungarian soldiers and civilians perished.[318] For Stalin, as for Alexander in Italy, the path to Vienna proved beyond the grasp of the Allies in 1944.

The temporary German stabilization of the front in Poland and East Prussia tempted Hitler to risk a strategic ploy that he had toyed with since August, when he called for a dedicated force to thrust into the rear and flank of the advancing American Twelfth Army Group from the area in front of the Vosges mountains. Task Group G was planned with six armoured divisions and six new armoured brigades, but with the continued retreat the counter-attack was abandoned.[319] By mid-September, Hitler had enlarged the plan with the idea of striking between the American and British army groups, forcing Montgomery's Twenty-first Army Group into a pocket, while driving on to Antwerp to end the prospect of closer Allied supply lines. Hitler hoped that the operation might even provoke a major political crisis between his Western enemies. 'Counter-offensive from the Ardennes: goal Antwerp,' he announced to his immediate circle on 16 September.[320] Coming so soon after the retreat across France and the battles at the German border, the plan was disliked by most army commanders, including von Rundstedt, recalled as supreme commander West early in September, and Model, commander of the campaign. Hitler's concept relied on a concentration of scarce forces, when the whole front required defence, and would work only if the army could capture stocks of fuel and live off Allied supplies. His commanders understood the risks in launching a major offensive with poor mobility (50,000 horses were needed for the operation), shortages of supplies of all kinds, and army units with only limited training, but they could not change Hitler's mind.

Hitler insisted on complete secrecy for Operation '*Wacht am Rhein*' ('Watch on the Rhine') and parried the obvious objections by insisting on his intuitive sense that whatever the problems, the campaign would transform the Western Front and 'perhaps the war as a whole'.[321] In mid-November he required an operation on his vocal cords, which contributed to postponing what was now called Operation '*Herbstnebel*' ('Autumn Mist') until he appeared again on 1 December able at least to whisper.[322] The date was pushed back, first to 10 December, then six days later, to take advantage of poor weather that would keep Allied air power grounded. On the morning of 16 December, 24 divisions of 410,000 men, 1,400 armoured fighting vehicles, 1,900 artillery pieces and more than 1,000 aircraft caught the Allied side entirely by surprise. They advanced on three axes: in the north, where Sepp Dietrich's Sixth SS Panzer Army was to drive through the Ardennes forest and capture Antwerp; in the centre, where General Hasso von Manteuffel was to drive towards the river Meuse and beyond; and in the south, where General Erich Brandenberger was to cover the flank of the operation. Within days a large salient had been formed, created chiefly on the central front, the 'bulge' that gave the battle its American name. Hitler, happy at last, as he told commanders at a briefing on 11 December, to be able to conduct a 'successful offensive' instead of a 'prolonged, stubbornly conducted defensive', told Goebbels that the effects on the Allies were 'colossal'.[323]

Hitler was right that the offensive would cause consternation on the Allied side. The day before it began, on 15 December, Montgomery had announced that the German army had no offensive capability left. Even on the day following the start of the German operation, Eisenhower described it as a 'rather ambitious counterattack' which would soon be cut off, but by the 18th it was clear that a major offensive was under way to divide Allied forces and drive to the Belgian coast.[324] Allied intelligence had warned Eisenhower's headquarters for the Allied expeditionary force (SHAEF) that a build-up of German reserves opposite the weakly held Ardennes sector of the front had been detected, but overconfidence that the German forces were in crisis left the warnings unheeded. Kenneth Strong, Eisenhower's intelligence chief at SHAEF, claimed that the German army was being destroyed in the war of attrition by twenty divisions each month; German reserve-building was assumed to be preparation for a final defence of the Rhine barrier, while an operation through the Ardennes forest seemed as implausible as it had been to the French high command in May 1940.[325] German preparations had been concealed as far as possible, with absolute radio silence and details of the plan revealed to only a small circle. Allied air reconnaissance, meanwhile, was hampered by persistent bad weather.

The operation began against the weakest sector of the American front line, where five First Army divisions, either resting or novice units, were spread across the Ardennes area. Neither Hodges, commander of First

Army, nor Bradley reacted firmly to the initial German thrusts (indeed Bradley stayed throughout at his headquarters in Luxembourg City, directing by radio and telephone), but local commanders succeeded in holding the key road junctions at St Vith and Bastogne against high odds, frustrating German progress. Patton had already prepared a contingency plan in case he was asked to move his forces north to help First Army, and six divisions were swiftly redeployed to threaten the southern wing of the salient. Along the Elsenborn Ridge to the north, Dietrich's Sixth SS Panzer Army was held back by determined anti-tank defences. Only von Manteuffel's Fifth Panzer Army made progress, reaching a point just 5 kilometres from the Meuse by 24 December, before it was halted and turned back. When the weather cleared on the 23rd, Allied air forces began a daunting assault on the German advance. The German air force, though on paper still a substantial size, was reduced in effect because of fuel shortages, poorly prepared forward airbases and the inexperience of hundreds of novice pilots with limited training. On 1 January an attempt was made to concentrate 1,035 fighters and fighter-bombers together for a major operation, codenamed 'Bodenplatte' ('Baseplate'), to attack Allied tactical airbases and make it possible finally to seize Bastogne. Exact figures for Allied losses have been hard to calculate but lie somewhere between 230 and 290 aircraft, most of them on the ground, uncamouflaged, but the German air force lost more than 300 aircraft, the largest single loss on any day of the war.[326] The Allies could afford the losses; the British and American air forces in the European theatre totalled in late 1944 no fewer than 14,690 aircraft.[327]

By this stage, a concerted drive chiefly by American forces slowly choked off the salient and began the laborious, costly and debilitating task of pushing the German army back. As German commanders had warned, shortages of fuel and equipment, and the untried nature of many of the new conscripts fighting in winter weather, produced high losses of men and machines, even though German troops fought, in Eisenhower's words, 'with a kind of fanaticism or "German fury"'.[328] By 3 January Hitler acknowledged that the offensive had failed, though he hoped that the bitter fighting in freezing conditions had absorbed Allied reserves, weakened the Allied front elsewhere and postponed the drive to the Rhine. For all its drawbacks, the German offensive had managed to achieve a significant degree of damage. Five days later Hitler accepted Model and Manteuffel's request to withdraw to avoid yet more destruction of their battered troops. Both sides had suffered heavy casualties: American forces from mid-December to late January lost 103,102 men, including 19,246 dead; German losses were estimated by OKW at 81,834, of which 12,642

were killed and 30,582 missing. Undeterred by failure, Hitler ordered a
second, smaller counter-offensive in Alsace, codenamed 'North Wind', but
it met the same fate as 'Autumn Mist'. OKW recorded in the war diary on
14 January that the initiative 'has passed to the Allies', as indeed it had
long beforehand.[329]

Although Hitler was not to know it, his gambit to divide the Western
Allies came closer to realization than the military contest. The tension
between Montgomery, the British Chiefs of Staff and Eisenhower was
exacerbated almost to breaking point during the Ardennes offensive. To
cope with the immediate threat, Eisenhower asked Montgomery to take
command of the American First and Ninth Armies to the north of the salient. Bradley was enraged by what he saw as a lack of confidence in his
leadership, but he was made to accept it. Montgomery certainly instilled
confidence on the north of the salient, but he contributed little from his
own British and Canadian forces, who suffered only 1,400 casualties, 200
of them dead. He was slow to order the counter-attack, which his American critics seized on to disparage his generalship. At the end of December,
Montgomery revived his earlier demand that he be allowed to assume
overall command of all ground forces, as he had for D-Day, or risk Allied
failure in the coming invasion of Germany. In private he told Alan Brooke,
the chief of the Imperial General Staff, that in his view Eisenhower 'doesn't
know what he is doing'. Marshall told Eisenhower to make no commitments, but both deeply resented the British implication that Eisenhower's
strategy was wrong.[330] A week later, following a press conference on 7
January in which Montgomery gave the impression, deliberately or not,
that the British had saved the day in the Battle of the Bulge, Eisenhower
warned Montgomery that if he persisted, it would 'damage the goodwill
and devotion to a common cause that have made this Allied force unique
in history'.[331]

Brooke reopened the issue of a single commander and a narrow thrust
into Germany from the British front during meetings of the Combined
Chiefs in late January on the island of Malta, a prelude to the Yalta summit. His intervention threatened an open rupture between the two allies.
In an ill-tempered meeting Marshall told the British chiefs that Eisenhower would have to resign if they continued to snipe at his conduct of
the campaign, but the following day, 1 February, Roosevelt insisted that
Eisenhower should stay. British persistence might well have provoked a
major crisis, but Churchill followed Roosevelt. The issues have remained
live long after the end of the war. There is something to be said for both
sides of the debate, but the governing factor was the presence of an American army much larger than the British, whose leaders would not accept

command by a British field marshal or a strategy that gave the glamour of defeating Germany to their British ally. 'The organization of command is, of course, not ideal,' Eisenhower wrote to Marshall, 'but it is the most practicable one, considering the questions of nationality involved and the personalities available . . .'[332] An open rift was just avoided, but it remains unclear still why Montgomery was unable to grasp the delicate politics of the Anglo-American alliance.

By January 1945, German and Japanese defeat was only a matter of time but the battles of the last months of conflict to subdue the crumbling enemy empires were among the bloodiest and costliest of the war for the Allies. Battle deaths for all American services in all theatres between December 1944 and May 1945 totalled 100,667, more than one-third of all wartime combat deaths; Soviet irrecoverable losses (dead and missing) for the main operations between January and May 1945 against German territory totalled 300,686. These were also the costliest months for German and Japanese dead, both servicemen and civilians. In the last four months of combat for the German armed forces 1,540,000 were killed, many of them teenagers or older men drafted in to fill the large gaps in German army units; at least 100,000 civilians perished in the bombing. The outcome was never in doubt. By early 1945 the Allies enjoyed overwhelming airpower – the German air force had just 15 per cent of the strength of the combined American and British forces by the end of December 1944 – while the ratio of tanks and self-propelled guns was four to one in the Allies' favour, six to one on the Western front. Resistance against such odds was close to suicidal, but it reflected the demand for a final extreme effort to preserve the imperial heartland. 'The principle of fanatical struggle for every metre of our homeland soil,' ran the order of the day to one German army group in January, 'must be for us a holy duty.'[333] On Iwo Jima, the first homeland territory of Japan to be invaded, the commander issued a list of 'Courageous Battle Vows' to his troops, which included the injunction that 'each man will make it his duty to kill ten of the enemy before dying.'[334]

Hitler had no doubt that he faced his *Endkampf*, the final moment of defeat. His air adjutant recalled a conversation with a despairing leader in January: 'I know the war is lost. The enemy superiority is too great . . . we will never capitulate, ever. We may go down, but we will take the rest of the world down with us.'[335] Although he would certainly have preferred victory, the alternative of absolute defeat was not in his distorted moral universe an unworthy outcome. This explains why he clung so desperately to the call for victory or destruction, because in his view it was essential for the German nation to be redeemed from the shameful surrender in

1918 by fighting to the last breath rather than giving up. To avoid shame was a trope in German historical culture with a powerful appeal not just to Hitler, but to those German circles still willing to sustain the war effort.[336] The redemptive sacrifice of absolute defeat was seen as a moral act of heroic proportions from which future generations of Germans would learn as they rebuilt the health and vigour of the race. In his 'political testament' dictated in the bunker in Berlin on 29 April 1945, Hitler claimed that the German war effort 'will go down in history as the most glorious and heroic manifestation of a people's struggle for life', and a prelude to the rebirth of a genuine 'people's community'.[337]

In the last months of the European war, the Allied air forces contributed a fittingly apocalyptic backdrop to Hitler's fantasies of the people's heroic destruction with the crumpled streets and raging fires that accompanied the final punishing campaign. Since September 1944, when Eisenhower released the heavy bomber forces back to air force control, both RAF Bomber Command and the American Eighth and Fifteenth Air Forces unleashed the heaviest bombing of the war, dropping three-quarters of Allied wartime bomb tonnage in just eight months against a German air defence severely depleted by the attrition of fighter forces in German air space, whose loss rate reached 50 per cent a month.[338] Both Henry Arnold, commander of the US Army Air Forces, and Harris hoped that the bombers might be able to inflict the knockout blow that had so far eluded Allied armies, but bombing against cities that had already been bombed repeatedly was also justified from fear that Germany might find ways to reverse its fortunes with novel weapons of war or an industrial revival if the air war was not carried on relentlessly. The power available was now awesome: United States air forces had 5,000 heavy bombers in Europe, supported by 5,000 fighter aircraft for escorting the bombers and suppressing the residual German air force; Bomber Command had around 1,500 bombers, chiefly the heavy Avro Lancaster. Operational losses, which had almost ended the campaigns late in 1943, were now on average just 1 or 2 per cent of all sorties.[339]

The bombers were to be unleashed in Operation 'Hurricane' to meet Eisenhower's requirement to achieve as much dislocation of military and transport targets in western Germany as possible for the imminent Allied invasion, but the objectives were not defined with much clarity. Uncertainty about what were now priority targets was resolved by Strategic Directive No. 2 from SHAEF on 1 November 1944, which called on maximum effort against oil targets and communications of all kinds, while in poor weather the bombers could continue area attacks on 'industrial centres'.[340] Harris was sceptical of bombing precise targets, though

Bomber Command contributed to the oil and transport plans. Most of the time his forces battered away at cities, including many smaller ones not yet incinerated, in the belief that a point must come when the social and psychological damage would make it impossible to continue the war. American bombers, dropping loads largely through cloud with radar guidance, did succeed in inflicting serious dislocation of communications and reducing Germany's domestic oil output by almost two-thirds from the level a year before. Yet the knock-out blow was not in the end delivered, even though the cumulative damage to German cities, industry and civilian population reached an exceptional threshold by the spring of 1945, including the firestorm at Dresden on the night of 13/14 February which killed (according to recent estimates) 25,000 people.

In March 1945, the German armaments minister, Albert Speer, warned Hitler that the collapse of transport and key industrial sectors meant that war production would survive perhaps six weeks. Whether this would have meant a German surrender is unlikely, given Hitler's obsessive determination to go down fighting rather than give in. Nor in the end would the ground invasion have been averted. The bombers were viewed by the ground force commanders as a contribution to the ground war, easing the path for Allied armies, including the Red Army. Dresden was part of a pattern of bombing cities in eastern Germany to help the Soviet advance, a decision agreed at the Yalta Conference in early February following a British suggestion and accepted by the Soviet side only if an adequate bomb line could be agreed which would prevent friendly fire on the Red Army.[341] It seems unlikely that Allied bombing contributed directly to the rapid Soviet advance. The key factor was reducing mobility for Germany's armed forces across the whole of the narrowing field of conflict.

By the time of the Allied summit at Yalta, which convened between 4 and 11 February 1945 in the Livadia Palace amidst the ruins of the Crimean town, Stalin had finally launched the long-expected operation to cross the Vistula in central Poland in the direction of the German capital. Planning began back in October 1944, but the need to establish new supply lines, to replenish depleted units and to train conscripts rounded up in the rush across Belorussia and eastern Poland, all contributed to a delay of three months before it could begin. Stalin now assumed direct command of the Red Army, and ordered Zhukov, his deputy, to take control of First Belorussian Army Group for the main thrust, with Konev's First Ukrainian Army Group to the south, attacking out of the Sandomierz bridgehead across the Vistula. The initial aim was as optimistic as Montgomery's had been: a drive to the Oder River by 3 February, then on to Berlin and the Elbe River by the beginning of March, carried out in one sweeping advance. The first ambition was clearly realistic, given the over-whelming material advantage on the Soviet side. Zhukov and Konev between them commanded 2.2 million men, 33,000 artillery pieces and mortars, 7,000 tanks and 5,000 aircraft. Facing them in German Army Groups A and Centre, according to Russian figures, were 400,000 troops, 5,000 guns, 1,220 armoured fighting vehicles and 650 aircraft.[342] Further north, to undertake simultaneous thrusts into East Prussia and Pom-erania, were the Second and Third Belorussian Army Groups, with 1.67 million men and 3,800 tanks between them.

The vast offensive was finally launched between 12 and 14 January. Zhukov and Konev made rapid progress against a disintegrating defence. The Red Army reached the Oder at the fortress city of Küstrin by 31 Janu-ary, fighting across 300 kilometres of territory in just two weeks to reach within 65 kilometres of the German capital; in the south Konev's forces reached the Oder at Breslau by 24 January, breached the river and cap-tured a major part of the Silesian industrial district by the end of the month. In the north, progress was slower against determined German opposition, but the Baltic coast was reached by 26 January and East Prus-sia cut off; the provincial capital at Königsberg, one of the fortress cities created in 1944, was surrounded and besieged three days later, though it held out for more than two months. In the three weeks before Yalta, the Red Army liberated western Poland, captured Silesia and cut off German forces in East Prussia.

Whether or not Stalin intended the rapid success of the campaign to strengthen his bargaining position with his allies, the result of the initial breakthrough in the East contrasted with the slower progress of British and American armies as they cleared the west bank of the Rhine and the *Westwall* defences during January and February. Montgomery's principal operations on the north of the front, Operation 'Veritable' to force a path through the Reichswald forest, and Operation 'Grenade' for the United States Ninth Army to force the line of the river Roer, only began as the Yalta Conference drew to an end, on 8 February. The three Allied leaders arrived at Yalta no longer concerned primarily with the course of the war, which was now predictable, but with the problems of the peace that fol-lowed. Much of the agenda was designed to satisfy Stalin. Unlike earlier encounters, the Western delegates found a congenial, restrained dictator, prepared 'in many instances', recalled the chair of the American Joint Chiefs, 'to compromise in order to reach agreement'.[343] Appearances were deceptive. A few weeks before, he had told a Yugoslav delegation in Mos-cow that with 'bourgeois politicians you have to be very careful . . . we are led not by emotions but by reason, analysis and calculation.' Stalin might have added by espionage as well, since many of the sensitive documents prepared for Roosevelt and Churchill were already in Soviet possession, while the Livadia Palace bristled with hidden microphones.[344] Roosevelt was exhausted and evidently very ill after his 9,500-kilometre trip, with a halt first at Malta to meet with Churchill. Anthony Eden, Churchill's foreign secretary, considered him to be 'vague, loose and ineffective', but he came knowing that he needed to impress the American public with a show of unity and commitment to a peaceful and democratic post-war order. This he broadly achieved with general agreement on the organization of the United Nations and a final-day signing of a Declaration on Liberated Europe, a commitment of the three powers to governments based on free elections and the will of the people. He also got agreement from Stalin that the Soviet Union would enter the war against Japan after Germany's defeat, a promise that still looked strategically necessary to the Americans in order to finish the Pacific war.[345]

The Declaration was in reality an effort to paper over obvious cracks between the Allies. Unknown to Roosevelt, Churchill had already written off most of Eastern Europe when he met Stalin the previous October in Moscow, where he produced an informal list of relative Soviet and Western shares – the so-called 'percentages agreement' – granting Stalin Romania and Bulgaria as long as the British had the main say in Greece. Churchill was concerned to ensure continued British dominance in the Mediterranean and to allow France a role in an occupied post-war Germany, which Stalin grudgingly conceded. The stumbling block was the future of Poland, all of which was now under Soviet occupation. Roosevelt and Churchill reluctantly agreed that the Soviet Union should keep the areas occupied in 1939, but there was no firm agreement on where Poland's compensating frontier in the West, carved out of eastern Germany, was to be fixed. The new Poland was already under the provisional rule of a committee of communists set up by Stalin in 1944 as a government-in-waiting, but neither Churchill nor Roosevelt was prepared to accept the new regime as it stood and wanted to involve other non-communist Poles. Stalin insisted that he wanted a democratic and independent Poland, but one friendly to Soviet interests, and in practice there was no means available to the Western Allies to compel a different outcome since the Soviet side was determined not to give way on Soviet security. A temporary compromise was reached when Stalin agreed to allow a commission, composed of Molotov and the British and American ambassadors, to meet in Moscow and work out a formula for a 'democratic' Poland, but the commission soon reached stalemate when the three men met, and Poland, the initial cause of war in 1939, was left to its communist fate.

Despite the publicity given to Yalta as an expression of Allied unity and post-war collaboration, captured in the many photographs of the three smiling leaders, relations between them deteriorated rapidly in the months down to German defeat. Stalin continued to worry that his partners might still reach a separate settlement with Germany. In late March he told a Czech delegation in Moscow that it was possible that 'our allies will try to save the Germans and come to an arrangement with them'. Roosevelt soon understood that the 'Declaration' at Yalta meant little to Stalin. On 24 March, told yet again that Stalin had obstructed American requests to help repatriate American POWs in Poland, the president banged his fists on his wheelchair in frustration: 'We can't do business with Stalin. He has broken every one of his promises he made at Yalta.'[346]

The public face of the alliance remained, however, unaltered by the growing climate of distrust and recrimination. The ring around Germany was closed from west, east and south over the following two months. Unlike the Allies, German armed forces faced insuperable barriers to any reversal of military fortunes. The transport system, which ought to have helped with internal lines of supply and communication, was too damaged to fulfil what was needed; military supplies were moved to the front in many cases by horse; air support was now merely residual for Germany's ground armies; German divisions were short of manpower, and replacements were fed in randomly, many drawn from age groups unfit or untrained; *Volkssturm* units were given an odd mix of uniforms, a few rifles and machine guns, and, in the case of one unit, 1,200 grenades with no fuses.[347] Allied soldiers reported that German resistance now diverged, as one put it, between 'savage determination and utter apathy'.[348] Above all, Hitler lost what little sense of reality he still retained in his final weeks as supreme commander, sacking senior officers who failed to stand fast and insisting that 'every block of flats, every house, every floor, every hedgerow, every shell-hole is defended to the utmost'.[349] He failed to allow the German armies trapped on the Courland Peninsula or cut off in East Prussia to leave by sea, when it was still possible, in order to strengthen defence of the German heartland. He refused to allow the German army to pull back the front line behind the barrier of the Rhine, or in Italy behind the river Po. In February and again in March he sent forces desperately needed in Germany to try to break the Soviet siege of Budapest, in the hope that they could then regain the area of Hungarian oil production at Lake Balaton, with predictable disaster. Finally, on 19 March, he published a decree usually known as the *Nerobefehl* (Nero Order) for a scorched-earth policy in remaining German territory to leave nothing intact, from bridges to food stocks, that the Allied military could use. The decree has been

interpreted as a rejection of the German people who had failed his sum-
mons to imperial glory, leaving them with nothing, but it is clear that the
wording referred only to military equipment, production and transport
and was consistent in Hitler's view with the way the Soviet authorities
had destroyed everything in the path of German armies four years
before.[350] By this stage, local military and Party authorities acted on their
own instincts and in many cases refused to implement the decree, since it
clearly did affect the survival of the civilian population; in the major cities there was in truth little left that Allied air forces had not already
scorched.

When the collapse came, it came suddenly. At Yalta the Allied leaders
discussed when they thought the European war would end and concluded
that it would not be before 1 July, but more certainly by 31 December. The
brittle defence that still shielded Germany, and German forces in Italy,
proved to have little depth to it. On the Western Front, Eisenhower's ambition to clear the western bank of the Rhine of enemy forces was completed
by 10 March, by which time the Allies calculated that one-third of German
army strength had been lost, including a net of 250,000 prisoners. On the
western side of the river there now stood 4 million Allied troops in 73 divisions (by the German surrender, 4.5 million in 91 divisions).[351] Eisenhower
once again faced conflicting pressure from Montgomery and Bradley over
where the Rhine should be crossed first, and although he supported the
British plan Operation 'Plunder' (supported by an airborne Operation
'Varsity') to begin on 23 March, he did nothing to stop Bradley's Twelfth
Army Group from exploiting the defeat of German forces along the central
sector of the front. On 7 March, a reconnaissance force of the Ninth
Armoured Division captured the Ludendorff Bridge at Remagen intact,
and Bradley got Eisenhower's permission to move forces across the Rhine.
The subsequent bridgehead moved only a short way and was contained
until the end of March, but Patton decided that rather than wait for Montgomery and a British operational coup, he would move first. He captured
Koblenz on 7 March with his US Third Army, after moving 88 kilometres
in 48 hours, and on 22 March crossed the Rhine at Nierstein and Oppen-
heim, just ahead of the British further north.

A day later, following a barrage from 3,500 artillery pieces, Montgomery's Twenty-first Army Group crossed the Rhine at Wesel. Resistance
here and further south was now limited and patchy after the defeats west
of the river; there were bitter and tenacious pockets of fighting, but also a
growing willingness on the part of German soldiers to surrender. Although
it took time to get the force across the Rhine, completed by the 28th, from
then on progress was as rapid as Zhukov's had been in January. The

Second Army was sent towards the Elbe and Hamburg, the Canadian First Army to the Netherlands. The United States Ninth Army was returned to Bradley's command for the encirclement of the Ruhr–Rhineland industrial region. Field Marshal Brooke deplored the 'nationalistic outlook of allies', which left Montgomery's army group weaker, and left the British with the more limited role of securing the Allies' left flank.[352] Progress was rapid across the flat northern plain as one town after another came under occupation, but it was not uncontested. Bremen was reached on 20 April and resisted British forces for six days; Montgomery was under orders to proceed rapidly to Denmark, and the Baltic port of Lübeck, in this case to forestall the Red Army since no agreement had been made with Stalin about the occupation of Denmark or the Netherlands. On 2 May Second Army entered Lübeck and the war in northern Germany came virtually to an end.

Further south, Bradley's army group crossed the Rhine in strength and again faced little serious opposition as he moved the Ninth Army from the north and the First Army from the south to surround and then divide the Ruhr pocket. The 317,000 men of German Army Group B finally laid down their arms on 17 April when their commander, Field Marshal Model, dissolved the organization rather than have to surrender. He shot himself four days later in a wood near the city of Duisburg.[353] At this point Eisenhower and Bradley initiated a sudden change in American strategy. Although the original ambition had been to drive to Berlin once the Rhine was breached – 'a rapid thrust to Berlin', Eisenhower had announced the previous September – a confused intelligence picture emerged suggesting that remaining elite German troops, principally Waffen-SS units, were concentrating in the south to create an *Alpenfestung* (Alpine fortress), supported in the mountains by hidden stores of food and equipment and even underground aircraft factories.[354] After the shock of the Ardennes attack, American commanders were wary of being caught out again. The apparent signs of reinforcement and fear that the large force still in Italy might move to the Alps were, as Bradley claimed in his memoirs, 'too ominous a threat to ignore', and on 28 March Eisenhower wrote directly to Stalin, and to Marshall and Montgomery, that he was ordering the Sixth Army Group and Patton's Third Army to go south and south-east to cut off the prospect of a last German stand in the mountains.[355] 'Berlin as a strategic area,' he told the Combined Chiefs of Staff, 'is discounted as it is now largely destroyed.'[356] The other American armies were ordered to move on to the Elbe after reducing the Ruhr pocket, and to stop there to await the Russians.

That the *Alpenfestung* was an intelligence fantasy is clear with hindsight, but there were enough Waffen-SS units and armour in the south to make the fear more plausible than it now seems. Churchill and the British Chiefs of Staff were dismayed by the changed priority but Eisenhower angrily insisted that this time he would brook no objection from his awkward ally. American forces moved quickly from the Rhine to the Tauber River in Franconia, but in the Steigerwald and along the Franconian heights they encountered improvised defensive lines, manned in many cases by military cadets and Hitler Youth units, where the fighting took on a murderous quality with little quarter given on either side. It took three weeks to break through to the Danube, but the remnants of the exhausted German defence could no longer offer any co-ordinated resistance. 'It was a picture of misery,' recorded one onlooker at the sight of German soldiers, 'to see these exhausted, tattered, and for the most part weaponless remains of the German army in flight.'[357] American forces moved through Austria, sealed the Brenner Pass to Italy and swept on into Czechoslovakia, where a common front was established with the Red Army to the west of Prague. Where they could avoid the terror inflicted by their own side on anyone who surrendered, German soldiers abandoned the fight in the south, reaching a total of 600,000 German POWs by the end of April.

Eisenhower might well have been less concerned over a final Alpine stand if he had understood the situation on the Italian front. Here too German forces dug in to contain the enemy on the final mountain ridges before the Po Valley and along the Adriatic coast. Field Marshal Kesselring, German commander in Italy, was moved on 10 March to become supreme commander West in place of von Rundstedt, and his replacement, Colonel General Heinrich von Vietinghoff-Scheel, had some twenty-three understrength divisions (including four from Mussolini's remnant Italian army) to hold the line from Liguria in the west to Ravenna in the east. Stretched taut, his defences now faced an enemy with overwhelming air superiority, a two-to-one advantage in artillery and three-to-one in armoured fighting vehicles. After the stalemate in the winter, the Allies prepared for a final battle. The Eighth Army began its assault on 9 April following a fearsome raid by 825 heavy bombers dropping fragmentation bombs; the Santerro River was reached and crossed two days later against a faltering enemy, and New Zealand advanced units moved rapidly towards Bologna.[358] On 14 April, General Lucian Truscott, now commander of the American Fifth Army after Clark was made overall army group commander in Italy, launched the breakout from the northern Apennines, meeting patchy but fierce opposition until the final Genghis Khan Line was broken on 19 April. Both wings of the Allied offensive could now move towards Bologna and on to the Po River, which was reached by the 22nd. Once the last defensive lines were breached, German units retreated like the army in France in August 1944 in a desperate effort to avoid collapse. They crossed the Po and those that could raced for the north-east and a possible path to Austria. By this time German army garrisons in the main northern cities were faced with partisan revolt. Surrenders multiplied as Allied armies approached, but the German high command had already begun to explore a general surrender through secret negotiations. Although the gauleiter of Tirol-Vorarlberg, Franz Hofer, had proposed some months before to Berlin the idea of creating an Alpine redoubt, he found little interest there because it suggested a defeatist outlook. By late April, with German forces in Italy facing collapse, any idea of a last stand evaporated.

For Stalin, American anxiety about the *Alpenfestung* was a relief because it meant that an inter-Allied race to Berlin could be avoided. Although he let it be known to his Allies that Berlin was not considered important by the Soviet side either, the capture of Hitler's capital was a political rather than a military priority. Stalin announced in January that he wanted to capture the German leader in his lair, and Soviet troops reacted by using the Russian word for lair, *berlog*, as their destination, instead of Berlin.[359] There was nevertheless an unexpected delay once the Oder line was reached. Zhukov told Stalin in early February that he could capture Berlin 'with a swift rush' by the middle of the month; while Stalin was at Yalta, Zhukov asked again for permission for an immediate campaign. Further south, Konev too was impatient to move, promising to reach the Elbe by the last days of February.[360] Stalin hesitated, then decided, with the Western Allies still apparently bogged down on the far side of the Rhine, to clear the Red Army flanks first where there were still heavy concentrations of enemy forces. His motives are not known with certainty, though clearing the flanks to avoid any risks in the capture of Berlin made strategic sense. The Soviet leader, after investing so much in invading and occupying the German heartland, could not afford an assault on Berlin that misfired. Zhukov was sent north to help clear Pomerania and reach the Baltic coast, and spent two months aiding Rokossovskii's Second Belorussian Army Group to defeat the remaining German armies in East Prussia and the former Polish 'corridor'. Danzig fell to the Red Army on 30 March. The fighting in the two months broke any further German resistance from the north but cost three times as many casualties as the Vistula–Oder operation in January. Further south, Konev was forced to fight major battles against General Ferdinand Schörner's Army Group Centre in Silesia, while on the Danube front the final German wartime counter-offensive, Operation 'Spring Awakening', led by Sepp Dietrich's Sixth Panzer Army, designed to recapture the Hungarian oilfield, had to be beaten back in mid-March with high casualties.[361] The way now lay open to Vienna, encircled and captured on 13 April, and to Prague where some of the last fighting of the European war took place in May after the German surrender.

As it became clear that the successful crossing of the Rhine in late March was the prelude to a rapid Western advance, Stalin ordered immediate preparations for an offensive towards Berlin and beyond it, to the line of the Elbe. The operation had to be developed quickly, while large forces were redeployed back from the flanks. Stalin wanted the German capital captured in five days and a vast military host was assembled for the task: the three army groups of Zhukov, Konev and Rokossovskii had between them 2.5 million men organized in 171 divisions and 21 mobile units, 6,250 tanks, 7,500 aircraft, 41,000 artillery pieces and mortars; the German Ninth and Third Panzer Armies defending on the Oder had 25 divisions with 754 tanks, while the Twelfth Army defending Berlin, commanded by Lieutenant General Walther Wenck, had 6 scratch divisions put together hastily in April with few heavy weapons. Altogether, German forces could muster only 766,000 men, many of them ineffective combatants due to injury, battle fatigue, or age. Both sides waited in high suspense for what was evidently the final major campaign of the war. On 16 April the offensive opened on Zhukov's front, facing the Seelow Heights as the most direct route to Berlin. Zhukov deployed 143 searchlights to dazzle the German defenders, but the massive preliminary artillery barrage not only churned up the ground at the expense of the advancing armour but created a thick pall of smoke that reflected the glare of the lights back onto the oncoming Red Army.[362] The heights were stormed at great cost by the end of the second day, but Stalin reacted to the information from Zhukov about the stalled attack by encouraging Konev, who had had more success further south, to swing northward to take Berlin from the south in a race to seize the city. Konev's army group had faced a difficult river crossing over the Neisse, but on 16 April, under a hail of artillery and artificial smoke, a swarm of small boats crossed and seized space on the far side within an hour. The enemy was driven back 13 kilometres on the first day, and then German resistance crumpled as the First Ukrainian Army Group swung west and north-west towards Berlin. By 18 April, Konev's vanguard captured the German army headquarters at Zossen, and was approaching Berlin. On 25 April, part of Konev's force, bypassing the capital, forged on to the Elbe River where, at a village near Torgau, Soviet and American forces finally met.

Around Berlin the final fragile defensive lines were breached one after another. Konev was poised to win the race as Third and Fourth Guards Tank Armies pushed into the suburbs of Berlin and made for the government centre and Hitler's lair. By the 25th, he was in a position to order the storming of the government centre and the Reichstag when his forward troops found themselves firing on General Chuikov's Eighth Guards Army, part of Zhukov's army group, which had managed to speed its advance to arrive in the centre of the capital just hours ahead of Konev. Chuikov's men were given the honour of seizing the lair and on 30 April a small detachment stormed into the Reichstag building and hoisted aloft a large red flag.[363] A few hundred metres away, Hitler and a small entourage huddled in the bunker built under the Reich Chancellery. He was entirely out of touch with the reality around him, creating fantasies that defeat could be averted by Providence. When news arrived on 12 April that Roosevelt had died of a cerebral haemorrhage, Hitler briefly imagined a reversal of fortune: 'Now that fate has rid the world of the greatest war criminal of all times, there will come a turning point in the tides of war.'[364] Hitler for days sustained the delusion that rescue might still be possible, and on 24 April issued an order to the German armies around the city 'to reestablish a broad link with Berlin and thus decide the battle of Berlin victoriously.'[365] On the 28th, as Soviet artillery battered the buildings overhead, Goebbels issued one more rallying cry, published in an improvised Berlin newspaper, the *Panzerbär*, to fashion the myth of Hitler as Germanic folk-hero: 'His orders are still being emitted from Berlin in a battle for freedom that is making world history . . . He is standing on the hottest battlefield man has ever known. And around him have gathered the most fantastic soldiers there have ever been . . .'[366] There was no way out. When interrogators asked Jodl why Hitler had not simply given up sooner when faced with catastrophic defeat, he replied: 'But can you give up an empire and a people, before you have lost a war? A man like Hitler could not do that.'[367]

Japan's 'final struggle' never materialized on the German scale because the home islands were not invaded, but it was the intention of the hardline military leadership that a similar redemptive battle should take place to save the honour of the empire as it went down to defeat. In January 1945 the Allies were still sufficiently far away to allow a degree of confidence that the tough battles in store might yet deliver the ambition, maintained since 1942, that the cost of defeating Japan would simply prove too great for the Allies, and finally allow a compromise peace to be negotiated. An inner defensive zone was established from Taiwan and eastern China, through southern Korea to the Pacific Bonin Islands. Yet in this case too, there was no doubt about the outcome, given Allied material superiority and the gradual collapse of the Japanese war economy under the impact of the air and naval blockade of Japanese trade. Only the pace of Allied progress was in question, and this proved slower in 1945 than expected as Japanese garrisons in the empire devised ways of ensnaring the enemy in long battles of attrition on ground of their choosing.

The tension in American planning for the final campaigns resurfaced over the slow progress made by MacArthur's large American commitment in the Philippines, which he considered the best staging post for the eventual invasion of the Japanese home islands. Admiral King hoped that a combined air and sea blockade, now made possible by bombing from bases in the Marianas, would render the invasion unnecessary, but both Nimitz and MacArthur were convinced that Japan would not give in until the home islands were invaded and occupied. For this purpose, Nimitz and Arnold, the commander of the army air forces, needed the island bases of Iwo Jima and Okinawa as forward air and naval staging bases. Capture of Iwo Jima would also prevent Japanese aircraft from regularly attacking the B-29 heavy bombers now based in the Marianas.[368] Before this could be done, MacArthur had to complete as soon as possible the occupation of the main island in the Philippines chain, Luzon. The invasion here began on 7 January, with 175,000 American troops, fewer than the 267,000 Japanese under the command of Lieutenant General Yamashita Tomoyuki, a statistic that MacArthur unhelpfully referred to as 'bunk' when he was informed.[369] Yamashita saw his objective as a deliberate delaying action to hold up any possible invasion of Japan and held back his forces in the hills and mountains surrounding the main valley area on Luzon. As a result, combat was limited in the first week while MacArthur urged his army commander, General Walter Krueger, to speed up the seizure of the capital, Manila, so that he could announce a definite victory and return in triumph to the city he had made his home before 1941.

The fight for Manila, chiefly against a naval ground force under Rear Admiral Iwabuchi Sanji, developed into a long and brutal campaign, in which the American commanders were told to change the rules of engagement to allow artillery to fire on civilian areas, while the Japanese command issued the order that 'all civilians on the battlefield will be killed'.[370] Japanese soldiers repeated the rampage against Nanjing, tying men together in groups and setting them alight, killing women and children in grotesque sprees of violence, raping women and young girls. The central and southern areas of the city had to be destroyed block by block and the Japanese garrison liquidated. Amidst the destruction was MacArthur's former penthouse suite atop the Manila Hotel. An estimated 100,000 Filipinos died from artillery fire, bombing and Japanese savagery; 16,000 Japanese were killed in the defence of Manila, but only 1,010 Americans died – an unusually small number for the Pacific war.[371] Under the circumstances, MacArthur cancelled a victory march he had planned through the centre of the capital, liberated in ruins on 3 March. Although Luzon's ports and airfields could now be used for the projected invasion, Yamashita retreated to mountain redoubts where he held out until the Japanese surrender in August. The cost of the combat that followed was exceptionally high among troops on both sides struggling in the tropical climate, in tough terrain ideal for concealed defence, weakened by disease and battle fatigue. By the end of the battle for the islands, Japanese casualties amounted to 380,000, most of them dead, while Allied losses amounted to 47,000 in battle, but a further 93,000 from illness, combat fatigue and psychiatric breakdown.[372] The cost was higher than anticipated, and it both delayed and weakened the capacity to mount the next stage of the invasion strategy, as Yamashita had intended.

The capture of Iwo Jima, one of the Bonin Islands south of Japan, and of Okinawa, largest of the Ryūkyū Islands, proved among the costliest of the Pacific war. Operation 'Detachment' against Iwo Jima was to begin in February 1945, followed by Operation 'Iceberg' against Okinawa in April. Both islands were technically Japanese territory, and soldiers were told that defence of Japanese soil was a sacred obligation. Iwo Jima has become notorious as the one island campaign where American casualties exceeded Japanese. Since the Japanese leadership expected the island to be a target, Iwo Jima's commander, Lieutenant General Kuribayashi Tadamichi, used his 20,000 men to build an island fortress, using the caves and volcanic rocks to create a network of defensive installations, connected by tunnels, where men, guns and stores could be concentrated almost invisible to the enemy. Kuribayashi had his headquarters built 22 metres underground, with a blockhouse on top protected by a roof of reinforced concrete 3 metres thick; the island was only 10 kilometres long and 3 kilometres wide, but there were 17 kilometres of tunnels built under its rocky surface. One of the three airfields was surrounded by no fewer than 800 pillboxes.[373]

Thus fortified, the island presented a complete field of fire from which there was scant protection for the three marine divisions of 70,647 men who made up the invasion force for D-Day, 19 February. They were given a three-day bombardment by Spruance's Fifth Fleet instead of the ten days asked for, because the navy wanted to move north to undertake direct attacks on the Japanese coastline. Although an estimated half of the heavy guns on the island were neutralized, and a quarter of the pillboxes and gun emplacements, the defence retained formidable firepower. Kuribayashi waited until the landing had been accomplished before unleashing a fierce barrage, a prelude to a six-week campaign in which the marines were subject to constant artillery, machine-gun and mortar fire. Although the airfields were secured within days, clearing the island proved to be an exceptional challenge. The iconic flag raised on the southernmost peak of Mount Suribachi on 23 February (captured for posterity by an Associated Press photographer in a re-enactment three hours later), was followed by six more days flushing Japanese soldiers out from the mountain's caves.[374] Further north, the marines moved slowly through the most heavily defended part of the island, destroying enemy installations with grenades, dynamite and flamethrowers, and in the process taking heavy casualties as the men became more exhausted and disoriented by a month of continual combat. Kuribayashi's blockhouse was finally detonated with dynamite while inside he committed ritual suicide. By the time the island was declared secure, on 27 March, a total of 6,823 American servicemen were dead and 19,217 wounded or incapacitated; of the 20,000-strong Japanese garrison, only 1,083 became prisoners.[375] The island became an American airbase from where P-51 long-range fighters escorted daylight raids on Japan's cities and hundreds of B-29 bombers stopped to refuel, or to cope with technical problems or combat damage.

Okinawa was an operation on an altogether larger scale. As part of Japan's territory, it was seen in Tokyo as a test of what might happen when the Allies invaded the main islands. The commander, Lieutenant General Ushijima Mitsuru, followed the new 'sleeping tactics' used on Iwo Jima, which allowed the amphibious landing to take place, luring the invaders to the heavily defended south of the island where around 83,000 combat troops, principally from the Thirty-second Army, were concentrated in another network of caves, tunnels and pillboxes.[376] American intelligence on the Japanese strategy on Okinawa was limited, but this time the navy took fewer chances, bombarding the island for ten days while a small force captured the peripheral islands at Kerama Retto to use as a seaplane base and naval staging post. The Americans put together a vast armada for the invasion of more than 1,200 ships of all kinds, but even before the troops landed, Vice Admiral Ugaki Matome had formally established on 5 March the Special Attack Force of suicide aircraft and sent off the first of an almost three-month campaign of suicide attacks against the approaching United States fleet. One succeeded in hitting the fleet commander's flagship *Indianapolis* on 30 March, two days before the invasion, and he had to transfer to the *New Mexico*. A total of 1,465 suicide aircraft were despatched, sinking 36 ships and damaging 300, including ships of the much smaller British Pacific Fleet which had finally joined under American command, only to be sent off to conduct minor operations before returning to Australia in May for refitting.[377]

On 1 April, the invasion force of 173,000 army and marine troops arrived in seven divisions under the command of General Simon Bolivar Buckner. They faced almost no opposition other than the suicide attacks, and within days had secured the airfield area. First contact with Japanese units was made by 8 April as American troops fanned out into the north and south of the island. It was on the mountainous southern zone that Ushijima had concentrated his concealed forces and once again the enemy was forced to move forward with painful slowness against defences that had to be eliminated one at a time, even after the artillery and naval support pumped 2.3 million shells into the hillsides.[378] It was as slow as the drive across Iwo Jima, and again taxed American forces to the limit in a hundred days of non-stop combat in weather that by late May turned the hillsides into pools of deep mud, where decomposing bodies filled the air with a putrid stench. It took until June to drive the remaining garrison into the south-west of the island, where they were slowly eliminated as they ran short of ammunition and food and medical supplies. Resistance finally ceased on 21 June, three days after Buckner was killed by a shell blast visiting the front lines. Ushijima followed Kuribayashi in committing suicide. Some 92,000 Japanese soldiers and Okinawan militia died, alongside a large civilian population, estimated at anywhere between 62,000 and 120,000. United States casualties for navy, army and marines numbered 12,520 dead and 36,613 wounded, but there were 33,096 non-battle casualties from fatigue and illness, giving a total not far short of Japanese losses.[379] It was these casualty figures from Okinawa and Iwo Jima that prompted growing protest at home over the cost of securing small islands whose strategic worth was hard to understand, and they fuelled anxiety in Washington that the costs of invading mainland Japan might be more than the American public would support.

Fierce Japanese resistance from prepared positions has to be set in the context of Japan's faltering war effort as the sea blockade and, from March 1945, heavy air attacks created a growing crisis for Japanese industry and the home population. The submarine and air campaign against Japanese ocean and coastal traffic peaked in 1944 and 1945. Japan's merchant marine was reduced from 5.9 million tons to 890,000 between 1942 and 1944, but by 1945 much of the remaining tonnage could not be used to transport goods from the south or from continental Asia because of the threat from submarines and mines.[380] Heavy mining of coastal areas around Japan in 1945 led to a final collapse of essential imports of raw materials, coal and food. Overall, bulk imports were 20 million tons in 1941, 2.7 million by 1945. Iron-ore imports for Japan's steel industry fell to just 341,000 tons in the last six months of the war, from 4.7 million tons in 1942; rubber imports fell to zero; coal imports, chiefly from the Asian mainland, totalled 24 million tons in 1941, but only 548,000 tons in the final six months of war.[381] Starved of resources, Japanese war industry was close to collapse in summer 1945.

The onset of heavy bombing by Twenty-first Bomber Command, operating from bases in the Marianas, complemented the impact of the blockade, although much of the fundamental damage to Japan's war effort and the reduction of provisions for the home population pre-dated the systematic bombing of Japanese cities. The bombing of precision targets in the aircraft and shipbuilding industries began in January and February 1945, but the tactic proved ineffective using the B-29 bombers in daylight at high altitude with a persistent strong airstream over Japan. In early March the new commander of the bombers, Lieutenant General Curtis LeMay, turned American tactics upside-down by initiating night-time raids from low altitude (5–8,000 feet instead of 33,000) using large loads of the M-69 incendiary bomb clusters, which contained the highly effective napalm incendiary gel developed by chemists at Harvard, deadly against Japanese cities with largely wooden structures.[382] The first raid against Tokyo on the night of 9/10 March 1945, with 325 B-29s, carrying 1,665 tons of incendiaries, was the deadliest air raid of the war, destroying over 40 square kilometres of the city in a firestorm that killed, according to police estimates, 83,793 people.[383] Between March and June, LeMay's force dropped 41,592 tons of incendiaries on Japan's most important urban-industrial areas, burning out half the urban area; from June to August, the B-29s pounded smaller cities with less industrial importance, in some cases burning 90 per cent of the urban area.[384] A post-war survey showed that by this time Japanese output in war factories in bombed areas was down to an average of 27 per cent of the wartime peak; in those undamaged it was down to an average of 50 per cent.[385] LeMay tried to convince Marshall and the Joint Chiefs that a concentrated campaign against the Japanese rail network would complete the destruction and make invasion unnecessary.

Both navy and air force commanders endorsed the claim that the damage inflicted by the air–sea blockade would be sufficient to force Japan's surrender, but the American planners remained convinced that only an invasion would make capitulation certain. Both sides prepared for what seemed an unavoidable final confrontation. In spring 1945, the Japanese army began to organize for Operation 'Ketsu-gō' ('Decisive Operation').

Two theatre commands were established: First General Army for the defence of central and north Honshu; Second General Army for western Honshu, Shikoku and the southern island of Kyushu. The aim was to establish a force of sixty divisions, thirty-six for counter-attack against invasion fronts, twenty-two for immediate coastal defence, and two mobile armoured divisions. Where useful, both the army and navy favoured suicide (*tokko*) tactics, including suicide swimmers of the Water's Edge Surprise Attack Force, as well as small suicide boats packed with explosive.[386] On 8 June, in the presence of the emperor, the 'Fundamental Policy' was laid down for a final fight to the death. An imperial rescript the following day called on the people to 'smash the inordinate ambitions of the enemy nations' in order 'to achieve the goals of the war'. Only a week before, the American Joint Chiefs had called for a formal invasion plan and MacArthur, the designated ground commander, drew up Operation 'Downfall', divided into two parts: an invasion of southern Kyushu (Operation 'Olympic') on 1 November, followed by invasion of the Tokyo area (Operation 'Coronet') in the early spring of 1946. The first required up to seventeen divisions, the second twenty-five, both supported by a vast armada of warships and amphibious vessels, including twenty-two United States carriers.[387] By this time, British leaders had offered to participate in the hope that evidence of good faith would keep alive Anglo-American post-war co-operation, but the five Commonwealth divisions to be made available (only one of them entirely British), represented a contribution that Marshall dismissed as 'an embarrassment'.[388] The offer of RAF bombing squadrons was treated summarily – 'the Goddam Lancaster outfit', complained Stilwell, now honing his acid tongue as Buckner's successor on Okinawa – and little progress could be made before the war ended.[389]

At a meeting between the new president, Harry S. Truman, and the Joint Chiefs on 17 June, a decision had to be reached. Truman favoured keeping pressure on Japan through the naval blockade and bombing, but, like the army chiefs, he believed invasion had to be attempted as long as the casualties could be reduced from the levels of bloodletting on Iwo Jima and Okinawa. Although much has been made of his fear for 500,000 to 1 million casualties, a figure plucked out of the air by an American journalist in May 1945, and later repeated in Truman's memoirs, the army estimates he was given at the time were less alarmist.[390] MacArthur supplied statistics that suggested a probable figure of dead and missing of 105,000, spread over a ninety-day campaign; the Joint Staff Planners suggested 43,500 dead or missing for both operations, while in conference with Truman and William Leahy, chair of the Joint Chiefs, Marshall suggested a total of 31,000 to 41,000, though he regarded all projections as speculative, as indeed they were. By August, the Japanese Fifty-seventh Army, under Lieutenant General Kanji Nishihara waited on Kyushu with 150,000 men for the axe to fall, perhaps as soon as October.[391] Truman approved invasion of the island (codenamed 'Diabolic' by the American side) to begin in November. From June onwards, after the fall of Okinawa and the virtual end of resistance in the Philippines and Burma, both sides waited for a showdown that could only be averted if Japanese leaders abandoned '*Ketsu-gō*' and accepted unconditional surrender.

THE LAST ACT: UNCONDITIONAL SURRENDERS

After war on such a scale, the act of surrender in 1945 for Germany and Japan was a moment of bathos amidst the intense drama of battles fought to the bitter end. In a few cases, fighting continued for days or even weeks after the surrenders were announced, but for the overwhelming majority of servicemen and women, surrender was a sudden release from the long ordeal of violence. Compelling surrender was nevertheless a complex process, both political as well as military, and for both sides. The announcement made by President Roosevelt at the Casablanca Conference in January 1943 that the Allied powers would accept nothing less than unconditional surrender was made partly to prevent any deviation by one of the Allied partners in seeking a separate peace, but also to ensure that the Axis enemy understood that nothing was to be gained by negotiation, which all three attempted. There were certainly conditions on the Allied side. Roosevelt added that victory would allow 'the destruction of a philosophy in Germany, Italy and Japan which is based on the conquest and subjugation of other peoples' – as indeed was empire everywhere.[392] Over the following two years further conditions were spelt out: military occupation and government, disarmament, the trial of war criminals, the purge of officials and politicians who ran the war effort, and the establishment under Allied eyes of a democratic political and social system. The Axis states knew that if they surrendered unconditionally as required, these were the likely conditions, but both leaders and populations expected much worse. It remains a moot point whether the Allied demand made the war last longer, but a willingness to compromise would have undermined the Allies' agreed purpose and endorsed aggressive regimes.

Neither Hitler nor Mussolini wanted to be the ones responsible for agreeing and signing unconditional surrender terms, and neither in the end did so. In Japan, surrender – unconditional or not – was not in the nation's

lexicon; no one should or could surrender without the intervention
mperor. Only an imperial rescript could end the state of war but
Emperor Hirohito voluntarily to take this unprecedented step was
an extremely delicate political, military and constitutional issue. Such complexities were already evident for the Allies when Roosevelt announced
he would only accept an unconditional surrender. The term was not, as
Roosevelt later suggested, one that 'just popped into my head'. Unconditional surrender had been canvassed as an Allied demand by American
State Department officials since at least May 1942 and it was to be distinct
from an armistice, which might be negotiated, as the Germans had tried to
do after signing the armistice in November 1918. In a meeting with the
American Joint Chiefs on 7 January 1943, shortly before leaving for Casablanca, Roosevelt assured them that he would bring up unconditional
surrender as the basis of the American wartime position.[393] Churchill would
have preferred a solution that left open the prospect of a separate peace
deal with Italy brokered with an anti-Mussolini faction, but his War Cabinet overruled him, insisting that Italy too would have to accept unconditional
surrender.[394] Stalin made no comment on the proposal until 1 May 1943,
when he used the term for the first time in a speech, but it was not a commitment to which he attached as much significance as his Western partners,
who needed continued Soviet belligerence, and in the end all three Axis
powers surrendered in the first instance to the Americans.[395]

The concept was to be tested for the first time only a few months later
when it became clear by the summer of 1943 that Italy might well be the
first of the Axis to collapse. There were significant Anglo-American disagreements over the attitude to take to an Italian government negotiating
for peace and to the survival of the Italian monarchy, both of which
Churchill was willing to accept while the Americans remained uncertain.
In discussion, the British used the term 'armistice', which the Americans
rejected. It was agreed to use the more neutral expression 'surrender
terms'. By the summer of 1943, when crisis in Italy seemed imminent, the
two Allies finally agreed to a joint military government following Italy's
'total surrender with no commitments', the same line adopted for Germany through to 1945.[396]

After the overthrow of Mussolini's government on 25 July, neither the
new regime under Marshal Pietro Badoglio nor the Allies quite understood
how to proceed. Badoglio announced that the war would continue, though
it was not what he wanted. Both sides harboured illusions about what
might be possible. The Allies even hoped that the Italian army would drive
the Germans out of Italy before agreeing to surrender, while King Vittorio
Emanuele was confident that Italian soldiers would still 'resist and fight'

long enough to find a negotiated solution. The Allies began to use the term 'honourable capitulation' to lure the Italians to surrender, but this term seemed to imply room for manoeuvre which Italian leaders hoped to exploit. Tension remained between the British and Americans over the terms of the surrender document and Eisenhower finally produced in early August a 'short armistice' covering military surrender and disarmament only, while the British 'long armistice', with harsher political and economic conditions, was only agreed between Churchill and Roosevelt at the Quebec Conference later in August. Badoglio sent emissaries to contact the Allies in order to discuss possible military collaboration, but with no offer yet of surrender. General Giuseppe Castellano, the principal contact, understood that the Allies were happy to have the promise of Italian military assistance, and persuaded Badoglio and the army chiefs that the short armistice ought to be signed quickly so that Italy would have a chance of changing sides. On 31 August Castellano went to Allied headquarters at Cassibile in Sicily where, on 3 September, the military surrender was signed. Eisenhower wanted it kept secret until the Allied invasion at Salerno was under way a few days later, in case the Germans occupied Italy.

Badoglio refused to tell his colleagues what had happened or to order preparations to confront the Germans in order to aid the Allies, whose plans for a landing at Salerno were known to the Italian side. On the night of 7/8 September he was woken at home in his pyjamas to be confronted by an irate American general, commander of the paratroop division that was supposed to arrive in Rome to support Italian defence of the capital against the Germans the following day. He had been smuggled into Rome to judge the Italian military position. Badoglio was forced to reveal that the Italian armed forces had done nothing and asked for the publication of the armistice to be postponed. Finally realizing the extent of Badoglio's duplicity, an incandescent Eisenhower announced on 8 September that Italy had surrendered unconditionally and forced the Italian government to do the same. On the evening of the 8th Badoglio announced the armistice (but avoided the word surrender) over the radio.[397] A formal surrender ceremony, including the forty-four conditions of the 'long armistice', was signed in Malta on 29 September by Badoglio and the king, who had fled south from Rome on 10 September. This was not the end of the difficulties. The Soviet government could see no reason why the Soviet Union should be kept out of the proceedings for surrender and the subsequent military control of Italy, since the Red Army had been fighting Italian forces since 1941 on the Russian front. The Western Allies refused the Soviets direct participation but offered a consultative role on an Allied Advisory Council for Italy. Soviet objections were relatively muted, but

Stalin drew the obvious lesson. When the Red Army forced armistices on Romania and Bulgaria in 1944, and Hungary in 1945, the Western Allies were excluded.[398] Subsequent peace treaties for the three states were imposed on Soviet terms, but in return Stalin allowed the United States to organize the occupation and peace settlement with Japan.[399]

The unconditional surrender in 1943 did not end Italy's war. It was the German armed forces who disarmed almost all the Italian military units and imposed harsh rule across most of the peninsula following the announcement of surrender on 8 September. The new Italian regime under Mussolini, established under German protection, was not party to the armistice. Unconditional surrender in Italy of all Axis forces, including Italians still fighting for Mussolini, was postponed until 1945, when once again the effort to secure surrender was complex and drawn out. Leading German officers on the Italian front began discussing early in 1945 the possibility of ending the war, and in March SS General Karl Wolff secretly visited the American Office for Strategic Services (OSS) representative in Bern, Allen Dulles, through the offices of a Swiss go-between, Gero von Gaervenitz. Wolff returned to Italy, promising to recruit the German supreme commander there, Field Marshal Kesselring, to support the idea of surrender. The British and Americans reacted positively to what they called Operation 'Sunrise' (Churchill insisted on calling it 'Crossword') but on 20 April Dulles was instructed to terminate the contacts since it was evident that the army commander in Italy, von Vietinghoff-Scheel, hoped to secure agreement that he could lead his armies back to Germany with their honour intact, rather than surrender unconditionally. A few days before, Wolff had flown to Berlin to meet Hitler face to face, where he was told to keep open contacts with the Americans to get better terms for an armistice: 'to capitulate unconditionally', Wolff reported Hitler's words, 'would be preposterous'.[400] Wolff returned to Italy, fortunate to survive the encounter, but orders from Hitler's Supreme Headquarters insisted that German forces stay in Italy and fight to the death.

News of the secret negotiations was passed to Moscow in March by Soviet spies and Stalin again feared that the West was seeking a separate peace, this time as a prelude to turning the armies in Italy against the Soviet advance in Central Europe. Soviet Foreign Minister Molotov immediately demanded that Soviet representatives be included in any negotiation, but he was told that on an Anglo-American front, only the British and Americans could be responsible – a similar rebuff to the one in 1943. There followed an acrimonious exchange in which the Western Allies were accused of working 'behind the back of the Soviet government'. On 3 April, Stalin complained that the West was planning 'to ease the armistice terms for the Germans' so that Anglo-American armies could then move eastwards. Two days later, in a reply to Roosevelt's firm rebuttal, Stalin explained that the surrender problem had opened up very different views of 'what an Ally can allow himself to do in respect of the other Ally'.[401] This was not yet an open rift, but it presaged the widening gulf in the alliance that turned step by step into the post-war confrontation that followed. Moscow was mollified again, at least formally, by the decision to allow a Soviet presence at any surrender ceremony to ensure that the Germans were not given an easy peace, and on 25 April, Major General Aleksei Kislenko, the Soviet representative on the Allied Advisory Council that had been set up in 1943, arrived at Allied headquarters in Caserta.[402]

By this stage, defeat was imminent so surrender was only a matter of time. Mussolini did not want to surrender. He arrived in Milan from his seat of government at Salò in mid-April to discover that his German ally was negotiating surrender without him. Though he complained of being 'betrayed', his instinct was to flee, and he was driven towards the Swiss border disguised as a German soldier. On 28 April he and other Fascist leaders were caught and executed by partisans. Their bodies were hung upside down in a square in Milan, like butcher's meat. Marshal Graziani, commander of the scattered Italian forces and Fascist militia still fighting against the Allies, asked the Germans to sign on behalf of the Italians, so as to avoid signing a second Italian unconditional surrender.[403] On 25 April, von Vietinghoff sent two emissaries to meet Dulles again in Bern, this time to agree to surrender unconditionally; Churchill was told at once and he immediately cabled Stalin to get agreement that the surrender could now be accepted. Stalin unexpectedly concurred and on the 27th two German officers arrived at the Allied headquarters to complete formalities. By this stage 40,000 Axis soldiers had already agreed to local surrenders and by the end of the month a further 80,000 had done so.[404] On the 29th the seventeen-page surrender document was finally signed, to come into force only three days later to give German commanders time to warn their scattered forces.[405] The surrender was not yet watertight because it had to be formally ratified in person by von Vietinghoff as overall commander in his headquarters in Bolzano, capital of the *Operationszone Alpenvorland* (Operational Zone, Pre-Alps). To avoid alerting Berlin to the surrender the emissaries were flown to Lyons and then driven by car across Switzerland to Bolzano. By the time they arrived at midnight on 30 April, Hitler had learned of the capitulation from Gauleiter Franz Hofer, who was also supreme commissar for the *Operationszone*. In one of his last acts before his suicide, Hitler ordered von Vietinghoff's arrest and replacement with Major General Paul Schultz, who was ordered to organize a fighting retreat into Austria. Schultz was arrested by Wolff's Waffen-SS troops when he arrived and on 1 May von Vietinghoff finally sent out orders to all military units to cease fighting. On 2 May Kesselring, now overall commander-in-chief West, reluctantly accepted that with Hitler's death further resistance was futile and approved capitulation. The Allied high command monitored German radio to make sure that surrender messages were indeed being relayed to German forces and at 6.30 on the evening of 2 May the second unconditional surrender in Italy was announced.[406]

The actual surrender proved in the end a messy affair. Some Axis forces – including the Cossack units that had murdered and raped their way across northern Italy in pursuit of partisans – refused to give up and fought their way to Austria through the valleys of Friuli on the northern Italian border. They were ambushed by partisans and in retaliation perpetrated the final acts of atrocity, massacring fifty-one villagers in Avanzis and twenty-three at Ovaro. Fighting here only ended on 14 May, a week after the general German surrender, and one sniper group, led by a last-ditch Fascist leader, was snuffed out only on 29 May.[407] Other units refused to disarm. When on 4 May an Allied commission drove to von Vietinghoff's headquarters in Bolzano, they passed through roadblocks manned by surly German soldiers and Waffen-SS still carrying weapons as if the war had been paused rather than ended. German commanders claimed that their soldiers kept their guns from fear of partisan vengeance, and it took ten days for the Allied commission, now supported by armed force, to insist that the weapons should be turned in. Some units continued to resist and for a month or more isolated pockets of German, Russian and Italian Fascist soldiers holed up in the thick woods and steep mountains around the Merano valley, foraging for food at the point of a gun. The local Allied commanders ended the fiasco only after weeks of improvised banditry. The local population, reported a British SOE officer, considered themselves 'worse off than they had been under the German occupation'.[408]

There were further complexities with the eventual unconditional surrender of all remaining German forces in Europe, while the tension between the Allies surfaced again within days of the crisis over the surrender in Italy. By spring 1945 there was no doubt about Germany's comprehensive military defeat and occupation as vast Allied forces converged on the German heartland. Efforts to open channels of communication with the Western Allies had no prospect of success, and after the problems in Italy, the West wanted to give no hint that separate negotiations might be under way. The instrument of unconditional surrender had already been drawn up and agreed in 1944 by the three major Allies and it followed closely the pattern for the Italian 'long armistice', although the version initially signed, as in Italy, was a short one. In addition, the Allies had agreed on Germany's territorial division, with a zone for each, although this was left out of the final surrender document. But who would surrender, and under what circumstances, was still far from clear. The possibility of a popular revolt in Germany to end the war had often been canvassed by Western intelligence but by spring 1945 such an outcome had been shown to be a political fantasy. The German people, concluded a report for Churchill from the Joint Intelligence Committee, lacked 'the energy, the courage or the organization to break the reign of terror'.[409] There was little confidence that Hitler himself would be caught and forced to sign the surrender document and speculation that he would probably commit suicide rather than face the humiliation of capture. Hitler indeed had no intention of becoming a prisoner. When the news of Mussolini's murder arrived in the Reich Chancellery bunker on 28 April, he was horrified that his body too might be desecrated and displayed to an angry German crowd. His decision to commit suicide, taken at some time on the 29th, avoided any danger, in his view, that his historical image would be tarnished by capture, murder or trial. On the afternoon of 30 April, he and Eva Braun, his bride for a day, killed themselves, she with a cyanide capsule, he with a shot through the head. He had ordered his body to be burnt, recalled his adjutant Otto Günsche, rather than have it 'taken back to Moscow to exhibit in a cabinet of curiosities'.[410]

Hitler had, nevertheless, thought about how the war might end. He continued to hope that Germany might still have some room for manoeuvre. Karl Wolff told Dulles after his visit to Hitler in the bunker on 18 April that the German leader explained how German forces would be concentrated in a series of redoubts until Soviet and American armies inevitably clashed when the Red Army tried to press on beyond the demarcation line agreed at Yalta. He expected to hold out in Berlin for six to eight weeks, and would then choose to join one side or the other in the war between the United States and the Soviet Union, evading surrender altogether.[411] His air adjutant recalled in his memoirs Hitler's hope that the West 'will no longer insist on unconditional surrender'.[412] On 20 April, he told his foreign minister that if he died defending Berlin, von Ribbentrop should engage in peace negotiations with the West to find grounds for a comprehensive agreement. In a letter for his headquarters chief, Field Marshal Keitel, sent in the last days from the bunker but never delivered, Hitler returned to his central belief that the nation's future aim was 'still to win territory in the East for the German people', even if he was no longer destined to deliver it.[413] These and other fantasies accompanied Hitler's last days. He cared nothing for the fate of the people he had led to the edge of disaster because surrender would mean that they 'had forfeited their right to existence'.[414] His suicide was a final abdication of any responsibility for the end of hostilities. This left open the question of how unconditional surrender could be enforced against a governmental system in the throes of collapse and armed forces that were surrendering in large numbers to local Allied commanders. The surrender in Italy on 2 May was followed two days later by the surrender to Montgomery of all German forces in northern Germany, the Netherlands and Denmark. This area included the town of Flensburg, near the German–Danish border, and it was here that a reorganized German government now operated. Hitler had provided in his final testament for his successors: Grand Admiral Karl Dönitz was to assume the German presidency, propaganda minister Joseph Goebbels the Chancellorship. Goebbels committed suicide in the bunker after Hitler, leaving Dönitz as the titular head of the collapsing German state and the 'Flensburg government'.

The new government functioned in a state of constitutional limbo, but Montgomery failed to order the occupation of Flensburg or the arrest of the new government, many of whom were on the Allies' list of major war criminals. The result was to arouse once again deep Soviet suspicion that Dönitz would become the German Badoglio. On 6 May, the Red Army deputy chief of staff, Aleksei Antonov, told Allied representatives in Moscow that the Soviet side refused to acknowledge that there was a new German government and insisted that unconditional surrender must be made by the German high command. Otherwise, continued Antonov, circles in Moscow would continue to believe that the Western Allies were negotiating a separate truce so that German forces could concentrate their efforts against the Red Army.[415] Dönitz knew surrender was inevitable, but, as the Soviets feared, he would have preferred to surrender to the Western powers and continue fighting in the East. He had delayed an immediate acceptance of surrender to allow time for German soldiers and refugees to flee from the advancing Soviet forces, until Eisenhower told him on 5 May that he had to surrender all forces unconditionally, not in fragments. Dönitz finally sent the chief of operations at OKW, Colonel General Jodl, to Eisenhower's SHAEF headquarters in the French city of Reims to sign a surrender, still in the forlorn hope that it might only involve the war in the West. He arrived to find that there was no room for manoeuvre. In the early hours of 7 May, without Stalin being informed, the document was signed.[416] A Soviet observer who was present, General Ivan Susloparov, could not decide whether to sign without instructions and did so, in the end, in trepidation at his possible fate. Stalin was predictably infuriated and insisted that the document in American hands was not the act of unconditional surrender but only what he later called a 'preliminary protocol'. The Soviet side demanded that a formal surrender ceremony take place in Berlin.[417] Eisenhower sent his British deputy, Air Marshal Tedder, to represent him in Berlin, together with a senior American and French commander as witnesses, and late on the evening of 8 May at Karlshorst, Hitler's military chief of Supreme Headquarters, Field Marshal Keitel, signed the document that the Allies could regard unanimously as unconditional surrender. The difference between the two sides remained enshrined in the days designated as VE-Day: 8 May in the West, 9 May in the Soviet Union – a distinction maintained down to the present day.

As in Italy, this was not the decisive end that unconditional surrender implied. Fighting continued in the Czech lands until 12 May, when the final embattled German forces were overwhelmed. The Dönitz government remained in place and a stream of American and British visitors arrived from the post-war bombing survey teams to discuss the campaign with German ministers. They found a city still bristling with armed soldiers and SS guards.[418] On 12 May, Montgomery's headquarters agreed with the German regime that Field Marshal Ernst Busch, based in Flensburg, should assume command of the province of Schleswig-Holstein to keep order and help provision the population, an act tantamount to acknowledging the authority of the new regime. Churchill favoured retaining Dönitz, whatever the political difficulties, because the regime might assist in stabilizing an occupied Germany. If he was 'a useful tool for us,' Churchill wrote, his 'war atrocities' could be overlooked.[419] The result was a renewed wave of protest from the Soviet regime and the Soviet press that the West was planning to give the new German regime legitimacy in order to form an anti-Soviet alliance. To add fuel to the fire, Stalin allowed a press campaign to suggest that Hitler had not died in Berlin after all, but had fled, and was probably being shielded by the Western Allies. The taunt prompted a concerted effort by British intelligence to confirm that Hitler had indeed committed suicide, but Stalin already knew as much from forensic evidence gathered in the garden of Hitler's Chancellery, where his body had been burnt.[420] The accusations of bad faith were not accidental. For two years Stalin had harboured deep suspicions about how his Allies would handle German defeat. The survival of the Dönitz regime confirmed his worst fears. In the end, Eisenhower, as military supreme commander in Europe, overrode Churchill and a prevaricating Combined Chiefs of Staff to authorize the occupation of Flensburg and the arrest of Dönitz and his Cabinet. On 23 May, more than two weeks after the original signature of surrender, a unit of British soldiers took the German leaders in Flensburg prisoner.[421] Only then did it prove possible to establish the joint Allied Control Council and to make a formal Allied declaration on 5 June 1945 of German defeat and unconditional surrender.

The complications in Europe paled in comparison with the difficulty of forcing a Japanese surrender, since for the Japanese military the concept was unthinkable, a state of mind confirmed by the hundreds of thousands of Japanese servicemen who had already been killed rather than give up a hopeless contest. For the Japanese leadership, the whole strategy of the Pacific war had been predicated on the idea that after initial victories a compromise would be reached with the Western enemies to avoid any prospect of having to fight to a surrender. Switzerland was thought of as a possible neutral intermediary; so too the Vatican, for which reason a Japanese diplomatic mission was established there early in the war. The Japanese government watched the Italian surrender in 1943 closely, and it encouraged the view that if Badoglio could modify unconditional surrender by retaining the government and the king, then a 'Badoglio' solution in Japan might ensure the survival of the imperial system.[422] When a new Cabinet was formed in April 1945, after months of military crises, the new prime minister, seventy-eight-year-old Suzuki Kantarō, announced on the radio that 'the current war has entered a serious stage in which no optimism whatsoever is permissible'. After hearing the broadcast, the former premier, Tōjō Hideki, told a journalist: 'This is the end. This is our Badoglio government.'[423] Suzuki was appointed after discussion with the emperor and the Council of Elders because he was among the circle in Japan that favoured finding a way to end the war on acceptable terms, but, like Badoglio, he also endorsed the continuation of the war to satisfy the military hardliners in the government who would brook no prospect of surrender. Throughout the months leading to the final capitulation, Japanese politics remained torn between the desire for peace and the imperative to fight if peace proved too costly.

Formal and informal approaches were made to both the United States and the Soviet Union to test whether a negotiated peace might be possible, even though the serial rejection of all Japanese efforts since 1938 to reach a compromise peace agreement with Chiang Kai-shek's government ought to have dampened expectations. In April 1945, while Wolff was in discussion with Dulles, feelers were put out to see if the same Swiss avenue could be used for Japan. The Japanese naval attaché in Berlin sent his assistant, Commander Fujimura Yoshikazu, to Switzerland where he succeeded in meeting Dulles on 3 May. Impressed by the success of the negotiations to bring surrender in Italy, Fujimura hoped that he could persuade Dulles that a compromise peace could be brokered with Tokyo which allowed the imperial system to survive and permitted Japan to continue to occupy the islands of Micronesia. The talks soon petered out once the US State Department made it clear that only unconditional surrender was acceptable, while the authorities in Tokyo distrusted any negotiation not under their direct control.[424] Similar efforts in Stockholm collapsed (as they had done with German approaches earlier in the year). That left the Soviet Union as a possibility since the two countries were not yet at war.

Japanese views on Soviet intervention in East Asia were mixed. It was generally expected that at some point Moscow would abandon the Non-Aggression Pact signed in 1941, but whether or when that might result in war was very uncertain. If the Soviet Union would not be willing to broker a peace with the Allies, there was hope that Soviet involvement in Asia might restore the balance against overwhelming American power and perhaps create post-war conditions in which Japan's national future could be preserved more easily than under American domination of East Asia. As with Hitler and the German leadership, there flourished the hope that conflict between the two wartime allies might leave room for manoeuvre for Japan (as it eventually did).[425] In July the Japanese ambassador in Moscow sounded out Soviet willingness to broker a settlement and found the Soviet side understandably cool. By this stage, a Soviet military build-up on the Manchurian border was evident, although the possible date for a Soviet invasion was speculative. The idea of using Soviet intervention to moderate the expected draconian American peace was exceedingly risky, given the fact that the Japanese Thought Police detected rising communist sentiment in Japan and Korea, but it was one of the ways in which the Japanese leadership hoped to avoid a surrender that was rigorously unconditional.[426]

By June, the Japanese government faced an impasse. There was no outlet through neutral powers for a negotiated end to the war; the army insisted on maintaining preparations for the final showdown with the American invasion of the home islands; and there was growing evidence, passed on by Hirohito's confidant, Kido Kōichi, lord keeper of the privy seal, of popular unrest, even of sentiment hostile to the emperor himself scrawled in graffiti on what was left of the city walls after three months of bombing. On 8 June, Hirohito approved the armed forces' 'Fundamental Policy for the Conduct of the War' because he still thought that some sign of military success was needed before considering an end to the conflict, but by the 22nd, with the fall of Okinawa, Hirohito finally directed the Supreme War Council to 'give immediate and detailed thought to the ways of ending the war ...' because 'conditions internal and external to Japan grow tense'.[427] Over the following weeks the stalemate continued but all parties, including the emperor, wanted concessions from the Allies. These varied from retaining the colonial empire and interests in China, avoiding occupation, allowing Japan to disarm its forces and punish its own war criminals, and – above all – retaining the imperial system and the *kokutai*, the national body. That negotiation might indeed be possible was sustained by regular news from the United States about growing war-weariness and the dislocation caused by demobilization and redeployment, which was an evident reality by the summer of 1945. The Supreme War Council was informed before the meeting on 8 June to confirm military plans that it might be possible, in the light of American domestic difficulties, 'to diminish considerably the enemy's will to continue the war'.[428]

Although Japanese leaders could not know it, there had been much debate in the United States from spring 1942 onwards about the status of unconditional surrender in relation to Japan, where there had been none with Germany. State Department officials who favoured a 'soft peace' worried that, if the Allies insisted on abolishing the imperial institution, it would provide 'a permanent incentive for insurgency and revenge'.[429] By summer 1945, American leaders did want to bring the war to a speedy conclusion, and did not relish the prospect of an amphibious invasion of the Japanese home islands once intelligence sources indicated a heavy deployment of Japanese troops and equipment to the southern island of Kyushu, where an American landing would take place. Conservatives around the secretary of war, Henry Stimson, feared that the longer the war went on, the greater the risk of Soviet intervention, even Soviet occupation of Japan; a longer war might also mean the prospect of a radical, even communist, movement in Japan, echoing the anxieties in Tokyo. Stimson favoured a statement defining unconditional surrender, which would include the 'soft peace' that retained the imperial system. Opponents who favoured a 'hard peace', led by the recently appointed secretary of state, James Byrnes, labelled this appeasement and refused to allow Japan the offer of any conditions. President Truman was against defining a term that seemed self-explanatory, but he was eventually persuaded that a declaration might focus the Japanese desire for peace. The draft was taken to the inter-Allied conference that convened in Potsdam on 17 July to iron out the remaining issues between the Allies on the future of Europe, and here Stimson's effort to include a clause protecting the status of the emperor was finally frustrated. Truman, who regarded Hirohito as a war criminal, agreed to replace it with the provision that 'the Japanese people will be free to choose their own form of government', which, as it turned out, left considerable room for interpretation.[430] The Potsdam Declaration, signed by the United States, Britain and China, was published on 26 July and promised instant destruction if Japan did not surrender unconditionally. It would have been published a week sooner but it took that time to send the document to Chiang Kai-shek's field headquarters near Chongqing, decrypt and translate it, and secure approval.[431] The Soviet Union was not yet at war with Japan, so did not sign. Stalin did agree to fulfil the promise made at the Yalta Conference that the Soviet Union would go to war with Japan and told his allies that a campaign was planned for mid-August. Neither side quite trusted the other's intentions in Asia, and they fought in effect two separate wars.[432]

By the time the declaration was published, Truman knew that the 'prompt and utter destruction' threatened was about to assume a literal form. On 16 July he received news at Potsdam that the first test of a nuclear bomb at the Alamogordo airbase in New Mexico had taken place successfully, the culmination of the codenamed 'Manhattan Project', which had begun three years before, aided by research material supplied from an earlier British project. The development required an industrial effort on a scale that only the United States could undertake. The Japanese physicist Nishina Yoshio had embarked on an experimental programme to isolate the vital U235 isotope in uranium necessary to make a bomb, but his wooden laboratory burnt to the ground in an air raid with the research project stalled. In the United States the 'Manhattan Project' was generously resourced, led by an international field of top physicists, and given high priority. Two bomb models were developed, one based on enriched uranium, one on plutonium, an artificial element derived from U239 isotopes of uranium. If Germany had not surrendered in May 1945, the first bomb might have been used in Europe, as originally intended by the British. The American Joint Chiefs of Staff were divided over whether it should be used at all, but in the end the decision was a political, not a military one.[433] In late July 1945 there were just two bombs ready, one of each kind, and Truman, with Churchill's approval, prepared to use them on two of a selection of Japanese cities preserved from the bombing campaign as possible demonstration targets. 'We have discovered,' wrote Truman in his diary, 'the most terrible bomb in the history of the world.' Whatever moral scruples might have brought him to hesitate in granting approval were set aside by the belief that the war with Japan might be speedily ended. He added in his diary, 'but it can be made the most useful'.[434] From his viewpoint, the whole purpose of the years spent developing the bomb was to use it once it was ready.

When it was learned that Suzuki had dismissed the Potsdam Declaration two days later – 'the government will ignore it', he claimed – the decision was confirmed to go ahead with the nuclear attacks. The rejection was taken as evidence that the Japanese were not serious about seeking peace, though it seems more likely that the declaration was regarded in Tokyo simply as a reiteration of the demand for unconditional surrender, which both sides understood, and which seemed to require no reply. From the list of cities noted down by the army air forces' commander, Henry Arnold – Hiroshima, Kokura, Niigata, Nagasaki, Kyoto – the first was chosen.[435] On 6 August, a B-29 bomber, the *Enola Gay*, flying from Tinian Island in the Marianas dropped the first bomb, insensitively nicknamed 'Little Boy' by the Americans. At 8.15 in the morning it exploded 1,800 feet above the ground, melting all human life within 1.5 kilometres of the epicentre of the explosion, burning those within 5 kilometres, and then, when the massive blast-wave followed, tearing off the skin and destroying the internal organs of those who had survived the initial flash. The crew of the bomber watched the huge ball of fire and the mushroom cloud as they flew back to base. 'If I live a hundred years,' wrote the co-pilot, Robert Lewis, in his diary, 'I'll never quite get those few minutes out of my mind.'[436]

Three days later the Japanese Supreme War Council met for a day of debate about how the war should end. The common assumption by Western leaders, endorsed many times since 1945 by the histories of the Japanese surrender, was to see the nuclear attack as the decisive factor that pushed the Japanese to capitulate. The pattern of cause and effect seems entirely plausible, yet it masks a more complex Japanese reality. In the context of the conventional bombing offensive, the impact on the ground at Hiroshima did not seem very different from the aftermath of a devastating attack with incendiaries, which had already burnt out almost 60 per cent of Japan's urban area and killed over 260,000 civilians. By the time the Council met there was also the Soviet invasion of Manchuria to consider. On 8 August, the Soviet foreign minister informed the Japanese ambassador in Moscow that a state of war would exist between the two countries the following day. Suzuki saw this as decisive because it ended any hope of Soviet mediation and ran the risk of a Soviet invasion of Korea or the home islands.[437] On the morning of 9 August, the Supreme War Council assembled and a long argument ensued. The military half of the council wanted to continue the fight unless the Allies abandoned plans for occupation, allowed the Japanese to disarm themselves and punish their own war criminals, and kept the imperial system intact. The other half followed Foreign Minister Tōgō Shigenori in accepting the Potsdam Declaration so long as the imperial system could be retained, 'one condition' against the army's 'four conditions'.[438] None of those present favoured surrendering unconditionally, even after news arrived that a second bomb, this time the 'Fat Man' plutonium bomb, had been dropped on Nagasaki that morning (rather than the intended target of Kokura, which was obscured by cloud). The deadlock was only resolved late on the 9th when Hirohito, lobbied by Suzuki and Kido, agreed to call a late-night Imperial Conference. The Privy

Council president, Hiranuma Kiichirō, told the meeting that the domestic situation was reaching crisis point: 'continuation of the war will create greater domestic disorder than termination of the war.' Hirohito had for weeks been warned that popular feeling against the war and his own person was fuelled by the bombing and a widespread food crisis, and this almost certainly weighed with him as much as the bomb and the Soviet invasion.[439] When Suzuki finally asked Hirohito to intervene in the early hours of the 10th, the emperor announced that he sanctioned the decision to accept the Potsdam Declaration, so long as the imperial system was retained. The following day the Allies were notified formally of the conditional acceptance of their terms.

The American reply was ambiguous because Truman and Byrnes were under strong pressure in Washington to accept the Japanese request in order to prevent further bloodshed. The note confirmed that the emperor and the Japanese government would be subject to the authority of the Allied supreme commander in Japan under the terms of unconditional surrender, but it did not specify that the imperial system would be suspended or abolished. On 14 August a second Imperial Conference was called, at which Hirohito insisted, against army objections, that the American version be accepted. All military leaders were now bound by the imperial decision. That day Hirohito recorded an imperial rescript to be broadcast on the following morning. The Allies were notified through Swiss intermediaries of the emperor's decision later in the day. The Japanese population was alerted by a radio announcement to expect an important broadcast at noon on the 15th. People gathered during the morning wherever a radio could be set up; the emperor had never before been heard by the wider public. When the 'Jewelled Voice' finally spoke, the words were difficult to understand, not only because Hirohito spoke in an archaic, formal Japanese, but on account of generally poor radio reception. He spoke, as one listener observed, with 'high-pitched, unclear and faltering words', but 'the sombre tone made it clear that he was informing us of defeat', even if the words were hard to comprehend.[440]

Hirohito did not say the word 'surrender', merely that he would accept the Potsdam Declaration and 'bear the unbearable' with his people. Why he took the unprecedented step of intervening to cut through the political arguments of his government and to announce in person the decision to surrender unconditionally will remain open to conjecture, but there seems little reason to favour one explanation over another. He feared the bombing (both nuclear and conventional), he understood that Japan was defeated comprehensively in the field, he did not want a Soviet occupation, and he could see that a major social crisis was erupting. He was also a product of his imperial past, which Western historians have been too loath to take at face value. In July he expressed his private fear that the imperial regalia (mirror, sword and jewel), handed down over centuries to protect the *kokutai* and the imperial family, could easily fall into the hands of the invading Allies. In his post-surrender 'monologue' he returned to the theme that Allied seizure of the sacred regalia would mean the end of historic Japan: 'I determined that, even if I must sacrifice myself in the process, we had to make peace.'[441]

This was the start of a process of surrender, not the surrender itself. A 'Badoglio government' was established as an interim measure on 15 August, led by Hirohito's uncle, Prince Higashikuni. Efforts were made on the 17th to get the Americans to agree to a limited occupation of certain specified points, but it was rejected. Most of Japan's far-flung empire was still in Japanese hands, unlike the aftermath of German defeat, and members of the imperial family were sent west and south to order local commanders to surrender their troops. In Saigon, Singapore and Nanjing separate surrender ceremonies took place. Forces in the Pacific surrendered to Admiral Nimitz; forces in Korea south of the 38th parallel, the Philippines and Japan to MacArthur. In Singapore, the Japanese surrendered to Mountbatten's South East Asia Command.[442] On 9 September in Nanjing, the overall Japanese commander in China, General Okamura Yasuji, surrendered his forces in mainland China, Taiwan and northern Vietnam to Chiang Kai-shek's representative, General He Yingqin; ignoring the Allied agreements, Mao Zedong's Communist armies organized the surrender of Japanese forces in north-west China as they fought to seize Japanese weapons and supplies.[443] The first American occupation forces arrived in Japan on 28 August. The supreme commander, General MacArthur, arrived two days later. The main surrender document was signed by Foreign Minister Shigemitsu Mamoru on board the American battleship *Missouri* in Tokyo harbour on 2 September. Although Stalin had hoped to share the occupation of Japan by sending forces to the northern half of Hokkaido, Truman brusquely rejected the claim. The Soviet war instead developed its own trajectory as the Red Army pushed on, after the emperor's broadcast, into the rest of Manchuria and eventually into Korea. The Japanese army in Manchuria finally signed an armistice on 19 August, but the battle for the southern Sakhalin Islands went on to 25 August, while at the same time Stalin ordered Soviet forces to occupy the Kurils, including the southern islands assigned at Yalta to the American zone of occupation. These conquests were only completed by 1 September, the day before the surrender ceremony; ceasefires were agreed independent of the surrenders already taking place further south.[444]

The unconditional surrenders brought to an end all the wars fought in Europe and East Asia and the imperial projects with which they began, but in each case ending war proved to be less straightforward than the plain term 'unconditional' might have suggested. In Germany and Japan, the surrender prompted a wave of suicides among those who feared retribution, or who were shamed by the comprehensive defeat of the nation-empire, or who could not cope with the extreme emotional and psychological turmoil provoked by the wasted effort to build the new order, or finally those who believed the propaganda about the barbarities that would be meted out by the enemy. Hitler's suicide was one of thousands during the final period of fighting and the weeks that followed, including Admiral Hans-Georg von Friedeburg, who had the misfortune to be present at all three German surrenders, and finally shot himself when the Dönitz government was arrested. Eight Party gauleiters committed suicide, seven senior SS leaders, fifty-three generals, fourteen air force commanders and eleven admirals. Josef Terboven, Reich commissioner in Norway, blew himself up on 8 May with 50 kilograms of dynamite.[445] Among the Party and SS faithful, suicides were common in the months just before and after surrender; among the major war criminals arraigned at Nuremberg, Hans Frank tried to commit suicide, while Robert Ley and Hermann Göring succeeded. Himmler avoided trial by swallowing cyanide when he was captured and identified.

A similar reaction followed surrender across Japan and its imperial outposts, where the honourable thing to do following defeat was to commit *gyokusai* (collective suicide) or *seppuku* (ritual suicide). In Okinawa, the first Japanese territory to be conquered by American forces, the local population as well as the soldiers were ordered to commit mass suicide rather than fall into enemy hands. Some civilians were issued with grenades, but others used razors, farm implements or sticks. One young Okinawan later recalled stoning his mother and younger siblings to death.[446] Among the Japanese elite, suicide was widespread. Nine senior generals and admirals killed themselves immediately after the surrender, including the war minister, Anami Korechika, and his predecessor General Sugiyama Hajime, who shot himself a day before his wife, dressed all in white, committed ritual suicide; Tōjō tried to commit *seppuku*, but failed and stood trial in 1946.[447] For millions of others, on both sides, the surrenders meant relief from the all-embracing demands of total war, but the many arguments between the Allies surrounding the surrenders and their aftermath anticipated the coming Cold War, while the unresolved crises generated by imperialism in Europe, the Middle East, Africa and Asia meant that years of violence and political conflict still lay ahead.

4

Mobilizing a Total War

'I was 16 years old in 1941. I was short and thin . . . I worked at a machine that made cartridges for automatic guns. If I could not reach the machine, they put me on a box . . . The workday was 12 hours or more. And so it went on for four years. Without any days off or holidays.'

Elizaveta Kochergina, Cheliabinsk[1]

Mobilizing the resources for global war could make exceptional demands, as it did for the young Soviet worker cited above. In the city of Cheliabinsk, deep inside Soviet Russia, labour decrees compelled women with children, youths and old men to work without a break making munitions. When another young woman, Vera Sheina, who welded fins on rocket cases, was sent home after hot metal had badly burnt her legs, the overseer came to her house, dragged her back to work with bandaged legs and forced her to carry on welding.[2] The Soviet Union exacted the harsh maximum from its population during the war, demanding levels of endurance that no Western worker would have tolerated. The experience of mobilization, whether into the armed services or wartime industry and agriculture, varied widely from one warring state to another, but everywhere it was governed by the near-universal belief that national survival in total war depended on utilizing the human and material resources of the nation to the fullest possible extent. Failure to do so meant probable defeat. In Cheliabinsk production failures were regarded as treason and punished accordingly.

The view of the Second World War as a war of mass mobilization is a commonplace, but it begs many questions. The scale of wartime commitment was unique, building on the experience of the Great War during which mass mobilization had only gradually emerged as strategically unavoidable. During the wars from the 1930s to 1945 the major powers put more than 90 million men and women in uniform; worldwide the number certainly exceeded 120 million. The mobilization of economic resources was equally colossal. The proportion of national income spent on waging war varied between the major combatants, but even the lower figures indicate an extraordinary shift in priorities. In Japan, in 1944 the war claimed 76 per cent of the entire national income, in Germany the same year more than 70 per cent – exceptional peaks that indicated the desperate efforts to stave off defeat. Among the Allied powers the peak proportion varied, from almost two-thirds in the Soviet Union, 55 per cent in Britain, and 45 per cent of national income in the resource-rich United States. The exception was Fascist Italy, where no more than one-fifth of the national product was devoted to war, an outcome that reflected Mussolini's reluctance to squander popular support by imposing too heavy a burden of mobilization, but also a consequence of a debilitating shortage of resources.[3] Home front commitment to war meant that most industrial workers were producing something for the war effort, from weapons to uniforms, paper and mess tins. Apart from the supply of basic foodstuffs, all civilian output was categorized as inessential and could be shut down. Mobilization on this scale was a unique historical phenomenon and it can only be understood by recalling the broader context in which it took place.

Mass mobilization was an expression of modernity. Only modern states with a substantial industrial and commercial base, a large technically trained workforce, a developed scientific establishment, and access to adequate resources and finance could engage in large-scale warfare and supply the weapons and equipment to sustain it. A modern bureaucratic state structure was required, capable of developing administrative and statistical practices that embraced every member of society. The ability of states to understand the composition and size of the aggregate economy was in its infancy even in the 1930s, yet the capacity to construct a statistical image of the workforce and of industrial output was essential for any macroeconomic planning of manpower and resource allocation between armed forces and war industries. The statistical revolution of the early decades of the century made this possible as states developed complex reporting and recording systems for a whole range of social and economic data. Extensive mass-production of weapons and military equipment lay at the heart of economic mobilization, but once again this was only possible because of the production and managerial revolutions in the early years of the century that had transformed the nature of manufacturing and distribution. Industrialized warfare depended on a cluster of modern weapons that were easily reproducible and relatively cheap so that it was possible to sustain large forces in the field and to resupply them over years of warfare – a phenomenon beyond the capacity of states today because of the escalating cost and technical complexity of current weapons. Modern warfare also required a sufficient level of education among recruits and workers as the handling and production of weapons became more sophisticated and warfare more bureaucratized. In Japan, for example, 30 per cent of army recruits were illiterate or semi-literate in 1900; thanks to expanded primary education, the figure by 1920 was negligible.[4] The range of weapons used in the two world wars – aircraft, radio, vehicles of all kinds, high performance artillery – meant that substantial numbers of skilled workers were needed both by the armed forces and by industry, and this too was possible only in a context of societies with advanced technical training and a precise division of labour. States that lacked all the hallmarks of modernity, like Nationalist China, could sustain warfare only with external aid, and could not, despite China's great size, achieve victory. None of the combatant states could have fought the world wars on the same scale a generation earlier.

These elements of modernity explain why mobilization was possible, but not why it happened. The willingness of governments to embrace almost unlimited mobilization, and of peoples to submit to it, was shaped by the emergence of modern nationalism and changing perceptions of citizenship. The modern nation was an exceptionally powerful mobilizing entity, and national competition, economic, imperial or military, came to be regarded as an inevitable consequence of the national struggle for existence. The Darwinian paradigm of the struggle for survival in nature was widely understood to apply with equal force to the contest between peoples, empires and nations.[5] During both world wars, one of the driving forces in sustaining the conflict, irrational though it might now appear, was fear of national extinction and the collapse of empire. Since in both wars efforts to find a negotiated peace proved futile, regimes and peoples assumed that defeat would be absolute unless the entire resources of the nation were fully mobilized. At the same time, the emergence of the modern nation or nation-empire introduced a different view of citizenship. One of the responsibilities for membership of the nation was to serve in its defence, and a lengthy period of compulsory military service, widely introduced from the last decades of the nineteenth century (except in Britain and the United States), was one way of building popular identity with the nation and preparing for large-scale mobilization.

The Great War was a watershed in the evolution of mass mobilization. Though none of the nations involved expected the war to develop into a war of attrition and national survival, fighting could only be sustained by large incremental increases in military manpower and through the

organized exploitation of industry and agriculture to supply weapons, feed
the armed forces and sustain popular commitment at home. The wartime
experience cemented the idea that victory in modern, industrialized, 'total'
war depended on the unrestricted mobilization of national resources, and
that responsibility for conducting such a war extended to the whole
national community, men and women, rather than simply the current
armed forces. This was particularly so in Germany, whose military leaders
assumed that defeat in 1918 represented a failure of national mobilization.
General Erich Ludendorff, who coined the term 'total war' in his post-war
memoirs, argued that nations in the future had to be prepared to put their
'mental, moral, physical, and material forces in the service of war'.[6] Twenty
years later, Adolf Hitler explained to his generals in a meeting in May 1939
that if a major war occurred they should not expect a quick victory as the
army had hoped for in 1914: 'every state will hold out as long as it can . . .
the unrestricted use of all resources is essential . . . The idea of getting out
cheaply is dangerous, there is no such possibility.'[7] A month later the Reich
Defence Council, chaired by Hermann Göring, the commander-in-chief of
the German air force, started planning on the basis that if a general war
between the great powers happened again, then the entire active population of 43.5 million men and women would have to be mobilized, at least
7 million of them in the armed forces, the rest producing food, equipment
and weapons for the war effort.[8]

   This was not a view confined only to Germany. The victors in 1918
also believed that straining every national (and imperial) effort had
brought them victory. Marshal Pétain, hero of Verdun, urged his countrymen to see that modern war 'demanded the mobilization of all the
resources of a country'.[9] The British strategist Cyril Falls in a lecture on
'The Doctrine of Total War' defined the new concept as 'the devotion of
every section of the nation, every phase of its activity, to the purpose of
war'.[10] In the inter-war years the 'democratic' character of future war
between the great powers was widely assumed to be inevitable. As a result,
the barrier between serviceman and home-front civilian that had existed
in 1914 was eroded; workers in industry, agriculture and transport could
all be deemed to be an integral part of the war effort, male or female. And
if the civilian population was as much an element in future war as the
armed forces, it should no longer expect immunity from enemy action. A
senior British airman explained to an audience at the Naval Staff College
in 1936 that the 'power of democracy' made the enemy's population a
legitimate object of attack; it was 'not possible,' he concluded, 'to draw a
line between combatant and non-combatant'.[11] American airmen in the
1930s also endorsed a view of warfare in which 'the ultimate aim of all

military operations is to destroy the will of those people at home', the 'civil mass – the people in the street'.[12]

What is now known as the 'civilianization' of warfare had its roots in the Great War, but it was augmented by the experience of civil war in Russia in 1918–21, in China in the 1920s, and in Spain between 1936 and 1939, in all of which civilians became combatants as well as victims. By the 1930s, the militarization of peacetime societies reflected the widespread view that conflict was expected to involve the whole community and that the whole community expected to be included. In the Soviet Union, Germany, Italy and Japan the prevailing political and ideological framework was predicated on the participation of the community in defence of the nation. Soviet citizens were expected to defend the revolutionary state alongside the armed forces, and yearly cohorts of the Communist youth league (*Komsomol*), male and female, were given rudimentary paramilitary training; in National Socialist Germany, the racial community (*Volksgemeinschaft*) was obligated as a whole to struggle for the nation's future existence. Japan was already fighting a total war in the 1930s against China, a commitment expressed through the National Total Mobilization Decree, issued in 1938. Japanese citizens organized thousands of local community associations to encourage support for Japanese imperialism and to cement popular identity with the national military effort.[13] The Chinese government eventually followed suit with a General State Mobilization Law in March 1942 'to concentrate and use all human and material forces in the country', giving the regime extraordinary powers over all aspects of military, economic and social life.[14]

In Britain, France and the United States, with low levels of popular militarization (though strong military cultures, thanks to the experience of the Great War), future war was also imagined as 'total war', not only because it would utilize 'all the resources of the nation', as one British military writer put it, but because of 'the unlimited issues at stake'.[15] Plans for extensive industrial war mobilization existed in America from the early 1930s; British and French governments in the late 1930s planned, if war came, to pick up the threads of economic and military mass mobilization dropped at the end of the Great War. The concept of 'total war' became a self-fulfilling prophecy, an infectious cliché, like the 'war on terror' or 'cyberwar' in the twenty-first century. As a result, no state or armed force thought they could risk avoiding the mobilization of all the social, material and psychological energies of the nation in the pursuit of victory in a modern war. Even the United States, which mobilized its resources less stringently than the other warring powers, and whose civilians were untouched by the physical reality of conflict, used the language of 'total war' to define the American war effort. In a speech in July 1942, Secretary of State Cordell Hull told his audience that the current war was 'a life-and-death struggle for the preservation of our freedom, our homes, our very existences'.[16] Here, as in every warring state, mobilization for total war represented a complex interplay between the existing structures of modernity, the perceived nature of a modern war between peoples, and the willingness of populations to identify their own interests with the broader concern for national or imperial survival.

MILITARY MOBILIZATION

The mobilization of military personnel in the Second World War was the first priority for all warring states, but mobilization was conditioned by a number of factors beyond the obvious realities of population size or the nature of the campaigns being fought. In the first place, modern warfare required large managerial, bureaucratic, service and training structures that mirrored peacetime society and absorbed millions of those in uniform. In the Pacific war there were eighteen American men and women in uniform for every man actually in combat.[17] Secondly, loss rates dictated the demand for additional recruits. Losses could be the result of intense combat with a high ratio of battle deaths and injuries, or prisoner losses, or desertions. High loss rates explain the extreme rates of mobilization in the Soviet Union, Germany and Japan, which between them mobilized 60 million service personnel. Relatively lower losses explain why the United States and Britain relied on the first waves of recruitment and never had to resort to emergency levels of mass conscription. In the Soviet Union, 34.5 million were mobilized, representing some 17.4 per cent of the pre-war population (or 25 per cent of the population that remained after the German conquest of the western Soviet Union); in Germany, including the areas annexed between 1938 and 1940, a total of 17.2 million were mobilized, approximately 18 per cent of the pre-war population. In Britain (but not including the Dominions and Empire) the figure for those mobilized was 5.3 million, in the United States 16.1 million – respectively 10.8 and 11.3 per cent of the pre-war population.

Military mobilization was also conditioned by the competition between military and civilian labour. In the First World War, the initial wave of recruitment pulled in large numbers of skilled workers and professional engineers and scientists, leaving the war economy short of essential qualified personnel. In the Second World War it was understood that military demands had to be balanced against the needs of industry and agriculture.

Men in reserved occupations could be exempted from conscription. In Germany by 1941, some 4.8 million workers were kept back from the draft, with an emphasis on skilled metalworkers; in Britain, some 6 million were exempted, predominantly skilled workers in engineering, shipbuilding and chemical plants, but also including Britain's 300,000 farmers.[18] Draft boards in the United States had greater difficulty because so little preparation had been made for a major war. In the initial programme of registration millions were exempted not only on occupational grounds, but also for family commitments, or illiteracy or psychiatric risk, even poor teeth. The federal authorities eventually compiled a list of 3,000 reserved occupations, which by 1944 kept at least 5 million young men out of the armed forces.[19] Only in the Soviet Union was exemption rarer, because of exceptional military losses; half the adult male workforce ended up at some point in the Soviet armed forces. Domestic production relied heavily on young women like Elizaveta Kochergina, who replaced the conscripted men.[20]

Estimating the necessary volume of military labour was a challenging undertaking, governed by expectations about future conflict and the capacity of the military to absorb large numbers of conscripts or reservists. In most major states it was assumed that something like the mass mobilization of the Great War would be necessary, and German and French reserves were mobilized with that in mind in the opening phase of the war. Reservists recalled to the colours were usually older age groups. The average age of 1.6 million French soldiers made prisoners of war in 1940 was thirty-five. In the early phase of the Sino-Japanese war, the Japanese military called up a million reservists; almost half of the army in China in May 1938 was composed of men between the ages of twenty-nine and thirty-four. An initial reluctance in Japan to conscript younger men was set aside only in the last two years of war, when cohorts aged nineteen and twenty were finally mobilized.[21] The Chinese government of Chiang Kai-shek ordered all men from eighteen to forty-five to be liable for military service (except for only sons and the disabled), but from a very large population only an estimated 14 million were actually enlisted since it was recognized that universal conscription was beyond the regime's capacity to enforce. Following an initial wave of patriotic volunteers in the early years of war, evasion of the draft became widespread. The rich could buy their sons out of enlistment, while others were hired as mercenaries rather than conscripts. In provinces where annual quotas could not be met, army recruiters toured the villages rounding up young peasants at gunpoint. Roped together and force-marched long distances to the training camps, Chinese conscripts were subjected to a brutal and demoralizing regime that reduced their value as soldiers from the outset.

An estimated 1.4 million died of disease, hunger and mistreatment even before they reached their front-line units.[22]

In the United States, which lacked a significant reserve of former conscripts, initial planning in the so-called 'Victory Program' in autumn 1941 was on the assumption that the armed forces could conscript and train a force to match the mass conscription of the enemy. The predicted strength of the ground army was 215 divisions with 9 million men, though if the Soviet Union failed to survive army planners imagined the nightmare scenario of an American army of 25 million organized in 800 divisions.[23] Thanks to Soviet survival, only ninety enlarged divisions were eventually raised. These were joined late in the war by units from Latin America, keen to help the United States if it meant a role in the post-war order. Mexico declared war on the Axis states in May 1942, Brazil six months later. In 1945, a group of Mexican airmen, the 'Aztec Eagles', saw combat in the Philippines; a division of Brazilian troops and a Brazilian air force detachment, despite British objections, arrived in Italy from July 1944, where they joined the combat in September through to German defeat eight months later.[24]

From the initial stages of mobilization, the combatant powers expanded the size of the armed forces incrementally, as the scope of the war expanded and losses mounted. The statistics on the size of military forces during the war are set out in Table 4.1.

Table 4.1   Total Armed Forces of the Major Powers 1939–45 (,000s)[25]

	1939	1940	1941	1942	1943	1944	1945
Germany	4,522	5,762	7,309	8,410	9,480	9,420	7,830
Italy	1,740	2,340	3,227	3,810	3,815	-	-
Japan	1,620	1,723	2,411	2,829	3,808	5,365	7,193
Britain	480	2,273	3,383	4,091	4,761	4,967	5,090
Soviet Union	-	5,000	7,100	11,340	11,858	12,225	12,100
United States	-	-	1,620	3,970	9,020	11,410	11,430

These figures replicated, then exceeded the scale of mobilization during the First World War. By 1945 in the final stages of the conflict in Europe and Asia, the major powers across the globe had 43 million men and women in uniform, transforming the familiar social landscape. This figure also included the Polish armed forces, who in 1939–40, and again in 1942 when Stalin allowed Polish prisoners of war to join the Allies in North

Africa, continued to fight under Allied command. There were 67,000 in the re-formed Polish army by May 1940; there was a small Polish navy, which flew the Polish flag, and Polish flyers in the Royal Air Force. In April 1944 there were 50,000 Poles fighting in the Allied ranks in Italy.[26]

These raw figures convey the dimensions of mass mobilization, but they fail to reveal the nature of the military societies that mass conscription produced. The armed forces were not a mass. Although they are often treated as quite distinct from civilian life once in uniform, the armed forces were, in reality, mirrors of the societies from which they were recruited. They were complex social organizations, a complexity that reflected the many forms of military labour made necessary by modern warfare. Many of these forms of labour were familiar from civilian life, the difference simply being that men and women now wore uniform. The link with civilian life was magnified by the fact that most of those who served were civilian volunteers or conscripts. The loss of many regular servicemen in the early stages of the war increased the military dependence on the wider population, who brought to the military a range of skills and aptitudes acquired in peacetime. The ancillary and support services for the armed forces were huge, in most cases relying on older men, or soldiers who had been wounded, as well as women volunteers. Those who actually saw combat were always a fraction. The rest of military society was made up of clerks, storemen, labourers, engineers, logistic personnel, signals and radio services, intelligence organizations, maintenance staff, archivists and record keepers, medical and veterinary services, food supply and preparation, the pay corps, and so on. This vast community of occupations explains why mobilization was so extensive. In the German army in 1943 there were 2 million men at the front line, but 8 million carrying out other designated military tasks. The United States army in December 1943 had 7.5 million men enlisted, but only 2.8 million assigned to combat units – of whom a significant proportion were in non-combat support roles. The American Eighth Air Force stationed in Britain in late 1943 had around 25,000 flying crew, but 283,000 employed in one of the many non-combat professions. A typical British infantry division numbered 15,500 men, but only 6,750 were front-line fighters.[27] Such ratios were less marked in Japan and the Soviet Union, with desperate shortages of manpower for the front line, but the military establishment everywhere relied for the effective organization of combat on millions who were not fighting.

As in civilian society, the military needed specialist skills or the ability to impart those skills quickly through training. Selection procedures were generally geared to finding the recruits with established skills and higher educational qualifications and allocating them to more technically complex branches of the services. The US Army Air Forces took two-fifths of those who scored highest in the standard Army General Classification Test. In Canada, the air force took only 90,000 out of 600,000 volunteers, using a special Visual Link Trainer designed by medical and psychological experts to distinguish a potential flyer.[28] British recruitment was initially poorly managed, with large numbers of skilled men in roles where their skills were not exploited. Psychological testing was slowly introduced in 1940, and finally, in 1941, a Directorate for Selection of Personnel was set up, modelled on the peacetime National Institute of Industrial Psychology. The new system relied on aptitude testing to ensure that skills acquired in civilian life were properly allocated to the many different military branches.[29] The systems were certainly far from perfect, and they reflected the prevailing class realities; poorly graded recruits, often with low educational achievements, ended up universally in the infantry. Sometimes training had to be extremely basic. In Italy, thousands of illiterate recruits from the countryside could not tell left from right and had to have a coloured band wound round one arm to help them remember which was which.[30] All conscripts underwent basic training, even if they were to serve subsequently in a service or auxiliary branch. Because of the sheer scale of mobilization, the training regimes had to be constructed to match the demand for manpower. The RAF, for example, relied on the British Commonwealth Air Training Plan, agreed with the Canadian government in December 1939, under whose auspices 131,000 aircrew from 97 Canadian training schools eventually graduated.[31] When the United States began recruiting in large numbers in 1942 an emergency training system had to be established at 242 different sites; officer training places expanded from 14,000 in 1941 to 90,000 a year later. Training even extended to some of the 1.6 million illiterates identified by the draft boards, who were to be taught reading and writing alongside regular military instruction.[32] The most remarkable training programme was achieved in the Soviet Union with the decree of 17 September 1941 on Universal and Obligatory Military Training of Citizens of the USSR, which required all men not yet in the armed forces to attend 110 hours of training courses after work to learn how to handle rifles, mortars, machine guns and grenades, and how to prepare a military trench.[33]

The second variable affecting the scale of mobilization was the cumulative impact of losses. Here there was a marked contrast between the Western democracies and the dictatorships. In Britain and the United States there was a widespread desire to avoid the debilitating losses dictated by the immobile trench warfare of the Great War. Greater emphasis was placed on

air and naval strategy, and although the loss of highly trained manpower
could be considerable (41 per cent of the crew of RAF Bomber Command),
the overall impact on manpower numbers was more modest. Both states
were engaged in large-scale ground combat only from 1944 onwards. By
the end of 1944, American absolute military losses on all fronts (dead, missing, POWs) amounted to 168,000, less than the losses sustained on the
Eastern Front in a single battle.[34] High casualties during the final months of
assault in Europe and the Pacific pushed the overall number of combat
dead to 292,000 (an additional 114,000 died of disease and injury).[35] British military dead amounted to 270,000 over six years of conflict. This scale
of loss allowed British conscription to decline steadily over the war years:
3 million were recruited by 1941, but in 1942 only 547,000, in 1943 a further 347,000 and 254,000 in 1944.[36] The slowdown in the end produced a
crisis of manpower in the second half of 1944, when losses were at their
highest and commanders were expected to try to keep casualty rates down.[37]
Survival for longer had the effect of producing more experienced and
resourceful soldiers and airmen, though it was found that even among those
who survived, servicemen became burnt out by continuous combat. It was
well known that novice aircrew were much more at risk in the bombing
war, while the American decision to feed in replacements in ground combat
piecemeal exposed the 'rookie' soldiers to much greater danger. Nevertheless, the relatively modest levels of loss year on year meant that British and
American populations were not exposed to the same imperative demand
for military manpower as their allies and enemies, although in both states
even these more modest levels of recruitment raised anxiety about the possibility of replenishment.

The great battles of attrition in the Second World War were fought out
on the Eastern Front. Without these catastrophic levels of loss, Germany's
war effort would have been less constrained and the war in the West more
dangerous for the democracies. Overall irrecoverable losses on the Soviet
side totalled 11.4 million, including 6.9 million dead from combat or
disease or accident, and 4.5 million POWs or missing. In addition, 22
million Soviet military suffered injury, frostbite or sickness. If the wounded
and sick are added to Soviet casualties, the Red Army suffered 11.8 million in just the first eighteen months of the war. Irrecoverable losses for
the German armed forces, fighting in three different theatres, reached 5.3
million, including 4.3 million killed and missing and 548,000 who died
from disease, injury or suicide. Soviet loss rates declined as the war went
on but still remained severe; German losses progressively increased, to
reach 1.2 million dead in the final battles of 1945.[38] All but 36,000 of the
Soviet casualties were endured in the war with Germany (the rest in the

conquest of Manchuria in August 1945). The best estimates suggest that 75 per cent of all German irrecoverable losses came from the war in the East. The statistics on annual military deaths are set out in Table 4.2.

Table 4.2 Comparative Statistics of German and Soviet Military Deaths 1939–45[39]

	1939/1940	1941	1942	1943	1944	1945
Germany	102,000	357,000	572,000	812,000	1,802,000	1,540,000
Soviet Union	-	802,000	1,743,000	1,945,000	1,596,000	732,000

Losses on this scale forced both states to recruit men from older or younger age groups and to return the wounded rapidly to combat. In Germany, almost 50 per cent of those who served in the armed forces had been born before 1914, 7 per cent after 1925.[40] The German government began to comb out 'surplus' labour from army offices and rear services following a decree in November 1943, but instead of the 1 million aimed for only 400,000 more were mustered for front-line duty.[41] In the Soviet Union older age was not regarded as a barrier to service any more than youth or disablement. The wounded were returned to combat, often in an unfit state, though few probably matched the legendary Marshal Rokossovskii, wounded forty-six times, who contested the siege of Stalingrad from a hospital bed. As the army advanced in 1943–4, desperately short of infantry, it recruited any men still left in the German-occupied areas and put them in uniform with only the most rudimentary training. The Red Army was forced to be indiscriminate with recruitment, but the declining levels of competence and health that this produced were masked by the massive output of weapons, which shifted the capital–labour ratio in the Soviet forces decisively in favour of equipment. This was a development common to most armed forces during the war as greater quantities of higher-quality weaponry became available for the new waves of conscripts. The military labour force inevitably suffered from pressures on the training system and the effort to mobilize more marginal recruits. In this sense, mass mobilization placed evident limits on military performance the longer the war continued.

This was, nevertheless, an imperial war. Exceptional demands on national manpower could be supplemented by those combatant states which were also empires, old or new. They were able to mobilize the populations under their control, the majority as auxiliary or service troops but, as the war went on, in combat units as well. The Japanese army began recruiting Korean and Taiwanese volunteers in 1937 and introduced conscription from 1942 onwards. Around 200,000 Koreans served with the Japanese army, 20,000 with the navy. More than 100,000 were integrated into Japanese army units, although only a fraction achieved officer status.[42] The Italian army employed East African colonial troops, *askari*, in large numbers, as well as Libyan horsemen. The new German empire in Europe was a source of wide recruitment. Thousands joined the army, the Waffen-SS and the security forces as volunteers to fight against what was presented as a Bolshevik menace to Europe, including 60,000 Estonians, 100,000 Latvians, 38,000 Belgians, 14,000 from Spain, 12,000 from Norway and Denmark, even 135 Swiss and 39 Swedes.[43] This was not always a profitable source. The Legion of French Volunteers against Bolshevism, recruited in 1941 among the French extreme right, arrived in Russia in time for the drive on Moscow in 1941 but proved a disaster. Poorly led by incompetent and venal officers, short of even the most basic resources, and offered a brief and rudimentary training, the legion was decimated in its first days of combat and never returned to the front line.[44] From the conquered areas of the Soviet Union more than 250,000 men joined the German war effort as combatants, recruited chiefly among the anti-Communist peoples of southern Russia and Ukraine, while as many as 1 million Russians worked for the German army behind the lines as *Hilfswillige* (voluntary helpers) performing a wide range of non-combatant and security roles. One of the converts to the German side, the Soviet general Andrei Vlasov, captured by a Dutch Waffen-SS unit, wanted to form a Russian liberation army to fight alongside the Germans, but the Vlasov army never materialized as a useful force. The two divisions finally formed in haste in January 1945 saw action in Prague in the last days of the war, where they turned their guns on their German allies to protect fellow Slavs from the final rampage of the local Waffen-SS.[45]

Of all the imperial powers, Britain was by far the most successful beneficiary of empire manpower. Indeed, much of Britain's war, particularly for the defence of the empire, was fought by non-Britons, a fact still too readily forgotten in British narratives of the conflict. The four Dominion countries – Canada, Australia, New Zealand and South Africa – between them mobilized 2.6 million men and women, India some 2.7 million. In 1945, Britain still had 4.6 million in uniform, India and the Dominions 3.2 million.[46] New Zealand had the highest rate of mobilization of any empire area, with 67 per cent of men aged eighteen to forty-five enlisted. In Canada, over 1 million men, or 41 per cent of those aged eighteen to forty-five, served in the forces. Dominion recruits supplied a significant proportion of the aircrew flying in RAF Bomber Command's strategic air offensive against Germany, the largest number of them Canadians, flying in their own squadrons alongside the British crews. The Dominions counted for a further 96,822 war dead fighting on Britain's behalf, India for 87,000. The largest single volunteer force during the war was raised in the subcontinent. Most Indian volunteers served at home, maintaining domestic security and facing the Japanese threat, but numerous divisions served in the South East Asian campaigns, the Middle East and, eventually, in Italy. By 1943 there were six divisions overseas, twenty divisions and fourteen brigades at home. Indian mobilization suffered in the early years from a shortage of equipment, but there was little shortage of volunteers. The British authorities preferred to recruit from the so-called 'martial races' first, principally from the Punjab (a mixture of Muslims and Sikhs), the Northwest Frontier Province and Nepal. Among the Sikh population, some 94 per cent of all recruitable males volunteered for the Indian army. But as the flow of recruits dried up among the 'martial races', recruitment was spread further south, to reach a peak in 1942, at which point the 'martial races' made up just 46 per cent of the Indian armed forces. Four-fifths of the army came from rural villages, since the British distrusted more urbanized and educated Indians, and almost all were illiterate.[47]

The importance of the Dominion and Indian contribution can be gauged by the proportion of non-British forces used for what were essentially imperial campaigns. The British Eighth Army in North Africa in 1941 was one-quarter British, three-quarters imperial. Under the South East Asia Command in 1945, four-fifths of the troops were Indian and African units.[48] The African divisions represented the rest of the colonial empire, which supplied more than half a million volunteers and conscripts for the armed forces. The King's East African Rifles, a force that dated back to 1902, eventually supplied 323,000 troops; the Royal West African Frontier Force, founded in 1900, a further 242,600. The southern African High Commission territories of Bechuanaland (Botswana), Swaziland and Basutoland (Lesotho) supplied 36,000 more. By the end of the war the African empire had supplied a grand total of 663,000 black labourers and soldiers for the armed forces.[49] Most of them did not see combat, but the divisions that saw service did so protecting the threats to empire – the East African Rifles in Ethiopia, Madagascar and Burma; the West African Force in Ethiopia, then Burma; the Bechuana in the Middle East. The Caribbean colonies raised an estimated 12,000 volunteers, most of whom also served as non-combatants. A Caribbean Regiment was raised in 1944 and posted to Italy, though it did not in the end see any fighting.[50]

Although British colonial recruitment relied at first on ostensible volunteers, for which there was a long imperial tradition, the urgent need for local military recruits for a variety of auxiliary roles encouraged a shift to recruitment strategies that were in little meaningful sense voluntary. In

West Africa, local chiefs were used as intermediaries by the British and allocated quotas for men to be rounded up from their villages; men on a court charge could be offered an army posting instead of prison; workers were sometimes loaded onto trucks on a pretext and driven to the local army camp; in Swaziland, press gangs were used. The shortage of recruits for a distant war, whose purpose was dimly understood, led to the introduction of colonial conscription, which proved widely unpopular. Rioting against the draft in the Gold Coast (now Ghana) town of Winneba left six of the protesters dead. The colonial authorities preferred to take men from more remote villages among peoples they regarded once again as 'martial races': as one white officer put it, 'the blacker their face – the better soldier they made'. Preference was given to those who had had little contact with the modern world, with the result that 90 per cent of the African recruits were illiterate.[51]

A small number of black volunteers, some of them already living in Britain, wanted to be able to join the regular British armed forces. Until October 1939 the ruling prevailed that only British subjects of British parents of European descent could serve in the British armed forces. The ruling was overturned following a campaign in the autumn of 1939 by the British-based League of Coloured People led by a black doctor, Harold Moody. The services nevertheless generally remained resistant to a black presence, except for the RAF, which recruited around 6,000 Caribbean blacks to augment the groundcrew at British airbases, and eventually allowed around 300 black volunteers to fly as aircrew.[52] A small handful of black recruits achieved 'emergency officer' status, though they had to run the gauntlet of persistent, though far from universal, racial prejudice ('I had never been called darkie before', one black officer later recalled). At the end of the war the British government tried to repatriate all black volunteers remaining in Britain, but once again popular protest allowed a number to stay in the motherland they had chosen to defend.

In the United States, race was an awkward issue for the predominantly white armed services. Black recruits had served in the First World War chiefly as military labourers and auxiliaries. Between the wars, combat units were all white. The rapid expansion of the American armed forces from 1941 onwards raised the question of whether the 10 per cent of black Americans would be allowed to bear arms. Roosevelt insisted that the navy and army accept black recruits, though it was agreed that the number would not exceed the proportion in the population, while both services retained the right to segregate black and white recruits in separate training facilities, camp amenities and military units.[53] The policy produced unfortunate anomalies. Black recruits from northern states, where segregation had long disappeared, were forced to accept racial discrimination. Bizarrely, the army believed that southern whites would make better officers of black units because they were more familiar with the black communities. The policy provoked wide resentment and occasional violent protest from recruits who were no longer accustomed to segregation.[54] The conflict persisted among the troops posted overseas, where white soldiers and officers tried to sustain military apartheid. In the English port of Bristol, a full-scale riot erupted in July 1944 between black and white American servicemen, leaving one black soldier dead and dozens injured.

The results of the programme of black recruitment were mixed. Like British colonial recruits, most black Americans were not in combat units. The great majority of the 696,000 conscripted into the army found themselves performing service and labouring duty. None of the services achieved the 10 per cent ratio agreed with Roosevelt.[55] The army claimed that black draftees performed poorly on the General Classification Test (around half failed it altogether by 1943), which explained their subordinate status. Only 1.9 per cent of the army officer corps was black, even fewer in the United States navy, where black conscripts made up just 6 per cent of naval personnel. The navy reluctantly agreed to admit black recruits in April 1942, but only on condition that they would not serve at sea, but in harbour and shore installations. By spring 1943, 71 per cent of the black personnel served in the Stewards Branch, waiting on their white officers.[56] The American army air forces also recruited few black airmen for combat; by the end of 1944 just 1 per cent of the 138,000 blacks in the air force had qualified as aircrew.[57] Black recruits for flying were trained in a separate all-black base at Tuskegee, Alabama, but few of them were allowed to fly in combat except for four squadrons of fighter pilots, the 'Tuskegee Airmen', sent to the Italian front in 1943–4, where they were constantly watched by their white superiors to see if their performance matched existing white prejudices. When they disembarked at Boston on their return home in 1945, there were separate gangplanks for white and black airmen who had fought together only weeks before. The 'Tuskegee Airmen' exposed the extent to which white prejudice hampered the full utilization of America's black population.[58] By contrast, the army's attitude to the Japanese-Americans interned in camps at the start of the war by presidential order was to offer them the prospect of proving their American credentials by volunteering. Around 22,500 Japanese-American men and women came forward, and 18,000 were organized into segregated military units that saw service in Europe, including the 422nd Regiment which became the most decorated unit in the American army.[59]

The same mix of prejudice and expediency extended to the recruitment of women into the armed forces. This, too, was not a new phenomenon. Women's service was introduced in the last years of the First World War to meet the manpower emergencies, but it was terminated in the years of peace. Total war, however, was far from gender-specific. The democratization of warfare implied by total war included women, whether as workers or civil defenders or, in a more limited way, as military personnel. There were few problems about recruiting women for war work or air raid precautions, since many women evidently shared the view that responsibility in modern war had to be shared across the community. Women also lobbied to be able to join the military effort, again reflecting the view of the conflict as a 'people's war' rather than a war conducted only by men. Male attitudes to recruiting women into the armed forces were more ambivalent. With the exception of the Soviet Union, none of the other major combatants allowed women to bear arms. Many of the tasks for which women replaced men in the military structure were those commonly undertaken by the female workforce in civilian life – stenographers, clerks, postal workers, cooks, telephone operators, librarians, dieticians, nurses.[60] The closest women usually got to military operations came through their role as radar plotters, or radio operators, or motor transport drivers, or routine intelligence personnel, but they were usually remote from the front line, except in the Soviet Union.

Only when the home front became the front line, as it did in the bombing war, did women see action. In Britain, Germany and the Soviet Union women joined anti-aircraft batteries, though only in the Soviet case were women allowed to fire the guns in the absence of men. In Britain, army regulations were changed in April 1941 to allow women from the Auxiliary Territorial Service to serve at anti-aircraft sites; by 1943 there was a peak of 57,000 women working as radar operators, spotters, height finders and searchlight crew. Despite resistance from men in the anti-aircraft crews, mixed units became the norm. Men did the heavy work of loading and firing. Under Royal Warrant issued in 1938, women were not allowed to bear arms and those who undertook guard duty at anti-aircraft posts could only carry axe handles and whistles. Women's participation was deliberately feminized – they had only two-thirds of male pay, extra time off and more comfortable accommodation than the usual tents for men. A 'female diet' of less meat, bread and bacon and more milk, eggs, fruit and vegetables was soon abandoned when it was discovered how hungry the women became.[61] In Germany the women air force auxiliaries operated searchlights, radio equipment and the telephone network in the German 'Kammhuber Line' of anti-aircraft defences stretching across the northern approaches to Germany. By 1944, the German air force had more than 130,000 female personnel, some of whom ended up helping to fire the guns as well. In March 1945, the German Supreme Headquarters finally conceded that these female auxiliaries could be supplied with handguns and the anti-tank *Panzerfaust*.[62]

There has survived a persistent myth that German women did not participate in the war effort because National Socialist ideology defined the woman's role as mother and housekeeper. The ideology was, in reality, never so inflexible. Women, but particularly young or single women, were expected to play a part as racial comrades along with the men. The armed forces recruited around half a million women as Armed Forces' Helpers (*Wehrmachthelferinnen*) to replace men in communication, clerical, administrative and welfare sectors. Thousands more worked as non-uniformed secretarial and office staff.[63] Approximately the same numbers were recruited to the British and United States armed forces. The three British services revived the First World War women's units following the outbreak of a second war. The Women's Royal Naval Reserve, the Auxiliary Territorial Service (Army) and the Women's Auxiliary Air Force expanded rapidly from a total of 49,000 in June 1940 to 447,000 by June 1944; three-quarters of them were volunteers, despite the introduction of female conscription in the National Service Act (2) introduced in December 1941, over half of them were under the age of twenty-two.[64] The Dominions also recruited women. In Canada, a Division of Volunteer Services was set up in 1941 to oversee the employment of women in volunteer roles. Unlike the British women's services, where women remained auxiliaries, the Canadian forces integrated the women as full military personnel and in 1942 the first female officers were commissioned.[65] Male distinction was sustained here – as everywhere in the Western war effort – by the exclusion of women from direct combat and the general practice that female officers could not give orders to fighting men.

In the United States there was stronger prejudice against recruiting women, though eventually the pressing need for labour forced the services' hand. Around 400,000 women served in the different branches of the armed forces, including 63,000 in the Women's Army Auxiliary Corps (from 1943 the Women's Army Corps). The Corps was only formed following legislation in May 1942, introduced into Congress by Republican representative Edith Rogers. There followed a lengthy argument against women's enlistment led by men who feared that female participation would result in the moral decline of the armed forces.[66] The army and air force insisted that women would be defined as 'with' the service rather than 'in' the service, until compelled by legislation introduced into

Congress in July 1943 – a second Rogers Bill – to allow full integration.[67] The change resulted in a simplified system of enlistment and prompted a flow of fresh volunteers. The army air forces, however, continued to bar women from the Auxiliary Air Corps for service with the American air warning and anti-aircraft system.[68] The United States navy was reluctant at the start of the war to employ women at all, but shortages of men for auxiliary roles finally produced a women's branch with the deliberately long-winded title 'Women Accepted for Volunteer Emergency Service' to allow the appropriate acronym WAVES. The new service was established by August 1942. Unlike the army, the naval authorities decided that the women should be integrated fully into the service ('in' rather than 'with') but commanded by a separate women's officer corps.[69] By the end of the war some 80,000 WAVES had graduated from the naval training schools. Few of the volunteers accepted for the American services were black, and those who were remained stationed in the United States until 1945, when a black unit of the Women's Army Corps, the 6888th Central Postal Directory Battalion, commanded by one of only two senior female black officers, was sent to Britain to sort out a mountain of unsent post.[70] It remains an open question whether the responsibilities taken over by women could not have been performed in part at least by men. In both Britain and the United States there was considerable pressure from women to be allowed to participate beyond the welfare and nursing work usually assigned to them, and since the democracies viewed the war as a genuinely shared commitment, the inclusion of women played a part in cementing domestic solidarity for the war effort by demonstrating that all citizens, men and women alike, shared a common responsibility.

Among the most dangerous tasks for which women volunteered in the democracies was the ferrying of aircraft on domestic flights from factory to airbase, or between training centres, or flying aircraft for target practice. The Air Transport Auxiliary, set up in January 1940 in Britain, recruited both qualified men and women. A total of 166 women served as pilot auxiliaries, and 15 lost their lives, including Britain's most famous aviatrix, Amy Johnson.[71] Another celebrity aviatrix, the American Jacqueline Cochran, volunteered to work with the British auxiliaries, and later returned to the United States to found the Women's Flying Training Detachment in September 1942, despite the initial reluctance of the army air forces' commander-in-chief, Henry Arnold. In 1943 the detachment merged with a Women's Auxiliary Ferrying Squadron under Cochran's command to form the Women Airforce Service Pilots (WASP). Female flying was more developed in America than anywhere else and there were 25,000 volunteers for training, though in the end only 1,074 qualified female pilots were selected, among whom 39 were killed in accidents. Like their British counterparts, they were refused full military status, and suffered petty male prejudice against including women in what pilots regarded as a male preserve. At some camps the women were given older or poorly serviced aircraft to fly for target practice, or were banned from bases altogether. No black applicant was admitted to WASP though they volunteered. In late 1944 the whole programme was summarily terminated, thanks to a growing surplus of trained male pilots and powerful lobbying against the alleged threat the women posed to male employment. By the end of the war women pilots had flown 12,652 ferrying missions in 78 different aircraft types, including the giant B-29 Superfortress which male pilots were hesitant to fly because of early technical problems. In 1977, after a long struggle for recognition, Congress finally approved legislation defining the women as war veterans.[72]

There was little hesitancy in the Soviet Union about female enrolment. The terrible haemorrhage of men in the first year of the war with Germany made recruitment of women a necessity. During the war around 850,000 served in the armed forces, 550,000 with the Red Army and Air Force regulars, 300,000 in anti-aircraft and home-front units. There were an estimated 25,000 women in uniform fighting with the partisans.[73] Despite the widespread pre-war rhetoric about the whole of society fighting to defend the Revolution, the Soviet regime was uncertain how to respond to the wave of young women volunteers who turned up at recruiting stations from the first days of the war asking to join the army. Girls in the Young Communist movement enlisted among the estimated 4 million civilian volunteers in 'people's corps' (*opolchenie*), which fought as militia against the onrushing Germans and were decimated by the enemy.[74] The Universal Military Training Programme was obligatory for men, but it did not preclude women if they could persuade local officials to let them attend. The first official recruitment of women came in October 1941, when Stalin allowed three combat air regiments with female crew to be mobilized. During the war female participation in the air effort expanded, and much of the night bombing of German bases was carried out by the women's units, including the legendary 46th Guards Night Bomber Aviation Regiment, whose crews flew 24,000 missions and won 23 medals as Heroes of the Soviet Union.[75] Just as famous was the Central Women's School of Sniper Training, set up in May 1943 following the success of women snipers over the previous year; a total of 1,885 snipers graduated from the school and saw front-line duty, killing an unrecorded number of German soldiers.[76]

By April 1942, the Soviet government finally accepted the need for female enlistment to replace the losses of men at the front. However, the proportion of women drafted into the kind of occupations reserved for Western women recruits was much lower in the Soviet Union. Out of 40,000 mobilized into the air force, only 15,000 took over work as clerks, librarians, cooks, or storekeepers, while 25,000 were trained for the front as drivers, armourers and communication troops. From the 520,000 who joined the armed forces, approximately 120,000 fought in ground and air combat and a further 110,000 as non-combat military specialists at the front.[77] Women shared the same hardships as the men but suffered additional deprivations because of the slow supply of female uniforms or hygienic and medical services adapted for female recruits. Unlike the Western forces, gender prejudices did not prevent women from commanding men on the front line, though prejudice remained. 'They've foisted girls on me,' one divisional commander complained. 'Corps de ballet! It's war, not a dance, a terrible war!'[78] Women nevertheless remained a feature of front-line combat throughout the war. Though the Soviet experience was the product of necessity as much as ideology, the extreme demands of the most total of wars matched the Soviet view that the struggle for survival in the Great Patriotic War required absolute levels of mobilization.

This was a necessity seldom if ever questioned among the military recruits of the warring powers. Mass military mobilization was largely taken for granted as a fact of life in total war by those who would do the fighting. There were remarkably few mutinies in the Second World War. Desertion or defection was more widespread but was a small fraction of the total number mobilized. Insubordination was frequent and widespread, but the many infractions of military life and discipline reflected the broad social net of recruitment and should not be interpreted as protest against mass mobilization. Cases that could be regarded as mutinous were usually the result of specific circumstances that prompted protest, rather than a rejection of service in wartime. In the Indian army, for example, there were numerous brief mutinies, some against the order to serve overseas, some in protest at the British insistence that Sikh soldiers should be compelled to cut their hair, remove their turbans and wear steel helmets. Sikh religious convention dictated that the turban and long hair were not negotiable, and mutinies occurred both in India and among Sikh servicemen in Hong Kong protesting against British enforcement of the policy. In the last case, eighty-three Sikhs were court-martialled for mutiny, and eleven given heavy sentences.[79] In the United States, racial segregation in the armed forces provoked widespread violence among black soldiers and airmen against their treatment. Mutinous violence began well before America was at war. In 1941, near Fort Bragg in North Carolina, white military police and black troopers fought a fierce gun battle that left two dead and five wounded. The worst violence occurred in 1943 where riots and shoot-outs occurred in at least ten different camps. A major conflict at Camp Van Dorn in Mississippi was sparked by the resentment of northern blacks in the 364th Infantry Regiment against unaccustomed segregation rules. After the mutiny was quelled, the unit was posted as a punishment to the Aleutian Islands in the far north Pacific for the rest of the war.[80]

The United States also witnessed the most active popular protest against the military draft. The Selective Service Bill of autumn 1940, and its renewal a year later, prompted nationwide protests from a range of isolationist and anti-war groups against the idea that large-scale recruitment was necessary. Polls in summer 1941 showed that almost half of those asked were opposed to extending the draft. Investigative journalists toured the draftees' camps where they found widespread disillusionment and resentment among young soldiers with little to do, poor combat training and few weapons. Half, it was estimated, were willing to desert if they could; 90 per cent of those interviewed expressed hostility to the government that put them in uniform. Violent riots at camps in the run-up to the renewal of the bill confirmed the extent of popular hostility to military service among the new recruits. The Selective Service Bill only passed the House of Representatives by one vote.[81] This was the most serious political crisis faced by any state on the issue of conscription. Draft-dodging certainly happened elsewhere but it was an individual decision, not the consequence of a collective campaign. Mass military service was eventually accepted in America as well after the outbreak of war in December 1941 as the only path to victory.

ECONOMIC MOBILIZATION

The primary concern for all the warring states was the ability to supply an adequate quantity of weapons, equipment and supplies to sustain the large fighting forces they recruited. Yet this priority raised fundamental questions about how warfare should be funded and about how the majority civilian population could be supplied and fed to a level sufficient to sustain national mobilization. The armed forces were exceptionally greedy consumers. The gigantic quantity of weapons produced by the major powers over the war years matched the extravagant mobilization of manpower. How military equipment was developed, produced and distributed is the subject of Chapter 6, but war production and mass military conscription had a very direct effect on the home population as taxpayers, savers, consumers and workers. The home front had to fund the war effort, work long hours on war orders, and watch a large proportion of the nation's food supplies and consumer goods disappear into military warehouses and canteens. National mobilization in general meant working harder and receiving less, while doing so without protest.

Armaments were the tip of a vast iceberg of military consumption. Typically, the acquisition of weapons took up between 15 and 20 per cent of the military budget. The armed forces were so large that they formed their own economies, importing not just weapons but food, consumer items of all kinds, textiles, chemicals, oil products, specialized equipment for haulage or maintenance and, in the case of the German and Soviet armed forces, large numbers of animals. The millions of service personnel and support staff had to be housed and military bases, airfields and supply depots constructed where they did not already exist. Great efforts were made to ensure that military personnel ate well, even if the civilian population went short. British soldiers were supposed to have a daily intake of 4,500 calories, well above the level of British civilian rations (and generally higher than the daily food supply for Indian and colonial troops).[82] German soldiers in the early years of war had three times the meat ration of civilians (later four times as much), and more than twice the volume of bread grains. Real coffee, chocolate, cigarettes and tobacco, jam and vegetables were also a priority for military personnel, but increasingly absent for ordinary German consumers.[83] Apart from food, the military economies absorbed a high proportion of all consumer goods. In Germany by 1941, half the production of the clothing industry was used for uniforms; the military took 80 per cent of all furniture produced, and the same proportion of all consumer chemical products (including toothpaste and shoe polish); they took 60 per cent of all paintbrushes, wooden boxes and barrels, 44 per cent of all leather goods, and so on. By 1941 an estimated half of all the civilian goods produced in Germany was taken by the military machine. So important was the supply of confectionery for the armed forces considered to be that the sector was given the highest priority ranking for the allocation of labour.[84]

The claims of these giant military consumers fundamentally distorted the economies of the warring powers even before the outbreak of war. The effect was already evident in the rearmament drive of the 1930s when the proportion of the national product devoted to military spending spiralled to unprecedented peacetime levels, reaching 17 per cent in Germany in 1938/9 and 13 per cent in the Soviet Union. On the eve of the First World War the proportions had been 3 per cent in Germany, 5 per cent in tsarist Russia, partly because the weaponry was less complex and expensive.[85] By

May 1939, almost one-third of the German industrial labour force was working on orders directly for the armed forces; two-thirds of German industrial investment in the years 1937–9 was devoted to military and war-essential projects. In the Soviet Union, the Third Five-Year Plan, begun in 1938, earmarked 21.9 billion roubles for defence investment against a figure of just 1.6 billion in 1936.[86] Spending programmes on this scale severely restricted what was available for the civilian consumer and the non-war sectors of the economy even in peacetime. But with the outbreak of war in Asia and Europe, governments had to confront the economic realities of total war and full-scale mobilization.

The experience of the First World War showed how important it was to balance military demands against the need for financial stability and adequate civilian living-standards. The largely improvised nature of the economic mobilization of the earlier conflict had generally produced high inflation, financial crisis and poorly managed distribution of resources between military and civilian needs. Food shortages had prompted widespread labour protest and social disaffection. The collapse of the Russian war effort in 1917 and the defeat of the Central Powers in 1918 were attributed in large part to economic and social crises. As a result, it was widely assumed that total war could only be waged successfully if the danger of social and financial crisis could be avoided a second time around. The critical problem was to understand the effects of the war effort on the structure of the national economy so that enough resources would be available for the military without undermining entirely the financial system, or the demands of consumers. For this, the mobilization of expertise was considered essential. The distinguished British economist John Maynard Keynes was attached as special adviser to the British Treasury in the summer of 1940 following publication of his seminal pamphlet 'How to Pay for the War', which directly addressed the problem of balancing consumption, savings and taxation without the risk of inflation.[87] In Germany, the economics minister, Walter Funk, established a 'Committee of Professors' in autumn 1939 to work out how to pay for the war and control consumption; German economists constructed provisional national income statistics to illustrate how taxation, savings and consumption could be balanced to suit military requirements.[88] The Japanese National Savings Promotion Council, established in June 1938, was staffed with social and economic experts briefed to find ways to encourage saving, limit consumption and avoid inflation.[89] Economists everywhere treated 'total war' as a distinct economic problem. There was little difference between the dictatorships and democracies on how the problem might be solved since some form of wartime 'command economy' was common to them both.

Financing a war on this scale, while avoiding runaway inflation, was the first challenge. There was no alternative with mobilization on this scale than to run a large deficit, although the deficit could be reduced by taxation or its economic effects postponed until after the war. Government long- and medium-term loans paid for around half the American war effort, raising the national debt to unprecedented levels; in Britain, loans of all kinds covered around 42 per cent of wartime expenditure, raising the current annual deficit from a modest £490 million in 1939 to £2.8 billion by 1943, and trebling the national debt; in Germany, government borrowing increased tenfold across the war years, from 30 billion marks to 387 billion, covering some 55 per cent of wartime expenditure; in Japan deficits by 1945 covered a similar proportion. Only in China did the government resort to simply printing money as states had done in the First World War: in 1945 the deficit amounted to 87 per cent of state spending.[90] The funds were in general raised from existing bank and credit institutions, which were given little alternative but to buy government paper. The exception was the Soviet economy, where central planning and pricing policy was designed to balance the books as far as possible from existing tax and tariff funds through a system of creative communist accounting. Loans accounted for only 100 billion roubles out of wartime government revenues totalling 1,117 billion roubles, or just 8.9 per cent.[91]

For some economies it was possible to postpone wartime payments by simply importing goods from occupied or empire areas and blocking payment for the duration. In Berlin the state held back a total of more than 19 billion marks owed to occupied states for vital war imports, to be repaid only after victory; a further 25.4 billion was extracted from occupied Europe as loans to pay for further goods.[92] Britain suspended payments to the sterling bloc for imported goods worth £3.4 billion by the end of the war – effectively a form of economic coercion.[93] Both states also relied on substantial contributions from the same imperial or occupied territories: the German war effort drew 71 billion marks towards wartime expenditure from the occupied areas, while Britain compelled India to pay for its role in the war, forcing the Indian government to run a large annual deficit from an economy that could ill afford the cost, and to accept sharp increases in taxation for the Indian population.[94] The German regime could also extract money and goods from the persecuted Jewish populations. Gold looted from Jewish owners, or gold teeth extracted in the extermination centres, was deposited in Swiss banks to help fund essential imports. In Germany, an estimated 7–8 billion marks' worth of Jewish property, including shares, precious metals and jewellery, was taken over by the state following legal restrictions on Jewish ownership of wealth, and programmes of compulsory 'Aryanization'. In the conquered areas, everything Jews owned could be seized and the proceeds taken by the state. Valuables were deposited in the Booty Office of the Reich Treasury in Berlin and used to boost state funds.[95]

High deficit spending ran the great danger of creating what Keynes christened the 'inflationary gap', the difference between the quantity of money in the economy and the quantity of goods available for the civilian population to buy. This gap, which had driven high inflation in the First World War, had to be made good in one way or another. All the warring states understood the problem, and all except China adopted very similar solutions: raising taxes, encouraging or insisting on high rates of personal saving, controlling wages and prices, and restricting access to the consumer goods left over after the military had taken their slice. In China raising taxes was a difficult option to enforce. Japanese occupation of the most productive parts of the country reduced customs receipts by 85 per cent and salt tax revenues by 65 per cent, both traditional sources of government funding. The wartime crisis made borrowing difficult, while reducing expenditure would expose China to defeat. Despite efforts to impose new taxes on income, landed estates and manufactures, the government was compelled to resort to the printing press, massively increasing the amount of money in circulation to the point of hyperinflation. Government banknote issues totalled 1.4 billion fabi in 1937, 462.3 billion in 1945.[96] Elsewhere, funding the war and reducing consumer purchasing power was far more effective, while populations were more willing to cooperate with government demands. Nevertheless, the increase in taxation, borrowing and savings had to be presented as a means to commit the citizen to the war effort in a very direct and personal way, by accepting economic sacrifices for the national good. This proved to be an unmanageable option in a divided and war-torn China.

Taxation as a way of coping with wartime expenditure had developed only slowly in the First World War, and with uneven effect. During the Second World War, tax yields rose dramatically, typically providing between one-quarter and one-half of government revenues. In the United States, where the war effort produced rapidly rising incomes across the board, taxation supplied 49 per cent of revenues, a large part from the unaccustomed imposition of income tax. In 1939, some 93 per cent of Americans paid no federal income tax, but by 1944 two-thirds of all earners were taxed, despite the many difficulties in setting up a complex fiscal structure for first-time taxpayers under wartime conditions. In order to make the sacrifices of war seem genuinely democratic, an excess profits tax was insisted on by Roosevelt, which became second only to income tax in supplying government funds.[97] In Japan, income tax payment also expanded rapidly among the employed population, rising from 6 per cent of personal income in 1939 to 15 per cent by 1944, but it was not enough to match rising expenditure. Unlike other war economies, under a quarter of Japan's wartime expenditure was covered by tax revenues.[98]

Britain and Germany had a longer tradition of income tax, and both regimes increased tax thresholds substantially during the war, as well as increasing indirect taxation. Commitment to the idea that citizens should share sacrifices equitably produced high rates of income tax for the highest earners. In Britain, the number of people with incomes of more than £4,000 a year after tax fell from 19,000 in 1939 to just 1,250 three years later. Total income tax revenues trebled, from £460 million in 1939/40 to £1.3 billion in 1944/45.[99] In Germany, an emergency surtax was imposed on personal incomes in 1939 and an excess profits tax on industry, which between them increased direct tax revenues from 8.1 billion marks in 1938 to 22 billion by 1943. Income tax thresholds again targeted the better off. Tax on incomes from 1,500–3,000 marks a year (the earnings of most semi-skilled and skilled workers) rose by one-fifth, but tax on those earning from 3,000–5,000 marks by 55 per cent. In the first war years half of German expenditure was met from taxes, a marked contrast with the failure to tax adequately in the Great War, although the regime worried a good deal over whether the German public would accept exceptionally high tax levels without protest.[100]

The issue of saving also suffered from the legacy of the earlier war, when patriotic campaigns had tried to rally subscriptions to war bonds whose value was rapidly eroded by inflation, or, in the German case, rendered completely worthless by the post-war collapse of the currency. In both Britain and Germany little reliance was placed on repeating the noisy fund-raising schemes. British Defence Bonds and National Savings Certificates were available for the public, but most of the increase in personal savings was diverted into small deposits in post office, savings bank or friendly society accounts, where it could be mobilized by the government without the need for persuasion or coercion.[101] The same system of what the German finance minister christened 'noiseless finance' was adopted in Germany. Encouraged to save by public propaganda, and with less to buy in the shops, small investors put their savings in savings banks or in post office savings accounts, whose holdings expanded from 2.6 billion marks in 1939 to 14.5 billion by 1941. The number of post office savings books increased from 1.5 million to 8.3 million.[102] The savings were then extracted by the government to help pay for the war, turning savers into involuntary subscribers to the war effort. The German public's distrust of war loans after the experience of the First World War was demonstrated when the regime tried to introduce a voluntary scheme of 'Iron Savings' in late 1941, to be deducted from income at source, and placed in special blocked accounts for use after the war. The scheme grew very slowly, while all other forms of personal savings quadrupled over the war years.[103] In both countries, savers were hoping to use rising earnings to provide a nest-egg after the war when economic conditions were expected to be tougher. Rather than accept financial risk for the sake of the nation, the savings boom showed that ordinary citizens, and not just capitalists, hoped to make money out of war.

In Japan and the Soviet Union, less affected by the legacy of the Great War, there was much greater reliance on patriotic appeals to buy government bonds or to increase personal savings for the war effort. In neither case could saving be regarded as an entirely voluntary act. In both states campaigns to encourage bond buying to support the modernization of the country had been policy since the 1920s, helping to create a social culture of thrift. In the Soviet case buying bonds was organized as a collective effort on farms and in factories, so that anyone standing out by refusing to comply ran the risk of public exposure and victimization. Saving was monitored by local Commissions for Contributions to State Credits and Savings, or *Komsody* for short. They encouraged workers to form small groups responsible for an allotted sum, which the workers or farmers then divided up between them. Because of the risks in non-compliance, bond issues were regularly oversubscribed. A new form of 'lottery' bond was introduced, which offered prizes of fur coats, jewellery, watches or cutlery for a people starved of even basic consumer goods, though there were regular complaints from prizewinners that the promised rewards never appeared.[104]

In Japan public campaigns to encourage saving and bond-buying were also accompanied by social strategies to minimize non-compliance by exploiting the idea of group saving. Savings associations were set up countrywide under government pressure in which the collective, as in the Soviet Union, took responsibility for a particular sum and made sure that all its members paid up. By 1944 there were 65,500 of these associations, with 59 million members. The same year a remarkable 39.5 per cent of the population's disposable income was devoted to saving. In every year except 1941, the state's target for saving was exceeded.[105] For workers, a savings sum was allocated on the basis of need and then deducted from wage packets like taxation.[106] In addition to personal savings, national bond drives were targeted at every neighbourhood association and quotas fixed. Neighbours met together to agree shares and each knew exactly what other households had pledged to buy. Failure to comply meant public shaming and the risk of more drastic discrimination, including the loss of entitlement to rations.[107] Saving was first and foremost regarded as a patriotic duty, but a state survey of motives organized in 1944 found that 57 per cent of respondents chose untimely needs as their motive, and 38 per cent a nest-egg for their children.[108]

Bond drives were central to the fundraising strategy in the United States. The bond campaigns were less coercive than in Japan or the Soviet Union, but the pressure to subscribe was widespread and relentless and resulted in a remarkable haul of $40 billion towards the cost of the war. As in Japan, there were schemes to deduct voluntary bond contributions from pay packets and around half of all bond sales were indirect. The rest was collected in small denominations – typically less than $100 – which meant that by the end of the war a remarkable 997 million bonds had been marketed. The bond drives were run as commercial projects. The object, as Treasury Secretary Henry Morgenthau put it, was 'to use *bonds* to sell the *war*, rather than vice versa'.[109] Modern advertising techniques were used, film stars recruited – including Bing Crosby who sang 'Buy a Bond' – and 6 million volunteers enlisted to visit households, factories and clubs. Like the Japanese neighbourhood associations, participation in many cases was only semi-voluntary. Here too, opinion polls found that patriotism played some part in the bond-buying, but up to two-thirds of respondents simply wanted to help buy the equipment needed at the front by husbands and sons overseas. The eight national bond campaigns helped to establish a direct link between a population distant from the battlefield and those doing the fighting.[110]

A further step in closing the inflationary gap came with a package of controls over prices, wages and consumer production, made necessary by the severe shortage of goods for consumers to buy. The controls over prices and wages were closely linked, since unregulated price inflation would, as in the Great War, drive down the value of wages and stimulate worker protest. Germany entered the war with a regime of price and wage controls that had already been in place for some years, to cope with the effects of high pre-war military spending. The Price Commissioner, appointed in 1936, had extensive powers to compel price stability across all areas of civilian spending and over the course of the war the cost-of-living index rose by less than 10 per cent, while average weekly earnings, boosted by longer hours at work, rose by just over 10 per cent.[111] Although the quality of many goods declined and long hours at work took a toll of the workforce, the effort to avoid inflation marked the German system as a model of stability compared with the inflationary spiral of the previous conflict. Japan also entered the world war with price and wage controls already in place in response to the war in China. Prices of food and textiles were controlled from 1937 onwards, and wages from April 1939. The price level nevertheless continued upwards in defiance of the regulations as the military and consumers competed for the same products. The government responded in September 1939 by issuing a general Price Freezing Ordinance, which covered not only most consumer products but also rents, fees, freight costs and wages, all of which were pegged at the level reached the day before the Ordinance came into force. By 1943 there were price controls on a remarkable 785,000 separate items, imposed by the main ministries and the local authorities. The new system stabilized the price index until 1943, but widespread shortages of even basic commodities, made worse by an extensive black market, fuelled growing inflation in the last months of the war which the Central Price Control Committee, set up in November 1943, proved unable to stem.[112] Despite a wage spiral encouraged by illicit competition between businesses for scarce labour resources, real wages by 1944 were down by a third from pre-war levels, and the following year down by half.[113] In China, where inflation ran out of control, average real wages by 1945 were down by almost two-thirds from before the war, forcing many workers below the subsistence level.[114]

For Britain and the United States, the war forced the abandonment of a free market in price and wage formation. Unlike in the authoritarian regimes, the introduction of state regulation had to take account of business interests and organized labour. In the first year of warfare the absence of effective control across the whole range of prices and wages stimulated the early signs of dangerous price inflation. By the end of 1940, the British cost-of-living index was almost a third higher than the year before, provoking demands for wage increases to compensate and inviting just the kind of crisis that Keynes, and others, had predicted. Despite the willingness of the trade unions to accept both wage restraint and the judgments of a new National Arbitration Tribunal set up in July, over the course of 1940 some 821,000 workers went on strike, the peak for the war years. The government priority, as the Ministry of Labour put it, was to find ways to ensure that 'the general body of the workers shall be contented', and over the course of the war years wage rates climbed faster than the cost of living. With longer hours, overtime payments and bonuses, average weekly earnings rose by almost 40 per cent, while the cost of living fo civilian households rose by a third. Price regulation was introduced pi meal: in August 1940 the government agreed to food subsidies to ke cost of all basic foodstuffs stable; in the 1941 budget, rents and fu were pegged; producers for the civilian market were enco concentrate and rationalize production to keep down costs. In July 1941 the government finally introduced the Goods and Services (Price Control) Act, which gave the state wide controls over maximum prices and maximum profit margins.[115] In all cases, both business and labour were involved in the decision-making to try to avoid any impression that state controls were imposed arbitrarily; the inflationary threat was tackled collectively, in a way, as Keynes put it, 'which satisfies the sense of popular justice'.[116]

Distrust of state power in the economy was much more embedded in the United States among the business community and among the wider public than it was in Europe, as the conflicts over the anti-Depression New Deal in the 1930s had made evident. Yet the Roosevelt administration had no choice but to find ways to control prices and wages in a context where the armed forces took around half of the goods usually designated for the civilian consumer. American rearmament from 1939 had already pushed up prices, but the government's initial response was simply to encourage business to limit price rises through voluntary restraint. Accelerated military spending in 1941 broke down whatever restraint might have existed. Despite insistence that strategic materials (steel, rubber, oil) should be subject to price controls, the government saw the consumer price index leap 12 per cent in one year, and wholesale prices by 17 per cent. Once at war, the administration recognized the need for urgent action. In April 1942, the Office of Price Administration introduced the General Maximum Price Regulation for all goods. 'General Max', as it was soon dubbed, forced firms to fix prices to an agreed base date, but since business was left to make the price calculation, there was plenty of room for creative capitalist accounting. Inflation continued into 1942, provoking a wave of labour unrest because the unions had agreed to wage restraint and a no-strike agreement. In April 1943, Roosevelt finally forced business and the unions to accept a wartime freeze on all prices and wages, to be enforced by a new Office of Economic Stabilization. 'Hold-the-line', as Roosevelt put it, worked well enough, partly because the price-fixing officials now relied on 6,000 local rationing boards to report violations, which were routinely penalized. Federal administrators determined the price of goods, abandoning what was left of the free market. In the last three years of war the consumer price index grew at the rate of only 1.4 per cent a year, lower than the rate recorded anywhere else among the warring states.[117]

These economic strategies were targeted at civilian populations that th ave to bear the brunt of the increase in military consumption and Un cline in the availability of civilian goods of all kinds. Only in the ible and Canada, with extensive economic resources, was it possible   bstantial increases in both guns and butter. Between 1939 and 1944 consumption of food in America increased by 8 per cent, but clothing and footwear increased 23 per cent, household goods (other than durables) by 26 per cent, and tobacco and alcohol by 33 per cent. By comparison, British food purchases were 11 per cent lower, clothing and footwear down by 34 per cent, and household goods by more than half.[118] Although there are conflicting estimates of the increase in personal consumption in the United States, they all indicate a significant increase over the war years compared with 1939, the peak year in the 1930s after the Depression. The official figures suggest that real spending per head of the population (excluding troops overseas and adjusted for price increases) was $512 in 1939 and $660 in 1945.[119] These figures are all the more significant because production of the major durable products, and in particular motor vehicles, was reduced to a trickle during the war. Americans instead spent more on clothes, shoes, drink and cigarettes, when they were not buying war bonds.

In all the other major warring states, personal consumption was cut back substantially in order to divert resources to the military effort. Like increased taxation and war bond campaigns, cuts in consumption were presented as an inevitable consequence of mobilization for war and seem generally to have been accepted as such by the civilian population. Limiting physical consumption, rather than soaking up surplus income, could be achieved in a number of ways: rationing consumer goods, particularly food and clothing; closing down inessential civilian production or converting it to war work; reducing quality through adulteration or standardization; or starving the manufacturers of consumer goods of materials and labour. In Britain and Germany, household items were produced to a standard cheap design – 'Utility' products for the British market, *Einheitsprodukte* (standard goods) for the German market – reducing choice but maintaining a minimum supply. British aggregate consumer spending fell from an index figure of 100 in 1938 to 86 in 1944, but the fall in consumption of non-food items fell faster: clothing down from 100 to 61, household goods from 100 to 73, and furnishings from 100 to 25.[120]

Contrary to a view still widely prevalent today, that the German people were not subjected to the economic demands of war until much later in the conflict, German civilian consumption was cut back even more extensively and systematically than in Britain from the very start of the war. From autumn 1939, all goods were either rationed or their output restricted or prohibited. Consumer spending per head was already declining before the war and fell rapidly in the first war years. Taking an index figure of 100 in 1938, price-adjusted consumption fell to 82 in 1941, and finally collapsed to 70 in 1944; if the poorer annexed areas of Greater Germany are included the figures are 74.4 and 67. The Hitler regime was determined to avoid any threat of social crisis, which was blamed for German defeat in 1918, but instead defined a 'minimum of existence' (*Existenzminimum*) for all civilians. This austere minimum was maintained through much of the wartime period, despite the heavy Allied bombing, but did not include any items of food or household goods deemed to be inessential. Life in Germany, observed an American journalist in 1941, was 'Spartan throughout', though bearable.[121] Civilians were expected, as they were in Britain, to 'make do and mend' by repairing old clothes, shoes and household furnishings. Heavy bombing of German cities in 1943 and 1944 forced a revival in consumer production to cope with the loss of household goods, but many of the bombed out were compensated with goods taken from warehouses full of furniture, clothes and shoes expropriated from deported and murdered Jews.

For the wartime consumer in Japan and the Soviet Union the story was entirely different. These were states with a relatively low standard of living where the demands of total war ate up a high proportion of the resources needed for the civilian population. In Japan, civilian supply had a low priority and had fallen steadily since the mid-1930s. Government propaganda stressed the need for an austere and thrifty lifestyle; in 1940, following new regulations restricting consumer production, the slogan 'Luxury is the enemy' became a standard trope in wartime culture.[122] Apart from the supply of food, civilian producers were either closed down or their resources transferred to war production. A Daily Necessities Plan drawn up in April 1943 focused on food, household fuel and textiles, but the same year the textile industry was allocated entirely for military production. The government aim was to reduce civilian consumption by one-third, but production of consumer goods fell dramatically the more the regime insisted on absolute priority for the failing war effort. By 1944 it was down to half the pre-war level and by the end of the war it was around one-fifth.[123] In the Soviet Union civilian supplies also took second place to war industry, falling to around a third of pre-war levels. Retail trade at constant prices fell from 406 billion roubles in 1940 to a wartime low of 147 billion in 1943; estimates of average household consumption, already very low by European standards, suggest a fall to 60 per cent of the pre-war figure by 1943. The problem for most consumers was the government decision to allow differential price levels. Rationed food and war goods were controlled, but all other goods were subject to the pressure of demand and experienced a rapid inflation. Wages failed to keep pace, leaving most Russian consumers much worse off than the official figures suggest.[124] All accounts of wartime life in the Soviet Union highlight the desperate poverty of the civilian population, but unlike the home front crisis that overwhelmed the tsarist state twenty years before, just enough food and fuel (and state terror) was available to prevent social collapse.

The Japanese and Soviet examples show, above all, the central importance of food as the key to sustaining work and war-willingness among the civilian population. Governments everywhere would have echoed Churchill's insistence that 'Nothing must interfere with the supplies necessary to maintain the stamina and resolution of the people of this country.'[125] Control over agricultural output and the survival of trade in food were critical explanations for the wider success of the mobilization effort. Only in the United States and the British Dominions, all of them food surplus zones, was the problem of feeding the population less urgent, though high military demands and extensive food exports forced even surplus areas to introduce limited rationing and controls over food supply. In the United States most of the population ate as well, if not better, during the war than before it. Average calories consumed per day actually rose from the level of the 1930s: 3,260 per head in 1938 to a wartime peak of 3,360 in 1943.[126] Although meat, coffee, sugar and dairy products were eventually subject to rationing, the rations were generous by international standards. Annual meat consumption per head rose from 143 pounds (65 kilos) to 154 pounds (70 kilos) by 1944, pushing the protein content of the American diet to record levels, though the official figures understated black market meat consumption in so-called 'meateasies', outlets supplied by farmers and abattoirs outside the system of state control.[127] More important for the Allied war effort was the willingness of the United States, through the Lend-Lease programme, to supply large quantities of food and fodder at no cost; for the Soviet war effort the 4.4 million tons of food did not solve the Soviet food problem, but for hungry soldiers and civilians it was an important margin for survival.[128]

In the food deficit areas, which included the Soviet Union after the loss of three-fifths of the Soviet cultivated area and two-thirds of grain supply in 1941–2, all governments tried to maintain adequate calorie intake, particularly for industrial workers and miners, and to ensure through rationing an equitable distribution of a shrinking quantity of foodstuffs. The rationing shares were never equal – German miners and steelworkers got 4,200 calories per day, the 'normal' consumer only 2,400 – and as the war continued it proved difficult in the Soviet Union, Japan and Germany to guarantee even the ration entitlement, but food supply broke down completely only in Japan in the last months of the war. Once the armed forces had taken their share, there was no question of being able to maintain pre-war food standards. All governments opted for an increase in high-calorie foods rather than proteins, fats and fresh produce, which meant for most urban consumers a monotonous and starchy diet with declining vitamin content. This was enough to survive on, though it served to undermine long-term health. The key staple for northern Europe was the potato, for Italy wheat, and for Japan and China, rice. Potatoes were easily grown, even on marginal soils, and nutritious. In Britain output increased by more than 50 per cent between 1940 and 1944; in Germany consumption increased 90 per cent against the pre-war level.[129] In the Soviet Union output by 1944 was 134 per cent higher than before the war, since for many Russians, even those working on collective farms, this was the only form of nourishment. In April 1942 the Soviet president, Mikhail Kalinin, even issued a national appeal on the potato: 'If you wish to take part in the victory over the German fascist invaders, then you must plant as many potatoes as possible.'[130]

Other staples proved difficult to maintain. In Italy, where maize and wheat were critical ingredients of the diet, agricultural production fell steadily from pre-war levels, made worse by the need to export foodstuffs to secure the oil and raw materials needed for the war effort; net output was down by a quarter by 1943, reducing the calorie content of rationed food to a paltry 990, though most food was produced and consumed outside the ration regime at rapidly inflated prices.[131] Rice proved the most challenging product not only for Japanese consumers, but throughout the area affected by the Asian war. Urban consumers in Japan had a daily ration of 330 grammes from April 1941, which provided a basic 1,158 calories, supplemented by small rations of other foods. Rice supply from the empire collapsed in 1944–5 as a result of the American sea blockade, reducing food consumption by almost a quarter from pre-war levels, by which time daily calorie intake for urban consumers had fallen to between 1,600–1,900 a day, insufficient to sustain the long hours of work.[132]

Agriculture in the food deficit regions faced many common problems. The male workforce was recruited in large numbers for the armed forces; agricultural machinery and equipment was worn out, and in many cases could not be replaced; chemical fertilizers competed with explosives for the same ingredients; draft animals and tractors were requisitioned by the army. In Germany, the supply of artificial fertilizers was halved during the war years, iron quotas for agricultural equipment fell from 728,000 tons to 331,000 between 1941 and 1944, and some 45 per cent of the male workforce was recruited in the first years of mobilization, leaving women to run many of the farms. By 1945, 65.5 per cent of the native German workforce in agriculture was female, assisted by large numbers of foreign workers and prisoners of war.[133] In the Soviet Union, machinery disappeared from the collective farms, fertilizers were low priority, and the male workforce shrank to a fraction. By 1944, four-fifths of the rural workforce were female; teams of women strapped themselves together to pull ploughs that should have been drawn by animals.[134] The exception was the British experience. Before the war Britain relied for 70 per cent of its supply on food from overseas. Shortage of shipping space and the German submarine campaign forced the government to introduce a programme to expand domestic output rapidly, and to do so meant investing in machinery, equipment and fertilizers to help the transition. Tractor production increased by 48 per cent, the output of threshing machines by 121 per cent, potato spinners by 381 per cent; draft animals were in general not requisitioned because the British Army was almost fully motorized. Domestic output of cereals increased from 4.2 million tons in 1939 to 7.4 million in 1944, bridging the gap sufficiently to avoid bread rationing throughout the war.[135] Agricultural modernization and policies to support enhanced nutrition, begun before the war, were sustained enough to ensure that the British population ate better than consumers in any of the other deficit areas.

Since food supply was so critical, ways were found – some legal, many not – to supplement the supply of rationed goods and increase the daily supply of calories for the home populations. The need for staple foods saw a decline in animal farming and an increase in the arable area. The results could be startling. In Britain the calorific value of farm produce almost doubled between the last peacetime years and 1944. In Japan, high-calorie crops were insisted on, and fifty different plant products were restricted or prohibited, including fruit, flowers and tea.[136] It was also possible to expand the area under cultivation by the simple remedy of encouraging the population, and the urban population in particular, to grow their own food. 'Victory Gardens' were widely promoted in the United States and 20 million of them planted (where record crops of tomatoes were recorded in 1943), while the British public was exhorted to 'dig for victory' by turning lawns and allotments over entirely to vegetables and fruit. By 1943 there were 1.5 million allotments in Britain, providing essential seasonal supplements to a dull diet. In Japan, food could be found growing alongside railway tracks or in school playgrounds.[137] Allotments proved to be the salvation of the Soviet workforce. A Kremlin decree in April 1942 allowed city workers to exploit uncultivated land and by 1944 there were 16.5 million allotments, where vegetables, fruit and even meat could be produced. A small army of 600,000 armed volunteers acted as guardians against pilfering by the hungry population.[138]

Where deficiencies could not be made good, there always remained adulterated and *ersatz* options. British white bread turned beige in 1942 when millers were ordered to extract more residue from the grain; Japanese white rice turned a brown colour for the same reason. Efforts in Japan

by the Substitute Food Section of the Ministry of Agriculture to develop a
'pulverized diet' by using dried acorns, vines, or mulberry leaves mixed
with flour largely failed, but in Germany *ersatz* products, from textiles to
coffee, were widespread, though hardly popular. Tea was made from wild
plants and berries, coffee chiefly from barley. Berliners quickly found
derogatory nicknames for the results: 'nigger sweat' for the coffee, 'cadaver
juice' for the adulterated milk powder they had to put in it. A pamphlet
titled 'Don't Waste' was circulated in Italy in 1941, introducing the population to recipes for 'fake fish' or 'fake meat' made from breadcrumbs,
'autarkic' desserts without sugar or eggs, and coffee without coffee.[139]

When all else failed, there were the temptations of the black market. In
reality most of the markets outside the controlled food and rationing sectors were more grey than black. In the Soviet Union the regime was content
for food outside the rations, grown chiefly on smallholdings, to be sold
without price controls. Non-rationed food rose in price more than tenfold,
out of the reach of most of the urban workforce. In Italy and Japan, with
a large rural population like the Soviet Union, authorities could turn a
blind eye to the foraging trips into the countryside, where the hungry town
populations traded what they could for extra food. In Japan children were
often sent, not only because they elicited more sympathy from farmers, but
because the police were less likely to punish them as they did other offenders. The Japanese black market operated from the 1930s onwards as food
scarcity developed. In 1938 the 'Economy Police' (*Keizai Keisatsu*) were
established to control evasion and price manipulation and in the first fifteen months they arrested 2 million people. Illicit trading became a part of
life if urban families wanted to survive, and in the end police curbs and
controls had little effect.[140] In China the secret police (*Juntong*) also took
on responsibility for pursuing hoarders, smugglers and black marketeers
who operated in an economic no man's land between the Chinese regime,
the local warlords and the Japanese occupiers. Here too the millions of
fines imposed did little to limit illegal trading.[141]

In societies where the rationing system worked more effectively and
controls were better organized, illicit trade was regarded as criminal and
dealt with accordingly. In Germany, a decree against economic crime was
published as early as 4 September 1939 and included any attempt to circumvent controls over the supply of food and the rationing regime. The
highest penalty was death, and a number of conspicuous cases were
treated as treason against the people and the culprits executed.[142] But here
too a grey area emerged in which small infractions could be carried out
between friends or with reliable shopkeepers, even though the risks were
always high. In Britain, where rationing covered a smaller range of

foodstuffs, the problem was to curb unofficial price hikes by local retailers which would fuel inflation. This proved difficult to enforce until a proper system of inspection was set up, but once this was in operation the number of prosecutions increased rapidly. Over the war years the Ministry of Food initiated no fewer than 114,488 cases for violation of market controls and illicit trading, but punishments involved no more than a fine or a brief spell in prison and violations continued to rise through the war years in the one European country at war where, paradoxically, food supply was more generous and wide-ranging.[143]

Official fears that failures in food supply would compromise the mobilization of the population for the war effort proved unfounded and there was no repeat of the revolutionary crises at the end of the First World War. But that did not mean that food was available to all on an equal basis. Political and business elites could eat well and did so conspicuously, as any onlooker at one of the Kremlin banquets or at dinner with Winston Churchill could see. Party bosses in Germany had access to sealed warehouses where tobacco, coffee and luxury foods were stored. Smart restaurants in Tokyo continued to serve Japan's wealthy while outside the wider population grew emaciated. There was also a marked contrast between the towns and the countryside, except in the Soviet Union, where collective farmers were allowed to keep only a fraction of their crop and had to forage for any extra food. Efforts were made to control the amount that rural 'self-suppliers' (the German term) could keep from their produce through a complex set of regulations that set quotas per head for bread, meat, butter, eggs and milk. In Japan, the rice market was government controlled, with quotas fixed for each farmstead as a way to limit the amount of produce consumed by the farm population.[144] Nevertheless, ways were found to circumvent the rules; when evacuees from bombing arrived in the German and Japanese countryside, they found a variety and quantity of foodstuffs long unavailable in the city and farmers willing to run the serious risks associated with illegal slaughtering and hoarding.

In the most vulnerable states, the urban consumer kept going on a severely impoverished diet. Post-war calculations in Italy suggested that anywhere between 7 and 13 million urban inhabitants had a food supply 'below the physiological minimum' by 1942-3; Soviet and Japanese rations in the middle years of the war were insufficient to maintain a normal physical state.[145] Starvation was kept at bay in the Soviet Union and Japan, and only just in the latter case, but in both countries, workers laboured away on a diet that meant continual hunger and declining health. Ration quotas here defined entitlement but did not mean that the food would actually be available. In some cases, officials siphoned off for their own use food allocated to hungry factory workers.[146] Soviet citizens who did not work had no entitlement at all and an unknown number died of hunger during the war. How workers kept going on a meagre diet, working often in cold and insanitary conditions for ten to fourteen hours a day, is difficult to explain. In both countries, workers were observed to die of malnutrition and overwork next to the machines they were operating, a consequence of the severe social pressure to support the collective, backed up by a strictly coercive state.

The situation improved for Soviet workers as territory was recaptured from the Germans, but by 1945 the Japanese urban population faced starvation. Japanese rice imports from the empire fell to just 236,000 tons in 1944/5, from 2.3 million tons in 1941/2, and home production from 10 million tons to 5.8 million in the last year of war.[147] Imports were hit by the American submarine and air blockade which, by 1945, had destroyed four-fifths of the Japanese merchant fleet; bombing sent a flow of 8 million refugees into the countryside and disrupted the harvest cycle and food distribution. By the summer months average per capita consumption was down to 1,600 calories a day, but the average concealed wide differences. The crisis prompted fears among the conservative elites in Japan that the food shortage might trigger social upheaval, even a communist revolution as in tsarist Russia. Emperor Hirohito was warned by his personal adviser, Kido Kōichi, in June 1945 that the food crisis might well mean that 'the situation will be beyond salvation'. Despite widespread social dislocation caused by conventional and atomic bombing, no revolutionary crisis materialized, but Hirohito's final decision for surrender taken on 10 August was prompted, at least in part, by the desire to avert the social consequences of a famine disaster that might destroy the Japanese empire from within before the military conflict was over.[148]

Famine was the ultimate consequence of wartime disruption in both Europe and Asia. Although in some cases nature played a part, the largest famines were chiefly man-made. In occupied Greece, the German armed forces were supposed to live off the land, which meant from April 1941 seizing all food stocks and the pack animals to carry them. German requisitioning was ruthless and in complete disregard for the needs of the Greek urban population. Efforts by the Greek puppet government to organize rationing broke down on the resistance of the 1.3 million peasant smallholders to providing grain at fixed prices when it could be hoarded and sold on the black market.[149] Less than a quarter of the food needed in the main urban area of Athens–Piraeus was available by the autumn of 1941. Bread rations, which could be supplied only irregularly, were cut from 300 grammes a day to 100; soup kitchens supplied by the Red Cross and other charities fed only 150,000 from a hungry population of more than a million.[150] In September, as famine loomed, the German occupiers refused to assist on the ground that this was an Italian conquest, for which Italy should take responsibility. Some food was shipped from Italy, but never enough to cope with the crises of supply and transport. Food from neutral countries was kept out by the British naval blockade. In Athens the death rate over the winter of 1941-2 rose more than sixfold as the most vulnerable died of hunger or of diseases to which they no longer had resistance. Only in February 1942 did the British government, under strong popular pressure, agree to relax the blockade, but not until June was a Swedish–Swiss Relief Commission established to organize the distribution of food sent through the blockade and only in the autumn were significant amounts of food finally available. By August 1942, 883,000 Athenians were fed at soup kitchens, some 80 per cent of the population.[151] Food deficit remained in place throughout the period of occupation, but famine receded over the course of 1942 and into 1943. The Red Cross calculated that at least 250,000 died of the direct or indirect consequences of starvation and malnutrition between 1941 and 1944.

In Asia, three major famines caused a wartime death toll estimated at more than 7 million people. Two occurred in areas still under Allied control, in Bengal in north-east India, and in Honan (Henan) province in Nationalist China; the third hit the Tonkin area of French Indochina, under Japanese occupation. The famines owed something to climate – frost, cyclones, or drought – but the loss of foodstuffs from natural causes was not enough to cause mass starvation. In all three cases, the food deficit was the result of market distortion and uneven distribution caused by the war. Bengal was hit by the loss of rice supplies from Burma and, during the course of 1942, rice produced by small peasant farms was bought up by speculators and hoarded. The price rose from 9 rupees for a maund (37 kilos) of rice in November 1942 to 30 rupees the following May, beyond the reach of poorer landless labourers and of peasants who had sold their rice stocks early. The Indian government made the situation worse by buying up grain to feed the Calcutta workforce and allowing a free market in rice. When famine hit the region, the government failed to acknowledge the seriousness of the situation and shipping that might have taken rice from surplus areas had either been immobilized to prevent the Japanese from seizing the boats (around two-thirds of the 66,500 available) or was being used for the war effort.[152] Surpluses available in other provinces were not mobilized to help Bengal. The authorities took time to acknowledge that there was a problem: the British governor deplored the images of dead and dying in the Indian press and called for propaganda to counter the 'unhelpful tales of horror'. Not until October 1943 were measures finally taken to ration and distribute available rice, by which time an estimated 2.7–3 million Bengalis had died.[153]

In the north-central Chinese province of Honan, the loss of rice imports from Burma and Vietnam exacerbated a lower than usual harvest in 1942. Richer landlords and speculators hoarded grain bought up from poorer peasants, while the loss of plough-oxen and male labourers reduced local productivity. Neighbouring provinces refused to release grain surpluses and the Nationalist government provided little effective relief. Between October 1942 and spring 1943 some 2–3 million died, an estimated one-third of the population. Much the same pattern occurred in Indochina where Japanese requisitions, after an agreement signed with the local Vichy French authorities in August 1942, took a million tons of the best rice each year. The colonial state imposed a grain levy on the millions of small producers, while price inflation encouraged the richer merchants to hoard. In Tonkin, the population faced famine or near-famine conditions from late 1943 until the summer of 1945, by which time one-fifth of the people were dead.[154] In all four cases of major famine, the food deficit was artificially created by military seizures, the greed of middlemen and the incompetence or indifference of the authorities.

MANPOWER AND WOMANPOWER

Beyond finance and food, mass mobilization for total war meant mass mobilization of the entire able-bodied civilian workforce. This phenomenon lay at the heart of pre-war definitions of total war: all human resources were to serve the single goal of achieving victory. This was an extraordinary claim, rooted once again in perception of the successes and failures of the Great War, but it was not just a rhetorical flourish. All warring governments sought to mobilize the entire working population with a common sense of purpose, and when the labour resources proved insufficient, as they did almost everywhere, they searched for ways to mobilize new sources of labour at the margins of the employable population. Workers fought on a different front line from the military, but they were defined in similar terms. American propaganda called on workers to see themselves as 'soldiers of production' alongside the GI overseas. Soviet labour law really did define workers as soldiers. A decree of 26 December 1941 established absence from work as 'desertion', punishable with up to eight years in a prison camp. Although German workers were not militarized in any formal sense, the introduction of harsh Gestapo-run 'Work

Education Camps' (*Arbeitserziehungslager*) was to remind the population 'that in war each has to contribute the utmost of their labour' or
suffer the consequences.[155]

There was no alternative but for the state and its agencies to organize
the mobilization and distribution of the workforce. So important was
labour strategy deemed to be that agencies for labour allocation enjoyed
virtually absolute powers. They were in most cases independent of the rest
of the structure for controlling the war economy so integrating labour
allocation with production programmes was seldom a straightforward
process. In some cases, the regime for labour allocation was itself divided.
The National War Labor Board in the United States had to reconcile policy with the War Manpower Commission (two out of a remarkable 112
new agencies created for the American war effort). In Germany, the Ministry of Labour had to compete with two agencies run by Party bosses, the
German Labour Front under Robert Ley, and the office of the Plenipotentiary for Labour Allocation under Fritz Sauckel, set up in 1942 to increase
the conscription of foreign labour. In both cases, the lack of a unified
labour programme undermined the drive to maximize production.

In Britain, labour policy was more centralized. Labour allocation (soon
to be changed to conscription) was covered by the National Labour
Conscription Ordinance in April 1939 and the People's Mobilization
Ordinance published three months later, which between them established
a nationwide labour programme for the war effort. Following the appointment of the trade union leader Ernest Bevin as minister of labour in
Churchill's 1940 Cabinet, the National Service Act was used to allocate
labour where it was needed, giving Bevin a degree of executive power, as
he admitted to his Cabinet colleagues, 'which had no precedent in the
country'.[156] The introduction of a national Register of Employment gave
Bevin an overview of the whole manpower structure, simplifying the
redistribution of labour resources as the war progressed. No such power
was possible in the United States, with a strong tradition of resistance to
state control. A frustrated Roosevelt finally tried to introduce a National
Service Bill into Congress in January 1944 to resolve shortages of labour,
but it was widely resisted, and in the end failed on a Senate vote in April.
One journalist hailed the vote as a decision 'that the country should not
go under a dictatorship'. Nevertheless, there were programmes of labour
allocation to encourage movement into wartime employment. The American War Manpower Commission allocated workers to no fewer than 35
million different placements, but as volunteers, not conscripts.[157]

The employment structures of the warring states differed chiefly in the
degree of labour concentrated in agriculture, which was high in Japan,

Italy and the Soviet Union, and very low in Britain, where industry and services made up the bulk of the workforce. For the more heavily industrialized and urbanized economies, the central issue was to redirect labour within industry from civilian production to war-related contracts rather than absorbing labour from outside industry. In Germany, the percentage of the industrial workforce producing directly for the war effort increased from 22 per cent in 1939 to 61 per cent by 1943, in manufacturing from 28 per cent to 72 per cent; in Britain, the less essential industrial sectors lost 40 per cent of their labour, while by 1943 one-third of the industrial workforce was concentrated in the direct production of weapons.[158] Where there existed a large agricultural sector, rural labour was recruited and, if necessary, retrained for industry. Japanese labour conscription drew 1.9 million workers from agriculture into armaments during the war; in the Soviet Union almost half a million youths were moved from the countryside to labour reserve schools in 1941, where they learned skills needed in the key wartime industries; in Italy, the shortage of engineering workers saw wartime training programmes drawing in men from the countryside and craft trades.[159] In the United States, farm labour declined by almost 1 million between 1940 and 1945, but the so-called Group I industries (which included most armaments production) expanded from 5.3 million in 1940 to 11 million three years later, absorbing not only farm workers but those in consumer or white-collar sectors. Economies also differed in the degree of unemployed or underemployed human resources available. Germany faced completely full employment by 1939, even before the outbreak of war; the Soviet Union also claimed to have no unemployed resources, which is why young girls found themselves working ten-hour days in grim conditions. In Britain on the other hand there were still 1 million unemployed in the summer of 1940; in the United States over 8 million, with millions more on short hours. By the end of the war, American unemployment was negligible – 670,000 alongside an employed population of 65 million – while in Britain unemployment in 1944 averaged just 0.6 per cent of the workforce.[160]

Whatever the differences in the structure of the labour force, the one common feature for all the combatant economies as the war went on was a shortage of workers. The claims of the armed forces and the need to keep at least a minimum of supplies for the rest of the population circumscribed the size of the workforce available to supply the armaments, equipment and materials for the war effort. Urgent shortages, for skilled workers in particular, became evident within the first months of war. The problem was made worse because the demand for labour encouraged workers to move where wages were higher or conditions better, and despite efforts to control labour mobility by tying workers to their current jobs, employers or plant managers colluded with workers who arrived without proper paperwork because they needed the extra labour urgently. In the Soviet Union reported cases of 'desertion' from work, despite the harsh penalties, reached 1.88 million during the war years, but many absentees found a new job somewhere else, continuing to contribute to the war effort.[161] 'Desertion' from work was also widespread in Japan, as major employers found ways to induce labourers to risk the unauthorized transfer to a new job and forged the necessary paperwork. Black market wages (*yamich-ingin*) were paid in defiance of the efforts of the Welfare Ministry both to peg wages and to control the movement of workers through a National Workbook System, introduced in October 1941, and the Labour Turnover Control Ordinance four months later.[162] In the United States, where workers were not threatened with legal sanctions or the labour camp, it proved difficult to enforce the wartime agreement with the unions that jobs would not be changed without approval. Some 25 million Americans moved across county and state boundaries in search of better work, including a million black Americans from the south searching for opportunities in the industrial cities of the north. In this last case, prejudice followed the black migrants; only 3 per cent of employees in armament firms were black because employers claimed they lacked sufficient technical skills.[163]

There were many ways in which these shortages could be tackled. The simplest was to extend working hours and introduce additional shifts. Ten- to twelve-hour shifts for men and women of all ages became for many workers the wartime norm, day and night. In Japan and the Soviet Union workers were supposed to work seven days a week with no holidays, a requirement that left many of them regularly debilitated by exhaustion and illness. The reallocation of workers in the so-called 'combing out' of labour from inessential occupations in the consumer, artisan or service sectors yielded both conscripts for the forces and additional workers for war industry. The British 'Concentration of Production' programme, begun in March 1941, gave the government the power to close down businesses in twenty-nine industrial branches and reallocate their resources to a nucleus of the largest and most efficient firms in each sector.[164] German 'combing out' operations went on throughout the war but the largest transfers of labour occurred in the first two years. In the large craft sector in Germany, 40 per cent of the workforce had been transferred to war work by 1942, many of them older skilled workers; male employment in the consumer industries fell by more than half a million by the summer of 1940 as men left for the services or war industry.[165]

Much could also be achieved by the 'rationalization' of production.

More efficient plant layout, more extensive use of specialized machine tools, and economies of scale from using larger factories laid out for conveyor-belt production were among many ways to reduce labour input and so increase output per worker. In Britain and Germany, state inspectors toured from factory to factory, noting poor practice and compelling firms to adopt methods used by the star firms in each sector. Efficiency gains were substantial in the defence industries, many of them prompted by suggestions from the factory workforce. In Germany, 3,000 firms had suggestion systems in place by 1941, 35,000 by 1943. Workers could be rewarded with bonuses or extra rations for suggestions that worked.[166] The production of Halifax bombers at the English Electric Company required 487 workers for every aircraft delivered in April 1942, but a year later needed only 220. When conveyor-belt production was introduced for manufacture of the German Panzer III tank in 1943, man-hours per vehicle declined from 4,000 to 2,000; rationalization of the output of German aero-engines saw the number of man-hours per engine at BMW fall from 3,260 in 1940 to 1,250 in 1943.[167] The result was a significant gain in productivity (measured by output per head) in the industries working for the war effort. In the Soviet Union, where mass-production methods were widely adopted to cope with wartime demands, the value added per worker in the defence sector was 6,019 roubles in 1940 and 18,135 in 1944. These figures were replicated across all the war economies, while productivity in agriculture and the consumer industries generally stagnated or declined as untrained workers replaced the mobilized men.[168]

The mobilization of women was of primary importance in coping with the loss of men to the armed forces and the high demands for wartime industrial and agricultural labour. Just as women volunteered to join the military services, so women on the home front understood that they were an integral part of any total-war effort rather than mere wartime substitutes for the missing men, though that is the impression often given in wartime accounts of female recruitment. Women as workers, or voters, or party members, or welfare volunteers were part of the fabric of pre-war society as much as men. Women made up a sizeable proportion of the pre-war workforce everywhere, lower in Britain and the United States (approximately 26 per cent at the start of the war), higher in Germany and Japan (37 per cent and 39 per cent respectively), and highest in the Soviet Union at 40 per cent. The war years saw considerable expansion of female employment in both the democracies, but elsewhere there was much less slack to take up and women were either redeployed from civilian production to war work or simply continued to run shops, offices or farms on their own, without the help of men. The chief influence on the differing scale of female employment in industry lay once again in the nature of the agricultural sector. In the Soviet Union, Japan and Germany, rural labour was somewhere between a third and a half of the working population and a large slice of the rural workforce was female. The ratio of women to men increased as the war continued: in the Soviet Union half the collective farm workforce was female in 1941, 80 per cent in 1945; in Japan, women made up 52 per cent in 1940, 58 per cent in 1944; German women constituted 54.5 per cent of the native rural workforce in 1939, 65.5 per cent by 1944.[169] These women were indispensable to the war effort because of the high priority placed on food supply and as a result there was no question of redeploying them to industry. In the context of total war, female farm workers were as much a part of the production front line as women in industry.

In Britain and the United States, the mobilization of women repre-sented a substantial net gain as millions of women, and married women in particular, chose to take up employment. In America the female work-force expanded by 5.2 million between 1940 and 1944 and of this number 3.4 million were married, mostly with older children, and 832,000 were single.[170] Impressive though the expansion was on paper, the great major-ity of American women remained at home, many of them doing volunteer work with the Red Cross, or collecting bond contributions, or helping with childcare. During the war 2 million actually left full-time employ-ment, while many women chose to move in and out of work when it suited them; only one-fifth of the female workforce worked in manufac-turing. Most of the women who made up for the missing men took jobs in offices, banks, shops and the federal bureaucracy.[171] The American gov-ernment rejected any idea of conscripting women. The initial reaction to the flood of women seeking war work was as half-hearted as it was for the military. Only gradually, as defence firms from necessity began to recruit and train women, did male managers overcome their prejudice.

Women were soon found to be more reliable workers – conscientious, organized, dexterous, patient – than many men and were recruited into war work in increasing numbers from 1942. 'To hell with the men,' one aviation industry director told a journalist, 'give me the women.'[172] By this stage women made up more than half the workforce in some of the large new aircraft plants in California, where mass production processes were adapted to cater for less skilled female workers and to reduce the physical strain of the work.[173] Much the same pattern developed in Britain, where recruiting additional female workers netted only 320,000 in the first year of war as employers in war plants hesitated to take on women who would have to be trained to work alongside men, while in many cases male workers resented the so-called 'dilution' of the labour force. Female employment rose from 6.2 million in 1939 to 7.7 million in 1943, but as in the United States, many women new to working preferred to replace men in white-collar occupations. To cope with wartime demands a limited conscription was introduced in 1942 and 1943: first, young single women and childless widows, then in 1943 childless wives. Most of the female factory workforce was found by redeploying women who were already working in civilian industry into factories producing military equipment.[174]

Redeployment was also characteristic of the German and Soviet economies where the proportion of working women was already very high, indeed higher at the start of the war than the level eventually reached in the democracies (see Table 4.3). The participation ratio (i.e., those in employment) of women aged fifteen to sixty in Germany was already 52 per cent in 1939, but in the United States the wartime peak was 36 per cent, while in Britain it was 45 per cent.

Table 4.3 The Proportion of Women in the Native Workforce 1939–44 (%)

Country	1939	1940	1941	1942	1943	1944
Britain	26.4	29.8	33.2	36.1	37.7	37.9
United States	-	25.8	26.6	28.8	34.2	35.7
Soviet Union: I	-	38.0	-	53.0	57.0	55.0
Soviet Union: II	-	-	52.0	62.0	73.0	78.0
Germany	37.3	41.4	42.6	46.0	48.8	51.0
Japan	-	37.8	-	42.0	-	-

(Soviet figures: I = all public sector employment; II = collective farm labour.)

In the Soviet Union female participation in all branches of the workforce was exceptional by international standards: 41 per cent of the industrial workforce in 1940, 53 per cent in 1943; 21 per cent of transport workers before the war, 40 per cent by 1943; and so on. In both Germany and the Soviet Union, most additional female war workers were found by transfers from civilian to defence contracts as factories were converted or inessential businesses closed down, rather than from net additions. Women were subject to labour conscription in the Soviet Union and those not working were too old or ill or burdened by childcare.

In Germany, the regime toyed with the idea of conscripting the whole female population but in the end relied on recruiting young single women, who were given no real option but to work, and encouraging married women with children to do half-shifts of six or seven hours, an option taken up by 3.5 million women by 1944 in addition to the 14.8 million already working. Millions of women undertook volunteer work in civil defence and first aid services or the Party welfare organization. Efforts to recruit more women than the 51 per cent in the native workforce finally achieved by 1944 were undermined by the Allied bombing campaign which sent millions of women and children to the countryside, removing mothers from the prospect of useful war work. By the time Japan was subjected to heavy bombing in 1945, women made up 42 per cent of the domestic workforce, chiefly in agriculture and commerce. Conscription for young women aged sixteen to twenty-five was introduced in 1941 and 1 million were mobilized; in September 1943 conscription was extended to girls of fourteen and fifteen, adding 3 million more. Women were even sent to work in mines, where female employment doubled over the war years.[175]

The recruitment of millions of women into work for the war effort did not end gender discrimination or encourage greater gender equality. Women seldom assumed supervisory or managerial roles or performed the most skilled work. Those working in white-collar occupations usually occupied low-paid clerical, secretarial or service jobs. The proportion of American women workers who were classified as craftsmen, foremen or skilled workers only increased from 2.1 to 4.4 per cent during the war. Women's average earnings in 1944 were $31 a week, male earnings $55, even when doing much the same work. In Britain, average wage rates for women were still only half those for men.[176] Conditions of work for women and girls were often beyond what many could endure for years, except for those like Elizaveta Kochergina and millions of other Soviet workers who were compelled to work continuously until they physically collapsed. Firms used to employing mainly men were often slow to provide rest rooms or medical facilities for women and expected them to cope with ten-hour shifts. When women showed higher than average absenteeism rates from exhaustion or illness or family problems, male prejudices were hardened against them. Many women faced pressures much greater than men as they coped with childcare, hunted for rationed goods, and completed household chores in the hours still left them between work and sleep. To help with these dual responsibilities, the state supplied day-care for children. By 1944 there were places for 1.2 million infants in German nurseries; in the United States over 30,000 day-care centres were set up, despite the reluctance of the government to see this as a state responsibility, though they attracted only 130,000 children. Media publicity highlighted a number of centres that were badly run by staff indifferent to the children's needs, with the result that some working mothers preferred to leave their young children on their own at home, sparking a nationwide debate about the plight of 'latchkey children' and the wave of juvenile delinquency that neglect was said to encourage.[177]

For the 'New Order' empires there remained one further resource to exploit. Workers could be recruited from conquered territories, by compulsion in most cases, to fill the gaps in the native workforce. Millions more worked for the occupiers in the occupied areas on construction sites, or building roads and railways, or in farms and factories. There were an estimated 20 million in Europe working to German orders and an unknown number in the case of Japan's new empire in Asia. Chinese workers were conscripted in large numbers to work for the Japanese war effort in Manchuria, Inner Mongolia, Korea and in the Japanese home islands. Between 1942 and 1945 some 2.6 million Chinese were taken as virtual slaves, working in poor conditions for no pay.[178] Workers in the Japanese colony of Korea fared better because of the high demand for local labour as industries were set up in the peninsula to serve Japanese war needs. Only 214,000 Koreans worked in industry, construction and transport in 1933, but by 1943 there were 1.75 million, including 400,000 in the manufacturing sector. Almost all Koreans were classified in the lowest grades for labour, but there were a growing number of Korean engineers and businessmen who profited from the demands of wartime production.[179] Other Koreans were less fortunate. The forced labour programme was also extended to the Japanese colonies and by the end of the war an estimated 2.4 million Koreans, one-quarter of the industrial workforce, worked in Japanese factories and mines in far less favourable conditions.[180]

The German war economy was much larger than the Japanese and the need for labour consequently more acute. Throughout the war the country relied on using non-German labour as an increasingly large fraction of the workforce. By the end of 1944 there were 8.2 million foreigners working in Germany and the annexed areas – so-called 'Greater Germany' – alongside a native workforce of 28 million. Over the course of the whole war, it has been estimated that between 13.5 and 14.6 million foreign workers, prisoners of war and labour camp prisoners contributed to the German manpower pool in the Reich itself, more than one-fifth of the civilian workforce by 1944.[181] The foreign workforce embraced a wide range of nationalities, organized in distinct categories to be treated by the Hitler regime in different ways. A small portion of the foreign workforce comprised volunteer labour. There were already 435,000 foreign workers in Germany by spring 1939 in response to the job opportunities and higher earnings generated by large-scale rearmament. Many came from neighbouring countries that would soon become conquered German territory within a year; a large fraction migrated from Germany's Italian ally, reaching a total of 271,000 by 1941.[182] After the conquest of the Netherlands and France in 1940, significant numbers of additional volunteers crossed the frontier to work in German firms: around 100,000 Dutch workers and 185,000 French. In the annexed areas taken from Poland in 1939, an estimated 3 million Poles worked for the Reich.[183] Much of this volunteer labour was voluntary in only a limited sense. Economic coercion occasioned by rising unemployment as output declined in the occupied countries pushed workers to take jobs in Germany. In Italy, Mussolini promised Hitler a flow of Italian migrant workers in return for German supplies of essential war materials. Local Fascist officials then encouraged, or pressured, Italian agricultural and factory workers into making the move. A wartime agreement between the two dictators compelled the Italian government to fund the wages sent back home to families left behind in Italy. The German economy not only got the labour but also avoided having to pay for it in full.[184]

The same held true for the exploitation of prisoner-of-war labour. The Geneva Convention of 1929, ratified by all the warring powers save the Soviet Union and Japan, restricted the use of prisoner labour to sectors not directly related to the war effort. These restrictions were observed more or less scrupulously by the Germans in the case of British and American prisoners. They also applied at first to the 300,000 Polish prisoners of war taken into the Reich in 1939 who were put to work on German farms, which was permitted under the Convention. Nine months later the German army captured 1.6 million French prisoners of war, one-third of them agricultural workers. More than a million were kept in Germany and half put to work, like the Poles, in German agriculture. As labour needs rose in industry, however, ways were found to get around the Geneva restrictions. Since the Polish state had in German eyes ceased to exist, it was argued that prisoners could be given civil status and used for tasks in defiance of the Convention. To avoid the limitations of international law in the French case, a special category was created in April 1943 of a 'transformed' prisoner. In return for every worker sent from France to the Reich under compulsion, a volunteer prisoner would be classified as a 'civilian worker' in Germany and thus qualify for industrial labour and a regular wage. By mid-1944 around 222,000 French prisoners had taken advantage of the agreement.[185]

The case was very different for prisoners taken in Eastern and Southern Europe. With Soviet prisoners of war there was no legal problem because the Soviet Union had not ratified the Geneva Convention. Most prisoners died or were killed in the first year of the German–Soviet war and only with reluctance did Hitler finally agree to use Soviet captives inside Greater Germany. The number remained small – by August 1944 there were 631,000 Soviet prisoners of war working in Germany – because many prisoners worked for the German armed forces and occupation authorities in the East. The Convention gave no protection either to the Italian soldiers taken prisoner by their former ally when Italy surrendered in September 1943. The 600,000 Italians deported to the Reich were classified as 'military internees' rather than prisoners of war, and so could be used for any kind of labour. Vilified by the German authorities and much of the German public as traitors to the Axis cause, Italian internees were poorly fed, badly housed, bullied and harassed at work. By the end of the war 45,600 had died in captivity.[186]

The shortages of labour by 1942 could not be satisfied by voluntary migration or by using prisoners of war. In the spring of 1942, the regime opted for compulsory labour service in the Reich from populations throughout the German-occupied area. The change was signalled in March 1942 by the appointment of the National Socialist gauleiter of Thuringia, Fritz Sauckel, to the post of Plenipotentiary for Labour Allocation. Forced labour had already been imposed on the Polish population and by the end of 1941 there were over 1 million Poles working in Germany, mostly in agriculture and mining.[187] Sauckel's responsibility was to find many more workers for the expanding armaments sector. In the East the strategy was easier to implement than in the Western occupied areas. In December 1941, a general obligation for labour service was introduced for all men aged fifteen to sixty-five and women aged fifteen to forty-five. There were some volunteers, and photographs of smiling Ukrainians and Belorussians boarding trains to Germany were used to encourage others to follow. Few did, and in spring 1942 compulsory labour was imposed in regular armed round-ups of young Soviet men and women, many carried out by local collaborators who were given quotas of the number of workers wanted by the German authorities and were free to use whatever methods were needed to deliver them. In the first year 1.48 million were shipped to Germany, but 300,000 were sent back because they were too old, or too ill, or pregnant. The round-ups persisted throughout the following years and by August 1944 there were 2.1 million Soviet workers in Germany, just over half of them women. They were all compelled to wear an armband with a prominent 'O' sewn on it to indicate *Ostarbeiter*, eastern worker.[188]

The recruitment of compulsory labour in Western and Southern Europe was more problematic because the existing states had not been eliminated by conquest. The conscription of French labour had to be negotiated with the government of Marshal Pétain based in the town of Vichy. In June 1942, Sauckel reached an agreement with the French prime minister, Pierre Laval, to supply 150,000 workers for German industry. Laval still hoped for a German victory and agreed to authorize the French labour authorities to begin compulsory registration and allocation of workers for two years of work in the Reich (the *relève*). It proved difficult to enforce, so in February 1943 the French state established the *Service du travail obligatoire* (STO), making all men aged between twenty and fifty liable for labour service for the Germans, either in France or in Germany. By 1944 some 4 million worked directly for the German occupation forces, while the four so-called 'Sauckel Actions' ('recruitment' drives) between 1942 and 1944 netted 728,000 men and women for transfer to Germany.[189] 'Actions' in the Netherlands and Belgium netted approximately half a million more. When Italy surrendered to the Allies, Sauckel travelled to Rome in September 1943 to demand a similar programme for the two-thirds of the peninsula now occupied by German forces. His aim was to extract 3.3 million additional Italian workers, but the end result was a negligible 66,000 to add to the Italian military internees and the 100,000 volunteer migrants who were stranded in Germany when Italy abandoned the fight.[190] By this time local populations understood what labour conscription meant. In Italy and France young men and women left their homes to join the resistance movements or found other ways of evading the draft. The poor returns from the later 'Actions', and the remorseless bombing of the home front, provoked a change in German policy. Contracts were now decentralized to the occupied areas so that fewer workers would have to be conscripted under coercion to work in the Reich.

Conditions varied for the different groups of foreign workers, but they were tough enough in the worst cases to produce a wartime mortality rate of 18 per cent of all those forced to work.[191] Those from Western Europe fared better, with levels of food rations comparable with German levels, at least until the widespread food shortages that developed in the last year of war. They were not slave workers, as is often implied, but were paid regular wages. After deductions of special taxes and the cost of feeding and housing, they were left on average around 32 marks a week, compared with a German worker on 43 marks. They also enjoyed the same welfare benefits in the event of illness or accident. They were subject to curfews and controls over which amenities and shops they could use, and subject to the same harsh regulations as German workers in cases of indiscipline or contract violation, though they could also end up in a concentration camp for persistent misconduct.

For Eastern workers, on the other hand, conditions were very different. They were generally housed in crude camp barracks near their place of work, had strict regulation of their movement, and after deductions for poor quality food and shelter were paid no more than 6 marks a week for a ten- to twelve-hour day. Though many would have found conditions substantially better than those they left behind in the Soviet Union, and the discipline little different, the productive performance of Eastern workers was at first well below that of German workers or workers from Western Europe. A survey of foreign workers carried out in 1942 found that French workers (most of them were still volunteers at this point) had a productivity record around 85–88 per cent of a German worker, the figure for Russians was only 68 per cent and for Poles 55 per cent.[192] It was soon realized that improving the food supply and raising wages would improve productive performance. Pay for Eastern workers increased to an average of 9.8 marks in 1942, and to 14 marks a week in 1943 for workers who achieved the norms. The most successful Eastern workers were women, who were soon allocated in large numbers to produce armaments and military equipment. Sauckel was keen to recruit Soviet women because, in his view, they displayed a healthy stamina when it came to industrial labour. 'They can hold out for ten hours,' he told an audience of German officials in January 1943, 'and can do every kind of man's work.' If they became pregnant once they had begun work, they were forced to have an abortion or to place the baby in a home, after which they were then brought straight back to the factory.[193] By 1944 their productivity was calculated at between 90 and 100 per cent of a German worker; Soviet male workers, chiefly in construction and mining, could achieve 80 per cent.

All the surveys showed that workers from Southern Europe could not be made to work so effectively, least of all the Greek forced labourers. Productivity levels remained anywhere between 30 and 70 per cent of German levels. Among prisoners of war put to work on building sites, British prisoners were among the worst, with less than half the productive level of a German worker.[194] In many of these cases, slow work and indiscipline reflected protest against the compulsion to work and the tough regime imposed on foreigners. Nevertheless, non-German labour was indispensable. To try to extract more from the foreign labour force, the German Labour Front got the Institute for Work Psychology to carry out aptitude tests on half a million of them to make sure they were allocated to tasks that suited their capabilities. The programme was even extended to debilitated concentration camp prisoners sent to work in industry, where they might survive little more than a few weeks.[195] All foreign workers could be disciplined more easily than German workers, particularly the high proportion of female workers. Average daily absenteeism at the Ford plant in Cologne in 1944 reached a peak of 25 per cent of German workers but averaged only 3 per cent among foreign workers.[196] By August 1944 foreign workers made up 46 per cent of the rural workforce, 34 per cent of all mineworkers and a quarter of all workers in industry.[197] In the armaments sector a third of the workforce was made up of foreign workers, forced to build military equipment for a state whose aggression had put them in that position in the first place.[198]

As the conscription of foreign workers tailed away in 1944 and resistance and evasion became more widespread, so the number of workers supplied from the system of concentration camps was expanded. In August 1942 there were 115,000 prisoners in the German camp system, but by August 1944 525,286 and by January 1945 714,211. Almost all the prisoners were non-German by this stage – a mix of resistance fighters, political opponents, recalcitrant foreign workers, and Jews who survived the deportations and mass murder of the extermination centres. In spring 1942, Heinrich Himmler's SS organization set up a Main Office of Economic Administration to exploit the labour resources available in the camps and the Jewish deportees more fully. Around one-fifth of the Jews deported to the killing camps were selected for labour, mainly young men and women. These prisoners *were* in effect slave workers, used as labour in SS enterprises or hired out in small numbers to hundreds of German firms who paid the Reich Treasury 6 marks a day for skilled camp workers, 4 marks for unskilled men and women.[199] By the end of the war there were thousands of camps across Germany, their columns of tired and emaciated labourers in striped uniforms, bludgeoned, bullied or murdered by their German guards, a familiar sight. Conditions were deliberately atrocious, though the object was to extract as much labour power as possible from the hapless prisoners, a cruel parody of total war.

On the bottom rung of the ladder stood the Jewish victims of labour mobilization. A programme of Jewish forced labour run by the German labour administration had been introduced as early as 1938. Jewish men were forced to register for compulsory labour and by summer 1939 there were 20,000 Jews working in segregated units, chiefly at construction sites in Germany; by 1941 there were 50,000 in a wide network of camps and sub-camps, some holding only a handful of workers at a time. The pattern was repeated in occupied Poland, where some 700,000 Jews worked in the forced-labour programme independent of the camp system run by the SS.[200] They were not yet prisoners, but in 1941 the SS took over the Jewish forced labour programme from the regular labour administration; the segregated work details were absorbed into the wider camp system alongside the Jews selected at the extermination camps for labour rather than immediate death. Labour shortages meant that around 400,000 Jewish forced labourers were still working in Greater Germany and occupied Poland even as late as the start of 1943. The conditions for Jewish labour were intentionally worse than for other prisoners or compulsory workers, though economic pressures meant that they were not usually worked to death at once. Death came slowly from malnutrition and disease as the last ounce of work was forced out of men and women deemed to be mortal enemies of the Reich. Exact figures for the number of deaths from all the different forms of forced and slave labour are difficult to calculate, but for workers in the SS camp system life expectancy was less than a year. Many of the estimated 2.7 million dead workers were from the camp system, a significant proportion of them Jews from all over Europe.[201] This level of mortality showed that total war had its irrational limits, as the regime wrestled with the conflict between its racist priorities and wartime economic necessity.

The Soviet exploitation of prisoner labour exposed the same paradox. In the national network of fifty-nine Gulag concentration camps, as well as the sixty-nine provincial camps and forced labour colonies first set up in the decade before the war, long days of labour were compulsory. During the war years, around two-thirds of the prisoners worked in industry, the rest in mining and forestry under debilitating and brutal conditions. Camp authorities were ordered to demonstrate that maximum labour was extracted and to minimize 'lost labour days', but during the war the shortage of food, workdays up to sixteen hours in length, and minimal healthcare meant that on average around a third of inmates were invalids or incapable of further work or dead.[202] Stalin himself regularly monitored the productive performance of the inmates to make sure they did not evade work for the war effort. Prisoners who failed to meet the norms they had been set were slowly starved of provisions while those who exceeded the work schedule were rewarded with time off and extra rations. Those who became too ill were released to make way for workers who still had some labour capacity to exploit. In April 1943, a government decree 'On Measures for Punishing German Fascist Villains, Spies, and Traitors to the Motherland and their Accomplices' established special hard-labour camps (*katorga*) where prisoners worked longer, in all temperatures, with no days off, on the most physically demanding sites. These prisoners, like Jews in the German slave-labour system, were literally worked to death, eking out what last labour they could supply for a Soviet war effort acutely short of workers. Between January 1941 and January 1946, 932,000 prisoners perished, testament to the fundamental inefficiency of a prison regime dedicated to extracting labour for total war.[203]

PROTEST AND SURVIVAL

Manpower and womanpower worked under very different conditions one country from another. In the United States and Britain (though not in the wider Empire), workers enjoyed reasonable wartime living standards, rising earnings and savings, improved conditions as the war continued and the right, if they chose it, to union representation. The German work-force (not including the prisoners and forced labourers) ate less well, had no union protection, and faced sharply deteriorating conditions once the city-bombing campaign began. The Soviet and Japanese workforces faced problems throughout the war of poor nutrition, long hours at work, tough supervision and rapidly declining living standards. In Cheliabinsk workers kept going through the biting cold with deficient heating, little sense of factory safety, and the constant threat of punishment. Girls could be seen working without shoes or boots, their feet blistered and festering from the cold and frostbite.

Across this broad spectrum of experience workers and consumers shared one important thing in common: they had to cope with a tough work regime, long hours and endless shortages not just for weeks or months but for years on end, with no idea when their ordeal would finish. Mobilization for total war placed exceptional pressures on civilians as the war efforts soaked up more and more of the resources that would usually supply the civilian economy. There is no easy explanation for how they coped, certainly not one that could cover such different political regimes, social structures and economic systems without distortion. For millions, total war became a way of life. Patriotism or hatred of the enemy might keep workers going for a time, but they are hardly sufficient to explain motivation for any extended period. The prospect of victory or defeat clearly played a part, although German and Japanese populations kept going doggedly in the face of imminent military collapse, while the British and American public showed signs of growing demoralization as victory approached in 1944.

It is more useful to understand that most workers were motivated by their own concerns as wage-earners rather than manipulated by propaganda to identify fully with the war effort. The war provided full employment, the opportunity for extra earnings (even in the Soviet Union, where those who surpassed their production norms got extra rations and other privileges), the possibility of saving for a time when peacetime spend-ing was restored, the opportunity to learn new skills and move up the wage ladder, or, for women workers, the prospect of earning higher than pre-war wages as a step to greater independence. One example might serve to illustrate the extent to which workers rationalized their mobilization in their own terms. In 1943 a Swedish businessman interviewed a cross-section of Hamburg dockworkers to try to find out what motivated them to carry on working for a regime that few of them identified with politically. His interviewees were unanimous that they worked hard for a German victory because they did not want to return to the unemployment and hardships of the Depression years. Allied victory, they claimed, would probably result in the fragmentation of Germany (as indeed it did) and their own impoverishment. German workers, above all, did not want to risk the accusation again that they had betrayed the army by 'stabbing it in the back'. British political propaganda tried to encourage German workers to rebel against their dictatorship in the last year of war, but reports smuggled out of the Ruhr–Rhineland in early 1945 made clear that workers were neither willing nor able to repeat 1918. There was 'no revolutionary situation in Nazi Germany', ran one report, 'neither leaders nor organisation'. Workers waited to rebuild a new Germany after defeat.[204]

The question can be turned the other way round. What prospects were there for the home front population to protest against the long years of war and the hardships they suffered? This was precisely the outcome that all wartime governments wanted to avoid. However, worker protest operated in the Second World War in inverse relation to the social and economic conditions workers experienced. In the United States and Britain, where conditions were the least onerous, labour protest was regular despite the early wartime agreement by the labour unions that they would suspend strike activity and collaborate with government, if the government respected worker interests. In Britain, an average of 1.8 million days were lost each year in unauthorized strike activity; there were 940 stoppages in 1940, but 3,714 in 1944, although 90 per cent lasted less than a week. Some were for trivial reasons ('the dictatorial attitude of a forewoman' or 'objection to working with Irishmen'), but they all reflected narrow worker interests in disputes about job demarcation, discipline, dilution of skills or wage rates, rather than opposition to the war.[205]

In the United States, labour unions tried to maintain the commitment not to strike but rising prices in the first war years and the uneven improvement in wage rates provoked unofficial labour protest. During the war there were 14,471 'wildcat' strikes, though once again few lasted longer than a week and only 6 per cent more than two weeks. In the United States, strikes were also about pay and conditions, not about the war, but the government response was more robust than in Britain.[206] Even before the war, a major stoppage at a North American Aviation plant in California, making one-quarter of American fighter aircraft, was ended when 2,500 soldiers were ordered to take over the plant and put workers back to work at gunpoint. Labour protest during the war was treated by much of the public as tantamount to treason. In 1943, in response to a major strike in the anthracite coalfield in Pennsylvania, and against Roosevelt's advice, Congress passed the Smith–Connally War Labor Disputes Act, which gave the government the right to take control of firms essential to the war effort and to take criminal proceedings against the leaders of unofficial strikes. The new law was tested that December when a defiant railroad strike prompted a federal take-over of the entire network for three weeks, until the unions backed down and accepted a state-imposed wage deal.[207] Even business leaders were not immune. Later in the war, when one company president refused to accept the provision that new workers in unionized plants would have to join the union (raising union membership from 10 million to 15 million over the war years), the American attorney-general in person led a squad of uniformed soldiers to expel him from his office and take over the company.

Nothing approaching this level of worker protest was possible in the authoritarian regimes, Axis or Allied. Strikes were outlawed in them all and the risks involved in industrial action well understood. Protest was interpreted in political terms not as a defence of worker interests, but as a challenge to the war effort and the regime. In Germany and the Soviet Union persistent offenders ended up in concentration camps. The harsh labour conditions in Japan, China and the Soviet Union nevertheless evoked spontaneous disaffection, or efforts to evade the tough conditions and low pay by moving job. Japanese trade unions had been restricted even before 1939 and in 1940 were suspended altogether; in 1939 there were 365,000 union members, in 1944 none. Police records nevertheless reveal 216 cases of industrial protest in 1944, though they involved no more than 6,000 workers in total, a tiny fraction of the workforce. Some workers responded to the absence of representation with go-slows or shoddy work, even occasional acts of sabotage.[208] The workforce was closely monitored for any possible hint of communist sympathy and all suspects arrested and mistreated. Exaggerated reports were produced on the slenderest evidence by the security forces to suggest that communist infiltration was mounting, but the revolutionary threat was a chimera.[209] In the Chinese defence industry workers were under military law and a tough factory regime, but nevertheless thousands ran the risk of desertion as an indirect form of protest. Firms reported that half the skilled work-force had to be replaced each year and blamed Communist agitation for luring their labour to areas under Communist control, but in many cases workers left to find any job where they would suffer less repression and receive more money or rice. Those caught were brought back under armed

guard and punished with the loss of pay and food.[210] In the Soviet Union
it was possible for workers to air grievances with the factory Communist
officials, though it was always risky. Workers were tied to their plant unless
told to move, but unofficial absenteeism became one indirect way of challenging poor conditions of work or exceptional mistreatment. On paper
the risks were very great: according to a secret government resolution in
January 1942, any worker in defence industries absent without leave had
to be reported to the military prosecutors within a day, and they could
impose a maximum punishment of between five and eight years in a labour
camp. It was a clumsy process and in the end most convictions were made
in absentia as the absconded workers could not be found; in some cases,
prosecution was begun against workers who were actually dead, or conscripts who had left for the army; in others, prosecutors blamed
management for the failure to supply decent conditions and let the workers go free.[211]

Working conditions for German workers were almost universally better
than conditions in the Soviet Union. All German workers and employers
were represented by the vast German Labour Front organization founded
in 1933 after Hitler came to power, and although workers had no right to
strike or protest, it was possible to get Labour Front officials to insist that
employers provide decent work facilities or maintain effective air-raid shelters. The system was otherwise as coercive as the Soviet model. Infractions
of work discipline, narrowly defined, were few: in 1940, 1,676 cases, in
1941, 2,364. In 1942 indiscipline was redefined to penalize a wider range
of infractions and the number of cases rose that year to 14,000. A rising
proportion of cases involved women workers, whose tough double life of
work and household duties made absenteeism or negligence more likely.
Most workers accused of indiscipline were given a warning, a fraction sent
to prison and a very small number to a concentration camp. In May 1941,
Himmler introduced a new punishment, 'Work Education Camps', for all
workers judged by their behaviour to be a recalcitrant threat to the war
effort. They were run by the Gestapo and by 1944 there were over a hundred of them, housing not only German workers but thousands of foreign
forced labourers judged to be guilty of sabotage or slow work. 'Work education' was a euphemism for extreme conditions and mistreatment, making
the camps little different from concentration camps.[212] Foreign workers,
whose conditions were generally poorer, did sometimes risk a strike. Six
hundred Italian workers at the Krupp complex in Essen downed tools in
April 1942 in protest at poor food and the lack of tobacco; Italians went on
strike at a firm in Hannover the same month over the poor supply of wine
and cheese. They were dealt with by the work police assigned to firms to

maintain order. Between May and August 1942 an average of 21,500 workers were arrested each month, 85 per cent of them foreign workers. Italians regarded as troublemakers were sent back to Italy where they were arrested by the Fascist police on their return. Among German workers, acts of indiscipline declined from 1942 onwards. In the first half of 1944, only 12,945 German workers were involved in protests, in contrast to 193,024 foreign workers. Evidence suggested a growing loyalty to the German war effort, a consensus not provoked by the coercive nature of the regime alone.[213]

The limited extent of protest by the working populations of the warring states demonstrated the growing power of the state to enforce a genuinely national commitment to the strategy of total mobilization. This outcome did not rely solely on coercion, though that was an ever-present reality, even in democracies. States proved their capacity to mobilize on a mass scale by ensuring the regular supply of food, responding flexibly where necessary to the needs of the workforce, and spreading the net of recruitment as widely as necessary or possible. Their success in this ensured that nothing like the revolutionary turmoil of the First World War and its aftermath was repeated except in Italy, where imminent defeat, bombing, inflation and food shortages fuelled growing social protest in the months before Mussolini's overthrow in July 1943. Mass mobilization depended on making a compact between state and people which underlined the total character of modern warfare. In the military and on the home front, the argument that total war required national mobilization was never seriously questioned. Those who failed to comply or to understand the implications of total war were bombarded with propaganda organized to challenge each individual to contribute something to the war effort and to isolate those who did not as unpatriotic, even treasonous, like the Soviet workers and managers accused of slacking or negligence, or the 18,000 Americans denounced by their countrymen to the FBI for alleged acts of sabotage.[214] Total war wherever it was organized required everyone's participation, but it worked only to the extent that the people could be persuaded to recognize its imperatives themselves. In 1945, the American critic Dwight Macdonald summarized the relationship between citizen and state in the war that had just ended: 'precisely because in this sphere the individual is most powerless in reality, do his rulers make their greatest efforts to present the State not only as an instrument for *his* purposes but as an extension of *his* personality.'[215] Macdonald might well have added '*her*' to his reflection. Total war made demands on all, men and women, young and old, free and unfree, to contribute what they could to the common effort to fight and work. This was a unique historical moment, scarcely possible beforehand, and now beyond the realms of possibility.

5

Fighting the War

'Some day a great story of the war in the Soviet Union can be built around a simple account of what happened to the twenty-five armoured divisions that Adolf Hitler sent across the Russian frontier. They were the blade of his sword, the machines that carved the way for his infantry and artillery. When they won, the Germans won. When they lost, the Germans lost.'

Walter Kerr, *The Russian Army*, 1944[1]

There is a tempting simplicity in the judgement that defeating German armoured divisions was enough to explain why Germany and the European Axis lost the Second World War. Walter Kerr represented the *New York Herald Tribune* in Moscow, and spent his years there during the war talking to Red Army commanders about their experiences until his return to the United States after Stalingrad. He relied on hearsay and military speculation to form his views of German armour. The twenty-five divisions were a popular exaggeration in Moscow; so too the common view that the Germans had launched Operation 'Barbarossa' with 18,000 tanks. Yet for all the misinformation, the focus on the armoured division as the central player in a modern ground war was not so wrong, even if the argument is incomplete. Of all the innovations in the Second World War, imitated by almost all the fighting powers, the organization of fully mechanized army units, combining tanks, motorized infantry and artillery, was among the most significant in explaining the outcome of ground combat. By 1945 the Red Army had activated forty-three tank corps, and it was their turn to do what the German army had done in 1941.

Inside Kerr's observation lies the larger question of why the Allied powers eventually won on the fighting front and why the Axis powers, after a string of initial victories, lost. The answer can be found in the extent to which each side learned to develop and exploit a range of what are called 'force multipliers' – operational organization, equipment, tactics, intelligence – that greatly increase the impact an army, air force or navy might have, particularly when at an initial disadvantage. If much of the marine and ground battlefield continued to be the preserve of more traditional arms whose importance should not be underestimated – battleships, infantry, artillery, even cavalry – it was the force multipliers that in general made the difference in battlefield performance. First among these was the development of mechanized warfare and the tactical, ground-support aviation that accompanied it. The organization and integration of armoured forces into the order of battle transformed the way the war was fought on land, first for the German army, then for the Allies. Tactical air forces were widely used in the First World War, but the advent of fast monoplane fighters, ground-attack aircraft and high-performance medium bombers, all armed with increasingly lethal weaponry, transformed the battlefield potential of aircraft as well. At sea, air power contributed to the revolution in amphibious warfare, first in the Pacific war with the Japanese advance and the Allied counter-offensive, then in Europe with amphibious landings in North Africa, Sicily, Italy and Normandy. These were complex combined operations in which air, sea and ground forces collaborated to find a way to springboard onto a heavily defended enemy shore in order to create a permanent lodgement. For the Allied sea powers, amphibious warfare was the only way to come to grips with their enemies on the territory they occupied. Learning how to project force from the sea onto land gave the Allies the successful means for doing so.

The evolution and application of electronic warfare accompanied the development of armour, air and warfare at sea. Radio and radar emerged as essential components of the modern battlefield and have remained so ever since. Modern radio technology permitted centralized control of aircraft units; it allowed commanders to manage a complex and fast-moving battlefield more effectively; the global sea war was led by radio communications; and radio was a lifeline for small units as they summoned assistance or co-ordinated their local operations. Radio-wave research led to the development of radar, which was initially introduced for the early warning of approaching enemy aircraft from across the sea, but soon had a range of further significant applications in the field. Among other things, radar gave advance warning of tactical attack aircraft, contributed critically to the success of anti-submarine warfare, gave notice of attacks on a fleet at sea, and allowed artillery to be ranged with deadly accuracy whether on land or aboard ships. Over the course of the conflict the advantage in electronic warfare shifted decisively to the Allies as they learned how to produce and use a technology at the cutting edge of the scientific war.

Radio was also central to the practice of wartime intelligence and counter-intelligence, including the development of complex deception operations. These are the final 'force multipliers' considered here. The intelligence war operated in a range of fields, some more useful in promoting fighting power, some less so. Operational and tactical intelligence were the most significant in helping armed forces to fight more efficiently. For much of the war the Allies enjoyed fuller access to intelligence and more effective evaluation than their enemies, even if it remains difficult to judge just how significant the impact of intelligence was on operations. So, too, with deception, which was widely exploited but often an evident failure. Nevertheless, where deception worked well the impact could be operationally decisive. Soviet forces were masters of deception. The devastating defeat of Axis armies during Operation 'Uranus' in November 1942 and the annihilation of German Army Group Centre in June 1944 were testament to its effects. The value of Allied deception before the Normandy invasion can be open to question, but it certainly reinforced Hitler's predisposed view that Normandy would be a feint and the Pas de Calais the primary invasion site. For the Allies, sound intelligence and successful deception helped to counteract the high fighting skills of an enemy determined to cling on to every square kilometre of the new empires. In this case, as with armour, air, amphibious operations and electronic warfare, the explanation for eventual victory or defeat in the Second World War hinges on the extent to which armed forces learned to exploit them.

ARMOUR AND AIR

When German forces invaded Poland in 1939, the world witnessed at first hand the revolution in military organization epitomized by the six armoured divisions deployed for the assault and the air-force battering ram of dive-bomber, bomber and fighter aircraft that supported them. But the success of the German assault on Poland generated much exaggeration. The tank was seen as the battle-winner in what came to be called *Blitzkrieg* (lightning war), a term widely current in the West then and now, though not a term used by the German army. Tanks enjoyed an almost legendary reputation; so too the Junkers Ju87 dive-bomber, with its terrifying 'Horn of Jericho' siren that blared out as the aircraft swooped down on its target. In the popular mind the German tank arm, as Walter Kerr described it, was a tremendous force 'of iron, steel and flame', waging war 'according to the Nazi pattern'.[2]

The tank was neither a new weapon, nor the monopoly of the German armed forces. The campaign in Poland could be traced back to German army evaluations in the 1920s of what had gone wrong in the last year of the Great War, when Allied tanks and aircraft had spearheaded the drive against the German western front in the '100 days campaign'. Under the terms of the Versailles Treaty the German army was prohibited from developing or possessing tanks and came to the weapon late, in the mid-1930s. Elsewhere tanks were widely developed during the inter-war years, most of them light tanks or 'tankettes' armed with just a machine gun, like the Japanese Type 94, the most numerous combat tank of the 1930s.[3] Heavier tanks began to appear only in the last half of the 1930s, more generally armed with a medium-calibre 37mm gun and a machine gun. The French army was alone in 1940 with the first heavy tank, the Char B1-Bis, which fielded 75mm and 47mm cannons and two machine guns. Only over the course of the war were tanks and self-propelled artillery upgraded to mount guns of 75mm or more.[4] Most early tanks were intended for infantry support or reconnaissance duties. As an offensive weapon, opinions varied. Where the tank arm grew out of the traditional cavalry force, as it did in Britain and the United States, there lingered on a preference for using tanks like traditional cavalry; in most cases, tanks were parcelled out among the infantry divisions to provide additional mobile firepower and to protect the infantry's flanks. The idea of using tanks as the core of an armoured fist to punch through and envelop an enemy line flourished briefly in the Soviet Union in the early 1930s under the influence of the Red Army chief of staff, Mikhail Tukhachevsky, until he was purged in 1937; it finally surfaced in the German army in the last years of peace.

As a battlefront weapon tanks had advantages and disadvantages. They were mobile, unlike most artillery, they could traverse a wide range of obstacles and uneven terrain, they could be used against enemy artillery, machine-gun posts or light fortifications, and, more rarely, against other tanks. Light tanks, armed only with machine guns, could be used against enemy infantry, as Japanese tanks were in the war with China. The tank was nevertheless a vulnerable weapon. They were generally slow-moving, and more so the heavier tanks became during the war. The German Panzer VI 'Tiger' tank weighed 55 tons and had a maximum speed of around 30 kilometres an hour with limited range and so much need for regular maintenance that it could not in practice be used as a vehicle to break through an enemy front and exploit the breach, as originally intended.[5] The vulnerability of all tanks to mechanical failure made it necessary to keep a maintenance battalion close behind, or else to abandon tanks that developed mechanical flaws or minor damage. Although wartime tanks were upgraded to have stronger armour, even the heaviest tanks were vulnerable to fire directed at the treads or the rear and sides of the hull. Conditions for the tank crews were demanding in the extreme. Smaller tanks had little room for the crew, who were expected to perform a number of tasks in a cramped space, but even in medium and heavy tanks, with four or five crew members, the claustrophobic interior made effective firing, loading and radio communication a constant challenge; visibility was restricted and the roar of the engine drowned out sounds from outside of enemy action or friendly fire; the tank hull filled with fumes, making a hot interior even more obnoxious; all the time the possibility of being hit brought the danger of fire or shards of sharp metal followed by the struggle to escape through the narrow exit. 'Our faces are bloody,' wrote one Soviet tank commander of the experience, '... small steel slivers flaked off and embedded themselves in cheeks and foreheads. We are deaf, poisoned by gun smoke, worn out by turbulence ...'[6]

Above all, tanks were vulnerable to a wide variety of anti-tank weapons. For all the fear that tanks engendered in soldiers as they rumbled remorselessly towards them, they could be immobilized by heavy anti-tank artillery, by other tanks, and by dedicated anti-tank guns, grenades, rocket launchers, limpet mines or anti-tank rifles. As tanks were upgraded during the war, so too were anti-tank weapons and munitions. Armies developed small 'tank hunter' infantry units that moved about the battlefield to engage isolated or immobilized tanks, using close attack weapons for the kill, such as the Japanese 'lunge mine' attached to a wooden pole that blew up the soldier holding it as he struck the tank (the American troops called it the 'idiot stick'), or the German 'double-charge' bags that were slung dangerously over the gun barrel of enemy tanks to detonate a few minutes later with disabling effect.[7] The majority of tanks allocated to front-line combat were damaged or destroyed. Even the heavily armoured 'Tiger' and 'King Tiger' tanks lost 1,580 destroyed out of the 1,835 produced.[8] The life expectancy of a Soviet T-34 tank in combat was no more than two to three days. Out of 86,000 tanks produced in the Soviet Union, 83,500 were lost or damaged and only the rapid recovery and repair of vehicles made it possible to sustain mechanized warfare at all.[9] The armour revolution prompted the evolution of its nemesis, anti-armour. The capacity to defend against armour assumed a significance comparable with armour itself, just as anti-aircraft fire increased in scale and effectiveness against the threat of tactical air power. Armoured divisions commonly had both the capacity for mobile offensive operations and the capacity for mobile defence against enemy armour and air. This proved to be an essential combination for survival.

On their own tanks were of limited usefulness. When in battle tanks outran the infantry they could be isolated and destroyed by anti-tank fire. Tanks could not occupy territory, any more than aircraft could. The success of armour during the war depended on the development of combined arms combat, in which tanks were the core of an armoured unit working closely together with motorized infantry, motor drawn or self-propelled artillery and anti-tank guns, field anti-aircraft batteries, a mobile engineer battalion and a maintenance unit. It was this combination, not the tank itself, that gave armoured formations their formidable striking power. Combined arms combat was the key to the ultimate success of armoured forces, and it depended to a high degree on extensive mechanization and mobility. To succeed, all arms allocated to support armoured warfare needed to have the trucks, field cars, armoured personnel carriers and towing vehicles necessary to move forward together, rather than trailing behind the tanks.

This was the factor that inhibited Germany's two major allies, Japan and Italy, from developing a full commitment to armoured warfare. Initial experiments in both countries recognized the virtues of combined arms organization, but they both lacked the industrial resources (particularly oil) necessary to motorize and mechanize their armed forces more extensively. In 1934, Japan developed one of the first dedicated armoured forces, the Japanese Independent Mixed Brigade, which had a battalion of tanks, motorized infantry, an engineer and artillery company and a mobile reconnaissance unit, but the field army's hostility to the idea of an independent force ended the brief career of the brigade at the start of the Sino-Japanese war. It was disbanded and the light tanks allocated in small numbers to support individual infantry divisions. Three combined arms armoured divisions were finally activated in 1942 in response to the evident success of the German example, and a fourth was added later for the defence of the home islands. They were difficult to deploy in the Pacific island war, which explains the low priority allocated to tanks in Japanese war production. In 1944 only 925 were produced, in 1945 only 256. The divisions were used piecemeal to support infantry; one was destroyed in the Philippines in 1944, one surrendered in Manchuria in August 1945, and the third collapsed with inadequate replacements and maintenance after a 1,300-kilometre trek across southern China.[10]

In Italy, an initial combined arms mechanized unit was formed in 1936, the *Brigata motomeccanizzata*, with a battalion of tanks, two of infantry and an artillery battery. The brigade was upgraded to the status of a division and more supporting arms added but, like the Japanese, the Italian army only activated three armoured divisions throughout the war, fighting as part of larger infantry corps. Infantry, according to Italian army doctrine, was 'the decisive element in combat', not the fighting vehicle.[11] The armoured element was initially composed of the Fiat 3000B light tank, with an ineffective 37mm gun, and turretless machine-gun carriers, the CV33 and CV35, whose value in mobile armoured warfare was negligible. In 1940 the M11/39 medium tank was introduced but soon withdrawn because of limited armour protection; the M13/40 followed in 1941 with an improved 47mm high-velocity gun, but armour no thicker than 30mm. No Italian tank proved adequate to the requirements of modern armoured warfare and during the entire war only 1,862 were produced. Two of the three divisions were destroyed at the Battle of El Alamein when by the end they had not a single tank between them. Neither Japan nor Italy developed a mature doctrine for armoured warfare. In the few mobile engagements in the Pacific war, Japanese tanks drove at the enemy line in the armour equivalent of a *banzai* charge and were wrecked by American anti-tank fire.

It was in Germany, starved for years after 1919 of the right to develop a modern army, that the operational advantages of a mechanized and motorized force were first successfully exploited. The German army had searched after defeat in 1919 for ways to improve the speed and hitting power of forces needed for the decisive battle (*Entscheidungsschlacht*) that had eluded them in the Great War. Even before Germany possessed modern tanks, armoured doctrine took shape. The army manoeuvres of 1932, using dummy vehicles, demonstrated the potential of mobile operations. Inspired by Major General Oswald Lutz, the inspector of motorized troops, and the young Major Heinz Guderian, the organization of an armoured (Panzer) division was worked out over the next three years, and in 1935 the first three were activated. The priority was to ensure that the tank was not held up by the limited mobility of supporting arms; the motorcycle, infantry, artillery, reconnaissance, engineer and communications units were all motorized, giving the division self-contained fighting power.[12] The decision was taken to place the tanks in a hard-hitting armoured core, against the resistance of some army leaders who wanted mechanization and motorization spread across the army as a whole. 'Concentration of the available armoured forces,' wrote Guderian in 1937, 'will always be more effective than dispersing them.'[13] In any event the limited number of vehicles available from a motor industry still modest in scale, and the speed with which rearmament was driven, precluded a broader base of motorization. The German armed forces entered the Second World War with essentially two armies: one modern and mobile; the other still based on slow-moving infantry, reliant on horse and rail for movement. When Hitler's armoured divisions battered their way into the Soviet Union, they were followed by an army with an estimated 750,000 horses (together with their grooms, ostlers, fodder trains and veterinary staff). In 1942, an additional 400,000 horses were requisitioned from across occupied Europe to pull artillery and heavy weapons because there were not enough vehicles.[14]

The six Panzer divisions available for the war against Poland, and the ten used against the West in May 1940, were the armoured fist of a long arm of infantry. Victory in both campaigns alerted the rest of the world to the radical impact of German mobile warfare and encouraged imitation, but it also masked problems derived from the rapid development of armoured forces and the difficulty of supplying the equipment needed. Among the 2,574 tanks used in the invasion of France and the Low Countries, 523 were PKW (*Panzerkraftwagen*) I armed only with machine guns, 955 were PKW II with an ineffective 20mm main gun, 334 were captured Czech tanks, and only 627 were the PKW III and IV with larger calibre guns, neither of which could easily hit or disable heavier enemy tanks. Many of the accompanying infantry and engineers were in trucks rather than armoured personnel carriers. The French army fielded a total of 3,254 tanks, many of them heavier and better armed.[15] The victory in France was secured in spite of the inferiority in numbers and quality of German armour, partly because of air support, partly because the French army dispersed a large proportion of its tanks among the infantry armies rather than concentrating them, but chiefly because the mobile supporting arms in the Panzer divisions, held together by good communications, played their intended role of occupying ground and combating enemy vehicles. In the one major tank-versus-tank engagement of the Battle of France, around the Belgian town of Gembloux, German commanders found that, because of the lack of radio, French tanks manoeuvred poorly, that they worked in small, dispersed groups rather than in a mass, and delivered slow and inaccurate fire – a problem exacerbated in smaller French tanks because the one-man turret required the tank commander to fire the gun as well as direct the tank's movement.[16] The battle exemplified the advantages of combined arms doctrine and the limitations of tanks trying to fight on their own.

For the Soviet invasion in 1941, the army was compelled to expand the number of armoured divisions while accepting a reduction in their strength. The twenty-one Panzer divisions, organized in four main Panzer groups, had only 150 tanks each instead of the 328 they had had in September 1939. Out of 3,266 tanks mobilized, 1,146 were PKW III and IV, the remainder Czech models and the PKW II with its inadequate armament. The complete collapse of the Red Army's order of battle in the opening months of 'Barbarossa' flattered German armour. Soviet losses in the first six months of the war amounted to a remarkable 20,500 tanks and self-propelled guns out of the 28,000 available, but German losses mounted steadily.[17] By August German tank strength was reduced by half; by November out of half a million vehicles of all kinds committed to the campaign, only 75,000 were still in working order. The German mechanized force suffered a progressive decline in the last years of war, with high losses and sluggish production at home limiting what could be done. In 1943 only 5,993 tanks of all kinds were produced; the same year the Soviet Union and the United States between them produced 53,586. At Kursk in July 1943 the mechanized divisions had an average of 73 tanks each, though some had considerably more for the assault phase, but the Ninth Army at Kursk needed 50,000 horses, the Fourth Panzer Army, 25,000.[18]

The German doctrine on tank use had to be modified as a result of the shifting balance of forces against the Allies. From an arm intended to break an enemy front followed by exploitation and envelopment, German armour was forced from mid-1943 on to the defensive. Even in defence, armour could be used offensively. On the Eastern Front, mechanized units were concentrated into *Panzerkampfgruppen* (armoured battle groups) composed of tanks, armoured infantry and towed artillery, to be allocated to key danger-points where they sustained the model of independent, combined arms combat. But the emphasis now shifted to the destruction of approaching enemy armour using a mix of tanks, tank-hunting infantry units, and anti-tank weaponry, including the self-propelled artillery piece, the *Sturmgeschütz*, with its armour-piercing 75mm gun, which by the end of the war was the most numerous armoured fighting vehicle of the German army.[19] The new PKW V 'Panther', with a high velocity 75mm gun, and the PKW VI 'Tiger' armed with a tank-busting 88mm gun, briefly used at the Battle of Kursk in the last German strategic offensive, were re-deployed as vehicles for limited counter-offensives or, on occasion, dug in as defensive artillery rather than used in their mobile role. There is a supreme irony in the shift in German priorities. The army that pioneered offensive armoured operations became adept in the last two years of war at defensive anti-tank combat. In 1943, the army organized dedicated *Pakfronten* (anti-tank defence fronts) with anti-tank guns dug in at concealed points to ambush advancing armour on their predicted routes, mimicking the earlier Soviet 'fire sack' – an area flanked by mines and natural obstacles, where Red Army anti-tank units tried to lure German armour into the zone of fire. In the same year, two new anti-tank weapons were introduced, the 88mm RPzB 43 rocket projector, commonly known as the *Panzerschreck* (tank terror), and the *Panzerfaust* (armour fist) one-time anti-tank gun that fired a warhead capable of penetrating more than 140mm of armour plate. They were both hand-held and light and could be used by any trained soldier to immobilize all types of medium and heavy tank. More than 8 million *Panzerfaust* were produced, giving German forces as they retreated effective weapons with which to slow down the advance of the heavily armoured enemy, turning on its head the operational strategy with which the army had begun the war.[20]

The Allies, by contrast, following the disasters in France in 1940 and in the initial stages of the invasion of the Soviet Union, had to rethink armoured doctrine and organization by looking closely at German practice. In Britain and the United States, the development and expansion of armoured forces had to begin almost from scratch; in the Soviet Union, the destruction of the large tank arm in summer 1941 forced a profound change in the way Soviet armour was deployed. Britain and the United States both enjoyed the advantage that they were the most heavily motorized of all the powers between the wars and could draw on a large motor industry and vehicle stock for modernizing the army in depth. American and British infantry were carried by truck and armoured personnel carriers; horses were a rarity. Yet their armoured forces grew out of the tradition of the horse cavalry. In both cases this tradition encouraged the development of mainly all-tank armoured units rather than combined arms, using tanks in mass, like horses, to pursue the enemy or exploit a break in the enemy line.

In Britain, early experiments in the 1920s with combined arms were replaced by the idea of the all-armoured force without infantry or artillery. The Tank Brigade, formed in 1931, was an all-tank unit, and it supplied the core of the later Mobile Division (soon to be called the British Armoured Division).[21] In 1939 it was decided to divide the tank forces in two: tank brigades, using the more heavily armoured medium tanks ('Matilda', 'Churchill' and 'Valentine') as infantry-support weapons, were attached to infantry divisions; armoured divisions with faster 'cruiser' tanks would continue to play the mobile role traditionally played by cavalry. The infantry tank brigades were regularly upgraded with higher calibre guns to engage enemy armour, but they remained tied to the infantry they supported. Between 1940 and autumn 1941 seven more armoured divisions were formed after Britain's First Division was destroyed in France. Their painful vulnerability without the support of other arms brought a final reorganization in 1942, with the reduction in the number of tanks and the addition of motorized infantry and greater anti-tank and anti-aircraft capability. When the Sixth Armoured Division was formed in 1943 from South African forces who had served in North Africa, it comprised a tank brigade, a motorized infantry brigade, three artillery regiments, a regiment of anti-tank guns and one of anti-aircraft guns, and eventually a regiment of self-propelled 25-pounder guns – a model Panzer division.[22] Nevertheless, by comparison with Germany and the Soviet Union, Britain's commitment to armour was modest and British tank quality widely regarded as inadequate. By the end of the war there were only five armoured divisions and eight army tank brigades, each heavily reliant on the American M4 'Sherman', which was supplied in large quantities from 1942 onwards through Lend-Lease.[23] Much more of Britain's fighting effort was devoted to air and sea.

The United States had almost no armoured forces before 1939, and like the British, developed the first armoured unit in 1939, the Seventh Cavalry Brigade, by replacing horses with 112 small armoured cars for scouting. In July 1940, following assessment of German success in Poland and France, the first two armoured divisions were activated, but they had too heavy a complement of tanks. Exercises in 1941 held in Louisiana showed how easily tanks massed on their own could be eliminated by anti-tank weapons. The divisions were hastily reformed to incorporate a balanced combined arms force with the addition of infantry, artillery, anti-tank weapons, a reconnaissance battalion, engineers and services. The divisions were entirely motorized and mechanized, each with 375 tanks and 759 other tracked and armoured vehicles, and were designed, like German armour, to punch through the enemy line. 'The role of the armored divisions', according to the field manual produced under General Adna Chaffee, first commander of the Armored Force, 'is the conduct of highly mobile warfare, particularly offensive in character, by a self-sustained unit of great power and mobility . . .'[24] However, the problems experienced in the initial American campaign in Tunisia forced major change. The number of armoured divisions planned was reduced from sixty-one to sixteen, and their role was changed to pursuit and exploitation of an initial breach in the enemy line achieved by heavily armed infantry, a doctrine successfully demonstrated in the breakout from Normandy in late July 1944.

Instead of more armoured divisions, seventy tank battalions were formed, one for each infantry division, effectively turning the whole American ground army into a Panzer force. No urgent requirement was issued for a heavy tank to match German and Soviet developments because rapid mobility was seen as the key to success, and heavy tanks were too slow. The M4 Sherman medium tank, and its many variants, was designed both to support infantry and to act in pursuit, but it could also be adapted to a wide range of other roles, as it was in the Pacific war against numerous Japanese bunkers and pillboxes. Although it was outclassed in tank-on-tank combat with the German Panther or Tiger, it was a robust vehicle, with high rates of serviceability. It was also produced in quantities that simply overwhelmed the enemy. In December 1944 the German army fielded 500 Panthers in the West, the Allied armies 5,000 M4s.[25] In addition, American mobile forces developed a range of weapons to knock out enemy tanks, including the hand-held 'Bazooka' rocket-launcher primed with anti-tank munitions. The M1 Bazooka (it got its name from a comedy musical instrument, which it closely resembled) was first used during Operation 'Torch', and a much-improved version with a more lethal warhead, the M9A1, was introduced two years later. Over 476,000 were produced, generously distributed across the armoured and infantry divisions. The formidable combination of tanks, 'tank-killer' self-propelled guns, dedicated anti-tank artillery, Bazookas and tank-busting aircraft frustrated enemy armour operations, most famously in the German counter-offensive at Mortain in August 1944.[26]

The most significant transformation in armoured capability came in the Soviet Union. It was here along the wide Soviet–German front that most German armour was deployed, and here that the German armoured force was finally blunted. The defeat of Soviet armoured forces in 1941 exposed many shortcomings. A high percentage of the very large number of Soviet tanks available on the eve of the invasion were not fully serviceable – only 3,800 out of the 14,200 available – and most were not the famed T-34 but smaller and lighter models, an easy match for German armour and artillery.[27] A report prepared by Major General Rodion Morgunov, commander of a mechanized corps in the Ukraine in June 1941 (where Panzer divisions with 586 German tanks helped to destroy all but 300 of the 3,427 Soviet tanks they confronted), deplored the failure to concentrate mechanized forces, the poor level of intelligence and communication, the lack of radios, spare parts and fuel, and the absence of any clear tactical plan.[28] From the spring of 1942, Soviet armour was reorganized from the dispersed pattern established in 1940, when mechanized units were attached to infantry armies. The basic operational unit was now the tank corps, equipped with 168 tanks, anti-tank and anti-aircraft artillery, and a battalion of Katyusha rocket batteries; two tank corps were joined with a rifle division to create a tank-infantry army, the equivalent of a Panzer division. They performed poorly at first from lack of experienced commanders, but as more were activated and the armoured force concentrated, the Red Army became capable of replicating German practice. From September 1942, tank armies were supplemented by combined arms mechanized corps with up to 224 tanks but a higher proportion of infantry, supported by extensive anti-tank and anti-aircraft artillery. Both tank armies and mechanized corps were upgraded as the supply of military resources expanded.[29] The number of tanks for a tank corps was raised in 1943 from 168 to 195, and during 1944 they began to receive the upgraded T-34 medium tank and IS-1 and IS-2 heavy tanks with 100mm and 122mm guns, the most advanced tanks of the war.

A total of forty-three tank corps and twenty-two mechanized corps were activated, giving the Red Army the largest concentration of armour of any of the combatant states. The new tank armies were used to pierce weaker points on the enemy line and then to pursue and envelop enemy forces as the Germans had done in 1940–41. Mobility was improved by conversion from petrol to diesel engines, which trebled tank range; command and control was revolutionized by the introduction of radio. Although hampered still by limited training and technical deficiencies, improved tactical deployment was evident in the ratio of losses between the two sides. In 1941–2, Soviet armoured forces lost six vehicles to every one German; by 1944 the ratio was one-to-one, helped by the evolution of more effective anti-tank artillery on the Soviet side, the 76mm ZiS-3 and the giant 100mm BS-3. Sustained production and an effective repair system meant that by the end of 1944 the Red Army possessed over 14,000 tanks to field against 4,800 German tanks and self-propelled guns; in the West, the Allies had 6,000 tanks against 1,000 German. The lessons of 1940 and 1941 had been learned in full.

Much the same story unfolded in the development of ground-support aviation in which the German air force enjoyed a substantial lead in 1939 in both doctrine and equipment. The German air force, like the armoured force, was formed only in the last years before the outbreak of war, but thinking about what German airmen called 'operational air war' drew on the experience of the First World War and the lessons they learned from it. The German Defence Ministry in the 1920s established more than forty study groups on the air war, almost all of them devoted to how to win and maintain air superiority over the battlefront in support of a ground offensive.[30] The 1936 manual 'Conduct of the Air War' defined the role of the air force as essentially offensive, working with army and navy in combination to defeat the enemy armed forces. Aircraft were to be used first to destroy the enemy air force and its organization in order to establish air superiority over the principal battlefield; once that was achieved, it was possible to support the ground offensive, first indirectly by isolating the battlefield through the interdiction of enemy supplies, communications and reserves up to a depth of 200 kilometres behind the front line, then through direct support for ground forces using medium bombers and ground attack aircraft.[31] This was the classic statement of tactical air power. The arsenal of new aircraft designs developed between 1935 and the outbreak of war – the Junkers Ju87 dive-bomber, the Heinkel He111, Dornier Do17 and Junkers Ju88 medium bombers, the Messerschmitt Bf109 and Bf110 fighters – were all designed with 'operational air war' in mind. They still formed the core of the German tactical air forces down to the end of the war, by which time, despite regular upgrading, most were well behind Allied air technology. The organization of the air force reflected these operational priorities. Behind each major army group was an air fleet composed of all air arms – reconnaissance aircraft, fighters, dive-bombers, bombers and transport aircraft – designed to follow the ground offensive; they were independently commanded, centrally controlled, mobile, and had by 1939 an effective web of radio communication both between air units and between air and ground.

The organization for supporting the fighting front remained virtually unchanged over the course of the war. Its success was evident during the invasion of France, when the concentration of more than 2,700 combat aircraft suppressed Allied air forces, attacked rear supplies, reinforcements and services, and gave direct support on the battlefield against enemy troops and artillery. Ground forces could call up air support within minutes thanks to close liaison between ground and air forces, whereas it took the RAF in France up to three hours to respond to a call for help from the army. The psychological shock of dive-bomber raids on enemy troops could be devastating, even if bombing accuracy was difficult to achieve. One French lieutenant caught under a hail of bombs during the German crossing of the Meuse River later wrote: 'we were there, immobile, silent, backs bent, shrunken into ourselves, mouths open so as not to have the eardrums burst.'[32] For the invasion of the Soviet Union there were 2,770 aircraft, scarcely more than a year before thanks to the sluggish expansion of aircraft production, but they achieved the same dramatic effect as in France, destroying Soviet air power in a matter of weeks and lending direct support to the major offensive thrusts of the armoured forces as they pushed deep into Soviet territory. Aircraft raided airfields, communications, troop concentrations and battlefield strongpoints using a mix of bombs and ground-strafing with machine-gun and cannon fire. Aircrew were instructed to attack enemy armour dangerously close to advancing German forces, but they learned to distinguish German armour from Soviet. 'The cumulative effect of our attacks,' wrote a BF110 pilot in his memoirs, 'could be seen from the growing numbers of burning vehicles and immobile or abandoned tanks littering the battlefield below.'[33] The concentration of air forces, like the concentration of German armour, maximized their impact. The German air force maintained front-line air superiority against the poorly organized and poorly trained Soviet air forces until the battle of Stalingrad, when the balance became for the first time less one-sided.

The German recipe for successful tactical air power might seem with hindsight straightforward common sense. Yet no other major air force developed an effective doctrine for tactical air power by the outbreak of war. This was due to two conflicting pressures. In the first place, armies wanted aircraft to provide very close support of ground forces by maintaining a defensive 'air umbrella' over them, and in cases when the army was able to dictate its requirements, air power was decentralized and subordinated to local army groups. By contrast, some air force commanders were anxious to develop independent air strategy, exploiting the flexibility and range of aircraft for operations far from the battlefield, even directed against the enemy home front. The army view of air power in the 1930s reflected the evident drawback of the aeroplane as an instrument of war. In 1935 American Brigadier General Stanley Embick summed up the 'inherent limitations' of the aircraft:

> They cannot occupy nor control permanently either land or sea areas, they are impotent and helpless save in flight and must depend largely upon land and sea forces in their protection. They are fragile, vulnerable to the smallest missile, inoperable in bad weather, and exceedingly costly.[34]

Like the tank, aircraft were also faced with increasingly sophisticated anti-aircraft artillery designed to shoot them down or to force them away from more fruitful targets. Embick might well have added that prevailing technology made air operations against ground targets inherently inaccurate unless undertaken at very low altitude. The idea of the aircraft as a 'tank-buster' during the war exaggerated the extent to which a small target could be hit from the air until the development of much improved ground attack weapons and munitions.

In Japan, Italy, France, the Soviet Union and the United States, aircraft were regarded by the army at best as an auxiliary arm, best suited to close support of ground units under army control, and the organization of air forces reflected that priority. Only in Britain did the air force, established as the first independent air service in 1918, develop a strategic profile that largely ignored commitment to the ground war, as it fought a long struggle to retain its autonomy against both the army and the navy. The RAF instead gave priority to air defence against a future bombing offensive and the development of an air striking force for carrying the bombing war to the enemy home front. These were both functions that exploited the difference between the exercise of air power and the exercise of land power, and they matched Britain's geopolitical position in the 1920s and 1930s, secure from invasion and unwilling to imagine a second major ground conflict after the bloodletting of the Great War. The focus on air defence and strategic bombing militated against the emergence of 'operational air war' which was prefigured in German planning and successfully demonstrated in the first years of war.

The failure of the British and French air forces in the Battle of France in 1940 highlighted the contrast with German practice. Neither air force was prepared as a first priority to attack the enemy air force and its supporting organization in order to achieve air superiority. The 1937 'Instruction on the Tactical Employment of Major Air Units' issued by the French Air Ministry insisted that 'Participation in ground operations counts as the most fundamental task of the air force.'[35] The army wanted an air force tied closely to individual armies and army groups and expected reconnaissance of enemy artillery, together with air force protection of troops on the ground, to be the priorities. The result was an air element in 1940 that was inflexible and decentralized, a situation made worse by the primitive state of French communications.[36] In Britain there had been remarkably little preparation for combined operations between army and air. In 1938 a tentative manual on 'The Employment of Air Forces in the Field' was devised by the RAF director of plans, John Slessor, and the army's Lieutenant Colonel Archibald Nye, but the 'Slessor/Nye' proposal for an army air component of fighters, bombers and army co-operation aircraft subordinate to the army commander was rejected by the Air Ministry as a backdoor attempt to create a separate army air force. Despite pressure after the outbreak of war from the War Office and the Imperial General Staff to create what the war minister, Leslie Hore-Belisha, called 'an Air Arm under Army Control', the air staff persisted in rejecting any attempt to subvert the independence of the RAF.[37]

In the end, the army had to make do with an Advanced Air Striking Force of obsolescent light bombers that were decimated by the German air force, and a small air component of fighters and reconnaissance aircraft under the control not of the army but of the air staff and the RAF commands for bombers and fighters. There was no joint headquarters for army and air force, poor communication between ground and air, and no attempt to engage in concerted counter-force operations. Like the French air force, the RAF was forced to act defensively in the face of the German assault with inadequate equipment against both enemy fighters and the numerous field anti-aircraft batteries, which the Allies lacked. The RAF viewed participation in the land battle in entirely negative terms. Slessor's argument that 'the aeroplane is not a battlefield weapon' was echoed by RAF commanders in the field. Attacks on enemy airfields were regarded as 'uneconomical expenditure' of effort, given the ease with which air resources could be concealed or redeployed.[38] In mid-May 1940 the RAF was given the opportunity to begin bombing German industrial cities as an indirect way of reducing German fighting strength in France. The poor experience of tactical air power appeared to confirm that 'strategic' attacks against the enemy home front in the future would be a more profitable use of air resources.

It was a long learning curve for the RAF to move from its strategic preferences to develop a tactical capability that by 1945 was extensive and effective. In the aftermath of failure in France, the army set up a committee under Lieutenant General William Bartholomew to review what went wrong and what needed to be done. The army laid substantial blame on the RAF for failing to provide an air umbrella over British forces to protect them from enemy aircraft, and for the following three years an unusually bitter argument continued between army and air force over control of battlefield air resources.[39] The emergence of a tactical capability was forced in the end by circumstances. The only place where the British ground forces could engage with the Axis was in North Africa. Here there was no possibility of long-range attacks against the enemy homeland, so RAF Middle East Command had to concentrate on creating 'operational air war' or risk simply being swallowed up by the army whose overall commander, General Archibald Wavell, wanted close army control of the air to prevent accidental attacks on British Empire forces. First under Air Vice Marshal Arthur Longmore, then from June 1941 Air Marshal Arthur Tedder, the Middle East Air Force began to develop something more closely resembling German 'operational air war'. They insisted that only an air commander could control and command air resources and attempted to concentrate air forces as the Germans had done. This was the recipe that had secured German success, but it proved difficult to replicate. Army commanders continued to demand close air protection, wasting resources on defensive patrols, or attacks on heavily defended ground targets where aircraft losses were magnified. Tedder wanted air and army headquarters to be located next to each other to better co-ordinate operational strategy, but during the battles of 1941 and the first half of 1942 they were sometimes as many as 130 kilometres apart.[40] The RAF worked in the first years with a motley collection of British and American aircraft, no dedicated ground attack units, and few effective medium bombers. Shaping 'operational air war' out of this unpromising mix was one of the more remarkable achievements of Britain's war effort.

The successful creation of a tactical air force owed much to the appointment in September 1941 of the New Zealander Air Vice Marshal Arthur 'Mary' Coningham as commander of the Western Desert Air Force under Tedder. His key contribution was a vigorous rejection of the army preference for close air protection. In a pamphlet on air–army co-operation drafted after victory at El Alamein, Coningham argued that air power had to be centralized to be effective, and had to be under direct air force command and control. 'The soldier,' he continued, 'must not expect or wish to exercise direct command over air striking forces' – a conclusion already arrived at by Churchill when he sent Wavell in November 1941 a firm rebuke for continuing to argue for an army air force. 'Never more,' wrote Churchill, 'must the ground troops expect, as a matter of course, to be protected against the air by aircraft,' a rare moment of direct political intervention in matters of doctrine.[41] The resolution of the dispute between the two services finally paved the way for fruitful combined operations.

Coningham and Tedder developed the three-tier operational strategy devised by the German air force: to achieve air superiority, to isolate the battlefield, and then to give direct support to the ground battle. For this last stage great attention was paid to marking a clear 'bomb line' so that friendly troops would not be hit, a problem that had plagued close air support until the summer of 1942. Air and army headquarters were at last placed side by side and with new radio equipment, mobile radar and a system of Air Support Control units to accompany the army into battle, the time taken to summon battlefront air support fell from an average of two to three hours to just thirty minutes.[42] The RAF was now armed with the Hurricane IID with powerful cannon fire for close support against tanks, the first effective British ground attack aircraft, and the American Lend-Lease fighter-bomber, the P-40D, renamed the Kittyhawk. In the late summer of 1942, as Rommel was poised to attack into Egypt, British and Commonwealth air forces achieved complete domination of the air. The damage inflicted on the enemy echoed the success of the German Air Force in France two years before. Rommel's offensive at Alam el Halfa in August was halted by British tactical air power, and during Montgomery's counter-offensive at El Alamein two months later command of the air was complete. Rommel later claimed that any army forced to fight against an enemy with air superiority 'fights like a savage against modern European troops'.[43]

The lessons carefully learned in the Western Desert campaign had to be painfully learned again when in November 1942 a combined American–British expeditionary force landed in north-west Africa in Operation 'Torch'. Neither the RAF component, dubbed the Eastern Air Force, nor the US Twelfth Air Force under Major General James Doolittle had detailed information about how tactical air power had succeeded in Egypt and Libya, despite Churchill's renewed intervention in October to insist that army and air force should adopt 'the Libyan model'.[44] The initial air campaign against the German and Italian air forces in Tunisia made all the mistakes slowly ironed out in the Western Desert: there was almost no communication between the British and American air commanders, since each was assigned to give close support to their respective ground forces; Eisenhower, overall expeditionary commander, insisted that the army should have the right of direct command over air units; there was almost no attempt at a co-ordinated campaign against the enemy air force, while ground commanders, both American and British, insisted on fighter patrols along the front line to supply an air umbrella; there were few dedicated ground attack aircraft, and American fighter pilots had no experience of ground strafing, and initially no external bomb racks for interdiction operations. Only five all-weather airfields were captured, severely limiting air force mobility during a season of torrential rain. Losses were high, while army commanders complained that their inexperienced troops, suffering high rates of psychiatric casualties in their first exposure to real fire, needed close air support at all costs.[45] The failures exposed the extent to which neither air force, distant from the reality of battle in Africa, had absorbed or understood the 'Libyan model'.

The American view on tactical air power before the war was dominated by the army requirement for close support of the ground forces under army control. Army commanders were hostile to air force arguments for greater independence, but extensive air-ground exercises conducted in Louisiana in 1941 showed that the army had few ideas about how an air force worked. The Air Corps Tactical School had already arrived at the conclusions adopted by the German air force for the three-tier operational air war, but the army view that close support was the priority could not be challenged. The first wartime field manual that addressed tactical air power, FM-31-35 published in April 1942, insisted that 'the ground force commander ... decides the air support required'. Eisenhower's headquarters issued 'Combat Aviation in Direct Support of Ground Forces' prior to 'Torch' which made explicit that air forces were subordinate to ground command.[46] The British army commander, Lieutenant General Kenneth Anderson, brought with him British army prejudice against independent air operations, and as a result supported the American insistence that air was commanded by ground. Within weeks it was possible to see that Allied tactical air power in north-west Africa was a disaster. Doolittle, who had been allowed only an advisory role even though he commanded the Twelfth Air Force, demanded that the Allies 'abandon our present 100 percent bitched up organization' and use air power as it should be used.[47] Eisenhower swiftly realized that he had misunderstood the nature of tactical air power and at the Anglo-American conference in Casablanca late in January 1943, the organization was radically overhauled as a prelude to adopting the tactical lessons of the Western Desert. Centralization of the command structure was the first step. Tedder was named overall commander-in-chief of Mediterranean air forces, the American air force general Carl Spaatz was made commander of the North-West African Air Forces, and joint control over tactical air power was vested in Coningham. They immediately ended the use of the 'air umbrella', overturned the right of army commanders to order air support, and introduced an offensive tactical air campaign against the Axis air force.

The 'Libyan model' was taken over entirely following a summit meeting in the Libyan port of Tripoli in February 1943 between the leaders of the Allied air and land forces in which Montgomery lectured the assembly on the necessity for an independent air arm pursuing its own version of air superiority. A new American field manual was introduced a few months later, FM-100-20, 'Command and Employment of Air Power', which opened in capital letters 'LAND POWER AND AIR POWER ARE CO-EQUAL ... NEITHER IS AN AUXILIARY OF THE OTHER.' The manual reproduced Coningham's idea of three tiers of operation, which American air force officers had taken back with them to Washington.[48] Although residual distrust between air and ground survived into later campaigns, the organizational and doctrinal changes brought about in North Africa dictated the use of tactical air power down to the end of the war. Improved communications, intelligence and equipment, including the American P-51 Mustang fighters (also designated the A-36 Apache as a ground attack aircraft), and the RAF rocket-firing Hawker Typhoon, magnified the impact of Anglo-American tactical air power. The American Ninth Air Force and the British Second Tactical Air Force mobilized to support the invasion of France in June 1944 were unrecognizable from the incoherent air forces that had contested 'Torch'. Allied tactical air power proved to be as decisive as mechanized warfare in explaining Allied victory. By contrast, the German air force as a tactical force collapsed. It was compelled to devote two-thirds of its fighter force and most anti-aircraft artillery to defend against the Allied bomber offensives. Short of all types of battlefield aircraft and fuel, it had to send pilots into combat with insufficient training.[49] Hitler's chief of operations, Colonel General Alfred Jodl, gave his opinion to interrogators in June 1945 that 'in the end the winning of complete air superiority in the whole area of the war has altogether decided the war'.[50]

If Soviet tactical air forces in late 1944 were added to the Western figures, the disparity would be greater still. Although German military leaders both during and after the war played down the significance of Soviet air power, the changes in the way the Red Air Force conducted tactical air war in response to early German victories can be compared with the great qualitative improvement in the Anglo-American air forces. Soviet air power suffered, like armoured doctrine and organization, from the reforms of the late 1930s when air forces were tied to individual armies and under direct army command. Soviet doctrine emphasized the role of aviation in direct support of ground forces as a combined air-ground offensive force. Unlike the German 'operational air war' or the 'Libyan model' in the West, the Red Air Force did not see the achievement of air superiority as doctrinally distinct from close support for ground forces because it was to be won not by bombing distant airfields and supplies but by destroying enemy fighters and bombers in combat over the battlefield. In the 'Combat Regulations for Fighter Aviation' published in 1940, the fighter was the principal instrument for gaining air superiority in combat.[51] Although some attempt was made in June 1941 to attack German rear areas, unescorted slow-moving bombers were mercilessly shot down by German fighter aircraft, encouraging the army to limit air support to tactical operations on the battlefield, dispersing and restricting what Soviet aviation was able to achieve. The emphasis on close battlefield support was retained throughout the conflict. Limited interdiction strikes behind the immediate front line were also considered in Soviet doctrine to be ground-support operations. Later in the war, Soviet pilots could follow so-called 'free hunter' tactics (*okhotniki*), pursuing targets of opportunity on the ground, but they were confined to distances of no more than 24 kilometres from the front line.[52] Unlike the practice of all the other major powers, tactical aviation was confined largely to supporting ground forces. Ironically, as German air resources dwindled and the ground fighting became more bitter and prolonged, German air fleets moved away from the pattern of 'operational air war' to concentrate more on close support for the army, now imitating the Soviet air force rather than the other way around.

The poor performance of Soviet aviation in the summer of 1941, when almost all the aircraft assigned to the western military districts were destroyed, prompted reform of the way battlefield support was organized even if the doctrine remained the same. In April 1942, the young air general Aleksandr Novikov, who had distinguished himself in the air defence of Leningrad and Moscow, was appointed air force commander-in-chief and he immediately set out to change the way air forces were organized.

The 'army aviation' and 'troop aviation' tied to individual armies and divisions, and subject to army command, were abolished and in their place came the air army, organized like the German air fleet with a corps of fighters, bombers and ground attack aircraft. The seventeen air armies were centrally controlled by air force officers who worked in headquarters alongside the army group commander whose forces they were assigned to support. The air army allowed battlefield aviation to be concentrated for the first time. To increase the degree of concentration at critical points in the offensive, Stavka (the Soviet supreme command) organized reserve corps of fighters, bombers and ground attack aircraft to be moved where they were needed. Air armies were completely mobile, like armoured units, with 4,000 vehicles apiece for rapid movement to forward airbases, or rapid retreat. Novikov and his staff introduced other reforms to increase fighting effectiveness. Communications and intelligence gathering were overhauled using radio and radar; maintenance and repair became a priority; effective camouflage and deception was practised to avoid the devastating destruction experienced in 1941. Most significant was the improvement in equipment. The Yak-3 and La-5 fighter/fighter-bombers could match the latest mark of the German Me109 and Fw190 fighter aircraft and could be modified to carry bombs or rockets. The Il-2 'Sturmovik' – nicknamed the 'Black Death' by German soldiers – was the most numerous ground attack aircraft of the war; it could be armed with rockets, bombs (particularly a fragmentation anti-personnel bomb that German soldiers came to dread) or grenade launchers, and in 1943 was modified with a 37mm cannon for destroying tanks. Produced in large numbers, they were used almost exclusively over the fighting front, where they destroyed German armour and demoralized the soldiers they bombed.

The Red Air Force took time to adjust to the reorganization, the new web of communications and the new aircraft models. Limited training regimes, which saw pilots in 1942–3 receive little more than a few hours of flying time in combat aircraft, resulted in high losses at the front; the focus on battlefield flying also resulted in dangerous operations against German anti-aircraft defences and ground fire from infantry. Soviet pilots took time to learn to rely on radio communication, and out of an astonishing 8,545 airfields constructed during the war, 5,531 were simple dirt tracks, dangerous to land on. Nevertheless, the contest between the two air forces became more even at Stalingrad and at Kursk while Soviet air tactics reached greater maturity in the long offensive against the German armed forces from mid-1943 onwards. Soviet ground attack aircraft worked well in support of major armoured thrusts, carving out a channel for the advancing ground units while fighters kept the enemy air force at bay by continuous offensive patrols. By 1945, with the German enemy much reduced in size and capability, it was possible to engage in wider interdiction operations behind the enemy front line, but these were still regarded as direct support for the battle zone. At this stage the Red Air Force had a front-line strength of 15,500 aircraft, a ten-fold advantage over the German enemy. The air–armour combination in the Soviet war effort, for all the deficiencies identified by subsequent research, was an irresistible force essential to overall Allied victory, just as air and armour had served German victories four years before.

RISE OF THE AMPHIBIANS

'To launch and maintain an amphibious operation,' wrote Admiral Lord Keyes in an edition of his Lees-Knowles lectures, delivered at Cambridge in 1943, 'it is necessary to possess Sea Supremacy in the theatre of the enterprise, and with the advent of Air Power it can only be obtained by a Navy possessing the means to fight, not only on the surface and sub-merged, but also in the air above.'[53] If ground and air warfare were ineluctably bound together in the Second World War, so too were sea and air, above all in the successful conduct of amphibious operations which, unlike the First World War, were a major element of the conflict in both Europe and the Pacific and a key to eventual Allied victory.

Amphibious warfare was a hybrid, requiring all three services to com-bine their operations for the initial assault and to maintain and extend the lodgement area until the enemy was defeated. It was distinct from a mere landing of troops unopposed, which happened commonly. Amphibious warfare meant what it said – fighting from the sea onto land. It was a low priority for most navies and armies in the inter-war years, partly because of service prejudices against a concept that compelled inter-service col-laboration, partly because of a prevailing view that with modern weaponry, including aircraft, it was impossible to storm a defended shoreline. The Allied disaster at Gallipoli in 1915–16 was a telling reminder of the dif-ficulty and a regular reference point in the inter-war years for critics of amphibious warfare. Only in Japan and the United States, face-to-face across the wide Pacific Ocean, was amphibious warfare taken seriously as a strategic and operational necessity in any future war between them. Geography dictated that both would need outlying bases among the island chains of the western Pacific and these could only be assaulted and captured from the sea.

American thinking about such a contest went back before the First

World War with the drafting of 'War Plan Orange' for a possible war with Japan, but the amphibious nature of any future campaign was only confirmed once Japan was rewarded in 1919 with the German island territories (the Marshall, Mariana and Caroline Islands) as League Mandates. In defiance of the League, Japan began secretly to build naval facilities and airfields in the 1920s, creating in effect the first stage of what would become in the Second World War a long defensive perimeter in the Pacific. In the light of Japan's new strategic position astride the western Pacific, the United States navy undertook to revise Plan Orange. Among the many contributions to the 1922 revision was a paper by Lieutenant Colonel Earl 'Pete' Ellis, a Marine Corps intelligence officer, titled 'Advance Base Operations in Micronesia', which laid the foundation for American doctrine on amphibious warfare. Ellis understood that attacking from the sea was fundamentally different both from war on land and conventional naval warfare. His description of future operations against defended shores anticipated in detail the conflict across the central Pacific twenty years later: the need for a large trained force of marines; channels cleared of mines and obstacles for the approach of landing craft to the shore; flanking support from naval gunfire to supress enemy fire; ground support from the naval air arm; artillery and signal battalions brought ashore to assist the marines in building a beachhead; beaches to be marked and controlled as men and supplies came ashore; and rapid ship-to-shore movement to maximize the initial impact of the assault. Amphibious operations, Ellis concluded, would 'entirely succeed or fail practically on the beach'.[54] Although both the navy and the army avoided commitment to amphibious warfare for much of the 1920s and 1930s, Ellis's prescription was taken up by the small Marine Corps as it prepared the first 'Tentative Manual for Landing Operations' issued in 1934. The manual in turn formed the core of the navy's 'Fleet Training Publication 167, Landing Operations Doctrine', first published in 1938 and retained (with some amendment) throughout the war in the Pacific. Ellis did not live to see his views vindicated. A career alcoholic, he died in unexplained circumstances on a spying trip to the Japanese-held Caroline Islands in 1923.[55]

The Japanese development of an amphibious capability was the mirror image of American planning. Since the 1890s and the nation's first steps in building an overseas empire, it was evident that Japan's army and navy would have to learn how to project force from the sea against any potential enemy, either in mainland Asia or the islands of the Pacific. In 1918, a joint navy–army manual, 'Outline of the Employment of Forces', included a possible amphibious invasion of the American Philippines; a version in 1923 added the American base at Guam. Close study of the Gallipoli campaign persuaded the Japanese army that it could not rely on the navy to conduct amphibious operations. Army training for attacks on a defended shoreline began in 1921, the first comprehensive army manual 'Summary of Amphibious Operations' was issued in 1924, and a final 'Outline of Amphibious Operations', jointly drafted with the navy, appeared in 1932. Japanese doctrine emphasized the need for rapid ship-to-shore movement, naval and air support to protect the landing, and specialized landing craft to move troops and supplies from the transports to the beach, preferably at night to disorient the defenders, using markers with luminous paint to guide the landing craft. But both the army and navy assumed that relatively small forces could be deployed. The navy developed Special Naval Landing Forces of battalion strength (approximately 1,000 officers and men) intended for operations against weakly-held Pacific bases; the army expected to undertake assaults at division strength or more, but in widely dispersed landings, each of more limited size.[56]

The critical factor in amphibious warfare identified very early on by the Japanese army was the need for specialized landing craft and landing ships designed to bring men, vehicles and supplies to the shoreline for rapid disembarkation. The evolution of dedicated vessels for amphibious operations was the major factor governing their future success, both Axis and Allied. By 1930, the Japanese army had two motorized landing craft, the Type I (*daihatsu*) to carry one hundred troops, fitted with a ramp for easy access to the beach, and the smaller Type II (*shōhatsu*) for thirty men, or ten men and ten horses, but without a ramp. Both were armed and armoured for protection from hostile fire. To transport the landing craft, army engineers developed the 8,000-ton landing ship, *Shinsu-maru*, which contained a well-deck with stern doors. After flooding the well-deck, the landing craft stored there could float out and make direct for the beach. The larger *Akitsu-maru*, introduced in 1941, could also carry aircraft.[57] American and British observers in China in the first year of the Sino-Japanese war watched the *Shinsu-maru* and *daihatsu* at work. Among them was a young American marine lieutenant, Victor Krulak, who sent a report to the Marine Corps commander, Thomas Holcomb, together with his own model of the landing craft. Holcomb immediately lobbied for a shallow-draft vessel with a bow ramp to disgorge troops directly onto the beach, but it took more than two years to persuade the navy that the concept was essential for amphibious operations, not least because assault craft would be greeted negatively by the isolationist lobby in Congress. The eventual Landing Craft, Vehicle, Personnel and Landing Ship, Dock, both in service by 1943, owed their origins to the Japanese innovations of the 1930s.[58]

The Pacific front line made sense of amphibious preparations in Japan and the United States, but in Europe there was little imperative to prepare forces and equipment for an unlikely wartime scenario. The expectation was for major ground war. Even in Britain, with the world's foremost navy and a global empire, landings against a defended shore were not regarded as likely. The lessons of Gallipoli were explored at length after 1918, but an Inter-Departmental Committee on Combined Operations set up in 1920 concluded that the services should remain independent and avoid planning for opposed landings. The 9,000-strong Royal Marines were tasked with defending existing naval bases overseas rather than forming the core of an amphibious assault force. A 'Manual of Combined Operations', first issued in 1922, gave little operational guidance. When planning for war in Europe began in 1939, the army assumed that British forces would be fighting alongside the French in imitation of 1918. No thought was given to the prospect that Britain would be expelled from the European mainland with no alternative but to prepare for a major amphibious assault against prepared defences, but by summer 1940 that was now the only option. The sole preparation made for amphibious operations was to develop small motorized landing craft in the 1920s under the auspices of a Landing Craft Committee, but by 1938 the navy possessed only eight. That same year orders went out to develop a Landing Craft, Assault for troops and Landing Craft, Tank for vehicles, a fortuitous decision that resulted in two standard vessels for the operations in 1943 and 1944.[59] Beyond that, Britain's capacity to mount major amphibious operations lay in a doubtful future.

The German enemy faced even greater restraints. The occupation of Norway came at a great cost in naval vessels and was not organized as a full-scale amphibious assault. The preparation of Operation 'Sea Lion' in summer 1940 for a landing in southern Britain began from a virtual blank slate. Although German army preparations were as thorough as they could be (including the allocation of extensive cargo space for fodder to feed the horses to be carried across the Channel), the army and navy lacked dedicated landing craft or transport vessels, flank support from heavy warships, experience in disembarking across a defended beach, and effective ship-to-shore communication. A plan to move 22 divisions across the Channel using 3,425 improvised steamers and towed barges was exceptionally ambitious and it relied entirely on establishing air supremacy over southern England. The army chief of staff, Franz Halder, scribbled on his copy of the operational plan beside the paragraph on air supremacy 'conditio sine qua non' – impossible without it.[60] Even with air supremacy the risks were very great. What might have been the first major amphibious operation in the European theatre foundered not only on failure in the air battle over England but also on the absence of secure doctrine, specialized equipment and adequately trained forces. The same problem applied to Hitler's Italian ally when Mussolini in March 1942 decided to capture Malta – 'a surprise with formidable results'.[61] There were plans already in place for invading and capturing the island, a thorn in the side of Axis forces as they ferried men and supplies across the Mediterranean to the North African front. The operational plan, 'Requirement C.3', had been drafted in the 1930s and was updated in 1942 to take account of Malta's significant defences. Hitler endorsed the idea without much enthusiasm, so long as it did not interrupt Rommel's operations in the desert. When the Italian navy began exploring the reality, they quailed at what they described as 'one of the greatest concentrations of defensive power in the world'.[62] Italian forces lacked dedicated landing craft or any experience at launching an amphibious assault against a well-defended shoreline, supported by the island's air power and the numerous British submarines operating around the island. The Italian navy certainly exaggerated the strength of the British garrison, but the risk of failure was high, and the operation petered out at the planning stage.

The first real test of amphibious warfare and the doctrine and equipment that supported it came with the onset of the Pacific war in December 1941. Japanese forces launched a series of operations from the sea against the Malay peninsula, the Dutch East Indies, the Philippines and the islands of the central and south Pacific under British, Australian or American rule. Japan had the advantage of local naval and air superiority, considered essential for successful amphibious assault, and years of experience in launching landings on China's coast and river deltas. The invasions were for the most part unopposed on the shoreline, despite Japanese expectations. The cover of night and sound pre-invasion intelligence maximized the impact of the landings against limited and unprepared forces. The first operation, against the north-east coast of Malaya, near the town of Kota Bahru, was opposed by a thin line of Indian troops manning pillboxes. Despite the loss of a number of landing craft and intermittent bombing from the nearby airbase, Japanese forces were miles inland from the beaches within hours, infiltrating behind the defenders and strongly supported by aircraft. The amphibious phase was quickly over. The most striking case of a defended coastline was the invasion of Singapore Island a few weeks later by Lieutenant General Yamashita's outgunned and outnumbered Twenty-fifth Army. The operation mounted across the Johore Strait on the night of 8/9 February 1942 was a model of amphibious assault, though it owed much to improvisation rather than doctrine. A deception plan succeeded in confirming the British commander's conviction that the north-east of the island was the main target. The more weakly held north-west was the real Japanese destination. Heavy shelling and bombing preceded the attack to soften up the defences; using inflatable dinghies and motor launches, a first wave of 4,000 infantry was ferried across the strait in the late evening darkness to the shoreline where the opposition was thinnest. Infiltrating between defensive positions, wave after wave of Japanese troops waded ashore and by morning the Allied front in the north had caved in. More than 20,000 troops, together with supplies and weapons, including 211 light tanks, were ferried ashore. Six days later Singapore was surrendered to Yamashita.[63]

The successful seizure of the entire south-central Pacific area down as far as the Solomon Islands and part of the island of New Guinea presented the Western Allies with a situation as intractable as that in Europe. Forcing the Japanese to abandon the conquests could only be done by amphibious operations against entrenched garrisons. For the Japanese, however, pioneers of amphibious warfare, it proved to be the end of the amphibious phase. Apart from a limited number of failed counter-offensive landings in the Solomon Islands and New Guinea, there was no repeat of the early operations. The army developed a new transport vessel, the Type 101, designed to resupply isolated garrisons in the conquered area rather than launch fresh amphibious assaults on islands recaptured by the Allies; the navy's new First Class Transport was designed to do much the same thing, capable of high speed to evade American aircraft and submarines. But too few were produced to make possible a major amphibious operation against stiff American defences even if the Japanese armed forces had willed it.

The initiative now passed to the United States. By late 1941 an amphibious capability was much closer to achievement than it had been two years before. In 1933, the navy had authorized the Marine Corps to activate a Fleet Marine Force dedicated to amphibious operations. Only 17,000 strong in 1936, the force was transformed under the command of the marines' toughest general, Holland 'Howlin' Mad' Smith, into effective combined arms units, supported by Marine Corps aviation. The Fleet Marine Force was the world's sole dedicated amphibious assault force and by late 1941 it numbered 55,000, by summer 1942, 143,000, and by the end of the war 385,000.[64] A long series of annual fleet exercises from 1936 to 1941 mimicked amphibious operations and provided a solid opportunity to learn from many mistakes. By the seventh exercise, in 1941, the complexities of a landing against opposition were fully understood. The American army, realizing that regular troops would also be needed in future amphibious operations, adopted the navy's FTP-167 manual almost verbatim as field manual FM-31-5, and began training its own dedicated forces. In 1940, the United States navy finally approved the production of a landing craft, designed by the New Orleans boat-builder Andrew Higgins, with room for troops and a vehicle. Landing Craft, Vehicle, Personnel (LCVP) became the standard, upgraded to a larger craft in 1943 with a landing ramp; more than 25,000 were pro-duced during the war. The second innovation was the Landing Vehicle, Tracked (LVT) developed from the 'Alligator' tractor produced by Don-ald Roebling to navigate the Florida Keys, and generally known as 'Amphtracks'. The amphibious vehicle, armed and armoured, could carry men or a vehicle across the shallow coral reefs that bordered many Pacific islands and proved to be the mainstay of the later operations; some 18,600 were built during the war, later versions modified with a bow ramp to allow for swifter disembarkation. Finally, the marine force needed trans-port ships that could carry cargoes, men, vehicles and landing craft. American cargo vessels were requisitioned and converted in the year before war, but a dedicated Landing Ship, Tank (LST) was designed with large bow doors, capable of reaching the shallows by the shore to offload men, vehicles and supplies. This trio of amphibious vessels bore the brunt of the wartime landings.[65]

Few of these dedicated amphibious resources were available for the first major assault ordered, at Roosevelt's insistence, to take place in sum-mer 1942 against the island of Guadalcanal in the southern Solomons. Translating doctrine into practice involved a complicated learning curve, not least for the commanders and thousands of fresh marine volunteers who had no real experience of amphibious operations. The naval officer appointed to command the amphibious force, Rear Admiral Richmond 'Terrible' Turner – yet another commander with a reputation for ill temper – thought the mission doomed in the absence of air and naval superiority. A major amphibious exercise conducted in Chesapeake Bay in January 1942 resulted in a chaotic landing, with no unit finding their assigned beach. When the marine force was finally embarked on its way to Guadalcanal from its temporary base in New Zealand, a major prac-tice run at Koro Island in Fiji proved even more disastrous, with not a single landing craft crossing the coral reef to arrive on the beach.[66] The hurried planning resulted in a shortage of shipping; the marines had to leave behind in New Zealand three-quarters of their vehicles, half the necessary ammunition, and one-third of their rations. The main landing on the morning of 7 August near the Japanese airfield nevertheless fol-lowed the Ellis pattern, with heavy gunfire support from the warships and carrier aircraft, followed by the launch of an organized line of landing craft towards the beach once men had scrambled down the netting slung over the side of the transports. The landing turned out to be unopposed on the shoreline, and the marines soon captured the airfield, but the small bridgehead immediately became the object of repeated Japanese air, naval and ground assault so that for six months, until the Japanese abandoned the island, the amphibious nature of the operation remained a reality.

The landing, though ultimately successful, exposed numerous shortcomings. The Japanese failure to attack the transport ships or blow up the supplies piled up on the sand was a matter of luck, but the operation might well have been a disaster, undermining commitment to future amphibious plans. Careful study of the campaign highlighted areas for correction. The most significant was the issue of command. Turner, as amphibious force commander, could not command the naval task force that accompanied the amphibious assault, and after two days Vice Admiral Frank Fletcher withdrew his carriers from fear of Japanese torpedo bombers, leaving the marine force exposed to Japanese air attack until American aircraft could be flown into the repaired airfield. In turn, Turner insisted on his right, according to FTP-167, to command both the landing and the marine force when it was ashore. The marine commander, Major General Alexander Vandegrift, objected to a naval officer commanding marine ground forces once they were established on land because the latter had no experience of ground combat. In November, following pressure from the marines' high command, Nimitz, the commander of the Pacific Fleet, obtained permission from the naval commander-in-chief, Admiral King, to alter doctrine, giving the navy the right of command ship-to-shore, but the marine or army commander the right to command once established on land. The reform proved difficult to implement against naval objection but nevertheless proved essential in later operations, particularly in the south-west Pacific where MacArthur's army command undertook twenty-six shore landings, almost all with little or no opposition from the beach.

The second issue concerned logistics. Too little attention was paid in loading cargo at distant ports to the doctrine that the most important goods should be the first to be unloaded and shipped to shore. At Guadalcanal ships unloaded when and where they could, causing a pile-up of goods on the shore; the failure of beach parties to organize the shoreline effectively resulted in large stacks of munitions and oil mixed with food and medical supplies, uncamouflaged and unprotected. After three days, Turner also withdrew the endangered transports, leaving the marines isolated for six days with no additional supplies. In the end, Turner used this early inexperience to reform the logistical chain. By November 1942 fuller instructions were in place to maximize the speed of ship-to-shore unloading: beaches had to be clearly marked with large signboards; beach parties to organize the distribution of supplies had to be landed first; stores had to be moved to safety as rapidly as possible. The proper organization of the beach, as Ellis had predicted twenty years earlier, was key to amphibious success.[67]

The first amphibious operations in the European theatre betrayed the same Allied inexperience. In 1940, Churchill insisted on creating a Combined Operations Headquarters to oversee his idea of regular raiding by special forces against the European coastline. First under Admiral Roger Keyes, then from 1942 Vice Admiral Louis Mountbatten, the headquarters not only developed commando raids but began to plan and train forces for an eventual amphibious re-entry to the Continent. To test how combined British forces actually were, a major raid was planned on the port of Dieppe in August 1942. A port was chosen because it was assumed that any future invasion could not be conducted and supplied across a beach. On 19 August, as Vandegrift's marines were digging in on Guadalcanal, a small flotilla of transports and landing craft, escorted by only four destroyers, approached the French coast. Operation 'Jubilee' was a chaotic disaster. Heavy German defences were alerted early on and rained fire on the unfortunate landing craft and their cargo. All twenty-seven tanks landed were knocked out or disabled, thirty-three landing craft were destroyed and one warship sunk. From 6,086 British and Canadian forces who went ashore, 3,623 were killed, wounded or captured. Naval and air casualties amounted to a further 659. As a learning experience it was exceptionally costly, but lessons were obvious. The British review of the disaster emphasized the essential nature of powerful naval gunfire support, together with aerial bombardment of the defences and air support against enemy aircraft; poor communications led to the conclusion that a dedicated amphibious command ship should co-ordinate any assault (a decision arrived at after Guadalcanal, for much the same reason); finally, that special vehicles should be designed to penetrate and clear beach defences. The Royal Navy also developed 'Force J', a naval assault force used for developing amphibious techniques and for training, which functioned for the rest of the war.[68]

Dieppe was a reminder that conducting an amphibious operation in Europe was entirely different from the operations against Japan's island perimeter. In Europe, the enemy had the advantage of long internal lines of communication for potential reinforcement and supply on a large scale; even in the event of a successful landing, this was only a prelude to a major ground campaign, leaving the amphibious war behind. By contrast, in the Pacific, the enemy garrisons were isolated from the Japanese main force, reliant on long and uncertain lines of supply and reinforcement across the sea. Here the amphibious operation was the source of the victory, island by island. This helps to explain the substantial resources devoted to amphibious warfare against Japan. After Guadalcanal, the United States navy and Marine Corps built up an operational force well beyond the scale available to the enemy, to ensure the necessary level of local naval and air superiority for each assault. For Guadalcanal there were 76 ships assigned; for the invasion of Okinawa in April 1945, a total of 1,200. It also explains the great efforts made to evaluate what went wrong in earlier operations. Even then, the first major attack against a heavily defended shore, which took place in November 1943 against Betio Island off the coast of the Tarawa atoll in the Gilbert Islands, showed that lessons still needed to be learned. The assault on Betio and its Japanese airbase by the Second Marine Division was deemed essential to open the way to the campaign against the Mandate Islands anticipated years before, but it presented a quite different challenge from Guadalcanal. Japanese defences on the tiny territory were dense: a field of rifle and machine-gun fire covering the whole island from 500 reinforced pillboxes covered with logs, steel beams, concrete and coral rock, almost invisible from above ground, supported by heavy coastal guns, light tanks, field artillery and mortars. On the beach, barbed wire, mines and concrete tetrahedron blocks were in place, and behind the beach a solid wall of coconut tree logs. It was the most heavily defended of Japan's necklace of occupied islands. The island commander, Rear Admiral Shibasaki Keiji, famously predicted that 'a million Americans could not take Tarawa in 100 years'.[69]

Tarawa could in fact be taken in three days of costly fighting, but the first assault against a heavily defended objective stretched current amphibious practice to its limit. It was not helped by a renewal of the argument about who had command between Admiral Turner, the amphibious force commander again, and 'Howlin' Mad' Smith, who was allowed to observe but not to direct the marine operation. Command and control on the morning of the assault on 20 November was compromised at once when the battleship *Maryland*, acting as the amphibious command ship, unexpectedly lost radio communication as a result of its heavy gunfire. The naval gunfire support and air attacks that preceded the landing had little effect on the heavily reinforced bunkers on the island. There was no inshore gunfire support from smaller vessels as the landing craft approached, leaving the Japanese defences approximately twenty minutes to recover from the bombardment and man their guns. The coral reef that bordered the island could not be crossed by the landing craft, leaving the marines reliant on a small number of Amphtracks – only 125, despite Smith's angry demand for more – to reach the shore. The cargo ships under fire from Japanese shore batteries had difficulty co-ordinating the unloading and lost communication with the marines ashore. Supplies came in haphazardly, but the artillery and vehicles could not easily cross the reef. Although 732 vehicles were assigned to the assault only a few were able to reach land on the first day. Troops on the beach struggled to clear the obstacles under a hail of continuous fire. When the Higgins landing craft brought in the second wave of troops, they had to unload the men 800 metres from the shore, where they struggled through the water with their weapons held aloft under a hail of machine-gun fire. The one positive result of the otherwise ineffective bombardment was the destruction of Japanese telephone line communications, leaving Shibasaki unable to co-ordinate the defence. Victory on Betio resulted chiefly from the initiative and courage of the marines assigned to the task against an enemy committed to death rather than surrender. The marines suffered 992 dead, almost as many in three days as they suffered in six months on Guadalcanal. From the 2,602 Japanese sailors from the navy's Seventh Special Naval Landing Force and Third Special Base Force, only 17 were captured; the 2,217 unfortunate Korean labourers on the island died in large numbers too, leaving just 129 still alive when the fighting was all over.[70]

The many failures at Tarawa generated a searching review of what had gone wrong. The assault was close to defeat on the first day. Almost all the subsequent operations against the island chains were opposed by forces dug in for defence, but the lessons learned at Tarawa contributed to the final reform of amphibious doctrine and practice to ensure that nothing so chaotic occurred again. Rear Admiral Alan Kirk, assigned to command the Western Task Force for the invasion of France, visited the Pacific theatre to learn at first hand what had gone wrong and what needed to be done to avoid making the same mistakes. The first step was to improve the command structure. After Tarawa, the division between the naval amphibious force commander and the commander of ground forces was insisted upon. To co-ordinate the assault, a dedicated assault command ship, with better radio communication equipment, replaced the converted battleships used in the initial operations. Gunfire support, which had been generous but ineffective at Tarawa, was to be increased substantially with a longer initial bombardment using armour-piercing shells to cope with the thick defensive carapace on the gun emplacements. Close-in gunfire support, together with dive-bomber attacks, was to keep up pressure on the defenders as the invasion force approached. Changes in equipment proved critical in future operations. Many more Amphtracks were needed (and the next major marine assault at Cape Gloucester had more than 350 for each division); light tanks were replaced by Sherman medium tanks, some of them equipped with flamethrowers. These were found to be the most effective way of clearing pillboxes and bunkers, and troops were also issued with portable backpack versions. Logistics were overhauled once again after the crisis at Betio. The flow of supplies was now to be controlled offshore with dedicated transfer points to ensure they arrived at the right point on the beach; rafts with floating dumps of essential supplies were set up at the departure line for landing craft for rapid movement to shore; shore parties were to be strengthened to give adequate support for the men shifting the supplies; finally, it was decided, when possible, to transport fully loaded trucks that could drive from the boats right onto the beach.[71]

The lessons drawn from Tarawa were essential to the evident improvement in American amphibious practice down to the final assault in April 1945 on Okinawa, the largest of the Ryūkyū islands 1,125 kilometres south of Japan, as a prelude to the expected landing on the Japanese home islands at some point later in the year. Okinawa was an operation approaching in scale the larger continental invasions in Europe. There were 433 assault transport and landing ships loaded at 11 different ports around the Pacific rim. Men, vehicles and supplies were uncomfortably convoyed over thousands of kilometres of ocean, many in shallow-draft boats that rose and fell with a resounding smack on every wave as they made their slow way to the destination, awash with vomit from the seasick soldiers. There were 183,000 assault troops (two marine divisions, three army), the largest force yet gathered in the Pacific for an opposed landing. Off the coast of Okinawa, a massive naval gunfire barrage was unleashed, supported by the marines' own Air Ground Task Force, now trained to give direct support to the troops as they landed and established the beachhead. Underwater demolition teams helped to clear obstacles to the landing.[72] The assault forces were generously supplied with LVTs, medium tanks and flamethrowers. The shore parties for controlling and distributing equipment as it landed numbered 5,000 men, supported by a Joint Assault Signal Company that ensured this time that communication on the beach and shore-to-ship functioned effectively. Some 313,000 tons of cargo were unloaded, stored according to plan, and moved forward on time to support advancing forces.

This time the Japanese army command had learned lessons too. Lieutenant General Ushijima Mitsuru, the island commander, abandoned the idea of defence on the beach, which had failed in every case, including Tarawa, and built inland lines of defence in caves and concealed bunkers

manned by more than 100,000 Japanese troops. Against American expectations, the initial landings were virtually unopposed. The subsequent
conquest of the island became in effect a ground operation, ably supported by seaborne logistics. Unlike earlier operations, it took eighty-two
days to clear Okinawa of the enemy. There were 7,374 American dead,
but an estimated 131,000 Japanese and Okinawans were buried alive in
destroyed bunkers and caves, or incinerated, or mown down by infantry
fire. The greatest Pacific amphibious operation, however, still lay in the
future. In September 1944, the American Joint War Plans Committee produced an invasion plan for the southern Japanese island of Kyushu: a
13-division invasion, supported by 7,200 naval and army air force aircraft, and 3,000 ships. The invasion force would land at three separate
beach areas, seize airfields and establish strong air support on the island.
In the end, Operation 'Olympic', and the follow-up amphibious invasion
of the main island of Honshu, never materialized following the Japanese
surrender in August 1945. The amphibious naval force instead ferried the
Allied occupation army to Japan in August and September and helped to
move Chinese forces back to the coastal areas occupied by Japan.[73]

The largest amphibious operation of the war remained Operation
'Neptune', the codename given to the amphibious phase of the Allied
invasion of north-west France, Operation 'Overlord', in June 1944. This
was an undertaking distinct from the smaller island and coastal operations in the Pacific theatre. The scale was enormous by comparison, and it
was to be undertaken against a heavily defended coastline where the
enemy had concentrated in summer 1944 some thirty-four divisions (with
more to be called up if needed), had spent two years constructing the
Atlantic Wall of powerful coastal defences, and under the direction of
Field Marshal Rommel, commander of the defence preparations, had
introduced beach and underwater obstacles, minefields and a lethal field
of fire. Reinforcement from interior lines of communication all the way
back to Germany was, at least in theory, a key advantage. The ghost of
Gallipoli hung over the operation, which perhaps explains the weak
enthusiasm of Churchill and the British military leadership for the enterprise. Churchill had behind him not only the legacy of Gallipoli, but
Norway, Dunkirk, Crete and Dieppe. On the other hand, despite the many
problems encountered, the American leadership could cite the successful
invasion of North Africa, Sicily and Italy, and the triumph against the
odds in the capture of Guadalcanal. The strategic risk, however, was
greater than the risks run in the island campaign or the earlier European
invasions. The failure to take Betio Island would not have damaged critically the advance across the Pacific, but the failure of 'Neptune' would

have faced the Western Allies with a strategic calamity, undermining relations with Stalin, making a second attempt doubtful, and demoralizing to an unpredictable degree public opinion in the United States, Britain and Canada. If, in retrospect, the success of the operation seems assured, the experience of amphibious warfare in Europe in the year and a half before 'Neptune' gave grounds for British reservation.[74]

Allied amphibious operations in Europe had begun with Operation 'Torch' in November 1942. The landings in Morocco and Algeria demonstrated even more than the raid on Dieppe how much there still was to learn, although the 'enemy' in this case constituted the limited garrisons and naval shipping kept by Vichy France in the empire areas of North Africa. It was hoped that the French might be persuaded not to oppose the landings, but the military authorities treated the Allied operation as an invasion of French territory. 'Torch', like Operation 'Watchtower' on Guadalcanal, was prepared at short notice with a good deal of improvisation. Most of those manning the landing ships and transports that crossed the Atlantic already loaded for combat were raw recruits with little training in amphibious warfare. One later recalled how 'green' the crews were: 'we had never seen an ocean before, let alone been on a ship.'[75] Training was hurriedly undertaken on board with models of beaches and landing craft but the army forces, unlike the marines in the Pacific, had not been fully prepared for an opposed landing. In the absence of boats, some of the recruits had been trained in motor cars driven across an undulating surface in pale imitation of waves. The landings in Morocco were chaotic, with too many landing craft controlled by coxswains with little experience, no proper maps, and no effective marking of the lanes of approach. Troops were slow to disembark down metal nets, slippery with the sea, carrying at army insistence 40 kilos of equipment, a policy abandoned by the marines in the Pacific. Engine failure, collisions, and French air activity played havoc with the craft that reached the shore. One transport lost eighteen out of twenty-five landing craft in the first wave, and five from the nine that remained in the second. The effort to bring ashore tanks in heavy seas left many of them stuck in the wet sand. On the first day only 2 per cent of stores made it to the shore. The Anglo-American landings in Algeria were less chaotic thanks to better marking of the approach lanes with beacons, but British insistence that ports mattered repeated the problems at Dieppe. Neither Oran nor Algiers could be taken, until forces landing on the beaches arrived.[76] Opposition against all the landings was finally overcome, helping to allay the belief that amphibious operations were destined to fail, but between 'Torch' and 'Neptune' there was much to learn, as there was between Guadalcanal and Okinawa. The many

problems that remained were dangerously exposed in the landings at
Salerno in September 1943 and Anzio a few months later.

The first hurdle to overcome for the invasion of France was the issue of
command. The decision was agreed between the Western Allies that General Eisenhower would exercise supreme command, but the operation
itself would have a naval commander for the amphibious landing, and an
army commander for the operations on land, a distinction already practised in the Pacific. Both were British, Admiral Bertram Ramsay to
command 'Neptune', Field Marshal Montgomery to command the ground
forces for 'Overlord'. Tactical air forces, essential to the amphibious operation, were centrally controlled by an air force commander, Air Marshal
Trafford Leigh-Mallory; strategic bomber forces, against the advice and
instincts of the bomber commanders, were placed directly under Eisenhower, to use as he saw fit. The planning and organization of the whole
operation from sea to shore was undertaken on a hitherto unimaginable
scale. Nine million tons of supplies were shipped across the Atlantic to
Britain to support the invasion. Some 350,000 men and women, military
and civilian, worked to organize the supply lines, to undertake the training and deployment of the millions of men destined for the European
campaign, and to develop the specialized equipment needed if a major
landing were not to be repelled on the beaches.[77] When the number of
divisions planned in the first wave was raised from three to five, across a
broader front in Normandy, the amount of shipping required escalated to
a point where competition for supply and reinforcement with the Mediterranean and Pacific theatres threatened to undermine the entire
amphibious plan. Shipping had been one of the arguments against
attempting a major landing in France in 1943, and although 'Neptune'
was the major operation of the Western war effort, a shortage of warships, transports and landing craft remained a critical constraint.

The initial plan for 'Neptune', drafted in 1943, called for a total of
2,630 assorted landing craft and no fewer than 230 of the most important
transports (Landing Ship, Tank) with their heavy load of vehicles and supplies. In relation to overall production, these requirements seem modest
enough. Construction of American landing craft from 1940 to 1945
totalled a remarkable 63,020, although 23,878 were produced after June
1944 to meet high demand in the Pacific theatre. Nevertheless, high losses
in the Pacific and Mediterranean, and the continued demand for landing
craft in both these theatres for operations that were not strategically necessary (including Churchill's stubborn insistence that he wanted an
amphibious invasion of Rhodes in 1944 even if it meant postponing 'Neptune' by two months) presented an awkward balancing act between the

many demands.[78] The enlarged number of divisions in the first wave increased the pressure on shipping resources still more. Landing ships and landing craft were finally given a special urgency rating for production only in August 1943, but it took time for new craft to be produced, and after the crisis at Tarawa, many additional resources were urgently allocated to production for the Pacific.

In the end, around 4,000 landing craft were made available – enough, as it turned out, to achieve the initial beachhead. The more critical shortage concerned the larger Landing Ship, Tank, most of which were produced in American shipways along the Ohio River. The vessels could land directly on the beach to unload vehicles and stores and in the absence of a port were vital to keep the forces ashore adequately supplied. Eisenhower wanted at least 230, but by 1944, with too many still in the Mediterranean to meet expected amphibious operations there, he regarded the available numbers as insufficient to transport the necessary supplies. A crash programme of production from October 1943, on the direct orders of Roosevelt and King, produced 420 new LSTs between November 1943 and May 1944, but many crossed the Atlantic too late for the invasion, though in time for the programme of resupply. The cancellation of operations in Burma and the Mediterranean added more, and by D-Day Eisenhower had 234. To cope with the operation the army insisted on loading to capacity, even overloading, while an urgent effort was made to ensure that all LSTs were serviceable. By 1 June, with five days to go, no fewer than 229 of the transports were ready for operations.[79]

The preparations for 'Neptune' had none of the urgent improvisation of many operations in the Pacific. The millions of troops to be conveyed across the English Channel spent long months of regular and intensive training, starting with small-scale practice to learn how to disembark and run up a beach, and finishing in early May 1944 with a series of full-scale exercises, codenamed 'Fabius', along the English south coast, using live ammunition and mines. 'Neptune' did however suffer from a severe shortage of trained seamen for the transports and landing craft. Many of the officers came straight from a short course in the United States to command the boats; others were trained at the Amphibious Training School at Slapton Sands on the south Devon coast. The Royal Navy established a temporary naval cadet school where junior officers were trained for managing an amphibious assault boat, but not for deep sea sailing. Once trained, the young recruits were expected to master limitless instructions from Ramsay's headquarters. The volume of directives numbered almost 1,200 pages covering every aspect of the amphibious stage of the assault. Specialized teams and equipment were also developed for the operation, imitating the shore and beach parties in the Pacific. To cope with the beach defences, thirty-two Naval Combat Demolition Units were established; pilots from all the tactical air forces were trained as artillery spotters; a number of Liberty cargo ships were converted into radar plotting units to direct fighter interception; and intensive cover by aerial reconnaissance produced a much fuller intelligence picture than for other amphibious operations. To get tanks quickly to the beaches, an amphibious 'duplex drive tank' was devised able, in theory, to swim to shore under its own power. So-called 'Rhino' ferries, large rafts with an outboard motor, were built to lift cargo onto the beach. Finally, amphibious cargo vehicles – DUKWs – were built not only to bring cargo across the shoreline, but to deliver it where the troops were fighting. When Ramsay announced to Eisenhower on 15 May that the operation was ready to go, the largest amphibious assault in history was about to unfold. On 28 May, Ramsay sent out the order to the vast force under his command, 'carry out Operation Neptune'.[80]

The invasion of Normandy showed how far Allied amphibious capability had matured from its first uncertain steps. It had much in common with the doctrine first articulated by Ellis and the Marine Corps in the 1920s. The prerequisite was sea and air superiority, and both were assured by June 1944. The invasion was supported by more than 1,000 warships of every kind and Allied air forces could muster 12,000 aircraft of all types. The German air force had been forced back to defence of the Reich, where it suffered debilitating losses during the first half of 1944. In northern France, German Air Fleet 3 on the eve of 'Neptune' could muster only 540 aircraft of all types, including just 125 fighters.[81] Allied naval supremacy was total. German fast motor torpedo boats (E-boats) and submarines attempted to intervene, but from the vast armada of 7,000 assorted vessels only 3 small cargo ships and a dozen minor naval vessels were lost, while from the 43 German submarines sent to intervene, 12 were damaged and 18 were sunk.[82]

The object of the initial assault on 6 June was the violent and rapid seizure of a secure beachhead, elimination of the shore defences, and enough logistical back-up to ensure that any concerted counter-offensive could be contained. Five separate beaches had been selected on a broad front across the Normandy coast – 'Gold', 'Juno' and 'Sword' for the combined Anglo-Canadian force, 'Utah' and 'Omaha' for the American forces. After the beach obstacles had been cleared by the special demolition teams, 200 minesweepers cleared marked channels through the minefields, and landing craft packed with seasick and nervous men began a voyage to the shore that in some cases involved a journey of more than 15 kilometres. The German defensive line was bombarded by naval vessels, a heavy assault by the larger four-engine bombers, and then by an inshore fusillade of rockets from converted landing craft supported by tactical strikes by dive-bombers and medium bombers. The bombardment did not destroy the defences, but the object was to neutralize them sufficiently to allow the shock of the beach invasion to disorient the defenders. The heavy bombers and naval gunfire did relatively little damage, but shore parties and aircraft 'spotters' were able to direct shelling behind the beaches where German forces were retreating. The landings were more orderly than might have been expected from the inexperience of many of the crews. Although it looked as if landing craft, amphibious tanks and piles of boxes had arrived in apparent confusion on the shore, order was soon imposed so that supplies and men could be rapidly brought in to strengthen the initial landing. By midday, all three beaches in the British sector were secured and troops began to move inland to create a more robust lodgement. At the Americans' 'Utah' beach, the troops landed some distance from their intended destination because of the pall of smoke from the bombardment, but by chance the site was weakly defended. By evening American forces on 'Utah' were 10 kilometres inland.

The principal battle on D-Day took place on the second of the American beaches. 'Omaha' was the Tarawa of the European war. As in the Pacific operation, everything that could go wrong did so, even if the beach was eventually secured against the odds. The initial naval bombardment was too brief, as it had been on Betio Island; the rocket salvoes fell short of their target; the heavy bombers dropped their bombs too far behind the defences, so that as the landing craft made their long way towards the beach, the German defenders had time enough to recover from the bombardment to man their guns. As the first wave of troops hit the beach, German mortar, artillery and machine-gun posts created a wall of fire, destroying landing craft and decimating the first to land. The rough sea swamped the amphibious tanks, sending them to the seabed with their doomed crews trapped inside. Only two out of twenty-nine launched reached the shore, whereas on 'Sword' thirty-one out of thirty-four arrived and on 'Juno', the Canadian beach, twenty-one out of twenty-nine.[83] The Naval Combat Demolition Units landed in the first hail of fire and lost so many men and so much equipment that only five narrow lanes could be opened before the second and third waves of infantry arrived. At the shoreline, damaged landing craft and equipment blocked the way for those coming after, breaking up the orderly wave of craft into a confused melee, disgorging men amidst the wreckage and the bodies as best they could. Retracting from the beach proved in many cases impossible or hazardous in the extreme.

German fire remained relentless. After two hours it seemed probable that the assault at 'Omaha' would fail. As on Tarawa, the courage and determination of American troops who had survived overcame the obstacles. Following an urgent call for destroyer support, a dozen vessels detached from the main fleet and, despite the shallow sea, closed to within a few hundred metres of the beach, firing all guns at German emplacements. Close-in bombardment was one of the lessons learned in the Pacific and it proved again much more effective than the heavier naval guns. Because the shore parties to direct gunfire had suffered severe casualties, the destroyers fired as opportunity dictated. The result of adopting inshore fire support, improvised though it was, was decisive in allowing American forces to advance from the narrow strip of shingle.[84] By the evening the worst disaster had been avoided and a small beachhead had been secured as it was at Tarawa. The cost in dead, wounded and missing is still unclear, but estimates agree that there were well over 2,000 casualties, matching the losses endured by the marines on Betio.

No amphibious landing against determined opposition can ever go perfectly to plan, and mistakes were made all along the stormed coastline. But in the end a secure lodgement was achieved on the first day. Even the loss of 'Omaha' beach would almost certainly not have imperilled the entire enterprise. The quantity of men, equipment and stores unloaded across the beaches in the opening week was enough to ensure that, even if the Germans had not divided their forces between Normandy and an anticipated landing in the Pas de Calais, throwing Allied forces 'back into the sea', as Hitler directed, was beyond their military means. By 11 June the armada of ships had brought 326,000 men, 54,000 vehicles and 104,000 tons of supplies to the beachhead; even across the battered shoreline on 'Omaha', some 50,000 tons were unloaded by the 17th, when Admiral Ramsay declared the amphibious phase of the invasion to be completed successfully.[85] This was the last major amphibious operation in Europe. In both theatres, European and Pacific, the Allies had been exposed to a long learning curve in turning amphibious doctrine into trained forces, pertinent equipment and tactical awareness. This was an essential element in their eventual victory, for without the means to invade a defended shore and capture a permanent foothold there was no way to dislodge the enemy from conquered territory. The Gallipoli albatross was finally laid to rest.

FORCE MULTIPLIERS: RADIO AND RADAR

In a 1945 publication by the American Joint Board of Scientific Information it was claimed that 'Radio detection and ranging' – better known by the American acronym Radar – 'more than any other development since the airplane, changed the face of warfare.'[86] This was a large claim but the mature development during the war of armoured warfare, tactical air power, amphibious warfare and naval-air combat relied a great deal on the evolution of front-line electronic warfare using radio and radar. The science of radio waves had reached a climactic moment in the second half of the 1930s. In a single year in the United States, the first American pulse radar was demonstrated by the Naval Research Laboratory, FM (frequency modulation) radio was discovered by a former Signal Corps officer, Edwin Armstrong, and the US army designed a pulse radar system for aircraft detection. The year was 1936, but only five years later, when the United States was forced into war, there already existed a defensive radar network from the Panama Canal to the Aleutian Islands, naval radar to detect surface vessels and to direct gunfire automatically, ASV (air-to-surface-vessel) radar in carrier aircraft, FM radios for all tanks and AI (air interception) radar for army aircraft. Development in the field was exponential and continued to be so across the war years.

Radio had been little used in the First World War. The static fronts relied on wire communications and the telephone, or used runners, flag signals and carrier pigeons. The advent of armour and aircraft made imperative a new form of communication since static telephone networks were of little use. The inter-war development of civilian radio technology had an obvious military application. By the 1930s, military research establishments worldwide explored the possibility of using radio for battlefield communication on land and at sea, both to command the battlefront directly and to allow front-line units of infantry, artillery and armour to communicate at a local level. Most armies initially remained attached to the idea of wire communications because they were more secure and the sound quality better, but air forces everywhere required radio because there was no other means of communicating between aircraft or between ground control and airborne planes. Shipboard radio for surface vessels and submarines became essential for operational communication between fleet units and with command centres. Nevertheless, radio had disadvantages that had to be overcome. Early sets were heavy and the aerials and antennae conspicuously long. AM (amplitude modulation) radios, standard in the 1930s, were subject to interference, frequency drift and static noise. The range for battlefront radios was short, sometimes little more than a kilometre or so. In a moving vehicle, AM radio was almost impossible to use. On board ship, radio could suffer concussion effects from the power of the naval guns. In extreme temperatures, high humidity, or heavy rain radios could become inoperable, or the delicate circuits might corrode. Radio communication was also insecure, since it could easily be intercepted and exploited by the enemy (unless the messages had previously been enciphered) or be subject to jamming by enemy signal troops. Using radio *en clair* made sense only in fast-moving battles on the ground or in the air where enemy message interception would make little difference. Most of these disadvantages were confronted during the war years as the need for radio became more urgent, but radio security and survivability were never fully resolved.

The creation of armoured forces in the second half of the 1930s went hand-in-hand with the search for better communication. German armed forces were the first to explore the prospect of using radio to control a battlefield from higher command down to small front-line units. In June 1932 a large-scale army manoeuvre titled *Funkübung* (Radio Exercise) tested communication in an imagined scenario of a Czechoslovak invasion of Germany. The exercise proved to be the foundation of a sophisticated signals doctrine and practice in which radio was to play a crucial part. Experience gained in the Spanish Civil War by German forces sent to aid Franco confirmed that armoured vehicles worked to best advantage when they were linked by radio.[87] By 1938, each armoured unit was co-ordinated by a *Befehlspanzerwagen* (armoured control vehicle) in which the unit commander, accompanied by a range of radio equipment, maintained control over his force and contact with tactical headquarters. By 1940 there were 244 control vehicles, by the invasion of the Soviet Union 330 – an innovation fundamental to the effective operation of armoured formations.[88] Standard two-way radio communication was installed in all German tanks and proved to be a decisive advantage in the invasion of France and the Low Countries in 1940, when four-fifths of French tanks had no radio. To control a force of French tanks sometimes involved an officer running from one tank to the next, shouting through the hatches to be heard.[89] By contrast, each German armoured division enjoyed a dedicated and well-equipped battalion of signal troops to sustain radio contact across the force. Radio training was rigorous. All signals had to employ codenames ('Lion', 'Eagle', 'Sparrowhawk', and so on), and be kept as brief as possible, using phrases listed in a 'brevity table' to avoid cluttering the airwaves and betraying position to the enemy.[90] The high standard of German radio signalling remains an important explanation for the ability of the German army, even in retreat, to sustain its fighting power.

Radio in battlefield situations where armour and vehicles were the core element proved to be essential for establishing what is now called 'command and control'. Tanks left to fight on their own, or artillery with no central direction, were at a permanent tactical disadvantage. Nevertheless, it took time before German practice was replicated in other armoured forces. British army field regulations issued as late as 1935 carried no mention of radio. Radios were rapidly developed in the first year of war, but in 1940 runners and telephone remained the principal means for front-line communication. Tanks eventually received the standard WS 19 AM radio, which allowed two-way communication between tanks and with the higher command posts, despite the difficulties using AM in a moving vehicle.[91] Soviet and Japanese tanks generally had no radios except for the tank commander of front-line units, and those that did exist were of poor quality and performance or in short supply. In Japanese armoured operations instructions were commonly given by hand signal, flares or an elaborate system of coloured and patterned flags.[92] Soviet defeat in 1941 owed a good deal to the lack of radio at all levels. The situation improved over time with the generous supply of 245,000 field radios from the United States and Britain. Radios down to small-unit level were fitted in the commander's tank, but command and control of tank forces by radio never matched German practice.

The United States army in the 1930s, like the British, assumed that telephone lines and conventional messaging would be adequate means for communication, as they had been for the American wartime expeditionary force in 1918. But under pressure from the newly created Mechanized Corps (soon to be the Armored Force), the army Signal Corps Laboratory began to develop high-quality FM radio sets for use in tanks and vehicles, using quartz crystals to create stable frequencies, good reception and immunity from jamming and interference. Major army exercises in Louisiana in the summer of 1940 showed that FM radio functioned well to create an effective web for controlling battlefield armour. The SCR-508 became the standard tank radio for two-way communication between tanks and with tactical command posts and proved its worth in the major armoured operations in Europe in 1944.[93] The only problem proved to be the vulnerability of FM quartz crystals to sudden failure due to a phenomenon known as ageing. The American physicist Virgil Bottom, recruited to the Quartz Crystal Section of the Signal Corps Laboratory, discovered the cause and the cure in time for the fighting in Normandy. By 1944, United States forces had not only the largest number of radios per unit of any of the warring powers, but radios of high reliability and performance.[94]

For infantry units, particularly for those detailed to support advancing tanks, communication was more problematic. Early radios were heavy, cumbersome and difficult to operate on the move. But because most operations were mobile, it was necessary to find a means to allow troops on the ground to communicate with armour and artillery and to establish 'voice control' over forward infantry units to ensure more effective tactical deployment. The idea that an integrated web could be constructed linking command with small units and small units with each other proved difficult in practice, chiefly because armour, artillery and infantry used different radios tuned to different frequencies. A common frequency was introduced for British forces only in 1945; common infantry–armour radio arrived in American units only in the final months of 1944. For American operations, in which infantry and tanks were supposed to work forward together, the problem was a real one. The typical infantry radios – the SCR-586 AM 'handie-talkie' (primitive ancestor of the mobile phone) and the larger SCR-300 AM 'walkie-talkie', operated by two men – were both incompatible with the tank's SCR-508 FM set. To summon assistance or to provide intelligence, infantry had to route messages through tactical command centres, a procedure that was too slow to allow the immediate response needed. Improvisations were used to try to circumvent the problem. Infantry radios were sometimes placed inside the tanks, where their performance was limited by noise and movement. The most common solution was the use of a field telephone welded to the rear of the tank and linked to the tank's intercom system. An infantryman could talk directly to the crew with instructions about targets and risks, though he remained dangerously exposed to enemy sniper fire.[95]

The front line of radio communications, though vital to help small units co-ordinate actions and summon assistance, was fraught with obvious difficulties. Apart from the technical problems encountered with unstable frequencies, broken valves or shoddy engineering, radio contact was easily disrupted by heavy rain, sea and river water, and an unfavourable topography. Mountains and hills limited range or cut out communication altogether, as Allied forces found in Tunisia in early 1943 and in Italy throughout the campaign along the peninsula. Radios had to be strapped to mules and carried to hilltops to help them function. Radio operators also faced greater vulnerability in combat. The heavy equipment occasionally dragged them under the water as they approached shore in amphibious operations; enemy marksmen looked for the telltale antennae that betrayed the signals operative as a primary target. Nevertheless, as radios became more reliable and lighter to carry, they were regularly distributed to small units in the field for operation by one or two men. The German Torn Fu. d ('Dora') and Torn Fu. g ('Gustav') were reliable portable sets with a range of up to 10 kilometres. British units had the less effective WS 38 walkie-talkie with a range of less than a kilometre, and the larger WS 18, operated by two men, with a range of up to 8 kilometres. Although regarded as an unreliable tool, 187,000 of the portable WS 38 were produced during the war and saw service across Europe. During the whole course of the war, the British army was supplied with 552,000 radios, testament to their indispensable value in combat.[96]

The advent of front-line radio required a steep learning curve. In the Pacific theatre, poor radio communication in the early American operations contributed to unnecessarily high casualties. For the assault on Tarawa in November 1943 the command ship USS *Maryland* had inadequate radio equipment for communicating with the marines as they were landed on the beaches. Radio suffered from the concussion effect of the battleship's huge guns, while ashore the portable marine radios, the navy TBX and TBY sets, functioned poorly because of water damage and short battery life. By the invasion of Okinawa in April 1945, dedicated command ships with better radio controlled the invasion movements ship-to-shore, where improved portable radio sets helped to organize the tactical battlefield with fewer casualties.[97] The use of radio in the first Anglo-American amphibious landing in North Africa in November 1942 also failed to establish a workable communications network. The AM sets were affected by torrential rain and the crowded frequencies. Many of the radio operators had been hastily trained on the ships crossing the Atlantic, while the supply of adequate equipment and replacements fell short of requirements. American and British radio systems were incompatible and had to be adjusted to be able to communicate between the two forces. So poor was the performance that the British set up a committee under Major General Alfred Godwin-Austen to evaluate lessons learned so that radio could play a more effective role. The conclusions were distributed in March 1944 in time to improve the use of radio in the invasion of Normandy.[98] By 1944 radio was finally embedded in British and American military practice. There were ten times as many radios for the British army as there had been in 1940; American army units had 90,000 radio transmitters on D-Day, the bulk of them the more reliable FM crystal-controlled radios, all tuned to new frequencies to confuse German signals intelligence. By that stage American industry was producing 2 million crystal units a month, against a pre-war output of 100,000 a year. Radio proved itself in the long pursuit of German forces across France in July and August 1944 and, in harness with ground radar, was essential in the effective fire direction and control of the Allies' formidable artillery.[99]

Radio was even more essential for the evolution of tactical air power during the war. Air forces asked for and were given priority in the allocation of high-performance radio. British very high frequency (VHF) radios were installed in all aircraft for the Battle of Britain in the summer and autumn of 1940, allowing pilots to communicate with each other and with the ground control stations that directed them to the target area once radar or ground observation had identified intruding aircraft. Radio was the only way to hold together the aerial zone of combat for defending aircraft. In the field, air offensives were more difficult to organize, relying not only on the establishment of forward ground control centres, to maintain voice control of attacking aircraft, but on the development of radio contact between aircraft and the army (or a fleet at sea) when a surface target needed to be neutralized. German air forces succeeded in doing this in the early campaigns in Poland and France, even though army and air force radios operated on different frequencies. Air force liaison officers were attached to major army units and played a critical role in melding air and ground operations together; for the invasion of the Soviet Union, Air Signal Liaison Detachments were assigned to each armoured division for the purpose of summoning air support. By the battles in 1943 on the Eastern Front, direct radio contact was available between tank commanders and supporting aircraft using the same radio frequency.[100]

Once again, it took some years before radio control of tactical air forces was perfected to the same degree by the Allies. In Britain, following the calamity in France, a joint army–air force team led by Lieutenant Colonel J. Woodall worked out a means to co-ordinate the role of air and ground forces. The subsequent 'Woodall report', completed in September 1940, recommended joint control centres capable of receiving detailed information on targets from signals units with the front-line troops, and rapidly despatching aircraft where they were needed. The system was formally approved, but in the desert war in North Africa radio control of aircraft in a war of rapid movement proved difficult to operate until there were enough aircraft and skilled radio operators and in the face of much remaining army prejudice.[101] Not until autumn 1941, with the creation of Forward Air Support Lines, did it prove possible for the front line to summon air strikes by radio, but the request had to go all the way back to RAF headquarters for approval, slowing down any operational response. Finally, in early 1942 a more sophisticated network of radio communication was established with Advanced Air Headquarters moving with the army, able – with VHF radio – to direct aircraft while still airborne from one ground target to the next. Some 400 VHF signals vehicles moved with the army, providing detailed information by radio of enemy positions to be attacked from the air, at last imitating and then surpassing German communications.[102]

The Soviet air force too had to learn from German practice. The absence of radios for aircraft in the first years of the war meant that on occasion reconnaissance aircraft had to land at airfields to alert the pilots for an operation, and then lead them visually to the target. Without radios, air units operated a follow-my-leader formation, which made them easy targets for their German opponents who could operate more flexibly thanks to radio. The poorly co-ordinated control of aircraft operations was highlighted in the reports of the War Experience Analysis Section of the Red Army, and in late 1942 Novikov, the new air force commander-in-chief, introduced a centralized radio-vectoring system on the Stalingrad front, using radio and radar to direct aircraft to targets in the air and on the ground. Auxiliary ground control posts, linked by radio to airbases and to Soviet aircraft, were established 2–3 kilometres behind the front line and 8–10 kilometres apart. A new field manual was produced on 'Instructions to the Air Force on Controlling, Informing and Guiding Airplanes by Radio' and German airmen began almost immediately to observe more effective and targeted Soviet interception. It took time for the radio networks to be installed across the wide fighting front, and for Soviet pilots to understand and to rely on radio control. They also sent messages *en clair*, which were easy for German signals intelligence to intercept. At the Battle of Kursk in July 1943 the system worked less well in defence, but for the long counter-offensive that followed in the summer and autumn the introduction of American-supplied radio stations and 45,000 Lend-Lease aircraft radios made it possible to use the Soviet Union's growing numerical superiority with greater effect.[103]

The United States army and navy air forces, like the Soviet air force, experienced a difficult apprenticeship. In the battle for Guadalcanal from August 1942 it was essential to be able to call up air support, but the navy, Marine Corps and army air forces all used different radio frequencies. An improvised solution was found in a system of 'air forward observers', who called back to a modified radio attached to two microphones so that a nearby naval radio could also hear the report.[104] During the landings in north-west Africa in November 1942 the air component functioned poorly chiefly because of the difficulty in rapidly establishing a reliable radio and radar network with inadequate supplies and personnel. The result, as the air commander Carl Spaatz complained, was a 'feeble and inept communications system', made worse by the failure to integrate the British and American air control frequencies.[105] The lessons learned in North Africa eventually produced a more workable signals system. For ground support operations in the invasion of France, Air Support Parties accompanied major army units so that they could provide immediate requests for air action to Air Support Control posts. By the late summer of 1944, Air Support Parties stationed a radio operator with VHF radio in lead tanks, able to call up support from aircraft patrolling above using the same SCR-522 radio sets used by the air force. The relative absence of German aircraft by that stage of the campaign meant that it was also possible to employ the small L-5 'Horsefly' liaison aircraft to fly in front of advancing ground forces to radio back potential targets.[106] Radio now worked as part of an elaborate web that linked ground control stations with aircraft, aircraft with each other and aircraft with ground forces. The systems were never perfect on either the Axis or the Allied side, but radio magnified the impact that aircraft enjoyed in battle, to the growing advantage of the Allies as they neared the end of their learning curve.

The advent of effective radio for controlling aircraft, whether in aerial combat or in support of surface forces, was intimately linked to the evolution and development of radar. The first tentative steps in exploiting radio waves for detection were prompted by the search for some means of advanced warning of approaching hostile aircraft other than the conventional use of large acoustic sensors, which were of little operational use since they could indicate nothing more than the presence of faint noise. Research on radio waves was universal and the technology needed to develop radar genuinely international. Two key components were Japanese and German in origin – the Yagi antenna, developed by Yagi Hidetsugu in 1926, and the Barkhausen–Kurz tube (or magnetron) invented in 1920 for use in receivers and transmitters – but they were also patented abroad and the research made readily available to others. The commercial development of television in the late 1920s and early 1930s, again common across the industrialized world, contributed in important ways to the evolution of radar, including the cathode ray tube, which was used in radar installations to provide an easily read image of the object detected. Civilian industry played an important part in supplying the engineering innovation that made radar possible: Telefunken in Germany, General Electric in the United States and Britain, Nippon Electric Company in Japan, and so on. Given the transnational nature of the science, it is not surprising that the observations that gave rise to radar occurred almost simultaneously in all the major states that later fought the war. No single person or single country 'invented' radar.

If the development of radar was inevitable by the 1930s, its early origins were the result of serendipity as much as foresight. In late 1934 the director of scientific research at the British Air Ministry, Henry Wimperis, impressed by the claim of the Hungarian physicist Nikola Tesla that concentrated radio waves could act as a 'death ray' to approaching aircraft, asked the superintendent of the Radio Research Station, Robert Watson-Watt, to investigate the claim. Watson-Watt reported that the claim was scientifically implausible, but that a radio beam might be used for 'radio detection as opposed to radio destruction'. Based on his work in measuring the ionosphere using radio pulses and the reflected echo, Watson-Watt organized an experiment a few miles from the BBC transmitter at Daventry on 26 February 1935. A Handley Page Heyford aircraft flew along the beam returning clear signals to the ground receiver. Excited by the result of the experiment, which at last promised protection against attack by hostile aircraft, Watson-Watt exclaimed 'Britain has become an island again!'[107]

Unknown to the British team, who have regularly been regarded as the inventors of what they called 'range and direction finding', the US navy's Bureau of Engineering had filed a patent in November 1934 for 'detecting objects by radio', while a month later the Naval Research Laboratory demonstrated that pulse radar could detect an aircraft at the distance of 1½ kilometres; the American army Signal Corps Laboratory had already begun a programme for 'radio position finding' in the same year. The German physicist Rudolf Kühnhold, director of the German navy's Radio Research Institute, used radio waves to detect shipping in 1934 and the following May, less than three months after the experiment at Daventry, successfully demonstrated the use of pulse radar.[108] Research in the Soviet Union began even earlier when in August 1933 the Central Radio Laboratory in Leningrad was authorized by the Main Artillery Administration to work on radio detection to help anti-aircraft defences. An experiment conducted on 3 January 1934 by Pavel Oshchepkov from the roof of a building in Leningrad showed that radio signals could be reflected by distant objects.[109] In almost all cases the military application of the discoveries was immediately understood, and radar suddenly became shrouded in a cloak of secrecy.

While the discovery of radar was universal, subsequent developments were less straightforward. There was a significant operational difference between the pulsed radar, adopted at once in Britain, the United States and Germany, and radio detection based on continuous wave transmission instead of interval pulses. True radar transmitted a pulse at around a millionth of a second's duration and received back an echo from the object detected in the interval between the pulses at several millionths of a second. This process increased the power of the radio beam and allowed measurement of the distance between the receiver and the object (a critical factor in air defence) as well as direction of flight. The estimate of height – or azimuth – was more difficult but was solved by adding an additional component (in the British case a goniometer which calculated the bearing of the aircraft). Continuous wave transmission could indicate range, height and direction imperfectly or not at all. Soviet research was complicated by the insistence of the air force on pulse radar and the army view that continuous wave would satisfy the requirements of anti-aircraft artillery, a conviction that proved a dead end since aircraft range could not be estimated. Politics intervened in the Great Terror in 1937–8 when most of the senior radio and radar researchers were arrested, including the pioneer Oshchepkov, who was sent to a Gulag camp for ten years.[110] In Japan neither the navy nor the army could be convinced in the 1930s that radio detection had anything to offer, and when a primitive radar system was finally established along China's coastline and on the home islands in 1941, the continuous wave stations could only indicate the presence of an aircraft, not its range or direction, rendering the system operationally futile although it was retained throughout the war. Neither the army nor the navy would collaborate on radar development, while the small scientific and engineering community dedicated to radio research was marginalized by a military establishment distrustful of civilian intervention.[111] The situation in Italy was considerably worse. When Italy entered the war in 1940 there was no radar capability available at all and low priority for radio detection research. The military preferred continuous wave but no coastal network was established even of inadequate radar. In 1941 two sets employing pulse radar waves for coastal and shipboard defence, code-named 'Folaga' ('Coot') and 'Gufo' ('Owl'), were eventually ordered, but only twelve were ever produced. The army developed the 'Lynx' aircraft-detection apparatus, but only a few were available before the Italian surrender. The radar network eventually established in 1943 was a German one, to protect German forces.[112]

The initial military and naval interest in radio detection focused on the possibility of early warning of approaching enemy aircraft with enough information and time to activate anti-aircraft defences and to scramble aircraft for interception. In Britain this was seen in the mid-1930s as a vital means to reduce the potential threat of bombing attack, which politicians and public alike feared might have a decisive impact in a war they expected sooner rather than later. In late 1935, less than a year after the experiment at Daventry, the first orders went out for constructing five 'Chain Home' stations along the south and east coasts. By 1940 there were thirty stations stretched from Cornwall in the south-west to the far north of Scotland. To detect low-flying aircraft a cordon of thirty-one 'Chain Home Low' stations was established. They did not function perfectly. The early radar could only detect over the sea and could not follow aircraft inland because ground clutter interfered; height remained difficult to measure accurately, partly because many of the personnel were hastily trained and needed the apprenticeship of combat to exploit radar fully.[113] Nevertheless, radar, once integrated with the network of radio and telephone, played a central part in alerting the British fighter force in time to intercept the regular German daytime incursions in 1940. Over the wartime years the radar was continually improved in performance against a shrinking number of enemy sorties.

In the United States coastal defence radar began to be installed from the late 1930s from fear that the Japanese, or German aircraft based in Latin America, might spring a surprise attack. Radar for long-range detection was authorized in 1937, and by 1939 both mobile and fixed-site sets had been developed. The first fixed-site SCR-271 radar was set up to defend the Panama Canal in 1940; in February that year the Air Defense Command was activated to begin work on a network of radar stations linked to air interception forces, not unlike the British system. The structure took time to develop because of shortages of trained personnel and the competing demands of rearmament so that by the time of Pearl Harbor there were only two radar stations on the east coast, six on the Pacific. The radar was able to detect direction and distance but not height. Many had been poorly sited on hilltops on instructions from the War Department and had to be transported to lower sites to optimize their performance. Only gradually with modification of the equipment did coastal radar reach British standards, and in the end a comprehensive network of sixty-five sites on the Pacific coast and thirty on the east coast was established. By the later war years Ground Control Interception radar, the SCR-588, could track enemy and friendly aircraft on the same screen and supply range, direction and azimuth, while the SCR-516 provided the equivalent of the British Chain Home Low, capable of detecting low-flying aircraft at ranges of over 100 kilometres.[114] In the end neither American coastline was attacked from the air so that the elaborate structure of radar, fighter stations, radio communications and ground observation, so vital to British survival in 1940, was never tested. Instead, radar stations had to cope with the large number of domestic air force training flights. In July 1942 alone, the Los Angeles air defence region monitored 115,000 training sorties, but not a single enemy plane.[115] The irony of a system untested in wartime was underscored by the one time it was needed – in the pre-war Japanese attack on the Pearl Harbor naval base. Radar had been installed by December 1941 at Opana Ridge on the north coast of Oahu, and two radar operators duly reported a large body of approaching aircraft in the early morning of 7 December, only to be told by their superior officer that they were friendly bombers on their way to reinforce the Pacific bases. As the radar screen became cluttered by background interference, the two operators left the radar unattended and went to breakfast.[116]

The most sophisticated and extensive radar defensive screen was established by the German air force on Germany's western frontiers and along the northern coast of occupied Europe. Here air combat was continuous, from the first British raids in May 1940 through to the end of hostilities in May 1945. German air-warning radar was developed by two private German firms, GEMA and Telefunken, and then taken over by the air force chief of signals, General Wolfgang Martini, for use by the German air force, which was responsible for the air defence system. The GEMA company originated what became the 'Freya' radar, operating on a broad radio wavelength and with a coastal range of 130 kilometres. In place by 1939, the radar was improved by adding target height measurements to allow accurate vectoring of fighter aircraft for interception. Improved performance came in 1940 from putting eight Freyas together to form a radar codenamed 'Wassermann' with a range of 300 kilometres; in 1941, sixteen Freya radars were linked to form what was codenamed 'Mammoth' with a similar range. With the enhanced models, British aircraft could be detected as they took off from bases in eastern England. Wilhelm Runge, director of Telefunken's Radio Research Laboratory, developed a gun-laying radar for accurate anti-aircraft fire codenamed 'Würzburg'. Both radars became the standard sets used in the German air defence system. Later in the war Würzburg was supplemented by 'Würzburg-Riese' ('Giant Würzburg') and by 'Mannheim', a control radar for anti-aircraft artillery with a range of 30 kilometres and enhanced accuracy. In 1944, to cope with low-level fighter-bomber raids, a mobile surveillance radar, Fu MG407, was introduced. Mounted on a converted truck, the radar was moved from place to place to fill the gaps between the widely spaced Freya and Würzburg installations.[117]

The radar was integrated with fighter defences, searchlights and anti-aircraft posts in a line of defences codenamed 'Himmelbett' ('Heavenly bed'), but usually described as the 'Kammhuber Line' after the first commander of the Reich fighter defences, General Josef Kammhuber. The radar belt stretched from the Swiss frontier through northern France and Belgium on as far as the German–Danish border. The system, like the British and American, did not work perfectly. There were shortages of skilled operators and slow output of the radars needed. By the spring of 1942 only a third of anti-aircraft batteries had the Würzburg gun-laying system.[118] Later the radar proved to be highly susceptible to jamming, particularly by the small strips of metal foil (known as 'window' in Britain, 'chaff' in the United States) which from summer 1943 onwards were dropped in their hundreds of thousands to smother enemy radar screens. Nonetheless, the defensive belt with its long-range detection, radar-controlled guns, and radar control of fighter interception, both by day and by night, succeeded in taking a heavy toll of British and American bombers, and by winter 1943 had come close to stifling the bomber offensive altogether.

Naval radar followed swiftly on the early observations in the mid-1930s. Indeed, naval research institutes in Britain, the United States and Germany were central players in the evolution of a wide range of radar applications beyond the static coastal detection systems. The pace of research generally reflected the extent to which a navy was willing or not to accept that air power had changed the balance in the exercise of sea power between warship and aircraft. Radio detection of incoming attack aircraft was the only means to avoid the crippling effects of air attack by alerting carrier aircraft in time, or by mobilizing a warship's anti-aircraft defences. Radar could also aid navigation, help to avoid collisions in combat or convoy, and detect surface vessels and submarines. With gun-laying radar, an enemy vessel could be hit at night, or in fog and cloud, without the victim being aware that it was under threat – the destruction of Italian warships in the Battle of Cape Matapan on 28 March 1941 was an early example. The use of radar at sea, however, added fresh difficulties. It had to be kept free of water and ice; the antennae were vulnerable to the effects of weather and combat; radar needed a stable platform, but ships pitched and yawed with the ocean; radar could also be rendered inoperable by the vibrations caused when ships fired their main guns. Radar on the German battleship *Bismarck* was rendered useless after the first engagement with the Royal Navy, making it impossible to detect the Swordfish torpedo bomber that finally crippled the vessel.[119] Solutions were eventually found to all these problems to make radar a factor of critical importance for the war at sea, particularly for Britain and the United States, where naval radar research and development pioneered the many applications of the new technology.

In Britain, the Admiralty Experimental Department began an independent research programme in 1935 on the grounds that conditions on board ship required radar distinct from the system being developed for coastal early warning, and by September it had successfully replicated the Daventry experiment with pulse radar. In 1937 the navy's Signal School took over the research and a year later had developed the first operational naval radar for detecting aircraft and surface vessels, the Type 79 Y, installed experimentally on the battleship HMS *Rodney*. Over the next two years the system was modified and improved so that radar could also direct anti-aircraft fire at the right range or train the ship's main guns against a distant surface vessel. The 79 Y evolved into a number of different applications: Type 281 was employed for detecting ships; Types 282 to 285 were developed as armament rangefinders, though none of them worked perfectly until naval personnel became more accustomed to exploiting the capability of the new equipment; to detect low-flying aircraft an air force air-to-surface-vessel (ASV) radar was modified as Type

286.[120] Carrier aircraft were fitted with the ASV Mk II and it was this radar that permitted Swordfish torpedo bombers from HMS *Victorious* to find the *Bismarck* in May 1941 despite low cloud, stormy seas and impending dusk. The navy's role in stimulating German radar development was just as significant. The first German operational radar on shore and at sea was the DeTe-I, generally known as *Seetakt*. Upgraded to DeTe-II in 1938, it provided the model for the air force Freya. The radar was fitted first on the ill-fated pocket battleship *Admiral Graf Spee*. The navy also introduced Identification Friend or Foe (IFF) in 1938 (known as *Erstling*, 'firstborn'), which the air force then adopted.[121] Pilots used a pre-arranged pulse signal to the home radar to indicate that they were not hostile aircraft so that operators would know not to order fire. IFF became standard in all major air forces by 1940 although it could be subject to interception and used by an enemy, or, in the case of training flights in the United States near the coast, was dangerously ignored by most pilots because there were no enemy aircraft. The failure to develop IFF in Italy led to regular complaints that their German ally's anti-aircraft batteries fired indiscriminately at Italian planes.

The Naval Research Laboratory in the United States also began an independent programme of radar research in 1934 and by April 1937 tested equipment successfully on board a warship. The first American operational radar, XAF, was installed on the battleship *New York* in January 1939. The following year two naval officers coined the acronym RADAR and it was adopted as a cover name for the research, but it was soon used widely in the Anglophone world to describe all forms of radio detection. Progress was rapid in adapting radar to all naval requirements. In late 1941 the SK radar was introduced using another fundamental innovation, the Plan Position Indicator, which showed an image of the combat environment and the surrounding geography. It was important for carrier aircraft that the carrier could distinguish between them and the airborne enemy, and in 1937 development began on an American naval version of IFF. By 1941 all carrier aircraft were also fitted with ASV and work began on a radar-directed bombsight that would allow the bombing of enemy vessels even at night or through cloud. The American Fourteenth Air Force stationed in China in 1944 claimed to have sunk 110,000 tons of Japanese shipping using radar bombing of the small targets by night. By the end of the war 27,000 of the standard ASV radars had been produced.[122] Almost all of the naval applications were adapted for use by armies and air forces. Radar for accurate gun-laying was a vital adjunct of anti-aircraft artillery on land as well as at sea. The British radar-directed Gun Laying Mark II (GL-Mk II) made possible an average 4,100 rounds fired for each aircraft destroyed, against a prodigal 18,500 rounds for the original Mark I equipment without radar. Following naval practice, air interception (AI) radar to allow aircraft to close on the enemy at night or in poor weather, assisted by surface radar, became common across all major air forces. Once ground control interception was introduced early in 1941 for RAF night fighters, German average operational losses rose from 0.5 per cent to 7 per cent. The German Lichtenstein and SN2 air interception radars developed later in the war were essential to vector German night fighters successfully onto the bomber stream.

All the early applications of pulse radar were made on broad wavelengths. The German radar worked on decimetre, usually 50-centimetre, wavelengths, most other radar on anything from 1.5 to 3 metres. It was known from the early 1930s that microwaves might permit greater accuracy and versatility if applied to radar, but initial research in Germany and Japan showed that the existing vacuum tubes could not generate sufficient power to make microwave radar possible, and the attempt was abandoned. The critical breakthrough into microwave technology occurred, like the first observation of radio echoes, through a fortunate set of chances. In 1939 the British Committee for the Coordination of Valve Development sent out contracts to Oxford, Bristol and Birmingham universities to develop a high-powered valve capable of operating a 10-centimetre wavelength. At Birmingham, the Australian physicist Marcus Oliphant recruited two young doctoral students, John Randall and Henry Boot, to join his team of researchers. Not familiar with the long arguments about whether the klystron or the magnetron (two advanced vacuum tubes on which previous microwave research had been based) was capable of generating the necessary power for centimetric wavelengths, they took both and melded them together to form what became known as the resonant cavity magnetron. The first experiment showed that the new apparatus was capable of the output of a high level of power. On 21 February 1941 they demonstrated the magnetron to Oliphant and his staff and showed that it could produce wavelengths of 9.8 centimetres. Production was immediately turned over to the General Electric Company, whose laboratory had also been sponsored by the Royal Navy to work on klystrons and magnetrons. A working model was produced by May, and in August the Telecommunications Research Establishment staged a demonstration that showed without doubt that the resonant cavity magnetron used in a pulsed system produced clear returns, even from small objects (in this case a metal plate attached to a bicycle pedalled along a nearby clifftop). The cavity magnetron, designated E1198, was packed into a metal box and the same month was taken by a scientific mission, headed by the government scientist Henry Tizard, to the United States. On 19 September the secret was revealed to a meeting of leading scientists in Washington where it provoked a dramatic reaction. There was a sudden realization, recalled Edward Bowen, who had escorted the cavity magnetron from England, 'that what laid [sic]on the table in front of us might prove to be the salvation of the Allied cause'.[123]

The resonant cavity magnetron transformed British and American radar. The Tizard mission handed over the magnetron to the American Microwave Committee on the understanding that they would organize mass production. The Bell Telephone Laboratories were given the responsibility and by the end of the war over a million were produced, most of them the improved 'strapped' cavity magnetron developed in 1941 to improve frequency stability. Radar research now assumed a central importance for the American armed forces. A Radiation Laboratory was established at the Massachusetts Institute of Technology in Boston under the direction of Lee DuBridge where the development of microwave technology became the principal activity. To avoid the wasteful duplication of effort in the first year of America's war, a branch of the laboratory was established in Britain in the summer of 1943.[124] All the earlier developments in battlefield radar could now be set aside in favour of more precise and versatile equipment. The initial priority was to produce a microwave air interception radar and a microwave gun-laying radar for automatic ranging and firing of anti-aircraft artillery. The AI radar was developed by summer 1942 as SCR-520, and finally upgraded to SCR-720. The radar was introduced on all American aircraft and, because of its advanced performance, was adopted by the British air force as AI-Mk X to replace the microwave radar, AI-Mk VII, which had been introduced into operation in April 1942. The gun-laying radar, SCR-584, was one of the most successful radars of the war. Using an analogue computer installed in the M9 predictor to measure range and altitude, guns fired automatically and accurately at enemy aircraft. It was used not only for anti-aircraft fire but in ground combat, where it could be employed to track shell trajectories and to detect enemy mortars, vehicles, even a single soldier, through smoke, fog or darkness. On D-Day, thirty-nine of the sets were taken ashore. As a consequence, American artillery and anti-aircraft fire could be directed with pinpoint accuracy.[125]

Microwave radar wavelengths were developed first at 10 centimetres, then 3 and finally 1 centimetre by the end of the war. The 3-centimetre wavelength was used to develop a means of surveying the ground from a bomber aircraft to improve target location. This was one of the occasions on which friction emerged between the two Allies over competitive research.

The British developed the H2S equipment, the Boston Radiation Laboratory a version they called H2X, and neither side would agree to accept a common system. A more fruitful collaboration came with the microsystem designed for the fuses in anti-aircraft shells, which could track the target using a small radar and then explode at the right moment. Initially proposed in 1940 by William Butement, an Australian physicist working on radar in Britain, the planned invention was taken with the Tizard scientific mission to the United States, where the concept was fully developed over the following year. The 'proximity fuse' was first used to bring down an enemy aircraft in the Pacific in January 1943 and transformed ship-to-air combat in the theatre. However, the fuses were used sparingly in Europe from fear that the technology would fall into German hands. Nevertheless, they could be used in British airspace, and were utilized successfully in the country's air defence against the V1 cruise missile, shooting down an estimated 50 per cent of them. The fuses were eventually used in the campaign in France and Belgium late in 1944. During the Battle of the Bulge, proximity-fused shells were responsible for shooting down at least 394 German aircraft. By 1945 some 22 million proximity fuses had been produced.[126]

Microwave radar for the war at sea proved to be an invaluable asset. In Britain, the Admiralty promoted development of an ASV radar capable of detecting German submarines with greater accuracy. The Type 271 was ready by early 1941, the first microwave radar in operation. With microwaves it proved possible to detect not only the submarine, but even the periscope as it pierced the surface of the sea. The first submarine detected and sunk using microwave radar occurred on 16 November 1941 off Gibraltar. Microwave ship-borne radar for the Royal Navy included better gun-laying equipment, navigation aids and target indicators. The American navy insisted on continuing to develop naval radar at the Naval Research Laboratory, rather than at the Radiation Laboratory at MIT, and produced a wide variety of centimetric radar for carrier aircraft, carriers and warships. The SM and SP sets were introduced for major warships and for lighter carriers, capable of detecting aircraft in three dimensions. Gun-laying became a more sophisticated operation with the introduction from late 1942 of the 10-centimetre Mk 8 radar, allowing naval guns to fire blind and track the trajectory of a shell; it also showed the elimination of the target on the radar screen. It was first used at Guadalcanal when an unsuspecting Japanese vessel was sunk at night at a distance of over 12 kilometres, but the new technology proved too challenging for most ships' captains. In November 1942 Admiral Nimitz directed all major warships to introduce a Combat Operations Center to help co-ordinate and disseminate the radar information, leaving commanders free to command. Under the codename 'Project Cadillac', Combat Information Centers, as they came to be called, were introduced across the fleet. Each housed a large number of radio and radar operators, but the key figures were the 'evaluator', who assessed the operational situation, and the 'talker' who communicated information where it was needed for air operations, anti-aircraft artillery or the ship's main guns.[127] Once commanders were familiar with the new technology, it played a critical part in the last two years of the war. By 1944 the American naval war in the Pacific was an entirely electronic one for which the Japanese enemy had no equivalent.

Microwave radar took British and American electronic warfare to a level well beyond German and Japanese achievements. German radar research had by the beginning of the war produced excellent radar using 50-centimetre wavelengths, while research on microwaves in the early 1930s had proven fruitless and was not revived during the war with any enthusiasm. Radar development during the war suffered from the culture of secrecy that surrounded it in a dictatorship where any dereliction was likely to be penalized. The plenipotentiary for high frequency research, Hans Plendl, recruited by Göring in 1940, was sacked in 1944 for using Jewish scientists imprisoned in Dachau concentration camp to help repair radar on the grounds that he 'had passed secret material to non-Germans'. He was fortunate not to end in a camp himself, unlike Hans Mayer, director of research at the electronics firm Siemens, who was incarcerated in Dachau for 'incautious talk'. Development also suffered from the multiplicity of centres for research, the poor communication between them, and the failure to establish clear priorities. Even when a cavity magnetron fell into German hands, recovered from a crashed Stirling bomber in February 1943, little was made of it. Named the *Rotterdam-Gerät* after the city where the aircraft crashed, the magnetron was taken to the Telefunken laboratory where a number of microwave sets were produced by the summer of 1943 but not used. A 10-centimetre gun-laying radar codenamed 'Marburg' was developed, but only a few were deployed by German anti-aircraft batteries; another microwave radar, named 'Berlin', was developed for German night-fighters by January 1945 and became operational in March 1945, too late to make any difference to the air war.[128] No proximity fuse was produced, although it would have made a substantial, perhaps decisive, contribution to the defence against the Allied bombing campaign.

Japanese radar development suffered from the poor relationship between the army and navy research establishments and a general distrust of civilian interference by scientists from universities and commercial research laboratories, who were treated, according to Yagi Hidetsugu, as if they were 'foreigners'. Magnetron research was advanced by international standards, but the military showed no interest in exploiting it. Radar was only taken seriously following a visit by two Japanese delegations to Germany in 1940 and 1941 where they were shown a limited amount of German radar equipment. The capture of British and American radar at Singapore and Corregidor early in 1942 allowed Japanese laboratories to reverse engineer them in order to develop a Japanese version, but development was slow and the first radar using the captured technology began operation only in 1944. As in Germany, the research programmes were decentralized and secrecy a barrier to rational development. At the main radio research laboratory, half of the engineers working on magnetrons and radar were drafted into the army, where they could end up as little more than regular infantry. Shortages of materials and skilled personnel distorted the search for priorities. Many electronic components were of poor quality, subcontracted to inexperienced workshops where key metals were lacking. What radar existed was highly susceptible to jamming through American electronic countermeasures, a programme led by the American scientist Frederick Terman, who had been recruited in 1942 to head the Radio Research Laboratory. For air operations over the Japanese home islands in 1945, a jammer called Porcupine was used to produce powerful radio noise to interfere with Japanese defensive radar. Microwave radar with limited scope was eventually introduced by the Japanese armed forces late in the war, first for a single ship-borne radar, Type 22, and then for an airborne set, FD-3, for night-fighters, of which only a hundred were produced. These radars lacked a Plan Position Indicator – essential imaging for combat – until one finally became available in July 1945. A cavity magnetron capable of high-power output was in development when the war ended.[129] By a strange twist, the idea of a 'death ray', which had first prompted Robert Watson-Watt to investigate radio detection in 1934, was taken up by Japanese researchers in 1945 as a desperate ploy. A concentrated radio beam was used to kill a rabbit at 30 metres in 10 minutes. A few months later two atomic bombs were dropped on Hiroshima and Nagasaki, each primed with four radar fuses.[130]

For the Allies, radio and radar made a substantial contribution to enhancing their fighting power. The technologies did not win the war, as is sometimes implied, nor did they work with uniform efficiency or free of technical problems, but they did provide an important margin of advantage to the Allied armies, air forces and navies by the last years of the war. This was an advantage that reflected the close links between government, scientists, engineers and the military. Radio wave research was sponsored in Britain and the United States by government-appointed committees, ample funds were made available, and a significant level of open collaboration between the researchers and users was established even before the United States entered the war. Manufacturing capacity, thanks to the advanced nature of the American electronics industry, was enormous. The training of qualified personnel was on an ambitious scale. The Pacific Fleet Radar Center alone trained 125,000 officers and men between 1942 and 1945. The navy and army laboratories supporting radar and radio research employed over 18,000 people by the end of the war.[131] Few of these advantages were available to the Axis enemy.

FORCE MULTIPLIERS? INTELLIGENCE AND DECEPTION

On 23 June 1944, the Japanese transport submarine I-52, carrying a cargo through the Allied blockade of gold, tungsten, molybdenum, opium, quinine, rubber and tin for the German war effort, was sunk by an acoustic torpedo dropped by an American Avenger bomber as she sailed from a rendezvous with a German submarine on the approach to the Bay of Biscay. The submarine's exact position had been intercepted and tracked for weeks by the United States Combat Intelligence Division using the decrypts of the submarine's numerous radio signals. A reception party of German and Japanese dignitaries waited impatiently for the Japanese crew to arrive at Lorient on the west coast of France as a publicity stunt to celebrate the arrival of a successful blockade runner. But as time passed and no further radio transmissions arrived from the sunken boat, it was assumed to be lost and as Allied forces broke out from the Normandy bridgehead the celebrations were hastily abandoned. Signals intelligence had betrayed eighteen out of twenty-seven transport submarines in 1944 and they were all sunk. The last surface blockade runner was sunk in January 1944, victim of the same intelligence scanning.[132]

The fate of I-52 was sealed by the Allied exploitation of tactical intelligence derived from radio signals – usually described as SIGINT (though in this case more properly communications intelligence, or COMINT) – which constituted the single most important source of operational and tactical intelligence on the fighting front wherever it could be successfully intercepted and interpreted. Around two-thirds of intelligence information for the German army during the Allied invasion of France came from radio traffic; the head of the German intelligence branch Foreign Armies West considered SIGINT to be 'the darling of all intelligence men'.[133] It was not by any means the only source exploited for intelligence purposes, but it was by far the largest element. Otherwise military and naval intelligence relied on so-called 'human intelligence' from agents or from prisoners of war, which was often of dubious value (not least when the agent had been successfully recruited by the enemy to supply misinformation), or from captured documents, which usually supplied only a glimpse of enemy intentions or dispositions, or from aerial photo reconnaissance, which was at least second to SIGINT as a major source of ready information if the material could be adequately interpreted.[134] The advantage of radio interception lay in the fact that it covered all aspects of the enemy's operational and tactical activity over a wide geographical range and in significant volume. The US navy's decryption section, OP-20-G, recovered 115,000 German navy signals during the Battle of the Atlantic; the work of the British Government Code & Cipher School (GCCS) on German Enigma machine traffic accounted for 39,000 messages a month by early 1943, but an average of 90,000 a month from late 1943 to the end of the war.[135] Information from radio signals was plentiful, reflecting the extent to which radio had become embedded in military and naval operations in the Second World War.

Every warring power exploited tactical and operational intelligence. Broader 'strategic' intelligence about enemy plans, intentions and behaviour was far more difficult to obtain and on many famous occasions was a conspicuous failure – the incapacity of the United States' military and political leadership in December 1941 to anticipate an imminent Japanese attack, the misjudgement of the Japanese that the Americans could be discouraged from waging all-out war, the German underestimation of Soviet strength in 1941 and the devastating refusal of Stalin to heed the more than eighty warnings received that a German invasion was about to happen, the persistent expectation that Germany would collapse through bombing alone, and so on. Most of these convictions were fed by intelligence, but they were often influenced by wishful thinking, speculation, racial or political prejudice, or mere incredulity even in the many cases where the less secure diplomatic ciphers were easily broken – as was the case with the American reading of Japanese MAGIC communications before Pearl Harbor. Strategic intelligence was all too often the victim of hubris in situations where victory seemed assured. The initial success of the German counter-offensive, Operation 'Autumn Mist', in December 1944 stemmed from the Allied belief that the Germans were now too beaten down to retaliate effectively, even though high-grade communications intelligence provided evidence to the contrary; so, too, the German army's persistent conviction that the Soviet armed forces would crumble under attack, which endured well past the point when all evidence suggested the opposite.

In terms of a 'force multiplier', operational and tactical intelligence was far more significant than strategic or political intelligence. The organization and practice of operational intelligence reflected specific military cultures in the way they were established and operated, and the extent to which intelligence was integrated into the broader war-making apparatus, but no major power neglected it. Japanese military intelligence was divided between the army's Second Department of the General Staff and the Third Department of the naval staff. Neither service had much respect for intelligence when it came to organizing operations and they kept intelligence staff at a distance. The Combined Fleet had only one intelligence officer attached to headquarters, and there was just one for each of the separate fleets. Commanders of naval units in combat were expected to make their own judgements about the enemy.[136] There was no central agency or committee for co-ordinating intelligence, and the two services collaborated little with each other. When army cryptanalysis broke some of the American army's M-94 and M-209 machine ciphers, they deliberately withheld the information from the navy.[137]

The organization of German military intelligence betrayed a similar reluctance to involve intelligence personnel too closely with operations, or to recruit widely from among civilians. Branch 1c of the German army staffs dealt with intelligence and a range of other activities, including propaganda work with the troops. The air force had its own intelligence division, the navy another. The air intelligence branch, D5, had only twenty-nine staff in 1939 and expanded slowly during the war, with only limited influence on the operational commanders. As with the army, air intelligence personnel were also responsible for aircrew welfare, press releases, censorship and propaganda.[138] The intelligence staffs in all three services were small and their responsibilities large, but German commanders at all levels were expected to be able to make their own judgement about operations with or without reference to their intelligence staff. As in Japan, there was compartmentalization in intelligence gathering and dissemination and no central agency for co-ordinating it. In the interpretation of aircraft reconnaissance photographs, low-ranking staff served each local commander, but there was no equivalent of the British centralized interpretation centre at Medmenham, distributing intelligence across the armed forces.[139] Neither was signals intelligence for the services integrated in one national centre as it was in Britain. If German intelligence gathering at tactical level was often systematic and abundant, integration at the operational level was limited.

In Britain and the United States, intelligence assumed a larger role, and involved not only the armed services, each of which had its own intelligence branch, but the broader civilian war effort. Scientific intelligence to serve military needs became institutionalized in Britain in 1940, and in the United States a year later; the British Joint Intelligence Committee, established in 1936, supplied the War Cabinet and armed forces with regular intelligence appreciations on a wide range of subjects; intelligence was integrated into operational planning from the strategic down to the tactical level. Signals intelligence for all the services was centralized at Bletchley Park, home of GCCS, where at the peak there were 10,000 people employed, most of them civilians, the majority women. The involvement of civilian expertise reflected the nature of wartime mobilization in the democracies, where there was less military prejudice against involving intelligence personnel, military or otherwise, in operational planning and evaluation. Many of those recruited to work as translators or decrypters were university students with a flair for classics or modern languages. The RAF intelligence division recruited 700 personnel during the war, but only 10 were regular RAF officers.[140] Above all, intelligence appreciations and information were shared between the two democracies under formal agreements, eventually establishing a degree of (almost unrestricted) intelligence collaboration. Efforts were made to extend the sharing to the Soviet Union as well, but collaboration was almost always one-sided and carried the risk of compromising Western sources. Soviet reception of the intelligence was disconcertingly graceless.[141]

The system of American military intelligence was, of all the major powers, the least developed before the war. Combat units had no dedicated intelligence staff and there were no special training facilities. In 1941 both the army and the navy began expanding the intelligence sections, G-2 in the US army, the Office of Naval Intelligence for the navy, but like Japanese intelligence they were poorly integrated. In summer 1941, the army initiated the establishment of a separate air intelligence branch, A-2, which relied heavily at first on material supplied freely by the RAF and the cooperation of the Australian intelligence services. As with the British, there was no alternative to recruiting widely among civilian experts, academics or qualified students. The army established a Military Intelligence Service which eventually introduced teams for combat intelligence into every regiment, so that graduates from military language courses in German or Japanese could interrogate prisoners of war or translate captured documents on the spot. The navy's intelligence division focused on work in the Pacific, where little had been known in 1941. The manual produced on Japanese aircraft had a blank page for the Mitsubishi 'Zero' fighter, though detailed information was already available.[142] Naval intelligence was based in Washington, but in the field combat intelligence teams and photo reconnaissance fed information into the Joint Intelligence Committee Pacific Ocean Area, which in turn produced a large number of intelligence reports to be distributed across the fighting services in the Pacific theatre.[143] Signals intelligence for the army was established at Arlington Hall in Virginia, the American equivalent of GCCS. The navy had a separate signals intelligence site in Washington, DC, but the two services developed a close collaboration as the war went on. By the late stages of the war, intelligence was an indispensable element at every level of the American war effort.

The organization of Soviet military intelligence differed fundamentally from the other major combatants. Intelligence gathering, *razvedka*, was a central part of Soviet operational doctrine long before 1941. It was integral to the organization of every army and air force formation from high command down to the smallest tactical unit. For broader operational intelligence, material from the fronts was fed to the Chief Intelligence Directorate of the Red Army (GRU) to assist in creating a composite picture of enemy intentions; operational and tactical intelligence was otherwise gathered, analysed and disseminated at the level of army group, army and divisional headquarters. Each level of command had an intelligence chief and staff working closely with the operational commanders, who had to formulate what intelligence they needed, the means to acquire it, and the forces necessary. In combat, army group commanders expected intelligence reports every two to three hours, individual army commanders every one to two hours. The intelligence was effectively all combat intelligence, gathered at the fighting front, and the principal means were through air reconnaissance (when that was possible), raiding and ambush of the enemy front, and armed reconnaissance in strength. Agents and infiltrators, supported by partisan detachments from 1942 onwards, penetrated up to 15 kilometres behind the enemy front lines. Forward observers in hides dangerously close to enemy lines reported the position of enemy artillery and machine-gun posts. Raids involving between five and eight men were designed to seize documents, weapons and prisoners, who were then subjected to rigorous interrogation. Human intelligence made up a very large part of the information needed; SIGINT was used with greater frequency only in the last years of war. There was little of the German or Japanese distrust of intelligence because it was a seamless part of Soviet military operations.[144] The doctrine and organization of intelligence work were tightened up in 1942 alongside the other reforms of Red Army and Red Air Force practice, and from 1943 onwards intelligence collection became better co-ordinated and more systematic, though never perfect. In April 1943, a directive from Stalin to field intelligence agents called on them to improve efforts to determine the axes on which the enemy was concentrating their forces, but the balance of German forces for the Battle of Kursk was still dangerously misunderstood.[145]

Intelligence nevertheless had evident limits, inherent in the nature of its operation, which affected the degree of trust or scepticism among military commanders. The intelligence picture was often patchy or inconsistent, with long breaks in the capacity to read enemy signals, or flawed evaluation of the information supplied by agents or enemy defectors, or failures in the interpretation of air reconnaissance – most notoriously in the West when reports from pilots who saw German armour massed in the Ardennes in May 1940 failed to get a sympathetic hearing from French commanders. Those who evaluated all the available sources were subject to the usual range of human error – over-optimism, a desire to impose order on a confused picture, institutional self-interest, and so on. Secrecy was at a premium everywhere; even in Britain, where a wide circle was involved in intelligence activities, communication between different sections was banned. Those working at the GCCS on lower-grade ciphers were not allowed to know about Ultra in case of a security leak. Ultra messages could only be delivered in Britain by the Special Liaison Unit, and in the United States by Special Security Officers, and were to be destroyed once read.[146] Above all, the regular changes made by all sides to the codes and ciphers used in SIGINT meant long weeks or months before the new ones could be read. British and American cryptanalysts lost the German naval Enigma traffic from February 1942 to December that year, and again experienced a blackout in March 1943; German naval intelligence could read the British Naval Cipher No. 3 for most of 1942 and early 1943, but then faced their own blackout when Naval Cipher No. 5 replaced it in June.[147] Before D-Day the Allies could read the signals between Berlin and the German high command in Paris, but lost the link when the ciphers altered on 10 June at a critical point in the battle and did not recover the traffic until September.[148]

Even when messages could be read, the decrypts often arrived days afterwards, too late to be used in current operations. Most of the decrypts made available for the German submarine high command in France could not be used in time. Transcription was also a challenge. The final translated version of intelligence information from intercepted communications went through a number of distinct stages, from the initial enemy encipherment through the version heard at the radio reception station, the process of decryption, translation of the message and the final typing up before it ended on the desk of a service intelligence branch. Language skills had to be developed even before the intelligence could be used. British translators of German or Japanese messages were expected only to have a workable reading knowledge; those trained in Japanese initially had just a brief introductory course based on outdated textbooks and dictionaries. Mistakes were unavoidable, not least from the sheer scale of the task. The number of captured documents requiring translation at GCCS from an already overstretched staff grew exponentially over the course of the war. Naval intelligence had 1,000 to translate by early 1943, but 10,000 pending translation by the summer of the following year.[149] In the United States a desperate shortage of white Americans fluent in Japanese led the army to start recruiting Japanese-Americans in 1941 as translators and interpreters of Japanese, a programme that continued even after the forced internment of Japanese-Americans in 1942. By 1945, 2,078 Japanese-Americans had graduated from the Military Intelligence Service Language School, many of them sent into combat along-side the troops in the Pacific to interrogate captured Japanese while the island fighting went on, risking death and injury.[150] The navy refused to enlist Japanese-Americans, and instead the navy and Marine Corps relied primarily on college students who were pushed through the Naval Japanese Language School in Boulder, Colorado, and then, with limited understand-ing of Japanese military terms, sent into combat in the bitter fighting in the Pacific, where they struggled to persuade fellow marines not to kill every Japanese before they could be interrogated.[151]

The most significant factor inhibiting intelligence was the effort devoted to ensuring the security of all information relayed by radio that the enemy might intercept. The chief objective for those gathering intelligence was to be able to break down the barrier of enhanced security in a timely and comprehensive way, and this proved to be a giant task in the face of the growing sophistication of machine systems for generating radio traffic. Occasionally messages could be read *en clair*, which potentially solved the problem, though they could also be misinterpreted. Communicating *en clair* was particularly the case with aircrew who proved in many cases to be careless with radio security, particularly American and Soviet airmen, but it also applied to ground forces in combat, when enciphering was too long-winded, or when communicating routine messages between military units. German communications intelligence on the Soviet–German front secured around 95 per cent of intercepts uncoded; in September 1944 on the Italian front, the Germans intercepted 22,254 messages *en clair*, against 14,373 encrypted.[152] Even uncoded signals could present problems. At one British 'Y' radio interception station the pleasure at hearing the first uncoded radio messages between German airmen subsided after discovering that no one present could understand German.[153] The most important messages, how-ever, were almost always encrypted in ways designed to frustrate enemy listeners, some more secure than others. The permutations were challeng-ing. The German Enigma traffic had fifty-two variants; Japanese navy and army traffic at least fifty-five between them.[154] In the complex endeavour to unravel these secrets, the British and American intelligence services enjoyed over the war years a significant lead.

The Anglo-American effort devoted to breaking enemy signals stemmed from the nature of the global field in which they operated, and the priority accorded to naval and air power. For the RAF and the Royal Navy, access to enemy radio traffic in the first years of the war was a necessity to protect mainland Britain from air attack and to keep open the sea lanes in the face of German and Italian submarines, warships and merchant raiders. For the United States navy, reading Japanese codes was essential in the early stages of the Pacific war to avoid defeat, but became in turn a key offensive instrument in the eventual destruction of the Japanese navy and merchant marine. The story of British interception is always associated with 'Ultra', the name finally settled on in 1941 to describe the decrypts from German Enigma machine signals (the navy had called it 'Hush', Churchill insisted on 'Boniface'). The focus on Ultra, however, ignores not only the periods when changed keys meant that messages could not be read, but overlooks the extent to which other forms of signals intelligence complemented, supplemented or, at times, replaced the material from Ultra. Enigma decrypts were at first confined to the less secure German air force communications, first broken in May 1940 thanks to the supply of Enigma equipment and assistance from Polish cryptographers as they fled the German invasion in September 1939. It could only be read with a time lag which was gradually reduced with the application of electromechanical 'bombes', machinery designed to speed up the process of decryption, first for three-rotor Enigma traffic and then, with the arrival in 1943 of American 'bombes', for the more challenging four-rotor traffic. It was used little in the Battle of Britain and the German air 'Blitz', was of limited use in the Mediterranean until entry was finally achieved into German army communications in time for the battles at Alam el Halfa and El Alamein, was interrupted at the height of the Battle of the Atlantic for ten frustrating months, and was non-existent for Western Europe because communications in the occupied areas were confined to landlines. Enigma traffic was useful for the German order of battle and a range of logistical and organizational information, but it gave fewer clues to German strategic and operational intentions. When it worked, Ultra gave the Allies a window onto the enemy they would otherwise have lacked, but it had to be used very cautiously to ensure that the German side never understood that their communications were compromised.

The extent to which Ultra needs to be put in context can be illustrated by looking at the intelligence available for the Battle of Britain and the Battle of the Atlantic. On the British side, the air battle involved the RAF

'Y' service for listening into the radio frequencies used by the German air force, sometimes messages *en clair*, otherwise with low-grade ciphers and call signs, easier to decrypt. German-speakers were recruited as 'computors' [sic] to provide current information on German air units and movements. This source was supplemented by the Home Defence Units which used radio direction-finding techniques to provide current material on take-off, course and height of enemy aircraft, and could distinguish between bombers and fighters, which radar was unable to do. The principal 'Y' service base at Cheadle, near Manchester, provided a stream of vital information to RAF fighter stations throughout the battle, often at one minute's notice of incoming aircraft, where radar at best gave four. The Ultra intercepts provided little useful tactical information, though they contributed to building up the German order of battle. The commander-in-chief of Fighter Command was not even told about Ultra until October, when the German campaign was all but over.[155]

A similar mix of sources served the Battle of the Atlantic. Among the more important was High Frequency/Direction Finding (HF/DF) run from stations in Britain, the United States and Canada (and eventually spread worldwide). Since German naval signals were all high frequency to achieve the necessary distance, messages could be intercepted and the presence of a submarine or merchant raider located with ever greater accuracy as the war went on. In addition, the submarines regularly used brief 'Beta' signals taken from the naval *Kurzsignalheft* (short signal book) once they had sighted a convoy; when intercepted they did not need to be decrypted because it was evident that contact had been made and that evasion was a necessity. Both were essential in the period when Ultra could no longer supply decrypts of naval Enigma signals, but between them all a web of information was supplied that allowed regular 'traffic analysis' reports to show where submarines were operating and in what strength. While used at first defensively to allow convoys to avoid contact with submarines, radio intercepts came to be used offensively from the spring of 1943 to help aircraft and anti-submarine shipping to hunt down the German wolf packs. They proved to be an essential instrument in the defeat of the submarine threat.[156]

Allied signals intelligence in the Pacific theatre used the same code-name, 'Ultra', for intercepts of high-grade Japanese radio traffic. Signals intelligence had proved an abject failure before Pearl Harbor, when little effort was devoted to decrypting the principal Japanese naval code, JN-25b. The American interception unit at Station Cast in the Philippines could read fragments of the messages late in 1941 (though little use was made of it by naval intelligence), but a week before the Pearl Harbor attack the Japanese navy adopted a new cipher, which was unreadable.[157] In a few frantic weeks in spring 1942, the Fleet Radio Unit, Pacific, based on Hawaii, struggled to master the new cipher, and did so in time to anticipate the Japanese operation against Midway Island. Thereafter, JN-25 could be read almost continuously by the navy's communications intelligence division responsible for Japan, OP-20-GZ. This 'Ultra' supplied details of Japanese convoys, escort shipping and garrison strengths on the Pacific islands.[158] It even detected the flight of Admiral Yamamoto on a routine inspection of the Gilbert and Solomon Islands' defences. With the approval of Admiral Nimitz, P-38 fighters flew to intercept and shoot down the commander of Japan's Combined Fleet. Not even this alerted the Japanese to the fact that their principal naval codes were compromised. In June 1943, American cryptographers finally broke the Japanese army's Water Transport Code, used by the convoys supplying the army garrisons. Together, the radio intelligence enabled American and Australian submarines and aircraft to locate and destroy a high proportion of Japan's merchant shipping and naval escorts.

In general, it proved harder to gain the same degree of access to army radio traffic. Partly this reflected the army preference for landline communication, which could only be intercepted by the risky means of wiretapping behind enemy lines. Where the battle lines were more fluid, radio was more widely used, though seldom enough to gain regular and current intelligence. Aggressive scouting, photo reconnaissance or prisoner of war interrogations made up for the shortage of army communications intelligence. Japanese cryptanalysis broke the Soviet army cipher OKK5 in 1939, but benefitted little from it in their defeat at Nomonhan in August that year and did not need it again until the Soviet Union declared war in August 1945, by which time the cipher had changed.[159] The German army in the Soviet Union, with a limited number of personnel, broke lower-grade ciphers at the front, decrypting in 1943 and 1944 around one-third of the messages, but higher command communications proved a barrier.[160] In the war in North Africa, Rommel could not read British army traffic regularly, but did get access to the communications between the air force and army units until the cipher was altered in summer 1942. There was no German equivalent of Ultra to use against the Western Allies on any long-term or consistent basis. The alternative sources were unreliable. Aerial reconnaissance was compromised by the British use of elaborate deceptive camouflage of prime industrial and military targets and the growing vulnerability of German reconnaissance aircraft; agents were risky because they could be turned by enemy counter-intelligence or provide little more than impressionistic information.

The Allies relied on a variety of avenues into German, Italian and Japanese army communications. In the Pacific war, less attention was paid at first to decrypting army messages since much of the early campaign was against the Japanese navy. Only 25 cryptanalysts were working on army ciphers in the summer of 1942, but a year later there were 270. Army ciphers were much harder to break than JN-25, until codebooks were recovered in New Guinea from the retreating Japanese Twenty-first Division in early 1944. From then on, army messages could be decrypted on a regular basis.[161] In the Mediterranean theatre Italian ciphers – codenamed 'Zog' and then 'Musso' at Bletchley Park – proved almost impossible to break. They were randomly encoded and then randomly enciphered. However, the easier low-grade cipher for Italian shipping was broken in 1941 and allowed a steady build-up of information on supplies and convoys to the Axis armies in North Africa.[162] The German army Enigma in the desert was finally broken in summer 1942. A branch of GCCS was set up in Cairo to ensure that message content was relayed rapidly to the Allied forces before the battles of Alam el Halfa and El Alamein, but Ultra proved less useful for the long pursuit of Axis forces across the desert and their final defeat in Tunisia.[163]

At this point of the war, British codebreakers found a source even more important than Enigma decrypts. The German army developed a radio tele-printer link using the Lorenz company *Schlüsselzusatz* 40 (later model 42) for sending high-level traffic without resort to the Morse code characteristic of Enigma. Each teleprinter link had its own cipher; by 1943 there were ten such links, by early 1944 there were twenty-six. The German army used the links for operational and strategic messages and regarded them as entirely secure. At Bletchley Park the signals were codenamed 'Fish' (after the German codename '*Sägefisch*' – 'swordfish') and work began on them early in 1942 by hand with limited success. Each link was given a marine cover name – 'Turbot' for the Berlin–Copenhagen line, 'Jellyfish' for Berlin to Paris, 'Conger' for Berlin to Athens, and so on.[164] One cipher for traffic to the German army command in the Balkans was broken first, then the link with Field Marshal Kesselring's armies in Italy in May 1943. To speed up the process of decryption, the first operational computers were eventually developed. Although commonly associated with supplying Ultra decrypts, the Colossus I early in 1944 (followed by Mark II installed on 1 June 1944) was designed to decrypt 'Fish', not Enigma. Colossus II could process 25,000 alphabetical characters per second, making it 125 times faster than the mechanical processes initially employed.[165] By March 1944, operational communication between Berlin and the German army commander-in-chief in Paris was broken, and although regular changes to the ciphers led to periods of blackout until September 1944, for the last nine months of the war 'Fish' supplied a regular diet of high-level German signals at a time when new Enigma settings were reducing the value of Ultra.[166] 'Fish' in turn was supplemented by other sources. The 'Y' service intercepted and decrypted German army medium-grade traffic from April 1943, and low-grade traffic, including tank codes, was broken from the end of the year, helping to establish a fuller picture of German dispositions before the invasion on D-Day. Human intelligence from SOE agents in France and French resistance units completed the picture. In this case, as Montgomery's chief of intelligence acknowledged, 'very few armies ever went to battle better informed of their enemy'.[167]

The extent to which intelligence gathering – and in particular SIGINT – contributed to operational success remains a vexed question despite the great volume of historical literature that has sought to demonstrate its essential value. Clearly, to operate blindly against enemy forces is needlessly ineffective and no armed services during the Second World War ignored the need to build a picture of enemy dispositions, capabilities, technical innovations and, whenever possible, intentions. But the use to which intelligence is put depends on the extent to which the information is integrated into operational planning at all levels, or the degree to which it is believed by the commanders whose job it is to judge the current battlefront situation. Intelligence was all too often refracted through complex layers of decision-making that inhibited effective operational use. Even the best intelligence could prove fruitless. A warning derived from Ultra decrypts was sent out for the first time to British commanders in the field on the eve of the German operation to capture Crete, but it could not prevent British defeat; Wavell was sent an urgent message indicating Rommel's imminent attack on 30 March 1941 but chose to disregard it, to his own misfortune. Even the famous breakthrough in late 1940 by British scientific intelligence, when German air navigation beams were identified and then deliberately distorted, could not prevent months more of bombing. Indeed, the raiding of port and industrial targets was now even less accurate and in consequence imposed higher civilian casualties. The clearest examples of operationally effective intelligence are to be found in the naval war, where radio signals were the medium of communication, and interception and decryption essential for combat across a global marine battlefield. Allied success here contributed substantially to defeating Axis submarine campaigns, protecting convoys, and destroying enemy marine supply lines, all vital to the effective prosecution of the wider war. These were lengthy campaigns in which the intelligence war clearly proved a force multiplier for the Allies, but the intelligence success depended to some extent on the good fortune that neither the Japanese nor German navies discovered that their codes and signals were compromised. For all the glamour and daring associated with the world of spies and spying, secret intelligence and counter-intelligence, in the context of the war it was the routine work of analysis and interpretation, day after day, that made the difference.

The same ambivalence exists in assessments of deception during the Second World War. Deception was the other side of the intelligence coin. The object of deception is to confuse the enemy about intentions and force disposition to the extent that when the surprise operation is launched the enemy is thrown into confusion, maximizing the impact of the deceiver's forces and reducing the costs of battle. Deception can work in modern war only by convincing enemy intelligence that what is false is true and sustaining the fabrication for as long as it is necessary. During the Second World War deception ranged from veiling major strategic operations down to more modest programmes of camouflage to protect military bases, airfields and supply dumps from prying aerial observation. Although occasional deception operations were common in all theatres on both sides, deception was only institutionalized in two military establishments during the war, the British and Soviet. The surprise assault on the Soviet Union in June 1941 and the Japanese attack on Pearl Harbor and South East Asia in December 1941 were almost the only major attempts at strategic deception mounted by the Axis states. Neither was quite a surprise. Despite German efforts at concealment, the 'Barbarossa' campaign was so well known by June 1941, thanks to the extensive Soviet spy network, that only Stalin's intransigent refusal to face realities qualified the opening of the campaign as a surprise. Japan's Pearl Harbor operation was concealed by the almost total radio silence of the naval task force as it approached Hawaii, but no deliberate effort was made to deceive the American military in advance. In both cases the Soviet and American leaderships deceived themselves.

British deception operations became so widespread in the British war effort that they finally merited a volume of the post-war official histories all to themselves.[168] Deception moved from limited beginnings to grand strategic objectives over the course of the war. The first efforts were chiefly defensive in the face of a probable German bombing offensive, and then the threat of invasion in summer 1940. As early as 1936 the chiefs of staff established an Advisory Committee on Camouflage, principally to recommend how to protect vulnerable and important targets from enemy bombers. The Ministry of Home Security, activated after the outbreak of war in 1939, took up the committee's brief when it set up the Civil Defence Camouflage Establishment.[169] The camoufleurs, many of them recruited from the worlds of art, architecture, film and theatre, spent days masking important war factories or trying to paint railways green to blend with the countryside. The RAF set up its own deception unit under the Air Ministry director of works, Colonel John Turner, to organize the construction of dummy airfields to lure German aircraft to attack them rather than the real thing; more than a hundred were built complete with fake aircraft and hangars, and they attracted twice as many raids as the real ones.[170] One of those trained on the inter-service camouflage course set up in 1940, the film-maker Geoffrey de Barkas, was sent out late in 1940 in charge of a tiny unit of camoufleurs to the war in North Africa and it was here, under the command of General Wavell, that British deception as a serious branch of operations was first established.

Wavell had observed the success of deception against the Turks in the campaign in Palestine during the First World War and was convinced that it was a force multiplier: 'I have always believed in doing everything possible to mystify and mislead one's opponent.'[171] In December 1940 he persuaded Churchill, himself a believer in the value of deception, to authorize a new unit for the Middle East Command to be known as 'A Force', responsible for deception in all its many guises. Wavell appointed the colourful Lieutenant Colonel Dudley Clarke as its director. Clarke's brief was to use all means to mislead the enemy as an aid to operations, but principally agent activity, radio disinformation and Barkas's camouflage unit. The results at first were mixed, but Churchill was enthusiastic enough to recruit a former minister of war, Oliver Stanley, as nominal head of a London centre for co-ordinating deception. In May 1942, a formal office was finally agreed by the chiefs of staff following a strong memorandum from Wavell on the many virtues of deception. Stanley was replaced by Lieutenant Colonel John Bevan as head of what was now called the London Controlling Section, the main organization for planning, supervising and co-ordinating Britain's global deception operations. His brief was to find deceptive means 'of causing the enemy to waste his military resources'. Although the United States armed forces viewed deception with much scepticism, they agreed to set up a corresponding organization, the Joint Security Control (initially just two officers) to perform the same task for the American army and navy.[172] Most of the initial activity centred on finding ways to defeat Axis forces in the desert campaign. The nature of the barren terrain presented particular difficulties with camouflage, but it was essential to protect Allied forces from attack and to confuse the enemy. Huge quantities of dun-coloured paint covered harbour installations and runways; airbases were disguised as areas of housing with clever use of paint and shadow; so-called 'sunshields' were designed out of available local materials to turn a tank into a lorry when seen from the air – more challenging was to turn a lorry into a tank, but local wattle was used to achieve this as well. So successful were the subterfuges in shielding Allied forces from enemy reconnaissance that Barkas wrote up his work in a training pamphlet 'Concealment in the Field', which was adopted as an operational requirement and more than 40,000 copies printed.[173]

The success of deception was always difficult to measure, and, unknown to the Allied side, Rommel had intelligence access both to the American military attaché's messages from Cairo and to the radio link between the Desert Air Force and the Eighth Army to give him a fuller view of his enemy's intentions and dispositions. Deception came into its own only with the preparations for the second Battle of El Alamein in autumn 1942, by which time Rommel had lost both intelligence sources. This was by far the most elaborate deception of the Mediterranean war, and it was deemed necessary if the hitherto unbeatable Rommel and his Italian ally were to be kept away from Cairo and the Suez Canal. Codenamed 'Bertram', the deception plan had six separate ploys, all designed to persuade the enemy that the main Allied thrust would be on the southern sector of the front, while the reality was a mass attack with armour in the north. Camouflage was essential to success. In the north, large supplies of oil, food and ammunition were cleverly concealed as lorry parks; in the south dummy stores were constructed to look like the real thing from the air. Real lorries and tanks were parked in the south and then moved northwards at night with complete radio silence and dummies put in the spaces they had occupied. In the north 360 artillery pieces were covered to look like lorries. A total of 8,400 dummy vehicles, guns and stores were eventually crafted to confirm in the enemy's mind that Montgomery's battleplan was to attack in the south. Dudley Clarke organized twenty-five phantom radio stations that complemented the impression from German and Italian air reconnaissance that most Allied strength was concentrated there.[174] Like all deception, it was a plan that could have gone awry given its scale and complexity, but the bait was swallowed and Rommel concentrated armour in the wrong place. The subsequent battle was only narrowly won despite overwhelming Allied air superiority and more numerous tanks and vehicles. The margin of victory was secured in this case by deception. Captured German and Italian commanders confirmed that they expected the main offensive on the southern flank and continued to do so for several days into the battle, by which time it was too late to salvage the situation.

The success of 'Bertram' may well explain the decision to use deception more fully in Anglo-American strategy. In summer 1943, as part of the long-term preparation for an invasion of France in 1944, the British Chiefs of Staff approved a plan of 'cover and camouflage', Operation 'Cockade', whose object was to persuade the German armed forces that a cross-Channel invasion was planned for the late summer of 1943, tying down German forces in the West to the benefit of the Allied campaigns in Italy and the Soviet Union. American commanders were unenthusiastic about the plan. The German side saw through the flimsy attempts to use double agents to issue warnings and were unimpressed by the limited air and sea activity, codenamed Operation 'Starkey', designed to simulate preparations for an assault.[175] In this and many other failed attempts at wartime deception, it was the absence of a real operation to mask that undermined the credibility of any cover plan. The complete failure of 'Cockade', run by the London Controlling Section, might well have ended any prospect of trying to deceive the enemy in 1944. A second deception, Operation 'Jael', was dreamt up to try to convince the Germans that the Mediterranean would be the main strategic theatre for Anglo-American forces in 1944, supplemented by the bomber offensive rather than any invasion. American army commanders thought, rightly, that the proposal was entirely unconvincing, and 'Jael' was cancelled.[176] Yet a further plan, Operation 'Torrent', was drawn up in July 1943 for the actual invasion planned a year later in order to try to confuse the Germans about Allied intentions: while the main force would invade Normandy, a limited diversionary feint would be mounted against the Pas de Calais with a handful of divisions to keep reinforcements away from the main assault. This plan, too, soon collapsed because the planned feint was regarded as too small to hold down German forces for any useful length of time.[177]

Deception survived as an element in Allied strategy for the invasion thanks to Churchill who, following the conference at Tehran in which the Normandy invasion was confirmed, returned again to the idea that the success of invasion depended on misleading the enemy so that forces would be kept away from northern France, an argument that reflected his own uncertainty about the successful outcome of the amphibious operation. Bevan and the London Controlling Station were directed to mount a new deception, Operation 'Bodyguard', to try to persuade the Germans that major operations in 1944 would be directed against the Balkans, northern Italy and Scandinavia; an invasion of France was to be postponed until later in 1944 at the earliest. But like 'Torrent' and 'Cockade', 'Bodyguard' largely failed in its purpose. By late 1943 the German high command, and Hitler too, already understood that the great build-up of forces in the British Isles was aimed at an invasion of France at some point in the following spring or summer. A possible threat to Norway or the Balkans was not discounted, and substantial forces were retained in both areas, but it was always subsidiary in German calculations about Allied intentions.

The deception plan for the Normandy invasion relied in the end on personnel from the Mediterranean theatre with real operational experience of deception. Dudley Clarke's deputy, Colonel Noel Wild, was transferred to London in December 1943 to take up responsibility for deception at the headquarters of the newly appointed supreme commander, General Eisenhower. Montgomery's appointment to command Twenty-first Army Group for the invasion completed the transition. Eisenhower and Montgomery both favoured deception and had both profited from it. Wild and the Special Means division worked with the deception staff of Twenty-first Army Group, known as 'R' Group, led by Lieutenant Colonel David Strangeways, to produce a deception plan for the genuine operation, codenamed 'Fortitude South'. 'Bodyguard' was kept going with 'Fortitude North', a continuation of the idea developed in 1943 that a threat to Norway and the iron-ore fields in Sweden was a plausible operation, but like its predecessors this had little effect on German planning since significant forces were always present in Norway and were not likely to be reinforced.

'Fortitude South' was the central ploy, designed to persuade the German military and political leadership that the invasion of Normandy was only a prelude to a larger invasion force across the narrow neck of the English Channel towards the Pas de Calais. As in the case of 'Bertram' at El Alamein, the object was to simulate the primary threat from one area, while masking the scale and timing of the real threat from another. A notional First United States Army Group (FUSAG) was established in south-east England, given a real commander – General Patton – and sustained by phantom radio traffic and dummy equipment. The rows of fake tanks and guns in eastern England drew on the experience in the desert, except for the dummy landing craft which proved too flimsy and were easily beached or broken (though never spotted by the limited German aerial reconnaissance). The great merit of the deception, as at El Alamein, was to keep some real forces in south-east England until shortly before their transfer to south-west England for the invasion, and then to replace them with real reserve forces mixed together with divisional units that existed only on paper. The deception was worked out to the last detail and the strictest security maintained.

The use of double agents reinforced what German SIGINT and aerial reconnaissance might discover. By 1942, British inland security, MI5, had captured almost all German spies in Britain and turned many of them into agents working for the Allies. For 'Fortitude South', the agent codenamed 'Garbo' by the Allies (the Spanish spy Juan Pujol García) used his notional network of fictitious agents to supply high-level intelligence to the German *Abwehr* (counter-intelligence). Between January and June 1944 he supplied 500 messages designed to lodge in the minds of his German controllers the build-up of forces in south-east England and Scotland and, less successfully, the idea that invasion would come later in the year. The more remarkable aspect of the story is the extent to which the German secret service believed for years that their British counterparts were unable to track down and eliminate enemy spying when Allied spies in occupied Europe were regularly caught. Agent information still had to make its way to the operational commands, but it was discovered after the war that of 208 messages formally recorded in the position reports on Britain by OKW, 188 were from double agents.[178] The problem for German military intelligence was what to make of the large quantity of material available as the invasion approached. German army intelligence, Foreign Armies West, was completely misled about the size of the force gathered in Britain. Thanks to the FUSAG deception, Allied forces were overestimated by 50 per cent, making it likely that at least two separate operations were planned, one in Normandy, but a larger one against the Pas de Calais. Either was plausible, which is why it proved so difficult for Hitler and his commanders to be sure which was the feint and which was not, though assessments by April had come to favour Normandy or Brittany. But by mid-May the increase in intelligence on the FUSAG forces suggested instead that invasion from south-east England was more likely, with Normandy the first, but subsidiary, operation. Ultra and MAGIC decrypts allowed the deceivers to gauge whether the ploys worked and by late May it was evident, from Hitler downwards, that the threat to the Pas de Calais was the one now taken seriously. On 1 June, a decrypt of a message to Tokyo from the Japanese ambassador in Berlin, Ōshima Hiroshi, based on a recent conversation with Hitler, confirmed that he expected a diversionary assault in Normandy, to be followed by 'an all-out second front across the Straits of Dover'.[179]

The timing of the invasion was also a mystery, although German army intelligence did recognize that efforts through double agents to suggest a postponement to later in the year was nothing more than the 'intentional disguise of enemy intentions'.[180] But the actual date eluded German intelligence. German forces along the coast had been subjected to ten highest alert alarms between April and June, and by then were less inclined to listen to cries of wolf. A summary prepared for the commander-in-chief in the West, von Rundstedt, on 5 June, just hours before the invasion armada arrived off the coast, concluded that imminent invasion 'does not seem to be indicated as yet'.[181] The key element of the 'Fortitude South' deception, however, was to sustain the fiction of a second invasion by the phantom American army group at some time after Normandy. Fears of a subsequent landing did not prevent Rommel from moving armoured divisions hastily to Normandy, but the German high command was unwilling to run the risk of denuding north-east France. The continued use of radio deception, coupled with further apparently reliable information from the double agents, lodged FUSAG ever more firmly in the minds of German commanders. A jumble of intelligence information, not all of it from double agents, suggested that FUSAG was waiting until the Normandy lodgement had drawn in German reserves before launching a second operation against the north-east coast of France. Given the intelligence available this was a plausible scenario, but it meant that some twenty-two German divisions were retained in the Pas de Calais well into July, when the German commanders finally decided that the success of the Normandy front had encouraged the Allies to change their mind and feed the FUSAG forces into the existing campaign rather than open up a second, retaining to the last belief in the phantom army group. Hitler finally ordered the forces in the Pas de Calais to join the battle in Normandy in August but by then it was too late.[182] Right to the end, the deception proved successful, despite all the risks that Allied cover might be blown, because it confirmed in the enemy's mind a strategic calculation that appeared entirely rational. As a consequence, the most elaborate of all Western deception operations multiplied Allied strength by dividing that of the enemy. The result was to reduce the high element of risk for an operation in which the Western Allies could not afford to fail.

While 'Fortitude South' played out in the West, a second major deception operation was mounted on the Eastern Front by Soviet forces against German Army Group Centre in Belorussia. This deception matched the scale of that for 'Overlord' and its effects were devastating for the German front line in the Soviet Union. Like 'Fortitude', the deception plan for Operation 'Bagration', launched on 22/23 June 1944, represented the fulfilment of a long apprenticeship in mastering strategic and operational deception. The central importance of *maskirovka* (deception or concealment) and *vnezapnost* (surprise) was recognized in Soviet military doctrine in the 1920s. Successive Red Army field regulations emphasized the advantages of secrecy: 'Surprise has a stunning effect on the enemy.' The object was always to conceal intentions from the enemy by masking force concentrations and then launching an unexpected assault which, according to later wartime field regulations, 'dumbfounds the enemy, paralyses his will, and deprives him of the opportunity to offer organised resistance'.[183] It was therefore ironic that Soviet forces had been themselves caught off-guard in June 1941 and their organized resistance temporarily confounded. By September 1941, Soviet Supreme Headquarters insisted that *maskirovka* be practised at every level, strategic, operational and tactical, and it became embedded in almost all the subsequent 140 front-line operations. Camouflage was second nature to Soviet soldiers, and they became adept at tactical-level concealment and ambush. But broader operational deception relied on the careful movement of forces at night, strict security, absolute radio silence (less difficult with the initial dearth of radios) and exploitation of unexpected terrain. By the time the German army was poised before Moscow in late 1941, German intelligence had already missed the presence of three entire Soviet armies. By 1942 each operational headquarters had a dedicated deception staff to co-ordinate *maskirovka* with operational planning in the hope that concealment might help the Red Army restore the balance against advancing German forces.

The success of these reforms was evident with Operation 'Uranus' in November 1942, designed to cut off German forces in Stalingrad, in the Battle of Kursk eight months later, and in the stunning defeat of Army Group Centre in summer 1944. For the success of 'Uranus', it was essential to conceal as completely as possible. The commanders, staffs and troops moved into position to launch the counter-offensive against the stretched flanks of the Axis forces were not told why they were there. Stalin insisted that there should be only verbal instructions, no maps or printed material. Radio security was tightened by threat of punishment, and infantry were ordered not to fire at enemy aircraft when they appeared, as they were prone to do.[184] South and north of the German corridor to Stalingrad 300,000 men, 1,000 tanks, and 5,000 artillery pieces and mortars were invisibly moved into place. The Axis forces, Hungarian, Italian and Romanian, who manned most of the corridor did become aware of some of this movement but were assured by the head of the intelligence division Foreign Armies East, General Reinhard Gehlen, that no major attack could be expected. The army chief of staff, General Kurt Zeitzler, concluded that the apparent lack of any further Soviet reserves rendered the Red Army incapable of launching 'a large-scale offensive'. The day before 'Uranus' was launched, 18 November 1942, Gehlen's report for the threatened armies was vague and non-committal.[185] The subsequent Soviet operation succeeded in exploiting surprise to the maximum. By the time Axis armies had recovered, it was too late. German forces in Stalingrad were cut off and efforts to rescue them abortive.

For the Kursk battle in July 1943, the full repertoire of *maskirovka* was employed. For the defensive zone around the salient every effort was made to confuse German air reconnaissance by constructing numerous fake artillery posts, tank parks and command centres, while using sophisticated camouflage of everything real, including minefields so well disguised in the terrain that in some cases German armoured forces failed to detect them before the first tank exploded. False radio traffic fed into German misapprehensions of Soviet strength and dispositions while rigid radio discipline kept the actual scale and position of Soviet forces concealed. Dummy airfields were constructed with such success that out of the twenty-five German air force attacks on Soviet airbases before the launch of the operation, only three hit the genuine target.[186] The key element in the deception, however, was the concentration of large reserve forces behind the Kursk salient, disguised as part of the defence but in reality prepared to launch a large-scale counter-offensive once German forces had been blunted on the defensive field. Here too comprehensive concealment was ordered to mask real strengths and to convey to the enemy the idea that here were limited reserves, designed to boost the defenders in the salient. German intelligence failed entirely to predict the sudden counter-offensives towards Orel north of the salient and Belgorod and Kharkov to the south. Elaborate deception was again used to mask the move forward to the jump-off positions for the new offensives, while major feint attacks further south successfully diverted German armoured reserves. The success of *vnezapnost* was vindicated in the broad offensive that unfolded in August 1943 that drove German forces on the central front in Russia all the way back to the Dnieper River by November.

The deception for Operation 'Bagration' in June 1944 built on all these experiences. The Red Army Field Regulations for 1944 made concealment and deception 'mandatory forms of combat support for each action and operation', integral elements in Soviet operational art. Only five people knew everything about the operation – Zhukov, Vasilevskii and three others – and they were forbidden to mention 'Bagration' either by telephone, letter or telegraph. At the strategic level, every indication was presented to the German side that major offensive operations would be conducted in the south against the Axis Balkan states and in the north along the Baltic coast. German army intelligence had already assumed that the main weight of the summer campaigning would be against the south and as a result were easy victims of the deception. The commanders of Army Group Centre straddled across Belorussia, which was where the main Soviet offensive was in fact planned, were told by army intelligence not to expect an offensive.[187] The deception required the secret redeployment to the Belorussian front of nine armies and eleven corps of tanks, armour and cavalry, as well as the concealment of 10,000 artillery pieces, 300,000 tons of fuel and half-a-million cans of rations. In the south, dummy artillery, tanks and airfields were constructed, with protection from live anti-aircraft fire and fighter patrols to add realism to the deceit. The secrecy was a daunting task. The front was ordered to keep up 'normal' appearances by firing as usual and to sustain regular radio traffic. All the new forces that moved in had to keep complete radio silence and move only at night, were not allowed to join scouting forays in case they were caught, and were told nothing of what was planned (in case of defectors). Engineers managed to conceal the construction of wooden causeways through the swampy ground north of the Pripet Marshes, and, like Guderian's tanks bursting out from the Ardennes forest in the Battle of France, Soviet armour would unexpectedly pour along these causeways into the startled German defenders.[188] Although local commanders had tried to indicate that there were major offensive preparations in front of them, the army high command assumed this was a feint, and none of the extra resources needed by Army Group Centre were forthcoming. On the night of the 22/23 June the offensive opened and within weeks the German army was cleared from Belorussia and Red Army units pressed on to the banks of the Vistula River in sight of Warsaw, one of the greatest defeats inflicted on German forces during the war.

The embedding of deception in Soviet operations did not guarantee success, which relied on weeks of gruelling combat, but in all the major operations against German forces, deception achieved the object of disorienting the enemy sufficiently to make the task of the forces on the ground and in the air that much easier. If proof were needed of its value, the final offensive campaign of the Soviet war against the Japanese Kwantung Army in Manchuria supplied it. Japanese forces had not yet been the object of extensive deception operations. American commanders were not attracted to deception as an element of strategy, since they identified it with the underhand operation the Japanese had committed in December 1941. The Joint Security Control, established to match the British London Controlling Section in Europe, had difficulty persuading commanders in the Pacific to take deception seriously. Late in 1943 Joint Security Control officers were directed to write deception annexes for American operational plans, but their influence was resented by the field commanders. The few deception operations – 'Wedlock', 'Husband', 'Bambino', 'Valentine' and 'Bluebird' – had little effect, chiefly because Japanese intelligence failed either to detect or respond to what were entirely fictitious operations. The strengthening of Japanese forces in the northern Kurile Islands in 1944 and in Taiwan in 1945 were almost certainly pre-emptive moves assessed as necessary by the Japanese military, rather than the direct result of the deception operation 'Wedlock' (a phantom invasion from the Aleutian Islands) or 'Bluebird' (a phantom landing on Taiwan and the South China coast).[189] Efforts by the British to use Japanese spies caught in India as double agents largely failed because the agents had only intermittent contact with Japanese intelligence and there was no way of knowing if any misinformation had actually influenced Japanese operations or not.[190]

The Manchurian offensive, by contrast, was a model of Soviet *maskirovka*: the transfer of Soviet armies eastwards was detected by the Japanese, but the scale was not understood. Railway traffic moved only at night and rail routes nearer to Manchuria were covered over with improvised tunnels to mask the traffic beneath. Once in place, Soviet forces used the whole range of camouflage and concealment. The Kwantung Army underestimated Soviet strength by around half, and also failed to anticipate the direction of attack (the Red Army negotiated terrain the enemy considered impassable for armour) and the timing. Although it was clear that the Soviet forces intended to invade, estimates suggested that the Red Army would not be ready until the late autumn, or even the spring of 1946. When the attack came it was wholly unexpected and Japanese forces were unhinged by the rapid Soviet deployment and infiltration. A campaign designed to last thirty days was completed in fifteen with the annihilation of Japan's largest military concentration, the million-strong Kwantung Army that had begun hostilities fourteen years before, in 1931.[191]

There is a firm case for arguing that carefully planned and orchestrated deception played a significant role in securing Allied victories that might otherwise have resulted in a longer war effort and higher losses. At El Alamein, Stalingrad and Kursk, in the assaults on Normandy and Belorussia and in Manchuria there can be no doubt that deception proved a force multiplier, even if other factors were also essential to victory. In Britain and the Soviet Union, a string of major defeats made it imperative to find ways of securing advantage, and deception was one way of doing so. It worked also because of the advantages enjoyed by Allied intelligence, and weaknesses in intelligence evaluation in both the German and Japanese cases. Nevertheless, the extent to which both intelligence and deception helped to determine the outcome of operations remains a more open question for historians than it does in the case of armour and air power, radio and radar, or amphibious assault.

WINNERS AND LOSERS: THE WARTIME LEARNING CURVE

The 'learning curve' was a term contemporary with the wartime crisis, first coined in 1936 and applied during the war to assessments of productivity development in the American shipbuilding industry. Although intended as a way to measure the rate at which managers and workforce learned to reduce the hours spent producing a unit of output, it seems singularly appropriate as a metaphor for the way in which armed forces during the war improved their fighting capability. The theory posits two kinds of learning: organizational learning and labour learning. The managerial side is important because managers can innovate technically and look at performance indicators to see where remedies are needed; labour needs to adapt to unfamiliar circumstances and equipment and learn how to master them.[192] That is exactly what armed forces did during the war, if not always uniformly or well. Military managers assessed deficiencies, remedied tactics, and promoted innovative technology and organization, while the ordinary soldier, sailor and airman became with training more adept and, with the necessary technical aids, more efficient in combat. In assessing winners and losers in wartime fighting, the capacity to learn and adapt was pivotal.

The learning curve nevertheless implies time needed to assess results, identify correctives, and train the workforce. For the Allies it was critical that after the initial disasters there was time enough to work out what was needed to reverse their fortunes. Although all three major Allies suffered a string of early defeats, the Axis powers were never able to bring their military force to bear to impose an early and decisive defeat as German forces had done in France in 1940. Germany and Italy could not invade the British Isles and were held at bay in North Africa; Japan could not invade the United States or Britain; the Soviet Union proved too large a geographical entity to be swallowed in one bite. The Axis states all had space rather than time, and it was space that slowed down their advance and brought them to a halt in 1942. The Allies were no nearer invading the Japanese, German or Italian homelands in 1942, but they now had the time and the global reach to work out how to reorganize and improve their military capability so that they were in a position to do so over the last two years of war. Their military establishments became what the organizational theorist Trent Hone has described as 'complex adaptive systems', in which the learning curve could be worked through.[193]

It was also essential that the Allied powers understood how necessary it was to learn and to reform, and that they could develop the institutional mechanisms for doing so. The process of assessing and learning was central to Soviet survival after the catastrophic losses of material and regular soldiers in 1941. During 1942 the army general staff inaugurated a widespread review of what had gone wrong and what needed to be learned, drawing substantially on German practice. Far-reaching improvements in communications and intelligence-gathering followed, together with a radical reorganization of armoured forces, infantry divisions and air forces at both operational and tactical levels.[194] The transformative effect was profound as German commanders discovered to their cost. Britain's military and naval capability built on substantial organizational reform in developing a largely mechanized army, an effective tactical air force (where there had been virtually none in 1940), and the capacity to mount major amphibious operations after the disaster at Dieppe. Reform was in many cases prompted by committees dedicated to learning such lessons – the Bartholomew Committee on the aftermath of Dunkirk, the Woodall Report on air–ground collaboration, the Godwin-Austen Committee on communications – but chiefly by the long catalogue of humiliating failures up to the first victory at El Alamein and even beyond.[195] Moreover, although British ground forces continued to rely on heavy and accurate artillery fire, together with extensive air support, they became tactically more adept and less hamstrung by top-down command structures than they had been in the first years of war. The 'Brief Notes on the Conduct of Battle for Senior Officers', written and circulated by Montgomery in December 1942, allowed subordinate commanders much greater leeway in using their own judgement to achieve a particular mission, closer to the famous German concept of *Auftragstaktik* (mission-based tactics) than most modern critics of British army practice have allowed.[196]

For the United States armed forces, there was nothing to do but to start learning. Small, technically backward and poorly served by intelligence, the United States army and army air forces faced a formidable task in turning a hastily assembled, largely conscript armed force into a professional military organization. The US navy was larger and better resourced, but still with much to learn. The first campaigns on Guadalcanal and in North Africa exposed numerous shortcomings and prompted a rapid reassessment of what was needed. After the near disaster at the Kasserine Pass in Tunisia, Lieutenant General Lesley McNair, commander of Army Ground Forces called for a 'training based' army, one constantly learning. In the field great emphasis was given to identifying and disseminating tactical information about the enemy and how to react. Combat Intelligence Centers drew together information from battle experience and sent out digests of information and advice to units facing or about to face the enemy. Gradually in the Pacific (and in Europe), the culture of rigid command instructions from the top was transformed to allow small unit officers discretion in coping with the tactical situation of Japanese defence to the death.[197] In Europe, centralized command and control was not always possible. Instructions to II Corps, Fifth Army in Italy in June 1944 laid down that in such circumstances 'commanders must act on their own responsibility, initiative and judgment. Inactivity is inexcusable.'[198] The transformation of American and British fighting power was comprehensive, from the organization of a mechanized army, effective communications, better intelligence, greatly improved amphibious doctrine and practice, and aggressive tactical air power – each of them an essential step along the learning curve.

Axis forces learned as well, upgrading investment in military resources, and observing their enemies closely. But the glamour of the early victories blunted the search for more transformative changes. For much of the war (and post-war) years German commanders considered the military quality of the forces they faced on all fronts as generally inferior. The *Afrika Korps* in 1942 noted the enemy's 'slowness and clumsiness, the lack of initiative and tactical planning' just weeks before its near-total defeat at El Alamein.[199] On the Eastern Front the early Soviet failures coloured the German view of the opponent. 'Every German soldier,' wrote General Hermann Geyer in autumn 1941, 'has the right to feel superior to the Russian.'[200] By the time such views were changing, it was too late. The armour–air combination served the German army well through to Stalingrad, when it stagnated; German radio and radar was ahead of Allied practice early in the war, but the lead was lost by 1943; the German submarine war echoed that of the earlier Great War and ended with the same ultimate failure; the success of surprise in France in 1940, or in the launch of 'Barbarossa', was never repeated. A similar outcome held true for Japanese forces. Against the poorly equipped Chinese forces there was little pressure on the Japanese high command to reform; amphibious operations defined Japanese success in 1941–2 but faded away as soon as the Pacific perimeter was secure; and finally, Allied surrenders in early 1942 produced an entirely contemptuous view of the enemy among troops who were expected to die rather than give up.

By contrast, the force multipliers utilized by the Allies reflected the weakness of their military effectiveness in the early years of war and the necessity for adaptation. The process was uneven, still prone to error or waste or technological constraints, but it was enough to secure victory. There has been a long tradition of seeing the Axis forces as simply worn down by the huge military resources available to the Allies while remaining militarily effective, or, in the German case, evidently superior to any Allied armed forces they faced.[201] But resource advantage means little – as the Red Army discovered when its own great superiority in numbers of tanks and aircraft in 1941 was easily swept aside – unless it is exploited by better doctrine, organization, training and intelligence. The Allies needed to improve in all these areas for their resource advantage to be significant. Combat was the real test and across the Pacific, through North Africa, Italy and France, and along the vast Eastern Front, Axis forces were eventually outfought by armed forces that had learned the hard way. According to the theory, the industrial 'learning curve' flattens out towards the end of the process as managers and workforce successfully optimize what they have learned. Allied victory in 1945 was the flattened end of their learning curve.

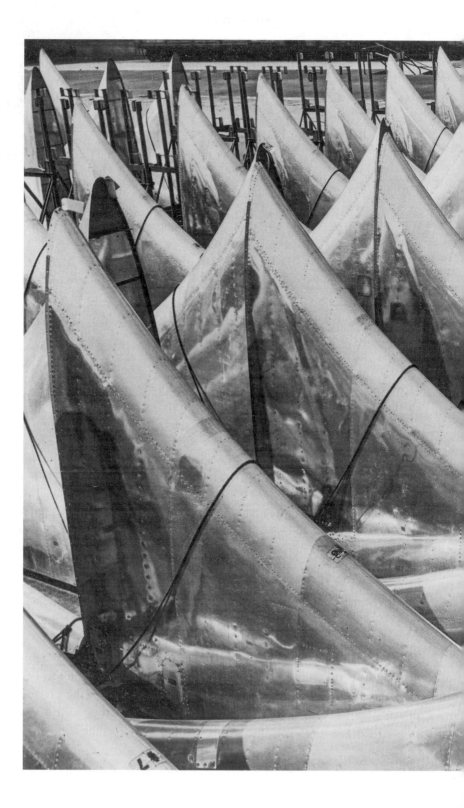

6

War Economies: Economies at War

'American industrial genius, unmatched throughout all the world in the solution of production problems, has been called upon to bring its resources and talents into action. Manufacturers of watches, of farm implements, of linotypes and cash registers and automobiles and sewing machines and lawn mowers and locomotives are now making fuses and bomb packing crates and telescope mounts and shells and pistols and tanks.'

Franklin Roosevelt, 'Fireside Chat', 29 December 1940[1]

'The necessary increase in efficiency of our production of weapons and equipment must therefore be achieved 1.) through a detailed correction in the construction of our weapons and equipment, in the sense of making possible mass production on modern principles, and by this method achieving the rationalization of our manufacturing methods.'

Adolf Hitler, 'Efficiency Decree', 3 December 1941[2]

In the United States the mass production of weapons and military equipment was taken for granted. President Roosevelt launched American air rearmament in May 1940 by calling for the production of 50,000 aircraft a year.[3] Later he intervened in planning tank production to insist on 25,000 a year. There were doubts at the time whether these goals could be achieved, but the 'American industrial genius' Roosevelt addressed in his 'fireside chat' in December 1940 rose to the demands of rearmament and war. By 1943 the United States alone already produced more than all the enemy states put together. Hitler had been warned by military experts not to underestimate the capacity of the United States to produce military goods, but this did not prevent him from declaring war. A few days before the Japanese attack on Pearl Harbor his headquarters issued a decree under his signature insisting that German war industry adopt a programme of simplification and standardization that would make German mass production possible too.

Hitler is not usually credited with much strategic grasp, but his recognition from early in the war that military output on the largest possible scale was an indispensable precondition for waging it successfully was borne out by events. The December 1941 decree followed months in which he had tried to intervene as supreme commander to get industry and the military to co-operate together to find ways to use Germany's extensive resources to maximize output. In May 1941 he held a conference with Munitions Minister Fritz Todt and the head of the armed forces' office for the war economy, General Georg Thomas, where he outlined his ideas for making the war economy more efficient. He blamed the military for over-burdening industry with complex technical demands, called for 'more primitive, robust construction', and the 'promotion of crude mass-production'.[4] A directive was issued calling on the three military services to reduce the number and complexity of weapons, followed by further directives across the summer and autumn to focus on weapons suitable for modern production methods, until the December decree finally spelt out what Hitler expected. 'It is significant,' recalled Albert Speer's deputy, Karl-Otto Saur, to his captors in 1945, 'that rationalization in Germany was only really put into operation for all practical purposes after Hitler's order of December 3 1941 and that his intervention was needed to carry it from theory to practice.'[5] The decree was not the end of the story, however. Two years later the head of aero-engine production in Germany, William Werner, complained that production was still 'strongly marked by craftsmanship' and called for assembly-line production 'according to the American model'.[6] The gulf between the two production cultures proved to be a challenging one to bridge and a major factor in the final outcome of the war.

WEAPONS OF MASS PRODUCTION

The military output of the warring powers dwarfed anything seen before or since. Large though the scale of output was, however, only some of the weapons, vehicles and vessels built were mass produced in the conventional view of the term. Mass production was associated with 'Fordism', whose origins lay in the revolution in production techniques ushered in by the American motor industry (and Henry Ford in particular) in the first decades of the century. Fordism was open to interpretation: in the United

States it was a means to maximize the output of cheap, standard consumer goods by applying rational control over the flow of resources and components to a production line where assembly was subdivided into easily learned and repetitive tasks; in the Soviet Union, Fordism was embraced by the young Communist regime not only as a symbol of Soviet modernity but because rational mass production would supply cheap commodities for the newly empowered proletariat. Only in Germany was Fordism viewed ambivalently. Although forms of mass production were adopted in the 1920s in a few sectors among the admirers of Ford's productivity model, the economic collapse after 1929 provoked a rejection of the American model of production in favour of a German emphasis on specialized production and high engineering quality, both factors that favoured the development of a sophisticated and technically advanced weapons sector. These different production cultures played out in the Second World War. They marked the difference between the volume production of the American Sherman and the Soviet T-34 tanks and the relatively modest output of the German Tigers and Panthers, both of which outperformed Allied mass-produced armour by a considerable margin but were produced in wholly inadequate numbers.

   In practice, mass production as it was understood in the output of standard consumer durables in the inter-war years had evident limitations when applied to the production of modern armaments. In the First World War, volume output of military equipment became essential, and in the production of small arms, munitions and artillery elements of modern factory practice were introduced in order to increase the productive efficiency of the workforce and to save resources.[7] But by the Second World War volume production meant expanding the output of complex engineering products, from tanks and armoured vehicles to aero-engines and airframes. A military aircraft typically required more than 100,000 separate parts, so that volume production represented an extraordinary challenge simply in terms of organizing the flow of parts from hundreds of subcontractors to ensure that final assembly could proceed relatively smoothly. Where a rifle or machine gun could be produced easily from a modest number of standard parts, replicating peacetime production practices, an aircraft or tank or submarine required an exceptional production process. The American Consolidated B-24 ('Liberator') bomber was put together using 30,000 production drawings; when Henry Ford tried to mass produce the bomber based on his experience of making cars and trucks, production was broken down into 20,000 separate operations, requiring the installation of 21,000 production jigs and fixtures and 29,000 dies. The project took so long to get running that the bomber was

obsolescent by the time production started.[8] Ford's confidence that peacetime mass production could be applied to weapons led him in 1940 to
offer to produce 1,000 fighter aircraft a day using standard machine tools,
but the offer was turned down after investigation because engineering
standards for a cheap family car did not remotely match the requirements
of modern aeronautical production. The same problem plagued the efforts
of General Motors to produce a fast modern fighter, the XP-75. The company tried to cut corners by buying in ready-made components from other
aircraft designs rather than engineering the entire product. After four years
the project was pronounced a complete failure and scrapped in the summer of 1945 – evidence of how difficult it was for a major mass-producer
to transfer peacetime practice to wartime needs, but also evidence that the
United States could expend effort and resources on futile projects while at
the same time outproducing every other economy.[9]

The many problems associated with volume output of advanced weaponry highlighted the difference between civilian, peacetime production,
where decisions about what to produce and in what quantity are dictated
by the consumer market and civilian tastes, and a war economy where
there is a single military customer whose requirements are uncertain, shifting and peremptory. The establishment of long production runs, and the
corresponding economies of scale, were regularly frustrated by unpredictable shifts in strategy, or the need to match or exceed enemy technical
accomplishments, or to interrupt production runs because of military
insistence on short-term tactical modifications to an established weapon.
Under these circumstances, standard models, interchangeable parts and
conveyor-line production were difficult to establish. Persistent modification was the enemy of wartime volume production. As Alec Cairncross, in
charge of planning components at the British Ministry of Aircraft Production, put it, 'life was one long battle with muddle'.[10] The German Junkers
Ju88 medium bomber had 18,000 design alterations in the first three years
of production, reducing completely any prospect of a long-settled production run. Design changes not only affected the final assembly of an aircraft
or a tank, but also affected the hundreds of component suppliers, whose
production had to be co-ordinated with the main assembly plants. There
was often a marked difference between the potential for volume production of individual suppliers since small companies were less able to adapt
flexibly to new requirements or to introduce more efficient forms of production. Tank output in the United States in 1942 fell short by 20,000
from the 42,000 tanks planned because of major component shortages. In
Germany in the middle years of the war an effort was made to ensure that
component subcontractors on military orders all adopted best practice.

The ratio between the best and worst performance was found to be 1:5; after the rationalization of factory practice the ratio was reduced to 1:1.5.[11]

All the major combatant powers, save Italy and China, eventually developed programmes of volume output, including elements of conventional 'mass production', despite the manifold problems associated with more complex and expensive military engineering. The wartime achievements are set out in Table 6.1. The aggregate statistics mask the effect that very different political and administrative regimes had on the production record, and the shifting strategic requirements that explain the priorities chosen. Japan and Britain focused volume production on aircraft and ships because, as island powers, this priority matched the nature of their chosen strategies; the Soviet Union and Germany produced modest quantities of naval equipment but exceptional levels of army and air force weapons; and only the United States, endowed with access to hemispheric resources, had the possibility of producing air, sea and army equipment on the largest scale. The figures also mask the differences in quality between different outputs. Although military authorities were generally committed to upgrading equipment to match the enemy, this was often difficult to do when production was already heavily committed to earlier versions, or simply beyond the engineering capacity of the economy. Qualitative difference was nevertheless seldom wide enough to compensate for a failure of quantity. As the wartime economies matured, so the military, business and governments each collaborated to focus on a cluster of weapons proven in combat which could be produced efficiently in volume, rather than dissipate effort among a large number of redundant models.

Table 6.1 The Military Output of the Major Warring Powers 1939–44

A: Aircraft	1939	1940	1941	1942	1943	1944
Britain	7,940	15,049	20,094	23,672	26,263	26,461
United States	5,836	12,804	26,277	47,826	85,998	96,318
Soviet Union	10,382	10,565	15,735	25,436	34,900	40,300
Germany	8,295	10,247	11,776	15,409	24,807	39,807
Japan	4,467	4,768	5,088	8,861	16,693	28,180
Italy	1,750	3,257	3,503	2,821	2,024	-
B: Naval Vessels						
Britain	57	148	236	239	224	188
United States	-	-	544	1,854	2,654	2,247
Soviet Union	-	33	62	19	13	23

Germany (U-Boats only)	15	40	196	244	270	189
Japan	21	30	49	68	122	248
Italy	40	12	41	86	148	-

C: Tanks

Britain	969	1,379	4,837	8,622	7,217	4,000
United States	-	331	4,052	24,997	29,497	17,565
Soviet Union	2,950	2,794	6,590	24,719	24,006	28,983
Germany (a)	794	1,651	3,298	4,317	5,993	8,941
(b)	-	394	944	1,758	5,941	10,749
Japan	559	1,023	1,216	1,271	891	371
Italy	(1940–43) 1,862 tanks, 645 self-propelled guns					

D: Artillery Pieces

Britain	1,400	1,900	5,300	6,600	12,200	12,400
United States	-	c.1,800	29,615	72,658	67,544	33,558
Soviet Union	17,348	15,300	40,547	128,092	130,295	122,385
Germany	c.2,000	5,000	7,000	12,000	27,000	41,000

Naval vessels exclude landing craft and small auxiliary vessels; German figures row (a) = for tanks, row (b) = self-propelled artillery and tank-killer armour; Soviet tank figures include self-propelled artillery; artillery pieces for Britain, United States and Germany are for medium and heavy calibre only, figures for the Soviet Union include all calibres.

The reduction in the number of different models produced and the more effective management of modification were significant multipliers in the volume production of weapons. Greater standardization had the advantage that volume output could be concentrated in the best and largest firms. This was an uneven process, particularly where competition for production resources between the different services discouraged co-operation. In Japan little control was exercised over the navy and army in their procurement policy and as a result the navy produced 53 basic aircraft models with 112 variations, and the army 37 basic models with 52 variants. The navy had by 1942 a total of fifty-two engine types. The result was to produce limited production runs and regular problems of spares and maintenance, although it did not prevent a sudden upsurge in aircraft and aero-engine production in the last two years of the war.[12] In Britain the process of settling on standard models took time as the technology rapidly altered, but by mid-war tank production was concentrated on the Churchill and the Cromwell (with the latter's derivatives, the

Comet and Challenger), and aircraft output on the Lancaster and Halifax bombers, the Spitfire and Hawker Tempest fighter/fighter-bombers, and the De Havilland Mosquito. Tank production was concentrated on just one engine, the Meteor, and aero-engine production on the Rolls-Royce Merlin. The United States undertook volume output of standard models from the outset of the conflict, focusing almost all tank production on the Sherman M4 and its derivatives, and army aircraft output on the B-17 and B-24 heavy bomber, the P-38, P-47 and P-51 fighter, and the Douglas DC-3 transport. The army and navy produced only eighteen aircraft models between them. Army truck production was based on just four tested models, while the ubiquitous Willys 'Jeep' was the principal small communications vehicle. Soviet tank output meant the T-34 and its upgrade models for the whole war period until the appearance of the JS-1 heavy tank in the last months of the conflict. For the Soviet air force, the Yak 1-9 fighter and the Ilyushin Il 2 'Sturmovik' dive-bomber were produced in huge quantities, 16,700 and 36,000 respectively.[13] One of the few German successes in standard production, the Messerschmitt Bf109 fighter, saw 31,000 produced over the war years. Economies of scale were derived almost automatically once a major model had been selected and allowed a long production run.

Even with a more stable programme of model selection and standardization, volume production was not free of problems. Modifications to models in production had to be negotiated with the military, whose priority was battlefield performance rather than uninterrupted production runs. In Britain, modification to aircraft models was carried out as far as possible on existing production lines through a policy of incremental design change to avoid too much disruption. The Spitfire went through twenty major upgrades in design without a break in output or a major redesign programme, but they were enough to make it a formidably more effective fighter in 1944 than in 1940. The American practice, by contrast, was to allow full volume production, with all the savings allowed by flow line manufacturing, but then to send the completed aircraft to one of twenty Modification Centers where it could take up to an additional 25–50 per cent of man-hours to complete the alterations on each aircraft, nullifying the advantage gained from mass producing the original. At the Ford Company's huge facility at Willow Run, Michigan, for the B-24 bomber, pre-production modifications transformed the aircraft and compelled regular changes to the machinery, jigs and fixtures that wasted both time and money even before production had begun. By 1944, the aircraft industry was encouraged to move to the British practice in order to avoid delays in supply and the confusion caused by gathering all the tactical demands from the forces in the field together for integration at the Modi-fication Centers.[14]

Volume production also affected the quality of the final product as a result of using cost-cutting practices and less-skilled labour. British tanks for most of the war years were notoriously poorly assembled, with break-downs frequent as a result. In September 1942, a Directorate of Fighting Vehicle Inspection was established, and the number of inspectors raised from 900 in 1940 to 1,650 in mid-1943, and by 1944 the number of reported mechanical failures declined. British forces found similar prob-lems with the Sherman tanks sent from the United States as Lend-Lease aid. A group of 38 sent to North Africa in 1942 were found to have 146 faults because of casual or poorly inspected assembly.[15] The rapid mass output of the Soviet T-34 tank saw the quality of workmanship slump. In the summer of 1943, at the time of the Kursk battle, only 7.7 per cent of tank output passed the factory tests for quality control.[16] When American engineers at the army's Aberdeen Proving Ground in Maryland examined the one example of the T-34 handed over by the Soviet side, they found a catalogue of shoddy engineering and poor finishing. After 343 kilometres of drive testing the tank broke down irreparably because the engine was destroyed by dirt coming through a poor-quality air filter; cracks appeared in the welded armour plates and water penetrated the tank interior when it rained; the steel tracks were made of low-quality material that fractured regularly; and so on.[17] Although volume production was the ideal, even the leading mass producers faced major hurdles in attempting to deliver a quality product.

The exception to the experience of volume output was the Sino-Japanese war. Chinese war production was limited by the immature state of indus-trial development and the loss to Japanese conquest of the northern and eastern regions, where much of the resource base and limited industrial capacity of China was to be found. In the face of invasion, a large-scale evacuation of machines and equipment from China's military arsenals was undertaken, shifted bodily to south-west China and the industrial zone around the new capital, Chongqing. The thirteen arsenals clustered around the city supplied at least two-thirds of all China's war output from the late 1930s onwards.[18] The subsequent wartime record was tiny by com-parison with the other warring powers. The arsenals lacked modern machinery or adequate supplies of materials and relied heavily on hand-work. The Guomindang Ordnance Department distributed only 12,000 tons of steel a year to the arsenals; at peak production there were no more than 56,500 armaments workers. The production effort was devoted largely to small arms and munitions, an 85mm mortar and hand grenades.

For an army estimated at 300 divisions of 3 million men, annual output in 1944 amounted to a meagre 61,850 rifles, 3,066 heavy machine guns, 10,749 light machine guns and 1,215 mortars. A 37mm artillery piece was developed in 1941 but only twenty to thirty were produced each year and the shells were of poor quality.[19] China produced no aircraft, no heavy guns, no tanks and no armoured vehicles. Such figures make it difficult to understand how the Nationalist armies could operate for years against a more heavily armed enemy, particularly once Japanese expansion severely restricted supply from abroad. Stocks of imported weapons from the pre-war years existed but these were small in scale and impossible to replenish. Chinese armies relied on waging an attrition war in circumstances where the geography favoured them, but in open combat this poor resource base usually exposed them to inevitable defeat.

Japanese war production for the conflict in China was similarly circumscribed, despite the call for a full-scale effort with the 1938 Total Mobilization Decree. Between 1937 and 1941, Japanese industry turned out an average of 600 light and medium tanks a year for the whole campaign, while aircraft production for the army and navy, based on a wide range of models for airframe and engine, averaged a little over 4,000 a year.[20] Greater resources were devoted to naval shipbuilding, though this had small effect on the war in China. The shipbuilding and aviation sectors were relatively modern in terms of organization and machine equipment, but volume production was limited by the clear division made by the army and navy between their separate spheres of production, and by the decentralization of production among a wide range of small subcontractors whose efficiency varied across a wide spectrum. The coming of war in the Pacific transformed war production. Investment poured into construction for the navy, merchant shipbuilding and aircraft. No attempt was made to increase the degree of mechanization or motorization of the Japanese army, most of which was still mired in the Chinese war. Over the years of the Pacific war, tank production declined from a peak of 1,271 in 1942 to a mere 371 in 1944; the production of armoured cars, begun in 1942, amounted to no more than 1,104 for the whole war. The Japanese vehicle industry was underdeveloped by American or European standards, producing just 5,500 large trucks in four years to serve both the military and the economy.[21] When ammunition in the field ran out, Japanese soldiers used swords and bayonets instead. Severe shortages of steel and other metals, exacerbated by the impact of the American sea blockade, partly explain the low level of wartime output, but it was also a result of strategic decisions about which goods a small industrial economy ought to focus on.

By 1943 absolute priority went to the aircraft needed to defend the empire's perimeter. The decision to maximize aircraft output placed severe pressure on the entire system of war production and in November 1943 the government finally, very late in the war, created a new Ministry of Munitions to oversee the aircraft effort. By 1944 aircraft production made up 34 per cent of all manufacturing, and elaborate plans were laid by the ministry for a real mass production of more than 50,000 aircraft in 1944.[22] An Aircraft Industrial Association was set up, divided into fourteen specialized associations for each major aircraft sub-assembly and component produced by the great increase in subcontracting.[23] Only by compelling every corner of the war economy to focus on aircraft did it prove possible to produce them in large volume in 1943 and 1944 before the supply of imported bauxite (for aluminium production) dried up. Production was nevertheless constrained by poor control over component suppliers, the limited durability and precision of home-produced machine tools, and the lack of production engineers with experience of volume output. Two large factories were planned in 1942 in which mass-production methods were to be employed, but the facility at Kouza, designed to produce 5,000 aircraft a year, yielded in the end just 60 fighters, while the aero-engine plant at Tsu failed to produce a single one before the end of the war.[24] The rest of the aircraft industry struggled to complete the programme; the urgency of production and the introduction of less skilled labour led to a decline in product quality, causing more casualties to the Japanese air force in the last years of war than aerial combat. Productivity remained low. By 1944, output of aircraft in pounds per man-day was 0.71; in the United States the equivalent figure was 2.76.[25] Even had there been higher levels of efficiency, material shortages would have limited what could be achieved. Throughout the war the Japanese economy produced just 10 per cent of the amount of war goods produced in the United States.

The real mass producers during the war were the Soviet Union and the United States. From 1941 to 1945 they produced between them 443,451 aircraft of all types, 175,635 tanks and self-propelled guns, and 676,074 artillery pieces, an achievement that dwarfed the output of the other major industrial powers and would dwarf military output today. The United States produced more aircraft than their wartime ally and the Soviet Union more tanks and artillery pieces, but both secured exceptional levels of output across the whole war. There were nevertheless profound differences in the circumstances facing the two major mass producers. The Soviet system was an authoritarian command economy, centrally organized, and policed with an exceptional rigour for any lapse by management or labour; the American economy was a free enterprise, capitalist system with a low level of state intervention, a wealth of

individual enterprise, and a free labour force. The Soviet Union had large
material resources available before the German invasion, but was then
reduced to a rump economy, losing two-thirds of steel and coal capacity.
In 1942 Soviet industry sustained war output with only 8 million tons of
steel, against production of 18 million tons in 1941, only 75 million tons
of coal instead of 150, and just 51,000 tons of aluminium, and so on. The
United States was by contrast more richly endowed with resources than
any other combatant power, producing in 1942 76.8 million tons of steel,
582 million tons of coal, and 521,000 tons of aluminium. Perhaps the
most significant contrast was the pre-war context of military production.
The Soviet Union had begun large-scale military output in the early 1930s
and by 1941 had, on paper, the world's largest air force and tank park.
Despite the crisis occasioned by the 'Barbarossa' campaign, Soviet engineers and workers had years of experience in volume production of
weapons. The United States had no such experience before 1941 except in
naval shipbuilding, so that rearmament began in most cases from a standing start. When engineers from the Chrysler Motor Corporation were
invited to visit Rock Island Arsenal in 1940 with a view to undertaking
tank production, not one of them had ever seen a tank.[26] Chrysler was
recruited, but a new facility had to be built on farmland in Michigan
before any production was possible – yet by the end of 1941 the plant was
turning out fifteen tanks a day, a monument to the depth of entrepreneurial and engineering strength in the American system.

The Soviet achievement was made possible by the nature of the Communist dictatorship. A State Defence Committee (GKO) was established on
30 June 1941, chaired by Stalin himself, with absolute power over the economy. All decisions about production and weapons were centralized on the
committee, which allocated responsibility for production to national commissariats. The GKO encouraged officials and engineers to display a degree
of flexibility and improvisation, in contrast to the tighter controls of peacetime. Any problem with a component or the supply of materials was
reported to the committee, which could act at once to try to unblock the
system, sometimes with no more than an irate and menacing phone call
from Stalin.[27] The priority for the war effort was also absolute, diverting all
investment in plant, machinery and raw material supply. The effectiveness
of the system was tested almost at once when a Council of Evacuation,
established two days after the German invasion, succeeded in moving eastwards 50,000 workshops and factories (including 2,593 major plants) and
16 million workers and their families to new sites in the Urals, Siberia and
southern Russia.[28] Dislocation was overcome only with extraordinary
efforts by engineers and workers, struggling to re-establish production in

freezing temperatures with scant amenities or housing. In 1942 the shrunken Soviet economy produced substantially more military equipment than in 1941, and throughout the subsequent war years industry turned out more aircraft, tanks, guns, mortars and shells than the Axis enemy. Moreover, these were weapons of solid combat quality. The soldiers and engineers who selected the weapons chose a narrow range of designs adapted for volume production, capable of holding their own against German technology and inflicting maximum damage to the enemy. The *katyusha* rocket was a good example. Mounted on the back of a lorry for easy deployment, the multi-barrel rocket-launcher sprayed enemy troops with a random load of high explosive. Easy to produce and use, the *katyusha* symbolized the blend of simplicity and impact of many Soviet weapons.

The scale of Soviet output was made possible by the characteristics of the productive system. Soviet factories were built on a huge scale, planned in many cases as integrated plants producing components and equipment as well as assembling the final product. Special machine tools made possible conveyor production, with parts and sub-assemblies fed into the assembly room, sometimes on conveyors made of hollowed-out wood. Plant was laid out by production engineers with a view to reducing waste of time or resources. The example of the Tractor Factory in the Urals city of Cheliabinsk illustrates the way Soviet production worked. In the months after the German invasion, the tractor factory was turned over to tank production under the direction of Isaak Zaltsman, deputy commissar for the tank industry. Some 5,800 machine tools were evacuated from Leningrad and installed in four giant new assembly halls where the roof had not yet been completed. Serial production was ordered to begin at once and the first KV-1 heavy tanks were ready for delivery by October 1941 but lacked starter motors. Zaltsman ordered the motors to be delivered to a station near Moscow, then sent the tanks off by rail to the capital, to have the motors installed on the way. In August 1942 the factory was ordered to convert to production of the T-34 medium tank and, despite all the problems of tooling up for a new model, the tractor plant was ready to produce the new tank in a month, and by the end of the year had delivered over 1,000.[29] The workforce of 40,000 included 43 per cent under the age of twenty-five and a third were women; mostly unused to factory work, they were given quick courses in new Trade and Industrial Schools, first set up in 1940, and were then introduced to relatively simple assembly-line tasks. Conditions were harsh and every dereliction punished, but as a result of large-scale standardized output, productivity per worker expanded significantly. The net value added per worker in the defence sector (at constant prices) was 6,019 roubles in 1940 but reached

18,135 roubles by 1944.[30] The capricious nature of the system was none-theless never far below the surface. Zaltsman's heroic efforts to transform Cheliabinsk into its nickname 'Tankograd' did not prevent Stalin from accusing him after the war of counter-revolutionary sympathies and ordering his demotion to the humble role of overseer.

American business operated with few of the resource constraints of their Soviet equivalent, and no threat of the Gulag. Yet there are grounds for comparison between the managerial energy and initiative displayed in reconstructing the Cheliabinsk Tractor Factory for conveyor tank assem-bly and the rapid building of the giant Chrysler tank plant, both of which began turning out ten tanks a day within months of their construction, both using less-skilled labour for many of the routine assembly roles. On the production front such similarities help to explain the successful achievement of volume production, but the system generating the achieve-ment in the United States was fundamentally at odds with its Soviet opposite number. Roosevelt hoped that the experience of the 1930s New Deal would make it possible to direct war production through federal agencies, but there was no tradition of state planning and scant under-standing about how to regulate the flow of materials and components usually dictated in peacetime by market forces. The need to recruit Ameri-can business to serve the war effort in the end resulted in a system where improvised, entrepreneurial initiatives created the conditions for volume production rather than the federal agencies formally responsible. The War Production Board, established in January 1942, had to concede to the army and navy their right to issue contracts for weapons and munitions without prior approval, nullifying the purpose of the board to oversee aggregate output. A Production Requirements Plan was instituted with the object of using rationing of raw materials as a way to limit the inde-pendence of the army and navy, but it lacked the necessary bureaucratic structure to enforce priorities. A Production Executive Committee was set up under the War Production Board to try to control and track the alloca-tion of standard, essential components. The committee produced a General Scheduling Order for eighty-six of them to make sure that they went where they were most needed and on time, but the results were mixed. A plethora of agencies emerged for controlling one or other part of the war economy, creating a system that was administratively confus-ing and all too often adversarial rather than co-operative.[31]

In the absence of tight planning and direction on the Soviet model, the war economy depended on the opportunism and ambition of American private business. The contrast was typified by one of the first actions of the War Production Board, which was run by the president of General Motors,

William Knudsen. He called together leading corporate directors, read out a list of priority contracts, and called for volunteers. The opportunities were snapped up by the major companies.[32] Four-fifths of the first wave of contracts went to just one hundred businesses, but the need to subcontract for thousands of components and new equipment brought smaller businesses into the rush for production and profits. General Motors used 19,000 suppliers to feed final assembly at the company's main plants, which included the output of 13,450 aircraft. The entire aircraft industry used an estimated 162,000 subcontractors.[33] Over the war years 500,000 new businesses were established, largely to meet the massive demand for specialized war material. Businessmen were also drafted in to help run the federal agencies, creating a formal link between the world of commerce and the efforts of government – Knudsen from General Motors, Donald Nelson (his successor) from Sears Roebuck, Charles Wilson from General Electric, the investment banker Ferdinand Eberstadt, and so on. Where the Soviet system depended on close monitoring of state managers, the American system relied on the traditions of anti-state voluntarism, vigorous competition and entrepreneurial imagination.[34] When Henry Ford made his unfulfilled offer to build 1,000 fighter aircraft a day, he added the caveat that he could only do so if there was no intervention at all from the federal state. Despite his prejudice against bureaucracy and red tape, Ford's company eventually became a major producer of a wide range of armaments: 277,896 jeeps, 93,718 trucks, 8,685 bombers, 57,851 aero-engines, 2,718 tanks, 12,500 armoured cars. The entire motor industry was converted almost completely to war orders. In 1941 over 3.5 million passenger cars were produced; at the height of the conflict, just 139.[35]

The many problems in trying to monitor war production – and the occasional examples of waste or corruption or incompetence that the competition between producers and agencies inevitably generated – mattered much less in the United States than they would have done anywhere else because there was an abundance of resources and money in an economy free of blockade or bombing. While Germany had to pour resources into defending its airspace and cities, the United States had to spend almost nothing. Most historians now consider that the production record might have been achieved more economically with greater centralization and coercion, but productivity nonetheless remained high enough in the arms sectors because of the economies generated by the sheer scale of output and the wide deployment of assembly line and flow production, even in the manufacture of shipping. The output of 303,713 aircraft and 802,161 aero-engines in four years reflected the positive strengths of the temporary alliance between the federal state and industry rather than its drawbacks. Per capita aircraft pounds produced each working day increased from 1.05 in July 1941 to 2.70 three years later. The scale of naval and merchant shipbuilding was also remarkable given the heavy commitment to army weapons. The launching of 1,316 naval vessels, from battleships to destroyer escorts, eclipsed anything produced by the other naval powers; in addition, there were 109,786 minor vessels, including 83,500 landing craft for amphibious operations.[36] The merchant shipbuilding industry turned out 5,777 major vessels, including the most famous example of American mass production, the 'Liberty Ship', produced by the quintessential American entrepreneur Henry Kaiser.

His was a classic rags-to-riches story, from running a small photographer's shop in New York to becoming head of a major construction company that built the Hoover Dam and the Bay Bridge. He liked the challenge presented by apparently impossible projects. He had no experience of shipbuilding, but when his construction company began to assemble new shipyards in 1940 he decided to build the ships as well, though he had never even seen one launched. At the Permanente Metals Yards in Richmond, California, he set out to mass-produce a standard 10,000-ton cargo ship to assist the replacement of merchant shipping sunk by German submarines. Simply designed with standard parts and assemblies, the 'Liberty Ship' moved along a production line several kilometres from the shore; components and sub-assemblies were fed in by 24-metre-long conveyors and giant pulleys, while workers with limited training, monitored by time-and-motion experts, were distributed along the line to perform repetitive tasks. The first ship launched in a Baltimore shipyard took 355 days to build and 1.5 million man-hours; by 1943, in Kaiser's California yards, a ship rolled off the assembly line in an average of 41 days, after just 500,000 man-hours. By the war's end his yards had built 1,040 Liberty ships, 50 escort carriers and a host of smaller vessels. Kaiser's construction of almost one-third of American wartime shipping was the product of a culture that flourished on individual entrepreneurial zeal and the cult of industrial rationalization.[37]

More questionable was the overall combat quality of some of the volume output. Even the 'Liberty Ship' with its novel all-welded hull could break up in mid-ocean in heavy seas. The military were committed to designs that were already in production or could be adapted quickly to volume output and it took the experience of combat to expose the drawbacks of this form of procurement. The B-17 and B-24 bombers proved to be vulnerable targets to the German air defence system and could only survive because they were escorted by more up-to-date fighter aircraft. These in turn could only engage in combat over Germany because of the introduction of extra fuel tanks, which were successfully mass-produced at very short notice in the United States late in 1943. The vanguard B-29 heavy bomber was only available for operations by late 1944, but was plagued by design problems once in combat. Despite a first jet-powered flight by the Bell XP-59A experimental aircraft in October 1942, development work was too slow to produce a jet aircraft in time for wartime combat.[38] The decision to stick with one medium tank design, the M4 Sherman and its derivatives, was approved by the army's Ordnance Department Technical Division, run by Major General Gladeon Barnes, because it could be produced quickly in volume, but it was inferior to the latest German and Soviet tank models. The Ordnance Department lacked any real experience in tank design or familiarity with the combat needs of armoured forces. The Sherman, despite limited upgrading, had ineffective armour protection, a vulnerable silhouette on the battlefield, and guns with insufficient velocity. M4 crews in combat in 1943 and 1944 had to devise tactics to hit a German tank at the side or rear, rather than head-on, when they were likely to be destroyed. 'We've got a good tank,' wrote a sergeant in an armoured division, 'for parades and training purposes, but for combat they are just potential coffins.' A heavier replacement, the T26 'Pershing', capable of combating the German Panther and Tiger tanks, was available only in the last weeks of the war in small numbers: 310 were delivered to the European theatre, 200 sent on to tank units.[39] American ground combat succeeded chiefly because there was simply so much equipment available to compensate for any deficiencies in the quality of the product.

The German economy during the war could potentially have become one of the main volume producers. Unlike Italy and Japan, relatively less developed industrially and with severe resource constraints, Germany had a depth of industrial, engineering and scientific strength to be mobilized for the purposes of war, and access by 1941 to the resources of most of continental Europe. Where the Soviet Union produced 8.5 million tons of steel in 1943, the German Empire produced 30.6 million; Germany had 340 million tons of coal available in 1943, the Soviet Union 93 million; aluminium output – essential for aircraft and many other war-related products – reached 250,000 tons in Germany in 1943, but Soviet production was just a fraction, at 62,000 tons. There can be no argument that the Third Reich did not enjoy adequate resources or industrial investment. But only by 1943–4 did the German economy, despite heavy bombing of the major industrial cities, begin to exploit these resources effectively enough to approach, though not to match, the volume output of the Allies. This paradox used to be explained by the reluctance of the Hitler regime to mobilize the economy fully from fear of alienating the working population until forced to do so in 1943 by the changing circumstances of war, a conclusion arrived at by the expert economists attached to the United States Strategic Bombing Survey in 1945 who were puzzled why Germany, with all the resources at the potential disposal of the military economy, had produced such modest numbers of aircraft, tanks and vehicles in the first years of war.[40]

The historical reality was very different. From the start of the war Hitler, as supreme commander-in-chief, expected war production to expand rapidly to exceed the levels achieved at the end of the First World War. The Army Armaments Bureau in December 1939 drew up a comparison of output in 1918, current output, and Hitler's *Endziel* (final goal) for munitions and weapons in 1940–42. Artillery produced in 1918 amounted to 17,453 pieces, Hitler's final aim was output of 155,000 a year; machine guns produced in 1918 numbered 196,578, Hitler's figure was over 2 million a year; output of gunpowder and explosives amounted to 26,100 tons a month in 1918, but Hitler wanted 60,000 tons a month. The order from Hitler's headquarters was to convert the German economy to war 'with all energy', to secure 'a programme with the highest possible figures'.[41] Hitler used these statistics as a benchmark in his complaints about the inefficiency of current military production. Albert Speer, appointed armaments minister in February 1942, told his post-war interrogators that Hitler 'knew the supply figures of the last war in detail and could reproach us with the fact that output in 1917/18 was higher than we could show in 1942'.[42] German war production expanded in 1939–42 but well below the level of possible volume production, given the fact that by 1942 almost 70 per cent of the manufacturing workforce laboured on orders for the armed forces (a level substantially higher than Britain or the United States ever achieved during the war), while three-quarters of Germany's substantial steel output was allocated to the military economy.[43] Britain and the Soviet Union in the first years of their wars produced more than the German economy but with fewer material resources and less labour.

There are many explanations for this disparity. Although Hitler had his own vision of where he wanted war production to go, he did not establish like Stalin (or indeed Churchill) a central defence committee in which strategy, industrial capacity and technical development could be integrated and matched. In the absence of a decision-making centre, the German system of war production remained stubbornly decentralized, with different elements of the administration operating in isolation – the Four-Year Plan controlled by Göring, the Economics Ministry, the Labour Ministry, the Munitions Ministry set up in spring 1940, the Air Ministry, and so on. The principal problem was the claim by the military authorities that they had an absolute right to control what was produced, by whom, and in what quantity. The military services failed to co-ordinate their planning, each branch claiming urgent needs on its own behalf, and with scant attention to what was industrially possible. The military instinctively distrusted mass production and preferred to use established contractors with a tradition of specialized, high-quality work and custom-built weapons. Modern armaments required a level of technical sophistication and precision finishing that volume output was expected to lose. Quizzed at the end of the war about the failure to fully mobilize the German motor industry with its potential for volume production, one senior official from Speer's ministry could still maintain that 'it was not suitable for war production ... We did not concentrate on one type to be produced in masses.'[44] Instead the military engineers and inspectors insisted that industry respond flexibly to endless demands for modification based on combat experience, while ordering a wide range of models and experimental projects that made standardization and long production runs difficult to establish. In 1942 Hitler observed that industry justifiably complained about a 'niggardly procedure – today an order for ten howitzers, tomorrow for two mortars and so on.'[45] Civilian industry was expected to obey orders; civilian engineers or designers were only tolerated at the front line if they put on a uniform; even the Armaments Ministry itself, run by civilian administrators intent on providing more weapons, was regarded by the Army Ordnance Office as 'an inexperienced intruder'.[46] The consequence of a largely planless war economy, buffeted by military demands that stifled the possibility of mass production, was a system that by 1941, according to Speer's deputy Saur, appeared 'completely unrationalized'.[47]

Hitler's decree on rationalization in December 1941 was an attempt to break the impasse and to insist that the military allow German industry to match Soviet practice in volume output. The results remained mixed. Shortly after Hitler's decree, the Munitions Ministry under Fritz Todt introduced a radical change in the way war production was organized. Main Committees were set up for each major class of weapon – armoured vehicles, small arms, munitions, machine tools, shipbuilding – to be staffed by engineers and industrialists rather than the military. However, aircraft production, which absorbed over 40 per cent of resources allocated to war production, remained independent of Todt's ministry. Erhard Milch, Göring's deputy at the Air Ministry, set up comparable production 'rings' for aircraft, aero-engines and components run by the main producers, although the 178 rings and committees that emerged by summer 1942 promised to swamp the system yet again.[48] The aim in both cases was to allow the most efficient firms to play the leading role. 'This idea of compelling firms under the leadership of the most competent one,' claimed Otto Merker, head of the Main Committee for ship construction, 'was the first big step towards the realization of successful rationalization.'[49] In February 1942 Todt was killed in an air crash and Hitler replaced him with his pet architect, the young Albert Speer, a civilian with no previous experience of arms production, as minister for armaments and war production. Speer continued Todt's work and in March introduced a Central Planning Board (*Zentrale Planung*) to try to regulate the supply of key raw materials, which had been allocated beforehand with little monitoring of priority and a good deal of waste. Following Hitler's decree, rationalization became not only an economic necessity but a political imperative. An efficiency expert, Theodor Hupfauer, was asked to report on the overall productive performance of the war industry. His survey, he told his interrogators in 1945, showed that 'the degree of efficiency in German industry and even in the most modern firms was bad'. He found that production times for individual processes could vary up to twentyfold between different firms, and for final assembly four or fivefold. The slogan for the rest of the war, he wrote, became 'INCREASED EFFICIENCY on as broad a basis as possible, using all possible means.'[50]

The attempt to exploit German industrial capacity for the war effort more rationally met resistance from the army, which continued to maintain the primacy of military procurement policies. Speer eventually established control over all branches of military output only by the summer of 1944, but the effort to rationalize had Hitler's direct backing and could not easily be challenged. One of the key changes introduced early in 1942 on Todt's initiative, but against the army's wishes, was the mandatory fixed-price contract to replace the system of cost-plus agreements for army contracts. A fixed price allowed manufacturers to cut costs in order to make an adequate profit, where cost-plus had encouraged less efficient factory practice as firms tried to evade the stringent military controls over prices and costs. Under the fixed-price regime, firms were given premiums if they could produce at a price 10 per cent below the agreed norm, or if they accepted a price well below the norm they could trim back costs by efficiency savings and take the margin as additional profit without having to pay the special war profits tax. As Todt told an assembly of German industrialists in January 1942, 'The firm that works most rationally has the largest profit.' The more successful a firm was in increasing efficiency, the higher the earnings.[51] The armed forces only reluctantly accepted that they no longer determined prices, and radicals in the National Socialist Party disliked the openly 'capitalist' nature of the Todt reform, but in May 1942 Speer introduced the new fixed-price system with the threat that firms who failed the test of greater productivity would be cut out of the circle of contractors. It is difficult to estimate how much of the improvement in productive performance was the result of the incentive to make profits, since some of the armaments firms were state owned, but the exclusion of the military from price formation freed businesses to make their own decisions about how they produced war goods.[52]

It proved more difficult to reorganize the confused state of military orders and to concentrate production on long runs of standard products, but the heavy losses from Stalingrad onwards made this essential. Speer succeeded by 1943 in concentrating component and machine-tool production, rewarding the more efficient and closing down the rest. Machine tools were produced in 900 firms in 1942, but only 369 by autumn 1943; the 300 different types of prismatic glass produced were reduced to 14, and the firms involved from 23 to 7.[53] An Armaments Commission, established by Speer to report on a better match between the technical demands of the military and industrial capabilities, resulted in agreement with the army to reduce the number of light infantry weapons from 14 to 5, anti-tank weapons from 12 to 1, anti-aircraft artillery from 10 guns to 2, vehicles from 55 to 14 and armour from 18 to 7. The army high command at last ordered 'simplification of construction' to assist in 'mass production'.[54] Aircraft models were reduced from 42 to 20, then to 9, and finally, under the supervision of an emergency 'Fighter Staff' set up in spring 1944 to help combat the bombing, to just 5.[55] The selected models and their components could then be produced in long runs, with the introduction of mechanized production using conveyors and pulleys. Modern factory methods were not universal and were undermined by heavy bombing and the need to disperse production. The German preference for general purpose machine tools rather than the specialized tools needed for flow production still encouraged over-reliance on skilled workers where that was possible, but by 1944, when high volume output was finally achieved, much of the workforce was semi-skilled foreign labour, more suitable for assembly line production. The performance of individual firms varied widely – annual productivity growth at the Junkers aircraft plants was 69 per cent, but at Heinkel only 0.3 per cent – but the overall statistics for labour productivity show the highest increases in the last two years of war.[56] Output per head in the German defence industry, according to one estimate, fell from an index figure of 100 in 1939 to 75.9 in 1941, and then rose to 160 in 1944; other estimates suggest a modest rise between 1939 and 1941 and then a sharper increase from 1942 to 1944 as the learning curve in war industry was finally mastered. The American post-war Bombing Survey, using official German statistics, found that productivity in related sectors – chemicals, iron and steel, liquid fuels – was substantially lower in 1944 than at the start of the war. In both cases, it was a less impressive achievement than either the Soviet or American experience.[57]

The final achievement of volume production arrived at just the point when the bombing and Allied advances on land reduced German access to resources and, like the expansion of Japanese production in 1944, came at the stage when Allied output vastly exceeded what the Axis could possibly produce. The large increase in the output of aircraft and vehicles in 1943–5 was as a result sucked into an attrition cycle in which rapidly rising losses nullified the military impact that higher volume output might have had. In the German case, the emphasis on the quality of weapons, so important to the military, was squandered by the disorganized nature of the war economy and failures in the development of new weapons. The air force made poor judgements about the evolution of a new generation of aircraft and ended up producing upgrades of the same models – the Me109, Me110, He111, Do17, Ju52, Ju87, Ju88 – that the air force had had in 1938. The heavy bomber Heinkel He177, and the heavy fighter Messerschmitt Me210, were both design disasters, absorbing large resources for little payback.[58] The jet-engine Me262 was developed rapidly in 1943–4 to replace the ageing piston-engine aircraft, because the engine needed fewer man-hours and used fewer scarce materials, but it was poorly made and tested. Out of 1,433 jet aircraft produced by the end of the war, only 358 saw service while hundreds had to be written off.[59] Aircraft research and development was isolated from the front and became fractured between a wide assortment of advanced projects that contributed little to the war effort, including the abortive 'People's Fighter', the rocket-powered Heinkel He162, which was hastily manufactured, like the Me262, in underground factories in the last months of war and introduced to operations in tiny numbers three weeks before the German surrender.[60]

In the naval war, the breakthrough in submarine design with the fully submersible Type XXI and Type XXIII, were not developed rapidly enough to see combat. The Tiger I and Tiger II heavy tanks, despite their formidable power, were not only produced in modest numbers but were also too technically complex and plagued with mechanical faults as a result of hurried production. Finally, Hitler's intervention in 1943 led to the decision to mass-produce the 'Vengeance Weapons', the V1 cruise missile and the V2 rocket, neither of which promised strategic dividends and both of which absorbed large production capacity that might have been devoted to weapons that did. For all the German military's emphasis on quality rather than quantity, the advanced technical threshold reached by 1944 was insufficient to compensate for the growing gap in battlefield resources between Germany and the Allies. German war production fell between the two stools of Soviet and American practice: on the one hand, a form of command economy without a central commander, and on the other a capitalist system in which entrepreneurial initiative was stifled by military intervention rather than liberated. The paradoxes this situation produced were resolved too late to realize Hitler's vision of mass production articulated in the 1941 decree.

ARSENALS OF DEMOCRACY:
LEASING AND LENDING

In early October 1941 British and American representatives reached a historic agreement in Moscow with the Soviet government to supply weapons and equipment to the Soviet war effort. In Moscow for the talks, Maxim Litvinov, about to take up the post of Soviet ambassador to Washington, leapt to his feet when agreement was reached and shouted, 'Now we shall win the war!'[61] Stalin was scarcely less enthusiastic about the accords after weeks of frosty exchanges over the lack of aid. In the midst of the battle raging near the Soviet capital, Stalin wrote to Roosevelt to express his 'deepest gratitude' for the promised supplies, and his 'sincere gratitude' that they would not have to be paid for, if at all, until after the war.[62] The same day, 7 November 1941, the American president formally directed that the Soviet Union would now be included as a recipient of Lend-Lease aid. The only way in which the other Allied powers could increase their access to war equipment beyond what was domestically possible was to rely on the United States' willingness to supply them without payment. The agreement in Moscow was part of an unprecedented worldwide logistic effort to redistribute resources among the states fighting the Axis. In a wartime appreciation of Lend-Lease, Charles Marshall, a professor of politics at Harvard and a temporary soldier, described 'a huge system of international economic strategy. Nations comprising two-thirds of the earth's land surface and of its population participate in it.'[63] The war economic potential of the Allies was transformed by the strategic choices made in Washington even before the United States was an active belligerent. Roosevelt's promise made in December 1940 that the United States would become 'the great arsenal of democracy' was redeemed by 1945 in an aid programme worth more than $50 billion.

The Axis allies enjoyed no comparable advantage. There was no 'arsenal of dictatorship'. Although the German war economy stood in relation to those of Italy and Japan like the American economy to the Allies, Germany was hard pressed to supply its own military needs without having to underpin the war economies of weaker partners. The small quantities of military deliveries to German allies, for which the allies had to pay, were dwarfed by American largesse. In 1943 Germany exported 597 aircraft, the majority of them non-combat, to Italy, Finland, Romania, Hungary, Bulgaria and Slovakia in return for much-needed oil, food and minerals; the United States allocated 43,000 aircraft and 48,000 aero-engines to its allies between 1941 and 1945.[64] There was no question that Italy and Japan would supply military aid to Germany, even if it had been logistically possible. Aid from the European Axis powers to Japan was circumscribed by geography and the fact of Anglo-American ocean-going naval power. Seven German aircraft and one BMW aero-engine made it to Japan in 1943. Japan finally agreed to supply materials from the captured Southern Region once it was clear that Germany would not make claims on them after conquering France and the Netherlands, and blockade-runners (so called *Yanagi-sen* or 'willow ships') delivered 112,000 tons of supplies, chiefly rubber and tin. Allied control of the oceans by 1943 made it impossible to continue. Out of 17,483 tons of supplies sent in 1943 through the Allied blockade only 6,200 tons arrived, a tiny fraction of inter-Allied tonnage. Instead, Japan used larger cargo submarines to send raw materials to Germany, but most were sunk in transit. Of 2,606 tons sent to Europe in 1944–5, only 611 tons got through.[65] Germany provided Italy chiefly with coal and steel, but the assumption in Berlin was that Italy ought to match its strategy to its resources rather than expect German deliveries. Only a fraction of the coal and steel Italy requested was actually supplied. German firms worried that any equipment sold or bartered with Italy would be imitated by Italian firms in the competitive post-war market. Italian officials were told that machinery for Italian war factories was at the bottom of the list because the priority was to supply industrial equipment to European firms working to German military orders. When the Italian air force asked for advanced radar equipment in 1942, Telefunken, the main supplier, insisted that it should be operated by German personnel in Italy to avoid commercial piracy.[66] There was very little direct technical or scientific aid between the three Axis powers. German engineers agreed to send an example of a Würzburg radar to Japan in 1942, but one of the two submarines carrying the equipment was sunk on the way.

The Axis states had to rely on the material resources of the areas they each conquered to fuel their domestic war effort. Additional military equipment could in general only be secured through the capture of enemy weapons, and this was at best an improvisation with unpredictable and short-term benefits. The most useful acquisition for the German armed forces was the addition of 200,000 French and British motor vehicles captured following the defeat of France, together with a quantity of requisitioned French aircraft. The German exploitation of the French aviation and motor-vehicle industries continued during the occupation. French firms supplied a total of 1,300 aircraft in 1942, 2,600 in 1943, though many of them were trainers and auxiliary aircraft. This constituted a tiny fraction of the aircraft produced in Germany over the course of the war and they had to be paid for.[67] Captured French armoured vehicles were used by German armies but once again the numbers were small: a German army report in May 1943 showed there were 670 French tanks active on all German front lines. Although the German army high command wanted as many Soviet tanks as possible put back into service, very few Soviet tanks were captured still fit for use. On the Eastern Front an estimated 300 Soviet T-34s were available at any one time with the German army or security forces, though the same report in May 1943 counted only 63 currently operating with army units. After heavy losses in combat, 310 captured tanks remained operational in April 1945. By that date the American wartime supply of tanks to the Allies numbered 37,323.[68]

The decision taken in the United States to supply aid to countries fighting the Axis without the promise of payment was nevertheless a difficult one, not only because the American military wanted to have first claim on military resources once rearmament was under way in 1940, but also because military aid raised important legal and constitutional issues in a nation still not at war. The decision arose from the irrefutable evidence that Britain would be unable to pay in dollars for any military orders much beyond the early months of 1941. For two years British contracts for military equipment, principally aircraft and aero-engines, had been paid for on a 'cash-and-carry' basis, following Roosevelt's successful modification of American neutrality legislation in 1939. By 1940 there were orders on hand for 23,000 aircraft from American factories, but the means to pay for them evaporated with the exhaustion of British reserves of dollars and gold, and without American supplies Britain's war effort was dangerously diminished. The United States had already sold large quantities of rifles, machine guns, artillery and ammunition during the summer to make good the losses of the British Expeditionary Force in France. In September 1940 Roosevelt approved the release of fifty rusting First World War destroyers to help the escort of British convoys, but only after the British government agreed to offer a string of military bases for American forces from Newfoundland to Bermuda. The deal was strongly opposed by the lobby groups hostile to intervention and Roosevelt assured Congress that the bases were outposts for the security of the Western

Hemisphere, not staging posts to American involvement in the European war. Although Roosevelt was entirely sympathetic to the British predicament, he understood that much American opinion was not only opposed to intervention but often Anglophobe in outlook. Even his close military advisers strongly disliked the idea that American assistance would help to preserve the British Empire. Their priority was the future security of the United States and assistance could only be expressed in these terms. The most ardent interventionist among senior military leaders, Admiral Harold Stark, argued that any aid for Britain was solely 'to assure the status quo of the Western Hemisphere, and to promote our national interests'.[69] When the bill to provide aid for Britain was introduced into Congress in January 1941 it was awkwardly titled 'A Bill to Promote the Defense of the United States and Other Purposes' and at the instigation of Felix Frankfurter, an American Supreme Court justice, it was given the patriotic (and anti-British) number H. R. 1776.[70]

The genesis of Lend-Lease was prompted by a letter from Churchill that was delivered to Roosevelt by seaplane on 9 December 1940 while aboard the USS *Tuscaloosa* in the Caribbean, on vacation following his unprecedented third presidential election victory in November. Churchill admitted that the moment had arrived when Britain could no longer pay cash for American supplies and shipping, and without that help 'we may fall by the way'.[71] The crisis had already been made clear more bluntly by the British ambassador to Washington, Lord Lothian, when he arrived at New York's La Guardia airport in late November. 'Well boys,' he told waiting pressmen, 'Britain's broke. It's your money we want.' In early December, Roosevelt's cabinet had debated the issue of whether the United States should bail Britain out to promote American security and decided in favour, despite residual scepticism that British assets really were as depleted as the government claimed.[72] The difficulty was to find a means to fund British orders without violating the neutrality legislation and the Johnson Act of 1934, prohibiting loans to any state, including Britain, which had reneged on repaying the loans from the First World War. The president was observed to read and re-read Churchill's letter on the deck of the *Tuscaloosa* until finally, on 11 December, he confided in Harry Hopkins, who was on board, the idea of leasing or lending the goods to Britain without, as he told a press conference a few days later, 'the silly, foolish old dollar sign'.[73] Roosevelt almost certainly hoped that by supporting British belligerency, America might avoid it; at the least the idea of Lease-Lend (as it was initially called) was designed to prevent a British collapse, or a British decision for an accommodation with the Axis. The 'fireside chat' of 29 December, in which Roosevelt coined the term 'arsenal of democracy', was used to assure

Americans that the United States would now be 'saved from the agony and suffering of war'.[74] Roosevelt ordered a bill to be drafted that reflected his decision and it was submitted to Congress on 6 January 1941.

Churchill was delighted with the outcome, 'tantamount to a declaration of war' he told his secretary.[75] This was not what most Americans wanted. The week the bill was finally approved by the House of Representatives in March 1941, opinion polling found 83 per cent of respondents opposed to American entry to the war. The Lend-Lease bill deeply divided American opinion. Opponents of intervention shared Churchill's view that it meant war in all but name. Even among those who had lobbied for several years to provide aid to the democracies there was fear that Lend-Lease was a step too far. The chairman of the Committee to Defend America by Aiding the Allies, William Allen White, resigned in protest at the bill, coining in the process the slogan 'The Yanks Are Not Coming'. One branch of the isolationist movement borrowed the slogan for the title of a pamphlet that sold 300,000 copies. Women demonstrated on the steps of Congress dressed in black carrying placards proclaiming 'Kill Bill 1776, not our sons'.[76] The bill also raised significant protests against the powers that the legislation would give to the president. Isolationists nicknamed it 'the Dictator Bill' because Roosevelt would enjoy the right to decide which nations qualified for Lend-Lease, what products they would be allowed to have, and on what scale, all without reference to Congress.[77] Executive discretion on this scale was unprecedented, but with polls showing that two-thirds of the population approved the bill, Roosevelt overrode objections. In the process he made two major concessions: he agreed that Lend-Lease would not commit the United States to convoying the material supplied under the programme, and that the bill would only last for two years. He also accepted that he would provide quarterly reports to Congress on the progress of the aid, while Congress enjoyed the right to vote the necessary funds under a series of 'Defense Aid Supplemental Acts'.[78]

On the issue of eventual repayment, Roosevelt relied on vague references to post-war recompense 'in kind'. Major concessions were expected from the British as well. Roosevelt ordered a number of British dollar assets to be seized and compelled the sale of others; Secretary of State Cordell Hull also extracted a grudging promise from London that the system of Imperial Preference would be replaced after the war with a more open trading regime, a concession that made explicit the changing power relationship between the two states and the American intention to eliminate the pre-war imperial economic blocs. This promise was not elicited without a struggle. Negotiation for what became the Master Lend-Lease Agreement dragged on for seven months while British

officials and politicians tried to resist Article VII, committing Britain to
free trade after the war. The agreement was signed on 23 February 1942
only after Roosevelt made it clear to the British that the consequences of
not doing so might stop the aid.[79] While in public Churchill praised Lend-
Lease as 'the most unsordid act', in private he worried that Britain would
not only be skinned 'but flayed to the bone'. There were also doubts that
Roosevelt would actually deliver what was promised. After fruitless lobbying in Washington, one British official complained that American
promises 'often peter out to nothing in practice'.[80] Similar doubts assailed
the Chinese, whose continued war effort against Japan was used by
Roosevelt as justification for extending Lend-Lease to China as well.
From the start Roosevelt promised extensive aid, to be channelled through
the China Defense Supplies Corporation established in Washington under
Chiang Kai-shek's brother-in-law, T. V. Soong. But pressure to supply
Western forces in the first instance kept aid for China to little more than
a trickle. So alienated was Chiang by the gulf between promise and reality
that he threatened in 1943 to reach a peace agreement with Japan if Lend-
Lease did not live up to his expectations.[81]

Lend-Lease was indeed slow to materialize everywhere. Out of the initial appropriation of $7 billion, only $1 billion had been spent by the end
of 1941. Most supplies to Britain from the United States in 1941 were still
paid for in cash; only 100 out of 2,400 aircraft that year came under
Lend-Lease provisions. American forces were committed to large-scale
rearmament and resented the diversion of military equipment to Britain
when their own air training schools had too few trainers and army exercises had to be conducted with dummy tanks. The Lend-Lease programme
was operated at first by an ad hoc committee chaired by Harry Hopkins
and backed by Roosevelt's new executive powers, but the system for
approving and procuring supplies under Lend-Lease was at best an
improvisation. On the issue of shipping the goods Britain needed,
Roosevelt was less helpful and public opinion much less enthusiastic,
since convoying ran the risk of conflict with German submarines. When
United States naval vessels began to venture further out into the Atlantic
to shield British convoys of Lend-Lease goods, Roosevelt insisted to the
public that these were 'patrols' not convoy protection; he also asked that
government publicity on Lend-Lease should say goods 'would be delivered', not that 'we were going to deliver', to avoid any suspicion that
American naval vessels were actually convoy escorts.[82] American supply
of merchant ships to the British merchant fleet was mainly limited in 1941
to allocating requisitioned Axis and neutral shipping in American ports to
sail on British trade routes.[83] Although it can be argued that Roosevelt did

see Lend-Lease as a stepping-stone to American intervention in the war in Europe, the evidence remains inconclusive. His regular assertion in public that Lend-Lease was a strategy to defend American interests by helping others do the fighting should not be set aside. It was a strategic outlook also evident in private. In a letter written to a congressman in May 1941 he cited a newspaper editorial reflecting on American strategy: 'We are not concerned with the affairs of the British Empire, but are concerned for our own safety, the security of our own trade and the integrity of our continent.' Roosevelt added, 'I think this is pretty good.'[84] American opinion remained solidly in favour of aid to Britain, but solidly against the idea of American entry to the war as a consequence.

The principle of aid to those fighting the Axis was tested once again when German and Axis forces invaded the Soviet Union on 22 June 1941. This was a more difficult decision because the 'arsenal of democracy' had not been intended to support totalitarian regimes, and popular hostility to the Soviet Union and domestic communism was widespread. One State Department official, Samuel Breckinridge Long, noted in his diary in July: 'the great majority of our people have learned that communism is something to be suppressed and the enemy of law and order. They do not understand how we can align ourselves even a little with it.'[85] Even interventionist organizations, content to aid Britain, were hostile to the idea of extending it to the Soviet Union since the object, according to a statement issued by the interventionist Fight For Freedom movement, was 'to extend democracy, not to limit it'.[86] The British response almost certainly helped Roosevelt to decide what to do. Churchill pledged unconditional support on 22 June and a week later Soviet officials in London provided an expansive list of the aid the Soviet Union wanted. The first goods released had still to be paid for, but on 4 September the British government agreed that a form of Lend-Lease in all but name would be used to cover the supplies to the Soviet Union, many of which would in practice be goods sent to Britain from the United States under the same scheme.

A few days after the German invasion, Roosevelt used a news conference to announce that the United States, too, was 'going to give all the aid we possibly can to Russia', and he ordered the unfreezing of $40 million of Soviet assets so that any goods supplied could be paid for. On 26 June the Soviet ambassador, Konstantin Oumansky, made a formal request for aid and a few days later an extravagant shopping list arrived from Moscow, which included not only requests for aircraft, tanks and munitions, but for entire factories for the production of light alloys, tyres and aviation fuel.[87] This was not only well beyond what the United States was capable of delivering in 1941, but there was no certainty that the Soviet Union would survive the German assault. The prevailing view in both London and Washington assumed a German victory within a few months, which would mean Western supplies falling into German hands. Only after Hopkins returned from a trip to Moscow in late July confident that the Soviet war effort was not about to collapse did Roosevelt finally agree on 2 August to give 'all economic assistance practicable', but as in the British case aid had to be paid for and was slow to materialize. In London there were fears that an American programme for the Soviet Union would mean less for Britain. Lord Beaverbrook, minister of supply, wanted British control over the flow of aid to the new ally by allocating a fraction of the Lend-Lease goods sent to Britain, but the American side refused.[88] Only following the meeting in Moscow in October was a firm commitment made by the two states under a First Protocol (there were to be four in all) together to supply a total of 1.5 million tons of goods and equipment between October 1941 and June 1942. As American opinion began to swing in favour of aid to the Soviet Union, Roosevelt asked and got approval from Congress to treat Soviet supplies as if they were Lend-Lease and thus 'vital to the defense of the United States', and from 7 November they no longer had to be paid for. The United States now became everyone's arsenal.

The scale and nature of the Lend-Lease programme exceeded anything that had been imagined when the legislation was introduced. By the end of the war more than $50 billion had been appropriated for Lend-Lease supplies, and goods were delivered to more than forty countries worldwide. American aid amounted to 16 per cent of all federal wartime expenditure; British Lend-Lease to the Soviet Union totalled a more modest £269 million, around 9 per cent of British wartime expenditure.[89] The programme became a joint one between Britain and the United States, with war production and raw material supplies overseen by two Combined Boards. British military missions in Washington negotiated priorities with American military leaders. Soviet allocations were separately agreed each year with Moscow officials. On 28 October 1941, Roosevelt created the Office of Lend-Lease Administration under the businessman Edward Stettinius and ended Hopkins's ad hoc committee. When American aid reached its peak in 1943–4 there were eleven different agencies engaged in producing, allocating and distributing the goods, creating a good deal of argument and duplication of effort. However, in March 1943, when the Lend-Lease Act came up for renewal, it was passed almost unanimously by Congress with none of the rancour of the debate two years earlier.[90] The principal beneficiary of American aid was the British Empire, which received some $30 billion, 58 per cent of the dollar value of all shipments, the great bulk of it for Britain, a fraction for the British Dominions.

Soviet aid amounted to $10.6 billion, 23 per cent of all expenditure, aid for the Free French forces some 8 per cent, and for China, where the aid was difficult to supply once the Japanese had occupied Burma, only 3 per cent. Around 1 per cent was supplied as aid to Latin American countries.[91]

One of the original intentions of the Lend-Lease scheme was for recipients to provide some form of recompense in kind for the generous supply of American goods and services, although Churchill was candid with Roosevelt that 'we aren't going to repay the Lend-Lease debts'.[92] Once the United States was at war, the idea of reciprocal or reverse Lend-Lease became a possibility. A formal 'Agreement on Mutual Aid' between Britain and the United States was signed on 28 February 1942. Britain paid for many of the resources and services needed by American army and air forces stationed in Britain from 1942 onwards, supplied oil and other services in North Africa, and shipping services when needed. The Australian government paid for many of the facilities and services needed by American forces stationed there during the Pacific war. British aid amounted to $5.6 billion during the war, Australian aid to $1 billion; total assistance from the British Empire reached $7.5 billion, some 15 per cent of the American total.[93] The Soviet Union made similar pledges under the terms of the aid Protocols but in the end supplied a paltry $2.2 million of reciprocal aid, an insignificant fraction of the aid sent between 1941 and 1945. All the Lend-Lease agreements stipulated, as Roosevelt intended from the outset, that goods should be returned where it was possible to do so after the war as if they really had been lent by the United States rather than gifted. Since almost all the weapons, raw materials and food were consumed by the insatiable demands of war and hungry populations, there was little left to give back. American War Department calculations suggested that an aggregate of $1.1 billion of supplies were returned, mainly for use by the United States armed forces. Chief among the states returning Lend-Lease was China, because it had proved too difficult to ship all the stockpiles of goods in India destined for China before the end of the war.

Not formally part of the Lend-Lease scheme was the aid programme negotiated between Canada and Britain. The Canadian contribution to global aid has often been ignored in accounts of Lend-Lease but it was a significant element in the economic assistance provided by the wider empire to Britain's imperial war effort. Canadian assistance, like American, was prompted by the exhaustion of Britain's capacity to pay in Canadian dollars for food and munitions, and by fears that Britain might divert orders instead to the United States on Lend-Lease terms. Canadian leaders did not want to imitate Lend-Lease, because it would pale by comparison with the larger American project, but they did want to remain one of the arsenals of democracy. After awkward arguments in the Canadian Cabinet, prompted by the opposition of Francophone Quebec to aid for Britain, it was decided that Canada would make a 'Billion Dollar Gift' to cover British orders from January 1942 to March 1943, when aid would have to be reassessed. Churchill was on a visit to Ottawa when the gift was revealed and was astonished by the generosity. Fearing that he had not heard the figure correctly, he asked for it to be repeated. Mackenzie King, the Canadian prime minister, told the Canadian parliament that 'Britain is receiving a reward for what she has done to ensure freedom', and the gift was presented to the Canadian public on those terms, but Gallup polls showed that only a narrow majority of Canadians approved. As a result, the gift was not repeated, but was replaced early in 1943 by a programme of Mutual Aid which, like Lend-Lease, would pool Canada's resources for the United Nations (as the Allies were now called) rather than Britain alone, but would keep a separate Canadian identity.[94]

The range of resources of all kinds made available under Lend-Lease – and other programmes of mutual or reciprocal aid – was enormous, but the core consisted of military equipment and munitions. The percentage of military supplies and shipping in Lend-Lease for Britain peaked at 70 per cent in 1943; the Soviet Union took larger proportions of industrial goods and food, so that military aid, though increased in quantity, fell from 63 per cent of the total in 1942 to 41 per cent in 1945. The total quantity of military goods supplied to the Allies from the United States is set out in Table 6.2. The non-military goods and services included oil, metals and large quantities of food. Since shipping was tight, ways had to be found to send food without taking up valuable cargo space. A key component was Spam – tins of compressed pork – nicknamed 'second fronts' by the Soviet soldiers who ate it. 'It would have been hard,' recalled the Soviet premier Nikita Khrushchev in his memoirs, 'to feed our army without it.' Almost 800,000 tons of tinned meat were sent to the Soviet Union by the end of the war.[95] Dehydration of fresh foods cut cargo space by more than half, but in the case of beef the saving was 90 per cent, with eggs and milk 85 per cent. The result was hardly appetizing when water was added before eating, but dried goods provided a vital supplement to the British diet. Britain in return supplied American forces stationed in Europe with most of their food undehydrated, and in addition large quantities of coffee, sugar, cocoa and jam, which British consumers could obtain for themselves, if at all, in small rationed packets. For American troops stationed in remote areas, the government requisitioned buses as 'Clubmobiles', bringing entertainment and food, including doughnuts, which were banned in British bakeries.[96]

Table 6.2 United States Supply of Military Equipment under Lend-Lease 1941–45[97]

Equipment Type	British Empire	Soviet Union	China	Others	Total
Tanks	27,751	7,172	100	2,300	37,323
Armoured cars	4,361	0	0	973	5,334
Armoured carriers	27,512	920	0	1,580	30,012
Scout cars	8,065	3,340	139	499	12,043
Light trucks	119,532	77,972	11,982	30,529	240,015
Medium trucks	97,112	151,053	2,616	9,167	259,948
Heavy trucks	64,646	203,634	10,393	13,768	292,441
Trailers	20,282	888	5,842	17,745	44,757
Anti-aircraft guns	4,633	5,762	208	888	11,491
Machine guns	157,598	8,504	34,471	17,176	217,749
Sub-machine guns	651,086	137,729	63,251	28,129	880,195
Rifles	1,456,134	1	305,841	126,374	1,888,350
Radio sets	117,939	32,169	5,974	7,369	163,451
Field telephones	95,508	343,416	24,757	14,739	478,420
Aircraft	25,870	11,450	1,378	4,323	43,021
Aero-engines	39,974	4,980	551	2,883	48,388

The supply of goods and services between Britain and the United States was supplemented by a significant sharing of technical and scientific innovation. Like Lend-Lease this was a product of strategic necessity. Once the United States was at war there was little reason not to share the information if it helped the common cause against the Axis, although in the particular case of the atomic programme the relationship was more fraught. Western leaders assumed for almost all the wartime period that German science and engineering was more sophisticated, more closely integrated with the military apparatus, and more capable of producing scientific inventions both unexpected and dangerous than was the technology available to the Allies. Although it is now clear that respect for Germany's scientific-military establishment was exaggerated, the anxieties at the time help to explain an unprecedented degree of collaboration across the Atlantic. What is more remarkable is that this collaboration began, like Lend-Lease, well before the United States joined the combat. In August 1940, the British

government scientist Sir Henry Tizard was sent to Washington at the head
of a British technical mission to provide secret technical and scientific information to American military and civilian scientists. The most important of
the mission's secrets was the cavity magnetron developed at Birmingham
University, which made possible the development of the much more effective microwave radar. The head of the recently inaugurated National
Defense Research Committee, Vannevar Bush, was granted the opportunity
to develop the new technology for the American armed forces. The Radiation Laboratory that he established at the Massachusetts Institute of
Technology became the foremost research institute for American radar. Following the Tizard mission, American and British scientists established
avenues for collaboration which lasted until the end of the war in all areas
of military research except for the development of nuclear weapons.[98]

The atomic, or nuclear, research programmes represented a vanguard
technology with both civilian and military implications too important to
share even with a potential ally. The decision to explore the possibility of
a bomb was taken in Britain when the Maud Committee was set up in
April 1940 to supervise the research. In July 1941 the committee reported
that a bomb was a practical proposition, a position that neither Tizard
nor the American scientists he encountered had thought possible in the
short term. In October 1941 Roosevelt suggested to Churchill that the
two countries co-ordinate their nuclear research, but the British side
refused from fear that secrets might be inadvertently released if their
research was communicated to American scientists. By summer 1942
American research had drawn ahead of progress in Britain, and the question of co-ordination was now broached by British scientists. This time
the Americans demurred from fear that their developments might be
exploited by Britain for post-war commercial motives. British and Canadian scientists then established the Montreal Laboratory to continue
nuclear research, using materials supplied from the United States but with
little access to American technical information. Only after Churchill gave
a firm commitment at the inter-Allied conference in Quebec in August
1943 that Britain would not exploit American research for its own purposes were some British scientists brought into the American programme
in ways that prevented them from seeing the entire process for developing
the bomb. In the United States there were fears that collaboration might
mean that other states would acquire nuclear weapons and undermine
American efforts to construct a new post-war order. Stalin was not told
that a bomb had been produced until July 1945, shortly before it was
used, but by then the Soviet programme under Igor Kurchatov had been
progressing since 1942, aided by a spy network in the United States that,

ironically, included Klaus Fuchs, one of the scientists supplied by the British under the Quebec agreements and a key Soviet source.[99]

If intellectual lend-lease was never an entirely straightforward exchange, the issues were nothing compared with the logistical problems and inter-Allied friction generated by the programme of material aid. The organization of a global system of distribution was a colossal task fraught with numerous difficulties. The Atlantic route to Britain was a battlefield for the first two years of Lend-Lease. The supply of merchant shipping was limited and until November 1941, when Congress agreed to modify the Neutrality Laws once again, American ships could not be used to transport war material. Neither German submarines nor the demands of the United States military after Pearl Harbor undermined the flow of Lend-Lease goods decisively, but the competing claims of both sides caused regular arguments over priorities and limited the quantity of goods reaching British ports. The major problem faced by the British merchant fleet, which was three times the size of the American in 1941, was the shipping tonnage under repair at any one time – an average of 3.1 million tons every month between 1941 and March 1943, when the German submarine threat subsided.[100] Much of the shipping was repaired in American dockyards under Lend-Lease but the schedule of repair continued to fall behind the requirement for cargo space. Only in 1943, when American merchant shipbuilding produced a remarkable 12.3 million tons of new shipping, was it possible for Roosevelt to promise that enough American ships would be diverted to British needs to ensure the flow of military aid and food. By summer 1943 there was more cargo space available than cargo to fill it.[101]

Even more demanding was the delivery of supplies to the Soviet Union, which took away both British and American shipping from the supply routes across the Atlantic. All three of the principal routes – the Arctic Sea route, the 'Persian Corridor' and the Alaska–Siberia passage – posed severe logistical challenges. The most dangerous route consisted of convoys across the Arctic seas to the northern Soviet ports of Murmansk and Archangel. Here the ships had to cope not only with atrocious weather and rough seas, the threat of on-board icing severe enough to topple a ship, and the occasional ice-flow and iceberg, but also with the persistent threat of German submarines, aircraft and surface vessels based in Norway. Under these harsh circumstances, losses were lower than might have been expected. Out of 848 sailings in 42 convoys on the Arctic route from ports in Scotland and Iceland a total of 65 ships were lost to accident, submarine and aircraft; a further 40 were lost on the return route.[102] The most notorious was the loss in June 1942 of twenty-four out of thirty-six ships of convoy PQ17 when it scattered to avoid a possible threat from

German warships. The disaster led to the postponement of Arctic convoys for several months across the summer of 1942, much to the anger of Soviet leaders. Better convoy protection from 1943 led to fewer casualties and ships continued to ply the route until the last wartime convoy from the Clyde in Scotland in April 1945. Some 4 million tons of supplies, 22.6 per cent of aid to the Soviet Union, was sent via the Arctic route.[103]

The other major routes for Soviet aid were less threatened by the presence of the enemy or the intervention of the elements. The most important was the relatively secure route across the northern Pacific, although even this became ice-bound during the winter months, leaving ships stranded in the ice where they occasionally broke up. Ships plying the route across the north of the Japanese island of Hokkaido, whether Soviet or American, sailed under the Soviet flag because the Soviet–Japanese Non-Aggression Pact, signed in April 1941, protected them from intervention, despite the fact that the goods were assisting the enemy of Japan's German ally. Some 8 million tons of supplies, 47 per cent of the total, came along the route, initially to the Soviet port of Magadan, then to new dock facilities built at Petropavlosk. Here goods were stored or taken by rail on the long route across Siberia to the industrial cities in the Ural region or to the more distant front line. The cost of constructing and operating the facilities along the routes from Alaska to Siberia exceeded by a considerable margin the actual value of the goods shipped.[104]

Almost a quarter of the military supplies came through the third route to be opened up to the Soviet Union across Persia (modern-day Iran), which began operation in early 1942. This was a perilous route because of the poor state of Iranian roads and the single rail track to Azerbaijan in the southern Soviet Union; it was also a route briefly threatened in the summer and autumn of 1942 as the German armed forces drove into the Caucasus region and towards the Volga River at Stalingrad. The British Persia and Iraq Command had responsibility for setting up the route, which required extensive work to expand port facilities in both Iran and Iraq, develop the rail links and make the roads fit for convoys of heavy trucks. The route crossed desert, stretches of land covered with salt (or a thick yellow slime known as *kavir*) and mountain passes with hundreds of zigzag bends; temperatures in one of the hottest places on earth could reach 49 degrees centigrade, but in the winter in the snowbound passes, temperatures could fall as low as -40. Drivers froze to death in their cabs in winter, or died from heatstroke in summer.[105] The Indian troops deployed to guard the railway from bandits could be murdered as they negotiated one of the 220 unlit tunnels, or risk suffocation from the smoke belching from slow-moving, overheated locomotives. Under such debilitating conditions, the troops, engineers and labourers achieved a miracle of supply. The railway carried 200 tons a day in 1941, but after the American Persian Gulf Command took control of the railways in 1942, daily tonnage rose to an average of 3,397. As the war neared its end, the Persian corridor was replaced by the easier route across the Black Sea to Russia's southern ports.[106]

To assist the Anglo-American effort, the Soviet transport authorities organized what was called a 'Special Mission' to carry goods and vehicles from ports in southern Iran to the Soviet Union along new highways constructed in 1942 and 1943. The distance was more than 2,000 kilometres, and the vehicle convoys were plagued by accidents, theft, dust storms and blizzards. British and American forces set up six assembly plants in southern Iran and Iraq where they put together the vehicles which had been packed into freighters, disassembled, for the long voyage around the Cape of Good Hope – a total of over 184,000 vehicle units. In August 1943, a Soviet 1st Special Motor Vehicle Detachment was established which succeeded in cutting delivery times from a month or more to an average of twelve to fourteen days. Along the dusty roads, rising in places to more than 2,000 metres, there were food stops and repair depots set up to speed the progress of the shipments. Once on Soviet territory there began a second long and arduous journey to the front-line units. The overall record for the Soviet Union from all three supply lines was a grand total of 16 million tons of supplies, transported in 2,600 sailings from ports around the North Atlantic and the western Pacific Rim.[107]

Scarcely less demanding were the routes for supplying Lend-Lease to Nationalist China. Although China was included as one of the initial states qualifying for aid, the priority accorded Chinese supply was very low compared with supplies for Britain and the Soviet Union. Many of these resources lay idle, first piled up on the docks and rail lines at Rangoon, then, after the Japanese invasion of Burma, at ports along the north-east Indian coastline, awaiting delivery on a limited transport network. Chinese aid could be sent across the Pacific until Pearl Harbor, but after that had to be routed across the Atlantic and Indian oceans. Once it arrived, there were profound geographical handicaps in getting the aid to the Chinese armies through some of the most inhospitable topography in the world, with inadequate roads and no effective railway. The effort in 1941 to construct a rail link from Lashio in northern Burma to Kunming in southern Yunnan province suffered from grim working conditions for around 100,000 Chinese and Burmese labourers, thousands of whom succumbed to malaria or typhoid, while an estimated half smoked opium to cope with their ordeal.[108] When the Burmese routes were lost, the only remaining prospect was to fly the supplies from bases in India across the Himalayas to

Kunming. This route, popularly dubbed 'The Hump', was perilous in the extreme: freezing temperatures at over 6,000 metres across the mountains, spectacular thunderstorms, strong winds that pushed up fuel use and forced emergency landings, and just two primitive landing strips in China made of crushed stone. At least 700 aircraft and 1,200 crew were lost over the course of the airlift. Until 1943 shortages of facilities, aircraft and crews kept the flow of supplies to a trickle; from 1943 the airlift expanded, but it was impossible to fly in heavy equipment or vehicles or machinery. By 1944 half of all supplies sent by sea were still awaiting shipment to China.[109] Most of the supplies that did get through were allocated to American forces in China, chiefly Chennault's Fourteenth Air Force. Chinese officials calculated that 98 per cent was used by the Americans, but even if this figure is too high, Stilwell, as Chiang's American chief of staff, saw to it that he could control the flow of Lend-Lease aid to suit American purposes.[110]

The logistical effort on all sides was prodigious but it was pursued not only because economic aid was understood to be a critical strand in Allied strategy but also because Allied national leaders were directly involved in negotiating the deals and monitoring the results. Yet despite the evident success of the logistic effort, there was persistent friction between the Allies over the pace of supply and the nature of the gifts. The British reception of American tanks was marred by complaints that the M3 and its successor, the M4 Sherman, needed modification for battle conditions; in 1944 there was a significant shortfall in tank supplies of more than 3,400, and in late 1944 all Lend-Lease tank shipments were abruptly cancelled because of unanticipated loss rates in American armoured units.[111] More significant were the arguments over the supply of aircraft. Because bombing Germany became a strategic priority in the summer of 1940, the RAF hoped that the American aviation industry would supply 500 heavy bombers a month by 1943, but delivery was compromised by the demands of the American air force for priority. When the first B-17 and B-24 bombers arrived, the RAF expressed disappointment at their combat potential and discussed using them only in subsidiary roles. Since these were the pet aircraft of the expanding American bomber arm, the criticisms were strongly resented and Henry Arnold, the army air forces' commander-in-chief, refused to promise more than 400–500 bombers for the whole of 1942, and eventually reneged on that. The obsolescent fighters and light bombers supplied in 1940 and 1941 were, according to the British air minister, Archibald Sinclair, 'almost valueless'.[112] Although in the end the United States supplied Britain and its empire with almost 26,000 aircraft, they included only 162 B-17s, but 3,697 light bombers, and 8,826 trainer and transport aircraft.[113]

Aid for the Soviet Union was accompanied by a litany of complaints from the Soviet side. The initial promises made by the British government in June 1941 were slow to materialize and much of the equipment that did arrive over the following months was regarded by the Soviet side as substandard. The Hurricane fighters were criticized for the lack of armour and weak armament; the British tanks, but particularly the Matilda, were regarded as inadequate for Russian conditions, under-armed and virtually immobilized in freezing temperatures. Serviceability of the British tanks averaged just 50 per cent. When the American Sherman tanks began to appear, Soviet engineers considered them to be poorly protected with armour and with a height that made them an easy target. Armoured forces nicknamed them (uncharitably) 'a grave for seven brothers' because of their vulnerability to enemy anti-tank fire.[114] It was certainly the case that both Western states preferred to send equipment that was not in the first rank unless it could not be avoided. Matilda tanks continued to be made in Britain and Canada in 1942–3 to supply Soviet forces when the model had been phased out of British armoured units; and when the Soviet side asked for the B-17 and B-24 heavy bombers, the Americans refused.[115]

The effective employment of Lend-Lease equipment was compromised by the persistent objection of the Soviet side to allowing Western personnel access to help with training and repair or to supply information on how the aid was being utilized. By 1943 large stockpiles of material had accumulated in the Soviet Union but it was impossible to check why this was or to limit further deliveries without Soviet co-operation. Soviet secretiveness made it difficult at the time to counteract the regular criticism of combat failures, while despite promises Soviet officials released little information on the development of Soviet tanks and aircraft, apart from the one T-34 tank sent to the United States in 1942. 'We still meet their requests to the limit of our ability,' complained the head of the American military mission in Moscow, John Deane, to General Marshall, 'and they meet ours to the minimum that will keep us sweet.'[116] Growing suspicion that Soviet requests for Lend-Lease supplies, which reached a peak in 1944 and 1945, included goods intended for Soviet post-war reconstruction led to political pressure in Washington to place limits on Soviet assistance. In August 1945, following the Japanese surrender, President Truman announced the immediate end of all Lend-Lease shipments without consulting either of the main recipients.[117]

Tensions in the Lend-Lease relationship were inevitable given the nature of the geographical scope involved and the contending requirements for urgent supply, but in the end vast resources, chiefly from the American productive surplus, were shared between the Allies. Was this record, in the words of Edward Stettinius, the Lend-Lease administrator, a 'weapon for victory'? The answer is more complicated than it seems. For years after the war the official Soviet line was to downplay or to ignore altogether the role of Lend-Lease in the Soviet war effort. This was a deliberate act of historical distortion. Shortly after the end of the war, informal guidelines were issued (which no sensible author could ignore under Stalin) that Lend-Lease 'did not play a somewhat noticeable part in Russian victory'.[118] The official line until the 1980s was to insist that Lend-Lease goods came late, were often of poor quality, and comprised only 4 per cent of the weapons produced by the Soviet Union's own efforts. During the war, however, Soviet leaders privately admitted how important all the forms of aid were. In the taped interviews for his memoirs, Khrushchev revealed the importance Stalin attached to the aid, but the following passage was only published in the 1990s: 'Several times I heard Stalin acknowledge [Lend-Lease] in the small circle of people around him. He said that . . . if we had had to deal with Germany one-to-one we would not have been able to cope.' Marshal Zhukov, victor in Berlin, toed the Party line in his memoirs published in 1969, but in a bugged conversation six years earlier he was overheard to say that without foreign aid the Soviet Union 'could not have continued the war'.[119]

The 4 per cent figure for Allied supplies as a percentage of Soviet output is not wrong, but it entirely masks what Lend-Lease actually achieved. In the early stages of the war, Lend-Lease tanks and aircraft supplied a higher percentage of Soviet equipment because of the exceptional losses in the first months of combat. As the war progressed, Soviet output revived, and Lend-Lease military equipment became correspondingly less significant. Up to the Battle of Stalingrad Lend-Lease tanks amounted to 19 per cent of Soviet production. But by the Battle of Kursk six months later, one of the largest tank engagements of the war, there were 3,495 Soviet-built tanks and only 396 Lend-Lease, around 11 per cent.[120] Tanks, aircraft and weapons, however, were not the decisive factor in Allied deliveries. Of much greater significance was the transformation of the Soviet communications system, support for the strained railway network, and large supplies of raw materials, fuel and explosives without which the overall Soviet war effort and military campaigns would have been less than adequate for the defeat of the great bulk of the German army. One of the major deficiencies in conducting air and tank combat in the early years of the war was the lack of electronic equipment; it was also a major problem for commanders trying to manage a vast battlefield with poor or little communication.

Under Lend-Lease the Western Allies together supplied 35,000 army radio sets, 389,000 field telephones and over 1.5 million kilometres of telephone cable.[121] By early 1943 the Red Air Force was at last able to operate centralized control of air combat units, while the simple device of installing radios in tanks proved a force multiplier. Radio also came to play a part in the Red Army's very effective use of deception and disinformation, which on numerous occasions left the German army unable to guess the size, the whereabouts or the intentions of enemy forces.

The supply position of the Red Army was above all transformed by the trucks and jeeps provided under Lend-Lease, which in the end amounted to more than 400,000, against domestic Soviet production of 205,000. By January 1945 one-third of Red Army vehicles were supplied by Lend-Lease.[122] American aid also broadened the range of vehicles serving the Soviet war effort: scout cars, armoured personnel carriers, half-tracks, the Ford amphibians and 48,956 jeeps, also fitted with radios so that Red Army commanders could control their forces with greater efficiency.[123] Shifting men and equipment by railway was also underpinned by the American provision of 1,900 locomotives (against Soviet output of just 92) and 56 per cent of all the rails used during the war. By late 1942 the Soviet rail system was able to supply front-line forces at Stalingrad with fifteen trains a day where German supply averaged twelve.[124] Finally, Allied aid provided almost 58 per cent of all aviation fuel, 53 per cent of all explosives and half the requirements of aluminium, copper and synthetic rubber tyres.[125] Allied supply on this scale was decisive. Soviet industry could concentrate on the mass production of weapons, leaving the supply of much else in the war economy to Allied assistance.

There is much less room for debate on the impact Lend-Lease made to the British war effort, although it seldom features as historically significant in popular memory of the war. Like Soviet treatment of Lend-Lease, memory of heavy reliance on another ally tarnishes the national record. Reliance was nevertheless absolute. Without generous United States aid from 1941 onwards, the British war effort would have foundered. There were no means to pay for more dollar resources, above all oil, and without access to American industrial production, food and raw materials the British wartime economy would have reached the limit of capacity well below what was necessary to sustain a global war effort or any prospect of defeating Germany. British military campaigns across the globe came to rely on American weapons and movement in American ships. In 1941 Lend-Lease made up 11 per cent of British military equipment, but by 1943 almost 27 per cent and in 1944, the peak year for British military campaigning, just under 29 per cent. By the Second Battle of El Alamein in late October 1942, the Americans had supplied to North Africa 1,700 medium and light tanks, 1,000 aircraft and 25,000 trucks and jeeps.[126] Altogether, the United States sent 27,751 tanks, 27,512 armoured personnel carriers and 25,870 aircraft to Britain and British theatres of war. As in the Soviet case, American supply allowed British industry to concentrate on the production of other weapons or, in some cases, to substitute capacity entirely. British tank production declined in 1944 because of American supplies and instead locomotive output was increased to ameliorate the strains on the British rail network.[127] Agreements between the Allies encouraged a rational allocation of resources, rather than duplication of effort. Both the British and Soviet productive record reflected the pattern of American aid. For both nations, knowledge that they did not have to rely just on their own resources was a psychological cushion which the Axis powers lacked. For the United States, allocating almost 7 per cent of domestic output to Lend-Lease was achieved with relatively little strain on the home economy, and it brought the great advantage that the principal Allied nations, as Roosevelt had intended from the outset, could defend American interests more effectively.

DENYING RESOURCES: BLOCKADE AND BOMBING

If mutual aid was an economic strategy to boost war supplies, economic warfare was the means to reduce both the finished weapons and material resources available to the enemy. The original sense of economic warfare as literally economic – freezing assets, pre-emptive purchases, interrupting and controlling trade with the enemy – was replaced in the Second World War by real economic wars, waged by submarine and bomber aircraft, with high losses of men and equipment to both sides in long battles of economic attrition. Conventional forms of economic warfare were still practised during the war, but their significance paled in comparison with the effort exerted to wage economic war with military means, either against resources in transit or against resources produced in the home economy. Unrestricted submarine warfare and the bombing of urban centres were common strategies of the economic war, Axis and Allied.

The potential success of economic warfare in this wider sense of the physical destruction of enemy resources before they reached the battlefield depended first on the degree of economic vulnerability exhibited by the warring states. On this measure there existed a marked contrast between the two sides as the war expanded in scope. The United States was almost immune to economic warfare: geography still protected American industry from any threat of bombing, while the vast resources of the Western Hemisphere shielded American war production from any but a few bottlenecks, particularly natural rubber, which was compensated for by an urgent and large-scale conversion to synthetic production. The brief period when German submarines in the first two months of 1942 were deployed along the American eastern coast to sink unescorted vessels was soon over, with little effect on the war effort. Across the Atlantic sea lanes, American shipping was vulnerable, but the overwhelming bulk of goods and military equipment convoyed over the ocean reached its destination. The Soviet Union, after the loss of the western area in 1941, might have been a victim of German long-range bombing of industrial areas, but the German Air Force lacked the means to carry it out and Soviet production continued without interruption. Rich domestic natural resources, together with the growing flow of Lend-Lease aid (despite the German attempt to interrupt the Arctic convoys) made it unlikely that economic warfare strategy against the Soviet Union would achieve very much. The most vulnerable ally was Britain, and it was against British production and trade that Germany directed the combined sea and air campaigns of 1940–43. This was the most serious attempt by the Axis to employ a strategy of economic warfare to undermine the war effort and will-to-war of a major enemy. British vulnerability, however, was relative. Heavy reliance on overseas supplies of food, raw materials and oil – and later military goods under Lend-Lease – meant that large resources were diverted to the battle to keep sea lanes open. Britain had by far the world's largest merchant-shipping fleet, and although not inexhaustible, it meant that a very high tonnage had to be sunk before British trade reached breaking point. With American assistance, a global network of merchant shipping was organized, giving the Allies the means to move material around the world wherever it could be found or was needed and to prevent the enemy from enjoying a similar advantage. To combat this system, the Axis would have required a corresponding global sea blockade and they lacked the means, even if it had been a strategic priority.

The Axis states had vulnerabilities in common. All three could be subjected to sea blockade because of the strength of British and then United States naval and air power. Italy and Japan, in particular, possessed weaker war economies, reliant on overseas supply because neither had a large foundation of natural raw materials. The Mediterranean was a closed sea where blockade could be imposed with relative ease (and indeed the British found that blockade worked both ways until 1943); Japan relied on long routes from the captured areas in South East Asia, but also on food and materials supplied from Taiwan, Manchuria and Korea. However, Germany's susceptibility to conventional blockade, asset-freezing and financial crisis, which had been a key element in Anglo-French strategy in 1939, turned out to be overestimated. Hitler's obsession with the effects of wartime blockade between 1914 and 1918 prompted the development of domestic self-sufficiency, or 'autarky' in the 1930s. By 1939 Germany produced 80 per cent of basic foodstuffs, and had synthetic programmes for oil, textiles, rubber and a range of other war-related products. The shortage of gold and foreign exchange for buying essential supplies for the military economy, evident in 1939, was overcome by a comprehensive strategy of looting European assets and putting pressure on Europe's neutral states.[128]

Once war with the West had broken out, the Allied sea blockade did cut Germany off from transoceanic shipping, but German territorial expansion from 1938 onwards was partly designed to make Germany *blockadefest*, free from the threat of blockade. Seizure of Norway made secure iron-ore supplies from Sweden; occupation of the Balkans secured further raw materials and access to Turkish trade. The German–Soviet Pact of August 1939 brought a significant flow of raw materials and food until June 1941: in 1940 617,000 tons of oil products, against 5,100 in 1939; 820,000 tons of grain against 200 tons the year before; and supplies of copper, tin, platinum, chromium and nickel up from zero in 1939.[129] Even without Soviet resources, the 'Great Area Economy' constructed between 1938 and 1941 effectively ended any prospect that conventional sea blockade would undermine the German war effort. The one resource that all three Axis states lacked was oil. This was a critical shortage since oil fired German mechanized warfare as it fired the Japanese Imperial Navy. The search for oil drove the Japanese to invade South East Asia and Hitler to attempt the seizure of the Soviet Caucasus region in 1942.[130] The Allies controlled or owned over 90 per cent of the world's output of natural oil; the Axis states controlled a mere 3 per cent of oil output, 4 per cent of oil-refining capacity. Germany produced synthetic fuel on a large basis, reaching 7 million tons a year in 1943, three-quarters of the oil Germany used, but more was always needed.[131] Oil vulnerability was to prove a central factor in the strategy of the Western Allies for denying resources and securing ultimate victory.

For the Axis states, absorbed by their imperial project, waging economic warfare had not been a part of their strategic planning for any larger war. Of the three, only Germany attempted to rectify the strategic gap by waging an air–sea blockade of Britain, but in 1939 the prospects were bleak. The German navy possessed only twenty-five ocean-going submarines, with a maximum at sea of six to eight at any one time, while the German air force was chiefly committed to achieving air superiority in support of ground operations, with no forward planning for conducting its own strategic campaign against either shipping or enemy industry. The German navy's 'Z-Plan' announced in 1939, for building an extensive ocean-going fleet, was years from fruition. Nonetheless, in November 1939 Hitler directed the armed forces to begin an economic war against Britain: 'To bring down England is the precondition for final victory. The most effective way of doing this is to degrade the English economy by striking at decisive points.'[132] The air force and navy were directed to collaborate in mining British trade routes, destroying harbour installations, warehousing, oil storage and food stocks, sinking shipping and bombing military industry, above all aircraft production. With an eye to the Allied food blockade of Germany in the First World War, Hitler put stress on blockading the supply of foodstuffs. After the brief interlude when the abortive invasion of Britain was planned, Hitler returned to the theme of a 'blockade decisive for the war' with aircraft and submarines collaborating in a campaign that in the foreseeable future would produce 'the collapse of English resistance'.[133]

Hitler's commitment to an economic war for which his forces were not prepared made little strategic sense at the time, but it reflected his own conception of war as a function of economic strength as much as military success. It was a view derived in part from the German submarine war between 1914 and 1918 which had come close to crippling the Allied war effort, when 6,651 ships with a gross tonnage of 12.5 million tons were sunk by submarines and mines.[134] This time round the German naval staff, encouraged by Hitler's optimism, hoped to wage what they called 'the greatest economic war of all time'. The belief that sinking tonnage was the key to defeating Britain was echoed by the commander of German submarines, Commodore (later Grand Admiral) Karl Dönitz, who made this the principal objective of his small submarine force.[135] Even after the United States' entry to the war, with a vast potential reservoir of new merchant shipping, Hitler continued to see economic warfare as a critical factor in denying resources. 'Fuehrer recognizes the fact,' reported the navy commander-in-chief, Grand Admiral Erich Raeder, in June 1942, 'that the submarine war will in the end decide the outcome of the war.'[136]

Despite the relative weakness of the resources available for a sea and air blockade, much was achieved in the first years of the war. Aircraft attacked shipping in the English Channel and North Sea, while in the Atlantic a combination of submarines, merchant raiders and the converted long-range airliner, the Focke-Wulf 200 'Condor', sank 1,207 ships between September 1939 and December 1940, helped by the ability of the German navy's intelligence service, the B-Dienst, to read British signal traffic on the convoys. By 1941 the Condor alone was sinking 150,000

tons of shipping a month, until British fighter aircraft were finally diverted
to hunting down and destroying the large slow-moving predator. In 1940,
580,000 tons were lost to aircraft, in 1941 over 1 million tons, a total of
500 ships. Submarines accounted for 869 ships over the same period, and
would have achieved much more were it not for the fact that the German
torpedo suffered serious technical deficiencies that were not finally recti-
fied until the autumn of 1942. Marine causes (collisions, wrecks, fires,
etc.) accounted for a further 653 vessels. British import tonnage fell
sharply, from 41.8 million tons in 1940 to 30.5 million tons in 1941.[137]

To the impact of the war at sea was added the blockade from the air,
which began in the summer of 1940 with raids on ports and dock facilities
in southern England and then spread out to the major port cities across the
British Isles once Hitler had postponed the Operation 'Sea Lion' invasion
in mid-September. Although those who experienced the German bombing
regarded it at the time as terror bombing aimed at breaking British morale,
the German air force was directed to support the sea campaign by destroying the port entry points for British overseas trade (with a primary focus
on London, Liverpool and Manchester), as well as warehouses, silos, oil
storage depots, shipping and ship-repair facilities; in addition military-
economic targets were to be raided, principally in the Midlands, where
aero-engine production was concentrated. The 'Blitz' was a form of economic warfare and was conducted throughout the nine months from
September 1940 to May 1941 with this perspective in mind. If blockade
succeeded, the effect was expected to be a decline in Britain's capacity to
wage war and a general decline in popular commitment to continuing the
conflict. Out of 171 major raids, 141 were directed at port cities, including
London, which in 1939 had handled the largest quantity of overseas trade.
Out of the 3,116 tons of incendiaries dropped, 86 per cent targeted ports;
of 24,535 tons of high explosive bombs the figure was 85 per cent.[138] From
January 1941 the German air force was instructed to use larger quantities
of incendiaries against port areas where British stocks of commodities
were vulnerable to fire. To counteract the British decision to switch incoming Atlantic trade to western ports, including Bristol, Clydebank, Swansea,
Cardiff and Liverpool, a new directive gave these ports priority.[139] By the
time the campaign was suspended, when air force units moved to the war
in the East, all the major port cities had been bombed heavily, and Hull,
Plymouth, London and Southampton repeatedly.

The bombing campaign proved much less effective than the war at sea,
although detailed intelligence on the damage inflicted was almost impossible
for the German high command to obtain. Hitler was soon disillusioned by
the results. In December 1940 he thought the impact on British war industry

minimal; two months later he agreed with Raeder's view that British morale had been 'unshaken' by the bombing, and on 6 February issued the directive that prioritized the submarine and aircraft campaign against shipping tonnage as the more decisive form of economic warfare.[140] The bombing was persisted with partly because it was difficult to explain to the German public, subjected for almost a year to raids from the RAF, why the campaign against Britain should be abandoned, partly in order to persuade Stalin that Britain was Hitler's primary concern while secret preparations went ahead for the invasion of the Soviet Union. In this case Hitler's instinct was right. Air Ministry calculations made later in 1941 showed that no more than 5 per cent of Britain's rapidly expanding war production was lost as a result of the bombing campaign; in raided cities, normal production rates were resumed from between three and eight days, except for the major raid on Coventry in November 1940, following which it took six weeks before pre-raid activity was restored. The effort to interrupt British stocks of oil and foodstuffs was equally limited. Only 0.5 per cent of stored oil was lost, 5 per cent of flour-milling capacity, 1.6 per cent of oilseed output and 1.5 per cent of cold-storage facilities. Water supply was nowhere interrupted for more than twenty-four hours, while rail communication continued an almost normal wartime service, with no line out of action for more than a day.[141] The cost to the German air force was substantial: between January and June 1941 572 bombers were destroyed, many lost to accidents, and 496 damaged. By May 1941 the bomber arm had 769 serviceable bombers, many fewer than had been available for the invasion of France a year before.[142] For the British side the heaviest cost was the death of 44,652 men, women and children in 1940–41, victims of an inconclusive air blockade.

Hitler abandoned the idea that bombing British targets would contribute to the blockade and the air force was never used again in that capacity. Instead, the blockade was concentrated on the submarine and air war at sea. The German surface fleet contributed little – accounting for only forty-seven ships throughout the war – and after the sinking of the modern battleship *Bismarck* in May 1941, major naval vessels were withdrawn from ocean-going operations in favour of protecting German supplies from Scandinavia and threatening the Arctic convoys to the Soviet Union. By summer 1941 conditions for the sea–air war had altered. Göring, the air force commander-in-chief, was unsympathetic to the diversion of air resources to support the sea campaign, even more so once the air force was heavily committed to the 'Barbarossa' campaign. The air unit designated to support the navy, *Kampfgruppe* 40, based in western France, was starved of adequate resources throughout its existence. Between July 1941 and October 1942 aircraft sank an average of only four ships a month.[143] The predominant instrument of the blockade became the submarine. Numbers increased considerably during 1941, from a total fleet of 102 in the first quarter to 233 by the end of the year, but the slow repair of damaged submarines, the heavy call for training boats, and the spread of operations between the northern, Atlantic and Mediterranean theatres, all meant that for the Atlantic assault on Britain's shipping lanes there were never more than a maximum of seventeen boats available for operations. A number of Italian submarines sent to help in the Atlantic proved unable to cope with the open ocean and were redeployed to safer and warmer zones. Only in 1942 did numbers begin to approach what Dönitz regarded as essential if the blockade were to work: 352 in July, 382 by the end of the year, and more than 400 for the whole of 1943. That year, the submarine fleet reached an operational peak of 110 boats at sea between January and March.[144]

By this stage Allied countermeasures had begun to have a significant effect on the submarine war. The British Admiralty set up the Western Approaches Command, based in Liverpool, which directed all incoming commercial maritime traffic in the war against the submarines. The Command used intelligence supplied by the Submarine Tracking Room on submarine movements culled from a wide variety of sources, including Ultra intercepts from German naval Enigma traffic between May 1941 and February 1942, when the German cypher was altered and for six months could no longer be read. The intelligence was designed to allow convoys to evade the waiting submarines. The 'Western Approaches Convoy Instructions' issued in spring 1941 made evasion the principal objective for the commander of the escorts, rather than hunting for the submarine. From the start of the war almost all shipping sailed in convoy except for vessels capable of 15 knots or more which could be routed independently. Escorts for convoys were greatly strengthened in 1941 while air cover, though far from complete, forced submarines to submerge for long periods. Escorts and aircraft were fitted with 1.7-metre radar to assist in detecting submarines and an advanced mark of ASDIC, the sound-detection device invented in the last year of the First World War. Neither worked perfectly in the conditions of frequent storms and the heavy swell of the ocean, but in 1940 a breakthrough occurred in radar development with the introduction of the cavity magnetron which allowed much narrower wavelengths. The Type 271 centimetric radar set was fitted to ships from mid-1941, and then to aircraft, allowing a much more accurate reading of the presence of a submarine, even in fog, low cloud, or at night. Improved anti-submarine measures did not lead to a significant increase in submarine losses (only nineteen in 1941, thirty-five in 1942), but it forced submarines away from their earlier hunting grounds further out to the mid-Atlantic 'gap', or south to the routes from Gibraltar and Sierra Leone. The success against coastal convoys in 1940 by aircraft and submarines was not repeated. Of the 608 convoys that plied between Scotland and London in 1941 and 1942, only 61 vessels were lost out of 21,570 sailings.[145] Tonnage lost in 1941 fell from a peak of 364,000 in March to just 50,682 in December.

The high point of the German blockade came between the spring of 1942 and spring 1943, when tonnage sunk suddenly expanded rapidly again. The reasons for the shift in fortunes were partly circumstantial, masking the extent to which the submarine and air campaign was in the long run compromised by the scale and inventiveness of the enemy's response. The declaration of war on the United States in December 1941 produced a sudden opportunity to exploit the almost unprotected western Atlantic coastal traffic. On 9 December Hitler lifted all remaining restrictions on submarine warfare now the United States was no longer neutral. Dönitz had been caught by surprise at the American entry, and at first there were only six boats available, and even by late January there were only ten. The long-range Type IXC were sent south to the Gulf of Mexico and the oil and bauxite route from Trinidad; the smaller Type VII sailed to the coast of the United States. Here they reaped an extraordinary harvest. There had been little thought in Washington that submarines posed a threat so close to home. City lights were still blazing along the coast, silhouetting the coastal traffic, while ships sailed independently with little radio restriction and fully lit. The commander-in-chief of the United States navy, Admiral Ernest King, refused to accept that convoys were necessary and there were few escorts or aircraft dedicated to anti-submarine warfare. The result was a carnage of Allied shipping for the first six months of 1942, setting a new record of sinking month on month – 71 vessels in February, 124 in June, the highest number of the war. Almost all were in American waters, 57 per cent of them oil tankers making their way to the north-west Atlantic for American industry and Lend-Lease supply to Britain.[146] Monthly tonnage losses began to approach the level of 700,000–800,000 tons that Dönitz considered necessary to undermine Allied shipping decisively. There was now a fresh urgency to the submarine campaign because with American entry the nature of the contest altered from an economic war to starve Britain of resources to a campaign to prevent the United States from sending men and equipment across the ocean for military operations in Europe.

Other factors played into German hands over the course of the year. The north-west Atlantic was the responsibility of the hastily expanded Royal Canadian Navy. A shortage of escort vessels, limited training for escort officers, an old-fashioned form of ASDIC and the demands of convoy patrols to the mid-Atlantic brought the service close to collapse. When German submarines moved to the north-west in the summer and autumn of 1942 for a campaign in the Gulf of St Lawrence they found only weak resistance: five submarines sank nineteen ships and forced the closing of the Gulf to merchant shipping.[147] After Admiral King finally introduced convoys and air/sea escort, attacks in American and Caribbean waters declined. Dönitz shifted the submarine 'wolf packs' back to the mid-Atlantic 'gap' which air patrols could not yet reach. The renewed campaign benefitted from the decision to change the settings on the naval Enigma, which left the British blind to Ultra intelligence from February to December, making evasion more challenging though still possible. Although escorts were stronger and primed with centimetric radar, the air gap was a critical factor. The Royal Navy pressed the RAF to release additional long-range aircraft to Coastal Command, principally the converted American B-24 'Liberator' bomber, but the chief obstacle to closing the gap proved to be Churchill. He insisted across the crisis months of 1942 that the bombing of Germany had the first call on air resources, preferring offensive economic warfare to the defensive needs of the convoys. He assumed, with the strong support of the commander-in-chief of Bomber Command, Air Marshal Arthur Harris, that bombing submarine production would achieve more than attacking submarines at sea, a view for which there was no credible evidence. Only when Churchill was presented with the stark reality that imports to Britain would fall to an insupportably low level in 1943 did he accept that more air resources should be diverted to the naval war, but only in the hope that this would not impair the bomber offensive. In the late spring of 1943, with shipping losses running at more than 600,000 tons a month, Churchill finally permitted the transfer of long-range aircraft; at the same time Roosevelt, aware of how severe the mauling of the convoys had become, compelled the army air forces to release fifteen Liberators to the Canadian air force to close the Atlantic gap from the west as well. By May, some forty-one very long-range aircraft finally covered the whole width of the ocean.[148]

The success of the submarines in 1942 and early 1943 was in many respects an optical illusion. It depended on the casual response to the submarine threat by the American navy and the temporary failure to supply the limited air resources needed to hound German wolf packs in the mid-Atlantic. Despite the heavy losses of merchant shipping, the statistics show that a great deal of shipping got through unscathed. Between May 1942 and May 1943, 105 out of 174 convoys on the Atlantic were undetected; out of the remaining 69 sighted by German submarines, 23 escaped any attack, 30 suffered minor losses, and only 10 were heavily damaged. For much of the period of German success the victims were stragglers or more vulnerable independents not sailing in convoy – 277 out of 308 ships sunk in American waters in the first half of 1942. On the main convoy routes from the base in Nova Scotia, convoys codenamed HX and SC, there were fewer losses in 1942 than in 1941: 69 ships instead of 116.[149] The record of tons sunk per submarine showed a sharp decline as the campaign continued: in October 1940 it amounted to 920 tons per day, in November 1942, with the peak of tonnage sunk in the Atlantic gap, the figure was only 220 tons.[150] Numerous technical and tactical advantages to the Allied side came on stream in 1942: centimetric radar, new High Frequency/Direction Finding equipment for an accurate bearing on any submarine using radio, the first escort carriers for convoys, better explosives, the Leigh Light for illuminating the sea ahead when an aircraft was too close for the radar to work effectively, and the discovery in October 1942 of the new 'Triton' codebooks on board U-559 captured in the eastern Mediterranean, which allowed Enigma traffic to be read again by December. Under a new commander, the submariner Admiral Max Horton, the Western Approaches Command transformed the training of escort commanders and introduced hard-hitting support groups of naval vessels to seek and destroy the wolf packs as they formed. Although two convoys were severely mauled in climactic battles in March 1943, SC121 and HX229, with the loss of twenty-one ships, submarine losses in all waters suddenly mounted to the highest so far in the war: nineteen in February and fifteen in March.

The combination of all these factors contributed to securing an abrupt end to the blockade threat. Additional merchant shipping from the United States saw an increase in British import tonnage from 22.8 million in 1942 to 26.4 million the following year. The 'import crisis' that so worried Churchill was a temporary crisis, caused largely by the diversion of shipping to the Pacific campaign and the Allied landings in North Africa. German naval intelligence estimated that the Allies would build no more than 5 million tons of new merchant shipping in 1942, but they built 7 million tons in 1942 and 14.5 million in 1943. Despite the shipping losses endured in 1942 and early 1943, Allied construction made it difficult for the German attrition campaign to sink enough to have a decisive effect. There were stocks in Britain totalling 18.4 million tons of accumulated food and materials available in December 1942, 17.3 million in February 1943, but 18.3 million again by June.[151] Thanks to American shipbuilding there was a surplus over losses in 1943 of 11 million tons of merchant shipping. In 1944 the German navy could do almost nothing to prevent the flow of equipment and men across the Atlantic for the invasion of France.

In the ocean battles the tables were entirely turned. On 11 May 1943 a

slow-moving convoy, SC130, was sent to Britain from Nova Scotia protected by a deliberately heavy naval escort. The convoy was met by wolf
packs in the mid-Atlantic where overhead the new Liberator patrols now
operated. Six submarines were sunk but not a single merchantman. In the
Atlantic that month thirty-three submarines were lost, forty-one in all
theatres. This represented a third of the operational boats. Dönitz drew
the conclusion that such losses were insupportable, and on 24 May
ordered submarines back to base until new equipment became available
to shift the battle again in his favour. On 31 May he reported the temporary defeat to Hitler who characteristically wanted no retreat: 'there can
be no talk of a let-up in submarine warfare. The Atlantic is my first line of
defence in the West …'[152] The blockade nevertheless remained broken
until the end of the war. More submarines than merchant ships were lost
in the second half of 1943, and in 1944 in all theatres the Allies lost only
170,000 tons of shipping, 3 per cent of the losses in 1942. The expansion
and upgrading of the anti-submarine forces made submarine operations
untenable and suicidal: some 237 were sunk in 1943, 241 in 1944. New
equipment was in the pipeline with the Type XXI and XXIII submarines,
which were genuine submersibles, able to operate undetected under water
and to fire submerged, with an operational range as far as Cape Town, but
development was slow, hit by Allied bombing and the diversion of
resources to other more pressing needs. The first of the new generation of
submarines became operational on 30 April 1945, making its way to the
Thames Estuary as the German war effort came to an end.[153]

Unlike that of the Axis powers, British and United States pre-war planning
contained a hard core of economic warfare, dictated largely by facts of
geography. Neither could be invaded by land, leaving them free to project
their main power by sea and air. United States planning for war against
Japan dated back to the years before the First World War, and it was predicated on exposing Japan to economic siege if ever it attempted to drive the
United States out of the western Pacific. War Plan Orange (the colour denot-
ing Japan) went through a number of iterations in the twenty-five years
after it was first conceived, but the commitment to unlimited economic
warfare was consistent throughout. The success of siege blockade against
the Confederacy in the American Civil War was the model. Denying all
overseas resources, the destruction of shipping, commercial and financial
isolation were all instruments designed to produce the 'impoverishment and
exhaustion' of the Orange enemy.[154] The strength of the American economy,
faced by a war to the limit against Japan, would ensure that Japan's economy would be destroyed. By the 1930s planners had built air power into

the equation as well, with bombing and blockade as complementary instruments of economic war. The version of War Plan Orange in 1936 foresaw long-range bombing of industrial and communications targets from Pacific island bases long before there was an aircraft with the range to attempt it, and it remained an aspiration until the means were finally available late in the campaign across the central Pacific.[155] Aircraft were also central to the plans for economic war in the European theatre once Germany had become a potential enemy. Here bombing was immediately possible and its purpose, agreed by American military planners in late summer 1941, would be 'the breakdown of the industrial and economic structure'.[156]

Britain's model for economic warfare was the First World War because it was assumed that one of the principal explanations for the collapse of the Central Powers had been the naval blockade, which denied resources and food, prompting industrial and social crisis by 1918. Towards the end of that conflict the prospect of bombing German industry was added to blockade as a form of economic warfare. Plans for a major Allied air offensive in 1919 with hundreds of multi-engine bombers were suspended by the armistice in November 1918, but the idea of laying an enemy economy to siege from the air remained a key plank of air force thinking for the next twenty years. In 1928 the chief of the air staff, Marshal of the RAF Hugh Trenchard, laid down that the central war aim of an air force was to attack an enemy's industrial cities and the war-willingness of their population: 'the points where defence is most difficult for him and where he is most vulnerable to attack'.[157] This ambition remained central to the air mission down to the onset of the wartime bomber offensive in May 1940 when it was integrated into the general blockade strategy. The formal blockade of enemy commerce by sea was also retained as a permanent option between the wars, and by 1937 planning was directed more specifically to a possible war with Germany. The Economic Pressure on Germany Committee was established in July 1937, and its deliberations on German economic weakness helped to shape the idea that economic warfare against Germany should become a major component of British grand strategy. A Ministry of Economic Warfare was temporarily activated at the time of the Munich crisis in September 1938. The title was deliberately intended to broaden the concept of economic warfare (a term first coined in 1936) from simple sea blockade, to include all possible forms of restricting German access to goods, finance and services, including offensive action as a 'fighting department'. These responsibilities eventually extended to defining and evaluating the economic targets for Bomber Command.[158] In September 1939 the ministry was formally established as an element in the machinery of Britain's war effort.

Western economic warfare was nevertheless potentially limited by legal
constraints on the use of submarines and aircraft against merchant shipping
and enemy industry. The 1936 London Submarine Protocol – agreed
between the major powers, including Germany and Japan – limited lawful
submarine attack to troopships, merchant ships in a convoy with naval
escorts, and any armed merchant ship that engaged in acts of war. Unrestricted submarine warfare was declared illegal. Merchant ships were
supposed to be brought to a halt, searched for contraband, and their crews'
safety respected. The same restrictions were applied to aircraft. Under British Air Ministry instructions issued in early 1940, only warships could be
attacked; if merchant ships were to be challenged from the air, the object
was to try to divert them from their intended course.[159] Since neither submarines nor aircraft could easily engage in the legal 'stop and search' policy,
their impact on economic warfare at sea was likely to be negligible. A similar issue faced the bombing of German targets. Instructions issued by the
government and the British Chiefs of Staff in 1939 declared all operations
illegal if they targeted civilians deliberately, if the targets were not readily
identifiable military targets (which meant no bombing through cloud or at
night), and if the death of civilians was likely to result from negligence.[160]

In both cases, the British government in the course of 1940 overturned
these restrictions. Bombing of industrial cities in Germany began in the
middle of May 1940 on the assumption that German forces had already
defied international law so blatantly that Britain was no longer bound to
observe it in the German case. By October all restrictions were lifted, paving the way for a strategy in mid-1941 that deliberately defined the civilian
population of industrial cities as a legitimate target.[161] The same reason-
ing was used with submarine warfare. Since Germany had evidently
adopted unrestricted submarine warfare – which was not quite the case –
there was no legal argument for not allowing unrestricted warfare against
German shipping. Beginning with the German campaign against Norway,
limited 'sink-on-sight' zones were established for British ships and aircraft. These zones were gradually extended over the following year, by
which time Axis shipping in general was subject to unrestricted warfare.
For the United States the legal issue was greatly simplified by the Japanese
operation against Pearl Harbor. The commanders at the stricken base
received a telegram six hours later: 'EXECUTE UNRESTRICTED AIR AND
SUBMARINE WARFARE AGAINST JAPAN.'[162]

Unrestricted economic warfare made its first appearance in the
Mediterranean theatre. On 13 June 1940 an Italian submarine sank a
Norwegian oil tanker without warning in an area of the sea the Italian
navy had designated as 'dangerous'. Italian minefields were apparently

laid without the formal declaration required under international law. In mid-July the British War Cabinet debated and approved the adoption of a 'sink-on-sight' instruction against Italian shipping, first off the Libyan coast, then 50 kilometres from the coast of any Italian territory. Submarines, surface vessels and aircraft were free to destroy Italian trade and the supply of military equipment and men to the fighting front in North Africa.[163] The British campaign nevertheless took time to materialize. In 1940 there were only ten submarines in the Mediterranean, all of them the older O- and P-class boats which were too large and dived too slowly for the shallower waters and clear visibility of the inland sea. Aircraft were too few and dedicated to the defence of Egypt. In 1941 the new T-class and smaller S- and U-class boats began to arrive in significant numbers, better suited to Mediterranean conditions. In October 1940 the British navy captured Italian submarine codebooks, and in June 1941 the Italian C38m cipher was broken, giving details of convoy sailings and routes.[164] Expanded air activity, more extensive mining, and surface forces dedicated to hunting convoys resulted in irreplaceable losses of Italian and German shipping (the latter loaned to the Italians but sailing under the German flag) and progressively destroyed the Italian merchant marine.

In the final dramatic few months between January and May 1943 Italian convoys braved the narrow channel between Allied minefields to supply Axis forces bottled up in Tunisia. They were battered from the air from nearby British and American bases and attacked by surface ships and submarines with scant chance of surviving unscathed. Italian seamen called it the 'death route'. Losses of naval vessels meant that there were never more than ten destroyer escorts available, working round the clock, and by February only five. By March and April 41.5 per cent of supplies ended up at the bottom of the sea; in May, shortly before the Italian surrender, the figure was 77 per cent. Over the lifespan of the 'death route' some 243 supply ships were sunk and 242 damaged.[165] Throughout the three-year campaign the Italian merchant marine was reduced by 2.8 million tons from the 3.1 million tons of Italian, German and captured tonnage available; a total of 1,826 ships and tankers were sunk, 42 per cent by submarines, 41 per cent by aircraft, and 17 per cent by surface vessels and mines.[166] The effect on the Axis war effort in North Africa was nevertheless mixed. Despite all the effort devoted to attacking the convoys, all but an estimated 15 per cent of supplies reached Africa. It was here, bottled up in small ports unused to the volume of goods, that ships and supplies were destroyed by relentless air attack from RAF units in the Middle East, or lost on the long vehicle routes to the front.[167] The problem was not the level of actual convoy losses at sea, but the growing shortage of ships to carry the goods. Thousands of tons were immobilized for repair in Italian shipyards that were short of resources. The peak monthly supply of goods to the North African front came between February and June 1941; by July to December 1942 the monthly average was only 62 per cent of the earlier figure while the force they were to supply was considerably larger.[168]

There is less room for dispute that the interruption of Italian merchant shipping contributed to the decline in Italian war production and short-ages of oil. The Allied blockade was directed not only at the traffic to Africa but also at the regular trade to Italian ports on which Italian indus-try depended for key materials and fuel, and the Italian population for supplies of food. The extent to which this was affected by the destruction or damage of Italian shipping has attracted less attention than the supply routes to Africa, and it is more difficult to demonstrate statistically. The armed forces estimated that 8.3 million tons of imported oil was needed each year, but the average delivered between 1940 and 1943 was 1.1 mil-lion; for copper and tin a requirement of 159,000 tons was met by average imports of 30,000 tons; for aluminium only 5,000 tons arrived per year instead of the 33,000 needed.[169] The supply of cotton and coffee in 1942 was just 1 per cent of the figure in 1940, wool was 4 per cent, wheat 11 per cent, iron and steel 13 per cent, and so on.[170] How much of these defi-ciencies was due directly to Allied economic warfare remains open to conjecture, but the loss by summer 1943 of 90 per cent of wartime ship-ping capacity tells its own story.

The conduct of economic warfare against Germany was on a signifi-cantly larger scale, and unlike the supply war in the Mediterranean was largely an air effort, pursued initially by RAF Bomber Command. From 1942 onwards it was joined by the United States Eighth Air Force, sta-tioned in Britain, and from late 1943 by the Fifteenth Air Force, based in southern Italy. The blockade of German sea traffic proved to be of limited use because of German access to the resources of occupied and neutral Europe. British submarines in northern European waters sank only 81 ships during the war, while Coastal Command aircraft accounted for a further 366, though many of these were light coastal vessels. Mines accounted for an estimated 638 more, mostly small boats.[171] Ocean-going merchant traffic to Germany was intercepted by British naval vessels in so-called 'contraband control' operations and war material impounded as prize cargo, but these cargoes soon declined in significance in the autumn of 1939. Blockade runners thereafter were few, some German, some Jap-anese, but a high proportion were sunk or impounded, and their strategic impact minimal. Even before the war, the denial of resources to the Ger-man war effort was deemed to be a strategy best conducted by attacks at source by long-range aircraft. In the months before the outbreak of war the British Air Ministry drew up the Western Air Plans, sixteen in number, a wish-list well beyond the capacity of Bomber Command to fulfil. The key plans were W. A. 5, 'Plans for attacking German manufacturing sources', including war industry in general, the Ruhr area, and German oil resources, and W. A. 8, for attacking German war stores by night. It was a fusion of the two plans that went into operation in mid-May 1940, once Churchill's new War Cabinet had given approval for night-time operations that would inevitably involve civilian casualties.[172] These early raids inaugurated a five-year campaign against the German home front and German production in occupied Europe, a campaign whose length and scale had scarcely been anticipated. Economic warfare from the air was expected by both the British and United States air forces to have an immediate impact, but, like the attrition war at sea, undermining economic resources proved to be a slow, frustrating and costly process.

In practice, Bomber Command was able to achieve almost nothing effective in the first two years of the campaign. Though Churchill threw his weight behind the offensive as the only way to bring the war home to the German people, the idea that German industry and communications could be heavily disrupted flew in the face of operational reality, and the evidence of the limited effect of German bombing on British output. Bomber Command had too few aircraft and no heavy bomber, lacked a modern bombsight or navigational aid, carried small-calibre high explosive bombs and few incendiaries, and faced a daunting number of anti-aircraft emplacements protecting the approaches to the key targets in western Germany. One Bomber Command pilot recalled that operations in 1940 against designated military-economic targets 'were pointless' when many crews could not even find the city they had been sent to bomb. A high proportion of bombs dropped on the open countryside; a significant number proved to be duds.[173] The failures were famously exposed when in August 1941 Churchill's scientific adviser, Frederick Lindemann, asked the young statistician David Bensusan-Butt to analyse 650 photographs taken by Bomber Command aircraft to measure accuracy. Butt found that only one in five aircraft got within 8 kilometres of the target, over the industrial Ruhr–Rhineland region only one in ten, and on moonless or misty nights, only one in fifteen. Two months later the Operational Research section of Bomber Command, recently inaugurated, found that autumn raids were even worse: only 15 per cent of aircraft bombed within 8 kilometres of the target.[174]

Even before the Butt Report the economic warfare strategy of Bomber Command had altered to take account of the problem that bombing in the current conditions was inherently inaccurate. From analysis of the impact of German bombing on Britain, the Air Ministry concluded that incendiary bombing was far more damaging than high explosive and should be given priority, and secondly that bombing the workers and their urban environment would be a more effective way of reducing enemy war production rather than fruitless attacks on a particular factory. In April 1941, a review of bombing policy recommended 'carefully planned, concentrated and continuous "BLITZ" attacks delivered on the centre of the working-class area of the German cities and towns'. Workers, it was argued by the director of Air Intelligence, were 'the least mobile and the most vulnerable to a general air attack'.[175] The Ministry of Economic Warfare at almost the same time concluded that economic warfare strategy would be more successful if directed at the destruction of 'workers' dwellings and shopping centres', rather than individual factories, and pressed the Air Ministry to adopt operations against whole cities.[176] Workers were transformed in British thinking into an abstract economic target. With this definition in mind, a fresh directive was issued to Bomber Command in July 1941 that three-quarters of operations should be against working-class and industrial areas, the rest when possible against transport targets. A second directive, on 14 February 1942, removed transport as a useful target (it had seldom been attacked with any success) and placed operations against the morale of the enemy civil population, and industrial workers in particular, as the primary objective. German industrial cities were zoned to highlight the vulnerable residential districts: 'Zone 1: central city area, fully built up; Zone 2(a): compact residential area, fully built up' down to 'Zone 4: industrial areas'. Bomber Command was expected to raid residential Zones 1 and 2(a) and to avoid wasting bombs on the more dispersed industrial zone.[177] The Ministry of Economic Warfare drew up a list of fifty-eight cities (the so-called 'Bomber's Baedeker') with an economic point score for each city based on an analysis of the number of key factories. Berlin had the highest key-point rating of 545; Würzburg, later destroyed in a firestorm, a key-point score of only 11. This was done not to encourage precision bombing, but to ensure that when an urban area was devastated many important producers would be affected by the death, injury and displacement of their workforce. The list was later extended to cover 120 cities. Following his appointment as Bomber Commander in February 1942, Harris kept the list with him and crossed through cities that he regarded as sufficiently obliterated. By April 1945, when the city-bombing finally ceased a few days before the German surrender, Harris had crossed through seventy-two of the cities on his list.[178]

The US Army Air Forces took a very different view of their economic warfare potential. In 1940, assisted by material produced by Air

Intelligence in Britain, the American air intelligence section drew up target folders on economic systems that they regarded as the most likely to undermine the German war effort decisively. When instructed by the War Department in August 1941 to draw up an air plan as part of Roosevelt's 'Victory Program', the analysts chose electric power, transport, fuel oils and morale (a tribute to British influence) as the primary targets of a strategic air offensive. Unlike all British planning, the American plan, AWPD-1, placed the German air force and its supporting industry and infrastructure as an essential 'intermediate target' whose destruction was sensibly regarded as the precondition for being able to destroy the other objectives effectively.[179] In 1942, as the Eighth Air Force was making its way across the Atlantic to bases in England, the initial plan was modified. In September 1942, AWPD-42 removed morale as a useful target, and added submarine production and synthetic rubber and aluminium as critical targets. The plans were precisely calculated, 154 individual targets in 1941, expanded to 177 in 1942.[180] Calculations were also made about the size of the bomber force necessary and the weight of attack. The assumption was that United States bombers, using an effective bombsight, could fly by day into Germany to launch precision raids on the plants identified as primary objectives. The American plan assumed that once the designated targets were destroyed the effect 'would be decisive and Germany would be unable to continue her war effort'.[181] The contrast with RAF night-bombing was institutionalized in the Combined Bomber Offensive finally agreed at the Allied Casablanca Conference in January 1943. The Pointblank Directive for the offensive, issued six months later, distinguished clearly between two forms of economic warfare – one based on specific industrial target systems attacked by day, the other on destroying by night-time raids the capacity and willingness of German workers to continue the war. These were separate but not incompatible strategies, though American air force leaders remained sceptical that the British offensive could achieve anything decisive in either political or economic terms. 'Morale in a totalitarian society is irrelevant,' concluded General Carl Spaatz, commander of American strategic air forces in Europe, 'so long as the control patterns function effectively.'[182]

For the first year the American Eighth Air Force experienced a difficult apprenticeship. The plans to immobilize the extravagant list of 177 specific targets proved to be impossible under prevailing conditions. The much-vaunted Norden bombsight turned out to be a poor tool for bombing from more than 4,500 metres; German industrial cities were regularly shrouded in cloud or industrial haze so that almost three-quarters of American bombs between 1943 and 1945 were dropped 'blind' using radar aids, little different from British area-bombing; and bombing by day without a fighter escort resulted in insupportable loss rates. Two major raids in August and October 1943 against just one key precision target, the ball-bearing works at Schweinfurt, resulted in a severe mauling of the bombers: 31 per cent were lost in the August raid, destroyed, heavily damaged or forced to fly on to North African bases; in October, 65 bombers were lost from a force of 229.[183] These rates could not be sustained and, until February 1944, the Eighth Air Force chose easier targets on the north German coast or in occupied Europe.

When the daylight offensive against German industry resumed in February 1944 it did so under very changed circumstances. Under the leadership of Spaatz, appointed commander of all the American strategic air forces in Europe in late 1943, and Major-General James Doolittle, who took command of the Eighth Air Force in January 1944, the economic war was made contingent on the military defeat of the German air forces defending German industry. This involved an economic dimension, since the aircraft industry was the priority industrial target. Between 19 and 26 February 1944 the Eighth Air Force in Britain and the Fifteenth Air Force flying from Italy undertook a wave of attacks against eighteen aircraft assembly plants in what was titled 'Big Week'. The damage was extensive but not yet critical. The real damage was done by the changed tactical picture. Like merchant ships at sea, the bomber convoys needed escort protection. From late 1943 American fighter aircraft – the P-38 Lightning, P-47 Thunderbolt, and the high-performance P-51 Mustang (powered by a British Merlin engine produced under licence in the United States) – were fitted with extra fuel tanks to allow them to penetrate far into German air space. Some protected the vulnerable bombers, but the fighters were also allowed to carry out 'freelance' operations, flying miles from the bomber stream to seek out enemy fighters, airbases and facilities. Despite very great increases in German fighter production during 1944, the attrition rate imposed by the aggressive American escorts proved disastrous. In February the German air force lost one-third of its fighter force, but by April the figure was 43 per cent of fighter strength.[184] The loss of experienced pilots could not be made good in time and training standards declined. This rate of loss proved insupportable, and, although aircraft production continued at a high level throughout 1944 despite the bombing, the German air force lost the contest for air superiority in German air space.

The defeat of the German air force allowed the American bomber forces to return to the economic war backed by a large expansion of bomber numbers. This time the wide range of target systems anticipated in the initial planning was abandoned in favour of an assault on German oil supplies. In March 1944 a report from the Enemy Objectives

Committee recommended oil as the most vulnerable target and one likely to have a significant effect on German fighting power in general. Although the bombing effort was supposed to be diverted to support the Allied invasion of France planned for June, Spaatz ordered the oil campaign to go ahead. In April devastating raids were made on the Romanian oilfield at Ploesti, the chief source of German natural oil. During May and early June heavy raids were made on the principal plants producing synthetic fuel and oil-refining facilities. Even though the great majority of bombs fell outside the target area, enough fell on the oil objectives to produce serious damage.[185] Aviation fuel output fell from 180,000 tons in March to 54,000 tons in June, and to 21,000 tons by October. Synthetic oil output was 348,000 tons in April, 26,000 tons by September. The decision to attack capital-intensive plant that could not easily be dispersed or concealed was extended to other basic chemicals needed for munition production. The output of nitrogen was reduced by three-quarters during 1944, that of methanol by four-fifths, soda by 60 per cent, sulphuric acid by 55 per cent, and so on. Synthetic rubber was added to oil as another key military resource and output here fell from 12,000 tons in March 1944 to 2,000 tons in November.[186] The cumulative effect was to erode remaining German stocks of key resources to levels that could not support continuous warfare for much beyond the spring of 1945.

The damage to the main oil and chemical plants was supplemented from September 1944 by a directive from Eisenhower to both the American and British air forces to focus on the bombing of communications as well as oil. Harris resisted any attempt to divert Bomber Command from bombing cities but did agree to area-bomb cities where there were also oil and rail targets. Most of the final campaign against designated target systems, including the continuous suppression of the German air force, was conducted by Spaatz. In economic terms, the wave of attacks launched against rail and canal targets from September 1944 onwards proved decisive. The Rhine waterway was blocked by a lucky strike on the Cologne–Mulheim bridge; the Mittelland Canal linking the Ruhr–Rhineland industrial region to central Germany was rendered virtually unusable in the last months of the year; out of 250,000 goods wagons available to the German railway, half were inoperable by November. Coal and steel could not be moved from the Ruhr and piled up at the railheads awaiting transport; total rail freight traffic declined by almost half between September 1944 and January 1945.[187] Germany was fragmented into economic zones where military output rapidly dwindled as resources dried up. In almost all the post-war interrogations of the officials and businessmen responsible for German war production, the decline of the transport system was highlighted as the principal explanation for economic crisis. By contrast, military leaders saw the loss of oil as the key element in the military collapse: 'without fuel,' observed Göring, 'nobody can conduct a war.'[188]

The post-war investigations of the economic war carried out by the United States Strategic Bombing Survey and the smaller British Bombing Survey Unit broadly confirmed the opinions extracted under interrogation. The surveys focused on the results of the economic warfare campaign rather than the political or military consequences. No attempt was made to disguise the fact that despite five years of bombing and 1.3 million tons of bombs, German war production had expanded significantly up to the autumn of 1944: fighter aircraft by a factor of thirteen, tanks by a factor of five, heavy guns by a factor of four.[189] The most rapid growth of output occurred precisely in the years when heavy and persistent bombing had become possible. No doubt without the bombing, more might have been produced, but bombing was only one of the factors affecting the performance of the war economy. The authors of the American 'Overall Report' calculated that bombing had cost the German economy 2.5 per cent of potential output in 1942, 9 per cent in 1943, and 17 per cent in 1944, when the American offensive against industrial targets finally became effective, although these statistics also included the output of non-war goods. The report, like the post-war interrogations, concluded that the oil campaign and the destruction of communications had been the chief factors undermining the German war effort, despite the fact that the report of the Survey's oil division showed that only 3.4 per cent of bombs aimed at oil installations actually hit the plant and pipelines, while 84 per cent landed outside the target.[190] The American report predictably argued that the British area-bombing campaign 'had little effect on production', but when the British Bombing Survey Unit compiled their report a year later the American assertion was proved broadly correct. A study of twenty-one industrial cities showed that area-bombing reduced output by only 0.5 per cent in 1942, and in 1944 by only 1 per cent. Output rose faster in the bombed cities than in fourteen unbombed cities which the survey also examined.[191] The British report concluded that the American strategy directed at transport had been the right choice. Area-bombing did destroy almost 40 per cent of the built-up area of Germany, and resulted in the deaths of more than 350,000 men, women and children, but even this unprecedented degree of damage did not prevent the upward trajectory of war output until autumn 1944.

The modest economic achievement of the bomber offensive until the assault on transport and oil can be explained by a number of factors. One of the economists drafted in to survey the German economy, Nicholas Kaldor, argued that modern industrial economies under wartime conditions had a degree of 'cushion' to absorb the impact of bombing. In Germany the cushion was partly supplied by the resources and labour extracted from occupied Europe, partly by rationalizing the system of war production, partly from the improvised dispersal of production.[192] The American economist J. K. Galbraith, also seconded to work on the survey, concluded that the German economy was 'expanding and resilient, not static and brittle', as Allied intelligence had suggested.[193] Even the strategy formulated in 1941 by the RAF and the Ministry of Economic Warfare that bombing would result in high absenteeism among a demoralized workforce failed in the end to materialize. Almost all heavily bombed cities returned to 80 per cent or more of their pre-raid output within three months, and to 100 per cent or more within six. In Hamburg after the firestorm in July 1943, over 90 per cent of the workforce was back at work by September.[194] In 1944, at the height of the bombing, absenteeism due to the raids constituted only 4.5 per cent of hours lost in industry, although rates were higher in targeted sectors such as submarine and aircraft production.[195] By this stage up to one-third of the workforce was composed of foreign forced labourers, who were compelled to work amidst the urban ruins and the raids. The chief cost to the German war economy came with the programmes of welfare and rehabilitation for bomb victims, and the labour lost through diversion to civil defence, rescue and repair. The extent to which this impeded the upward trajectory of war production before the destruction of the transport system is difficult to calculate statistically, and no attempt was made to do so in 1945, but it seems inherently unlikely that the post-raid resources would have contributed to raising war output to any significant degree had they been released.

The military cost to the Germans was much more substantial. By autumn 1944 80 per cent of the fighter force was concentrated in Germany for defence against bombing, while bomber production fell to only one-tenth of the number of fighters, leaving the fighting fronts denuded of both aircraft types. By 1944 there were 56,400 anti-aircraft artillery pieces in Germany, with output running at 4,000 guns a month; anti-aircraft armament consumed half the production of the electronics industry and one-third of the products of the optical industry.[196] This massive diversion of effort had not been anticipated by the Allies when the bombing began, but it resulted fortuitously in reducing the equipment available for German forces at the fighting fronts at the critical point of the war.

The economic war against Japan was, by contrast, a campaign fought principally at sea. The bases needed for heavy bombers to fly to the Japanese home islands became available only in late 1944 and early 1945, with the American capture of the Mariana Islands. Bombing as a strategy to undermine Japanese war production was only possible on any scale in the last six months of the Pacific war. The war at sea was a form of indirect economic warfare, denying the material resources for Japanese war industry, oil for the army and navy, and food for the Japanese population. This had been the intention of 'Plan Orange' but the assumption behind the original plan was an American presence in the western Pacific. The Japanese capture of the Philippines and American bases at Guam and Wake meant that any blockade would have to be conducted by submarine and by naval aircraft until such time that secure land bases and ports were again in American hands.

Japanese leaders understood that heavy dependence on imports, particularly from the areas conquered in the south Pacific and South East Asia, made it imperative to secure enough merchant shipping to compensate for possible losses. The Materials Mobilization Plans drawn up in 1941 and 1942 were based on the available supply of shipping, a factor that governed the development of the Japanese war economy down to 1945. Under the terms of the Wartime Ocean Shipping Control Order, published in March 1942, a Shipping Operation Committee was formed to control the requisition, movement and operation of all Japanese shipping.[197] Merchant shipping became a priority area of war production. The tonnage available in December 1941 was 5.2 million; by enlarging existing dockyards, building six large new yards, and standardizing the design and construction of boats, it proved possible to build an additional 3.5 million tons during the war.[198] For much of the war years the principal problem for the Japanese economy was the quantity of merchant shipping requisitioned by the army and navy to support operations across a vast expanse of sea, from the Aleutians in the far north Pacific to Burma in the Indian Ocean. The requirement to replenish troops and equipment was inexorable but the result was a level of military requisitioning that for most of the war left less than 2 million serviceable tons of civilian shipping to supply the home islands with food, materials and oil. The critical battle across the winter of 1942–3 on the island of Guadalcanal alone absorbed 410,000 tons of merchant shipping; for limited operations in Burma in June 1943, the military took away 165,000 tons of cargo space from the civilian sector.[199]

It took almost two years before United States forces could exploit the vulnerable state of Japanese overseas supply effectively. There were few submarines available in 1942 for the scale of the marine battlefield, and no clear strategy as to their use. For almost two years, the standard American torpedo suffered the same problem as the German, with regular failure of the magnetic and contact fuses. Over the war years it took 14,748 torpedoes to sink 1,314 merchant and naval vessels. In 1942 only 180 Japanese ships, totalling 725,000 tons, were lost.[200] But in 1943, under the command of Vice Admiral Charles Lockwood, with expanded bases at Pearl Harbor and the Australian ports of Freemantle and Brisbane, American submarines began to patrol the main supply routes around the Japanese Empire, hunting for merchantmen and oil tankers or, when possible, enemy naval vessels. That year a total of 1.8 million tons were sunk, and by the end of the year vessels sunk exceeded new replacements. Japanese import tonnage declined from 19.5 million tons to 16.4 million, a dangerous but not yet critical situation. The effectiveness of submarine operations was magnified by good intelligence from decrypts (also called Ultra in the Pacific), the development of radar detection, and the final development of torpedoes, the Mk XIV and Mk XVIII, that could sink a vessel more reliably with improved explosives and a more robust fuse. The submarine force was never large, but the standard American 1,500-ton fleet submarine was capable of ranges of up to 10,000 miles and carried supplies for 60 days at sea, both necessary conditions for the long trips across the Pacific. The heavy damage inflicted came from a force that by early 1944 still numbered only seventy-five boats. Over the course of the war the United States navy commissioned 288 submarines, a fraction of the number built by German industry for the war in the Atlantic.[201]

Despite the rapid decline of the merchant marine available – by the end of 1943 only 1.5 million tons remained for all non-military operations – the Japanese navy made few of the efforts the Western Allies had made in the Atlantic to protect their vulnerable overseas trade. Anti-submarine warfare was hampered by a lack of short-wave radar, which only became available in autumn 1944, and by a failure to work out the most effective tactics for using depth charges or radio direction finding. American submarine losses occurred most commonly when attacking more heavily escorted military supply convoys: fifteen were sunk in 1943, nineteen in 1944, but never enough to inhibit the long campaign of attrition against merchant shipping, which was the strategic priority. Only in 1943 did the Japanese begin regular convoys on the main routes, but priority was given to convoying supplies for the navy and army. A Grand Escort Fleet was established, supported by the 901st Air Squadron, but the ship and air escorts were spread too thinly to mount effective anti-submarine patrols. Most of the aircraft dedicated to anti-submarine operations were destroyed in 1944 by American carrier aircraft, while three out of four small escort carriers were sunk.[202] When in 1944 submarines were joined by aircraft in the hunt for merchant shipping, there was little the Japanese could do in response, and one after another major supply routes were

closed off. Iron-ore supplies shipped from the Yangtze River were interrupted by extensive mining, which reduced supply by three-quarters; the
flow of oil from the south was reduced from 700,000 tons a month to
200,000 by December 1944 and in February 1945 the oil route was suspended altogether.[203] Japanese improvisation was of little help. Materials
transported by rail to Chinese and Korean ports, rather than by sea, still
had to be shipped to the home islands with the risk of air and submarine
attack. Small vessels – junks and sampans – were requisitioned to increase
the tonnage available, and ships were built of wood to cope with the steel
shortage, but by 1944 American submariners were running out of useful
targets and began to sink even tiny vessels on the presumption that they
were carrying war goods, as many were.[204]

From November 1944 the American navy's air and sea campaign against
enemy shipping was joined by the army air forces' strategic bombing campaign against the Japanese home islands. Air force planners intended to add
the direct destruction of Japanese home industry to the effects of the wider
blockade but the early raids with the Boeing B-29 'Superfortress' were hampered by the difficulty of coping with the unanticipated weather conditions
over Japan (a powerful jet stream made accurate bombing from altitude
almost impossible) and the regular cloud and industrial haze over the target
cities, while the standard radar equipment developed from the H2X radar
used in Europe, the AN/APQ-13, failed to give a clear enough image of the
target area.[205] As in Europe, priority was given to destroying the aircraft
and aero-engine assembly plants, but by January 1945 not one designated
target had been hit effectively. These operational realities led to a revision
of priorities, as they had done in Britain in 1941. As early as 1943 the
American air force Committee of Operation Analysts had recommended
area attacks on Japan's six main industrial cities, deploying the same argument used by the RAF and the Ministry of Economic Warfare that industrial
workers and their milieu constituted a legitimate economic target, and it
was this recommendation, repeated as a priority in October 1944, that contributed to the decision to firebomb Japanese cities in spring 1945, beginning
with the Tokyo firestorm on the night of 10 March.[206]

Precision raids on aircraft plant continued through to the end of the war
when weather conditions permitted, but otherwise most of the subsequent
operations were area attacks. Unlike with the war in Europe, oil and communications were not singled out as potentially decisive. Instead, economic
intelligence on Japan suggested that production was widely dispersed into
small workshops concealed in the residential zones of the major cities. Area
incendiary attacks were designed to take account of the extreme flammabil-
ity of Japanese urban building, and their stated purpose was to kill or

disable workers, to destroy their housing and amenities, and to burn down the small workshops, all in the hope that the destruction would affect the productive performance 'at scores of war plants'.[207] General Curtis LeMay, commander of XXI Bomber Command stationed on the Mariana Islands, finally unleashed the incendiary raids at night from low altitude because the precision raids proved ineffective. He later defended the firestorms his force created on the grounds that this was the only way to cope with the Japanese strategy of industrial dispersal. 'All you had to do,' he wrote in his memoirs, 'was visit one of those targets after we'd roasted it, and see the ruins of a multitude of tiny houses, with a drill press sticking up through the wreckage of every home. The whole population got into the act and worked to make those airplanes or munitions of war . . .'[208] This proved in the end to be an unverifiable assertion, and both the Committee of Operation Analysts and the United States Strategic Bombing Survey, set up in the Pacific theatre in summer 1945, claimed later that home workshops were no longer widely used and should not have justified area attacks.[209] Nevertheless, the assertion gave an economic warfare gloss to what was in effect a lethal war on civilians and their urban environment.

It proved much more difficult than it had been in Germany to assess what impact strategic bombing had on the Japanese economy because by 1945 Japanese war production and the military effort were already close to collapse as a consequence of the tightening noose of the sea blockade, which reached its zenith in the year before Japan's surrender. The peak of Japanese munitions output was reached in September 1944 before the bombing started and could only be kept going by using up accumulated stocks of materials and cutting civilian consumption to the bone. Despite extensive new factory capacity and an expanding stock of machine tools, military production declined rapidly once the replenishment of materials from overseas dried up. The index of munitions output (1941 = 100) was 332 in September 1944, 156 by July 1945.[210] The import of bulk commodities fell to 10.1 million tons in 1944, half the figure for 1941, and in 1945 reached no more than 2.7 million tons. By the second quarter of 1945 there were only 890,000 tons of merchant shipping still available, but much of this was blocked in ports around the Sea of Japan as American submarines began to venture into Japanese home waters. As a supplement to the naval war, XXI Bomber Command began a mining campaign that deposited 12,000 mines around the Japanese coast, sinking a further 293 ships between March and August 1945. In total Japan lost 8.9 million tons of merchant shipping, or more than 90 per cent of the shipping made available between 1942 and 1945.[211] The loss of Japanese merchant tonnage and the effects on strategic imports are set out in Table 6.3.

Table 6.3 Japanese Merchant Shipping and Commodity Trade 1941–45 (1,000 m. tons)[212]

	1941	1942	1943	1944	1945
Merchant Shipping (grt)	5,241	5,252	4,170	1,978	1,547
Civilian, available for use	1,513	2,260	1,545	896	594
Merchant Shipping Built	210	260	769	1,699	503
Merchant Shipping Losses (grt)	–	953	1,803	3,834	1,607
Bulk Commodity Imports	20,004	19,402	16,411	10,129	2,743
Coking Coal	6,459	6,388	5,181	2,635	548
Iron Ore	6,309	4,700	4,298	2,153	341
Bauxite	150	305	909	376	15
Raw Rubber	67	31	42	31	18
Rice	2,232	2,269	1,135	783	151

Figure for merchant tonnage is the average for Oct.–Dec. each year, Aug. for 1945; commodity figures for 1945, Jan.–Aug. only; grt = gross registered tonnage.

The economic war took years of combat attrition but by the spring of 1945 Japanese industrial production and food supply were nearing exhaustion. There was little prospect that the economy could survive on a residue of industrial output much beyond the end of the year.

Economic warfare was by its nature a slow-burning strategy and its results ambiguous. 'You can't destroy an economy,' observed the British government scientist Sir Henry Tizard in a review of Britain's bombing campaign conducted in 1947.[213] And indeed, large modern industrial economies were more flexible in the face of attack than had been expected before the war. In all cases, there was an over-optimistic assessment of how rapidly and decisively economic warfare would work, particularly so in view of how little prepared for such campaigns the main belligerents were. The German air and sea blockade was supposed to finish British resistance in less than a year; both British and American air commanders hoped that bombing would unravel the enemy war effort within months. In practice, economic war worked best when very specific targets were selected that had a multiplier effect through the damage inflicted on the wider economy. This was the case with the successful assault on Japanese merchant shipping and the bombing of German oil and communications, but even in these cases the impact of economic war was felt very late, when both Germany and Japan were facing defeat on the military front for reasons other than the loss of economic resources. It is significant that the Soviet Union did not attempt to engage in economic war, partly because there was little opportunity given the geographical restrictions, but chiefly because Soviet military doctrine stressed the primacy of the battlefield and the defeat of the enemy's armed forces. The Soviet Union instead relied on mass production and Allied aid to create the economic conditions for victory. Even in the economic war, military conflict determined its course and outcome. The German blockade of Britain failed because of the defeat of the submarine arm by the Allied navies and air forces; the final success of the American bombing of Germany relied on the prior defeat and continued suppression of the German air force; the destruction of Japanese and Italian merchant tonnage was a consequence of years of small battles between warships, escort vessels and submarines. The front line of the economic war became, in effect, a military front line.

Economic warfare was also conducted at great cost to both sides. In the effort to deny resources to the enemy, ample resources had to be deployed. The bombing wars against Britain in 1940–41 and against Germany in 1940–45 diverted a significant proportion of military output, and in turn compelled the defender to allocate resources for air defence, even though in both cases the impact on the economy under attack was for much of the time limited or minimal. Bomber Command lost 47,268 killed in action, the American strategic air forces against Germany 30,099. The two bomber forces lost 26,606 aircraft between them.[214] The bombing war against the enemy economy and the morale of the workforce cost more than 650,000 German and Japanese civilian lives. German submariners were annihilated by the war, losing more than four out of every five of the men who had volunteered (and a remarkable 781 submarines) without in the end blockading the enemy successfully. Merchant seamen, who despite their civilian status were generally treated as if they were military personnel, suffered too. On British convoy routes, 29,180 seamen were killed; among Japanese merchant seamen total casualties ran to 116,000 killed, missing or incapacitated.[215] Despite their great success, American submariners experienced the highest loss rate in the United States armed services: 3,501 officers and men, or 22 per cent of the volunteer force.[216] At the same time thousands of bomber aircraft ended up as so much scrap on the ground and millions of gross tons of shipping sank to the ocean floor. Denying resources was consistent with the idea of total war, but in the end volume-production and the sharing of military goods proved to be the surer economic contribution to victory.

7

Just Wars? Unjust Wars?

'Moral and ethical questions have no validity in Total War except in as far as their maintenance or destruction contributes towards ultimate Victory. Expediency, not morality, is the sole criterion of human conduct in Total War.'

Dennis Wheatley, *Total War*, 1941[1]

Every combatant state in the Second World War thought that the war they fought was justified. They thought so for different reasons and with differing moral outlooks, but none of the participants had a guilty conscience. Justification for war was soon transformed into the belief that war must be just. The post-war literature has almost unanimously regarded the claims of the aggressor states to be fighting for a just cause as entirely spurious, but little sense can be made of the efforts of almost all populations to prosecute the war to the bitter end unless it is recognized that both sides believed right to be on their side. Both Axis and Allies made extensive efforts to persuade their peoples of the virtue of their cause and the vileness of the enemy and in doing so changed the conflict into a struggle of different versions of 'civilization', a struggle that had to be prolonged until complete victory had been sealed. Those who openly opposed the war on ethical grounds remained a tiny and isolated minority.

Dennis Wheatley, the popular British author whose view on wartime morality opens this chapter, was recruited in 1940 by the British military Joint Planning Staff to draft papers on the nature of a total war and its moral implications. His description might well have been appropriated by all the fighting powers at the height of the conflict. 'It must be clearly realized and it must be clearly stated,' wrote Wheatley, 'that Total War has only two possible alternatives for a Nation-at-War: they are Total Victory or Total Annihilation.' Under these stark circumstances, Wheatley concluded that any course of action that would shorten the war and achieve victory was morally justified 'irrespective of its "legal" or "illegal" implications'.[2] The absolute terms in which the Second World War was fought were historically unique. Regimes on both sides adopted the rhetoric of do or die, national extinction or national survival. The pursuit of victory at all costs was the moral cement that held the war effort together. Although the threat of complete annihilation was in most cases greatly exaggerated, the possibility supplied a ready moral imperative to compel absolute compliance with the war effort, and to justify the most extreme national exertion on both sides, Axis and Allied. The war for survival was everywhere viewed, by definition, as a just war, distorting the conventional legal and ethical description of the term which suggested that natural justice rather than Darwinian struggle ought to determine whether or not a war was just.

JUSTIFYING WAR

The absolute terms in which total war was defined had not been intended by the Axis aggressors in the 1930s when they began their imperial projects to seize territory in Asia, Africa and Europe. Their ambitions were regional and their justification for conquest rested on the assumption that they were each denied by the existing structure of world power a just share in the world's resources, and – in particular – adequate territory. Justice in this sense derived from a prior assumption that there were peoples fitted for empire, by reason of their racial and cultural superiority, and peoples fitted only to be colonized, a view evidently legitimated by the recent history of European expansion. The global order in the 1930s was regarded as illegitimate because it was designed to limit these claims; the wars of imperial conquest, from Manchuria in 1931 to Poland in 1939, promised to correct the injustice of denying vigorous peoples an outlet to empire and fairer access to the world's natural resources.[3] The Three Power Pact signed between the three Axis states in September 1940, assigning each a new imperial order in Europe, the Mediterranean basin and East Asia, declared that a lasting peace would be possible only once every nation in the world (that is, every 'advanced' nation) 'shall receive the space to which it is entitled', suggesting that the new order should be based on a firmer sense of international justice.[4] As one Japanese official complained, why was it regarded as morally acceptable for Britain to dominate India, but not for Japan to dominate China?

The pursuit of new regional empires was hesitant and improvised, not least because all three Axis states understood that their justification for aggressive expansion was unlikely to be endorsed by the wider world community. By the time war broke out in September 1939, the West had formed the view that Axis aggression was part of a larger plan to dominate the world, and the idea that the Axis were embarked on a global conspiracy of conquest became enshrined in the Allies' perception of the enemy down to the post-war trials of the major war criminals, in which conspiracy to wage aggressive war was a principal charge. The claim that the Axis, and in particular Hitler's Germany, sought 'world domination' was never clearly defined, but it was used as a rhetorical tool to maximize the menace posed by the aggressor states. In reality there was no coherent plan or deliberate conspiracy to achieve world domination, however it might be defined. Indeed, the Axis states saw the situation as the complete reverse. When their regional imperial ambitions were finally challenged by war in Asia and the Pacific from 1937 onwards and in Europe from 1939, they found that their justification for war had to be reconfigured as total wars of self-defence against the implacable hostility and naked self-interest of states that already enjoyed the fruits of empire, or abundant land and resources. In Germany, aggression against Poland was overshadowed by the British and French declaration of war, which was regarded as a renewed attempt to 'encircle' Germany and stifle its legitimate claims to imperial parity. The popular view in September 1939, recalled a young German, was that 'we had been attacked and we had to defend ourselves', and it was the Western powers who were engaged in conspiracy, not Germany.[5] Defence of the German core against its enemies became the overriding moral obligation on the German people, inverting the injustice of German aggression into a just war for national survival.

Such moral inversion was common to all the Axis states. In their view it was the Allied powers that were guilty of conspiring not only to limit their just claims to territory, but even to annihilate the national existence of the imperial core. Mussolini repeatedly claimed that Italy was imprisoned in the Mediterranean by the 'plutocratic powers' that colluded to deny the country its right as a civilizing power to *lo spazio vitale*, living space, where a new civilization could be founded. War was justified by the pursuit of empire.[6] In Japan, there was strong resentment that earlier Western willingness to involve Japan as an ally in the Great War, and to co-operate in imposing the 'unequal treaties' on China, had been transformed by the 1930s into strong prejudice against Japan's ambitions in Asia. Western support for China following the outbreak of the Second Sino-Japanese War was regarded as one element in a wider conspiracy that had taken shape since the occupation of Manchuria to frustrate Japan's rightful claim to empire. Among Japan's military, political and intellectual elite, this so-called 'white peril' threatened the very survival of the *kokutai*, the historic community of the Japanese, and with it the divine mission to bring the Asian people under the one roof of Japanese imperial protection. Japan's moral obligation, wrote Nagai Ryūtarō, was to 'overthrow the world-wide autocracy of the white man'.[7] Although the final decision to risk war with the United States and the British Empire had a solid military and economic rationale, it was expressed by Prime Minister Tōjō as a more fundamental defence of Japan's historic emperor-state against the threat that the West would create a 'little Japan' and end 2,600 years of imperial glory.[8] On the day of the Pearl Harbor attack, the government issued an 'Outline of Information and Propaganda Policies' that blamed the war on the West's 'selfish desire for world conquest'.[9] The ethical commitment of the Japanese people to total war was to be based on a similar inversion of reality to the German case, where aggression in China and the Pacific was transformed into a war of self-defence against encirclement by the white powers. In December 1941 the Japanese poet Takamura Kōtarō summed up the Japanese view of the conflict with the West:

> We are standing for justice and life,
> While they are standing for profits,
> We are defending justice,
> While they are attacking for profits,
> They raise their heads in arrogance,
> While we are constructing the Great East Asia family.

A year later the *Japan Times* reminded readers that the war of self-defence was 'absolutely just'.[10]

The most elaborate and pernicious conspiracy theory took hold in Germany. For Hitler and the National Socialist leadership, the real enemy conspiring to launch war against the German people was 'world Jewry'. From the outset of the European war in September 1939, Hitler coupled the war against the Western Allies with a broader war against the Jews. The national enemies were regarded as merely the instruments of a malign international network of Jews that conspired not only to frustrate Germany's rightful claim to an empire, but to annihilate the German people. This fantasy had firm pre-war roots. German defeat in 1918 had long been interpreted by the radical nationalist constituency as the consequence of an alleged stab in the back by Jewish defeatists and agitators on the home front. Hitler in his speeches in the early 1920s as leader of the tiny National Socialist Party broadened this allegation into a more apocalyptic 'life and death struggle', a real war 'between Jew and German'.[11]

Hitler and his fellow anti-Semites consistently viewed the conflict with the Jews in world-historical terms. For National Socialist propaganda, it was the Jews who sought 'world domination', not Germany; it was the Jews who sought world war, not the Germans. In 1936, years before the war, Heinrich Himmler, head of the SS and the later architect of the Jewish genocide, wrote that Germany's principal enemy was the Jew 'whose desire is world domination, whose pleasure is destruction, whose will is extermination ...' In November 1938 Himmler warned an audience of senior SS officers that if war broke out, the Jews would seek to annihilate Germany and exterminate its people: 'speaking German and having had a German mother would suffice.'[12] These two tropes, that the Jews wanted war with Germany and would conspire to provoke it, and that the Jews planned to exterminate the German – or 'Aryan' – people, made explicit the connection in the National Socialist mind between war and Jewish guilt. Hitler on 30 January 1939 finally chose to announce in public, in a speech to the Reichstag on the anniversary of his chancellorship, a notorious prophecy that if the Jews succeeded in plunging Europe once again into war (as they were alleged to have done in 1914), the consequence would be the annihilation of the Jewish race in Europe. Historians have been wary of taking this statement at face value, yet over the coming years Hitler returned again and again to the theme that behind the coming of war and its subsequent expansion lay the malign and deliberate efforts of 'world Jewry'.[13]

The intertwining of a war between states and a war with the shadowy conspirators of 'world Jewry' began from the very start of the conflict. In a radio speech to the German people on 4 September 1939, Hitler blamed the British and French declaration of war on a 'Jewish-democratic international enemy' which had harried the two Western powers into declaring a war they did not want.[14] The anti-Semitic *Weltdienst* journal went so far as to assert that the Seventh 'Protocol' on universal war in the fabricated *Protocols of the Learned Elders of Zion* (more than 150,000 copies of which had been sold in Germany) was realized in the Western declaration of war: 'Could the war plans of Jewry be more clearly expressed?'[15] When the head of the World Jewish Congress, Chaim Weizmann, publicly pledged support for the British cause later in September, the journal *Die Judenfrage* (*The Jewish Question*) told its readers that in Britain they faced 'the world enemy number 1: international Jews and the power-hungry, hate-filled world Jewry'.[16] The war of self-defence was two wars waged as one: war against the Allies, and war against the hidden Jewish enemy. The refusal of Britain to accept a peace agreement after the defeat of France was attributed to Jewish influence on Churchill (a regular theme). The attack on the Soviet Union, for which there were solid economic and territorial motives, was presented as a pre-emptive strike against an alleged Jewish plot between London and Moscow, an assertion that allowed German propaganda to play with an otherwise implausible alliance of plutocracy and Bolshevism.[17]

The final steps to global war, from the publication of the Atlantic Charter in August 1941 that signalled British–American collaboration, to the American entry into war in December that year, were publicly condemned by German leaders as final evidence, if evidence were needed, that Germany was the victim of a Jewish plot to annihilate the German people. When copies of a 100-page book, *Germany Must Perish*, self-published in the United States by the unknown Theodore Kaufman, reached Germany in July 1941, it was taken as definite proof that American leaders danced to a Jewish tune. The headline in the Party paper on 23 July trumpeted 'THE PRODUCT OF CRIMINAL JEWISH SADISM: ROOSEVELT DEMANDS THE STERILISATION OF THE GERMAN PEOPLE!' Following announcement of the Atlantic Charter on 14 August, the Party paper published the headline 'ROOSEVELT'S GOAL IS THE WORLD DOMINATION BY THE JEWS', while Hitler ordered that German Jews should now be forced to wear the yellow Star of David so that the German people would recognize for certain the enemy in their midst.[18] By the time Hitler declared war on the United States in a speech to the Reichstag on 11 December, it was taken for granted among the anti-Semitic faithful that the Jews had again conspired to push Roosevelt into war. On the day after Pearl Harbor, the daily press release for the German media claimed that the war in Asia 'is the work of the warmonger and world criminal Roosevelt, who as the acolyte of the Jews has striven ceaselessly for years together with Churchill for war.'[19] Rather than see American belligerency as the consequence of Japanese aggression, Hitler claimed in his Reichstag speech that 'It was the Jew, in his full satanic vileness' that explained it.[20] American entry into the war sealed the claim, repeated regularly in directives to the press from Hitler's press chief, that 'Bolshevism and capitalism are the same Jewish world deception only under different management . . .'[21]

The repeated emphasis on a Jewish world conspiracy to explain why Germany found itself in a war of self-defence against the threat of annihilation was evidently more than a rhetorical ploy to encourage the German people to see the war as a legitimate struggle for survival. That could have been achieved without reference to the Jews. The claims appear now – and must have appeared to many Germans at the time – as utterly preposterous, but it is difficult not to accept that Hitler and those around him actually wanted to believe them. The paradigm that was never questioned was the guilt of the Jews for German defeat in the First World War; the guilt of the Jews for the second war was established by analogy. The ish conspiracy became a powerful historical metaphor that allowed ___er and those around him to project their guilt for waging aggressive war onto the Jews. For the Party leadership and much of the rank and file, the Jewish conspiracy made explicable the unforeseen turn of events from the Anglo-French declaration of war, Britain's refusal to make peace in summer 1940, the necessary war with Russia, and American intervention in the war. 'To know the Jew,' claimed a propaganda circular for local Party speakers issued in autumn 1944, 'is to understand the meaning of the war.'[22] When Hitler dictated his final notes to Martin Bormann in the spring of 1945, he reflected that the role of the Jews explained why so many things had not gone as he had hoped. As early as 1933 'Jewry decided . . . tacitly to declare was on us'; peace with Britain was impossible 'because the Jews would have none of it. And their lackeys, Churchill and Roosevelt, were there to prevent it'; Roosevelt was not responding to the Japanese attack, but 'urged on by Jewry, was already quite resolved to go to war to annihilate National Socialism'. There had never been a conflict, Hitler concluded, 'so typically and at the same time so exclusively Jewish'.[23] Even with their captives after the war, Allied interrogators found the trope still alive, when it might prudently have been abandoned. Challenged by what he regarded as unfair accusations of anti-Semitism, Robert Ley, former head of the German Labour Front, wanted the Allies to understand why the Jews had been singled out: 'We National Socialists . . . saw in the struggles which now lie behind us, a war solely against the Jews – not against the French, English, Americans or Russians. We believed that they were only the <u>tools</u> of the Jew . . .'[24]

The alleged Jewish plot served to make the wars that Germany waged appear legitimate. The struggle between 'Aryan' and Jew was a struggle to the death and the moral responsibility of every German was to wage that struggle to the full. It served, too, to legitimize the shift to genocide in 1941; by painting the Jew as an enemy, at war with Germany, all Jewish communities became unwittingly militarized as irregular combatants, justifying their annihilation. By projecting onto 'world Jewry' the idea that Jews would exterminate Germans, the repeated public threats to annihilate, exterminate, destroy or root out the Jew appeared to be an entirely justified response, even a moral act in defence of the racial community. The real war and the fantasy war with the Jews created a terrible symbiosis in the mind of Hitler and his accomplices in genocide in which killing enemy soldiers and killing Jews attained a moral equivalence. Though the proximate cause for the shift from deportation and ghettoization to mass murder is still widely debated, the link between war seen by Hitler and his circle as a product of Jewish machination and what Himmler later called the 'iron reason' of extermination appears self-evident.[25] However improvised the final shift to mass killing, the explanatory framework that shaped the regime's view of the war was an essential precondition. Writing in his diary in May 1943, when the majority of Jewish victims had already been killed, Joseph Goebbels reflected that 'None of the Führer's prophetic words has come so inevitably true as his prediction that if Jewry succeeded in provoking a second world war, the result would be not the destruction of the Aryan race, rather the wiping out of the Jews.'[26]

The obsession with the fight against a world Jewish conspiracy had implications for the way Germany's allies, Italy and Japan, responded to the 'Jewish question'. For Japanese leaders, the absence of long contact with Jewish communities meant that they were largely neutral about the issue. Two dedicated anti-Semites, Colonel Yasue Norihiro for the army (who translated *The Protocols of the Learned Elders of Zion* into Japanese) and Captain Inuzuka Koreshige for the navy, were employed in the 1930s to study Jewish affairs, but although Inuzuka could describe Jews as a 'cancer in the world' neither he nor Yasue developed a coherent view of Jewish conspiracy, or enjoyed wide influence. Both hoped to exploit the 20,000 Jewish refugees from Europe, resident chiefly in Shanghai, to gain access to Jewish finance and to improve relations with the United States. When that prospect disappeared with the signing of the Three Power Pact with Germany and Italy, the official Japanese treatment of the Jewish refugees became more restrictive, but there was nothing in common with German treatment. A Jewish settlement was established in Shanghai for all refugees and although conditions were far from ideal, it did not operate like the ghettoes and camps in Europe and anti-Semitism did not become a theme of wartime propaganda.[27]

The situation differed in Italy, where racial laws against Jews were introduced in 1938 independent of any German pressure, creating the basis for a harsh regime of Jewish apartheid, but even here it was not until the founding of Mussolini's Italian Social Republic late in 1943 that Fascist justification for war came to include more explicitly the idea of a war against a Jewish world enemy, inspired by the rabidly anti-Semitic ex-priest Giovanni Preziosi (who published his translation of *The Protocols* in 1921). In the 'Verona Manifesto' drawn up by Mussolini's new republic in 1943, the Jews were identified specifically as an 'enemy nation'.[28] Propaganda posters used anti-Semitic images to brand Allied leaders as stooges of world Jewry. Fascist newspapers declared, along with allegations of spying and terrorism, that Jews were 'the greatest supporters of this war' and that Jews were 'pursuing a crazy project of world domination', but the propaganda was not systematic or linked, like Hitler's world view, to a central idea of conspiracy. Jews were blamed much more for 'treachery' in the overthrow of Mussolini in summer 1943, posing a domestic threat rather than an international one.[29]

For the Allies there was no necessity to pretend that wars of aggression were just wars of self-defence against an external menace, racial or otherwise. The justice of the Allied cause was taken for granted. Nevertheless, self-defence was a complicated argument for the British and French governments because they had declared war on Germany, not the other way around, and until September 1939 neither state had been directly threatened by German aggression. Self-defence was presented in these two cases as defence in a more generic sense against the territorial ambitions and naked violence of the Third Reich, which had to be stopped before German expansion really did challenge Western interests face to face. The defence of Poland was a subsidiary concern, one that neither state seriously contemplated before Poland was defeated; declaring war on Poland's behalf was nevertheless enough to put both France and Britain in the front line against German armed forces, and this confrontation was easily transformed into the rhetoric of self-defence once Hitler had decided that attack was preferable to a perfectly feasible defensive stand-off. The other Allied powers, major and minor, could present themselves unambiguously as the victims of unprovoked aggression waging wars of self-defence. There were, Stalin announced in his annual November speech in 1941 commemorating the Revolution, 'two kinds of war: wars of conquest, and consequently unjust wars, and wars of liberation, or just wars.'[30] The defence of the Motherland against fascist aggression became the central ambition in Soviet wartime rhetoric. The concept of the 'Great Patriotic War', the term used in the Soviet Union throughout the conflict, was coined in the official Party newspaper *Pravda* only a day after the opening of hostilities, on 23 June 1941.[31] In the United States, the attack on Pearl Harbor had an electrifying effect on American opinion, which had been sharply divided between isolationists and interventionists up to December 1941. The cement that held together an unlikely alliance of divergent political forces was the unequivocal commitment to defending the United States against what Roosevelt called 'powerful and resourceful gangsters', bent on enslaving the human race.[32] Self-defence was in all these latter cases consistent with the just war tradition.

The Allied states had no difficulty making a moral case for waging war. On 3 September 1939, Neville Chamberlain ended his radio broadcast on the British declaration of war with a clear statement of the case: 'It is evil things that we shall be fighting against – brute force, bad faith, injustice, oppression and persecution – and against them I am certain that the right will prevail.'[33] Stalin, in his 1941 commemorative speech, told his audience that the Germans' 'moral degradation' had reduced them 'to the level of wild beasts'. In 1942, Roosevelt, facing all three Axis enemies, defined America's war as a fight 'to cleanse the world of ancient evils, ancient ills'.[34] The same year Chiang Kai-shek, on the fifth anniversary of China's long war against Japan, announced that the Chinese people were also fighting a war 'between good and evil, between right and might' that gave China a position of 'moral ascendancy'.[35] Waging war against enemies perceived as irretrievably immoral provided a powerful negative justification for war throughout the ensuing conflict. The assumption of enemy wickedness rested on the evidence of the 1930s during which the Western states, while taking little action, had nevertheless deplored the violent expansion and repressive authoritarianism of the Axis states. The moral contrast was taken for granted by the time war broke out and the prevailing language of moral condemnation was mobilized remorselessly to provide a consistent narrative in which overcoming a wicked enemy justified any means used to achieve it. When the British War Cabinet debated in mid-May 1940 whether or not to allow bombing of German targets in which civilians would be killed, Churchill argued that the long catalogue of German crimes gave 'ample justification' for the operations.[36] For the British public, loathing for the German enemy gave the contest an almost biblical character. The pacifist author A. A. Milne dropped his objection to war in 1940 because fighting Hitler was 'truly fighting the Devil, Anti-Christ'. Another lapsed pacifist, the theologian Reinhold Niebuhr, thought that history had never presented decent men 'with a more sharply defined "evil"'.[37] In the United States, the semi-official narrative, captured in the first of Frank Capra's film series *Why We Fight*, began with a trailer claiming that the documentary was the greatest gangster movie ever made: 'More vicious ... more diabolical ... more horrible than any horror-movie you ever saw.'[38]

Forging positive justifications for war was more complex. Dennis Wheatley observed in *Total War* that, despite the near universal belief that Britain's war was just, there was what he called 'a lamentable lack of mental ammunition' on Britain's positive war and peace aims.[39] In the United States, Archibald MacLeish, the man chosen by Roosevelt to run part of the government's information service, wrote a memorandum in April 1942 trying to puzzle out what would provide an affirmative view of the war: '1. Should this war be presented as a crusade? 2. If so, a crusade for what? What do men want? a. Order and security? World order, etc.? b. Better life? 3. How do you get those things?'[40] The positive narrative on the moral nature of the conflict was in the end provided by the trope that the Allies were saving civilization and humanity from the barbarity and destructiveness of the Axis enemy. For Britain and France in 1939, the hubristic claim that they were defending civilized values reflected profound fears among the intellectual and political elite of both countries that the crisis of the 1930s posed by economic collapse, political authoritarianism and militarism might indeed mean that civilization as the West understood it was genuinely imperilled.[41] Hitler and Hitlerism became the lightning rod for a range of Western anxieties, so that war with Germany in 1939 was not simply about restoring a balance of power, but a fundamental contest to decide the future fate of the world. These were very grand terms. 'Our responsibility,' wrote the British MP Harold Nicolson late in 1939 in *Why Britain is at War*, 'is magnificent and terrible.' Britain, he continued, is fighting for its very life, but would also fight to the war's bitter end 'in order to save humanity'.[42] The same rhetoric was mobilized in France. Édouard Daladier, the French premier, in a speech to the French Senate in December 1939 explained that while fighting to the utmost for France, 'at the same time we are fighting for other nations, and, above all, for the high moral standard without which civilization would be no more.' The war was seen by definition as a just war, because, as the French philosopher Jacques Maritain put it in 1939, 'it is for the elementary realities without which human life ceases to be human.'[43]

There were nevertheless ambiguities in the way the British and French war to defend civilization was presented. There was criticism that the claims were too grandiose and too vague for populations that wanted definite promises for the post-war world of a better and more secure future. Civilization itself was seldom defined, on the assumption that Western publics would understand what it implied without having to interrogate the term too closely. Much of the rhetoric stressed the democratic way of life and the survival of conventional liberties, but there was an awkward contrast between those who saw the war as a form of crusade to save 'Christian civilisation', and those who took a more secular view of what modern civilization represented. Although Churchill used the term 'Christian civilisation' in his famous speech in June 1940 after the fall of France, announcing the coming 'Battle of Britain', he seldom expressed Britain's war aims in religious terms. Christian writers in both Britain and France were critical of any claim to be rescuing Christian civilization because of the extent to which Christian values had already evidently lapsed among Western populations.[44] In February 1945, an 'Appeal Addressed to All Christians' circulated in Britain by the Bombing Restriction Committee asserted that there existed 'a deeply distressed, widespread and unexpressed Christian conscience against the pursuit of victory by unlimited violence'.[45]

Above all there was the awkward double standard in the constant repetition that the two allies (together with the British white Dominions) were defending democratic values, when they both controlled large colonial empires in which they had little intention of instituting these values either during or after the war. The reality in 1939 was that both Britain and France went to war to defend not simply the democratic motherland but the wider empires as well. Without the empire, Nicolson wrote, Britain would lose not only 'her authority, her riches and her possessions; she would also lose her independence.'[46] Churchill throughout the war remained steadfast in his belief that the British Empire should long outlast the end of the conflict. The result was a persistent wartime tension between the claim to be defending democratic civilization and the desire to sustain British imperialism. While committed to saving Western democracy and the liberties of their citizens, colonial governance rested on a denial of those liberties and the repression of any protest against the undemocratic nature of colonial rule. The wartime propaganda on the significance of empire unity suggested that the colonial areas shared a common sense of moral purpose with the motherland, but this claim masked a less certain historical reality. 'The victory of the Allies,' claimed a Labour pamphlet in 1940, 'would mean the consolidation of the greatest Empire in the world, the Empire that taught the Nazis the use of concentration camps, the Empire in whose prisons men like Gandhi and Nehru have spent great parts of their lives ...'[47] India was an obvious wartime example. In autumn 1942, when Mahatma Gandhi launched the 'Quit India' movement in protest at the failure of the British government to offer the prospect of post-war self-government to India, thousands of Indian nationalists were imprisoned and hundreds killed when troops and police opened fire on protesters. The African American theologian Howard Thurman thought that Gandhi had 'reduced to moral absurdity' the British claim to 'fight a war for freedom'.[48]

In the United States, the initial uncertainty about how to present the war other than as a war of defence was gradually replaced by an unambiguous internationalism driven by Roosevelt's own view that defined liberties should be enjoyed by the wider world after victory. His moral commitment to create a better world was already in place well before the United States was forced into war. In January 1941, he defined what he saw as the essential freedoms – freedom from want, freedom from fear, freedom of religious conviction and freedom of speech. The Four Freedoms became the foundation stone of the public American wartime narrative about why the war was fought. They were illustrated by the artist Norman Rockwell and the four paintings were reproduced endlessly throughout the war; in 1943 2.5 million leaflets were distributed using the four pictures as an incentive to buy war bonds.[49] Two of the four freedoms were enshrined in Roosevelt's second pre-war statement of moral intent, the Atlantic Charter. The document was the fruit of the first summit meeting between Roosevelt and Churchill in Placentia Bay, Newfoundland, between 9 and 12 August 1941. It was at best an accidental statement, since neither Roosevelt nor Churchill had arrived for the meeting primed to produce it, though the president hoped that it might happen. Neither statesman had disinterested motives. For Roosevelt, making a statement of some kind was designed to strengthen the hand of domestic interventionists; for Churchill and the British government it was hoped that a statement, however non-committal, would indicate that the United States was publicly behind the Allied cause and might be drawn into full belligerency.[50]

The Charter itself was simply a list of eight statements of intent expressed in lofty internationalist language, consistent with much of Roosevelt's rhetoric on his hopes for a better world. The 'common principles' in the Charter included a desire for post-war disarmament, freedom of the seas and economic justice for victor and vanquished. The third statement was the most significant: 'the right of all peoples to choose the form of government under which they will live.' There was no explanation of how these might be achieved beyond defeat of 'the Nazi tyranny'.[51] The British reaction to the Charter was muted. Churchill especially was unwilling to apply the principles to the Empire. The Charter, he told the House of Commons on his return, was not 'applicable to coloured races in colonial empire' but only to the states and nations of Europe.[52] Stalin associated the Soviet Union with the Charter merely as a gesture of goodwill towards Allies already supplying the Soviet war effort. In China, the Atlantic Charter was regarded by Chiang Kai-shek as too exclusively European in intent, although he decided to interpret 'Nazi tyranny' loosely so as to include Japan. In January 1942 Chiang asked Roosevelt formally to apply the Charter to the peoples of Asia under colonial rule; disappointed, he again asked at a summit conference with Roosevelt and Churchill in Cairo in November 1943 for a Charter that applied to the whole world, but without success.[53]

Roosevelt nevertheless allowed the Charter to become a central reference point once the United States was in the war. It signalled American commitment to a more moral post-war order that served not only American interests but had global implications. In a 'fireside chat' broadcast in February 1942, Roosevelt told his American audience that in his view the Charter did apply not just to the states bordering the Atlantic but to the whole world, and he added the establishment of the 'Four Freedoms' as an Allied principle, though only fear and want had been included in the

Charter.[54] By this point Roosevelt had, with Churchill's grudging acceptance, renamed the Allied powers the 'United Nations' and invited them all to sign a Declaration, published on 1 January 1942, that reaffirmed the principles laid down in the Charter. This did not yet amount to an endorsement of a post-war international organization, since Roosevelt was hesitant to suffer what Woodrow Wilson had endured with American rejection of participation in the League of Nations. But by January 1943, he was fully persuaded by the State Department that American global interests could best be defended through a new international assembly to promote peace and human rights.[55] Roosevelt's object was to ensure that the Allies formally occupied the moral high ground whatever contradictions or ambiguities existed in uniting democracies, imperial powers and authoritarian dictatorships in a common endeavour. The call for unconditional surrender made at the Casablanca Conference in January 1943 underscored the ethical commitments made in the Charter and the Declaration by making it clear that there could be no agreement with states regarded as morally degraded. In January 1942, Roosevelt had already put on record, in his annual State of the Union address, his conviction that 'there never has been – there never can be – successful compromise between good and evil', a contrast that allowed the Allies to set aside any moral scruples they might have in the conduct of the war.[56]

As the war turned against the Axis, they made greater efforts to find a way to present their own justification for war in more international terms. German propaganda from 1943 onwards argued that the war of self-defence was a war to save European civilization from Bolshevik barbarism. Japanese propaganda sought to portray Japan as the saviour of Asia from the return of white oppressors. Neither claim was credible in the face of imminent defeat. By 1945 both states fought a final desperate struggle to avoid what they saw as the real prospect of national extinction. The major advantage enjoyed by the Allies in their public justification for war was the adoption of a language of universal rights, while the Axis claims were always for the defence of a particular people and its right to territorial conquest. This contrast was institutionalized in the military tribunals set up in Nuremberg in 1945 and Tokyo in 1946 (though not in Italy, which by 1945 had become an Allied co-belligerent). Churchill and some of his Cabinet had favoured declaring German leaders to be outlaws who could be executed as soon as they were properly identified.[57] But both the United States and the Soviet government wanted a formal trial so that the wartime claims of Axis wickedness and Allied justice could be publicly displayed for world opinion.

In both sets of trials the principal charge was the waging of aggressive war. Since waging war was not formally contrary to international law, the Allied prosecutors used the Kellogg–Briand Pact of 1928 which sixty-two states eventually signed, including all the major states later involved in the war. The pact was supposed to commit signatories to abandon war as an instrument of policy or be regarded as an 'offender against the Law of Nations'.[58] Although it was treated more as a statement of moral intent than an instrument of international law, it was considered to be robust enough for the case against German and Japanese leaders. The American chief prosecutor, Robert Jackson, opened the Nuremberg Trial on behalf of an undefined 'civilization' against defendants who were accused of perpetrating calculated, malignant and devastating crimes against the rest of the world. For all the many procedural and judicial problems presented by victors' justice, the trials were intended to define wars that were unjust and wars that were just. In December 1946 the principles enunciated at Nuremberg were enshrined in international law by the United Nations Organization, successor to the informal wartime United Nations, as a set of seven 'Nuremberg Principles', which are still in force in the twenty-first century.[59]

NOT SUCH A 'GOOD WAR'

The Axis states understood that in the eyes of most world opinion they occupied the moral low ground. But they were sceptical of the Allied assertion of moral ascendancy. In April 1945, shortly before German defeat, Hitler poured scorn on the 'puerile' claims of the United States to superiority, 'a kind of moral *vade mecum*, which is based on lofty but chimerical principles and so-called Christian Science.'[60] Japanese commentators contrasted the democratic rhetoric of the West with the reality of colonial oppression or domestic racism and delighted in reporting every act of imperial repression in India and every lynching or race riot in the United States as evidence of British and American hypocrisy. One newspaper expressed a common view in Japan of American 'barbarism': 'If one considers the atrocities which they committed against the American Indians, the Negroes and the Chinese, one is amazed at their presumption in wearing the mask of civilization . . .'[61] Critics on the Allied side were equally dismissive of what was regarded as special wartime pleading to cover over the moral ambiguity of Allied rhetoric. W. E. B. Du Bois, the veteran campaigner for civil rights in the United States, claimed after the war that 'There was no Nazi atrocity – concentration camps, wholesale maiming and murder, defilement of women or ghastly blasphemy of childhood – which the Christian civilization of Europe had not long been practicing against colored folk in all parts of the world.'[62] Above all, the Allied insistence that the post-war trials were a showcase for Axis crimes against humanity and crimes against peace raised the awkward question of how the Western states could make common cause with the savagely repressive dictatorship in the Soviet Union which had conspired with Germany to tear up the post-1919 settlement in Eastern Europe. The apparent incompatibility of an alliance between the two major capitalist states and the one communist one nourished Axis fantasies until the end of the war that the Grand Alliance would fall apart.

One of the remarkable consequences of the unexpected alliance between the Western Allies and the Soviet Union was the capacity of all three major states to set aside for the duration of the conflict the profound political and moral differences between them. Until the outbreak of the German–Soviet war, the Western powers treated the Soviet Union as little better than Hitler's Germany, and regarded communism, at home and abroad, as a profound threat to the democratic way of life and to democratic values. The German–Soviet Pact of August 1939, followed by the Soviet invasion of eastern Poland in September, and then aggression against Finland in late November 1939, reinforced the view that the dictators were two of a kind. Although there was sympathy for the Soviet experiment in both Britain and the United States among circles regarded as progressive, the prevailing view deplored a regime that could indulge in mass terror, commit acts of aggression, and collaborate with the fascist enemy. With the invasion of Finland, the Soviet ambassador to London, Ivan Maisky, observed a 'frenzied anti-Soviet campaign' among public and politicians. 'The question,' he wrote in his diary, is 'who is the No. 1 enemy? Germany or the USSR?'[63] He watched the angry parliamentary debate about the armistice forced on Finland in March 1940 during which MPs displayed '<u>fury</u> ... vivid, seething, overflowing fury'.[64] Finland proved a turning point for Roosevelt too, and for many pro-Soviet liberals. Stalin's Soviet Union, the president told an audience late in 1939, was 'a dictatorship as absolute as any other dictatorship in the world', and he called for a moral embargo on American export of arms and equipment to meet Soviet needs. He deplored what he called 'the dreadful rape of Finland'.[65] A brief 'Red Scare' revived in the United States, but popular hostility to communism was directed more at the Soviet system and at Stalin himself, who was, claimed the Catholic archbishop of Washington, 'the greatest murderer of men the world has ever known'.[66] The international community signalled its moral disapproval by expelling the Soviet Union from the League of Nations on 14 December 1939. There was

serious planning in the spring of 1940 in London and Paris for the possibility of conflict with the Soviet Union alongside its new German ally.
Roosevelt worried that a German–Soviet victory in Europe would imperil
civilization.[67]

If the Western world regarded the Soviet Union as morally beyond the
pale, Soviet leaders were equally harsh in their judgement of the capitalist
world beyond Soviet borders. The moral universe they inhabited was
divorced from the values of the liberal West, veiled in a language that
inverted historical reality. Stalin for years before the outbreak of war in
1939 assumed that at some point the capitalist states were bound by historical necessity to try to destroy the Soviet experiment. Repeated war
scares, irrational though they proved to be, kept alive the idea that capitalism was the principal threat to peace and bourgeois leaders the agents
of an immoral class repression.[68] From this perspective the pact with Hitler in August 1939 could be justified by the regime as the means to
frustrate bourgeois plans to turn German aggression against the Soviet
Union, just as the conclusion of the war with Finland was explained to the
Communist faithful as 'a victory for the Soviet Union peace policy'
because it pre-empted alleged British and French plans for a global war
against the Soviet–German alliance.[69] The war in the West was presented
as an imperialist war waged by the British and French ruling classes. The
British Communist Party was informed from Moscow that it was not
fascist Germany but 'anti-Soviet England, with its enormous colonial
empire, which is the bulwark of capitalism'. The 'liberation' of the working people of eastern Poland in September 1939 showed, by contrast, that
the Soviet Union was 'a powerful bulwark for all peace loving forces'.
During the period of the German pact, the Soviet line consistently maintained that the major enemy was British imperialism, while Germany was
regarded as a cause for peace, forced into defensive aggression by the
imperialist powers. In late 1940 Stalin even considered the possibility that
the Soviet Union might adhere to the Three Power Pact, signed by the
Axis powers in September.[70] Communist parties everywhere toed the
Party line. The British *Daily Worker*, on the day before it was closed down
by the government in January 1941, celebrated the fact that the masses
everywhere were 'seeking the way out of the imperialist war' through the
means of Leninist class struggle.[71]

The moral condemnation expressed by both sides evaporated with the
Axis invasion of the Soviet Union on 22 June 1941. Maisky noted a few
days after the attack that the British public was bewildered by the change:
'only recently "Russia" was considered a covert ally of Germany, all but
an enemy. And suddenly, within 24 hours, it has become a friend.'[72]

Churchill famously broadcast on the evening of 22 June his support for the struggle of the Russian people, though he added the caveat that he would take nothing back from his long and consistent opposition to communism. For Churchill, as for many in the West, Hitler was the world's greatest menace: 'Any man or State,' Churchill continued, 'who fights against Nazism, will have our aid.' Roosevelt shared the view that the German threat was immediate and greater and set aside his moral concern with Soviet aggression. In one of his regular 'fireside chats' to the American radio audience he claimed that no insoluble differences separated the United States and the Soviet Union: 'we are going to get along with him [Stalin] and the Russian people very well indeed.'[73]

In Moscow, the outbreak of war brought an immediate end to the campaign against imperialist capitalism. On the day of the invasion Stalin told the head of the Comintern, Georgi Dimitrov, that the new line was 'a matter of routing fascism' and all mention abroad of socialist revolution was to be abruptly ended. By turning the war into 'a defensive war against fascist barbarism', Soviet leaders hoped that the powerful wave of Western anti-fascism would immediately identify with the Soviet struggle and lend support.[74] In the end, both sides were prepared to use Beelzebub to drive out the German Satan. The resulting collaboration was never easy for either side, but it was driven by military necessity, and by the hope that perhaps communism and capitalism could find some common ground in building a peaceful post-war order.[75] The Soviet view of the West was soured by arguments over a Second Front in Europe and the pace of Lend-Lease deliveries; Western goodwill was tested by the many petty restrictions placed on their personnel in the Soviet Union and by the growing evidence that Soviet leaders intended to introduce 'democracy' in Eastern Europe on communist terms. Neither side entirely trusted that the other would not reach some agreement with Hitler. But Western leaders turned a blind eye, at least in public, to the record of Soviet aggression between 1939 and 1941 and to Soviet political repression at home and abroad because the central moral imperative shared by all three was the defeat of Germany.

The willingness of Western leaders to embrace the Soviet Union as a partner and ally was underpinned by a wave of popular support in both Britain and the United States for the Soviet war effort. Some of that enthusiasm was generated by official propaganda, both Western and Soviet. In Britain, this raised awkward questions about how to popularize the Soviet war effort without endorsing its ideology. This was achieved, as Churchill had done in his speech of 22 June, by talking of 'Russia' rather than the Soviet Union. The British Political Warfare Executive, in charge of political propaganda, was instructed to speak 'whenever possible of the "Russian

Government" instead of the "Soviet Government"' and to ensure that exhibitions and speeches stressed Russian history, arts and character, but avoided Russian politics.[76] In the United States, the Office of War Information, staffed by liberals generally more favourable to the Soviet experiment, created an idealized, sentimental image of the Soviet Union for the American public, reinforced by feature films that played on Russian heroism – *The North Star*, *Counter-Attack*, *Song of Russia* – and by the mass media. *Life* magazine in March 1943 told readers that the Soviet people 'look like Americans, dress like Americans and think like Americans', and made Stalin 'man of the year'.[77] The Soviet propaganda effort in the West played on this sentimental view of Russia and the image of Stalin as a man committed to peace and democracy, a view swallowed uncritically by the Western public whose knowledge of Soviet realities was gleaned entirely from the propaganda image. When the bishop of Chelmsford, president of the National Council for British–Soviet Unity, opened a congress in London in November 1944, he talked of the Allies as the 'three great democracies'. A second churchman at the congress spoke of the 'truly religious achievements of the Soviet Government' and the great contribution the Soviet regime had made 'to the ethical side of life'.[78]

Much popular support was nevertheless spontaneous, an exuberant celebration of Soviet resistance to the Axis invasion in contrast to the limited military successes of British and American arms. The recapture of Stalingrad was treated as if it had been a Western victory. Maisky noted in his diary in February 1942 'rapturous admiration' for the Red Army, 'fervent Sovietophilia' in June that year, and after Stalingrad universal delight, 'unreserved and unrestrained'.[79] In Britain committees and groups for 'friendship and aid' were established across the country from 1941 onwards; by 1944 there were more than 400 of them, organized under the umbrella of the National Council for British–Soviet Unity. It was estimated that around 3.45 million people were represented by organizations working for the Soviet war effort and Soviet amity.[80] In the United States the Committee for Soviet–American Friendship played a similar role in mobilizing popular enthusiasm, expressed across America with flag days, travelling exhibitions and fundraising committees. In both countries to be anti-Soviet was now treated as an act of bad faith, even treasonable. The House Committee for the Investigation of Un-American Activities, established in 1938 under Congressman Martin Dies principally to root out communist subversion, continued its work during the war to a chorus of hostile criticism and accusations of sympathy for fascism. Anti-Sovietism moved from the mainstream before 1941 to the fringes of wartime politics.[81]

The moral gloss placed on the Soviet Union and its struggle against fascism, both official and unofficial, did not exclude continued mistrust or hostility towards communism, particularly the home-grown movements. In Britain, MI5 (F Branch) continued its close surveillance of the Communist Party of Great Britain after the Soviet Union became an unexpected ally. In 1943 Douglas Springhall, the Communist Party national organizer, was charged with procuring secret information and sentenced to seven years in prison. Herbert Morrison, the home secretary, warned Churchill that extra vigilance was required because of the 'current sympathy' for the Soviet cause. Communists, he continued, 'had no obligation of loyalty to a "capitalist state"'.[82] Churchill needed little encouragement. Maisky recorded an after-dinner conversation in April 1943 in which Churchill expressed his admiration for Russia but his loathing for its current system: 'I don't want communism ... If anyone came here wishing to establish communism in our country, I would fight him just as ferociously as I'm fighting the Nazis now.'[83] Even the Labour Party, generally more sympathetic to the Soviet cause, published a wartime pamphlet on 'The Communist Party and the War: A Record of Hypocrisy and Treachery to the Workers of Europe'.[84] In the United States, where the Communist movement increased membership to around 100,000, supporters of the Soviet war effort were more wary of the threat that communism might pose at home. Anxious to be perceived as good patriots, the party abolished itself in 1944 and then re-formed as the Communist Political Association, but by then active support for domestic communism was on the wane, as it was in Britain.

By the last year of war, on both sides, Western and Soviet, the pre-war view of communism and capitalism as morally incompatible began to resurface. For Soviet leaders, the alliance was always what John Deane, head of the American Military Mission in Moscow, called 'a marriage of expediency'.[85] In Moscow there had never been much moral distinction made between the fascist and democratic states, since all were regarded as ultimately tarred with the same capitalist brush. With the imminent defeat of Germany, Soviet Foreign Minister Vyacheslav Molotov claimed 'now it is easier to fight capitalism'. Although Stalin hoped that some form of peaceful co-existence might be possible after the end of hostilities, he assumed by early 1945 that future conflict after the defeat of the fascist faction would be 'against the faction of capitalists', returning the Soviet Union to a familiar confrontation.[86] In autumn 1946, Nikolai Novikov, sent to Washington as ambassador in order to assess American intentions, reported back to Moscow that preparation for future war in the United States 'is being conducted with the prospect of war against the Soviet Union, which in the eyes of American imperialists is the main obstacle in the path of the United States to world domination.'[87]

In the United States, the evidence of Soviet unwillingness to establish genuine popular democracy in the states of Eastern Europe liberated by the Red Army alienated important sections of liberal and progressive opinion, which had previously accepted that Soviet rhetoric about peace and democracy was sincere. Louis Fischer, an editor on the left-wing journal *The Nation*, resigned in May 1945 in protest at his colleagues' determination to see Britain and the United States as 'the devils' and Stalin as 'the archangel'. Fischer supplied a long list of Soviet violations of the principles enshrined in the Atlantic Charter as justification for his decision.[88] Although Roosevelt reminded his critics that no one had signed or ratified the Atlantic Charter, its spirit was invoked regularly in arguments against uncritical co-operation with the Soviet Union. In 1944 ex-President Herbert Hoover complained that the Charter had been 'sent to the hospital for major amputation of freedom among nations'. Averell Harriman, Roosevelt's last ambassador in Moscow, and once a keen advocate of collaboration, warned his chief in 1945 that the Soviet programme 'is the establishment of totalitarianism, ending personal liberty and democracy as we know and respect it.' A few months later he asked Truman, Roosevelt's successor, to do what he could to avert a 'barbarian invasion' of Europe.[89] In the last months of war and the first months of peace, the popular Western honeymoon with the Soviet Union evaporated as both sides understood how difficult it was going to be to sustain the 'marriage of expediency'.

The blind eye to Soviet violations of peace and human rights nevertheless had to be sustained through the founding of the United Nations Organization and the post-war trial of the major German war criminals, in both of which the Soviet Union played a full and equal part with the other wartime Allies. The Soviet government refused to allow any discussion that touched on the pre-war record of unprovoked aggression against Poland and Finland, or the forcible annexation of Lithuania, Latvia, Estonia and the northern provinces of Romania. The secret protocol to the German–Soviet Pact that divided Poland between the two dictatorships was known to the American prosecution team (it had been supplied to the American ambassador in Moscow in 1939 by a German diplomat), but it was filed away with the word 'aggression' scribbled across the top and never used during the trial.[90] The Soviet team wanted the crime of conspiracy to wage aggressive war to apply only to the instances of German aggression, not to a more universal principle, and the Western prosecutors reluctantly agreed. A special security unit was sent to Nuremberg from Moscow in November 1945 to try to ensure that there would be no mention of Soviet international crimes. So sensitive was the regime that references to German aggression against Poland were eliminated from the Soviet prosecutors' opening address at the trial, in case it prompted awkward questions. The former Soviet procurator general, Andrei Vyshinsky, ordered Soviet lawyers during the course of the trial to shout down any attempt by the defence or the defendants to raise Soviet complicity in the territorial seizures in 1939–40. The one mention of the Soviet–Finnish war duly brought a noisy Soviet intervention.[91]

The Allies also agreed, despite Soviet reluctance, to charge the German defendants with 'crimes against humanity', in order to include in the indictment the terror the regime practised against the German people and the crimes committed against non-Germans, including deportation, forced labour and mass killings. Here the West was not only blind to the inhumanities of the Stalinist regime, but had very little hard information, since an almost impenetrable veil was drawn over the real treatment meted out to all those deemed to be hostile to or incompatible with the Soviet system, both in the Soviet Union and in the areas occupied in Eastern Europe, and both before the war and at its end. Except for systematic genocide, the Soviet repressive apparatus had engaged in almost all the other crimes against humanity listed at Nuremberg: mass deportations to labour and concentration camps on a vast scale; the operation of camps with a record of abuse and routine death that matched the worst camps in the German Empire; intolerance to all forms of religion; and none of the liberal freedoms of speech, association or respect for the rule of law.[92] While the Nuremberg tribunal was expressing outrage at the concentration camps of the defeated enemy, the Soviet security apparatus in the Soviet zone of Germany set up an isolation facility in a former German camp at Mühlberg on the river Elbe, where 122,000 German prisoners were sent without trial, of whom 43,000 perished or were killed.[93] Between a German camp and a Soviet camp, wrote Anatoli Bakanichev in a private memoir after his experience in both, 'the differences were only in the details.'[94]

The one instance that the West was fully aware of was the massacre of Polish officers by the Soviet NKVD in April 1940 in and around the Katyn forest, because German propaganda had made much of the discovery of the mass graves in 1943. Unknown at the time, the Soviet chief prosecutor at Nuremberg, Roman Rudenko, had actually been sent by Stalin to supervise the murder of Polish officers in Kharkhov, because the local NKVD officers proved to be squeamish about committing the crime. The Soviet authorities stuck rigidly to the story that this was a German atrocity, and although the British were almost certain that their ally had committed the offence, it was felt to be politically prudent not to interrogate the evidence too closely (and indeed the unassailable truth only

emerged after the collapse of the Soviet Union in 1990). Western reticence
on this and all the other evidence of Soviet crimes against humanity or
war crimes was deemed essential to prevent the German defendants from
exploiting what was a growing rift between the former wartime Allies.
Even by 1948, when the rift was explicit and the Cold War unavoidable,
the Soviet leadership maintained the fiction that they represented a
uniquely humane system. In arguments in Paris in 1948 about the drafting of a United Nations Declaration on Human Rights, Vyshinsky
suggested that it was an irrelevance as far as the Soviet Union was concerned, since the communist system as the primary agent of popular
liberation represented 'human rights in action'.[95]

None of the Western Allies matched the Soviet Union in the ruthless
way territorial aggression and mass repression was practised, and in the
moral inversions used to justify it, but the Axis taunt that they failed to
live up to their democratic self-image because of race exposed one of the
major fault lines in the moral position assumed by the West, and particularly by the United States, which, in contrast to Britain, placed particular
emphasis on defending democratic freedoms. The principal racial issue in
America was the long history of discrimination, segregation and violence
directed at the African American minority. The absence of full civil rights
and the social endorsement of racial segregation by white communities,
predominantly in the southern half of the United States, were issues that
the Roosevelt administration avoided in the decade before the war, not
least because the president depended on support in Congress from Southern Democrats who resolutely opposed any concessions to the black
minority. The coming of war, with the call for national unity and defence
of freedom, was understood by black leaders as an opportunity to express
their frustration with existing inequalities and their hope that war to protect 'democracy' would mean their liberation too. The war, declared an
optimistic Du Bois, was a 'war for Racial Equality'.[96]

In January 1942, the same month that the first wartime lynching took
place in Sikeston, Missouri, where 300 spectators watched as a black suspect was doused with five gallons of petrol and burnt to death, the
Pittsburgh Courier published a letter from a young black canteen worker,
James Thompson, calling on black Americans to fight for 'the double
VV for a double victory'. The first V, he explained, was for victory over
America's external enemies, 'the second V for victory over our enemies
from within.'[97] For many, black and white, who opposed the second-class
status of African Americans, the war to defend democracy against dictatorship was hollow without recognizing that democratic ideals had not
been extended to non-white minorities. 'I believe in democracy, so much /

That I want everybody in America / To have some of it / Negroes . . . They shall have some of it', wrote the poet Rhoza Walker in September 1942.[98] Black activists understood that unattractive comparison could be made with German racism at a time when the Roosevelt regime was pledging allegiance to the 'Four Freedoms' and the promises expressed in the Atlantic Charter. A wartime civil rights pamphlet in St Louis had the headline 'LET'S STOP WOULD-BE HITLERS AT HOME – Let's practice democracy as we preach it', a sentiment echoed throughout the civil rights movement.[99] When opinion polls run by the African American press asked if black Americans identified with the lofty sentiments expressed by Roosevelt and his government, 82 per cent said no.[100] The opportunity presented by the war to exploit the moral contrast between official wartime propaganda and the reality for millions of black Americans resulted in a substantial increase in black activism. The circulation of the black press increased by 40 per cent during the war; membership of the National Association for the Advancement of Colored People (NAACP), led by Walter White, grew tenfold across the war years; a more radical March on Washington Movement, founded in 1941 by A. Philip Randolph, spread branches across the country.[101] The demand for equality long pre-dated the war, but wartime provided an appropriate context in which to challenge more openly and extensively white assumptions about race.

The results of the growing activism were mixed. While black protest increased, white intransigence in many cases only hardened. Southern congressmen believed the rising demand for civil rights and economic equality to be a disaster for the country – 'no greater menace', as one put it.[102] In Southern states, black voters were kept away from the polls, while efforts were made to find ways of tying black rural labour to serve on white-owned farms. In some areas black men were forced to carry a badge with them wherever they went with the name of their employer and their work schedule or face the prospect of arrest. The 'work or jail' culture was calculated to suppress any prospect of black militancy.[103] For many black Americans from the North, wartime drafting into the armed forces, or work in the growing defence sector, exposed them to an unfamiliar level of segregation and discrimination. When employers relented to market pressure for labour, black workers were commonly given only unskilled labouring jobs, whatever their qualifications. In the armed forces, segregation was widely enforced. Black recruits were given poorer living conditions and made to carry out roles as mess attendants or labourers, and in parts of the South they even risked lynching if they were caught outside camp in uniform. 'If it ever been slavery it is now,' complained one soldier in a letter to the *Pittsburgh Courier*, writing from a camp where black draftees had to sleep on the floor and use buckets as latrines.[104] The separate treatment of black soldiers was reinforced by the prejudiced views of the administration. The United States army, wrote another disillusioned recruit, is 'about as Nazi-like as Hitler's'.[105] In 1944 the Office of War Information issued a confidential manual to white officers on 'Certain Characteristics of the Negro', which included the following: 'gregarious, extrovertive [sic] ... hot tempered ... mentally lazy, not retentive, forgetful ... ruled by instinct and emotion rather than by reason ... keen sense of rhythm ... evasive ... lies easily, frequently, naturally'.[106] One black soldier writing back from the European theatre at news of racial violence in the New York district of Harlem claimed that black fighters were asking themselves, 'what are we fighting for?'[107]

The contradictions exposed by the war finally prompted a wave of racial violence. White workers engaged in so-called 'hate strikes' directed at the employment of a growing number of blacks in the early war years. White segregationists engaged in violent confrontations in defence of all-white neighbourhoods or schools. As wartime labour mobility brought a million black migrants to northern and western cities, so racial tension was heightened, reaching a violent peak in 1943. That year, an estimated 242 racial confrontations were counted across 47 American cities.[108] Riots and street battles occurred in the shipyards at Mobile, Alabama, and Port Chester in Pennsylvania, in Centerville, Mississippi, in Los Angeles and in Newark, New Jersey. The deadliest occurred in summer 1943, first in Detroit, then in Harlem. The violence in Detroit exploded on 20 June from the simmering resentment by white workers at the influx of new black labour; the riots left 37 dead (25 of them black) and 700 wounded before order could be restored. On 1 August, rioting erupted in Harlem, leaving 6 dead and 1,450 stores burnt down or ransacked. Roosevelt was persuaded to make no public statement about the race issue, partly from concern for white opinion in the South, partly to avoid stoking further racial tension by admitting that the fault line existed. Instead, increased intelligence-gathering on potential crisis points was used to anticipate further violence, while local means were devised to defuse any social conflict before it disrupted the war effort.[109]

Roosevelt's subdued response to the evidence of mounting racial tension was indicative of his approach to the broader issue of civil rights and racial equality. Southern Democrat support in Congress was essential for his political position, and he was reluctant to offer anything to black opinion that might jeopardize that support. The one concession he made, in 1941, before the war, was to issue Executive Order 8802 founding the Fair Employment Practices Commission to try to erode race discrimination in the defence sector following lobbying by civil rights leaders (or as his press secretary Stephen Early put it, after a 'long howl from the colored folks'). Black wartime employment in the defence industries did increase from 3 per cent in early 1942 to a peak of 8 per cent in 1944, but black household incomes still averaged between 40 and 60 per cent of white earnings. In 1942 the new Fair Employment agency was absorbed by the War Manpower Commission, limiting the prospects for using the agency to combat race inequality. In the South, the administration offered subsidies and training programmes to help raise the productivity of white farms, while turning a blind eye to the increased control over black workers that wartime reforms made possible.[110] On the paradox presented by his rhetoric of freedom and the survival of racial segregation and discrimination at home, the president remained largely silent.

The same held true for Roosevelt's view of racism in the British Empire, which was prudently cautious in order not to undermine the wartime alliance, despite his private view that the colonial empires were morally bankrupt and ought to be brought under international trusteeship or granted independence. When the British authorities arrested Gandhi in August 1942, along with thousands of other Indian supporters of his 'Quit India' campaign, Roosevelt made no public statement condemning the decision or the violence that accompanied it. Walter White, secretary of the NAACP, cancelled a speech he was to make on behalf of the Office of War Information in protest, and sent a telegram to Roosevelt linking the civil rights movement to the wider world struggle for emancipation from Western imperialism: 'One billion brown and yellow people in the Pacific will without question consider ruthless treatment of Indian leaders and peoples typical of what white people will do to colored people if United Nations win.'[111]

The link between the struggle for civil rights in the United States and the wider global movement for colonial liberation became firmer as the war went on. After visiting the North African and European theatres of war in 1944, White wrote *A Rising Wind*, a memoir designed to show that 'the struggle of the Negro in the United States is part and parcel of the struggle against imperialism and exploitation in India, China, Burma, Africa, The Philippines, Malaya, West Indies and South America.'[112] When delegates met in San Francisco in May 1945 to agree the formation of the United Nations organization, black lobby groups tried to get the American delegation to include a statement on human rights that would not only embrace the rights of black Americans but also grant rights to 'colonies and dependent people', but the lobbying failed to produce a positive response to racial discrimination. John Foster Dulles, one of the United

States delegates, worried that human rights would highlight the 'Negro problem in the South'.[113] In 1948, when the United Nations met in Paris to discuss, among other things, the drafting of a Human Rights Declaration, the chair of the Human Rights Commission, Roosevelt's widow, Eleanor, refused to accept a petition drafted by Du Bois, 'An Appeal to the World', linking black oppression in the United States directly to the human rights agenda because of the political issues it raised. The delegates from the major states wanted to ensure that a statement of universal rights did not imply the right of intervention in countries where those rights were manifestly abused.[114] Despite the war waged to defend democracy, the United States and the imperial powers emerged in 1945 with discrimination still embedded in the Western view of race.

If the Allies' record on domestic racism failed to match the wartime rhetoric, there were further ambiguities in the way the racism of the enemy was confronted, above all in the case of anti-Semitism. The high profile now enjoyed by the Holocaust or Shoah in public memory of the Second World War has contributed to the assumption that a major factor in waging the war against Germany and its European Axis allies was to end the genocide and liberate the remaining Jewish populations. This is largely an illusion. The war was not fought to save Europe's Jews, and indeed the governments of all three major Allied powers worried lest the public should think this to be the case. Liberation when it came was a by-product of a broader ambition to expel the Axis states from their conquests and to restore the national sovereignty of all conquered and victimized peoples. Towards the Jews, the attitude of the Allied powers was by turns negligent, cautious, ambivalent or morally questionable.

The way that the Allied powers viewed the so-called 'Jewish question' was shaped on the one hand by pre-war responses to the challenges posed by German anti-Semitism and, on the other, by the rise of Zionism and assertions of Jewish nationhood. Soviet policy towards the Jews was dictated in particular by hostility to Zionist aspirations that challenged Jewish allegiance to the Soviet system. Stalin had a long-held view that Soviet Jews were unassimilable in the new Soviet Union and he resented what he saw as their desire for 'segregation'. Zionists were persecuted and driven underground; Jewish emigration was reduced to a trickle by the early 1930s, and from 1934 banned altogether; Jewish workers were not allowed time off to celebrate the Sabbath and hundreds of synagogues were closed down.[115] When 2 million additional Jews came under Soviet rule in 1939 and 1940, with the occupation of eastern Poland and the Baltic states, they were subjected to the destruction of their traditional way of life. Across the region an estimated 250,000 Jews were deported to the Soviet interior, thousands of rabbis and Jewish leaders were arrested and sent to the Soviet concentration camps, synagogues were closed or converted to other uses, businesses taken into state ownership, and Jewish public religious and cultural rituals suppressed. The traditional life of the small-town *shtetl* communities was emasculated long before the arrival of the Germans in 1941.[116]

In Britain and the United States, the Jewish question was bound up with anxieties about the effect of large-scale Jewish immigration prompted by increased persecution, and, in the British case, concern that Jewish migration should not upset the fragile security of their League Mandates in the Middle East. Although in neither case explicitly or overtly anti-Semitic, fear of the social or political consequences of opening the doors to Jewish refugees without restriction governed the response of both governments. During the 1930s substantial numbers of Jewish immigrants nevertheless succeeded in escaping from Germany and the areas annexed in 1938–9, a total of approximately 360,000 between 1933 and 1939. Of this number, 57,000 found sanctuary in the United States, 53,000 in Britain's Palestine mandate, and 50,000 in the British Isles. There was also substantial emigration of European Jews from other countries where anti-Semitism had become by the 1930s a more acute problem. The total number of Jewish immigrants to Palestine was 215,232 between 1933 and 1939, doubling the Jewish population of the region.[117] It was this influx that most affected the British government's approach to the problem of Jewish refugees. In 1936 a widespread Arab revolt was prompted by the arrival in Palestine of the fresh wave of Jews from Europe. The revolt tied down much of the small British army in the territory in 1936–9 and threatened Britain's strategic position in the Middle East. The result was a final decision in 1939, published in a White Paper in May, to limit further Jewish migration to 75,000 over five years, and then to suspend it entirely unless the Arab community acquiesced, which was an unlikely outcome. An initial six-month ban was imposed on all immigration as a penalty for large-scale illegal entry. In 1939 only 16,000 were allowed legally into Palestine, but there were 11,000 who managed to enter illicitly. To rub salt in the wound, the government paper also ruled out the prospect of a separate state for Jews, which was the principal Zionist ambition.[118] The guidelines laid down in spring 1939 governed British policy throughout the war, disastrously closing off what had been one of the most important escape routes for Jewish refugees.

Emigration to Britain itself was curtailed at just the point when German anti-Semitism reached a new level of intense discrimination and persecution following the *Kristallnacht* pogrom in November 1938. A number of unaccompanied children were allowed on the so-called 'Kindertransport', and by July 1939 7,700 had reached Britain, but adult refugees faced increased problems in meeting British criteria for entry and acquiring the necessary visas. The British authorities preferred Jewish immigrants who could be supported by Jewish organizations and had some useful skill, or filled a gap in the labour market, but the Home Office preference was for Jews who promised to re-emigrate after arrival in Britain. This was a prospect progressively reduced as the war approached. Quotas and restrictions on immigrants were shared across the Western world. In the United States these restrictions did not apply to Jews directly, because they were treated as citizens of their particular country, but this meant long waiting lists for visas for up to two years, and no exceptions once a country's quota was full. On this the United States government refused to make concessions to the particular crisis facing European Jews. When Roosevelt was pressured to allow easier entry for Jews after *Kristallnacht*, he merely commented 'the time is not ripe for that.' Opinion polls, to which Roosevelt was always alert, showed that 75 per cent of Americans considered that the Jews possessed 'undesirable traits', while 72 per cent were opposed to any additional Jewish immigration.[119] A bill introduced into Congress in January 1939 (the so-called 'Children's Bill') to allow 20,000 refugee children into the United States over a two-year period prompted no public response or support from the president and failed at the committee stage. Opinion polls again showed strong opposition from the public.

Rather than face the prospect of a potential flood of desperate refugees, proposals were raised in Britain to send Jews to the South American colony of British Guiana ('to salve the conscience of H. M. G. in relation to European Jewry', as one Foreign Office official bluntly put it), but fears of local opposition ended the speculation. In the United States it was proposed to create a Jewish enclave in Alaska, but Roosevelt vetoed the idea from fear of creating a Jewish state within a state.[120] What neither country wanted was an enlarged Jewish presence on the home front whatever the moral grounds for allowing it to happen. Roosevelt's ambassador in Moscow, Laurence Steinhardt, observing the pressure of the refugee movement in 1940, summed up the choice his government faced: 'I am of the opinion that when there is even the remote possibility of a conflict between humanitarianism and the welfare of the United States that the former must give way to the latter.'[121]

The coming of war only strengthened this conviction. From September 1939, no further Jewish emigration to Britain from Germany or German-occupied Europe was to be permitted. 'So far as we and France are concerned,' wrote a Foreign Office official, 'the position of the Jews in

Germany is now of no practical importance.'[122] In the United States, congressional opposition ensured that the existing tight quota system was not revised. The German authorities were keen to expel as many Jews as possible, right up to the moment in October 1941 when Himmler finally banned emigration in favour of annihilation. But the number fortunate enough to find an avenue to the West was a tiny fraction of those in need. Emigration to Palestine, which was still permitted by quota, never reached the levels permitted under the White Paper because no effort was made to facilitate the flight of Jews from Europe. In fifteen of the thirty-nine months in which it was possible for Jews to leave Germany and its new empire, all immigration was suspended by the British authorities as a punishment for a shrinking number of illegal immigrants. The number of Jewish emigrants to the United States in 1940 was 36,945, but thousands more waited in Europe because the quotas were full. Those who managed to reach Britain suffered further indignity when the British government ordered in June 1940 that most should be interned as enemy aliens, following a public panic about 'fifth columnists'. Most detainees were later released, but the conditions they suffered in temporary camps in Britain, Canada and Australia were initially harsh and humiliating.[123]

The overwhelming crisis faced by the Jewish population of Europe spurred on the search for escape in defiance of the regulations imposed by the West. Here the British authorities displayed a callousness that entirely belied the claim that the British were fighting for decent values. When three overladen ships sailing from Romania, full of hungry and fearful Jewish refugees from Central Europe, arrived off the coast of Palestine, the fugitives were first denied the right to disembark, then brought ashore and interned in crude camps while efforts were made to find some way of forcing them out of Palestine. The authorities decided to send some on to the island colony of Mauritius but the refugees, desperate and demoralized by their mistreatment, refused. On the day they were to be deported they lay naked on their beds in protest. Colonial police beat the men with sticks and then carried the naked men and women to the ship, where their possessions were dumped in the sea or seized and sold off for Palestine government funds. On the way to the island over forty died of typhoid or debilitation; on arrival, they were interned behind barbed wire with armed guards, trading one harsh regime for another. They remained imprisoned, the men separated from their wives and children, until the last months of the war. Sir John Shuckburgh, deputy under-secretary at the Colonial Office, thought the protests showed that 'The Jews have no sense of humour and no sense of proportion.'[124] From spring 1941 illegal entry to Palestine dried up.

Official indifference to the fate of the Jews was difficult to sustain once the genocide began in earnest from the summer of 1941, first on the Eastern Front, then across Axis Europe. Although it was challenging at first to pin together the many different strands of intelligence reaching London and Washington, by the early summer of 1942 the systematic mass murder of Europe's Jews seemed the unambiguous conclusion. In May 1942, the Polish underground sent a report to the Polish government-in-exile, the so-called 'Bund Report', detailing the extermination of Polish Jews. In June the BBC was allowed to broadcast to Europe the report's conclusion that 700,000 Jews had already been killed, but the Foreign Office thought the information doubtful and worried that it might be a device to justify further emigration to Palestine.[125] In early August 1942 the representative of the World Jewish Congress in Geneva, Gerhart Riegner, sent a long telegram via the Foreign Office to the British MP Sydney Silverman with details of the extermination camps and the gassing, supplied from a German source. It was sent on 8 August; the Foreign Office, despite persistent scepticism about unverified intelligence, passed the telegram to Silverman on the 17th with the warning that he should not make too much of the news.[126] The telegram was also sent to the State Department in Washington to pass on to Rabbi Stephen Wise, head of the World Jewish Congress, but officials decided that the 'fantastic nature of the allegation' precluded sending it any further. American censors missed a second telegram sent directly to Wise by Silverman, enclosing the Riegner report. But when Wise tried to get permission from the State Department to publicize the news, it took three months before it was reluctantly granted.[127] Officials in both countries were wary of what was still regarded as unsubstantiated intelligence and anxious lest Jewish lobby groups use the grim news to demand government action.

By December 1942 there was sufficient information publicly available to increase popular pressure on both Western governments. A British Gallup poll showed 82 per cent of respondents willing to admit more Jewish fugitives.[128] To allay the protests at Allied inaction, the British foreign secretary, Anthony Eden, proposed to issue a statement in the House of Commons on behalf of the Allied powers, highlighting the German murder of the Jews and promising post-war retribution against those responsible. In Washington, the State Department thought the statement would only encourage more Jewish protest which might adversely 'affect the war effort'. In the end American officials acquiesced, but only after 'reports from Europe which leave no room for doubt' about extermination was modified to read 'numerous reports from Europe', which still left room for doubt. A week before the statement, Roosevelt had his only meeting during the war with Jewish leaders to discuss response to the genocide. He spoke for four-fifths of the time, devoted only two minutes to the real subject of the meeting, and promised nothing.[129] In Moscow, where since summer 1941 there had been plentiful direct evidence of the genocide collected and written up by the NKVD security service (though not relayed to the West), there existed similar ambivalence about an Allied statement that singled out Jews as victims, rather than Soviet victims in general, but the Soviet Union joined the list of signatories for what turned out to be the only major wartime statement on the Jewish catastrophe.[130] On 17 December Eden read the statement to the House of Commons, where members rose spontaneously for two minutes of silence. For Jewish organizations worldwide it seemed possible that the Allies might relax their restrictions and respond positively to the plight of Europe's Jews. For Jews trapped in the Axis net, Allied publicity was a mixed blessing: 'We should be happy at the "concern" for our fate,' wrote Abraham Lewin in his diary in the Warsaw Ghetto, 'but will it be of any use to us?'[131]

The statement in December 1942 proved to be the high point of government response to news of the Holocaust and it resulted in almost no significant change in Allied policy towards those European Jews who remained alive. In the Soviet Union, the Jewish Anti-Fascist Committee (set up in 1942 with Stalin's approval under the watchful supervision of the security service) was tolerated because it attracted American money, but it was not intended to support an active strategy to rescue or support Soviet Jews under German occupation, most of whom were by the end of 1942 already dead. In Britain, Home Secretary Herbert Morrison rejected calls to admit more Jewish refugees and asked the Foreign Office to consider some other remote destination, including Madagascar, which had briefly been a German idea in 1940. To still further criticism, the War Cabinet set up a Committee for the Reception and Accommodation of Jewish Refugees, but the word 'Jewish' was then dropped from the title from a desire not to appear to privilege a particular victim group. The committee in January 1943 saw its purpose as largely negative, 'to kill the idea that mass immigration to this country and the British colonies was possible'. Morrison's only offer was the possibility of taking in a further 1,000–2,000 if the refugees could be shown to be useful to Britain's war effort.[132]

In America, the December statement was followed by no immediate practical steps. Suggestions from Jewish lobbies were sidelined or ignored by Roosevelt and the State Department. Washington received a proposal in January from the British government to consider a top-level summit on the refugee problem, and after much American foot-dragging a conference finally assembled in mid-April 1943 on the British island colony of

Bermuda in the Caribbean. Both sides agreed that they would discuss refugees in general rather than just the Jews, and that they would not discuss what were viewed as Utopian suggestions about rescue. The results, reported the head of the British delegation, were 'meagre'. The conference agreed to reconstitute an Intergovernmental Committee on Refugees first established in 1938, but its role in assisting Jews in the years that followed was negligible. No concession was made to take more Jewish refugees in Britain, Palestine or the United States beyond the existing quota, although Roosevelt was eventually pressured in 1944 to offer wartime sanctuary to just 1,000 refugees in Fort Ontario, New York. The idea mooted at Bermuda that a camp could be set up in Allied-occupied North Africa for Jewish refugees from Spain took a year to materialize. Anxiety about the effect on Muslim opinion, coupled with French obstruction, eventually resulted in a camp which housed not thousands as intended but a modest 630.[133] The main conclusion of the conference was that nothing could be done, in Eden's words, 'until final victory is won'. By coincidence, the conference convened at the moment when the Jewish fighters in the Warsaw Ghetto launched their abortive revolt. While delegates debated in a Bermuda hotel about how to contain the refugee problem, Jewish rebels fought their final doomed battle against their oppressors, little assisted by the Polish Home Army and assisted not at all by the Allies. One of the last messages from the stricken ghetto simply stated, 'the world of freedom and justice is silent and does nothing.'[134]

This was a harsh judgement but not an unreasonable one. Jewish persecution and extermination did not elicit from the Western Allies a response equal to the horrors of the Holocaust. Instead, Jewish refugees who hoped to flee Europe and Jewish organizations that tried to pioneer rescue operations were faced with endless obstacles or blank refusal and only occasionally grudging support. In the full knowledge of what happened, post-war generations have been equally harsh in judging the moral failure of the Allied cause. The reasons for that failure are many. In the first place, the problem of coping with the Jewish refugees in the 1930s had prompted, particularly for the British administration in Palestine, strong negative reaction against providing further assistance. Secondly, there was the problem of credibility. As the horrors unfolded, the glimpses afforded to the Western public seemed to defy belief, even among Jewish communities. 'Believe the unbelievable', wrote the World Jewish Congress bureau in London to the New York headquarters.[135] The atrocity stories in the West were treated with caution after the experience of the First World War, and journalists who filed the details from Europe had to break through what Leon Kubowitzki, addressing the World Jewish Congress in 1948, termed 'a crust of skepticism'. The press was shy of repeating the same story again and again, because its news value was rated poorly in comparison with war news. The *New York Times*, America's foremost daily paper, ran 24,000 front-page articles during the war years, but only 44 covered Jewish issues. The Jewish-American owner, Arthur Sulzberger, hesitated to use his paper to push the Jewish tragedy too far, from fear of alienating his readership or generating an anti-Semitic response. As a result, public knowledge of the Holocaust was patchy and episodic, and likely to inspire incredulity rather than empathy. 'The death struggle in which the Jewish people were engaged,' continued Kubowitzki in his speech, 'was not only incredible to the human mind, it was also incomprehensible.'[136]

The failure might also be explained by anti-Semitism, but this too is more complex an issue than it seems. In all three major Allied states anti-Semitism in its crude racist form was present, though not as a mainstream movement, and not at the level of government. In the United States popular anti-Semitism increased during the 1930s. The slogan 'New Deal = Jew Deal' was thrown by the extreme right at Roosevelt's economic reforms in the 1930s. Populist anti-Semitism was represented by William Pelley and his 15,000 fascist 'silver shirts'; by the Revd Gerald Winrod, whose anti-Semitic paper *Defender* was read by 100,000 Americans; and by Father Charles Coughlin, the radio priest and a believer in the 'Protocols' of the 'Elders of Zion', whose anti-Semitic tirades reached an audience of millions until he was silenced by his archbishop in 1942. Desecration of synagogues and regular attacks on Jews continued through the war years.[137] British anti-Semitism existed on the right-wing fringe, but this was marginalized in the late 1930s and in 1940 activists from the British Union of Fascists were interned. It is nevertheless evident that many politicians and officials in the West who confronted the 'Jewish question' did so from a position of prejudice or intolerance, as did much of the public. The stereotypical view of the 'Jew' provoked a passive anti-Semitism that adversely affected the prospect of a more positive response to the Jewish crisis. Anthony Eden, who master-minded the declaration in December 1942, had told his private secretary a year before 'If we must have preferences ... I prefer Arabs to Jews.' The officials in the Foreign Office and Colonial Office who had to deal with Palestine, or the refugee problem, peppered their minutes with a casual racism. 'In my opinion,' wrote one in 1944, 'a disproportionate amount of the time of this office is wasted on dealing with these wailing Jews.'[138] Churchill was unusual among his Cabinet colleagues in his unconcealed support for Zionism and his concern for the Jewish people caught in the Axis net, but he was unable during the war to overturn the indifference or hostility of those around

him. Roosevelt, by contrast, did little to address the problem of Jewish
refugees or to respond to the Jewish crisis unless he felt that public opinion required it, in the end substituting political calculation for humanitarian
concern.

There was yet another sense in which anti-Semitism contributed to
explaining the Western response. Among Jewish organizations and lobby-
groups there was a persistent fear that Jewish activism before and during
the war would provoke an anti-Semitic backlash and make conditions
worse for Jews everywhere. Jewish leaders in Britain and the United States
were not enthusiastic about the prospect of large numbers of additional
Jewish immigrants from Central and Eastern Europe who might dislocate
the established Jewish communities and who would be difficult to integrate. There were fears, too, that Jewish agitation might create the idea
that Jews were a disloyal minority, which was the view Stalin had formed
of the Soviet Jewish population. When Rabbi Wise addressed the American Jewish Congress in August 1943, he announced: 'We are Americans,
first, last and all the time.'[139] Among non-Jewish politicians there was a
similar anxiety about prompting anti-Semitism if a flood of Jewish refugees, encouraged by German design, suddenly demanded entry. In Britain,
the prospect of such an influx remained alive for much of the war, even
when most of the Jews in Hitler's Europe were dead. In both countries,
identifying Jews as the principal victims of the European war was regarded
as politically problematic because it seemed to privilege Jews at the expense
of other victim groups in the occupied territories of Europe. (Hence the
decision to delete the word 'Jewish' from the emergency committee for
refugees set up in Britain in January 1943.) Finally, both Jewish and non-
Jewish leaders were concerned that a more positive response to the Jewish
crisis would play into the hands of German propaganda by appearing to
show that the war against Germany was, indeed, a 'Jewish war'.

The response to the Holocaust was, above all, conditioned by political
expediency and military necessity. The issue of Jewish refugees had a low
priority for Western populations concerned with the outcome of the wider
war. Even where sympathy for the Jewish crisis existed, it was treated in
general as part of a broader concern with all victims of Axis occupation. In
propaganda to Europe, British officials were anxious not to create the
impression that the Jews, who did not constitute a 'nation', should enjoy
priority over the peoples who did. The European governments-in-exile in
London shared this concern that their captive populations might resent
attention to the Jews at the expense of their own plight. General de Gaulle,
leader of the Free French, was advised that he 'must not be the man who
brings back the Jews'. The French right blamed Jews for defeat in 1940,

just as Polish nationalists blamed the Jews for betraying the country to the Russians in September 1939. Exile governments were anxious not to create their own 'Jewish problem' during and after the war, and British propaganda respected these political concerns.[140] Even when Germany offered neutral states the opportunity to repatriate Jews holding their passports or papers, the response was a cautious procrastination in deference to domestic nationalist opinion. Of the 5,000 Jews who held Spanish papers, only 667 arrived in Spain in 1943 and 1944, and only on condition that they re-emigrate. Thousands were murdered while neutral officials haggled over entry requirements and the verification of documents.[141]

The ambiguous response to the Jewish catastrophe continued after the victory which was supposed to be the key to liberation. The introduction of the term 'genocide' in the deliberations of the International Military Tribunal to arraign the major German war criminals in 1945 was inspired by a Jewish lawyer from Poland, Rafael Lemkin, who arrived in the United States in 1941. He defined the term not to deal with the fate of his fellow Jews, but to describe the political, cultural and social emasculation of the national identity of the conquered peoples. The inclusion of the mass murder of the Jews in the indictment came at the last moment because of the difficulty in defining the Jews as a 'nation' and Soviet hostility to the idea that the Jews should be singled out collectively rather than be included among the total of national victims.[142] The term genocide was used sparingly during the trials and in the final judgment not at all. Lemkin campaigned to get the United Nations to define genocide as an international crime, but it was sponsored not by the major powers but by India, Panama and Cuba. The final Genocide Convention was adopted in December 1948 at the same time as the Universal Declaration of Human Rights, but not without resistance from Britain, France, the Soviet Union and the United States, all of which worried that the Convention could be used to apply to the treatment either of colonial populations or of oppressed minorities at home. Stalin at the time had authorized an anti-Semitic purge that led to the murder or incarceration of thousands of Soviet Jews, including those who had run the wartime Jewish Anti-Fascist Committee. In the United States the reluctance to ratify the Convention was linked to fear of further civil rights agitation. And indeed in 1951 the civil rights campaigners Paul Robeson and William Patterson presented the United Nations with a petition, 'We Charge Genocide', over the treatment of American blacks. Lemkin regretted comparing the plight of the Jews with that of blacks: 'To be unequal is not the same as to be dead.' In the end, the United States government did not ratify the Genocide Convention until 1986.[143]

The morally relative position taken during the war on collaboration between the Allies, or on domestic racism, or on assisting Europe's Jews did not make the Allies the same as the Axis states, but it did challenge the universal claim made by the Allied powers to be representing collectively a set of progressive and humane values. The narrative of the Allies' 'Good War' was already under construction while the conflict was going on and has remained a central trope ever since in memory of the war.[144] The reality was less clear-cut. Wartime moral and political expediency produced a history in which the Allied powers, driven by what was seen as strategic and political necessity, or by ideological conviction, made moral choices that have tarnished the wartime narrative.

PEOPLES' WARS: FORGING THE 'MORAL COLLECTIVE'

The moral expediency displayed by all the powers when justifying the purpose of the conflict and the sacrifices demanded of their populations made it essential to persuade the great majority of the people that the war was a contest worth supporting. If asked, the great majority would almost certainly have preferred not to be at war, either on practical or on moral grounds. 'We must, first of all, realize,' wrote the leaders of the British Parliamentary Peace Aims Group in 1943, 'that the common people in any civilized country share little responsibility for the war. They are dragged into it by their rulers, pacified with cheap phrases and made to suffer all the horrors and indignities . . .'[145] If this judgement seems more applicable to the Axis states than to the Allies, there was an impelling need for all warring regimes to ensure that the people identified with a conflict not of their making and that they sustained a moral commitment to the war effort even in the face of crisis or defeat. The First World War demonstrated the costs of failing to do so.

The principal means of ensuring such commitment was the construction of a 'moral collective' in which the entire population was ostensibly united in prosecuting the war to the end. The collective reflected the idea that modern war was total war, waged by whole societies, not simply by governments and armed forces. The concept of the collective as an organic wartime community dominated by an ethic of duty and sacrifice was universal, not a phenomenon confined to the dictatorships. The essential features of the moral construct were captured by Chiang Kai-shek in an address to the Chinese nation early in 1942:

You must all be aware that modern war is not a mere matter of military operations. It involves the whole strength and all the resources of the nation. Not only soldiers, but also all citizens without exception, take part. The latter must conceive the national peril as affecting them personally, and must consent to the endurance of all necessary hardships, and must abandon private freedom and satisfaction when discipline and the public interest demand it . . . In a society where this is so, life will conform to the exigencies of wartime; that is, the nation's interest will be held supreme and victory will be held the proper goal of all citizens' efforts.[146]

The moral collective was captured in the language used to define the war effort. In Britain the war was early on christened a 'People's War', to distinguish it from wars fought in the past on behalf of a more narrowly defined elite; the 'common people' united against tyranny became the central feature of the wartime narrative.[147] In Germany, the popular idea of the racially exclusive 'People's Community' (*Volksgemeinschaft*), a dominant feature of National Socialist ideology and propaganda during the 1930s, was easily transformed during the war into the concept of a 'Fighting Community' (*Kampfgemeinschaft*) defending the people and, as defeat drew near, as a 'Community of Fate' (*Schicksalsgemeinschaft*), dedicated to enduring the hardships of the final struggle.[148] The Soviet Union was supposed to become, in Stalin's words, a single 'armed camp', waging the Great Patriotic War to drive out the fascist invader. The idea of a people's war was captured in a popular song in the first weeks of war, '*voina narodnaia*', a war of the people. In September 1942 Stalin announced that the Soviet Union was also fighting a 'People's War' in which every able-bodied citizen, male or female, should be willing to fight.[149] In the United States, with its prevailing ethic of individualism, constructing the moral wartime community was more problematic, but it was articulated in Roosevelt's first wartime broadcast after Pearl Harbor: 'We are all in it – all the way. Every single man, woman and child . . .'[150]

An exception here was the experience in China and Italy, where wars had already been fought during the 1930s at great cost for relatively weak economies. By 1940, when Mussolini decided finally to risk a war against other major powers, the appetite of important sections of the Italian military and political elite, and of much of the public, for further warfare was limited. Instead of prompting a new moral solidarity, as major war did elsewhere, conflict from 1940 onwards exposed a widening gap between regime and population. Early defeats fuelled wide public pessimism; police reports showed declining confidence in victory, fear of American entry, and a longing for an end to the conflict. A typical report from Genoa in November 1940 highlighted 'an absolute lack of enthusiasm about the war and its aims'.[151] Mussolini, as a consequence, hesitated to impose total mobilization, with the result that many more Italians could stand aside from the conflict than was the case in Britain, or Germany, or the Soviet Union. In China, identification with the war effort, despite Chiang's understanding of what was necessary to achieve it, remained limited. Later in 1942, Chiang chided his countrymen in an address to a plenary session of the People's Political Council in Chongqing for failing to embrace his call for total war: 'To a considerable degree social life is as lax now as in peacetime ... Enthusiastic patriotism is widely absent among the people and self-seeking habits and neglect of the public interest remain as obstacles ...'[152] China's problems provide enough explanation for the absence of a proper sense of collective endeavour. Half the nation was occupied by the Japanese, where there was widespread opportunistic collaboration with the enemy; there existed a state of latent conflict between Chiang's Nationalist regime and the Chinese Communist Party, which was generally more successful in its appeal for an 'All-People's war against Japan' in the base areas it occupied; in the villages, millions of Chinese peasants struggled with the flood of refugees and the search for food or defence against widespread banditry and were little moved by the idea of fighting for a national community; and throughout unoccupied China corruption was rife at the highest level, while merchants took advantage of shortages, or the rich bought their sons out of conscription.[153] Chiang deplored the display of disunity, which he described with the Chinese phrase 'a tray of loose sand', each man for himself.[154]

Where it was successfully constructed, the wartime moral collective was intended to be inclusive, except for those regarded by definition as excluded, like the 120,000 Japanese residents in the United States who were rounded up in 1942 and placed in camps, or Jews and foreign workers in Germany, or the broad category of 'enemies of the people' in the Soviet Union. Every member of the population, including children and adolescents, was expected to play some part, however minor or passive, in sustaining the war effort and coping with the necessary sacrifices. In Germany, the Soviet Union and Japan participation was part of the broader regimentation of the community, in which active involvement for much of the population on behalf of community goals was unavoidable. In these cases, creating the wartime collective, with a shared moral consensus, was an extension of established forms of community commitment. The population in Germany organized in one or other of the associations for youth, the Party, welfare provision, civil defence and labour service has been estimated to number by 1939 some 68 million out of a population of 80 million.[155] All these organizations assumed a share of the war effort on the home front once war had begun. In Japan, the Home Ministry in 1940 established a network of 'community councils' (*chōnaikai*) to create a formal structure for involving the population in the war effort. By the end of the year there were 180,000 of them, each one based in the cities around several hundred households, in the countryside on each village. At the same time, more than a million smaller neighbourhood associations were set up, commonly of eight or nine families, which were supposed to bind local communities even more tightly to the wider purposes of the war and to isolate easily anyone who failed to accept the moral obligation to comply.[156] In Britain and the United States, on the other hand, the creation of commitment depended much more on exhortatory appeals to individual conscience rather than on pre-existing collectivities. The American wartime narrative contrasted the organic nature of Japanese society, with its narrow conception of citizenship, with the idea of civic voluntarism in which the individual would come to understand his obligation to others. 'What did you do today for Freedom?' asked one American poster.[157] Propaganda to encourage inclusion complemented strong social pressure to comply. A failure to accept sacrifices willingly or to participate in local community activity was observed and reported. In Britain, despite evident differences of class or region, there existed a shared commitment to the idea that the temporary wartime collective placed a moral obligation to work for victory on everyone able to do so.

These wartime collectives were peculiarly powerful moral and emotional constructs. It was difficult to stand aside or outside the fighting community, and in the authoritarian states it was dangerous to do so. In the majority of warring states, there was widespread endorsement of the moral obligation to take part, whatever private reservations individuals might have. Alleged shirkers, defeatists and pacifists were moral outcasts; in the Soviet Union they were likely to be executed. Propaganda was indispensable, but constructing the wartime community also depended on developing a broader culture of participation in which the media, youth organizations, churches, women's groups and, in the Western states, commercial advertising all played a part. The involvement of children in the wartime community presents a particularly telling example of the way the discourse on the wartime collective was constructed and absorbed. Published in the United States shortly after Pearl Harbor, a primer for schools on *Education for Victory* suggested that teachers should try to encourage children to understand the current moral discourse: 'Sensing what America is fighting for by developing an understanding of democratic ideals ... Sensing that America's fight for democratic principles is but one part of mankind's long struggle for freedom.' Half-a-million copies of 'The Children's Morality Code' were distributed, exhorting children to be loyal to family, school, state and nation, and above all 'loyal to humanity'. When Treasury Secretary Henry Morgenthau called on 30 million young Americans to join the fight for freedom under the slogan 'Save, Serve, Conserve', some 28,000 schools enrolled. Pupils saved war-bond stamps, undertook house-to-house collections of scrap metal, paper and grease, and joined local community projects.[158]

In Japan, children were brought up to acknowledge moral commitments to the community. School pupils had been instructed for decades with ethics textbooks issued by the Ministry of Education to encourage obedience, loyalty and courage. The textbook editions published in 1941 were redrafted to include nationalist symbols and sentiments ('Japan is a fine country / a pure country. / The only divine country / in the world.') and a range of references to ordinary citizens willing to die for the emperor. Exemplary stories encouraged children to collect salvage for the war effort, write letters to soldiers abroad, and to be thankful to be part of the great imperial family. The teachers' manual accompanying the textbook explained that the new 'national morality' now absorbed both the social and the individual moral sphere. By 1945 children also found themselves regularly singing war songs in class and taking part in military training to prepare them for the final defence of Japan. One young schoolgirl recorded in her diary a day of 'spiritual training' that included hand-to-hand combat, throwing balls as hand-grenade practice, wooden sword-fighting, and finally practising spearing an opponent: 'it was really fun. I was tired, but I realized that even one person can kill a lot of the enemy.'[159]

The creation of the wartime collective nevertheless had clear limits. There was nothing automatic about sustaining wartime commitment among populations with a wide range of differing perspectives, ages, interests and expectations. To ensure that the overarching narrative of a war fought for just causes by a wartime moral community was sustainable, all wartime regimes engaged in the systematic monitoring of public opinion, censorship and selective propaganda to ensure that any conspicuous areas of dissent, or manifestations of temporary scepticism and disenchantment, could be identified and measures taken to mollify or suppress them. The fashionable term to describe the popular state of mind in wartime was morale. Used widely in the First World War, the concept became embedded during the inter-war years in popular perception of the potential resilience or otherwise of the home population. In 1940, for example, the Yale scholar Arthur Pope established an unofficial Committee of National Morale to examine the ways in which American morale might be sustained in wartime; the resulting research helped the government shape its own thinking on how to sustain American commitment to war.[160] Morale was difficult to define with any precision, and even harder to measure. Opinion polls in Britain to test public satisfaction with the war effort displayed wide swings over the war years, from a low point of 35 per cent in early 1942 to peaks of 75–80 per cent in the last year of war, yet there was no sustained crisis in popular support for prosecuting the war through to the end.[161] In the Soviet Union there was widespread evidence of defeatism in the first crisis year of the war, not least among the estimated 200,000 soldiers who defected to the German side. Harsh policing by the NKVD ensured that defeatist sentiment would find no mass base.[162] In all cases, popular unease about the course of the war did not necessarily translate into damaging demoralization, except in the case of Italy. Nevertheless, monitoring morale, however loosely defined, was regarded as an essential tool in keeping the moral collective in being; the role of the state in surveying its own citizens vastly exceeded the experience of the First World War in its scope and ambition.

The task of assessing the popular mood was considerably easier in the authoritarian states because they had established structures in place before the war for supplying the regime with detailed reports on public opinion and behaviour. In the absence of a free press and a liberal political system, the dictatorships relied on a wide network of informers to report public reaction to government initiatives at home and abroad. The German system was a model of careful organization. One branch of the *Sicherheitsdienst* (Security Service) in the 1930s was devoted to reporting inland news. It was reorganized in September 1939 as Department III of the newly established Reich Main Security Office under the SS commander Otto Ohlendorf, and from 9 October the office began to compile the first formal 'Reports on the Internal Political Situation'. In November the title was changed to 'Reports from the Reich', which continued to be compiled under that name down to the summer of 1944 when the pessimistic tone of the intelligence brought accusations of defeatism, and an end to the regular reporting. Ohlendorf's office was divided into eighteen (later twenty-four) subgroups for gathering intelligence on every possible aspect of opinion and morale. The information was gathered by an estimated 30,000 to 50,000 informers, whose reports were filtered by local and provincial offices before forwarding to Berlin. There, an overall report was produced and distributed to Party leaders and the Propaganda Ministry. Informers were recruited from a largely professional background – doctors, lawyers, civil servants, police officials – and their task, according to one regional office, was to engage family, friends and work colleagues in conversation on topical issues, and to overhear conversations at work, on the bus, in shops, at the hairdresser, in markets or at the local bar.[163] The reports were comple-mented by the work of the Gestapo, whose own network of informers identified potential harm from defeatist or dissenting voices, which could then be stifled at source.

Similar systems operated in Italy and the Soviet Union. The Italian secret political police (OVRA) used a network of informers and agents to return regular weekly reports from the summer of 1940 onwards on the state of popular opinion (*lo spirito pubblico*). The number of informers was hastily expanded once it became evident just how pessimistic and disaffected much of the public was.[164] Secret police intelligence was supplemented by reports from the local prefectures, all of which ended up at the Ministry of the Interior in Rome and eventually on Mussolini's desk. In the Soviet Union, local communities were constantly scrutinized by local Communist Party officials and members and by the large network of NKVD informers. Any hint of defeatism or criticism of the regime was denounced to the police authorities. Denunciation became institutionalized to such an extent that every Soviet citizen became a potential informer.[165] However demoral-ized in reality Soviet citizens might be by the demands made of them during the war, it was universally known that the risks of complaint were enough to sustain at the least a negative state of morale. Nevertheless, in all three dictatorships a balance was struck between coercion and concession. Pub-lic concerns were often over far lesser issues than the prosecution of the war or its moral conduct and could be alleviated through appropriate responses by the state authorities or by targeted coercion.

For Britain and the United States the situation was very different. There was no established network for intelligence-gathering on the state of pub-lic opinion. Opinion polling began in the late 1930s but was still an immature tool for testing public morale when war broke out. Roosevelt had his own system at the White House for monitoring opinion, based on careful analysis of the thousands of letters that arrived every day, and a daily scrutiny by his staff of more than 400 American newspapers. In September 1939 an Office of Government Reports was set up, designed, despite its title, to track changes in public opinion. In 1940, Roosevelt reached a private agreement with Hadley Cantril, one of the pioneers of selective polling, to provide him with regular polls on popular opinion, and by 1942 he was receiving polling results every two weeks.[166] Over the war years the government set up a number of offices designed both to monitor opinion and to educate the public with appropriate information. The Office of War Information, set up in June 1942 under the CBS news-man Elmer Davis, had a Domestic Intelligence Division to report regularly on the state of the nation's morale. Local informers were recruited among businessmen, clergymen, editors and labour leaders ('the alert and articulate fraction' of the people, the Office claimed) who reported regularly on local opinion and undertook where possible to shape it.[167] Informers organized by the Office of Civilian Defense, set up in May 1941 under the mayor of New York, Fiorello La Guardia, acted as so-called 'morale wardens', reporting to the Office of War Information on local conditions. Opinion surveys were complemented by numerous programmes designed by the Office of War Information to help shape opinion: the Office's Bureau of Radio (which reached an audience of 100 million); the Bureau of Motion Pictures (which were watched by an estimated 80–90 million a week); and the Bureau of Graphics and Printing, responsible for posters and images that proliferated in every public space. Rather than resorting to crude propaganda, the American morale programme focused on providing clear information that would help to educate opinion rather than lecture to it, and on encouraging the private commercial sector to reinforce the moralizing message through advertising.[168]

The British monitoring system was built up only slowly from the early months of war. In December 1939 Mary Adams, a BBC producer, was appointed to head a Home Intelligence branch of the Ministry of Information, briefed to supply 'a continuous flow of reliable information' as a basis for government publicity, and 'an assessment of home morale'. Home Intelligence began issuing daily reports in May 1940, then from September onwards weekly reports, which were distributed to the main ministries and the War Cabinet.[169] Since there was little experience in the systematic gathering of intelligence on opinion, Adams recruited the privately run Mass-Observation in April 1940 to supply detailed surveys on morale and to report on evidence of defeatism. Mass-Observation had been founded in 1937 by the scientist Tom Harrisson and the poet Charles Madge to provide surveys of social behaviour and attitudes, using methods of interview sampling to provide the raw material. The methods were immediately applied to the task of assessing morale. Around sixty interviews were conducted for each report, based on general questioning about current news and events. The sample was tiny, and regionally specific, which should have undermined its credibility, but the Mass-Observation 'News Quota', filed each Monday and Thursday, continued to be supplied down to May 1945 as a key source for the Ministry of Information's own morale reports.[170]

These reports were supplemented by the Ministry's own informers, recruited once again from among doctors, lawyers, civil servants, clergymen, shopkeepers and publicans, and by the work of the Wartime Social Survey, established in June 1940 by academics at the London School of

Economics to supply detailed reports not only on morale, but also on a range of social issues. Staffed mainly by social psychologists, the Wartime Survey provided a more professional assessment of popular outlook. By October 1944 it had conducted 101 surveys, involving no fewer than 290,000 doorstep interviews.[171] By this time regular morale reports to Cabinet had been suspended in view of the fact that from late 1942 onwards most of the war news was positive. The Ministry of Information, controlled from July 1941 by Churchill's close confidant Brendan Bracken, learned from the intelligence on opinion to adapt wartime publicity, as in the United States, from exhortatory calls to participate to straightforward explanatory and educational material. In Britain, as in all the major states, the issues raised by monitoring morale operated at a level below the master narrative of a moral community committed to seeing the war through to the end. Popular criticism and concern were more often than not directed at making the war effort more effective, or its social effects more equitable, rather than undermining the broader moral framework of collective effort.

The close surveillance of popular attitudes to war raises the question of just how effective states were in embedding the grand narrative justifying war among the wider population. If there was in most cases general endorsement of the idea of a wartime community prosecuting a just war, comprehension of the more specific moral purposes of the war, regularly articulated in wartime rhetoric, appears more problematic. For a great many ordinary people caught up in a war that lasted for years, comprehension of its course and purposes could be partial, unclear, poorly informed and unstable over time. If the historical perspective now renders the war as a comprehensible whole, people at the time viewed it from subjective perspectives on the shape of wartime events and the unpredictable future of the conflict. They were inherently limited by what they were allowed to know and what they were allowed to say, a condition that varied greatly between the different warring nations. News was invariably censored, both by the military and by the civil authorities; in the dictatorships, the news was managed by central agencies responsible for dictating what the public could read; in the democracies, the press and media were not centrally controlled, but they could not publish or broadcast entirely as they liked. In Australia, for example, where the government remained very sensitive to criticism, particularly of the American ally, there were no fewer than 2,272 instructions to censor press material between 1942 and 1945.[172] The press everywhere depended on official communiqués that were more or less economical with the truth, and seldom entirely trusted. A report from Milan in February 1941 observed how the city population was 'bitterly disappointed' by press coverage that was full of 'big words, groundless or obsolete predictions . . . childish arguments'.[173] In China, the collapse of the regular daily press after the Japanese occupation led to a proliferation of small local broadsheets that reproduced the bland government notices or, in the absence of dedicated war correspondents, made up the news from a mix of rumour and supposition. Even among the small number who could read, the credibility of news media was low. For the illiterate majority, news came by word-of-mouth from activists who read out the news reports to villagers, or it was spread by rumour.[174]

Rumour – or 'false news' – everywhere played an important part during the war in supplementing official news. Rumours of all kinds supplied what one historian has called a 'clandestine universe' that gave ordinary people, either at the front line or at home, a certain power over the way the war and its purposes were presented.[175] In the dictatorships, rumour was one way of challenging the necessity for prudent silence in public places and reasserting some sense of autonomy. The German SD office for domestic news counted 2,740 reported rumours between October 1939 and July 1944. They varied from the trivial to rumours that Hitler was dead, or the government overthrown, and they could move with lightning speed across the whole country. A decree of 13 March 1941 distinguished between rumours and jokes, deeming the latter to have some positive value but mandating harsh penal measures against anyone caught spreading rumours 'of a spiteful character detrimental to the state'.[176] Rumours were rife in Italy in the absence of reliable news, and local Fascists were encouraged if they caught rumour-mongers (*vociferatori*) to beat them or dose them with castor oil.[177] The Soviet response was to hunt down defeatists and 'disseminators of provocative rumours'. In the six months from June to December 1941, a total of 47,987 people were arrested as rumour-mongers and defeatists.[178]

In Britain, rumours were investigated by the Ministry of Information, and the police were encouraged to prosecute 'malicious rumour-mongers', but an initial spate of harsh sentences in the summer of 1940 provoked strong public protest and prosecutions ceased in August. Rumour was henceforth to be countered by better information.[179] In the United States, particularly in more isolated communities far removed from the reality of wartime, rumours were widespread. The Office of War Information established a rumour control group in the Bureau of Public Inquiries under Eugene Horowitz, tasked with investigating rumour sources and supplying the information necessary to quash them. Volunteer 'rumour clinics' were set up where local civic figures identified and reported rumours and, where possible, used local press and radio to correct the illusions rumour created.[180] Rumours were widespread in Japan, partly explained by the mendacious reports in the press about Japanese 'successes' which were hard to believe. Between autumn 1937 and spring 1943, 1,603 rumours that violated the Military Code were investigated and 646 people prosecuted. Hundreds more were investigated from 1942 under a 'peace and order ordinance' to prevent rumours from exciting public concern.[181] Fantastic rumours served the same function as the many superstitions that flourished in wartime as an antidote to fear. The American 'rumour clinics' found that belief in rumour fluctuated between one-fifth and four-fifths of those who heard them, on a scale of plausibility. The authorities took them seriously, which explains the effort to monitor their source and their course, but there is little evidence that they challenged the prevailing narratives in any dangerous way.

The limits on understanding the war in the grand terms in which it was prosecuted were reflected in the uneven way in which the moral justification for war was appropriated by the wider public. Official wartime rhetoric can be found repeated in the diaries and correspondence of ordinary civilians and soldiers as they searched for ways to articulate attitudes and feelings. The language generated by wartime propaganda on the moral purposes of war was nevertheless more abstract and speculative than the public wanted. Opinion polling in the United States found a disappointingly small proportion of respondents who had absorbed Roosevelt's grand narrative: some 35 per cent had heard of the Four Freedoms, but only 5 per cent could recall that they included freedom from fear and want; by summer 1942 only one-fifth of respondents had even heard of the Atlantic Charter.[182] In 1943 *Life* magazine observed 'the bewilderment of the boys in the armed forces concerning the meaning of the war.' The winner of an essay competition for American soldiers in Italy on the reason they were fighting contained just two short sentences: 'Why I'm fighting. I was drafted.'[183]

A more compelling example is the extent to which the German public believed the claims by Party and government that the Jews were responsible for the war and that the German people had a moral obligation to defend the nation against the Jewish threat. There can no longer be any doubt that a high proportion of the German population knew about the deportations of the Jewish communities, and through rumour, or word of mouth from the Eastern Front, or by taking literally the threats of annihilation made publicly by German leaders, understood that the Jews were being systematically murdered. One estimate suggests a third of the population knew about or suspected the genocide, though the figure may well be higher. But whether that meant acceptance of the argument is much more open to doubt.[184] Few Germans could be unaware of the smothering embrace of anti-Semitic propaganda associated with the shift to genocide. During the middle years of the war, the public was bombarded with official material on the Jewish threat. In November 1941 Goebbels ordered a small black leaflet with a Jewish Star of David and the words 'Germans, this is your deadly enemy' sent out with the weekly ration cards. Posters that winter explained that the Jews 'wanted this war in order to destroy Germany'.[185] Millions of wall posters and pamphlets repeated the message; a *Handbuch der Judenfrage* (*Handbook on the Jewish Question*) sold 330,000 copies; a booklet produced by Goebbels' ministry in autumn 1941 on 'The War Aims of World Plutocracy', based on Kaufman's *Germany Must Perish*, had a print-run of 5 million.[186]

Yet the evidence of the extent to which the German public believed the propaganda and used it to justify the war in their minds remains ambiguous. There is no shortage of quotations from diaries or correspondence to show that a fraction, certainly among Party members, but also among the military, did absorb as true the struggle against a Jewish world enemy. A typescript written in 1944 by Georg Mackensen, a senior civil servant who had not joined the Party, reveals the extent to which the culture created by the regime of German versus Jew could become embedded in popular perceptions of the war: 'This war is no ordinary war – waged for dynasties or fought to gain territories. No! It is a struggle between two opposing ideologies, between two races ... Here we have Aryans – there Jews. It is a fight for the survival or extinction of our occidental civilization ...'[187] On the other hand, there is wide evidence of scepticism, uncertainty, even hostility over the regime's Jewish policies and, by implication, of the claim that the war was a just war against the Jewish world enemy rather than a conventional war of defence against real enemies. A reserved attitude towards the master narrative did not exclude anti-Semitic sentiment, or a desire to profit from Jewish exclusion, or a state of indifference to the fate of the Jews – which was widespread – but it did indicate that Hitler's view of the war as 'typically Jewish' was not readily endorsed. The two approaches came together only in the final years of the war when the remorseless propaganda claim that if the war was lost the Jews would take a frightful revenge was believed more readily as the Allied bombing intensified and the Red Army drew nearer, but these fears were largely dictated by firm or partial knowledge of what Hitler's Germany had already done to Europe's Jews, rather than a late acceptance of the theory of a world Jewish conspiracy.[188]

For the wider population at war everywhere, moral concerns were generally more limited and particular than those presented by the dominant narrative. Military and civilians alike constructed for themselves subjective private narratives to make sense of the war going on around them and their place in it. Identification with the national cause gave families a way of coping with the death of loved ones as valuable, even noble, rather than capricious or pointless. The key imperative was to bring the war to an end, which is why the broader collective effort was generally supported, even in the Soviet Union where there was wide latent hostility to Stalin and Communist rule, or in Japan where there existed a layer of private reservation about the war and the claims of the state.[189] Beyond compliance, voluntary or otherwise, it became necessary to find ways of accommodating to wartime conditions that still preserved the private sphere. Moral obligations here extended to family and friends, to colleagues and to the absent fighting men and women; for servicemen and women it extended to the immediate unit, whether an infantry company, a bomber crew or the men of a submarine. In the United States, much of this private wartime narrative was devoted to protecting the family and regular home life, turning abstract obligation into a personal sense of responsibility. Norman Rockwell's illustrations for the Four Freedoms played on conventional domestic scenes – a Thanksgiving dinner, small children in bed, a town meeting – linking the private sphere in a comprehensible way with the broader ethical message.[190] For Western populations, whose expectations could be examined and expressed freely, research found that what the majority wanted was a return to normality, a life with no war. In Britain, the Nuffield College Social Reconstruction Survey, conducted in the middle years of war, found little enthusiasm for great post-war plans, but a widespread desire for a return to a regular private life free of too much state interference, and with the promise of greater economic security. In the United States, opinion surveys found a similar desire for more immediate and empirical goals concerning employment, housing and personal security and less desire to act as the world's conscience.[191]

There is no reason not to believe that German, Soviet or Japanese populations also separated out the private sphere of obligation and their private expectations and hopes from the public world of war. Soviet citizens hoped that their sacrifices might earn a better life after the war, freer from Communist control and economic hardship. From early in the conflict, the Soviet authorities recognized that appeals to fight for Marxist-Leninist ideals were not what ordinary people wanted. Instead, propaganda reflected a prevailing reality that Soviet soldiers and workers saw their war in private rather than state terms – defence of the family, home and home town. The state press allowed the publication of private letters that featured filial affection and loyalty to loved ones that would have been ignored in the

1930s, but which evidently suited a popular mood in which fighting for private motives transcended any ambivalence in fighting for the Communist state.[192] Private anxieties and hopes in Germany were difficult to express openly but were also real enough. A bugged conversation between German prisoners of war in the Mediterranean theatre in 1945 reveals how one young German lieutenant viewed the tension between the duty to fight and the violation that war represented for ordinary lives:

> When I think of what the war has cost me and my generation I am appalled! ... The best years of my life have been thrown away – six precious years in which I should have achieved my Doctor's degree in chemistry, married, and begun raising my family, and contributed something to my age and my country. In the things that really matter I am much poorer now than I was six years ago.[193]

Such sentiments could not have been openly expressed while he was still fighting. As a result, there was little serious incompatibility even in the dictatorships between the public ethic of duty and sacrifice needed to sustain the war effort and the existence of a wide range of private perceptions of the war that were more critical or sceptical or incredulous or indifferent. Only in Mussolini's Italy did private grievances rupture the collective, and then only in the face of imminent invasion and defeat. Elsewhere, to break the moral bonds that kept societies fighting, by rejecting participation in the war, was a choice made by only a handful.

AGAINST WAR: THE DILEMMAS
OF PACIFISM

In 1942, the Revd Jay Holmes Smith, founder of the Community Church in New York and an American follower of Mahatma Gandhi's call for non-violent resistance, suggested that what was needed to oppose total war was 'total pacifism'.[194] This proved to be a challenging claim. Absolute pacifist rejection of war was an ethical position taken by a small minority even in states where it was permissible to appeal to conscience when rejecting military service. Participation in total war became a moral imperative that overrode conscientious rejection of violence, even by churches and churchmen that before the war condemned the drift to renewed conflict. Pacifism nevertheless survived the coming of war, for all the stifling effects of the propaganda to participate. The moral rejection of wartime violence was a dissenting voice with strong pre-war roots and a long post-war history after 1945.

That so few took a moral stance against war after 1939 is something of a historical paradox, given the widespread popular anti-war sentiment evident in the 1920s and 1930s across the Western world. In the 1920s, the rejection of war was both a reaction against the conflict just ended and an endorsement of the new wave of international idealism embodied in the creation of the League of Nations. The anti-war movement was a broad church, embracing radical pacifists utterly opposed to any manifestation of militarism, Christian pacifists who argued that war and the teachings of Christ were fundamentally incompatible, socialists and communists for whom peace was an ideal aspiration, and a more conservative anti-war lobby that was not formally pacifist, but nevertheless worked hard for a world at peace. The profound differences in outlook between the many components of the anti-war lobby were veiled only by the shared desire to avoid war at all costs. There otherwise existed persistent tension between those who stressed ethical rejection of violence, particularly Christian pacifists, those whose radical pacifist activism was linked to a broader political rejection of systems and regimes that made war possible, and those whose desire for peace did not exclude the possibility of war in a just cause.

The largest anti-war lobbies were to be found among the victor powers of 1918, although in defeated Germany there also developed in the 1920s a broad range of pacifist groups loosely organized under the *Deutsches Friedenskartell* (German Peace Cartel). The most successful was the German branch of the 'No More War Movement' led by Fritz Küster, founder of the journal *Das andere Deutschland* (*The Other Germany*), until like all peace organizations it was closed down by the Hitler regime, and the leaders imprisoned.[195] In France, Britain and the United States pacifist and anti-war sentiment reached a twentieth-century peak in the 1920s and 1930s. French pacifism embraced a wide constituency, including former soldiers of the Great War, the *anciens combattants pacifistes*, who rejected the prospect of ever repeating the conflict. By the early 1930s there were at least fifty groups that claimed some form of pacifist programme, from those opposed politically to 'imperialist war' to those who rejected on moral grounds all forms of violence, preaching what was called 'integral pacifism'. One of the most successful movements was the International League of Fighters for Peace founded in 1930 by Victor Méric, with 20,000 members. In its first appeal the League insisted that politics, philosophy and religion were distractions from the principal aim: 'Only one thing counts – <u>Peace</u>.'[196] In 1936 the French socialist leader and prime minister, Léon Blum, led a million people through Paris in a mass demonstration in favour of peace. French pacifists helped to found the

International Peace Campaign (*Rassemblement pour la paix*) in September that year, uniting the anti-war activities of the Western democracies, including the British League of Nations Union, whose nominal membership of around 1 million made it the largest anti-war group in Europe.

British support for peace was well established in the 1920s with the creation of the National Peace Council, an umbrella organization that represented numerous affiliated organizations, including the No More War Movement, but excluding the more radical War Resisters' International, organized by the British pacifist H. Runham Brown from his home in north London. The War Resisters held rigidly to the principle that 'War is a crime against humanity' and participation in any kind of war, direct or indirect, should be rejected absolutely.[197] The popular commitment to peace in Britain was widespread and non-partisan. In 1934 the League of Nations Union, together with other peace movements, launched a national campaign for voters to register their support for League internationalism. Quickly christened the 'Peace Ballot', the organizers succeeded in getting almost 12 million people to vote in favour of the work of the League in promoting peace. As a symbol of British pacifist sentiment, it was hailed as a triumph. The choice facing the world, wrote the president of the Union, Lord Robert Cecil, in 1934, was 'cooperation and peace, or anarchy and war'.[198] The same year saw the launch of what became the largest absolute pacifist lobby, the Peace Pledge Union. The Anglican clergyman Dick Sheppard asked men (women were later included, though few participated) to sign a pledge that they would never take part in or assist a future war. By 1936, when the pledge movement was formally constituted as the Peace Pledge Union, there were 120,000 members. By 1939 there were 1,150 branches across the country. Sheppard died at his desk in October 1937, and for two days queues filed past his body as it lay in state. His funeral procession to St Paul's Cathedral was flanked by huge crowds. Though absolute pacifism was a minority voice among the anti-war constituency, it articulated a much broader longing for peace among the British public.[199]

In the United States, commitment to peace was institutionalized in reaction to the experience of the Great War. There was a widespread belief that America had been tricked into participation by guileful Europeans, who took money and men from the New World and gave nothing back. Although the United States Senate in 1920 rejected participation in the League of Nations, the pursuit of peace was seen as central to American values. The Carnegie Endowment for International Peace and the World Peace Foundation, both founded in 1910, became major institutions pursuing a war-less world after 1919; a National Committee on the Cause and Cure of War represented around 6 million women; in 1921 the Chicago lawyer Solomon

Levinson founded the American Committee for the Outlawry of War; the Women's Peace Group tried unsuccessfully to get Congress to add a constitutional amendment that 'war for any purpose shall be illegal'.[200] When in 1928 the American secretary of state, Frank Kellogg, together with the French foreign minister Aristide Briand, persuaded fifty-nine countries to sign a pact that did outlaw war as a means of settling disputes, the peace movement appeared to have achieved what the League powers had failed to do. 'Today,' claimed the American journal *Christian Century*, after the Senate ratified the Pact, 'international war was banished from civilization.'[201]

In the 1930s, popular anti-war sentiment expanded in reaction to the evident international crisis and the political campaigns for isolation and neutrality. The major pacifist organizations – the War Resisters' League, the Fellowship of Reconciliation, the Women's International League for Peace and Freedom – all expanded their membership over the decade. The Women's International League, founded in 1915, had 50,000 members by the 1930s, organized in twenty-five countries.[202] Its founder, American sociologist Jane Addams, was awarded the Nobel Prize for Peace in 1931. To demonstrate the unwillingness of the current generation to embrace war, 750,000 college students staged a walk-out for peace, picketing professors who disagreed with their stand. An informal lobby organized by Princeton students under the ironic banner 'Veterans of Future Wars' was soon copied at 300 campuses across America. A poll of 21,000 students found that 39 per cent were 'uncompromising pacifists'.[203] President Roosevelt was not a pacifist, but he shared his public's longing to avoid war. When he gave the opening address at the New York World's Fair in April 1939, he saw America's future hitched to a star, 'a star of international good will, and, above all, a star of peace'. As the world crumbled into war, the organizers of the fair changed its title from 'the World of Tomorrow' to the fair for 'Peace and Freedom'.[204]

The rejection of war, embracing millions on both sides of the Atlantic, did not survive the crisis that engulfed the world. In the British parliament there was only one vote against war on 3 September 1939, by the pacifist socialist John McGovern. Explaining his stand, he told the House that he could see no idealism at work in declaring war, but only 'a hard, soulless, grinding materialist struggle for human gain'.[205] In the United States, where anti-war agitation had reached a frenzy of activity throughout 1941, there was again only one vote against war following the attack on Pearl Harbor, by the veteran pacifist and Republican representative from Montana, Jeannette Rankin. The collapse of the anti-war movement was already evident well before the coming of the European war in September 1939. In the dictator states, with political cultures dedicated to the idea of struggle, whether for the future of the race or the future of the revolution, there was no room for pacifist or anti-military sentiment in the 1930s. In Hitler's Germany, prominent pacifists were forced into exile or sent to prison or a concentration camp, since their anti-war convictions were seen as politically unacceptable in a newly militarized community. In 1939 Hitler, asked about how to treat those who objected on moral grounds to military service, replied that in times of national emergency personal conviction had to give way to a 'higher ethical purpose'.[206] Pacifism was given the same short shrift in Stalin's Soviet Union where anti-militarism was regarded as a bourgeois deviation. The principal surviving pacifist organization, the Tolstoyan Vegetarian Society, was closed down in 1929; other religious sects where pacifism was a central principle were forced to abandon their position or suffer like German pacifists a sentence in the Soviet concentration camps.[207]

Pacifism in the democracies did not suffer direct persecution, but the growing war crisis opened up irreconcilable rifts in the broad anti-war movement. The Spanish Civil War proved a watershed for many secular pacifists who found it difficult to reconcile their moral rejection of war with their loathing for fascism. Prominent pacifist leaders abandoned the cause and embraced the idea of a just war against tyranny. 'I could no longer justify pacifism,' wrote the veteran peace campaigner Fenner Brockway in his memoirs, 'when there was a fascist threat.'[208] French pacifism evaporated in 1939 with the renewed German menace. 'The appeal of force,' claimed Léon Blum, 'is today the appeal for peace.'[209] In the United States, the prominent theologian and pacifist Reinhold Niebuhr abandoned his pacifism and founded the Union for Democratic Action, calling for 'full military participation' to eradicate the menace of fascism. A United Pacifist Committee, set up in 1940 to combat American conscription, found support foundering in 1941 on confused accusations that pacifism was either a front for communist infiltration, or a stalking horse for the American extreme right.[210]

For the more moderate anti-war lobby everywhere, the failure of the League of Nations and the onset of competitive rearmament posed a dilemma that could only be resolved by the paradoxical argument that war might prove unavoidable in order to return to a state of peace. This had already been evident in the Peace Ballot when, in answer to the question whether war should be used as an ultimate resort to prevent aggression, 6.8 million voted yes. A large majority of those who joined anti-war movements were not pacifist, and when confronted with the reality of war accepted that there was little to be done but to wind down the organizations and plan for a better post-war world. Absolute pacifists became a shrinking minority, regarded with increasing suspicion that they

were, wittingly or not, helping the enemy's cause. Public unease over the
activity of the PPU in London after the outbreak of war led to calls for
the organization to be closed down, and although the government refused
an outright ban, absolute pacifists were watched closely by the secret service. Six officials were prosecuted for distributing the poster 'War will
Cease when Men Refuse to Fight'.[211] In December 1942, the PPU general
secretary, Stuart Morris, was arrested under Regulation 18B and charged
with violating the Official Secrets Act.[212] Membership of the main absolute pacifist groups was difficult to sustain in the face of the manifest
failure of the inter-war movement to save the peace, and popular hostility
to wartime dissenters. Even fellow pacifists could resent the problems
caused by an uncompromising stance. The 'incurable minoritarians', complained the British pacifist Vera Brittain, were inclined to do more harm
than good to the efforts to keep alive a moral commitment to peace.[213]

The surviving pacifist constituency might well have expected support of
some kind from the Christian churches, since many churchmen had played
a part in the 1930s in shaping the moral rejection of war. 'As Christians,'
announced William Inge, dean of St Paul's in London, 'we are bound to be
pacifists.'[214] Christian pacifists drew their inspiration from the teachings of
Jesus, and particularly the 'doctrine of non-resistance to evil'. American
Methodists formally declared in 1936 that war is 'a denial of the ideals of
Christ'.[215] In October 1939, in reaction to the outbreak of war, the American Federal Council of the Churches of Christ passed a resolution that war
'is an evil thing contrary to the mind of Christ'.[216] The Anglican pacifist
clergy in England, lobbying the archbishops for an appeal for peace in the
summer of 1940, claimed that opposition to war expressed 'the truth and
clarity of Jesus Christ'.[217] The Anglican hierarchy, however, was never formally pacifist. When challenged earlier in 1935 to explain the paradox of
Christians accepting participation in war, the archbishop of Canterbury,
Cosmo Lang, argued that without the possibility to coerce, the result
would be anarchy: 'I cannot believe that Christianity compels me to this
conclusion.' A year later Lang and the archbishop of York, William Tem-
ple, explained to pacifist clergy that circumstances might well arise in
which 'participation in war would not be inconsistent with their duty as
Christians'.[218] Even George Bell, bishop of Chichester and a leading English critic of modern war, argued in 1940 that the current war had
descended as the 'Judgement of God', an inescapable consequence of the
current 'reign of violence, cruelty, selfishness, hatred among men and
nations' against which Christians could take up arms with a clear conscience. He cited the 37th Article of Religion of the Anglican Church that
it was lawful for Christian men 'at the command of the magistrate, to wear

weapons and serve in wars', all the more so, he thought, in a war against the 'barbarian tyrant'.[219] Only one Anglican bishop, Ernest Barnes of Birmingham, retained his pacifist convictions in wartime: 'for the time being,' he complained, 'Christianity is being prostituted' for the sake of the war.[220]

Like the Anglican Church, national Christian churches everywhere rallied to offer moral and practical support to the national war effort, as they had done during the First World War. This was the case even where the churches were the object of discrimination or persecution by the secular state authorities. Churches looked to institutional self-interest, in addition to the more conventional moral commitment to provide solace to their suffering congregations and patriotic prayer for the national war effort. Unconditional support for war promised to integrate religion and state and to protect church interests, an attitude that explains more fully the willingness of churches to endorse war. In Germany, the churches generally supported the war effort despite the anti-clerical nature of the Hitler regime. The Lutheran bishops saw nothing unjust about the war with Poland when they offered in September 1939 'intercessions for our *Führer* and Reich, for the armed forces, and for those who do their duty for the Fatherland'. The Confessing Church, a breakaway church founded in 1934 by Protestant clergy critical of the state's religious policy, nevertheless supported the war at every stage, as required under St Paul's injunction (Romans 13) to give absolute obedience to the constituted authority. There remained uncertainty about whether the war was really a 'just war' in theological terms, but even the most radical clergy accepted that the faithful had to display 'obedience to God's command' and obey the state.[221] The Confessing Church's members willingly joined the armed forces and condemned conscientious objection, an alignment with the regime that ensured the church suffered less from state hostility in wartime. Catholic clergy, who suffered more than Protestants under the regime's anti-Christian campaigns in the 1930s, were more cautious in supporting the war effort – conspicuously not offering prayers for victory, but instead for a 'just peace' – but even in this case Catholic bishops saw the war in the tradition of 'just war' and accepted their role as patriotic supporters for those who performed their soldierly duty. Bishop Galen, famous for condemning the 'euthanasia' programme for killing the disabled, could praise the soldiers dying on the Eastern Front as crusaders against 'a Satanic ideological system'.[222] The crusading image was widely used to define the war against the atheist Soviet Union. In Finland, the first field bishop appointed to the army in 1941, Johannes Björklund, called on the Finnish Lutheran clergy to share in 'the all-European crusade against Bolshevism', binding army and church together in a 'holy war'. Finnish field chaplains sustained the image of God's war waged, as one of them claimed, by 'a crusading warrior, a soldier whose flag is marked by the cross'.[223]

In the Soviet Union and Japan, states not nominally Christian, the churches used support for the war as a way of displaying loyalty and averting further state repression or supervision. The position of the Patriarchal Russian Orthodox Church by the outbreak of war in 1941 was parlous in the extreme. Some 70,000 clergy and lay officials had died in the Great Terror and 8,000 churches and religious houses had been closed down. Yet on the first day of the war, Metropolitan Sergei of Leningrad urged his countrymen to defend the motherland, and to 'grind the hostile forces of fascism into the ground'.[224] Orthodox patriotism was real enough, continuing a long tradition of church support for Russia at war. From the start of the war the church began to collect donations from the Orthodox faithful to provide welfare and hospital facilities for the wounded, clothing for soldiers and refugees, and money to buy weapons, including the air squadron 'For the Motherland'. The church donated an estimated 300 million roubles over the course of the conflict. The spontaneous demand by Orthodox Christians, long denied effective religious freedom, for the reopening of churches, prompted Stalin to relax the antireligious campaign and to appoint a new patriarch of the church. The moral support for the war did not at the same time lead the church to endorse the Communist regime. At a church *Sobor* (council) in February 1945, the hierarchy called on all Christians worldwide to remember Christ's words, 'that he who raises the sword shall perish by the sword', turning the war into a Christian crusade against fascism rather than the triumph of Soviet communism.[225] Even during the war Communist religious persecution continued. The breakaway Orthodox Josephite sect, who remained uncompromisingly opposed to the dictatorship, were hunted down by the security police and sent to the Gulag camps. Unsurprisingly, Stalin's religious thaw ended two years after the end of the war, but church endorsement helped the war effort by offering another way for the Orthodox faithful to view the war as just.[226]

The Japanese case was more complex. Under the Shōwa emperor Hirohito, the native Shinto religion was transformed into 'State Shinto' and all Japanese were supposed to display their loyalty to the god-emperor by ritual worship at a Shinto shrine. The culture of obedience to the emperor-state became embedded in Japanese society. For the major Christian denominations in Japan this posed less of a challenge to Christian belief than the glorification of the state in the European dictatorships. Christian loyalty to God and to the emperor were treated as parallel rather than rival commitments. During the long Asian war, all but one of the Christian churches accepted the war as a just war or holy war to rid Asia of European claims, in order to establish what was called 'Pure Christianity', shed of its European baggage. The link between the war and the establishment of a Japanese form of the Christian religion was explicit in a statement issued by the Association for the Attainment of Church Unity in October 1942:

> We who believe in Christ are convinced together of our great responsibility to serve and to contribute to the establishment of a Pure Christianity by destroying the intent of the enemy's thoughts and intelligence, by eradicating the British and American colour, smell and taste, and by sweeping away religions, theology, thoughts and organizations which are dependent on Britain and the USA.[227]

Only the Holiness Church, waiting for the Second Coming, and the Jehovah's Witnesses refused to accept the idea of the emperor-god, or to support the war effort, and were imprisoned for their challenge to the Religious Organization Law of 1928 and to the sanctity of the state.

The situation for the Catholic Church differed fundamentally because the papacy was an international authority, not the representative of a particular nation. The pope and his hierarchy represented an important fraction of those fighting in the war on all sides. During the war the Vatican proved unwilling either to condemn aggression, or to suggest that there was anything inconsistent about Catholics fighting in a war that challenged Christian values. The pope elected in 1939, just before the outbreak of war, Pius XII, took as his starting point the importance of remaining non-partisan, as Pope Benedict XV had done in the First World War. His principal concern, he claimed, was 'the salvation of souls' wherever Catholics fought and the path to salvation was through penance and prayer, but he was also aware of the risks involved to the institution of the Church if he provoked the dictators too far. The Vatican was situated physically in the Fascist capital; from September 1943, the capital was in German hands. Pius did condemn injustices and mistreatment, except in the signal case of the persecution of the Jews, but he wanted to distance the Church from any initiatives that would force him to take sides. The one major intervention made by Pius came on Christmas Eve 1939, when he proclaimed to the College of Cardinals his five postulates for the basis of an honourable and just peace. The first postulate clearly had in mind the recent fate of Catholic Poland: 'an assurance for all nations great or small, powerful or weak, of their right to life and independence.' The fifth called on statesmen to bear in mind Christ's Sermon on the Mount and the 'moral thirst for justice', to be guided by universal love, and to display a sense of responsibility founded on the 'sacred and inviolable standards of the law of God'.[228] The peace plan implicitly condemned Axis aggression, but following the subsequent failure of his initiative, Pius was reluctant to be drawn again into efforts to end the conflict.

His private view of Hitler was of a man possessed by the devil. In secret, Pius conducted a number of long-range exorcisms to free Hitler from his grip, but only in 1945 after the war was over did he inform the College of Cardinals that in his view Hitler was truly Satanic.[229] Nevertheless, the wartime stance of the Vatican was complicated by the Axis invasion of the Soviet Union, because many in the Catholic hierarchy and among the Catholic clergy hoped the Axis would destroy atheistic Bolshevism. Catholic anti-communism made it difficult to condemn what the German invaders and their Axis allies were doing, even after the dimensions of the German genocidal programme became clear to the Vatican authorities. 'The whole world is in flames,' complained the bishop of Trieste after meeting Pius to discuss the Jewish question; 'in the Vatican they meditate on the eternal truths and pray ardently.'[230] Pius in this case too believed discretion to be the better part of valour. He told Father Scavizzi, an Italian military hospital chaplain, that on the fate of the Jews 'he was in anguish for them and with them' but feared a papal intervention would do more harm than good, prompting 'a more implacable persecution'.[231] In the field, Catholics came to terms with their own consciences, but on the issue of whether they should be fighting the war or not, the Vatican remained prudently neutral while national Catholic churches sought to avoid any indication that they were anything less than patriotic.

There were more profound moral dilemmas for those churches, Protestant and Nonconformist, where pacifism was a theological imperative. Quakers, Methodists, Seventh Day Adventists, Mennonites, Congregationalists and Baptists were all opposed to war as such, but in a war commonly defined as a clash between Christian civilization and the forces of darkness, pacifist churches found themselves forced to make compromises. Mennonites in the Soviet Union became combatants in 1941 to avoid persecution. The small number of Quakers in Germany issued a 'Peace Testimony' in 1935, reaffirming the Religious Society of Friends' commitment to pacifism, but it was not made binding on members and all but one of those conscripted undertook military service as non-combatants.[232] In Britain the main Nonconformist churches were divided over their approach to a war whose justice seemed irreproachable. The Baptists took four years to decide if their congregation could take part in war, Methodists left the decision open, while the Quakers were allowed to retain their rejection of violence because at the same time they encouraged active participation in civil defence and medical relief both at home and in the field as an example of what was called, paradoxically, 'front line pacifist service'.[233] A similar ambivalence characterized the response of the American Protestant churches as they contemplated in the years immediately before Pearl Harbor the strong possibility of war. Not all the so-called 'Peace Churches' were strictly pacifist, but they embraced the doctrine of 'non-resistance' to evil, rejecting the use of violence. The Methodist General Conference in 1940 resolved that the church 'will not officially endorse, support, or participate in war', but after 1941 Methodists were free to make their own choice whether to take part on the ground that, although they were not formally *at* war, God and the church were *in* the war. At the Methodist Convention in 1944 delegates finally rejected the decision not to bless the war and accepted that they could 'pray for victory'.[234] The Presbyterian Church General Assembly accepted that the war was 'necessary and right' only in 1943, by which time many of their congregation were already in uniform. The Congregational Christians at their assembly in 1942 voted by 499 to 45 to support the war effort, because 'the aggressions of the Axis powers are so unspeakably cruel and ruthless, and their ideologies are destructive of those freedoms we hold dear . . .'[235] Mennonites and Seventh Day Adventists kept their commitment to non-resistance, but members of both denominations served in other ways for the war effort. Religious pacifism in Britain and the United States avoided the direct rejection of participation in war and, by implication, endorsed its moral purpose.

Only one church across the divide between Allies and Axis rejected absolutely any participation in the war. The Bible Students' Association, better known as Jehovah's Witnesses, the name adopted when the denomination established a headquarters in New York in 1931, was unconditionally opposed not only to war and war service, but to the demands of the state. The movement was nevertheless not absolutely pacifist because Witnesses waited for Armageddon, the final battle between the satanic forces and the godly. They would serve only in 'God's army', not as conscripts for a godless state, and remained intransigent in their opposition to the war.[236] They were penalized everywhere for their conscientious convictions, not least because they insisted that the war was a manifestation of the powers of darkness, even in Britain and the United States where their convictions were tolerated in peacetime. In Germany, the sect was banned in late 1933 and had to meet and organize in secret. An estimated 10,000 of the 23,000 Witnesses were imprisoned or sent to a concentration camp, including women, while children were taken into state custody. Only those who recanted were freed, but few did. Refusal of military service carried a one-year prison sentence before 1939, but a new decree on 26 August 1939 on military service introduced mandatory capital punishment for refusal to serve. Witnesses made up a high proportion of those tried by the *Reichskriegsgericht* (Reich Military Court) and of 408 Witnesses prosecuted for 'subverting the nation's military strength', 258 were executed. The court, under the director Admiral Max Bastian, could impose a lesser punishment if a Witness recanted, but traditions in German and Prussian military law encouraged judges to be harsh.[237] In Japan, the Witnesses denied the concept of the god-emperor as the work of the devil and suffered the consequences for refusal to serve in the armed forces, although in this case they numbered only five.[238] In Britain and the United States, the Witnesses were singled out among the pacifist and anti-war groups for particularly harsh treatment. Two-thirds of those imprisoned in America for refusing the draft were Jehovah's Witnesses; mob violence was directed at Witnesses for their alleged lack of patriotism (in Flagstaff, Arizona, a crowd cornered one Witness, baying 'Nazi spy! String him up! Chop his head off!').[239] In Britain, the Witnesses' claim that each one of the 14,000 members was a minister of the church, charged with the task of conversion, was ignored and their organization was denied recognition as a religious denomination. Witness meetings were banned under Defence Regulation 39E.[240] The distinction Witnesses made between ungodly and godly wars was taken as evidence that they were not opposed to war as such, implausible though the final battle with the Anti-Christ might be, and therefore had no right to conscientious objection to the current conflict.[241]

The moral rejection of participation in the war was in the end confined to men (and a number of women) prepared as individuals to declare their conscientious objection. This was a courageous stance in the face of firm public disapproval and the coercive nature of the wartime state. How many more might have expressed their moral qualms at being trained and ordered to kill will never be known, but more certainly existed. The stigma of cowardice and the threat of punishment were powerful dissuaders. Moreover, the obligation on citizens to defend their state and their community in wartime was regarded as the proper expression of conscience; those who refused to do so were deemed to have violated that higher moral commitment. Objection was only formally possible in the United States and the British Commonwealth, though under strict conditions. In the dictatorships the status of conscientious objection had been erased by the time war broke out. In the Soviet Union conscientious objection had been allowed under a liberal decree dating from 1919, but the growing hostility of the state towards pacifist sentiment meant that by 1930 objection had almost ceased. Those who objected were sent to prison or the Gulag for up to five years. Between 1937 and 1939, the years of the Great Terror, there were no applications, and in

1939 the original right was deleted from the statute book.[242] In the Third Reich, the conscription law introduced in 1935 had no provision for conscientious objection, and those who did object were treated as deserters and imprisoned. The regime overrode military justice and insisted that objectors be sent to concentration camps, a majority of them Jehovah's Witnesses. The first execution of an objector took place at the Sachsenhausen camp in September 1939; over the war years an estimated 300 more were killed. In a regime where execution was regarded as the antidote to moral objection to military service, it required profound conviction and a special courage to persist.[243]

The decision to allow conscientious objection in Britain, the United States, and the British Dominions reflected not only concern over the way objectors were treated in the First World War, but also the challenge of creating conscript armies in liberal democracies with vocal pacifist minorities. In all the democracies, freedom of conscience was contrasted with the regimentation of the Axis enemy, which made it difficult to deny that some citizens could exercise that freedom by refusing military service on grounds of conscience. William Beveridge, author of the wartime plan for a postwar welfare state, considered the willingness of the state to allow objection 'the extreme case of British freedom'.[244] This view sat uneasily with the way objectors were treated. In Britain, as in the United States, secular objection to military service was not generally regarded as an acceptable moral position. Although the chairman of one of the local tribunals set up to judge objectors' sincerity asked his tribunal colleagues to bear in mind that 'a belief that war is horrible, or futile, or unnecessary may lead to a conviction that it is wrong', other judges were sceptical about secular pacifism. The most convincing political objector, claimed one tribunal judge, would be a fascist.[245] Most objectors who were registered and taken before a tribunal were expected to be able to prove the sincerity of their religious convictions, since religious objection was taken to be an acceptable moral position.

Very few of the 60,000 British conscientious objectors were given unconditional release from any form of wartime activity. At tribunals objectors were given a tough cross-examination to try to expose the moral ambiguities in their outlook. It was never enough to claim, as one objector did, 'Love and not force is the ultimate power in the universe'; lengthy adherence to a pacifist church and the support of the clergy were paramount in securing either unconditional status, granted to just 4.7 per cent of applicants, or the right to undertake other forms of service in agriculture or civil defence, secured by a further 38 per cent. Of the rest, 27 per cent were assigned to non-combatant service with the armed forces, and the remaining 30 per cent were removed from the register because they could not make an adequate case to convince the tribunals. Of those who persisted in refusing service, 5,500 were sent to prison, including 500 women, and 1,000 were court-martialled by the military authorities and sent to military prisons. Since the civilian workforce was also subject to conscription, a further 610 men and 333 women were convicted for refusing work in war industry.[246] For some objectors whose status was conditional on undertaking community work, there were small rural communities set up by pacifists where objectors could work in what one of the staff of the Central Board for Conscientious Objectors later called 'anti-war islands in a martial sea'.[247] The Christian Pacifist Forestry and Land Units, set up before the war, offered objectors an environment free of the popular hostility they experienced elsewhere. The Peace Pledge Union ran a 300-acre farm where objectors were trained by the Community Land Training Association to fit them for rural work.[248] For those directed to the civil defence services there were other obstacles to overcome because of the quasi-military nature of civil defence employment. Some 2,800 were convicted for refusing to take the civil defence medical examination because it replicated the military procedure they had already rejected; some objectors who volunteered for the fire service found that they might be required to use a gun to defend the fire station.[249] The Central Board, set up in 1939, pressured the home secretary, Herbert Morrison (a former objector from the First World War), to ensure that pacifists would not be asked to do anything that compromised their objection and in late 1943 he finally agreed that no one with objector status would be required to do anything 'repugnant to their consciences', a recognition that their moral stance was to be treated with respect.

In the United States, conscientious objection was more politically charged. The Selective Service Act of 1940 was amended under pacifist and church pressure to include the right to objection on religious grounds, which would otherwise have been illegal.[250] A National Service Board for Religious Objectors was established by the major pacifist churches and treated by the government as representative of all those who registered objection. Although objection was legally permitted, it was unpopular with the public, and won scant support from the political leadership. Roosevelt wanted to avoid making 'it too easy for them' and hoped they would be drilled by the army; his successor as president, Harry Truman, thought the objectors he had met 'were just plain cowards and shirkers'.[251] General Lewis Hershey, in charge of the Selective Service programme, thought for their own good the objector 'is best handled if no-one hears of him'.[252] Draft boards were uncertain how to treat those who claimed a moral rejection of service. 'Conscience,' observed one official, 'is an undiscernible and undescribable something hidden in the heart and soul of man.' Because it was assumed that only religious objection could have a genuine moral basis, very few secular applicants were granted objector status. Those who did object on political grounds commonly did so as black conscripts protesting against race discrimination. In one such case the Board judge read sections from Hitler's *Mein Kampf* on the dictator's attitude to blacks. 'How can you sit idly by,' the judge continued, 'and say "I will not raise a finger against the man who thinks my race only half human?"' to which he received the disconcerting response, 'There are a lot of people over here that agrees with him.'[253] Political protest, if persisted in, would earn a prison sentence, but only 6 per cent of those imprisoned were classed as secular cases.[254]

A total of only 43,000 Americans refused military service out of the 12 million mobilized. There was no category of unconditional objection as in Britain. Category I-A-O directed objectors to non-combatant service; category IV-E allowed objectors to carry out work 'of national importance'. In either category the army defined the objectors as draftees whether they liked it or not.[255] For those who refused absolutely to serve, 6,000 were imprisoned with lengthy sentences. Of the rest, 25,000 were granted non-combatant status in the armed forces, while a new institution was created, the Civilian Public Service, which absorbed around 12,000 objectors for work on projects that were deemed to be useful to society, but not directly related to the war effort. The CPS programme was run by the peace churches through the National Service Board, though under the overall control of the military authorities, and 151 camps were eventually set up where objectors had to pay $35 a month for their keep.[256] Conditions in the deliberately isolated sites were generally considered poor and the unskilled work on the land or in forests scarcely of national importance. In 1942 there was a wave of protests against what was regarded by the objectors as forced or slave labour (since the men were not paid), and against military control of the system.[257] Protesters ended up in prison, together with the absolute pacifists and Jehovah's Witnesses. In the prisons, objectors continued their protests with hunger strikes and non-violent confrontation, aimed in part at challenging racial segregation among the internees. In Chicago in 1942, encouraged by the protests, black pacifist James Farmer founded the Congress for Racial Equality to campaign against racial discrimination using Gandhian methods of non-violence.[258] Moral rejection of wartime service thus became entwined with broader issues about the moral claims of the United States at war. In 1945 President Truman refused amnesty for the 6,000 objectors still in prison, prompting a further wave of protests led by the Committee for Amnesty.

A demonstration outside the White House in October 1945 carried placards claiming 'Federal Prisons – American Concentration Camps'. Truman continued to reject a general amnesty, though many were eventually freed under his presidency. Igal Roodenko, an objector who conducted a long hunger strike, later wrote that 'Freedom and democracy can become exportable commodities only insofar as we practice them at home.'[259] Small though their numbers were, conscientious objectors, where they could, defended the principle that even in total war it was possible to defy the moral imperatives imposed by the community in favour of individual moral choice.

During the war, pacifists continued to bear witness, often at great sacrifice, to what they regarded as the futility and moral degradation of war. The overwhelming majority of the warring populations endorsed willingly or not the moral claims of their state by their silence, complicity, enthusiasm, or indifference. Powerless though the broad pre-war anti-war movement proved to be, pacifism was one of the factors that impelled states to embrace strategies of control, surveillance and morale-building to ensure that their war effort was regarded as legitimate and just, even in those many cases where it was not.

8

Civilian Wars

'Wars today are not fought or won on battlefields alone or decided in encounters between the great battle fleets of the warring nations. They are fought by ministries of propaganda, by loyal civil servants, by men and women working at menial tasks in factories; by clerks and aldermen, by farmers tilling their fields by day ... and by humble housewives who, after their day's work is done, leave their homes and patrol the blacked-out streets ... Wars today are fought by all sorts of people in all sorts of humdrum ways.'

Raymond Daniell, 1941[1]

It is now well known that millions more civilians died in the Second World War than military servicemen, the reverse of the First World War. When the American journalist Raymond Daniell found himself in London covering the German bombing of the 'Blitz', approximately ten British civilians had been killed for every British soldier. A joke circulated in bombed London about a girl who gave a white feather to her boyfriend when he said he was going to join the army. Military personnel who returned to cities under air attack were found to be more anxious than the civilians around them. Civilians had hardly been immune in the war waged between 1914 and 1918, particularly in territory occupied by the enemy, or in states where the war ended in violent revolution, but the direct involvement of civilians in wartime violence was limited. The Russian Civil War of 1918–21 and the Spanish Civil War waged from 1936 to 1939 anticipated the 'civilianization' of warfare between 1939 and 1945, when civilians fought, and died, in defence of their communities and their beliefs.

If civilians are all too often painted as passive victims of the violence that flooded over and around them during wartime, a significant fraction engaged in their own defence or their own liberation, changing from witnesses of war to active participants. A remarkable feature of the wartime years was the willingness of civilians to act on their own behalf against air attack, or invasion and occupation, or, in the extreme case of the Jewish genocide, against the menace of extermination. They did so while running exceptional risks with little protection, legal or otherwise, unlike their military counterparts. Civil defence personnel were exposed every night of an air raid to the prospect of sudden death; resistance fighters, whether regular partisans or irregular insurgents, knew that they had no defence under the laws of war if they were caught and could be shot at will by their captors; where occupation encouraged racial or ideological divisions among the occupied population, civilian fighters often found themselves fighting a brutal civil war against fellow civilians even while engaged in resistance against the occupying enemy. The battle lines involving civilians were, as a result, more incoherent and more dangerous than service in the military war effort. The violence generated by resistance and civil war was also more visceral and immediate than in most military engagements, while the aftermath of a heavy bombing raid exposed civil defenders to an utterly unaccustomed level of physical damage to the human body. Civilian wars were fought as part of the broader conflict, but they had their own distinct character.

What made some civilians into fighters varied with circumstance, opportunity and disposition. The great majority of civilians did not become civil defenders or resisters or partisans but instead sought other ways to accommodate their private world to the war going on around them. In Britain and Germany between 1 and 2 per cent of the population enrolled in formal civil defence roles; some estimates suggest that only between 1 and 3 per cent of the French population took part in some form of active resistance, although such statistics are impossible to verify.[2] For the fraction that did, there was a generally shared conviction that this war above all did not end on the battlefield but ought to be waged on the home front, whether defending against the bombing, or engaging in political subversion, or fighting as a partisan. Among resisters of every kind, including defeated soldiers who founded or led partisan detachments, there was a refusal to accept that military defeat or surrender meant that the war was over, subverting the military convention that an armistice or military occupation brought hostilities to an end. The logic of total war as a conflict that embraced whole societies explains why civilians saw their struggle as an integral part of the broader military conflict, not as an aberration. The result was not so much the civilianization of war as the militarization of civilians.

For those who dared to cross the threshold into active civilian engagement, there were individual motivations so numerous that any generic explanation is fruitless. Patriotism, ideological conviction, the pursuit of a new post-war order, profound hatred for the enemy, desperation, a long-ing for revenge, even self-interest, could all play a part in explaining why those who did participate chose to do so. In some cases, civilians were pressured into participation rather than expressing voluntary commit-ment. Assisting with civil defence was in many cases mandatory rather than a free choice. Support for armed resistance could be coerced as much as willing. Soviet partisan units routinely rounded up potential recruits from among local villagers who would not otherwise have joined. An order to enlist posted by partisans in Diakivka, a village in Ukraine, sim-ply stated that those who refused to comply 'will be shot, and their homes will be burned'.[3] Still others were pushed into resistance as a means to escape the occupiers' labour levies or the threat of deportation and could be reluctant civilian warriors. In those cases where civilian violence was transformed into civil war, civilians on both sides of the divide could find themselves unexpectedly turned into combatants, whether they sought it or not. One woman partisan in the Greek Civil War later claimed that circumstances pushed people reluctantly into action: 'life forcing you to be a hero, nobody wanted to be one.'[4] Civilians faced with such unex-pected demands found themselves compelled to make stark moral choices over whether to participate or to stand aside, and on what terms.

CIVIL DEFENDERS

The wartime civil defence effort was the single largest context in which civilians could shed their previous immunity and participate directly in the prosecution of war. The long-range bombing of cities, either because they were military-economic targets or as an act of deliberate demoralization, transcended the line that separated the urban civilian population and the civilian milieu from the fighting at the front line. Bombing away from the front lines had occurred on a small scale in the First World War: German bombing by airship and aeroplane of British coastal cities and London; British bombing of towns in western Germany; and occasional Austrian and Italian bombing of more distant urban targets. Limited though the early experiments were, the advent of aerial bombing in the war of 1914–18 opened up an imaginative vista in the inter-war years about future war in which bombing cities might quickly provoke social and political upheaval and bring the war to a rapid conclusion. The most famous of these predictions came from the Italian general Giulio Douhet in his book *The Command of the Air*, published in Italy in 1921, in which he argued that only air power directed ruthlessly at enemy cities, infrastructure and population could win a future war, and win it quickly, by turning the civilian home front into the main strategic objective, and rendering void the efforts of the army to defend the people.[5] Apocalyptic visions of war on civilian populations were universal, though they bore scant relation to the reality of conventional air power before 1939. The culture of future disaster, however, focused not on current military capabilities, which were technically limited, but on the belief that modern urban populations were uniquely susceptible to the panic and despair brought on by an air raid because the modern city lacked a firm sense of community.[6] The British military theorist J. F. C. Fuller thought an air attack on London would turn the capital into 'one vast raving Bedlam ... traffic will cease, the homeless will shriek for help, the city will be pandemonium.'[7] Another British catastrophist, the Cambridge philosopher Goldsworthy Lowes Dickinson, commenting on the claim that enemy aircraft could in three hours poison the entire population of London, reasoned that the air war now signified extermination, 'not of soldiers only, but of civilians and of civilisation'.[8]

Fear of the dramatic effects of bombing on urban society was widely shared among the populations of the major powers, but it exposed a paradox in the projection that future war would be total war: if urban society was so easy to tear apart in a few days of bombing, then it made little sense to prepare for the total mobilization of national resources since the war would be over before they could be fully exploited. The gap between these two different views of future war was filled by the advent of civil defence measures in the 1930s as the prospect of major war became more likely. Although civil defence was introduced in the First World War on a small scale in reaction to the early experience of long-range (soon to be called 'strategic') bombing, the establishment of nationwide civil defence organizations dated from the decade before the onset of the Second. This was a novel and, as it turned out, unique experience, prompted not only by the threat posed by bombing but also by widespread endorsement of the view that civilians should not expect to be immune in the next war. Civil defence linked civilians intimately with the reality of the conflict and gave them a sense of participation and worth that had been lacking in the First World War. The purpose was to mobilize civilians in defence of their own communities, in order to avert the kind of crisis that more catastrophic forecasts suggested. This was an ambition that had no precedent. Mass civilian mobilization in defence of modern society was made necessary by the advent of the bomber, but it also followed the logic of total war. Civil defence became, as a result, another means for the state to monitor on a regular basis civilian engagement with the total war effort, whether through obedience to the compulsory blackout of all lighting, or

compulsory air-defence drill, or participation in rotas for fire-watching. To
link fighting front and civilian front, civil defenders were themselves transformed into paramilitary personnel, with military-style discipline, uniforms
and training. In Italy, they were defined from August 1940 as 'mobilized
civilians', to give a more formal military status to the home front and to
prevent civil defenders from absconding.[9] When Herbert Morrison, the
British minister for home security, reflected at the end of the war on the
millions who had served in civil defence roles, he described them as a 'citizen army', made up of 'rank-and-file warriors', men and women alike.[10]

Civil defence measures were eventually introduced across the globe,
even in areas remote from the real prospect of bombing. No aggregate
figure of the numbers involved can easily be calculated, chiefly because a
distinction needs to be made between those civilians who undertook full-
time or part-time civil defence tasks as air-raid wardens, auxiliary firemen,
shelter guardians, first-aid trainees and welfare personnel, and those millions of householders and young people who were co-opted to undertake
air-raid training and air-raid duties, but who were not formally uniformed
civil defenders. This second category embraced a vast urban (and in some
cases rural) constituency that numbered tens of millions; residents were
expected to play a part as civilians in what the German authorities called
'self-protection' of homes and workplaces under the supervision of the
formal civil defence organizations. Civil defenders and their numerous
auxiliaries were usually tasked with protecting their own community and
were rarely transferred away from the region or town in which they lived,
a factor that played an important part in explaining their commitment
through difficult years to saving a place that was familiar. Civil defence
was socially inclusive and made no distinction of gender, giving women
an important part to play in community defence, in contrast to their more
restricted role in the regular military apparatus. Women volunteered in
large numbers for the many civil defence services as local communities
were denuded of younger men. In Germany around 200,000 of the full-
time officials in the civil defence organization were women; in Britain by
1940 there were 151,000 full-time and part-time women civil defence
workers, including the auxiliary fire service, and a further 158,000 supporting the first-aid services.[11] In the United States, almost two-thirds of
Washington's home defence volunteers were women; in Detroit, around
half.[12] Schoolboys and girls were also recruited for particular tasks: Boy
Scout volunteers in Britain bravely cycled between air-raid posts with
emergency messages; the Soviet Union recruited from *Komsomol*, the
Soviet youth movement, for youngsters to join rescue teams or to spot
incendiaries on rooftops; in the final months of the bombing over

Germany, Hitler Youth members were posted as *Flakhelfer* (anti-aircraft auxiliaries) to man the anti-aircraft guns in the absence of regular air force troops.

The largest civil defence organizations were founded in Japan, Germany and the Soviet Union, where the defence of local communities from the effects of bombing became an almost universal obligation. Japanese preparations dated back to the late 1920s, with blackout practices and air-raid drills in major cities involving the entire urban population. In April 1937, a National Air Defence Law introduced a nationwide programme through which local urban 'block associations' and smaller neighbourhood groups in towns and villages became responsible for ensuring that all civilians were transformed into potential civil defenders. Two years later the government established auxiliary fire and police forces recruited from civilian communities to help cope with raiding. Civil defence was based on traditions of collective commitment that left little room for dissent. The large civil defence organizations established in the Soviet Union and in Germany were similarly authoritarian and collectivist, reflecting the ambition in both dictatorships to mobilize their citizens for a wide range of activities designed to cement their public commitment to the purposes of the national community. The Soviet 'Society for Assistance to Defence' (*Osoviakhim*), dating from 1927, had at least 15 million members by 1933, including 3 million women, when the threat from bombing was minimal. They were given rudimentary training in air-raid defence, on how to cope with a gas attack and on post-bombing first aid. In July 1941 a decree on 'universal and compulsory' anti-air-raid preparations turned every citizen into an impromptu civil defender. By 1944 it was claimed that a remarkable 71 million Soviet citizens of all ages had received some form of civil defence training. In cities closer to the threat of bombing, the authorities set up urban 'self-defence' units to assist in firefighting and rescue, and by the end of the war these units had 2.9 million members. Those recruited were expected to play a full part in preparing their communities for bomb attacks and in combating the after-effects of a raid. Alongside this army of civilian civil defenders, the state established in 1932 the Main Directorate of Local Air Defence (MPVO), which had formal responsibility for training civil defence personnel, creating a network of shelters, principally in residential buildings, and supplying fire and rescue services following a raid. The MPVO workers were paramilitary civil defenders, and at the wartime peak they numbered a further 747,000.[13]

The German Reich Air Defence League (*Reichsluftschutzbund*), set up in 1933 by the newly founded Air Ministry, was rapidly expanded as the principal agent for educating and training the public about air-raid precautions.

In May 1937 a law on 'self-protection' (*Selbstschutz*) was introduced, compelling all householders to prepare their homes and buildings against an air
attack, to assist with air-raid protection for public buildings and offices, or
to take part in 'work protection' for factories.[14] Because the regime insisted
that community self-defence was an obligation, as it was in the Soviet Union
and Japan, there were 11 million members of the League by 1937, 13 million by 1939 and 22 million by 1943, one-quarter of the German population.
The organization itself had 1.5 million office-holders by 1942 and ran a
system of 3,400 'air-raid schools' where basic training was undertaken.[15]
There was also a formal structure of air-raid protection supplied by Air
Protection Police and Fire Protection Police and by the regional German air
force commands, but their work depended a great deal on the voluntary
contribution made by League members in organizing and inspecting the
air-raid preparations of local communities to ensure that 'self-protection'
was being fully observed, and in supplying the men and women needed for
civilian civil defence roles.

By contrast the civil defence systems in the Western states relied more
heavily on volunteers in response to appeals by government to take up
civic duties in wartime. In Britain, civil defence recruitment on any scale
began only in the late 1930s. There was no equivalent mass organization
for air-raid protection to match the German or Soviet example, but once
bombing began in autumn 1940 the government moved from encouraging volunteers to making some elements of civil defence obligatory and
universal. Prompted by fear of an approaching war, the government in
late 1937 passed the Air Raid Precautions Act, which required all local
authorities to establish a civil defence scheme and to appoint an Air Raid
Precautions Controller (usually the senior municipal administrator), and
an Emergency or War Executive Committee to oversee civil defence once
bombing became a reality. In 1939 a network of Regional Commissioners
was established to co-ordinate local initiatives and to act as a bridge
between central government and local communities.[16] The structure was
almost entirely civilian in character; the army and air force were responsible only for the active anti-aircraft defences of guns and fighter aircraft.
To emphasize its civilian character, all civil defence was placed under a
civilian minister of home security when war broke out in September 1939.
By summer 1940 there were 626,000 civil defenders, one-fifth of them
full-time workers, and a further 354,000 part-time personnel to be mobilized during an emergency. In addition, the fire services expanded from
5,000 regular firemen in 1937 to a figure by 1940 of 85,000 full-time and
139,000 auxiliary firemen and women, while the Women's Voluntary Services for Air Raid Precautions, founded late in 1938, could boast almost

a million members at the wartime peak.[17] Following the introduction of compulsory fire-watching in factories and public buildings late in 1940, the number of additional part-time civil defenders reached more than 4 million, around one-tenth of the entire population.[18] Even where it was not compulsory, civilians were supposed to organize the defence of their residential communities street by street, challenging every household, as in Germany, to play some part in their own protection.

In France and Italy, both countries that by the late 1930s might have expected at some point to be bombed, the civil defence organizations were more modest in scale. A system of 'Passive Defence' was set up at government insistence in France in 1935, obliging all local communities, as in Britain, to establish air-raid protection and to train local civilians to fulfil civil defence roles. The system was never properly tested before the French surrender in June 1940. Under the Vichy regime, civil defence lapsed until first the British air force, then the American, began bombing targets in France. The Pétain government was reluctant to mobilize civilians when France was ostensibly no longer at war, or to bear the costs of an extensive civil defence system, but under pressure from the Germans the Passive Defence responsibilities of local prefects and mayors were once again revived, though they remained desperately short of funds and personnel.[19] In Italy, the regime issued a law in March 1934 mandating provincial prefects to establish a decentralized regional civil defence system, but the Provincial Inspectorates for Air Raid Protection that resulted remained a low priority for resources.[20] Italian civil defence relied on voluntary membership in the National Union for Anti-Aircraft Protection (UNPA), set up by the War Ministry in August 1934 to establish a corps of civil defenders, but they numbered only 150,000 by 1939 and in 1940, when war with Britain and France began, thousands abandoned the organization. Preference was given to Fascist Party members as civil defence officials, and little co-ordinated effort was made to mobilize and organize civilians in the main urban areas to undertake training and to embrace 'self-protection'.[21]

Away from the main threats in Europe and East Asia, civil defence was still regarded not only as strategically necessary, but as a way to mobilize and discipline populations to perform civic duties for the war effort. 'We have reached a moment in history, I believe,' General Marshall told an American radio audience in November 1941, 'when the civilian should definitely take his place in the general preparation of the country . . .'[22] An Office of Civilian Defense was established by presidential order in May 1941 to prepare civilian volunteers not only for the possible case that either the Japanese or the Germans would find a way to bomb the American west or east

coast, but also to encourage civilian participation for a variety of other wartime social programmes. Initially run by the mayor of New York, Fiorello La
Guardia, the office was taken over from February 1942 by Harvard law
professor James Landis, who oversaw the recruitment of millions of Americans into civil defence roles as air-raid wardens, auxiliary firemen, first-aid
volunteers and rescue teams. Altogether an estimated 7–8 million people
volunteered, while millions more, including schoolchildren, were introduced
to elementary civil defence drill in the workplace and at school.[23] The Civilian Defense journal was titled *Civilian Front* to make explicit the involvement
of civilians directly in America's total war. Civil defence, wrote Landis in
1943, 'is a military assignment as definite as that given an armed task force
ordered to take and hold an enemy position'.[24] Although the bombing of the
mainland United States never materialized, despite the unfulfilled ambition
of the German air force to find the ideal 'America bomber', civilian defenders
until the end of the war continued to be given training, while air-raid wardens patrolled the streets of America's coastal cities. The same held true for
the distant parts of the British Empire, where the menace of air attack was
not completely remote following the outbreak of the Pacific war in December 1941 (and in the case of Hong Kong, Singapore and northern Australia
real enough). In New Zealand, which like the United States was never
bombed, the Emergency Precautions Service established in March 1942 was
modelled on British civil defence, with wardens (one for every 500 people),
first-aid, welfare and rescue services. Here too civil defence was a constant
daily reminder for the population that modern war invoked civilian participation, not mere military effort. 'Citizens of the Commonwealth be prepared,'
ran the recruitment slogan. 'It can happen here.'[25]

In practice the demands made on civil defenders to protect their communities varied widely in time and space. Many places in Europe or Asia
were bombed only once, some not at all. Where there were more raids,
there could be long gaps of months or years between each experience. Cities in Germany – Hamburg, Cologne, Essen – bombed more than 200
times were the exception rather than the rule. In the war in Asia, only the
Nationalist Chinese capital at Chongqing, bombed 218 times between
1938 and 1941, matched the experience in Germany.[26] Bomb loads also
varied greatly: a force of 600 Lancaster heavy bombers could unleash a
devastating quantity of high explosive and incendiary bombs, enough to
burn down the whole centre of a city; a small force of fifty medium bombers carrying a relatively small bomb load could inflict serious local damage
but not large-scale destruction. For most civil defenders, action was spasmodic and brief; for many, there was little or no action to see, sometimes
for years. The Japanese civil defence system was kept in a constant state

of preparation for four or five years before the first raids hit late in 1944, prompting over time a mixture of apathy and resentment among some of those recruited. Only for the last six months of the Pacific war, once Japanese cities were in range, was civil defence at last tested. Civil defence regulations, enforced by the army of civil defenders, were nevertheless maintained in case the bombers ever came. Everywhere the imperatives of civil defence were an effective means to remind the population on a daily basis, as they drew the blackout blinds or checked the water and sand kept against the risk of fire, that they were on a new civilian front line. 'Each time there is an air-defence drill,' wrote one Tokyo woman in 1943, 'we are made to line up in single file, call out our names, and roll is taken, with lots of muttering about which houses are not represented ...'[27] Infractions of the blackout rules were regularly punished everywhere they occurred. The intervention of the wartime state became a direct reality in the daily lives of almost every citizen.

The difference in experience was also dictated by the nature of the air strategy deployed against civilians. Almost all bombing in the Second World War was inaccurate, often by a wide margin, but the aim was generally to undermine the military capability of the enemy by attacking distant military and military-economic targets. In only three cases was air strategy directed deliberately at the destruction of the civilian milieu and the death of civilians: the Japanese bombing of Chongqing; the strategy of area-bombing of German cities adopted by RAF Bomber Command from the summer of 1941; and the bombing of Japanese cities by the American XXI Bomber Command, beginning with the firebombing of Tokyo in March 1945 and ending with the two atomic bombs. The development of the RAF strategy of attacking enemy morale through deliberate destruction of the urban area had its roots in the 1930s, when the discussion of future bombing strategy assumed that in modern war there was no distinction any longer between combatant and non-combatant. Civilians were regarded as a target because they contributed materially to sustaining the enemy war effort, a mirror image of the popular civilian conviction that their own staying power was likely to be an objective in any future war. In 1944, Air Vice Marshal Richard Peck, responsible for RAF publicity, defended the indiscriminate attack of civilian urban areas with the argument that the workers

are the industrial Army – their overall is a uniform – each man has been reserved from the Army, by the Army; each woman takes a place that otherwise a man must fill – they are quartered nearby in the town – their house is the equivalent of the soldier's rest billet or reserve trench.[28]

Bombing operations against German industrial cities were designed to
cause maximum damage to working-class residential districts and amenities, and to kill workers, and this was most easily achieved by high
concentrations of incendiary weapons against the central residential zones
of the city.[29] This was a war against civil defence. Small quantities of high
explosive bombs were mixed in with the incendiary load to blow in win-
dows and roofs, and to deter the civil defenders. To discourage them further,
explosives were fitted to a number of the incendiaries (around 10 per cent
of the load) with fuses timed at different intervals. In 1942 small anti-
personnel bombs were added to the aircraft bomb loads. The intention was
to kill or maim any civil defenders unfortunate enough to be near them.[30]

The US Army Air Forces over Japan adopted a similar policy of disabling the Japanese civil defence system. The inflammability of Japanese
cities was well known. General Marshall, in a secret press conference
shortly before Pearl Harbor, told pressmen that if war came Japan's 'paper
cities' would be set on fire: 'There won't be any hesitation about bombing
civilians – it will be all-out.'[31] However, only in 1945 were American
bomber aircraft near enough to inflict heavy incendiary raids and their
explicit purpose was to destroy the urban environment, kill or maim Japanese labourers, and to demoralize the workforce. 'It made a lot of sense,'
observed General Ira Eaker, deputy commander of the army air forces in
1945, 'to kill skilled workers by burning whole areas.'[32] As with the RAF,
this involved careful research about the optimum operational conditions
for overwhelming the fire and emergency services. Research on how best
to burn down Japanese houses had begun several years before the raids,
aided by British experience in the scientific calculation of the nature of
incendiary damage, which was willingly passed on between the Allies. The
mass destruction of the civilian milieu and the urban civilian population
became an object in itself, as it had been for the RAF over Germany.
Here, too, was a direct war between air forces and civil defenders.

Civil defence was presented with its sternest test in these campaigns
that deliberately targeted the civilian population, but everywhere that
bombing was experienced civil defenders struggled to cope with the reality that during any determined bombing raid most bombers would get
through to disgorge their loads on the civilian areas below them. This was
true even of the most sophisticated air-defence system. By 1944 the German air-defence line of radar, anti-aircraft artillery, fighter and night-fighter
aircraft, the so-called 'Kammhuber Line' (after General Josef Kammhuber
who devised it), was unmatched anywhere, but night after night and day
after day the majority of Allied bombers reached the approximate target
area despite regular attrition of the attacking force. Where there were

weak or non-existent defences, bomber aircraft were free even of the threat of enemy fighters and effective anti-aircraft fire. Early Japanese raids on the Chinese Communist capital at Yan'an in late 1938 were virtually unopposed until a few anti-aircraft guns were installed in the city's Ming-era tower. At Chongqing the feeble Chinese fighter force was swept aside by the Japanese and anti-aircraft fire was limited, leaving Japanese bomber crew with the luxury to bomb almost at will.[33] Even in Britain, where by day the fighter force was able to inflict heavy damage on incoming German bombers in the first days of the Blitz in September 1940, the switch to night-bombing left British cities relying on the fire of anti-aircraft guns – which hit few bombers, but forced them to fly higher and to bomb with even less accuracy – and an entirely ineffective night-fighter force until the introduction of radar-directed interception in the spring of 1941.[34] As a consequence, civil defenders were willy-nilly the front line between the bombers and the bombed, a unique front line in which they never saw the face of the enemy that menaced them.

The bombing of British cities for nine months across the winter and spring of 1940–41 supplied civilian defenders with the opportunity to demonstrate what an organized civil defence force was capable of. The initial experience highlighted evident problems. There was little understanding of what constituted panic, or how it might be defused. One senior psychoanalyst, Edward Glover, writing in 1940 on fear of bombing, could only suggest as a mundane antidote to panic that citizens with sterner nerves should carry with them a hip flask of brandy or a packet of biscuits to calm down their more agitated compatriots.[35] In a number of cases there was widespread panic by the civilian population and an exodus from a city following a raid, though the rapid provision of shelter and welfare usually defused any potential social crisis. The issue of 'trekking', as it became known, was at its most serious in Plymouth, Southampton and Hull, all ports repeatedly bombed. The heavy bombing of Southampton in late November 1940 was so severe that the civil defence system temporarily collapsed, 'overwhelmed by the magnitude of the disaster', as the regional commissioner put it. An official from the Ministry of Food found the people on the day following the raid 'dazed, bewildered, unemployed and uninstructed'.[36] Civil defenders were hamstrung by the collapse of communications and the loss of the central air-raid precautions control room. The population de-camped to the nearby woods and villages, though the death toll of 244 from the two raids was modest compared with the losses inflicted in Allied bombing raids later in the war.

The early failures prompted rapid reform of the civil-defence system, with greater emphasis on effective communication and information, more and better-stocked welfare centres and emergency kitchens, and – above all – programmes for rapid rehabilitation in homes that could easily be repaired. For the army of air-raid wardens whose task it was to alert their communities once the warning siren sounded, a major difficulty was enforcing shelter discipline, which was the one clear way to reduce casualties. In Germany and the Soviet Union seeking shelter was compulsory, and the police were responsible for backing up the efforts of local wardens to maintain shelter discipline with as heavy a hand as they needed (which in Germany included the exclusion of Jews and foreign forced workers from shelters reserved for 'Aryan' Germans). On the other hand, British wardens had no legal sanction to resort to, so that compliance with sheltering was an individual decision rather than a legal obligation. The government also preferred a system of decentralized shelters in basements and cellars, or the domestic 'Anderson shelters' dug into gardens for those who had them. Only half the threatened population had access to a designated shelter, and almost none of them were in fact bombproof. Research later in the war revealed that of those families without a shelter facility at home, only 9 per cent sought to use public shelters.[37] Public shelters quickly proved to be poorly constructed and insanitary, almost all of them without proper sleeping facilities. Even when the government initiated from December 1940 an energetic programme to supply beds, welfare and proper hygiene in shelters, public confidence remained low. Thousands chose instead to defy the civil defence system and to remain in their homes in bed, or under the stairs, or under the table, a fact that helps to explain the high casualties suffered from a campaign that lacked the scale of the heavy saturation raids on Germany and Japan later in the war. In Britain only 3 per cent of the urban area was destroyed, but in Germany 39 per cent and in Japan an exceptional 50 per cent.[38]

The saturation raids were designed to break the enemy's civil defence structure and open the way to unlimited destruction, almost always by fire. Where major firestorms occurred – in Hamburg in July 1943, Kassel three months later, Dresden in February 1945 – civil defence was indeed overwhelmed. In Hamburg during the firebombing there were 34,000 firefighters, soldiers and emergency workers, but they could only work to limit the spread of the conflagration to the outer suburbs of the city. The police president of the city in his report of the firestorm on the night of 27/28 July acknowledged that civil defence was powerless in the face of a firestorm – 'speech is impotent,' he wrote, as he tried to describe what happened – but recommended major changes in the way civil defenders coped with the threat of fire: inspecting all domestic shelters (the 'bombproof room') to ensure that there was an emergency exit to prevent those inside from suffering asphyxiation as the fire sucked out the oxygen, as had been the case in Hamburg; and the construction of known escape routes in city centres so that the population could flee before the firestorm over-whelmed them.[39] Civil defence personnel were advised to train all householders to tackle incendiary bombs at once, in the middle of a raid, to prevent small fires from amalgamating into a conflagration, thus exposing many more civilians to all the dangers faced by the regular civil defenders. Civilian volunteers made up most of the 1.7 million firefighters in Germany by 1944, including 275,000 women and girls. Around 100,000 of the vol-unteers were organized in 700 emergency units, designed to move from place to place as required to combat the fires. In August 1943, special 'self-protection squads' were established to compel all civilians by law to take an active part in collective civil defence beyond the self-protection of individ-ual homes.[40] Hamburg also prompted greater attention to the supply of food, emergency shelter and medical assistance to bombed areas; as in Brit-ain, the supply of effective information, food and welfare, together with a programme of evacuation or rapid rehabilitation (carried out in part by concentration-camp labour), showed the extent to which civil defence and rescue services, properly organized, could challenge efforts to create social breakdown in the bombed cities. In Hamburg an estimated 61 per cent of the residential housing was damaged or destroyed, but within months 90 per cent of those who remained in the city, some 300,000 households out of half a million, were re-housed in repaired or prefabricated buildings.[41]

The firebombing of Japanese cities was again the point at which civil defence preparations broke down under extreme pressure. Japanese authorities had expected precision bombing of economic and military tar-gets, which the American air forces undertook in the first wave of bombing from late 1944 to February 1945, with little success. Firebombing, initi-ated with the major raid on Tokyo on the night of 9/10 March, created conflagrations that proved impossible to control. Civil defence volunteers had been trained to cope with more limited raids; the air-raid drill for civilian householders proved completely inadequate when fire rapidly consumed an entire urban zone. 'If there is an air raid,' wrote a Japanese mother to her evacuated daughter in May 1945, 'please think of the house as gone.'[42] There was secure shelter space for only 2 per cent of the urban population. Japanese cities were peculiarly vulnerable to firebombing with their wood and paper construction; some 98 per cent of buildings in Tokyo were built from flammable material, while population density in the main urban areas was exceptionally high.[43]

The earlier bombing of the Chinese capital at Chongqing by the Jap-anese naval air force in 1939 and 1940 had demonstrated how vulnerable such cities could be. The narrow, cramped streets, fronted by buildings mainly constructed of wood and bamboo, were ideal for spreading fires even during a limited incendiary attack. Some four-fifths of the commercial centre of the city was destroyed entirely by fire in a handful of raids by small groups of enemy aircraft.[44] In order to avert a similar disaster in mainland Japan, the civil defence authorities ordered the demolition of a remarkable 346,629 buildings in order to construct firebreaks across urban areas. American low-level bombing by the giant Boeing B-29 bombers, however, saturated the urban area with thousands of tons of incendiaries in a narrowly defined zone. Out of 160,000 tons of bombs dropped on Japan, 98,000 tons were incendiaries.[45] In the Tokyo raid the collapse of civil defence, welfare and first aid was exacerbated by the destruction of 449 out of 857 first-aid stations, as well as 132 out of 275 hospitals, and hundreds of the welfare stations prepared in advance. Units for maintaining morale and averting panic – the so-called 'Political Thought Squads' – were regarded as a priority, but as a result the rescue and fire services found themselves poorly resourced with insufficient personnel, heavy equipment or specialized rescue apparatus. The result was an exceptional level of casualties in Tokyo, where an estimated 87,000 died in the firestorm on 9/10 March. Throughout the bombed urban area, in just five months of bombing, the official statistics counted 269,187 killed, 109,871 seriously injured and 195,517 who suffered minor wounds.[46]

The high toll of chiefly civilian casualties was repeated across all heavily bombed areas, but even in more lightly bombed regions civil defence was unable to avert civilian losses and widespread destruction. In Germany, current estimates suggest that between 353,000 and 420,000 lost their lives (the official figure from 1956 claimed 625,000); the bombing of Britain resulted in 60,595 deaths from bombs, rockets and cruise missiles; the bombing of European states under German occupation, although designed to limit casualties where possible by avoiding the saturation of urban areas with incendiaries, produced estimated deaths in France of somewhere between 53,000 and 70,000 civilians, in Belgium an estimated 18,000 and in the Netherlands a further 10,000; in Italy both as an Axis enemy until its surrender in September 1943, and then under German occupation until May 1945, the official post-war figure for bombing dead amounted to 59,796; the official statistic from German bombing of Soviet targets, small-scale though the raiding was, accounted for a further 51,526 dead; the best estimate for Chinese deaths from bombing is 95,522.[47] In addition there were those seriously injured by the raids, in most cases approximately doubling the number of casualties. The figures of around 1 million killed and a similar number badly injured might suggest that on balance the vast civil defence effort was a straightforward failure. The battlefront was certainly a case of asymmetric warfare: bombers primed with a daunting array of aerial weapons against civil defenders who were unarmed and, in most cases, part-time civilian volunteers. Yet despite this disparity, civil defenders and the great array of civilians who played an auxiliary part in the many schemes of self-protection confronted enemy air power even in the firebombed cities in order to avert the uncontrollable social collapse that pre-war fiction and military futurology had predicted.

There can be little doubt that without the civil defenders the level of casualties and the social dislocation of urban communities would have been considerably worse, and the impact of bombing closer to Giulio Douhet's prognosis. Where civil defence broke down, as it did in a number of cases, particularly during the firestorm raids, the crisis could generally be localized with urgent help provided from outside the stricken city. The habit of trekking from bombed ports in Britain did not create a permanent social crisis. Welfare services established emergency 'cushion belts' in the surrounding countryside where families could live while the workers commuted into the town each day. Many more lives were saved by the formal and informal schemes of mass evacuation that were introduced in all stricken areas. In Germany almost 9 million people left the cities by early 1945; in Japan the figure approached 8 million by the war's end. But lives were also saved during the raids themselves because of the immediate effort on the part of civil defenders to ensure that where shelters were available, the population could be persuaded to make use of them in an orderly way. When a sudden panic did ensue, the results could be disastrous, as they were after a long Japanese raid on Chongqing on 5 June 1940. As people were leaving one tunnel shelter, others tried desperately to get in after a rumour that the Japanese were returning with gas bombs, crushing those in front of them. Police records showed 1,527 killed in the stampede.[48] A panic at the London Bethnal Green underground station on 3 March 1943 following an air-raid warning created too much human pressure down the wet and dimly lit staircase and resulted in 173 people trampled or suffocated to death.[49]

These examples proved the exception. Wardens played a courageous part in controlling threatened communities and ensuring orderly access to public shelters or monitoring the use of domestic shelter. Firefighters and first-aid workers risked their lives while the bombs were dropping. Even in Chongqing, where more than 1,000 tunnel shelters were hastily improvised in the city's hillsides, wardens generally succeeded in imposing order on their communities when the siren signalled the moment to retreat to the tunnels. In 1937 shelters could accommodate only 7,000 from a population of almost half a million, but by 1941 there was shelter for 370,000.[50] In 1939 there were eleven casualties for every two bombs dropped on the city; but by 1941 the figure was one casualty for every 3.5 bombs.[51] The peak weeks for casualties in the Blitz on Britain came between September and November 1940 as the system was learning to cope. Everywhere, civil defenders did what they could to ameliorate the worst effects of the bombing and its immediate aftermath. Contemporary accounts of air raids contain numerous stories of the personal heroism displayed by civilians. In Germany, civil defenders killed in the course of duty were, like fallen soldiers, allowed an iron cross next to their name in newspaper lists of the dead; heroes who survived could be decorated with the military iron cross. During the Blitz on Britain, King George VI instituted the George Medal for exceptional gallantry displayed by civilians, to reward the many examples of bravery displayed under the bombs. Among the first recipients were two fire officers and an auxiliary fireman from the Dover Auxiliary Fire Service, who worked to rescue a ship filled with explosives while it was being bombed, and two women ambulance drivers in Suffolk who had rescued a badly injured man during a raid.

Civil defenders and the millions of civilians who worked with them played a critical role in containing the demoralizing effects of bombardment and ameliorating the traumatic effects of a raid. In this, they acted as agents of the state, providing a layer of local civilian management that linked damaged communities with the wider national effort to sustain morale, and at the same time helped to contain the damage done by bomb destruction. This was certainly an uneven success story, but in general civil defence helped to maintain some sense of local community solidarity which the central state would not have been capable of achieving unaided. Dependence on the state increased as a result of bombing, but the means by which that dependence was secured lay in the efforts of all those engaged in civil defence, welfare and rescue to sustain community life even in the face of repeated raids. The civilian war against the bombing also linked local communities more intimately with the reality of the war, while the regular discipline involved through monitoring compliance with civil defence, and in training millions of civilians, turned the home front into a surrogate fighting front. In a speech to civil defence workers on 12 July 1941, Winston Churchill addressed them in military terms: 'train the civil troops, prepare the munitions for the battle against fire, mobilise, practise and equip the great army of fire-bomb fighters . . .'[52] Civilian volunteers were not, of course, soldiers, even when wearing a uniform, but unarmed citizens trained for a unique form of combat. Under the impact of bombing, civilians found themselves fighting an unequal war during which they themselves sustained substantial casualties, and often for years at a time. Nothing else quite represented the civilianization of warfare as explicitly as the war of civil defence.

THE MANY FACES OF WARTIME RESISTANCE

Civilian resistance constituted a front line of an altogether different kind from civil defence. It was not about sustaining community solidarity in the face of a shared threat, but about destabilizing societies under enemy occupation. Resistance was directed against an enemy that had defeated national or imperial armed forces and now controlled entire civilian areas as a conqueror. Yet while civil defence is relatively simple to define, civilian resistance has proved, then and now, elusive of any simple definition. Resistance could take many forms, covert or overt. Minor acts of non-compliance or dissent were widespread but scarcely matched the wartime image of resistance. The French journalist Jean Texcier published an anonymous '33 Conseils à l'occupé' ('33 Recommendations to the Occupied') in August 1940, but he simply enumerated ways in which the French public should avoid contact, sympathy or even conversation with the German enemy.[53] This passive attitude to occupation was the commonest form of behaviour. Most civilians waited to be liberated, an attitude dismissively described by the French resistance as *attentisme* and by the Italian partisans as *attendismo*, 'wait and see'.[54] The understandable desire somehow to survive under occupation without attracting attention or running risks was widespread across occupied Europe and Asia. The post-war view that occupied societies were bi-polar, either *résistants* or *collaborateurs* in the French case, or in occupied China *káng Ri* (resisters) or *hanjian* (collaborators), makes little historical sense.[55] The millions who did not actively resist found a wide space between these two poles, from which they sometimes ventured in one direction or another if they were compelled by circumstances to do so, but where they otherwise tried to shield the private sphere from the sufferings imposed by the occupiers and their local proxies. Resisters and collaborators alike, voluntary or involuntary, were always only a small fraction of the populations under occupation.

Resistance in a more active sense was a heterogeneous phenomenon. At root almost all major resistance movements were about achieving national liberation, an ambition reflected in the titles chosen: Committee for National Liberation in Italy, Council of National Resistance in France, the Greek National Liberation Front and National People's Liberation Army, the Yugoslav National Liberation Army, and so on. But these national movements masked a wide variety of different ways in which resistance might be expressed, and glossed over smaller, often local movements that did not necessarily identify with the broader campaign for national liberation on ideological or political or tactical grounds. Resistance can best be summarized as any form of active confrontation with the occupying authority that violated the occupiers' rules or challenged its political and military presence. In some cases that meant subversive political activity – publishing newspapers, pamphlets or wall posters, organizing illicit meetings and networks – without necessarily moving to the next step of organized guerrilla/terrorist activity. The most popular French resistance paper, *Défense de la France*, printed in a basement room at the Sorbonne, was a form of cultural confrontation with the occupying regime, but its publishers did not engage in active violence.[56] In China, popular village theatre based on the traditional *yangge* (rice-sprout songs) was used as a form of cultural resistance in the occupied areas, featuring short plays on resistance themes – 'Joining the Guerrilla Forces', 'Arresting Traitors' – which peasant audiences could easily understand.[57] In most cases, however, resistance involved acts of violence against the occupier, even for those organizations or groups that set out initially to engage in political struggle and to eschew terrorism. By March 1944, after years of brutal German repression, *Défense de la France* published a leading article on 'A Duty to Kill': 'Our duty is clear: we must kill. Kill the German to cleanse our territory, kill him because he kills our own people, kill him to be free.'[58]

Armed resistance took many distinct forms. There were spontaneous, individual acts of terror; there were groups that undertook sabotage and assassination, organized through a wider network of resisters; finally, there were major guerrilla/partisan units that formed in the rear of the enemy to harass and intimidate his forces. There remained a wide gap between the shadowy existence of a few hundred resisters operating an underground network with as much secrecy as possible, and the large partisan armies active by the war's end. The Chinese Communist Party armed forces numbered 900,000 by 1945; the Greek National Liberation Army (ELAS) fielded 80,000 in 1944, with 50,000 reservists; the Yugoslav National Liberation Army contributed 8 divisions to the re-conquest of Serbia, with up to 65,000 partisans supporting the Red Army in the capture of Belgrade.[59] These very different forms of armed resistance were dictated partly by geography, partly by the question of timing. For partisans fighting in Europe, it was possible to exploit the large areas of mountain and dense forest along the mountain ranges in Italy, the hills and mountains of Yugoslavia, Macedonia and Greece, or the vast forests and swamplands in eastern Poland and the western Soviet Union. Where resisters tried to operate in the urban areas in Western Europe or the broad steppes of Ukraine and Russia, they were easy prey. In France, resisters finally congregated in large numbers from 1943 onwards in the forests and mountains of the Massif Central or the French Alps, adopting the Corsican word *maquis* or 'scrubland' to define themselves in suitably topographical terms. In Asia, the jungles of the Philippines and Burma, or the vast areas of mountain, plateau and river valleys across north and central China provided a relative immunity from an enemy spread thin on the ground, and permitted the large build-up of resistance forces.

The issue of timing was one that all resistance movements, large or small, had to face. Early resistance was often a spontaneous reaction to invasion, doomed to ineffectiveness. Thereafter, resisters had to judge the way the war was going in order to decide how and when to act. Resistance continued even through the long period when the balance of the war seemed uncertain, but in some cases armed action was avoided as far as possible to conserve the manpower and equipment for a moment when Allied victory seemed more certain. The Polish *Armia Krajowa* (Home Army) built up a network of reserves across the occupied zones to be used only for a final revolt when liberation seemed imminent. The strategy, announced the commander-in-chief Stefan Rowecki in spring 1943, was 'to wait with arms in hand, and not to get caught up in hasty deeds that would result in bloody defeats'.[60] After defeat in pitched battle at the hands of the Japanese army in north China, Mao Zedong insisted that the Communist resistance be limited to small guerrilla attacks, even to long periods of inactivity, in order to conserve Communist forces for the end of the war of resistance and for the civil war to come: 'we believe in a strategy of drawn-out warfare and engagements with a quick decision . . .'[61] Other movements took the view that an attrition war against the occupier made greater sense, leaving aside the question of whether resistance long before liberation was futile or demoralizing. The Greek National Liberation Front published a manifesto in September 1941 on the aims of the movement: 'The struggle must go on at all times and in all places . . . in the market place, the café, the factory, the streets, the estates, and in all work.'[62]

Membership of resistance movements and military forces was equally heterogeneous and changed over time. Early resistance depended heavily on the contribution of small groups of intellectuals, professionals and students, who could all help to shape the aims of the movement, produce and publish resistance literature, and establish networks. Officers from the defeated armed forces also played a leading role in instigating resistance if they had avoided capture and a prisoner-of-war camp. The first

major French groups in the unoccupied south reflected the social character of the first activists: *Combat* was founded in summer 1941 by Henri
Frenay, an army captain with oddly radical views, *Libération-Sud* by a
left-wing journalist, Emmanuel d'Astier de la Vigerie. In the occupied
zone, *Libération-Nord* was formed in December 1940 by Christian
Pineau, a former official from the French Ministry of Information, together
with trade union officials.[63] As the war continued and resistance became a
mass movement, the social composition altered. Many of the early leaders
and activists were caught and executed, to be succeeded by younger activists. Thousands of young French men joined the guerrilla war in 1943 and
1944 to avoid being sent for compulsory labour in Germany; in Italy after
the surrender in 1943, thousands of young Italian men fled to the partisan
units to avoid conscription into the army of the rump Fascist state, or to
evade forced labour for the Germans.[64]

   The changing composition owed much to the willingness of communist
parties in Europe to engage in resistance once Axis forces had invaded the
Soviet Union and they were no longer hamstrung by the German–Soviet
Non-Aggression Pact. In the Italian partisan war, the communists contributed the largest number of units, their 'Garibaldi brigades' forming an
estimated 50 per cent of the guerrilla forces.[65] The French communist
resistance, *Francs-Tireurs et Partisans* (FTP), formed in 1942, became one
of the largest of the main resistance organizations with 60,000 active party
members by 1944.[66] In Greece, Yugoslavia and the Soviet Union, partisan
resistance was built around the efforts of the communist parties to organize and mobilize large numbers of predominantly peasant recruits into the
movement, to be organized by communist party officials and members
drawn in general, though not always, from a more urban or working-class
background. Although communist partisan fighters ended up in military-
style units, a high proportion of them were civilian volunteers or conscripts
who had to adapt to the rigours and regulations of paramilitary combat in
order to survive. In the Chinese Communist army, civilian recruits were
given barely a month's training, almost half of it devoted to political and
historical education rather than preparation for combat. Beyond the army
units, the Party organized local militia in the People's Self-Defence Corps
composed entirely of peasant villagers, including 'Vanguards to Resist
Japan' for young recruits aged eighteen to twenty-four, and 'Model Units'
for older men. The local civilian recruits numbered almost 3 million by
1945, dedicated to defence of their communities.[67]

   A significant proportion of resistance activists were women. Their
involvement signified clearly that the resistance war, like participation in
civil defence, was a choice made by civilians across the gender divide.

Women featured in every phase and every type of resistance, armed or unarmed. Although in resistance narratives women often appear as auxiliaries, helping to supply partisan units, acting as messengers and lookouts, providing 'safe' houses for those on the run, or caring for the wounded, all these activities were treated by the enemy as resistance acts, as indeed they were, and they punished them with much the same severity meted out to an armed partisan. There were nevertheless more specifically female concerns. Women were widely involved in protests against the poor supply of rationed food, or conditions of work and welfare for the thousands who now found themselves replacing men; for many women, inside and outside the resistance, protection for the family was a leading priority. In France, it has been calculated that there were at least 239 demonstrations by women protesting about issues related to the household.[68] For some women, political resistance was an additional means to challenge male domination and to pave the way for female emancipation, enabling them to pursue two forms of liberation simultaneously. Such concerns were not necessarily expressed in terms of active resistance, but the divide between women who protested over household or family issues and women who worked in resistance networks was a permeable one. Many of the men in the French resistance saw the work women did for them in providing food, shelter and medical care as an extension of the household rather than a step towards combat, which few French women took up.[69] In Yugoslavia, it was estimated that a million chiefly peasant women provided some form of illicit support for the much smaller number of active women fighters. Many belonged to the Anti-Fascist Women's Front, which by 1945 had over 2 million members, with regional and local committees and their own newspapers.[70] In Italy, the *Gruppi di defesa delle Donne* (Groups for the Defence of Women), established in November 1943 to provide, among other things, welfare and support for families, working women and the bombed-out, also engaged in the production and distribution of illegal papers and leaflets, as well as other more direct forms of assistance for the partisans. The founding charter stressed their resistance character: 'the barbarians steal and lay waste, ravage and kill. We cannot give in. We must fight for liberation.'[71]

Many women did fight alongside the men, invading what had been a male preserve. When challenged by a German court in Lyons to explain why she had taken up arms, Marguerite Gonnet, a local leader in *Libération-Sud*, replied 'because the men had dropped them'.[72] The iconic image of a young woman nestling a gun in her arms was not mere propaganda. In Italy, an estimated 35,000 women joined the partisans in the forests and mountains; between 9,000 and 10,000 were killed, wounded, arrested, deported or executed, a level of casualty that few regular armies could cope with.[73] In Greece, women joined the National Liberation Army in the partisan war against the Axis, and later made up an estimated 20 to 30 per cent of the Communist-led Greek Democratic Army, in both combat and ancillary roles.[74] In Yugoslavia, 100,000 women served in the National Liberation Army following the decision taken by the Yugoslav Communist leadership in February 1942 to allow women to bear arms, in addition to the conventional nursing and auxiliary roles they already occupied. The *partizankas* made up around 15 per cent of the partisan forces, taking part in combat in mixed male and female units, and taking heavy casualties, estimated at one quarter of those who joined. They were in general poorly trained, with little familiarity with the equipment they were using, and surrounded by men some of whom were hostile or unhelpful towards the influx of predominantly very young women. Veterans recall that they were expected by the men to undertake the regular camp chores, and nursing, alongside their role in combat. Women who became pregnant were obliged to abandon their babies or to kill them at birth, an imperative also imposed among women serving in the Soviet partisan movement.[75]

The world of resistance combat inhabited by men and women alike was a special form of warfare quite unlike the fight between regular military forces. Because of their isolation, it was difficult to get adequate intelligence on what other groups were doing or where they operated. Combat when it came was universally savage: kill or be killed. It was entirely lawless, not only because resisters were outside the realm of the existing laws of war and could be treated as the occupier saw fit, but because resisters committed acts that in peacetime would have been considered serious crimes. Indeed, after 1945, the Italian judicial system put on trial numerous former partisans on the grounds that the murder of Fascist officials and Fascist militia was contrary to existing law and should be punished. Resistance did have its own code of ethics, a product of the supremely dangerous environment in which resisters operated. In many cases they swore a blood oath, like some secret society, accepting that they would pay with their lives for any act of betrayal or desertion. Any resister suspected of treachery, or anyone whose carelessness might cost the lives of others, could expect only rough justice, like the young French communist Mathilde Dardant, whose shot and naked body was found in the Bois de Boulogne in Paris, victim of a Communist miscarriage of justice.[76] Real traitors, once detected, were killed outright or hunted down and assassinated, though the difference between being a resister and turning traitor could be a slender one for someone bribed, threatened, or disillusioned. Partisans were also expected to respect the local population or suffer the consequences, since crime was certain to alienate those whose help was needed, but many failed to live up to expectations. The Greek National Liberation movement set up local 'people's courts' in villages that they controlled, where partisans could be executed for stealing, or killing livestock, or rape.[77] There was a paranoid fear of subversion or spying; 'our gravest duty,' claimed one Greek resistance journal, 'is vigilance.'[78]

The tough justice imposed on their own recruits reflected the constant state of danger that resisters faced. Unlike regular soldiers, they knew that if they were caught they would be tortured, tried (if at all) by special tribunals with no prospect of appeal, and usually executed. In many cases they were simply shot or hanged on the spot, a reality that was in many cases reciprocated if enemy soldiers or militia were unlucky enough to be taken prisoner. One child partisan in Belorussia witnessed the execution of a group of seven German captives that mimicked the justice meted out to partisans: forced to strip naked, they were made to stand in a line and then shot.[79] The resistance war was merciless, from all sides and wherever it was fought. The fear inspired in the occupying forces and their collaborators stemmed from the complete unpredictability of terrorist attack or a guerrilla foray. Mao Zedong, after writing *On Protracted War* in 1938, became the leading exponent of guerrilla tactics in the war against Japan, insisting that his forces engage the enemy in small operations against isolated Japanese detachments, using ambush, the cover of night and surprise before melting away again into the countryside.[80] In cities, sabotage and killing depended on complete secrecy, the speed of the attack and a small number of perpetrators. The object was to avoid confrontation with the enemy in urban areas, where regular soldiers could bring their better training and weaponry to bear, and where escape was more difficult. Hit-and-run tactics gave resisters some form of compensation for their massive military inferiority.

The asymmetric character of all resistance warfare against heavily armed and organized opponents was exacerbated by the great difficulty of getting access to weapons and equipment, even uniforms. A great many of the familiar images of resistance fighters show groups of men and women clad in a wide assortment of clothing, some military, some not, most without protective helmets – the polar opposite of military spick and span. When General de Gaulle reviewed the French partisans in Toulouse after the city's liberation, he was horrified by the informal soldiery in front of him, dressed in the improvised costumes of guerrilla war. A British delegate to the Greek resistance recalled their sorry appearance: 'Their nondescript clothes were mostly in rags, and many were literally barefoot ... in snow. Their guns were old, some 60 years ...'[81] Weapons were scarce, but ammunition to keep the fighting going was even more difficult to acquire. Heavy weapons were a rarity except for some of the partisan units on the Eastern Front or in Yugoslavia, which were generally better equipped. Yet even the First Proletarian Division of the Yugoslav National Liberation Army could provide only half its 8,500 soldiers with a gun.[82] The Polish Home Army, which had stored weapons away for years until the moment to strike, was better resourced than most resistance movements, but when the Twenty-seventh Division finally went into action in January 1944, there were 4,500 rifles and 140 sub-machine guns for 7,500 men. In two months of fighting the unit was virtually destroyed.[83] The Communist army in northern China, though large on paper by 1940, could not provide even half the recruits with a battlefield weapon, and for those with guns, precious little ammunition.[84] When the British began to drop supplies to European resistance movements, they sent large quantities of plastic explosive and fuses, because sabotage was a British strategic priority, but far fewer battlefield weapons which was what the resistance wanted. Unlike a regular army, logistic back-up for resisters was irregular, unsystematic, and almost always inadequate.

The field of resistance combat was not confined only to the occupier. Resisters were harsh with the enemy, but they were also harsh with collaborators, and harsh on occasion with fellow resistance movements. The enemy could be defined in many different ways. Collaborators were a particular target, easier to hit, not necessarily armed, and their death a warning to others in occupied societies not to work for the enemy. In China collaboration was widespread as local elites or warlords strove to protect their interests under Japanese occupation. Statistics kept by one local Communist administration in north China showed for 1942 that 5,764 Chinese collaborators had been killed, but only 1,647 Japanese troops; the following year the figures were even more remarkable, 33,309 Chinese against 1,060 of the enemy.[85] Mao himself later claimed that only 10 per cent of the Communist resistance effort had been devoted to fighting the Japanese. In the Philippines, the communist-led Hukbalahap insurgents were feared more than the Japanese occupiers because of the violence meted out to alleged spies and collaborators, a high proportion of the 25,000 estimated victims of the Huk rebels.[86] Greek guerrillas in the National Liberation Movement took revenge in the areas they controlled on anyone suspected of collaborating with the puppet regime, a savage campaign of intimidation and murder that even included alleged Anglophiles, guilty, so it was said, of encouraging British interference in Greek affairs.[87]

In the guerrilla war on the Eastern Front, collaborators, alleged or otherwise, were routinely murdered along with their families. In the confused conflict against both the Germans and the nationalist Ukrainian National Army, Soviet partisans could be ruthless to excess. One partisan unit under the command of Oleksii Fedorov annihilated the village of Liakho-vychi because they thought the population collaborated with the insurgents. An eyewitness recalled the indiscriminate attack:

> They killed everyone they spotted. The first to be killed were Stepan Marchyk and his neighbor Matrena along with her eight-year-old daughter, Mykola Khvesyk and Matrena Khvesyk with their ten-year-old daughter . . . They killed the family of Ivan Khvesk (wife, son, daughter-in-law, and baby boy) and threw [them] into a burning house . . . Fifty innocent people perished.[88]

Although partisan detachments boasted to Moscow that they killed ten Germans for every collaborator, some German records suggest that the ratio was more like 1:1.5, while partisan memoirs suggest that the ratio was considerably higher. Collaborators were regularly tortured, even on occasion flayed or buried alive.[89] In Western and Southern Europe, an unquantifiable proportion of the resistance effort was spent assassinating or intimidating collaborators, or destroying equipment and plant working to produce goods for the German war effort.

Among those supposedly on the same side, facing common Axis enemies, the same ruthless treatment could be meted out. In Greece, the largest resistance movement, the National Liberation Front, effectively controlled by the Greek Communist Party, tried forcibly to compel the smaller non-communist resistance groups to merge with their larger competitor. In April 1944, partisans in the National Liberation Army attacked and eliminated the rival Greek National and Social Liberation movement, and executed its leader, Colonel Demetrios Psarros. The Greek Democratic National League survived, despite repeated armed clashes, only because its leader, General Napoleon Zervas, had strong support from the British. Greek Communists hunted down alleged Trotskyist resisters and assassinated them; French Communists did the same.[90] Rivalry was fuelled by very different ideological convictions and political agendas. In Yugoslavia, armed conflict between the Communist-led National Liberation Army and the 'Chetnik' insurgents led by Colonel Draža Mihailović was founded on contrasting visions of a post-war Yugoslav state, one communist, the other monarchist. Communist leaders in spring 1942 decided on a strategy of class terror against resistance rivals and in April murdered 500 leading Chetniks, the start of a prolonged civil war between the two sides.[91] In China, Chiang Kai-shek's Guomindang nationalists clashed repeatedly with Chinese Communists in the guerrilla war both were waging in the rear of the Japanese armies, despite the initial agreement to operate a United Front against the aggressor. Nationalist leaders privately viewed both the Japanese and Mao's Communists as enemies. When in January 1941 a division of the Communist New Fourth Army lost its way moving north through Jiangsu province to the rear of the Japanese, it was annihilated by units of the Guomindang armed forces and 10,000 killed. The United Front never recovered its shallow unity thereafter.[92] Political ambition and personal rivalry shaped resistance everywhere. Divided by a common enemy, resisters could kill each other just as they killed collaborators and the occupiers.

Within every resistance struggle there existed a form of civil war against collaborators and rivals, but in China, Yugoslavia and Greece resistance was bound up with civil war as Communist-led guerrillas exploited the wartime crisis to begin transforming the social and political landscape in the areas they came to control even while engaged in guerrilla war against the external enemy. These wars were about the political future of the nation, and their participants implicitly assumed that the Axis New Orders would fail. By 1945 the Chinese Communist Party ruled 100 million people in the large base areas from which it operated. Here the Communists forced surviving landlords to accept a general reduction in rents and interest payments on behalf of the peasant majority. Among the 'Ten Platforms for Resisting Japan and Saving our Nation' proclaimed by the Party Politburo in 1937 was a commitment to social equalization and greater local democracy. Reforms were imposed where local elites or landowners objected, while peasants were granted the unaccustomed right to participate in local political structures.[93] By 1945 the Party was primed for a more radical class confrontation waged with mounting violence against the old elites and the Guomindang regime, which was soon transformed into open civil war.

In Greece, a similar transformation of rural life was initiated by the Communist-dominated National Liberation Movement and its armed wing. Legend has it that in June 1942 the young Greek communist Aris Velouchiotis, entered the village of Domnista, in the mountains 300 kilometres from Athens, with fifteen armed men, a flag and a bugle, and declared the 'banner of revolt' not only against the enemy but against the old class system.[94] Whether true or not, in villages across the areas dominated by the guerrillas, local people's democracy was established on the model of the code of 'self-government and people's justice' first issued in the village of Kleistos. Each village had its own guerrilla commissariat and a local 'responsible one' (ipefthinos) for organizing village life, but the peasantry had the opportunity, as in China, to vote for the local council and committees, and to serve on them.[95] Each village had its own 'People's Court', which met regularly on a Sunday to hear local cases. The rhetoric of the National Liberation Movement underlined a commitment to 'people's rule', an idea that could be communicated easily to a largely illiterate rural population without having to define too closely what it might mean.[96] Those who resisted the new order or questioned its legitimacy faced the risk of arbitrary execution. Conditions were far from ideal even for those who complied, with levies on the harvest, taxes to pay for the guerrilla forces, and a regular settling of local scores between rival families caught up in the conflict.[97] Writing years later, the Communist leader Yiannis Ioannidis justified the widespread violence: 'When you are fighting a civil war you do not indulge in sentimentalities ... You wipe out the enemy by whatever means.'[98] The transformation aimed at creating the conditions for a fundamental social revolution and class war, and when the Germans finally abandoned their occupation in autumn 1944, the areas liberated by the guerrillas – known as 'Free Greece' by the resistance – became the base from which the Greek Communist Party launched its attempt to seize power nationally, turning the implicit civil war of the occupation years into an open post-war conflict. The battle for the future of Greece between the Communist insurgency and the Greek National Army, rebuilt in 1944–5, led to an estimated 158,000 deaths, all but 49,000 of them civilians, and to years of turmoil and displacement for those who survived.[99]

In Yugoslavia, explicit civil war raged side by side with the resistance war throughout the wartime years. The civil war was a complex mix of ethnic, religious and political conflict in which civilians became caught up in a web of extreme violence as participants or as victims. The best estimate suggests that just over 1 million Yugoslavs lost their lives during the war, the majority through the fighting between fellow Yugoslavs, rather than against the enemy. Resistance in Yugoslavia had a double meaning: resistance against the occupiers and resistance against internal enemies. The German invasion in April 1941 had destroyed the fragile Yugoslav state and replaced it with an occupation structure that invited domestic conflict. A nominally independent Catholic Croatia under the fascist leader Ante Pavelić contained large minorities of Bosnian Muslims and Orthodox Serbs; Italy controlled Slovenia and Montenegro, Germany a rump Serbian state with a pro-German puppet government under Milan Nedić, the Serbian Pétain. The new Croat regime wanted to maintain its independence and to create an ethnically cleansed nation; the Serbian Chetniks wanted a Greater Serbia that saw the monarchy restored but which excluded Muslims; the small Yugoslav Communist Party wanted a common front against the fascist enemy and a remorseless fight against all those movements whose vision of the future rejected any collaboration with communism.[100]

The civil war began almost at once. Croats murdered or expelled the Serbian population; Serb Chetniks murdered Bosnian Muslims and destroyed their villages, slitting the throats of their victims; communist partisans fought ruthlessly against Serb monarchists and Croat fascists.[101] Thousands of volunteers formed irregular armed forces to preserve their communities and their movements. The Chetnik Yugoslav Army of the Homeland devoted most of its efforts to killing Bosnians, Croats and communists. The Communist People's Liberation Army, led by Josip Broz (Tito), defended itself against German counter-insurgency but also actively fought against the Chetniks, the Croat Ustaša militia and the quasi-fascist Serbian Volunteer Corps. Everywhere civilians formed improvised self-defence groups to resist the many existential threats they faced – the Muslim Green Cadre, Muhamed Pandža's Muslim Liberation Movement, the anti-communist Slovenian Alliance.[102] The violence was persistent and savage. 'Death was nothing unusual,' wrote the communist Milovan Djilas in his memoir of the war. 'Life had lost all meaning apart from survival.'[103] The German and Italian occupiers played groups off against each other or reached temporary agreements to collaborate against the common communist enemy. By 1944 Tito's liberation movement began to attract wide support, even among former monarchists, because it promised a future in which religious and ethnic difference would be transcended by the establishment of a new federal national state that claimed to respect both. In rural and small-town areas controlled by the Communist partisans, social and political reforms were introduced as they were in Greece and China.[104] The final campaign in autumn 1944 to liberate Serbia, the region where Tito's movement had made least progress, was a fight between Yugoslavs. The Germans could mobilize only a few police and SS battalions and relied instead on thousands of Chetniks and the Serbian Volunteer Corps, supported by Russian anti-communist volunteers. The end of the war in Serbia in autumn 1944 was also the end of a civil war.[105]

The ideological and political divisions that fuelled civil war were just two of many obstacles resistance movements faced during the war. Because the overwhelming bulk of every population under occupation did not actively resist there remained a persistent ambivalence in popular attitudes towards those who did, and at times an overt hostility. Where major guerrilla movements emerged, resources and food had to be taken from local villagers. In some cases, farmers collaborated, but in China or in Ukraine, peasant producers saw the partisans as little better than the occupiers, seizing their limited food stocks and killing those who resisted. Isolated units of stragglers or deserters behind enemy lines in the Soviet Union could resort to open banditry to survive, shedding any resistance pretensions as they did so. Local, improvised bands emerged in the German rear, intent on survival at the expense of the communities around them. A report by a local Soviet partisan commander near Kiev condemned the 'familial partisan' units that operated independently: 'they engage in drunkenness, the confiscation of property from the population ... Disorder reigns in the detachments.'[106] The Ukrainian National Army under Stepan Bandera, the *banderivtsy*, were known locally by villagers simply as *bandity*, bandits. They stole livestock, murdered both non-Ukrainians and Ukrainians unsympathetic to the Bandera movement, burnt down hostile villages, and preyed on the society they were supposed to liberate.[107] In northern China banditry was rife even before the Japanese invasion, as local small-scale gangs took advantage of the absence of effective state power. In the war of resistance some bandit leaders pretended to offer security against the Japanese while pillaging and extorting from the villagers they guarded. Hu Jinxiu, one bandit leader happy to adopt the pretext, gathered around him 5,000 men who, instead of protecting the population, behaved like the outlaws they were, murdering and stealing, until a Japanese sortie destroyed his force.[108] For the Chinese peasantry under occupation, the priority was to find any form of stability, even if it meant supporting the Japanese against local guerrillas and bandits. The Communist New Fourth Army were surprised to find the inhabitants of one small town enthusiastically waving Japanese flags as they entered.[109] In these chaotic and violent conditions, the only state that still existed was the state of nature.

Local populations were also the regular victims of savage reprisals by the occupying powers in retaliation for resistance acts they regarded as mere criminal terrorism. The intended result was to encourage popular rejection of the resistance campaign, from fear of the consequences for the innocent. For every death of a German soldier in south-east or Eastern Europe, the German authorities were permitted to execute up to 100 innocent civilian hostages; in France, where occupation atrocity was more restrained, the ratio was fixed at five dead hostages for every dead German.[110] Public unease was evident under such circumstances about whether the cost of resisting was not too high. An early wave of assassinations in France in 1940 and 1941 was widely condemned by the public, and by the Free French authorities in London, because of the German practice of seizing large numbers of hostages and fulfilling their pledge to murder them. When a Dutch Resistance Council was founded in spring 1943, the government-in-exile refused their request to be allowed to engage in acts of violence against the Germans for much the same reason.[111] Resisters were constantly confronted with the moral dilemma that

their acts would harm innocent compatriots while inflicting only modest
or negligible damage on the occupier. Repression was from the outset
quite indiscriminate, since its object was to terrorize the rest of the population into compliance. By 1941, local Japanese commanders were so
frustrated with Communist guerrilla raids that they ordered their troops
to adopt the notorious 'Take all, burn all, kill all' in areas where it was
known that guerrillas operated, and there were many examples earlier in
the war where anti-partisan units destroyed all the villages in their path,
killed the inhabitants and stole all the produce.[112] In Europe, the reaction
was much the same. In cities, resisters were sent for trial, deported, or
executed, and hostages were shot in retaliation, often in public view. In
rural areas, whole villages were burnt to the ground and their inhabitants
murdered simply on suspicion that they gave sanctuary to partisans or
francs-tireurs. The destruction in 1942 of the Czech village of Lidice in
retaliation for the assassination of Reinhard Heydrich, or the annihilation
in June 1944 by a regiment of the SS *Das Reich* Division of the French
village of Oradour-sur-Glane along with all its inhabitants, women and
children included, were the tip of an iceberg of cruel collective punishment for individual acts of resistance. In Ukraine, German security and
military forces, led by the SS General Erich von dem Bach-Zalewski,
burnt down 335 villages and, according to their own precise but morbid
statistics, murdered 49,294 men, women and children, two-thirds of them
in 1943 at the peak of partisan activity. In Greece, 70,600 were executed
or murdered in reprisal operations.[113]

The occupiers also organized larger military operations against guerrilla activity that had severely damaging effects on resistance. In
Yugoslavia, Operation 'White', between January and March 1943, and
Operation 'Black', from May to June the same year, failed to eliminate the
National Liberation Army but inflicted heavy losses; in Ukraine, Operation 'Seidlitz' in June and July 1943 resulted in 5,000 partisan deaths. The
anti-partisan campaigns waged in northern Italy in the winter of 1944–5
decimated the brigades, with the loss of an estimated 75,000 men and
women. In France and the Low Countries, persistent detective work by
the Gestapo, regularly assisted by local police forces, had broken most of
the early networks and movements by the spring of 1944. Some of those
recruited to undertake the anti-resistance operations were freebooters –
Ukrainian militia, Bosnian Muslims in the SS Handžar Division, a Cossack
division in Italy – who from most accounts relished the savage nature of
the assignment. Against determined opposition, there were real limits to
what resistance could do. The longer it took for the Allies to roll back the
Axis advance, the more desperate the resistance effort appeared. The long

delay in liberation prompted demoralization, even antagonism towards the Allied powers, but the absence of sufficient heavy weapons and an effective force structure, even where a partisan army existed, meant that resistance had little if any prospect of securing liberation by its own means. This posed a challenging paradox: to be more effective required practical assistance and equipment from the Allies, but to accept such help compromised the ambition to liberate the nation from within and to mould its future. 'In reality,' wrote Henri Frenay, leader of *Combat*, 'we have created groups of partisans who want to fight even more for their liberation than against the invader . . .'[114]

RESISTANCE AND THE ALLIES

Supporting liberation movements was not the Allies' priority. Resistance mattered to them chiefly to the extent that it contributed to the defeat of the enemy. Assistance for resistance forces, when it was possible to provide it, was supplied on the understanding that equipment would be utilized for strategic ends and Allied strategic intentions respected. 'We had to judge every proposal and every enterprise,' recalled the chief of staff of Britain's special operations in Europe, 'from the severely practical point of view of the contribution it would make to winning the war.'[115] The Allies did not ignore the political implications of resistance when it came to thinking about the political aftermath of war, but military necessity governed wartime policies, as it did when the British government in 1943 shifted support from the monarchist Mihailović to the communist Tito only because his National Liberation Army was fighting the Germans more effectively. (Paradoxically, Stalin was not opposed to supporting Mihailović's Chetnik units, but wary of Tito's Communist Party ambitions in case they soured relations with his Western allies.) For the chief resistance movements, on the other hand, the defeat of the enemy was a means not an end. In China, Italy, France and the Balkans, liberation was about creating a different society once victory was assured, more democratic, more socially just and more inclusive than the societies overthrown or challenged by invasion. Michel Brut, head of the *Service National Maquis*, contrasted his view of the resistance effort with that of the Allies: 'There will be no liberation without insurrection . . . It is less a question of the immediate strategic value of these actions than of training the fighters for the insurrection.'[116]

There were, nevertheless, differences in the way the major Allied powers exploited resistance. In the Soviet case, partisan resistance on Soviet soil came to be closely integrated with the Soviet war effort on the other side of the front line. Here the expectation of liberation increased with every Soviet victory in 1943 and 1944 and, unlike the British and Americans, the Red Army and the partisans who aided its progress were liberating their own territory and peoples. Even before the original Soviet frontier was reached in 1944, the partisan resistance war was wound down and partisans were integrated into regular army units. Only then did the Soviet ally engage with the wider resistance war in Eastern Europe, with very mixed results. The Soviet partisans nonetheless faced many of the same difficulties as resistance elsewhere in Europe when it came to external assistance. As the Red Army retreated in 1941, the regime organized stay-behind units to constitute a partisan force, but they were difficult to sustain and Stalin was less interested in their potential than he was later in the war. Out of 216 detachments in Ukraine there were only 12 left by 1943 with just 241 men. Attempts to parachute in reinforcements were frustrated by the ease with which they were detected. Early civilian recruits were poorly trained, unused to the demands of guerrilla warfare, and prone to defect or desert.[117] Moreover the local population, although ostensibly supporters of a partisan war to speed up liberation and the restoration of Soviet power, displayed an evident ambivalence towards fighters who seized civilian food and resources, placed whole villages under threat of retaliation by the occupier, offered scant protection and would bring back harsh Communist rule.

The situation improved in May 1942 with the appointment of the Belorussian Party secretary, Panteleimon Ponomarenko, to head a central partisan staff in Moscow, but it still proved difficult to establish radio communication with all units or to supply adequate ammunition and explosive. Only after victory at Stalingrad did popular attitudes towards the partisans become less adverse, while the supply of Red Army equipment and the infiltration of Red Army specialists through the German lines increasingly militarized the irregular forces that made up the partisan detachments. Through the course of 1943, partisan units became more effective and numbers grew; by July there were 139,583 officially recorded, though losses remained high. Only a little more than half of those infiltrated into the German rear areas in 1943 survived, while among the many poorly trained peasants conscripted into the partisan detachments the loss rate was higher still.[118] However, partisan activity at last represented a clear strategic gain for the Soviet high command. By the spring of 1943 partisans controlled an estimated 90 per cent of the forested regions of Belorussia and two-thirds of the region's grain and meat production, denying these resources to the occupier.[119] Attacks on German communications reached a peak, with more than 9,000 in the second half of the year; in August 1943 alone, while the German army was reeling back from the disastrous defeat at Kursk, German records show more than 3,000 kilometres of track destroyed, and almost 600 locomotives put out of action. Statistics compiled on the Soviet side, which may well distort the reality, claimed that partisans destroyed 12,000 bridges and 65,000 vehicles during the period of peak activity.[120] The extent to which each partisan achieved the expected norm of exterminating 'at least five fascists and traitors' every month is beyond statistical recovery. In January 1944 the Central Partisan Staff was closed down, and partisan units in areas already liberated were incorporated into the Red Army.

By early 1944 Soviet forces had swept across Ukraine and reached the old Soviet border. Stalin was now faced with a novel resistance environment in Eastern and South-eastern Europe where communists competed with non-communist resistance movements that did not want Soviet victory to mean the imposition of a communist version of liberation. Even local communist armed resistance – principally in Yugoslavia and Greece – did not necessarily follow or even understand the Party line from Moscow. Soviet views of resistance could be dismissive or patronizing about the contribution resistance might make. One Soviet officer thought the Greek National Liberation Army was 'just a rabble of armed men, not worth supporting'; another Red Army commander thought that Tito's partisans were 'damned good amateurs', but amateurs nonetheless.[121] The most tragic example was Poland. Here the majority resistance organization, the *Armia Krajowa*, was strongly anti-communist and anti-Soviet yet was faced with the prospect that of the major Allies only the Soviet Union would be involved directly in the liberation of Poland. However, the *Armia Krajowa*, though the largest, was not the only resistance movement. The pre-war Peasant Party, with a radical anti-capitalist programme, set up *Bataliony Chłopskie* (peasant battalions) to protect peasant interests against the conservative social forces strongly represented in the *Armia Krajowa*. The Polish Communists had their own resistance movement, the *Armia Ludowa* (People's Army), which refused to co-operate with the rest of the resistance and by 1944 was drawing supplies from the approaching Red Army as the Soviet partisans had done in German-occupied Russia. The number of Communist fighters was small – around 1,500 nationally by 1943, 400 in Warsaw in 1944 – but they enjoyed the advantage that the military tidal wave sweeping the German army from Ukraine and Belorussia was a Communist one.[122]

Resistance in Poland was limited until 1944, chiefly because the *Armia Krajowa* wanted to avoid a premature insurrection. A significant fraction of the 400,000 potential fighters recruited by 1944 had experienced military training, though they were now civilians in all but name, including thousands of Polish women. The army was divided into conventional military units and stocks of weapons and food were concealed across the country to await the optimum moment to strike. This was difficult to determine since it depended on the course of the wider Allied war against the Germans. The Polish government-in-exile in London realized the paradox facing the main resistance movement. Political relations with the Soviet Union deteriorated rapidly during 1943 and by June 1944 Stalin had shifted support completely to a Committee of National Liberation composed of Polish Communists, the so-called Lublin Committee. Efforts by the *Armia Krajowa* headquarters to liaise with the approaching Red Army high command were ignored by the Soviet side and it was unclear what Soviet intentions might be. The commander of the *Armia Krajowa*, General Tadeusz Bór-Komorowski, was told from London to act 'without any consideration for the military or political attitude of the Russians'.[123] The Allies had no plans to support a Polish rising. Western supplies of equipment and arms amounted to no more than 305 tons between early 1941 and June 1944. A few hundred Polish volunteers had parachuted into Poland in 1943 and 1944 from the West, but their priority was sabotage to help the Allied military effort. Stalin told Churchill in summer 1944 that the non-communist resistance in Poland was 'ephemeral and lacking in influence'. General Vasily Chuikov, the defender of Stalingrad, whose army pushed into Polish territory in the Soviet summer offensive in June and July 1944, Operation 'Bagration', thought that the Polish Home Army 'simply did not fight the Germans at all'.[124]

In 1944 this was no longer true. Bór-Komorowski decided on his own initiative to order the *Armia Krajowa* and the peasant battalions to prepare battle stations against the retreating Germans. Arms caches were retrieved from their hiding places, food stocks set up, Molotov cocktails mixed. The army was poorly equipped, with crude uniforms adorned with an armband in the Polish national colours, red and white. In January 1944, the resistance launched Operation '*Burza*' ('Storm') against German forces in eastern Poland in the hope that Polish towns could be liberated by Polish fighters before the Red Army arrived. The campaign exposed the degree of wishful thinking in Poland about the possibility of achieving national liberation independent of the looming Soviet presence. Unknown to the resistance, Stalin had already approved an order to Red Army commanders in November 1943 to disarm all *Armia Krajowa* forces and to kill any who refused. Between January and October 1944 21,000 of the resistance army were arrested; their officers were deported to the Soviet Union, and the rank and file put in recently vacated German camps, including the labour and extermination camp at Majdanek, liberated by the Red Army in July.[125] Soviet repression of nationalist resistance was already known to Bór-Komorowski and the commander of the Warsaw region, General Antoni Chruściel. It was the same harsh punishment meted out to Ukrainian nationalists as the Red Army and the NKVD moved westward, deporting and murdering any of them in their path. Like the Polish state in September 1939, the Home Army in summer 1944 found itself trapped between Soviet and German forces equally hostile to its survival.

This stark reality makes it easier to understand the decision finally taken by Bór-Komorowski and his commanders to launch a major uprising in Warsaw on 1 August. The military situation was not entirely clear, but the Red Army was known to be only a matter of kilometres from the east bank of the Vistula River dividing Warsaw, while German military and civilian authorities in and around Warsaw appeared to be preparing to abandon the city. Radio broadcasts beamed from Moscow in late July exhorted the people of Warsaw to rise against their oppressors, though the appeals were aimed at the much smaller Communist *Armia Ludowa*, which might have alerted the rest of the resistance to the dangers they would certainly face under Soviet occupation. There were cautious voices from the Polish government in London, unsure of any kind of support from the Western Allies; Chruściel was against running risks with so few weapons and an unreliable number of resisters. The decision finally turned on an issue of principle: the resistance wanted to liberate Warsaw before Soviet armies arrived to show that Polish national sovereignty could be won with Polish blood alone, rather than relying on Allied assistance. The Home Army command calculated that they had no more than four or five days to drive the Germans out and welcome the Russians in as allies, but not as liberators. On these terms, the national uprising, Bór-Komorowski later wrote, 'appeared real and feasible'.[126] Resistance leaders met on 31 July to decide what to do. There was still no consensus on action until news arrived – false as it happened – that Soviet tanks were entering the eastern suburbs of Warsaw. The information triggered agreement that the moment was now or never. After the order to begin the uprising on the following day had been sent out, intelligence arrived that the Red Army was not on the move. Bór-Komorowski refused to rescind the order.[127]

In truth the uprising was doomed and the restoration of Polish national sovereignty a forlorn aspiration. But for the resistance this seemed a sublime moment of revenge. 'Our victory seemed assured,' recalled Kazik, a Jewish survivor posing as an ethnic Pole, '... an atmosphere of popular rebellion ... a time of elation.'[128] On 1 August at 5 p.m. the *Armia*

Krajowa launched multiple attacks on the startled Germans across the city. Estimates suggest that there were more than 50,000 recruits, of whom around 40,000 took part in the uprising. Arms were scarce, enough to provide perhaps 8,500 of the fighters with an effective weapon. Some of the volunteers were women. There were also thousands of children organized in the 'Grey Ranks', the paramilitary wing of the Polish Scouting Association; only those over sixteen were allowed to fight, and four-fifths of them were killed.[129] Against the resisters were arrayed German army and Waffen-SS forces which had been hurriedly sent to reinforce the Vistula line against the approaching Red Army. When news reached Hitler of the uprising, he ordered that Warsaw should be erased from the map and its citizens all murdered, the most pathologically extreme of all his reactions to resistance. Two brigades with savage reputations – one SS unit controlled by Oskar Dirlewanger, the other by the Russian renegade Bronislav Kaminsky – were drafted in to see that Hitler's orders were obeyed. In the areas where the *Armia Krajowa* failed to take control, the attackers engaged in a grotesque orgy of killing and destruction, driving the resistance into shrinking enclaves in the city. An unknown number of civilians took the risk of joining the uprising, but thousands did not. An estimated 150,000 were killed by bombing, shelling and mass murder, the largest single military atrocity of the war. Only with the arrival of SS General Bach-Zalewski, the veteran commander of the brutal anti-partisan war and now commander of the forces suppressing the uprising, was the deliberate murder of all the inhabitants altered to a policy of mass deportation for those who had survived the onslaught.

Allied assistance for the uprising was minimal. The optimistic expectation that the Red Army would arrive in Warsaw once the rebels had expelled the Germans was shown almost immediately to have been misplaced. On 1 August, the Soviet offensive ground to a halt after forty days of continuous and gruelling combat against the retreating German armies. Reaching the Vistula had exhausted Soviet efforts and there was no plan to push on to seize Warsaw; even had the Soviet high command ordered it, Marshal Rokossovskii's troops were beyond a further bruising assault across a river barrier that the German army was rapidly reinforcing for a major counter-offensive. As it was, a further six weeks of combat were required before the German response was beaten back; assistance for the uprising was not possible before mid-September. However, after smashing Army Group Centre in Belorussia, Stalin's aim was to advance on the northern axis towards the Baltic States and the easier southern axis towards the Balkans and Central Europe to ensure Soviet domination of the region.[130] He had no interest in aiding Polish nationalists, whose uprising he casually dismissed: 'What kind of army is it, without artillery, tanks, air force? They do not even have enough hand weapons. In modern war this is nothing . . .' In mid-August, a message from Stalin to Churchill described the uprising as nothing more than a 'reckless and fearful gamble'.[131] Only when, against all expectations, the Polish resistance fought on not for four or five days, but for weeks, did Stalin come under pressure from the Polish units fighting with the Red Army and from his Western allies to make a political gesture. Airborne supplies were dropped from the night of 13/14 September for a further two weeks, but the aircraft had to fly so low to identify the small pockets of resistance that many of the parachutes attached to the air drops failed to open and much of the equipment and food was ruined. Air drops by the British, flying from Italy, and American aircraft flying from Britain provided further supplies, but most canisters fell into German hands. Out of 1,300 dropped by the Third American Air Division, only 388 were successfully retrieved. British and Polish crews found it hard to reach Warsaw and took high casualties. Only 30 of 199 aircraft dropped supplies directly on Warsaw and of these the Polish resisters benefitted from only a fraction.[132]

Allied aid delayed the inevitable, but by 2 October the battle was over for the battered and desperate remnant of the resistance. Bór-Komorowski and 16,300 insurgents, including 3,000 women, went into captivity; they were granted prisoner-of-war status as a rare tribute for irregular forces. Estimates vary on the losses suffered by the resisters, but a conservative figure of 17,000 seems likely. Bach-Zalewski made the implausible claim after the war that his men suffered almost as heavily with 10,000 dead and 7,000 missing, but his original wartime report gave figures of 1,453 killed and 8,183 wounded. These figures in themselves were testament to the bitter nature of the contest, which, like Stalingrad, was fought house by house and street by street. The surviving youngsters of the Grey Ranks were sent to labour camps. By an awful irony, Allied bombers later hit by mistake one of the camps at Brockwitz, killing many of the young Poles who had managed to survive the insurrection.

The defeat of the uprising brought an end to organized Polish resistance. In the four months before the Red Army mounted a major operation across the Vistula in January 1945, Polish society retreated from the awful costs of failure. Some 350,000 of the capital's inhabitants were expelled to an uncertain fate as refugees, thousands more taken for forced labour in Germany. On 9 October, Hitler repeated his demand that Warsaw be physically erased; the Germans looted the city before systematically destroying more than 50 per cent of the buildings. Some 23,500 railway wagons filled with booty made their way back to Germany.[133] The effect on the rest of the resistance movement was entirely negative. Soviet repression of the *Armia Krajowa* in the areas occupied by the Red Army intensified following discovery of an appeal alleged to be from Bór-Komorowski: 'Actions in favour of Russia are treason to the motherland ... Time is coming to fight the Soviets.'[134] Peasant battalions and Home Army units in the German-held areas disbanded. The population responded to the horrors of Warsaw with growing resentment towards the resisters rather than the perpetrators. A report produced in November by the Polish underground government noted the popular 'feeling of powerlessness' and the widespread reaction against further resistance: 'The matter has gone on for too long. The number of victims is too large, the results are poor ...'[135]

Throughout the war the Soviet attitude even to resistance movements that were overtly communist was also far from clear-cut. Stalin even distrusted the Polish Communists fighting in the resistance in 1944 because they remained too independent of the 'Moscow Poles' he now supported. The messages from Moscow to communists everywhere were cautious, to avoid confrontation and to collaborate with non-communists. From the 1930s, Stalin was particularly wary of the Chinese Communist Party, which operated largely independently of the Communist capital in Moscow. Mao later complained to the Soviet ambassador that Stalin 'did not trust us very much. He considered us to be a second Tito, a backward nation.' The Soviet leader wanted Mao to avoid a civil war and to collaborate with Chiang Kai-shek in a common front against the Japanese enemy; once the war was over, Stalin remained half-hearted in supplying Mao's forces with military equipment and hostile to Chinese Communist ambitions to rule all of China.[136] The emphasis on a united front with non-communists was formal policy once the Soviet Union was invaded, and in Greece and Yugoslavia, where the main resistance movements were communist-led, Stalin wanted to avoid a revolutionary crisis, chiefly because he was anxious not to alienate the Western Allies by encouraging a communist takeover in an area of evident strategic priority for the British. For the Greek revolutionaries the Soviet regime had little respect.[137] Stalin wanted the Greek Communist Party to avoid revolutionary language or insurrectionary planning and to focus on self-defence. Almost no Soviet supplies were forthcoming for the Greek liberation army. In late 1944 Stalin advised the Communists to join a British-sponsored coalition government and refused to endorse the emerging civil war.[138]

In Yugoslavia, the Comintern tried to persuade Tito not to mount a campaign that was too communist and to collaborate with all the other movements opposing fascism, but the civil war had its own momentum, beyond Stalin's control. As a result, until 1944 Stalin continued to support the exiled king and his government and to encourage Tito to embrace all anti-Hitler elements, including the monarchist Chetniks. Only when it was clear that his Western allies would not disapprove did he recognize Tito's provisional government in June 1944.[139] At the point when Soviet military assistance might have helped the Yugoslav partisans, the directive to the Red Army from Stalin's Supreme Headquarters that September bluntly stated: 'Do not attack into Yugoslavia, since it would lead to dispersing our forces.'[140] After Tito visited Stalin later in the month, the Soviet leader agreed to release limited forces from the Red Army's advance on Hungary to help Tito capture Belgrade, but on the assumption that the Red Army would leave after the operation. Stalin was uncertain about the political outcome in Yugoslavia and allowed army units to collaborate with Chetniks as well as Tito's guerrillas.[141] Once Belgrade was captured in October 1944 the Red Army did move on, leaving Tito's guerrilla army to complete the liberation of the country. British unease about the imminent Communist takeover of Yugoslavia prompted Tito to finally break with the Western Allies, who had up until then supported his forces with supplies and air strikes. 'I, as president and supreme commander,' he told the British mission, 'am not responsible to anyone outside my country for my actions.'[142] In March 1945 Tito formed a government with twenty-three Communists out of a Cabinet of twenty-nine and left the Allies with little choice but to recognize it as the legitimate regime. After a bloody final assault on the German line along the river Sava, where fighting did not end until 15 May, a week after Germany's unconditional surrender, national liberation was finally achieved without a direct Allied military presence, a triumph unique among the chequered histories of wartime resistance.

In Western Europe the Allies did not isolate and persecute the resistance, as the Soviet Union continued to do with the Poles and other nationalities in Eastern Europe well after victory in 1945, but their attitude was governed by the pursuit of victory over Germany as a first priority. Resistance movements were otherwise treated with caution. The Western Allies wanted to disarm all partisans after liberation and to limit the power of the resistance to influence the political reconstruction of liberated areas, just as the Soviet Union did, though in this case the object was to limit the spread of communism, not to encourage it. The origins of Western support for resistance lay in the British decision in July 1940, in the absence of any alternative strategy, to find indirect ways of engaging with the German war effort. One course was sea blockade; another was the bombing of German industry. The third strand was to promote resistance movements that would engage in sabotage and terror against the occupier, or, in Churchill's well-known phrase 'set Europe ablaze'. This was a novelty in modern war strategy. The idea that civilian populations should engage in insurgency while waiting patiently to be liberated made little practical sense in 1940, and in truth the British made only limited efforts to promote resistance until the time came when re-entry to the European mainland became possible.

The strategy was nevertheless put into action at once. The minister of economic warfare, the Labour politician Hugh Dalton, was given responsibility for developing a secret organization that would send agents, money and supplies into occupied Europe. Neville Chamberlain was invited to draw up the founding document of the new department, and he coined the title Special Operations Executive to describe it.[143] Dalton, who imagined potential revolution among Europe's oppressed working classes, thought the prospects immense of 'this war from within'.[144] Alongside SOE, the government approved propaganda to occupied Europe to encourage resistance of all kinds, including radio broadcasts from the BBC and leaflets dropped from the air. At the wartime peak the BBC was broadcasting 160,000 words a day in 23 different languages, listened to across Europe by populations eager for more reliable news than Axis radio; and over the course of the war aircraft and balloons dropped nearly 1.5 billion leaflets, news-sheets and magazines. They were eagerly sought, even though possession of a piece of Allied propaganda could mean a death sentence.[145]

A second organization, the Political Warfare Executive, was established under the direction of the former diplomat Robert Bruce Lockhart to orchestrate the propaganda campaign from headquarters in the BBC's Bush House in central London. Political warfare was intended to sustain morale in the occupied areas and to encourage clandestine acts of resistance to 'injure or undermine' the enemy.[146] The ultimate aim was to promote a widespread resistance movement to be mobilized at the right moment to assist the Allies. Lockhart and his colleagues devised various programmes that it was hoped might stimulate opposition. A 'Peasants Revolt' campaign was targeted at European farmers with early morning broadcasts ('Dawn Peasants') calling on them to defy German demands for food. The campaign, like many others, was based on a mix of speculation and fantasy. 'If the peasants do not cooperate,' ran one optimistic report, 'the war machine of the National Socialist dictators will one day cease to function.'[147] A second campaign, codenamed 'Trojan Horse', was targeted at European workers conscripted for forced labour in Germany. The strategy document drawn up in 1944 claimed that the workforce constituted a 'unique revolutionary force' which could be called upon to revolt once the Allied invasion began. Despite the lack of any credible evidence, or any real understanding of the conditions under which compulsory labourers operated, the PWE succeeded in persuading Eisenhower's headquarters to adopt the campaign as policy.[148] The Czech foreign ministry in exile had a more realistic assessment when it warned Lockhart that British political warfare was 'twenty thousand miles' from European realities. At the end of the war the head of Britain's Joint Intelligence Committee, Victor Cavendish-Bentinck, concluded that it was doubtful if political warfare 'shortened the recent war by one hour'.[149]

After the United States joined the war, the Office of Strategic Services, set up in July 1942 under General William Donovan, established an American Special Operations branch (SO) to match SOE and a Morale Division (later the Political Warfare Division) to imitate the work of the Political Warfare Executive.[150] Both SOE and the American SO branch organized and trained special agents to be infiltrated into enemy-occupied territory and once there to establish contact with local resistance movements in order to undertake acts of sabotage or to gather intelligence. Left to their own devices, the Allies feared that civilian resisters would be ineffective amateurs. The two organizations operated worldwide and divided their activities geographically to avoid duplicating and confusing the secret war. In Asia, the SO Operational Groups played a larger part, except in Burma, where responsibility was shared. In Europe, SOE predominated and when SOE and SO were amalgamated in January 1944, American operatives were in many cases merged with the existing SOE units. SOE eventually comprised 13,200 men and women, around half of whom served as agents in the field, taking high casualties, like local resisters, through betrayal or detection. OSS by the end of the war employed 26,000, a part serving in SO, a part in the American Secret Intelligence branch.[151]

In some cases, the agents were native-speakers, recruited from among refugee populations in Britain or from among American immigrant communities, in some cases not. They lived a dangerous and deadly existence once parachuted into enemy-held territory, characterized, as the last wartime head of SOE, Major General Colin Gubbins, put it, by 'a continual anxiety, all day and every day'.[152] Their precarious position was due not only to the presence of the enemy, who treated them as terrorists, but also to the uncertain relations with local resisters, who collaborated with Allied agents chiefly because the Allies also supplied money, arms and explosives without which the resistance was severely handicapped. There otherwise existed a tension between the Allied desire for operations that suited their strategic and tactical priorities and the broader resistance campaigns for national liberation, which the Allies were less concerned to support. Peter Wilkinson, the first agent to establish face-to-face contact with Tito, reported back to SOE headquarters that the partisans seemed more interested in waging civil war than confronting the Germans. 'As it is,' his report continued, 'there is no, repeat no, sabotage work being done though the possibilities are enormous.'[153] Agents parachuted into Greece were even more dismissive of the fighting potential of the village guerrillas they were supposed to help, men and women casually dismissed by Churchill as 'miserable banditti'.[154] Western assistance was always conditional: sabotage of all kinds was expected to serve the central goal of defeating the Axis states. Arms were not intended to fuel civil wars. When civil war did break out in Greece following liberation in autumn 1944, the British army intervened in December 1944 to prevent a communist takeover of Athens by National Liberation Army units armed with Allied weapons. This was the one example of Allied forces fighting the very resistance groups they had supported through their struggle against the Axis enemy.[155]

The insistence that aid for resisters should principally match the strategic priorities of Western forces is evident from the statistics on the supply of resources and agents from the air. Between 1943 and 1945, 8,455 tons of supplies were dropped by the RAF from British bases to the French resistance, 484 tons for Belgium, 554 tons for the Netherlands, 37 tons for Poland and a single ton for Czechoslovakia, which was difficult to reach by air without undue risk to the crews and planes. For the Yugoslav partisans, holding down at least 6 German divisions, 16,500 tons were supplied, but for the Italian partisans, whose military worth was regarded more sceptically, only 918 tons were dropped during the critical months of battle on the Italian front between June and October 1944.[156] The timing was also determined by Allied military planning. Supplies to France were scanty until early 1944 when the resistance movements were expected to undertake sabotage in support of the Normandy invasion. From 1941 to the end of 1943, 602 tons of supplies were dropped, but between January and September 1944 the British and American air forces dropped 9,875 tons, of which almost two-thirds came after the landings in June. The number of agents parachuted in to assist with the Allied invasion matched the flow of supplies: some 415 were sent between 1941 and 1943, but 1,369 from January to September 1944, of whom 995 arrived after D-Day.[157] Assistance was also targeted at the areas near the front line even though resistance was countrywide. In Italy, aid to partisan units in the far north-east of the country was negligible. 'Was the RAF a myth . . . ?' wrote an irate SOE agent in Friuli back to headquarters. 'If the Command has no intention of being interested,' he continued, 'it should not have promised arms and materials . . . to give [the partisans] false hopes . . .'[158] In France, the resisters in Brittany, close to the Allied landing zones, were sent 29,000 weapons after D-Day, but in the distant

Alsace-Ardennes-Moselle region, on the French eastern border, only 2,000.[159] The priorities made operational sense for the Allies but left partisans who were isolated from the front line frustrated at what they saw as the deliberate neglect of their share in the struggle.

The ambiguous nature of the Allied response to the irregular forces behind enemy lines was evident in the case of Italy and France in the late stages of the war. In both cases the Allies wanted to be able to exercise some kind of direct control, even to command the partisans. In Italy this proved to be difficult because the Italian movement for national liberation preferred the possibility of popular, insurrectionary violence over formal allegiance to the Allied high command and its orthodox military planning. The major anti-Fascist resistance movements – the Italian Communist Party, the Action Party and the socialists – agreed in March 1943 on a united call for national insurrection, and the emphasis on a popular civilian war of liberation remained in place for the following two years. After the Italian surrender and Allied invasion of mainland Italy in September 1943, the first insurrectionary violence liberated the city of Naples from German occupation without Allied aid. The rising was a spontaneous reaction against the shortages of food, the deprivations of the German occupiers (who within hours of the surrender had begun to treat Italians as an enemy people) and against the German demand that all men of working age should be deported to Germany. What began on 28 September as an indecisive exchange of fire between German forces and a mix of armed civilians and deserters grew rapidly in scale. A German report the following day observed that the 'activity of the [partisan] bands has expanded to the point where it has been transformed into an insurrection of the entire population'.[160] In four days the improvised combat drove the Germans out of the city while the British, now established on the islands of Capri and Ischia in the Bay of Naples, looked on, refusing a request to supply men or ammunition for the rebels. The insurrection cost an estimated 663 Italian lives, one-fifth of them women, and the widespread destruction of the city, but it was a popular victory. The Neapolitan revolt, wrote the resistance leader Luigi Longo, was a 'guiding example', granting 'sense and value' to the call for insurrection in the rest of occupied Italy.[161]

The partisan movement in Italy that developed after the German occupation grew rapidly following the success in Naples. Estimates suggest that partisan units by the summer of 1944 comprised between 80,000 and 120,000 men and women.[162] They were loosely co-ordinated by the Committee of National Liberation for Upper Italy (CLNAI), created in September 1943, which operated independently from the main National Liberation Committee based in the southern, Allied-occupied areas.

Although in contact with SOE and the American OSS agents, the partisans operated largely outside the control of the Allies as they laboured to expel the Germans from the rest of the peninsula. The head of the OSS in occupied Italy, Max Corvo, later observed how difficult it was to persuade the CLNAI 'to control their paramilitary activities in conjunction with orthodox military plans . . .'[163] The Allied high command was wary of the political ambitions of the resistance, above all the prospect of communist-inspired social revolution. In liberated cities, the British tried to install local aristocrats as provisional authorities but were forestalled by the local committees of liberation and by popular resentment. A report from Number 1 Special Forces, the SOE headquarters in Italy, warned that 'communist bands were preparing themselves to seize power'. Aid to the partisans went where it was judged to be most useful militarily, but least threatening politically.[164] The result was an Allied approach to resistance that was largely instrumental. When resistance was not needed or its help regarded with suspicion, the Allied high command could act with indifference, even hostility. When an armed insurrection broke out in Florence on 8 August 1944, involving thousands of civilian volunteers alongside the partisans, the approaching Allied forces were reluctant to support it, and after the German withdrawal, they moved tanks to the outskirts of partisan camps to force the irregular forces to disarm. When the Allied advance finally stalled in October 1944 along the German Gothic Line, the resistance to the north was effectively abandoned. In October 1944 only 110 tons of supplies were dropped, against the original promise of 600 tons.[165] Worse still, as the Allied front line closed down for the winter months, German and Fascist forces were given notice that they could engage in a savage anti-partisan war without fear of intervention.

On 13 November 1944, General Harold Alexander, commander-in-chief of Allied armies in Italy, broadcast *en clair* on the resistance radio station 'Italia Combatte' ('Italy Fights') a proclamation announcing that Allied armies would halt the campaign for the winter months, with a recommendation that the guerrillas cease their attacks, conserve their weapons and wait for instructions in the spring.[166] The result was devastating for the resistance once the German army realized it could focus its efforts on combating the partisans. The German army, together with Fascist 'black brigades' and a Cossack volunteer division, had already begun a major campaign against the partisans in October once the front line had solidified. After Alexander's broadcast the counter-insurgency increased in intensity; special 'Counter-guerrilla' tribunals were set up, which targeted not only the armed resistance but anyone suspected of aiding or supporting the partisan movement. The mountain retreats were attacked and thousands of partisans killed, while thousands more either deserted or descended to the plains of the Po Valley, where they were an easy target for denunciation and pursuit. By the end of the year numbers were down to an estimated 20–30,000 still in arms.[167] The absence of support from the Allies led to a major crisis for guerrilla units short even of basic clothes, boots and food. The local communities that had supported the partisans over the summer were savagely victimized by the anti-partisan units, with the result that they showed a growing antipathy towards further partisan collaboration. The mood among the partisans, the official SOE narrative later admitted, was one of 'confusion and despair'. The Allies soon realized the misjudged nature of Alexander's appeal but left the resistance to its fate. The allegation that Alexander deliberately sacrificed the partisan movement to remove the prospect of a communist insurrection remains unproven, however plausible. The proclamation instead reflected the failure of the Allied high command to appreciate the true nature of irregular warfare, which could not be switched on or off to suit Allied intentions. 'There were no lulls in partisan warfare,' reflected Max Corvo in his memoir of the crisis, 'no rest – no respite.'[168]

In December CLNAI leaders travelled to Rome to press the Allies to provide more practical support and to acknowledge that their organization and its irregular army represented political authority behind the German front. The second was agreed warily, because the Allies did not want to encourage political radicalism in the areas they liberated; greater direct support was accepted, but only because by January 1945 the Allied armies were preparing the final assault on German forces in the Po Valley and now needed the partisans once again to sabotage German communications and supplies. The Rome Protocols, as they came to be called, mollified the effect of Alexander's blunder. Despite the severity of the crisis across the winter months, the prospect that Italians would soon be able to liberate their northern cities in advance of the renewed Allied offensive brought a wave of fresh recruits; Allied supplies suddenly flowed in abundance so that units starved of useful resources for months could now rearm themselves. By early spring more than 1,000 tons of supplies a month arrived for partisan forces that had swollen again to an estimated 80,000 by March, 150,000 a month later.[169] The Allies and the government authorities in Rome wanted the guerrilla army only to fight the Germans. The CLNAI agreed in March on the 'exclusive employment of military forces for purposes of warfare', but although there was an increase in sabotage operations against German lines of communication, the partisans were more concerned to prepare for a final wave of insurrectionary violence – fighters and civilians alike – against the occupiers and their Fascist allies.[170] When the Allied campaign began on 10 April, American General Mark Clark ordered the partisans to make no move 'without the authorization of the allied Supreme Command'. Partisan forces largely ignored the order.[171]

As Allied armies broke rapidly through the German line and began the advance across the Po Valley, the liberation movement, armed and unarmed, began planning ways to drive the Germans from the major cities before Allied armies reached them. If it proved possible, they hoped to take control of the local justice system, in order to purge, violently if necessary, those Italians who had supported the puppet Fascist regime. The CLNAI announced that anyone deemed to be a war criminal or a traitor could be summarily executed and among the victims of this rough justice were Benito Mussolini and his mistress, Clara Petacci, caught and shot on 28 April as they tried to flee across the Swiss border. In the last two weeks of April 1945, the armed resistance, supported by numerous volunteers from the local civilian population and a widespread strike movement, liberated city after city: Bologna on 20 April, Milan and Genoa (where 18,000 Germans surrendered to a smaller guerrilla force) on 25–26 April, Turin by 28 April. Many smaller cities and towns were freed across northern Italy by the insurrection or were liberated because of German retreat, altogether a remarkable total of 125.[172] Allied armies arrived within days, keen to supervise the establishment of administrative and judicial control and to avoid the prospect that a radical revolutionary movement would try to pre-empt them. Partisans were reluctant to surrender their weapons; thousands were hidden away, while damaged or obsolete guns were handed over instead. The Allies could not prevent a wave of violent revenge killings against Fascists and collaborators which washed across the whole of northern Italy, a total according to the best estimate available of between 12,000 and 15,000 deaths.[173] Whatever assistance the partisan war had provided for the Allied military cause, the resistance was principally concerned to eradicate Fascism and, like the Poles, to achieve national liberation before the Allied arrival and the end of the war. Instead of 2 May, when German forces formally surrendered to the Allies, Italy has celebrated victory ever since on 25 April, to make clear the distinction between the formal end to the military campaign and the insurrectionary moment of liberation a week before.

The Allied experience in France differed in many important respects from that in Italy. France was an occupied ally, Italy a former enemy; Britain hosted a French liberation movement under the leadership of General de Gaulle, while there was no external Italian liberation movement; the French resistance movements were eventually brought under the unified military command of de Gaulle's British-based Free French and their actions integrated as far as possible with Allied operations in 1944, while command in Italy, to the extent it could be exercised at all, remained with the national liberation movement; by 1944 there was an entire French army fighting side by side with the Western Allies to reassert the right of France to be considered a major power again, but liberated Italy contributed principally auxiliary forces with only a small number of combat troops. Finally, the Italian partisan movement seized the moment in 1945 to free Italy's northern cities by their own force, while most French cities were liberated by the Allies, including the revived French army.

The centralization of control over the resistance movements in France was not achieved easily and, as in Italy, was resented or rejected at local level because of the tension between those running the risks of combat every day and those in the safety of London trying to dictate resistance priorities. De Gaulle conducted a lengthy campaign not only to get his authority recognized in France, but to get his putative British and American allies to accept it as well. In October 1942 the major resistance movements – *Combat*, *Libération* and *Francs-Tireurs et Partisans* – were directed by the Free French to pool their resources and to accept the umbrella title *Armée Sécrete* (Secret Army), loosely commanded by the retired French general Charles Delestraint. In January 1943 the resistance groups formally united as the *Mouvements unis de la Résistance*. Numbers claimed for the secret army were at best speculative. In March 1943 there were supposedly 126,000 but those with weapons amounted to perhaps no more than 10,000; by January 1944, there were 40,000 under arms as Allied supplies multiplied. In 1943, Jean Moulin, de Gaulle's representative in France, founded the *Conseil national de la Résistance* to co-ordinate the political and military wings of the movement, but with Moulin's arrest and death in June 1943 and the discovery by the Gestapo of the archives of the *Armée Sécrete* and the *Mouvements unis*, the resistance movement again fragmented with many of its leading cadres victims of the terror. The *Conseil national* found shelter with the Allies and eventually constituted a government-in-waiting, installed in the recaptured city of Algiers. When the national movement revived, the Allies sought to integrate it more directly with the planned invasion of France.

Efforts to co-ordinate the Allies' plans for the period just before and after the Normandy landings had begun as early as the spring of 1943, when a joint planning committee was set up between SOE and the resistance Bureau of Intelligence and Action. The plans '*Vert*', '*Violet*', '*Tortue*' and '*Bleu*' were drawn up for sabotage of railways, telecommunications, troop reinforcement and electricity supply. Although the Allies distrusted de Gaulle's ambition and were guarded about the military worth of the resistance, they accepted the creation in March 1944 of the *Forces françaises de l'Intérieur* (FFI) under the Free French General Marie-Pierre Koenig, and effectively under de Gaulle's overall command. Eisenhower insisted on integrating the FFI with his Supreme Headquarters and put Koenig in charge not only of the French resistance forces, but also of Allied Special Forces; a French Committee of Defence was formed to control resistance action at and behind the fighting front on behalf of the Western Allies.

There were French resisters who disliked the outcome, but it suited both the Allied powers and de Gaulle's Free French not only because sabotage was an essential element in the strategy for the invasion, but because it created a central command structure over the resistance that favoured military operations over the contested politics of liberation. To ensure that the resistance effort, carried out in many cases by untrained civilians, would be effective, SOE and SO agents were infiltrated through the SOE's F Section to organize networks of resisters for sabotage operations and to train them in the use of explosives. By D-Day there were an estimated fifty networks in operation; after D-Day special three-man teams of agents, codenamed 'Jedburgh' (after a Scottish village), were sent into the occupied areas, a total of ninety-two teams infiltrated from Britain, and twenty-five from the Mediterranean.[174] The result was a significant increase in sabotage activity. From April to June 1944 there were 1,713 acts of sabotage against the French rail network; in the first six months of the year the resisters destroyed or damaged 1,605 locomotives and 70,000 goods wagons. Attacks by Allied aircraft removed a further 2,536 locomotives and 50,000 wagons.[175] The *'Tortue'* plan to hold up German reinforcements to the Normandy front relied more heavily on action by SOE and the resistance on the ground in destroying bridges and blocking roads. This had a significant impact: it took the Ninth and Tenth Panzer Divisions, arriving in Lorraine on 16 June, a further nine days to reach western France; it took the Twenty-seventh Infantry Division seventeen days to move 180 kilometres.[176]

Allied efforts to mobilize the resistance directly under their control resembled the way the Soviet armed forces and security system came to control the activity of Soviet partisans. In territory liberated during the Allied advance through northern France and, from August, in the south as well, those FFI fighters of combat age who volunteered were integrated into the French army as regular soldiers, as partisans were in Russia. Most French cities and towns waited to be liberated by the arrival of the Allies. Research on 212 locations has shown that 179 of them were freed by the

Allies or were liberated as a result of German retreat, while a further 28 engaged in limited insurrectionary violence to assist their approaching liberators.[177] Armed resistance at that stage was treated with a particular savagery by the German occupiers – SS, Gestapo and army alike – so that *attentisme* right to the end made practical sense.[178] Nevertheless, the revolutionary impulse that had mobilized support for resistance activity well before the invasion did not entirely disappear, spurred on by communist calls for a mass 'armed insurrection'. On 8 June 1944 the Parisian Committee of Liberation, dominated by the communist resistance, called on the population to begin a popular rising by killing the occupiers and their Vichy allies: 'Men and women of Paris: each one his Boche, his *milicien* [Vichy militia], his traitor!' Six days later, the Paris-based military committee of the resistance, which had rejected the Allied intention to control partisan activity, called on the FFI to collaborate with the 'popular masses' as a step towards 'national insurrection'.[179]

In Lille, Marseilles, Limoges, Thiers, Toulouse, Castres and Brive as well as a number of smaller communities, the resistance did succeed in liberating the town before the Allies arrived, but there was no general insurrection. In Toulouse, communist-dominated FFI units controlled the city after its liberation, but on the threat that a division of the regular French army would be drafted in to restore the authority of the provisional government, the communist leadership caved in.[180] The most significant insurrection took place in Paris, where an improvised force of civilian insurgents and FFI units decided they would rather defy instructions from Koenig and the Committee of National Liberation in Algiers to avoid an anarchic conflict with a large German garrison than wait for the Allies. The climax was reached in August as Allied forces burst out of the Normandy bridgehead across northern France. It was not Eisenhower's intention to liberate Paris but to move north and south to cross the Seine and encircle the German garrison. But news of the German defeat in north-western France accelerated the planning in the capital for a popular insurrection. On 17 August the resistance leaders held a meeting to discuss the possibility. Opinions were divided, the more prudent conscious not only that de Gaulle did not want popular violence, but also aware of the crisis currently faced by the resistance in Warsaw. In the end the insurrectionary option prevailed: 'cannot allow [Allied] entry without insurrection', ran the minutes of the meeting.[181]

On 18 August the communist leader of the Parisian resistance forces, Henri Rol-Tanguy, ordered placards posted all over the city calling on the population to inaugurate the insurrection the following day, even though he estimated that his force of perhaps 20,000 men and women had no

more than 600 weapons available. The fighting that followed was sporadic, unlike the bitter contest in Warsaw, and the outcome was indecisive.
A brief truce was declared, but the FFI fighters, eager to prove themselves,
violated it. Barricades, iconic symbol of the long revolutionary tradition in
Paris, were hastily constructed in the predominantly working-class *arron-
dissements*. 'Freedom is returning,' wrote the writer Jean Guénenno in his
diary. 'We don't know where it is, but it is all around us in the night.'[182]
Uncertain of the outcome, on the 20th Rol-Tanguy sent an emissary to the
Allied high command asking for help, and the following day de Gaulle
persuaded Eisenhower to divert a French division commanded by General
Philippe Leclerc to secure the liberation and avoid a communist takeover.
The regular troops arrived on the 24th, by which time the insurrection had
indeed finally achieved its goal against a demoralized German garrison.
The German commander in Paris, General Dietrich von Choltitz, ignored
Hitler's demand that the city be defended to the last man and reduced to
ashes like Warsaw and surrendered to Leclerc and Rol-Tanguy a day
later.[183] The simultaneous arrival of de Gaulle nevertheless compromised
the popular insurrection. The Parisian resistance had to accept the authority of Koenig, the integration of the FFI with the Allied armies, and a
French government organized by de Gaulle with the reluctant support of
the British and American authorities, who had initially wanted to exercise
military government in the French territory they liberated. In the end
thirty-five regiments and battalions of the FFI were amalgamated as units
of the French First Army, a total of at least 57,000 men. Thousands more
returned home rather than fight in a regular army, some to secure their
jobs, some too exhausted to continue, some unwilling to trade the glamour
and danger of clandestine resistance for the rigours of regular army life.[184]

For the Western Allies the value of the resistance was measured, as it
was in the Soviet Union, by the extent to which its activity undermined or
impeded enemy operations and reduced the enemy's resources. Extensive
supplies of equipment and the large-scale infiltration of agents occurred
only when Allied forces needed support for major operations of their own.
Few resisters would have agreed with the SOE chief of staff, Brigadier
General Richard Barry, when in 1958 during the first conference on the
history of resistance he informed his audience that, without Allied aid,
'little if any resistance would have been possible'.[185] Resistance went on
across Europe and Asia independent of Allied assistance and with a time-
scale and purpose dictated more by local conditions and possibilities than
by Allied needs. For those with the exceptional civil courage to resist, predominantly civilian men and women leavened with a core of former
soldiers and deserters, the aim was to demonstrate to the occupying

powers that they would not exercise authority unchallenged and that the liberation of local communities and of the nation would also be fought for from within. The ambition to play a part as civilian insurgents was a political and moral statement, not merely a contribution to victory, which is why in Warsaw or Milan or Paris insurrection was deemed preferable to the passive acceptance of liberation by Allied forces. The final acts of insurrection were a way of validating both those who resisted and the years of struggle in which they had taken part. A young woman partisan Léon Brescia, in northern Italy, recalled in her diary the day when partisans liberated the city ahead of the American army: 'our boys pass by proudly, their machine guns cocked. In their eyes shines the joy of victory. They have won the city and it is now in their hands ... the heart sings. The city is free.'[186]

'WE ARE LOST, BUT WE MUST FIGHT': THE RESISTANCE OF THE JEWS

The resistance of Europe's Jewish civilian communities differed fundamentally from all other forms of resistance. Unlike those resistance and partisan formations struggling to liberate the nation from occupation, or fighting each other over the issue of what that post-war nation should look like, European Jews were confronted with a regime that was committed to a war of extermination against the Jewish people. Resistance on these terms meant fighting back to limit or challenge the programme of annihilation, or, if possible, to find ways of evading an inevitable fate by strategies of concealment or flight. There was no Jewish nation or political future towards which the struggle could be directed. Jews who resisted as Jews did so because, doomed though the enterprise might be, they preferred a death of their own choosing, rather than the fate prepared by the German perpetrators and their accomplices. 'We are lost,' claimed Dr Icheskel Atlas, a Jewish partisan leader in 1942, 'but we must fight.' He died in the partisan battles in eastern Poland later that year.[187]

The issue of what constitutes Jewish resistance is nevertheless not straightforward. In the first place, a number of Jewish resisters saw themselves as part of the national resistance movement and hoped to avoid being seen as pursuing specifically Jewish needs. This was a common approach for Jews who were well integrated in the national community, as in France, where many Jewish resisters wanted to identify with the broader patriotic campaign rather than risk accusations that they served only Jewish interests. 'I am French,' wrote the Jewish resistance fighter Léon Nisand in his memoirs, 'and our family is French because ... we participate in the

fortunes and misfortunes of our Republic.'[188] French Jews played a prominent part in the early non-Jewish resistance movement in France, as
founder members of the Musée de l'Homme circle in 1940, as half the
group that launched *Libération* in July 1941, and as prominent active
resisters in Paris, where an estimated two-thirds of all attacks between July
1942 and July 1943 involved Jewish groups.[189] Jewish communists across
Europe were also divided between a desire to assist in some way the victimized Jewish communities and the need to remain primarily loyal to the
political class struggle against fascism. In the German-occupied areas of
the Soviet Union after 1941, some of the Jews who fled to the forests to
join or to form partisan units found that they could protect themselves
best by merging into non-Jewish units that fought to re-establish Soviet
power and which cared little for the fate of the Russian Jews. Young Jews,
if they escaped being shot as suspected German stooges, were encouraged
to adopt Russian pseudonyms to avoid the real danger of anti-Semitic violence. The result was a paradox in which they had to appear to be
non-Jewish to fight against the enemies of the Jewish people.[190]

The second problem is to define more precisely what resistance means
in the context of the Jewish genocide. Political resistance was limited, since
the Jewish persecution was not about political repression. It has often been
argued that armed struggle is the only proper definition of Jewish resistance. Yet because the purpose of the German machinery of extermination
was to kill every single Jew, except for the fraction kept alive long enough
to extract their diminishing labour power, resistance also embraced the
effort to hide Jews, to aid their flight, or to provide them with false
identities – acts that also included the contribution of many non-Jews. All
these strategies challenged a central priority of the regime by denying the
perpetrators the chance to murder their intended victims. Survival was, in
itself, a way of resisting the genocidal imperatives that the Jews confronted
everywhere across occupied or Axis Europe but, except for those who fled
to the forests and swamps of Eastern Europe and Russia, evasion depended
on non-Jewish civilians with the courage to defy the perpetrators. Rescue
was widespread in Western Europe, where Jewish communities were generally more integrated and the population more likely to reject German
demands; in France some 75 per cent of the native Jewish population survived the genocide, in Italy some 80 per cent.[191] By contrast, in the
conquered areas in the East the presence of a widespread, often visceral
dislike of the Jews made it much more difficult to find non-Jews willing to
run the many risks involved. Nevertheless, an estimated 28,000 Polish
Jews were hidden in Warsaw outside the ghetto, and around two-fifths of
them survived the war. Some Belorussian and Ukrainian households also

hid Jews, but not usually for any length of time, since Jews in flight in the East sought, if they could, to reach the relative safety of the small Jewish communities hiding in the shelter of the forests.[192]

Concealment as a form of resistance carried all the usual dangers associated with political and military opposition: house searches, police interrogations, denouncement by neighbours keen, at least in the East, to take the bag of sugar or salt offered as a reward for every Jew caught. Like the regular resisters, those in any household or institution found guilty of harbouring Jews were subject to the death penalty or incarceration in a camp. Estimates suggest that between 2,300 and 2,500 Poles were executed for aiding Jews, but since they could be killed summarily without any process of law, the figure is almost certainly much higher. Where networks of rescue were operated, the rescuers could be tortured to reveal other names and 'safe' houses, just as political resisters were treated. Gestapo searches focused particularly on children, who were easier to conceal and among those most likely to find an adoptive home. Some 2,500 Jewish children in Poland were rescued and hidden at great risk under the auspices of Żegota, the Council to Aid the Jews, either placed with families or in orphanages or in the care of the Catholic Church. Once caught, the children, in most cases orphaned or abandoned, would suffer like the non-Jews who had sheltered them, either shipped to the extermination camps, or killed on the spot. When the Gestapo discovered that monks of the Silesian Brotherhood in Warsaw were sheltering a number of Jewish children, they and their young charges were all hanged from a high balcony in full sight of a busy street below and their bodies left there to rot as a warning. Efforts were made by Żegota rescuers to ensure that young children who spoke only Yiddish would be taught Catholic prayers in Polish to aid their disguise, but one six-year-old girl, Basia Cukier, could not recite them in front of the Gestapo officials and was taken away to her death.[193] Under such circumstances where concealment of all kinds was criminalized and the penalties cruelly severe, both the rescued and the rescuer must be regarded in their own right as resisters.

Jewish armed resistance, like the efforts to conceal or rescue Jews, differed in important ways from other forms of confrontation with Axis occupation. Because it was a response to the changing pattern of German and Axis persecution, the timing of Jewish resistance was dictated not by the course of the wider world war, but by the course of Hitler's war against the Jews. In most of Europe and Asia, resistance peaked only in the last eighteen months of the conflict, once it became clear that the aggressor states faced certain defeat, sooner or later. Jewish resistance, by contrast, came chiefly in 1942 and 1943 as a reaction to the programme of mass deportation of Jewish populations from the ghettoes in the East and from the rest of Western Europe. Jewish armed resistance in France was most conspicuous in the middle years of the war when other resistance groups were more cautious. Jewish action in Poland ran directly against the interests of the Home Army, which wanted to avoid confronting the occupier until his defeat was imminent. There was no intention that Jewish resistance should help the Allied war effort, although in marginal ways it sometimes did so, nor did the Allies supply Jewish groups with weapons or money to sustain their activity as they did with other guerrilla movements. Out of 240 Jewish volunteers from Palestine, trained reluctantly by SOE, only 32 were parachuted into Europe in 1944, too late to help the beleaguered Jewish communities.[194] Jewish fighters were chiefly civilians, most with limited or no military experience, and poorly equipped to confront the well-armed German security apparatus and its numerous non-German auxiliaries – Lithuanian, Latvian, Russian, Ukrainian or Polish. Resistance was about confounding the remorseless process of genocide in one limited form or another, but most Jewish resisters understood that their opposition was doomed. War against the Germans, as one Jewish fighter put it, was 'the most hopeless declaration of war that has ever been made'.[195]

Active Jewish resistance was expressed in two contrasting ways: the first was to find means to ensure that at least a small fraction of the menaced Jewish population could be saved from deportation and, if geography allowed it, might establish self-protection groups or guerrilla bands to defend the outlawed communities; the second was to organize revolts which, though doomed from the start, would demonstrate to the German perpetrators that the Jewish populations were not universally passive in confronting their fate but, as the Zionist youth leader Hirsch Belinski put it, would 'die with dignity and not like hunted animals'.[196] In truth there was little difference in the fate of the Jews in either context. 'Every Jew carries with him a death sentence,' observed the chronicler of the Warsaw Ghetto, Emanuel Ringelblum.[197] The dangerous nature of active resistance and the tiny number of weapons available help to explain why only a very small minority of the doomed Jewish populations actually participated in combat. Of the remaining inhabitants of the Warsaw Ghetto in spring 1943, only an estimated 5 per cent actually fought in the uprising. By March 1943 the resistance movement in the large Vilna Ghetto could count on only 300 fighters.[198] Those who escaped from ghettoes and camps to join armed groups were a tiny fraction of the whole ghetto and camp population; those who made it to the relative sanctuary of the forests were a smaller fraction still, as militia and police hunted down the fugitives with a remorseless zeal.

Opportunity was certainly limited, but there were many other constraining factors to explain why more did not resist. Jewish communities everywhere had only limited or partial understanding of what was being done to them, and a strong predisposition to believe that the worst could not be true. One diarist in the Warsaw Ghetto deplored the 'terrifying rumours . . . the product of some inflated imagination.'[199] There was a realistic fear that armed action might make things worse by speeding up the deportations and killings, or by encouraging savage German reprisals. Potential resisters faced a hard moral choice between protecting their family and companions or abandoning them to take up arms. Preserving family, and in particular saving children, was a strong incentive among the ghetto communities not to resist with violence.[200] There were also profound political and religious divisions within Jewish communities, particularly between more conservative Jews and those in the various Jewish communist organizations, which made co-operation more complex and, at times, impossible. Many Orthodox Jews denied that there was any right to obstruct a fate that must be ordained by God, and called on congregations to focus on strengthening the spirit in the face of oppression.[201] Above all was the forlorn belief that by co-operating with the German authorities some of the ghetto inhabitants, particularly those labouring in German workshops, might survive long enough to see German defeat and liberation. The failure of the resistance movement in the Vilna Ghetto stemmed from the wide support among the population for the Jewish leader Jacob Gens, whose strategy of compliance seemed more likely to save lives than a fruitless revolt.[202] One Jewish ghetto policeman reflected that nobody would take the heroic step to resistance 'as long as one spark of hope existed that they would last out'. Hope, observed Herman Kruk in his diary of the Vilna Ghetto, is 'the worst disease in the ghetto'.[203]

Estimates for those who did succeed in escaping the round-ups or life in the ghettoes and camps vary widely between 40,000 and 80,000 people across German-occupied Europe, but they were overwhelmingly concentrated in Eastern Europe where the geographical conditions were the most favourable. In the Polish General Government, with a population by 1942 of around 3 million Jews, other estimates suggest that as many as 50,000 escaped as refugees to the forests around Lublin and Radom, though the figures are unverifiable.[204] Once there, the fugitives had a number of stark choices. Some formed independent Jewish guerrilla groups, numbering anything from a handful to hundreds, driven in many, perhaps most, cases by a longing for revenge against their tormentors.[205] Using arms stolen or occasionally bought, their object was to confront the enemy rather than simply to secure survival, engaging in small harassing attacks before melting back into the forests or swampland. Others formed so-called 'family units', where a Jewish community was built up in hiding with the chief purpose of ensuring that at least some survived the conflict. An estimated 6,000 to 9,500 lived in the family units in the conquered Soviet area.[206] These units were poorly armed and avoided direct combat when they could, using what limited military equipment they had in order to defend the community. The unit led by Shalom Zorin, for example, resisted pressure from Soviet partisans to join the military campaign by acting as a supply unit, helping to find food and providing medical and artisan services to the non-Jewish guerrillas. The famous Bielski brigade 'New Jerusalem', numbering at some points up to 1,200 refugees, moved regularly from one hiding place to another to avoid fighting. 'Don't rush to fight and die,' Tuvia Bielski is reported as saying, 'so few of us are left, we have to save lives.'[207]

Life in the forests and marshland, whether hiding or fighting, was difficult in the extreme. Most fugitives were from cities or towns and were unfamiliar with the demands of living in the wild. Food was difficult to obtain and the risks great in trying to persuade peasants, already subject to German demands or the depredations of Soviet or Polish partisans, to hand over any more of their produce. Since dependence on forest food – plants, nuts, fruit – was seasonal, food had to be stolen or occasionally bartered. Jewish fugitives gained an unwanted reputation, even among other non-Jewish resisters, as plunderers and criminals. One Jewish survivor later recalled that the fugitives were something between heroes and robbers: 'We had to live and we had to deprive the peasants of their meagre belongings.'[208] When food was found, the fugitives had to lay aside any scruples about only eating kosher food or the taboo against eating pork. A woman survivor recalled her introduction to the dilemma when she was offered and ate a pig's mouth. Cooking involved additional risks that fire would give away the hiding place. Peasant helpers taught the groups how to make fire using flints and moss, and which woods gave off little or no telltale smoke. Clothing had to be improvised, including shoes made from the bark of oak or birch trees.[209] Healthcare was rudimentary and disease, hunger and debilitation endemic. In winter weather, survival was a matter of chance.

All of these difficulties were eclipsed by the fear of discovery and the certain death that followed. The fugitives were hunted by German police units, the Polish collaborating 'Blue Police', and from 1942 onwards by Soviet auxiliaries in the so-called *Ostlegion* units, who treated Jewish captives with a particular savagery.[210] They were also the victims of other partisan groups, Polish, Ukrainian and Soviet, among whom anti-Semitism was widespread, including the Polish National Armed Forces (NSZ) and occasionally units of the Polish Home Army. One Jewish survivor in a Polish partisan unit had learned Christian rites in prison and passed himself off as a Catholic: 'I couldn't be a Jew,' he recalled, 'they would have killed me.' Estimates suggest that a quarter of the deaths of Jewish fugitives came at the hands of non-Jewish partisans.[211] Soviet partisans were told to distrust Jews as potential spies sent in by the Germans, which encouraged further grotesque violence. One group of Jewish women fugitives captured by partisans were stripped, raped, tied together with barbed wire and set alight.[212] For Jews in hiding, there was no easy way to distinguish between friend and foe, and few friends. Of those who fled the persecution, estimates suggest that between 80 and 90 per cent perished, from violence, disease, cold or hunger.

Active, armed resistance was little less dangerous. At least four-fifths of all those involved perished, alongside thousands caught in the crossfire or victims of harsh and indiscriminate retribution. The reaction of German leaders was to see all armed action as evidence of just how dangerous their Jewish enemy was, rather than a desperate effort to stave off the genocidal wave. 'One sees though what one may expect from the Jews when they manage to get their hands on weapons,' noted Joseph Goebbels in his diary in May 1943 during the Warsaw Ghetto uprising.[213] In France a number of Jewish resistance organizations emerged intent on pursuing Jewish interests. *La main forte* (Strong Hand) was founded in Toulouse in 1940 by a group of largely immigrant Jews, committed to combating the anti-Jewish policies of the Vichy regime; a year later, in August 1941, it was transformed into the *Armée juive*, and later still into the *Organisation juive de combat*. It answered not to the French resistance but to the Zionist Haganah movement, with its headquarters in Palestine.[214] The group was responsible not only for establishing rescue and welfare support for Jews in France, but for regular armed assaults against both German and Vichy French targets, including the assassination of those French individuals known to have betrayed Jews to the Gestapo. They faced exceptional risks and paid for it with regular denunciations, arrests and executions. Well before the Allied invasion, the *Armée juive* was finally broken by three waves of mass arrests in 1943. Efforts to re-form again in 1944 met with a similar fate.[215]

In Eastern Europe, armed resistance away from the forest hideouts consisted of numerous revolts that were largely spontaneous reactions to the fact of deportation, or the conditions in the labour and concentration camps, or, in the case of the Special Units (*Sonderkommando*) responsible for burning the bodies of the gassed victims in the extermination camps, revolt represented a brief effort to sabotage the killing machine. Such reaction was widespread. There were revolts in seven major ghettoes and forty-five smaller ones, and resistance movements in an estimated quarter of all ghettoes. In the concentration camps there were five uprisings, and in forced labour camps a further eighteen.[216] In the extermination camp at Sobibor, an uprising on 14 October 1943 resulted in the death of 11 SS men and the camp commandant and the escape of 300 prisoners to the forests; on 2 August 1943 in Treblinka rebels killed guards, set the camp on fire and allowed 600 to escape, only for most to be shot or recaptured later. At Auschwitz-Birkenau, a revolt by the *Sonderkommando* on 7 October 1944 left 450 of the 663 members dead; a further 200 were executed later.[217] Escapes were possible following a revolt, but for most participants, the gesture was their last. Himmler reacted to the violence by ordering the elimination of all Jewish workers. On 3 November 1943, 18,400 Jewish men and women were murdered at the Majdanek labour camp.[218]

The largest armed revolt illustrates the many problems confronting those Jews who decided that fighting back was a profound moral statement to recover, however briefly, their autonomy and some sense of self-worth against an enemy that valued them as less than human. The Warsaw Ghetto uprising, which began on 19 April 1943, followed the mass deportations from the ghetto inaugurated in the summer of 1942. In this case, the revolt was far from spontaneous. A Jewish Fighting Organization (ZOB) was established by left-wing Zionists in the autumn of 1942 under the leadership of Mordechai Anielewicz; distrust of its sympathy for communism led to the founding of the Jewish Military Union (ZZW) by Zionist Revisionists; the socialist Jewish Bund refused to join, but agreed to co-operate, while a number of 'wild' groups were established outside the main rebel organization. By the time of the rising the ZOB had some twenty-two combat groups, the ZZW ten, spread out in different districts of the ghetto. When the German authorities under SS Colonel Ferdinand von Sammern-Frankenegg began a new programme of deportations in January 1943, the insurgents were caught off-guard, but staged a brief four-day battle, enough to warn the Germans that the next stage of deportation was likely to be opposed more firmly. Himmler ordered the liquidation of the ghetto as soon as it was feasible. A large force of Waffen-SS, police and Ukrainian auxiliaries, supported by heavy weapons, was organized to carry out the next major deportation. Sammern-Frankenegg was replaced at the last moment by SS Major General Jürgen Stroop, who was expected to act ruthlessly, decisively and swiftly to stamp out any resistance.[219]

Warned in advance that a major move was planned, the two main fighting organizations finally collaborated in establishing resistance sites and garnering what limited weapons they could. By the time of the revolt the ZOB had only one sub-machine gun, a few rifles, and a greater number of handguns, grenades and Molotov cocktails. The Polish Home Army offered some limited training and a few arms for a largely inexperienced civilian force, but would not give more because they were needed for a future general rising.[220] When the German-led troop of an estimated 2,000 men entered the ghetto, they were faced by between 750 and 1,000 rebels stationed at key points. The subsequent battle frustrated German plans entirely. One survivor recalled his joy at the sight of 'German soldiers screaming in panicky flight' as they fled the mines and snipers they suddenly encountered.[221] Although the insurgents had pitifully few resources, careful use of what they had, and an initial element of surprise, meant that the rising continued on into the first week of May. German tactics changed with a reliance on artillery, bombing from the air and fire-raising, destroying the ghetto street by street. In one of the many vulnerable bunkers where the fighters sheltered, Anielewicz killed himself rather than be captured. Limited guerrilla actions lasted through the summer as the remains of the burnt-out ghetto were cleared and the final Jews were sent to Treblinka for extermination. An estimated 7,000 died in the fighting, including most of the ZOB and ZZW combatants, and perhaps 5–6,000 more in the fires. The great majority of the dead were Jews in hiding; they were flushed out by flamethrowers and gas grenades, or burnt alive in the widespread fires set by the attackers. Stroop claimed to have lost only sixteen men, which seems implausible given the length of the conflict, but higher figures are speculations.[222]

The rising did little to halt the deportations for more than a few weeks, though it did allow some further Jews to escape the ghetto. Doomed though it was, the rising also signalled clearly to the wider world what the Jews confronted. For the Germans, the rising was an inconvenient interruption to a programme that continued unabated through 1943 when the last inhabitants of the Warsaw Ghetto were eliminated. Jewish resistance, unlike the resistance movements across the rest of Europe and in Asia, mattered in the unique context of the genocide rather than the wider context of a world war in which the fate of the Jews was marginalized. Only when Jews served in the broader non-Jewish resistance and partisan movements did their role contribute to the struggle for liberation. In these cases, Jews suffered a double jeopardy both as resisters and as the alleged racial enemy of the Germans, who anyway regarded most armed resistance as inspired by the Jew. The separate war against the genocide was limited and self-defeating, pitting unarmed or poorly armed civilians against a heavily resourced security apparatus. It was a war that Jewish civilians had not expected to fight and for which they were inadequately prepared, in every sense. Of all the many civilian wars fought between 1939 and 1945, the Jewish resistance to the Holocaust was the most unequal and the most sacrificial.

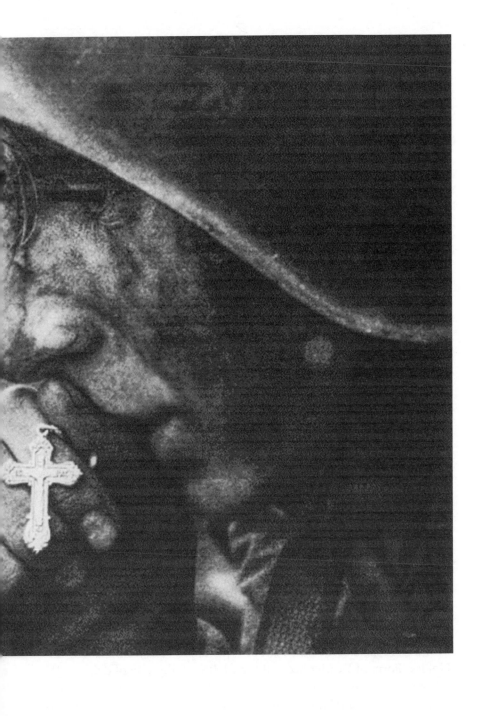

9

The Emotional Geography of War

'I have wept so much in the last few nights that even I find it unbearable. I have seen a comrade weeping, too, but he had a different reason. He was weeping over his lost tanks, of which he had been desperately proud . . . I have been weeping for the last three nights over the dead Russian tank driver whom I murdered . . . at night I cry as unrestrainedly as a child.'

A last letter from Stalingrad, January 1943[1]

The last letters sent by German soldiers from Stalingrad were never read by their families or friends. The German army was ordered to confiscate the final seven sacks of mail flown out of the Stalingrad pocket so that some assessment could be made of the state of morale of the doomed soldiers. The result was not quite what was hoped for. An analysis of the letters showed that only 2.1 per cent approved the conduct of the war, while 37.4 per cent appeared doubtful or indifferent, and 60.5 per cent were sceptical, negative or unequivocally opposed. When plans were made to use them for a propaganda book on the heroic struggle on the Volga, Joseph Goebbels rejected it: 'The whole thing is a funeral march!' On Hitler's orders all the letters were destroyed. Some thirty-nine letters were copied by the propaganda official who was supposed to write the book and later published after the war.[2] Like the weeping soldier who opens this chapter, the outlook and behaviour of the German soldiers conformed not at all to the image of heroic racial warriors, fighting to free Europe from the Bolshevik menace. The dead, wrote one survivor, 'are lying all around us – some without arms, legs or eyes and others with their bellies torn open. Someone ought to shoot a film of it, just to discredit the Noblest Form of Death once and for all. It's a filthy way of dying . . .'[3]

The emotional response of the men in Stalingrad was nothing unique in the Second World War. It was a reaction to the horrifying field of battle they inhabited and the bleak prospects for survival that they shared. In its most extreme form that reaction could result in severe psychiatric or psychosomatic responses that temporarily or permanently disabled hundreds of thousands of servicemen. The primary emotion shared by those who faced combat in all its many forms, including the civilians who experienced bombardment by aircraft or artillery, is usually defined as fear. As a generic term, fear is little more than a descriptive umbrella for a wide range of emotional states – prolonged anxiety, terror, hysteria, panic, acute depression, even aggression – and it can prompt an equally wide range of neuropsychiatric, psychotic or psychosomatic conditions. The reactions provoked by extreme forms of fear, more commonly understood today as traumatic stress, although universal in wartime combat, are not necessarily disabling for all those who experience them. Soldiers in combat are often faced with a bewildering range of emotions. One British soldier fighting in Burma was 'scared stiff but not witless' and described his emotional state as a confused mix of 'rage, terror, elation, relief and amazement'.[4] A Soviet woman in a front-line unit recalled that when an attack begins 'you begin to shake. To shiver. But that's before the first shot ... Once you hear the command, you no longer remember anything; you rise up with everybody and run. And you no longer think of being afraid.' Instead, she concluded, war exposed 'a glimpse of something bestial' in those who fought it.[5] For military commanders or for wartime governments the emotional states provoked by wartime violence became a problem only when they threatened to become disabling, either undermining military effectiveness or creating mass panic and debilitating demoralization on the home front. Managing the emotional response of soldiers and civilians to the visceral reality of combat became an important element in the war effort of every combatant state. Coping with wartime trauma, on the other hand, was the stark reality for tens of millions of ordinary men and women caught up in the coils of total war. Their psychiatric reactions usually went untreated and have generally been overlooked in post-war narratives of the war years.

'WAR NEUROSES ARE CAUSED BY WAR'

The experience of widespread emotional crisis in the armed forces has to be understood in the particular context of conflict in the Second World War. The armed forces were exceptionally large, relying almost entirely on civilian conscripts (a fraction of whom had done brief military service), whose expectations and values were shaped by a civilian milieu. In wartime the

armed forces represented a broad cross-section of the societies they were
drawn from, embracing wide differences in social class, education, personality and temperament. Despite the efforts of military institutions to shape
the men and women at their disposal, there was no such thing as a standard
military character. Young civilians were faced with the most extreme forms
of stress: the danger of being killed and the demand that they kill others.[6] It
was therefore certain that on a modern battlefield, service personnel would
display a wide range of physical and mental reactions. Conditions of combat also maximized the prospect of psychiatric casualties because of the
nature of advanced weaponry. Attacks by aircraft against troops in the field
and against civilians during the long-range bomber offensives evoked a particular terror provoked by the powerlessness of those on the ground and the
unpredictability of the target. In ground combat, the power of modern artillery in all its many forms, or the threat posed by tanks as they rolled through
exposed infantry positions, produced a scenario which tested the most courageous of men. The cumulative effect, wrote one wartime psychiatrist, of
'constant explosions, bangs, snaps of machine guns, whines of artillery
shells, rustle of mortars, drone of airplane engines, wears down resistance'.[7]
The average soldier (and the bombed civilian) had also to accept the regular
sight of dead and mutilated bodies, fields or streets strewn with body parts,
grisly scenes utterly alien to daily civilian life. The military environment
itself, with its rigid discipline, anti-individualism and suppression of identity provoked what one Australian psychiatrist described as a 'mental
shipwreck' long before the battlefield was ever reached.[8] The British army
based at home in 1941 had 1,300 psychiatric casualties a month. American
soldiers garrisoned on the far north Aleutian Islands were diagnosed with
'combat fatigue' when they had done no fighting. Psychiatric screening of
Australian soldiers returning from New Guinea found that two-thirds of
psychoneurotic casualties had not seen combat, prompting the conclusion
that there was no evidence to assume that it was combat alone that produced psychoneurosis.[9]

The scale of psychiatric casualty under these conditions was potentially
enormous, and so it proved in practice. The United States rejected around
2 million draftees on psychiatric grounds, but nevertheless had 1.3 million diagnosed psychiatric casualties throughout the conflict, 504,000 of
whom were discharged from the forces. In the European theatre 38.3 per
cent of all the American casualties were defined in one or other category
of psychoneurotic disorder. It was estimated that 98 per cent of all the
infantrymen who survived the Normandy campaign were at some point
psychiatric casualties.[10] In the same campaign between 10 and 20 per cent
of all British army casualties were defined as psychiatric, in the Canadian

army 25 per cent. Of those discharged on medical grounds from the British and American armies, one-third were psychiatric patients.[11] For the United States navy the proportion was much lower, partly because the field of combat was quite different, with no face-to-face killing and only short periods of intense combat. Only 3 per cent of those discharged from the navy had suffered psychoneurotic disorders.[12] Figures for the German and Soviet armies are more difficult to judge, since neurotic conditions were often ignored or treated as organic, and hence medical, casualties. One estimate suggests around 1 million Red Army psychiatric casualties, another, less plausibly, as few as 100,000.[13] For the German army, psychoneurotic cases in the early stages of the 'Barbarossa' campaign rose sharply to become the single most important source of casualty. By January 1944 estimates suggest that there were 20–30,000 psychiatric casualties per month, by the turn of 1944–5 perhaps as many as 100,000 a month. Figures up to 1943 suggest that among those discharged from military service, 19.2 per cent were psychoneurotic cases, but this statistic certainly rose in 1944–5 with tougher combat conditions, increasing prospects of death or injury, and the recruitment of ever younger and older men.[14] Italian records are too incomplete to provide aggregate statistics, but local evidence shows that Italian soldiers suffered the same debilitating range of psychiatric disorders as other armies.[15]

There were other ways in which combat, or the threat of combat, could be avoided that did not necessarily derive from any form of neurotic disorder, although it is likely that a substantial proportion of those who inflicted their own injuries, or those who deserted, or soldiers who surrendered also suffered to a greater or lesser degree from psychiatric reaction to fear, or a traumatic experience, or to the stifling effects of military life. Self-inflicted wounds carried many risks (and could occasionally be fatal). They were commonly inflicted by a shot through the hand or the foot. The record suggests that they occurred among most armed forces, but figures are scarce. In the campaign in North-west Europe, around 1,100 American servicemen chose this route to relative safety; the Canadian army in the same campaign recorded 232 cases in 1944. In the Red Army a self-inflicted wound might swiftly be followed by execution; they were always treated as examples of shameful abdication. In American military hospitals patients were separated off with the sign 'SIW' hung above the bed, and treated by the staff as pariahs, though not yet formally punished.[16]

Desertion was of a different order. In the Red Army, desertion (including those who went over to the enemy) reached the staggering figure of 4.38 million. Of the 2.8 million defined as deserters or draft dodgers on the Soviet side of the line, 212,400 were never caught (and may indeed have been dead). Many were not technically deserters, but lost touch with their units during the great retreats of 1941–2 or managed to slip through German lines in the battles of encirclement, and these soldiers were generally returned to units.[17] Among those classed as deserters were those who defected to the German lines, either from disillusionment with the Soviet system, or with poor conditions and leadership, or simply in the hope (forlorn as it turned out) of a better chance of survival. Estimates suggest at least 116,000 defections between 1942 and 1945, and perhaps as many as 200,000 in 1941, though both figures are subject to wide margins of error.[18] In the American army in Europe there were 19,000 deserters out of a total of 40,000 worldwide. For the British army, the wartime total was 110,350, peaking in the years of relative inactivity in 1941–2, prompted by frustration with lack of activity and the nearness of home, rather than the experience of battle. The figures known for the German army are limited to those caught and condemned to death as deserters, who alone numbered 35,000. Accounts of the war in Asia suggest that men caught running away in the Japanese or Chinese armies were usually shot, but the battlefield was too confused to expect accurate statistics. Official Japanese army figures for 1943 and 1944 claimed only 1,023 and 1,085 deserters respectively, plus 60 defectors, but by then many soldiers had escaped to jungle or mountain areas to hide from the enemy and could not be traced for the statistics.[19] Men deserted for many reasons, some on emotional grounds, some as a result of war-induced neurosis, some for criminal reasons, some as a political and conscientious protest, but they were all treated as men who wanted to shirk combat. The scale of desertions placed great pressure on the military system to avoid any mass panic and although most were not shot, desertion was punished and stigmatized to ensure that it did not reach epidemic proportions.[20]

The decision to abandon fighting or the retreat into psychiatric crisis was evidently not universal. Much depended on the particular circumstances that soldiers were confronted with rather than the nature of their personalities. In battle conditions with high losses, situations where men were trapped with little hope of help, the sudden death of close companions, or a near miss from a bomb or shell, the prospects of a stress reaction were very high. In the North African campaign in 1942, demoralization among British Empire and Commonwealth troops, fighting an enemy with better weaponry and generalship, led to a very great increase in the number who surrendered rather than fought on, or who went absent without leave. Between March and July 1942 there were 1,700 deaths in the Eighth Army, but 57,000 'missing', most as a result of surrender.[21] In a situation where the replacement system fed new soldiers piecemeal into unfamiliar units, as was the case with the American army, there was a high incidence among them of battle deaths or psychiatric breakdown. In some battle topographies conditions were much more demanding of the human capacity to endure – the web of rivers and mountains in China, jungle warfare in South East Asia, winter warfare on the Russian front, or the harsh conditions on the mountainous Italian front where frost, snow, mud and disease took a high toll. Psychiatric casualty rates in Allied armies climbed sharply across the first winter campaign in southern Italy; in the Burma campaign the frightening environment of the tropical forest, combined with diseases that typically produced stress reactions, provoked high casualty rates with an indeterminate diagnosis.[22]

The one common conclusion from every fighting front was that no one, under the most extreme conditions, was immune from breakdown. 'War neuroses,' wrote the American psychiatrists Roy Grinker and John Spiegel in 1943, 'are caused by war.'[23] The United States Research Branch, set up in October 1941 to monitor the sociological and psychological state of the army, concluded during the war that no man was immune from the psychologically distorting effects of combat. Following the report of a six-week field trip in Italy by the military psychiatrist John Appel, the American surgeon general, Norman Kirk, issued to all army commands in December 1944 the official view that 'psychiatric casualties are as inevitable as gunshot and shrapnel wounds'.[24] Even the German army command, generally hostile to the idea that proper men broke down under fire, produced guidelines for the treatment of neurosis in 1942 which acknowledged that 'outstandingly efficient soldiers' were no more immune from emotional stress than any other.[25] By 1944 military psychiatrists were arguing over just how many days of combat the average soldier could endure. The British estimate was around 400 days, but with regular breaks for short periods of rest; American doctors thought anywhere between 80 and 200 days would be the limit. In May 1945, the American army ordered a limit of 120 days. For bomber crew in the campaign against Germany fifteen to twenty sorties was suggested as a limit, but aircrew regularly flew thirty missions and some returned for a second thirty. Since only 16 per cent survived a second round of operations, most airmen were dead before they could be classified as psychiatrically worn out. Modern research has suggested that after sixty days in combat, a serviceman is no longer effective.[26]

For all military institutions in the Second World War it was necessary to establish and develop a system for coping with emotional casualty that would reduce the prospect of emotional 'contamination' of those not affected and return as many men as possible to the front line. The prior experience of battle exhaustion in the First World War (generally known as 'shell-shock') played a part in military expectations about the new conflict, but many of the lessons learned had been forgotten or had been overtaken by contemporary developments in psychiatric medicine and psychology.[27] The most important development came with the Freudian revolution in the inter-war years, which encouraged the widespread belief that certain personalities were predisposed to unconscious psychological conflicts brought on by experiences in childhood. Although medical psychiatrists distrusted the psychological claims made by Freud and his followers, the idea of predisposition was reinforced by the evolution of genetic thinking about the inheritance of mental defect, and this encouraged psychiatrists to assume that, in one way or another, predisposition determined psychiatric reactions.[28] Both psychiatry and psychology competed with neurology, whose medical practitioners argued that all psychiatric disorders had an organic origin in the operation of the brain and the nervous system and rejected the notion of psychological 'disease'. All these perspectives, and the scientists who represented and defended them, played a part in the development of wartime military psychiatry, but the result was a good deal of unresolved argument and confusion over the proper form of treatment. The situation was exacerbated by the distrust displayed by many military commanders towards any practitioner who encouraged the idea that psychiatric breakdown was an acceptable form of medical casualty. One psychologist recruited to assess draftees at an Idaho selection station was told bluntly by the officer in charge that his help was not needed: 'I know how to handle men with shit in their veins.'[29]

Different cultural and scientific approaches to the idea of emotional stress explain the substantial differences in the way military psychiatry was applied in the Second World War. It was integrated fully into the American military effort, a reflection of the wide public enthusiasm for developments in psychology. It was integrated least in the German, Soviet and Japanese military establishments.[30] In the American armed forces a neuropsychiatric department was established at the highest level for both the army and the navy. Before the war there were 3,000 practising psychiatrists in the United States, but only 37 in the Army Medical Corps.[31] The situation was transformed during the war, when 2,500 psychiatrists were recruited into the armed forces' sanitary and medical services. By 1943 there was one psychiatrist assigned to every army division. The navy set up a neuropsychiatry branch in 1940 and established psychiatric units throughout the service, each composed of a psychiatrist, a psychologist and a neurologist, perhaps to ease the theoretical tensions between them.[32] In the British armed forces the integration of psychiatry was a slower process. There were very few psychiatrists recruited at first, until in April

1940 it was decided to appoint a consultant psychiatrist to each army command. But it was not until January 1942 that a formal system was set up for the treatment and disposal of psychiatric cases, while a Directorate of Army Psychiatry was formed only in April that year, reflecting perhaps Churchill's prejudice that psychiatry 'may very easily degenerate into charlatanry'. By 1943 there were still only 227 psychiatrists attached to the entire British Army, of whom only 97 were overseas.[33] The RAF, which saw the bulk of combat in the early years of the war, established a neuropsychiatric branch in 1940 under a leading British neurologist to cope with the stresses of combat flying. The branch set up special centres, eventually twelve in number, to evaluate the emotional casualties under the presumptive title Not Yet Diagnosed Neurotic. The majority of doctors assigned to the RAF were psychiatrists or neurologists.[34]

In Germany and the Soviet Union psychiatrists were kept at arm's length by the military. This was partly a product of distrust of the psychological sciences in both the Soviet and German dictatorships, where the health of the collective was emphasized over the needs of the individual. The presumption was that servicemen (and women in the Soviet case) would be inspired by ideological commitment to overcome emotional crisis. The head of the psychiatric department of the Soviet Military-Medical Academy wrote in 1934 that the 'political morale level of the Red Army soldier, his durable political class consciousness, will enable him to more easily overcome psychotic reactions'.[35] For the German soldier, wrote one psychiatrist, the drive to mere self-preservation in situations of real danger 'is conquered and suppressed through his attachment to high values and ideals'.[36] In Germany psychiatrists and psychologists were recruited to assist with selection for the armed forces and, during the war, to act as consultant advisers (*Beratenden Psychiater*) to each main army group. There were eventually sixty psychiatrists under the control of the chief of the Armed Forces Sanitary Branch who provided advice on morale and medical treatment to the army and air force, but at ground level treatment was the responsibility of medical officers. Both psychologists and psychiatrists were integrated more fully into the air force medical services. A branch for psychotherapy was set up in 1939, and eventually eleven psychiatric hospitals were established for aircrew with debilitating stress symptoms. But in 1942, at just the point where the democracies were expanding their facilities, military psychology was wound up on Hitler's orders, first in the air force in May, then, two months later, in the army. Psychiatry maintained a precarious position at the front, where the assumption was that those who broke down needed a sterner education in soldierly values rather than extensive therapy.[37]

The situation for psychiatry was even more tenuous in the Soviet Union, where there existed a persistent shortage of any personnel with psychiatric training and a strong belief that psychiatric conditions had an organic root and could be treated by regular medical staff. Psychiatrists working under the Main Military-Sanitary Directorate were finally asked to establish psychiatric hospitals in September 1941, but they dealt with only the most intractable cases. Military hospitals allocated only thirty beds to psychiatric patients. A number of psychiatrists were attached to major army fronts in 1942 as advisers, some attached to individual army divisions. The vast majority of cases of emotional breakdown were dealt with at the front by doctors with little experience or sympathy.[38] The Japanese army assumed a priori that conscripts would display endurance to the death and so made almost no provision for psychiatric care. It was assumed that those who broke down were criminals or misfits, and they were sent to the army's 'Education Unit' where they were treated as mental degenerates. The few psychiatrists attached to the army were there specifically to explain why some soldiers displayed psychopathic criminal instincts (including the regular murder of officers), but not in order to maintain the mental health of the rest of the army.[39]

Psychiatry and psychology were exploited in the armed forces in two very different ways, reflecting the tension in the science between those who favoured the idea of a predisposition to emotional breakdown and those who saw psychiatric casualty as a result of the psychologically and physically demanding nature of combat. After the experience of the First World War, there was a widespread belief that more effective selection procedures for civilian recruits would eliminate in advance anyone whose background or personality traits indicated the possibility of emotional collapse. Once combat was under way, there existed an equally wide belief that those who exhibited disabling emotional states were pre-programmed to do so, or as one Australian officer put it, 'the weaker vessels are broken easily'.[40] Only the United States armed forces insisted that a psychiatrist or psychologist should be involved on every selection panel for the draft. Interviews for psychiatric profiling typically took from three to fifteen minutes, seldom long enough to establish whether anxiety states or abnormal psychology could really be detected. Interviewers were told to look out for men who displayed any of twenty-two possible conditions, from 'lonesomeness' to 'recognized queerness' or 'homosexual proclivities'. Such an arbitrary filter resulted in the rejection of over 2 million draftees. American psychiatrists generally agreed that home background and personality were paramount – 'war neuroses are "made in America"' – and that they could detect them with simple tests.[41] Psychiatrists in both the

Australian and American armed forces devised formulaic questions designed to weed out the potential emotional casualty. 'Do you worry very much?' or 'Do you get discouraged very easily?' were typical, but hardly likely to elicit frank or useful answers.[42] To help those who were selected, the US army provided a handbook, *Fear in Battle*, which explained that men were bound to feel fear but that fear could be surmounted through a process of emotional 'adjustment'.[43]

British forces were much slower to develop selection on psychiatric grounds and only 1.4 per cent of conscripts were rejected for obvious psychotic conditions, compared with 7.3 per cent of all American recruits. The British selectors were much more concerned that they matched particular aptitudes to the right job, though they did try to weed out those with an obvious 'timorous disposition and anxious temperament'.[44] In Germany, psychologists were attached to selection centres on the premise that it was both a racial and military necessity to eliminate all those defined as 'asocial' or with obvious personality defects, just as the wider regime was trying to eliminate or exclude them from the racial community. The prejudice against the 'war neurotics' among German veterans of the first conflict, encouraged by National Socialist efforts to mould a generation of 'manly' soldiers rather than potential hysterics, was reflected in military screening procedures. The army was anxious to avoid any repeat of the shell-shock panics provoked by trench warfare and was hostile to the prospect of having to cope with men they regarded as shirkers and 'pension-seekers'.[45] Otto Wuth, psychiatric adviser to the Army Sanitary Inspection, distinguished between the 'willing' and the 'unwilling' and psychiatrists were used to weed out those in the second category, among them alleged psychological failures and troublemakers. The low level of psychiatric casualty in the first two years of the war, with quick mobile victories and no repeat of the arduous trench warfare of 1914–18, seemed to confirm that screening had indeed eliminated the war neurotic. The cases that were recorded were attributed largely to predisposition: 'These people are not of full spiritual value,' wrote one psychiatrist in 1940. 'Here it does not concern an actual illness in a medical sense, but [persons] of lower worth.'[46]

The emphasis on the predisposition to fail psychologically as a serviceman was challenged by the widespread evidence that psychiatric breakdown occurred across the whole range of conscripts. But it was not eliminated entirely because there were evidently a number of men with serious psychotic disorders from among such a large population cohort, while the idea that some men were born cowards or shirkers chimed with existing military prejudices. The most famous example came at an American field hospital in the Sicilian town of Nicosia where the American commanding general in the invasion of Sicily, George Patton, slapped an apparent psychiatric casualty across the face for alleged malingering (in fact the soldier was suffering a misdiagnosed case of malaria). 'Such men,' he subsequently reported, 'are cowards.'[47] Patton was sidelined for his behaviour, but military intolerance of psychiatric casualties was instinctive. Arthur Harris, commander-in-chief of RAF Bomber Command, was notoriously dismissive of 'weaklings and waverers' who cracked under the strain of combat, but this prejudice was built into the RAF's treatment of flying crew from the point in April 1940 when the so-called 'waverer letter' was sent out to commands, recommending that they deal swiftly with any sign of emotional breakdown that might be defined as 'Lack of Moral Fibre'. LMF became the standard description for all crew released from the service for alleged malingering or cowardice, and although the majority of psychiatric casualties were treated by field psychiatrists with more sympathy, the onus was on the serviceman to convince his superiors that he was not a coward.[48] The RAF's priority was to identify and remove emotional cases before healthy aircrew were infected: 'The important task for psychologists is not to patch up inferior material but to eliminate it before it can fail.'[49] Psychiatrists working for the Australian army maintained the primacy of predisposition throughout the war. A study of Australian soldiers in New Guinea identified 51 per cent of cases as a result of psychological preconditions. The psychiatrists searched for men who had been in orphanages, or had a neurotic family history, or alcoholic parents. The object was to avoid pandering to 'wasters and psychopaths'.[50]

Nevertheless, as the war went on it became increasingly obvious that predisposition or character failings or alleged poor racial qualities could not explain the high levels of casualties defined as psychiatric, particularly for the American and German armed forces, where effort had been devoted to selecting conscripts on the basis of their psychological adaptability for military duty. For psychiatrists working in the field, it was obvious that what they were observing were stress reactions to extreme or prolonged combat, some simply the product of physical and mental exhaustion, some genuine traumatic shock reactions that provoked more serious psychotic disorders. The symptoms displayed were familiar from the First World War. 'Dark eyes that had a haunted look and were sunk way back in the head,' recalled one American soldier, 'in clothes too big, a chain smoker, shaking hands, nervous tics.'[51] Men trembled or wept uncontrollably, lost control of their motor skills, defecated or urinated involuntarily, curled up in foetal positions, or became unresponsive and apathetic. Many developed psychosomatic conditions – loss of hearing, mutism, stuttering, spasm attacks, peptic ulcers (an epidemic in the

German army). The physiological explanation for the effects of extreme fear on bodily functions was already understood by some neurologists before the war but was not applied to psychiatric casualties. Involuntary defecation, experienced by a quarter of American soldiers according to one survey, was a prime target for accusations of cowardice, but it was a normal physiological reaction prompted by the sympathetic nervous system. Gradually the military authorities came to recognize that most men in combat were neither cowards nor shirkers, but the victims of stress produced by prolonged danger. The answer was to develop appropriate treatment rather than to stigmatize servicemen with poor morale.[52]

The Soviet and German armed forces had a clearer view of the effects of combat than the democracies because they were more inclined to treat psychiatric reactions as organic conditions and to view only the smaller element of psychotic patients as true casualties of neurotic disorders. The German armed forces had already identified four categories for front-line treatment in the 1930s: nervous exhaustion and temporary psychogenic (experience-related) reactions, which were to be treated at or near the front; and strong hysterical reactions and psychoses, which were to be treated at rear hospitals or returned home. Once the war in the East began to impose high casualties in the autumn of 1941, psychologically induced functional disorders were treated first at front-line stations or rest centres, where food, sleep, narcotic treatment, counselling and the presence of companions were all designed to return men quickly to the front line. The air force set up rest centres further from the front line for airmen who were designated as *abgeflogen* (literally 'flown out' – flying stress), three in 1940 in Paris, Brussels and Cologne, eight more by 1943.[53] The Red Army employed the same system of forward medical centres where rest, decent food and sanitation were expected to turn men exhausted by combat into soldiers healthy enough to return to the front line. It took longer for the democratic armies to recognize the problem and then to provide what came to be called 'forward psychiatry'. The New Zealand army was the first to introduce field rest centres in North Africa in 1942, but it was quickly followed by the British and Americans fighting in the campaign for Tunisia. The director of the American Army Neuropsychiatric Division, Roy Halloran, approved the establishment of front-line units to provide psychiatric care because it was soon realized that men taken too far back from the front tended to get worse rather than better, as they found themselves defined as psychiatric cases. The first forward clinic was set up in Tunisia in March 1943 on an experimental basis. Its immediate success saw the establishment of forward treatment throughout the army.[54] The British army set up a similar system, starting with forward ambulance units for dedicated psychiatric care, followed in 1943 by forward filtration units and corps exhaustion centres. By the end of the war large numbers of those regarded as victims of combat exhaustion were treated at or just behind the battle lines.[55]

Even with forward treatment, the tension between different views of stress reactions and the most effective way to minister to them continued to produce friction and, in unnumbered cases, misdiagnosis (though few would have suffered the indignity of a casualty on the Burma front, whose preliminary medical record simply stated 'Lunatic').[56] Professional rivalry played a part in the attitude to constructive therapy. Military psychiatrists in Germany argued against the trend in air force hospitals for allowing lengthy therapy, influenced by psychoanalytical therapeutic practice, and suggested that many airmen had been the fortunate beneficiaries of what amounted to a 'failure of the medical art' and a contravention of 'military manly discipline'.[57] German psychiatrists were quick to penalize anything that smacked of simulation among psychiatric casualties; indeed the threat of a punitive regime of treatment seems to have played a part in encouraging voluntary return to the front. In the Red Army, too, the prevailing military culture insisted there was no place for shirkers or cry-babies, and knowledge of what might happen to them almost certainly helped to accelerate whatever recovery comradeship and sleep had already allowed.[58]

The very language used to describe psychiatric casualties reflected the confusion surrounding what psychiatry claimed to be treating and the sceptical views of the military leadership about what counted as an acceptable condition. In the first major battle in the Pacific at Guadalcanal the only psychiatrist attached to the Americal Division was so worried about attitudes to psychiatric breakdown that he diagnosed the men with the more military-sounding 'blast concussion'; Soviet medical services used the word 'contusion' for the same reason.[59] In Britain the term 'shell-shock' was abandoned well before the war, in case it encouraged soldiers to think that breakdown under fire was acceptable, but the new terms – effort syndrome, fatigue syndrome – were just as capable of exploitation, until 'battle exhaustion' was introduced for the campaign in Normandy.[60] In the United States forces the recognition that the great majority of cases were the result of combat conditions resulted in a regular diagnosis of 'combat exhaustion' for soldiers and 'operational fatigue' for airmen. Psychiatrists themselves divided the patients who did not recover at forward stations into a wide variety of different medical categories, reflecting the progress that had been made during the inter-war years in understanding the nature of psychiatric damage, but at the same time encouraging men who did not want to return to the front to see themselves as invalids with an approved specific condition.

In the end the test of psychiatric medicine in the war was the extent to which soldiers who displayed exhaustion symptoms, or more serious psychotic or psychosomatic states, could be returned to service. Psychiatrists and psychologists were under great pressure to show that their place in the military medical structure was deserved; professional anxiety almost certainly meant that men were returned to the front or to non-combat duties who were not in any sense 'cured', though no longer obviously incapacitated. A wide variety of therapies were employed to help overcome exhaustion and fear, including narcotics, suggestion therapy, insulin injections (to encourage weight gain) and, in some cases, initiating a drug-induced state in which specific traumas were re-lived by the patient at the prompting of the psychiatrist in order to release repressed terrors.[61] The rate of return to service claimed by the neuropsychiatric units varied widely, and most of those returned were allocated to non-combat roles at or just behind the front lines, though Italian front-line psychiatric hospitals returned only around 16 per cent to their units, while the great majority of casualties was sent back to Italy.[62] By March 1943, American military psychiatrists on the Tunisian front were claiming return rates of 30 per cent after just thirty hours of rest and treatment, and 70 per cent after forty-eight hours, but other estimates suggested only 2 per cent were actually back in combat.[63] Overall British return rates were estimated in 1943 at between 50 and 70 per cent within a week, but once again most went back to non-combat duties. The airmen not formally classified as LMF in the British air force still did not in general return to flying duties. Of those who did return, little effort was made to check on relapse rates. Some wartime studies suggested that only a small number became casualties again, but studies of individual units showed much less success. A study of 346 infantry casualties returned to fight again in Italy in 1943 showed that only 75 were still in combat three months later.[64] After weeks of tough combat in Normandy, only 15 per cent of those sent to front-line exhaustion centres could be returned to their units, while half were sent back to Britain.[65] Most of those returned to the front line as fit enough were ineffective fighters. The result was that fresh recruits, often lacking sufficient training and quickly immersed in the mess of front-line conflict, had to take the place of men no longer able to fight, with a high chance that they would in turn rapidly become emotional casualties.

For those who could not be helped at the forward psychiatric stations mixed fates awaited them as they made their way back through the chain of rear hospitals and psychiatric clinics. Some were simply recognized as burnt out and not subjected to any further effort. What came to be called the 'Old Sergeant Syndrome' (or in the British army, 'Guardsman's hysteria') was recognized by Allied forces in the Italian campaign in 1943 and 1944 as a growing number of officers and NCOs with impeccable combat records collapsed after months at the front. These were men regarded as untreatable, and they were honourably discharged from the forces.[66] In Britain those diagnosed with psychotic or psychopathic states were returned home for treatment and discharged if their condition was not likely to improve, or kept in the armed forces for work at bases and stores if they were judged capable enough of labour that would release fit men for the front.[67] In the dictatorships, on the other hand, the presumption was that those who suffered emotional collapse were likely to be simulating or exaggerating their symptoms as a form of what German psychiatrists called *Kriegsflucht*, flight from war. In the Red Army alleged shirkers or malingerers were sent to punishment battalions, where they were likely to be quickly eliminated. In Germany, those who returned to rear clinics were subjected to a deliberately painful form of electric shock therapy, during which heart attacks or broken bones were not unknown. If they remained resistant to treatment, or refused to return to service, they were placed in punishment 'special departments' in the rear, where conditions were similar to those in concentration camps, or, from April 1942, in punishment battalions at the front. In 1943 the army decided to put those suffering from psychosomatic stomach or hearing conditions into so called 'Battalions of the Sick' (*Krankenbatallionen*) to replace regular troops on garrison and fortification duty. A small minority of those deemed by their 'asocial' character to be beyond all hope made their way to the 'euthanasia' facilities and death.[68]

The high level of psychiatric casualty, the poor rate of return to combat duties, and the induction of new draftees unprepared for the searing demands of the front meant that all armed forces during the war became less effective as the conflict went on. The decline in the human element was masked by massive military production and substantial operational and tactical improvements in the way those forces fought, but prolonged combat in difficult conditions slowed down the capacity of forces to take full advantage of the material changes. Ground armies, in particular, staggered under the weight of losses and, like punch-drunk boxers, found it harder to land the knockout punch the longer combat was sustained. Numerous examples of front-line panic are to be found among small units across all the battlefronts. Contemporary accounts of the Sino-Japanese war are full of such moments on a fluid, confused battlefield, with men running away, as one Chinese officer put it, 'frightened as mice'.[69] There were, nevertheless, few examples of collective panic or the complete breakdown of discipline. The British retreat in Norway in 1940, or the collapse of discipline on Singapore Island in early 1942, or the Italian division at Tobruk that surrendered in fright as 6,000 Polish soldiers, out of ammunition, charged them with fixed bayonets, were unusual. Mass surrenders (at least until the very last days of the war) generally occurred early in the conflict – in France and Belgium in 1940, in East Africa and the Soviet Union in 1941 – or they happened when fighting could no longer be continued, as at Stalingrad. Even those cases where armies temporarily collapsed – the French army in 1940 or the Red Army in summer 1942 on the Don Steppe or the disorganized German retreat across France in 1944 – eventually ended with the establishment of a new line of defence as panicking soldiers were brought again under control and their fears disciplined. Men continued to fight despite the psychological effects of modern combat and the epidemic of psychiatric casualties, as they had done in the First World War.

MAINTAINING 'MORALE'

If wartime emotional pressures for hundreds of thousands of servicemen and women were too great to bear, for reasons that are not difficult to comprehend, the question remains about how the majority who did not succumb to psychiatric crisis, either temporary or long-term, managed to overcome their reactions to combat and continue to fight. This is a question usually presented as a matter of maintaining morale, but the term 'morale' is a nebulous one. It is used to cover not only a wide range of possible explanations for why men fight, but it is applied across the whole spectrum of possible reactions from men whose differences in intelligence, social background, psychological state or personal circumstances are certain to render any generic assumptions about their moral or emotional state untenable. Military organizations tended to assume during the Second World War that, with effective training and motivational education, servicemen could all be pressed into the same mould. The British adjutant general, Ronald Adam, writing in 1943, claimed that 'the vast majority of men can be trained to deal with fear as they can be trained to deal with Germans'.[70] Even psychiatrists imagined the existence of a normative individual who could adapt to modern warfare and military life, unlike those who were 'unobtrusive or shy, and self-conscious, but irresolute', as one British psychiatrist put it, who could not.[71] The prevailing assumption was that most men, when ordered to do so, could overcome their fears. 'Behind the belief is the idea,' wrote the consultant psychiatrist to the British army, J. R. Rees, 'that somehow courage and cowardice are alternative free choices that come to every man, overriding all emotional stress . . . and that he can be courageous if he is told he must be.'[72]

Any generic conclusion that all men can be prepared for combat, except the fraction whose emotional state rules them out, takes little account of broad cultural and social differences between the military environments of the fighting powers or of the differing conditions of combat. Much has been made in wartime narratives of the importance of sound leadership or of the moral enthusiasm engendered by the prospect of victory, but neither argument works any better as a general explanation than the claim that men can be trained to be courageous. German and Japanese forces continued to fight with grim determination in the face of imminent defeat; Allied troops became noticeably more cautious and unwilling to risk death the closer victory appeared to come. General George Marshall, the United States army chief of staff, introduced a Morale Division in the army only in 1944, when victory seemed assured.[73] In the Soviet Union the turning tide in 1943–4 made less difference to the state of the troops than might have been expected. 'After three years of war,' claimed one Red Army fighter in 1944, 'the Soviet soldier is tired, physically and morally.'[74] Poor overall command and operational misjudgement did not stop United States forces fighting in the Anzio bridgehead in southern Italy in 1943–4, or in the disastrous campaign in the Hürtgen Forest in late 1944 where both sides, American and German, took horrific casualties for a pointless operation. Armed forces kept fighting in the most demoralizing of circumstances for which no general argument about the nature of morale can provide a satisfactory explanation.

The obvious, if less fashionable explanation, is military coercion. All military organizations are by their nature coercive, though not equally punitive. In the Second World War they took a wide cross-section of civilian society and compelled it to accept the structures, discipline and daily demands of military life. The military justice system was expanded to cope with the problems this was likely to raise, but the concerns of military justice were quite distinct from the sphere of civil justice because they were designed to restrict almost any freedom of choice and to prescribe a narrow range of acceptable behaviour from training ground to battle-front. The daily habits of discipline were deliberately intrusive, inhibiting and ever-present, undermining the individual and emphasizing the power of the collective. At every level of military activity, in every theatre, and in all the services, military coercion maintained the organization and fighting power of the human material at its disposal. Discipline was supplemented by training (whose severity varied between military cultures), by programmes of political and ideological education, by deliberate campaigns to boost morale, and (for a fraction) the prospect of promotion and awards. These factors evidently mattered a great deal to those who lived and worked in the unfamiliar environment of modern combat, but coercion and the threat of punishment underlay the capacity of armed forces to recruit, train and discipline the tens of millions of former civilians who took part in the fighting.

The degree of coercion nevertheless differed from one military environment to another; armed forces in authoritarian regimes were in general significantly more punitive than the armed forces of the democracies. Military cultures in Germany and Japan were based around traditions of honour and obedience – in the case of Japanese soldiers to the death. Japanese soldiers could be publicly flogged for any hint of cowardice or disobedience, and even beaten by their fellow recruits for any dereliction of duty.[75] These were psychologically coercive cultures in which under the most strenuous of circumstances absolute obedience and unflinching duty, as the highest military values, were expected of every serviceman, even if they were not always fulfilled.[76] The military justice system and the patterns of military discipline were at their most extreme in the Soviet and German dictatorships, where desertion or psychiatric breakdown were tolerated least. The military penal system was an extension of the state terror practised by both dictatorships, where deviance of any kind from the ideological goals of the regime carried severe penalties. Failure or unwillingness to take part in fighting for the future of the German race or for the defence of the Soviet motherland was regarded as an unforgivable lapse in political motivation as well as defiance of military codes of conduct. In Italy, Fascism took much the same view. The 130 soldiers sentenced to death for desertion by the extraordinary military tribunals, though only a fraction of those caught deserting, were intended to be a 'pedagogic' example to the rest to encourage greater commitment to the cause.[77]

In the Soviet Union, orders to execute all deserters and cowards were sent from Moscow to army group councils in August 1941, then to army and corps level. To prevent mass desertion or retreat, the Red Army set up so-called 'blocking detachments' of rear troops or NKVD security men in September 1941. Their main task was to stop frightened and isolated soldiers as they streamed back from defeats and to return them to their units. In the first months of the German invasion the detachments caught 657,364 men, but most were restored to the front line except for 10,201 whose desertion was regarded as serious enough to merit execution. In July 1942 Stalin published Order No. 227, 'Not a Step Back', to make it clear that no soldier could abandon his position without punishment. Over the course of the war, it has been estimated that 158,000 were executed for desertion, cowardice, criminal activity or political deviance; a further 436,000 were sent to the network of Gulag camps, the equivalent of approximately 60 Soviet divisions.[78] From 1943 onwards, any lapse by Soviet service personnel was investigated by a new security organization set up under the title 'Death to Spies' (*Smersh*); alongside the hunt for signs of treason, *Smersh* officers also took over responsibility for deserters, cowards and those with self-inflicted wounds. The object was to instil a fear of punishment that was stronger than fear of the enemy.[79] Since the regime also threatened to punish the families of those who deserted or surrendered, Soviet soldiers had an additional pressure to overcome whatever emotional crises they faced and to continue fighting.

In the German armed forces it was assumed that those who abandoned the fight, either through physical desertion or an inner psychological desertion, were lesser racial comrades who deserved their punishment for abandoning the struggle to secure Germany's future. As the manpower shortages forced the military to recruit less able or adaptable soldiers to front-line service, so the threat of punishment – or 'special handling' (*Sonderbehandlung*) in the lexicon of the regime – was used more to enforce compliance. Military justice against 'flight from war' or the undermining of military discipline was enforced under Section 51 of the military penal code; cases often required a psychiatrist to submit a report to confirm that the culprit was not a severe psychiatric case and could be punished accordingly.[80] The punishment in many cases meant execution, and, as in the Soviet armed forces, fear of the consequences of dereliction of duty was intended to keep men fighting.[81] If the German armed forces were not quite as prodigal with their manpower as the Red Army, the total deaths dwarfed the forty-eight executions carried out in the First World War. An estimated 35,000 servicemen were condemned to death and 22,750 executed, of whom around 15,000 were deserters, but the figure of total military deaths is almost certainly larger than this.[82] In the last year of war absconded soldiers found in the Reich were hanged on lamp posts as an example to the rest or shot out of hand by the military police, leaving little statistical trail. Lesser offences were still more numerous, and the military prison service became a major institution. The total of prison sentences handed out for armed forces personnel during the war was around 3 million; of these some 370,000 were for periods of more than 6 months, and 23,124 were long sentences of hard labour.[83] The paradox presented by the statistics for both the Soviet and German armies is that fear of punishment did not work as a deterrent. The struggle on the Eastern Front was particularly long, bitter and bloody. Both armed forces used severe discipline as a way to ensure that all their troops knew the cost of dereliction of duty, but it was never enough to stem the flow of those too fearful or disenchanted to continue.

In the democratic armed forces, coercion existed as an organizational and daily reality but without the threat of excessively punitive military justice. Desertion and crime were both punished, but only one American soldier was shot for desertion during the war and no British soldier, despite the forceful request by the British army commander-in-chief in North Africa, General Claude Auchinleck, that the death penalty be restored for men who abandoned the fight.[84] More emphasis was placed on shaming those who abandoned fighting without good medical cause by dishonourable discharge or formal public ceremonies of demotion. Those British airmen investigated for LMF had their badges and insignia stripped from their uniform and were marched through local streets for the public to see, all before any formal decision had been taken about their mental or physical state.[85] For those who did abscond, there was still a regime of punishment, though no more danger. In the last year of war 8,425 British service personnel were convicted of desertion.[86] Over the whole course of the war there were 30,299 court-martial convictions; almost 27,000 were for desertion or absence without leave, 265 for self-inflicted wounds, but only 143 for cowardice.[87] The United States army held 1.7 million courts martial, mostly for trivial offences in the field, but imprisoned 21,000 for desertion.

Coercion was also supplemented by a more positive approach to maintaining morale, through programmes of orchestrated commitment. The attempt to motivate military manpower by providing regular political education and morale-lifting talks was again more obtrusive in the armed forces of dictatorship than the democracies. Each Soviet military unit had a military political commissar attached to it under reforms introduced in 1939, whose role was to raise the level of political consciousness among conscripts, identify any political lapses, and punish political wayward-ness. Issues for discussion and propaganda were sent out from Moscow and soldiers were supposed to participate when they could. Even when the operational role of the political commissar was downgraded in 1942 at the insistence of the army leadership, the role of political education was not abandoned. The army's *Red Star* news-sheet, with its mix of war news and lessons in current ideology, was published in its millions and distrib-uted to all troops. Soviet wartime culture traded on stories of remarkable heroism, few of which were fully truthful; the object was to create an emotional bond between the individual soldier and the idealized model which could only be redeemed by further acts of selfless courage. Millions of servicemen and women who distinguished themselves in combat were given a shortcut to membership of the Communist Party.[88] In the German armed forces political education and morale-building also played an

important part in encouraging identification with Germany's struggle for
survival, with the war against the Jewish enemy, and with the values of the
National Socialist 'People's Community'. In April 1939 an Armed Forces
Department for Propaganda was established, which organized propaganda companies to raise military morale and distribute front-line reading
material. In October 1940 guidelines on army education were published
based on four key elements: 'The German People' (Volk); 'The German
Empire'; 'German Living Space'; and 'National Socialism as the Foundation'.[89] In October 1943, at the point where political education in the
Soviet forces was being downgraded, Hitler ordered the creation of a
National Socialist Leadership Staff, whose task was to appoint political
commissars to military units. By December 1943 there were 1,047 full-
time commissars and a further 47,000 officers who combined their regular
military role with morale-raising activities.[90]

It is difficult to judge how effective these programmes of orchestrated
commitment actually were in helping soldiers identify with the cause and
maintain their discipline. At one level all armed forces understood the
enemy they were fighting and the necessity of victory, but this was not
something that sustained troops in any meaningful sense through the alter-
nating days of tedium or danger. Soviet soldiers were often so exhausted by
combat that prompting emotional commitment to the struggle was unlikely
to have made much difference, though they understood that defeatist talk
or political dissent would be penalized regardless: 'you become indifferent,'
claimed one Red Army soldier, 'you are not even happy to be alive any
more.'[91] German soldiers by 1944 were also at a point where fighting for
the early ideals, if they had had an impact at all, was almost extinguished.
One young tank soldier observed in his diary in July 1944 that he and his
companions were 'only fighting because of the sense of duty that has been
drummed into them'.[92] Ideals had certainly not sustained the men at Stalingrad. 'No one can tell me,' wrote one soldier among the last letters, 'that my
comrades died with words like "Germany" or "Heil Hitler" on their lips.'[93]
Only the American army surveyed the views of the soldiers on the extent of
their understanding about the cause they represented. Among those surveyed, 37 per cent in the Pacific and 40 per cent in Europe said it made no
difference at all to why they fought. When Gallup asked soldiers to state
what the Four Freedoms were that Roosevelt had pledged to defend through
war, only 13 per cent could name even one.[94] One veteran told the army's
Research Branch that he was 'patriotic as hell' when he joined up, but combat changed him: 'You're fighting for your skin ... There's no patriotism on
the line.'[95] In British units the army education service found soldiers much
more willing to discuss the world after victory, but the nature of the conflict

and commitment to the cause of winning the war met with more negative reactions. Orchestrated commitment may have made greater sense than a coercive framework of discipline, but its capacity to mobilize soldiers to overcome the immediate reaction to fear or despair or danger remains an open question.

Much the same can be said of efforts to mobilize collective hatred of the enemy. Hating might be assumed a priori to be a characteristic feature of war, and there is plenty of evidence that at certain moments hatred (or more properly a sudden burst of anger) motivated men to take revenge for the death of comrades, or against the remorselessness of sniper or machine-gun fire, or from evidence of war crimes. Diaries from the Sino-Japanese war are sprinkled with spontaneous expressions of hatred as a form of self-motivation against a dangerous and often hidden enemy.[96] There is, nevertheless, much evidence that formal efforts to instil hatred into troops had mixed fortunes. Hatred, as one leading British psychologist put it in 1940, is 'fitful and capricious', an emotion difficult to sustain over any length of time.[97] The British army decided to set up battle schools in 1942 with an element of hate-training, designed, as a BBC programme announced, 'to teach men ... to hate the enemy and how to use that hate'. There followed a public outcry when it became clear that hate-training involved visits to slaughterhouses where conscripts were deliberately spattered with blood. The practice was terminated at the insistence of Montgomery, then commander-in-chief South-East Region, who regarded hatred as a futile way to mobilize emotions for war.[98] The social anthropologist John Dollard, in a 1943 study of fear in battle, found that 'hatred of the enemy' ranked only eighth out of nine motivations, a few percentage points ahead of 'keeping busy'.[99] The American army surveys of morale found that 40 per cent of servicemen in Europe did not consider hatred as a motive at all; in the Pacific the figure was 30 per cent, but here the propaganda they were exposed to treated the Japanese as especially hateful.[100] The feeling was reciprocated. Japanese servicemen were exposed to regular hate propaganda against the 'barbarous' Americans. Post-war American surveys of Japanese morale found that 40 per cent expressed extreme hatred, anger and contempt for the enemy, and only one-tenth had none.[101]

A more convincing way to explain how servicemen coped with the emotional demands of conflict without breaking under the strain is to look at the ground level of daily experience. Mass armed forces are not, of course, a mass, but an amalgam of thousands of small military communities – an infantry company, a submarine crew, an artillery unit, a bomber crew. A great deal of the literature on wartime morale emphasizes the importance of the immediate unit as the focus of loyalty, commitment and emotional support. At the front line most servicemen, even officers, have little idea about how the rest of the force is fighting; they have little understanding of the wider strategy they are serving; information of all kinds is rationed to what they need to know to perform particular operations. For Japanese soldiers stationed on remote Pacific islands or in the jungles of New Guinea or Burma, there was no way of even understanding whether they were winning the war or not, though the official line, if it reached them, was always optimistic. Only historians have the luxury of seeing the whole and assessing the consequences. On the ground of day-to-day experience, the priority for most men (and women in the Soviet case) was to support the small collective they belonged to as the only means to ensure a chance of survival. What concerned fighting men were mundane issues, like the German tankman weeping at the loss of his tanks. Each small collective constituted what social psychologists call a 'universe of obligation' in which each member's survival depends on the mutual aid of the rest.[102] The primary moral and emotional commitment is to those immediately sharing the same dangers, not to any wider community of obligation. Though it is often assumed that morale is managed from the top down, it was as often self-managed from below.

This smaller context involved a set of different emotional reactions. Men stayed at the task through feelings of emotional commitment and loyalty to the group, and through real fear of the shame or guilt they might feel if they abdicated their responsibility or broke down. The test of true courage for millions was not some act of random heroism, but the ability to overcome the pervasive sense of fear and to carry on for the sake of those around them. 'I discover,' wrote one American veteran, 'the difference between being scared and being a coward is having other people find out.'[103] Even wounded men could be seen struggling to avoid tears because of the stigma that might attach to them in a military culture that encouraged displays of overt manliness.[104] Psychiatrists found that physical and psychiatric casualties were often wracked with guilt at their own incapacity to endure and keen to prove themselves again to their comrades. Surveys conducted with US servicemen found that 87 per cent, in both major theatres, believed that not letting down the men around them was of critical importance. However good the cause, as one veteran put it, 'it was not as important as the respect men had for one another.'[105] Studies of the sociology of both the Soviet and the German armies have confirmed that small-group cohesion was of great importance, and although high losses meant that groups often fragmented quickly, they could be re-formed from necessity as new men were drafted in to units that retained their identity regardless of losses.[106] Critics have rightly observed that bonds can also exist at the level of the regiment or even the division, or not exist at all, and can be encouraged by commitment to prevailing ideologies or value-systems, but these are factors external to the primary units which make up battle, and whose internal sense of commitment mattered most, however diverse one from another their origins, composition and outlook.[107] In the air war, bomber crews in the offensive against Germany suffered exceptional loss rates, but once aboard an aircraft, even with a crew that had not had time to bond, the enclosed community had no choice but to work together for its own survival. For this reason it was felt to be essential that a weak link in the crew, whatever the psychological explanation, had to be removed rapidly from combat to avoid affecting the rest.[108] No two of these small units were identical, and they could be disturbed by the familiar emotional tensions in any human group, or disrupted by psychological breakdown or military disaster, but fighting could only be sustained in mass armed forces by the myriad of small, temporary communities forged by the circumstances of war.

Within these small solidarities, daily life was governed by simple factors. The availability of food and resources was a constant concern (though shortages did not stop men fighting); the prospect of loot of any kind, but especially food, was always at hand, and looting was practised by every army, starting with the German invasion of Poland in 1939.[109] Small perquisites, however trivial, could have an important impact on the morale of each small unit. The British army's considerable efforts to supply tea even to the most remote fronts allowed the regular brew-ups that so surprised American and Commonwealth soldiers when they observed British soldiers drinking tea even during spells of combat. Soviet authorities decided that the mass distribution of free harmonicas might have an uplifting effect on tired and dejected troops.[110] Whenever they could be found, forces everywhere appropriated alcohol and drugs to dull the effects of fear. Soviet soldiers drank wood alcohol or anti-freeze and died from the after-effects; Allied servicemen in Italy could rely on a steady supply of illicit narcotics from ports in the Middle East; Japanese soldiers used copious quantities of alcohol distributed by the army to dull the horrors of the battlefield.[111] For men usually far from home, sexual deprivation was also an issue. Armies either turned a blind eye to local prostitution or set up controlled brothels and distributed prophylactics to avoid an epidemic of venereal disease. The Japanese army ruthlessly allowed the establishment of stations for sexual slavery across China and South East Asia, where so-called 'comfort women' were forced into virtual prisons and regularly raped by Japanese soldiers, while the Red Army's predatory search for sexual loot is well known. Both are explored in greater depth in the next chapter.[112] Pursuit of sex was not confined to single men, but married men faced a range of emotional issues if they joined in. Anxiety about wives and families, often very far away, with no prospect of leave, was observed to be one of the most demoralizing aspects of daily life in the military. American women were subject to wide public pressure to remain loyal to their partners sent overseas but with evidently mixed results. In January 1945, the American Red Cross publicly rebuked those civilians who sent letters to serving soldiers denouncing their wives' infidelity because it undermined military morale. Strenuous efforts were made to sustain the flow of mail between the home country and the front line. A special express service was set up for families in Germany to let men at the front know that they had survived bombing raids. Shortages of mail, or letters bringing bad news from home, seem to have had a more debilitating effect on morale than the prospect of immediate combat.[113]

Among the small anxieties and pleasures of daily military life, men and women developed coping mechanisms of one kind or another. Superstitions and talismans were common to all armed forces. American submariners took with them small models of the Buddha and rubbed the plump belly before combat as a symbol of good luck. Sometimes servicemen became convinced that a talisman would ensure their own invulnerability. Although psychiatrists thought such reliance was a dangerous sign of impending psychiatric crisis, akin to the fatalistic stupor found in other casualties as they contemplated their own death, the superstitions evidently helped some individuals to cope with the stresses they faced.[114] For some, though not all, armed forces religion assumed a growing importance as a way of coping with the fears prompted by combat. Japanese soldiers understood that their sacrifice in combat had a central religious significance, though whether that made the prospect of death easier to cope with must remain uncertain. In the Soviet army, religion was excluded by Communist ideology, but during the war Stalin relaxed the campaign against religious practice, churches were reopened and the violent atheist assaults on religious claims were toned down. Nevertheless, God was not the Soviet soldier's first court of appeal. In Germany, the regime's hostility to religion was reflected in the struggle experienced by the army high command in getting chaplains into military units. In the end only around 1,000 were recruited for an army of 6 million, and their access to the front was arbitrarily controlled.[115] That religion mattered to ordinary soldiers is evident from the surviving letters from Stalingrad, in which appeals to God's providence intermingled with claims that the experience had shattered belief.

The American and British Commonwealth armies were much better endowed with chaplains, and there was no prior prejudice against religious practice. There were 8,000 chaplains from a wide range of denominations attached to United States forces, 3,000 for British forces and 900 in the much smaller Canadian army. The British priests held regular discussions during 'Padre's hour', including one perhaps aptly titled, 'Can we believe in immortality?' The BBC Radio Padre had an audience of 7 million by 1941. American chaplains were inundated with requests for solace and support, some conducting as many as fifty interviews a day; General Eisenhower insisted that 'religious consolation' should be inscribed in military medical records. Surveys carried out in 1943–4 of American servicemen showed that 79 per cent of those asked said their faith in God had strengthened as a result of the war. A survey of troops in Europe found that 94 per cent thought prayer helped a great deal in coping with the stress of combat.[116] The obvious appeal of 'foxhole religion' for conscripts from a country with a strong culture of religiosity prompted debate about whether soldiers in a moment of crisis were capable of what one chaplain called 'true prayer', but the issue for soldiers was not their degree of faith but the extent to which prayer could temporarily ameliorate the states of chronic fear that they experienced in combat. Research carried out at the end of the war confirmed the link between prayer and stress.[117] This was one of many ways in which the debilitating psychological effects of war were mediated for those who survived at the front and continued to fight.

HOME FRONT EMOTION

The civilian populations of the warring states, from among whom the armed forces were recruited, endured their own share of emotional pressure, but it has attracted much less attention from historians than the psychological aspects of military morale. Fear and uncertainty were ever-present, though shared in different ways and seldom as a continuous emotional state. Separation anxiety, fear over news of deaths or injuries, anger at the enemy, despair over the future mingled with the day-to-day emotional reality of domestic life. The degree of danger or deprivation varied widely: American society was never directly affected by war, though preparations were made by the American Psychiatric Society in 1939 to help Americans face the 'insecurity and fear' prompted by war, while in 1940 a Committee for National Morale was set up by a group of academics to help create 'an intense and durable emotional unity'.[118] Soviet society, on the other hand, was steeped in nothing else but the struggle to survive long hours of labour, poor supplies of food, and a front line that absorbed the great majority of Soviet men. In between these poles were the states where civilian populations were subjected to bombing campaigns that brought a semblance of the front-line experience to the home front. Urban populations in Britain, Germany, Italy and Japan were bombed heavily for long periods of the war (and suffered cumulative deaths of around 750,000 civilians); France and much of the rest of Europe under Axis control suffered bombing of industrial or tactical targets but on such a scale that heavy civilian losses were unavoidable. Over the course of the war approximately a million civilians were killed from the air, and approximately the same number seriously injured for reasons already explored more fully in Chapter 8.[119] Only the conditions of the camps and the deportations generated an emotional experience as psychologically damaging as the experience of repeated bombardment from the air.

Before the coming of world war in 1939 it had been widely assumed that civilian morale was likely to be a target in any future war and that heavy bombing of city areas, using a mix of regular bombs, gas and biological warfare, would compel a terrified people to force their government to sue for peace. Much of the popular writing on future war highlighted the psychological vulnerability of civilians, who lacked a soldier's training, had no way of fighting back, and were expected to be easily susceptible to mass panic and emotional breakdown. Governments were aware of the potential damage to any future war effort if civilians were subject to bombing, and in particular the danger that terrified workers would engage in a form of 'economic desertion' from threatened factories and so undermine the war economy. Everywhere, civil defence preparations and anti-aircraft defences were introduced, along with preparations to provide welfare support and shelter for menaced communities, but medical services were also prepared for a possible wave of psychiatric bombing casualties. Psychologists in Britain and in Germany supported the idea that bombing would cause emotional breakdown apart from physical injury, and psychiatric hospitals were emptied of patients to make room for wartime casualties.[120]

When regular strategic, long-range bombing began in 1940 the emotional consequences appeared to be much less severe than had been expected. Urban populations did not engage in mass panics and psychiatric hospitals did not fill up with severely emotionally disturbed patients. During the German bombing 'Blitz' on Britain, psychologists and psychiatrists began to research the reasons why there were so few chronic or persistent disorders.[121] A study of 1,100 people who regularly occupied the same shelters in London found that only 1.4 per cent manifested any prolonged psychological problems. An official from the British Mental Health Emergency Committee who visited the areas of London's East End hit heavily in

September 1940 could find 'no obvious cases of emotional disturbance'.[122] When the British Ministry of Home Security organized a survey of the mental health of the heavily bombed port city of Hull in 1941, the psychiatrists reported that they could find almost no evidence of 'hysteria' (the condition most commonly anticipated) and concluded that the people of Hull were mentally stable.[123] Most British psychiatrists assumed that those few who did break down were, like military conscripts, predisposed to do so. A study of 'Air Raid Phobia' confirmed that those few psychiatric casualties admitted to hospital all had a previous history of neurotic disorders.[124] Some psychotic cases were actually observed to improve with the stress of bombardment; masochists, so it was argued, actually enjoyed the physical threat to their bodies.[125] The same phenomenon was observed among other bombed populations. In Germany, psychiatrists interviewed for the American bombing survey in 1945 confirmed that there had been remarkably few cases of 'organic neurologic diseases or psychiatric disorders' passing through their clinics. Even in Japan, researchers found that following the dropping of the two atomic bombs there was no exceptional level of depression, merely a sustained apprehensiveness. Admissions for psychiatric treatment during the whole bombing campaign were, like the British and German experience, regarded as unremarkable.[126]

The apparent absence of chronic disorders and high levels of hospitalization masked a much harsher reality. For a number of reasons, the full extent of the psychiatric casualties caused by bombing was understated by those with a professional interest in measuring it. This was partly because so many psychiatric medical staff were recruited into the armed forces, leaving a much smaller cohort to monitor the rest of the population. Unlike the growth of military psychiatry during the war, no regular provision was made for the civilian population and civilians were discouraged from overloading the existing hospital system. Some senior psychiatrists in Britain thought the civilian population too prone to exaggerate their symptoms, and that a cup of tea and a stiff talk would be sufficient remedy.[127] As a result, most of those civilians who became temporary psychiatric casualties, or who suffered severe psychosomatic reactions or even more prolonged disorder, nursed their emotional crises in private. As with soldiers, many of the shock reactions were treated as organic in origin, rather than psychological, and sufferers listed, if at all, as medical casualties. In one British survey of a hundred people in two bombed roads in Bristol, it was found that a high proportion suffered somatic reactions that they assumed could be treated by patent medicine, while some of those with evident psychiatric reactions were too ashamed to admit their condition.[128]

These casualties were classified as having 'temporary traumatic neuroses' in Britain or 'fleeting reaction symptoms' in Germany. Their number is impossible to calculate (one British psychologist suggested at least five times greater than the observed cases), but what evidence there is suggests that the emotional reaction to bombing resulted in widespread, if often temporary, psychiatric casualties. Like soldiers, those observed by psychiatrists to be most likely to suffer psychologically were not those necessarily predisposed, but those who had what one called a 'near miss' experience – buried alive, a house destroyed, or family killed. Personal involvement was a critical factor in precipitating severe emotional reactions, a factor that was also confirmed by German doctors when they were interviewed after the war.[129] The symptoms resembled in some ways those of soldiers subjected to heavy bombing or shelling: excessive trembling, loss of bladder control, sensory and motor disturbance, stupor states, pronounced depression and, among civilian women, amenorrhoea. Psychosomatic reactions were common, involving temporary mutism, loss of hearing, paralysis of the legs or arms or, in the German case, an epidemic of civilian peptic ulcers.[130] The case-study evidence accumulated during the survey of Hull showed, despite the optimistic conclusion of the psychiatrists, a wide range of emotional disorders. Some female victims revealed that they fainted or urinated or vomited at the sound of the air-raid siren; men admitted to pronounced dyspepsia, insomnia, depression, heavy drinking and irritability. Most had refused to see a doctor and the men had returned to work within days or weeks despite their anxious state.[131] The psychiatric costs of bombing were coped with here, as in all other bombed cities, as a private crisis, what the writer James Stern, one of the American morale team recruited to interview German bomb victims, called the 'hidden damage'.[132] Some post-war research, like Stern's experience of women interviewees in Germany who trembled and wept at every sudden noise, found that the effects of intense traumatic experience for civilians were long-lasting. Doctors working in Leningrad in 1948 identified the 'Leningrad hypertension' syndrome among survivors of the siege, where a mix of hunger, shelling and bombing had, unsurprisingly, produced severe psychological trauma.[133]

Nevertheless, the issue that concerned governments was the extent to which the psychological reaction to bombing might prompt mass panic and rapid demoralization. Yet, even under the most severe of circumstances, bombing did not become socially disabling. The fear engendered by the prospect and reality of bombing did provoke temporary evidence of panic, but it took the form of an understandable desire to flee the immediate site of the violence, an option seldom available to the military. In cases of heavy

bombing, populations streamed out of the cities into the nearby countryside and villages, a product of reason rather than panic. This was true of
British cities, particularly smaller conurbations hit heavily in the Blitz such
as Southampton, Hull, Plymouth or Clydebank; it was true of cities in
Germany where flight was disliked by the authorities, but in the short term
was unavoidable; it was true of cities in Japan in 1945 where firebombed
populations fled to the countryside. In every bombed state, formal programmes of evacuation were introduced to prevent flight from turning into
a social crisis. In Britain around 1 million women and children were evacuated, in Italy an estimated 2.2 million, but in Germany by the end of the
war, the figure was almost 9 million and in Japan 8 million. The fear that
these large transfers of population might undermine the war economy
proved unfounded. Studies of the workforce in Britain found that almost
all workers returned to work within a few days of a raid, even if they did
so by trekking back and forth between workplace and the surrounding
countryside. In Germany, the heavy and continuous bombing in 1943 and
1944 did not produce high levels of absenteeism. Only 2.5 per cent of
hours lost was directly attributable to bombing; overall hours worked in
the war-economy sectors actually rose between March and October 1944,
though much of the new labour in 1944 was made up of foreign workers
or concentration camp prisoners forced to work through raids.[134]

There were ample explanations for why bombed cities did not collapse
as social and economic units. Public authorities played a part in constructing 'emotional regimes' that encouraged civilians to accept sacrifices
and to avoid demoralizing displays of emotion. These regimes were not
the same, and indeed they reflected very specific cultural differences
between the warring states. In Japan, the culture of death and sacrifice
imbued the efforts of the authorities to establish a popular emotional
engagement with the war effort that matched that of the armed forces.[135]
In Britain, the prevailing propaganda trope during the Blitz that 'Britain
can take it' played up British stereotypes of calm resolve in the face of
crisis. Images from the bombed cities showed people still walking to work
through the morning rubble, or cheerful women handing round mugs of
tea.[136] In Germany, the dictatorship emphasized that the civilians were
bound together with the soldiers in a 'community of fate' in which personal anxieties had to be set aside in the struggle for the nation's existence.
The propaganda images showed the people's sombre resolve in the face of
the shared sacrifices of the collective, and a morbid obsession with heroic
death. The German army refused to discharge psychotic cases back to
Germany because of the effect it might have on the civilian population if
the reality of unheroic collapse became visible. The Soviet regime also

stressed collective sacrifice and heroic endeavour, but did so in ways that avoided the morbidness of the German enemy.[137]

Death, though an ever-present reality for bombed civilians and for soldiers' families, was kept at an emotional distance by set-piece funerals that expressed public resolve rather than public grief. In Japan whole communities celebrated lost 'heroic spirits' in elaborate, stage-managed ceremonies. Images of dead civilians were censored, while in Britain details of casualty figures were deliberately suppressed or restricted during the bombing campaign, ostensibly to avoid panic.[138] Displays of hysterical emotion were disapproved of, and when they occurred in public bomb shelters, civil defence personnel were encouraged to remove offenders. The 'emotional regimes' became models for the civilian populations against which they could test their own capacity for passive endurance and emotional stability. The extent to which individuals could adjust their emotional state to comply with wartime norms in reality varied widely, but the normative framework provided the scaffolding that held the construction of positive morale in place. The congruence between the public image and private behaviour was enforced by social pressure and official practice, so that those who could not cope with the stress became emotional deviants, to be helped or disciplined like the combat soldier.

Material aid was also essential for coping with the consequences of bombing. The psychiatrists at Hull concluded that 'the stability in mental health of the population depends much more on their nutritional state'. State efforts to supply food, welfare, compensation and programmes of rehabilitation proved generally to work well enough to prevent widespread social protest or demoralization. For the immediate victims, a form of 'forward psychiatry' operated, though chiefly by chance, in rest centres and first-aid posts that supplied food, sleep and the opportunity to talk through the worst of people's recent experience, though no formal psychiatric treatment. Psychiatrists in Britain adopted a no-nonsense approach to civilian suffering by suggesting banal forms of 'mental first aid' – firm words and a pat on the back. Concealing fear from others was considered a priority, but agitated individuals could be calmed down, so it was claimed, with a packet of biscuits or sweets, or a nip of brandy.[139] Communal shelters were also regarded as small self-support communities in which fear would be blunted by co-operation in the organization of an active underground community life. Even in the most heavily bombed areas of Germany, shelters were regarded by psychologists as 'psychotherapeutic' sites for controlling emotion and helping those who broke down to conquer the consequences of fear and shock.[140] Psychiatrists noted the capacity of civilians who were regularly bombed to become habituated to the experience, unlike those who experienced continual front-line combat where repeated exposure could produce the opposite effect. Post-war surveys conducted in Germany found that 66 per cent of respondents claimed to have the same or less fear after being bombed, while only 28 per cent were more fearful.[141] When British interviewees were polled during the Blitz about the worst thing they feared, the threat to food supplies came top on both occasions; bombing was rated the worst by only 12 per cent in November 1940, and 8 per cent four months later.[142]

Like servicemen in the field, many civilians relied on other coping mechanisms to come to terms with their fear. These took the form of superstitions, reliance on talismans, or a noticeable fatalism or apathy about the prospects of survival. Japanese civilians were told to place an onion on their head to ward off the menace of the bombs; in Britain shops filled with 'Good Luck' amulets and lucky charms. In 1941 the British Mass-Observation organization carried out a survey on superstitions and found that 84 per cent of women respondents and 50 per cent of the men admitted that they were influenced by them.[143] One prevailing superstition in Germany and in Italy was the idea that civilians were being punished for the crimes of their regimes and that only 'good behaviour' would keep the bombers at bay. In Italy there existed a powerful superstitious belief that a lone aircraft of indefinite origin, nicknamed 'Pippo', flew over the cities of the peninsula, looking for wrongdoers to punish, or, on some accounts, warning of an impending raid.[144] Bombed civilians could also cope fatalistically with their fear, either through the belief that a bomb 'with your name on it' was unavoidable, or through a psychological coping mechanism described by one psychiatrist as an 'invulnerability state', during which individuals took irrational risks because they attributed their personal survival to supernatural agency.[145]

Finally, some civilians, like servicemen, came to rely more heavily on religion as a safeguard and consolation under the hail of bombs. Observers everywhere found increased church attendance, or reliance on prayer, but bombing also inhibited religious practice as churches were destroyed and congregations scattered. In Germany, Hitler decreed that church services could not be held at times that clashed with the priorities of civil defence and post-raid recovery. In 1943, the Rhineland bishops petitioned Hitler to relax the restrictions to help people cope with 'the huge psychological and growing nervous strain' occasioned by the raids, but he refused.[146] By the 1940s Britain was too secular a country for religion to play the same role and although there was evidence of 'crisis praying', and a National Day of Prayer inaugurated for each September, church attendance declined from 1942 onwards.[147] Religion was a more useful source of consolation in Catholic communities, where the culture of solace through prayer, appeals for divine help, and the intervention of the saints was easily adapted to the conditions of the bombing war. In threatened Italian cities, households set up small altars to the Madonna or to local saints to ward off the danger of bombs; prayers were created for the air war, calling on the Virgin Mary to turn the bombers back. Where statues of the Madonna survived amidst the ruins, congregations regarded it as a miracle of deliverance. In Forlí in northern Italy, 40,000 people filed past the Madonna del Fuoco, still intact after the bombing. Marianism increased its appeal in both Germany and Italy. When a young village girl near the Italian town of Bergamo claimed to have had thirteen visions of the Madonna, tens of thousands of Italians flocked to the site in search of protection or consolation or the promise of an end to the war. The official line played down the evidence of visions and miracles, but for many Italian Catholics the church came to replace the state as the main source of both practical help and psychological succour under the bombs.[148]

At the extreme end of the spectrum of civilian suffering were those millions caught up in the maelstrom of deportation, genocidal killing, mass atrocity and war in the vast zone of the German–Soviet conflict. Here there was no 'forward psychiatry', no attempt to ward off the raw impact of traumatic stress at its most extreme, no concern with emotional regimes or managed morbidity. 'Death reigns,' wrote one survivor in the starving, bombed city of Leningrad: 'Death has become a phenomenon observable at every turn. People are used to it. They are apathetic . . . The feeling of pity has vanished. No one cares.'[149] Some knowledge of the emotional or psychological state of the millions of victims can be extracted from surviving memoirs, or from oral testimony, or from contemporary diaries and letters, but it was not a concern of the perpetrators and millions of those who died have left no record. Historians are left with inadequate records to trace the patterns of traumatic reaction at just the point where the unmediated violence, different from the controlled violence of the battlefield, pushed human beings to the primitive edges of human conduct. 'We have returned,' wrote the same Leningrad diarist, 'to prehistoric times.'[150]

In the Soviet Union psychiatrists were permitted a sudden opportunity to grasp the extent of the emotional damage when the Red Army liberated areas in the western Soviet Union that had experienced two years or more of German occupation. They focused on the state of the children that they found, thousands of whom had been deeply traumatized by the violence of the occupiers. The terror had been directed not only at the adult population, but also at their children. The German occupiers treated the young as partisan suspects, or potential forced labourers, even those as young as nine or ten, or murdered them for pleasure or, in the case of girls, sent them to field brothels. Many children were orphaned and forced to live on the streets and steal for food, creating a further target for the occupiers' careless mistreatment.[151] This was the day-to-day experience of life under occupation for millions caught in the crossfire of the war. In the liberated areas, Soviet doctors took the most extreme cases of psychiatric collapse for treatment and found children who had witnessed the murder of parents or neighbours, who had escaped from buildings where the whole village population was burnt to death, or who had watched scenes of torture and mutilation. A major study carried out in 1943–4 found that children lived with 'constant fear and anxiety', expressed either through conventional anxiety symptoms – fainting, sleep-walking, bed-wetting, headaches, extreme irritability – or through somatic reactions such as paralysis, nervous tics, stuttering, mutism, or stupor states. Reports showed that child patients responded reasonably well to rest and a secure environment, but reaction syndromes were persistent. Loud noises or explosions could bring on bouts of nausea, involuntary defecation, trembling and heavy perspiration, reactions very similar to those observed in the aftermath of bombing raids or among soldiers psychiatrically scarred by combat.[152] Psychogenic reactions to extreme fear continued to be manifested long after the dangers were past, but Soviet psychiatric units were too pressed for resources and personnel to be able to embrace more than a fraction of those who had suffered.

A small number of the Soviet children were Jews who had escaped annihilation, but only a fraction of those who suffered in the Holocaust, the *She'arit Hapleta* or 'surviving remnant', were still alive in 1945. Little effort seems to have been made either to treat or survey the emotional states of those survivors, since in most cases their needs appeared to be medical more than psychological, while the culture of 'liberation', even if it meant little to the starving and disoriented camp prisoners, created the illusion that the traumatic experience was now over.[153] At a 'liberation concert' held three weeks after the end of the European war, Zalman Grinberg, working at a hospital full of Jewish patients, tried to capture the emotional state of those who had come through the ordeal:

We belong to those who were gassed, hanged, tortured, starved, worked and tormented to death in the concentration camps . . . We are not alive. *We are still dead* . . . It seems to us that for the present mankind does not understand what we have gone through and experienced during this period. And it seems to us that neither shall we be understood in the future. We have unlearned

to laugh; we cannot cry any more; we do not understand our freedom; this
is probably because we are still among our dead comrades.[154]

For survivors there were also feelings of guilt or shame that they lived
while the great majority had been killed, emotions that competed with the
anguish of discovery, often long afterwards, that family or friends were
indeed dead. In the camps for Displaced Persons (DPs), where Jewish
survivors lived at first in demoralizing conditions, they existed, according
to one observer, in 'a constant state of fear, anxiety, and uncertainty'. Officials trying to cope with management of the camps found among the
survivors evidence of disruptive, neurotic and uncooperative behaviour,
including bed-wetting, infantile regression, petty theft and poor hygiene,
which evidently reflected the psychiatric response to severe trauma and
continued uncertainty.[155] What is more surprising is the evidence in the
camps for Jewish survivors of an energetic re-establishment of Jewish culture and community. Despite anxieties that the psychiatric damage of the
camps might have induced impotence or a permanent state of amenorrhoea, the birthrate among the Jewish survivors by 1948 was among the
world's highest, seven times the rate among the surviving Germans.[156]

Not until a year after the end of the war were psychologists allowed to
visit the DP camps in Germany that now housed the great majority of the
remaining Jewish survivors. In the West more interest had been shown in
trying to understand the emotional state of the perpetrators by identifying
and describing a 'Nazi mind' rather than in defining what persecution had
meant in emotional terms to the victims.[157] In April 1946 a Polish psychologist, Tadeusz Grygier, keen to study the 'impact of oppression on the
human mind', was allowed to find a group of former camp prisoners and
forced labourers as his raw material, but Jewish DPs rejected his request,
an outcome that Grygier attributed to the influence of 'extreme oppression'.[158] In July 1946 a Russian-American physiological psychologist,
David Boder (born Aron Mendel Michelson), was also given permission to
carry out a programme of interviews in the DP camps. He was interested
in studying 'personality under unprecedented stress' and saw the Jewish
camp survivors as an obvious cohort. As a Jew himself, he faced none of
the problems Grygier had experienced and he studied a range of survivors, both Jews who had survived the camps and foreign forced labourers
who had lived in wartime Germany under far easier conditions.[159]

Boder began by using a standard 'Thematic Apperception Test' in which
a selection of images was shown to interviewees to which they were supposed to respond with associated reactions. He soon found that the test
told him very little since his interviewees were often non-committal or

sceptical that a proper understanding of the emotional world of persecution could ever be achieved. 'Are the psychologists so far advanced,' asked
the eighteen-year-old Abe Mohnblum, 'that they really know human
nature so well?' When Boder demurred that psychology was in the process
of exploring fresh avenues, his interviewee retorted that psychologists 'are
absolutely incapable of appraising what can really happen'.[160] Boder was
evidently humbled by the disjuncture between his aims as a psychologist
and the unimaginable reality confronted by his cohort of survivors, retold
to him at great length. He titled the eventual publication of a selection of
his recordings in 1949 *I Did Not Interview the Dead*. In it he established
what he called a 'Traumatic Index' (in later editions changed to 'Traumatic
Inventory'), containing twelve categories within which he defined 'psychologically what has happened to these people'. The index covered all areas
of their experience that stripped away from them the emotional and physical world of the cultured present and replaced it with a primitive past,
including as item 7: 'chronic overloading of the physical and mental ability
to endure'.[161] Although Boder used the term 'trauma' rather differently from
its current usage as a description of a repressed reaction to stress, his intention was nevertheless to describe the cumulative psychological damage
that the experience of persecution had left in that fragment of victims who
survived. He eventually tried to quantify their suffering by measuring it in
'catastrophic units' and found, not surprisingly, that camp survivors bore
a traumatic load at least three times greater than the foreign workers.[162]

Millions of those who suffered emotional crisis during the war failed to
survive either at the fighting front or under the bombs or among the civilian victims of atrocity, starvation and genocide. From the German, Soviet
and Japanese armed forces around 18 million were dead by the end of the
war, in contrast to around 1 million from Western armed forces. This meant
that many more millions from the democratic armies returned home to be
reintegrated back into civilian society. Like the treatment of survivors from
the camps, this was not a straightforward process as servicemen and
women now used to a world of quite different values, carrying with them
the emotional and psychiatric baggage of distant battlefields, tried to cope
with re-establishing normative civilian behaviour and conventional emotional bonds. Only in the United States was psychiatric adjustment regarded
as an urgent issue. Numerous guidebooks were published in 1945, including a *Psychiatric Primer for the Veteran's Family and Friends*, which
explained that returning service personnel were likely to be 'restless, aggressive and resentful'.[163] Widespread fears that returning servicemen might
prompt a crime wave, or that their psychiatric disorders would challenge

the revival of peacetime communities, led the United States army to fund two publicity films in 1945, one on 'combat exhaustion', the other inaptly named *The Returning Psychoneurotics*. The second film, directed by John Huston, explored the therapies for rehabilitating seriously disordered patients in a New York psychiatric hospital, but the army decided that the images were too morbid for an American public not yet aware of how much emotional damage the war had inflicted on what the screenplay chose to call 'human salvage'. Although the film was renamed *Let There Be Light*, the army banned its screening until 1981.[164]

The few surveys carried out among servicemen after the war showed how the emotional scars of the conflict survived the peace. In the United States, 41 per cent of veterans received disability compensation for psychiatric disorders. Another survey published by the War Department in 1946 showed that between 40 and 50 per cent of all those who had received medical care during the war were cases of combat exhaustion.[165] In Britain, a number of small investigations were carried out to follow up psychiatric cases discharged back into the community during the war. They showed that many of these men found it difficult to hold down a job, or to revive their self-esteem. Although systematic surveys seem not to have been conducted on veterans returning to civilian life in Germany, the Soviet Union or Japan, the process of emotional reintegration was difficult, or in the German and Japanese case sometimes long delayed by the decisions in Britain, France and the Soviet Union to keep German or Japanese prisoners for labouring tasks in post-war reconstruction long after the period stipulated under the Geneva Convention.[166] When Japanese prisoners were finally sent back from the Soviet Union to Japan in the early 1950s, there was widespread public concern at men who had not only been dishonourably captured but who now also proved to be disruptive and 'argumentative' in their return to civilian life.[167]

The United States was unique in its requirement that where possible the remains of those who died in combat abroad should be returned home after 1945. Allied and Axis servicemen and women who served overseas were generally buried in the theatre where they died. The overwhelming desire of the American public, whose servicemen died across thousands of miles of ocean, was to rebury the dead in American soil. The effect was to suspend the emotional regime of wartime America, where the official line was to veil the reality and extent of battle deaths, and for once allow a moment of collective, if orchestrated, grief. In October 1947 the first 6,200 coffins returned from Europe. One Unknown Soldier was chosen at random and his coffin paraded in a solemn cavalcade along Fifth Avenue in New York in front of half-a-million people; in Central Park a service was held for 150,000 of the onlookers.[168] Some crying, some unable to watch, the moment captured the pent-up emotions of the wartime years. 'There goes my boy,' cried a woman from the crowd. For years, millions of servicemen and women had had to cope with the tension between their private fears and anxieties and a military regime of discipline and self-sacrifice, while for their part civilians across the world had lived with the contradiction between public cultures of endurance and the private reality of grief and loss.

10

Crimes and Atrocities

'When the Jews were taken from their apartments to be shot, Liza Lozinskaya, a schoolteacher, was hiding somewhere. The next day, after the mass shootings, the Gestapo cutthroats caught her. The bandits dragged her onto the market square, tied her to a telegraph pole, and began throwing sharp daggers at her. The monsters hung a placard around her neck with the inscription "I impeded German officials from carrying out laws and regulations."'

Recorded testimony, 'The Germans in Mozyr'[1]

'Once a German soldier was caught and brought to the [partisan] base. They didn't even manage to interrogate him. People basically tore him to pieces. That was a horrible picture; they ripped his hair out, women, elderly people. And everybody shouted "for my son, for my husband," etc.'

Interview with Leonid Okon[2]

The Second World War was an atrocious conflict. From its beginning to its end, crimes and atrocities punctuated the conduct of soldiers, security personnel and civilians on a scale and with a relentless energy that could scarcely have been imagined beforehand. Atrocity bred atrocity in a vicious cycle of retribution. The villager who recalled the fate of Liza Lozinskaya also remembered a female Soviet partisan caught and punished in the same way for 'impeding' the work of German policemen and local auxiliaries, whose task it was to herd the nearby Belorussian Jews to pits outside the village and shoot them, a layer at a time.

The young Leonid Okon, an escapee from the Minsk Ghetto, joined the partisans with one thought: 'I wanted to fight the whole time. I wanted revenge.'[3] The Germans and their helpers lived in fear of that revenge, and their anxiety fuelled further waves of cruel violence to try to keep the threat at bay. This was one front line among many in the narrative of wartime atrocity. There was no single theatre to which it was confined and no single cause that explains it; the dark underside of the Second World War was made of many parts. Some of the atrocities were regular war crimes that flouted the established laws and customs of war. Some were the product of profound racial hatreds or prejudices. Some, easier to conceal, were the fruit of persistent male violence towards women.

For contemporaries, the concept of 'war crime' was usually understood as a violation of the annexes of the 1907 Hague Convention on Land Warfare governing the 'laws and customs of war on land' and the Geneva Convention on the International Red Cross, agreed originally in 1864. On this definition, war crimes were carried out by armed forces either against enemy armed forces in the field and as prisoners, or against enemy civilians who were supposed to be protected from violation under the 'laws of humanity' existing among 'civilized peoples'.[4] The Convention did not apply to colonial populations defined as 'semi-civilized' or 'uncivilized'. The nature of the crimes was not defined very precisely, nor was it evident how they might be investigated or punished, since no international court was ever established to enforce the agreements. During the Great War, the customs and usages of war were violated by both sides, though not systematically since for long periods the zones of combat were limited to trench warfare, without partisan war or civilians in the firing line. The war nevertheless prompted the classification of other 'crimes' deemed to be violations of the Hague Conventions. A catalogue of thirty-two offences was drawn up at the end of the war by the victors as an indicative list of conduct regarded as criminal, including 'murder and massacres' (directed particularly at the Turkish killing of the Armenians), 'systematic terrorism', 'torture of civilians' and the deportation and forced labour of non-combatants.[5] A Commission on the Responsibilities for the War and Its Conduct was appointed by the Allies in February 1919, which in turn established a subcommittee on the violations of the laws of war which was to report on the prosecution of known enemy war criminals. The United States, however, vetoed the idea of an international tribunal to try alleged German and Turkish war crimes and in the end the German and Turkish governments conducted a few token trials at Allied encouragement, while the French and Belgians tried and convicted 1,200 prisoners still in their hands. A German Bureau of Investigation had in turn compiled 5,000 wartime dossiers on Allied war crimes, but justice in 1919 lay with the victors, not with the defeated enemy.[6]

The obvious failures of definition and procedure exposed in 1919 led to efforts over the following ten years to reach more precise international agreement about acceptable wartime conduct. During the war, bombing of civilians had been carried out by both sides, but although 'aerial bombing' was prohibited under the 1907 Convention, there was no specific body of international law governing the conduct of air warfare. In 1923, following a decision taken at the Washington Naval Conference the previous year, an international committee of jurists at The Hague drew up the Hague Rules for Air Warfare. Though the rules were never ratified by any government, they were regarded as having the force of international law, particularly the provision that no attack should be made on civilian lives and property but only on identifiable military objectives.[7] In 1925, agreement was reached at Geneva for a convention outlawing the use (though not the possession) of gas and bacteriological weapons. Four years later a further convention was drawn up governing the treatment of prisoners of war, amplifying the protection already awarded under the Hague Treaties. In 1936 new rules were drawn up for naval warfare, outlawing the unrestricted submarine warfare practised during the Great War; naval vessels were required to stop and search merchant ships suspected of supplying the enemy, and to provide safety for their crews rather than sinking ships on sight.

Many of these additional safeguards were already violated during the 1930s. Italy and Japan used poison gas in the invasions of Ethiopia and China; Japanese aircraft bombed civilians in the war in China, and Italian and German aircraft did so in Spain during the Civil War; Chinese prisoners of war were killed out of hand by the Japanese army. During the Second World War every international agreement was violated by one or other party to the conflict, in many cases gross violations on a scale never even contemplated when the instruments of international law were drafted. As the evidence of atrocity on an unimaginable scale emerged, the twentieth-century idea of a war crime was stretched to its limit and beyond. By the end of the war a new concept was devised to cope with the consequences of such an atrocious conflict so that it would be possible to penalize the mass deportation, exploitation and murder of civilian populations. These outrages were now classified under the umbrella term 'crimes against humanity'.[8] In 1945 the Allied victors once again defined the nature of wartime crime. In addition to the so-called Class A war criminals, charged with plotting aggressive war, there were Class B criminals (violators of the customs and usages of war) and those arraigned under Class C, charged with crimes against humanity.

VIOLATING THE 'LAWS AND CUSTOMS OF WAR'

War crimes in the narrower sense of illegitimate violence between rival armed forces or between armed forces and the civilian population proved impossible to restrict by paper agreements. Battlefield violations were numerous for obvious reasons. Unlike the trench warfare of the First World War, there were regular pitched battles in open, mobile warfare. In such circumstances it sometimes proved simpler to shoot surrendering soldiers, or the enemy wounded, rather than divert men and effort to transfer them to the rear. In infantry combat, soldiers who tried to surrender minutes after killing the enemy might well be killed outright; snipers were regularly executed when caught because they were regarded as a special kind of murderous killer. In the Soviet–German war and the war in Asia, the wounded were routinely butchered where they fell. In the heat of battle, soldiers did not have the Geneva Convention at the front of their minds, and officers in all armies seem to have exercised little restraint of their men and, in some cases, actively encouraged and abetted war crimes. At sea the battlefield was very different, but here too there were opportunities to violate established agreements when sailors and troops were left struggling in the water, or lifeboats were deliberately fired on, or survivors machine-gunned. Only in air-to-air combat were rules more closely observed, though all sides were guilty at times of machine-gunning parachuting airmen; air-to-ground combat, on the other hand, raised awkward issues because of the inaccurate, even at times random nature of bombing and strafing during ground operations. Above all, long-range 'strategic' bombing raised profound ethical issues because operations killed civilians in large numbers, in some cases deliberately so, as well as destroying indiscriminately hospitals, schools, churches and cultural treasures.

Most Class B war crimes were committed in ground combat, where soldiers came face to face with the prospect of killing or being killed. 'There is one rule here,' an American engineer in the Pacific war wrote in his journal, 'KILL, KILL, KILL.'[9] Although violations in the heat of the moment were routine, the scale and nature of wartime atrocities between armed forces were determined by a wide range of factors in each theatre of war – geography, ideology and propaganda, military culture, the absence of restraint, and so on. It is unlikely that any except the lack of restraint was in the minds of those who committed the violence at the time it was perpetrated. Where restraint was absent, or the rules deliberately flouted by the military authorities, soldiers were free to behave with an instinctive violence on the battlefield. In December 1941, for example, Hitler told the army fighting in the Soviet Union that the war there had nothing to do with 'soldierly chivalry or with the agreements of the Geneva Convention' and expected his troops to draw their own conclusions. But in the war against the Western powers, he wanted his forces to observe as far as possible the agreed rules of combat, a view he reiterated to the army when news reached him of the massacre of American soldiers by the Waffen-SS at Malmédy late in 1944.[10] Though much rarer among Western forces, it was still possible at times for the rules to be suspended. Before the American invasion of Guam in 1944, cheering marines and soldiers were told that no prisoners were to be taken.[11]

The broader context within which campaigns were fought nevertheless explains the wide differences in the scale and barbarity of battlefield crime one theatre from another. In the war in Western Europe and the Mediterranean, the opposing armed forces generally observed the conventions laid down by international agreement. The one exception was Western combat against the Waffen-SS, who were widely regarded as a law to themselves, fanatically committed to Hitler and unscrupulous in their conduct. During the bitter battles in Italy and along the German frontier in 1944–5, captured Waffen-SS were sometimes despatched where they were caught. When news filtered out to the troops about Waffen-SS atrocities, they drew their own conclusions. In the Battle of the Bulge, very few Waffen-SS made it to the prisoner pens. 'War being what it is and people being what they are,' an American veteran later recalled, 'a lot of times a fellow gets so angry he just loses control of himself and emotions take over.'[12] British forces occasionally responded in kind too, and the Special Air Service, first set up in 1941, seldom took prisoners. German war crimes against other soldiers in North Africa, Italy and Western Europe were also relatively isolated examples when compared with anything of the scale of atrocity in the Soviet Union and China. Victims in these theatres were numbered in tens or hundreds, while in Russia and Asia there were hundreds of thousands. In the war at sea, both sides adopted unrestricted submarine warfare in defiance of the 1930 London Naval Treaty, but in general both sides refrained from killing those who had abandoned ship, while the Royal Navy in all but a few cases rescued those in the water.[13]

The Eastern European theatre and the war in Asia had a completely different complexion. In both regions the defending armies quickly came to understand the terms in which the advancing enemy was prepared to fight and reacted in kind. The result was a crescendo of atrocity, each vicious reprisal prompting a further degeneration of behaviour on the part of the troops of both sides. The 'barbarisation of warfare' – a term coined by the historian Omer Bartov to describe the savage war waged by the German army in Russia – was deliberate in the German and Japanese cases, but there were also many circumstantial pressures on both sides to transform men who would otherwise not have committed atrocities into vicious killers.[14] Not least was the role of geography. Soldiers found themselves fighting in the most inhospitable of conditions, far from home, with little prospect of leave. The demands made on troops in the jungle conditions of Burma or the remote islands in the South Pacific, or among the mountains and rivers of central China, or on the vast Russian steppe, burning hot and dusty in summer, freezing in winter, evidently played a part in encouraging harsh combat. In these remote zones, the pervasive reality of mass death from combat or disease or injury contributed to a profoundly morbid culture in which enemy deaths were treated with complete indifference. German soldiers found the almost suicidal tactics of the Red Army difficult to comprehend, but the result was to treat Soviet soldiers as so much cannon fodder. Japanese soldiers fought to the death in a military system in which the principle of *gyokusai* (glorious self-annihilation) was instilled into every recruit.[15] Suicidal attacks and suicidal defence blunted American, Australian and British attitudes to Japanese deaths. On roads where Japanese bodies lay unburied, Allied traffic soon reduced any corpse to a flattened, desiccated shadow.

The Japanese war in China was waged from the outset with little or no regard for the conventions of modern warfare. Chinese soldiers who surrendered were routinely shot or beheaded on the spot as the Japanese army advanced. The wounded were finished off by bayonet or swords, weapons Japanese infantry exploited with relish. Although leaflets were dropped by aircraft encouraging Chinese Nationalist soldiers to surrender with the promise that the Japanese army 'will not harm prisoners', diary accounts from Japanese soldiers make clear that the promise was no more than a ruse. One Japanese soldier in the assault on the province of Hebei recorded his pleasure at beating Chinese wounded with a stone and slicing open a prisoner with his sword. As his unit followed the retreating Chinese forces into Shanxi province he wrote that killing fleeing enemy soldiers was fun: 'Also playing around with the wounded and making them kill themselves was fun.'[16] The diaries also reveal the profound insecurity and fear that plagued the advancing Japanese soldiers as they were subjected to regular ambushes by Chinese soldiers who had melted away from the battlefield and now resorted to irregular guerrilla tactics. The Japanese army took high casualties as it moved forward, and soldiers took their revenge on the enemy with calculated sadism.

The high point of atrocity was reached in the assault and capture of the Nationalist Chinese capital of Nanjing, where an estimated 20,000 Chinese soldiers were butchered alongside thousands of civilians. Although the senior Japanese command in China wanted soldiers to show restraint, the long months of difficult combat in an endless landscape encouraged a yearning for reprisal. Two Japanese soldiers became overnight celebrities in Japan as news was relayed about a competition to see which of them could cut off 100 Chinese heads first; the 'Hundred man killing contest' carried on into 1938, and by March one of the lieutenants had beheaded 374 men. Poems, songs, even children's books celebrated the 'Patriotic Hundred-Man Killings'.[17] Everywhere, Chinese soldiers were hunted down and slaughtered using a variety of cruel forms of execution – prisoners hanged by the tongue, buried alive, burnt alive, used for bayonet practice, dropped naked into holes in the winter ice to 'go fishing'.[18] One Japanese soldier passed by a group of 2,000 dead and mutilated Chinese in Nanjing who had surrendered with a white flag. They were, he noted, 'killed in all different kinds of ways' and left to rot on the road.[19] The unrestrained violence stemmed from the decision by the Japanese military to define Chinese soldiers as bandits, removing any legal barrier to their murder when they were caught. The Geneva Convention on prisoners had not been ratified by the Japanese government, but even if it had been, the limits imposed by international law enshrined in the Geneva agreements were not communicated even to senior Japanese commanders.[20] As Japanese soldiers became hardened to a life of savage combat, the habit of killing wounded and captured enemy became a way of life. 'I trod on the corpses of Chinese soldiers without care,' wrote one witness of Nanjing in his journal, 'for my heart had become wild and disturbed.'[21]

When Japan attacked American, British and Dutch possessions in South East Asia and the South Pacific in December 1941 most of the soldiers employed had seen service already in the China war, unlike the Allied armies they confronted who had no or little battle experience. Japanese soldiers transferred the habits of four years of combat to the war against the colonial powers. The reputation for savagery preceded them, but the impact was nevertheless a shock for Western servicemen who not only underestimated the tactical fighting skills of the Japanese enemy, but assumed that in combat with white armies the Japanese would observe the conventions restraining unlimited violence. When the British governor surrendered Hong Kong to the Japanese on Christmas Day 1941, the invading force rampaged through the settlement, killing prisoners, bayoneting the wounded in the hospitals, raping and murdering nurses (though only a few days before, British troops and police had mown down Chinese looters with machine-gun fire, and, in one case, lined up seventy alleged fifth columnists, placed sacks over their heads and shot them one at a time).[22] In the invasion of Malaya Japanese soldiers killed prisoners taken as they advanced down the peninsula and slaughtered the wounded, a pattern that was to be repeated across the combat in the Pacific. In the fighting in New Guinea, with Japanese forces often close to starvation, and poorly supplied with munitions, captured Australian soldiers were later found tied naked to trees for bayonet practice, or slashed to ribbons with swords and, in a number of cases, butchered to supply human flesh for hungry Japanese troops.[23] American forces found dead comrades mutilated and tortured, or trophies taken from Americans in the pockets of Japanese dead. At sea, the Japanese navy sank ships on sight and either left the survivors to drown or machine-gunned them in the water; naval personnel ashore during the invasion of the East Indies (present-day Indonesia) massacred hundreds of captured Australian and Dutch soldiers on Amboina Island, giving the execution detail the choice of beheading each prisoner or stabbing them in the chest with a bayonet.[24] The US navy also adopted unrestricted submarine warfare from the start of the war. By 1945 there was little left to sink, and submariners turned to fishing vessels and coastal sampans, in violation of their rules of engagement. Whether Japanese survivors struggling in the sea or scrambling into lifeboats were abandoned or killed was a matter of conscience for individual commanders, rather than a matter of law.[25]

For the Japanese invaders, atrocious behaviour towards Allied forces proved completely counterproductive. Since the Japanese made no attempt to sustain the conventions of war, the forces facing them in the field retaliated in kind. Not every Allied soldier, nor every Japanese soldier, committed acts in defiance of the laws of war, but in the Pacific conflict such violation was commonplace and soldiers and marines did not expect to be disciplined for doing so. The attitude of American servicemen was conditioned by the wave of spontaneous anger at the attack on Pearl Harbor. The director of naval operations, Admiral Harold Stark, announced within hours of the outbreak of war that American forces could undertake 'unrestricted air and submarine warfare against Japan', overturning international commitments even before combat had started. Roosevelt's personal adviser, William Leahy, also made clear that when fighting 'Japanese savages' established rules of warfare 'must be abandoned', while Vice Admiral William Halsey signalled to the crews of his carrier fleet: 'Kill Japs, Kill Japs, Kill More Japs.'[26] Under these circumstances, there was no prospect that American servicemen would be held back by legal constraints, even less so when they witnessed at first hand the reality of Japanese violations. 'Kill the Bastards' became a standard motif in the literature read by United

States servicemen. Japanese forces in defence obeyed no rules, even in defiance of all reason: they used flags of truce to ambush the approaching enemy; lay still on the battlefield to simulate death before opening fire; surrendered with a live grenade strapped to their arms to kill both themselves and their captors; and, on rare occasions, charged en masse with swords drawn against enemy machine guns.[27]

American marines and infantry held a widespread loathing and contempt for the enemy, fuelled by propaganda that painted them as inhuman animals, products of an exotic and unfathomable culture. In the field the 'good Jap' was the 'dead Jap', and few prisoners were taken. The wounded might be finished off with a slit throat. Trophy parts were cut from bodies, some of the dead scalped and gold teeth prised out, to be kept in small trophy pouches. So widespread was physical mutilation that the War Department in September 1942 ordered all commanders to ban the gruesome souvenirs, but with little effect. When Japanese skeletons were repatriated from the Marianas Islands after the war, 60 per cent were found to have no skulls. A letter opener carved from a Japanese bone was even presented to Roosevelt, who insisted that it should be returned to Japan.[28] Some Japanese captives, unable to accept their failure to die in combat, struggled so violently that their wish was granted by their captors. So difficult did it become in the battle for the Solomon Island of Guadalcanal to find a live Japanese to interrogate that men of the Americal Division were promised whiskey and extra beer if they brought one in.[29] By October 1944, after three years of combat, there were just 604 Japanese in Allied hands. In the whole Pacific theatre only 41,000 Japanese soldiers and sailors were eventually taken prisoner, almost all of them at the end of the war. Knowledge that the Americans and Australians did not generally take prisoners simply reinforced the Japanese Field Service Code requiring death rather than dishonour. The same held true for the war in Burma, where British, West African and Indian forces so regularly killed prisoners and wounded Japanese after witnessing Japanese atrocities that there was no inducement for Japanese soldiers to surrender. On one occasion Indian soldiers burnt alive 120 wounded Japanese, on another they buried alive more than 20. Wounded Japanese were routinely bayoneted or shot, dead soldiers bayoneted to be sure they were dead. Remarked one brigade major, 'they were animals and as such they were treated.'[30]

The war on the Eastern Front displayed many of the same elements. The German army had already acted severely in the war in Poland in 1939, when around 16,000 captured Polish soldiers were shot in reprisal actions. Even before the conflict with the Soviet Union began, German forces were instructed with a pamphlet 'Do You Know the Enemy?' to prepare them to expect Soviet troops to be 'unpredictable, underhand and callous' in the way they fought, a prejudice based in part on memory of the Russian army's practices in the First World War.[31] A blend of racial prejudice and hostility to 'Jewish-Bolshevism' encouraged army commanders to concur with Hitler's claim, communicated to them in March 1941, that the campaign in Russia was a 'war of extermination' in which Germans needed to 'move away from the idea of soldierly camaraderie'. General Georg von Küchler, commander of Eighteenth Army for the invasion, told his officers that they would be fighting against 'racially foreign soldiers' who deserved 'no mercy' in battle.[32] Major General Eugen Müller described the way German soldiers were to fight in Russia as a return to 'an earlier form of warfare' before the rules of combat were codified at The Hague and Geneva.[33] Three directives issued from Hitler's Supreme Headquarters in May and June, shortly before the invasion, defined what this 'earlier form' would be. The Guidelines for the Conduct of the Troops in Russia called for complete ruthlessness in eliminating all forms of resistance; the Commissar Order gave instructions to pass all captured Soviet military commissars – personifications of the 'Asiatic form of warfare' – directly to the SS for execution; the final directive on Curtailment of Military Jurisdiction gave a blanket amnesty to any soldier who committed what international law defined as a crime against soldiers or civilians. Though some German commanders worried that the directives would encourage what Field Marshal Walter von Reichenau described as an undisciplined 'delirium of shooting', most seem to have approved and later carried out the war without mercy.[34]

The war that unfolded from June 1941 confirmed German prejudices about the way Soviet forces would fight. German soldiers as they advanced found the mutilated corpses of their companions – soldiers whose tongues were nailed to a table, prisoners hanged on meat hooks, others stoned to death. Stories of Soviet atrocities, true or not, soon spread through the advancing German units, and in the opening weeks of the campaign captured Red Army soldiers in small groups were commonly shot when they surrendered. In September 1941, the army high command defined all Soviet soldiers found behind German lines as partisans, to be executed without further ado.[35] Like the Japanese, Soviet soldiers often fought in hopeless situations to the last man, or hid in ambush to attack German forces from the rear, or played dead before opening fire, or continued to fight even when severely wounded. Soviet soldiers were expected, like Japanese, not to be taken prisoner, and to underline the ethos of self-sacrifice for the sake of the collective, the Soviet regime issued Order 270 in August 1941, condemning all those who surrendered or became a prisoner as 'traitors to the motherland', with penalties for their families.[36] In the early desperate battles, the Red Army seldom took prisoners; later in the war, when the Red Army was advancing rapidly, captured enemy soldiers were a handicap. One young German soldier, lost in a forest late in 1944, avoided the fate of the remainder of his unit; when he found his companions again they were laid out in a row in a field, their heads crushed and their stomachs slit open by bayonet.[37]

Soviet soldiers were under no obligation to abide by the rules. They fought with any means, fair or foul, because the central moral commitment to which they were supposed to subscribe was to save the Soviet motherland from the fascist invaders. Stories of German atrocities spread through the ranks, reinforcing the view that the enemy deserved little mercy.[38] Their task was to kill Germans. Like the American literature in the Pacific war, Red Army journals carried hate-filled exhortations to kill. 'Nothing gives us so much joy,' wrote the poet Ilya Ehrenberg in *Red Star*, 'as German corpses.' Soldiers were encouraged to kill at least one German a day if they could. Stragglers in the retreats in 1941 formed partisan units which constantly harassed the German lines of communication and regularly tortured and killed any Germans they caught. Under these circumstances, abiding by notional laws of war was meaningless for troops struggling desperately to turn the tide against an unexpected aggressor. Millions were nevertheless captured in the great encirclement battles of 1941 and news soon spread back that thousands of the prisoners were systematically murdered by their German captors. The German army proved generally loyal to the directive to kill commissars, Communists and Jews among those taken prisoner, murdering an estimated wartime total of 600,000. In turn, German soldiers found prisoners, as the German Foreign Office protest to Moscow put it, 'murdered and tortured in bestial and indescribable fashion'.[39] For both military organizations, no effort was made to restrain the violence because it was sanctioned from above. Prisoner killing declined from 1942–3 only because both regimes wanted to use prisoner labour in their war economies, but by then half of all Germans captured were already dead, and two-thirds of the Soviet troops in German hands.

The fate of prisoners of war away from the front line reflected the different approaches to the rules of war at the front itself. Survival rates give a clear indication of this difference. Prisoners in British Empire and American hands were not subject to severe punishment or torture, or brought close to starvation, though the large number taken prisoner in 1945 as the war ended presented unexpected problems in housing and feeding them, and higher-than-expected levels of mortality in the makeshift camps that were set up. Out of the 545,000 Italians in British and American hands, all but 1 per cent survived.[40] Western prisoners in German or Italian hands were treated under the terms of the Geneva Convention and from 353,474 prisoners, 9,300 died, most from wounds or sickness (2.7 per cent); by contrast, of the 132,134 prisoners taken by the Japanese, 35,756 died or were killed (27 per cent). American and Australian captives in the Pacific fared worst: one-third of the 43,000 prisoners taken died.[41] Relatively few Japanese became prisoners before the war ended, since most died or were killed on the front line. In Burma, 1,700 Japanese were taken prisoner, but 185,000 died. Only 400 of the survivors were fit, and all of them tried to commit ritual suicide.[42] Because of the sheer scale of the German–Soviet war, and despite the regular murder of surrendering soldiers, very large numbers became prisoners during the war. Of the 5.2 million Soviet soldiers captured, estimates range between 2.5 and 3.3 million who perished in captivity (43–63%); of the 2.88 million Germans who eventually ended up in Soviet captivity, 356,000 died (14.9%). A further 1.1 million Axis prisoners were captured from Italy, Romania, Hungary and Austria (counted separately from Germans), of whom 162,000 died (14.7%). From the 600,000 Japanese captured in the conquest of Manchuria in August 1945, 61,855 died (10.3%).[43] The exception in Soviet hands was the fate of Italians sent by Mussolini in 1941 to fight against Bolshevism: of 48,947 who ended up in prison camps, some 27,683 (56.5%) perished.[44]

The exceptional level of mortality of Soviet prisoners in German hands and Allied prisoners in Japanese hands was a consequence of decisions deliberately taken to mistreat, neglect or kill those who survived the murderous encounters on the battlefield. The attitude of the Japanese military to prisoners of war was entirely negative by the 1930s when the ideology of undergoing heroic death for the emperor rather than surrender reached its high point. The moral failure in becoming a prisoner was drilled into every Japanese recruit. In January 1941, the Japanese army minister, General Tōjō Hideki, issued a booklet for all soldiers on 'Instructions for the Battlefield' which reiterated the warning 'Do not suffer the shame of being captured alive.'[45] As a consequence, Japanese forces regarded enemy prisoners as entirely unworthy. Captured Chinese could be killed as 'bandits', regarded not as human beings, as one Japanese officer put it, but as 'pigs'.[46] When large numbers of Allied prisoners fell into Japanese hands after the surrenders at Singapore in February 1942 and Corregidor three months later, they were regarded with a mixture of incredulity and contempt by their captors and subject to routine mistreatment. Japan had signed but not ratified the 1929 Geneva Convention on prisoners of war, although in January 1942 the government did offer to abide by its stipulations if the Allies did the same. Significantly, the Japanese offer excluded the clauses prohibiting the use of prisoner labour for the enemy war effort and Tōjō, now prime minister, issued an order that prisoners of war should be used as a resource for building roads, airfields and railways for the Japanese military. In reality, Allied prisoners were granted none of the safeguards of the Geneva Convention, and those charged with running the camps and guarding them were not instructed to enforce them. The head of the Japanese POW Information Bureau, Lieutenant General Uemura Mikio, favoured harsh treatment as a way to demonstrate to the populations of the conquered colonies the 'superiority of the Japanese race' and the downfall of the Caucasians.[47]

The high mortality rate that followed had a number of causes. The guards for much of the camp system were recruited among Korean and Taiwanese conscripts, who were taught to regard the prisoners as animals and left largely free to deal with them as they saw fit. Treated brutally by Japanese soldiers and officers, often short of food and medical supplies themselves, the guards took out their frustrations on the men they guarded. The view was widespread that prisoners of war deserved conditions inferior to the already tough conditions imposed on Japan's own soldiers. The priority for the camp commanders and staff was to complete the work assignments rather than protect the prisoners from abuse. Prisoners were denied adequate food rations or medical supplies and almost all suffered from tropical diseases and endemic dysentery. The work details were subject to random brutality, beaten with staves and whips, tortured if they were thought to be slacking and subject to long spells in the punishment cell for minor infractions of the regulations. In the punishment cell men were denied water for three days, food for seven. If they tried to escape they could be shot. If the Special Service of the *Kempeitai* (Military Police), responsible for political surveillance, suspected plans for resistance by prisoners, they could be tortured into confession. The methods used were intended for results. They included the 'rice torture' in which the victim would be force fed large quantities of uncooked rice, followed by a hoseful of water; the rice expanded in the stomach, causing agonizing pain for days. To make beatings more unbearable, wet sand was rubbed into the victim's skin, creating bloody abrasions across the whole of the pummelled area.[48] The tortured either died as they were interrogated or confessed to bizarre conspiracies. Once they had confessed, a kangaroo court pronounced either their execution, or a lengthy prison sentence. These exactions were imposed on men already debilitated by long-term hunger and disease. Survival was a lottery, dependent on the whim of local Japanese officers or the luck of a placement where disease was less rife or the guards less sadistic.

Ideology played a major part in the high mortality rate among prisoners in the war between the Axis states and the Soviet Union. Because the German armed forces were instructed to ignore the Hague and Geneva Conventions, they were under no obligation to treat captured Soviet soldiers and airmen decently. In September 1941, when millions of Soviet soldiers had already been captured, Reinhard Heydrich, head of the Reich Main Security Office (RSHA) issued a directive that since Soviet prisoners of war were no better than criminals, they had no claim 'to treatment as an honourable soldier' and would be dealt with accordingly.[49] Little provision had been made for the sheer numbers captured. The Soviet troops were herded into makeshift camps, often forced to walk hundreds of miles to their destination. The camps were little more than fields surrounded by barbed wire and machine guns; there was little water, food was scant and of poor quality, and medical care denied unless carried out by captured Soviet medical personnel. Uniforms and boots were stolen by German guards. Men who tried to escape were shot; shooting in the camps included not only the Jews and Communist Party members hunted out by the security forces, but any soldier who infringed the crude camp rules, including in one case two prisoners shot for cannibalism instead of dying of starvation as the rest were doing.[50] Those who were still fit enough were put to work, but the cold and hunger did its work along with an epidemic of typhus fever. Some of those who survived captivity in 1941–2 did so only because they agreed to work for the German army as *Hilfswillige*, volunteer auxiliaries, but a great many captives within weeks of their incarceration were beyond the capacity to do useful work and were left to die. By February 1942 2 million Soviet prisoners were dead; little effort had been made to keep them alive.[51]

Like Japan, the Soviet Union had not ratified the Geneva Convention of 1929 and regarded all pre-revolutionary agreements made by the tsarist regime, including the two Hague Conventions, as no longer valid. In late June 1941, the Soviet government tried to use the offices of the International Red Cross to get German agreement that both sides should nevertheless respect the terms in which prisoners were supposed to be treated, but the German government refused. By that stage both armies had already violated any terms likely to be agreed. Because the war was unexpected, the Soviet armed forces had made no provision at all for housing prisoners. By the end of 1941 only 3 camps were available, capable of housing the 8,427 German soldiers who had managed to survive the front-line killing; by 1943 the number of camps had increased to 31, with capacity for up to 200,000. The prisoners were put to work under a decree of 1 July 1941 on the use of prisoner labour. They were classified on the same lines as Soviet prisoners in the Gulag concentration camps, and received the same camp rations. Like Soviet prisoners, they could earn more food by working hard but the harsh conditions in tents and rough barracks, with shrinking supplies of food, left many prisoners too debilitated to labour. German prisoners were not deliberately left to starve, like Soviet prisoners, but the food supply system broke down in 1942–3, leaving hundreds of thousands of Soviet Gulag convicts dead as well. In the winter of 1942–3 the mortality rate of Axis prisoners reached 52 per cent; 119,000 died from extreme dystrophy. Over the whole period from June 1941 to April 1943, 171,774 prisoners died, out of the 296,856 captured, victims of disease, cold and medical neglect.[52]

From spring 1943 the poor conditions were gradually ameliorated on the orders of the Soviet Defence Committee and the Commissariat of the Interior (NKVD), and by the end of the war the death rate was down to 4 per cent. By then the Soviet authorities were trying to re-educate the German prisoners to turn them from fascism to communism; one-fifth of those left alive enrolled in a Communist-inspired 'Free Germany' movement.[53] The mass death of Italian prisoners of war was also not deliberate policy, but the result of neglect, hunger and cold. In the initial camps set up after the Axis defeat at Stalingrad, the mortality rate was exceptional. Prisoners arrived already weakened by weeks short of both food and adequate protection from the freezing temperatures. In the camp at Chrenovoe 26,805 prisoners were held in late January 1943, but only 298 remained alive two months later. In this case the camp commandant was arrested for ignoring NKVD directives on the treatment of prisoners, whose labour was now essential to the Soviet war effort. Italian prisoners were poorly prepared for their ordeal and the camps they were concentrated in were among the worst. Between January and June 1943, a further 31,230 died, some on the way to the camps, some in the initial holding centres, most in the destination camps from hunger, hypothermia and an epidemic of typhus, as had so many of the Soviet prisoners in German hands.[54]

The failure to observe agreed rules of combat or to respect prisoner-of-war status exposed the fragile nature of all international agreements limiting the possibility of crime in war. One of the main concerns in the original Hague Conventions had been to secure some agreed measure of civilian immunity in war, but just as crimes between military personnel flourished under the conditions of combat in the Second World War, so too did the crimes perpetrated by the military against civilians. Civilian immunity was compromised by the imperatives of total war, not only because civilians could be considered a full part of the enemy war effort, but because in many cases civilians chose to confront an occupying force with their own violence. It was also compromised by the sheer scale of military power as armies rampaged across hostile or friendly territory in millions, regardless of the unfortunate civilian populations in their path. Those who drafted the Hague Convention in 1907 could not have imagined the extent to which civilian immunity would be violated by the states who signed it.

The violation common to all armed forces was looting, although in the circumstances of combat in the world war, states were chiefly the culprits responsible. Articles 46 and 47 of the Hague 'Laws and Customs of War on Land' stipulated that 'private property cannot be confiscated' and that 'pillage is formally forbidden'.[55] The definition of what constituted looting was shady at the edges. Under international law, a conqueror had the right to make use of the public assets of the conquered state, including gold bullion and currency reserves, but was nevertheless supposed to ensure that the economic and social needs of the occupied population were fully met. While the state could take a great deal, the individual soldier was supposed to respect the private property of civilians by abstaining entirely from plundering them.[56] This was an idealistic aspiration even when it was drafted. In the Second World War, legal restraint was almost impossible to impose and for officers and military police who might have enforced restrictions, the task was simply beyond the means available even when the will existed. General Eisenhower, the Allied supreme commander in Europe, ordered the American army not to loot, but soldiers did so on a large scale, even from among the civilians the army was liberating.[57] In the opening weeks of the invasion of the Soviet Union, German army commanders ordered units to pay farmers for the goods they seized rather than simply loot them, but within weeks plundering was accepted as unavoidable and uncontrollable.[58] The extent and nature of the looting or pillaging varied with circumstances and opportunity. It ranged from petty pilfering of goods and food and alcohol from civilian houses used as billets, to wholesale and destructive ransacking. Looting was in some cases commonly associated with the rape of the women and girls of the household, abused as sexual booty; in the case of Jews robbed of their last possessions by the soldiers and militia in Germany's war in the East, it was the prelude to their murder. Here were composite atrocities; they form the subject matter of the later sections of this chapter.

The conquering states looted as a matter of course. From the first days of the German campaign in Poland in 1939 soldiers helped themselves to Polish possessions. A Polish doctor, Zygmunt Klukowski, noted the depredations day after day in his diary: 'general destruction and looting of stores'; 'the Germans . . . especially look for good food, liquor, tobacco, cigarettes and silverware'; 'today even the German officers began searching Jewish homes, taking all cash and jewelry'. He watched as German soldiers stole treasures from local Catholic churches. The military police, he observed, stood by and did nothing.[59] In the conquest of Western Europe, looting was in general more restrained, but trainloads of foodstuffs, drink and furnishings made their way back to German families. In the conquest of the Balkans, looting repeated the Polish experience. In Greece, looting in the cities of everything from museum treasures to household goods was indulged in by officers and men alike. A shocked onlooker in Athens puzzled over why the Germans 'have all become thieves'. He watched as 'they empty the houses of whatever meets their eye ... From the poor houses in the area they seized sheets and blankets ... even the metal knobs from the doors.'[60]

The comprehensive pillaging of the civilian population in both town and countryside was reserved for the Soviet population in the wake of the invasion in 1941. The German forces were expected, as the Japanese in China and South East Asia, to live as far as possible off the land. Across the vast swathes of conquered territory in Russia and China, armies stole whatever they found from the poor farmers in their path and no effort was made to sustain local living standards. These were areas where living standards were already low and the prospects of booty-hunting correspondingly poorer. Nevertheless, German and Japanese forces descended like locusts on the occupied zones. Japanese forces were encouraged by instructions issued in 1940 in response to Chinese guerrilla attacks, to respond with terror against the local population, or 'take all, burn all, kill all' as the Chinese victims described it.[61] Through the provinces of central and southern China where the war raged, the countryside was devastated as livestock was stolen, villages burnt to the ground, and towns ground to rubble by bombing. In Russia, the armies on the move seized whatever they needed as supplies, while German soldiers helped themselves to warm Russian clothing to offset the bitter weather. Looting was systematic, to sustain the German offensive. The troops, observed one German soldier on the advance to Leningrad, 'had no choice but to plunder the gardens ... The poor population then had more items absolutely necessary for their livelihood taken by the baggage units. Behind us came other organizations who took up the cause ...' Another officer, watching the troops seize all the fodder and animals from impoverished peasants, realized how little there was to take, 'and when we are gone, there is nothing left.'[62]

When Allied armies looted on a large scale, as they did in the months leading to the final defeat and occupation of Germany, the motives were more mixed. British and American forces began unauthorized looting as they moved across France in the second half of 1944. British looting had been difficult to control in 1940, when the expeditionary force alienated the local French population by regular stealing, but the scale was much greater in 1944. The British government eventually paid £60,000 in compensation for thefts by British soldiers. American servicemen took food and drink, and warm clothing or blankets to help deal with the extreme cold in the winter of 1944–5; houses left empty by refugees were an open invitation to looters. But once on German soil, looting was no longer regarded by the troops as theft, but as justified booty for the victor, 'liberating the Germans' as it came to be called. Only those caught directly in the act by the military police were likely to be punished, if at all. 'We are devastation,' wrote an American sergeant in a letter in April 1945. 'Where we have passed little remains – no cameras, no pistols, no watches, very little jewelry, and damn few virgins.'[63] Large caches of alcohol already looted in France by the Germans were, in turn, appropriated by the liberators. In Koblenz, even while the final fighting was going on, one young soldier found a wine cellar packed with champagne. His unit filled the bath with it and took turns to wash in wine 'like one of those naked movie stars', hoping there would not be a German counter-attack.[64]

Soviet soldiers as they marched into German territory also ransacked supplies of any kind of alcohol they found, even when the effects were poisonous. Soldiers were found drowned in cellars filled with wine from bullet holes in the casks. Hospitals were vandalized in search of anything that tasted alcoholic. But Soviet soldiers also had other motives for comprehensive looting. After years of hardship, booty was regarded as an irrepressible perquisite of war. The homes and farmsteads in their path were pillaged, often wantonly destroyed. What aroused the anger of the ordinary Red Army soldiers was the evident gulf between Soviet life and the relative prosperity of the Germans. It was difficult for them to understand why the limited possessions of the Soviet people had been seized by invaders who already enjoyed such a well-endowed existence. The same contrast had fuelled Soviet looting six years before in the occupation of eastern Poland and the Baltic States; now it unleashed an orgy of plunder, by officers as well as ordinary soldiers.[65] The thieving was officially endorsed, allowing soldiers to send back to Russia a 5-kilogramme package each month, officers a 14.5-kilogramme parcel. The military postal system was swamped with the flood of goods sent back to families in the Soviet Union, who had been denied the prospect of decent food and consumer goods for years.[66]

Looting was the mere tip of an iceberg of crime against civilian populations. Over the course of the years from the mid-1930s to the late 1940s millions of civilians were killed or starved to death, an unknown

proportion of them the victims of atrocities perpetrated by the armed
forces and the security services that waged war across their territories. Like
the crimes between armed forces, civilian deaths were a consequence of a
range of different motives and circumstances. Reconstructing the numbers
killed and the purpose of the atrocities has nevertheless proved difficult in
contexts where few accurate records of the numbers killed, or the damage
inflicted, were ever made. The one exception is the pattern of atrocity in
Italy, where both the number of victims and the variety of circumstances
have been charted across the whole peninsula. Between 1943 and 1945,
there were 5,566 cases of violence against civilians by German forces and
Italian Fascist militia (mobilized by Mussolini's puppet Italian Social
Republic), resulting in 23,479 victims. They were killed in retaliation
against attacks by Italian partisans, as collective punishment for acts
deemed to be rebellious, or in some cases because the village populations
refused to move when ordered from front-line areas. Almost a third of the
victims were men and women partisans caught unarmed in round-ups,
who had no legal protection. Although women and children were murdered in a number of notorious cases, 87 per cent of the victims in Italy
were men, most of military age.[67] The murder of women and children
occurred in a number of exceptionally violent punitive massacres, including the Monte Sole atrocity near Bologna, where the 770 victims represented
the largest number killed in a single atrocity in the Western European theatre.[68] The most notorious atrocity in France, the murder and destruction of
the village of Oradour-sur-Glane by units of the Second SS Panzer Division
Das Reich, resulted in the murder of 642 inhabitants, 247 of them women,
205 of them children, allegedly in retaliation for local French resistance
activity. The killing of French civilians followed an escalation in French
partisan attacks during the Allied assault on Normandy after years in
which atrocities had been, as far as possible, avoided. In June 1944, 7,900
were killed, 4,000 by the *Das Reich* Division alone.[69]

The statistics of civilians murdered, starved or tortured in the war in
Eastern and South-eastern Europe, or the war in Asia, utterly dwarf the
violence in Western Europe. Civilian deaths in the Axis–Soviet war totalled
an estimated 16 million (of whom 1.5 million were Soviet Jews); deaths in
Poland amounted to 6 million, of which half were Jewish victims. There are
no exact figures for the deaths of Chinese civilians but estimates range
between 10 and 15 million. In the Pacific war, civilians perished in their
hundreds of thousands in the Japanese-occupied territories, 150,000 in the
final stages of Japanese occupation in the Philippines. Around 100,000
Okinawans, citizens of Japan, died in the brutal defence and conquest of
the island, at the hands of both Japanese and American forces; they were

caught in a savage front line, killed by air and artillery, deprived of food by both sides, forced out of their refuges to be mown down by machine-gun fire, or bayoneted and blown up by Japanese soldiers if they tried to surrender.[70] In the partisan wars, civilians could be the victims of partisan violence if they were suspected of collaborating with the enemy, or tried deliberately to withhold food from scavenging partisan units. In northern Burma, Chinese partisans, part guerrilla fighters, part bandits, preyed on the local population, razing villages to the ground and murdering peasants who resisted their depredations. Russian partisans in Ukraine were ruthless towards the population they were trying to liberate, publicly hanging alleged collaborators.[71] Soviet and Chinese civilians were also victims of their own regimes in their war against communities suspected of aiding the enemy. During the war years millions were deported to internal exile in the Soviet Union, including hundreds of thousands of Poles and Baltic peoples under Soviet occupation in 1939–41: in 1941 descendants of the Volga Germans (a population that had moved to Russia in the eighteenth century) were accused as a whole of fifth-column activity. The women and children were sent to makeshift camps in central Asia, the men to forced labour camps, where thousands died of hunger and mistreatment. In 1944 it was the turn of non-Russian peoples in the Crimea and the Caucasus, who were brutally uprooted and deported to Siberia. Every Soviet citizen risked accusations of sabotage or defeatism for the slightest infraction or dereliction of duty, which might earn a spell in the Gulag concentration camps, where some 974,000 died between 1940 and 1945.

The overwhelming majority of the civilian casualties in Europe and Asia were nevertheless victims of the conquering German and Japanese armed forces. The effort to capture Eurasia presented inevitable difficulties. Japanese forces found themselves occupying a territory containing 160 million people with an army and military administration stretched taut across the conquered region; German and Axis forces occupied a Soviet area of 60 million people, policed by military and security units that numbered a few hundred thousand. Pacification was a priority for both Japanese and German commanders, but the scale of the task was daunting and acts of resistance widespread and unpredictable. Across Russia and China there existed apparently endless space that was endlessly dangerous. The invaders treated the local population with a toxic mix of fear and contempt; these were areas regarded as ripe for colonization and the harsh treatment of civilians mirrored the long history of violent colonial expansion. For peoples who resisted the colonizing project there was no protection in international law. German treatment of populations in the East differed fundamentally from the treatment of Western and Northern Europeans.[72]

The colonial paradigm was also at work in the Italian atrocities committed against civilian pre-war resistance in Ethiopia and wartime insurgency in Libya, where the army and the brutal *Polizia dell'Africa italiana* suppressed Arab and Berber insurgency with methods regarded as acceptable colonial practice – mass executions, public hangings and flogging. Local colonists took their own revenge on insurgents, some of whom were killed with grenades or burnt alive or used as target practice.[73] The Italian colonial police collaborated with the German security forces by providing advice and training for Germany's own colonial policing in the East. Similar security practices were extended to Italy's rule in Greece and Yugoslavia, where the burning of villages and the execution of civilian subjects mirrored the African experience.[74]

The pacification strategies in both Russia and China were governed by the need to create a secure rear area for the bulk of the army fighting along a distant front line. In both cases the invaders found themselves facing not only the regular units of the enemy but irregular resistance from soldiers isolated from their own forces, or civilian militia, or from civilians dedicated to obstructing the colonizing project. In China regular soldiers shed their uniforms and blended into the civilian population or joined the numerous guerrilla groups or bandit gangs that operated in the Japanese rear. In the Soviet Union it was difficult to police communities in which resisters could pass as ordinary workers, like the young maid who assassinated Wilhelm Kube, commissar for Belorussia, at his headquarters in Minsk. In both cases, the Japanese and German armed forces saw irregular insurgency as a profound threat to the security and well-being of their own troops, and one to be dealt with resolutely and harshly. In Japan, the army was given permission to combat insurgency with 'severe punishment by law' (*genju-shobun*) or in the field by 'on-the-spot punishment' (*genchi-shobun*). Local commanders, faced with routine threats of ambush, assassination and sniping, took matters largely into their own hands, giving free rein to troops to murder civilians, burn villages, and execute hostages without restraint. German forces, from the outset of the wars in the Soviet Union, were given permission to use all means to ensure pacification. In July 1941 at his East Prussian headquarters, Hitler urged his commanders to pacify the conquered region as rapidly as possible, 'shooting anyone who even looks askance'. On 25 July, the army high command issued a directive that all attacks and acts of violence against German forces by irregulars should be 'ruthlessly put down', and if the perpetrators could not be found, 'collective violent measures' were called for. These instructions opened the way from the start of the campaign to extreme violence towards any alleged threat. Civilian irregulars were publicly hanged as a warning, villages razed to the ground, and thousands of hostages executed within weeks of the invasion. Reinhard Heydrich, head of the security forces, issued a directive the same month permitting the execution in the field of all 'radical elements (saboteurs, propagandists, snipers, assassins, agitators etc)', giving free rein to unlimited violence.[75]

As the campaigns in Russia and China reached stalemate, so the treatment of the civilian population and the partisan threat became radicalized. By May 1941 there were an estimated 467,000 guerrillas in the Chinese theatre, some little more than bandit gangs profiting from the lawless zones in the Japanese rear, some of them Communists, some of them units infiltrated from the Nationalist south-west to harass Japanese communications.[76] The heightened insecurity and fear experienced by Japanese soldiers was projected onto the hapless civilians among whom the guerrillas operated. Japanese treatment of Chinese civilians in punitive expeditions was extreme. Although some of the later testimony no doubt played up the savage nature of Japanese occupation, there are too many accounts of civilians buried alive, burnt to death, decapitated, or drowned, or of babies thrown live into boiling water, or women staked to the ground through the vagina, for this to be only the product of rumour or invention. Japanese soldiers not only chose to vent their frustration, brutal conditioning and permanent anxieties on civilians in their path, but often to do so with calculated and grotesque sadism. Occasionally this was the product of a sudden spasm of violence as troops moved forward, like the toxic mix of victory euphoria and vengeance that animated the orgy of killing in Nanjing. Sometimes it seems to have been merely for the pleasure derived from gruesome spectacle, like the young girl from an American mission house on New Guinea who was held down screaming while her head was cut off, or the Dutch children made to scramble up palm trees until they slid down exhausted onto bayonets awaiting them below. Sometimes it was the product of bizarre planning, none stranger than the death of thirty interned civilians on the South Pacific island of New Ireland, including seven German clergymen, natives of Japan's German ally. Instead of simply shooting them, the officers involved choreographed a chilling murder. The internees were told to pack a bag and arrive at the quayside for shipping to another destination. They were then led forward one at a time, concealed from the others, and made to sit on the quay edge. Here a hood was placed over their head, followed by two nooses that were swiftly pulled tight by men standing on either side. After the act of silent strangulation, the bodies were strapped with wire to a large block of concrete, taken out to sea and pushed into the ocean.[77]

German counter-insurgency was also radicalized by the growing threat of irregular resistance, and as in Japan, harsh collective punishments were meted out as a warning to the population not to oppose German instructions or to provide any succour for the partisans. The German reaction combined the work of regular army and police units working behind the front, whose task was to maintain order and combat partisan activity, with the efforts of the security police and security service (*Sicherheitspolizei* and *Sicherheitsdienst*), who rounded up suspects, interrogated and tortured them, and in most cases executed the prisoners.[78] The German authorities saw themselves engaged in an earlier version of the war on terror, for which they were legally entitled to respond with measures of terror severe enough to inhibit further terrorism. The insurgents everywhere in German-occupied territory were designated from 1941 as 'bandits' or 'gangs' to avoid any danger that they might be granted combatant status and to emphasize their criminal status. The language of counterterrorism permeated the long line of orders and directives that flowed from Hitler's headquarters and down the command chain. In August 1942, Hitler deplored the 'unbearable scope' of terror attacks and ordered a policy of 'extermination', an injunction vague enough to allow units in the field to slaughter without restraint. In December 1942, Hitler finally approved 'the most brutal means . . . against women and children also', though German troops and security men had been killing women and children in anti-partisan sweeps long beforehand. On 30 July 1944 Hitler's Supreme Headquarters issued a further directive on 'The Struggle against Terrorists and Saboteurs' to make it clear that there should be no regard for civilians when drastic action was required.[79] At local level, commanders interpreted the central directives in their own way. For the major counter-insurgency operations in Croatia in 1943, the German commander issued the following instruction: '*Every* measure that ensures the security of the troops . . . is justifiable . . . No-one should be held to account for acting with excessive harshness.' General Karl Kitzinger, transferred from command in Ukraine to command in France, directed that 'the harder method' is always 'the correct one'.[80] Research has shown that not every unit operated in the same way, but there was strong pressure on officers not to shy away from committing civilian killing. Field Marshal Hugo Sperrle, the air force officer second-in-command in France, warned commanders that if they acted 'softly or irresolutely' they would be penalized, but 'too severe measures' would be tolerated. Soldiers were told that those with moral scruples committed 'a crime against the German people and the soldiers at the front'.[81]

The radicalization of German anti-terrorist policy to include whole communities, men, women and children, did not take place in a vacuum.

Insurgents did use terrorist tactics against the occupier, anticipating the pattern of asymmetric warfare that developed globally after 1945. The profound sense of fear and insecurity felt by the occupying forces, particularly in the areas behind the fighting, stemmed from the unpredictable behaviour of an enemy hidden from view among distant mountains and forests, or invisible among the urban crowds. Insurgents knew that they had no legal protection if caught, and so gave no quarter to the enemy. In the Soviet Union, German soldiers captured by partisans were routinely executed. One young partisan later recalled when two German soldiers were caught that even 'children wanted to at least hit them with a stick'. This was mild retribution compared with accounts of Russian partisans flaying prisoners alive, gouging out eyes, cutting off ears and tongues, beheading or drowning their captives. [82] One Italian partisan, Giovanni Pesce, wrote a post-war account of a conflict in which no quarter was given by either side: 'We had met the enemy's terror with terror, his retaliation with reprisal, his roundup with ambush, his arrest with surprise action.'[83] His brigade's achievements in a few weeks of the struggle in Milan showed the nature of the terror campaign Pesce waged:

> On July 14 (1944), two Gappisti seriously wounded Odilla Bertolotti, a Fascist spy and that same evening, two Gappisti destroyed a large German truck on Viale Tunisia. A German officer who attempted to intervene was killed. Between July 20 and August 8, eight large trucks and two German staff cars were destroyed. Three large trucks were set on fire with Molotov cocktails. On Via Leopardi, a German tank was set on fire. Two officers were killed.[84]

The cost of the terrorist activities that Pesce and others engaged in was met by local civilians, 'bandit accomplices' according to German instructions to the armed forces, whose villages were destroyed and populations decimated by regular atrocity. In the end, the Axis war on terror resulted in the death of millions of civilians in an effort to stamp out the thousands who terrorized their forces.

Allied ground forces did not routinely murder civilians in their path because they fought as liberators and expected that the population would treat them that way. The Red Army did take revenge on Soviet collaborators with the Axis occupiers, but usually in staged trials and executions. The first Red Army units to arrive on German soil in East Prussia engaged in spasmodic but extreme violence against the first towns and villages they encountered, infuriated by the devastation of the Soviet countryside through which they had passed. 'Happy is the heart as you drive through a burning German town,' a soldier wrote home. 'We are taking revenge for everything, and our revenge is just. Fire for fire, blood for blood, death for death.'[85] But after the first days of violence, the Soviet commanders began to impose greater discipline to reduce the destruction of property and murder of German civilians (but turned a blind eye to the multiple victims of rape). How many civilians died in the initial thirst for revenge is unknowable, but later on German civilians who had served the Hitler dictatorship in one capacity or another were rounded up and put in a former German concentration camp, where more than 43,000 died in the course of 1945–6, principally from malnutrition and disease.

The Allied air forces, on the other hand – British, American and Canadian – did kill approximately 900,000 civilians in bombing offensives in Europe and the Pacific; more than 140,000 of the victims were among the populations to be liberated, adding another layer of complexity to any legal or ethical judgement on the failure to respect civilian immunity. The extent to which the killing of enemy civilians constituted a war crime has remained a contentious issue. There is little doubt that the bombs resulted in atrocious conditions on the ground as whole city centres were set ablaze and thousands died from the effects of high explosives, asphyxiation or severe burns. More than 18,000 Germans in Hamburg were incinerated in a single night of attacks on 27/28 July 1943, consumed in the firestorm that resulted, which left streets littered with carbonized corpses and bunkers full of people who had been slowly asphyxiated as the oxygen was sucked out of the air. The death of 87,000 civilians in the Tokyo raid of 10 March 1945, or the 200,000 who died in the atomic bombings of Hiroshima and Nagasaki in August that year, set wartime records for the number of civilians killed in one operation by any combatant.

All the states that engaged in long-range strategic air attacks during the war knew that the prevailing legal view was to condemn bombing in which civilians and the civilian milieu would be the deliberate or 'negligent' victims of air assault. The Hague Rules had prioritized protection for civilians from air attack by closely limiting what could be regarded as a legitimate target. Though not formally ratified, these were treated as having the force of international law. Western opinion regarded Japanese attacks on cities in China in the 1930s, or Italian and German bombing in the Spanish Civil War, as terror attacks which clearly flouted not only the Hague Rules but the international laws of war as they were generally understood. The British position on legality was explicit. The Air Ministry and the chiefs of staff announced at the start of the European war in autumn 1939 that bombing operations against military targets in civilian urban areas, or bombing by night where targets could not be distinguished, or the deliberate targeting of civilians and their milieu, were all illegal under the prevailing laws of war.[86] These legal restrictions imposed on British airmen were lifted progressively in 1940 as night-bombing became the norm against an enemy now demonized as barbaric, while they featured hardly at all in American assessments of what was acceptable in the bombing campaign.[87] 'I never felt there was any moral sentiment among the leaders of the Army Air Forces,' claimed Ira Eaker, commander of the US Eighth Air Force in 1942–3. 'A military man has to be trained and inured to do the job . . .'[88] Bombing in which civilians would evidently be killed in large numbers, whether deliberately or not, became accepted practice by all air forces that conducted long-range strategic air attacks. The legal implications of operations in which civilians and their milieu would be victimized were largely set aside in favour of pragmatic arguments about how to conduct air operations most effectively against the enemy home front.

In judging the legal position, it is usually maintained that there are evident differences between the face-to-face killing of civilians in Axis counter-insurgency operations and the death of civilians through bombing. Bombed cities were almost always defended by fighter aircraft and anti-aircraft fire (though ineffectively in the case of Chinese cities), and airmen saw themselves engaged in a regular military conflict when they flew, rather than as agents of civilian destruction. In bombing operations there was a long distance, both literal and psychological, between those doing the bombing and those on the ground, a distancing that created the illusion that bombing was in some sense independent of human agency. In theory, populations were free to leave the threatened areas, while victims of reprisal atrocities were not. In reality this was a very limited freedom, given the scale of the problem presented by complete evacuation, but it did alter the way in which civilian victims were viewed. Finally, most air forces directed bomber formations to bomb military targets in the broadest sense, including industrial and transport targets that sustained the domestic war effort, and not to target civilians deliberately. This was done in the knowledge that civilians would be killed, probably in large numbers, which certainly violated the Hague Rules of 1923, but the intention was to damage the physical infrastructure, not to kill people as such – a fine legal distinction that meant little to those being bombed.

The principal exceptions were the British bomber offensive against Germany and the United States city-bombing of Japan in 1945. Despite the early wartime directives that bombing 'negligently' to cause civilian casualties was illegal, the RAF, with government approval, stretched the definition of military target to embrace whole cities working for the war effort, and their civilian populations. Beginning with directives in July

1941 and February 1942, bomber aircraft were instructed to undermine the morale of the working-class population by attacking them and destroying the civilian milieu. Although the shift in strategy was dressed up with the argument that killing and 'dehousing' workers was a function of economic warfare, and therefore not deliberate civilian bombing, the private directives from the Air Ministry, endorsed by Churchill's intermittent enthusiasm for bombing 'every Hun hole', made clear that killing civilians and burning down residential areas was the operational object. In December 1942, the chief of the air staff, Air Marshal Charles Portal, explained to his fellow chiefs of staff that over the following year the ambition was to kill 900,000 Germans and maim a further million.[89] One of the scientists attached to Bomber Command, writing in the autumn of 1943, expressed regret that recent raids had failed to produce an 'all-consuming holocaust' in a German city.[90] The radicalization of British bombing strategy found in Arthur Harris, commander-in-chief of Bomber Command from February 1942, the ideal agent. He had no scruples about proclaiming that the aim was widespread urban destruction and the death of civilians. When asked near the end of the war why he was still bombing areas that had already been all but obliterated through earlier raids, he scribbled on the side of the letter that he did it simply 'to kill Boche'.[91] Killing French, Dutch, Belgian and Italian civilians was more ethically problematic. Here the British, and American, high commands used military necessity as the explanation, since the civilians being killed in order to liberate their compatriots were not in this case the deliberate target. The killing of German civilians was deliberate, and a good deal of scientific and technical effort went into finding the best way of killing more of them. The strategy was a clear violation of the legal restraints governing the use of air power that British political and military leaders had first announced in 1939 and a violation of the spirit of the pre-1914 Hague Conventions on protecting civilians from deliberate harm.

The same legal and moral restraints might have held back the United States bombing of Japanese cities with mass incendiary attacks designed, as the wartime air force planners intended, to kill and maim Japanese civilian workers and to destroy the residential-industrial milieu in which they worked.[92] Carl Spaatz, the overall commander of American strategic air forces in Europe, was shocked by the firebombing raids on Japan: 'I never have favored,' he wrote in his diary in August 1945, 'the destruction of cities as such with all their inhabitants being killed.'[93] The American secretary of war, Henry Stimson, later complained to President Truman about bombing that he did not want 'to have the United States get the reputation of outdoing Hitler'.[94] Yet from the outset of the war, when

General Marshall ordered unrestricted air and sea warfare against Japan, any legal or ethical scruples were removed. The cities of Japan were viewed as especially vulnerable because of the close-packed housing and preponderance of wooden construction. In February 1944 Henry Arnold, commander-in-chief of US Army Air Forces, recommended to Roosevelt starting 'uncontrollable conflagrations' to burn down Japanese cities and the military industries scattered among them. Japanese workers, like German workers, were regarded as a legitimate target as part of the enemy war effort. 'THERE ARE NO CIVILIANS IN JAPAN', wrote an air force intelligence officer in July 1945 after the Japanese government declared the mobilization of all civilians for the war effort.[95] Over Japan, American airmen did not think they were engaged in crime when incinerating Japanese civilians, but were instead speeding up the end of the war against an enemy demonized as barbaric, fanatical and criminal. 'We knew we were going to kill a lot of women and kids when we bombed that town [Tokyo],' wrote General Curtis LeMay, commander of XXI Bomber Command in the Pacific theatre. 'Had to be done.'[96] In reality, such attacks not only violated the conventional laws of war, but also the spirit of Roosevelt's appeal to the belligerent powers in September 1939 to restrain from bombing enemy cities. They also contrasted with the effort in the European theatre to distance American bombing practice from British bombing of civilian zones in German cities, which was regarded as militarily inefficient. Against Japan, urgent military necessity was used to justify setting aside conventional moral concerns about the killing of civilians. For both the British and American leadership there was understandable reluctance after the war to cite bombing as an indictable offence in the post-war trial of war criminals. When it was mooted in summer 1945 in London, the British Foreign Office insisted on deleting a charge that would otherwise have made the Western Allies equally culpable of major crime.[97]

RACE CRIMES

Among the many atrocities committed against civilian communities was a core of extreme violence that was racially based. That racial or ethnic difference could give rise to a specific category of war crimes had not been anticipated in any of the international legal instruments drawn up before the First World War. In 1919, however, the victorious Allies explored the prospect of indicting Turkish perpetrators of the Armenian massacres, an initiative that might have enshrined racial atrocity in international law.

There was no concept of genocide – a term first coined at the end of the Second World War – and no widespread expectation that racial extermination should be dealt with by international legal process. The Turkish precedent in the end proved too complex to enforce in the absence of a body of agreed law and a competent international court. Racial violence was a difficult thing to condemn in a world dominated by empires where racial difference was a defining characteristic and racialized, even genocidal violence common. When the Japanese delegation at Versailles in 1919 wanted a race-clause inserted in the section of the treaty establishing the League of Nations as a guarantee that racial discrimination would not be used against them as an Asian people, the other Allies refused. Differentiation between races was embedded in an imperial world dominated by white Europeans. Modern biological science was mobilized to confirm that there were superior races and inferior races, but racial discrimination relied chiefly on perceived cultural differences. Europeans in the imperial states regarded much of the rest of the world as semi-civilized, even uncivilized, and assumed that, even with European rule, races could not become equal.[98] This racialized view of the world encouraged deep prejudices about the racial other, not only in empire areas but in the ethnic melting pot of Eastern and Central Europe, where the 1919 settlement forced large ethnic fractions to live under the rule of the dominant national group, and left the Jewish Pale of Settlement in the former tsarist empire, where the majority of Europe's Jews lived, straddled across new and unfamiliar national borders.

In a world where racial difference and racial hierarchies played such a defining role, race was certain to be an issue in the effort to build new empires in the 1930s or to defend the old; it was inevitable with the profound dislocations of war that race hatreds would be one of the factors that encouraged atrocious crime. Hitler's Germany was by no means the only regime to promote a racialized view of the enemy or to use race as a justification for extreme violence. Japanese and Italian empire-building in the 1930s and 1940s was also racially constructed, sharing with earlier European imperialism the view that the newly subjected peoples were inherently inferior to the colonizing race, and could be treated with the violent contempt reserved for the colonized. In the Pacific war, the savage behaviour of the two sides reflected competing racial ideologies – Japanese hostility towards their white opponents and Allied racial contempt for the Japanese. In most of these cases racism was not the sole explanation for the violence, but it gave a justification that ordinary servicemen could understand, while at the same time legitimizing military violence that might otherwise have been regarded by the perpetrators as clearly criminal.

In the Asian and Pacific wars, perception of the enemy in racial terms permeated all levels of combat and the harsh treatment meted out to civilian populations. The attitude of the Japanese military to the Chinese population in the occupied territories was rooted in the belief that the Japanese were a special race, historically destined to dominate the imperial region they occupied and the races they ruled. The Chinese were commonly regarded as little more than animals, to be treated harshly if they opposed the Japanese imperial project. In the areas conquered in South East Asia, the local Chinese communities were the one racial group singled out for atrocious victimization. In Singapore, after the British surrender in February 1942, the Japanese army and secret police, in a deliberate 'purging of overseas Chinese' (*kakyō shukusei*), massacred up to 10,000 Chinese residents in acts of gruesome ferocity. In fighting the European powers and the United States, Japanese anxieties about the 'white united front' intent on emasculating Japan's racial future gave way to growing contempt for the white enemy and an indifference to battlefield violations. America was presented in the Japanese media as a barbarous country, its barbarism exemplified by the photos displayed in the press of Roosevelt holding the letter opener carved from a Japanese forearm.[99] Japanese racial hostility to the white enemy was framed by decades of resentment against the presence of the Western powers in East Asia and the persistent racial denigration of the Japanese in the West's racialized view of the world. The menace of the 'white peril' was to be overturned by the Japanese conquest of South East Asia.[100] After the fall of Hong Kong, a bedraggled column of white colonists was paraded through the streets to demonstrate to the outside world the hollow nature of the white man's claims to superiority.

American and Australian views of the Japanese also derived from long decades of prejudice, but the racial basis of the war waged by both states in the Pacific was ignited by the Japanese invasions and the savage nature of Japanese fighting. The attitude owed something to the heritage of exterminatory violence against the native Americans or the Australian Aboriginal peoples. The historian Allan Nevins concluded that probably 'no foe has been so detested as were the Japanese ... Emotions forgotten since the most savage Indian wars were awakened ...'[101] The American public and American forces shared the exterminatory vision of the Japanese enemy; in one poll of Pacific veterans, 42 per cent wanted the Japanese to be wiped out. The unrestrained violence directed at the Japanese in the Pacific was framed by the extreme racial prejudice expressed by the Allied media and absorbed by the troops. Japanese soldiers, wrote one American lieutenant, 'live like rats, squeal like pigs, and act like monkeys'. An army training pamphlet on 'The Jap Soldier' claimed that he typically gave off 'the gamey smell of animals'.[102] Soldiers responded by seeing the Japanese as game, to be hunted for sport. 'Open season for Japs' became a popular vehicle sticker, along with numerous hunting metaphors that underlined the connection between America's frontier legacy and the new frontier in the Pacific.[103] Australian troops responded with a similar racialized hostility against 'ugly yellow' or 'dirty yellow bastards', who behaved, as one soldier put it, like 'clever animals with certain human characteristics'. In an address to Australian troops in 1943, General Thomas Blamey told his men that the Japanese were 'a curious race – a cross between the human being and the ape'.[104] Against an enemy defined in such derogatory racial terms, excessive violence became normalized, as it had been for decades in contact between Asian peoples and the West.

The war in Europe was racialized in a different way. War in Western Europe generated strong hostilities, some of which were the result of crude stereotyping of the enemy, but the conflict was not a racial one. American polls showed that only one-tenth of respondents thought that Germans should be exterminated or sterilized out of existence. The one exception was the German response to the French employment of black troops in the Battle of France in 1940, which involved regular, though unorchestrated, atrocity on grounds of race. Hostility to the French use of black colonial soldiers went back to the First World War and to the French occupation of the Ruhr–Rhineland in 1923, when black soldiers were used to enforce French claims for reparations. When German units encountered the West African *Tirailleurs Sénéglais*, they took few prisoners, murdering perhaps as many as 1,500 in a series of atrocities in May and June 1940. Black soldiers fought tenaciously, sometimes lying low to attack German troops from the side and rear. German officers regarded the blacks as savages who used their traditional *coupe-coupes* knives to mutilate German captives. Not every German unit killed black soldiers, but they suffered poorer conditions of captivity than white soldiers and were the butt of racially motivated discrimination. Dead *Tirailleurs* were refused burial or a grave marking.[105]

The German wars in the East, from Poland to the 'Barbarossa' campaign against the Soviet Union, were racialized from the outset. Atrocity in this case was not only prompted by conditions in the field but was a deliberate policy dictated by the German political and military leadership and carried out by agents of the state. The German imperial project, with its core commitment to ethnic cleansing and brutal colonization, has already been described (see Chapter 2), but the crimes committed in the field by soldiers, policemen and security agents against the Jewish population of the Soviet

Union in face-to-face killings in 1941–2 were uniquely racial atrocities reflecting the racial priorities of the regime. The killing of non-Jews in the counter-insurgency and pacification campaigns had racial implications, but they were killed as part of savage and indiscriminate security operations, not principally on grounds of race. The murder of an estimated 212,000 Roma and Sinti in Europe reflected a prejudice that nomadic peoples were likely to be spies or criminals or saboteurs, though racial prejudice evidently played a part in their persecution. In the East, they were treated as partisans or their accomplices, which meant 'to be treated as Jews', with entire families murdered, often in the company of Jewish victims.[106] For the perpetrators, even the murder of Soviet Jews, which soon extended to the elimination of every man, woman and child, was not based entirely on race. The identification of Soviet Jews as the bearers of the Bolshevik virus gave a spurious political gloss to the genocidal project, while the fiction that Jews were the chief insurgents harassing German forces was used to justify mass killings from the start. 'Where there are partisans,' announced SS General Erich von dem Bach-Zalewski in September 1941, 'there are Jews, where there are Jews, there are partisans.'[107] This crude syllogism masked the reality over the summer and autumn of 1941 that Jews, irrespective of age or gender, were to be slaughtered as Jews.

The atrocities against the Jews began from the very first days of the campaign against the Soviet Union using the slender excuse that they had sought to obstruct the advance of the German army. The reasons are still not clear, though the army had always exaggerated the potential threat from the civil population. The 'criminal orders' from Hitler's Supreme Headquarters specified elimination of male Jews in the Soviet Communist Party or state employment, but no order has come to light directing the military and security forces to murder Jews indiscriminately. Very soon all Jewish men of military age were added to the list of approved victims. Even though killing selected Jewish targets had Hitler's and Himmler's approval, in the first weeks the German leadership was concerned whether the German public, and rank-and-file soldiers in the East, would react negatively to the evidence of mass atrocity. It soon became clear that this was far from the case, and from July 1941 onwards security, police and military units, as well as the four *Einsatzgruppen* allocated to the Eastern campaign, were all encouraged to collaborate in identifying and eliminating Jews as part of a wider cleansing operation in the whole occupied zone.[108]

By this stage the mass murder of Jews had already begun. On 23 June in the Lithuanian town of Gargždai, the SD arrested 201 Jews (including a woman and a child) for crimes against the German army and the following day they were executed by units of the local police. On 27 June in

Białystok, in what had been eastern Poland before the Soviet invasion in 1939, 2,000 Jews were killed by a battalion of the regular German Order Police, working on orders from the army's 221st Security Division, including 500 men, women and children who were burnt alive in the synagogue. No instructions about killing women and children had yet been issued, but by late July, probably at Himmler's insistence, the practice was approved as standard. That month, Friedrich Jeckeln, commander of *Einsatzgruppe* C, ordered the First SS Brigade to murder 1,658 Jewish women and men in a cleansing operation near Zhytomyr. On 30 July, *Einsatzkommando* 9 shot 350 Jewish men and women at Vileyka, after the commander had been reprimanded for his failure to follow the new course. From August onwards, women and children were routinely included in the massacres.[109]

The rapid escalation of the murder of Jews took place against a background of so-called 'self-cleansing', in which non-Germans in the Baltic States, Poland and Romania used the sudden collapse of the Soviet presence to vent their own savage revenge on local Jewish populations who were blamed, among other accusations, for collaborating with the Soviet occupiers. These atrocities were in some cases spontaneous, in some the result of German pressure. In north-eastern Poland, where the Soviet presence between 1939 and 1941 had been harsh, the local population murdered Jews in at least twenty towns during the interregnum between the Soviet retreat and the establishment of German authority. As German forces swept eastwards, Poles formed vigilante groups to take revenge. At Kolno on 23 June, German soldiers watched local Poles butchering entire Jewish families; in Grajewo, according to post-war testimony, hundreds of Jews were incarcerated in the synagogue where they were tortured in grotesque ways, their hands tied with barbed wire, some with their tongues and nails pulled out, and all subjected to 100 lashes every morning. In Radziłów, Poles murdered and raped their Jewish neighbours, then forced those who survived into a barn that was set on fire; when more Jews were found in hiding, they were made to climb up a ladder and leap into the flames. In some cases, the local Polish officials asked the Germans if killing Jews was permitted before embarking on the pogroms. Jews, replied one German officer, were 'without any rights' (*rechtlos*) and could be dealt with as the Poles saw fit.[110] The German authorities in Berlin kept a close watch on the violence, but did nothing to obstruct it. 'No obstacles should be put in the way of the "self-cleansing efforts",' Heydrich informed the *Einsatzgruppen* in June 1941, '. . . on the contrary, they are to be instigated, of course imperceptibly, intensified and directed into the right course.'[111]

A spasm of savage violence was also directed at Jews by the Romanian army and police when Romania joined the invasion of the Soviet Union on 2 July 1941. As the Red Army hastily withdrew from the former Romanian provinces of Bessarabia and Northern Bukovina, occupied by the Soviet Union in June 1940, local communities began a series of pogroms against their Jewish neighbours who in this case too were blamed for having helped the 'Jewish-Bolshevik' invader. When the Romanian army arrived a few days later the massacres were well under way; estimates for the number of dead in the opening days of the war range between 43,500 and 60,000. The arrival of the Romanian army and gendarmes escalated the violence. At Storojinet in Northern Bukovina on 4 July, soldiers shot 200 men, women and children while the victims' neighbours pillaged their homes. Ukrainian farmers from the province engaged in particularly savage revenge, murdering their Jewish neighbours with their farm tools; still alive, a kosher slaughterer was sawn in pieces with his own equipment.[112] Elements of the German *Einsatzgruppe D* accompanied the Romanians, but the violence was beyond provocation by the SS. Even the German observers were shocked by the level of brutality and indiscipline displayed by the Romanian forces and their local accomplices, which continued unabated up to and including the Romanian–German capture of the city of Odessa.

The Polish and Romanian violence was a mixed product of a pre-war culture of anti-Semitism and visceral resentment at the role Jews were alleged to have played in the Soviet occupation. The German authorities soon moved to end the unlimited violence and the extensive plundering of Jewish property, but the manifestations of hostility to the Jews across the whole area occupied between June and September 1941 eroded any remaining doubts about the feasibility of escalating German violence against the Jews. Indeed, a case can be made that German security forces, observing the unrestrained massacre of Jewish communities, were encouraged to embrace a more exterminatory practice themselves. It also proved easy to find enthusiastic anti-Semitic volunteers among the police and militia forces in the Baltic States, and from the occupied Soviet zone in Bessarabia and Ukraine, once it became clear that there was simply not enough German manpower to expand the killing. Auxiliary formations were established to assist with identifying, rounding up and guarding Jews, then herding them to the execution sites. By late 1941 there were 33,000 auxiliaries (*Schutzmänner*), by summer 1942 165,000, and at the peak in 1943 300,000. Occasionally Belorussians took the initiative in killing local Jewish populations, as was the case with the liquidation of the Borisov Ghetto in Belorussia in October 1941 and the massacre of its

6,500–7,000 inhabitants.[113] The denunciation of Jews in hiding or those who tried to conceal their Jewish identity was so widespread that the German authorities set up formal information posts (*Anzeigestellen*) to encourage betrayal; accurate information was rewarded with a hundred-rouble bounty, occasionally with the promise of a former Jewish home.[114]

The hands that pulled the trigger in the massacre of Soviet Jews were almost invariably German. From July 1941, Himmler and the chief of the Order Police, Kurt Daluege, substantially expanded the numbers involved in killing. To the original 3,000 members of the *Einsatzgruppen* were added around 6,000 Order Police in reserve police battalions, and 10,000 from the Waffen-SS. The personnel were regularly relieved and replaced, but the figure of approximately 20,000 German perpetrators remained more or less constant over the year of massacres that followed. These units were helped by SD and Security Police when the need arose, and by the military Secret Field Police and Field Gendarmerie. Less commonly, the army could be asked to supply not only weapons, ammunition and supplies, which it willingly did, but also on occasion soldiers to do the killing. By no means all army commanders collaborated with enthusiasm once it was clear that the killing of Jews was indiscriminate, but the views of the commander of the Sixth Army, Field Marshal von Reichenau, were not unusual. In October 1941 he announced to his men the 'necessity of tough but just atonement to be extracted from the sub-human Jewish race'.[115] Units of von Reichenau's army had collaborated in early August 1941 with *Sonderkommando* 4a, a sub-unit of *Einsatzgruppe C*, in rounding up 402 mainly elderly male Jews in Zhytomyr for execution following the arrest of two Jewish men as alleged NKVD agents. The killing in a local cemetery highlighted some of the problems already encountered in earlier massacres: victims were shot by firing squad in front of a prepared pit, but around a quarter were observed to still be alive when they fell in; shooting the victims in the head proved difficult as the killers were sprayed with brain and blood; in the end the half-dead were left to be covered by the next bodies and layers of soil. After the execution, SS and army officials met to discuss more effective ways to carry out the killings and reduce the psychological pressure on their men.[116]

Over the months that followed, the SS, police and army gradually developed an ordered set of procedures for each killing site. In September 1941, a course was staged in the captured city of Mogilev, at the instigation of the army commander of the area, on how to deal with Jews/partisans. The course concluded with a practical demonstration of the execution of thirty-two Jewish men and women. Learning by example was widespread. The killing of women and children was difficult for some of the perpetrators, so permission was given to allow women to hold their children, who would be shot before the parent was despatched. When the order to murder women and children came through to the *Einsatzgruppe* units, the head of *Sonderkommando* 11b personally demonstrated the method to his men, first shooting an infant, then the mother.[117] In Order Police units it was common at first for one of the officers to show his men how to kill with a shot to the back of the head, and then invite them to follow his example. During the second wave of mass killings that began in the early spring of 1942, the experience of the previous year was used to ensure that massacres were conducted in ways that reduced the pressure on the perpetrators and maximized the efficiency of the killing. The killing involved a precise division of labour between those designated the 'shooters' for the day, those who guarded the convoy of victims to the pits, those who drove the lorries, and those who kept the bodies in the pit stacked in enough order to allow room for the next layer. A Jew murdered at Tarnopol left behind an unposted letter describing how structured the killing seemed to be: 'Moreover, they have to sort the first, the executed, in the graves so that the space is well used and order prevails. The entire procedure does not take long.'[118] Mistakes in the theatre of execution were frowned upon (though not usually punished), while the killers were expected to remain detached and clinical, as if performing a difficult surgical operation rather than a messy atrocity. SS men who exhibited excessive brutality – and there were a great many – sometimes ran the risk of discipline if they were felt to undermine the ethos of the organization by behaviour unbecoming an SS man. Still, in passing judgment on one SS officer in 1943, the Munich SS Court observed that, however demeaning his conduct, 'the Jews must be annihilated; there is no great loss when it comes to any of them.'[119]

The atrocities performed in the field against the Jewish population of the Soviet Union continued well into 1942, overlapping the operation of the death camps set up early that year for the programme of genocidal destruction of Europe's Jewish populations. The death camps were established by the SS leadership partly to reduce the psychological strain on the thousands of German perpetrators in the massacres in Russia. Yet killing in the field continued as the German army advanced over the course of the year, catching in the genocidal net Jews who had managed to flee as refugees from the areas conquered the previous year. In the remote village of Peregruznoe on the approach to Stalingrad, a small signals unit of the Fourth Panzer Army in September 1942 rounded up all the Jewish inhabitants and refugees – men, women, children and babies – on the pretext that they were taking information to the distant Soviet lines. The commander, Lieutenant Fritz Fischer, had no orders from above. A convinced National

Socialist and anti-Semite, he may well have wanted to make his own small contribution to the wider programme of extermination. The Jews were loaded into trucks overnight, then driven out to the steppe by a small group of soldiers who had volunteered or not resisted their officer's request. The first truck stopped, the Jews were allowed to climb out, and were then shot while they ran or staggered away. To avoid the unpleasant task of killing the next group amidst the pile of dead and dying, the trucks were driven 200 metres further down the road to a clean killing field. The men finished their task and returned in time for breakfast.[120]

The killing at Peregruznoe is one example among thousands, and it raises the same questions that apply to the German killing of Jews in all the face-to-face executions. These killings were unlike the pogroms in Poland, or Romania or the Baltic States, where communities killed the Jews in their midst in a spasm of extreme violence and expropriation that lasted a day or days at most, fired by ethnic hatreds. The German killing was systematic and persistent. Order Police units, who carried out much of the killing, found themselves responsible not just for one massacre, but for one after another. Reserve Police Battalion 101 began its murderous career with the killing of around 1,500 Jews from the Józefów Ghetto on 13 July 1942, but nine months later the unit had participated in killing more than 80,000 Jewish men, women and children.[121] Unlike the instigators of the pogroms, the German perpetrators did not know their victims (though they relied on local informers to help find them) and had no intrinsic reason to hate them. The murders were carried out in cold blood, the opposite of the other examples of twentieth-century genocidal violence, and unlike the many other categories of crime described in this chapter. How it was possible for the perpetrators to kill abstractly and without discrimination, pursuing every single Jew that could be found with a remorseless forensic energy, challenges historical and psychological explanation.

The temptation is to assume that the anti-Semitic ideology of the regime was sufficiently embedded among the different perpetrator cohorts to allow them to justify their actions and quash any scruples they might harbour. Evidently all those engaged in the killing were aware that they served an anti-Semitic regime in which the demonization of the Jew as the arch-enemy of the German people was a central trope. Propaganda was directed at the men in the field to underline, as one publication in December 1941 put it, that a central war aim was now 'a Jew-free Europe'.[122] The extent to which ordinary soldiers and policemen could relate the idea of the Jew as Germany's *Weltfeind* or 'world enemy' to the huddles of frightened, disoriented and impoverished people they slaughtered is more open to question. Most accounts of the killing units in the East emphasize the importance of the instigators, the middle- and lower-ranking officers in the security services and police force, who were given additional political training, including regular courses in which the malign nature of the Jewish world conspiracy was a central ingredient. Fantasies about the Jewish menace crop up sufficiently often in the conversations and correspondence of the security forces, the SS and the army to show how readily the paranoia of the regime could be appropriated to sanction mass murder. 'The Jews will then fall on us,' reflected a German infantry-man in 1944 on the prospect of defeat, 'and exterminate everything that is German, there will be a cruel and terrible slaughter.'[123] Some units had a high proportion of National Socialist or SS members among the officers and NCOs, and among them there was clearly an element of competition or emulation in carrying out their tasks with harsh efficiency.[124] For the rank-and-file killers in the police or army no generalization can easily be made. They represented a cross-section of German society, some of them dedicated to the causes of the regime, some not. But whether sceptical, enthusiastic or indifferent, very few of those recruited to the unantici-pated role of killer refused to participate.

The social psychology of perpetration suggests that the men found a variety of ways of coping with the task they were ordered to perform, for they were not simply obeying orders.[125] The killers came from diverse backgrounds, with a wide range of personality types, and they accommo-dated themselves to the killing each in their own way. Once a standard procedure was in place, the division of labour allowed some of each unit to avoid killing at all by volunteering as drivers or guards or clerks. It was possible to refuse to take part, but some who refused one day might accept the next from a sense of shame that their companions had had to take their part. Others displayed a positive enthusiasm for killing after the initial blooding and at times had to be reined back. It is likely that some developed a hatred for victims whose fate forced them to become reluc-tant killers in the first place, blaming the Jews for what was happening, but not themselves. Evidence of gratuitous cruelty is widespread, and so too the element of spectacle as soldiers and police took pictures of the torments inflicted on the victims. The number of onlookers brought a directive from the head of the Gestapo, Heinrich Müller, in August 1941 telling the *Einsatzgruppen* 'to prevent the crowding of spectators during the mass executions'.[126] At Himmler's insistence, the perpetrators were supplied with generous measures of alcohol, often available before and during the killing. Ukrainian auxiliaries were notorious for their drunken cruelty, allegedly throwing children in the air to be shot at like birds. After killing sprees, the men were encouraged to spend evenings together carousing and drinking. Following the mass execution of 33,000 Jews and Soviet prisoners in the ravines at Babi Yar near Kiev, the killers enjoyed a banquet to mark the occasion. These evenings were designed by the SS leadership to blunt the psychological impact of the executions, which might otherwise harm 'the mind and character' of the men. Himmler hoped that they would bond together as decent Germans doing a hard job and resist the drift to brutalization and 'melancholia'.[127] Some of the killers did succumb to the pressure of routine murder and suffered nervous collapse. They were sent back to Germany, treated as victims of a tough and nerve-wracking assignment.

The view that the perpetrators were in some sense victims of the acts they perpetrated, in need of solace and recuperation, was only one of the many moral inversions that made the German killings possible. Concern for the well-being of the men involved left the actual victims entirely excluded, all but invisible in the distorted moral universe that the perpetrators and their commanders inhabited. The Jewish communities were represented as outside the moral sphere of the killers, whose primary obligations were to the rest of their unit, and to the fulfilment of their task. The consequences of a psychological process described by modern neuroscience as 'otherization' were profound. The Jewish victims became mere objects in the cruel ceremonies of their obliteration. In all the surviving accounts and testimony from the killing units, there are almost no examples of killers making even the slightest gesture of compassion for those they were to kill, because to do so would readmit the victim to a shared moral sphere. Instead, the perpetrators set aside feelings of guilt, and replaced them with anxieties in case they displayed any sign of scruple or softness or let down their companions. Belonging to the group that shared the crimes made it possible to stop viewing them as conventional crimes at all.

GENDER VIOLENCE AND WAR

Crimes committed against women in the Second World War hover uncertainly between war crimes as they have been narrowly defined and crimes against humanity. The treatment of women victims by enemy forces was certainly inhuman, and the examples plentiful. In the German invasion of Latvia in June 1941, a group of men from the Württemberg-Baden Grenadier regiment seized two female students from Riga University, tied them naked to two chairs whose cushioned seats had been replaced by tin sheets, lit two primus stoves beneath them, and then danced in a circle round the writhing victims. A year later, when German troops retook towns in the

Crimea, they found the bodies of Red Cross nurses stripped and raped, tortured by Soviet soldiers, some with their breasts cut off, some with broomsticks rammed into their vaginas. In the Asian war, atrocities against women were routine. In a northern Chinese village in Beipiao, Japanese forces raped all the women in front of their families. One pregnant woman was stripped, tied to a table, raped and then bayoneted to remove the foetus. Soldiers took photographs as souvenirs of the grisly scene.[128]

These sordid stories betray unrestricted sadism; they have in common the cruel exploitation of women for the entertainment of men, which makes such atrocities unique. Though taken at random, these examples could be multiplied many times and in many different contexts. Because of the nature of the crimes and the victims, international law was largely silent about the sexual abuse of women in wartime. In the Hague Convention of 1907, the protection of 'family honour and rights' was one of the directives for civilian immunity, and it was generally understood by 'honour' that women should not be violated in war. The 1929 Geneva Convention speci-fied that female prisoners should be treated with 'all considerations due to their sex'. But not until sexual crime was defined in the Fourth Geneva Convention in 1949 were 'rape, enforced prostitution, or any form of inde-cent assault' finally spelt out as illegal.[129] Rape was nevertheless considered a crime in most military judicial systems. Just as soldiers were not supposed to pillage enemy or ally, sexual predation was regarded as a crime that brought military dishonour and threatened military discipline. Nonetheless, sexual crime, like looting, was widespread, though its scale is impossible to measure. Women victims of sexual crimes, or other forms of what has been defined as 'molestation', were reluctant to talk of their ordeal, or unable to find avenues where their violation would be taken seriously.[130] The culture of shame was reinforced by social disapproval of the public exposure of sexual crime, and the strategies of male denial.

Sex was certain to be a major wartime problem. Tens of millions of men were taken away from their home communities for years, inhabiting almost entirely male institutions and with declining prospects of leave to return to families or partners at home. Many of them were subjected to long periods of high stress and unnatural levels of aggression, enhancing their sex drive and sense of sexual frustration. The military authorities understood these issues, but also the dangers that arose from epidemics of venereal disease if sexual opportunities were not regulated, or the men not supplied with adequate quantities of prophylactics. The Japanese Ministry of War regarded the provision of brothels for the troops as 'espe-cially beneficial' for the psychological health and fighting spirit of the men. A War Ministry directive claimed that the supply of sexual comfort would 'affect the raising of morale, the maintenance of discipline, and the prevention of crime and venereal disease'. During the war over 32 million condoms were issued to the troops to try to prevent the spread of disease, but their distribution was irregular and soldiers were encouraged to wash and reuse them.[131] Heinrich Himmler thought that regular sex in brothels would increase the efficiency not only of German soldiers, but forced labourers and concentration camp prisoners as well. Ten brothel barracks were set up in camps in Germany, Austria and Poland for privileged prisoners.[132] It was also a way of controlling sexual disease. To ensure that soldiers and SS men did not rely on fake remedies, Himmler banned all forms of prophylactic aids except condoms, which were made freely available.[133] The guidelines issued to the troops about sexual behaviour called for 'restraint with respect to the other sex', but the armed forces and SS also organized sanitation houses for the treatment of venereal disease, since the priority was not to stigmatize lack of restraint, but to get men back into fighting units.[134]

The British army did not supply brothels, though troops were not generally prevented from using them, except in the Cairo red-light 'Berka' district, where venereal disease was rife. The attitude of the army medical authorities was to assume that British soldiers would do the decent thing and abstain from using the services of prostitutes, or indeed from any kind of sex. Officers were not expected to visit prostitutes as a point of honour, and could be cashiered for doing so. Sexual continence, announced the director of medical services in the Middle East, Major General E. M. Cowell, 'is a duty to oneself, to one's family and one's comrades'. Energetic sports were encouraged as a substitute, though prophylactic sets (soap, cotton wool, antiseptic cream) were available for those soldiers who failed to resist temptation, 'the rather stupid sensual fellow', as a senior venereologist put it. If soldiers contracted venereal disease and had it treated, they were forced to wear a red tie as a mark of shame; if they contracted a disease and failed to report it, they would lose pay or suffer a rank's demotion. In the Middle Eastern theatre, the rate of infection varied over time from 34 in every 1,000 in 1940 to 25 in every 1,000 in 1942, but in Italy by the end of the war the rate was 71 per 1,000. These were relatively low levels, which suggest that the appeal for self-restraint and healthy sports in the British case was not entirely misplaced.[135]

For the German and Japanese armed forces, brothels became a central feature of wartime military culture. As early as 1936 the German military authorities decided that military brothels were 'an urgent necessity'. On 9 September 1939 the German Interior Ministry ordered the construction of barracks where prostitutes could be concentrated to serve the troops.

Here they were subject to regular medical inspection and the soldiers' access regulated to an average of five to six sessions a month. Military brothels proliferated in the Eastern campaigns, in contrast to the situation in Western Europe where soldiers could exploit the existing network of red-light districts. The prostitutes rounded up for military service were effectively incarcerated; refusal to accept military prostitution carried the threat of a concentration camp, where some prostitutes had already been sent as so-called 'asocials' in the 1930s. To fill the quotas of prostitutes, the police sent women and girls whose allegedly loose living and flagrant sexuality defined them as candidates for enforced prostitution. Increasingly the brothels were filled with women from the occupied East, Sinti and Roma women, even Jewish women, despite the fact that sexual relations with Jews were prohibited under the 1935 Nuremberg Laws. The difficulty of finding Soviet women from a society where prostitution was now uncommon meant that many of those who 'volunteered' for the brothels did so only from the desperation of hunger and deprivation. An Italian policeman serving alongside the Italian army in Russia described one bleak visit to a brothel filled with local women: 'Thin, underfed, awkward bodies, spruced up in rags, with frightened eyes, sat in cold, squalid alcoves.' A high proportion of the young girls forced by hardship to come forward to work as prostitutes were virgins, and were, in many cases, turned away. German organizers began to recruit Polish women, while Italian brothel keepers imported girls from Romania.[136] As the military retreated in 1943–4 across the occupied Soviet Union, the scorched-earth policy could be extended to the women forced into prostitution. The bodies of a hundred prostitutes were flung into the ravines at Babi Yar as German troops moved out of Kiev in November 1943.[137]

By far the largest and most coercive military prostitution service was set up by the Japanese armed forces. From the early months of the war in Manchuria and northern China in 1931–2 to the very end of the war, when thousands of enforced prostitutes were murdered in a climax of violence at the shame of defeat, the Japanese military set up a vast network of permanent military brothels, improvised or temporary sex stations that moved with the front lines, or smaller and often unauthorized holding centres where women were imprisoned and raped. Some were operated by Chinese collaborators who used local prostitutes or kidnapped women and girls to satisfy Japanese demand. The wide variety of different institutions is usually covered by the single, ironic term 'comfort station' (*ianjo*), occupied by the so-called 'comfort women' (*ianfu*). The very term 'comfort' suggests that the men were the victims of war rather than the women who suffered enforced prostitution or sexual slavery. The system operated on a very large scale. The military authorities calculated that around 20,000 women would be needed for every 700,000 Japanese servicemen. The average number of men a woman was expected to 'service' each day ranged between thirty and thirty-five. [138] Some of the women were recruited by the Japanese police from among Japan's large prostitute population; Korean prostitutes were also conscripted into military sexual service whether they wanted to or not, alongside an unknown number of Korean women kidnapped or tricked into prostitution. Estimates suggest there were anywhere between 80,000 and 200,000, with four-fifths of them from Korea.[139] Japanese prostitutes enjoyed the best conditions, signed a contract, and received small fees; many were reserved for comfort stations set up for officers, who paid more for their services. They were not free to come or go and bizarrely, like the military, could be punished for deserting their post.

For tens of thousands of the women and girls incarcerated in the wider and often informal network of sex stations, prostitution was enforced. Throughout occupied China, then later in Malaya, Burma, the Dutch East Indies and the Philippines, women were abducted, lured under false pretences by job offers, or sold by their families to meet the expanding sexual demands of Japanese forces. A number of captured European women were forced into prostitution or threatened with death. All these women victims were literal sex objects. They were classified by the Japanese logistics organization as 'military supplies'. In China, where perhaps as many as 200,000 women were abused in sex stations, women were held as prisoners and punished severely if they tried to escape. In some cases, a woman's entire family would be decapitated as a punishment and a warning to other women. There was little or no supervision of the many front-line stations set up by individual army units; some holding stations, or 'fortresses' as they were sometimes called, held a handful of women who would be raped repeatedly by the local soldiers. Accounts from Chinese survivors tell of routine brutality, poor food and the rapid collapse of health. On the occupied Chinese island of Hainan there were over sixty stations serving the small occupation force. Out of 300 Chinese women forced into sexual slavery on the island, 200 were dead by the end of the war. There was little control over the way women were treated, since they could be replaced by the next wave of abductions. Women who became pregnant or diseased were routinely killed. At one 'comfort station' in central China, women who became pregnant from the multiple rapes they were subjected to were tied naked to stakes and used for bayonet practice by the soldiers who had previously abused them.[140] No amount of special pleading or linguistic sleight-of-hand can mask the terrible toll taken of the women forced to supply sex. They were the victims of rape from the first soldier to the last; any one of the women forced into prostitution who survived 100 days of abuse might be raped as many as 3,000 times.

One of the many cruel ironies of the Japanese 'comfort' system was the hope expressed by the military authorities that it would reduce the risk of unregulated rape and the spread of disease and at the same time reassure the local population that pacification would not lead to unrestricted sexual crime. Instead, Japanese forces combined the comforts of military brothels with random and universal rape in all the areas they occupied. Rape was the most extreme form of suffering imposed on women during the war, but there were other forms of sexual molestation that fell short of actual violation. Women prisoners were often forced to strip for interrogation to increase their anxiety and humiliation; intimate body searches by men violated female integrity; the torture of women commonly involved inflicting pain on the genitals or the threat of rape.[141] The definition of rape, however, is straightforward, despite the regular male arguments about what does and does not constitute consent: rape is the sexual violation of a woman without her consent. Contemporary judicial approaches to rape nevertheless left many grey areas in assessing the degree of crime and influenced the way rape was regarded by the male military establishment. The novelist and war veteran William Wharton later recalled that there was not a wide difference between the Russian soldiers who ran down women 'the way you would a deer or a rabbit' and the American GIs who used the offer of cigarettes and food to seduce desperate women, 'as close to rape as you can get, but not too much rampant violence'.[142] Indeed, thousands of women resorted to temporary prostitution to alleviate hardship and hunger, stretching the idea of consensual sex to its limit.

Rape was also difficult to report to a male establishment, and it was difficult to get adequate redress. In the Soviet Union, the German military judicial authorities insisted that rape would only be investigated if a woman made a formal complaint and could identify the culprit, a decision that meant in effect that most rapes went unreported and uninvestigated.[143] A sense of shame or the disapproval of families also limited the willingness of victims to come forward to expose their abuse. As a result, the number of rapes committed during the war in all theatres is unknowable. Estimates of the number of German women raped by Soviet soldiers in 1945 range from 200,000 to 2 million. One of the current estimates of rapes by American servicemen in Europe, approximately 18,000, is based on a criminological investigation from the 1950s that claimed only 5 per cent of rapes were ever reported, an extrapolation that is impossible to verify.[144] A more recent estimate, based on the number of illegitimate children recorded in

Germany, suggests that there were 190,000 American rapes during the occupation period. All these estimates are statistical guesswork.[145] Only 904 American rape cases were actually investigated but clearly many more went unrecorded. In a forensic survey of four Chinese provinces under Communist control in 1946, the figure of 363,000 rapes by the Japanese occupiers was arrived at, but in the Asian theatre, thousands of women were raped and then murdered, leaving little or no post-war trace.[146]

If rape is simple to define, it nevertheless took many forms in wartime and was the product of a variety of motives. Of the many rape crimes for which there is historical record, gang rapes (or 'buddy rapes') were widespread, sometimes involving only two or three men, sometimes many more, repeatedly abusing a victim. In the New Guinea campaign, Australian soldiers came across the body of a Papuan woman tied down spread-eagled on a veranda, surrounded by a litter of seventy used condoms.[147] In the China war, Japanese soldiers commonly shared their victims, sometimes holding them in their own homes for repeated rapes over days. Soviet soldiers in the first weeks of the invasion of Germany could be seen huddled in groups around German women and girls laid out along the highway, eagerly awaiting their turn.[148] There were rapes conducted by a lone rapist, acting opportunistically, that resembled more closely rape in peacetime communities, but gang rapes served a purpose beyond mere sexual gratification, by bonding men as a group and reinforcing a masculinity challenged by the fears and dangers of war. Where one soldier hesitated to join his companions, he could be pressured into participation rather than leave open the question of his own male credentials, or the implicit condemnation of the act. One Soviet officer writing after the war recalled his anxiety when he hesitated to accept the offer of a German girl from among a huddle of victims, in case he was considered impotent or a coward.[149] Mass rapes were often fuelled by alcohol, when any remaining inhibitions were quickly extinguished, and in many cases they constituted a sadistic spectacle, to be enjoyed by the soldiers who watched as well as by those who took part, like the rape and murder of Red Cross nurses in Warsaw during the 1944 uprising by the psychopathic Dirlewanger Brigade. After their mass rape, the naked nurses were hanged by the feet on Adolf Hitler Platz and shot in the stomach, watched by a leering crowd of German soldiers, Russian freebooters and Hitler Youth.[150]

Rape in recent conflicts has been exploited as a deliberate strategy for exerting male power and to dominate or menace the enemy community. It is more difficult to be certain about the motives that underlay the incidence of mass or systematic rape during the Second World War. What is called 'compensation rape' clearly played a part as frustrated and tense soldiers seized sexual booty that they regarded as a male perquisite of war.[151] The use of rape as an expression of complete domination over the enemy community represented a more overt use of rape as strategy. In China and in Germany, Japanese and Soviet soldiers commonly raped women and young girls in front of their families, shooting or beheading any men who intervened, highlighting the powerlessness of the males and the power of the perpetrators. Mass rape in Berlin in 1945, wrote one of the many victims, constituted nothing less than 'the defeat of the male sex'. Since women of any age or condition could be subjected to rape, the desire to dominate was indiscriminate.[152] Other examples of rape on a large scale came with the release of tension after months of harsh combat and the sudden prospect of victory. The rape of Italian women in central Italy by French forces, and particularly by French colonial troops from North Africa, was a reaction to the collapse of the German front and the sudden opportunity that opened to loot and violate the local population – a prospect that some colonial troops took for granted after their own experience of colonial violence. The sudden increase in the reported incidence of rape by American soldiers in Germany in 1945, and later the same year in Japan, was a product of the same victory lust. In Germany there were 552 reported American rapes, against the 181 committed in France and Belgium. In the American conquest of Okinawa, an estimated 10,000 women were raped, kidnapped, occasionally murdered.[153] When the Japanese home islands were occupied, there followed a spasm of gang rapes by American and British Commonwealth soldiers against an enemy whose own sexual violence seemed to justify repayment in kind. In one Japanese prefecture there were 1,336 reported cases in the first 10 days of occupation. To protect Japanese women from further violation, the Japanese authorities in late August 1945 authorized the establishment of 'comfort houses' under the euphemistic title 'Recreation and Amusement Association', populated by 20,000 Japanese prostitutes as a surrogate for rape.[154] In one port city, prostitutes were told that they had to satisfy American lust to save the Japanese race: 'This is an order coming from the Gods ... The destiny of all Japanese women is the burden on your shoulders.'[155]

That rape was a crime was not in doubt in all military jurisdictions, but there was a wide gap between its illegal status and the willingness of the military to take the crime very seriously. Out of the 904 American soldiers actually accused of rape in the European theatre, there were only 461 convictions. Sexual offences made up just 3.2 per cent of American courts martial. Punishment for those convicted was nevertheless tough, to discourage further crime, and seventy of those convicted were executed. The bulk of convictions involved black or Hispanic soldiers (72 per cent),

suggesting that policing sexual crime had a strongly racist character.[156] In
Italy, the French military authorities reacted to the wave of rapes by also
penalizing North African troops heavily. Local Italian communities
blamed 'the Moroccans' as a general rule, although white French soldiers
were also involved, sometimes in 'buddy rapes' with their North African
companions. The wave of sexual violence occurred chiefly in the Italian
provinces of Lazio and Tuscany in May–July 1944; the Italian authorities
counted 1,117 rapes or attempted rapes across the three-month period
between the breaching of the German Gustav Line, the capture of Rome
and the advance on Florence. The effort to re-establish discipline involved
the conviction of only 156 soldiers – considerably less than the number of
rapes – of whom 144 were colonial troops from Morocco, Algeria, Tunisia and Madagascar. Over the same period the Italian authorities reported
only thirty-five rapes by American soldiers and eighteen by troops of the
British Empire; forty of these cases involved black or Indian perpetrators,
once again a disproportionate number in relation to the number of white
servicemen.[157]

The German military also condemned rape as a crime, but the approach
to the issue of sexual crime was based less on concern for the victims than
anxiety about military honour and the threat that rape posed to strategies
of pacification. Rape was of more concern in the Western theatre, where
the crimes were very evident and local protest possible – though as one
German officer told a French investigating magistrate: 'We are the victors!
You have been beaten! . . . Our soldiers have the right to have fun.'[158] In
France there were nevertheless only sixteen cases of rape brought to court,
resulting in six convictions with penal servitude; in Italy there were also
few cases, because the German military wanted to avoid turning the population against the German occupation that was imposed in September
1943.[159] Rape was more common in the war in the East, where close
supervision was more difficult and the attitude to Soviet and Polish
women framed by the colonization project. German soldiers knew that
legislation on race defilement was supposed to limit their sexual appetites
in the East, but evidence suggests that much of the time the military turned
a blind eye to the law. Race defilement was exploited as a regulatory
mechanism in the Reich itself, where Polish and Russian prisoners of war
or forced labourers were hanged or sent to a camp if they were found to
have had intercourse with a German. Guidelines from the Ministry of
Justice in January 1943 warned German women who entered a sexual
relationship with enemy prisoners of war that they 'have betrayed the
front, done gross injury to their nation's honour'. The women, if found
guilty, lost their civil rights and could face a prison sentence.[160]

In the broad area of German occupation in the East, however, there were many more opportunities for sexual crime, though there is little evidence of gang rape. German soldiers and security men used the excuse to search for insurgents to molest women they arrested or searched; sexual torture was used without compunction. German soldiers had a particular hatred for Soviet women snipers, the so-called *Flintenweiber*, shotgun wives. When caught they faced the prospect of sexual torture, genital mutilation and rape. Their bodies could sometimes be seen spread-eagled on the street clothed only in their uniform jacket as a warning to women not to challenge men in a man's world.[161] The military judicial system did investigate and punish a number of rape cases, particularly if the rape involved other forms of gratuitous violence or murder, and in some cases imposed a heavy sentence. But most sexual crimes earned punishment from two months to two years, much of the time spent serving in a penal battalion where distinguished service could earn remission. Returning men to active service was a higher priority. Rape was not designated a 'primary crime' and there was little sympathy for Soviet women, who lacked, according to German views of Russian society, 'sexual integrity'. Surviving case notes show that the men convicted were guilty not only of rape, but dereliction of duty or anti-social behaviour that reflected poorly on the armed forces and undermined efforts to pacify the vast Eastern region: 'damaged the interests of the German armed forces', 'damaged the reputation of the armed forces', undermined 'pacification work', and so on. These 'asocial' soldiers were given much heavier penalties.[162] Here, as elsewhere, sexual crime was deplored for its impact on the reputation of the male armed forces in the occupied zone, not for the moral lapse of the perpetrator or the terror of the victim.

In two cases sexual crime was widespread and unpunished because the military institutions involved tolerated the sexual excesses and made little effort to restrain them. Although rape contravened the Japanese military code, it was designated a subcategory in the code of conduct, and only 28 soldiers were convicted for rape by military courts during the war, and a further 495 by the domestic criminal courts.[163] In the field, soldiers took whatever advantage they could of the vulnerability and powerlessness of the women whose territory they occupied. In Nanjing an estimated 20,000 women were violated, mutilated or murdered, though this figure is unverifiable. When complaints were made to one Japanese officer about the mass rape of nurses in the city, he retorted that 'they should be honoured to be raped by an officer of the Japanese imperial army,' a view surely not intended to be ironic.[164] Rape became an endemic feature of Japanese military culture during the long wartime period, aided by the general view of the Japanese high command that sex, even under conditions of uncontrolled atrocity, helped to renew the fighting spirit of the men. Since the Japanese armed forces had access to the largest organization of military brothels of any armed force, the persistence of mass rape outside the regular system of 'comfort stations' suggests more fundamental issues concerning contemporary Japanese attitudes to women, and the enemy's women in particular, who were treated simply as objects for cruel gratification rather than as human beings. Since rape was so widespread, it was evidently not regarded as a crime in any conventional sense. Japanese soldiers were taught to operate in a closed moral universe of collective loyalty to the emperor in which respect for the humanity of those outside the closed moral order was largely absent.

Mass rape by the Soviet military differed from the Japanese experience, not least because it was largely confined to a year of extreme sexual violence as the Red Army penetrated into Eastern Europe and Germany in the final drive for victory. Although rape was also a designated crime in the Soviet military code, it was scarcely used as a charge against soldiers who violated the enemy. Sexual crime was tolerated at the very apex of the dictatorship. When the prominent Yugoslav communist Milovan Djilas complained to Stalin in 1945 about the rape of Yugoslav women by Red Army soldiers, Stalin explained that after all the horrors the Red Army soldier had gone through 'what is so awful in his having fun with a woman'.[165] One Russian officer, Lev Kopelev, who tried to prevent soldiers raping, was accused of 'bourgeois humanism' and 'pity for the enemy' and sentenced to ten years in a labour camp. Here too a closed moral universe applauded the ruthlessness with which the enemy was punished and absolved the perpetrators of guilt. Rape was only reined back by the military authorities where they could because of the indiscipline it encouraged and the hostility it provoked, but not because they necessarily disapproved of it.[166] Red Army propaganda prepared the way for the violation to come. 'Break with force the racial arrogance of Germanic women!' Ilya Ehrenburg exhorted. 'Take them as the legitimate spoils of war!'[167] Red Army men needed little prompting. Rapes began even before they reached the Soviet frontier, against collaborators or non-Russians in their path. After the occupation of Bucharest in 1944 and Budapest in early 1945, soldiers went on a sexual rampage through the cities, fuelled by any supplies of alcohol they could find. In Hungary, an estimated 50,000 women and girls were raped, though for years after the war the Communist regime in Budapest insisted that the Red Army had been model liberators and the sex consensual.[168] Across East Prussia and on into Berlin, women and girls of all ages were gang raped, sometimes

mutilated and murdered if they resisted, sometimes tortured and mutilated for amusement. 'There weren't enough women,' recalled one veteran,
'we found very young ones. Twelve or thirteen years old ... If she cried,
we'd beat her, stuff something into her mouth. It was painful for her, but
funny for us.'[169] Red Army soldiers were also fired by a raw hatred for the
enemy, and saw women not simply as an object to satisfy pent-up lust but
as a way of stamping their conquest on the bodies and body of the nations
that had violated Soviet society. Rape was also a way of stripping away
spurious German claims to racial superiority. The violence was uncontrollable and indiscriminate, targeted in many cases at women refugees, who
were more vulnerable away from their home communities. Even female
prisoners found in camps were not immune, nor a number of Jewish
women who had managed to hide through the years of Jewish persecution
only to emerge from concealment to be raped by their liberators.

For Jewish women the war years exposed them to double jeopardy,
both as victims of racial persecution and as victims of sexual abuse.
Although the German laws on race defilement had been initially enacted
specifically to ban sexual relations between Germans and Jews, there were
few cases where soldiers, SS or police were punished for flouting the law.
One of the Jewish community leaders in Warsaw, Henryk Szoszkies, was
told by a German officer trying to recruit young Jewish girls for a military
brothel: 'Don't let the race laws bother you. War is war and in such a situation all theories die out.'[170] Because sexual abuse of Jewish women was
regarded as transgressive, much of the evidence has disappeared. In the
East it was easier to conceal the abuses, and since Jews were slated for
extermination, many women could be raped first before being killed, like
the gang rape and murder of two Jewish girls by seven soldiers witnessed
near the ravine at Babi Yar, outside Kiev.[171] Jewish women were sometimes kept as concubines by SS officers, and later killed or sent to the
camps; in the Jewish ghettoes there are records of SS men and soldiers on
marauding raids to find Jewish girls to rape; some Jewish women were
sent to the army brothels for enforced prostitution, their racial identity
concealed from the military authorities; Jews in hiding could be threatened by their male protectors.[172]

Because Jews were defined as victims outside the scope of normative
justice, there was no redress for rape and abuse. Their isolation and persecution made them an easy target for non-Germans too, whether Ukrainian
militia and guards working for the Germans during the Holocaust or local
anti-Semites in the 'liberated' areas in the Baltic States. In Romania, the
army and police indulged in massive sexual violence against Jewish communities following the invasion and reoccupation of Bessarabia and

Northern Bukovina and the deportations of Romanian Jews to Transnistria. Romanian soldiers roamed the streets and markets of the ghettoes kidnapping young women for the local military bases. From the Bershad Ghetto in summer 1942, a group of girls was seized and forced to go 'through the ranks' in the barracks, where they were reportedly raped to death.[173] Much post-war testimony of the rape of Jewish women has focused on the camps, where Jewish women were entirely isolated and helpless, the victims of random and degrading sexual violence. In this terrifying twilight world of race-based sexual crime, Jewish women were forced to endure their double victimhood.

CRIME AND PUNISHMENT

The overwhelming majority of all the war crimes committed went unpunished and generally unrecorded, except through the surviving testimony of eyewitnesses. Not all military personnel committed crimes by any means. A rough calculation of war crimes attributed to American servicemen in the Pacific theatre has suggested that no more than 5 per cent were perpetrators; in a wartime survey, only 13 per cent of United States servicemen admitted to having witnessed crimes, though 45 per cent had heard of them.[174] In armed forces of great size, even 5 per cent would produce a worldwide figure of perhaps 5 million crimes, from irregular battlefield violence to looting, rape, mass execution and murder. Only the police and security forces assigned to the military theatres in Russia and Asia committed regular atrocities, above all in their role in the 'wild killing' of Jews in Eastern Europe and Russia, but also in the context of savage counter-insurgency operations. In neither case would they have regarded their own activities as criminal.

The attitude of the ordinary serviceman to crime varied widely, from strong disapproval to cynical acceptance that the frictions of total war made crime inevitable; at the other end of the spectrum was the refusal to accept that what had been done could be defined unambiguously as criminal. Memoir accounts of excessive wartime brutality commonly blamed wartime conditions for the distorting effect on human nature. 'How low human beings can come,' wrote William Wharton, 'when you take the leash off them.'[175] In many cases perpetrators could justify their actions as though they were the consequence of an abstract, external compulsion under which individual moral choice vanished. Writing of the murder of 7,000 Chinese prisoners in the diary he later published, Azuma Shirō could not think of the crime as 'inhuman or horrible'. 'On the battlefield,' he continued, 'life has no more value than a fistful of rice. Our lives are discarded in a great trash bin called war . . .'[176]

In the murder of the Jews in Eastern Europe, the emphasis at the many face-to-face murder sites was on maintaining a sense of order in the choreography of killing, even to the extent of issuing instructions for the precise size of the trenches in which the victims were to be buried and insisting that Jews awaited their execution in an orderly line.[177] When a policeman accompanying a column of Jews from the Riga Ghetto to the killing site was asked why he was shooting the old or infirm along the way, he replied: 'We are acting in complete accordance with the instructions we have received. We must adhere strictly to the schedule for moving the column to its designated site; therefore we are culling from the ranks everyone who might slow the pace.'[178] Order and orders dictated the sense of obligation experienced by the perpetrators, and obviated the need to respect the humanity of the victims. 'But someone must do it,' a police officer in the East responded to the question why. 'Orders are orders.'[179] This displacement of individual agency was also evident in the bombing war. Aircrew, whether German, British or American, did not see themselves as the agents of mass civilian killing (although that is what resulted), but as servicemen whose job was to take bombs from base to target as ordered, avoid the threats from anti-aircraft fire and hostile aircraft, drop the bombs and return home. Almost none of the memoirs by bomber crew dwell on any sense of moral lapse in violating civilian immunity, but they do reveal the powerful moral commitment that the crew members had to each other, and the priority of their own survival.

The millions of perpetrators of crimes, great or small, were not career sadists or psychopaths, but in general normal men (and a few women) who would not have contemplated theft, rape or murder in their own home communities. They were not quite 'ordinary men', as Christopher Browning claimed in a ground-breaking book on genocidal crime in Eastern Europe, because they were soldiers and security personnel, selected and trained to kill the enemy, or to combat insurgency ruthlessly, or to obey orders to exterminate any putative threat to the race. Some among the millions of military and police personnel evidently did have psychopathic tendencies, as they might well have had in civilian life, though military organizations in general tried to eliminate anyone from the ranks who was manifestly insane. The change in 'normal men' was brought about by the exceptional circumstances in which they found themselves, where the moral compass that dictated behaviour at home was weakly present or altogether absent. In the moral desert of combat in Asia and the Pacific or in Eastern Europe, perpetrators became inured to a distorted world of extreme violence where the normal constraints on sadistic behaviour or killing were reversed; such behaviour became an object of approval, even entertainment in what one historian has called 'execution tourism'.[180] In these alien environments, brutalization was a cumulative process, each unpunished act pushing the threshold of what was permissible further forward. By the end of his murderous career on the Eastern Front, one German policeman told his wife, 'he could shoot a Jew while eating a sandwich.'

The absence of a secure moral compass meant that few perpetrators expressed much regret either at the time or subsequently. Many of the atrocities were collective acts, in which responsibility was distributed across the group, freeing individuals from the usual burden of guilt. Battlefield crimes in particular supplied a sort of rough justice in the absence of any formal policing. One American submarine captain claimed after the war that when he was asked if he had conscientious qualms about all the sailors and soldiers he left to their fate in the water he would reply 'no, as a matter of fact, I considered it a great privilege to kill those bastards.'[181] Among the many depositions from the security policemen who murdered Jews in the East collected at their trials in the 1960s, any sense of moral failure is reserved not for the victims, but for moments when they let down their companions or failed in their duty.[182] In oral testimony taken from a wide selection of surviving RAF bomber crew in the 1990s, only one admitted to regret that he had behaved 'like a terrorist' in dropping bombs on civilians.[183] In all these cases, the idea of criminality was largely absent from post-war reflections. In wartime, criminality was projected instead onto the victim community as an object of profound resentment. Insurgency was regarded as illegal, and the harsh punishment meted out therefore morally justified; the Jews were defined in the National Socialist world view as conspirators bent on destroying the German people, their crime justifying the extreme nature of the German response; even sexual crime could be presented as something that the women deserved, not unmerited violence inflicted on them.

The perpetration of crime and atrocity did not follow any universal pattern. It was lesser in scale and intensity in Western and Northern Europe, where the local state structure and justice system remained in place under occupation, and crimes were more easily observed and reported. The most atrocious theatres of war, where battlefield war crimes, race crimes and sexual crime overlapped on a large scale, were areas where state structures were weak or overturned by invasion and occupation, where there was large-scale displacement of populations as refugees or deportees, and where normative justice was difficult to maintain or largely absent. In these exceptional circumstances, local communities were extremely vulnerable as enemy armed forces flooded across them. The sheer scale of the campaigns ensured that the military police and judicial authorities would be unable to restrain all incidence of crime. However, the factor that made the behaviour of the military and security forces in Asia and Eastern Europe particularly toxic was not the absence of restraint, though that played a part, but the active direction, approval, or tolerance of violence from the military and political leadership. The German 'criminal orders', the Japanese strategy of 'take all, kill all, burn all', Stalin's injunction to the Red Army in November 1941 to match German violence with their own 'war of extermination' all contributed to the degeneration of the contemporary customs and laws of war. In turn, the savagery of one side provoked, as it did with American servicemen, a reactive savagery that was largely tolerated by commanders in the field. 'The soldiers we faced I did not consider as people,' recalled a veteran of the Americal Division on Guadalcanal. 'They tortured ... prisoners and mutilated our dead and wounded. We thought of them as the lowest form of life.'[184] In these atrocious theatres of war, the victims of crime were effectively dehumanized. The same diarist who wrote of the murder of Chinese prisoners described them as 'a pack of beasts', whose status as a human enemy was 'unthinkable'.[185] Admiral William Halsey thought the Japanese were 'like animals ... They take to the jungle as if they had been bred there, and like some beasts you never see them until they are dead.'[186] Even the bombing war masked the human target in euphemistic language. When asked by the general secretary of the Federal Council of the Churches of Christ to justify the dropping of atomic bombs, President Truman famously responded: 'When you have to deal with a beast you have to treat him as a beast.'[187]

Most perpetrators of crimes and atrocities who survived the war avoided any punishment. Allied victory in 1945 swept aside any claims that might have been made against Allied forces, leaving only the handful of soldiers caught and convicted of serious crimes in prison. In the Soviet Union, justice was meted out to critics of Soviet crimes, or to returning prisoners of war accused of cowardice or collaboration with the enemy, but not to any perpetrator. Many of those guilty of war crimes and crimes against humanity on the Axis side were themselves dead by the end of the war, making the task of tracking down and indicting known offenders in many cases redundant. Most surviving perpetrators melted back into civilian society, once again within the conventional framework of normative justice and moral restraint, with their looting, raping or murdering behind them. It took twenty years before the Federal German judicial authorities began to arrest and then prosecute the hundreds of reserve policemen who had taken part in the mass murder of Jews in Poland and Russia, but their short prison sentences belied the reality that many had helped to murder tens of thousands of men, women and children. In Japan, little effort was made to indict any soldier or sailor for their war-time crimes, though the Japanese police authorities had to co-operate with the Allied hunt for servicemen regarded by the victors as criminal. For years after 1945, Japanese society continued to assume that the actions of the military were justified in service to the imperial ideal, and so could not be deemed crimes at all. One officer writing after the end of the war deplored the Western fashion of describing the massacres he had taken part in as 'atrocities': 'In times of peace, these acts would be totally unthinkable and inhuman, but in the strange environment of the battle-field, they are easy.'[188]

The victorious Allies nevertheless wanted to use their victory to under-line the wickedness of their former enemies. In lieu of finding the many millions of participants in crime, they focused on senior and middle-rank commanders who could be held responsible for what the forces under their command perpetrated in the field. That named individuals rather than abstract states or institutions were to be prosecuted under international law was in itself a remarkable innovation. There were, nevertheless, major dif-ficulties in the case of war crimes and crimes against humanity, because the Hague Convention of 1907 did not explicitly define the acts it proscribed as criminal, but simply as wartime violations that the signatory powers agreed to avoid. These limitations on the treatment of prisoners of war and on pillage (Articles XXII, XXIII and XXVIII) were used as the starting point for the discussion of war crimes, but the International Military Tribu-nals (IMT) set up to try the major war criminals in Germany and Japan had to define their actions as criminal. Allied jurists argued that there existed common and customary understanding of the violation of the laws of war and that conventional military courts straightforwardly treated such viola-tions as criminal without reference to the Convention.[189] The London Charter, agreed between the major Allies in 1944, retrospectively defined war crimes under Article 6 (b) so that the tribunals would have something with which to charge the defendants. The general definition remained 'vio-lations of the customs and usages of war', but this was to include, though not be limited to, 'murder, ill-treatment or deportation to slave labour' of a civilian population under occupation, the murder or ill-treatment of prison-ers of war or 'persons on the seas', the killing of hostages, plunder of private and public property and the wanton destruction of cities, towns or villages, or any other devastation not justified by military necessity. This was a bold step since the Soviet government and Soviet forces in the field had also indulged at some point in many of the violations on the list, while the atomic attacks still to come would stretch the idea of military necessity beyond any legal limit. When the Charter for the IMT for the Far East was announced in 1946, the complexity of the definition was side-stepped in clause 5 (b) 'Conventional War Crimes' by publishing only the opening general principle: 'violations of the customs and usages of war'. By this stage the idea of 'crimes against humanity' to include all gross forms of racial and political persecution, 'murder, extermination, enslavement, deportations', had been separated out from conventional war crimes in the final indictment presented for the European tribunal to ensure that every aspect of the war's atrocious consequences would be criminalized, and the Tokyo tribunal adopted the same distinction.[190]

These definitions were utilized in many contemporary or subsequent trials held in Asia and Europe to prosecute known perpetrators from among the military commanders, security men and policemen who had ordered or organized war crimes. In Asia there were additional tribunals in Yokohama, Manila, Luzon, Nanjing, Guangzhou and other cities, in which 5,600 were put on trial, 4,400 convicted and 920 executed. The French government established a Permanent Military Tribunal in Saigon to pursue Japanese soldiers who had murdered French troops and civilians in the last six months of the war, but it was the killing of French nationals that concerned the tribunal, rather than the persistent and widespread atrocities committed against the non-white population of Indochina. Over four years the French tried 230 defendants, and condemned 63 to death, including 37 *in absentia*, an indication of how difficult it proved to track down and extradite the accused. By the late 1940s the French authorities lost interest in pursuing war crimes, and prominent known offenders were recruited to serve French interests in the war against the Vietminh.[191] Around the same aggregate number were tried in Europe, where there were similar difficulties in tracking down known and named defendants, some of whom had fled abroad, some of whom were now in Soviet-occupied Europe where their fate or whereabouts were uncertain. In the subsequent IMT trials in Germany, conducted by an American prosecution team, 177 were tried, 142 convicted and 25 executed. The other European states conducted their own trials of war criminals accused of violations against the military or against civilians: British military courts convicted 700 and sentenced 230 to death; French courts tried 2,100, convicted 1,700 and executed 104. In all the war crimes trials between 1947 and 1953 a total of 5,025 accused were convicted and a tenth of them sentenced to death.[192] By this stage death sentences were regularly commuted to modest prison terms, while others guilty of major crimes found strategies for avoiding indictment or were treated leniently by the courts. When Lieutenant Fischer was finally arrested and tried in 1964 for the murders at Peregruznoe, the court decided – against all the evidence – that he had not committed murder as defined in the Federal German penal code, because his acts had not been deliberately cruel, were not the product of base motives, and displayed none of the 'reprehensible characteristics that distinguish deliberate and illegal killing . . .'[193]

The Allied effort to define war crimes in international law was formalized in the United Nations Charter Clause 6, where the so-called 'Nuremberg Principles' were enshrined, defining crimes against peace, war crimes and crimes against humanity. The principles were endorsed by the UN Assembly on 14 December 1946. The same month Resolution 96 (1) defined genocide as a crime under international law, and two years later the Genocide Convention was published. In 1949 new Geneva Conventions were agreed: Convention No. III, 'Relative to the Treatment of Prisoners of War', and Convention No. IV, 'Relative to the Protection of Civilian Persons in Time of War'. Additional protocols were agreed in 1977, when for the first time more explicit protection was accorded the potential victims of future bombing. Under the fourth convention in 1949, women were given for the first time specific international recognition that attacks 'on their honour' were illegal; the stipulation included rape, although it was still treated as a moral violation rather than an act of extreme physical and psychological violence. Only in the 1977 Additional Protocols to the Geneva Convention Nos. I and II was the idea of 'honour' replaced with 'outrages upon personal dignity', including rape, enforced prostitution and any other form of indecent assault.[194] Specific focus on the violence directed at women was enshrined in the United Nations Declaration on the Elimination of Violence against Women, published in 1993, but it was not legally binding. Sexual abuse as a war crime was prosecuted for the first time only in the 1990s in the special tribunals for former Yugoslavia and Rwanda.

It remains a matter of speculation whether more solid agreements on the laws of war, or an agreed body of international humanitarian law, might have limited the crimes and atrocities of the Second World War, since they have failed to do so in most of the conflicts that have occurred subsequently. It seems improbable, since even where the existing Geneva or Hague Conventions were known and understood, they had no force of law. When one wounded Japanese officer was captured on Okinawa, he informed his captors that under the Geneva Convention he was entitled to be taken to a hospital and given medical treatment. 'Piss on you shit-head,' was the reply and he was shot where he lay.[195] The widespread criminality of the Second World War reflected its vast scale, and the ferocity and determination with which it was fought. Above all it reflected the diversity of different forms of conflict and violence, from savage battlefield encounters to counter-insurgency, civil wars, colonial pacification, genocide and sexual crime, each of which generated distinct forms of atrocity and a wide spectrum of hapless victims.

11

Empires into Nations:
A Different Global Age

'The old order is crumbling and a new order is arising in its place.
Throughout the world the foundations of the old society in which
one set of people rode happily on the backs of others are being
shattered. The downtrodden peoples of the earth are turning in
their misery and degradation and are fighting back . . . Imperialism
does not liquidate itself.'
Amanke Okafor, *Nigeria: Why We Fight for Freedom*, 1949[1]

Four years after the end of the war, the Nigerian law student and communist George Amanke Okafor, his activities closely monitored by the
British security services, wrote and published a pamphlet in London setting out the post-war case for African independence from colonial
domination by Europeans.[2] A foreword was added by the American civil
rights campaigner and singer Paul Robeson, endorsing the movement
across Africa to 'shake off the shackles of colonialism'. The defeat and
liquidation of the Italian, Japanese and German empires by 1945 prompted
a widespread popular rejection of the imperialism still practised by the
British and French victors, and by the liberated Belgians and Dutch.
Despite the determination of the victor powers to cling on to imperial rule
over people still living, according to the post-war Labour minister Lord
Pethwick-Lawrence, 'in a state of primitive civilisation', the most significant geopolitical consequence of the war was the collapse within less than
two decades of the entire European imperial project and the establishment of a world of nation states. In 1960, Nigeria, Britain's largest
remaining colonial possession, was granted independence, restoring, in
Okafor's words, 'the dignity of the African peoples'.[3]

The history of the immediate post-war years has been dominated by
the vast humanitarian crisis generated by the conflict, the development of
a renewed global system of economic collaboration and international

co-operation, dominated by the West, and – above all – by the onset of the Cold War between the Second World War's erstwhile allies. Less attention has been given to the end of imperialism, yet the unravelling of empire, old and new, was the context which shaped the humanitarian crisis, the new internationalism, and the emerging Cold War. The defeat and disappearance of the Axis empires was swiftly followed by the final death throes of the older empires that the Axis had sought to supplant. In Asia, the Middle East and Africa the geopolitical structure was radically altered with the retreat of the European powers and Japan, to be replaced by a political geography that has persisted into the twenty-first century.

ENDS OF EMPIRE

The defeat and surrender of Germany and Japan in 1945, and the earlier surrender of Italy in 1943, brought to a sudden and dramatic end the fourteen years of violent empire-building begun in 1931 with the invasion of Manchuria. In none of the three Axis states did the circles who had supported the new imperialism try to revive it, or seek to sustain the radical nationalism that had fuelled it. The destruction of all three empires exposed the enormous human cost that this imperialism had carried in its wake, a cost that was now visited upon the large populations of Germans, Japanese and Italians stranded in what had briefly been colonial or imperial territory. The destruction of the new empires had been a central aim of what came to be called from January 1942 onwards the 'United Nations', a term Roosevelt dreamt up during Churchill's visit to Washington in late December 1941, but one that soon came to define the Allies as a whole.[4] In discussions about Axis surrender it was assumed that Germany (and its European allies Romania, Bulgaria and Hungary) would have to abandon all its territorial gains; that Italy would forfeit its colonies in Africa and the territories seized in Europe; and that Japan would lose all the colonies, mandated territories and protectorates occupied in East Asia and around the Pacific. All three would be confined within their national boundaries as defined by the victors. They would be nations but no longer 'nation-empires'.

The most radical national reconstruction took place in Germany. Not only were the Allies determined to restrict Germany to the territory held after the Versailles Treaty of 1919, but, following agreement with Stalin at the Yalta Conference, Poland was to be compensated for the loss of the eastern territories occupied by the Soviet Union in September 1939 by a large slice of eastern Germany. The three major Allies had also agreed that

what was left of Germany would be partitioned between them in three
zones of military government, with the final constitution of a new German nation left indefinite; after pressure from the provisional French
government in 1944, France was also allotted a small zone of occupation
in the south. There were even suggestions in London that Germany be
turned temporarily into a British dominion while Germans learned the
lessons of democracy.[5] In the end, the occupying powers failed to agree on
a united German future and in 1949 created two separate nations: the
German Democratic Republic in the Soviet zone, and the Federal Republic of Germany constructed from a union of the three Western zones. The
situation was simpler in Japan. There was only one occupation authority
under the Allied supreme commander, Douglas MacArthur. Korea, Taiwan, Manchuria and the pre-war League mandate islands were no longer
Japanese. Okinawa, the largest of the Ryūkyū Islands, was taken under
American administration until 1972. By agreement between the United
States and the Soviet Union, Korea was divided at the 38th Parallel, as it
had been in 1904 when Japan and Russia had first delimited zones of
influence. Soviet forces occupied the north, American forces the south.
Taiwan and Manchuria were awarded to Chiang Kai-shek's China, with
concessions to the Soviet Union in Manchuria, while the Pacific islands
were awarded to the United States as United Nations' trust territories.

The treatment of Italy was a more delicate matter because from September 1943 onwards Italy had been a co-belligerent with the Allies, and
in May 1945 it became a united country again within the frontiers of
1919. A military stand-off as the war ended between the British army and
Tito's Yugoslav partisans over the future of the Adriatic port of Trieste
ended with the city once again in Italy; a second stand-off with French
forces in the Val d'Aosta in the western Alps prevented a French annexation of Italian territory.[6] The former Italian colonies were all under British
military administration, while Ethiopia had been restored as an independent nation in 1941 under the reinstated emperor, Haile Selassie. There
existed a nationalist lobby in Rome that hoped to take back some or all
of Italy's former colonies as a measure of prestige in a renewed world of
empire, but the situation in 1945 was entirely different from 1919. The
post-war wave of anti-colonial sentiment meant there was scant international sympathy for Italian efforts, and article 23 of the Treaty of Peace
signed with Italy in February 1947 specifically ruled out any return to an
imperial role. But that did not resolve serious arguments between the former wartime Allies over what to do with Italy's lost colonies. At the
Potsdam Conference in July 1945, the Soviet government requested trusteeship of at least one Italian territory. Britain and the United States did

not want a Soviet foothold in Africa and persisted in refusing Soviet involvement, an attitude that added one more nail in the coffin of possible post-war co-operation between them. Neither did the United States want a solution that strengthened Britain's imperial position in Africa, and so it rejected British proposals for the Horn of Africa and the future of Libya which would have given the British a continued presence there.[7] In the end, failure to reach an acceptable compromise led the Allies to hand the issue over to the United Nations. In May 1949 the UN General Assembly rebuffed both Italian diplomatic efforts to overturn the ruling in the peace treaty and British hopes to reorganize the region in their interest. Libya was granted independence, Eritrea was eventually federated with Ethiopia, and finally, in December 1950, the Assembly agreed to grant Italy United Nations' trusteeship of Somalia, the poorest and smallest of Italy's former colonies. Faced with numerous difficulties in finding the funds and personnel to run the trusteeship in the face of organized Somali nationalism, Italian officials prepared the trust territory for independence and the last vestige of Italian imperialism was extinguished on 30 June 1960.[8]

The end of Axis empire was accompanied by an exodus, partly voluntary but in the most part coerced, of the Italians, Germans and Japanese who still lived in the territories of the now defunct empires. Most were not recent colonists but long-established communities dating back well before the onset of violent expansion in the 1930s (in the German case some were hundreds of years old) but they were penalized as somehow representative of these imperial ambitions, as some were.[9] Many Italian emigrants had already returned well before 1945, including 50,000 from Ethiopia, but in Italian Somaliland there were more than 4,000, in Eritrea 37,000 and in eastern Libya some 45,000, so that by the end of the 1940s the total of those returning to Italy reached over 200,000. An additional 250,000 fled or were driven out of Italy's brief European empire in Istria and Dalmatia. The colonists were difficult to reintegrate into Italian society; many were placed in refugee camps, which were only cleared by the early 1950s.[10] The numbers were nevertheless small compared with the millions of Japanese and Germans who were uprooted and returned to the motherland. When the war ended in August 1945 there were an estimated 6.9 million Japanese military and civilians spread out across China, South East Asia and the Pacific. The Allies planned for the repatriation of military personnel, but for civilians there was no clear-cut policy. The United States took the lead in assuming that the deportation of civilian Japanese was necessary, in part to protect them from violence and in part to signal the demise of the imperial project.[11] Many of the civilians had long roots in the colonies and lost possessions and wealth when they were ordered to leave; the rest were recent migrants to Manchuria and north China, or officials and businessmen running the empire.

The experience of those repatriated or deported varied widely. In Manchuria, the majority were women and children who were given little assistance, were harassed or violated by Soviet forces, and possessed few means of transport or access to food. Their ordeal was the harshest, abandoned for nine months or more among a hostile population and occupying force. The 223,000 peasant settlers began a flight eastward when the Red Army arrived, but many, perhaps most, had their goods and food stolen, leaving tens of thousands to beg or steal. Only 140,000 ever returned to Japan; 78,500 died from violence, disease or starvation.[12] Organized repatriation of the rest of the Japanese population in Manchuria began only in the summer of 1946, when over a million civilians were moved to camps in Japan. In the regions under American and Chinese control the programme of repatriation began earlier and was less arduous than in Manchuria, thanks to the supply of American shipping, but it nevertheless involved compulsory resettlement and the loss of home and goods. In the half of Korea occupied by American forces, repatriation of Japanese troops and civilians was declared mandatory on 17 September 1945, shortly after the surrender, and the transport to Japan began that same month; however, many civilians chose to remain, so in March 1946 they were ordered to leave by the beginning of April or face punishment. The small amount of money and possessions they could take was prescribed by the American military government. In Taiwan, the Nationalist Chinese gave similarly short notice, announcing in March 1946 there would be compulsory deportation, to be completed by the end of April. Within a matter of weeks 447,000 Japanese were shipped to Japan, abandoning their colonial past. On the home islands there began a long period of readjustment from the repatriation centres to regular civilian life. Mainland Japanese put an invisible barrier between themselves and the expellees, who remained a symbol of the failed imperial project and its grim costs.[13]

On mainland China, the deportation of civilians, chiefly in American boats, began in November 1945 and was largely completed by the following summer; numerous Japanese military units, by contrast, were kept by the Chinese government to provide public order in Shanghai and Beijing, and to combat the insurgent Chinese Communists. The slowest repatriation took place in the area under Lord Louis Mountbatten's South East Asia Command. Conditions for Japanese soldiers and civilians were deliberately poor. Military captives were redefined as 'Surrendered Military Personnel' rather than prisoners of war so that the British authorities could avoid the requirements of the Geneva Convention. They were kept as forced labourers, and even when the bulk of Japanese forces were finally repatriated in summer 1946, using American shipping again, 100,000 were kept as labourers until early 1949 in defiance of the Convention.[14] Civilians had a difficult transition. Many were placed in badly run camps with tough labour regimes. One Japanese government official in Indonesia recalled the gruelling routine at the British prison camp in which he was interned, where semi-naked prisoners were forced to clean airbase runways with a wire brush in full sun with little water or food; later he was transferred to Galang Island near Singapore, in an isolated camp with no shelter from the sun, no natural water supply, and a ration of less than half a cup of rice a day. Conditions improved only following an inspection by the Red Cross.[15]

By far the largest movement of deportees and refugees from the new empires involved those Germans who had found themselves involuntarily part of the new Reich as it spread out across Central, Eastern and Southeastern Europe, including the German inhabitants of lands lost under the Versailles settlement but regained after 1939, and now lost again. The number of those displaced to occupied Germany is estimated to be between 12 and 14 million (more precise figures are beyond historical recovery); they came predominantly from Czechoslovakia and the Polish 'Recovered Territories' in what had been eastern Germany but was now transferred to Poland. There were also expulsions to German territory from Romania, Yugoslavia and Hungary, together with an unknown number of the Soviet Volga Germans who had managed to flee westwards with the retreating German armies. The Soviet army deported 140,000 Germans from Romania and Hungary the other way, eastwards to camps inside the Soviet Union.[16] The bulk of expellees were women, children and the elderly; many fit men were kept back by the authorities to provide labour for the economic recovery of the region. Despite the Allied hope expressed at Potsdam that expulsions should be 'orderly and humane', the wave of retributive violence that followed German defeat was visited indiscriminately on German minorities with little order or humanity. Estimates of the deaths among the expellees vary widely, from half a million to 2 million, but what is not in doubt is that hundreds of thousands did die from hunger, hypothermia, disease and deliberate killing.[17] The first six months after the end of the war was a period of so-called 'wild expulsions', when German communities were forced to march across the frontier into the four Allied zones of occupation or were crammed into insanitary trains with little food or clothing for lengthy and debilitating journeys to German territory. In the first wave of retribution, police and soldiers treated the Germans as the Jews had been treated in the deportations to the East. In one atrocity in June 1945, Czech soldiers forced 265 Sudeten Germans from a train at Horní Moštěnice. The group, including 120 women and 74 children, were forced to dig a mass grave behind the station and were then shot in the back of the neck into the pit.[18] In many cases, expellees were given only a few hours' notice, sometimes only a few minutes', and could take little with them. Boxcars were filled up so that the expellees could only stand, crushed against each other, and trains were sent off with no water or food on board; the dead were removed at stations along the way. Some were at first confined in makeshift camps where the men did forced labour in conditions familiar from all concentration camps – poor food, lice, typhus, routine brutalities.

For the Allies the first waves of expulsion were challenging to deal with in zones where problems of food and rehabilitation were difficult enough for the existing German population. There were occasions when the reception authorities refused entry. American officials worried that they were colluding with what one called 'these terrible and inhumane things'. British officials reported back to London the routine atrocities they witnessed, but the Foreign Office view was to avoid condemning the Czechs or Poles lest the British got the reputation 'of being unnecessarily softhearted with the Germans'.[19] Eventually, the Allies agreed to impose some order on the expulsions. In October 1945, a Combined Repatriation Executive was established, responsible for the logistical programme of moving expellees to Germany and 'Displaced Persons' back to their countries of origin, a total of more than 6 million people. In November, an Allied Control Council agreement was announced, allocating numbers of expellees for each zone (2.75 million for the Soviet Zone, 2.25 million for the American, 1.5 million for the British, and 150,000 for the French), and for the following year the expulsions continued under Allied supervision. Conditions remained poor for the deported Germans despite efforts to establish regulations about their treatment and transfer, but conditions in Germany were seldom better. The Allies had not anticipated the vast exodus of Germans from Eastern and Central Europe, and they were settled in makeshift camps, even former concentration camps, with limited food and welfare and poor prospects of employment. In the Soviet Zone there were 625 camps by the end of 1945, in the Western zones thousands more. As in Japan, reintegrating the expellees proved a long and strenuous process among the resident German population many of whom distrusted the new arrivals and disapproved of the cost of keeping them.[20]

While the flow of expellees from the new empires moved one way, millions of men, women and children displaced by the war as refugees, orphans, forced labourers or prisoners moved in the opposite direction, either to return home or to seek a new home overseas. These victims of the new wave of empire-building numbered tens of millions, victims of an unprecedented scale of forced displacement. In East Asia, the greatest displacement occurred in China, where Chiang Kai-shek's government estimated that 42 million ended the war having, in the official term, 'fled to another place'. Post-war estimates for the entire refugee population, including those who moved more than once, suggest that 95 million people, a quarter of the population, were displaced at some point during the war. From the occupied provinces in the north and east, between 35 and 44 per cent of the population moved away. Most returned as best they could to the former occupied areas, often after months of further movement, but state aid was provided for fewer than 2 million of them. Some abandoned the effort and remained permanently displaced. Refugees who did return found the family networks broken up and their homes and possessions taken over by those who had stayed behind, an outcome that provoked a growing resentment at the communities that had not fled the Japanese but, by implication, had collaborated.[21] The return of forced labourers, colonial troops mobilized for the Japanese armed forces, and the numerous 'comfort women' forced into prostitution was the responsibility of the American and British occupation authorities and was carried out during 1945 through a programme of repatriation based on a rough estimate of assigned nationality.

In the European theatre, the wartime Allies had realized long before the end of the war that the new German empire, through the exploitation of slave labour, racial deportation and terror, had created a potentially unlimited problem of displacement. In this case, the DPs were not refugees from the German new order but were mostly taken from their home communities to service the German war machine or to fill up the concentration camps. Some were volunteers for the German military machine from the occupied East, now stranded by German defeat. In 1943, two years before the formal United Nations Organization was established, the probationary 'United Nations' inaugurated the Relief and Rehabilitation Administration (UNRRA) to try to anticipate the issues to be confronted once Germany and its allies were defeated. Welfare was to help, in Roosevelt's words, 'the victims of German and Japanese barbarism'.[22] UNRRA operated in the end in sixteen countries in Asia and Europe, distributing food aid between 1945 and 1947 valued at $10 billion. In Western Europe the administration was organized in small teams of thirteen people, composed of medical, welfare, clerical and organizational staff, more than half of them from continental Europe to help with the anticipated language problems. In the Soviet Zone, UNRRA missions collaborated with local authorities in Poland, Czechoslovakia, Ukraine and Belorussia, but goods had to be handed over at ports or at the frontier, to be distributed by government agents rather than by UNRRA.[23] By summer 1945 there were 322 teams administering some 227 centres in the Western zones of Germany and 25 in Austria; by 1947 there were 762 DP centres in Italy, Austria and Germany.[24]

The total number of the displaced non-German population has been estimated at 14 million, but once again precise figures are impossible to calculate. Figures for the areas occupied by the Red Army are uncertain since UNRRA did not operate directly in the Soviet zones. Millions made their way home in the weeks following the end of the war, aided by American trucks and priority trains. Out of the 1.2 million French deportees and prisoners in Germany, only 40,550 were left by June 1945. By July 3.2 million DPs had returned home, leaving 1.8 million in the centres run by UNRRA. Conditions at first were chaotic as the displaced were housed and fed in improvised barracks. Food was scarce despite the priority given to DPs and by 1947, when there were still more than half a million DPs in the camps, daily calorie intake was down to 1,600 per head, well below the level necessary to sustain full health.[25]

The Western Allies assumed that all those displaced would want to return home after their ordeal, but in practice the issue of repatriation was far from straightforward. Jewish DPs were given a special status as 'United Nations nationals' to protect them from being returned to areas where they had been the victims of persecution.[26] The principal problem was the reluctance of millions of East Europeans to return to life under Communist rule. By September 1945 some 2 million Soviet citizens had been returned home from across Europe, but the West had little understanding of what the transfer meant for men and women who were treated on their return as if they were contaminated by their contact with fascism. Screened by the NKVD or the military intelligence agency *Smersh*, some were allowed home, others exiled to remote parts of the Soviet Union, while thousands were sent to the Soviet concentration and labour camps. From the 5.5 million soldiers and civilians who were repatriated, some 3 million were punished in one way or another. Around 2.4 million were allowed home, but of these 638,000 were later rearrested.[27] Soviet officials and officers toured the Western DP camps seeking out those they classified as Soviet citizens for repatriation. Western armies initially collaborated in forcing reluctant deportees into Soviet hands, with the single exception of nationals from the Baltic republics, whose independence had been destroyed in 1939–41 through Soviet occupation. Thousands of Yugoslavs who had fought against Tito's partisans or who supported the royalist cause were returned by the British army against their will and were slaughtered or imprisoned on their return.[28]

By October 1945 there was enough evidence of systematic abuse of those who returned into Communist hands that Eisenhower, as supreme commander in the West, formally directed that DPs from the region could choose whether to return or not, despite vigorous Soviet protests, and the decision was confirmed by the United Nations' General Assembly in February 1946 'This so-called tolerance,' bemoaned the Soviet delegate, Andrei Vyshinsky, 'is known to history in one word: Munich!'[29] Nevertheless, over the following two years great efforts were made by UNRRA and its successor, the International Refugee Organization, to persuade Russians, Poles and Yugoslavs to return home. A hard core of 450,000 Soviet soldiers and civilians refused to return. In the end, Western states allowed large numbers of DPs to emigrate, stimulated by post-war labour shortages. In Britain, 115,000 veterans of the Polish units that fought in the West were allowed to stay; Canada took 157,000 by the end of 1951, Australia a further 182,000. Under pressure from a cross-party lobby group, the Citizens' Committee on Displaced Persons, President Truman was persuaded to pass two enabling acts in June 1948 and June 1950 to allow 400,000 DPs to settle in the United States. By 1952 there were only 152,000 dependent DPs left, most of them the elderly, disabled or those with chronic tuberculosis. The last centres were closed down by the Federal German government in 1957.[30]

'MERDEKA DENGAN DARAH' – INDEPENDENCE THROUGH BLOOD

The early involvement of the United Nations in coping with the aftermath of the Axis empires anticipated a broader commitment, enshrined in Article 1 of the founding Charter, finally agreed in June 1945, to respect the self-determination of peoples. This was more than a response to the destruction of nations at the hands of the Axis empires. It implied that the other, older colonial empires should see the destruction of German, Japanese and Italian colonialism as a prelude to a wider global programme eventually to end all territorial empire. 'The colonial days are past,' declared Roosevelt's Republican rival Wendell Willkie on a world tour in 1942, '. . . this war must mean an end to the empire of nations over other nations,' and few Americans would have disagreed.[31] 'Imperialism is imperialism whether it is old or new,' ran an editorial in the *American Mercury* in February 1945, 'and the daily routine violence necessary to maintain old tyrannies is almost as inexcusable as new aggression.'[32]

The end of the war in 1945 produced a fundamentally different

outcome from 1919, when popular demands for self-determination evaporated in the face of resistance from the imperial powers. Three out of the
four major victors in 1945 – the United States, the Soviet Union and
China – were opposed to the survival of imperial power and colonial possession. Although Britain and France hoped that as senior members of the
United Nations, and permanent members of the Security Council, the new
international organization might help to protect and revitalize their
empires after years of wartime crisis, they were quickly disabused. The war
was a watershed for the European empires. Anti-colonial critics argued
that the war against the Axis had been about securing political independence for all peoples, not just the liberated states of Europe. Drawing on the
language of the 1941 Atlantic Charter and Woodrow Wilson's Fourteen
Points, the Nigerian nationalist Nnamdi Azikiwe (later the first president
of independent Nigeria) drafted a 'Freedom Charter' in 1943 that included
a right to life, freedom of expression and association, and the right to self-
determination. Both the earlier documents, so Azikiwe argued, confirmed
'the right of all people to choose the form of government under which they
may live.'[33]The Iraqi premier, Nuri al-Sa'id, wrote to Churchill that he
hoped 'the authors of the Atlantic Charter will not fail to find a way for the
United Nations to secure [independence] for the Arabs . . .'[34] In the event,
the United Nations did not define 'self-determination' as a substantive
right until December 1950, and then it was not legally binding until UN
Resolution 1514 was passed in December 1960, by an overwhelming
majority, under the title 'Declaration on the Granting of Independence to
Colonial Peoples and Countries'. This became, the British Colonial Office
noted, a 'sacred text of the United Nations'.[35]

This was not the outcome that the European imperial powers wanted.
They assumed that 1945 would be very like 1919, with self-determination
re-established in Europe (though in a very different guise in the area dominated by the Soviet Union) but not applied to empire territories. In the
aftermath of war, all the imperial powers had a priority in rebuilding the
peacetime economy and in exploiting empire as a way to re-establish
political credibility and prestige after the sudden wartime lapse of political and moral authority. An OSS report to Washington warned that the
British Labour government that replaced the wartime coalition in July
1945 'is as empire-minded as was its Conservative predecessor under
Churchill'.[36] The new British prime minister, Clement Attlee, thought the
'simple surrender' of colonial territories to be both 'undesirable and
unpractical'. When Montgomery, now head of the Imperial General Staff,
went on a tour of Africa in November and December 1947, he reported
to the government that he considered the African to be still 'a complete

savage'. He favoured exploiting the empire 'in order that Britain may sur-vive'.[37] In 1944 General de Gaulle, at the Brazzaville Conference in French Congo, called for greater integration between the colonies and France, while ruling out 'any idea of autonomy, any possibility of evolution out-side the French bloc of empire'.[38] The Dutch government on its return to the Netherlands set out at once to develop a new form of Dutch 'com-monwealth' in a restructured empire, now that all prospect of Dutch settlement in the conquered German East had disappeared.[39] All the war-time imperial allies understood that to be respectable in the new post-war order, they would have to emphasize their commitment to the economic and social development of their empires, as they had done in the inter-war years, while at the same time avoiding the promise of independence.

For Britain and France, the changed balance of power at the end of the war was difficult to accept. They had been the two major global powers in 1939 thanks to empire, and empire might again restore their great-power status. The British delegate at the founding conference of the United Nations could even claim that the empire had been 'one vast machine for the defence of liberty' and should be retained.[40] Both govern-ments feared that the United States might insist at the founding of the United Nations in May 1945 that all colonies become trustee territories under international supervision. Their success at the San Francisco Con-ference in introducing Article 2 (7) to the Charter, confirming that colonial rule was an internal affair and not subject to interference, allowed them to develop empire again to underpin their global status. The British for-eign secretary, Ernest Bevin, was a consistent defender of empire as a means to create a 'third power' between the Soviet Union and the United States, taking up the idea of a 'tripartite system' already developed by the Foreign Office in May 1945 to ensure that the European victors were treated as equals.[41] Bevin opposed independence for India, hoped to extend the British Empire to Libya, and disliked the UN trusteeship scheme. There was strong preference for expanding the idea of 'Common-wealth', a loose (and loosely defined) association of independent states, dominated by Britain, as a global third force. (The prefix 'British' was dropped from the Commonwealth's title in 1949 to avoid accusations of neo-colonialism.)[42] Bevin took up another Foreign Office idea for a bloc of European imperial powers – Britain, France, Belgium – exploiting 'Eurafrica' to help secure, he told the British Cabinet in January 1948, 'an equality with the Western hemisphere and the Soviet blocs'.[43] Hugh Dal-ton, chancellor of the exchequer, thought that with the exploitation of African resources 'we could have the US dependent on us'.[44] The project petered out because of lukewarm support from the French government.

The French planned instead to create a new constitutional framework for their empire which would bind the colonies more closely to metropolitan France, by promising citizenship status to colonial subjects and a limited version of local autonomy. The French Union was founded following a plebiscite in 1946, but it soon became clear that its purpose was to ensure the long-term survival of a colonial relationship in which colonial subjects would not enjoy the same suffrage, civil rights, welfare provision or economic opportunities enjoyed by the French. There was no intention that the Union would allow national independence; Union meant ties that bound the empire more tightly.[45]

Much of the programme to revitalize empire was wishful thinking. Britain, France and the Low Countries faced severe problems of economic recovery. Britain was almost bankrupted by the war, the French economy undermined by years of occupation. Reliance on the United States for economic assistance was unavoidable, and the revival of empire as a source of economic strength was compromised by American insistence after the Bretton Woods agreement in 1944 that closed imperial trading systems and currency areas would have to be dismantled in favour of a global system of freer trade. The introduction of the European Recovery Program in 1947, generally known as the Marshall Aid plan, tied the European empires more closely to reliance on America. When Britain denied the United States unconditional access to Jamaican bauxite, the Marshall Aid loan of 1949 was made conditional on British compliance.[46] If empire was a source of markets and materials, it was also costly. To appear less colonial both Britain and France established development programmes – the British Colonial Development and Welfare Act in 1945, the French Economic and Social Development Fund a year later – but much of the money was to encourage economic projects in the empire that would benefit the revival of living standards for the home population, rather than contribute to projects for the subject peoples. The money used by the British came from colonial credits blocked in London for the duration of the war, a sleight-of-hand that avoided having to use British taxpayers' money.

Nor did the imperial powers realize the extent to which the survival of empire would become a battleground at the United Nations and a major factor in the transition from wartime alliance to Cold War. From 1946 onwards the Soviet Union chose to renew the campaign against imperialism that had dropped away at the start of the German–Soviet war. In a widely publicized speech in 1947 to representatives of communist organizations in Europe (Cominform), Andrei Zhdanov announced the Soviet view that there were now 'two camps' in the world, the imperialist and anti-democratic camp, and the anti-imperialist and democratic camp. The

Soviet aim was to fight against 'new wars and imperialist expansion'.[47] The British Colonial Office began to monitor Soviet activity as a 'champion of colonial peoples' and instructions were sent by Bevin to all diplomatic missions in 1948 on 'Countering Soviet Attacks on Colonialism'.[48] A French Interior Ministry official warned the American ambassador in April 1947 that one of the principal aims of Soviet communism was 'the disintegration of existing colonial possessions' in order to enfeeble the colonial powers and make them easy prey 'for ultimate Communist domination'.[49] The Soviet delegation to the United Nations was at the forefront of criticism of colonialism and demands for self-determination, including sponsorship of Resolution 1514 in 1960 by the Soviet premier, Nikita Khrushchev, but the prevailing sentiment of the Assembly was anyway hostile to the survival of empire, and even more so with the passing of the Declaration on Human Rights in 1948, which was regularly invoked in the anti-colonial campaign thereafter. A British official observed in 1947 that, ever since the founding of the United Nations two years before, 'world attention has been focused on colonial questions'. A decade later a British report on work at the United Nations concluded, rightly, that it was 'infinitely less favourable to the interests of Western Europe than the composition of the League . . .'[50]

The main impulse for the collapse of the old empires came, however, from the growth of nationalist and anti-colonial sentiment across the colonized world encouraged by the course and consequences of the war. Even without the war, demands for self-government and independence would have challenged the imperial systems, as they had done in 1919, but the speed with which the old empires disappeared after 1945 was the product of a worldwide hostility to empire in its traditional form and the establishment of networks of anti-imperialists in the wake of wartime mobilization. The change was symbolized by the organization of a Pan-African Congress in Manchester in October 1945, where representatives from sixty countries and anti-colonial movements met to stimulate the demand for emancipation from colonial rule and an end to racial discrimination. Wartime recruitment into trade unions or labour corps in the empire gave an additional foundation for organized protest, which linked up with the campaign of Marxists, such as the Trinidadian George Padmore, to see the struggle against empire in terms of economic entitlement.[51] The Jamaican founder of the People's National Party, Norman Manley, worked with the Jamaican Progressive League founded in New York's Harlem, and exhorted black American workers to battle not only for their own rights but for 'minority and colonial groups all over the world'.[52] Networks could reach even the most remote corners of the empire. In

1945, on Guadalcanal, scene of one of the most dramatic battles of the war, Jonathan Fifi'i, a sergeant in the wartime Solomon Islands Labour Corps, wanted to create a national political movement after working side by side with American black soldiers: 'We felt angry,' he later recalled, 'that we had been treated like rubbish' by the British. Citing the UN Charter in support, he and others helped to found *Maasina Ruru* (Rule of Brotherhood), which set up an alternative tribal system of authority, refused to pay taxes and boycotted British 'native councils'. The British authorities responded in the Solomons with Operation 'De-Louse', to suppress the movement. Thousands were imprisoned for sedition until the early 1950s.[53]

The wave of anti-imperial nationalism proved this time to be irreversible, and it was met by the old imperial powers with an uneven mix of expedient compromise and extreme violence. The crises of empire when they came were not unpredictable, like an earthquake, but their effects were seismic. The collapse of the European Asian empires between 1946 and 1954 ended centuries of empire-building in eight years. For Britain, this was a central concern because the great arc of empire from India through Burma to Malaya and Singapore was the largest and richest part of the whole; essential, so it was argued, to the continuation of a secure British presence in Asia and a global status. The wartime crisis in India prompted by the Quit India campaign in 1942 had been suppressed, but the war years created a mass movement dedicated to the idea that after the obligations and sacrifices of war, *azadi* (freedom) and *swaraj* (self-rule) must follow. 'We suffered in the war,' one Indian soldier claimed in 1946, '... we bore with this that we might be free.' More than a million were demobilized in 1945 to return to villages and towns dislocated by war.[54] The desire for independence from British rule, sustained by political elites in the 1930s, was now a populist demand on a large scale. The All-India Muslim League grew from a party with little more than 1,000 members in the late 1920s to a mass party of 2 million by 1946. In 1940, the League published the Lahore Resolution, setting out the aspiration for a sovereign Muslim Pakistan.[55] The Indian National Congress became an alliance of popular nationalist forces by the war's end with a mass rural and urban following. When, on 14 June 1945, Congress leaders were finally freed from prison to continue the campaign for an end to British rule, they found a changed movement. Jawaharlal Nehru, the freed Congress president, warned Stafford Cripps, now President of the Board of Trade in the new Labour government, that independence was now unavoidable: 'People have grown desperate ... there must be no prevarication.'[56]

The attitude of the Attlee government was uncertain, but the magnitude of the impending crisis was beyond doubt. Food shortages, widespread labour protests, and a full-scale naval mutiny in spring 1946 by Indian sailors stationed at Bombay (Mumbai) were all linked by the popular press and local Indian politicians with the broader issue of freedom for India. The Indian government's ill-judged decision to put on trial members of the Indian National Army because of their association with the Japanese enemy became a national cause célèbre, prompting violent protests. The British presence was in truth too weak to hold on to a subcontinent seething with hostility to the continuation of the Raj. By 1946 there were only an estimated 97,000 Britons in the whole of India, while the great bulk of the army and police force was Indian. Elections held in the spring of 1946 gave an overwhelming mandate for change. Muhammad Jinnah's Muslim League won all the majority Muslim provinces, the Congress Party the rest. Indians now ruled in all the provinces. The viceroy, Field Marshal Wavell, communicated the unfolding political drama to London with a mounting pessimism; India was close to ungovernable by the summer of 1946. The extent to which the government in London understood how parlous the situation had become was limited, but the decision was finally taken to send a Cabinet Mission to India, headed by the secretary of state for India, Lord Pethwick-Lawrence, to work out a constitutional future for an independent Indian dominion under the crown. In June 1946 the mission finally proposed a complicated federal structure of a central all-India government responsible for defence and foreign policy, with provincial federations representing majority Muslim or Hindu populations responsible for most domestic issues. A constituent assembly was to be elected and an interim Indian government installed. The proposal quickly broke down: Congress feared that the British planned to 'Balkanize' India; the All-Muslim League wanted a firm commitment to Pakistan and began to advocate partition. The British found it impossible to police the growing violence and local government passed rapidly into the hands of Indians.

Evidence that the crisis in India was beyond redemption by the British regime came in mid-August 1946, when savage rioting broke out in Calcutta (Kolkata) between rival Muslim and Hindu followers during the Direct Action Day called for by Jinnah in response to the British proposals. The violence replicated clashes that had been seen across northern India for more than a year on the religious fault lines in Punjab and Bengal, but it was on a more vast and more lethal scale. Gangs roamed the city murdering and mutilating each other with improvised weapons, burning stores and houses together with their inhabitants, abducting and raping women and girls, but it was not until six days later that the viceroy finally ordered in British, Indian and Gurkha troops. Estimates on the deaths range widely from the official figure of 4,000 to as many as 15,000, with more than 100,000 injured. The subsequent Calcutta Disturbances Commission of Enquiry decided nothing, and there was nothing the British could do with limited military power to stem the spread of further violence.[57] Killings escalated across the winter of 1946–7 fuelled partly by the continuing uncertainty over what the British intended to do after the failed Cabinet Mission and by the fear generated in minority Hindu and Muslim communities that they might end up on the wrong side of any religious demarcation line.

In March 1947 Wavell was replaced by Lord Mountbatten as viceroy with a brief from London to find any solution that would allow British withdrawal. He decided that partition into two states, one Muslim and one Hindu, was unavoidable and, once the British Cabinet was persuaded, he announced on radio on 3 June 1947 that the subcontinent would be divided into two sovereign British dominions, India and Pakistan. The decision was implemented with indecent haste. Independence Day was set for 15 August 1947 and British forces and officials began to pull out at once. The partition boundaries were defined at speed and millions of Muslims, Hindus and the minority Sikhs (whose views had largely been ignored) found themselves in a state of virtual civil war. No precise estimate of the subsequent death toll can be made, but it fluctuates between half a million and 2 million; there were 3 million refugees crossing the religious divide. It took years before the legacies of Britain's sudden abdication in India were overcome. In 1949 both new states became republics, rejecting continued status as British dominions under the crown.

Nothing confirmed the end of empire quite so decisively as the independence of India and Pakistan. The following year Ceylon (Sri Lanka) became the first crown colony to be granted independence. While India was in the throes of independence, Burmese nationalists began a campaign to oust the British, spurred on by the brief period of 'independence' experienced under the Japanese. The Burmese National Army, which under Aung San (popularly known as Bogyoke) had switched sides from support for Japan to fight with the Allies, expected Britain to relinquish its discredited rule. Aung San headed the main nationalist political party, the quaintly titled Anti-Fascist People's Freedom Movement. Under its auspices, paramilitary People's Volunteer Organizations were set up to mobilize the countryside for the national cause, hoarding British and Japanese weapons left over from the war. The evidence of what was happening in India spurred Burmese nationalists on. Burma, too, became almost ungovernable during the course of 1946 with large areas of the country virtually out of British control. A wave of strikes in the autumn threatened to cripple the country, while the evidence was all around that an armed rebellion against British rule was likely. Montgomery told the chiefs of staff that Britain simply lacked the manpower to hold on to Burma since Indian forces could no longer be used to suppress an anti-British insurgency. On 20 December 1946, Attlee announced in Parliament that Britain would now 'hasten forward the time when Burma shall realise her independence', though he still hoped Burma would remain in the Commonwealth and be tied closely to Britain with trade and defence deals.[58] In January 1947 Aung San visited London, where agreement was reached on Burma becoming independent in January 1948. Aung San was assassinated in July 1947 by a squad of heavily armed militia working for the corrupt right-wing politician U Saw, who hoped to maintain close business ties to Britain. He was tried, found guilty, and hanged. On 4 January 1948 Burma became an independent state, but a republic, outside the Commonwealth. Only then did the unstable mix of nationalist, communist and separatist forces in the country descend into a long period of violent confrontation. In this case, as in India, Britain left before the violence had to be confronted by British forces.[59]

The same was not the case in South East Asia where the colonies captured by the Japanese were reoccupied with waves of violent repression, in Malaya, French Indochina and the Dutch East Indies. In contrast to the loss of south Asia, the British, French and Dutch sent large armed forces in the years following 1945 to recapture the colonies and to prevent nationalist movements from swiftly ending colonial rule. For all three imperial powers, South East Asia retained its importance as an economic resource, particularly for generating much needed dollar earnings; for all three, fear of the spread of communism, now the new global enemy after the defeat of the Axis, helps to some extent to explain the degree of violence eventually exerted. Above all, the violence displayed by the insurgent groups against the returning colonizers prompted savage wars to re-establish control that in many ways resembled the counter-insurgency campaigns waged by the Axis in Europe and Asia. In Indonesia, the Japanese patronage of the independence movement and eventual granting of 'independence' to the nationalist leaders Sukarno and Muhammad Hatta on the eve of the Japanese surrender, led to the declaration of an independent Indonesia on 17 August 1945. As in Burma and India there was a broader populist movement that blossomed during the war, committed to the ideal of *merkeda*, freedom from colonial oppression. Among young Javanese, the *pemuda* movement created a radical, rebellious generation, committed to violent rejection of a Dutch return: 'we extremists,' broadcast a charismatic *pemuda* leader, Bung Tomo, '. . . would rather see Indonesia drowned in blood and sunk to the bottom of the sea than colonized once more!'[60] The Allies nevertheless assumed that they would restore some form of Dutch rule and British Empire forces were despatched to Java and Sumatra in September 1945, to be followed by the first Dutch contingents the following spring. British commanders found the returning Dutch officials intransigent on the question of resuming control. Many of them had sat out the war in 'Camp Colombia' in Australia waiting for the chance to resume old colonial habits and had little sense of the changed popular mood. When the short-sighted lieutenant governor, Hubertus van Mook, arrived in October 1945 to resume his duties, he was greeted by placards that he was unable to read. 'Death to van Mook,' his aides discreetly informed him.[61]

British forces remained until November 1946, caught between a Republican government that the Dutch would not accept, Dutch military and police units which behaved with conspicuous violence against the Indonesian population, and a disorganized insurgency that took a continuous toll of Dutch lives. This did not stop the *pemuda* from assuming that the British were a barrier to independence too. Before the evacuation of British Empire forces, they fought a pitched battle in November 1945 against nationalist forces in the port city of Surabaya, where *pemuda* militia, heavily armed by the outgoing Japanese, seized the town, killed the local British commander and engaged in grotesque acts of murderous vengeance against the Dutch and Eurasians trapped in the city, severing heads, limbs and genitalia.[62] The response was nevertheless out of all proportion. A naval barrage, followed by an assault by 24,000 troops, 24 tanks and 24 aircraft reduced much of Surabaya to rubble, killing an estimated 15,000 Indonesians, most of them caught in the crossfire, but leaving 600 dead from British forces. There was less fallout than expected from the destruction; a ceasefire with the insurgents was negotiated, and a semi-independent status offered to the Republic, but talks broke down by the summer of 1947.

Dutch hardliners insisted on a military response. The Dutch sent 160,000 troops and 30,000 militarized police to Indonesia between 1945 and 1949, and a body of 'shock troops' (the *Depot Speciale Troepen* led by Raymond Westerling) to instil terror into the nationalist resistance.[63] Little connection was made between the Dutch wartime resistance and the savage repression of Indonesians, even though politicians who endorsed the repression had themselves been resisters.[64] A popular saying – 'If the Indies are lost, ruin will follow' – kept the Dutch public committed to a war whose conduct violated conventional rules of engagement. To avoid accusations of war crimes, the Dutch forces called their campaign 'police actions'. Detention without trial, torture during interrogation and arbitrary killings became structural elements of the counter-insurgency. 'You need to be as hard as stone here,' wrote one Dutch soldier, 'and you mustn't let the suffering and misery get to you.' The watchword for soldiers who arrived from the Netherlands was 'Shoot before you are shot and don't trust anyone black!'[65] Over the course of the four years of conflict an estimated 100,000–150,000 Indonesians were killed, some caught in the crossfire, others the victims of inter-ethnic violence, in a war that proved in the end too costly in lives and money for the Dutch government to justify to an increasingly critical public. On 27 December 1949, Queen Juliana formally presided over the transfer of power to President Sukarno following agreement that they would be equal partners in a 'commonwealth'.[66] The agreement soon foundered on Dutch insistence on retaining the remnant Western New Guinea as a sop to the disappointed colonial lobby. Plans to turn it into a model settler colony failed to materialize, and Indonesian claims almost brought the two sides to war until the Netherlands relinquished the territory to the United Nations Organization, which promptly granted it to Indonesia in 1963.[67]

Mountbatten's South East Asia Command was in the initial firing line in Vietnam as well, when British Empire troops occupied the south of the country up to the 16th Parallel, while Chinese Nationalist forces occupied the north. Here, as in Indonesia, the Japanese surrender was used as the opportunity for nationalists grouped in the Communist-led Vietminh to declare independence as rapidly as they could. The Communist leader Ho Chi Minh arrived in Hanoi in late August 1945 and on 2 September, the date of the formal Japanese surrender, citing the United Nations commitment to self-determination and equality of peoples, he declared the independent Democratic Republic of Vietnam to a vast and emotional crowd.[68] A provisional government for the whole of occupied Vietnam was established. A few days later the British General Douglas Gracey assumed command of the south, to be followed by the French General Philippe Leclerc with an expeditionary force whose purpose was ostensibly to re-establish, in his words, 'the future of the white race in Asia'.[69] One of the first acts of liberated French soldiers was to hang some of the Vietminh 'People's Committee' set up in Saigon to represent the Hanoi government. The British reacted violently to the advance of poorly armed Vietminh towards Saigon, imposing martial law and ordering troops to shoot on sight any 'armed Annamese'.[70] The British repression was soon eclipsed by a ferocious counter-offensive by French colonial forces ordered by the man chosen as French high commissioner, Admiral Georges-Thierry

d'Argenlieu, a fervent Catholic and former monk who wanted the Vietnamese to accept the authority of Christian civilization. In defiance of
instructions from Paris, d'Argenlieu established a separate Republic of
Cochin China (the core of later South Vietnam) and stamped a brutal
French authority on the south of the country. In the north, a National
Assembly called by the Vietminh met in October 1946 in Hanoi and
elected Ho Chi Minh as president. When it was clear that the French
wanted Vietnam to become an associate member of the French Union and
not an independent state, an open war broke out between the Vietminh
and the French, which continued, despite sporadic attempts at compromise, for the following eight years.

The French, with growing United States support, fought a draining war
against the guerrilla forces of the Vietminh. In 1949, in an attempt to find
a compromise, the French authorities chose the former emperor of Annam,
Bao Dai, who had briefly been installed by the Japanese in 1945, as leader
of a unitary state within the French Union. The provisional central government was formally established on 2 July 1949. France still effectively
controlled Vietnam, and the appointment of Bao Dai made little difference to the war, since the Vietminh refused to accept the absence of full
independence. By the early 1950s, there were 150,000 French and colonial troops in Vietnam, supported by a probationary national Vietnamese
army around 100,000 strong, trained and officered by the French army to
wage what for these soldiers was a civil war.[71] Military units were inse-
curely stationed in central and northern areas where the Vietminh, with
its largely Communist core, controlled wide areas of the peasant countryside. By this time the insurgents had the support of China, after Mao
Zedong's victory over Chiang's Nationalists in the civil war, and from
Stalin, who until 1950 had refused to recognize the Democratic Republic
of Vietnam. As a result the conflict now assumed a Cold War dimension.[72]
The region operated under two different regimes, one based on Saigon,
and the other in the regions dominated by Ho Chi Minh in the centre and
north of the country. In early 1954 the French military commander, General Henri Navarre, planned a final showdown with Vietminh forces; the
small village of Dien Bien Phu, near the border between northern Vietnam
and Laos, was chosen as the site, designed to tempt the enemy into a
major battle. The area was turned into a large fortress, and 13,200 paratroops were flown in to stiffen the local force. Navarre hoped the Vietminh
would assault the fortress in futile frontal attacks and be mown down.

Navarre expected the battle to be decisive for the future of France in
Vietnam, and so it proved to be. Reinforced with heavy weapons supplied
by the Chinese, the Vietminh commander, Vo Nguyen Giap, brought

100,000 soldiers and auxiliaries across the mountains surrounding Dien Bien Phu and in March 1954 began a siege of the French base rather than a frontal assault. Heavy artillery ruined the makeshift landing strip, preventing further air supplies. The small artillery redoubts outside the main fortress were picked off one by one; persistent shelling wore down the defenders, who were short of food and ammunition and medical supplies. On the night of 6/7 May the French surrendered. The following day was the start of negotiations in Geneva in a summit called by Britain and the Soviet Union to try to resolve the crisis in Vietnam. French defeat made it inevitable that colonial aspirations would finally be dashed. Agreement was reached to divide Vietnam into two states. France abandoned Indochina, and North Vietnam, South Vietnam, Laos and Cambodia became independent sovereign states. The cost in casualties was large for both sides, though uneven. An estimated 500,000 Vietnamese died in the first war for independence, while 46,000 French and colonial troops were killed – not far short of the losses sustained in the defeat of 1940.[73]

While the French fought a full-scale war in Vietnam, the British reimposed colonial possession of Malaya and Singapore. Although the success in Malaya in avoiding anything on the scale of insurgency in Indonesia and Vietnam has often been attributed to British efforts to win 'hearts and minds' instead of engaging in brutal and failed campaigns of pacification, in this case, too, insurgency encouraged a protracted and brutal war from 1948 until the late 1950s, the last colonial war in Asia. The Japanese presence created the conditions that prompted the rejection of colonial rule. The large Chinese population of the peninsula, around 38 per cent of the total, had played a major part in opposing the Japanese occupation through the Malayan People's Anti-Japanese Army and the Malayan Communist Party. At the end of the war the army was disbanded but the radicalism of the war years remained, encouraged by widespread hunger and unemployment resulting from the dislocation caused by Japanese occupation. Over the two years following the end of the war there were regular strikes and protests at the poor conditions existing under a British Military Administration, and then under a renewed civilian colonial regime. The war generated a similar crisis of legitimacy for the returning colonial power and resentment at the reimposition of British commercial exploitation of the peninsula. Alongside the Communist Party, the Malayan Nationalist Party and the 'Generation of Aware Youth' (API), modelled on the Indonesian *pemuda* movement, called for an end to empire under the slogan *Merkuda dengan darah*, 'independence through blood', a text used to convict the API leader Ahmad Boestamam in 1947.[74] The British counted on the political and ethnic divisions in Malaya to prevent a united rebellion and in 1947 created a Federation of Malaya that favoured the Malay majority, but the breakdown of order in parts of the peninsula was already evident. A full clash developed only in 1948 as the colonial regime became more illiberal in its treatment of the press and the political parties. In June 1948, the governor declared a 'State of Emergency', a legal device based on the British 1939 Emergency Powers Act passed at the start of the war, which allowed the colonial regime here (and later in Kenya, Cyprus and Oman) to arrest without trial, hold suspects in detention camps, employ torture during interrogations, impose curfews, criminalize 'seditious literature' and even to kill wanted suspects on the spot. One of the first murders, in an armed police raid on an isolated hut in July 1948, was of the former commander of the anti-Japanese guerrilla force, who had led the Malayan contingent at the victory parade in London three years before.[75]

The emergency lasted for a further ten years during which British and Malay security forces used every measure to extinguish resistance. The active insurgent groups of the Malayan Races Liberation Army never numbered more than 7–8,000 but they had wide support among the population. Most were Chinese, as they had been in the anti-Japanese war, but not all. Although not all were communists, the British authorities assumed this was the case, so this insurgency too became linked to wider Cold War fears for empire. The reaction here, as in Indonesia, was entirely disproportionate. Despite persistent claims at the time and since that the British employed only 'minimum force', field manuals made reference only to the minimum force necessary, which was open to wide interpretation. Necessary force, as the British secretary of state for war told Parliament, 'will be quite a lot of force'.[76] It included regular naval gunfire aimed speculatively at small guerrilla camps; for eight months in 1955 during Operation 'Nassau', naval bombardment was conducted almost every night.[77] By the peak in 1952, there were 40,000 British troops, 67,000 police and 250,000 armed Malayan 'Home Guard', recruited largely from Malays hostile to the Chinese and to communism, to enforce the emergency. This was an exceptional level of security in a population of only 6 million.[78]

The rebels were treated with scant regard for legality. To justify the repression the Colonial Office revoked the term 'insurgent' and substituted 'bandit', as the Germans had done fighting partisans in Europe during the war. Sir Henry Gurney, the governor general in 1949, admitted privately that 'the police and the army are breaking the law every day'.[79] Only in 1952 did the Colonial Office finally ban the practice of bringing back severed heads from anti-guerrilla operations for purposes of identification, the same year that 'bandit' was dropped in favour of the Cold

War acronym CT (communist terrorist). Emergency regulations ostensibly legalized 'reasonable force', which was taken to mean that suspects could be shot in so-called 'free fire zones' without recrimination; detention camps were set up for suspects held without trial; under regulation 17C deportation was authorized, allowing the authorities to deport 20,000 Chinese to mainland China.[80] To prevent the local population from providing support for the insurgents, the British finally authorized a compulsory resettlement scheme. Some half a million Chinese were moved from the forest fringes to 'New Villages', surrounded by barbed wire, with gun towers and a guarded entrance. The villagers were supposed to provide information on the whereabouts of guerrilla fighters and failure to do so was penalized by reduced rations, shop closures and curfews. By 1954, there were 480 New Villages, while a further 600,000 labourers had been relocated to make it easier to control them. Three years later more than two-thirds of the insurgents were dead and the communist threat was deemed to be ended. Malaya was granted independence in 1957 under the rule of Tunku Abdul Rahman, winner of the first national elections in 1955 with an overwhelmingly Malay electorate.

The end of empire in South East Asia sustained wartime violence and coercion for a decade after the end of the war. Independence was won as much as granted by imperial powers uncertain how to recolonize lost territories. The collapse of empire across Asia was finally celebrated as a historic landmark with the Bandung Conference of Afro-Asian states held in the Indonesian city of Bandung from 18–24 April 1955. The 29 states present, including Communist China, represented 1.5 billion people, more than half the world's population. The conference summed up the rejection of 'Westernism' made explicit through the movements for independence. The final communiqué called for an end to all surviving colonialism or attempts at neo-colonialism. The organizers saw the conference as a symbolic landmark of the changing post-war order. The conference organizer, Indonesia's President Sukarno, hailed a 'departure in the history of the world', when Asian and African countries could finally meet as 'free, sovereign and independent'.

The freedom of colonies, protectorates and trust territories in Africa was still to be won. After the first wave of decolonization, this remained the only region of the world where the imperial powers still exercised significant colonial rule. Here they believed they were on safer ground once the disruption of war was over. Where Asian nationalism was a force difficult to confront, national movements in Africa were less developed. Although France, Britain and Belgium paid lip service to the idea that they were developing African territories as examples of 'liberal imperialism', it was widely assumed that self-determination was a distant goal for peoples not yet fit to govern themselves. Some territories, claimed the British colonial minister Henry Hopkinson in 1954, 'can never expect to be fully independent'.[81] The British historian Hugh Seton-Watson lamented that extending democracy to Africans would indicate the 'tragic decay of civilization' and 'a reversion to barbarism'. Europeans, he continued, will be replaced by 'the goat, the monkey, and the jungle'.[82] Nevertheless, the imperial powers were expected under the terms of the United Nations' Charter to 'accept the obligation . . . to assure the progress of dependent populations', and this included progress towards self-government. Once independence had been granted across Asia, resisting the extension of self-determination to African colonies and protectorates became difficult to defend politically. This was all the more true of the United Nations' Trust Territories, most of which were in Africa. The trustee powers were the same powers that had operated the territories as League of Nations Mandates, but this time their activity as trustees was to be supervised by a United Nations' Special Committee on Information from Non-Self-Governing Territories and a Trusteeship Council. The Council consisted of eight members who were trustees, but a further eight were chosen from among the states of the United Nations' General Assembly. The Special Committee became a battleground between the colonizers and their critics, since many of the members came from territories recently independent. The British and French refused to supply information on political and constitutional issues in the mandatory annual report, arguing that these were internal affairs not subject to interference, but in 1951 a resolution was passed asking the trustees to submit additional information on human rights. The imperial powers now found themselves subject to scrutiny on the way they treated African peoples, a factor that contributed to the final scramble in the late 1950s and early 1960s to abandon the colonial model.[83]

Even under scrutiny, political repression was possible in the Trust Territories. In French Cameroon, the Union of the Peoples of Cameroon, the independence movement founded in 1948 on the basis that self-determination was now a formal human right, was pursued relentlessly by the French colonial administration and in 1955 was banned as a communist organization, the first political party proscribed in a trust territory. The movement's leaders fled to the neighbouring Trust Territory of British Cameroon where the French hunted down and assassinated the party's president. The British followed suit in banning the party, in June 1957, and deported the party's leaders to Sudan. The New York human rights watchdog, the International League of the Rights of Man, calculated that France and Britain had violated at least five of the principal articles of the UN Declaration on Human Rights. In 1956 alone, there were 45,000 petitions concerning human rights abuse sent to the United Nations from Cameroon.[84]

Away from the scrutiny of the trusteeship committee, colonial governance could be as harsh as it was in South East Asia. In Kenya a rebellion by elements of the Kikuyu people against loss of land and exploitation by the white settler community prompted another state of emergency, declared in October 1952. The 'Mau Mau' (literally 'greedy eaters' of traditional tribal authority) organized a Land Freedom Army, some of whose leaders had fought with the British against the Japanese in Burma. 'We could no longer accept,' claimed one, 'the belief that a *mzungu* [European] was better than an African.'[85] They settled scores with white farmers and their families through random killings by groups armed with a mix of modern and traditional weapons.[86] The reaction of the authorities to the rebellion was the most extreme of all Britain's counter-insurgencies. The Kikuyu were blamed indiscriminately for the violence, even though some served in a local 'Home Guard' in support of the colonial regime, responsible for much of the violence unleashed on the rebels in yet another example of colonial civil war.[87] As in Malaya, a 'New Village' system was enforced and 1 million Kikuyu forced to inhabit them; detention centres were set up in remote areas where at the peak there were 70,000 detainees, subject to debilitating labour and regular violence, chiefly imposed by other Kenyans working for the colonial authorities.[88] Over 1,000 Mau Mau leaders were hanged, and 11,503 (the official figure) killed in free fire zones and security sweeps. The detainees were officially screened to extract confessions from those who had taken the Mau Mau oath, but screening involved routine torture, beatings, threats of castration, and hanging by the arms or upside down. A blind eye was turned by the authorities until news of the beating to death of eleven detainees at Hola Camp – notorious for years of abuse – in 1959 finally reached the public.[89] After years of repression, the rebel Kikuyu had been bludgeoned into submission and moderate nationalists led by Jomo Kenyatta bargained with the government, promising to respect the rights of white settlers in return for independence, granted in 1963. By this stage, the British and French governments had come to realize that independence could no longer be reasonably denied, and twenty-three African states became independent between 1959 and 1961.

The one exception provided the most violent drama of the end of empire. French governments in the 1950s had moved from the idea of French Union to a French Community of former colonies, which would collaborate together as nominally independent states while keeping close links with France, and it was this structure, following local referenda, that allowed almost all French African colonies to achieve independence by 1962.

Algeria in North Africa was the exception. It was not a colony, even if its Arab and Berber populations were treated as if it were, but an integral part of France, divided into administrative departments, with a largely French settler electorate. During the war Algeria had remained loyal to the Vichy regime until Allied occupation in November 1942, when thousands of Algerians were mobilized to join the Free French armies. In 1945, on the day Victory in Europe was celebrated, a violent clash between French settlers (the *pieds noirs* – 'black feet', so-called because of European shoes) and Arab protesters at Sétif resulted in the deaths of around 3,000 Algerian rebels in the repression that followed and marked the onset of the long struggle for Algerian independence that did not end until 1962.[90]

Because Algeria was regarded by Paris politicians as part of France, Algerian nationalism was regarded as a profound internal threat, even though Algeria's indigenous society was far removed from the reality of metropolitan France. When Jacques Soustelle was appointed governor general of Algeria in January 1955, he announced that Algeria and France were indivisible: 'France will not leave Algeria any more than she will leave Provence and Brittany.'[91] A few months before, a National Liberation Front (FLN), some of its leaders veterans of the Sétif rising and long spells in prison, began a campaign of sporadic terrorist violence against the administration, settlers and Algerian 'collaborators'. The French responded with a renewed wave of violent repression, urged on, as in Kenya, by a large settler community that wanted effective protection. This was the onset of a familiar counter-insurgency, with arbitrary detention, free fire zones, regular killing of unarmed suspects and the routine torture of guerrillas and their alleged accomplices. The effect proved counterproductive; FLN forces grew in number and capability, forcing local communities to assist them and placing them in the firing line between both sides. By 1956, there were 450,000 French troops in Algeria, most of them conscripts. The scale of the response can be measured by the final tally of 2.5 million French soldiers serving at some time in the Algerian war. Of these, over 18,000 were killed. The number of Algerian dead has been calculated as half a million, through war, revenge killings, famine and disease.[92]

Algerian society was devastated by the decision to mimic the resettlement schemes in South East Asia. Under the direction of Maurice Papon, responsible during the war for sending French Jews to their death, the regime inaugurated a programme to isolate the rebels from the wider population by a policy of *regroupement*, forced resettlement into crude modern villages that destroyed traditional village or nomadic life. Around these villages scorched-earth policies were pursued, with free fire zones for anyone foolish enough to trespass into them. By 1961 there were 2,380 centres of *regroupement*; official figures suggested that 1.9 million had been moved, but more recent estimates suggest 2.3 million, or a third of the rural population. Some 400,000 nomads from the Saharan fringes were moved and lost 90 per cent of their livestock. The massive dislocation undermined Algerian agriculture: wheat and barley crops declined by three-quarters between 1954 and 1960, exposing thousands to the threat of famine. An estimated 75 per cent of Algeria's forested area was destroyed by the use of napalm.[93] The strategy of isolation and the massive deployment of soldiers eventually eroded the military base of the FLN, whose size in 1958 was an estimated 50,000. Pursued by the French army, 60,000 *harkis* (Algerian militia working for the French) and settler vigilantes, the guerrilla units were halved by 1959.[94] But by then the intractable and costly nature of the counter-insurgency had led to the fall of the French Fourth Republic and the recall of the wartime leader, Charles de Gaulle. He understood that the French public had had enough of an unwinnable colonial war that now pointlessly defied the wave of decolonization. On 16 September 1959 he announced that he would seek a ceasefire, authorize an amnesty, call elections and begin the move to self-determination. Bitter opposition from the settler community peaked in a wave of violence and a failed coup in 1960–61 launched by generals who supported the vicious counterguerrilla campaign of the *Organisation de l'armée secrète* (OAS). In July 1962 Algeria became independent under the FLN leader Ahmed Ben Bella, a veteran of the wartime Italian campaign, decorated for his role at the Battle of Monte Cassino.

Like the end of Axis empire, the drawn-out collapse of the old empires provoked a further wave of resettlement as British, French, Dutch and Belgian colonists, officials and police sought a new home. The *pieds noirs* left Algeria, 1.38 million to settle in France, 50,000 in Spain; 300,000 Dutch left Indonesia; and 90,000 Belgians abandoned the Belgian Congo when independence was finally granted in 1960. Estimates suggest that between 5.4 and 6.8 million people from the former empire territories returned to Europe following the war and its long, violent aftermath. For the colonized, the last fling of empire produced high levels of death in all the insurgent areas, a result of war, inter-ethnic and inter-religious conflict, hunger and disease – perhaps as many as 1 million from Indonesia to Algeria, though most statistics remain speculative. In addition, forced labour, detention without trial, compulsory resettlement, exile and deportation all dislocated local communities and permitted routine abuse of power on a remarkable scale. These were the West's first 'wars on terror' and they violated not only the UN Declaration on Human Rights, but the

Nuremberg principles approved after the trial of the major German war criminals. The abuses generally went unpunished and unpublicized. The colonial 'wars after the war' provided a messy and violent coda to the era of new territorial imperialism that began in the 1870s, peaked in the 1940s, and collapsed by the 1960s.

A WORLD OF NATION STATES

The end of empire in Asia and Africa transformed the nature of the United Nations. 'Nation' had been the defining term for Roosevelt and Churchill when the United Nations front was set up in 1942, even though Britain and France were empires. Neither leader thought very much beyond the established nations of Europe and the New World, but within two dec-ades decolonization gave the organization an overwhelming majority from the 'Third World' of independent states in Asia, Africa and the Mid-dle East. Even though the frontiers of the imperial world had been drawn up with little regard for cultural or ethnic differences, most of the inde-pendence movements after 1945 were forced to work with boundaries set by the colonial powers. Ideas of federation or community that transcended the straitjacket of nationhood, popular particularly in Francophone Africa, failed in the end to undermine the seductive appeal of national identity.[95] At the founding conference there had been fifty-one nations represented. The test of inclusion was a declaration of war against the Axis states no later than 8 March 1945. Those present included, after much argument between the Allies, Ukraine and Belorussia, which were not strictly nations, India, which was not yet independent, and Poland, whose admission was a bone of Cold War contention despite its status as the first to fight. By 1955 and the time of the Bandung Conference there were seventy-six states, including the former Axis states of Austria, Hun-gary, Romania and Italy. By the time Algeria and Kenya had been granted independence in 1962 and 1963, there were 112, including all the major colonial territories except for Portuguese Angola and Mozambique, finally independent in 1975 and 1976 respectively. Japan was admitted in 1956, the two German states only in 1973. The United Nations Organization, for all the criticism then and now of its capacity to ensure peace and pro-mote human rights, symbolized in a very palpable form the shift from a world of global empires to a world of nation states.

Among the world of sovereign nations at the founding meeting in San Francisco in 1945 were the states of the Middle East: Egypt, Iraq, Iran, Syria and Lebanon. Their presence masked a different reality, for all of them in 1945 were occupied by British Empire forces and officials, a wartime outcome that effectively compromised their sovereignty; one half of Iran was still occupied by the Soviet Union under the terms of the agreement reached in autumn 1941. During the war, securing the region had been a central priority in British grand strategy and the nominal independence of all five states had been trampled over by British forces. In addition, Palestine and Transjordan were still held as Mandated Territories of the League of Nations, a status that temporarily survived the founding of the United Nations. It was nevertheless evident in 1945 that the pre-war domination by Britain and France could no longer be sustained. Syria and Lebanon had declared their independence after the Vichy French were defeated by British forces in 1941, and in 1944 both states were recognized by the Soviet Union and the United States. The Free French under de Gaulle hoped to restore the French position in Syria when the war ended and in late May 1945 the local French garrison began a bombardment of central Damascus, in retaliation against anti-colonial demonstrations, only to be halted by the British army, whose commander declared martial law and confined the French troops to barracks. Neither the British nor the Americans had any desire to see France re-established in the Middle East and were happy to endorse independence. On 21 June 1945 the Syrian and Lebanese governments joined forces in rejecting any French claim to residual authority in the Mandates and independence was assured. The last Allied troops left in summer 1946.[96] The British League Mandate in Transjordan was also quickly terminated after agreement with King Abdullah that Britain would continue to enjoy the right to base troops there and might even support the king's private ambition to create a 'Greater Syria' out of adjoining territory, until the American State Department rejected any prospect of Jordanian expansion. Transjordan became an independent state in March 1946, but because it remained closely tied to British interests, the United States and the Soviet Union did not recognize the new state until 1949, when Jordan, as it was now called, took its place in the United Nations.[97]

Once France was expelled from the region, Britain's principal concerns in the Middle East reflected wartime priorities: to prevent Soviet infiltration into the region, to protect British oil interests in Iraq and Iran, and to maintain a strategic grip on the Suez Canal as the route to the eastern empire. The situation appeared most dangerous in Iran, where fear of the Soviet presence and the threat to Iranian oil supplies were closely linked. The wartime agreement stipulated that British and Soviet forces would leave Iran six months after the end of the war. The British pulled out in March 1946, but the Soviet forces remained. The Soviet government tried to pressure the Iranian government, now led by the nationalist Ahmad Qavam, to grant an oil concession in the north of the country and backed the efforts of the Azerbaijani population in the north to set up an autonomous zone. In May 1946 Soviet forces withdrew on the assumption that Qavam had agreed to a treaty accepting the Soviet demands, but under strong American and British pressure the Iranian government rejected the treaty. Once again Stalin backed down, because he wanted to avoid a conflict while preoccupied with the political reconstruction of Eastern Europe.[98] The communist threat remained, however, with the rise of the Tudeh (Masses) Party and a wave of strikes and popular protests. The British Foreign Office and the local officials from the Anglo-Iranian Oil Company launched an anti-communist propaganda campaign, bribing officials and newspaper editors, and when a major strike, prompted by Tudeh, hit the Abadan oilfield in July 1946, Bevin ordered troops to the British Iraqi base at Basra as a threat. The strike evaporated, but the following month Qavam rejected further foreign interference in Iranian affairs.[99] Three years later, in March 1951, the new prime minister, Mohammad Mosaddeq, won the support of the Iranian parliament to nationalize British oil holdings. Herbert Morrison, the new British foreign minister following Bevin's death, wanted to send 70,000 troops to protect British interests, but the United States urged caution – 'sheer madness' according to Secretary of State Dean Acheson – and in October 1951 the British were expelled from Iran. 'Their prestige in the Middle East,' ran an Egyptian newspaper report, 'is finished.'[100] The judgement was premature. In 1953, the British secret service, working closely with the American CIA, prompted a coup in Tehran to overthrow Mosaddeq's regime. Oil continued to flow to British and American companies in Iran until the Islamic revolution in 1979.[101]

Iraq was also in the front line for British hopes to contain the Soviet threat by maintaining airbases there for possible operations against Soviet targets. Iraq, although nominally independent, had been run as if it were a mandate from the suppression of the revolt in 1941 to the end of the war. Client politicians accepted the British presence, which remained in place after the war had ended with the restoration, at least in name, of Iraqi independence. Iraq was a prime example of Bevin's ambition to create 'empire by treaty' in the Middle East. Although British administrators and most British Empire forces left Iraq by 1947, a new treaty to supplant the 1930 treaty of independence was negotiated aboard HMS *Victory* in Portsmouth harbour, a symbolic imperial setting. The Treaty of Portsmouth (not to be confused with the treaty of 1906 signed at Portsmouth, Maine, to end the Russo-Japanese war) was agreed in January 1948, giving Britain continued military concessions in Iraq. But the British here, as elsewhere, had under-estimated the strength of anti-imperial sentiment. Following widespread anti-British rioting, the Iraqi regent, Abd al-Ilah, rejected the treaty and British interests in the country dwindled. In 1948 Iraq left the sterling currency bloc, and four years later negotiated a deal to take half the oil revenues from the British oil concession. In 1955 the two British airbases, from which putative bombing raids were to be mounted against the Soviet threat, were handed over to Iraqi control, and in 1958 an army coup finally ended what was left of the residual British connection.[102]

Nothing mattered more for the British than retaining a presence astride the Suez Canal, which they had defended stoutly throughout the early years of the war. The chiefs of staff saw the canal as an essential artery linking Britain with the Asian empire, and continued to do so even after India and Pakistan had become independent on the grounds that combating communism required bases from which to project air and ground forces against possible Soviet threats. The obsession with a military presence placed a premium on reaching agreement with the Egyptian government and, above all, stabilizing the British Mandate in Palestine after years of argument about the future of the Arab and Jewish populations. Relations with the Egyptian king and government had been poor during the war, and deteriorated rapidly after Allied victory as the United States replaced Britain as a major source of investment and commercial assistance.[103] King Farouk wanted an end to the 1936 mutual defence treaty which had allowed British Empire forces to campaign on Egyptian soil throughout the war. In 1945 the British-controlled Suez Canal Zone was the largest military base in the world, with 10 airfields, 34 army camps and 200,000 troops.[104] The numbers did decline with demobilization, and in 1946 British Empire forces left the rest of Egyptian territory, leaving only the Canal Zone under occupation. But the Egyptian government insisted on complete evacuation and abrogated the 1936 treaty of mutual defence, prompting an expansion of British forces once again at Suez to 84,000. The area became difficult to defend against persistent attacks by Egyptian irregulars, including the Muslim Brotherhood, while the violent counter-attacks by British forces that these incursions provoked were strongly condemned by the United States.

After Farouk was overthrown in 1952 in an army coup, Britain continued to negotiate to retain its presence in the country, in order to avoid what Churchill, now prime minister again, called 'a prolonged humiliating scuttle before all the world'.[105] He nevertheless agreed two years later to terminate the Canal base and British forces left in October 1955. This was not the end of the story. In July 1956 the Egyptian government under Colonel Gamal

Abdel Nasser nationalized the Suez Canal, prompting the last fling of Anglo-French imperialism in the Middle East. The decision to seize the Canal Zone by force in co-operation with the Israeli government was a disaster. War began on 24 October, but by 6 November universal pressure, both from domestic opinion and from the United Nations, forced a cease-fire and withdrawal.[106] The Commonwealth threatened to collapse as the former dominions condemned British action – 'like finding a beloved uncle arrested for rape,' complained Canada's prime minister.[107] The Suez crisis really was the end of the British effort to remain a major Middle Eastern player, and the last feeble fling of an older imperial tradition.

Given the problems in occupying Egypt, the British government had sought from 1945 to exploit the Palestine Mandate as an alternative strategic base and one that would be under direct British control, rather than reliant on treaty. This was in reality a strategic fantasy. Palestine was the site of a prolonged military crisis from 1945 with the end of the war and a resumption of the popular demand from the Arab population for an independent Arab Palestine, alongside Jewish hopes to turn their presence in the Jewish homeland into a national Jewish state. The issue of what to do with Palestine had been postponed until the end of hostilities. The British preference was to avoid doing anything that would alienate Arab opinion, on which the continued British presence in the Middle East would rely, and that meant making no concession to Jewish demands for a state. Policy was still governed by the White Paper of May 1939, restricting Jewish immigration into Palestine and denying the right to Jewish autonomy. Nonetheless, during the war, the Jewish Agency as representative of approximately 650,000 Jews living in the Mandate, prepared for the possibility of statehood. 'The Jews should act as if they were the state in Palestine,' declared the Agency head, David Ben-Gurion, 'and should so continue to act until there will be a Jewish state there.'[108] The Agency had a Jewish 'parliament', an executive and the illegal Haganah, a paramilitary force with the potential to mobilize at least 40,000 fighters. In May 1942, Zionists meeting at a hotel in New York drew up the 'Biltmore Declaration', calling for the creation of a Jewish commonwealth in Palestine and Jewish control of immigration. American support came not only from the numerous Jewish Americans who provided generous funding for the Agency, but from the American leadership. In October 1944 Roosevelt called for 'the opening of Palestine to unrestricted Jewish immigration', a policy that the British opposed emphatically then and in the immediate post-war years.[109] The radical wing of the Jewish nationalist movement came to see the British as a greater enemy to Jewish statehood than the Germans. During the war two organizations, the *Lohamei Herut Israel* (better known as the Stern gang after their leader, Abraham Stern) and the *Irgun Zvai Leumi* (led, among others, by Menachem Begin, the future Israeli prime minister), began a terrorist campaign against British targets. Haganah publicly opposed the violence, but in private supported the aim of the terrorists. In November 1944, Lord Moyne, deputy minister of state in Egypt, was assassinated by members of *Lohamei Herut Israel*, and even Churchill, who had supported the Zionist cause, was shocked into reconsidering his loyalty 'maintained so consistently in the past'.[110]

British sympathies lay more generally with the Arab cause. In March 1945, Egypt, Syria, Lebanon, Iraq and Saudi Arabia founded the Arab League, one of whose priorities was to campaign for genuine sovereignty for all Arab states, including a future Palestine.[111] After Britain permitted political parties again in the Mandate, six Arab organizations emerged, the most significant among them the Palestine Arab Party, led by Jamal al-Husayni, which demanded the maximum – an independent Arab Palestine. In the months after the end of the war, with British approval, small groups of Arab *al-Najjda* (literally 'ready for succour') militants emerged under the guise of a network of sports clubs, which were actually units for paramilitary training against the coming crisis. In February 1946 the Arab League encouraged the Palestinian nationalists to work together under a Higher Committee, then under an Arab Higher Executive, led by Grand Mufti Amin al-Husayni. Other paramilitary units emerged, among them the Army of Sacred Jihad, and the Rescue Army based in Syria and composed chiefly of exiled Palestinians and Syrian volunteers, each force dedicated to eradicating the threat of a Jewish state with violence, but each too poorly trained and armed for serious conflict.[112] Faced with incipient civil war, the British government reacted by stationing 100,000 troops in Palestine, supported by 20,000 armed police. So dangerous did it become for British service personnel to appear in the streets that their bases were nicknamed 'Bevingrads' in honour of the man who had sent them there.

Jewish terrorist attacks increased in intensity. On a single night in October 1945 there were 150 attacks on the local rail network. In June 1946 the British high commissioner was given discretionary powers to deal with the emergency of Jewish violence. Montgomery, chief of the imperial general staff, insisted with impolitic directness that the Jews 'must be utterly defeated and their illegal organisations smashed forever'.[113] By the summer of 1946, British agents had linked the Jewish Agency directly with the terrorist campaign and on 29 June the army of occupation launched Operation 'Agatha', raiding the Agency headquarters and arresting 2,700 suspects. British soldiers carrying out the raid, frustrated by the terrorism, chanted 'what we need are gas chambers' and

scrawled 'death to the Jews' on raided buildings. In reaction, Begin ordered
the bombing of the British headquarters at the King David Hotel in Jerusalem, which was blown up on 22 July resulting in the deaths of ninety-one
people trapped inside, twenty-eight of them British. The bombing was a
turning point, alienating the British public from the cost and sacrifice of
occupation and leaving the British forces stationed in Palestine with the
prospect of conducting a harsh counter-insurgency operation in the full
glare of public scrutiny. When a few months later martial law was proclaimed, it was suspended after two weeks because of the political risks
involved.

This did not prevent the British authorities from ruthless action in trying to prevent illegal Jewish immigration into Palestine to circumvent the
rigid restrictions still in place. Ships, including the *Ben Hecht*, paid for
with Zionist donations in the United States, were intercepted illegally outside Palestinian territorial waters, the crews imprisoned and the refugees
sent to camps in Cyprus. Secret instructions from Bevin, appropriately
codenamed Operation 'Embarrass', allowed British agents to sabotage
ships in port in Europe for the transport of Jewish refugees, including the
contamination of food and water supplies, and the use of limpet mines.
Most famously the *Exodus 1947*, packed with refugees chosen for their
vulnerability – the elderly, pregnant women, children – was rammed and
damaged by two British destroyers (after narrowly escaping a plan to
mine it). It was towed into port in Palestine, where the passengers were
forced to disembark, re-embarked on three deportation ships and sent on
to Hamburg, to be greeted by British police and soldiers armed with
hoses, teargas and truncheons employed to force the exhausted and debilitated Jews off the boat and back into camps in Germany.[114] The result
was a public relations disaster. 'The plain truth to which we so firmly shut
our eyes,' wrote an official at the Colonial Office, 'is that in this emergency Detention business we are taking a leaf out of the Nazi book . . .'[115]

The immigration issue became central to the final collapse of British
responsibility for the Mandate. It divided American from British responses
to the crisis in Palestine and damaged Britain's international reputation.
Initially there were only some 27,000 Jewish Displaced Persons in the western zones of Germany and Austria in summer 1945, but they were soon
supplemented by a flow of Jews from Eastern Europe sent by the Polish and
Soviet governments as 'unrepatriable', ostensibly on humanitarian grounds
but in truth to export the Jews in order to avoid the problems of integration
in a climate of post-war anti-Semitism. By summer 1946 there were an
estimated 250,000 Jewish DPs, most of them in the more sympathetic environment of American camps. Among the camp population there was an

overwhelming desire to emigrate to the British Mandated Territory. UNRRA
circulated a questionnaire among 19,000 Jewish DPs to find out their stated
preference for a new home and 18,700 wrote Palestine. 'We have worked
and struggled too long on the lands of other peoples,' an elderly Jew
explained in 1945. 'We must build a land of our own.'[116] President Truman
sent Earl Harrison, a delegate on the Inter-Governmental Committee on
Refugees, to investigate the Jewish plight in Europe. His report was a devastating indictment of their condition and an unequivocal endorsement of
their right to emigrate to Palestine. Truman asked Attlee to accept 100,000
immigrants but the British government prevaricated. Bevin wanted to send
just enough 'to appease Jewish sentiment', but the entry of a vast number
into Palestine would exacerbate the crisis and alienate Arab opinion.[117]
Although Truman's initiative has been seen as a political gambit to mollify
the large Jewish voting bloc in the United States and to avoid taking in large
numbers of Jewish refugees, American opinion was generally critical of the
British position and expected the British government to respond more fully
and humanely to the Jewish desire to emigrate. Refugee organizations in
Europe came to define the Jewish DPs first as stateless, then as a 'non-
territorial nation', effectively granting national status. On 4 October 1946,
Truman called for a 'viable Jewish state' to meet the Jewish demand for
nationhood. For the British government the intractable conflict in Palestine,
like the crisis in India, was impossible to resolve unilaterally. In February
1947, Bevin proposed a bi-national Palestine ruled by Britain as trustee for
at least five years, but it was already evident that neither side in the territory
would accept this. The same month the British handed the problem to the
United Nations to solve. 'Nature may partition Palestine,' was Bevin's part-
ing shot.[118]

The UN Special Committee for Palestine concluded that partition into
Jewish and Arab states was the only solution. Their report, strongly supported by the United States and the Soviet Union, was approved in a
dramatic General Assembly vote on 29 November 1947 after strong pressure had been applied by the United States to ensure compliance from
states in Latin America and Western Europe. The British abstained and
refused to implement the partition terms drawn up by the Special Committee. Instead, the government announced that Britain would withdraw
unilaterally from the Mandate on 15 May 1948 and the vast military presence in Palestine remained confined to barracks. The result was civil war
as Jews and Arabs began to fight over areas designated for one side or the
other in the partition map drawn up by the Special Committee. The Rescue
Army infiltrated Palestine from Syrian bases, accompanied by an assortment of Bosnian, German, British and Turkish anti-Semitic volunteers.

King Abdullah's Arab Legion, trained by British officers, moved into the west bank area of the Jordan River to defend Jerusalem from Jewish attack. The Jewish Agency directed Haganah, now numbered between 35,000 and 40,000 armed men, including the 5,000 veterans of the wartime Jewish Brigade, to take the offensive. In a series of small but bloody battles they took control of the partition areas and attacked Arab settlements in an effort to acquire further territory.[119] The Jewish forces were better armed, better disciplined and better led than their Arab opponents, and by the time Ben-Gurion declared the state of Israel on 14 May, the day before the British withdrawal, the partition state was consolidated enough to begin operation at once. The Arab League then declared war to eliminate the newcomer, but the Arab armies were too poorly resourced and failed to co-operate together. Temporary truces were imposed by the United Nations, but largely ignored. By 1949 there were 650,000 Palestinian Arab refugees, more than half the Arab population. A separate Arab state failed to materialize; Jordan took over the West Bank, where most Palestinian refugees had fled, and Egypt the Gaza strip. A series of armistice agreements was finally brokered by the United Nations in 1949, and on 11 May that year Israel was admitted to the United Nations. Between 1948 and 1951, 331,594 European Jews emigrated to Israel.[120]

The one major state absent from the early decades of the United Nations was the People's Republic of China, founded in October 1949 after victory for Mao Zedong's Communist liberation armies in the civil war. China was represented by Taiwan, where Chiang Kai-shek had taken refuge in 1949 with a small rump of his Nationalist party and army. Among all the upheavals after 1945 that helped to shape the new post-war global order, the most significant in both the short and long term was the Communist Party's achievement in creating a unitary nation state out of the conflict-ridden and divided China that emerged from the war of resistance to Japanese aggression. When the war against Japan ended, both Chiang and Mao imagined that they could exploit the wartime chaos and dislocation to create a new order. From late August 1945, Mao and Zhou Enlai, the Communists' principal negotiator, spent six weeks as Chiang's guests at the Nationalist capital Chongqing, to see whether negotiation could bring about a new China through collaboration, but the talks exposed an obvious gulf between their visions of what a new China meant. Mao refused to limit the size of the Communist army, soon to be named the People's Liberation Army, or to integrate it with Chiang's army under Nationalist command. Nor would the Communists relinquish their demand to govern five northern provinces which they had secured in the last year of war.[121] Although Mao had been warned by Stalin to avoid a civil war and the probable disintegration of China, the refusal to give up control over an armed force with more than a million recruits made civil war almost inevitable. Even as the talks were proceeding, fighting broke out between the two sides in the Yangtze valley and the northern provinces, while Communist armies began to pour into Manchuria under the watchful gaze of the occupying Red Army.

Given the presence of Soviet forces in Manchuria and American military advisers and equipment in the south, the future of post-war China was also a major international issue. Chiang's wartime Western allies had differing views of how China would fit into a new world order. Roosevelt had insisted that China be one of the 'Four Policemen' enforcing post-war security, and China became a member of the United Nations' Security Council in 1946.[122] For Churchill, China's claim to be a great power was a mere 'affectation'. British officials continued to view China in much the same way, and assumed that it would be possible to reassert British 'informal empire', which had been reluctantly abandoned in 1943 when Chiang insisted on abrogating the 'unequal treaties' that gave Westerners the right to extra-territoriality in China's major trading ports.[123] The British Cabinet's Far Eastern Committee recommended every effort to 'recover as much as possible of our previous influence in China', but principally economic concessions. The test of British intentions came with the reoccupation of Hong Kong in September 1945, carried out by the Royal Navy in defiance of an agreement with Chiang to allow Chinese forces to take it back. The United States objected to the fait accompli and every effort was made to ensure that Britain would not attempt to resuscitate its former status. Roosevelt had sent General Patrick Hurley as his special envoy to China late in 1944 with express instructions to 'keep an eye on European imperialism'.[124] The large American military and business presence obstructed British activity, but the main obstacle was Chiang, who had no intention of reversing the Nationalist insistence that the old order of European and Japanese influence was now dead.

The British after 1945 preferred the idea of a weak, divided China, where regional concessions might still be extracted, but they faced an American administration committed to what General George Marshall, successor to Hurley as special envoy, described as a China 'strong, democratic, unified'.[125] Where the British presence was attenuated and barely tolerated, American involvement in post-war China was extensive. Aid packages totalling $800 million were distributed between 1945 and 1948, more than the value of the entire wartime aid to China. American military advisers trained sixteen divisions of the Nationalist army, and gave preliminary training to a further twenty, while 80 per cent of Chiang's military equipment came from the United States.[126] American policy was predicated on support for Chiang rather than the Communists, but support was conditional on the Chinese leader's willingness to progress China rapidly to the American model of democracy, a requirement that indicated how little the United States had learned about China in four years of wartime alliance. In December 1945, Truman sent Marshall to Chongqing as a mediator to avert civil war and bring the two main political movements into coalition 'by peaceful, democratic means'.[127] He established a 'Committee of Three', consisting of Marshall, Zhou Enlai and the Guomindang minister Zhang Qun, to thrash out agreement once again. In January, the committee brokered a deal on a ceasefire between the two sides, a coalition government, and the integration of the two armies. Chiang undertook to begin the work of democratizing China, while Mao wrote promising that 'Chinese democracy must follow the American path'.[128] Marshall was delighted with the outcome: 'very remarkable how we could straighten out what seemed impossible conditions . . . until we arrived, nothing could be done.' His optimism was premature. Chiang confided to his diary in late January 1946 that Marshall did not understand Chinese politics well at all. 'The Americans,' he wrote, 'tend to be naïve and trusting . . . taken in by the communists.' Mao's real view was that all agreements with imperialists were scraps of paper. 'Everything,' he told his army commanders, 'is decided by victory or defeat on the battlefield.'[129]

While Marshall thought he had a solid agreement, the civil war opened up in North China and Manchuria, ignoring the ceasefire that nominally came into effect in mid-January. Manchuria became the principal battleground, far from the discussions in Chongqing. For Chiang control of the region was a priority, not least because it was here that the long Second World War had begun in 1931, when the Nationalist response had been a complete failure. In August 1945, Chiang succeeded in reaching agreement with Stalin that Soviet-occupied Manchuria would be returned to Chinese sovereignty. The Sino-Soviet Treaty of 14 August gave the Soviet Union control of two key ports in Manchuria, but otherwise promised Chiang 'moral, military and other material assistance' in establishing his undisputed rule over a united China.[130] The Chinese Communists were not party to the agreement and were uncertain of Stalin's attitude. In the first months after the end of the war more than half a million Communist troops moved into the region under the command of Lin Biao, introducing land ownership reform and developing local party cadres in the countryside. Efforts to enter the cities in Manchuria were resisted by the Red Army because Stalin had promised the region to Chiang. From late 1945 onwards the United States navy helped to ship 228,000 Nationalist troops and their equipment to Manchuria, including Chiang's best forces, the New First and New Sixth armies; over the months that followed 70 per cent of Chiang's army arrived in Manchuria.[131] Skirmishes soon developed into major battles once Soviet forces began to withdraw in March and April 1946. The Communists were driven from Shenyang (Mukden) in March but in April the Communist Liberation Army destroyed a Nationalist garrison in Changchun. The ceasefire was a failure as both Mao and Chiang knew it would be. Marshall found the following months disillusioning and finally persuaded Truman to impose an arms embargo on supplies to Chiang's armies, leaving them in the campaigns that followed short of ammunition and spare parts for their American weapons. The civil war now had its own momentum, beyond control from either the United States or the Soviet Union.

The outcome of the conflict for the future of China was not a foregone conclusion. For the eighteen months after the breakdown of the ceasefire, Nationalist forces seized back control of cities, towns and rural areas occupied by the Communists in the south, east and north as far as the Great Wall. By the end of 1946, the Communists had lost control of 165 towns and 174,000 square kilometres of territory. In March 1947, the Nationalist general Hu Zongnan launched a major offensive into Shaanxi to capture the Communist capital at Yan'an. Warned in advance by a spy at Hu's headquarters, Mao and the Communist leadership moved everything out of the city to bases to the north and east. A token force was left to defend Yan'an and was swept aside, but Hu's forces entered a city deserted of Communists. The capture was hailed by the Nationalist leadership and press as a historic victory, even the successful climax of the war.[132] The victory was a delusion, however, for despite heavy losses in the eighteen months of the war, the Chinese Communist Party remained embedded in much of rural China in the north and in Manchuria. As with the war against Japan, Communist strategy was to establish and protect base areas and to engage in what General Zhu De called 'sparrow warfare', wearing down the enemy by short, surprise attacks against isolated units before melting back into the surrounding area. 'The countryside surrounds the cities' ran the Communist slogan and it was here, in stimulating a social revolution, that the eventual success of communism in China was to be found.[133]

The post-war situation in China favoured the Communist vision of the future more than it did the Nationalist. The upheaval of war had led to widespread dislocation and dispossession; the conventional Confucian values governing family life and attitudes to authority broke down as families became separated and as trust in the regime evaporated under the weight of Japanese occupation and an ineffective Nationalist war effort. Young Chinese in particular were affected by the breakdown of order and a new sense of liberation from traditional social bonds. Half of the recruits to the Communist Party and the Liberation Army were under twenty years old. For the peasantry in much of China, the war had been a negative experience. In Hunan province between 2 and 3 million had died of famine in 1944–5; in 1946, 4 million more died. Landlords, black-marketeers and bandits exploited and preyed on villagers across China. In areas where the Communists could achieve it, peasants were protected and land reform introduced. The 'Directive concerning the Land Issue', published by the Communist Party on 4 May 1946, called for the expro-priation of the landlord class and redistribution to those who worked the land. The class war that had been suspended during the conflict with Japan became the central plank of communist appeal. In the villages of the north a programme of 'speaking bitterness' was introduced, where local peasants and labourers were encouraged to come forward to denounce those who had oppressed them. The object was to raise aware-ness among the rural poor of the reasons for their poverty and to focus on the class enemy. Trained 'bitterness speakers' were sent to communities by the Party, with instructions to wear a sad expression and to give vent to a simulated anger.[134] Reprisals against the exploiters were harsh, often a summary execution; collaborators with the Japanese or the Nationalists were punished with arbitrary violence. Communists traded above all on hostility to Chiang and the Nationalist regime who were blamed for hold-ing back the building of a new China out of the ruins of war.

For Chiang and the Nationalist movement, the post-war years merely exacerbated the financial and social crises generated by the wartime emer-gency. The inflationary spiral continued, made worse by military requirements which ate up almost two-thirds of state spending. The Chi-nese *fabi* exchange rate against the American dollar deteriorated from 2,655 in June 1946 to 36,826 one year later and 180,000 in January 1948. The hyperinflation affected consumers and savers in Nationalist-dominated urban China but had less effect in the more self-sufficient rural areas where communism was now rooted. When Chiang insisted on a conversion of Japanese occupation currency into *fabi* at a rate of 1:200, thousands who had worked for the Japanese occupiers or had grown rich on black-marketeering were ruined.[135] Those who had collaborated with the Japanese, or were judged to have done so, were driven from their homes and their property seized by incoming Guomindang supporters, alienating and impoverishing many in the old commercial and bureaucratic elite, but benefitting a new elite grown rich on confiscations. The corruption and criminality that had prejudiced the war effort persisted into the post-war years, as people competed for advantage or simply sought to survive. The dedicated Chinese branch of UNRRA saw corruption on a wide scale as goods were looted or sold privately to businesses, rather than supplied to the destitute refugees who needed them.[136] Despite the success on the battlefield, China's population was alienated by continuous warfare and the Chiang regime that sustained it. In February 1948, Chiang observed in his diary: 'the people are losing confidence everywhere.'[137]

The greatest difficulty facing Chiang was to consolidate his victories in northern China and Manchuria by eliminating Communist resistance. The strategic choice of Manchuria made sense to Chiang because conflict there would ensure that Stalin's promise of Chinese sovereignty for the province would be redeemed, while Communist armies could be destroyed by American-trained troops and American equipment. Nevertheless, Manchuria proved difficult to reinforce at such a long distance along a single rail line that was easily sabotaged by the enemy, while the American arms embargo nullified the advantage of American weapons if they could not be supplied with ammunition. Marshall became despondent about his role in 'message-carrying' and was relieved to return to America in early January 1947 as secretary of state.[138] The American administration began to distance itself from direct support for Chiang, since the cost of further military aid seemed dangerously open-ended. Supplies began to arrive again only in September 1948, by which time it was too late.[139]

Since the Communist threat had retreated to the countryside, Nationalist armies were locked up in the main cities, unable to return to southern China until victory was complete and increasingly demoralized by the harsh climate and conditions in the north. After the defeats of 1946–7, the Communist Party reorganized, recruited further waves of volunteers from among the impoverished and alienated urban young, and rebuilt the Liberation Army with the help of Soviet equipment supplied across the Manchurian–Soviet border, whither Communist armies had retreated in 1946. By autumn 1947 there were once again an estimated 1 million men and women in the Liberation Army in Manchuria. In December 1947, in temperatures of –35°C, 400,000 Communist troops began the reconquest of urban Manchuria when they crossed the frozen Sungari River to besiege the city of Shenyang. The ten-month encirclement of around 200,000 Nationalist troops in a city of 4 million led to a desperate shortage of food and fuel. Communist units cut the main rail link, isolating Manchuria from possible aid. A fourfold superiority in artillery compensated for the lack of Communist air power, while Soviet technical advisers helped to turn a guerrilla force into a modern army capable of large-scale warfare.[140] In

May 1948, Lin Biao laid siege to Changchun, further north. When the Nationalist commander refused to surrender, Lin Biao ordered his forces to turn Changchun into 'a city of death'.[141] From May to October a total siege was imposed. The city was surrounded at a distance by defensive lines of barbed wire, pillboxes and trenches. Refugees from the starving population tried to navigate the barren no man's land between the city and the Communist lines, but they could neither advance past Communist guards nor were they allowed back into the stricken city. Bloated corpses piled up in the summer heat; an estimated 160,000 died outside and inside the city. When Chiang ordered the Nationalist commander, Zheng Dong-guo, to try to break out, half his force mutinied, and the city surrendered on 16 October 1948.[142]

The fall of Changchun was followed rapidly by the capture of Jinzhou, then Shenyang, which surrendered after bitter hand-to-hand fighting on 1 November. In the city battles, Chiang lost most of his best armies, an esti-mated total of 1.5 million men. Each Communist success brought a swarm of defectors from the enemy side, while many elite Chinese – the so-called 'wind faction' – changed allegiance in the hope of gaining more from Com-munist order. Defeat in Manchuria made defeat elsewhere almost inevitable. What followed mirrored remarkably the geographical pattern of the Jap-anese advance ten years before. Beijing was subjected to a forty-day siege which ended with surrender on 22 January 1949. The 240,000 Nationalist troops were absorbed into the People's Liberation Army. A hastily drawn portrait of Mao was hung up in Tiananmen Square to replace the image of Chiang. Unable to bear the loss of Beijing, and facing defeat everywhere, Chiang stepped down as president on 21 January, handing over to his deputy, Li Zongren, as 'acting' president, with the forlorn task of negotiat-ing the end of the civil war. In April, Mao demanded unconditional surrender, which Li Zongren could not accept. Chiang complained in his diary that defeat had come from the perennial failure to build an effective 'system and structure' out of the unruly Guomindang party and an unre-formed army.[143] Communist forces now fanned out across northern China. The largest battle of the civil war took place to capture the rail junction in the city of Xuzhou. Almost 2 million men fought for the gateway to the south, but the Nationalist armies crumbled again. Further south, Chiang's capital Nanjing fell on 23 April, followed by Wuhan, and then Shanghai in May 1949. Although Chiang had gone to the city earlier in the month, before the arrival of the enemy, to declare that Shanghai would be the Stalingrad of China, there was only sporadic resistance. Lionel Lamb, the British ambassador, wrote back to London that the Chinese people in the south now regarded 'the collapse of the central government a foregone conclusion.'[144] One million Communist troops, strengthened by hundreds of thousands of defectors from the enemy side, now stood on the northern banks of the Yangtze poised to invade the south.

A few months earlier, Stalin had intervened again to ask Mao to hold back from crossing the Yangtze pending Soviet mediation. He preferred a north–south division, like Korea. His motives seem to have been fear that a unified communist China might not only prove indigestible for him but would also alienate the United States and cut across agreed spheres of interest. The idea of 'Two Kingdoms' resonated with Chinese history, and both the British and American governments wondered if division might not be preferable if Chiang could rally the south.[145] Mao rejected the proposal and Communist forces, though weakened by months of gruelling campaigning and uncertain how the southern population would react, swarmed across the Yangtze. By October they had captured the major southern port of Guangzhou (Canton). Chiang fled again to Chongqing, but, unlike the Japanese, the Liberation Army captured the former capital. Chiang flew to Taiwan on 9 December 1949. Fighting continued into 1950 in areas where the Nationalists refused to surrender, but a new unitary state was a reality. In a speech in September to the People's Consultative Conference, an assembly set up originally by Chiang to satisfy Marshall's demand for democracy on the American model, Mao triumphantly proclaimed the end of the Nationalist regime and its imperialist backers: 'Ours will no longer be a nation subject to insult and humiliation. We have stood up.'[146]

Arriving in Beijing, Mao declared to an enthusiastic gathering in Tiananmen Square on 1 October 1949 the founding of the People's Republic of China. The young doctor Li Zhisui, who became Mao's personal physician, recalled in his memoirs that he had been that day 'so full of hope, so happy, that the exploitation and suffering, the aggression from foreigners, would be gone forever.'[147] The civil war was near its end, but the task of building a Communist society promised no end to the suffering imposed on those who failed the Communist test of 'good class', to be classified instead as 'middle class' or 'bad class'. Ironically, one of the first Western nations to recognize the new Chinese state, on 6 January 1950, and in defiance of the United States, was Britain, China's imperial nemesis for more than a century, still hoping for trading opportunities. Recognition of China's new status at the United Nations had to wait a further twenty years. Following a motion introduced by Albania in July 1971, the General Assembly voted on 15 October 1971 for the People's Republic to be the only legitimate Chinese state. The representatives of Chiang's Republic of China argued that the Nationalists' contribution to winning the Second World War justified their membership, but they were overruled and stormed out of the session. In November, Mao's China took up a seat in the Assembly and on the Security Council.

NEW EMPIRES FOR OLD?

The war created two superpowers, the United States and the Soviet Union. They both became embroiled in the reconstruction of the post-imperial order, and established as the principal adversaries in a Cold War that owed much to the crises surrounding the end of empire. Soon after 1945, contemporaries began to reflect on whether the two superpowers might themselves become 'empires' as successors to the defunct order, and over the decades that followed the terms 'Soviet Empire' and 'American Empire' have become a commonplace description of the hegemonic power exercised by the two federal states in the context of the Cold War. Many of the leaders at the Afro-Asian Conference in Bandung in 1955 feared that the end of the old colonialism would pave the way for new forms of empire. The Iraqi delegate, Djalal Abdoh, warned fellow leaders of new communist aggressors 're-inventing colonialism under new forms' to subvert hard won 'sovereignty and freedom of peoples'.[148] Marxist sympathizers in turn viewed the emerging global power of the United States after 1945 as empire in a different guise. Soviet accusations that the United States now practised a worldwide imperialism became embedded in communist discourse until the end of the Soviet bloc in 1990. American liberal critics of empire were equally willing to apply the term to the United States' long involvement in post-colonial wars in Vietnam. The term has become widely accepted in the context of American uni-polar power after 1990 and the collapse of the Soviet bloc.[149]

There is no argument that the Soviet Union and the United States became hegemonic powers in the post-war world based upon their massive military superiority inherited from the wartime years and shared political ambitions to project that influence globally. But they were both anti-colonial powers in wartime and over the post-war years. Stalin deplored colonialism and accepted Roosevelt's idea at the Tehran Conference in November 1943 that colonies should all be handed over to international supervision after the end of the war. With the onset of the Cold War, Soviet leaders wanted not just trusteeship but universal self-determination. The bi-polar contest between 'socialism' and 'imperialism' was the central pillar of Soviet strategic planning and thinking from the late 1940s onwards.[150] At a stormy session of the United Nations in November 1960, the Soviet delegate Valerian Zorin denounced colonialism as 'the most shameful phenomenon in the life of mankind' and demanded independence for all colonial peoples within a year. The British delegate deplored the repetition of 'worn-out Leninist slogans', and highlighted the absence of self-determination for Soviet republics, but the Soviet Union was formally committed to the ideology and to the practical strategy of intervening, where it was expedient to do so, in colonial liberation struggles.[151]

American wartime leaders were opposed to colonialism not only because of the liberal idealism espoused by Roosevelt, but also from a pragmatic desire to create an open global economy by dismantling the special trade preferences embedded in the pre-war imperial economies. Roosevelt's envoy to the Middle East in 1943, General Hurley, complained that Britain took American aid 'not for the purpose of building a brave new world based on the Atlantic Charter and the Four Freedoms, but for British conquest, British imperialistic rule, and British trade monopoly.'[152] The establishment of the International Monetary Fund and the World Bank following the economic summit at Bretton Woods in 1944, and the later General Agreement on Tariffs and Trade in 1947, were important elements in American efforts to subvert the closed blocs and trade and currency restrictions characteristic of the imperial systems before and during the war. Economic ambitions were closely interwoven with plans for decolonization. A State Department territorial committee began in 1942 to explore ways in which dependent territories after the war might be de-coupled from enclosed colonial rule. By November of that year the committee had arrived at the idea of 'International Trusteeship', later enshrined in the new United Nations Trusteeship organization.[153] Roosevelt was the leading spokesman for an end to traditional colonialism. He favoured universal trusteeship for all dependent territories, and planning before 1945 was clearly aimed at ending the traditional imperial structures despite the resistance of his British ally. By the end of the war some form of trusteeship was envisaged in Washington for the dependent world based on the ideal of development towards self-determination combined with international economic assistance.

Strong opposition from Britain and France meant that in the end a system of universal trusteeship was abandoned during the opening conference of the United Nations, but Roosevelt's successor, Harry Truman, was no more attached to the idea of restoring the old empires than his predecessor, evident in his government's hostility to British efforts to reassert traditional informal empire in China and Iran. American opposition to the restoration of colonies was nevertheless equivocal, because growing fear of Soviet communism made American leaders less insistent on the issue of universal trusteeship as a rapid route to independence. In the

Caribbean, despite lobbying to end all New World colonialism by the Organization of American States, formed in 1948, the United States worried that its southern flank might be threatened if the British were pressed too hard to decolonize, and so supported British efforts to identify and combat 'enemy penetration' by communists agitating for independence.[154] In Indochina, Roosevelt's strong aversion to restoring the colonies to French rule was compromised by fears after 1945 that without American support a communist Vietnam would result. In Indonesia, on the other hand, the absence of a major communist threat gave Truman more leeway in encouraging Dutch efforts to offer self-government and end the counter-insurgency, or face possible sanctions.

The anti-colonial focus of American policy was also evident in the process of decolonization of American dependent territories after 1945, where wartime disruption and poverty fuelled radical protests against the American presence and those who collaborated with it. In 1946 the Philippines were granted independence as promised in 1934, before the war, but social conflict resulted in a civil war that ended in 1954 with a strengthened Filipino nationalism. Puerto Rican nationalists, led by Pedro Albizu Campos, embarked on a campaign of violent protest, including a shooting attack in the US House of Representatives and a plan to assassinate President Truman.[155] The territory was granted the status of a 'commonwealth' in 1952, while development funds were pumped in to keep radical demands at bay. The islands of Hawaii moved from being a protectorate to becoming a full state of the Union in 1959, following victory by the Democratic party in the 1954 island elections. Cuba, captured in the Spanish–American war of 1898, was nominally independent but closely tied to the United States until the revolution of 1959 brought Fidel Castro to power, rupturing the relationship between the two states for more than half a century. Convinced that this was communist 'enemy penetration' in the Caribbean, the Eisenhower administration pursued policies to isolate or eliminate the Castro regime. The result was a close if temporary alignment with Moscow where few such links had previously existed.[156]

The denomination of the Soviet Union and the United States as 'empires' is evidently not straightforward. Empire is an elastic term, applied with little precision to a wide range of historical examples from the classical world to the twenty-first century. The change that occurred in 1945 ended empire of a more precisely defined character: territorial empires that involved direct subjugation and loss of sovereignty of the indigenous population, whether in colonies, protectorates, mandated territories, special settlements, or territorial condominiums. The German, Italian and Japanese wartime empires shared these characteristics with the older European empires, some of which dated back some 400 years. The hegemonic status enjoyed by the two superpowers was not based on this form of territorial empire and it has not been revived since 1945. As it turned out, neo-colonialism was practised much more widely by the former imperial powers, which in many cases succeeded, even long after independence, in sustaining cultural, economic and defence interests in former colonial territory.

The case for Soviet empire rests chiefly on the power relationship established between the Soviet Union and the areas in Eastern and Central Europe liberated from German empire in 1944–5. Here the Red Army and Soviet security forces fought a protracted war against national movements in Ukraine, Poland, Slovakia and the Baltic States whose members did not want to be ruled by communists. These were major counter-insurgency campaigns begun in 1944 as Soviet troops regained Belorussian and Ukrainian territory, and continued as Estonia, Latvia and Lithuania were reincorporated into the Soviet Union, and in Poland where nationalists from the Home Army continued to fight against the prospect of communist rule. The reaction by the Red Army and the NKVD security forces showed the same disdain for legality in conducting anti-guerrilla operations that characterized the colonial counter-insurgencies. Insurgents in turn engaged in savage acts of violence to intimidate the local population into passive or active support. The Organization of Ukrainian Nationalists boasted of their disregard for the people they were trying to liberate. 'Not intimidate but destroy,' exhorted the commander of the OUN's military wing. 'We should not be concerned that people might damn us for brutality.'[157] The liberation wars came at a high cost to both sides. In 1944–6, guerrilla resistance resulted in the death of 26,000 police, soldiers, Soviet officials and civilians; in 1945–6, an estimated 100,000 insurgents were killed, a high proportion in the area of western Ukraine. The wars continued until the early 1950s when the final guerrilla groups were hunted down and eliminated. Between 1944 and 1953, 20,000 Lithuanian guerrillas were killed, but only 188 in the last year of resistance.[158] The chief difference between the Soviet counter-insurgencies and those of the imperial states lay in the strategy of mass deportation of insurgents and their families to penal colonies in the Soviet Union. This was conducted on a major scale not only to rid the region of nationalist resistance, but to carry out the social reconstruction of Eastern Europe by eliminating 'class enemies' – richer peasants, landlords, clergy, nationalist politicians and alleged German collaborators. Between 1945 and 1952 108,362 people were deported from Lithuania; from western Ukraine (Polish territory incorporated into the Soviet Union), 203,662 'bandit accomplices' and rich peasants were exiled to Soviet 'special settlements'.[159]In Latvia, a mass deportation to Siberia of 43,000 nationalists, captured guerrillas, richer peasants and their families took place in March 1949. A further 150,000 were punished for political crimes as defined by the Soviet occupiers.[160]

Together with the deportation of class enemies and 'bandits' – the near-universal term applied to guerrillas fighting for liberation – the Soviet authorities embarked on a major programme of ethnic reconstruction in the conquered areas to avoid the possibility of post-war resistance on grounds of ethnic conflict, which had bedeviled the new states of Eastern Europe after 1919. By November 1945, 1 million Poles had been deported from Ukraine and Belorussia to the new Polish state, while 518,000 Belorussians and Ukrainians were sent from Poland to the Soviet Union. After annexing Transcarpathian Ukraine from Czechoslovakia, a Soviet–Czech agreement was reached to repatriate up to 35,000 Czechs and Slovaks from the area.[161] The programmes of ethnic and social reconstruction were intended to underpin the emergence of people's democracies in the areas of Eastern and South-eastern Europe liberated by communist forces. Stalin's initial response was not to impose communist rule but to encourage broad coalitions from which support for communism would develop naturally as a result of social and economic reform on socialist lines. Stalin told the Czech Communist leader, Klement Gottwald, in July 1946 that 'after the defeat of Hitler's Germany, after the Second World War . . . which destroyed the ruling class . . . the consciousness of the masses of people was raised.'[162] The multiple paths to socialism proved difficult in practice, and conflicted with Stalin's priority to construct a barrier of pro-Soviet states to ensure that there would be no further threat to Soviet security from former enemies.[163] Communists came to dominate the new regimes in Bulgaria, Romania, Poland and Hungary. The Soviet leadership became preoccupied with the possibility of Western intervention as the Cold War solidified in 1947, a fear symbolized for Stalin in the Marshall Plan for European recovery, in which the Czechoslovak regime was keen to participate. The Plan was rejected for the Communist bloc as an instrument to 'strengthen imperialism, prepare a new imperialist war'.[164] In February 1948, the coalition Czech government of President Beneš was overthrown and a hardline Communist regime installed. When in 1949 the Soviet Zone in Germany was converted into the German Democratic Republic, the states of Eastern Europe were all pro-Soviet and Communist-led.

Did this amount to a Soviet empire? There are clear arguments against the claim. The Baltic States were forcibly incorporated into the Soviet Union as federal socialist republics. The reconstituted states in Eastern Europe, which had been part of a colonial project under the Third Reich, were restored as sovereign states, their populations treated as citizens, not subjects, despite the absence of conventional civil rights. The object, according to Stalin in a speech in February 1946, was to 'restore democratic liberties', in the communist sense of the term, and part of the initiative in constructing the 'people's democracies' came from local communists, asserting their right to determine their future.[165] At the Bandung Conference, Nehru had defended the Communist bloc, in spite of his dislike of communism, because 'it is not colonialism if we recognize their sovereignty'. While the political system imposed was not democratic in any recognizable Western form, and violated human rights routinely, it was not the same as rule by a governor general over subject peoples. Although Communist economic development figures can be viewed sceptically, the new states of Eastern Europe did experience the rapid development of industry and urbanization and the introduction of welfare and social policies that were universal.

There were also limits to how far Soviet ambitions might go. Stalin refused to help the Greek communists in the civil war after 1945; Tito's Yugoslavia broke with Stalin's authority in March 1948 and was expelled from Cominform (the successor to Comintern) in June; Albania followed by 1961, accusing the Soviet Union of deviation from the anti-imperialist line. Stalin respected Finnish independence, and insisted that the large Communist parties in Italy and France co-operate in restoring conventional Western democracy. Outside Europe, Stalin displayed a reluctance to be drawn into the battles of decolonization. He agreed to hand back Manchuria after Soviet occupation to Chiang Kai-shek rather than to Mao Zedong; he only recognized Ho Chi Minh's Democratic Republic of Vietnam after five years, and gave little direct support, unlike Mao's China; he shied away from confrontation with the British in Iran; while encouraging North Korea to test American resolve in 1950, he stepped back from direct involvement in the subsequent war, which once again brought Communist China into the conflict; in South Asia, the Middle East and Africa, the Soviet Union contributed little to the nationalist and liberation movements, despite persistent Western fears. The Soviet security service, the KGB, only opened a department for sub-Saharan Africa in 1960, during the final wave of decolonization and independence.[166]

The case for American empire is equally problematic. America's newfound power was expressed through political pressure, economic threats, worldwide intelligence surveillance and a global military presence, but it was not a territorial empire. In the occupied areas of Germany, Italy and Japan, the military governments helped to restore services, provide capital for reconstruction projects, and prepare the former enemy states for regaining full sovereignty under parliamentary regimes. The United States' presence thereafter consisted of air and ground forces in dedicated bases, but since these also existed in Britain, they were hardly evidence of imperialism except by crude analogy. American empire has nevertheless been described as an 'empire of bases'. By the twenty-first century they numbered at least 725 in 38 different countries, each global region with its own commander-in-chief.[167] The military presence allowed the United States to project power globally but not in the same way as the British or French had done as colonial powers. When Roosevelt reflected on whether it might not be better to take over British colonial possessions in the Caribbean in order to safeguard the new military facilities agreed in the destroyers-for-bases deal in 1940, he rejected the idea as contrary to the spirit of American anti-colonialism. Like Stalin, American leaders were most concerned with security, particularly against the perceived threat of communism, rather than empire in any historically meaningful sense. Hence the regional security pacts, the largest and most enduring of which is the North Atlantic Treaty Organization, founded in 1949.

The United States faced the greatest challenges in trying to cope with post-colonial conflicts. In Korea, the agreed partition at the 38th Parallel in 1945 left American forces responsible for a former colony suddenly bereft of its colonial masters. The XXIV Corps posted to southern Korea under General John Hodge faced a daunting task. Almost none of the officers could speak Korean or had any detailed knowledge of the country and its recent past. Koreans clamoured to be able to organize political parties at last, but by October 1945 there were 54 of them, and by 1947 some 300.[168] The Americans established a Military Government under Major General Archibald Arnold but the early organization relied heavily on the assistance of former Japanese officials, who supplied 350 detailed memoranda for the new administration before they were repatriated. Koreans demanded self-determination and economic reform and within months there were widespread strikes and rural protests. An opinion poll in October 1946 showed that almost half those polled preferred Japanese rule to American.[169] In the north, Soviet forces installed as the local Communist leader the former anti-Japanese guerrilla Kim Il Sung, who had lived out the war years in Siberia. Fear of communist infiltration in the many people's committees that emerged in the south Korean countryside diverted American attention from the widespread demand for self-government from Japan's former subjects.

In September 1945 nationalists in the south had declared a Korean People's Republic, but Hodge proscribed it three months later because he thought it too communist. At a conference in Moscow on 27 December 1945, the Soviet Union, Britain, China and the United States agreed to operate a joint trusteeship for Korea to last for at least four years. Wide hostility from Korean nationalists to the idea that the country would have to wait for its independence led to deadlock. Under Soviet supervision, Kim Il Sung and fellow Communists initiated sweeping reforms in the north, above all land redistribution, which peasants on both sides of the 38th Parallel wanted. A Korean National Democratic Front was established late in 1946 and the future Communist state began to take shape. In the south the Military Government banned trade unions and the right to strike, and in September 1946 a rebellion in the city of Taegu was violently suppressed. Further talks with the Soviet Union over creating a unified and independent Korea broke down and in September, anxious to disengage from a costly and challenging occupation, the United States asked the United Nations to assume responsibility. A UN Temporary Committee on Korea moved to hold national elections to a new assembly, but the Soviet Union refused to acknowledge its authority. Elections were held in the south and a National Assembly, representing only a fraction of the Korean population, approved a constitution and elected the veteran nationalist Syngman Rhee, who had begun his campaign for independence by petitioning Woodrow Wilson in 1919, as the first president of what became, on 15 August 1948, the Republic of Korea. The north also called 'national' elections and the Supreme People's Assembly, which included communists from the south of the country, inaugurated the Democratic People's Republic on 9 September 1948. The division matched the arrangement a year later of the two Germanies. Both sides claimed to represent a national Korea, but only the Republic of Korea was regarded by the United Nations as the lawful government.[170] A United Nations Commission for the Unification and Rehabilitation of Korea was created in 1950 but any prospect of success disappeared with the Korean War and its long aftermath. Not until September 1991 were the two Korean republics granted membership of the United Nations.[171]

The United States withdrew from the Republic of Korea in 1949 but was back again within a year. In both the south and the north of the peninsula there remained the objective of national unity, but the south had no desire to be communist, and the Communist north no desire to be reunited with Rhee's nationalist and anti-communist regime. In June 1950, the Korean People's Army invaded the south in the hope of unifying a communist Korea. The Republic's limited forces were pushed back to a small area around the port of Pusan in the far south. The United Nations' Security Council, in the temporary absence of the Soviet Union, resolved to send military forces to assist the south. The invaders were repelled in turn far into the north, and Rhee in turn hoped to create a unified Korea as Communist resistance wilted. Chinese intervention in November 1950 forced a United Nations retreat once again, but by April 1951 the front line had stabilized approximately where the war had started and negotiations began to end the conflict. Not until July 1953 was an armistice finally signed, while in the interim the United States Strategic Air Forces had dropped more bombs on the Democratic Republic than had been dropped on Germany during the war. Major cities in the north suffered between 75 and 90 per cent destruction. The cost of the conflict far outstripped any of the other colonial and post-colonial wars: an estimated 750,000 military deaths and somewhere between a low of 800,000 and a high of almost 2 million dead civilians.[172]

The war in Korea demonstrated the extent to which the wider Cold War confrontation was fuelled by the crisis points of decolonization, as in the later Vietnam War. But the outcome reflected to only a limited extent the suggestion that this was also a clash of Soviet and American 'empires' rather than an ideological confrontation. This is not merely a semantic difference. Korea was divided into two independent sovereign states after thirty-five years as a colony and they remained independent after four years of war. The Soviet and American hegemons played their part in the outcome and aftermath, as did newly Communist China, but the end of Japanese empire in 1945 was not an invitation to recolonize.

The long Second World War, from the 1930s to the violent post-war years, ended not only a particular form of empire, but discredited the longer history of the term. In her 1961 Reith Lectures for the BBC, the Oxford Africanist Margery Perham observed that, of all the 'old authorities' currently condemned following the war, 'none has fared worse than imperialism'. This was, she believed, a profound historical shift. 'All through the sixty centuries of more or less recorded history,' she continued, 'imperialism, the extension of political power by one state over another, was ... taken for granted as part of the established order.' The only authority that people would now accept since the war 'is that which arises from their own wills, or can be made to appear to do so'.[173] Hence the scramble for the status of nation, 193 in total at the United Nations in 2019. The new body of nation states, represented by international institutions and regional pacts, has evidently not ended conflict, either international or domestic, but it is a different age from the one that existed before the onset of the last imperial war. The Second World War, more than the Revolutionary and Napoleonic wars, or the First World War, created the conditions for transforming not just Europe, but the entire global geopolitical order. That final stage of territorial empire was not, as Leonard Woolf had speculated in 1928, to be 'buried peacefully', but with a surfeit of 'blood and ruins'.

Notes

ABBREVIATIONS

AHB   Air Historical Branch, Northolt, Middlesex
BAB   Bundesarchiv- Berlin
BA-MA   Bundesarchiv- Militärarchiv, Freiburg
CCAC   Churchill College Archive Centre, Cambridge
IWM   Imperial War Museum, Lambeth, London
LC   Library of Congress, Washington, DC
NARA   National Archives and Records Administration, College Park, MD
TNA   The National Archives, Kew, London
TsAMO   Central Archive of the Russian Ministry of Defence, Podolsk
UEA   University of East Anglia, Norwich
USMC   United States Marine Corps
USSBS   United States Strategic Bombing Survey

Preface

1. Frederick Haberman (ed.), *Nobel Lectures: Peace, 1926–1950* (Amsterdam, 1972), 318. 2. Christopher Browning, *Ordinary Men: Reserve Police Battalion 101 and the Final Solution in Poland* (London, 1992). See too Richard Overy, '"Ordinary men", extraordinary circumstances: historians, social psychology, and the Holocaust', *Journal of Social Issues*, 70 (2014), 515–30. 3. See recently Gordon Corrigan, *The Second World War: A Military History* (London, 2010), Antony Beevor, *The Second World War* (London, 2013), Max Hastings, *All Hell Let Loose: The World at War 1939–1945* (London, 2011) and Andrew Roberts, *The Storm of War: A New History of the Second World War* (London, 2009). The best of the books with a less military focus are Gerhard Weinberg, *A World at Arms: A Global History of World War II* (Cambridge, 1994), Evan Mawdsley, *World War Two: A New History* (Cambridge, 2012) and the classic study by Gordon Wright, *The Ordeal of Total War, 1939–1945* (New York, 1968); more recently Andrew Buchanan, *World War II in Global Perspective: A Short History* (Hoboken, NJ, 2019) and Victor Hanson, *The Second World Wars: How the First Great Global Conflict was Fought and Won* (New York, 2019). A stimulating addition to the debate about the military outcome is Phillips O'Brien, *How the War was Won* (Cambridge, 2015). 4. Reto Hofmann and Daniel Hedinger, 'Axis Empires: towards a global history of fascist imperialism', *Journal of Global History*, 12 (2017), 161–5. See too Daniel Hedinger, 'The imperial nexus: the Second World War and the Axis in global perspective', ibid., 185–205. 5. On the Great War and its consequences for empire see Robert Gerwarth and Erez Manela, 'The Great War as a global war', *Diplomatic History*, 38 (2014), 786–800; Jane Burbank and Frederick Cooper, 'Empires after 1919: old, new, transformed', *International Affairs*, 95 (2019), 81–100. 6. On the limits of 'military' history see the stimulating lecture by Stig Förster, 'The

Battlefield: Towards a Modern History of War', German Historical Institute, London, 2007 Annual Lecture, and Jeremy Black, *Rethinking World War Two: The Conflict and its Legacy* (London, 2015).

Prologue

1. Leonard Woolf, *Imperialism and Civilization* (London, 1928), 17. **2.** Ibid., 9–12. **3.** Birthe Kundrus, *Moderne Imperialisten: Das Kaiserreich im Spiegel seiner Kolonien* (Cologne, 2003), 28. See too Helmut Bley, 'Der Traum vom Reich? Rechtsradikalismus als Antwort auf gescheiterte Illusionen im deutschen Kaiserreich 1900–1938', in Birthe Kundrus (ed.), *Phantasiereiche: zur Kulturgeschichte des deutschen Kolonialismus* (Frankfurt am Main, 2003), 56–67. **4.** Nicola Labanca, *Oltremare: Storia dell'espansione coloniale Italiana* (Bologna, 2002), 57. **5.** Louise Young, *Japan's Total Empire: Manchuria and the Culture of Wartime Imperialism* (Berkeley, Calif., 1998), 12–13, 22–3; Frederick Dickinson, 'The Japanese Empire', in Robert Gerwarth and Erez Manela (eds.), *Empires at War 1911–1923* (Oxford, 2014), 198–200. **6.** The idea of the 'nation-empire' has been widely discussed. See in particular the essay by Gary Wilder, 'Framing Greater France between the wars', *Journal of Historical Sociology*, 14 (2000), 198–202 and Heather Jones, 'The German Empire', in Gerwarth and Manela (eds.), *Empires at War*, 56–7. **7.** Birthe Kundrus, 'Die Kolonien – "Kinder des Gefühls und der Phantasie"', in *idem* (ed.), *Phantasiereiche*, 7–18. **8.** Paul Crook, *Darwinism, War and History* (Cambridge, 1994), 88–9. See too Mike Hawkins, *Social Darwinism in European and American Thought 1860–1945* (Cambridge, 1997), 203–15. **9.** Friedrich von Bernhardi, *Germany and the Next War* (London, 1914), 18. **10.** Benjamin Madley, 'From Africa to Auschwitz: how German South West Africa incubated ideas and methods adopted and developed by the Nazis in Eastern Europe', *European History Quarterly*, 35 (2005), 432–4; Guntram Herb, *Under the Map of Germany: Nationalism and Propaganda 1918–1945* (London, 1997), 50–51. **11.** Timothy Parsons, *The Second British Empire: In the Crucible of the Twentieth Century* (Lanham, Md, 2014), 8; Troy Paddock, 'Creating an oriental "Feindbild"', *Central European History*, 39 (2006), 230. **12.** Madley, 'From Africa to Auschwitz', 440. **13.** A useful discussion on the conceptual view of empire is found in Pascal Grosse, 'What does German colonialism have to do with National Socialism? A conceptual framework', in Eric Ames, Marcia Klotz and Lora Wildenthal (eds.), *Germany's Colonial Pasts* (Lincoln, Nebr., 2005), 118–29. **14.** Martin Thomas, *The French Empire between the Wars: Imperialism, Politics and Society* (Manchester, 2005), 1; Wilder, 'Framing Greater France', 205; Parsons, *Second British Empire*, 5, 83–4. **15.** Giuseppe Finaldi, '"The peasants did not think of Africa": empire and the Italian state's pursuit of legitimacy, 1871–1945', in John MacKenzie (ed.), *European Empires and the People: Popular Responses to Imperialism in France, Britain, the Netherlands, Germany and Italy* (Manchester, 2011), 214. **16.** Kundrus, *Moderne Imperialisten*, 32–7; Bernhard Gissibl, 'Imagination and beyond: cultures and geographies of imperialism in Germany, 1848–1918', in MacKenzie (ed.), *European Empires and the People*, 175–7. **17.** Kristin Kopp, 'Constructing racial difference in colonial Poland', in Ames, Klotz and Wildenthal (eds.), *Germany's Colonial Pasts*, 77–80; Bley, 'Der Traum von Reich?', 57–8; Kristin Kopp, 'Arguing the case for a colonial Poland', in Volker Langbehn and Mohammad Salama (eds.), *German Colonialism: Race, the Holocaust and Postwar Germany* (New York, 2011), 148–51; 'deepest barbarism' in Matthew Fitzpatrick, *Purging the Empire: Mass Expulsions in Germany, 1871–1914* (Oxford, 2015), 103. **18.** Kopp, 'Constructing racial difference', 85–9; Gissibl, 'Imagination and beyond', 162–3, 169–77. **19.** Robert Nelson, 'The Archive for Inner Colonization, the German East and World War I', in *idem* (ed.), *Germans, Poland, and Colonial Expansion to the East* (New York, 2009), 65–75. See too Edward Dickinson, 'The German Empire: an empire?', *History Workshop Journal*, 66 (2008), 132–5. **20.** Young, *Japan's Total Empire*, 89–90. **21.** Daniel Immerwahr, 'The Greater United States: territory and empire in U. S. history', *Diplomatic History*, 40 (2016), 377–81. **22.** Figures from Parsons, *Second British Empire*, 32. **23.** Finaldi, '"The peasants did not think of Africa"', 214; see too Lorenzo Veracini, 'Italian colonialism through a settler

colonial studies lens', *Journal of Colonialism and Colonial History*, 19 (2018), 2 for the idea that Italians contrasted their 'proletarian' imperialism with 'aristocratic' and 'bourgeois' imperialism. **24.** Labanca, *Oltremare*, 104–17. **25.** Richard Bosworth and Giuseppe Finaldi, 'The Italian Empire', in Gerwarth and Manela (eds.), *Empires at War*, 35; Finaldi, ' "The peasants did not think of Africa" ', 210–11; Labanca, *Oltremare*, 123–4. **26.** The best recent analyses of the 1914 crisis can be found in Christopher Clark, *The Sleepwalkers: How Europe Went to War in 1914* (London, 2012); Margaret MacMillan, *The War that Ended Peace: How Europe Abandoned Peace for the First World War* (London, 2013). **27.** See the discussion in Robert Gerwarth and Erez Manela, 'The Great War as a global war', *Diplomatic History*, 38 (2014), 786–800. **28.** William Mulligan, *The Great War for Peace* (New Haven, Conn., 2014), 91–2, 104–6; Bosworth and Finaldi, 'The Italian Empire', 40–43; Labanca, *Oltremare*, 117–27. **29.** Details in Jones 'German Empire', 63–4. **30.** Dickinson, 'The Japanese Empire', 199–201; Nicholas Tarling, *A Sudden Rampage: The Japanese Occupation of Southeast Asia, 1941–1945* (London, 2001), 24–6. **31.** John Darwin, *The Empire Project: The Rise and Fall of the British World System, 1830–1970* (Cambridge, 2009), 315–18; David Fieldhouse, *Western Imperialism and the Middle East, 1914–1958* (Oxford, 2006), 47–51. **32.** Jones, 'German Empire', 62; details on the German programme for destabilizing enemy empires in Jennifer Jenkins, 'Fritz Fischer's "Programme for Revolution": implications for a global history of Germany in the First World War', *Journal of Contemporary History*, 48 (2013), 399–403; David Olusoga, *The World's War* (London, 2014), 204–7, 224–8. **33.** Fieldhouse, *Western Imperialism*, 57–60. **34.** Vejas Liulevicius, *War Land on the Eastern Front: Culture, National Identity and German Occupation in World War I* (Cambridge, 2000), 63–72. **35.** Cited in Jones, 'The German Empire', 59, from Andrew Donson, 'Models for young nationalists and militarists: German youth literature in the First World War', *German Studies Review*, 27 (2004), 588. **36.** Paddock, 'Creating an oriental "Feindbild" ', 230; Vejas Liulevicius, 'The language of occupation: vocabularies of German rule in Eastern Europe in the World Wars' in Nelson (ed.), *Germans, Poland, and Colonial Expansion*, 122–30. **37.** Cited in Darwin, *The Empire Project*, 313. On Africa, see Jones, 'The German Empire', 69–70. **38.** Robert Gerwarth and Erez Manela, 'Introduction', in *idem* (eds.), *Empires at War*, 8–9; Philip Murphy, 'Britain as a global power', in Andrew Thompson (ed.), *Britain's Experience of Empire in the Twentieth Century* (Oxford, 2012), 39–40. **39.** Richard Fogarty, 'The French Empire', in Gerwarth and Manela (eds.), *Empires at War*, 109, 120–21. A higher figure of 607,000 soldiers conscripted is given in Berny Sèbe, 'Exalting imperial grandeur: the French Empire and its metropolitan public', in MacKenzie (ed.), *European Empires and the People*, 34. **40.** Erez Manela, *The Wilsonian Moment: Self-determination and the International Origins of Anticolonial Nationalism* (Oxford, 2007), 23–4, 43–4; Trygve Throntveit, 'The fable of the Fourteen Points: Woodrow Wilson and national self-determination', *Diplomatic History*, 35 (2011), 446–9, 454–5. **41.** Manela, *The Wilsonian Moment*, 37; Marcia Klotz, 'The Weimar Republic: a postcolonial state in a still colonial world', in Ames, Klotz and Wildenthal (eds.), *Germany's Colonial Pasts*, 139–40. **42.** Edward Drea, *Japan's Imperial Army: Its Rise and Fall, 1853–1945* (Lawrence, Kans, 2009), 142–5. On fear of Bolshevism in Europe see Robert Gerwarth and John Horne, 'Bolshevism as fantasy: fear of revolution and counter-revolutionary violence, 1917–1923', in *idem* (eds.), *War in Peace: Paramilitary Violence in Europe after the Great War* (Oxford, 2012), 40–51. **43.** Manela, *The Wilsonian Moment*, 59–65, 89–90. **44.** Cited in Manela, *The Wilsonian Moment*, 149. **45.** Ibid., 60–61. **46.** For full details see Susan Pedersen, *The Guardians: The League of Nations and the Crisis of Empire* (Oxford, 2015), 1–4, 29–32. **47.** Ibid., 2–3, 77–83. **48.** Ibid., 24–6. **49.** Wilder, 'Framing Greater France', 204–5; Thomas, *French Empire between the Wars*, 31–4. **50.** Thomas, *French Empire between the Wars*, 94–8, 103. **51.** Henri Cartier, *Comment la France 'civilise' ses colonies* (Paris, 1932), 5–6, 24. **52.** Sèbe, 'Exalting imperial grandeur', 36–8; Thomas, *French Empire between the Wars*, 199–202. **53.** Brad Beaven, *Visions of Empire: Patriotism, Popular Culture and the City, 1870–1939* (Manchester, 2012), 150–51, 164; Matthew Stanard, 'Interwar pro-Empire propaganda and European colonial culture: towards a comparative research agenda', *Journal of Contemporary History*, 44 (2009), 35. **54.** William Fletcher, *The Search for a New Order: Intellectuals and Fascism in Prewar Japan* (Chapel Hill, NC,

1982), 31–2; Dickinson, 'The Japanese Empire', 203–4; John Darwin, *After Tamerlane: The Global History of Empire since 1405* (London, 2007), 396–8; Hosoya Chihiro, 'Britain and the United States in Japan's view of the international system, 1919–1937', in Ian Nish (ed.), *Anglo-Japanese Alienation 1919–1952: Papers of the Anglo-Japanese Conference on the History of the Second World War* (Cambridge, 1982), 4–6. **55.** Tarling, *A Sudden Rampage,* 26. **56.** Sarah Paine, *The Wars for Asia 1911–1949* (Cambridge, 2012), 15–16; Jonathan Clements, *Prince Saionji: Japan. The Peace Conferences of 1919–23 and their Aftermath* (London, 2008), 131–6. **57.** Fletcher, *Search for a New Order*, 29–33, 42; Tarling, *A Sudden Rampage*, 25–7; Paine, *Wars for Asia*, 21–2; Young, *Japan's Total Empire*, 35–8. **58.** MacGregor Knox, *Common Destiny: Dictatorship, Foreign Policy and War in Fascist Italy and Nazi Germany* (Cambridge, 2000), 114–15. **59.** Bosworth and Finaldi, 'The Italian Empire', 41. **60.** Spencer Di Scala, *Vittorio Orlando: Italy: The Peace Conferences of 1919–23 and their Aftermath* (London, 2010), 140–41, 170–71. **61.** Claudia Baldoli, *Bissolati immaginario: Le origini del fascism cremonese* (Cremona, 2002), 50–53; Mulligan, *The Great War for Peace*, 269, 275–7, 281. **62.** Di Scala, *Vittorio Orlando*, 156–7, 173. **63.** See John Gooch, *Mussolini and His Generals: The Armed Forces and Fascist Foreign Policy, 1922–1940* (Cambridge, 2007), 62–8. **64.** Greg Eghigian, 'Injury, fate, resentment, and sacrifice in German political culture, 1914–1939', in G. Eghigian and M. Berg (eds.), *Sacrifice and National Belonging in Twentieth-Century Germany* (College Station, Tex., 2002), 91–4. **65.** Dirk van Laak, *Über alles in der Welt: Deutscher Imperialismus im 19. und 20. Jahrhundert* (Munich, 2005), 107; Shelley Baranowski, *Nazi Empire: German Colonialism and Imperialism from Bismarck to Hitler* (Cambridge, 2011), 154–5. **66.** Wolfe Schmokel, *Dream of Empire: German Colonialism, 1919–1945* (New Haven, Conn., 1964), 18–19. **67.** Christian Rogowski, '"Heraus mit unseren Kolonien!" Der Kolonialrevisionismus der Weimarer Republik und die "Hamburger Kolonialwoche" von 1926', in Kundrus (ed.), *Phantasiereiche*, 247–9. **68.** Uta Poiger, 'Imperialism and empire in twentieth-century Germany', *History and Memory*, 17 (2005), 122–3; Laak, *Über alles in der Welt*, 109–10; Schmokel, *Dream of Empire*, 2–3, 44–5; Andrew Crozier, 'Imperial decline and the colonial question in Anglo-German relations 1919–1939', *European Studies Review*, 11 (1981), 209–10, 214–17. **69.** David Murphy, *The Heroic Earth: Geopolitical Thought in Weimar Germany, 1918–1933* (Kent, Ohio, 1997), 16–17; Woodruff Smith, *The Ideological Origins of Nazi Imperialism* (New York, 1986), 218–20. **70.** Murphy, *The Heroic Earth*, 26–30; Smith, *Ideological Origins*, 218–24; Laak, *Über alles in der Welt*, 116–19. **71.** Herb, *Under the Map of Germany*, 77. **72.** Ibid., 52–7, 108–10. **73.** Vejas Liulevicius, *The German Myth of the East: 1800 to the Present* (Oxford, 2009), 156. **74.** Pedersen, *The Guardians*, 199–202; on decolonization see Laak, *Über alles in der Welt*, 120. It was coined by the economist Moritz Julius Bonn. **75.** Fletcher, *The Search for a New Order*, 40–41; Hosoya Chihiro, 'Britain and the United States', 5–6, 7–10. **76.** Knox, *Common Destiny*, 121–2, 126–8. **77.** Labanca, *Oltremare*, 138–9, 149–52, 173–5; A. de Grand, 'Mussolini's follies: Fascism and its imperial and racist phase', *Contemporary European History*, 13 (2004), 128–32; Gooch, *Mussolini and His Generals*, 123–6. **78.** This view is sustained in the best recent account of the crisis: see Robert Boyce, *The Great Interwar Crisis and the Collapse of Globalization* (Basingstoke, 2012), esp. 425–8. **79.** Laak, *Über alles in der Welt*, 127–8. **80.** Boyce, *Great Interwar Crisis*, 299. **81.** Jim Tomlinson, 'The Empire/Commonwealth in British economic thinking and policy', in Thompson (ed.), *Britain's Experience of Empire*, 219–20; Thomas, *French Empire between the Wars*, 93–8. **82.** Takafusa Nakamura and Kōnosuke Odaka (eds.), *Economic History of Japan 1914–1955* (Oxford, 1999), 33–7. **83.** Paine, *Wars for Asia*, 22–3; Fletcher, *Search for a New Order*, 40–42. **84.** On the German case see Horst Kahrs, 'Von der "Grossraumwirtschaft" zur "Neuen Ordnung"', in idem (ed.), *Modelle für ein deutschen Europa: Ökonomie und Herrschaft im Grosswirtschaftsraum* (Berlin, 1992), 9–13. **85.** Joyce Lebra, *Japan's Greater East Asia Co-Prosperity Sphere in World War II: Selected Readings and Documents* (Oxford, 1975), 74–5. **86.** 'Report on the work of the Central Committee to the Seventeenth Congress of the CPSU, 26 January 1934', in Joseph Stalin, *Problems of Leninism* (Moscow, 1947), 460.

1. Nation-Empires and Global Crisis

1. Cited in Louise Young, *Japan's Total Empire: Manchuria and the Culture of Wartime Imperialism* (Berkeley, Calif., 1998), 57–8. 2. Ibid., 39–41; Sarah Paine, *The Wars for Asia, 1911–1949* (Cambridge, 2012), 13–15; Edward Drea, *Japan's Imperial Army: Its Rise and Fall, 1853–1945* (Lawrence, Kans, 2009), 167–9. 3. A. de Grand, 'Mussolini's follies: fascism and its imperial and racist phase', *Contemporary European History*, 13 (2004), 137. 4. Young, *Japan's Total Empire*, 146–7. 5. Nicholas Tarling, *A Sudden Rampage: The Japanese Occupation of Southeast Asia, 1941–1945* (London, 2001), 28. 6. See Michael Geyer, '"There is a land where everything is pure: its name is land of death": some observations on catastrophic nationalism', in Greg Eghigian and Matthew Berg (eds.), *Sacrifice and National Belonging in Twentieth-Century Germany* (College Station, Tex., 2002), 120–41. 7. Steven Morewood, *The British Defence of Egypt 1935–1940: Conflict and Crisis in the Eastern Mediterranean* (London, 2005), 25–6. 8. CCAC, Christie Papers, 180/1/4, 'Notes of a conversation with Göring' by Malcolm Christie (former British air attaché, Berlin): 'Wir wollen ein *Reich*' [Christie's emphasis]. 9. Aurel Kolnai, *The War against the West* (London, 1938), 609. 10. De Grand, 'Mussolini's follies', 136; Davide Rodogno, *Fascism's European Empire: Italian Occupation during the Second World War* (Cambridge, 2006), 44–6. 11. Gerhard Weinberg (ed.), *Hitler's Second Book* (New York, 2003), 174. 12. Young, *Japan's Total Empire*, 101–6, 116–32. 13. Rainer Zitelmann, *Hitler: The Politics of Seduction* (London, 1999), 206–7; on anti-Westernism see Heinrich Winkler, *The Age of Catastrophe: A History of the West, 1914–1945* (New Haven, Conn., 2015), 909–12. 14. Patrick Bernhard, 'Borrowing from Mussolini: Nazi Germany's colonial aspirations in the shadow of Italian expansionism', *Journal of Imperial and Commonwealth History*, 41 (2013), 617–18; Ray Moseley, *Mussolini's Shadow: The Double Life of Count Galeazzo Ciano* (New Haven, Conn., 1999), 52. 15. Nicola Labanca, *Oltremare: Storia dell'espansione coloniale Italiana* (Bologna, 2002), 328–9; De Grand, 'Mussolini's follies', 133–4. By 1935 Italy's empire provided only 4.8 per cent of Italy's imports. On Albania see Bernd Fischer, *Albania at War, 1939–1945* (London, 1999), 5–6. 16. Ramon Myers, 'Creating a modern enclave economy: the economic integration of Japan, Manchuria and North China, 1932–1945', in Peter Duus, Ramon Myers and Mark Peattie (eds.), *The Japanese Wartime Empire, 1931–1945* (Princeton, NJ, 1996), 148; Paine, *Wars for Asia*, 13–15, 23; Tarling, *A Sudden Rampage*, 27–8. 17. Karsten Linne, *Deutschland jenseits des Äquators? Die NS-Kolonialplanungen für Afrika* (Berlin, 2008), 39. 18. CCAC, Christie Papers, 180/1/5, 'Notes from a conversation with Göring', 3 Feb. 1937, p. 51. 19. Weinberg (ed.), *Hitler's Second Book*, 16–18, 162. On the change in German economic thinking see Horst Kahrs, 'Von der "Grossraumwirtschaft" zur "Neuen Ordnung"', in Kahrs et al., *Modelle für ein deutsches Europa: Ökonomie und Herrschaft im Grosswirtschaftsraum* (Berlin, 1992), 9–10, 12–14; E. Teichert, *Autarkie und Grossraumwirtschaft in Deutschland, 1930–1939* (Munich, 1984), 261–8. On Hitler's economic thinking see Rainer Zitelmann, *Hitler: Selbstverständnis eines Revolutionärs* (Hamburg, 1989), 195–215. 20. On this see Patricia Clavin, *The Failure of Economic Diplomacy: Britain, Germany, France and the United States, 1931–1936* (London, 1996), chs. 6–7. 21. Otto Tolischus, *Tokyo Record* (London, 1943), 32. 22. George Steer, *Caesar in Abyssinia* (London, 1936), 401. 23. Malcolm Muggeridge (ed.), *Ciano's Diplomatic Papers* (London, 1948), 301–2. 24. Drea, *Japan's Imperial Army*, 182–6. 25. Wilhelm Treue, 'Denkschrift Hitlers über die Aufgaben eines Vierjahresplan', *Vierteljahreshefte für Zeitgeschichte*, 3 (1954), 204–6. 26. Kathleen Burke, 'The lineaments of foreign policy: the United States and a "New World Order", 1919–1939', *Journal of American Studies*, 26 (1992), 377–91. 27. G. Bruce Strang, 'Imperial dreams: the Mussolini–Laval Accords of January 1935', *The Historical Journal*, 44 (2001), 807–9. 28. Richard Overy, 'Germany and the Munich Crisis: a mutilated victory?', *Diplomacy & Statecraft*, 10 (1999), 208–11. 29. Susan Pedersen, *The Guardians: The League of Nations and the Crisis of Empire* (Oxford, 2015), 289–90, 291–2. 30. Paine, *Wars for Asia*, 25. 31. Benito Mussolini, 'Politica di vita' [*Il popolo d'Italia*, 11 Oct. 1935] in *Opera Omnia di Benito Mussolini: vol. XXVII* (Florence, 1959), 163–4. 32. Chad Bryant, *Prague in Black: Nazi Rule and Czech Nationalism* (Cambridge, Mass., 2007), 41–4.

33. Kristin Kopp, 'Arguing the case for a colonial Poland', in Volker Langbehn and Mohammad Salama (eds.), *German Colonialism: Race, the Holocaust and Postwar Germany* (New York, 2011), 150–51; David Furber, 'Near as far in the colonies: the Nazi occupation of Poland', *International History Review*, 26 (2004), 541–51. **34.** James Crowley, 'Japanese army factionalism in the early 1930s', *Journal of Asian Studies*, 21 (1962), 309–26. **35.** Drea, *Japan's Imperial Army*, 183–6; Tarling, *A Sudden Rampage*, 40–43. **36.** Details from Paine, *Wars for Asia*, 34–40; Takafusa Nakamura, 'The yen bloc, 1931–1941', in Duus, Myers and Peattie (eds.), *Japanese Wartime Empire*, 1789. **37.** Paine, *Wars for Asia*, 15. **38.** Takafusa Nakamura and Kōnosuke Odaka (eds.), *Economic History of Japan 1914–1945* (Oxford, 1999), 49–51; Paine, *Wars for Asia*, 24–30; Myers, 'Creating a modern enclave economy', 160. **39.** Yoshiro Miwa, *Japan's Economic Planning and Mobilization in Wartime, 1930s–1940s* (Cambridge, 2015), 62–4; Nakamura and Odaka (eds.), *Economic History of Japan*, 47–51; Akira Hari, 'Japan: guns before rice', in Mark Harrison (ed.), *The Economics of World War II: Six Great Powers in International Comparison* (Cambridge, 1998), 283–7. **40.** Hans van de Ven, *China at War: Triumph and Tragedy in the Emergence of the New China 1937–1952* (London, 2017), 58–64. **41.** Ibid., 66–70; Paine, *Wars for Asia*, 128–9. **42.** Rana Mitter, *China's War with Japan 1937–1945: The Struggle for Survival* (London, 2013), 73–4. **43.** Van de Ven, *China at War*, 68–76; Odd Arne Westad, *Restless Empire: China and the World since 1750* (London, 2012), 256–7. **44.** Paine, *Wars for Asia*, 128–9. **45.** Hans van de Ven, *War and Nationalism in China, 1925–1945* (New York, 2003), 194–5. **46.** Paine, *Wars for Asia*, 181–2. **47.** Mitter, *China's War with Japan*, 128–35; on the massacres see Iris Chang, *The Rape of Nanking: The Forgotten Holocaust of World War II* (New York, 1997), chs. 3–4. **48.** Van de Ven, *War and Nationalism*, 221–6. **49.** Diana Lary, *The Chinese People at War: Human Suffering and Social Transformation, 1937–1945* (Cambridge, 2010), 60–62; Mitter, *China's War with Japan*, 158–61. **50.** Paine, *Wars for Asia*, 134–5, 140–42; Mark Peattie, Edward Drea and Hans van de Ven (eds.), *The Battle for China: Essays on the Military History of the Sino-Japanese War of 1937–1945* (Stanford, Calif., 2011), 34–5. **51.** Dagfinn Gatu, *Village China at War: The Impact of Resistance to Japan, 1937–1945* (Copenhagen, 2007), 415–17. **52.** Paine, *Wars for Asia*, 165–7. **53.** MacGregor Knox, *Common Destiny: Dictatorship, Foreign Policy and War in Fascist Italy and Nazi Germany* (Cambridge, 2000), 69. **54.** Morewood, *British Defence of Egypt*, 32–45; Labanca, *Oltremare*, 184–8. **55.** Alberto Sbacchi, *Ethiopia under Mussolini: Fascism and the Colonial Experience* (London, 1985), 13–14; Morewood, *British Defence of Egypt*, 25–7. **56.** Claudia Baldoli, 'The "northern dominator" and the Mare Nostrum: Fascist Italy's "cultural war" in Malta', *Modern Italy*, 13 (2008), 7–12; Deborah Paci, *Corsica fatal, malta baluardo di romanità: irredentismo fascista nel mare nostrum (1922–1942)* (Milan, 2015), 16–19, 159–67. **57.** Matteo Dominioni, *Lo sfascio dell'impero: gli italiani in Etiopia 1936–1941* (Rome, 2008), 9–10; Sbacchi, *Ethiopia under Mussolini*, 15–18. **58.** Steer, *Caesar in Abyssinia*, 135–6, 139; Sbacchi, *Ethiopia under Mussolini*, 16–18. **59.** Angelo Del Boca, *I gas di Mussolini* (Rome, 1996), 76–7, 139–41, 148. There were in all 103 attacks using 281 mustard gas bombs and 325 phosgene bombs. **60.** On the war see Labanca, *Oltremare*, 189–92; Giorgio Rochat, *Le guerre italiane 1935–1943* (Turin, 2005), 48–74; Sbacchi, *Ethiopia under Mussolini*, 25–8. **61.** Figures from Sbacchi, *Ethiopia under Mussolini*, 33. **62.** Labanca, *Oltremare*, 200–202; Sbacchi, *Ethiopia under Mussolini*, 36–7. **63.** Giulia Barrera, 'Mussolini's colonial race laws and state-settler relations in Africa Orientale Italiana', *Journal of Modern Italian Studies*, 8 (2003), 429–30; Fabrizio De Donno, '"La Razza Ario-Mediterranea": Ideas of race and citizenship in colonial and Fascist Italy, 1885–1941', *Interventions: International Journal of Postcolonial Studies*, 8 (2006), 404–5. **64.** John Gooch, *Mussolini and His Generals: The Armed Forces and Fascist Foreign Policy, 1922–1940* (Cambridge, 2007), 253. **65.** Vera Zamagni, 'Italy: How to win the war and lose the peace', in Harrison (ed.), *The Economics of World War II*, 198; Rochat, *Le guerre italiane*, 139. There are different estimates of the cost of the Ethiopian war, ranging from 57.3 billion lire to 75.3 billion, depending on what is counted as a contribution to the war effort and subsequent pacification. **66.** Haile Larebo, *The Building of an Empire: Italian Land Policy and Practice in Ethiopia* (Trenton, NJ, 2006), 59–60. **67.** Sbacchi, *Ethiopia under Mussolini*, 98–100; De Grand, 'Mussolini's follies', 133; Haile Larebo,

'Empire building and its limitations. Ethiopia (1935–1941)', in Ruth Ben-Ghiat and Mia Fuller (eds.), *Italian Colonialism* (Basingstoke, 2005), 88–90.   68. Barrera, 'Mussolini's colonial race laws', 432–4.   69. Alexander Nützenadel, *Landwirtschaft, Staat und Autarkie: Agrarpolitik im faschistischen Italien (1922–1943)* (Tübingen, 1997), 144, 317, 394.   70. Rochat, *Le guerre italiane*, 117–21.   71. De Grand, 'Mussolini's follies', 128–9; Rodogno, *Fascism's European Empire*, 46–7.   72. De Donno, 'La Razza Ario-Mediterranea', 409.   73. Fischer, *Albania at War*, 5–7; Moseley, *Mussolini's Shadow*, 51–2.   74. Nicholas Doumanis, *Myth and Memory in the Mediterranean: Remembering Fascism's Empire* (London, 1997), 41–4.   75. Fischer, *Albania at War*, 17–20.   76. Ibid., 20, 35, 37–40, 90–91; Moseley, *Mussolini's Shadow*, 53–5; Rodogno, *Fascism's European Empire*, 59–60.   77. Albert Speer, *Inside the Third Reich* (London, 1970), 72.   78. Christian Leitz, 'Arms as levers: *matériel* and raw materials in Germany's trade with Romania in the 1930s', *International History Review*, 19 (1997), 317, 322–3.   79. Pierpaolo Barbieri, *Hitler's Shadow Empire: Nazi Economics and the Spanish Civil War* (Cambridge, Mass., 2015), 180–82, 260.   80. Treue, 'Denkschrift Hitlers', 204–5, 206.   81. BAB, R261/18, 'Ergebnisse der Vierjahresplan-Arbeit, Stand Frühjahr 1942', for a summary of the Plan's activities since 1936.   82. Richard Overy, *War and Economy in the Third Reich* (Oxford, 1994), 20–21.   83. Manfred Weissbecker, '"Wenn hier Deutsche wohnten": Beharrung und Veränderung im Russlandbild Hitlers und der NSDAP', in Hans-Erich Volkmann (ed.), *Das Russlandbild im Dritten Reich* (Cologne, 1994), 9.   84. Milan Hauner, 'Did Hitler want a world dominion?', *Journal of Contemporary History*, 13 (1978), 15–32.   85. 'Colloquio del ministro degli esteri, Ciano, con il cancelliere del Reich, Hitler', 24 October 1936, in *I documenti diplomatici italiani, 8 serie, vol v, 1 settembre–31 dicembre 1936* (Rome, 1994), 317.   86. Bernhard, 'Borrowing from Mussolini', 623–5.   87. Wolfe Schmokel, *Dream of Empire: German Colonialism, 1919–1945* (New Haven, Conn., 1964), 21–2, 30–32; Willeke Sandler, *Empire in the Heimat: Colonialism and Public Culture in the Third Reich* (New York, 2018), 3, 177–83.   88. Robert Gordon and Dennis Mahoney, 'Marching in step: German youth and colonial cinema', in Eric Ames, Marcia Klotz and Lora Wildenthal (eds.), *Germany's Colonial Pasts* (Lincoln, Nebr., 2005), 115–34.   89. Linne, *Deutschland jenseits des Äquators?*, 39.   90. CCAC, Christie Papers, 180/1, 'Notes of a conversation with Göring', 3 Feb. 1937, pp. 53–4.   91. Colonel Hossbach, 'Minutes of the conference in the Reich Chancellery, November 5 1937', *Documents on German Foreign Policy*, Ser. D, vol. I, (London, 1954), 29–39.   92. Geoffrey Megargee, *Inside Hitler's High Command* (Lawrence, Kans, 2000), 41–8.   93. Bryant, *Prague in Black*, 29–45; Alice Teichova, 'Instruments of economic control and exploitation: the German occupation of Bohemia and Moravia', in Richard Overy, Gerhard Otto and Johannes Houwink ten Cate (eds.), *Die 'Neuordnung' Europas: NS-Wirtschaftspolitik in den besetzten Gebiete* (Berlin, 1997), 84–8. See too Winkler, *Age of Catastrophe*, 658–60.   94. Teichova, 'Instruments of economic control', 50–58.   95. Full details can be found in Ralf Banken, *Edelmetallmangel und Grossraubwirtschaft: Die Entwicklung des deutschen Edelmetallsektors im 'Dritten Reich', 1933–1945* (Berlin, 2009), 287–91, 399–401.   96. Overy, *War and Economy*, 147–51.   97. Ibid., 319–21; Teichova, 'Instruments of economic control', 89–92.   98. Bryant, *Prague in Black*, 121–8.   99. Teichova, 'Instruments of economic control', 103–4.   100. Roman Ilnytzkyi, *Deutschland und die Ukraine 1934–1945*, 2 vols. (Munich, 1958), i., 21–2.   101. This view has been argued most forcefully by Gerhard Weinberg, *The Foreign Policy of Hitler's Germany: Starting World War II, 1937–1939* (Chicago, Ill., 1980), and Adam Tooze, *The Wages of Destruction: The Making and Breaking of the Nazi Economy* (London, 2006), 332–5, 662–5. For a different perspective see Overy, *War and Economy*, 221–6.   102. Overy, *War and Economy*, 238–9.   103. IWM, Mi 14/328 (d), OKW minutes of meeting of War Economy Inspectors, 21 Aug. 1939; OKW, Wehrmachtteile Besprechung, 3 Sept. 1939.   104. Richard Overy, *1939: Countdown to War* (London, 2009), 31–40.   105. Hildegard von Kotze (ed.), *Heeresadjutant bei Hitler 1938–1945: Aufzeichnungen des Majors Engel* (Stuttgart, 1974), 60, entry for 29 August; IWM, FO 645, Box 156, testimony of Hermann Göring taken at Nuremberg, 8 Sept. 1945, pp. 2, 5.   106. Cited in John Toland, *Adolf Hitler* (New York, 1976), 571.   107. Vejas Liulevicius, 'The language of occupation: vocabularies of German rule in Eastern Europe in the World Wars', in Robert Nelson (ed.), *Germans,*

Poland, and Colonial Expansion in the East (New York, 2009), 130–31.   **108.** Alexander Rossino, *Hitler Strikes Poland: Blitzkrieg, Ideology, and Atrocity* (Lawrence, Kans, 2003), 6–7.   **109.** Ibid., 7, 24–5, 27.   **110.** Winfried Baumgart, 'Zur Ansprache Hitlers vor den Führern der Wehrmacht am 22 August 1939', *Vierteljahreshefte für Zeitgeschichte*, 19 (1971), 303.   **111.** Elke Fröhlich (ed.), *Die Tagebücher von Joseph Goebbels: Band 7: Juli 1939–März 1940* (Munich, 1998), 87, entry for 1 Sept. 1939; Christian Hartmann, *Halder: Generalstabschef Hitlers 1938–1942* (Paderborn, 1991), 139.   **112.** On the military balance see Klaus Maier, Horst Rohde, Bernd Stegmann and Hans Umbreit, *Das Deutsche Reich und der Zweite Weltkrieg: Band II: Die Errichtung der Hegemonie auf dem europäischen Kontinent* (Stuttgart, 1979), 102–3, 111.   **113.** Halik Kochanski, *The Eagle Unbowed: Poland and the Poles in the Second World War* (London, 2012), 84–5.   **114.** Ibid., 84; Maier et al., *Das Deutsche Reich und der Zweite Weltkrieg: Band II*, 133. Soviet figures in Alexander Hill, 'Voroshilov's "lightning" war – the Soviet invasion of Poland, September 1939', *Journal of Slavic Military Studies*, 27 (2014), 409.   **115.** On the air force see Caius Bekker, *The Luftwaffe War Diaries* (London, 1972), 27–78, 466.   **116.** Jürgen Zimmerer, 'The birth of the *Ostland* out of the spirit of colonialism: a postcolonial perspective on the Nazi policy of conquest and extermination', *Patterns of Prejudice*, 39 (2005), 197–8.   **117.** Furber, 'Near as far in the colonies', 552, 570. On the colonial paradigm see Shelley Baranowski, *Nazi Empire: German Colonialism and Imperialism from Bismarck to Hitler* (Cambridge, 2011), 237–9.   **118.** M. Riedel, *Eisen und Kohle für das Dritte Reich* (Göttingen, 1973), 275–6, 301–2; Kochanski, *The Eagle Unbowed*, 100.   **119.** Catherine Epstein, *Model Nazi: Arthur Greiser and the Occupation of Western Poland* (Oxford, 2010), 135–7, 140.   **120.** Lora Wildenthal, *German Women for Empire, 1884–1945* (Durham, NC, 2001), 197–8.   **121.** Rossino, *Hitler Strikes Poland*, 10–13; Edward Westermann, *Hitler's Police Battalions: Enforcing Racial War in the East* (Lawrence, Kans, 2005), 124–8.   **122.** Jürgen Matthäus, Jochen Böhler and Klaus-Michael Mallmann, *War, Pacification, and Mass Murder 1939: The Einsatzgruppen in Poland* (Lanham, Md, 2014), 2–7.   **123.** Ibid., 20.   **124.** Timothy Snyder, *Bloodlands: Europe between Hitler and Stalin* (London, 2010), 126–8.   **125.** Furber, 'Near as far in the colonies', 562–3; Robert van Pelt, 'Bearers of culture, harbingers of destruction: the *mythos* of the Germans in the East', in Richard Etlin (ed.), *Art, Culture and Media under the Third Reich* (Chicago, Ill., 2002), 100–102, 127–9; Kopp, 'Arguing the case for a colonial Poland', in Langbehn and Salama (eds.), *German Colonialism*, 146–8, 155–7.   **126.** Christian Ingrao, *The Promise of the East: Nazi Hopes and Genocide 1939–43* (Cambridge, 2019), 5.   **127.** Isabel Heinemann, '"Another type of perpetrator": the SS racial experts and forced population movements in the occupied regions', *Holocaust and Genocide Studies*, 15 (2001), 391–2; Michael Burleigh, *Germany Turns Eastwards: A Study of Ostforschung in the Third Reich* (Cambridge, 1988), 159–60, 162–3; Baranowski, *Nazi Empire*, 243–52.   **128.** For a recent account of Nomonhan see Alistair Horne, *Hubris: The Tragedy of War in the Twentieth Century* (London, 2015), 133–56.   **129.** Keith Neilson, *Britain, Soviet Russia and the Collapse of the Versailles Order, 1919–1939* (Cambridge, 2005), 328–9.   **130.** Ibid., 257–61.   **131.** London School of Economics archive, National Peace Council papers, 2/5, minutes of Executive Committee, 13 Mar., 17 Apr. 1939.   **132.** Josef Konvitz, 'Représentations urbaines et bombardements stratégiques, 1914–1945', *Annales*, 44 (1989), 823–47.   **133.** Daniel Hucker, 'French public attitudes towards the prospect of war in 1938–39: "pacifism" or "war anxiety"?', *French History*, 21 (2007), 439, 441.   **134.** Gerald Lee, '"I see dead people": air-raid phobia and Britain's behaviour in the Munich Crisis', *Security Studies*, 13 (2003), 263.   **135.** Lawrence Pratt, *East of Malta, West of Suez: Britain's Mediterranean Crisis 1936–1939* (Cambridge, 1975), 3.   **136.** Ibid., 239–40.   **137.** Hucker, 'French public attitudes', 442–4; Donald Watt, 'British domestic politics and the onset of war', in Comité d'Histoire de la Deuxième Guerre Mondiale, *Les relations franco-brittaniques de 1935 à 1939* (Paris, 1975), 257–8; Charles-Robert Ageron, 'Vichy, les Français et l'Empire', in Jean-Pierre Azéma and François Bédarida (eds.), *Le Régime de Vichy et les Français* (Paris, 1992), 122.   **138.** Donald Low, *Eclipse of Empire* (Cambridge, 1991), 11, 29.   **139.** Matthew Hughes, *Britain's Pacification of Palestine: The British Army, the Colonial State and the Arab Revolt, 1936–1939* (Cambridge, 2019), 377–84.   **140.** League Against Imperialism, 'The British Empire', July 1935,

4–5. **141.** Martin Thomas, *The French Empire between the Wars: Imperialism, Politics and Society* (Manchester, 2005), 226–32; Timothy Parsons, *The Second British Empire: In the Crucible of the Twentieth Century* (Lanham, Md, 2014), 86–96. **142.** Claude Quétel, *L'impardonnable défaite* (Paris, 2010), 206–7. **143.** TNA, AIR 9/8, Air Staff memorandum, 15 Jan. 1936; Air Ministry (Plans) to Deputy Chief of Air Staff, 24 Sept. 1936. **144.** On the historical approaches to appeasement see Brian McKercher, 'National security and imperial defence: British grand strategy and appeasement 1930–1939', *Diplomacy & Statecraft*, 19 (2008), 391–42; Sidney Aster, 'Appeasement: before and after revisionism', ibid., 443–80. **145.** See for example Martin Thomas, 'Appeasement in the late Third Republic', *Diplomacy & Statecraft*, 19 (2008), 567–89. **146.** See for example Pierre Guillen, 'Franco-Italian relations in flux, 1918–1940', in Robert Boyce (ed.), *French Foreign and Defence Policy, 1918–1940: The Decline and Fall of a Great Power* (London, 1998), 149–61; Greg Kennedy, '1935: a snapshot of British imperial defence in the Far East', in Greg Kennedy and Keith Neilson (eds.), *Far-Flung Lines: Essays on Imperial Defence in Honour of Donald Mackenzie Schurman* (London, 1996), 190–210; Thomas, 'Appeasement', 578–91. **147.** Sidney Paish, 'Containment, rollback, and the origins of the Pacific War, 1933–1941', in Kurt Piehler and Sidney Paish (eds.), *The United States and the Second World War: New Perspectives on Diplomacy, War and the Home Front* (New York, 2010), 42–3, 45. **148.** Orlando Pérez, 'Panama: nationalism and the challenge to canal security', in Thomas Leonard and John Bratzel (eds.), *Latin America during World War II* (New York, 2006), 65–6. **149.** Neill Lochery, *Brazil: The Fortunes of War* (New York, 2014), 39–40, 61–2, 70. **150.** Sean Casey, *Cautious Crusade: Franklin D. Roosevelt, American Public Opinion and the War against Nazi Germany* (New York, 2001), 23. **151.** Chamberlain Papers, University of Birmingham, NC 18/1/1108, Chamberlain to his sister, Ida, 23 July 1939. **152.** George Peden, 'Sir Warren Fisher and British rearmament against Germany', *English Historical Review*, 94 (1979), 43–5; Robert Shay, *British Rearmament in the Thirties* (Princeton, NJ, 1977), 159, 223; Joe Maiolo, *Cry Havoc: The Arms Race and the Second World War 1931–1941* (London, 2010), 99–101. **153.** Morewood, *British Defence of Egypt*, 1, 95–6, 180–86. **154.** Franco Macri, *Clash of Empires in South China: The Allied Nations' Proxy War with Japan, 1935–1941* (Lawrence, Kans, 2012), 119–20, 154–7; Ashley Jackson, *The British Empire and the Second World War* (London, 2006), 17–19. **155.** Eugenia Kiesling, '"If it ain't broke, don't fix it": French military doctrine between the wars', *War in History*, 3 (1996), 215–18; Robert Doughty, *The Seeds of Disaster: The Development of French Army Doctrine, 1919–39* (Mechanicsburg, Pa, 1985), 95–105, 108–10. **156.** Thomas, *French Empire between the Wars*, 312–13, 323–5, 333–4. **157.** Morewood, *British Defence of Egypt*, 37–48. **158.** Peter Jackson, *France and the Nazi Menace: Intelligence and Policy Making 1933–1939* (Oxford, 2000), 289–96. **159.** Hans Groscurth, *Tagebuch eines Abwehroffiziers* (Stuttgart, 1970), 124. For this perspective on Munich see Overy, 'Germany and the Munich Crisis', 193–210. **160.** *Akten zur deutschen Auswärtigen Politik*, Series D, vol. 2, 772, minutes of meeting between Hitler and Horace Wilson, 27 Sept. 1938; Wacław Jędrzejewicz (ed.), *Diplomat in Berlin, 1933–1939: Papers and Memoirs of Józef Lipski* (New York, 1968), 425, letter from Lipski to Josef Beck. **161.** H. Michaelis and E. Schraepler (eds.), *Ursachen und Folgen vom deutschen Zusammenbruch 1918 bis 1945. Vol. 12: Das sudetendeutsche Problem* (Berlin, 1976), 438–40, Fritz Wiedemann über seine Eindrücke am 28 Sept. 1938. **162.** Groscurth, *Tagebuch*, 128, entries for 28, 30 Sept. 1938. **163.** André Maurois, *Why France Fell* (London, 1941), 21–2. **164.** Jean Levy and Simon Pietri, *De la République à l'État français 1930–1940: Le chemin de Vichy* (Paris, 1996), 160–61. **165.** TNA, AIR 9/105, chiefs of staff, 'British Strategical Memorandum, March 20 1939', pp. 6–7. On joint planning see William Philpott and Martin Alexander, 'The Entente Cordiale and the next war: Anglo-French views on future military cooperation, 1928–1939', *Intelligence and National Security*, 13 (1998), 68–76. **166.** John Darwin, *The Empire Project: The Rise and Fall of the British World-System, 1830–1970* (Cambridge, 2009), 494–7; Christopher Waters, 'Australia, the British Empire and the Second World War', *War & Society*, 19 (2001), 93–4. **167.** Thomas, *French Empire between the Wars*, 314–25; Martin Thomas, 'Economic conditions and the limits to mobilization in the French Empire 1936–1939', *Historical Journal*, 48 (2005),

482–90. 168. Hucker, 'French public attitudes', 442, 446; George Gallup (ed.), *The Gallup International Public Opinion Polls: Great Britain, 1937–1975* (New York, 1976), 10, 16, 21. 169. Richard Overy, *The Morbid Age: Britain and the Crisis of Civilization between the Wars* (London, 2009), 21–2. 170. Neilson, *Britain, Soviet Russia*, 314–15. 171. TNA, PREM 1/331a, note on Italian proposals, 2 Sept. 1939. 172. Brian Bond (ed.), *Chief of Staff: The Diaries of Lieutenant General Sir Henry Pownall: Volume One* (London, 1972), 221. 173. TNA, PREM 1/395, translation of Hitler speech of 6 Oct. 1939 for the prime minister, p. 18. 174. Winkler, *The Age of Catastrophe*, 670–71. 175. Quétel, *L'impardonnable défaite*, 216–17. 176. Maurois, *Why France Fell*, 73. 177. Speer, *Inside the Third Reich*, 163. 178. Megargee, *Inside Hitler's High Command*, 76; Nicolaus von Below, *At Hitler's Side: The Memoirs of Hitler's Luftwaffe Adjutant 1937–1945* (London, 2001), 40–41. 179. TNA, PREM 1/395, Lord Halifax, draft response to Hitler, 8 Oct. 1939; Churchill to Chamberlain, 9 Oct. 1939; minute for Chamberlain from Alexander Cadogan (Foreign Office), 8 Oct. 1939. 180. Willi Boelcke (ed.), *The Secret Conferences of Dr. Goebbels 1939–1943* (London, 1967), 6, directive of 16 Dec. 1939; *Fuehrer Conferences on Naval Affairs 1939–1945* (London, 1990), 60, Conference of Department Heads, 25 Nov. 1939. 181. Megargee, *Inside Hitler's High Command*, 76. 182. Karl-Heinz Frieser, *The Blitzkrieg Legend: The 1940 Campaign in the West* (Annapolis, Md, 2012), 63–8; Mungo Melvin, *Manstein: Hitler's Greatest General* (London, 2010), 136–7, 142, 149–51, 154–5; von Below, *At Hitler's Side*, 40–41. 183. Martin Alexander, 'The fall of France, 1940', *Journal of Strategic Studies*, 13 (1990), 13–21; Julian Jackson, *The Fall of France: The Nazi Invasion of 1940* (Oxford, 2003), 75–6. 184. TNA, PREM 1/437, press communiqué on meeting of the Supreme War Council, 15 Nov. 1939. 185. Brian Bond, *France and Belgium 1939–1940* (London, 1990), 40–41, 49–51, 58–9. 186. Martin Alexander, '"Fighting to the last Frenchman?" Reflections on the BEF deployment to France and the strains in the Franco-British alliance, 1939–1940', in Joel Blatt (ed.), *The French Defeat of 1940: Reassessments* (Providence, RI, 1998), 323–6; Bond, *France and Belgium*, 76–7. 187. Quétel, *L'impardonnable défaite*, 237; Robert Desmond, *Tides of War: World News Reporting 1931–1945* (Iowa City, Iowa, 1984), 93. 188. Gallup (ed.), *International Opinion Polls*, 22, 30. 189. Quétel, *L'impardonnable défaite*, 246; Alan Allport, *Browned Off and Bloody-Minded: The British Soldier Goes to War 1939–1945* (New Haven, Conn., 2015), 44. 190. Talbot Imlay, 'France and the Phoney War 1939–1940', in Boyce (ed.), *French Foreign and Defence Policy*, 265–6. 191. TNA, WO 193/144, War Office Memorandum for the Supreme War Council, 15 Dec. 1939; Director of Military Operations report, 'Operational Considerations affecting Development of Equipment for Land Offensive', 12 Apr. 1940. 192. Richard Overy, 'Air Power, Armies, and the War in the West, 1940', 32nd Harmon Memorial Lecture, US Air Force Academy, Colorado Springs, 1989, 1–2. 193. Guillen, 'Franco-Italian relations in flux', 160–61. 194. Morewood, *British Defence of Egypt*, 139–47. 195. Macri, *Clash of Empires in South China*, 195–201, 214–15. 196. Geoffrey Roberts, 'Stalin's wartime vision of the peace, 1939–1945', in Timothy Snyder and Ray Brandon (eds.), *Stalin and Europe: Imitation and Domination 1928–1953* (New York, 2014), 234–6; Martin Kahn, *Measuring Stalin's Strength during Total War* (Gothenburg, 2004), 87–9. 197. TNA, WO 193/144, War Office memorandum 'Assistance to Finland', 16 Dec. 1939 ('we cannot recommend that we should declare war on Russia'); Kahn, *Measuring Stalin's Strength*, 90–92. 198. Gabriel Gorodetsky (ed.), *The Maisky Diaries: Red Ambassador at the Court of St James's, 1932–1943* (New Haven, Conn., 2015), 245, entry for 12 Dec. 1939. 199. Patrick Salmon, 'Great Britain, the Soviet Union, and Finland', in John Hiden and Thomas Lane (eds.), *The Baltic and the Outbreak of the Second World War* (Cambridge, 1991), 116–17; Thomas Munch-Petersen, 'Britain and the outbreak of the Winter War', in Robert Bohn et al. (eds.), *Neutralität und totalitäre Aggression: Nordeuropa und die Grossmächteim Zweiten Weltkrieg* (Stuttgart, 1991), 87–9; John Kennedy, *The Business of War* (London, 1957), 47–8. 200. TNA, PREM 1/437, Reynaud to Chamberlain and Lord Halifax, 25 Mar. 1940. 201. TNA, PREM 1/437, memorandum for the prime minister, 'Possibilities of Allied Action against the Caucasus', March 1940, p. 3. For details of the operation see C. O. Richardson, 'French plans for Allied attacks on the Caucasus oil fields January–April 1940', *French Historical Studies*, 8 (1973),

130–53. **202.** Edward Spears, *Assignment to Catastrophe* (London, 1954), 102–6; Jackson, *Fall of France*, 82–4. **203.** Walter Warlimont, *Inside Hitler's Headquarters 1939–45* (London, 1964), 66–72. **204.** *Fuehrer Conferences on Naval Affairs*, 63–7, 80–84. **205.** Maier et al., *Das Deutsche Reich und der Zweite Weltkrieg: Band II*, 212–17; British Air Ministry, *The Rise and Fall of the German Air Force* (London, 1983), 60–63. **206.** Maier et al., *Das Deutsche Reich und der Zweite Weltkrieg: Band II*, 224. **207.** Robert Rhodes James (ed.), *The Diaries of Sir Henry Channon* (London, 1993), 244–50, entries for 7, 8, 9 May 1940. **208.** Frieser, *Blitzkrieg Legend*, 36–48. The statistics on air power are subject to some variation, depending on levels of serviceability on particular days and the classification of reserves. Patrick Facon, *L'Armée de l'Air dans la tourmente: La Bataille de France 1939–1940* (Paris, 1997), 151–69, arrives at rather different figures: 5,524 aircraft for the Allies, 3,959 for the German side. See too Ernest May, *Strange Victory: Hitler's Conquest of France* (New York, 2000), 479, who gives figures for bombers and fighters for the two sides: 2,779 German against 5,133 Allied. **209.** Frieser, *Blitzkrieg Legend*, 45; Facon, *L'Armée de l'Air*, 169, 205; Jackson, *Fall of France*, 15–17. **210.** Jackson, *Fall of France*, 21–5. On the German horse-drawn tail see Richard Dinardo, *Mechanized Juggernaut or Military Anachronism? Horses and the German Army of WWII* (Mechanicsburg, Pa, 2008), 24–6. **211.** Quétel, *L'impardonnable défaite*, 246. **212.** Frieser, *Blitzkrieg Legend*, 93. **213.** Henri Wailly, 'La situation intérieure', in Philippe Ricalens and Jacques Poyer (eds.), *L'Armistice de juin 1940: Faute ou necessité?* (Paris, 2011), 48–9. **214.** Von Below, *At Hitler's Side*, 57. **215.** Frieser, *Blitzkrieg Legend*, 107–12. **216.** Ibid., 161. **217.** Jackson, *Fall of France*, 45–7. **218.** David Dilks (ed.), *The Diaries of Sir Alexander Cadogan 1938–1945* (London, 1971), 284, entry for 16 May; Spears, *Assignment to Catastrophe*, 150. **219.** Megargee, *Inside Hitler's High Command*, 85. **220.** Hugh Sebag-Montefiore, *Dunkirk: Fight to the Last Man* (London, 2006), 3. **221.** Max Schiaron, 'La Bataille de France, vue par le haut commandement français', in Ricalens and Poyer (eds.), *L'Armistice de juin 1940*, 3–5. **222.** Stephen Roskill, *Hankey: Man of Secrets, Volume III 1931–1963* (London, 1974), 477–8. **223.** Claude Huan, 'Les capacités de transport maritime', in Ricalens and Poyer (eds.), *L'Armistice de juin 1940*, 37–8. **224.** Frieser, *Blitzkrieg Legend*, 301–2. **225.** Allport, *Browned Off and Bloody-Minded*, 55–6. **226.** Sebag-Montefiore, *Dunkirk*, 250–53. **227.** Paul Gaujac, 'L'armée de terre française en France et en Afrique du Nord', in Ricalens and Poyer (eds.), *L'Armistice de juin 1940*, 15–16. **228.** Huan, 'Les capacités de transport maritime', 38–9. On Polish soldiers see Kochanski, *The Eagle Unbowed*, 212–16. **229.** Jacques Belle, 'La volonté et la capacité de défendre l'Afrique du Nord', in Ricalens and Poyer (eds.), *L'Armistice de juin 1940*, 150–57; Gaujac, 'L'armée de terre française', 20–22. **230.** Schiaron, 'La Bataille de France', 7–8. **231.** Ibid., 9–11; Elisabeth du Réau, 'Le débat de l'armistice', in Ricalens and Poyer (eds.), *L'Armistice de juin 1940*, 65–9. **232.** Schiaron, 'La Bataille de France', 11–12; Jackson, *Fall of France*, 143. **233.** Gilles Ragache, 'La bataille continue!', in Ricalens and Poyer (eds.), *L'Armistice de juin 1940*, 142–5. **234.** Rochat, *Le guerre italiane*, 239. **235.** Gooch, *Mussolini and His Generals*, 494–8, 508–11; Robert Mallett, *Mussolini and the Origins of the Second World War, 1933–1940* (Basingstoke, 2003), 214–17. **236.** Gooch, *Mussolini and His Generals*, 510. **237.** Galeazzo Ciano, *Diario 1937–1943*, ed. Renzo di Felice (Milan, 1998), 429, 435, 442, entries for 13 May, 28 May, 10 June 1940. **238.** Rodogno, *Fascism's European Empire*, 25–6. Ciano, *Diario*, 444, entry for 18/19 June 1940. **239.** Ciano, *Diario*, 443, entry for 18/19 June 1940. **240.** Ragache, 'La bataille continue!', 143–4. **241.** Rochat, *Le guerre italiane*, 248–50. **242.** Karine Varley, 'Entangled enemies: Vichy, Italy and collaboration', in Ludivine Broch and Alison Carrol (eds.), *France in an Era of Global War, 1914–1945: Occupation Politics, Empire and Entanglements* (Basingstoke, 2014), 153–5; Rodogno, *Fascism's European Empire*, 26–7. On German terms see Thomas Laub, *After the Fall: German Policy in Occupied France 1940–1944* (Oxford, 2010), 36–9. **243.** Roberts, 'Stalin's wartime vision of the peace', 236–7. **244.** Ciano, *Diario*, 443, entry for 18/19 June 1940. **245.** Randolph Churchill (ed.), *Into Battle: Speeches by the Right Hon. Winston S. Churchill* (London, 1941), 255–6, 259. **246.** John Colville, *The Fringes of Power: Downing Street Diaries 1939–1955: Volume 1 1939–October 1941* (London, 1985), 267, entry for 20 Aug. 1940. **247.** Gorodetsky, *Maisky Diaries*, 304, entry for 20 Aug.

1940. **248.** Ibid., 287, entry for 17 June 1940. **249.** Hastings Ismay, *Memoirs* (London, 1960), 153. **250.** James (ed.), *The Diaries of Sir Henry Channon*, 261–2. **251.** Srinath Raghavan, *India's War: The Making of Modern South Asia, 1939–1945* (London, 2016), 47–8. **252.** On Soviet views see Sergei Kudryashov, 'The Soviet perspective', in Paul Addison and Jeremy Crang (eds.), *The Burning Blue: A New History of the Battle of Britain* (London, 2000), 71–2. On France see Robert Tombs and Isabelle Tombs, *That Sweet Enemy: Britain and France* (London, 2007), 10, 571–3. **253.** Colville, *Fringes of Power*, 176, entry for 6 June 1940. **254.** Robert Self, *Neville Chamberlain: A Biography* (Aldershot, 2006), 434; for the Churchill quotation, Spears, *Assignment to Catastrophe*, 70, who reported Churchill's remark that 'We were quite capable of beating the Germans single-handed'. **255.** Paul Addison and Jeremy Crang (eds.), *Listening to Britain: Home Intelligence Reports on Britain's Finest Hour May–September 1940* (London, 2011), 80, 123, 126, entries for 5 June, 17 June and 18 June 1940. See too Richard Toye, *The Roar of the Lion: The Untold Story of Churchill's World War II Speeches* (Oxford, 2013), 51–9. **256.** John Charmley, *Lord Lloyd and the Decline of the British Empire* (London, 1987), 251. **257.** John Ferris and Evan Mawdsley, 'The war in the West', in *idem* (eds.), *The Cambridge History of the Second World War: Volume I: Fighting the War* (Cambridge, 2015), 350. **258.** Richard Toye, *Lloyd George and Churchill: Rivals for Greatness* (London, 2007), 342, 363–9, 380; Antony Lentin, *Lloyd George and the Lost Peace: From Versailles to Hitler, 1919–1940* (Basingstoke, 2001), 121–7. **259.** Self, *Neville Chamberlain*, 433. **260.** Richard Hallion, 'The American perspective', in Addison and Crang (eds.), *The Burning Blue*, 83–4. **261.** Richard Overy, *The Bombing War: Europe 1939–1945* (London, 2013), 252–4. **262.** Toye, *Roar of the Lion*, 54. **263.** Richard Toye, *Churchill's Empire: The World that Made Him and the World He Made* (New York, 2010), 203–4. **264.** Jackson, *The British Empire and the Second World War*, 21–3. **265.** Parsons, *The Second British Empire*, 108–9; K. Fedorowich, 'Sir Gerald Campbell and the British High Commission in wartime Ottawa, 1938–40', *War in History*, 19 (2012), 357–85; Toye, *Churchill's Empire*, 209; Jonathan Vance, *Maple Leaf Empire: Canada, Britain, and Two World Wars* (Oxford, 2012), 149–50, 179; Darwin, *The Empire Project*, 495–7. **266.** Clair Wills, *The Neutral Island: A History of Ireland during the Second World War* (London, 2007), 41–8; Toye, *Churchill's Empire*, 196–7, 207. **267.** Raghavan, *India's War*, 13–16, 38–9, 52–60, 69–70. **268.** Dilks (ed.), *Diaries of Sir Alexander Cadogan*, 311, entry for 5 July 1940; Tarling, *A Sudden Rampage*, 54–5. **269.** Morewood, *British Defence of Egypt*, 174–7, 193–8. **270.** Ageron, 'Vichy, les Français et l'Empire', 122. **271.** Schmokel, *Dream of Empire*, 144–54. **272.** Gerhard Schreiber, Bernd Stegemann and Detlef Vogel, *Germany and the Second World War: Volume III* (Oxford, 1995), 282–8; Schmokel, *Dream of Empire*, 140–44. **273.** Donald Nuechterlein, *Iceland: Reluctant Ally* (Ithaca, NY, 1961), 23–36. **274.** William Roger Louis, *Imperialism at Bay: The United States and the Decolonization of the British Empire, 1941–1945* (Oxford, 1977), 158, 175–7; Neil Smith, *American Empire: Roosevelt's Geographer and the Prelude to Globalization* (Berkeley, Calif., 2003), 353–5. **275.** Guy Vanthemsche, *Belgium and the Congo 1885–1980* (Cambridge, 2012), 122–6, 130. **276.** Jonathan Helmreich, *United States Relations with Belgium and the Congo, 1940–1960* (Newark, NJ, 1998), 25–40. **277.** Jennifer Foray, *Visions of Empire in the Nazi-Occupied Netherlands* (Cambridge, 2012), 3–5. **278.** Ibid., 50–51, 54, 109–15. **279.** Ibid., 50–53; Tarling, *A Sudden Rampage*, 66–8. **280.** Marcel Boldorf, 'Grenzen des nationalsozialistischen Zugriffs auf Frankreichs Kolonialimporte (1940–1942)', *Vierteljahresschrift für Wirtschafts-Sozialgeschichte*, 97 (2010), 148–50. **281.** Ageron, 'Vichy, les Français et l'Empire', 123–4, 128–9; Frederick Quinn, *The French Overseas Empire* (Westport, Conn., 2000), 219–20. **282.** Tarling, *A Sudden Rampage*, 53–4; Martin Thomas, *The French Empire at War 1940–45* (Manchester, 1998), 45–6. **283.** Charmley, *Lord Lloyd*, 246–7. **284.** Tombs and Tombs, *That Sweet Enemy*, 561, 572–3. **285.** Ibid., 562–3; Christopher Bell, *Churchill and Sea Power* (Oxford, 2013), 197–9; Raymond Dannreuther, *Somerville's Force H: The Royal Navy's Gibraltar-based Fleet, June 1940 to March 1942* (London, 2005), 28–34. **286.** Martin Thomas, 'Resource war, civil war, rights war: factoring empire into French North Africa's Second World War', *War in History*, 18 (2011), 225–48. **287.** Varley, 'Entangled enemies', 155–6. **288.** Quinn, *French Overseas Empire*, 221–2; Thomas, *French*

Empire at War, 52–8.   289. Robert Frank, 'Vichy et les Britanniques 1940–41: double jeu ou double langage?', in Azéma and Bédarida (eds.), Le Régime de Vichy et les Français, 144–8. On Dakar see Thomas, French Empire at War, 75–6; Bell, Churchill and Sea Power, 209.   290. Foray, Visions of Empire, 93, 103.   291. Varley, 'Entangled enemies', 155–8.   292. Ciano, Diario, 449, 452, entries for 2 July, 16 July 1940.   293. Max Domarus, Hitler: Reden und Proklomationen 1932-1945, 3 vols. Volume II, Untergang (Munich, 1965), 1538.   294. Elke Fröhlich (ed.), Die Tagebücher von Joseph Goebbels: Sämtliche Fragmente, 4 vols. (Munich: K. G. Saur, 1987), iv, 221, 227, entries for 28 June, 4 July 1940. On the 'go-betweens' see Karina Urbach, Go-Betweens for Hitler (Oxford, 2015).   295. Domarus, Reden und Proklomationen, ii, 1537–8, Halder's notes of meeting at the Berghof, 13 July 1940; von Below, At Hitler's Side, 67–8.   296. Gerwin Strobl, The Germanic Isle: Nazi Perceptions of Britain (Cambridge, 2000), 84, 92–4.   297. Domarus, Reden und Proklamationen, ii, 1557–8.   298. Fröhlich (ed.), Tagebücher: Sämtliche Fragmente, iv, 246–7, entry for 20 July 1940.   299. Colville, Fringes of Power, 234, entry for 24 July 1940.   300. Fröhlich (ed.), Tagebücher: Sämtliche Fragmente, iv, 250, entry for 24 July 1940.   301. Walter Hubatsch (ed.), Hitlers Weisungen für die Kriegführung (Frankfurt am Main, 1962), 71–2, Directive No. 16.   302. Von Below, At Hitler's Side, 68–9, entry for 21 July 1940.   303. Domarus, Reden und Proklamationen, ii, 1561, General Halder's report on meeting with the Führer, 21 July 1940.   304. Toye, Lloyd George and Churchill, 376.   305. Domarus, Reden und Proklamationen, ii, 1561; Fröhlich (ed.), Tagebücher: Sämtliche Fragmente, iv, 249.   306. BA-MA, I Fliegerkorps, 'Gedanken über die Führung des Luftkrieges gegen England', 24 July 1940. On German preparations see Horst Boog, 'The Luftwaffe's assault', in Addison and Crang, Burning Blue, 40–41.   307. Bell, Churchill and Sea Power, 199.   308. Overy, The Bombing War, 251–2.   309. TNA, AIR 16/212, No. 11 Group Operational Orders, 'Measures to Counter an Attempted German Invasion, Summer 1940', 8 July 1940, p. 2.   310. AHB, 'Battle of Britain: Despatch by Air Chief Marshal Sir Hugh Dowding', 20 Aug. 1940, 569.   311. Hubatsch (ed.), Hitlers Weisungen für die Kriegführung, 75–6; AHB, German Translations, vol. 1, VII/21, OKW directive 'Operation Sea Lion', 1 Aug. 1940.   312. TNA, PREM 3/29 (3), Fighter Command Order of Battle, 6 Sept. 1940.   313. TNA, AIR 22/72, report on German propaganda, Aug. 1940.   314. Percy Schramm (ed.), Kriegstagebuch/OKW: Band 1, Teilband 1 (Augsburg, 2007), 59–60, entry for 3 Sept. 1940.   315. TNA, AIR 16/432, Home Security intelligence summary, 'Operations during the Night of 5/6 September'.   316. Ibid., reports for 24/25, 25/26 and 28/29 Aug. 1940. The first night three London boroughs were hit, the second night five, and the third night eleven.   317. Overy, The Bombing War, 83–4; Fröhlich (ed.), Tagebücher: Sämtliche Fragmente, iv, 309.   318. Allport, Browned Off and Bloody-Minded, 68.   319. David French, Raising Churchill's Army: The British Army and the War against Germany 1919–1945 (Oxford, 2000), 185, 189–90; Alex Danchev and Daniel Todman (eds.), War Diaries: Field Marshal Lord Alanbrooke, 1939–1945 (London, 2001), 108, entry for 15 Sept. 1940.   320. TNA, AIR 8/372, minute by chief of the air staff, 22 May 1940; Cripps to War Cabinet, 26 June 1940; Foreign Office minute for Churchill, 3 July 1940.   321. TNA, INF 1/264, Home Intelligence, Summary of daily reports, 4 Sept. 1940.   322. Virginia Cowles, Looking for Trouble (London, 1941), 448–9, 452.   323. Warlimont, Inside Hitler's Headquarters, 114.   324. Ibid., 115–7; von Below, At Hitler's Side, 72.

2. Imperial Fantasies, Imperial Realities

1. F. C. Jones, Japan's New Order in East Asia (Oxford, 1954), 469. This is a translation from the German text. The original was in English and this version had 'each its own proper place' rather than 'the space to which it is entitled . . .' The term 'Raum' (space) was inserted in the German version to make the nature of the New Order more explicitly territorial.   2. Galeazzo Ciano, Diario 1937-1943, ed. Renzo de Felice (Milan, 1998), 466–7; William Shirer, Berlin Diary: The Journal of a Foreign Correspondent 1934–1941 (London, 1941), 417–20, entry for 27 Sept. 1940.   3. On the English version see Akten der deutschen auswärtigen Politik: Band XI:I (Göttingen, 1964), 153–4, von Mackensen to the German Foreign Office, 24 Sept.

1940, and 140–41, von Ribbentrop to von Mackensen, 24 Sept. 1944; Otto Tolischus, *Tokyo Record* (London, 1943), 30 (speech of 27 Jan. 1941).   **4.** Horst Kahrs, 'Von der "Grossraum-wirtschaft" zur "Neuen Ordnung"', in Kahrs et al., *Modelle für ein deutsches Europa: Ökonomie und Herrschaft im Grosswirtschaftsraum* (Berlin, 1992), 17–22; Gustavo Corni, *Il sogno del 'grande spazio': Le politiche d'occupazione nell'europa nazista* (Rome, 2005), 61–8; Paolo Fonzi, *La moneta nel grande spazio: Il progetto nazionalsocialista di integrazione monetaria europea 1939–1945* (Milan, 2011), 116–17, 121, 167–9.   **5.** Geoffrey Megargee, *Inside Hitler's High Command* (Lawrence, Kans, 2000), 90–91; Nicolaus von Below, *At Hitler's Side: The Memoirs of Hitler's Luftwaffe Adjutant 1937–1945* (London, 2001), 72–3.   **6.** The best account of these negotiations can be found in Norman Goda, *Tomorrow the World: Hitler, Northwest Africa, and the Path toward America* (College Station, Tex., 1998). See too H. James Burgwyn, *Mussolini Warlord: Failed Dreams of Empire 1940–1943* (New York, 2012), 22–9.   **7.** Gabriel Gorodetsky, *Grand Delusion: Stalin and the German Invasion of Russia* (New Haven, Conn., 1999), 17–18.   **8.** Joachim von Ribbentrop, *The Ribbentrop Memoirs* (London, 1954), 149–52.   **9.** Von Below, *At Hitler's Side*, 74–5.   **10.** Sönke Neitzel, *Der Einsatz der deutschen Luftwaffe über dem Atlantik und der Nordsee 1939–1945* (Bonn, 1995), 55–6, 68.   **11.** Christopher Bell, *Churchill and Sea Power* (Oxford, 2013), 215.   **12.** W. J. R. Gardner, *Decoding History: The Battle of the Atlantic and Ultra* (Basingstoke, 1999), 177; Marc Milner, *The Battle of the Atlantic* (Stroud, 2005), 40, 46.   **13.** Milner, *Battle of the Atlantic*, 40–41; Bell, *Churchill and Sea Power*, 216, 224.   **14.** Milner, *Battle of the Atlantic*, 43–4.   **15.** Figures calculated from Arnold Hague, *The Allied Convoy System 1939–1945: Its Organization, Defence and Operations* (London, 2000), 23–5, 107–8.   **16.** Ralph Erskine, 'Naval Enigma: a missing link', *International Journal of Intelligence and Counter-Intelligence*, 3 (1989), 497–9.   **17.** Richard Overy, *The Bombing War: Europe 1939–1945* (London, 2013), 84–5; Percy Schramm (ed.), *Kriegstagebuch/OKW: Band 1, Teilband 1* (Augsburg, 2007), 76, entry for 14 Sept. 1940.   **18.** BA-MA, RL2 IV/27, 'Grossangriffe bei Nacht gegen Lebenszentren Englands, 12.8.1940–26.6.41'.   **19.** TsAMO, f.500, o. 725168, d. 110, Luftwaffe Operations Staff report on British targets and air strength, 14 Jan. 1941; *Fuehrer Conferences on Naval Affairs, 1939–1945* (London, 1990), 179, 'Basic Principles of the Prosecution of the War against British War Economy'.   **20.** Michael Postan, *British War Production* (London, 1957), 484–5; Klaus Maier, Horst Rohde, Bernd Stegmann and Hans Umbreit, *Das Deutsche Reich und der Zweite Weltkrieg: Band II: Die Errichtung der Hegemonie auf dem europäischen Kontinent* (Stuttgart, 1979), 402–4.   **21.** C. B. A. Behrens, *Merchant Shipping and the Demands of War* (London, 1955), 325. In 1941 there were almost 17 million tons of food and imported materials in stock.   **22.** John Darwin, *The Empire Project: The Rise and Fall of the British World-System 1830–1970* (Cambridge, 2009), 510–11.   **23.** Warren Kimball, '"Beggar my neighbor": America and the British interim finance crisis 1940–41', *Journal of Economic History*, 29 (1969), 758–72; idem (ed.), *Churchill & Roosevelt: The Complete Correspondence*, 3 vols. (London, 1984), i, 139, Churchill memorandum, 1 Mar. 1941.   **24.** Nigel Nicolson (ed.), *Harold Nicolson: Diaries and Letters 1939–45* (London, 1967), 144–5, letter to W. B. Jarvis.   **25.** Orio Vergani, *Ciano: una lunga confessione* (Milan, 1974), 97.   **26.** Davide Rodogno, *Fascism's European Empire: Italian Occupation During the Second World War* (Cambridge, 2006), 38, diary entry by General Bongiovanni.   **27.** Mario Cervi, *Storia della Guerra di Grecia, ottobre 1940–aprile 1941* (Milan, 1986), 51.   **28.** Vergani, *Ciano*, 88.   **29.** Marco Bragadin, *The Italian Navy in World War II* (Annapolis, Md, 1957), 28–9; Simon Ball, *The Bitter Sea* (London, 2009), 52–3.   **30.** Lucio Ceva, 'Italia e Grecia 1940–1941. Una guerra a parte', in Bruna Micheletti and Paolo Poggio (eds.), *L'Italia in guerra 1940–43* (Brescia, 1991), 190; Burgwyn, *Mussolini Warlord*, 38–9.   **31.** Ceva, 'Italia e Grecia', 191–2.   **32.** Cervi, *Storia della Guerra di Grecia*, 40, 51–2; Ball, *Bitter Sea*, 50–52; Giorgio Rochat, *Le guerre italiane 1935–1943: Dall'impero d'Etiopia alla disfatta* (Turin, 2005), 261.   **33.** Ceva, 'Italia e Grecia', 192; Rodogno, *Fascism's European Empire*, 29–30.   **34.** Mario Luciolli, *Mussolini e l'Europa: la politica estera fascista* (Florence, 2009), 220 (first published in 1945).   **35.** Ceva, 'Italia e Grecia', 193–201; Rochat, *Le guerre italiane*, 262–3, 274.   **36.** Bragadin, *Italian Navy in World War II*, 41–2; Gerhard Schreiber, Bernd Stegmann and Detlef Vogel, *Germany and the Second World War: Volume*

III: *The Mediterranean, South-east Europe and North Africa, 1939–1941* (Oxford, 1995), 426–9. 37. Leland Stowe, *No Other Road to Freedom* (London, 1942), 182–3. 38. Ceva, 'Italia e Grecia', 201–2; Bragadin, *Italian Navy in World War II*, 42, 79. 39. Rochat, *Le guerre italiane*, 279–80. Ceva, 'Italia e Grecia', gives a higher total of 40,000 Italian dead. Thousands died of frostbite and disease away from the front, which may account for the wide discrepancy in statistics of the dead. 40. Jack Greene and Alessandro Massignani, *The Naval War in the Mediterranean* (London, 1998), 103–7; Bragadin, *Italian Navy in World War II*, 44–6. 41. Bragadin, *Italian Navy in World War II*, 90–95. 42. On the failure to take Tripoli see Klaus Schmider, 'The Mediterranean in 1940–1941: crossroads of lost opportunities?', *War & Society*, 15 (1997), 27–8. 43. Schreiber, Stegmann and Vogel, *Germany and the Second World War: Volume III*, 92–5. On the conduct of operations see Rochat, *Le guerre italiane*, 268–77. 44. Richard Carrier, 'Some reflections on the fighting power of the Italian Army in North Africa, 1940–1943', *War in History*, 22 (2015), 508–14. 45. Schreiber, Stegelmann and Vogel, *Germany and the Second World War: Volume III*, 454–6. 46. Walter Warlimont, *Inside Hitler's Headquarters 1939–45* (London, 1964), 128. 47. John Kennedy, *The Business of War: The War Narratives of Major-General Sir John Kennedy* (London, 1957), 72–5. 48. Vergani, *Ciano*, 100. 49. Kennedy, *Business of War*, 101–3. 50. Nicolson, *Diaries and Letters*, 161, entry for 4 Apr. 1941; Daniel Todman, *Britain's War: Into Battle 1937–1941* (London, 2016), 565. 51. Ashley Jackson, *Persian Gulf Command: A History of the Second World War in Iran and Iraq* (New Haven, Conn., 2018), 56–7. 52. Jeffrey Herf, *Nazi Propaganda for the Arab World* (New Haven, Conn., 2009), 60–61. 53. Jackson, *Persian Gulf Command*, 88. 54. Ibid., 99. 55. Ibid., 94–104; Herf, *Nazi Propaganda*, 57–8, 61. 56. Walther Hubatsch (ed.), *Hitlers Weisungen für die Kriegführung 1939–1945* (Munich, 1965), 139–41, 'Weisung Nr. 30: Mittlerer Orient'; 151–5, 'Weisung Nr. 32: Vorbereitungen für die Zeit nach Barbarossa'. 57. Herf, *Nazi Propaganda*, 36–9. 58. David Motadel, *Islam and Nazi Germany's War* (Cambridge, Mass., 2014), 84–9. 59. Ibid., 107–9. 60. Ibid., 111–12, 130. On Italian treatment of the Libyan population see Patrick Bernhard, 'Behind the battle lines: Italian atrocities and the persecution of Arabs, Berbers, and Jews in North Africa during World War II', *Holocaust and Genocide Studies*, 26 (2012), 425–46. 61. Nicholas Tamkin, 'Britain, the Middle East, and the "Northern Front" 1941–1942', *War in History*, 15 (2008), 316. 62. David Fieldhouse, *Western Imperialism in the Middle East 1914–1958* (Oxford, 2006), 325–6. 63. Stefanie Wichhart, 'Selling democracy during the second British occupation of Iraq, 1941–5', *Journal of Contemporary History*, 48 (2013), 515. 64. Ibid., 523. 65. Gerry Kearns, *Geopolitics and Empire: The Legacy of Halford Mackinder* (Oxford, 2009), 155. 66. W. H. Parker, *Mackinder: Geography as an Aid to Statecraft* (Oxford, 1982), 150–58; Geoffrey Sloan, 'Sir Halford J. Mackinder: the heartland theory then and now', in Colin Gray and Geoffrey Sloan (eds.), *Geopolitics, Geography and Strategy* (London, 1999), 154–5. 67. Geoffrey Sloan, *Geopolitics in United States Strategic Policy 1890–1987* (London, 1988), 31–6; Kearns, *Geopolitics and Empire*, 15–17. 68. Benjamin Madley, 'From Africa to Auschwitz: how German South West Africa incubated ideas and methods adopted and developed by the Nazis in Eastern Europe', *European History Quarterly*, 35 (2005), 432–4. 69. Andrew Gyorgy, *Geopolitics: The New German Science* (Berkeley, Calif., 1944), 207–8, 221. 70. Kearns, *Geopolitics and Empire*, 20; L. H. Gann, 'Reflections on the German and Japanese empires of World War II', in Peter Duus, Ramon Myers and Mark Peattie (eds.), *The Japanese Wartime Empire, 1931–1945* (Princeton, NJ, 1996), 338. 71. Volker Ullrich, *Hitler: Downfall 1939–45* (London, 2020), 145; Warlimont, *Inside Hitler's Headquarters*, 140. 72. Max Domarus, *Hitler: Reden und Proklamationen 1932–1945*, 3 vols., *Volume II, Untergang* (Munich, 1965), 1731, Hitler's Proclamation to the German People, 22 June 1941. 73. Warlimont, *Inside Hitler's Headquarters*, 139. 74. Von Ribbentrop, *Memoirs*, 153. 75. Ullrich, *Hitler: Downfall*, 145. 76. Albert Kesselring, *The Memoirs of Field Marshal Kesselring* (London, 1953), 87. 77. Michael Bloch, *Ribbentrop* (London, 1992), 317. 78. Hugh Trevor-Roper (ed.), *Hitler's Table Talk 1941–1944: His Private Conversations* (London, 1973), 15, entry for 27 July 1941. 79. Stephen Fritz, *The First Soldier: Hitler as Military Leader* (New Haven, Conn., 2018), 132–8. 80. David Stahel, *Operation Barbarossa and Germany's Defeat in the East* (Cambridge, 2009), 47–53.

81. Megargee, *Inside Hitler's High Command*, 114–15. 82. Fritz, *First Soldier*, 151–2. 83. Warlimont, *Inside Hitler's Headquarters*, 140. 84. Jürgen Förster, 'Hitler turns East: German war policy in 1940 and 1941', in Bernd Wegner (ed.), *From Peace to War: Germany, Soviet Russia and the World, 1939–1941* (Oxford, 1997), 129; Andreas Hillgruber, 'The German military leaders' view of Russia prior to the attack on the Soviet Union', in Wegner (ed.), *From Peace to War*, 171–2, 180. On the use of racial pejoratives see Andrei Grinev, 'The evaluation of the military qualities of the Red Army in 1941–1945 by German memoirs and analytic materials', *Journal of Slavic Military Studies*, 29 (2016), 228–9. 85. Fritz, *First Soldier*, 124–5; Elke Fröhlich (ed.), *Die Tagebücher von Joseph Goebbels: Sämtliche Fragmente: Band 4* (Munich, 1987), 695, entry for 16 June 1941. 86. Stahel, *Operation Barbarossa*, 74. 87. R. L. Dinardo, *Mechanized Juggernaut or Military Anachronism? Horses and the German Army of WWII* (New York, 1991), 36–9. 88. Stahel, *Operation Barbarossa*, 78, 132–3. 89. Klaus Schüler, 'The eastern campaign as a transportation and supply problem', in Wegner (ed.), *From Peace to War*, 207–10. 90. F. Seidler and D. Zeigert, *Die Führerhauptquartiere: Anlagen und Planungen im Zweiten Weltkrieg* (Munich, 2000), 193–6; Warlimont, *Inside Hitler's Headquarters*, 162. 91. Johannes Kaufmann, *An Eagle's Odyssey: My Decade as a Pilot in Hitler's Luftwaffe* (Barnsley, 2019), 97. 92. Christian Ingrao, *The Promise of the East: Nazi Hopes and Genocide 1939–43* (Cambridge, 2019), 21–2, 99–101. 93. Horst Boog et al., *Das Deutsche Reich und der Zweite Weltkrieg: Band 4: Der Angriff auf die Sowjetunion* (Stuttgart, 1983), 129–35. 94. Stephen Fritz, *Ostkrieg: Hitler's War of Extermination in the East* (Lexington, Ky, 2011), 61–2; Alex Kay, '"The purpose of the Russian campaign is the decimation of the Slavic population by thirty million": the radicalization of German food policy in early 1941', in Alex Kay, Jeff Rutherford and David Stahel (eds.), *Nazi Policy on the Eastern Front, 1941: Total War, Genocide, and Radicalization* (Rochester, NY, 2012), 107–8. 95. Stahel, *Operation Barbarossa*, 114–16. 96. Oula Silvennoinen, 'Janus of the North? Finland 1940–44: Finland's road into alliance with Hitler', in John Gilmour and Jill Stephenson (eds.), *Hitler's Scandinavian Legacy* (London, 2013), 135–6. 97. Joumi Tilli, '"Deus Vult!": the idea of crusading in Finnish clerical rhetoric 1941–1944', *War in History*, 24 (2017), 364–5, 372–6. 98. Silvennoinen, 'Janus of the North?', 139–40. 99. Dennis Deletant, 'Romania', in David Stahel (ed.), *Joining Hitler's Crusade: European Nations and the Invasion of the Soviet Union, 1941* (Cambridge, 2018), 66–9. 100. Ibid., 9, 69–70. 101. Jan Rychlík, 'Slovakia', in Stahel (ed.), *Joining Hitler's Crusade*, 123–4; Ignác Ramsics, 'Hungary', ibid., 88–9, 92–5, 100–101. 102. Jürgen Förster, 'Freiwillige für den "Kreuzzug Europas" gegen den Bolschewismus', in Boog et al., *Das Deutsche Reich und der Zweite Weltkrieg: Band 4*, 908–9. 103. Thomas Schlemmer, *Invasori, non Vittime: La campagna italiana di Russia 1941–1943* (Rome, 2019), 9–12. 104. Von Below, *At Hitler's Side*, 111. 105. Alessandro Massignani, 'Die italienischen Streitkräfte unde der Krieg der "Achse"', in Lutz Klinkhammer, Amadeo Guerrazzi and Thomas Schlemmer (eds.), *Die 'Achse' im Krieg: Politik, Ideologie und Kriegführung 1939–1945* (Paderborn, 2010), 123–6, 135–7. 106. Eugen Dollmann, *With Hitler and Mussolini: Memoirs of a Nazi Interpreter* (New York, 2017), 192–3. Dollmann used papers he wrote at the time to record the events. 107. K. Arlt, 'Die Wehrmacht im Kalkul Stalins', in Rolf-Dieter Müller and Hans-Erich Volkmann (eds.), *Die Wehrmacht: Mythos und Realität* (Munich, 1999), 107–9. 108. David Glantz, *Stumbling Colossus: The Red Army on the Eve of World War* (Lawrence, Kans, 1998), 95–6, 103–4; R. E. Tarleton, 'What really happened to the Stalin Line?', *Journal of Slavic Military Studies*, 6 (1993), 50; C. Roberts, 'Planning for war: the Red Army and the catastrophe of 1941', *Europe-Asia Studies*, 47 (1995), 1319. 109. Glantz, *Stumbling Colossus*, 239–43; Christopher Andrew and O. Gordievsky, *KGB: The Inside Story* (London, 1990), 209–13; David Glantz, *The Role of Intelligence in Soviet Military Strategy in World War II* (Novato, Calif., 1990), 15–19. 110. This is now an old debate. See Klaus Schmider, 'No quiet on the Eastern Front: the Suvorov debate in the 1990s', *Journal of Slavic Military Studies*, 10 (1997), 181–94; V. Suvorov, 'Who was planning to attack whom in June 1941, Hitler or Stalin?', *Military Affairs*, 69 (1989). 111. R. H. McNeal, *Stalin: Man and Ruler* (New York, 1988), 238. 112. Georgii Zhukov, *Reminiscences and Reflections: Volume I* (Moscow, 1985), 217–29; Alexander Hill, *The Red Army and the Second World War* (Cambridge, 2017),

205–7. **113.** Von Below, *At Hitler's Side*, 103. **114.** J. Schecter and V. Luchkov (eds.), *Khrushchev Remembers: The Glasnost Tapes* (New York, 1990), 56. **115.** Henrik Eberle and Matthias Uhl (eds.), *The Hitler Book: The Secret Dossier Prepared for Stalin* (London, 2005), 73; von Ribbentrop, *Memoirs*, 153. **116.** W. J. Spahr, *Zhukov: The Rise and Fall of a Great Captain* (Novato, Calif., 1993), 43; A. G. Chor'kov, 'The Red Army during the initial phase of the Great Patriotic War', in Wegner (ed.), *From Peace to War*, 417–18. **117.** Victor Kamenir, *The Bloody Triangle: The Defeat of Soviet Armor in the Ukraine, June 1941* (Minneapolis, Minn., 2008), 247–54. **118.** Von Below, *At Hitler's Side*, 107. **119.** Evan Mawdsley, *Thunder in the East: The Nazi–Soviet War 1941–1945* (London, 2005), 19. **120.** Kamenir, *The Bloody Triangle*, 21–5. **121.** Roberts, 'Planning for War', 1307; Chor'kov, 'Red Army', 416; R. Stolfi, *Hitler's Panzers East: World War II Reinterpreted* (Norman, Okla, 1991), 88–9. **122.** James Lucas, *War on the Eastern Front: The German Soldier in Russia 1941–1945* (London, 1979), 31–3. **123.** G. F. Krivosheev, *Soviet Casualties and Combat Losses in the Twentieth Century* (London, 1997), 96–7, 101. **124.** Trevor-Roper (ed.), *Hitler's Table Talk*, 17, 24, entries for 27 July, 8/9 Aug. 1941. **125.** Megargee, *Inside Hitler's High Command*, 132–3. **126.** Martin Kahn, 'From assured defeat to "the riddle of Soviet military success": Anglo-American government assessments of Soviet war potential 1941–1943', *Journal of Slavic Military Studies*, 26 (2013), 465–7. **127.** Johannes Hürter (ed.), *A German General on the Eastern Front: The Letters and Diaries of Gotthard Heinrici 1941–1942* (Barnsley, 2015), 68, letter of 6 July 1941. **128.** Ibid., 73–4, letters of 1 and 3 Aug.; 78, letter of 28 Aug. 1941. **129.** Hans Schröder, 'German soldiers' experiences during the initial phase of the Russian campaign', in Wegner (ed.), *From Peace to War*, 313. **130.** Stahel, *Operation Barbarossa*, 182. **131.** Dinardo, *Mechanized Juggernaut*, 45–9; Stahel, *Operation Barbarossa*, 183–5. **132.** Dinardo, *Mechanized Juggernaut*, 53; Stahel, *Operation Barbarossa*, 234. **133.** Fritz, *Ostkrieg*, 129–32. **134.** Peter Longerich, *Hitler: A Biography* (Oxford, 2019), 753. **135.** Dmitri Pavlov, *Leningrad 1941–1942: The Blockade* (Chicago, Ill., 1965), 75, 79, 84, 88; N. Kislitsyn and V. Zubakov, *Leningrad Does Not Surrender* (Moscow, 1989), 116–18. The figure for deaths during the winter of 1941–2 in the total blockaded area is approximate, but is now generally agreed to be the best estimate available from current evidence. See Richard Bidlack and Nikita Lomagin, *The Leningrad Blockade 1941–1944* (New Haven, Conn., 2012), 270–73. **136.** Megargee, *Inside Hitler's High Command*, 135. **137.** Domarus, *Reden und Proklamationen*, ii, 1758–67. **138.** Jack Radey and Charles Sharp, 'Was it the mud?', *Journal of Slavic Military Studies*, 28 (2015), 663–5. **139.** Ibid., 667–70. **140.** Fritz, *Ostkrieg*, 161. **141.** Klaus Reinhardt 'Moscow 1941: the turning point', in John Erickson and David Dilks (eds.), *Barbarossa: The Axis and the Allies* (Edinburgh, 1994), 218–19; Fritz, *Ostkrieg*, 189–90. **142.** Fritz, *Ostkrieg*, 187–9. **143.** Spahr, *Zhukov*, 74–5. **144.** *Kriegstagebuch des Oberkommandos der Wehrmacht*, 5 vols. (Frankfurt am Main, 1961–3), i, 1120; statistics from Fritz, *Ostkrieg*, 192. **145.** On Soviet deficiencies see Hill, *Red Army*, 302–3. **146.** Christian Hartmann, *Operation Barbarossa: Nazi Germany's War in the East 1941–1945* (Oxford, 2015), 54–5. **147.** Hürter (ed.), *A German General on the Eastern Front*, 126, letter of 2 Jan. 1942. **148.** Carl Boyd, *Hitler's Japanese Confidant: General Ōshima Hiroshi and Magic Intelligence 1941–1945* (Lawrence, Kans, 1993), 27–30. **149.** Klaus Reinhardt, *Moscow – The Turning Point: The Failure of Hitler's Strategy in the Winter of 1941–42* (Oxford, 1992), 58. **150.** Gerhard Krebs, 'Japan and the German–Soviet War', in Wegner (ed.), *From Peace to War*, 548–50, 554–5; John Chapman, 'The Imperial Japanese Navy and the north–south dilemma', in Erickson and Dilks (eds.), *Barbarossa*, 168–9, 177–9. **151.** Warlimont, *Inside Hitler's Headquarters*, 207–9. **152.** Eri Hotta, *Japan 1941: Countdown to Infamy* (New York, 2013), 6–7. **153.** Hans Boberach (ed.), *Meldungen aus dem Reich: Die geheimen Lageberichte des Sicherheitsdienst der SS 1938–1945* (Herrsching, 1984), viii, 3073, report for 11 Dec. 1941; ix, 3101–2, report for 19 Dec. 1941; Will Boelcke (ed.), *The Secret Conferences of Dr. Goebbels 1939–1941* (London, 1967), 194, conference of 18 Dec. 1941. **154.** *Fuehrer Conferences on Naval Affairs*, 245, Report by the C-in-C Navy to the Fuehrer, 12 Dec. 1941. **155.** Eberle and Uhl, *The Hitler Book*, 79. **156.** Ben-Ami Shillony, *Politics and Culture in Wartime Japan* (Oxford, 1981), 134–6, 142–5; Nicholas Tarling, *A Sudden Rampage: Japan's Occupation of Southeast Asia 1941–1945* (London, 2001),

127–8.   157. Boyd, *Hitler's Japanese Confidant*, 44.   158. Friedrich Ruge, *Der Seekrieg: The German Navy's Story 1939–1945* (Annapolis, Md, 1957), 252–5.   159. Dollmann, *With Hitler and Mussolini*, 204. This is the argument presented in Tobias Jersak, 'Die Interaktion von Kriegsverlauf und Judenvernichtung: ein Blick auf Hitlers Strategie im Spätsommer 1941', *Historisches Zeitschrift*, 268 (1999), 345–60.   160. Christian Gerlach, 'The Wannsee Conference, the fate of the German Jews, and Hitler's decision in principle to exterminate all European Jews', *Journal of Modern History*, 70 (1998), 784–5. For the meeting on 12 December see Martin Moll, 'Steuerungsinstrument im "Ämterchaos"? Die Tagungen der Reichs und Gauleiter der NSDAP', *Vierteljahreshefte für Zeitgeschichte*, 49 (2001), 240–43.   161. Tolischus, *Tokyo Record*, 30, citing speech to the Diet, 20 Jan. 1941.   162. Sean Casey, *Cautious Crusade: Franklin D. Roosevelt, American Public Opinion and the War against Nazi Germany* (New York, 2001), 39.   163. Jonathan Marshall, *To Have and Have Not: Southeast Asian Raw Materials and the Origins of the Pacific War* (Berkeley, Calif., 1995), 36–41; Sidney Pash, 'Containment, rollback, and the origins of the Pacific War, 1933–1941', in Kurt Piehler and Sidney Pash (eds.), *The United States and the Second World War: New Perspectives on Diplomacy, War and the Home Front* (New York, 2010), 43–4.   164. Pash, 'Containment, rollback', 46–51; Sarah Paine, *The Wars for Asia 1911–1949* (Cambridge, 2012), 175–82; Tarling, *A Sudden Rampage*, 71–3. Grew quotation in Joseph Grew, *Ten Years in Japan* (London, 1944), 257.   165. Hotta, *Japan 1941*, 4–7.   166. Krebs, 'Japan and the German–Soviet War', 550–51.   167. Tarling, *A Sudden Rampage*, 73–4; Sarah Paine, *The Japanese Empire: Grand Strategy from the Meiji Restoration to the Pacific War* (Cambridge, 2017), 147–8, 153.   168. Pash, 'Containment, rollback', 53–5, 57–8; Marshall, *To Have and Have Not*, 147–50.   169. Marshall, *To Have and Have Not*, 163.   170. Hotta, *Japan 1941*, 265–8.   171. Tarling, *A Sudden Rampage*, 77.   172. Krebs, 'Japan and the German–Soviet War', 558–9.   173. Alan Zimm, *Attack on Pearl Harbor: Strategy, Combat, Myths, Deceptions* (Philadelphia, Pa, 2011), 15.   174. Hotta, *Japan 1941*, 234–5; Chapman, 'Imperial Japanese Navy', 166.   175. Richard Hallion, 'The United States perspective', in Paul Addison and Jeremy Crang (eds.), *The Burning Blue: A New History of the Battle of Britain* (London, 2000), 101–2.   176. Zimm, *Attack on Pearl Harbor*, 151–4; Paine, *Wars for Asia*, 187–8.   177. Zimm, *Attack on Pearl Harbor*, 223–4, 228–9.   178. David Roll, *The Hopkins Touch: Harry Hopkins and the Forging of the Alliance to Defeat Hitler* (Oxford, 2015), 158.   179. Andrew Buchanan, *American Grand Strategy in the Mediterranean during World War II* (Cambridge, 2014), 23–4, 31–2; Mark Stoler, *Allies in War: Britain and America against the Axis Powers* (London, 2005), 42–5.   180. Debi Unger and Irwin Unger, *George Marshall: A Biography* (New York, 2014), 148–9   181. Tarling, *A Sudden Rampage*, 81–2.   182. Evan Mawdsley, *December 1941: Twelve Days that Began a World War* (New Haven, Conn., 2011), 230–34.   183. Tarling, *A Sudden Rampage*, 91–2; David Kennedy, *The American People in World War II: Freedom from Fear* (New York, 1999), 102–5.   184. Alan Warren, *Singapore 1942: Britain's Greatest Defeat* (London, 2002), 46, 301–2; Christopher Bayly and Tim Harper, *Forgotten Armies: The Fall of British Asia 1941–1945* (London, 2004), 146.   185. Warren, *Singapore 1942*, 272–4, 290–92; Richard Toye, *Churchill's Empire: The World that Made Him and the World He Made* (New York, 2010), 217–18.   186. Bayly and Harper, *Forgotten Armies*, 156.   187. Hans van de Ven, *China at War: Triumph and Tragedy in the Emergence of the New China 1937–1952* (London, 2017), 162–3; Tarling, *A Sudden Rampage*, 95–6.   188. William Grieve, *The American Military Mission to China, 1941–1942* (Jefferson, NC, 2014), 188–90.   189. Ibid., 108–16, 191.   190. Jay Taylor, *The Generalissimo: Chiang Kai-Shek and the Struggle for Modern China* (Cambridge, Mass., 2011), 190.   191. Van de Ven, *China at War*, 164; Grieve, *American Military Mission*, 196–7, 202.   192. Taylor, *Generalissimo*, 197–200.   193. Srinath Raghavan, *India's War: The Making of Modern South Asia, 1939–1945* (London, 2016), 209.   194. Rana Mitter, *China's War with Japan 1937–1945: The Struggle for Survival* (London, 2013), 256–61; Tarling, *A Sudden Rampage*, 98–100; Francis Pike, *Hirohito's War: The Pacific War 1941–1945* (London, 2016), 303.   195. Bayly and Harper, *Forgotten Armies*, 169, 177–8, 196–7; Pike, *Hirohito's War*, 299–300.   196. Mitter, *China's War with Japan*, 260.   197. Paine, *Wars for Asia*, 128.   198. Daniel Hedinger, 'Fascist warfare and the Axis alliance: from *Blitzkrieg* to total war', in

Miguel Alonso, Alan Kramer and Javier Rodrigo (eds.), *Fascist Warfare 1922–1945: Aggression, Occupation, Annihilation* (Cham, Switzerland, 2019), 205–8.   **199.** Warren, *Singapore 1942*, 60; Ken Kotani, *Japanese Intelligence in World War II* (Oxford, 2009), 111–13.   **200.** Bayly and Harper, *Forgotten Armies*, 5–7; Kotani, *Japanese Intelligence*, 116–17.   **201.** Gerald Horne, *Race War: White Supremacy and the Japanese Attack on the British Empire* (New York, 2004), 72–4; Philip Snow, *The Fall of Hong Kong: Britain, China and the British Occupation* (New Haven, Conn., 2003), 66–72.   **202.** David Horner, 'Australia in 1942: a pivotal year', in Peter Dean (ed.), *Australia 1942: In the Shadow of War* (Cambridge, 2013), 18–19.   **203.** Craig Symonds, *World War Two at Sea: A Global History* (New York, 2018), 235–7.   **204.** Arthur Marder, M. Jacobsen and J. Horsfield, *Old Friends, New Enemies: The Royal Navy and the Imperial Japanese Navy, 1942–1945* (Oxford, 1990), 155–9; James Brown, *Eagles Strike: South African Forces in World War II, Vol. IV* (Cape Town, 1974), 388–400.   **205.** Horne, *Race War*, 217–18.   **206.** Neil Smith, *American Empire: Roosevelt's Geographer and the Prelude to Globalization* (Berkeley, Calif., 2004), 349–50; William Roger Louis, *Imperialism at Bay: The United States and the Decolonization of the British Empire 1941–1945* (Oxford, 1977), 173–6.   **207.** Simon Rofe, 'Pre-war postwar planning: the phoney war, the Roosevelt administration and the case of the Advisory Committee on Problems of Foreign Relations', *Diplomacy & Statecraft*, 23 (2012), 254–5, 258–9.   **208.** Louis, *Imperialism at Bay*, 149.   **209.** Roll, *The Hopkins Touch*, 188–9; M. Subrahmanyan, *Why Cripps Failed* (New Delhi, 1942), 5–11, 25.   **210.** Horne, *Race War*, 215–17.   **211.** Yasmin Khan, *The Raj at War: A People's History of India's Second World War* (London, 2015), 191; Kaushik Roy, *India and World War II: War, Armed Forces and Society, 1939–45* (New Delhi, 2016), 176.   **212.** Roy, *India and World War II*, 177–8; Raghavan, *India's War*, 272–4.   **213.** Khan, *The Raj at War*, 191.   **214.** Louis, *Imperialism at Bay*, 156–7, 181.   **215.** Matthew Jones, *Britain, the United States and the Mediterranean War 1942–44* (London, 1996), 223.   **216.** Mitter, *China's War with Japan*, 216–19; Timothy Brook, 'The Great Way government of Shanghai', in Christian Henriot and Wen Hsin Yeh (eds.), *In the Shadow of the Rising Sun: Shanghai under Japanese Occupation* (Cambridge, 2004), 67–8.   **217.** David Barrett, 'The Wang Jingwei regime, 1940–1945: continuities and disjunctures with Nationalist China', in David Barrett and Larry Shyu (eds.), *Chinese Collaboration with Japan, 1932–1945: The Limits of Accommodation* (Stanford, Calif., 2001), 104–12.   **218.** Timothy Brook, *Collaboration: Japanese Agents and Local Elites in Wartime China* (Cambridge, Mass., 2005), 35–8.   **219.** Ibid., 41–7.   **220.** Mark Peattie, 'Nanshin: the "Southward Advance" 1931–1941, as a prelude to the Japanese occupation of Southeast Asia', in Duus, Myers and Peattie (eds.), *The Japanese Wartime Empire*, 236–7.   **221.** Takuma Melber, *Zwischen Kollaboration und Widerstand: Die japanische Besatzung Malaya und Singapur (1942–1945)* (Frankfurt am Main, 2017), 186–9; Paul Kratoska, *The Japanese Occupation of Malaya 1941–1945* (London, 1998), 52–4.   **222.** Tarling, *A Sudden Rampage*, 84–5; Kratoska, *Japanese Occupation of Malaya*, 85–7.   **223.** Kiyoko Nitz, 'Japanese military policy towards French Indo-China during the Second World War: the road to *Meigo Sakusen*', *Journal of South East Asian Studies*, 14 (1983), 331–3.   **224.** Melber, *Zwischen Kollaboration und Widerstand*, 189; Tarling, *A Sudden Rampage*, 127, 133–4.   **225.** Peter Duus, 'Imperialism without colonies: the vision of a Greater East Asia Co-prosperity Sphere', *Diplomacy & Statecraft*, 7 (1996), 58–9, 62, 68–9.   **226.** Ethan Mark, *Japan's Occupation of Java in the Second World War* (London, 2018), 116–19, 163.   **227.** Tarling, *A Sudden Rampage*, 127–8.   **228.** Mark, *Japan's Occupation of Java*, 1, 129–30.   **229.** Ibid., 232.   **230.** Ibid., 107–8.   **231.** Melber, *Zwischen Kollaboration und Widerstand*, 325–33; Kratoska, *Japanese Occupation of Malaya*, 94–7.   **232.** Tarling, *A Sudden Rampage*, 167–8.   **233.** Melber, *Zwischen Kollaboration und Widerstand*, 289.   **234.** Chong-Sik Lee, *Revolutionary Struggle in Manchuria: Chinese Communism and Soviet Interest 1922–1945* (Berkeley, Calif., 1983), 271, 291–4.   **235.** Li Yuk-wai, 'The Chinese resistance movement in the Philippines during the Japanese occupation', *Journal of South East Asian Studies*, 23 (1992), 308–9.   **236.** Melber, *Zwischen Kollaboration und Widerstand*, 520.   **237.** Ibid., 521.   **238.** Li, 'The Chinese resistance movement', 312–15.   **239.** Ben Hillier, 'The Huk rebellion and the Philippines' radical tradition: a people's war without a people's victory', in Donny Gluckstein (ed.), *Fighting on All*

Fronts: Popular Resistance in the Second World War (London, 2015), 325–33. **240.** Melber, *Zwischen Kollaboration und Widerstand*, 545, 549–53. **241.** Tarling, *A Sudden Rampage*, 152. **242.** Kratoska, *Japanese Occupation of Malaya*, 223–44. **243.** USSBS, *The Effects of Strategic Bombing on Japan's War Economy* (Washington, DC, 1946), 121, 190; Nicholas White, J. M. Barwise and Shakila Yacob, 'Economic opportunity and strategic dilemma in colonial development: Britain, Japan and Malaya's iron ore, 1920s to 1950s', *International History Review*, 42 (2020), 426–33. **244.** Kratoska, *Japanese Occupation of Malaya*, 223, 241. **245.** Robert Goralski and Russell Freeburg, *Oil and War: How the Deadly Struggle for Fuel in WWII Meant Victory or Defeat* (New York, 1987), 150–52; Daniel Yergin, *The Prize: The Epic Quest for Oil, Money, and Power* (New York, 1991), 355–66. **246.** USSBS, *Effects of Strategic Bombing*, 135 (figures for fiscal years 1940/41 and 1944/5). **247.** Gregg Huff and Sinobu Majima, 'The challenge of finance in South East Asia during the Second World War', *War in History*, 22 (2015), 192–7. **248.** Ibid.; Paul Kratoska, '"Banana money": consequences of demonetization of wartime Japanese currency in British Malaya', *Journal of South East Asian Studies*, 23 (1992), 322–6. **249.** Paul Kratoska (ed.), *Food Supplies and the Japanese Occupation in South East Asia* (London, 1998), 4–6. **250.** Kratoska, *Japanese Occupation of Malaya*, 183–200. **251.** Mark, *Japan's Occupation of Java*, 263–5. **252.** Ju Zhifen, 'Labor conscription in North China 1941–1945', in Stephen MacKinnon, Diana Lary and Ezra Vogel (eds.), *China at War: Regions of China 1937–45* (Stanford, Calif., 2007), 217–19. **253.** Tarling, *A Sudden Rampage*, 230, 238; Mark, *Japan's Occupation of Java*, 259–65. **254.** Kratoska, *Japanese Occupation of Malaya*, 44–5; Joyce Lebra, *Japan's Greater East Asia Co-Prosperity Sphere in World War II: Selected Readings and Documents* (Kuala Lumpur, 1975), 92. **255.** Tarling, *A Sudden Rampage*, 128. **256.** Raghavan, *India's War*, 284–94; Kratoska, *Japanese Occupation of Malaya*, 104–8. **257.** Tarling, *A Sudden Rampage*, 155–7; Joyce Lebra, 'Postwar Perspectives on the Greater East Asia Co-Prosperity Sphere', 34th Harmon Memorial Lecture, US Air Force Academy, Colorado Springs, 1991, 5–6. **258.** Tarling, *A Sudden Rampage*, 167–72. **259.** Mark, *Japan's Occupation of Java*, 271–2. **260.** Nitz, 'Japanese military policy', 337–46. **261.** Trevor Barnes and Claudio Minca, 'Nazi spatial theory: the dark geographies of Carl Schmitt and Walter Christaller', *Annals of the Association of American Geographers*, 103 (2013), 676–7; Timothy Snyder, *Black Earth: The Holocaust as History and Warning* (London, 2015), 144–5. **262.** Wolfgang Benz, 'Typologie der Herrschaftsformen in den Gebieten unter deutschen Einfluss', in Wolfgang Benz, Johannes ten Cate and Gerhard Otto (eds.), *Die Bürokratie der Okkupation: Strukturen der Herrschaft und Verwaltung im besetzten Europa* (Berlin, 1998), 15–19. **263.** Karen Gram-Skjoldager, 'The law of the jungle? Denmark's international legal status during the Second World War', *International History Review*, 33 (2011), 238–46. **264.** Nicola Labanca, David Reynolds and Olivier Wieviorka, *La Guerre du désert 1940–1943* (Paris, 2019), 188–9, 193–7. **265.** Rodogno, *Fascism's European Empire*, 36–8. **266.** For this and other details on annexations, ibid., 9–10, 73–102. **267.** Srdjan Trifković, 'Rivalry between Germany and Italy in Croatia, 1942–1943', *Historical Journal*, 31 (1995), 880–82, 904. **268.** Alessandra Kersevan, *Lager italiani: Pulizia etnica e campi di concentramento fascisti per civili jugoslavi 1941–1943* (Rome, 2008), 100–103. **269.** Rodogno, *Fascism's European Empire*, 168–71, 177–8, 357–9. **270.** Jürgen Förster, 'Die Wehrmacht und die Probleme der Koalitionskriegführung', in Klinkhammer et al. (eds.), *Die 'Achse' im Krieg*, 113. **271.** M. Pearton, *Oil and the Romanian State* (Oxford, 1971), 231; Anand Toprani, 'Germany's answer to Standard Oil: the Continental Oil company and Nazi grand strategy 1940–1942', *Journal of Strategic Studies*, 37 (2014), 956–9. **272.** Dieter Eichholtz, *Deutsche Ölpolitik im Zeitalter der Weltkriege: Studien und Dokumente* (Leipzig, 2010), 345–9. **273.** Trifković, 'Rivalry between Germany and Italy', 884–7. **274.** Rodogno, *Fascism's European Empire*, 232–40. **275.** Nuremberg Trials, Case XI, Prosecution Document Book 113, pp. 1–3, Göring decree on the distribution of smelting works in Lorraine and Luxembourg, 5 Feb. 1941. **276.** Patrick Nefors, *La collaboration industrielle en Belgique 1940–1945* (Brussels, 2006), 180–82, 223–5, 236–7. **277.** Henry Picker (ed.), *Hitlers Tischgespräche im Führerhauptquartier* (Wiesbaden, 1984), 62, 69, entries for 1 Aug. and 8/9 Aug. 1941; Trevor-Roper (ed.), *Hitler's Table Talk*, 15, 33, 35, 68–8, entries for 27 July, 17 Sept. and 17 Oct. 1941. **278.** Brendan

Simms, *Hitler: Only the World was Enough* (London, 2019), 422–3. **279.** Jürgen Matthäus and Frank Bajohr (eds.), *The Political Diary of Alfred Rosenberg and the Onset of the Holocaust* (Lanham, Md, 2015), 239, entry for 11 Apr. 1941. **280.** Karel Berkhoff, *Harvest of Despair: Life and Death in Ukraine under Nazi Rule* (Cambridge, Mass., 2004), 50. **281.** Klaus Arnold, 'Die Eroberung und Behandlung der Stadt Kiew durch die Wehrmacht im September 1941: zur Radikalisierung der Besatzungspolitik', *Militärgeschichtliche Mitteilungen*, 58 (1999), 35. **282.** Ben Kiernan, *Blood and Soil: A World History of Genocide and Extermination from Sparta to Darfur* (New Haven, Conn., 2007), 422. **283.** Elissa Mailänder Koslov, '"Going East": colonial experiences and practices of violence among female and male Majdanek camp guards (1941–44)', *Journal of Genocide Research*, 10 (2008), 567–70. **284.** Johannes Enstad, *Soviet Russians under Nazi Occupation: Fragile Loyalties in World War II* (Cambridge, 2018), 51–3, 66–8. **285.** Jonathan Steinberg, 'The Third Reich reflected: German civil administration in the occupied Soviet Union, 1941–4', *English Historical Review*, 110 (1995), 628. **286.** Trevor-Roper (ed.), *Hitler's Table Talk*, 34, entry for 17 Sept. 1941. **287.** Nicholas Terry, 'How Soviet was Russian society under Nazi occupation?', in Claus-Christian Szejnmann (ed.), *Rethinking History, Dictatorship and War* (London, 2009), 134–6. **288.** Berkhoff, *Harvest of Despair*, 48–9. **289.** Grzegorz Rossoliński-Liebe, 'The "Ukrainian National Revolution" of 1941: discourse and practice of a fascist movement', *Kritika*, 12 (2011), 83, 93–106. **290.** Matthäus and Bajohr (eds.), *Political Diary of Rosenberg*, 253–7. **291.** Theo Schulte, *The German Army and Nazi Policies in Occupied Russia* (Oxford, 1989), 65–8. **292.** Roland Clark, 'Fascists and soldiers: ambivalent loyalties and genocidal violence in wartime Romania', *Holocaust and Genocide Studies*, 31 (2017), 411. **293.** Steinberg, 'Third Reich reflected', 615. **294.** Theo Schulte, 'Living standards and the civilian economy in Belorussia', in Richard Overy, Gerhard Otto and Johannes Houwink ten Cate (eds.), *Die 'Neuordnung Europas': NS-Wirtschaftspolitik in den besetzten Gebieten* (Berlin, 1997), 176; Steinberg, 'Third Reich reflected', 635. **295.** Wendy Lower, 'The *reibungslose* Holocaust? The German military and civilian implementation of the "Final Solution" in Ukraine, 1941–1944', in Gerald Feldman and Wolfgang Seibel (eds.), *Networks of Nazi Persecution: Bureaucracy, Business and the Organization of the Holocaust* (New York, 2005), 246–7. **296.** Terry, 'How Soviet was Russian society?', 131; Kim Priemel, 'Occupying Ukraine: great expectations, failed opportunities, and the spoils of war, 1941–1943', *Central European History*, 48 (2015), 39. **297.** Richard Overy, *Goering: The Iron Man*, 3rd edn (London, 2020), 131–2. **298.** Kim Priemel, 'Scorched earth, plunder, and massive mobilization: the German occupation of Ukraine and the Soviet war economy', in Jonas Scherner and Eugene White (eds.), *Paying for Hitler's War: The Consequences of Nazi Hegemony for Europe* (Cambridge, 2016), 406–7. **299.** Overy, *Goering*, 132–3. **300.** Priemel, 'Occupying Ukraine', 37–9, 48, 50–52. **301.** Eichholtz, *Deutsche Ölpolitik*, 450–60. **302.** Priemel, 'Occupying Ukraine', 42–8. **303.** Christoph Buchheim, 'Die besetzten Länder im Dienste der deutschen Kriegswirtschaft während des Zweiten Weltkrieges', *Vierteljahrshefte für Zeitgeschichte*, 34 (1986), 123, 143–5. **304.** Arnold, 'Die Eroberung und Behandlung der Stadt Kiew', 36. **305.** Ibid., 39. **306.** Sergei Kudryashov, 'Labour in the occupied territory of the Soviet Union 1941–1944', in Overy, Otto and ten Cate (eds.), *Die 'Neuordnung Europas'*, 165–6; Schulte, 'Living standards and the civilian economy', 179–80. **307.** Priemel, 'Scorched earth, plunder', 405–6. **308.** Schulte, *German Army and Nazi Policies*, 96–7. **309.** Gustavo Corni and Horst Gies, *Brot, Butter, Kanonen: Die Ernährungswirtschaft in Deutschland unter der Diktatur Hitlers* (Berlin, 1997), 553–4, 574. **310.** Stephan Lehnstaedt, *Imperiale Polenpolitik in den Weltkriegen* (Osnabrück, 2017), 433. **311.** Isabel Heinemann, '"Ethnic resettlement" and inter-agency cooperation in the Occupied Eastern Territories', in Feldman and Seibel (eds.), *Networks of Nazi Persecution*, 217–22; *idem*, '"Another type of perpetrator": the SS racial experts and forced population movements in the occupied regions', *Holocaust and Genocide Studies*, 15 (2001), 391–2. **312.** Dietrich Beyrau and Mark Keck-Szajbel, 'Eastern Europe as "sub-Germanic space": scholarship on Eastern Europe under National Socialism', *Kritika*, 13 (2012), 694–5. **313.** Barnes and Minca, 'Nazi spatial theory', 670–74; Ingrao, *Promise of the East*, 99–100, 144–8. **314.** Lehnstaedt, *Imperiale Polenpolitik*, 447; on Moscow and Leningrad 'den Erdboden gleichzumachen', Arnold, 'Die

Eroberung und Behandlung der Stadt Kiew', 27. **315.** Ingrao, *Promise of the East*, 101. **316.** Gerhard Wolf, 'The Wannsee Conference in 1942 and the National Socialist living space dystopia', *Journal of Genocide Research*, 17 (2015), 166; Andrej Angrick, 'Annihilation and labor: Jews and Thoroughfare IV in Central Ukraine', in Ray Brandon and Wendy Lower (eds.), *The Shoah in Ukraine: History, Testimony, Memorialization* (Bloomington, Ind., 2008), 208–11. **317.** Markus Leniger, *Nationalsozialistische 'Volkstumsarbeit' und Umsiedlungspolitik 1933–1945* (Berlin, 2011), 89. **318.** Ingrao, *Promise of the East*, 108–9. **319.** Heiko Suhr, *Der Generalplan Ost: Nationalsozialistische Pläne zur Kolonisation Ostmitteleuropas* (Munich, 2008), 18–20; Lehnstaedt, *Imperiale Polenpolitik*, 450. **320.** Daniel Siemens, '"Sword and plough": settling Nazi Stormtroopers in Eastern Europe, 1936–43', *Journal of Genocide Research*, 19 (2017), 200–204. **321.** Kiernan, *Blood and Soil*, 452. **322.** Geraldien von Frijtag Drabbe Künzel, '"Germanje": Dutch empire-building in Nazi-occupied Europe', *Journal of Genocide Research*, 19 (2017), 241, 248–51; Siemens, '"Sword and plough"', 204. **323.** Ingrao, *Promise of the East*, 108–14; Michael Wildt, *Generation des Unbedingten: Das Führungskorps des Reichssicherheitshauptamtes* (Hamburg, 2002), 663–5, 669–70. **324.** www.holocaustresearchproject.org, Speech of the Reichsführer-SS at the SS Group Leader Meeting in Posen, 4 Oct. 1943, p. 16. **325.** http://prorev.com/wannsee.htm, Wannsee Protocol, 20 Jan. 1941, p. 5. **326.** Snyder, *Black Earth*, 5–8. **327.** Wilhelm Treue, 'Hitlers Denkschrift zum Vierjahresplan, 1936', *Vierteljahrshefte für Zeitgeschichte*, 3 (1955), 204–5. **328.** Peter Longerich, *The Unwritten Order: Hitler's Role in the Final Solution* (Stroud, 2001), 155. **329.** Alon Confino, *A World without Jews: The Nazi Imagination from Persecution to Genocide* (New Haven, Conn., 2014), 195. **330.** Domarus, *Reden und Proklamationen*, ii, 1866–7, speech of 26 Apr. 1942 (author's translation). **331.** Gustavo Corni, *Hitler's Ghettos: Voices from a Beleaguered Society 1939–1944* (London, 2002), 23–5. **332.** Leni Yahil, *The Holocaust: The Fate of European Jewry 1932–1945* (New York, 1990), 164. **333.** Wolf Gruner, *Jewish Forced Labour under the Nazis: Economic Needs and Racial Aims, 1938–1944* (Cambridge, 2006), 232–52. **334.** Ullrich, *Hitler: Downfall*, 251–3. **335.** Ibid., 267. **336.** Lower, 'The *reibungslose* Holocaust?', 250. **337.** Waitman Beorn, 'A calculus of complicity: the Wehrmacht, the anti-partisan war, and the Final Solution in White Russia 1941–42', *Central European History*, 44 (2011), 311–13. **338.** Christian Ingrao, *Believe and Destroy: Intellectuals in the SS War Machine* (Cambridge, 2013), 148–50. **339.** Leonid Rein, 'The radicalization of anti-Jewish policies in Nazi-occupied Belarus', in Kay, Rutherford and Stahel (eds.), *Nazi Policy on the Eastern Front*, 228. **340.** Walter Manoschek, *'Serbien ist judenfrei': Militärische Besatzungspolitik und Judenvernichtung in Serbien 1941/42* (Munich, 1993), 102–8. **341.** Alexander Kruglov, 'Jewish losses in Ukraine, 1941–1944', in Brandon and Lower (eds.), *The Shoah in Ukraine*, 278–9. **342.** Stephen Lehnstaedt, 'The Minsk experience: German occupiers and everyday life in the capital of Belarus', in Kay, Rutherford and Stahel (eds.), *Nazi Policy on the Eastern Front*, 244–5. **343.** Corni, *Hitler's Ghettos*, 34–6. **344.** Kruglov, 'Jewish losses in Ukraine', 275. **345.** Berkhoff, *Harvest of Despair*, 75. **346.** Matthäus and Bajohr (eds.), *Political Diary of Alfred Rosenberg*, 263–4. **347.** Christian Gerlach, *The Extermination of the European Jews* (Cambridge, 2016), 84–8; Wolf, 'Wannsee Conference', 165–6, 167–8. **348.** Robert Gerwarth, *Hitler's Hangman: The Life of Heydrich* (New Haven, Conn., 2011), 206–7. **349.** Bertrand Perz, 'The Austrian connection: the SS and police leader Odilo Globocnik and his staff in the Lublin district', *Holocaust and Genocide Studies*, 29 (2015), 400. **350.** Gerlach, *Extermination of the European Jews*, 90. **351.** Dieter Pohl, 'The murder of Ukraine's Jews under German military administration and in the Reich Commissariat Ukraine', in Brandon and Lower (eds.), *The Shoah in Ukraine*, 50–52. **352.** Gruner, *Jewish Forced Labour*, 258–62, 270. **353.** Frediano Sessi, *Auschwitz: Storia e memorie* (Venice, 2020), 279–80. **354.** William Brustein and Amy Ronnkvist, 'The roots of anti-Semitism in Romania before the Holocaust', *Journal of Genocide Research*, 4 (2002), 212–19. **355.** Dennis Deletant, 'Transnistria and the Romanian solution to the "Jewish question"', in Brandon and Lower (eds.), *The Shoah in Ukraine*, 157–8; Clark, 'Fascists and soldiers', 409–10, 417–21; Waitman Beorn, *The Holocaust in Eastern Europe: At the Epicentre of the Final Solution* (London, 2018), 185–7. **356.** Deletant, 'Transnistria', 172–9. **357.** Eduard Nižňanski,

'Expropriation and deportation of Jews in Slovakia', in Beate Kosmola and Feliks Tych (eds.), *Facing the Nazi Genocide: Non-Jews and Jews in Europe* (Berlin, 2004), 210–23, 230. **358.** Krisztian Ungváry, 'Robbing the dead: the Hungarian contribution to the Holocaust', in Kosmola and Tych (eds.), *Facing the Nazi Genocide*, 233–44; Pohl, 'The murder of Ukraine's Jews', 29–31. **359.** Gerlach, *Extermination of the European Jews*, 114–15. **360.** Frederick Chary, *The Bulgarian Jews and the Final Solution, 1940–1944* (Pittsburgh, Pa, 1972), 35–8, 41–4, 54–5, 58–9, 184–7; Beorn, *Holocaust in Eastern Europe*, 195–9. **361.** Peter Staubenmaier, 'Preparation for genocide: the "Center for the Study of the Jewish Problem" in Trieste, 1942–44', *Holocaust and Genocide Research*, 31 (2017), 2–4. **362.** Jonathan Steinberg, *All or Nothing: The Axis and the Holocaust 1941–43* (London, 1991), 54–61. **363.** Liliana Picciotto, 'The Shoah in Italy: its history and characteristics', in Joshua Zimmerman (ed.), *Jews in Italy under Fascist and Nazi Rule, 1922–1945* (Cambridge, 2005), 211–19. **364.** Liliana Picciotto, 'Italian Jews who survived the Shoah: Jewish self-help and Italian rescuers 1943–1945', *Holocaust and Genocide Studies*, 30 (2016), 20–28; Simon Levis Sullam, 'The Italian executioners: revisiting the role of Italians in the Holocaust', *Journal of Genocide Research*, 19 (2017), 21–7. **365.** Gerlach, *Extermination of the European Jews*, 375–6. **366.** Anne Grynberg, *Les camps de la honte: les internés juifs des camps français 1939–1944* (Paris, 1991), 151–3. **367.** Michael Meyer, 'The French Jewish Statute of October 5 1940: a reevaluation of continuities and discontinuities of French anti-Semitism', *Holocaust and Genocide Studies*, 33 (2019), 13. **368.** Ibid., 6–7, 15. **369.** Julian Jackson, *France: The Dark Years, 1940–1944* (Oxford, 2001), 354–9. **370.** Ibid., 362; Gerlach, *Extermination of the European Jews*, 95–6. **371.** Orna Keren-Carmel, 'Another piece in the puzzle: Denmark, Nazi Germany, and the rescue of Danish Jewry', *Holocaust Studies*, 24 (2018), 172–82; Gerlach, *Extermination of the European Jews*, 301–3. **372.** Simo Muir, 'The plan to rescue Finnish Jews in 1944', *Holocaust and Genocide Studies*, 30 (2016), 81–90. **373.** Hugh Trevor-Roper (ed.), *The Testament of Adolf Hitler: The Hitler–Bormann Documents* (London, 1959), 105, notes of 25 Apr. 1945.

3. The Death of the Nation-Empire

1. Carl Boyd, *Hitler's Japanese Confidant: General Ōshima Hiroshi and Magic Intelligence 1941–1945* (Lawrence, Kans, 1993), 72. **2.** Gerhard Krebs, 'Gibraltar oder Bosporus? Japans Empfehlungen für eine deutsche Mittelmeerstrategie im Jahre 1943', *Militärgeschichtliche Mitteilungen*, 58 (1999), 66–77. **3.** Boyd, *Hitler's Japanese Confidant*, 94. **4.** John Gooch, *Mussolini's War: Fascist Italy from Triumph to Collapse 1935–1943* (London, 2020), 325. **5.** Ikuhiko Hata, 'Admiral Yamamoto's surprise attack and the Japanese war strategy', in Saki Dockrill (ed.), *From Pearl Harbor to Hiroshima: The Second World War in Asia and the Pacific, 1941–45* (London, 1994), 66. **6.** Sarah Paine, *The Wars for Asia 1911–1949* (Cambridge, 2012), 192; Hans van de Ven, *China at War: Triumph and Tragedy in the Emergence of Modern China 1937–1952* (London, 2017), 162; Edward Drea and Hans van de Ven, 'An overview of major military campaigns during the Sino-Japanese War 1937–1945', in Mark Peattie, Edward Drea and Hans van de Ven (eds.), *The Battle for China: Essays on the Military History of the Sino-Japanese War of 1937–1945* (Stanford, Calif., 2011), 38–43. **7.** Ronald Lewin, *The Other Ultra: Codes, Ciphers, and the Defeat of Japan* (London, 1982), 85–106. **8.** Craig Symonds, *World War II at Sea: A Global History* (New York, 2018), 283–92; J. Tach, 'A beautiful silver waterfall', in E. T. Wooldridge (ed.), *Carrier Warfare in the Pacific: An Oral History Collection* (Washington, DC, 1993), 58. **9.** Symonds, *World War II at Sea*, 332–3, 345–6. **10.** Lucio Ceva, *Storia delle Forze Armate in Italia* (Turin, 1999), 315–17. **11.** Niall Barr, *Pendulum of War: The Three Battles of El Alamein* (London, 2004), 12–13. **12.** Ibid., 16–21. **13.** Andrew Buchanan, 'A friend indeed? From Tobruk to El Alamein: the American contribution to victory in the desert', *Diplomacy & Statecraft*, 15 (2004), 279–89. **14.** Gabriel Gorodetsky (ed.), *The Maisky Diaries: Red Ambassador to the Court of St. James's 1932–1943* (New Haven, Conn., 2015), 442, entry for 3 July 1942. **15.** Bernd Wegner, 'Vom Lebensraum zum Todesraum. Deutschlands Kriegführung zwischen

Moskau und Stalingrad', in Jürgen Förster (ed.), *Stalingrad: Ereignis, Wirkung, Symbol* (Munich, 1992), 20–21. **16.** Geoffrey Roberts, *Stalin's Wars: From World War to Cold War, 1939–1953* (New Haven, Conn., 2006), 123–4. **17.** Robert Citino, *Death of the Wehrmacht: The German Campaigns of 1942* (Lawrence, Kans, 2007), 102–8. **18.** Wegner, 'Von Lebensraum zum Todesraum', 23–4; Citino, *Death of the Wehrmacht*, 108–14. **19.** David Glantz, *The Role of Intelligence in Soviet Military Strategy in World War 2* (Novato, Calif., 1990), 49–51. **20.** Citino, *Death of the Wehrmacht*, 266. **21.** Walther Hubatsch, *Hitlers Weisungen für die Kriegführung 1939–1945* (Munich, 1965), 227–30. **22.** Mikhail Heller and Aleksandr Nekrich, *Utopia in Power: The History of the Soviet Union from 1917 to the Present* (London, 1982), 391; David Glantz and Jonathan House, *When Titans Clashed: How the Red Army Stopped Hitler* (Lawrence, Kans, 1995), 121. **23.** Joachim Wieder, *Stalingrad und die Verantwortung der Soldaten* (Munich, 1962), 45. **24.** David Horner, 'Australia in 1942: a pivotal year', in Peter Dean (ed.), *Australia 1942: In the Shadow of War* (Cambridge, 2013), 18–20, 25. **25.** Debi Unger and Irwin Unger, *George Marshall: A Biography* (New York, 2014), 173–6. **26.** Mark Stoler, *Allies and Adversaries: The Joint Chiefs of Staff, The Grand Alliance and U.S. Strategy in World War II* (Chapel Hill, NC, 2000), 76–8. **27.** Maury Klein, *A Call to Arms: Mobilizing America for World War II* (New York, 2013), 302–3; John Jeffries, *Wartime America: The World War II Home Front* (Chicago, Ill., 1996), 153–5; Sean Casey, *Cautious Crusade: Franklin D. Roosevelt, American Public Opinion and the War against Nazi Germany* (New York, 2001), 48–50. The average of polls from Dec. 1941 to Mar. 1942 showed 62 per cent in favour of concentrating on Japan, 21 per cent for Germany. **28.** David Roll, *The Hopkins Touch: Harry Hopkins and the Forging of the Alliance to Defeat Hitler* (New York, 2013), 183–4. **29.** Ibid., 197–8. **30.** David Kennedy, *The American People in World War II* (New York, 1999), 148–50. **31.** Matthew Jones, *Britain, The United States and the Mediterranean War 1942–44* (London, 1996), 19. **32.** Unger and Unger, *George Marshall*, 150–55, 171–2; Roll, *The Hopkins Touch*, 204–8. **33.** Stoler, *Allies and Adversaries*, 88. **34.** Kennedy, *The American People in World War II*, 153–4; Stoler, *Allies and Adversaries*, 79–85; Unger and Unger, *George Marshall*, 172–7; Roll, *The Hopkins Touch*, 214–21; Andrew Buchanan, *American Grand Strategy in the Mediterranean during World War II* (Cambridge, 2014), 48–9. **35.** Hastings Ismay, *The Memoirs of Lord Ismay* (London, 1960), 279–80. **36.** This description from the official history: Frank Hough, *The Island War: The United States Marine Corps in the Pacific* (Philadelphia, Pa, 1947), 41, 61, 84–5. **37.** John Lorelli, *To Foreign Shores: U.S. Amphibious Operations in World War II* (Annapolis, Md, 1995), 43–4; Richard Frank, *Guadalcanal* (New York, 1990), 33–44. **38.** David Ulbrich, *Preparing for Victory: Thomas Holcomb and the Making of the Modern Marine Corps, 1936–1943* (Annapolis, Md, 2011), 130–32. **39.** Lorelli, *To Foreign Shores*, 46–50; Hough, *Island War*, 45–8. **40.** Meirion Harries and Susie Harries, *Soldiers of the Sun: The Rise and Fall of the Imperial Japanese Army* (London, 1991), 339–40. **41.** Symonds, *World War II at Sea*, 328–9. **42.** Ibid., 366–71; Trent Hone, '"Give them hell": the US Navy's night combat doctrine and the campaign for Guadalcanal', *War in History*, 13 (2006), 188–95. **43.** Frank, *Guadalcanal*, 559–61, 588–95. **44.** Harries and Harries, *Soldiers of the Sun*, 341–2; Hough, *Island War*, 79–85; Frank, *Guadalcanal*, 611–13; Francis Pike, *Hirohito's War: The Pacific War 1941–1945* (London, 2016), 574–5. Frank gives a slightly lower figure for Japanese deaths of 30,343. **45.** Frank, *Guadalcanal*, 618–19. **46.** Ashley Jackson, *Persian Gulf Command: A History of the Second World War in Iran and Iraq* (New Haven, Conn., 2018), 254. **47.** Glyn Harper, '"No model campaign": the Second New Zealand Division and the Battle of El Alamein, October–December 1942', in Jill Edwards (ed.), *El Alamein and the Struggle for North Africa: International Perspectives from the Twenty-first Century* (Cairo, 2012), 88. **48.** John Kennedy, *The Business of War: The War Narrative of Major-General Sir John Kennedy* (London, 1957), 251. **49.** Gooch, *Mussolini's War*, 312–13. **50.** Jonathan Fennell, *Fighting the People's War: The British and Commonwealth Armies and the Second World War* (Cambridge, 2019), 179–80. **51.** Nigel Hamilton, *Monty: Master of the Battlefield 1942–1944* (London, 1983), 9; Harper, '"No model campaign"', 75. **52.** Fennell, *Fighting the People's War*, 268–9. **53.** Richard Hammond, *Strangling the Axis: The Fight for Control of the Mediterranean during the Second World War* (Cambridge, 2020),

141–3.   54. Barr, *Pendulum of War*, 218–19.   55. Fennell, *Fighting the People's War*, 268; Citino, *Death of the Wehrmacht*, 213–14.   56. David French, *Raising Churchill's Army: The British Army and the War against Germany 1919–1945* (Oxford, 2000), 256.   57. Horst Boog et al., *Das Deutsche Reich und der Zweite Weltkrieg, Band 6: Der globale Krieg* (Stuttgart, 1990), 694.   58. French, *Raising Churchill's Army*, 243.   59. Peter Stanley, '"The part we played in this show": Australians and El Alamein', in Edwards (ed.), *El Alamein*, 60–66 on the Australian experience; Harper, '"No model campaign"', 73–5, 86–8, on the New Zealand division.   60. French, *Raising Churchill's Army*, 246–54; Fennell, *Fighting the People's War*, 276–8, 283–90.   61. Buchanan, 'A friend indeed?', 289–91.   62. Fennell, *Fighting the People's War*, 301; Ceva, *Storia delle Forze Armate in Italia*, 319–20; Boog et al., *Das Deutsche Reich und der Zweite Weltkrieg: Band 6*, 694, which notes that RAF strength in the Middle East theatre as a whole was over 1,500 aircraft.   63. Barr, *Pendulum of War*, 276–7; Richard Carrier, 'Some reflections on the fighting power of the Italian Army in North Africa, 1940–1943', *War in History*, 22 (2015), 508–9, 516; Domenico Petracarro, 'The Italian Army in Africa 1940–1943: an attempt at historical perspective', *War & Society*, 9 (1991), 115–16.   64. Rick Stroud, *The Phantom Army of Alamein: The Men Who Hoodwinked Rommel* (London, 2012), 183–209. The deception plan is dealt with in more detail in Ch. 5.   65. Simon Ball, *Alamein* (Oxford, 2016), 16–22.   66. Fennell, *Fighting the People's War*, 308–12; Ball, *Alamein*, 37–41; Barr, *Pendulum of War*, 398–401.   67. Barr, *Pendulum of War*, 404; Ceva, *Storia delle Forze Armate in Italia*, 320; Ball, *Alamein*, 47; Gooch, *Mussolini's War*, 322.   68. Barr, *Pendulum of War*, 406–7.   69. David Glantz, *Colossus Reborn: The Red Army at War, 1941–1943* (Lawrence, Kans, 2005), 37.   70. Boog et al., *Das Deutsche Reich und der Zweite Weltkrieg: Band 6*, 965–6; Citino, *Death of the Wehrmacht*, 254.   71. Citino, *Death of the Wehrmacht*, 257.   72. Geoffrey Megargee, *Inside Hitler's High Command* (Lawrence, Kans, 2000), 181–7.   73. Alexander Statiev, *At War's Summit: The Red Army and the Struggle for the Caucasus Mountains in World War II* (Cambridge, 2018), 130–31, 264.   74. Roberts, *Stalin's Wars*, 142.   75. Evan Mawdsley, *Thunder in the East: The Nazi–Soviet War 1941–1945* (London, 2005), 205–7.   76. Alexander Hill, *The Red Army and the Second World War* (Cambridge, 2017), 392–3.   77. Stephen Fritz, *Ostkrieg: Hitler's War of Extermination in the East* (Lexington, Ky, 2011), 291–2.   78. Wegner, 'Vom Lebensraum zum Todesraum', 32.   79. Vasily Chuikov, *The Beginning of the Road: The Story of the Battle of Stalingrad* (London, 1963), 14–27, 93–102.   80. Fritz, *Ostkrieg*, 295.   81. Roberts, *Stalin's Wars*, 145–7.   82. Kurt Zeitzler, 'Stalingrad', in William Richardson and Seymour Frieden (eds.), *The Fatal Decisions* (London, 1956), 138.   83. Boog et al., *Das Deutsche Reich und der Zweite Weltkrieg: Band 6*, 995–7.   84. Hill, *Red Army*, 395–7; Roberts, *Stalin's Wars*, 151.   85. John Erickson, *The Road to Stalingrad* (London, 1975), 447–53; Glantz and House, *When Titans Clashed*, 133–4.   86. Williamson Murray, *Luftwaffe: Strategy for Defeat* (London, 1985), 141–4.   87. Fritz, *Ostkrieg*, 316.   88. Ibid., 319–20.   89. Ibid., 318–19.   90. Thomas Kohut and Jürgen Reulecke, '"Sterben wie eine Ratte, die der Bauer ertappt": Letzte Briefe aus Stalingrad', in Förster (ed.), *Stalingrad*, 464.   91. Soviet losses calculated from G. Krivosheev, *Soviet Casualties and Combat Losses in the Twentieth Century* (London, 1997), 124–8; German losses from Rüdiger Overmans, *Deutsche militärische Verluste im Zweiten Weltkrieg* (Munich, 2004), 279; Italian losses in Gooch, *Mussolini's War*, 296.   92. David Glantz, 'Counterpoint to Stalingrad: Operation "Mars" (November–December 1942): Marshal Zhukov's greatest defeat', *Journal of Slavic Strategic Studies*, 10 (1997), 105–10, 117–18, 133   93. *La Semaine*, 4 Feb. 1943, p. 6.   94. TNA, WO 193/856, Military attaché Ankara to the War Office, 23 July 1943.   95. Henrik Eberle and Matthias Uhl (eds.), *The Hitler Book: The Secret Dossier Prepared for Stalin* (London, 2005), 91, 130, 133.   96. Fabio De Ninno, 'The Italian Navy and Japan: the Indian Ocean, failed cooperation, and tripartite relations', *War in History*, 27 (2020), 231–40, 245.   97. Bernd Martin, 'The German–Japanese alliance in the Second World War', in Dockrill (ed.), *Pearl Harbor to Hiroshima*, 158–9.   98. Rotem Kowner, 'When economics, strategy, and racial ideology meet: inter-Axis connections in the wartime Indian Ocean', *Journal of Global History*, 12 (2017), 237–42; Bernd Martin, 'Japan und Stalingrad: Umorientierung vom Bündnis mit Deutschland auf "Grossostasien"', in Förster, *Stalingrad*, 242–6.   99. Jones, *Britain, The United States and the*

Mediterranean War, 38–9. 100. Buchanan, *American Grand Strategy*, 72–4; Martin Thomas and Richard Toye, *Arguing about Empire: Imperial Rhetoric in Britain and France, 1882–1956* (Oxford, 2017), 184–6. 101. Jones, *Britain, The United States and the Mediterranean War*, 75–6. 102. Ibid., 33. 103. Buchanan, *American Grand Strategy*, 70. 104. Ibid., 76–80. 105. Ibid., 21; Stoler, *Allies and Adversaries*, 117; Richard Toye, *Churchill's Empire: The World that Made Him and the World He Made* (New York, 2010), 245–6. 106. Stoler, *Allies and Adversaries*, 168. 107. Marco Aterrano, 'Prelude to Casablanca: British operational planning for metropolitan Italy and the origins of the Allied invasion of Sicily, 1940–1941', *War in History*, 26 (2019), 498–507. 108. Steve Weiss, *Allies in Conflict: Anglo-American Strategic Negotiations 1938–1944* (London, 1996), 70–71. 109. Gooch, *Mussolini's War*, 342–5; Giorgio Rochat, *Le guerre italiane 1935–1943: Dall'impero d'Etiopia alla disfatta* (Turin, 2005), 358. 110. Jones, *Britain, The United States and the Mediterranean War*, 50–52. 111. Fennell, *Fighting the People's War*, 317–18; Megargee, *Inside Hitler's High Command*, 194. There are various estimates for the number of prisoners which range from 220,000 to 275,000, but the higher figure now seems more likely. 112. Symonds, *World War II at Sea*, 423–4. 113. Jones, *Britain, The United States and the Mediterranean War*, 57–9; David Jablonsky, *War by Land, Sea and Air: Dwight Eisenhower and the Concept of Unified Command* (New Haven, Conn., 2010), 95–6. 114. Symonds, *World War II at Sea*, 424–5. 115. Alfred Chandler (ed.), *The Papers of Dwight David Eisenhower. The War Years: IV* (Baltimore, Va, 1970), 1129, Eisenhower to Marshall, 13 May 1943. 116. Gooch, *Mussolini's War*, 378–80. 117. Symonds, *World War II at Sea*, 438–9; Stoler, *Allies and Adversaries*, 118. 118. Jones, *Britain, The United States and the Mediterranean War*, 62. 119. Gooch, *Mussolini's War*, 383. 120. Philip Morgan, *The Fall of Mussolini* (Oxford, 2007), 11–17, 23–6. 121. Eugen Dollmann, *With Hitler and Mussolini: Memoirs of a Nazi Interpreter* (New York, 2017), 219. 122. Helmut Heiber and David Glantz (eds.), *Hitler and his Generals: Military Conferences 1942–45* (London, 2002), 252, 255, Meeting of the Führer with Field Marshal von Kluge, 26 July 1943. 123. Megargee, *Inside Hitler's High Command*, 198; Gooch, *Mussolini's War*, 389, 404. 124. Elena Rossi, *Cefalonia: La resistenza, l'eccidio, il mito* (Bologna, 2016), 53–60, 113–15. 125. Lutz Klinkhammer, *L'occupazione tedesca in Italia, 1943–1945* (Turin, 1996), 48–54; Frederick Deakin, *Storia della repubblica di Salò*, 2 vols. (Turin, 1963), ii, 740–48. 126. Deakin, *Storia della repubblica di Salò*, ii, 766, 776–8, 817. 127. Jones, *Britain, The United States and the Mediterranean War*, 146–8. 128. Ibid., 150, Montgomery diary entry for 26 Sept. 1943. 129. Symonds, *World War II at Sea*, 454–8; Carlo D'Este, *Eisenhower: Allied Supreme Commander* (London, 2002), 452–3. 130. Lorelli, *To Foreign Shores*, 94–6. 131. Ibid., 163–4; Symonds, *World War II at Sea*, 488–9. 132. Lorelli, *To Foreign Shores*, 94–5, 98–9. 133. Symonds, *World War II at Sea*, 475. 134. Pike, *Hirohito's War*, 671–2, 695; Lorelli, *To Foreign Shores*, 156–61. 135. Pike, *Hirohito's War*, 680–91, 695. 136. Hough, *Island War*, 126. 137. Ibid., 146. 138. Ibid., 145. 139. Lorelli, *To Foreign Shores*, 117. 140. Ibid., 193–4. 141. Ibid., 193–204. 142. Kennedy, *The American People in World War II*, 162. 143. David Reynolds and Vladimir Pechatnov (eds.), *The Kremlin Letters: Stalin's Wartime Correspondence with Churchill and Roosevelt* (New Haven, Conn., 2018), 263–9, Churchill to Stalin, 20 June 1943; Stalin to Churchill, 24 June 1943. 144. Roberts, *Stalin's Wars*, 165–6. 145. Reynolds and Pechatnov, *Kremlin Letters*, 354; Roberts, *Stalin's Wars*, 180. 146. Reynolds and Pechatnov, *Kremlin Letters*, 269. 147. Mawdsley, *Thunder in the East*, 252–6. 148. Megargee, *Inside Hitler's High Command*, 193–4. 149. Fritz, *Ostkrieg*, 336–8. 150. Roman Töppel, 'Legendenbildung in der Geschichtsschreibung – Die Schlacht bei Kursk', *Militärgeschichtliche Zeitschrift*, 61 (2002), 373–4. 151. Valeriy Zamulin, 'Could Germany have won the Battle of Kursk if it had started in late May or the beginning of June 1943?', *Journal of Slavic Military Studies*, 27 (2014), 608–9; Lloyd Clark, *Kursk: The Greatest Battle* (London, 2011), 188–90. 152. Georgii Zhukov, *Reminiscences and Reflections: Volume II* (Moscow, 1985), 168–79; Konstantin Rokossovskii, *A Soldier's Duty* (Moscow, 1970), 184–90; Clark, *Kursk*, 211. 153. Töppel, 'Legendenbildung', 376–8; Fritz, *Ostkrieg*, 339–40. 154. Clark, *Kursk*, 199; Fritz, *Ostkrieg*, 343. Of these 200 were 'Panthers', 128 'Tigers'. 155. William Spahr, *Zhukov: The Rise and Fall of a Great Captain* (Novato, Calif., 1993), 119–21. 156. Glantz,

The Role of Intelligence, 100–103; Zhukov, *Reminiscences*, 180–83.   **157.** Hill, *Red Army*, 439–40; Von Hardesty and Ilya Grinberg, *Red Phoenix Rising: The Soviet Air Force in World War II* (Lawrence, Kans, 2012), 226 for air figures; Alexander Vasilevskii, 'Strategic planning of the Battle of Kursk', in *The Battle of Kursk* (Moscow, 1974), 73. Slightly different figures in Clark, *Kursk*, 204.   **158.** Fritz, *Ostkrieg*, 343.   **159.** Charles Sydnor, *Soldiers of Destruction: The SS Death's Head Division 1933–1945* (Princeton, NJ, 1977), 233–8.   **160.** Töppel, 'Legendenbildung', 381–5; Hill, *Red Army*, 450–52; Fritz, *Ostkrieg*, 349–50.   **161.** Valeriy Zamulin, 'Soviet troop losses in the Battle of Prochorovka, 10–16 July 1943', *Journal of Slavic Military Studies*, 32 (2019), 119–21.   **162.** Clark, *Kursk*, 402.   **163.** Töppel, 'Legendenbildung', 389–92; Clark, *Kursk*, 399–402.   **164.** Hill, *Red Army*, 454; Fritz, *Ostkrieg*, 367; Töppel, 'Legendenbildung', 396–9.   **165.** Fritz, *Ostkrieg*, 378.   **166.** Hill, *Red Army*, 466.   **167.** Alexander Werth, *Russia at War 1941–1945* (London, 1964), 752–4.   **168.** Mawdsley, *Thunder in the East*, 273–5.   **169.** Boris Sokolov, *Myths and Legends of the Eastern Front: Reassessing the Great Patriotic War* (Barnsley, 2019), x.   **170.** Glantz, *Colossus Reborn*, 60–62.   **171.** Stoler, *Allies and Adversaries*, 165–6; Theodore Wilson, 'Coalition: structure, strategy and statecraft', in Warren Kimball, David Reynolds and Alexander Chubarian (eds.), *Allies at War: The Soviet, American and British Experience 1939–1945* (New York, 1994), 98.   **172.** Robert Dallek, *Franklin D. Roosevelt: A Political Life* (London, 2017), 533; Jones, *Britain, The United States and the Mediterranean War*, 153.   **173.** Buchanan, *American Grand Strategy*, 159.   **174.** Sally Burt, 'High and low tide: Sino-American relations and summit diplomacy in the Second World War', *Diplomacy & Statecraft*, 29 (2018), 175–8.   **175.** Jay Taylor, *The Generalissimo: Chiang Kai-Shek and the Struggle for Modern China* (Cambridge, Mass., 2009), 247–8.   **176.** Valentin Berezhkov, *History in the Making: Memoirs of World War II Diplomacy* (Moscow, 1983), 282.   **177.** Ibid., 287; Keith Eubank, *Summit at Teheran* (New York, 1985), 350–51.   **178.** Wenzhao Tao, 'The China theatre and the Pacific war', in Dockrill (ed.), *Pearl Harbor to Hiroshima*, 137–41.   **179.** Taylor, *Generalissimo*, 256–61.   **180.** Alex Danchev and Daniel Todman (eds.), *War Diaries 1939–1945: Field Marshal Lord Alanbrooke* (London, 2001), 458, 490, entries for 7 Oct., 3 Dec. 1943.   **181.** Keith Sainsbury, *The Turning Point: Roosevelt, Stalin, Churchill, Chiang Kai-Shek, 1943* (Oxford, 1986), 288–96.   **182.** John Buckley, *Monty's Men: The British Army and the Liberation of Europe* (New Haven, Conn., 2013), 253–4.   **183.** Hough, *Island War*, 298–300; Waldo Heinrichs and Marc Gallicchio, *Implacable Foes: War in the Pacific 1944–1945* (New York, 2017), 160–63.   **184.** Douglas Delaney, 'The Eighth Army at the Gothic Line, August–September 1944: a study of staff compatibility and coalition command', *War in History*, 27 (2020), 288–90.   **185.** Wang Qisheng, 'The Battle of Hunan and the Chinese military's response to Operation Ichigō', in Peattie, Drea and van de Ven (eds.), *Battle for China*, 404–10; Hara Takeshi, 'The Ichigō Offensive', ibid., 392–5.   **186.** Rana Mitter, *China's War with Japan 1937–1945: The Struggle for Survival* (London, 2013), 327–9.   **187.** Hara, 'Ichigō Offensive', 399–401; Wang, 'Battle of Hunan', 410–12.   **188.** Christopher Bayly and Tim Harper, *Forgotten Armies: The Fall of British Asia 1941–1945* (London, 2004), 381–2, 388.   **189.** Srinath Raghavan, *India's War: The Making of Modern South Asia* (London, 2016), 427–8.   **190.** Taylor, *Generalissimo*, 280–86.   **191.** Mitter, *China's War with Japan*, 334–5; Peattie, Drea and van de Ven (eds.), *Battle for China*, 486.   **192.** Louis Allen and David Steeds, 'Burma: the longest war, 1941–45', in Dockrill (ed.), *Pearl Harbor to Hiroshima*, 114.   **193.** Lorelli, *To Foreign Shores*, 208–9.   **194.** Heinrichs and Gallicchio, *Implacable Foes*, 62–7.   **195.** Lorelli, *To Foreign Shores*, 234–5.   **196.** Richard Muller, 'Air war in the Pacific, 1941–1945', in John Olsen (ed.), *A History of Air Warfare* (Washington, DC, 2010), 69–70.   **197.** Heinrichs and Gallicchio, *Implacable Foes*, 103–8.   **198.** Hough, *Island War*, 245–6.   **199.** Heinrichs and Gallicchio, *Implacable Foes*, 115–23; Lorelli, *To Foreign Shores*, 243–7.   **200.** Boyd, *Hitler's Japanese Confidant*, 157.   **201.** Frederick Morgan, *Overture to Overlord* (London, 1950), 134–6, 142–4; John Ehrman, *Grand Strategy: Volume V: August 1943 to September 1944* (London, 1946), 54–6.   **202.** TNA, AIR 8/1103, CCS meeting minutes, 4 June 1943; Charles Webster and Noble Frankland, *Strategic Air Offensive against Germany: Volume IV* (London, 1961), 160, Directive to Harris, 3 Sept. 1943.   **203.** TNA, AIR 14/783, Portal to Harris encl. 'Extent to which the Eighth U.S.A.A.F and Bomber

Command have been able to implement the G.A.F. Plan', p. 1. **204.** TNA, AIR 14/739A, 'Conduct of the Strategic Bomber Offensive before Preparatory Stage of "Overlord"', 17 Jan. 1944; LC, Spaatz Papers, Box 143, Arnold to Spaatz, 24 Apr. 1944. **205.** Air Force Historical Research Agency, Maxwell, Ala, Disc A1722, 'Army Air Forces Evaluation Board, Eighth Air Force "Tactical Development August 1942–May 1945"', pp. 50–55; Stephen McFarland and Wesley Newton, *To Command the Sky: The Battle for Air Superiority over Germany, 1942–44* (Washington, DC, 1991), 141, 164–6. **206.** Horst Boog et al., *Das Deutsche Reich und der Zweite Weltkrieg: Band 7: Das Deutsche Reich in der Defensive* (Stuttgart, 2001), 11; Richard Davis, *Carl A. Spaatz and the Air War in Europe* (Washington, DC, 1993), 322–6, 370–79; Murray, *Luftwaffe*, 215. **207.** Boog et al., *Das Deutsche Reich unde der Zweite Weltkrieg: Band 7*, 293. There were 198 serviceable bombers. **208.** Günter Bischof and Rolf Steininger, 'Die Invasion aus der Sicht von Zeitzeugen', in Günter Bischof and Wolfgang Krieger (eds.), *Die Invasion in der Normandie 1944* (Innsbruck, 2001), 68. **209.** Ian Gooderson, *A Hard Way to Make a War: The Italian Campaign in the Second World War* (London, 2008), 260; Jones, *Britain, The United States and the Mediterranean War*, 154–6. **210.** Lorelli, *To Foreign Shores*, 187–8. **211.** Jones, *Britain, The United States and the Mediterranean War*, 157. **212.** Lorelli, *To Foreign Shores*, 188–90; Gooderson, *Hard Way to Make a War*, 268–71. **213.** James Parton, *'Air Force Spoken Here': General Ira Eaker and the Command of the Air* (Bethesda, Md, 1986), 363–5. **214.** Gooderson, *Hard Way to Make a War*, 271–8; Peter Caddick-Adams, *Monte Cassino: Ten Armies in Hell* (London, 2012), 211–12. **215.** Caddick-Adams, *Monte Cassino*, 225–7; Halik Kochanski, *The Eagle Unbowed: Poland and the Poles in the Second World War* (London, 2012), 473–5. **216.** Jones, *Britain, The United States and the Mediterranean War*, 163–5; Gooderson, *Hard Way to Make a War*, 278–9. **217.** Stephen Roskill, *The War at Sea: Volume IV* (London, 1961), 25–8. **218.** TNA, AIR 37/752, Harris memorandum, 'The Employment of the Night Bomber Force in Connection with the Invasion of the Continent', 13 Jan. 1944; LC, Spaatz Papers, Box 143, Spaatz to Eisenhower [n.d. but April 1944]. **219.** Stephen Ambrose, *Eisenhower: Soldier and President* (New York, 1991), 126; Davis, *Carl A. Spaatz*, 336–8. **220.** Andrew Knapp and Claudia Baldoli, *Forgotten Blitzes: France and Italy under Allied Air Attack, 1940–1945* (London, 2012), 29; death figures in Richard Overy, *The Bombing War: Europe 1939–1945* (London, 2013), 574. **221.** Wesley Craven and James Cate, *The Army Air Forces in World War II: Volume III* (Chicago, Ill., 1983), 158. On the bridge campaign see Stephen Bourque, *Beyond the Beach: The Allied War against France* (Annapolis, Md, 2018), ch. 9. **222.** Detlef Vogel, 'Deutsche Vorbereitungen auf eine alliierte Invasion im Westen', in Bischof and Krieger (eds.), *Die Invasion in der Normandie*, 52. **223.** Bischof and Steininger, 'Die Invasion aus der Sicht von Zeitzeugen', 56. **224.** Vogel, 'Deutsche Vorbereitungen', 45; Olivier Wieviorka, *Histoire du Débarquement en Normandie: Des origins à la liberation de Paris 1941–1944* (Paris, 2007), 191–3. **225.** Vogel, 'Deutsche Vorbereitungen', 46–8. **226.** Gordon Harrison, *Cross Channel Attack: The United States Army in World War II* (Washington, DC, 1951), 154–5, 249–52; Friedrich Ruge, *Rommel und die Invasion: Erinnerungen von Friedrich Ruge* (Stuttgart, 1959), 174–5. **227.** Danchev and Todman (eds.), *War Diaries*, 554, entry for 5 June 1944. **228.** D'Este, *Eisenhower*, 518–22. **229.** Eberle and Uhl (eds.), *The Hitler Book*, 149. **230.** *Report by the Supreme Commander to the Combined Chiefs of Staff on the Operations in Europe of the Allied Expeditionary Force* (London, 1946), 32. **231.** Vogel, 'Deutsche Vorbereitungen', 50–51; Bischof and Steininger, 'Die Invasion aus der Sicht von Zeitzeugen', 66. **232.** Fennell, *Fighting the People's War*, 534. **233.** Volker Ullrich, *Hitler: Downfall 1939–45* (London, 2020), 427–9. **234.** Alistair Horne and David Montgomery, *The Lonely Leader: Monty, 1944–1945* (London, 1994), 207; L. Ellis, *Victory in the West: Volume I: The Battle for Normandy* (London, 1962), 329–30. **235.** Percy Schramm (ed.), *Kriegstagebuch des Oberkommandos der Wehrmacht*, 4 vols. (Munich, 1963), iv, 326; Eddy Bauer, *Der Panzerkrieg*, 2 vols. (Bonn, 1965), ii, 104–5, 125–6; John English, *The Canadian Army and the Normandy Campaign* (New York, 1991), 227–31. **236.** Joachim Ludewig, *Rückzug: The German Retreat from France, 1944* (Lexington, Ky, 2012), 34–5, 40. **237.** Ralph Bennett, *Ultra in the West: The Normandy Campaign of 1944 to 1945* (London, 1979), 112–16; Martin Blumenson, *Breakout and Pursuit: U.S. Army in World War II* (Washington,

DC, 1961), 457–65. **238.** Klaus-Jürgen Müller, 'Die Zusammenbruch des deutschen Westheeres: Die operative Entwicklung im Bereich der Heeresgruppe B Juli bis Ende August', in Michael Salewski and Guntram Schulze-Wegener (eds.), *Kriegsjahr 1944: im Grossen und im Kleinen* (Stuttgart, 1995), 31–2. **239.** D'Este, *Eisenhower*, 572. **240.** Milton Shulman, *Defeat in the West* (London, 1947), 175. **241.** Jones, *Britain, The United States and the Mediterranean War*, 183. **242.** Ludewig, *Rückzug*, 58–62. **243.** D'Este, *Eisenhower*, 567. **244.** Ludewig, *Rückzug*, 73. **245.** On the role of de Gaulle and the Fighting French, Wieviorka, *Histoire du Débarquement*, 402–8. **246.** Fennell, *Fighting the People's War*, 565. **247.** Bischof and Steininger, 'Die Invasion aus der Sicht von Zeitzeugen', 65. **248.** David Kahn, *Hitler's Spies: German Military Intelligence in World War II* (London, 1978), 440–41. **249.** John Erickson, *The Road to Berlin: Stalin's War with Germany* (London, 1983), 253; David Glantz, 'The red mask: the nature and legacy of Soviet deception in the Second World War', in Michael Handel (ed.), *Strategic and Operational Deception in the Second World War* (London, 1987), 213–17; S. L. Sokolov and John Erickson, *Main Front: Soviet Leaders Look Back on World War II* (New York, 1987), 177–8, 192. **250.** Stephen Fritz, *The First Soldier: Hitler as Military Leader* (New Haven, Conn., 2018), 320–21; Gerd Niepold, 'Die Führung der Heeresgruppe Mitte von Juni bis August', in Salewski and Schulze-Wegener (eds.), *Kriegsjahr 1944*, 61–3; Rolf Hinze, 'Der Zusammenbruch der Heeresgruppe Mitte', ibid., 97. **251.** Fritz, *First Soldier*, 296; for slightly lower figures from Soviet sources see Hinze, 'Der Zusammenbruch der Heeresgruppe Mitte', 79–80. **252.** Paul Winterton, *Report on Russia* (London, 1945), 23. **253.** Karl-Heinz Frieser et al., *Das Deutsche Reich und der Zweite Weltkrieg: Band 8: Die Ostfront 1943/44* (Munich, 2007), 814–15. **254.** Oula Silvennoinen, 'Janus of the North? Finland 1940–44', in John Gilmour and Jill Stephenson (eds.), *Hitler's Scandinavian Legacy* (London, 2013), 141–2; Juhana Aunesluoma, 'Two shadows over Finland: Hitler, Stalin and the Finns facing the Second World War as history 1944–2010', ibid., 205–7. **255.** Deborah Cornelius, *Hungary in World War II: Caught in the Cauldron* (New York, 2011), 256–9, 271–80. **256.** Peter Sipos, 'The fascist Arrow Cross government in Hungary (October 1944–April 1945)', in Wolfgang Benz, Johannes Houwink ten Cate and Gerhard Otto (eds.), *Die Bürokratie der Okkupation: Strukturen der Herrschaft und Verwaltung im besetzten Europa* (Berlin, 1998), 50, 53–5. **257.** Ben-Ami Shillony, *Politics and Culture in Wartime Japan* (Oxford, 1981), 62–3. **258.** Theodore Hamerow, *On the Road to the Wolf's Lair: German Resistance to Hitler* (Cambridge, Mass., 1997), 320–21; Klemens von Klemperer, *German Resistance against Hitler: The Search for Allies Abroad* (Oxford, 1992), 432–3. **259.** Randall Hansen, *Disobeying Hitler: German Resistance in the Last Year of WWII* (London, 2014), 38–44. **260.** Ullrich, *Hitler: Downfall*, 475–7. **261.** Sönke Neitzel, *Tapping Hitler's Generals: Transcripts of Secret Conversations, 1942–45* (Barnsley, 2007), 263, recording a conversation between father and son, Gen. Heinz Eberbach and Lt Heinz Eugen Eberbach, 20/21 Sept. 1944. **262.** Nick Stargardt, *The German War: A Nation under Arms, 1939–45* (London, 2016), 452–3; Ian Kershaw, *The End: Hitler's Germany 1944–45* (London, 2011), 31–3. **263.** Shillony, *Politics and Culture in Wartime Japan*, 51–2, 59–60, 71–4. **264.** John Dower, *Japan in War and Peace: Essays on History, Race and Culture* (London, 1993), 102–7. **265.** Ibid., 129. **266.** Frank Gibney (ed.), *Sensō: The Japanese Remember the Pacific War* (New York, 2007), 169–78; Samuel Yamashita, *Daily Life in Wartime Japan 1940–1945* (Lawrence, Kans, 2015), 163–72. **267.** Alfons Kenkmann, 'Zwischen Nonkonformität und Widerstand', in Dietmar Süss and Winfried Süss (eds.), *Das 'Dritte Reich': Eine Einführung* (Munich, 2008), 150–52. **268.** Kershaw, *The End*, 36–7. **269.** Hansen, *Disobeying Hitler*, 209–10. **270.** Ralf Bank, *Bitter Ends: Die letzten Monate des Zweiten Weltkriegs im Ruhrgebiet, 1944/45* (Essen, 2015), 232. **271.** Michael Sellmann, 'Propaganda und SD – "Meldungen aus dem Reich"', in Salewski and Schulze-Wegener (eds.), *Kriegsjahr 1944*, 207–8. **272.** Stargardt, *The German War*, 477–80. **273.** Benjamin Uchigama, *Japan's Carnival War: Mass Culture on the Home Front 1937–1945* (Cambridge, 2019), 241. **274.** Ibid., 242–3. **275.** Aaron Moore, *Writing War: Soldiers Record the Japanese Empire* (Cambridge, Mass., 2013), 237–8. **276.** Thomas Kühne, *The Rise and Fall of Comradeship: Hitler's Soldiers, Male Bonding and Mass Violence in the Twentieth Century* (Cambridge, 2017), 160, 171. **277.** Thomas Brooks, *The*

War North of Rome: June 1944–May 1945 (New York, 1996), 363. **278.** Stargardt, *The German War*, 476. **279.** Jeffrey Herf, *The Jewish Enemy: Nazi Propaganda During World War II and the Holocaust* (Cambridge, Mass., 2006), 257–61. **280.** Robert Kramm, 'Haunted by defeat: imperial sexualities, prostitution and the emergence of postwar Japan', *Journal of World History*, 28 (2017), 588–91. **281.** Richard Frank, *Downfall: The End of the Japanese Imperial Empire* (New York, 1999), 188–90. **282.** Stargardt, *The German War*, 456–7; Stephen Fritz, *Endkampf: Soldiers, Civilians, and the Death of the Third Reich* (Lexington, Ky, 2004), 91. **283.** Kennedy, *The American People in World War II*, 358. **284.** Klein, *A Call to Arms*, 681–6. **285.** Daniel Todman, *Britain's War: A New World 1943–1947* (London, 2020), 582, 591, 654. **286.** Martha Gellhorn, *The Face of War from Spain to Vietnam* (London, 1967), 142. **287.** Geoffrey Picot, *Accidental Warrior: In the Front Line from Normandy till Victory* (London, 1993), 196–7, 201. **288.** Paul Fussell, *The Boys' Crusade: American GIs in Europe: Chaos and Fear in World War II* (London, 2003), 93–9. **289.** Catherine Merridale, *Ivan's War: The Red Army, 1939–45* (London, 2005), 230–32, 242–3. **290.** Klein, *A Call to Arms*, 676–83, 717–19. **291.** Heinrichs and Gallicchio, *Implacable Foes*, 424–6. **292.** Todman, *Britain's War*, 655–6. **293.** Heinrichs and Gallicchio, *Implacable Foes*, 422. **294.** Fritz, *First Soldier*, 336–7. **295.** Mitter, *China's War with Japan*, 342. **296.** Van de Ven, *China at War*, 196–7. **297.** Shillony, *Politics and Culture in Wartime Japan*, 76. **298.** Tohmatsu Haruo, 'The strategic correlation between the Sino-Japanese and Pacific wars', in Peattie, Drea and van de Ven (eds.), *Battle for China*, 438–9. **299.** Christopher Baxter, 'In pursuit of a Pacific strategy: British planning for the defeat of Japan, 1943–45', *Diplomacy & Statecraft*, 15 (2004), 254–7; Nicholas Sarantakes, 'The Royal Air Force on Okinawa: the diplomacy of a coalition on the verge of victory', *Diplomatic History*, 27 (2003), 481–3. **300.** Mark Jacobsen, 'Winston Churchill and a Third Front', *Journal of Strategic Studies*, 14 (1991), 349–56. **301.** Todman, *Britain's War*, 673; Sarantakes, 'Royal Air Force on Okinawa,' 486. **302.** Heinrichs and Gallichio, *Implacable Foes*, 150–54. **303.** Ibid., 180–90. **304.** Symonds, *World War II at Sea*, 585–7. **305.** Chandler (ed.), *Papers of Dwight David Eisenhower*, 2115, Eisenhower to all commanders, 4 Sept. 1944. **306.** Ibid., 2143–4, Eisenhower to Marshall, 14 Sept. 1944; Eisenhower to Montgomery, 15 Sept. 1944. **307.** Gooderson, *Hard Way to Make a War*, 281–4. **308.** Brooks, *The War North of Rome*, 254–8, 304. **309.** Chandler (ed.), *Papers of Dwight David Eisenhower*, 2125–7, Eisenhower to the CCS, 9 Sept. 1944. **310.** Buckley, *Monty's Men*, 240. **311.** Fennell, *Fighting the People's War*, 582. **312.** D'Este, *Eisenhower*, 626–7. **313.** Ludewig, *Rückzug*, 206–7. **314.** Alistair Noble, *Nazi Rule and the Soviet Offensive in Eastern Germany 1944–1945* (Eastbourne, 2009), 102–17. **315.** Bastiann Willems, 'Defiant breakwaters or desperate blunders? A revision of the German late-war fortress strategy', *Journal of Slavic Military Studies*, 28 (2015), 353–8. **316.** Fritz, *Ostkrieg*, 432–4; Mawdsley, *Thunder in the East*, 303–5. The Soviet side claimed to have captured 274,000 when Courland was surrendered on 10 May 1945. **317.** Krisztián Ungváry, *Battle for Budapest: 100 Days in World War II* (London, 2019), 4–6, 49–56. **318.** Ibid., 330–31. **319.** Ludewig, *Rückzug*, 204–5. **320.** Ullrich, *Hitler: Downfall*, 507. **321.** Ibid., 508. **322.** Ibid., 509. **323.** Walter Warlimont, *Inside Hitler's Headquarters 1939–45* (London, 1964), 486; Ullrich, *Hitler: Downfall*, 514. **324.** Buckley, *Monty's Men*, 259; Chandler, *Papers of Dwight David Eisenhower*, 2355, Eisenhower to Brehon Somervell, 17 Dec. 1944. **325.** D'Este, *Eisenhower*, 635–6. **326.** Charles MacDonald, *The Battle of the Bulge* (London, 1984), 608; British Air Ministry, *The Rise and Fall of the German Air Force 1933–1945* (London, 1986), 376–80. **327.** Richard Overy, *The Air War 1939–1945* (London, 1980), 77. **328.** Chandler (ed.), *Papers of Dwight David Eisenhower*, 2407, Eisenhower to the CCS. **329.** Warlimont, *Inside Hitler's Headquarters*, 487–9. **330.** Jablonsky, *War by Land, Sea and Air*, 129–30. **331.** D'Este, *Eisenhower*, 658; Harry Butcher, *Three Years with Eisenhower: The Personal Diary of Captain Harry C. Butcher, 1942–1945* (London, 1946), 626–8. **332.** Chandler (ed.), *Papers of Dwight David Eisenhower*, 2419, Eisenhower to Marshall, 10 Jan. 1945. **333.** Heinrich Schwendemann, 'Strategie der Selbstvernichtung: Die Wehrmachtführung im "Endkampf" um das "Dritte Reich"', in Rolf-Dieter Müller and Hans-Erich Volkmann (eds.), *Die Wehrmacht: Mythos und Realität* (Munich, 1999), 228. **334.** Hough, *Island War*, 732–3. **335.** Nicolaus von Below, *At Hitler's Side: The Memoirs of Hitler's Luftwaffe Adjutant 1937–1945* (London, 2001), 223.   **336.** Michael Geyer, '*Endkampf* 1918 and 1945: German nationalism, annihilation, and self-destruction', in Alf Lüdtke and Bernd Weisbrod (eds.), *No Man's Land of Violence: Extreme Wars in the 20th Century* (Göttingen, 2006), 45–51.   **337.** Werner Maser (ed.), *Hitler's Letters and Notes* (New York, 1974), 346–50.   **338.** Boog et al., *Das Deutsche Reich und der Zweite Weltkrieg: Band 7*, 105.   **339.** Davis, *Carl A. Spaatz*, Appdx. 8; Henry Probert, *Bomber Harris: His Life and Times* (London, 2006), 305–6.   **340.** Webster and Frankland, *Strategic Air Offensive*, 174–6, Directive from Bottomley to Harris, 13 Oct. 1944; pp. 177–9, '1st November 1944: Directive No. 2 for the Strategic Air Forces in Europe'.   **341.** Overy, *The Bombing War*, 391–4.   **342.** Mawdsley, *Thunder in the East*, 325.   **343.** S. M. Plokhy, *Yalta: The Price of Peace* (New York, 2010), 330.   **344.** Roberts, *Stalin's Wars*, 235; Plokhy, *Yalta*, xxv.   **345.** Fraser Harbutt, *Yalta 1945: Europe and America at the Crossroads* (Cambridge, 2010), 305, 313–17.   **346.** Plokhy, *Yalta*, 331–4, 343–4.   **347.** Richard Bessel, *Germany 1945: From War to Peace* (New York, 2009), 21–2.   **348.** Brooks, *War North of Rome*, 371; L. P. Devine, *The British Way of Warfare in Northwest Europe, 1944–5* (London, 2016), 163–7.   **349.** Bessel, *Germany 1945*, 17–18.   **350.** Martin Moll (ed.), *Führer-Erlasse: 1939–1945* (Stuttgart, 1997), 486–7, 'Zerstörungsmassnahmen im Reichsgebiet', 19 Mar. 1945.   **351.** Buckley, *Monty's Men*, 278; D'Este, *Eisenhower*, 681.   **352.** Buckley, *Monty's Men*, 286.   **353.** Kershaw, *The End*, 304–5.   **354.** D'Este, *Eisenhower*, 683, 696–7.   **355.** Fritz, *Endkampf*, 15–19.   **356.** Chandler (ed.), *Papers of Dwight David Eisenhower*, 2569, Eisenhower to the CCS, 31 Mar. 1945.   **357.** Fritz, *Endkampf*, 40–41.   **358.** Brooks, *The War North of Rome*, 363–6.   **359.** Merridale, *Ivan's War*, 243.   **360.** Mawdsley, *Thunder in the East*, 355–6.   **361.** Hill, *Red Army*, 523–31.   **362.** Zhukov, *Reminiscences*, 353–5.   **363.** Ivan Konev, *Year of Victory* (Moscow, 1969), 171–2; Erickson, *The Road to Berlin*, 809–11.   **364.** Eberle and Uhl (eds.), *The Hitler Book*, 219.   **365.** Moll (ed.), *Führer-Erlasse*, 495–6, Directive, 24 Apr. 1945.   **366.** Ibid., 241, footnote 2.   **367.** Geyer, '*Endkampf* 1918 and 1945', 51.   **368.** Alvin Coox, 'Strategic bombing in the Pacific 1942–1945', in R. Cargill Hall (ed.), *Case Studies in Strategic Bombardment* (Washington, DC, 1998), 296–7. Japanese bombers attacked the B-29 airfields from Nov. 1944 to Jan. 1945.   **369.** Heinrichs and Gallicchio, *Implacable Foes*, 231–3.   **370.** Ibid., 248–55.   **371.** Ibid., 255–6.   **372.** Ibid., 358–9.   **373.** Ibid., 265–6.   **374.** Hough, *Island War*, 342–3.   **375.** Heinrichs and Gallicchio, *Implacable Foes*, 281–3; Symonds, *World War II at Sea*, 606.   **376.** Frank, *Downfall*, 69–70.   **377.** Symonds, *World War II at Sea*, 619–26.   **378.** Frank, *Downfall*, 70.   **379.** Ibid., 271; Heinrichs and Gallicchio, *Implacable Foes*, 400–401.   **380.** Theodore Roscoe, *United States Submarine Operations in World War II* (Annapolis, Md, 1949), 523.   **381.** USSBS, *The Effects of Strategic Bombing on Japan's War Economy* (Washington, DC, 1946), 180–81; Akira Hari, 'Japan: guns before rice', in Mark Harrison (ed.), *The Economics of World War II: Six Great Powers in International Comparison* (Cambridge, 1998), 245; Roscoe, *United States Submarine Operations*, 453.   **382.** Barrett Tillman, *Whirlwind: The Air War against Japan 1942–1945* (New York, 2010), 139–45.   **383.** Coox, 'Strategic bombing in the Pacific', 317–21.   **384.** Ibid., 340–48.   **385.** USSBS, Pacific Theater, Report 1, 'Summary Report', Washington, DC, 1 July 1946, p. 19.   **386.** Frank, *Downfall*, 84–5, 182–4.   **387.** Ibid., 96–8.   **388.** Thomas Hall, '"Mere drops in the ocean": the politics and planning of the contribution of the British Commonwealth to the final defeat of Japan, 1944–45', *Diplomacy & Statecraft*, 16 (2005), 101–4, 109.   **389.** Sarantakes, 'Royal Air Force on Okinawa', 479.   **390.** Barton Bernstein, 'Truman and the A-bomb: targeting non-combatants, using the bomb, and his defending his "decision"', *Journal of Military History*, 62 (1998), 551–4.   **391.** Frank, *Downfall*, 134–45.   **392.** Heinrichs and Gallicchio, *Implacable Foes*, 515.   **393.** Elena Agarossi, *A Nation Collapses: The Italian Surrender of September 1943* (Cambridge, 2000), 14–22.   **394.** David Ellwood, *Italy 1943–1945* (Leicester, 1985), 22–3.   **395.** Agarossi, *A Nation Collapses*, 14–26.   **396.** Ibid., 28–32.   **397.** Ibid., 64–72, 80–87; Morgan, *Fall of Mussolini*, 91–3; D'Este, *Eisenhower*, 449–52.   **398.** Ellwood, *Italy*, 41–6.   **399.** Marc Trachtenberg, 'The United States and Eastern Europe 1945: a reassessment', *Journal of Cold War Studies*, 10 (2008), 106, 124–31.   **400.** Allen Dulles, *The Secret Surrender* (London, 1967), 97–100, 177–8.   **401.** Reyonolds and Pechatnov (eds.), *The*

Kremlin Letters, 570–71, 578–9, Stalin to Roosevelt 3 Apr. 1945; Stalin to Roosevelt, 7 Apr. 1945. **402.** TNA, WO 106/3974, Military Mission Moscow to AGWAR, 24 Apr. 1945; Moscow Mission to SHAEF, 25 Apr. 1945. **403.** Giorgio Bocca, *Storia dell'Italia partigiana, settembre 1943–maggio 1945* (Milan, 1995), 506, 519–20; Max Corvo, *OSS Italy 1942–1945: A Personal Memoir of the Fight for Freedom* (New York, 2005), 267–9. **404.** J. Lee Ready, *Forgotten Allies: Volume 1, European Theater* (Jefferson, NC, 1985), 426–7. **405.** TNA, CAB 106/761, Instrument of Local Surrender of German and Other Forces, 29 Apr. 1945; PREM 3/198/3, Churchill cable to Stalin, 29 Apr. 1945. **406.** TNA, PREM 3/198/3, Alexander to Eisenhower, 2 May 1945; Richard Lamb, *War in Italy 1943–1945: A Brutal Story* (London, 1993), 293–5; Bocca, *Storia dell'Italia partigiana*, 523. **407.** David Stafford, *Mission Accomplished: SOE and Italy 1943–1945* (London, 2011), 325; Bocca, *Storia dell'Italia partigiana*, 521–2; Lamb, *War in Italy*, 262–5. **408.** Stafford, *Mission Accomplished*, 318–19. **409.** TNA, PREM 3/193/6°, JIC report 'German strategy and capacity to resist', 16 Oct. 1944, p. 2. **410.** Eberle and Uhl (eds.), *The Hitler Book*, 269. **411.** Dulles, *Secret Surrender*, 176–8. **412.** Von Below, *At Hitler's Side*, 239. **413.** Brendan Simms, *Hitler: Only the World was Enough* (London, 2019), 516; TNA, FO 1005/1701, CCG (British Element), Bulletin of the Intelligence Bureau, 28 Feb. 1946, interrogation of von Below (Hitler's air adjutant). **414.** Dulles, *Secret Surrender*, 178. **415.** TNA, PREM 3/197/4, telegram from John Deane to the British Foreign Office, 7 May 1945. **416.** Kershaw, *The End*, 367–70. **417.** TNA, WO 106/4449, Moscow embassy to Foreign Office, 12 May 1945; Eisenhower to the CCS, 7 May 1945. **418.** John Galbraith, *A Life in Our Times: Memoirs* (London, 1981), 221–2; Albert Speer, *Inside the Third Reich* (London, 1970), 498–9. **419.** TNA, PREM 3/197/4, minute from Churchill to Orme Sargent, Foreign Office, 14 May 1945; Foreign Office minute on General Busch, 12 May 1945. **420.** Richard Overy, '"The chap with the closest tabs": Trevor-Roper and the hunt for Hitler', in Blair Worden (ed.), *Hugh Trevor-Roper: The Historian* (London, 2016), 192–206. **421.** TNA, WO 219/2086, SHAEF G-3 Report, 'Arrest of members of Acting German Government', 23 May 1945. **422.** Gerhard Krebs, 'Operation Super-Sunrise? Japanese–United States peace feelers in Switzerland 1945', *Journal of Military History*, 69 (2005), 1081, 1087, 1115–17. **423.** Shillony, *Politics and Culture in Wartime Japan*, 77–8, 81. **424.** Krebs, 'Operation Super-Sunrise?', 1087–96. **425.** These ideas are developed more fully in Yukiko Koshiro, 'Eurasian eclipse: Japan's end game in World War II', *American Historical Review*, 109 (2004), 417–26, 434–7. **426.** Jeremy Yellen, 'The specter of revolution: reconsidering Japan's decision to surrender', *International History Review*, 35 (2013), 209–10, 213–14. **427.** Shillony, *Politics and Culture in Wartime Japan*, 85; Yellen, 'The specter of revolution', 214. **428.** Heinrichs and Gallicchio, *Implacable Foes*, 523–6. **429.** Eric Fowler, 'Will-to-fight: Japan's imperial institution and the United States strategy to end World War II', *War & Society*, 34 (2015), 47–8. **430.** Heinrichs and Gallicchio, *Implacable Foes*, 512–13, 541; Andrew Rotter, *Hiroshima: The World's Bomb* (Oxford, 2008), 162–4. **431.** Michael Neiberg, *Potsdam: The End of World War II and the Remaking of Europe* (New York, 2015), 244–5. **432.** David Holloway, 'Jockeying for position in the postwar world: Soviet entry into the war with Japan in August 1945', in Tsuyoshi Hasegawa (ed.), *The End of the Pacific War: Reappraisals* (Stanford, Calif., 2007), 172–5. **433.** Phillips O'Brien, 'The Joint Chiefs of Staff, the atom bomb, the American military mind and the end of the Second World War', *Journal of Strategic Studies*, 42 (2019), 975–85. **434.** Heinrichs and Gallicchio, *Implacable Foes*, 552. **435.** LC, Arnold Papers, Reel 199, note 'Atomic Bomb Cities' [n.d.]. **436.** Rotter, *Hiroshima*, 191–3. **437.** Sumio Hatano, 'The atomic bomb and Soviet entry into the war', in Hasegawa (ed.), *End of the Pacific War*, 98–9. **438.** Ibid., 99–101. **439.** Yellen, 'The specter of revolution', 216–17. **440.** Yamashita, *Daily Life in Wartime Japan*, 173–9; Gibney (ed.), *Sensō*, 215. **441.** Cited from the Japanese in Yellen, 'The specter of revolution', 219. **442.** Ronald Spector, 'After Hiroshima: Allied military occupation and the fate of Japan's empire', *Journal of Military History*, 69 (2005), 1122–3; Shillony, *Politics and Culture in Wartime Japan*, 89. **443.** Van de Ven, *China at War*, 203–5, 209–13. **444.** Sarah Paine, *The Japanese Empire: Grand Strategy from the Meiji Restoration to the Pacific War* (Cambridge, 2017), 167–70. **445.** Christian Goeschel, *Suicide in Nazi Germany* (Oxford, 2009), 149–52. **446.** Haruko Cook and Theodore Cook (eds.), *Japan at War: An Oral History* (New York, 1992), 364–5. **447.** Yamashita, *Daily Life in Wartime Japan*, 188.

4. Mobilizing a Total War

1. Cited in Lennart Samuelson, *Tankograd: The Formation of a Soviet Company Town: Cheliabinsk 1900–1950s* (Basingstoke, 2011), 230. **2.** Ibid., 229, 231. **3.** National Income figures from Mark Harrison (ed.), *The Economics of World War II: Six Great Powers in International Comparison* (Cambridge, 1998), 21. **4.** Edward Drea, *Japan's Imperial Army: Its Rise and Fall, 1853–1945* (Lawrence, Kans, 2009), 160. **5.** Thomas Hippler, *Governing from the Skies: A Global History of Aerial Bombing* (London, 2017), 15–16, 112–13. **6.** Erich Ludendorff, *The Nation at War* (London, 1935), 22–3. **7.** *Akten zur deutschen auswärtigen Politik*, Ser. D, vol. vi (Göttingen, 1956), 481, Führer conference with military commanders, 29 May 1939. **8.** Rudolf Absolon, *Die Wehrmacht im Dritten Reich: Band IV, 5 February 1938 bis 31 August 1939* (Boppard-am-Rhein, 1979), 9–11. **9.** Roxanne Panchasi, *Future Tense: The Culture of Anticipation in France between the Wars* (Ithaca, NY, 2009), 81, 84. **10.** Cyril Falls, *The Nature of Modern Warfare* (London, 1941), 7. **11.** TNA, AIR 9/39, Air Vice-Marshal Arthur Barrett, 'Air Policy and Strategy', 23 Mar. 1936, pp. 5–6. **12.** United States Air Force Academy, Colorado Springs, McDonald Papers, ser. V, Box 8, 'Development of the U.S. Air Forces Philosophy of Air Warfare', pp. 13–15. **13.** On Japan see Samuel Yamashita, *Daily Life in Wartime Japan 1940–1945* (Lawrence, Kans, 2015), 11–14; on Germany and the Soviet Union, Richard Overy, *The Dictators: Hitler's Germany and Stalin's Russia* (London, 2004), 459–67. **14.** Hans van de Ven, *War and Nationalism in China 1925–1945* (London, 2003), 279–81. **15.** Stephen King-Hall, *Total Victory* (London, 1941). **16.** *Total War and Total Peace: Four Addresses by American Leaders* (Oxford, 1942), 29, from a speech given on 23 July 1942. **17.** USSBS, Pacific Theater, Report 1, 'Summary Report', Washington, DC, 1 July 1946, pp. 10–11. **18.** IWM, Speer Collection, Box S368, Schmelter interrogation, Appendix 1, 'The call-up of workers from industry for the Armed Forces', pp. 7–8; Alan Bullock, *The Life and Times of Ernest Bevin: Volume II. Minister of Labour 1940–1945* (London, 1967), 55. **19.** Maury Klein, *A Call to Arms: Mobilizing America for World War II* (New York, 2013), 340–41, 691–4. **20.** Anna Krylova, *Soviet Women in Combat: A History of Violence on the Eastern Front* (Cambridge, 2010), 146–51; John Erickson, 'Soviet women at war', in John Garrard and Carol Garrard (eds.), *World War 2 and the Soviet People* (London, 1993), 50–76. **21.** Drea, *Japan's Imperial Army*, 198–9, 234. Only 11 per cent were regulars in May 1938, 22.6 per cent first reserve (age 24–28), 45.2 per cent second reserve (age 29–34). **22.** Diana Lary, *The Chinese People at War: Human Suffering and Social Transformation 1937–1945* (Cambridge, 2010), 160–61; van de Ven, *War and Nationalism in China*, 255–8, 269–71; Joshua Howard, *Workers at War: Labor in China's Arsenals, 1937–1953* (Stanford, Calif., 2004), 171–2. **23.** Mark Stoler, *Allies and Adversaries: The Joint Chiefs of Staff, the Grand Alliance, and U. S. Strategy in World War II* (Chapel Hill, NC, 2000), 48–9, 54–5. **24.** Stephen Schwab, 'The role of the Mexican Expeditionary Air Force in World War II: late, limited, but symbolically significant', *Journal of Military History*, 66 (2002), 1131–3; Neill Lochery, *Brazil: The Fortunes of War: World War II and the Making of Modern Brazil* (New York, 2014), 230–34. **25.** Harrison (ed.), *The Economics of World War II*, 14, 253. **26.** Halik Kochanski, *The Eagle Unbowed: Poland and the Poles in the Second World War* (London, 2012), 209–10, 467. **27.** David French, *Raising Churchill's Army: The British Army and the War against Germany 1919–1945* (Oxford, 2000), 186; Ulysses Lee, *The Employment of Negro Troops* (Washington, DC, 1994), 406. **28.** Wesley Craven and James Cate, *The Army Air Forces in World War II: Volume VI: Men and Planes* (Chicago, Ill., 1955), 429–30; Allan English, *The Cream of the Crop: Canadian Aircrew, 1939–1945* (Montreal, 1996), 19. **29.** Emma Newlands, *Civilians into Soldiers: War, the Body and British Army Recruits 1939–1945* (Manchester, 2014), 31–2; Jeremy Crang, *The British Army and the People's War 1939–1945* (Manchester, 2000), 7–11, 14–15. **30.** Domenico Petracarro, 'The Italian Army in Africa 1940–1943: an attempt at historical perspective', *War & Society*, 9 (1991), 104–5. **31.** Parliamentary Archives, London, Balfour Papers, BAL/4, 'The British Commonwealth Air Training Plan, 1939–1945', Ottawa, 1949, pp. 3–8. **32.** Klein, *A Call to Arms*, 340–41; Steven Casey, *Cautious Crusade: Franklin D. Roosevelt, American Public Opinion and the War against Nazi Germany* (New York, 2001), 86. **33.** Krylova, *Soviet Women in Combat*, 114. **34.** Klein, *A Call to Arms*, 694. **35.** Hugh Rockoff, *America's Economic Way of War: War and the US Economy from the Spanish–American War to the Persian Gulf War* (Cambridge, 2012), 160. **36.** *Statistical Digest of the War* (London, 1951), 11. **37.** French, *Raising Churchill's Army*, 244–6. **38.** Rüdiger Overmans, *Deutsche militärische Verluste im Zweiten Weltkrieg* (Munich, 2004), 261–6; G. F. Krivosheev (ed.), *Soviet Casualties and Combat Losses in the Twentieth Century* (London, 1997), 85, 87; David Glantz, *Colossus Reborn: The Red Army 1941–1943* (Lawrence, Kans, 2005), 135–9. **39.** Overmans, *Deutsche militärische Verluste*, 266; Krivosheev, *Soviet Casualties and Combat Losses*, 96–7. **40.** Bernhard Kroener, 'Menschenbewirtschaftung. Bevölkerungsverteilung und personelle Rüstung in der zweiten Kriegshälfte', in Bernhard Kroener, Rolf-Dieter Müller and Hans Umbreit, *Das Deutsche Reich und der Zweite Weltkrieg: Band 5/2: Organisation und Mobilisierung des deutschen Machtbereichs* (Stuttgart, 1999), 853–9; Overmans, *Deutsche militärische Verluste*, 244. **41.** Geoffrey Megargee, *Inside Hitler's High Command* (Lawrence, Kans, 2000), 202. **42.** Carter Eckert, 'Total war, industrialization, and social change in late colonial Korea', in Peter Duus, Ramon Myers and Mark Peattie (eds.), *The Japanese Wartime Empire, 1931–1945* (Princeton, NJ, 1996), 28–30. **43.** Rolf-Dieter Müller, *The Unknown Eastern Front: The Wehrmacht and Hitler's Foreign Soldiers* (London, 2012), 169, 176, 212, 223–4; David Stahel (ed.), *Joining Hitler's Crusade: European Nations and the Invasion of the Soviet Union, 1941* (Cambridge, 2018), 6–7. **44.** Oleg Beyda, '"La Grande Armée in field gray": the legion of French volunteers against Bolshevism, 1941', *Journal of Slavic Military Studies*, 29 (2016), 502–17. **45.** Joachim Hoffmann, *Die Geschichte der Wlassow-Armee* (Freiburg, 1984), 205–6; Müller, *Unknown Eastern Front*, 235. **46.** F. W. Perry, *The Commonwealth Armies: Manpower and Organisation in Two World Wars* (Manchester, 1988), 227. **47.** Kaushik Roy, *India and World War II: War, Armed Forces, and Society, 1939–1945* (New Delhi, 2016), 12, 16–17, 28, 35, 37, 53, 80; Tarak Barkawi, *Soldiers of Empire: Indian and British Armies in World War II* (Cambridge, 2017), 51–4. **48.** Ashley Jackson, *The British Empire and the Second World War* (London, 2006), 1–2. **49.** David Killingray, *Fighting for Britain: African Soldiers in the Second World War* (Woodbridge, 2010), 44. **50.** Stephen Bourne, *The Motherland Calls: Britain's Black Servicemen and Women 1939–1945* (Stroud, 2012), 10–12. **51.** Killingray, *Fighting for Britain*, 35–40, 42, 47–50, 75. **52.** Bourne, *The Motherland Calls*, 11, 23–4. **53.** Morris MacGregor, *Integration of the Armed Forces, 1940–1965* (Washington, DC, 1985), 17–24. **54.** Sherie Merson and Steven Schlossman, *Foxholes and Color Lines: Desegregating the U. S. Armed Forces* (Baltimore, Md, 1998), 67, 77–8, 82–3; Chris Dixon, *African Americans and the Pacific War 1941–1945* (Cambridge, 2018), 59–60. **55.** Dixon, *African Americans*, 53, 63–5 **56.** Lee, *Employment of Negro Troops*, 411–16; MacGregor, *Integration of the Armed Forces*, 24; Mershon and Schlossman, *Foxholes and Color Lines*, 64–5. **57.** Mershon and Schlossman, *Foxholes and Color Lines*, 63. **58.** Lee, *Employment of Negro Troops*, 286; MacGregor, *Integration of the Armed Forces*, 28–30. On the Tuskegee Airmen see J. Todd Moye, *Freedom Flyers: The Tuskegee Airmen of World War II* (New York, 2010); William Percy, 'Jim Crow and Uncle Sam: the Tuskegee flying units and the U. S. Army Air Forces in Europe during World War II', *Journal of Military History*, 67 (2003), 775, 786–7, 809–10; Stanley Sandler, *Segregated Skies: All-Black Combat Squadrons in World War II* (Washington, DC, 1992), ch. 5. **59.** Robert Asahima, *Just Americans: How Japanese Americans Won a War at Home and Abroad* (New York, 2006), 6–7; Brenda Moore, *Serving Our Country: Japanese American Women in the Military during World War II* (New Brunswick, NJ, 2003), xi–xii, 19. **60.** See for example the list of standard roles in Rosamond Greer, *The Girls of the King's Navy* (Victoria, BC, 1983), 14–15, 144. **61.** Gerard DeGroot, 'Whose finger on the trigger? Mixed anti-aircraft batteries and the female combat taboo', *War in History*, 4 (1997), 434–7. **62.** Birthe Kundrus, 'Nur die halbe Geschichte: Frauen im Umfeld der Wehrmacht', in Rolf-Dieter Müller and Hans-Erich Volkmann (eds.), *Die Wehrmacht: Mythos* *und Realität* (Munich, 1999), 720–21. **63.** Franz Siedler, *Blitzmädchen: Die Geschichte der Helferinnen der deutschen Wehrmacht* (Bonn, 1996), 169. **64.** *Statistical Digest of the War,* 9, 11; Jeremy Crang, *Sisters in Arms: Women in the British Armed Forces During the Second World War* (Cambridge, 2020), 2–3, 30, 36, 310. **65.** Greer, *Girls of the King's Navy,* 14– 16. **66.** Klein, *A Call to Arms,* 352–3. **67.** Jeanne Holm, *In Defense of a Nation: Servicewomen in World War II* (Washington, DC, 1998), 1, 41, 75. **68.** Craven and Cate, *Army Air Forces: Volume VI,* 102–4. **69.** Holm, *In Defense of a Nation,* 48–9, 57–9. **70.** Bourne, *The Motherland Calls,* 121. **71.** Helena Schrader, *Sisters in Arms: The Women who Flew in World War II* (Barnsley, 2006), 8–16. **72.** Kathleen Cornelsen, 'Women Airforce Service Pilots of World War II', *Journal of Women's History,* 17 (2005), 111–12, 115–16; Bourne, *The Motherland Calls,* 120–21; Schrader, *Sisters in Arms,* 138–45. **73.** Krylova, *Soviet Women in Combat,* 3; Erickson, 'Soviet women at war', 52, 62–9. **74.** Roger Reese, *Why Stalin's Soldiers Fought: The Red Army's Military Effectiveness in World War II* (Lawrence, Kans, 2011), 104–5, 114. **75.** Reina Pennington, *Wings, Women and War: Soviet Airwomen in World War II* (Lawrence, Kans, 2001), 1–2. **76.** Krylova, *Soviet Women in Combat,* 158–63. **77.** Ibid., 151–2, 168–9. **78.** Svetlana Alexievich, *The Unwomanly Face of War* (London, 2017), 8, from the testimony of Maria Morozova. **79.** Roy, *India and World War II,* 96–9. **80.** Sandler, *Segregated Skies,* 68–72. **81.** Lynne Olson, *Those Angry Days: Roosevelt, Lindbergh, and America's Fight over World War II, 1939–1941* (New York, 2013), 351–2. **82.** Newlands, *Civilians into Soldiers,* 57; Roy, *India and World War II,* 128– 30. **83.** USSBS, Special Paper 4, 'Food and Agriculture', exhibits G. J. M; BAB, R26 iv/51, Four Year Plan meeting, Geschäftsgruppe Ernährung, 11 Mar. 1942. **84.** IWM, FD 5444/45, Protokoll über die Inspekteurbesprechung, 22 Feb. 1942, 'Ersatzlage der Wehrmacht'; IWM, EDS Al/1571, Wirtschaft und Rüstungsamt, Niederschrift einer Besprechung, 9 Jan. 1941. **85.** Overy, *The Dictators,* 452–3. **86.** IWM, FD 3056/49, 'Statistical Material on the German Manpower Position', 31 July 1945, Table 7; Lennart Samuelson, *Plans for Stalin's War Machine: Tukhachevskii and Military-Economic Planning 1925–1941* (London, 2000), 191–5; N. S. Simonov, '*Mobpodgotovka*: mobilization planning in interwar industry', in John Barber and Mark Harrison (eds.), *The Soviet Defence Industry Complex from Stalin to Khrushchev* (London, 2000), 216–17. **87.** Richard Toye, 'Keynes, the labour movement, and "How to Pay for the War"', *Twentieth Century British History,* 10 (1999), 256–8, 272–8. **88.** BAB, R7 xvi/7, Report from the 'Professoren-Ausschuss' to Economics Minister Funk, 16 Dec. 1939. **89.** Sheldon Garon, 'Luxury is the enemy: mobilizing savings and popularizing thrift in wartime Japan', *Journal of Japanese Studies,* 26 (2000), 51–2. **90.** Jingping Wu, 'Revenue, finance and the command economy under the Nationalist Government during the Anti-Japanese War', *Journal of Modern Chinese History,* 7 (2013), 52–3. **91.** Rockoff, *America's Economic Way of War,* 166–7; Stephen Broadberry and Peter Howlett, 'The United Kingdom: victory at all costs', in Harrison (ed.), *The Economics of World War II,* 50–51; *Statistical Digest of the War,* 195; Willi Boelcke, 'Kriegsfinanzierung im internationalen Vergleich', in Friedrich Forstmeier and Hans-Erich Volkmann (eds.), *Kriegswirtschaft und Rüstung 1939–1945* (Düsseldorf, 1977), 40–41; Akira Hara, 'Japan: guns before rice', in Harrison (ed.), *The Economics of World War II,* 256–7; Mark Harrison, 'The Soviet Union: the defeated victor', in *idem* (ed.), *The Economics of World War II,* 275–6. **92.** Jonas Scherner, 'The institutional architecture of financing German exploitation: principles, conflicts and results', in Jonas Scherner and Eugene White (eds.), *Paying for Hitler's War: The Consequences of Nazi Hegemony for Europe* (Cambridge, 2016), 62–3. **93.** Hein Klemann and Sergei Kudryashov, *Occupied Economies: An Economic History of Nazi-Occupied Europe, 1939– 1945* (London, 2012), 210–11; Broadberry and Howlett, 'United Kingdom', 52–3. The sterling debt included £1,321 million owed to India, the largest of the blocked debts. **94.** Karl Brandt, Otto Schiller and Franz Ahlgrimm (eds.), *Management of Agriculture and Food in the German-Occupied and Other Areas of Fortress Europe,* 2 vols. (Stanford, Calif., 1953), ii, 616–17; Srinath Raghavan, *India's War: The Making of Modern South Asia* (London, 2016), 342–7. **95.** Sidney Zabludoff, 'Estimating Jewish wealth', in Avi Beker (ed.), *The Plunder of Jewish Property during the Holocaust* (New York, 2001), 48–64; H. McQueen, 'The conversion of looted Jewish assets to run the German war machine', *Holocaust and Genocide*

Studies, 18 (2004), 29–30. **96.** Lary, *The Chinese People at War*, 36, 157; Jingping Wu, 'Revenue, finance and the command economy', 49–50. **97.** Rockoff, *America's Economic Way of War*, 166–7; James Sparrow, *Warfare State: World War II America and the Age of Big Government* (Oxford, 2011), 123–5. **98.** Bruce Johnston, *Japanese Food Management in World War II* (Stanford, Calif., 1953), 167; Bernd Martin, 'Japans Kriegswirtschaft 1941–1945', in Forstmeier and Volkmann (eds.), *Kriegswirtschaft und Rüstung*, 280; Garon, 'Luxury is the enemy', 55. **99.** 'National finances in 1944', *The Banker*, 74 (1945), 66; Sidney Pollard, *The Development of the British Economy 1914–1967* (London, 1969), 308; R. Sayers, *Financial Policy* (London, 1956), 516. **100.** BAB, R7 xvi/8, Statistisches Reichsamt report, 'Zur Frage der Erhöhung des Eikommens-und Vermögenssteuer', 3 Feb. 1943; NARA, microfilm collection T178, Roll 15, frames 3671912–7, Reich Finance Ministry, 'Statistische Übersichten zu den Reichshaushaltsrechnungen 1938 bis 1943', Nov. 1944. **101.** Pollard, *Development of the British Economy*, 328; H. Durant and J. Goldmann, 'The distribution of working-class savings', in University of Oxford Institute of Statistics, *Studies in War Economics* (Oxford, 1947), 111–23. **102.** BAB, R7 xvi/22, memorandum 'Die Grenzen der Staatsverschuldung', 1942, p. 4; R28/98, German Reichsbank, 'Die deutsche Finanz-und Wirtschaftspolitik im Kriege', 8 June 1943, pp. 11–12. On 'noiseless finance' see Willi Boelcke, *Die Kosten von Hitlers Krieg* (Paderborn, 1985), 103–4. **103.** Wolfgang Werner, '*Bleib übrig*': *Deutsche Arbeiter in der nationalsozialistischen Kriegswirtschaft* (Düsseldorf, 1983), 220–21. **104.** Kristy Ironside, 'Rubles for victory: the social dynamics of state fundraising on the Soviet home front', *Kritika*, 15 (2014), 801–20. **105.** Garon, 'Luxury is the enemy', 42–6, 56–7. **106.** Martin, 'Japans Kriegswirtschaft', 280; Takafusa Nakamura and Konosuke Odaka (eds.), *Economic History of Japan 1914–1945: A Dual Structure* (Oxford, 1999), 82. **107.** Yamashita, *Daily Life in Wartime Japan*, 30–32. **108.** Garon, 'Luxury is the enemy', 61. **109.** Sparrow, *Warfare State*, 127–9. **110.** Ibid., 129, 134–46; Theodore Wilson, 'The United States: Leviathan', in Warren Kimball, David Reynolds and Alexander Chubarian (eds.), *Allies at War: The Soviet, American, and British Experience 1939–1945* (New York, 1994), 182. **111.** BAB, RD-51/21–3, Deutsche Reichsbank, 'Deutsche Wirtschaftszahlen', Mar. 1944, p. 2. **112.** Johnston, *Japanese Food Management*, 170–73. **113.** Richard Rice, 'Japanese labor in World War II', *International Labor and Working-Class History*, 38 (1990), 38–9; Benjamin Uchiyama, 'The munitions worker as trickster in wartime Japan', *Journal of Asian Studies*, 76 (2017), 658–60, 666–7. **114.** Howard, *Workers at War*, 138–9. **115.** Ina Zweiniger-Bargielowska, *Austerity in Britain: Rationing, Controls and Consumption 1939–1945* (Oxford, 2000), 46–7. **116.** *The Collected Writings of John Maynard Keynes, Volume XXII* (Cambridge, 2012), 223, 'Notes on the Budget', 28 Sept. 1940. **117.** Rockoff, *America's Economic Way of War*, 174–8; Wilson, 'The United States', 178–80. **118.** Zweiniger-Bargielowska, *Austerity in Britain*, 54. **119.** Hugh Rockoff, 'The United States: from ploughshares to swords', in Harrison (ed.), *The Economics of World War II*, 90–91. **120.** Zweiniger-Bargielowska, *Austerity in Britain*, 53–4. **121.** Richard Overy, *War and Economy in the Third Reich* (Oxford, 1994), 278–85. 'Spartan throughout' from Lothrop Stoddard, *Into the Darkness: Nazi Germany Today* (London, 1941), 80. **122.** Garon, 'Luxury is the enemy', 41–2. **123.** Akira Hara, 'Wartime controls', in Nakamura and Odaka (eds.), *Economic History of Japan*, 271–2, 282; Martin, 'Japans Kriegswirtschaft', 279. **124.** Harrison, 'The Soviet Union', 277–9, 290–91. **125.** C. B. Behrens, *Merchant Shipping and the Demands of War* (London, 1955), 198. **126.** Rockoff, 'The United States', 93. **127.** Rockoff, *America's Economic Way of War*, 179; Wilson, 'The United States', 179. **128.** Mark Harrison, *Soviet Planning in War and Peace, 1938–1945* (Cambridge, 1985), 258–9; William Moskoff, *The Bread of Affliction: The Food Supply in the USSR during World War II* (Cambridge, 1990), 121–2. **129.** Gustavo Corni and Horst Gies, *Brot. Butter. Kanonen. Die Ernährungswirtschaft in Deutschland unter der Diktatur Hitlers* (Berlin, 1997), 478–9; Zweiniger-Bargielowska, *Austerity in Britain*, 37. **130.** Moskoff, *Bread of Affliction*, 222–4. **131.** Alberto De Bernardi, 'Alimentazione di guerra', in Luca Alessandrini and Matteo Pasetti (eds.), *1943: Guerra e società* (Rome, 2015), 129–30; Vera Zamagni, 'Italy: how to lose the war and win the peace', in Harrison (ed.), *The Economics of World War II*, 191. **132.** Takafusa Nakamura, 'The age of turbulence:

1937–54', in Nakamura and Odaka (eds.), *Economic History of Japan*, 71–3; Johnston, *Japanese Food Management*, 161–4; Yamashita, *Daily Life in Wartime Japan*, 38–9. **133.** Corni and Gies, *Brot. Butter. Kanonen*, 424–38; Freda Wunderlich, *Farm Labor in Germany 1810–1945* (Princeton, NJ, 1961), 297–9. **134.** Alec Nove, 'The peasantry in World War II', in Susan Linz (ed.), *The Impact of World War II on the Soviet Union* (Totowa, NJ, 1985), 79–84. **135.** Broadberry and Howlett, 'The United Kingdom', 59, 61–3. **136.** Johnston, *Japanese Food Management*, 116–18. **137.** On Britain and the United States, Lzzie Collingham, *The Taste of War: World War Two and the Battle for Food* (London, 2011), 390, 418; on Japan, Yamashita, *Daily Life in Wartime Japan*, 55. **138.** Moskoff, *Bread of Affliction*, 108–9, 175. **139.** Collingham, *Taste of War*, 388–9; De Bernardi, 'Alimentazione di guerra', 131; William D. Bayles, *Postmarked Berlin* (London, 1942), 18–20, 24; Johnston, *Japanese Food Management*, 202. **140.** Owen Griffiths, 'Need, greed, and protest: Japan's black market 1938–1949', *Journal of Social History*, 35 (2002), 827–30. **141.** Van de Ven, *War and Nationalism in China*, 285–6. **142.** Corni and Gies, *Brot. Butter. Kanonen*, 414–15. **143.** Zweiniger-Bargielowska, *Austerity in Britain*, 54. **144.** Corni and Gies, *Brot. Butter. Kanonen*, 494–7; Johnston, *Japanese Food Management*, 169–70. **145.** De Bernardi, 'Alimentazione di guerra', 131 (based on research by the demographer Luzzatto Fegiz in post-war Trieste). **146.** Wendy Goldman, 'The hidden world of Soviet wartime food provisioning: hunger, inequality, and corruption', in Hartmut Berghoff, Jan Logemann and Felix Römer (eds.), *The Consumer on the Home Front: Second World War Civilian Consumption in Comparative Perspective* (Oxford, 2017), 57–65. **147.** Johnston, *Japanese Food Management*, 136; Yamashita, *Daily Life in Wartime Japan*, 37. **148.** Jeremy Yellen, 'The specter of revolution: reconsidering Japan's decision to surrender', *International History Review*, 35 (2013), 213–17. **149.** Klemann and Kudryashov, *Occupied Economies*, 281–2. **150.** Mark Mazower, *Inside Hitler's Greece: The Experience of Occupation 1941–1944* (New Haven, Conn., 1993), 27–30. **151.** Violetta Hionidou, 'Relief and politics in occupied Greece, 1941–4', *Journal of Contemporary History*, 48 (2013), 762–6. **152.** Roy, *India and World War II*, 129–30; Sugato Bose, 'Starvation among plenty: the making of famine in Bengal, Honan and Tonkin, 1942–45', *Modern Asian Studies*, 24 (1990), 715–17. **153.** Yasmin Khan, *The Raj at War: A People's History of India's Second World War* (London, 2015), 208. **154.** Bose, 'Starvation among plenty', 718–21. **155.** Sparrow, *Warfare State*, 161–2; Martin Kragh, 'Soviet labour law during the Second World War', *War in History*, 18 (2011), 535; Werner, *'Bleib übrig'*, 178. **156.** TNA, LAB 8/106, memorandum by the minister of labour for the War Cabinet, 'Labour Supply Policy since May 1940', 17 July 1941; Bullock, *Life and Times of Ernest Bevin*, ii, 55. **157.** Sparrow, *Warfare State*, 163; Klein, *A Call to Arms*, 626–88, 748–50. **158.** IWM, FD 3056/49, 'Statistical Material on the German Manpower Position during the War Period 1939–1943', FIAT report EF/LM/1, July 1945, table 7; G. Ince, 'The mobilisation of manpower in Great Britain in the Second World War', *The Manchester School of Economic and Social Studies*, 14 (1946), 17–52; William Hancock and Margaret Gowing, *British War Economy* (London, 1949), 453. **159.** Johnston, *Japanese Food Management*, 95, 99. **160.** British unemployment was just 54,000 in 1944. See Henry Parker, *Manpower: A Study of Wartime Policy and Administration* (London, 1957), 481. **161.** Kragh, 'Soviet labour law', 540. **162.** Rice, 'Japanese labor', 31–2; Uchiyama, 'The munitions worker as trickster', 658–60. **163.** Sparrow, *Warfare State*, 113–14. **164.** G. C. Allen, 'The concentration of production policy', in Norman Chester (ed.), *Lessons of the British War Economy* (Cambridge, 1951), 166–77. **165.** IWM, EDS/AL 1571, 'Arbeitseinsatz und Einziehungen in der nicht zum engeren Rüstungsbereichgehörenden Wirtschaft', OKW report, 9 Jan. 1941, p. 3; Rolf Wagenführ, *Die Deutsche Industrie im Kriege* (Berlin, 1963), 47–8. **166.** Lutz Budrass, Jonas Scherner and Jochen Streb, 'Fixed-price contracts, learning, and outsourcing: explaining the continuous growth of output and labour productivity in the German aircraft industry during the Second World War', *Economic History Review*, 63 (2010), 131. **167.** British figure from TNA, AVIA 10/289, memorandum for Ministry of Aircraft Production, 'The supply of labour and the future of the aircraft industry programme', 19 May 1943; German figures in IWM, Box 368, Report 65, interrogation of Ernst Blaicher, head of Main Committee Tanks, p. 12; IWM, 4969/45, BMW report, 'Ablauf der Lieferungen seit

Kriegsbeginn', n.d., p. 25.   168. German figures from Rüdiger Hachtmann, *Industriearbeit im 'Dritten Reich'* (Göttingen, 1989), 229–30; Soviet figures in Harrison, 'The Soviet Union', 285–6.   169. Harrison, 'The Soviet Union', 284–5; Wunderlich, *Farm Labor in Germany*, 297–9; Johnston, *Japanese Food Management*, 244.   170. Rockoff, 'The United States', 101–3.   171. John Jeffries, *Wartime America: The World War II Home Front* (Chicago, Ill., 1996), 95–6, 102; David Kennedy, *The American People in World War II* (New York, 1999), 351–3.   172. Klein, *A Call to Arms*, 354.   173. Gerald Nash, *World War II and the West: Reshaping the Economy* (Lincoln, Nebr., 1990), 77–8.   174. Geoffrey Field, *Blood, Sweat and Toil: Remaking the British Working Class, 1939–1945* (Oxford, 2011), 129–30, 145.   175. Yamashita, *Daily Life in Wartime Japan*, 16; Martin, 'Japans Kriegswirtschaft', 281; Johnston, *Japanese Food Management*, 244.   176. Parker, *Manpower*, 435–6; Jeffries, *Wartime America*, 96.   177. Leila Rupp, *Mobilizing Women for War: German and American Propaganda* (Princeton, NJ, 1978), 185; Jeffries, *Wartime America*, 90–91; Klein, *A Call to Arms*, 710.   178. Lary, *The Chinese People at War*, 161.   179. Eckert, 'Total war in late colonial Korea', 17–21, 24–5.   180. Hara, 'Japan: guns before rice', 246; Michael Seth, *A Concise History of Modern Korea: Volume 2* (Lanham, Md, 2016), 83.   181. Mark Spoerer, *Zwangsarbeit unter dem Hakenkreuz* (Stuttgart, 2001), 221–3; Johann Custodis, 'Employing the enemy: the economic exploitation of POW and foreign labor from occupied territories by Nazi Germany', in Scherner and White (eds.), *Paying for Hitler's War*, 79.   182. Ulrich Herbert, *Fremdarbeiter: Politik und Praxis des 'Ausländer-Einsatzes' in der Kriegswirtschaft des Dritten Reiches* (Bonn, 1985), 56–8; Gustavo Corni, 'Die deutsche Arbeitseinsatzpolitik in besetzten Italien, 1943–1945', in Richard Overy, Gerhard Otto and Johannes Houwink ten Cate (eds.), *Die 'Neuordnung Europas': NS-Wirtschaftspolitik in den besetzten Gebieten* (Berlin, 1997), 137–41.   183. Spoerer, *Zwangsarbeit*, 50, 59–60, 66; Bernd Zielinski, 'Die deutsche Arbeitseinsatzpolitik in Frankreich 1940–1944', in Overy, Otto and ten Cate (eds.), *Die 'Neuordnung Europas'*, 119.   184. Corni, 'Die deutsche Arbeitseinsatzpolitik', 138–9.   185. Spoerer, *Zwangsarbeit*, 45–7, 62–5; Zielinski, 'Die deutsche Arbeitseinsatzpolitik', 111–12.   186. Corni, 'Die deutsche Arbeitseinsatzpolitik', 143–9.   187. Herbert, *Fremdarbeiter*, 83–90, 99.   188. Spoerer, *Zwangsarbeit*, 73–80; Herbert, *Fremdarbeiter*, 157–60, 271.   189. Zielinski, 'Die deutsche Arbeitseinsatzpolitik', 121–3, 131; Spoerer, *Zwangsarbeit*, 64–5. Zielinski gives figures of 850,000–920,000 deportees, which includes those taken outside the four 'actions'.   190. Corni, 'Die deutsche Arbeitseinsatzpolitik', 150–60.   191. Custodis, 'Employing the enemy', 95.   192. Cesare Bermani, Sergio Bologna and Brunello Mantelli, *Proletarier der 'Achse': Sozialgeschichte der italienischen Fremdarbeiter in NS-Deutschland 1937 bis 1943* (Berlin, 1997), 222.   193. Elizabeth Harvey, 'Last resort or key resource? Women workers from the Nazi-occupied Soviet territories, the Reich labour administration and the German war effort', *Transactions of the Royal Historical Society*, 26 (2016), 163.   194. Spoerer, *Zwangsarbeit*, 186. The figures are based on four separate German surveys carried out in 1943–4.   195. Rüdiger Hachtmann, 'Fordism and unfree labour: aspects of work deployment of concentration camp prisoners in German industry between 1942 and 1944', *International Review of Social History*, 55 (2010), 496.   196. IWM, Speer Collection, FD 4369/45, British Bombing Survey Unit, 'Manuscript Notes on Ford, Cologne'.   197. Spoerer, *Zwangsarbeit*, 226; Herbert, *Fremdarbeiter*, 270–71.   198. Custodis, 'Employing the enemy', 72.   199. Hachtmann, 'Fordism and unfree labour', 505–6. For the debate on whether the term 'slave' is appropriate see Marc Buggeln, 'Were concentration camp prisoners slaves? The possibilities and limits of comparative history and global historical perspectives', *International Review of Social History*, 53 (2008), 106–25.   200. Wolf Gruner, *Jewish Forced Labor under the Nazis: Economic Needs and Racial Aims, 1938–1944* (New York, 2006), 63–75, 282.   201. Spoerer, *Zwangsarbeit*, 228–9.   202. Golfo Alexopoulos, *Illness and Inhumanity in Stalin's Gulag* (New Haven, Conn., 2017), 160–61, 208–9, 216.   203. Ibid., 197–8; Wilson Bell, *Stalin's Gulag at War: Forced Labour, Mass Death, and Soviet Victory in the Second World War* (Toronto, 2019), 8–9, 157–8.   204. TNA, FO 371/46747, Col. Thornley to G. Harrison (Foreign Office), enclosing the 'Jupp Report', 26 Feb. 1945.   205. TNA, LAB 10/132, Trade Stoppages: weekly returns to the Ministry of Labour 1940–1944; Field, *Blood, Sweat, and Toil*, 102–3.   206. James Atleson, *Labor and the Wartime State:*

Labor Relations and Law during World War II (Urbana, Ill., 1998), 142; Richard Polenberg, *War and Society: The United States 1941–1945* (Philadelphia, Pa, 1972), 159–72.   **207.** Kennedy, *The American People in World War II*, 213–19; Klein, *A Call to Arms*, 624–6.   **208.** Rice, 'Japanese labor in World War II', 34–5, 38.   **209.** Martin, 'Japans Kriegswirtschaft', 282; Yellen, 'The specter of revolution', 207–11.   **210.** Howard, *Workers at War*, 172–5.   **211.** Kragh, 'Soviet labour law', 537–40.   **212.** Werner, '*Bleib übrig*', 172–89.   **213.** Bermani, Bologna and Mantelli, *Proletarier der 'Achse'*, 210–11, 220–22; Werner, '*Bleib übrig*', 189–92.   **214.** Sparrow, *Warfare State*, 82–3.   **215.** Robert Westbrook, *Why We Fought: Forging American Obligations in World War II* (Washington, DC, 2004), 11.

5. Fighting the War

1. Walter Kerr, *The Russian Army* (London, 1944). 69.   **2.** Ibid., 69–70.   **3.** Steven Zaloga, *Japanese Tanks 1939–1945* (Oxford, 2007), 7–10.   **4.** Peter Chamberlain and Chris Ellis, *Tanks of the World 1915–1945* (London, 2002), 39.   **5.** Christopher Wilbeck, *Sledgehammers: Strengths and Flaws of Tiger Tank Battalions in World War II* (Bedford, Pa, 2004), 182–9.   **6.** Victor Kamenir, *The Bloody Triangle: The Defeat of Soviet Armor in the Ukraine, June 1941* (Minneapolis, Minn., 2008), 187.   **7.** Gordon Rottman, *World War II Infantry Anti-Tank Tactics* (Oxford, 2005), 19–20, 57.   **8.** Wilbeck, *Sledgehammers*, 186; Markus Pöhlmann, *Der Panzer und die Mechanisierung des Krieges: Eine deutsche Geschichte 1890 bis 1945* (Paderborn, 2016), 527.   **9.** Gary Dickson, 'Tank repair and the Red Army in World War II', *Journal of Slavic Military Studies*, 25 (2012), 382–5.   **10.** Gordon Rottman and Akira Takizawa, *World War II Japanese Tank Tactics* (Oxford, 2008), 3–6.   **11.** MacGregor Knox, 'The Italian armed forces, 1940–3', in Allan Millett and Williamson Murray (eds.), *Military Effectiveness: Volume III: The Second World War* (Cambridge, 1988), 151.   **12.** Pöhlmann, *Der Panzer*, 190–91, 207–12; Richard Ogorkiewicz, *Tanks: 100 Years of Evolution* (Oxford, 2015), 129–30; Robert Citino, *The Path to Blitzkrieg: Doctrine and Training the German Army, 1920–39* (Mechanicsburg, Pa, 2008), 224–31.   **13.** Heinz Guderian, *Achtung-Panzer!* (London, 1992), 170 (translated from the 1937 German edition).   **14.** R. L. Dinardo, *Mechanized Juggernaut or Military Anachronism? Horses and the German Army of WWII* (Mechanicsburg, Pa, 2008), 39, 55–7.   **15.** Karl-Heinz Frieser, *The Blitzkrieg Legend: The 1940 Campaign in the West* (Annapolis, Md, 2005), 36–42.   **16.** Jeffrey Gunsburg, 'The battle of the Belgian Plain, 12–14 May 1940: the first great tank battle', *Journal of Military History*, 56 (1992), 241–4.   **17.** G. F. Krivosheev, *Soviet Casualties and Combat Losses in the Twentieth Century* (London, 1997), 252.   **18.** Dinardo, *Mechanized Juggernaut*, 67; Richard Ogorkiewicz, *Armoured Forces: A History of Armoured Forces & Their Vehicles* (London, 1970), 78–9; Matthew Cooper, *The German Army 1933–1945* (London, 1978), 74–9. For tank figures at Kursk see Lloyd Clark, *Kursk: The Greatest Battle* (London, 2011), 197–9.   **19.** Ogorkiewicz, *Tanks*, 1523; Pöhlmann, *Der Panzer*, 432–4.   **20.** Rottman, *World War II Infantry Anti-Tank Tactics*, 46–7, 49–52.   **21.** Giffard Le Q. Martel, *Our Armoured Forces* (London, 1945), 40–43, 48–9.   **22.** Willem Steenkamp, *The Black Beret: The History of South Africa's Armoured Forces: Volume 2, The Italian Campaign 1943–45 and Post-War South Africa 1946–61* (Solihull, 2017), 35–9.   **23.** Ogorkiewicz, *Tanks*, 120–23; Wilbeck, *Sledgehammers*, 203–4.   **24.** Steven Zaloga, *Armored Thunderbolt: The U.S. Army Sherman in World War II* (Mechanicsburg, Pa, 2008), 16–17.   **25.** Ibid., 24, 329–30.   **26.** Rottman, *World War II Infantry Anti-Tank Tactics*, 29–32.   **27.** Krivosheev, *Soviet Casualties*, 241. Alexander Hill, *The Red Army and the Second World War* (Cambridge, 2017), 691, has a figure of 12,782 tanks available, of which only 2,157 were new issue requiring no service.   **28.** Kamenir, *Bloody Triangle*, 255–6, 280–81.   **29.** David Glantz, *Colossus Reborn: The Red Army at War, 1941–1943* (Lawrence, Kans, 2005), 225–34.   **30.** James Corum, 'From biplanes to Blitzkrieg: the development of German air doctrine between the wars', *War in History*, 3 (1996), 87–9.   **31.** Karl-Heinz Völker, *Dokumente und Dokumentarfotos zur Geschichte der deutschen Luftwaffe* (Stuttgart, 1968), 469, doc. 200 'Luftkriegführung'; Michel Forget, 'Die Zusammenarbeit zwischen Luftwaffe und Heer bei den französischen und deutschen Luftstreitkräfte im Zweiten Weltkrieg', in Horst Boog (ed.), *Luftkriegführung im Zweiten Weltkrieg* (Herford, 1993), 489–91. **32.** Ernest May, *Strange Victory: Hitler's Conquest of France* (New York, 2000), 429. **33.** Johannes Kaufmann, *An Eagle's Odyssey: My Decade as a Pilot in Hitler's Luftwaffe* (Barnsley, 2019), 117. **34.** NARA, RG 165/888.96, Embick memorandum, 'Aviation Versus Coastal Fortifications', 6 Dec. 1935. **35.** Forget, 'Zusammenarbeit', 486 (emphasis in original). **36.** P. Le Goyet, 'Evolution de la doctrine d'emploi de l'aviation française entre 1919 et 1939', *Revue d'histoire de la Deuxième Guerre Mondiale*, 19 (1969), 22–34; R. Doughty, 'The French armed forces 1918–1940', in Alan Millett and Williamson Murray (eds.), *Military Effectiveness: Volume II: The Interwar Period* (Cambridge, 1988), 58. **37.** David Hall, *Strategy for Victory: The Development of British Tactical Air Power, 1919–1945* (Westport, Conn., 2007), 30–42. **38.** Slessor comment in Peter Smith, *Impact: The Dive Bomber Pilots Speak* (London, 1981), 34; TNA, AIR 9/99, 'Appreciation of the Employment of the British Air Striking Force against the German Air Striking Force', 26 Aug. 1939, p. 5; TNA 9/98, 'Report on Trials to Determine the Effect of Air Attack Against Aircraft Dispersed about an Aerodrome Site', July 1938. **39.** Matthew Powell, 'Reply to: The Battle of France, Bartholomew and Barratt: the creation of Army Cooperation Command', *Air Power Review*, 20 (2017), 93–5. **40.** David Smathers, '"We never talk about that now": air–land integration in the Western Desert 1940–42', *Air Power Review*, 20 (2017), 36–8. **41.** Richard Hallion, *Strike from the Sky: The History of Battlefield Air Attack, 1911–1945* (Washington, DC, 1989), 131–3, 182. **42.** Smathers, '"We never talk about that now"', 40–43; Robert Ehlers, 'Learning together, winning together: air–ground cooperation in the Western Desert', *Air Power Review*, 21 (2018), 213–16; Vincent Orange, 'World War II: air support for surface forces', in Alan Stephens (ed.), *The War in the Air 1914–1994* (Maxwell, Ala, 2001), 87–9, 95–7. **43.** Hallion, *Strike from the Sky*, 159–61. **44.** David Syrett, 'The Tunisian campaign, 1942–43', in Benjamin Cooling (ed.), *Case Studies in the Development of Close Air Support* (Washington, DC, 1990), 159–60. **45.** B. Michael Bechthold, 'A question of success: tactical air doctrine and practice in North Africa', *Journal of Military History*, 68 (2004), 832–8. **46.** Ibid., 830–34. **47.** Syrett, 'The Tunisian campaign', 167. **48.** Hallion, *Strike from the Sky*, 171–3; Syrett, 'The Tunisian campaign', 184–5. **49.** Richard Overy, *The Air War 1939–1945* (3rd edn, Dulles, Va, 2005), 77. The figures were 46,244 US aircraft, 8,395 British and 6,297 German. **50.** NARA, United States Strategic Bombing Survey, Interview 62, Col. Gen. Jodl, 29 June 1945. **51.** Kenneth Whiting, 'Soviet air–ground coordination', in Cooling (ed.), *Case Studies in Close Air Support*, 117–18. **52.** Von Hardesty and Ilya Grinberg, *Red Phoenix Rising: The Soviet Air Force in World War II* (Lawrence, Kans, 2012), 204–5, 261–2. **53.** Lord Keyes, *Amphibious Warfare and Combined Operations* (Cambridge, 1943), 7. **54.** Edward Miller, *War Plan Orange: The U.S. Strategy to Defeat Japan 1897–1945* (Annapolis, Md, 1991), 115–19; John Lorelli, *To Foreign Shores: U.S. Amphibious Operations in World War II* (Annapolis, Md, 1995), 10–11. **55.** Allan Millett, 'Assault from the sea: the development of amphibious warfare between the wars – the American, British, and Japanese experiences', in Allan Millett and Williamson Murray (eds.), *Military Innovation in the Interwar Period* (Cambridge, 1996), 71–4; Lorelli, *To Foreign Shores*, 13–14; Miller, *War Plan Orange*, 174. On the fate of Ellis, John Reber, 'Pete Ellis: Amphibious warfare prophet', in Merrill Bartlett (ed.), *Assault from the Sea: Essays on the History of Amphibious Warfare* (Annapolis, Md, 1983), 157–8. **56.** Hans von Lehmann, 'Japanese landing operations in World War II', in Bartlett (ed.), *Assault from the Sea*, 197–8; Millett, 'Assault from the sea', 65–9. **57.** Lehmann, 'Japanese landing operations', 198; Millett, 'Assault from the sea', 81–2. **58.** David Ulbrich, *Preparing for Victory: Thomas Holcomb and the Making of the Modern Marine Corps, 1936–1943* (Annapolis, Md, 2011), 95, 187–8. **59.** Millett, 'Assault from the sea', 59–60, 78–9. **60.** TsAMO, Sonderarchiv, f.500, o. 957972, d. 1419, Army commander-in-chief, von Brauchitsch, 'Anweisung für die Vorbereitung des Unternehmens "Seelöwe"', 30 Aug. 1940, pp. 2–5, Anlage 1; OKH, general staff memorandum 'Seelöwe', 30 July 1940, p. 4. See too Frank Davis, 'Sea Lion: the German plan to invade Britain, 1940', in Bartlett (ed.), *Assault from the Sea*, 228–35. **61.** Renzo de Felice (ed.), *Galeazzo Ciano: Diario 1937–1943* (Milan, 1990), 661, entry for 26 May 1942. **62.** IWM, Italian Series, Box 22, E2568, 'Esigenza "C.3" per l'occupazione dell'isola di Malta', pp. 25–7; see too Mariano Gabriele, 'L'operazione "C.3" (1942)', in Romain Rainero and Antonello Biagini (eds.), *Italia in guerra: Il terzo anno, 1942* (Rome, 1993), 409 ff. **63.** Alan Warren, *Singapore: Britain's Greatest Defeat* (London, 2002), 60–64, 221–32. **64.** Ulbrich, *Preparing for Victory*, xiii, 123; Robert Heinl, 'The U.S. Marine Corps: author of modern amphibious warfare', in Bartlett (ed.), *Assault from the Sea*, 187–90. **65.** Craig Symonds, *Operation Neptune: The D-Day Landings and the Allied Invasion of Europe* (New York, 2014), 149–52; Ulbrich, *Preparing for Victory*, 61–2, 84; Frank Hough, *The Island War: The United States Marine Corps in the Pacific* (Philadelphia, Pa, 1947), 212–15. **66.** Lorelli, *To Foreign Shores*, 38, 49; Hough, *The Island War*, 36. **67.** Lorelli, *To Foreign Shores*, 53–6; Ulbrich, *Preparing for Victory*, 130–32, 138–9. **68.** Lorelli, *To Foreign Shores*, 58–9; Symonds, *Operation Neptune*, 75–6. **69.** USMC Command and Staff College paper, 'Tarawa to Okinawa: The Evolution of Amphibious Operations in the Pacific during World War II', 9. **70.** Ibid., 9–11, 17–20; Lorelli, *To Foreign Shores*, 162–76; Hough, *The Island War*, 132–8. **71.** USMC Command and Staff College, 'Tarawa to Okinawa', 14–25; Lorelli, *To Foreign Shores*, 178–81. **72.** Hough, *The Island War*, 215–16; USMC Command and Staff College, 'Tarawa to Okinawa', 11–12. **73.** Lorelli, *To Foreign Shores*, 307–13. **74.** Frederick Morgan, *Overture to Overlord* (London, 1950), 146–8. **75.** Lorelli, *To Foreign Shores*, 63. **76.** Ibid., 71–9; Symonds, *Operation Neptune*, 88–91. **77.** Robert Coakley and Richard Leighton, *Global Logistics and Strategy: Volume 2, 1943–1945* (Washington, DC, 1968), appendix D-3, 836, appendix D-5, 838; Dwight D. Eisenhower, *Report by the Supreme Commander to the Combined Chiefs of Staff* (London, 1946), 16. **78.** Coakley and Leighton, *Global Logistics*, 805–7, 829; Symonds, *Operation Neptune*, 163–4. **79.** Coakley and Leighton, *Global Logistics*, 309–11, 348–50, 829; Lorelli, *To Foreign Shores*, 215–16, 222. **80.** Symonds, *Operation Neptune*, 196–210, 220–21; Lorelli, *To Foreign Shores*, 215–22. **81.** British Air Ministry, *Rise and Fall of the German Air Force 1919–1945* (Poole, 1983; orig. publ. 1947), 323–5, 327–32. **82.** Friedrich Ruge. 'The invasion of Normandy', in Hans-Adolf Jacobsen and Jürgen Rohwer (eds.), *Decisive Battles of World War II: The German View* (London, 1965), 336, 342–3; Royal Navy Historical Branch, Battle Summary No. 39, *Operation Neptune* (London, 1994), 132; British Air Ministry, *Rise and Fall of the German Air Force*, 329. **83.** Symonds, *Operation Neptune*, 256–7. **84.** Ibid., 291–9. **85.** Eisenhower, *Report by the Supreme Commander*, 32. Hitler's directive in Hugh Trevor-Roper (ed.), *Hitler's War Directives 1939–1945* (London, 1964), 220, Directive 51, 3 Nov. 1943. **86.** Joint Board on Scientific Information, *Radar: A Report on Science at War* (Washington, DC, 1945), 1. **87.** Citino, *The Path to Blitzkrieg*, 208–11; Pöhlmann, *Der Panzer*, 269. **88.** Riccardo Niccoli, *Befehlspanzer: German Command, Control and Observation Armored Combat Vehicles in World War Two* (Novara, 2014), 2–6, 88. **89.** Karl Larew, 'From pigeons to crystals: the development of radio communications in U.S. Army tanks in World War II', *The Historian*, 67 (2005), 665–6; Gunsburg, 'The battle of the Belgian Plain', 242–3. **90.** Wolfgang Schneider, *Panzer Tactics: German Small-Unit Armor Tactics in World War II* (Mechanicsburg, Pa, 2000), 186–91. **91.** Richard Thompson, *Crystal Clear: The Struggle for Reliable Communications Technology in World War II* (Hoboken, NJ, 2012), 5–6; Simon Godfrey, *British Army Communications in the Second World War* (London, 2013), 6–12. **92.** Rottman and Takizawa, *World War II Japanese Tank Tactics*, 27–8. **93.** Thompson, *Crystal Clear*, 13–14, 20–22 **94.** Ibid., pp. 145–57. **95.** Zaloga, *Armored Thunderbolt*, 151–3. **96.** Godfrey, *British Army Communications*, 233; Gordon Rottman, *World War II Battlefield Communications* (Oxford, 2010), 29–30, 35–6; Anthony Davies, 'British Army battlefield radios of the 1940s', *Proceedings of the International Conference on Applied Electronics*, 2009, 2–4. **97.** USMC Command and Staff College, 'Tarawa to Okinawa', 14–15. **98.** Godfrey, *British Army Communications*, 12–13, 144; Thompson, *Crystal Clear*, 51–2. **99.** Thompson, *Crystal Clear*, 163–7; Larew, 'From pigeons to crystals', 675–7. **100.** Williamson Murray, 'The Luftwaffe experience, 1939–1941', in Cooling (ed.), *Case Studies in Close Air Support*, 79, 83, 98; Hermann Plocher, *The German Air Force Versus Russia, 1943* (New York, 1967), 263–4. **101.** Smathers, '"We never talk about that now"', 33–6, 42–3. **102.** Robert Ehlers, *The Mediterranean Air War: Air Power and Allied Victory in World War II* (Lawrence, Kans, 2015), 103, 186; Hallion, *Strike from the Sky*, 154. **103.** Hardesty and Grinberg, *Red Phoenix Rising*, 121, 129–31, 147–9, 257–8; Whiting, 'Soviet air–ground coordination', 130–34, 139–40; Hallion, *Strike from the Sky*, 241–2, 183.   104. Hallion, *Strike from the Sky*, 165.   105. Thompson, *Crystal Clear*, 49–52.   106. Bechthold, 'A question of success', 831–2; W. Jacobs, 'The battle for France, 1944', in Cooling (ed.), *Case Studies in Close Air Support*, 254–6, 265, 271–2; Hallion, *Strike from the Sky*, 181, 199.   107. Raymond Watson, *Radar Origins Worldwide: History of Its Evolution in 13 Nations through World War II* (Bloomington, Ind., 2009), 43–6.   108. Ibid., 115–25, 233–41; H. Kummritz, 'German radar development up to 1945', in Russell Burns (ed.), *Radar Development to 1945* (London, 1988), 209–12.   109. John Erickson, 'The air defence problem and the Soviet radar programme 1934/5–1945', ibid., 229–31; Watson, *Radar Origins Worldwide*, 280–87.   110. Louis Brown, *A Radar History of World War II: Technical and Military Imperatives* (London, 1999), 87–9.   111. Watson, *Radar Origins Worldwide*, 319–20; Shigeru Nakajima, 'The history of Japanese radar development to 1945', in Burns (ed.), *Radar Development*, 243–58.   112. Watson, *Radar Origins Worldwide*, 342–5; M. Calamia and R. Palandri, 'The history of the Italian radio detector telemetro', in Burns (ed.), *Radar Development*, 97–105.   113. Colin Dobinson, *Building Radar: Forging Britain's Early Warning Chain, 1935–1945* (London, 2010), 302–5, 318.   114. Wesley Craven and James Cate, *The Army Air Forces in World War II: Volume 6, Men and Planes* (Chicago, Ill., 1955), 82–5, 89, 96–8.   115. Ibid., 103–4.   116. Takuma Melber, *Pearl Harbor: Japans Angriff und der Kriegseintritt der USA* (Munich, 2016), 129–30.   117. G. Muller and H. Bosse, 'German primary radar for airborne and ground-based surveillance', in Burns (ed.), *Radar Development*, 200–208; Watson, *Radar Origins Worldwide*, 236–41; Kummritz, 'German radar development', 211–17.   118. Alfred Price, *Instruments of Darkness: The History of Electronic Warfare, 1939–1945* (London, 2005), 55–9.   119. Alan Cook, 'Shipborne radar in World War II: some recollections', *Notes and Records of the Royal Society*, 58 (2004), 295–7.   120. Watson, *Radar Origins Worldwide*, 73–85.   121. Ibid., 236–8; Kummritz, 'German radar development', 211, 219–22.   122. Watson, *Radar Origins Worldwide*, 115–29; Joint Board on Scientific Information, *Radar*, 19–22, 26–7.   123. Watson, *Radar Origins Worldwide*, 142–7, 157–8; Russell Burns, 'The background to the development of the cavity magnetron', in Burns (ed.), *Radar Development*, 268–79.   124. Chris Eldridge, 'Electronic eyes for the Allies: Anglo-American cooperation on radar development during World War II', *History & Technology*, 17 (2000), 11–13.   125. Brown, *A Radar History*, 398–402; Watson, *Radar Origins Worldwide*, 210–12; Eldridge, 'Electronic eyes for the Allies', 16.   126. Edward Bowen, 'The Tizard Mission to the USA and Canada', in Burns (ed.), *Radar Development*, 306; Brown, *A Radar History*, 402–5; Guy Hartcup, *The Effect of Science on the Second World War* (Basingstoke, 2000), 39–43.   127. Trent Hone, *Learning War: The Evolution of Fighting Doctrine in the U.S. Navy, 1898–1945* (Annapolis, Md, 2018), 206–14; Watson, *Radar Origins Worldwide*, 167–9, 185–6, 208–10; Joint Board on Scientific Information, *Radar*, 20–21, 40–41; Brown, *A Radar History*, 368–70.   128. Watson, *Radar Origins Worldwide*, 250–60; Kummritz, 'German radar development', 222–6.   129. Nakajima, 'History of Japanese radar development', 244–52, 255–6.   130. Brown, *A Radar History*, 424–5.   131. Joint Board on Scientific Information, *Radar*, 44; Watson, *Radar Origins Worldwide*, 223.   132. Carl Boyd, 'U.S. Navy radio intelligence during the Second World War and the sinking of the Japanese submarine I-52', *Journal of Military History*, 63 (1999), 340–54.   133. David Kahn, *Hitler's Spies: German Military Intelligence in World War II* (New York, 1978), 210.   134. On the issues surrounding the importance of photo-reconnaissance see Taylor Downing, *Spies in the Sky: The Secret Battle for Aerial Intelligence in World War II* (London, 2011), 327–34.   135. Jeffrey Bray (ed.), *Ultra in the Atlantic: Volume 1: Allied Communication Intelligence* (Laguna Hills, Calif., 1994), 19; F. H. Hinsley, 'An introduction to FISH', in F. H. Hinsley and Alan Stripp (eds.), *Code Breakers: The Inside Story of Bletchley Park* (Oxford, 1993), 144.   136. John Chapman, 'Japanese intelligence 1919–1945: a suitable case for treatment', in Christopher Andrew and Jeremy Noakes (eds.), *Intelligence and International Relations 1900–1945* (Exeter, 1987), 147, 155–6.   137. Ken Kotani, *Japanese Intelligence in World War II* (Oxford, 2009), 122, 140, 161–2.   138. Samir Puri, 'The role of intelligence in deciding the Battle of Britain', *Intelligence and National Security*, 21 (2006),

420–21. **139.** Downing, *Spies in the Sky*, 337–9. **140.** Sebastian Cox, 'A comparative analysis of RAF and Luftwaffe intelligence in the Battle of Britain, 1940', *Intelligence and National Security*, 5 (1990), 426. **141.** For a full account of a tortuous relationship see Bradley Smith, *Sharing Secrets with Stalin: How the Allies Traded Intelligence 1941–1945* (Lawrence, Kans, 1996). **142.** Douglas Ford, 'Informing airmen? The US Army Air Forces' intelligence on Japanese fighter tactics in the Pacific theatre, 1941–5', *International History Review*, 34 (2012), 726–9. **143.** Wilfred J. Holmes, *Double-Edged Secrets: U.S. Naval Intelligence Operations in the Pacific War During World War II* (Annapolis, Md, 1979), 150–53; Karl Abt, *A Few Who Made a Difference: The World War II Teams of the Military Intelligence Service* (New York, 2004), 3–4. **144.** David Glantz, *The Role of Intelligence in Soviet Military Strategy in World War II* (Novata, Calif., 1990), 109–12, 219–20. **145.** Valerii Zamulin, 'On the role of Soviet intelligence during the preparation of the Red Army for the summer campaign of 1943', *Journal of Slavic Military Studies*, 32 (2019), 246, 253. **146.** Alan Stripp, *Codebreaker in the Far East* (Oxford, 1989), 117–18. **147.** W. Jock Gardner, *Decoding History: The Battle of the Atlantic and Ultra* (London, 1999), 137–9. **148.** Hinsley, 'Introduction to FISH', 146–7. **149.** Hilary Footitt, 'Another missing dimension? Foreign languages in World War II intelligence', *Intelligence and National Security*, 25 (2010), 272–82. **150.** James McNaughton, *Nisei Linguists: Japanese Americans in the Military Intelligence Service during World War II* (Washington, DC, 2006), 18–23, 328–9, 331. **151.** Roger Dingman, 'Language at war: U.S. Marine Corps Japanese language officers in the Pacific war', *Journal of Military History*, 68 (2004), 854–69. **152.** Kahn, *Hitler's Spies*, 203–4. **153.** Footitt, 'Another missing dimension?', 272. **154.** Stripp, *Codebreaker*, 65–6. **155.** Arthur Bonsall, 'Bletchley Park and the RAF "Y" Service: some recollections', *Intelligence and National Security*, 23 (2008), 828–32; Puri, 'The role of intelligence in deciding the Battle of Britain', 430–32; Cox, 'A comparative analysis of RAF and Luftwaffe intelligence', 432. **156.** Ralph Erskine, 'Naval Enigma: a missing link', *International Journal of Intelligence and Counterintelligence*, 3 (1989), 494–504; Gardner, *Decoding History*, 126–31; Bray (ed.), *Ultra in the Atlantic*, xiv–xx, 19–24. **157.** Brian Villa and Timothy Wilford, 'Signals intelligence and Pearl Harbor: the state of the question', *Intelligence and National Security*, 21 (2006), 521–2, 547–8. **158.** Edward Van Der Rhoer, *Deadly Magic: Communications Intelligence in World War II in the Pacific* (London, 1978), 11–13, 49, 138–46; Stephen Budiansky, *Battle of Wits: The Complete Story of Codebreaking in World War II* (London, 2000), 320–23. **159.** Kotani, *Japanese Intelligence*, 122. **160.** Kahn, *Hitler's Spies*, 204–6. **161.** Budiansky, *Battle of Wits*, 319–22. **162.** Patrick Wilkinson, 'Italian naval decrypts', in Hinsley and Stripp (eds.), *Code Breakers*, 61–4. **163.** F. H. Hinsley, 'The Influence of Ultra', in Hinsley and Stripp (eds.), *Code Breakers*, 4–5. **164.** Jack Copeland, 'The German tunny machine', in idem (ed.), *Colossus: The Secrets of Bletchley Park's Codebreaking Computers* (Oxford, 2006), 39–42. **165.** Thomas Flowers, 'D-Day at Bletchley Park', in Copeland (ed.), *Colossus*, 80–81. **166.** Hinsley, 'Introduction to FISH', 141–7. **167.** F. H. Hinsley et al., *British Intelligence in the Second World War: Volume 3, Part 2* (London, 1988), 778–80; David Kenyon, *Bletchley Park and D-Day* (New Haven, Conn., 2019), 246. **168.** Michael Howard, *Strategic Deception in the Second World War* (London, 1990). **169.** Rick Stroud, *The Phantom Army of Alamein* (London, 2012), 23–8. **170.** Charles Cruickshank, *Deception in World War II* (Oxford, 1981), 4–5. **171.** Michael Handel, 'Introduction: strategic and operational deception in historical perspective', in idem (ed.), *Strategic and Operational Deception in the Second World War* (London, 1987), 15–19. **172.** Howard, *Strategic Deception*, 23–8. **173.** Stroud, *Phantom Army*, 80–86; Cruickshank, *Deception*, 20–21. **174.** Niall Barr, *Pendulum of War: The Three Battles of El Alamein* (London, 2004), 299–301; Cruickshank, *Deception*, 26–33; Stroud, *Phantom Army*, 193–7, 212–18. **175.** John Campbell, 'Operation Starkey 1943: "a piece of harmless playacting"?', in Handel (ed.), *Strategic and Operational Deception*, 92–7. **176.** Howard, *Strategic Deception*, 104–5. **177.** Campbell, 'Operation Starkey', 106–7. **178.** Handel, 'Introduction', 60. **179.** Thaddeus Holt, *The Deceivers: Allied Military Deception in the Second World War* (London, 2004), 565–6. **180.** Howard, *Strategic Deception*, 122. **181.** Ibid., 122, 132. **182.** Ibid. 186–93; T. L. Cubbage, 'The German misapprehensions regarding Overlord: understanding failure in estimative process', in Handel (ed.), *Strategic and Operational Deception*, 115–18.   **183.** David Glantz, 'The Red mask: the nature and legacy of Soviet military deception in the Second World War', in Handel (ed.), *Strategic and Operational Deception*, 175–81, 189.   **184.** Hill, *The Red Army*, 399–400; Glantz, 'Red mask', 204–5.   **185.** Glantz, 'Red mask', 206–9; Kahn, *Hitler's Spies*, 437–9.   **186.** David Glantz, *Soviet Military Deception in the Second World War* (London, 1989), 152–3; Hill, *The Red Army*, 444–5.   **187.** Kahn, *Hitler's Spies*, 440–41.   **188.** Jonathan House and David Glantz, *When Titans Clashed: How the Red Army Stopped Hitler* (Lawrence, Kans, 1995), 205–6.   **189.** Katherine Herbig, 'American strategic deception in the Pacific', in Handel (ed.), *Strategic and Operational Deception*, 260–75; Holt, *The Deceivers*, 730–43.   **190.** Cruickshank, *Deception*, 214–15; Handel, 'Introduction', 50–52.   **191.** Glantz, 'Red mask', 192, 233–8.   **192.** Louis Yelle, 'The learning curve: historical review and comprehensive survey', *Decision Sciences*, 10 (1979), 302–12.   **193.** Hone, *Learning War*, 3.   **194.** Glantz, *Colossus Reborn*, 123–41.   **195.** See David French, *Raising Churchill's Army: The British Army and the War against Germany 1919–1945* (Oxford, 2000), 212–35 for an account of British combat deficiencies in the desert campaign.   **196.** Patrick Rose, 'Allies at war: British and US Army command culture in the Italian campaign, 1943–1944', *Journal of Strategic Studies*, 36 (2013), 47–54. See too L. P. Devine, *The British Way of Warfare in Northwest Europe, 1944–5* (London, 2016), 178–82.   **197.** Douglas Ford, 'US assessments of Japanese ground warfare tactics and the army's campaigns in the Pacific theatres, 1943–1945: lessons learned and methods applied', *War in History*, 16 (2009), 330–34, 341–8.   **198.** Rose, 'Allies at war', 65.   **199.** French, *Raising Churchill's Army*, 5.   **200.** Andrei Grinev, 'The evaluation of the military qualities of the Red Army in 1941–1945 by German memoirs and analytic materials', *Journal of Slavic Military Studies*, 29 (2016), 228–32.   **201.** John Cushman, 'Challenge and response at the operational and tactical levels, 1914–45', in Millett and Murray (eds.), *Military Effectiveness*, iii, 328–31; Richard Carrier, 'Some reflections on the fighting power of the Italian Army', *War in History*, 22 (2015), 193–210; French, *Raising Churchill's Army*, 4–10.

6. War Economies

1. Russell Buhite and David Levy (eds.), *FDR's Fireside Chats* (Norman, Okla, 1992), 172.   **2.** IWM, EDS Mi 14/433 (file 2), Der Führer, 'Vereinfachung und Leistungssteigerung unserer Rüstungsproduktion', 3 Dec. 1941, p. 1.   **3.** Jeffery Underwood, *Wings of Democracy: The Influence of Air Power on the Roosevelt Administration 1933–1941* (College Station, Tex., 1991), 155. Roosevelt also wanted the strength of the army and navy air forces to reach 50,000.   **4.** IWM, EDS Mi 14/463 (file 3), OKW 'Aktenvermerk über die Besprechung bei Chef OKW, Reichskanzler, 19 Mai 1941', pp. 2–3.   **5.** IWM, Speer Collection, Box 368, Report 901, 'The Rationalisation of the German Armaments Industry', p. 8.   **6.** Rüdiger Hachtmann, 'Fordism and unfree labour: aspects of the work deployment of concentration camp prisoners in German industry between 1941 and 1944', *International Review of Social History*, 55 (2010), 501. For a general discussion of the issue see Richard Overy, *War and Economy in the Third Reich* (Oxford, 1994), ch. 11.   **7.** Charles Maier, 'Between Taylorism and technocracy: European ideologies and the vision of industrial productivity in the 1920s', *Journal of Contemporary History*, 5 (1970), 33–5, 45–6.   **8.** Jonathan Zeitlin, 'Flexibility and mass production at war: aircraft manufacturers in Britain, the United States, and Germany 1939–1945', *Technology and Culture*, 36 (1995), 57.   **9.** Irving B. Holley, 'A Detroit dream of mass-produced fighter aircraft: the XP-75 fiasco', *Technology and Culture*, 28 (1987), 580–82, 585–91.   **10.** Alec Cairncross, *Planning in Wartime: Aircraft Production in Britain, Germany and the USA* (London, 1991), xv.   **11.** IWM, Speer Collection, Box 368, Report 90 IV, 'Rationalization of the Munitions Industry', p. 4.   **12.** Yoshiro Miwa, *Japan's Economic Planning and Mobilization in Wartime: The Competence of the State* (New York, 2016), 413–15.   **13.** John Guilmartin, 'The Aircraft that Decided World War II: Aeronautical Engineering and Grand Strategy', 44th Harmon Memorial Lecture, United States Air Force Academy, 2001, pp. 17, 22.   **14.** Zeitlin, 'Flexibility and mass production', 53–5, 59–61; John

Rae, *Climb to Greatness: The American Aircraft Industry 1920–1960* (Cambridge, Mass., 1968), 147–9; Wesley Craven and James Cate, *The Army Air Forces in World War II: Volume VI, Men and Planes* (Chicago, Ill., 1955), 217–20, 335–6. **15.** Benjamin Coombs, *British Tank Production and the War Economy 1934–1945* (London, 2013), 91–3, 102. **16.** Steven Zaloga, *Soviet Lend-Lease Tanks of World War II* (Oxford, 2017), 31–2. **17.** Boris Kavaler-chik, 'Once again about the T-34', *Journal of Slavic Military Studies*, 28 (2015), 192–5. **18.** Joshua Howard, *Workers at War: Labor in China's Arsenals, 1937–1953* (Stanford, Calif., 2004), 51–5. **19.** Ibid., 64–73. **20.** USSBS, Pacific Theater, 'The Effects of Strategic Bombing on Japan's War Economy, Over-All Economic Effects Division', Dec. 1946, p. 221. **21.** Ibid., pp. 220–22. **22.** Tetsuji Okazaki, 'The supplier network and aircraft production in wartime Japan', *Economic History Review*, 64 (2011), 974–9, 984–5. **23.** Akira Hara, 'War-time controls', in Takafusa Nakamura and Kōnosuke Odaka (eds.), *Economic History of Japan 1914–1955* (Oxford, 1999), 273–4. **24.** Miwa, *Japan's Economic Planning*, 422–3, 426–7; Masayasu Miyazaki and Osamu Itō, 'Transformation of industries in the war years', in Nakamura and Odaka (eds.), *Economic History of Japan*, 289–92. **25.** Bernd Martin, 'Japans Kriegswirtschaft 1941–1945', in Friedrich Forstmeier and Hans-Erich Volkmann (eds.), *Kriegswirtschaft und Rüstung 1939–1945* (Düsseldorf, 1977), 274–8; Jerome Cohen, *Japan's Economy in War and Reconstruction* (Minneapolis, Minn., 1949), 219; Irving B. Hol-ley, *Buying Aircraft: Material Procurement for the Army Air Forces* (Washington, DC, 1964), 560. **26.** Maury Klein, *A Call to Arms: Mobilizing America for World War II* (New York, 2013), 252–4. **27.** S. R. Lieberman, 'Crisis management in the USSR: the wartime system of administration and control', in Susan Linz (ed.), *The Impact of World War II on the Soviet Union* (Totowa, NJ, 1985), 60–61. **28.** F. Kagan, 'The evacuation of Soviet industry in the wake of Barbarossa: a key to Soviet victory', *Journal of Slavic Military History*, 8 (1995), 389–406; G. A. Kumanev, 'The Soviet economy and the 1941 evacuation', in Joseph Wieczyn-ski (ed.), *Operation Barbarossa: The German Attack on the Soviet Union, June 22 1941* (Salt Lake City, Utah, 1992), 161–81. **29.** Lennart Samuelson, *Tankograd: The Formation of a Soviet Company Town: Cheliabinsk 1900s to 1950s* (Basingstoke, 2011), 196–204. **30.** Mark Harrison, 'The Soviet Union: the defeated victor', in *idem* (ed.), *The Economics of World War II: Six Great Powers in International Comparison* (Cambridge, 1998), 285–6; Mark Harrison, *Accounting for War: Soviet Production, Employment and the Defence Bur-den 1940–1945* (Cambridge, 1996), 81–5, 101. **31.** Hugh Rockoff, *America's Economic Way of War* (Cambridge, 2012), 183–8; Theodore Wilson, 'The United States: Leviathan', in Warren Kimball, David Reynolds and Alexander Chubarian (eds.), *Allies at War: The Soviet, American and British Experience 1939–1945* (New York, 1994), 175–7, 188. **32.** Alan Clive, *State of War: Michigan in World War II* (Ann Arbor, Mich., 1979), 25. **33.** Craven and Cate, *Army Air Forces, Volume VI*, 339. **34.** For a good example see Jacob Meulen, *The Politics of Aircraft: Building an American Military Industry* (Lawrence, Kans, 1991), 182–220. **35.** Allen Nevins and Frank Hill, *Ford: Decline and Rebirth 1933–1961* (New York, 1961), 226; Francis Walton, *Miracle of World War II: How American Industry Made Victory Possible* (New York, 1956), 559; Clive, *State of War*, 22. **36.** *U. S. Navy at War: 1941–1945. Official Reports to Secretary of the Navy by Fleet Admiral Ernest J. King* (Washington, DC, 1946), 252–84. **37.** Kevin Starr, *Embattled Dreams: California in War and Peace 1940–1950* (New York, 2002), 145–9; Frederic Lane, *Ships for Victory: A History of Shipbuilding under the U.S. Maritime Commission in World War II* (Baltimore, Md, 1951), 53–4, 224ff.; Walton, *Miracle of World War II*, 79; David Kennedy, *The American People in World War II* (New York, 1999), 225–8. **38.** Hermione Giffard, *Making Jet Engines in World War II: Britain, Germany and the United States* (Chicago, Ill., 2016), 37–41. **39.** Steven Zaloga, *Armored Thunderbolt: The U.S. Army Sherman in World War II* (Mechanicsburg, Pa, 2008), 43–5, 289–90; David Johnson, *Fast Tanks and Heavy Bombers: Innovation in the U.S. Army 1917–1945* (Ithaca, NY, 1998), 189–97. **40.** Overy, *War and Economy in the Third Reich*, 259–61; USSBS, 'Overall Report: European Theater', Sept. 1945, 31. **41.** IWM, Speer Collection, FD 5445/45, OKW Kriegswirtschaftlicher Lagebericht, 1 Dec. 1939; EDS, Mi 14/521 (part 1), Heereswaffenamt, 'Munitionslieferung im Weltkrieg'; BA-MA, Wi I F 5.412, 'Aktenver-merk über Besprechung am 11 Dez. 1939 im Reichskanzlei'. **42.** IWM, Speer Collection,

Box 368, Report 54, Speer interrogation 13 July 1945. **43.** On labour see IWM, FD 3056/49, 'Statistical Material on the German Manpower Position during the War Period 1939–1944', 31 July 1945, Table 7. The proportions were 28.6 in 1939, 62.3 in 1940, 68.8 in 1941 and 70.4 in 1942. Figures for 31 May each year. **44.** NARA, RG 243, entry 32, USSBS Interrogation of Dr Karl Hettlage, 16 June 1945, p. 9. **45.** Hugh Trevor-Roper (ed.), *Hitler's Table Talk 1941–44* (London, 1973), 633. **46.** IWM, Speer Collection, Box 368, Report 83, 'Relationship between the Ministry and the Army Armaments Office', Oct. 1945. It was Speer's view that the General Staff 'lacked any understanding of technical and economic matters'. **47.** IWM, Speer Collection, Box 368, Report 90 I, interrogation of Karl-Otto Saur, p. 4. **48.** Lutz Budrass, *Flugzeugindustrie und Luftrüstung in Deutschland 1918–1945* (Düsseldorf, 1998), 742–6; Rolf-Dieter Müller, 'Speers Rüstungspolitik im totalen Krieg: Zum Beitrag der modernen Militärgeschichte im Diskurs mit der Sozial-und Wirtschaftsgeschichte', *Militärgeschichtliche Zeitschrift*, 59 (2000), 356–62. **49.** IWM, Speer Collection, Box 368, Report 90 IV, 'Rationalization of the Munitions Industry', p. 44. **50.** IWM, Speer Collection, Box 368, Report 85 II, p. 4 (capitals in original). **51.** Lotte Zumpe, *Wirtschaft und Staat in Deutschland: Band I, 1933 bis 1945* (Berlin, 1980), 341–2; Müller, 'Speers Rüstungspolitik', 367–71. **52.** Müller, 'Speers Rüstungspolitik', 373–7. **53.** Dieter Eichholtz, *Geschichte der deutschen Kriegswirtschaft 1939–1945: Band II: Teil II: 1941–1943* (Munich, 1999), 314–15; IWM, Speer Collection, Box 368, Report 90 V, 'Rationalization in the Components Industry', p. 34. **54.** IWM, EDS, Mi 14/133, Oberkommando des Heeres, 'Studie über die Rüstung 1944', 25 Jan. 1944. **55.** IWM, EDS AL/1746, Saur interrogation, 10 Aug. 1945, p. 6; see too Daniel Uziel, *Arming the Luftwaffe: The German Aviation Industry in World War II* (Jefferson, NC, 2012), 85–90. **56.** Lutz Budrass, Jonas Scherner and Jochen Streb, 'Fixed-price contracts, learning, and outsourcing: explaining the continuous growth of output and labour productivity in the German aircraft industry during the Second World War', *Economic History Review*, 63 (2010), 124. **57.** Eichholtz, *Geschichte der deutschen Kriegswirtschaft: Band II*, 265. This figure is an estimate based on an armaments index constructed by officials in the Reich Statistical Office. The USSBS calculated a 48 per cent increase in output per head over the same period for the metalworking sectors. The Survey figures in 'Industrial Sales, Output and Productivity Prewar Area of Germany 1939–1944', 15 Mar. 1946, pp. 21–2, 65. See too Adam Tooze, 'No room for miracles: German output in World War II reassessed', *Geschichte & Gesellschaft*, 31 (2005), 50–53. **58.** Willi Boelcke, 'Stimulation und Verhalten von Unternehmen der deutschen Luftrüstungsindustrie während der Aufrüstungs- und Kriegsphase', in Horst Boog (ed.), *Luftkriegführung im Zweiten Weltkrieg* (Herford, 1993), 103–4. **59.** Hermione Giffard, 'Engines of desperation: jet engines, production and new weapons in the Third Reich', *Journal of Contemporary History*, 48 (2013), 822–5, 830–37. **60.** Uziel, *Arming the Luftwaffe*, 259–61. On the isolation of the research community see Helmut Trischler, 'Die Luftfahrtforschung im Dritten Reich: Organisation, Steuerung und Effizienz im Zeichen von Aufrüstung und Krieg', in Boog (ed.), *Luftkriegführung*, 225–6. **61.** W. Averell Harriman and Elie Abel, *Special Envoy to Churchill and Stalin, 1941–1945* (London, 1945), 90–91. **62.** David Reynolds and Vladimir Pechatnov (eds.), *The Kremlin Letters: Stalin's Wartime Correspondence with Churchill and Roosevelt* (New Haven, Conn., 2018), 62–3, Stalin to Roosevelt, 7 Nov. 1941. **63.** Charles Marshall, 'The Lend-Lease operation', *Annals of the American Academy of Political and Social Science*, 225 (1943), 187. **64.** German figures from IWM, Reich Air Ministry records, FD 3731/45, Deliveries to neutrals and allies, May 1943–Feb. 1944; US figures from Office of Chief of Military History, 'United States Army in World War II. Statistics: Lend-Lease', 15 Dec. 1952, 33. **65.** IWM, FD 3731/45, Position of deliveries to neutrals and allies, 18 June 1943, 18 Aug. 1943; Berthold Puchert, 'Deutschlands Aussenhandel im Zweiten Weltkrieg', in Dietrich Eichholtz (ed.), *Krieg und Wirtschaft: Studien zur deutschen Wirtschaftsgeschichte 1939–1945* (Berlin, 1999), 277; Rotem Kowner, 'When economics, strategy and racial ideology meet: inter-Axis connections in the wartime Indian Ocean', *Journal of Global History*, 12 (2017), 231–4, 235–6. **66.** Richard Overy, *The Bombing War: Europe 1939–1945* (London, 2013), 515–16. **67.** Figures from Combined Intelligence Objectives Sub-Committee, 'German Activities in the French Aircraft Industry', 1946, Appendix 4, pp. 79–80. **68.** Jochen

Vollert, *Panzerkampfwagen T34-747 (r): The Soviet T-34 Tank as Beutepanzer and Panzerattrappe in German Wehrmacht Service 1941–45* (Erlangen, 2013), 16, 33–4; US figure from Office of Chief of Military History, 'Statistics: Lend-Lease', p. 25. 69. Mark Stoler, *Allies and Adversaries: The Joint Chiefs of Staff, the Grand Alliance, and U.S. Strategy in World War II* (Chapel Hill, NC, 2000), 29–30; Matthew Jones, *Britain, the United States and the Mediterranean War, 1942–44* (London, 1996), 6, 11–13. 70. Ted Morgan, *FDR: A Biography* (New York, 1985), 579; Klein, *A Call to Arms*, 134–5. 71. Warren Kimball (ed.), *Churchill & Roosevelt: The Complete Correspondence: Volume 1, Alliance Emerging* (London, 1984), 102–9, Churchill to Roosevelt by telegram, 7 Dec. 1940. 72. Kennedy, *The American People in World War II*, 40–42. 73. David Roll, *The Hopkins Touch: Harry Hopkins and the Forging of the Alliance to Defeat Hitler* (New York, 2013), 74–5. 74. Buhite and Levy (eds.), *FDR's Fireside Chats*, 164, 169–70. 75. John Colville, *The Fringes of Power: The Downing Street Diaries, 1939–1955* (London, 1986), 331–2, entry for 11 Jan. 1941. 76. Andrew Johnstone, *Against Immediate Evil: American Internationalism and the Four Freedoms on the Eve of World War II* (Ithaca, NY, 2014), 116–21; Morgan, *FDR*, 580–81. 77. Kennedy, *The American People in World War II*, 45–6. 78. Hans Aufricht, 'Presidential power to regulate commerce and Lend-Lease transactions', *Journal of Politics*, 6 (1944), 66–7, 71. 79. Richard Overy, 'Co-operation: trade, aid and technology', in Kimball, Reynolds and Chubarian (eds.), *Allies at War*, 213–14. 80. Gavin Bailey, '"An opium smoker's dream": the 4000-bomber plan and Anglo-American aircraft diplomacy at the Atlantic Conference, 1941', *Journal of Transatlantic Studies*, 11 (2013), 303; Kennedy, *The American People in World War II*, 50. On British concessions see Cordell Hull, *The Memoirs of Cordell Hull*, 2 vols. (New York, 1948), ii, 1151–3. 81. William Grieve, *The American Military Mission to China, 1941–1942: Lend-Lease Logistics, Politics and the Tangles of Wartime Cooperation* (Jefferson, NC, 2014), 155–7. 82. J. Garry Clifford and Robert Ferrell, 'Roosevelt at the Rubicon: the great convoy debate of 1941', in Kurt Piehler and Sidney Pash (eds.), *The United States and the Second World War: New Perspectives on Diplomacy, War and the Home Front* (New York, 2010), 12–17. 83. Kevin Smith, *Conflicts Over Convoys: Anglo-American Logistics Diplomacy in the Second World War,* (Cambridge, 1996), 67–9. 84. Elliott Roosevelt (ed.), *The Roosevelt Letters: Volume Three, 1928–1945* (London, 1952), 366, letter to Senator Josiah Bailey, 13 May 1941. 85. Fred Israel (ed.), *The War Diary of Breckinridge Long: Selections from the Years 1939–1944* (Lincoln, Nebr., 1966), 208. 86. Johnstone, *Against Immediate Evil*, 156–7. 87. *Foreign Relations of the United States (FRUS), 1941*, 1, pp. 769–70 and 771–2, Memorandum of conversation with Soviet Ambassador, 26 June 1941; letter from Steinhardt to Cordell Hull, 29 June 1941. 88. Richard Leighton and Robert Coakley, *Global Logistics and Strategy, 1940–1943* (Washington, DC, 1955), 98–102; *FRUS, 1941*, 1, pp. 815–16, Sumner Welles to Oumansky, 2 Aug. 1941. 89. Ministry of Information, *What Britain Has Done, 1939–1945*, 9 May 1945 (reissued, London, 2007), 98–9. 90. Aufricht, 'Presidential power', 74. 91. Chief of Military History, 'Statistics: Lend-Lease', 6–8. 92. Cited by Edward Stettinius in his wartime diary, *The Diaries of Edward R. Stettinius, Jr., 1943–1946* (New York, 1975), 61, entry for 19 Apr. 1943. 93. H. Duncan Hall, *North American Supply* (London, 1955), 432; British Information Services, 'Britain's Part in Lend-Lease and Mutual Aid', Apr. 1944, 3–4, 15–16. 94. Hector Mackenzie, 'Transatlantic generosity: Canada's "Billion Dollar Gift" for the United Kingdom in the Second World War', *International History Review*, 34 (2012), 293–308. 95. Alexander Lovelace, 'Amnesia: how Russian history has viewed Lend-Lease', *Journal of Slavic Military Studies*, 27 (2014), 593; 'second fronts' in Alexander Werth, *Russia at War, 1941–1945* (London, 1964); H. Van Tuyll, *Feeding the Bear: American Aid to the Soviet Union 1941–1945* (New York, 1989), 156–61. 96. British Information Services, 'Britain's Part', 6–8; Marshall, 'The Lend-Lease operation', 184–5. 97. Chief of Military History, 'Statistics: Lend-Lease', 25–34. 98. David Zimmerman, 'The Tizard mission and the development of the atomic bomb', *War in History*, 2 (1995), 268–70. 99. John Baylis, *Anglo-American Defence Relations 1939–1984* (New York, 1984), 4–5, 16–32; Donald Avery, 'Atomic scientific co-operation and rivalry among the Allies: the Anglo-Canadian Montreal laboratory and the Manhattan Project, 1943–1946', *War in History*, 2 (1995), 281–3, 288. 100. Smith, *Conflicts Over Convoys*, 61–7. 101. Ibid., 177–83.

102. Arnold Hague, *The Allied Convoy System 1939–1945* (London, 2000), 187.   103. V. F. Vorsin, 'Motor vehicle transport deliveries through "lend-lease"', *Journal of Slavic Military Studies*, 10 (1997), 154.   104. Ibid., 155; Zaloga, *Soviet Lend-Lease Tanks*, 43.   105. British War Office, *Paiforce: The Official Story of the Persia and Iraq Command 1941–1946* (London, 1948), 97–105.   106. Ashley Jackson, *Persian Gulf Command: A History of the Second World War in Iran and Iraq* (New Haven, Conn., 2018), 297–307, 348–9.   107. Vorsin, 'Motor vehicle transport', 156–65.   108. Grieve, *American Military Mission*, 32–3, 135–8.   109. Ibid., 151–5; Edward Stettinius, *Lend-Lease: Weapon for Victory* (London, 1944), 166–70.   110. Jay Taylor, *The Generalissimo: Chiang Kai-Shek and the Struggle for Modern China* (Cambridge, Mass., 2011), 271.   111. Coombs, *British Tank Production*, 109, 115, 125.   112. Bailey, '"An opium smoker's dream"', 294–8.   113. Chief of Military History, 'Statistics: Lend-Lease', 33–4.   114. Alexander Hill, 'British Lend-Lease aid to the Soviet war effort, June 1941–June 1942', *Journal of Military History*, 71 (2007), 787–97; Zaloga, *Soviet Lend-Lease Tanks*, 10–11, 26–7, 31–2.   115. Coombs, *British Tank Production*, 109; Robert Coakley and Richard Leighton, *Global Logistics and Strategy 1943–1945* (Washington, DC, 1968), 679.   116. John Deane, *The Strange Alliance: The Story of American Efforts at Wartime Co-Operation with Russia* (London, 1947), 84.   117. G. C. Herring, 'Lend-Lease to Russia and the origins of the Cold War 1944–1946', *Journal of American History*, 61 (1969), 93–114.   118. Lovelace, 'Amnesia', 595–6.   119. Boris Sokolov, 'Lend-Lease in Soviet military efforts, 1941–1945', *Journal of Slavic Military Studies*, 7 (1994), 567–8; Jerrold Schecter and Vyacheslav Luchkov (eds.), *Khrushchev Remembers: The Glasnost Tapes* (New York, 1990), 84.   120. Denis Havlat, 'Western aid for the Soviet Union during World War II: Part I', *Journal of Slavic Military Studies*, 30 (2017), 314–16; Zaloga, *Soviet Lend-Lease Tanks*, 30.   121. Van Tuyll, *Feeding the Bear*, 156–7; Joan Beaumont, *Comrades in Arms: British Aid to Russia, 1941–1945* (London, 1980), 210–12.   122. Vorsin, 'Motor vehicle transport', 169–72.   123. Alexander Hill, 'The bear's new wheels (and tracks): US-armored and other vehicles and Soviet military effectiveness during the Great Patriotic War', *Journal of Slavic Military Studies*, 25 (2012), 214–17.   124. H. G. Davie, 'The influence of railways on military operations in the Russo-German War 1941–1945', *Journal of Slavic Military Studies*, 30 (2017), 341–3.   125. Sokolov, 'Lend-Lease', 570–81.   126. Havlat, 'Western aid', 297–8.   127. Coombs, *British Tank Production*, 122–3.   128. Neville Wylie, 'Loot, gold and tradition in the United Kingdom's financial warfare strategy 1939–1945', *International History Review*, 31 (2005), 299–328.   129. Edward Ericson, *Feeding the German Eagle: Soviet Economic Aid to Nazi Germany, 1933–1941* (Westport, Conn., 1999), 195–6.   130. See Dietrich Eichholtz, *Krieg um Öl: Ein Erdölimperium als deutsches Kriegsziel (1938–1943)* (Leipzig, 2006), 90–100.   131. USSBS, Report 109, Oil Division Final Report, 25 Aug. 1945, 18–19.   132. Walther Hubatsch (ed.), *Hitlers Weisungen für die Kriegführung, 1939–1945* (Munich, 1965), 46, Weisung Nr. 9 'Richtlinien für die Kriegführung gegen die feindliche Wirtschaft', 29 Nov. 1939.   133. Ibid., 118–19, Weisung Nr. 23 'Richtlinien für die Kriegführung gegen die englische Wehrwirtschaft', 6 Feb. 1941.   134. Hague, *Allied Convoy System*, 19.   135. Sönke Neitzel, *Der Einsatz der deutschen Luftwaffe über dem Atlantik und der Nordsee 1939–1945* (Bonn, 1995), 49–50.   136. *Fuehrer Conferences on Naval Affairs, 1939–1945* (London, 1990), 285, Report on a conference between the C.-in-C. Navy and the Fuehrer, 15 June 1942.   137. Smith, *Conflicts Over Convoys*, 249; Hague, *Allied Convoy System*, 107–8; Edward von der Porten, *The German Navy in World War II* (London, 1969), 174–8; Stephen Roskill, *The War at Sea 1939–1945*, 4 vols. (London, 1954–61), i, 500, 603.   138. BA-MA, RL2 IV/7, Otto Bechtle lecture 'Grossangriffe bei Nacht gegen Lebenszentren Englands, 12.8.1940–26.6.1941'.   139. TsAMO, Moscow, Fond 500/725168/110, Luftwaffe Operations Staff, report on British targets, 14 Jan. 1941.   140. Nicolaus von Below, *At Hitler's Side: The Memoirs of Hitler's Luftwaffe Adjutant, 1937–1945* (London, 2001), 79; *Fuehrer Conferences on Naval Affairs*, 177–8.   141. Overy, *The Bombing War*, 113–14.   142. AHB Translations, vol. 5, VII/92, 'German Aircraft Losses (West), Jan–Dec 1941.   143. Neitzel, *Einsatz der deutschen Luftwaffe*, 125.   144. David White, *Bitter Ocean: The Battle of the Atlantic 1939–1945* (New York, 2006), 297–8.   145. Hague, *Allied Convoy System*, 120.   146. Marc Milner, *Battle of the Atlantic* (Stroud, 2005), 85–9; Michael Hadley,

U-Boats against Canada: German Submarines in Canadian Waters (Montreal, 1985), 52-5. **147.** Hadley, U-Boats against Canada, 112-13. **148.** Christopher Bell, Churchill and Sea Power (Oxford, 2013), 259-79. **149.** Hague, Allied Convoy System, 116; Milner, Battle of the Atlantic, 85-9; Jürgen Rohwer, The Critical Convoy Battles of March 1943 (Annapolis, Md, 1977), 36; Patrick Beesly, Very Special Intelligence: The Story of the Admiralty's Operational Intelligence Centre 1939-1945 (London, 1977), 182. **150.** Karl Dönitz, Memoirs: Ten Years and Twenty Days (London, 1959), 253, 315. **151.** Smith, Conflicts Over Convoys, 257. **152.** Fuehrer Conferences on Naval Affairs, 334, minutes of the conference of the C.-in-C. Navy with the Fuehrer, 31 May 1943. **153.** Milner, Battle of the Atlantic, 251-3. **154.** Edward Miller, War Plan Orange: The U.S. Strategy to Defeat Japan, 1897-1945 (Annapolis, Md, 1991), 21-8. **155.** Ibid., 344, 348-50. **156.** Conrad Crane, American Airpower Strategy in World War II: Bombs, Cities, Civilians and Oil (Lawrence, Kans, 2016), 30. **157.** TNA, AIR 9/8, 'Note upon the Memorandum of the Chief of the Naval Staff', May 1928. **158.** William Medlicott, The Economic Blockade: Volume I (London, 1952), 13-16. **159.** Richard Hammond, 'British policy on total maritime warfare and the anti-shipping campaign in the Mediterranean 1940-1944', Journal of Strategic Studies, 36 (2013), 792-4. **160.** TNA, AIR 14/429, 'Air Ministry Instructions and Notes on the Rules to be Observed by the Royal Air Force in War', 17 Aug. 1939; AIR 41/5, J. M. Spaight, 'International Law of the Air 1939-1945', p. 7. **161.** Joel Hayward, 'Air power, ethics and civilian immunity during the First World War and Its aftermath', Global War Studies, 7 (2010), 127-9; Peter Gray, 'The gloves will have to come off: a reappraisal of the legitimacy of the RAF Bomber Offensive against Germany', Air Power Review, 13 (2010), 13-14, 25-6. **162.** Clay Blair, Silent Victory: The U.S. Submarine War against Japan (Philadelphia, Pa, 1975), 106. **163.** Hammond, 'British policy on total maritime warfare', 796-7. **164.** Jack Greene and Alessandro Massignani, The Naval War in the Mediterranean 1940-1943 (London, 1998), 266-7; Hammond, 'British policy on total maritime warfare', 803. **165.** Marc'Antonio Bragadin, The Italian Navy in World War II (Annapolis, Md, 1957), 245-9. **166.** Ibid., 364-5; Hammond, 'British policy on total maritime warfare', 807. There are a number of different estimates of Axis losses in the Mediterranean. Admiralty estimates showed 1,544 sunk for the whole war period, but totalling 4.2 million tons. See Robert Ehlers, The Mediterranean Air War: Airpower and Allied Victory in World War II (Lawrence, Kans, 2015), 403. **167.** This is the conclusion of Martin van Creveld, Supplying War: Logistics from Wallenstein to Patton (Cambridge, 1977), 198-200. **168.** Bragadin, Italian Navy, 356. The figure for 1941 was 89,563, for 1942 56,209. **169.** Vera Zamagni, 'Italy: how to win the war and lose the peace', in Harrison (ed.), The Economics of World War II, 188 **170.** Istituto centrale di statistica, Statistiche storiche dell'Italia 1861-1975 (Rome, 1976), 117. **171.** Hammond, 'British policy on total maritime warfare', 808; Christina Goulter, Forgotten Offensive: Royal Air Force Coastal Command's Anti-Shipping Campaign, 1940-1945 (Abingdon, 2004), 296-8, 353. **172.** Charles Webster and Noble Frankland, The Strategic Air Offensive against Germany 1939-1945: Volume IV (London, 1961), 99-102, 109. **173.** Cited in Edward Westermann, Flak: German Anti-Aircraft Defences, 1914-1945 (Lawrence, Kans, 2001), 90. **174.** Webster and Frankland, Strategic Air Offensive, iv, 205, 'Report by Mr. Butt to Bomber Command, 18 August 1941'; Randall Wakelam, The Science of Bombing: Operational Research in RAF Bomber Command (Toronto, 2009), 42-6. **175.** CCAC, Bufton Papers, 3/48, Review of the present strategical air offensive, 5 Apr. 1941, App. C, p. 2. **176.** TNA, AIR 40/1814, memorandum by O. Lawrence (MEW), 9 May 1941. **177.** Richard Overy, "The weak link"? The perception of the German working class by RAF Bomber Command, 1940-1945', Labour History Review, 77 (2012), 25-7. **178.** RAF Museum, Hendon, Harris Papers, Misc. Box A, Folder 4, 'One Hundred Towns of Leading Economic Importance in the German War Effort', n.d. **179.** Haywood Hansell, The Air Plan that Defeated Hitler (Atlanta, Ga, 1972), 81-3, 298-307. **180.** Stephen McFarland and Wesley Newton 'The American strategic air offensive against Germany in World War II', in R. Cargill Hall (ed.), Case Studies in Strategic Bombardment (Washington, DC, 1998), 188-9. **181.** Crane, American Airpower Strategy, 32-3. **182.** LC, Spaatz Papers, Box 67, 'Plan for the Completion of the Combined Bomber Offensive. Annex: Prospect for Ending War by Air Attack against

German Morale', 5 Mar. 1944, p. 1. **183.** Friedhelm Golücke, *Schweinfurt und der strate-gische Luftkrieg* (Paderborn, 1980), 134, 356–7; Richard Davis, *Bombing the European Axis Powers: A Historical Digest of the Combined Bomber Offensive, 1939–1945* (Maxwell, Ala, 2006), 158–61. **184.** Richard Davis, *Carl A. Spaatz and the Air War in Europe* (Washington, DC, 1993), 322–6, 370–79; Williamson Murray, *Luftwaffe: Strategy for Defeat 1933–1945* (London, 1985), 215. **185.** Overy, *The Bombing War*, 370–71. **186.** USSBS, Oil Division Final Report, 17–26, figs. 49, 60. **187.** Alfred Mierzejewski, *The Collapse of the German War Economy: Allied Air Power and the German National Railway* (Chapel Hill, NC, 1988), 191–3; AHB, German translations, vol. VII/23, 'Some Effects of the Allied Air Offensive on German Economic Life', 7 Dec. 1944, pp. 1–2 and vol. VII/38, Albert Speer to Wilhelm Keitel (OKW), 'Report on the Effects of Allied Air Activity against the Ruhr', 7 Nov. 1944. **188.** LC, Spaatz Papers, Box 68, USSTAF HQ, Ninth Air Force Interrogation of Hermann Göring, 1 June 1945. **189.** Webster and Frankland, *Strategic Air Offensive*, iv, 469–70, 494, Appendix 49 (iii) and 49 (xxii); Rolf Wagenführ, *Die deutsche Industrie im Kriege 1939–1945* (Berlin, 1963), 178–81. **190.** USSBS, Overall Report (European Theater), 25–6, 37–8, 73–4; USSBS, Oil Division Final Report, Fig. 7. **191.** Sebastian Cox (ed.), *The Strategic Air War against Germany, 1939–1945: The Official Report of the British Bombing Survey Unit* (London, 1998), 94–7, 129–34, 154. **192.** UEA, Zuckerman Archive, SZ/BBSU/103, Nicholas Kaldor typescript, 'The Nature of Strategic Bombing', pp. 4–6; Kaldor typescript, 'Capacity of German Industry', pp. 2–5. **193.** LC, Spaatz Papers, Box 68, Galbraith memorandum, 'Preliminary Appraisal of Achievement of the Strategic Bombing of Germany', p. 2. **194.** Werner Wolf, *Luftangriffe auf die deutsche Industrie, 1942–45* (Munich, 1985), 60, 74. **195.** BAB, R3102/10031, Reichsministerium für Rüstung und Kriegswirtschaft, 'Vorläufige Zusammenstellung des Arbeiterstundenausfalls durch Feindeinwirkung', 4 Jan. 1945. **196.** Webster and Frankland, *Strategic Air Offensive*, iv, 494–5, 501–2; Cox (ed.), *The Strategic Air War*, 97. **197.** Miwa, *Japan's Economic Planning*, 240; Akira Hara, 'Japan: guns before rice', in Harrison (ed.), *The Economics of World War II*, 241–3. **198.** Miyazaki and Itō, 'Transformation of industries in the war years', in Nakamura and Odaka (eds.), *Economic History of Japan*, 290–91; Theodore Roscoe, *United States Submarine Operations in World War II* (Annapolis, Md, 1949), 523. **199.** Hara, 'Wartime controls', in Nakamura and Odaka (eds.), *Economic History of Japan*, 271, 277; idem, 'Japan: guns before rice', 245. **200.** Blair, *Silent Victory*, 118–19, 361. **201.** Samuel Eliot Morison, *The Two-Ocean War: A Short History of the United States Navy in the Second World War* (Boston, Mass., 1963), 494–9; Blair, *Silent Victory*, 552. **202.** Roscoe, *United States Submarine Operations*, 215–17. **203.** USSBS, Pacific Theater, 'The Effects of Strategic Bombing', 35–42; Blair, *Silent Victory*, 816. For a full account see Phillips O'Brien, *How the War Was Won* (Cambridge, 2015), pp. 432–44. **204.** Michael Sturma, 'Atrocities, conscience, and unrestricted warfare: US submarines during the Second World War', *War in History*, 16 (2009), 455–6; Hara, 'Wartime controls', 277. **205.** Thomas Searle, '"It made a lot of sense to kill skilled workers": the firebombing of Tokyo in March 1945', *Journal of Military History*, 66 (2002), 108–12. **206.** William Ralph, 'Improvised destruction: Arnold, LeMay, and the firebombing of Japan', *War in History*, 13 (2006), 502–3. **207.** Searle, '"It made a lot of sense to kill skilled workers"', 119–21. **208.** Conrad Crane, 'Evolution of U.S. strategic bombing of urban areas', *Historian*, 50 (1987), 36–7. **209.** Ralph, 'Improvised destruction', 521–2. **210.** USSBS, Pacific Theater, 'The Effects of Strategic Bombing', 205. **211.** Roscoe, *United States Submarine Operations*, 523; Hara, 'Japan: guns before rice', 245; Barrett Tillman, *Whirlwind: The Air War against Japan 1942–1945* (New York, 2010), 194–9. **212.** Roscoe, *United States Submarine Operations*, 453; Hara, 'Japan: guns before rice', 245; USSBS, Pacific Theater, 'The Effects of Strategic Bombing', 180–81. **213.** UEA, Zuckerman Archive, SZ/BBSU/3, Rough Notes on Exercise Thunderbolt, 13–16 Aug. 1947. **214.** TNA, AIR 20/2025, Casualties of RAF, Dominion and Allied Personnel at RAF Posting Disposal, 31 May 1947; AIR 22/203, War Room Manual of Bomber Command Operations 1939–1945, p. 9; US figures in Davis, *Carl A. Spaatz*, App 4, 9. **215.** Hague, *Allied Convoy System*, 107; Roscoe, *United States Submarine Operations*, 523. **216.** Roscoe, *United States Submarine Operations*, 493; Blair, *Silent Victory*, 877.

7. Just Wars? Unjust Wars?

1. Dennis Wheatley, *Total War: A Paper* (London, 1941), 17.   2. Ibid., 18, 20.   3. Davide Rodogno, *Fascism's European Empire: Italian Occupation during the Second World War* (Cambridge, 2006), 44–9.   4. F. C. Jones, *Japan's New Order in East Asia* (Oxford, 1954), 469. This is a translation from the German text of the agreement. The original was drafted in English and this version had 'each its own proper place' rather than 'the space to which it is entitled'. The idea of 'space' was inserted in the German version to make the nature of the New Order more explicitly territorial.   5. Eric Johnson and Karl-Heinz Reuband, *What We Knew: Terror, Mass Murder and Everyday Life in Germany* (London, 2005), 106. See too Nick Stargardt, *The German War: A Nation under Arms, 1939–45* (London, 2015), 15–17.   6. Rodogno, *Fascism's European Empire*, 46–50.   7. Peter Duus, 'Nagai Ryutaro and the "White Peril", 1905–1944', *Journal of Asian Studies*, 31 (1971), 41–4.   8. Sidney Paish, 'Containment, rollback and the origins of the Pacific war 1933–1941', in Kurt Piehler and Sidney Paish (eds.), *The United States and the Second World War: New Perspectives on Diplomacy, War and the Home Front* (New York, 2010), 53–5, 57–8.   9. John Dower, *War without Mercy: Race and Power in the Pacific War* (New York, 1986), 205–6.   10. Ben-Ami Shillony, *Politics and Culture in Wartime Japan* (Oxford, 1981), 136, 141–3.   11. Werner Maser (ed.), *Hitler's Letters and Notes* (London, 1973), 227, 307, notes for speeches 1919/20.   12. André Mineau, 'Himmler's ethic of duty: a moral approach to the Holocaust and to Germany's impending defeat', *The European Legacy*, 12 (2007), 60; Alon Confino, *A World without Jews: The Nazi Imagination from Persecution to Genocide* (New Haven, Conn., 2014), 152–3.   13. Randall Bytwerk, 'The argument for genocide in Nazi propaganda', *Quarterly Journal of Speech*, 91 (2005), 37–9; Confino, *A World without Jews*, 153–5.   14. Heinrich Winkler, *The Age of Catastrophe: A History of the West, 1914–1945* (New Haven, Conn., 2015), 87–91.   15. Randall Bytwerk, 'Believing in "inner truth": The Protocols of the Elders of Zion and Nazi propaganda 1933–1945', *Holocaust and Genocide Studies*, 29 (2005), 214, 221–2.   16. Jeffrey Herf, *The Jewish Enemy: Nazi Propaganda during World War II and the Holocaust* (Cambridge, Mass., 2006), 61–2.   17. Ibid., 64–5.   18. Tobias Jersak, 'Die Interaktion von Kriegsverlauf und Judenvernichtung: ein Blick auf Hitlers Strategie im Spätsommer 1941', *Historische Zeitschrift*, 268 (1999), 311–74; Bytwerk, 'The argument for genocide', 42–3; Herf, *The Jewish Enemy*, 110.   19. Helmut Sündermann, *Tagesparolen: Deutsche Presseweisungen 1939–1945. Hitlers Propaganda und Kriegführung* (Leoni am Starnberger See, 1973), 203–4.   20. Confino, *A World without Jews*, 194.   21. Sündermann, *Tagesparolen*, 255, press directive of 13 Aug. 1943.   22. Bytwerk, 'The argument for genocide', 51, citing a *Sprechabendsdienst* (evening discussion service) circular for Sept./Oct. 1944.   23. François Genoud (ed.), *The Testament of Adolf Hitler: The Hitler–Bormann Documents February–April 1945* (London, 1961), 33, 51–2, 76, entries for 1–4 Feb., 13 Feb., 18 Feb. 1945.   24. NARA, RG 238 Jackson Papers, Box 3, translation of letter from Ley to attorney Dr Pflücker, 24 Oct. 1945 (not sent).   25. Mineau, 'Himmler's ethic of duty', 63, from a speech to Abwehr officers in 1944: 'The only thing that had to prevail was iron reason: with misplaced sentimentality one does not win wars in which the stake is life of the race'; see too Claudia Koonz, *The Nazi Conscience* (Cambridge, Mass., 2003), 254, 265; Christopher Browning, 'The Holocaust: basis and objective of the *Volksgemeinschaft*', in Martina Steber and Bernhard Gotto (eds.), *Visions of Community in Nazi Germany* (Oxford, 2014), 219–23.   26. Bytwerk, 'The argument for genocide', 49.   27. Gao Bei, *Shanghai Sanctuary: Chinese and Japanese Policy toward European Jewish Refugees during World War II* (Oxford, 2013), 20–25, 93–4, 104–7, 116–25.   28. Amedeo Guerrazzi, 'Die ideologischen Ursprünge der Judenverfolgung in Italien', in Lutz Klinkhammer and Amedeo Guerrazzi (eds.), *Die 'Achse' im Krieg: Politik, Ideologie und Kriegführung 1939–1945* (Paderborn, 2010), 437–42.   29. Simon Levis Sullam, 'The Italian executioners: revisiting the role of Italians in the Holocaust', *Journal of Genocide Research*, 19 (2017), 23–8.   30. Joseph Stalin, *The War of National Liberation* (New York, 1942), 30, speech of 6 Nov. 1941.   31. Oleg Budnitskii, 'The Great Patriotic War and Soviet society: defeatism 1941–42', *Kritika*, 15 (2014), 794.   32. R. Buhite and D. Levy (eds.), *FDR's Fireside Chats* (Norman, Okla, 1992), 198, talk of 9 Dec. 1941.   33. Keith

Feiling, *The Life of Neville Chamberlain* (London, 1946), 416. **34.** Stalin, *War of National Liberation*, 30; Susan Brewer, *Why America Fights: Patriotism and War Propaganda from the Philippines to Iraq* (New York, 2009), 87. **35.** Chinese Ministry of Information, *The Voice of China: Speeches of Generalissimo and Madame Chiang Kai-shek* (London, 1944), 32–3, address to the Chinese people, 7 July 1942. **36.** Martin Gilbert, *Finest Hour: Winston S. Churchill, 1939–1941* (London, 1983), 329–30. **37.** Keith Robbins, 'Britain, 1940 and "Christian Civilisation"', in Derek Beales and Geoffrey Best (eds.), *History, Society and the Churches: Essays in Honour of Owen Chadwick* (Cambridge, 1985), 285, 294. **38.** Dower, *War without Mercy*, 17. **39.** Wheatley, *Total War*, 33, 54. **40.** Brewer, *Why America Fights*, 88. **41.** On the anxieties of the age see Richard Overy, *The Morbid Age: Britain and the Crisis of Civilization* (London, 2009); Roxanne Panchasi, *Future Tense: The Culture of Anticipation in France between the Wars* (Ithaca, NY, 2009). **42.** Harold Nicolson, *Why Britain is at War* (London, 1939), 135–6, 140. **43.** Jacques Maritain, *De la justice politque: Notes sur la présente guerre* (Paris, 1940), 23; Hugh Dalton, *Hitler's War: Before and After* (London, 1940), 102. **44.** Robbins, 'Britain, 1940 and "Christian Civilisation"', 279, 288–91; Maritain, *De la justice politique*, ch. 3, 'Le renouvellement moral'. **45.** Friends House, London, Foley Papers, MS 448 2/2, 'An Appeal Addressed to All Christians', 8 Feb. 1945. **46.** Nicolson, *Why Britain is at War*, 132–3. **47.** University Labour Federation, 'How we can end the War', Pamphlet No. 5, 1940, 4–5. **48.** Penny Von Eschen, *Race against Empire: Black Americans and Anticolonialism 1937–1957* (Ithaca, NY, 1997), 31 (quoted in the American newspaper *Courier*). **49.** James Sparrow, *Warfare State: World War II Americans and the Age of Big Government* (New York, 2013), 44–5; Robert Westbrook, *Why We Fought: Forging American Obligation in World War II* (Washington, DC, 2004), 40–46. **50.** David Roll, *The Hopkins Touch: Harry Hopkins and the Forging of the Alliance to Defeat Hitler* (New York, 2013), 142–5. **51.** H. V. Morton, *Atlantic Meeting* (London, 1943), 126–7, 149–51. **52.** Von Eschen, *Race against Empire*, 26. **53.** Gerhard Weinberg, *Visions of Victory: The Hopes of Eight World War II Leaders* (Cambridge, 2005), 86–9; Jay Taylor, *The Generalissimo: Chiang Kai-Shek and the Struggle for Modern China* (Cambridge, Mass., 2011), 186. **54.** Buhite and Levy (eds.), *FDR's Fireside Chats*, 217, broadcast of 23 Feb. 1942. **55.** Stephen Wertheim, 'Instrumental internationalism: the American origins of the United Nations, 1940–3', *Journal of Contemporary History*, 54 (2019), 266–80. **56.** Michaela Moore, *Know Your Enemy: The American Debate on Nazism, 1933–1945* (New York, 2010), 119. **57.** Richard Overy, *Interrogations: The Nazi Elite in Allied Hands* (London, 2001), 6–8. **58.** International Law Association, *Briand–Kellogg Pact of Paris: Articles of Interpretation as Adopted by the Budapest Conference 1934* (London, 1934), 1–2, 7–10. **59.** Howard Ball, *Prosecuting War Crimes and Genocide: The Twentieth-century Experience* (Lawrence, Kans, 1999), pp. 85–7. **60.** Genoud (ed.), *The Testament of Adolf Hitler*, 108, entry for 2 Apr. 1945. **61.** Ben-Ami Shillony, *Politics and Culture in Wartime Japan* (Oxford, 1981), 146. **62.** David Mayers, 'Humanity in 1948: the Genocide Convention and the Universal Declaration of Human Rights', *Diplomacy & Statecraft*, 26 (2015), 464. **63.** Gabriel Gorodetsky (ed.), *The Maisky Diaries: Red Ambassador to the Court of St. James's, 1932–1943* (New Haven, Conn., 2015), 244–5, entry for 12 Dec. 1939. **64.** Ibid., 258–9, entry for 13 Mar. 1940. **65.** Elliott Roosevelt (ed.), *The Roosevelt Letters: Volume Three, 1928–1945* (London, 1952), 290, Roosevelt to Lincoln MacVeagh, 1 Dec. 1939. **66.** George Sirgiovanni, *An Undercurrent of Suspicion: Anti-Communism in America during World War II* (New Brunswick, NJ, 1990), 33–4, 36; David Mayers, 'The Great Patriotic War, FDR's embassy Moscow and US–Soviet relations', *International History Review*, 33 (2011), 306–7. **67.** Roosevelt (ed.), *Roosevelt Letters*, 292–3, letter from Roosevelt to William Allen White, 14 Dec. 1939. **68.** James Harris, 'Encircled by enemies: Stalin's perception of the capitalist world 1918–1941', *Journal of Strategic Studies*, 31 (2008), 534–43. **69.** Fridrikh Firsov, Harvey Klehr and John Haynes, *Secret Cables of the Comintern 1933–1943* (New Haven, Conn., 2014), 140–41, 175. **70.** Ibid., 153–7, 164. **71.** *Daily Worker*, 21 Jan. 1941, 4. **72.** Gorodetsky (ed.), *The Maisky Diaries*, 368, entry for 27 June 1941. **73.** Sirgiovanni, *Undercurrent of Suspicion*, 3–5; Buhite and Levy (eds.), *FDR's Fireside Chats*, 277–8, broadcast of 24 Dec. 1943. **74.** Firsov, Klehr and Haynes, *Secret Cables of the Comintern*, 184–5. **75.**

On hopes for collaboration see Martin Folly, *Churchill, Whitehall, and the Soviet Union, 1940–1945* (Basingstoke, 2000), 78–9, 165–6. **76.** TNA, FO 800/868, Desmond Morton to Lord Swinton, 11 Nov. 1941; Morton to Robert Bruce Lockhart, 15 Nov. 1941. **77.** Sirgiovanni, *Undercurrent of Suspicion*, 3–5; Frank Warren, *Noble Abstractions: American Liberal Intellectuals and World War II* (Columbus, Ohio, 1999), 181–4. **78.** 'Britain, Russia and Peace', Official Report of the National Congress of Friendship and Co-operation with the USSR, 4–5 Nov. 1944, 14–15. **79.** Gorodetsky (ed.), *Maisky Diaries*, 411, 436, 475, entries for 15 Feb., 24 June 1942, 5 Feb. 1943. **80.** 'Britain, Russia and Peace', 3–4. **81.** Sirgiovanni, *Undercurrent of Suspicion*, 49–56. **82.** Daniel Lomas, 'Labour ministers, intelligence and domestic anti-communism 1945–1951', *Journal of Intelligence History*, 12 (2013), 119; Christopher Andrew, *The Defence of the Realm: The Authorized History of MI5* (London, 2009), 273–81. **83.** Gorodetsky (ed.), *Maisky Diaries*, 509–10. **84.** Andrew Thorpe, *Parties at War: Political Organisation in Second World War Britain* (Oxford, 2009), 39–40. **85.** John Deane, *The Strange Alliance: The Story of American Efforts at Wartime Co-Operation with Russia* (London, 1947), 319. **86.** Jonathan Haslam, *Russia's Cold War: From the October Revolution to the Fall of the Wall* (New Haven, Conn., 2011), 23–32; Geoffrey Roberts, 'Stalin's wartime vision of the peace, 1939–1945', in Timothy Snyder and Ray Brandon (eds.), *Stalin and Europe: Imitation and Domination 1928–1953* (New York, 2014), 249–59. **87.** John Iatrides, 'Revolution or self-defense? Communist goals, strategy and tactics in the Greek civil war', *Journal of Cold War Studies*, 7 (2005), 24. **88.** Warren, *Noble Abstractions*, 172–4. **89.** Sirgiovanni, *Undercurrent of Suspicion*, 58, 85–6; Mayers, 'The Great Patriotic War', 318–24. **90.** NARA, RG 238, Box 32, translation of 'Secret Additional Protocol to the German–Soviet Pact of 23.8.39'; Mayers, 'The Great Patriotic War', 303. **91.** Arkady Vaksberg, *The Prosecutor and the Prey: Vyshinsky and the 1930s Show Trials* (London, 1990), 259; S. Mironenko, 'La collection des documents sur le procès de Nuremberg dans les archives d'état de la federation russe', in Anna Wiewiorka (ed.), *Les procès de Nuremberg et de Tokyo* (Paris, 1996), 65–6. **92.** For two excellent recent accounts of Soviet inhumanity see Golfo Alexopoulos, *Illness and Inhumanity in Stalin's Gulag* (New Haven, Conn., 2017) and Jörg Baberowski, *Scorched Earth: Stalin's Reign of Terror* (New Haven, Conn., 2016), esp. chs. 5–6. **93.** Achim Kilian, *Einzuweisen zur völligen Isolierung. NKWD-Speziallager Mühlberg/Elbe 1945–1948* (Leipzig, 1993), 7. **94.** Andrew Stone, '"The differences were only in the details": the moral equivalency of Stalinism and Nazism in Anatoli Bakanichev's *Twelve Years Behind Barbed Wire*', *Kritika*, 13 (2012), 123, 134. **95.** Mayers, 'Humanity in 1948', 462–3. **96.** Ronald Takaki, *Double Victory: A Multicultural History of America in World War II* (New York, 2000), 6. **97.** David Welky, *Marching Across the Color Line: A. Philip Randolph and Civil Rights in the World War II Era* (New York, 2014), 86–9. **98.** Thomas Sugrue, 'Hillburn, Hattiesburg and Hitler: wartime activists think globally and act locally', in Kevin Kruse and Stephen Tuck (eds.), *Fog of War: The Second World War and the Civil Rights Movement* (New York, 2012), 91. **99.** Welky, *Marching Across the Color Line*, 89. **100.** Sugrue, 'Hillburn, Hattiesburg and Hitler', 91–2. **101.** Ibid., 93–4; Welky, *Marching Across the Color Line*, xx–xxi, 112. **102.** Julian Zelizer, 'Confronting the roadblock: Congress, Civil Rights, and World War II', in Kruse and Tuck (eds.), *Fog of War*, 38–40. **103.** Daniel Kryder, *Divided Arsenal: Race and the American State during World War II* (Oxford, 2000), 208–10, 248–9. **104.** Takaki, *Double Victory*, 28–9. **105.** Chris Dixon, *African Americans and the Pacific War 1941–1945: Race, Nationality, and the Fight for Freedom* (Cambridge, 2018), 68. **106.** Welky, *Marching Across the Color Line*, 112. **107.** Takaki, *Double Victory*, 53. **108.** Kryder, *Divided Arsenal*, 3. **109.** Ibid, 229–32; Welky, *Marching Across the Color Line*, 121–2; Robert Dallek, *Franklin D. Roosevelt: A Political Life* (London, 2017), 520. **110.** Kryder, *Divided Arsenal*, 208–10; Takaki, *Double Victory*, 43–4. **111.** Kenneth Janken, 'From colonial liberation to Cold War liberalism: Walter White, the NAACP, and foreign affairs, 1941–1955', *Ethnic and Racial Studies*, 21 (1998), 1076–8. **112.** Ibid., 1079; Von Eschen, *Race against Empire*, 2–5 **113.** Elizabeth Borgwardt, 'Race, rights and nongovernmental organisations at the UN San Francisco Conference: a contested history of human rights without discrimination', in Kruse and Tuck (eds.), *Fog of War*, 188–90, 192–6; Von Eschen, *Race against Empire*, 81–2. **114.** Janken, 'From colonial liberation', 1082; Mayers,

'Humanity in 1948', 457–9. **115.** J. B. Schechtman, 'The USSR, Zionism and Israel', in Lionel Kochan (ed.), *The Jews in Soviet Russia since 1917* (Oxford, 1978), 118; Nora Levin, *Paradox of Survival: The Jews in the Soviet Union since 1917*, 2 vols. (London, 1990), i, 275–6. **116.** Ben-Cion Pinchuk, *Shtetl Jews under Soviet Rule: Eastern Poland on the Eve of the Holocaust* (London, 1990), 39, 55, 129–31. **117.** Bernard Wasserstein, *Britain and the Jews of Europe 1939–1945* (Oxford, 1979), 7, 11. **118.** Ibid., 18–20; Louise London, *Whitehall and the Jews 1933–1948: British Immigration Policy, Jewish Refugees and the Holocaust* (Cambridge, 2000), 140. **119.** Takaki, *Double Victory*, 195; Joseph Bendersky, 'Dissension in the face of the Holocaust: the 1941 American debate over anti-Semitism', *Holocaust and Genocide Studies*, 24 (2010), 89. **120.** Wasserstein, *Britain and the Jews*, 46–7; Takaki, *Double Victory*, 195–6. **121.** Mayers, 'The Great Patriotic War', 305. **122.** Wasserstein, *Britain and the Jews*, 52. **123.** Leah Garrett, *X-Troop: The Secret Jewish Commandos who Helped Defeat the Nazis* (London, 2021), 26–41. **124.** Wasserstein, *Britain and the Jews*, 54–76. **125.** Michael Fleming, 'Intelligence from Poland on Chelmno: British responses', *Holocaust Studies*, 21 (2015), 172–4, 176–7; Jan Láníček, 'Governments-in-exile and the Jews during and after the Second World War', *Holocaust Studies*, 18 (2012), 73–5. **126.** Fleming, 'Intelligence from Poland', 174–5. **127.** David Wyman, *The Abandonment of the Jews: America and the Holocaust 1941–1945* (New York, 1984), 43–5; Zohar Segev, *The World Jewish Congress during the Holocaust: Between Activism and Restraint* (Berlin, 2017), 23–6. **128.** London, *Whitehall and the Jews*, 207–8. **129.** Wyman, *Abandonment of the Jews*, 73–5. **130.** Leonid Smilovitskii, 'Antisemitism in the Soviet partisan movement 1941–1945: the case of Belorussia', *Holocaust and Genocide Studies*, 20 (2006), 708–9; Jeffrey Herf, 'The Nazi extermination camps and the ally to the East: could the Red Army and Air Force have stopped or slowed the Final Solution?', *Kritika*, 4 (2003), 915–16; Alexander Gogun, 'Indifference, suspicion, and exploitation: Soviet units behind the front lines of the Wehrmacht and Holocaust in Ukraine, 1941–44', *Journal of Slavic Military Studies*, 28 (2015), 381–2. **131.** Láníček, 'Governments-in-exile', 76. **132.** London, *Whitehall and the Jews*, 205–6, 218; Wasserstein, *Britain and the Jews*, 183, 188. **133.** Wasserstein, *Britain and the Jews*, 190–203; Shlomo Aronson, *Hitler, the Allies and the Jews* (New York, 2004), 85–100; Takaki, *Double Victory*, 205–6. **134.** Wasserstein, *Britain and the Jews*, 304. **135.** Segev, *The World Jewish Congress*, 26–30. **136.** Laurel Leff, *Buried by the Times: The Holocaust and America's Most Important Newspaper* (New York, 2005), 330–41. **137.** Bendersky, 'Dissension in the face of the Holocaust', 89–96; Takaki, *Double Victory*, 189–91. **138.** Wasserstein, *Britain and the Jews*, 34, 351. **139.** Segev, *The World Jewish Congress*, 41. **140.** Láníček, 'Governments-in-exile', 81–5; Wasserstein, *Britain and the Jews*, 295–302. **141.** Rainer Schulze, 'The *Heimschaffungsaktion* of 1942–3: Turkey, Spain and Portugal and their responses to the German offer of repatriation of their Jewish citizens', *Holocaust Studies*, 18 (2012), 54–8. **142.** Overy, *Interrogations*, 48–9, 178–9. **143.** Bendersky, 'Dissension in the face of the Holocaust', 108–9; Mayers, 'Humanity in 1948', 448–55. **144.** Kenneth Rose, *Myth and the Greatest Generation: A Social History of Americans in World War II* (New York, 2008), 1–7. **145.** Parliamentary Peace Aims Group, 'Towards a Total Peace: A Restatement of Fundamental Principles', 1943, 4. **146.** Chinese Ministry of Information, *The Voice of China*, 12, broadcast to the nation, 18 Feb. 1942. **147.** Sonya Rose, *Which People's War? National Identity and Citizenship in Wartime Britain 1939–1945* (Oxford, 2003), 286–9. **148.** Frank Bajohr and Michael Wildt (eds.), *Volksgemeinschaft: Neue Forschungen zur Gesellschaft des Nationalsozialismus* (Frankfurt/Main, 2009), 7–9; Detlef Schmiechen-Ackermann, 'Social control and the making of the *Volksgemeinschaft*', in Steber and Gotto (eds.), *Visions of Community*, 240–53. **149.** Michael David-Fox, 'The people's war: ordinary people and regime strategies in a world of extremes', *Slavic Review*, 75 (2016), 552; Anika Walke, *Pioneers and Partisans: An Oral History of Nazi Genocide in Belorussia* (New York, 2015), 140. **150.** Buhite and Levy (eds.), *FDR's Fireside Chats*, 199, broadcast of 9 Dec. 1941. **151.** Luigi Petrella, *Staging the Fascist War: The Ministry of Popular Culture and Italian Propaganda on the Home Front, 1938–1943* (Bern, 2016), 142–3; Romano Canosa, *I servizi segreti del Duce: I persecutori e le vittime* (Milan, 2000), 387–93. **152.** Chinese Ministry of Information, *The Voice of China*, 40, speech by Chiang Kai-shek, 22 Oct. 1942.

153. On the issues facing Chiang's efforts see Rana Mitter, *China's War with Japan 1937–1945* (London, 2013), 177–82; on collaboration see the outline in David Barrett and Larry Shyu (eds.), *Chinese Collaboration with Japan, 1932–1945* (Stanford, Calif., 2001), 3–12; on Communist mobilization, Lifeng Li, 'Rural mobilization in the Chinese Communist Revolution: from the anti-Japanese War to the Chinese Civil War', *Journal of Modern Chinese History*, 9 (2015), 97–104. **154.** Chinese Ministry of Information, *The Voice of China*, 46, speech by Chiang Kai-shek, 31 Oct. 1942. **155.** Bajohr and Wildt (eds.), *Volksgemeinschaft*, 7. **156.** Samuel Yamashita, *Daily Life in Wartime Japan* (Lawrence, Kans, 2015), 13–14. **157.** Sparrow, *Warfare State*, 72–3; Westbrook, *Why We Fought*, 8–9. **158.** William Tuttle, *'Daddy's Gone to War': The Second World War in the Lives of American Children* (New York, 1993), 115–16, 118, 121–3. **159.** Yamashita, *Daily Life in Wartime Japan*, 66–70, 87. **160.** Sparrow, *Warfare State*, 65. **161.** Ian McLaine, *Ministry of Morale: Home Front Morale and the Ministry of Information in World War II* (London, 1979), endpapers. **162.** Budnitskii, 'The Great Patriotic War', 771–81; Mark Edele, *Stalin's Defectors: How Red Army Soldiers became Hitler's Collaborators, 1941–1945* (Oxford, 2017), 21, 29–31. There are no precise figures for defection and 200,000 represents a probable upper limit. **163.** Hans Boberach (ed.), *Meldungen aus dem Reich: Die geheimen Lageberichte des Sicherheitsdienstes der SS 1938–1945: Band I* (Herrsching, 1984), 11–16, 20; David Welch, 'Nazi propaganda and the Volksgemeinschaft: constructing a people's community', *Journal of Contemporary History*, 39 (2004), 215. **164.** Mimmo Franzinelli, *I tentacoli dell'Ovra: agenti, collaboratori e vittime della polizia politica fascista* (Turin, 1999), 386–8; Canosa, *I servizi segreti*, 380–85. **165.** Amir Weiner, 'Getting to know you: the Soviet surveillance system 1939–1957', *Kritika*, 13 (2012), 5–8. **166.** Sparrow, *Warfare State*, 43. **167.** Ibid., 69; Brewer, *Why America Fights*, 93–6, 103. **168.** Neil Wynn, 'The "good war": the Second World War and postwar American society', *Journal of Contemporary History*, 31 (1996), 467–70; Sparrow, *Warfare State*, 67–8, 87–8; Westbrook, *Why We Fought*, 49–50, 69–70. **169.** Paul Addison and Jeremy Crang (eds.), *Listening to Britain: Home Intelligence Reports on Britain's Finest Hour, May to September 1940* (London, 2011), xi–xii. **170.** James Hinton, *The Mass Observers: A History, 1937–1949* (Oxford, 2013), 166–7 **171.** McLaine, *Ministry of Morale*, 256–7, 260; Addison and Crang (eds.), *Listening to Britain*, xiii–xiv; Hinton, *Mass Observers*, 179–80. **172.** John Hilvert, *Blue Pencil Warriors: Censorship and Propaganda in World War II* (St Lucia, Qld, 1984), 220–22. **173.** Petrella, *Staging the Fascist War*, 136. **174.** Chang-tai Hung, *War and Popular Culture: Resistance in Modern China, 1937–1945* (Berkeley, Calif., 1994), 181–5. **175.** Peter Fritzsche, *An Iron Wind: Europe under Hitler* (New York, 2016), 10–13. **176.** Boberach (ed.), *Meldungen aus dem Reich: Band I*, 25. **177.** Petrella, *Staging the Fascist War*, 136–8. **178.** Budnitskii, 'The Great Patriotic War', 791. **179.** McLaine, *Ministry of Morale*, 80–84. **180.** Sparrow, *Warfare State*, 86–8. **181.** John Dower, *Japan in War and Peace: Essays on History, Race and Culture* (New York, 1993), 129. **182.** Sparrow, *Warfare State*, 45. **183.** Rose, *Myth and the Greatest Generation*, 64. **184.** Johnson and Reuband, *What We Knew*, 194, 224. **185.** Frank Bajohr and Dieter Pohl, *Der Holocaust als offene Geheimnis: Die Deutschen, die NS-Führung und die Alliierten* (Munich, 2006), 35–6, 56–7; Herf, *The Jewish Enemy*, 114–22. **186.** Bytwerk, 'The argument for genocide', 43–4; Bytwerk, 'Believing in "inner truth"', 215. **187.** Schmiechen-Ackermann. 'Social control and the making of the *Volksgemeinschaft*', 249. **188.** Peter Longerich, *'Davon haben wir nichts gewusst!': Die Deutschen und die Judenverfolgung, 1933–1945* (Munich, 2006), 317–21, 326–7; Bytwerk, 'The argument for genocide', 53–4. **189.** See Edele, *Stalin's Defectors*, 169–74; Yamashita, *Daily Life in Wartime Japan*, 165–71. **190.** Westbrook, *Why We Fought*, 8–9, 40–50. **191.** José Harris, 'Great Britain: the people's war', in Warren Kimball, David Reynolds and Alexander Chubarian (eds.), *Allies at War: The Soviet, American and British Experience 1939–1945* (New York, 1994), 244–51; Brewer, *Why America Fights*, 115–17. **192.** Lisa Kirschenbaum, '"Our city, our hearths, our families": local loyalties and private life in Soviet World War II propaganda', *Slavic Review*, 59 (2000), 825–30. **193.** LC, Eaker Papers, Box I:30, MAAF Intelligence Section, 'What is the German saying?' [n.d. but March 1945], entry (g). **194.** Timothy Stewart-Winter, '"Not a soldier, not a slacker:" Conscientious objection and male citizenship in the United States during the Second World War', *Gender & History*, 19 (2007),

533; Barbara Habenstreit, *Men Against War* (New York, 1973), 142–3. **195.** Rennie Smith, *Peace verboten* (London, 1943), 45–8. **196.** Norman Ingram, *The Politics of Dissent: Pacifism in France 1919–1939* (Oxford, 1991), 134–9. On the International Peace Campaign (in French the *Rassemblement universel pour la Paix*) see Overy, *The Morbid Age*, 257–9. **197.** H. Runham Brown, *The War Resisters' International: Principle, Policy and Practice* (London, 1936 [?]), 1–5. **198.** Storm Jameson (ed.), *Challenge to Death* (London, 1935), p. xii. On the 'Peace Ballot' see Martin Caedel, 'The first referendum: the Peace Ballot 1934–35', *English Historical Review*, 95 (1980), 818–29. **199.** Overy, *The Morbid Age*, 243–50; D. C. Lukowitz, 'British pacifists and appeasement: the Peace Pledge Union', *Journal of Contemporary History*, 9 (1974), 116–17. **200.** Habenstreit, *Men Against War*, 126–33. **201.** Gerald Sittser, *A Cautious Patriotism: The American Churches and the Second World War* (Chapel Hill, NC, 1997), 18–19. **202.** Ibid., 133–4; Scott Bennett, 'American pacifism, the "greatest generation", and World War II', in Piehler and Pash (eds.), *The United States and the Second World War*, 260–61. **203.** Haberstreit, *Men Against War*, 138–9. **204.** *The Public Papers and Addresses of Franklin D. Roosevelt: 1939 Volume: War and Neutrality* (New York, 1941), 300, 'President Opens the New York World's Fair, April 30 1939'; Marco Duranti, 'Utopia, nostalgia, and world war at the 1939–40 New York World's Fair', *Journal of Contemporary History*, 41 (2006), 663. **205.** *Parliamentary Debates*, vol. 351, col. 298, 3 Sept. 1939. **206.** Graham Jackman, '"Ich kann nicht zwei Herren dienen": conscientious objectors and Nazi "Militärjustiz"', *German Life and Letters*, 64 (2011), 205. **207.** Peter Brock, *Against the Draft: Essays on Conscientious Objection from the Radical Reformation to the Second World War* (Toronto, 2006), 329–31, 340. **208.** Tobias Kelly, 'Citizenship, cowardice and freedom of conscience: British pacifists in the Second World War', *Comparative Studies in Society and History*, 57 (2015), 701. **209.** Mona Siegel, *The Moral Disarmament of France: Education, Pacifism and Patriotism 1914–1940* (Cambridge, 2004), 192–201. **210.** Carrie Foster, *The Women and the Warriors: The U. S. Section of the Women's International League for Peace and Freedom 1915–1946* (Syracuse, NY, 1995), 263–4, 284–5. **211.** Neil Stammers, *Civil Liberties in Britain during the Second World War* (London, 1989), 93–4; Lukowitz, 'British pacifists and appeasement', 115–28. **212.** TNA, MEPO 3/3113, extract from parliamentary debates, 6 Mar. 1940, 26 Nov. 1941; MEPO 3/2111, file on trial of Stuart Morris. **213.** Martin Caedel, *Pacifism in Britain, 1914–1945: The Defining of a Faith* (Oxford, 1980), 299; Vera Brittain, *One Voice: Pacifist Writings from the Second World War* (London, 2005), 39, 'Functions of a Minority'. **214.** Peter Brock and Nigel Young, *Pacifism in the Twentieth Century* (Syracuse, NY, 1999), 165. **215.** Sittser, *A Cautious Patriotism*, 19. **216.** Ray Abrams, 'The Churches and the clergy in World War II', *Annals of the American Academy of Political and Social Science*, 256 (1948), 111–13. **217.** John Middleton Murry, *The Necessity of Pacifism* (London, 1937), 106; London School of Economics Archive, Women's International League for Peace and Freedom Papers, 21AW/2/C/46, 'Report of a deputation of Pacifist Clergy to the Archbishops of Canterbury and York', 11 June 1940. **218.** Overy, *The Morbid Age*, 242–3. **219.** George Bell, *Christianity and World Order* (London, 1940), 78–81. **220.** Stephen Parker, 'Reinvigorating Christian Britain: the spiritual issues of the war, national identity, and the hope of religious education', in Tom Lawson and Stephen Parker (eds.), *God and War: The Church of England and Armed Conflict in the Twentieth Century* (Farnham, 2012), 63. **221.** Donald Wall, 'The Confessing Church and the Second World War', *Journal of Church and State*, 23 (1981), 19–25. **222.** Thomas Brodie, 'Between "national community" and "milieu": German Catholics at war 1939–1945', *Contemporary European History*, 26 (2017), 428–32. **223.** Jouni Tilli, '"Deus Vult!": the idea of crusading in Finnish clerical war rhetoric', *War in History*, 24 (2017), 369–75. **224.** Roger Reese, 'The Russian Orthodox Church and "patriotic" support for the Stalinist regime during the Great Patriotic War', *War & Society*, 33 (2014), 134–5. **225.** Jan Bank with Lieve Grevers, *Churches and Religion in the Second World War* (London, 2016), 506. **226.** Reese, 'The Russian Orthodox Church', 144–5. **227.** For this paragraph see John Mitsuru Oe, 'Church and state in Japan in World War II', *Anglican and Episcopal History*, 59 (1990), 202–6. **228.** Bell, *Christianity and World Order*, 98–100. **229.** Frank Coppa, 'Pope Pius XII: from the diplomacy of impartiality to the silence of the Holocaust', *Journal of Church and State*, 55

(2013), 298–9; Gerard Noel, *Pius XII: The Hound of Hitler* (London, 2008), 3–4. **230.** Bank and Grevers, *Churches and Religion*, 483–94. **231.** Coppa, 'Pope Pius XII', 300. **232.** Brock, *Against the Draft*, 350–52; Anna Halle, 'The German Quakers and the Third Reich', *German History*, 11 (1993), 222–6. **233.** Kelly, 'Citizenship, cowardice and freedom of conscience', 701–2; Richard Overy, 'Pacifism and the Blitz, 1940–1941', *Past & Present*, no. 219 (2013), 217–18. **234.** W. Edward Orser, 'World War II and the pacifist controversy in the major Protestant Churches', *American Studies*, 14 (1973), 7–10; Sittser, *A Cautious Patriotism*, 35–6. **235.** Orser, 'World War II and the pacifist controversy', 12–18. **236.** Gabriele Yonan, 'Spiritual resistance of Christian conviction in Nazi Germany: the case of the Jehovah's Witnesses', *Journal of Church and State*, 41 (1999), 308–9, 315–16; Stewart-Winter, '"Not a soldier, not a slacker"', 532. **237.** Thomas Kehoe, 'The Reich Military Court and its values: Wehrmacht treatment of Jehovah's Witness conscientious objection', *Holocaust & Genocide Studies*, 33 (2019), 351–8; Yonan, 'Spiritual resistance', 309; Jackman, '"Ich kann nicht zwei Herren dienen"', 189, 193. **238.** Oe, 'Church and state in Japan', 210. **239.** Sittser, *A Cautious Patriotism*, 186–7. **240.** Denis Hayes, 'Liberty in the War', pamphlet published by *Peace News*, Sept. 1943, 5–6. **241.** Bennett, 'American pacifism', 267; Stewart-Winter, '"Not a soldier, not a slacker"', 532; Kelly, 'Citizenship, cowardice and freedom of conscience', 710. **242.** Brock, *Against the Draft*, 329–30. **243.** Jackman, '"Ich kann nicht zwei Herren dienen"', 189–93, 197–8. **244.** Kelly, 'Citizenship, cowardice and freedom of conscience', 699. **245.** National Library of Wales, Stanley Jevons Papers, I IV/103, Notes by the Chairman of the South-East Tribunal (n.d. but Sept.–Oct. 1941); Kelly, 'Citizenship, cowardice and freedom of conscience', 709. **246.** Brock and Young, *Pacifism in the Twentieth Century*, 158–9; the quotation is from Kelly, 'Citizenship, cowardice and freedom of conscience', 694. **247.** Denis Hayes, *Challenge of Conscience: The Story of Conscientious Objectors of 1939–1949* (London, 1949), 210. **248.** Andrew Rigby, 'Pacifist communities in Britain during the Second World War', *Peace & Change*, 15 (1990), 108–13. **249.** Rachel Barker, *Conscience, Government and War: Conscientious Objection in Britain, 1939–45* (London, 1982), 58; Overy, 'Pacifism and the Blitz', 222–3. **250.** Sittser, *A Cautious Patriotism*, 131–2. **251.** Scott Bennett, '"Free American political prisoners": pacifist activism and civil liberties, 1945–48', *Journal of Peace Research*, 40 (2003), 424; Stewart-Winter, '"Not a soldier, not a slacker"', 527–8. **252.** Stewart-Winter, '"Not a soldier, not a slacker"', 522. **253.** Ibid., 522–6. **254.** Bennett, 'American pacifism', 267. **255.** Nicholas Krehbiel, *General Lewis B. Hershey and Conscientious Objection during World War II* (Columbia, Miss., 2011), 5–6, 97. **256.** Ibid., 260, 265–6; Stewart-Winter, '"Not a soldier, not a slacker"', 521. **257.** Krehbiel, *General Lewis B. Hershey*, 112–16. **258.** Habenstreit, *Men Against War*, 151–2; Bennett, 'American pacifism', 264, 272–3, 275–7; Bennett, '"Free American political prisoners"', 414–15. **259.** Bennett, '"Free American political prisoners"', 413–14, 423–30.

8. Civilian Wars

1. Raymond Daniell, *Civilians Must Fight* (New York, 1941), 4–5. **2.** Mark Edele, *Stalin's Defectors: How Red Army Soldiers became Hitler's Collaborators, 1941–1945* (New York, 2017), 177; on British civil defence statistics, Fred Iklé, *The Social Impact of Bomb Destruction* (Norman, Okla, 1958), 163–4. **3.** Alexander Gogun, *Stalin's Commandos: Ukrainian Partisan Forces on the Eastern Front* (London, 2016), 155–7. **4.** Margaret Anagnostopoulou, 'From heroines to hyenas: women partisans during the Greek civil war', *Contemporary European History*, 10 (2001), 491, from the author's interview with a veteran partisan. **5.** Giulio Douhet, *The Command of the Air* (Maxwell, Ala, 2019), 14–24; see too Thomas Hippler, *Bombing the People: Giulio Douhet and the Foundations of Air-Power Strategy, 1884–1939* (Cambridge, 2013), ch. 4. **6.** On these tropes see John Konvitz, 'Représentations urbaines et bombardements stratégiques', *Annales*, 44 (1989), 823–47; Susan Grayzel, '"A promise of terror to come": air power and the destruction of cities in British imagination and experience, 1908–39', in Stefan Goebel and Derek Keene (eds.), *Cities into Battlefields:*

Metropolitan Scenarios, Experiences and Commemorations of Total War (Farnham, 2011), 47–62. 7. Ian Patterson, *Guernica and Total War* (London, 2007), 110. 8. Goldsworthy Lowes Dickinson, *War: Its Nature, Cause and Cure* (London, 1923), 12–13. 9. Franco Manaresi, 'La protezione antiaerea', in Cristina Bersani and Valeria Monaco (eds.), *Delenda Bononia: immagini dei bombardamenti 1943–1945* (Bologna, 1995), 29–30. 10. Foreword to Stephen Spender, *Citizens in War – and After* (London, 1945), 5. 11. Terence O'Brien, *Civil Defence* (London, 1955), 690, Appendix X. On the issue of gender roles see Lucy Noakes, '"Serve to save": gender, citizenship and civil defence in Britain 1937–41', *Journal of Contemporary History*, 47 (2012), 748–9. 12. Matthew Dallek, *Defenseless Under the Night: The Roosevelt Years and the Origins of Homeland Security* (New York, 2016), 248–9. 13. Richard Overy, *The Bombing War: Europe 1939–1945* (London, 2013), 215–17. 14. BAB, R 1501/823, Luftschutzgesetz, 7 Durchführungsverordnung, 31 Aug. 1943. 15. Bernd Lemke, *Luftschutz in Grossbritannien und Deutschland 1923 bis 1939* (Munich, 2005), 254–6. 16. O'Brien, *Civil Defence*, chs. 3–5; Lemke, *Luftschutz*, 342–62. 17. TNA, HO 186/602, Statistics on Civil Defence Personnel, Summary of all Services, 30 June 1940, 14 Nov. 1940; HO 187/1156, historical survey, 'Manpower in the National Fire Service'; Shane Ewen, 'Preparing the British fire service for war: local government, nationalisation and evolutionary reform, 1935–41', *Contemporary British History*, 20 (2006), 216–19; Charles Graves, *Women in Green: The Story of the W. V. S.* (London, 1948), 14–20. 18. O'Brien, *Civil Defence*, 548–58, 690. 19. Claudia Baldoli and Andrew Knapp, *Forgotten Blitzes: France and Italy under Allied Air Attack, 1940–1945* (London, 2012), 51–5, 92–3; Service historique de l'armée de l'air, Vincennes, Paris, 3D/44/Dossier 1, 'Formations et effectifs réels, Défense Passive', 15 Jan. 1944. 20. Nicola della Volpe, *Difesa del territorio e protezione antiaerea (1915–1943)* (Rome, 1986), 194–203, doc. 17 'Istruzione sulla protezione antiaerea'. 21. Ibid., 46–8; Baldoli and Knapp, *Forgotten Blitzes*, 54. 22. Larry Bland (ed.), *The Papers of George Catlett Marshall: Volume 2 'We Cannot Delay'* (Baltimore, Md, 1986), 607–8, Radio broadcast on the Citizens' Defense Corps, 11 Nov. 1941. 23. Dallek, *Defenseless Under the Night*, 223–5. 24. NARA, RG107, Lovett Papers, Box 139, James Landis, 'We're Not Safe from Air Raids', *Civilian Front*, 15 May 1943. 25. Cambridge University Library, Bernal Papers, Add 8287, Box 58/2, E.P.S. Bulletin No. 1, March 1942. 26. Tetsuo Maeda, 'Strategic bombing of Chongqing by Imperial Japanese Army and Naval Forces', in Yuki Tanaka and Marilyn Young (eds.), *Bombing Civilians: A Twentieth-century History* (New York, 2009), 141. 27. Samuel Yamashita, *Daily Life in Wartime Japan, 1940–1945* (Lawrence, Kans, 2015), 28. 28. RAF Museum, Hendon, Bottomley Papers, AC 71/2/31, Address to the Thirty Club by Richard Peck, 8 Mar. 1944, p. 8. For a full discussion of the shift to area-bombing of industrial cities see Richard Overy, '"The weak link"? The perception of the German working class by RAF Bomber Command, 1940–1945', *Labour History Review*, 77 (2012), 24–31. 29. TNA, AIR 14/783, Air Staff memorandum, 7 Oct. 1943: the aim of area attacks was 'the destruction of workers' housing, the killing of skilled workers, and the general dislocation of public services.' 30. Overy, *The Bombing War*, 328–30. 31. Bland (ed.), *The Papers of George Catlett Marshall: Volume 2*, 678, report of press conference, 15 Nov. 1941. 32. Thomas Searle, '"It made a lot of sense to kill skilled workers": the firebombing of Tokyo in March 1945', *Journal of Military History*, 66 (2002), 116–19. 33. Rana Mitter, *China's War with Japan 1937–1945: The Struggle for Survival* (London, 2013), 191–2; Maeda, 'Strategic bombing of Chongqing', 146–9. 34. Overy, *The Bombing War*, 99–105. 35. Edward Glover, *The Psychology of Fear and Courage* (London, 1940), 35, 63. 36. TNA, HO 186/608, Report of the Regional Commissioner South, 14 Dec. 1940; Ministry of Food report, 'Brief Visit to Southampton, December 3 1940', 5 Dec. 1940. 37. Dietmar Süss, 'Wartime societies and shelter politics in National Socialist Germany and Britain', in Claudia Baldoli, Andrew Knapp and Richard Overy (eds.), *Bombing, States and Peoples in Western Europe, 1940–1945* (London, 2011), 31–3; University of East Anglia, Zuckerman Archive, OEMU/59/13, draft report 'Shelter Habits', Table B, Table C. 38. Kevin Hewitt, 'Place annihilation: area bombing and the fate of urban places', *Annals of the Association of American Geographers*, 73 (1983), 263. 39. TNA, AIR/20/7287, 'Secret Report by the Police President of Hamburg on the Heavy Raids on Hamburg July/August 1943', 1 Dec. 1943, pp. 22–3,

67–8, 87–99. 40. Hans Rumpf, *The Bombing of Germany* (London, 1957), 186–7; Andreas Linhardt, *Feuerwehr im Luftschutz 1926–1945: Die Umstruktierung des öffentlichen Feuerlöschwesens in Deutschland unter Gesichtspunkten des zivilen Luftschutzes* (Brunswick, 2002), 171–82. 41. Iklé, *Social Impact of Bomb Destruction*, 67–8. 42. Yamashita, *Daily Life in Wartime Japan*, 102, from a letter sent in May 1945. See too Aaron Moore, *Bombing the City: Civilian Accounts of the Air War in Britain and Japan 1939–1945* (Cambridge, 2018), 112–14. 43. USSBS Pacific Theater, Report 11, 6, 69. 44. China Information Committee, *China After Four Years of War* (Chongqing, 1941), 174–5. 45. USSBS Pacific Theater, Report 11, 69, 200. 46. Ibid., 2, 9–11. 47. Statistics from the following: France, Jean-Charles Foucrier, *La stratégie de la destruction: Bombardements allies en France, 1944* (Paris, 2017), 9–10; China, Diana Lary, *The Chinese People at War: Human Suffering and Social Transformation, 1937–1945* (Cambridge, 2010), 89. 48. Mitter, *China's War with Japan*, 231–2. 49. Bernard Donoughue and G. W. Jones, *Herbert Morrison: Portrait of a Politician* (London, 2001), 316–18. 50. Edna Tow, 'The great bombing of Chongqing and the Anti-Japanese War, 1937–1945', in Mark Peattie, Edward Drea and Hans van de Ven (eds.), *The Battle for China: Essays on the Military History of the Sino-Japanese War of 1937–1945* (Stanford, Calif., 2011), 269–70, 277–8. 51. China Information Committee, *China After Four Years of War*, 179. 52. CCAC, CHAR 9/182B, Notes for a speech to civil defence workers, County Hall, London, 12 July 1940, pp. 4–5. 53. Matthew Cobb, *The Resistance: The French Fight against the Nazis* (New York, 2009), 39–40. 54. Tom Behan, *The Italian Resistance: Fascists, Guerrillas and the Allies* (London, 2008), 67–8; Cobb, *The Resistance*, 163–4. 55. On the Chinese case see Poshek Fu, 'Resistance in collaboration: Chinese cinema in occupied Shanghai, 1940–1943', in David Barrett and Larry Shyu (eds.), *Chinese Collaboration with Japan 1932–1945* (Stanford, Calif., 2002),180, 193. 56. Robert Gildea, *Fighters in the Shadows: A New History of the French Resistance* (London, 2015), 70–71, 143–4. 57. Chang-tai Hung, *War and Popular Culture: Resistance in Modern China, 1937–1945* (Berkeley, Calif., 1994), 221–30. 58. Cobb, *The Resistance*, 223–4. 59. Gaj Trifković, '"Damned good amateurs": Yugoslav partisans in the Belgrade operation 1944', *Journal of Slavic Military Studies*, 29 (2016), 256, 270; Yang Kuisong, 'Nationalist and Communist guerrilla warfare in north China', in Peattie, Drea and van de Ven (eds.), *The Battle for China*, 325; John Loulis, *The Greek Communist Party 1940–1944* (London, 1982), 153. 60. Shmuel Krakowski, *The War of the Doomed: Jewish Armed Resistance in Poland 1942–1944* (New York, 1984), 5. 61. Svetozar Vukmanović, *How and Why the People's Liberation Struggle of Greece Met with Defeat* (London, 1985), 41, citing Mao Zedong in *The Strategic Problems of the Chinese Revolutionary War*. 62. L. S. Stavrianos, 'The Greek National Liberation Front (EAM): a study in resistance organization and administration', *Journal of Modern History*, 24 (1952), 43. 63. Cobb, *The Resistance*, 60–63. 64. Olivier Wieviorka and Jack Tebinka, 'Resisters: from everyday life to counter-state', in Robert Gildea, Olivier Wieviorka and Annette Warring (eds.), *Surviving Hitler and Mussolini; Daily Life in Occupied Europe* (Oxford, 2006), 158–9. 65. Behan, *The Italian Resistance*, 45–8. 66. Philippe Buton, *Les lendemains qui déchantant: Le Parti communiste français à la Libération* (Paris, 1993), 269. 67. Kuisong, 'Nationalist and Communist guerrilla warfare', 323–5; Daoxuan Huang, 'The cultivation of Communist cadres during the war of resistance against Japanese aggression', *Journal of Modern Chinese History*, 10 (2016), 138. 68. Julia Ebbinghaus, 'Les journaux clandestins rédigés par les femmes: une résistance spécifique', in Mechtild Gilzmer, Christine Levisse-Touzé and Stefan Martens, *Les femmes dans la Résistance en France* (Paris, 2003), 141–4, 148–50; Jean-Marie Guillon, 'Les manifestations de ménagères: protestation populaire et résistance féminine spécifique', ibid., 115–20. 69. Julian Jackson, *France: The Dark Years 1940–1945* (Oxford, 2001), 491–4. 70. Barbara Jancar, 'Women in the Yugoslav National Liberation Movement: an overview', *Studies in Comparative Communism*, 14 (1981), 150, 155–6. 71. Jomane Alano, 'Armed with the yellow mimosa: women's defence and assistance groups in Italy 1943–45', *Journal of Contemporary History*, 38 (2003), 615, 618–20. 72. Gildea, *Fighters in the Shadows*, 131. 73. Alano, 'Armed with the yellow mimosa', 616. 74. Anagnostopoulou, 'From heroines to hyenas', 481–2. 75. Jelena Batinić, *Women and Yugoslav Partisans: A History of World War II Resistance* (Cambridge, 2015), 128–9, 143–8,

156–7; Jancar, 'Women in the Yugoslav National Liberation Army', 155–6, 161.   76. Cobb, *The Resistance*, 185.   77. Stavrianos, 'The Greek National Liberation Front', 45–50; Dominique Eudes, *The Kapetanios: Partisans and Civil War in Greece, 1943–1949* (London, 1972), 22–3.   78. Spyros Tsoutsoumpis, *A History of the Greek Resistance in the Second World War* (Manchester, 2016), 226.   79. Anika Walke, *Pioneers and Partisans: An Oral History of Nazi Genocide in Belorussia* (New York, 2015), 191–2.   80. Hans van de Ven, *China at War: Triumph and Tragedy in the Emergence of the New China, 1937–1952* (London, 2017), 139–41; Kuisong, 'Nationalist and Communist guerrilla warfare', 309–10.   81. Eudes, *The Kapetanios*, 22.   82. Trifković, '"Damned good amateurs"', 271.   83. Halik Kochanski, *The Eagle Unbowed: Poland and the Poles in the Second World War* (London, 2012), 389–90.   84. Kuisong, 'Nationalist and Communist guerrilla warfare', 319–20.   85. Peter Seybolt, 'The war within a war: a case study of a county on the North China Plain', in Barrett and Shyu (eds.), *Chinese Collaboration with Japan*, 221.   86. Ben Hillier, 'The Huk rebellion and the Philippines radical tradition', in Donny Gluckstein (ed.), *Fighting on All Fronts: Popular Resistance in the Second World War* (London, 2015), 327.   87. Mark Mazower, *Inside Hitler's Greece: The Experience of Occupation, 1941–44* (New Haven, Conn., 1993), 289–90, 318–20.   88. Gogun, *Stalin's Commandos*, 109.   89. Hans-Heinrich Nolte, 'Partisan war in Belorussia, 1941–1945', in Roger Chickering, Stig Förster and Bernd Greiner (eds.), *A World at Total War: Global Conflict and the Politics of Destruction, 1937–1945* (Cambridge, 2005), 268–70, 271–3.   90. Loulis, *The Greek Communist Party*, 85–90, 122; Stavrianos, 'The Greek National Liberation Front', 42–3; John Iatrides, 'Revolution or self-defense? Communist goals, strategy, and tactics in the Greek civil war', *Journal of Cold War Studies*, 7 (2005), 7–8.   91. Stevan Pavlowitch, *Hitler's New Disorder: The Second World War in Yugoslavia* (London, 2008), 114–15.   92. Van de Ven, *China at War*, 146–9.   93. Lifeng Li, 'Rural mobilization in the Chinese Communist Revolution: from the anti-Japanese war to the Chinese civil war', *Journal of Modern Chinese History*, 9 (2015), 97–101.   94. Eudes, *The Kapetanios*, 5–6, 13–14.   95. Stavrianos, 'The Greek National Liberation Front', 45–8.   96. Mazower, *Inside Hitler's Greece*, 265–79.   97. Tsoutsoumpis, *History of the Greek Resistance*, 8–9, 214–18.   98. Iatrides, 'Revolution or self-defense?', 6.   99. André Gerolymatos, *An International Civil War: Greece, 1943–1949* (New Haven, Conn., 2016), 287–8.   100. John Newman, *Yugoslavia in the Shadow of War* (Cambridge, 2015), 241–61.   101. David Motadel, *Islam and Nazi Germany's War* (Cambridge, Mass., 2014), 178–83; Pavlowitch, *Hitler's New Disorder*, 115–17, 124–32.   102. Motadel, *Islam and Nazi Germany's War*, 183, 212; Pavlowitch, *Hitler's New Disorder*, 142–5.   103. Pavlowitch, *Hitler's New Disorder*, 106.   104. Blaž Torkar, 'The Yugoslav armed forces in exile', in Vít Smetana and Kathleen Geaney (eds.), *Exile in London: The Experience of Czechoslovakia and the Other Occupied Nations 1939–1945* (Prague, 2017), 117–20.   105. Gaj Trifković, 'The key to the Balkans: the battle for Serbia 1944', *Journal of Slavic Military Studies*, 28 (2015), 544–9.   106. Gogun, *Stalin's Commandos*, 10.   107. Jared McBride, 'Peasants into perpetrators: the OUN-UPA and the ethnic cleansing of Volhynia, 1943–1944', *Slavic Review*, 75 (2016), 630–31, 636–7.   108. Seybolt, 'The war within a war', 205–15.   109. Li, 'Rural mobilization', 98–9.   110. Geraldien von Künzel, 'Resistance, reprisals, reactions', in Gildea, Wieviorka and Warring (eds.), *Surviving Hitler and Mussolini*, 179–81.   111. Mark Kilion, 'The Netherlands 1940–1945: war of liberation', in Gluckstein (ed.), *Fighting on All Fronts*, 147–8.   112. Seybolt, 'The war within a war', 219–20.   113. Gogun, *Stalin's Commandos*, 187–8; Wieviorka and Tebinka, 'Resisters', 169.   114. Cobb, *The Resistance*, 163.   115. *European Resistance Movements 1939–1945: First International Conference on the History of the Resistance Movements* (London, 1960), 351–2.   116. Cobb, *The Resistance*, 183–4.   117. Gogun, *Stalin's Commandos*, 45–6.   118. Ibid., 56–9.   119. Nolte, 'Partisan war in Belorussia', 274–5.   120. Gogun, *Stalin's Commandos*, xv–xvi; A. A. Maslov, 'Concerning the role of partisan warfare in Soviet military doctrine of the 1920s and 1930s', *Journal of Slavic Military Studies*, 9 (1996), 892–3.   121. Trifković, '"Damned good amateurs"', 261; Loulis, *The Greek Communist Party*, 81–2.   122. Anita Prazmowska, 'The Polish underground resistance during the Second World War: a study in political disunity during occupation', *European History Quarterly*, 43 (2013), 465–7, 472–4.   123. Tadeusz Bór-Komorowski, 'Le mouvement de Varsovie', in *European Resistance Movements*, 287. **124.** Kochanski, *The Eagle Unbowed*, 385–6, 395. **125.** Ibid., 390–92, 396–7. **126.** Bór-Komorowski, 'Le mouvement de Varsovie', 288–9. **127.** Alexandra Richie, *Warsaw 1944: The Fateful Uprising* (London, 2013), 176–80. **128.** Kazik (Simha Rotem), *Memoirs of a Warsaw Ghetto Fighter* (New Haven, Conn., 1994), 119, 122. **129.** Ewa Stańczyk, 'Heroes, victims, role models: representing the child soldiers of the Warsaw uprising', *Slavic Review*, 74 (2015), 740; Kochanski, *The Eagle Unbowed*, 402, 424–5. **130.** David Glantz, 'Stalin's strategic intentions 1941–45', *Journal of Slavic Military Studies*, 27 (2014), 687–91; Alexander Statiev, *The Soviet Counterinsurgency in the Western Borderlands* (Cambridge, 2010), 120–22. **131.** Valentin Berezhkov, *History in the Making: Memoirs of World War II Diplomacy* (Moscow, 1983), 357–8; David Reynolds and Vladimir Pechatnov (eds.), *The Kremlin Letters: Stalin's Wartime Correspondence with Churchill and Roosevelt* (New Haven, Conn., 2018), 459, Stalin to Churchill 16 Aug. 1944. **132.** TNA, AIR 8/1169, Despatches from MAAF on Dropping Operations to Warsaw [n.d.]; Norman Davies, *Rising '44: The Battle for Warsaw* (London, 2003), 310–11; Kochanski, *The Eagle Unbowed*, 408–11. **133.** Richie, *Warsaw 1944*, 610, 617. **134.** Statiev, *Soviet Counterinsurgency*, 122. **135.** Krakowski, *War of the Doomed*, 8–9. **136.** Dongill Kim, 'Stalin and the Chinese civil war', *Cold War History*, 10 (2010), 186–91. **137.** Loulis, *The Greek Communist Party*, 81–2. **138.** Iatrides, '"Revolution or self-defense?"', 11–12, 16–18, 19–21. **139.** Tommaso Piffer, 'Stalin, the Western Allies and Soviet policy towards the Yugoslav partisan movement 1941–4', *Journal of Contemporary History*, 54 (2019), 424–37. **140.** Glantz, 'Stalin's strategic intentions', 690, Directive of 5 Sept. 1944. **141.** Trefković, '"Damned good amateurs"', 254–5, 276–7. **142.** Pavlowitch, *Hitler's New Disorder*, 236. **143.** Michael Foot, *SOE: The Special Operations Executive 1940–46* (London, 1984), 20–21. **144.** Olivier Wieviorka, *The Resistance in Western Europe 1940–1945* (New York, 2019), 27. **145.** TNA, FO 898/457, 'Annual Dissemination of Leaflets by Aircraft and Balloon 1939–1945'. **146.** Richard Overy, 'Bruce Lockhart, British political warfare and occupied Europe', in Smetana and Geaney (eds.), *Exile in London*, 201–4. **147.** TNA, FO 898/338, PWE 'Special Directive on Food and Agriculture', 1 Aug. 1942; PWE memorandum 'The Peasant in Western Europe', 5 Apr. 1943; Major Baker to Ritchie Calder (PWE), 'The Peasant Revolt', 13 Feb. 1942. **148.** TNA, FO 898/340, Patrick Gordon-Walker, 'Harnessing the Trojan Horse', 31 Mar. 1944; SHAEF Political Warfare Division, 'Propaganda to Germany: The Final Phase', 4 July 1944. **149.** TNA, FO 800/879, Dr Jan Kraus to Lockhart, 10 Nov. 1942; FO 898/420, 'Suggested Enquiry into the Effects of British Political Warfare against Germany', 12 July 1945. **150.** Ian Dear, *Sabotage and Subversion: The SOE and OSS at War* (London, 1996), 12–13. **151.** Ibid., 12–14. **152.** Foot, *SOE*, 171. **153.** Peter Wilkinson, *Foreign Fields: The Story of an SOE Operative* (London, 1997), 148. **154.** Mazower, *Inside Hitler's Greece*, 297–8, 352. **155.** Gerolymatos, *An International Civil War*, 138–41. **156.** Mark Seaman, '"The most difficult country": some practical considerations on British support for clandestine operations in Czechoslovakia during the Second World War', in Smetana and Geaney (eds.), *Exile in London*, 131–2; David Stafford, *Mission Accomplished: SOE and Italy 1943–45* (London, 2011), 225. **157.** Michael Foot, *SOE in France* (London, 1966), 473–4. **158.** Stafford, *Mission Accomplished*, 223. **159.** Olivier Wieviorka, *Histoire de la résistance 1940–1945* (Paris, 2013), 498–9. **160.** Gabriella Gribaudi, *Guerra Totale: Tra bombe alleate e violenze naziste: Napoli e il fronte meridionale 1940–44* (Turin, 2005), 197. **161.** Ibid., 197–8; Behan, *The Italian Resistance*, 37–8. **162.** Santo Peli, *Storia della Resistenza in Italia* (Turin, 2006), 121–3. **163.** Max Corvo, *OSS Italy 1942–1945* (New York, 1990), 215. **164.** Peli, *Storia della Resistenza*, 152–3. **165.** Tommaso Piffer, *Gli Alleati e la Resistenza italiana* (Bologna, 2010), 177–81; Stafford, *Mission Accomplished*, 226; Behan, *The Italian Resistance*, 89–2. **166.** Corvo, *OSS Italy*, 227; Peli, *Storia della Resistenza*, 113–14. **167.** Peli, *Storia della Resistenza*, 114, 123–5, 139. **168.** Corvo, *OSS Italy*, 228. **169.** Stafford, *Mission Accomplished*, 217; Peli, *Storia della Resistenza*, 137–9, **170.** Claudio Pavone, *A Civil War: A History of the Italian Resistance* (London, 2013), 603–4. **171.** Peli, *Storia della Resistenza*, 160–61. **172.** Piffer, *Gli Alleati e la Resistenza*, 227–8. **173.** Pavone, *A Civil War*, 609–10. **174.** Dear, *Sabotage and Subversion*, 155, 182–3. **175.** Georges Ribeill, 'Aux prises avec les voies ferrées: bombarder ou saboter? Un dilemme revisité', in Michèle Battesti and Patrick Facon (eds.), *Les bombardements alliés sur la France durant la Seconde Guerre Mondiale: stratégies, bilans matériaux et humains* (Vincennes, 2009), 162; CCAC, BUFt 3/51, SHAEF report 'The Effect of the Overlord Plan to Disrupt Enemy Rail Communications', pp. 1–2. **176.** Wieviorka, *Histoire de la résistance*, 504–5. **177.** Buton, *Les lendemains qui déchantent*, 104–5. **178.** Thomas Laub, *After the Fall: German Policy in Occupied France 1940–1944* (Oxford, 2010), 277–80 for details of reprisal policy in 1944. **179.** Wieviorka, *Histoire de la résistance*, 507, 522–3; Buton, *Les lendemains qui déchantent*, 91–2. **180.** Raymond Aubrac, *The French Resistance, 1940–1944* (Paris, 1997), 35–7; Gildea, *Fighters in the Shadows*, 386–8. **181.** Gildea, *Fighters in the Shadows*, 394–5. **182.** Jean Guéhenno, *Diary of the Dark Years, 1940–1944: Collaboration, Resistance, and Daily Life in Occupied Paris* (Oxford, 2014), 270, entry for 21 Aug. 1944. **183.** Jean-François Muracciole, *Histoire de la Résistance en France* (Paris, 1993), 119–20; Gildea, *Fighters in the Shadows*, 395–401. **184.** Philibert de Loisy, *1944, les FFI deviennent soldats: L'amalgame: De la résistance à l'armée régulière* (Paris, 2014), 187–9, 192–3, 258–9. **185.** Richard Barry, 'Statement by U.K. representatives', in *European Resistance Movements*, 351. **186.** Maria Pasini, *Brescia 1945* (Brescia, 2015), 40–41. **187.** Nechama Tec, *Defiance: The Bielski Partisans* (New York, 1993), 81–2. **188.** Léon Nisand, *De l'étoile jaune à la Résistance armée: Combat pour la dignité humaine 1942–1944* (Besançon, 2006), 21. **189.** Renée Poznanski, 'Geopolitics of Jewish resistance in France', *Holocaust and Genocide Studies*, 15 (2001), 256–7; idem, 'Reflections on Jewish resistance and Jewish resistants in France', *Jewish Social Studies*, 2 (1995), 129, 134–5. **190.** Walke, *Pioneers and Partisans*, 132–4; Zvi Bar-On, 'On the position of the Jewish partisan in the Soviet partisan movement', in *European Resistance Movements*, 210–11. **191.** Christian Gerlach, *The Extermination of the European Jews* (Cambridge, 2016), 407, 409–10. **192.** Kochanski, *The Eagle Unbowed*, 303; on Belorussia, Walke, *Pioneers and Partisans*, 121–5. **193.** Kochanski, *The Eagle Unbowed*, 319–21; Janey Stone, 'Jewish resistance in Eastern Europe', in Gluckstein (ed.), *Fighting on All Fronts*, 113–18. **194.** Philip Friedman, 'Jewish resistance to Nazism: its various forms and aspects', in *European Resistance Movements*, 198–9. **195.** Rachel Einwohner, 'Opportunity, honor and action in the Warsaw Ghetto 1943', *American Journal of Sociology*, 109 (2003), 665. **196.** Ibid., 661. **197.** Krakowski, *War of the Doomed*, 163–5. **198.** Gustavo Corni, *Hitler's Ghettos: Voices from a Beleaguered Society 1939–1944* (London, 2002), 306–7. **199.** Ibid., 293–7. **200.** James Glass, *Jewish Resistance During the Holocaust: Moral Uses of Violence and Will* (Basingstoke, 2004), 21–2; Friedman, 'Jewish resistance', 196–7. **201.** Friedman, 'Jewish resistance', 201–2; Corni, *Hitler's Ghettos*, 303. **202.** Eric Sterling, 'The ultimate sacrifice: the death of resistance hero Yitzhak Wittenberg and the decline of the United Partisan Organisation', in Ruby Rohrlich (ed.), *Resisting the Holocaust* (Oxford, 1998), 59–62. **203.** Ibid., 63; Einwohner, 'Opportunity, honor and action', 660. **204.** Suzanne Weber, 'Shedding city life: survival mechanisms of forest fugitives during the Holocaust', *Holocaust Studies*, 18 (2002), 2; Krakowski, *War of the Doomed*, 10–11. **205.** Glass, *Jewish Resistance*, 3, 14. Revenge featured widely in the oral testimony Glass gathered from Jewish survivors of the guerrilla movement. **206.** Walke, *Pioneers and Partisans*, 164–5; Glass, *Jewish Resistance*, 80. **207.** Walke, *Pioneers and Partisans*, 180–81; Tec, *Defiance: The Bielski Partisans*, 81–2; Friedman, 'Jewish resistance', 191; Glass, *Jewish Resistance*, 9–10. **208.** Tec, *Defiance: The Bielski Partisans*, 73; Krakowski, *War of the Doomed*, 13–16. **209.** Weber, 'Shedding city life', 5–14, 21–2. **210.** Krakowski, *War of the Doomed*, 12–13; Weber, 'Shedding city life', 23–4. **211.** Glass, *Jewish Resistance*, 3, 93; Bar-On, 'On the position of the Jewish partisan', 235–6. **212.** Amir Weiner, ' "Something to die for, a lot to kill for": the Soviet system and the barbarisation of warfare', in George Kassimeris (ed.), *The Barbarisation of Warfare* (London, 2006), 119. **213.** Stone, 'Jewish resistance in Eastern Europe', 102; Saul Friedländer, *The Years of Extermination: Nazi Germany and the Jews 1939–1945* (London, 2007), 525. **214.** Gildea, *Fighters in the Shadows*, 229–30. **215.** Poznanski, 'Geopolitics of Jewish resistance', 250, 254–8. **216.** Stone, 'Jewish resistance in Eastern Europe', 104; Rohrlich (ed.), *Resisting the Holocaust*, 2. **217.** Frediano Sessi, *Auschwitz: Storia e memorie* (Venice, 2020), 316. **218.** Friedländer, *The Years of Extermination*, 557–9. **219.** For a detailed description see

Krakowski, *War of the Doomed*, 163–89; Friedländer, *The Years of Extermination*, 520–24. **220**. Kochanski, *The Eagle Unbowed*, 309–10. **221**. Kazik, *Memoirs of a Warsaw Ghetto Fighter*, 34. **222.** Krakowski, *War of the Doomed*, 211–13; Stone, 'Jewish resistance in Eastern Europe', 101–2; Friedman, 'Jewish resistance', 204; Corni, *Hitler's Ghettos*, 317–20.

9. The Emotional Geography of War

1. *Last Letters from Stalingrad*, trs. Anthony Powell (London, 1956), 61–3. **2**. Ibid., v–vii. **3**. Ibid., 24–5. **4**. Cited in Pat Jalland, *Death in War and Peace: A History of Loss and Grief in England 1914–1970* (Oxford, 2010), 172–3. **5**. Svetlana Alexievich, *The Unwomanly Face of War* (London, 2017), 135–6, interview with Olga Omelchenko. **6**. David Grossman, 'Human factors in war: the psychology and physiology of close combat', in Michael Evans and Alan Ryan (eds.), *The Human Face of Warfare: Killing, Fear and Chaos in Battle* (London, 2000), 10. Psychiatrists and neurologists now agree that the threat of being killed and killing others are the principal 'stressors' in combat situations. **7**. Thomas Brown, '"Stress" in US wartime psychiatry: World War II and the immediate aftermath', in David Cantor and Edmund Ramsden (eds.), *Stress, Shock and Adaptation in the Twentieth Century* (Rochester, NY, 2014), 123. **8**. Ann-Marie Condé, '"The ordeal of adjustment": Australian psychiatric casualties of the Second World War', *War & Society*, 15 (1997), 65–6. **9**. Emma Newlands, *Civilians into Soldiers: War, the Body and British Army Recruits 1939–1945* (Manchester, 2014), 156; Condé, '"The ordeal of adjustment"', 64–5; Walter Bromberg, *Psychiatry Between the Wars 1918–1945* (New York, 1982), 162. **10**. Grossman, 'Human factors in war', 7; Paul Wanke, '"Inevitably any man has his threshold": Soviet military psychiatry during World War II – a comparative approach', *Journal of Slavic Military Studies*, 16 (2003), 92; Paul Wanke, 'American military psychiatry and its role among ground forces in World War II', *Journal of Military History*, 63 (1999), 127–33. **11**. Robert Ahrenfeldt, *Psychiatry in the British Army in the Second World War* (London, 1958), 175–6, 278; Terry Copp and Bill McAndrew, *Battle Exhaustion: Soldiers and Psychiatrists in the Canadian Army* (Montreal, 1990), 126. **12**. Frederick McGuire, *Psychology Aweigh! A History of Clinical Psychology in the United States Navy 1900–1988* (Washington, DC, 1990), 99–100. **13**. Wanke, '"Inevitably any man has his threshold"', 94, who suggests a comparison with the rate of American casualty, producing from 18,319,723 Red Army casualties a total of 1,007,585 on psychiatric grounds. For the more modest figure, see Catherine Merridale, *Ivan's War: The Red Army 1939–1945* (London, 2005), 232. The true figure is certainly higher since many cases went undiagnosed, or men were killed or captured before their symptoms could be medically ascertained. **14**. Peter Riedesser and Axel Verderber, *'Maschinengewehre hinter der Front': Zur Geschichte der deutschen Militärpsychiatrie* (Frankfurt/Main, 1996), 146–7, 168; Klaus Blassneck, *Militärpsychiatrie im Nationalsozialismus* (Würzburg, 2000), 35–7. **15**. Paolo Giovannini, *La psichiatria di guerra: Dal fascismo alla seconda guerra mondiale* (Milan, 2015), 73–6. **16**. Bromberg, *Psychiatry Between the Wars*, 163; Copp and McAndrew, *Battle Exhaustion*, 135; Roger Reese, *Why Stalin's Soldiers Fought: The Red Army's Military Effectiveness in World War II* (Lawrence, Kans, 2011), 238–9. **17**. Reese, *Why Stalin's Soldiers Fought*, 173–5. **18**. Mark Edele, *Stalin's Defectors: How Red Army Soldiers Became Hitler's Collaborators, 1941–1945* (Oxford, 2017), 30–31, 111. **19**. Samuel Yamashita, *Daily Life in Wartime Japan 1940–1945* (Lawrence, Kans, 2015), 159. **20**. US figures from Paul Fussell, *The Boys' Crusade: American G.I.s in Europe: Chaos and Fear in World War Two* (London, 2004), 108; British figures from Ahrenfeldt, *Psychiatry in the British Army*, Appendix B, 273; German figures from Dieter Knippschild, '"Für mich ist der Krieg aus": Deserteure in der deutschen Wehrmacht', in Norbert Haase and Gerhard Paul (eds.), *Die anderen Soldaten: Wehrkraftzersetzung, Gehorsamsverweigerung und Fahnenflucht im Zweiten Weltkrieg* (Frankfurt/Main, 1995), 123, 126–31; on Italy, Mimmo Franzinelli, *Disertori: Una storia mai racconta della seconda guerra mondiale* (Milan, 2016), 133–49. **21**. Jonathan Fennell, 'Courage and cowardice in the North African campaign: the Eighth Army and defeat in the summer of 1942', *War in History*, 20 (2013), 102-5. **22.** On Italy see Albert Cowdrey, *Fighting for Life: American Military Medicine in World War II* (New York, 1994), 149-50; Copp and McAndrew, *Battle Exhaustion*, 50-51. On the Indian front, B. L. Raina, *World War II: Medical Services: India* (New Delhi, 1990), 40-41. **23.** Brown, '"Stress" in US wartime psychiatry', 127. **24.** Cowdrey, *Fighting for Life*, 151; G. Kurt Piehler, 'Veterans tell their stories and why historians and others listened', in G. Kurt Piehler and Sidney Pash (eds.), *The United States and the Second World War: New Perspectives on Diplomacy, War, and the Home Front* (New York, 2010), 228-9; Rebecca Plant, 'Preventing the inevitable: John Appel and the problem of psychiatric casualties in the US Army in World War II', in Frank Biess and Daniel Gross (eds.), *Science and Emotions after 1945* (Chicago, Ill., 2014), 212-17. **25.** Blassneck, *Militärpsychiatrie im Nationalsozialismus*, 20. **26.** Grossman 'Human factors in war', 7-8; Edgar Jones, 'LMF: the use of psychiatric stigma in the Royal Air Force during the Second World War', *Journal of Military History*, 70 (2006), 449; Cowdrey, *Fighting for Life*, 151; Ahrenfeldt, *Psychiatry in the British Army*, 172-3; Plant, 'Preventing the inevitable', 222. **27.** On emotional crisis in the First World War see, for example, Michael Roper, *The Secret Battle: Emotional Survival in the Great War* (Manchester, 2009), 247-50, 260-65. **28.** On changes in German attitudes to 'shell-shock' see Jason Crouthamel, '"Hysterische Männer?" Traumatisierte Veteranen des Ersten Weltkrieges und ihr Kampf um Anerkennung im "Dritten Reich"', in Babette Quinkert, Philipp Rauh and Ulrike Winkler (eds.), *Krieg und Psychiatrie: 1914-1950* (Göttingen, 2010), 29-34. On the arguments in the United States see Martin Halliwell, *Therapeutic Revolutions: Medicine, Psychiatry and American Culture 1945-1970* (New Brunswick, NJ, 2013), 20-27, and in Britain, Harold Merskey, 'After shell-shock: aspects of hysteria since 1922', in Hugh Freeman and German Berrios (eds.), *150 Years of British Psychiatry: Volume II: The Aftermath* (London, 1996), 89-92. **29.** Bromberg, *Psychiatry Between the Wars*, 158. **30.** Paul Wanke, *Russian/Soviet Military Psychiatry 1904-1945* (London, 2005), 91-2. **31.** Wanke, 'American military psychiatry', 132. **32.** Gerald Grob, 'Der Zweite Weltkrieg und die US-amerikanische Psychiatrie', in Quinkert, Rauh and Winkler (eds.), *Krieg und Psychiatrie*, 153; Cowdrey, *Fighting for Life*, 139; McGuire, *Psychology Aweigh!*, 35-41. **33.** Edgar Jones and Simon Wessely, *Shell Shock to PTSD: Military Psychiatry from 1900 to the Gulf War* (Hove, 2005), 70-71, 76; Ben Shephard, *A War of Nerves: Soldiers and Psychiatrists, 1914-1994* (London, 2000), 195. **34.** Jones, 'LMF', 440, 445; Sydney Brandon, 'LMF in Bomber Command 1939-1945: diagnosis or denouement?', in Freeman and Berrios (eds.), *150 Years of British Psychiatry*, 119-20. **35.** Wanke, '"Inevitably any man has his threshold"', 80-81. **36.** Blassneck, *Militärpsychiatrie im Nationalsozialismus*, 21. **37.** Geoffrey Cocks, *Psychotherapy in the Third Reich: The Göring Institute* (New Brunswick, NJ, 1997), 308-16; Blassneck, *Militärpsychiatrie im Nationalsozialismus*, 41-5; Riedesser and Verderber, 'Maschinengewehre hinter der Front', 135-8. **38.** Wanke, '"Inevitably any man has his threshold"', 92-7. **39.** Janice Matsumura, 'Combating indiscipline in the Imperial Japanese Army: Hayno Torao and psychiatric studies of the crimes of soldiers', *War in History*, 23 (2016), 82-6. **40.** Condé, '"The ordeal of adjustment"', 65. **41.** Brown, '"Stress" in US wartime psychiatry', 123-4 (the quotation is from a 1944 publication by Merrill Moore and J. L. Henderson); Bromberg, *Psychiatry Between the Wars*, 153-8; Halliwell, *Therapeutic Revolutions*, 25; Ellen Herman, *The Romance of American Psychology: Political Culture in the Age of Experts* (Berkeley, Calif., 1995), 86-8. On homosexuality see Naoko Wake, 'The military, psychiatry, and "unfit" soldiers, 1939-1942', *Journal of the History of Medicine and Allied Sciences*, 62 (2007), 473-90. **42.** McGuire, *Psychology Aweigh!*, 101-2; Condé, 'The ordeal of adjustment', 67-8. **43.** Herman, *Romance of American Psychology*, 110-11; Shephard, *War of Nerves*, 235. **44.** R. D. Gillespie, *Psychological Effects of War on Citizen and Soldier* (New York, 1942), 166-72; Shephard, *War of Nerves*, 187-9. **45.** Crouthamel, '"Hysterische Männer?"', 30-34; Manfred Messerschmidt, *Was damals Recht war ... NS-Militär- und Strafjustiz im Vernichtungs krieg* (Essen, 1996), 102-6. **46.** Riedesser and Verderber, 'Maschinengewehre hinter der Front', 103-5, 115-17; Blassneck, *Militärpsychiatrie im Nationalsozialismus*, 17-20, 22-3. **47.** Cowdrey, *Fighting for Life*, 138-9. **48.** Jones, 'LMF', 439-44; Brandon, 'LMF in Bomber Command', 119-23. For a full account of psychiatry and the bomber crews see Mark Wells, *Courage and Air Warfare: The Allied Aircrew Experience in the Second World War* (London, 1995), 60–89. 49. Allan English, 'A predisposition to cowardice? Aviation psychology and the genesis of "Lack of Moral Fibre"', *War & Society*, 13 (1995), 23. 50. Condé, '"The ordeal of adjustment"', 65–72. 51. John McManus, *The Deadly Brotherhood: The American Combat Soldier in World War II* (New York, 1998), 193. 52. Grossman, 'Human factors in war', 9–10, 13–15; Brown, '"Stress" in US wartime psychiatry', 130–32. 53. Blassneck, *Militärpsychiatrie im Nationalsozialismus*, 55–6; Cocks, *Psychotherapy in the Third Reich*, 309–12; Riedesser and Verderber, '*Maschinengewehre hinter der Front*', 145–6. 54. Hans Pols, 'Die Militäroperation in Tunisien 1942/43 und die Neuorientierung des US-amerikanischen Militärpsychiatrie', in Quinkert, Rauh and Winkler (eds.), *Krieg und Psychiatrie*, 133–8. 55. Edgar Jones and Simon Wessely, '"Forward psychiatry" in the military: its origin and effectiveness', *Journal of Traumatic Stress*, 16 (2003), 413–15; Mark Harrison, *Medicine and Victory: British Military Medicine in the Second World War* (Oxford, 2004), 171–3. 56. Raina, *World War II: Medical Services*, 41. 57. Riedesser and Verderber, '*Maschinengewehre hinter der Front*', 135–7. 58. Catherine Merridale, 'The collective mind: trauma and shell-shock in twentieth-century Russia', *Journal of Contemporary History*, 35 (2000), 43–7. 59. Merridale, *Ivan's War*, 232; Cowdrey, *Fighting for Life*, 137. 60. Gillespie, *Psychological Effects of War*, 32–3, 191–4; Edgar Jones and Stephen Ironside, 'Battle exhaustion: the dilemma of psychiatric casualties in Normandy, June–August 1944', *Historical Journal*, 53 (2010), 112–13. 61. Pols, 'Die Militäroperation in Tunisien', 135–7. 62. Giovannini, *La psichiatria di Guerra*, 74–6. 63. Ibid., 137–9. 64. Ahrenfeldt, *Psychiatry in the British Army*, 168–70; Jones and Wessely, '"Forward psychiatry"', 411–15. 65. Jones and Ironside, 'Battle exhaustion', 114. 66. Cowdrey, *Fighting for Life*, 149–50; Pols, 'Die Militäroperation in Tunisien', 140–42; Harrison, *Medicine and Victory*, 114. 67. Ahrenfeldt, *Psychiatry in the British Army*, 155–6. 68. Blassneck, *Militärpsychiatrie im Nationalsozialismus*, 47–53, 73–85; Riedesser and Verderber, '*Maschinengewehre hinter der Front*', 118–23, 140–43, 153–6. 69. Aaron Moore, *Writing War: Soldiers Record the Japanese Empire* (Cambridge, Mass., 2013), 94, 95, 127. 70. Harrison, *Medicine and Victory*, 177. 71. Gillespie, *Psychological Effects of War*, 166. 72. Ahrenfeldt, *Psychiatry in the British Army*, 167. 73. Halliwell, *Therapeutic Revolutions*, 27. 74. Merridale, *Ivan's War*, 282. 75. Matsumura, 'Combating indiscipline', 82–3, 90–91. 76. This is evident in the tape-recorded conversations of German prisoners when they talked of military virtues. See Sönke Neitzel and Harald Welzer, *Soldaten: Protokolle vom Kämpfen, Töten und Sterben* (Frankfurt/Main, 2011), 299–307. 77. Franzinelli, *Disertori*, 115–16. 78. Reese, *Why Stalin's Soldiers Fought*, 161–5, 173–5. 79. Ibid., 171. 80. Blassneck, *Militärpsychiatrie im Nationalsozialismus*, 47–50; Riedesser and Verderber, '*Maschinengewehre hinter der Front*', 109, 115–16, 163–6. 81. Omer Bartov, *Hitler's Army: Soldiers, Nazis, and War in the Third Reich* (New York, 1991), 96–9. 82. Knippschild, '"Für mich ist der Krieg aus"', 123–6. 83. Fietje Ausländer, '"Zwölf Jahre Zuchthaus! Abzusitzen nach Kriegsende!" Zur Topographie des Strafgefangenenwesens der deutschen Wehrmacht', in Haase and Paul (eds.), *Die anderen Soldaten*, 64; Jürgen Thomas, '"Nur das ist für die Truppe Recht, was ihr nützt . . ." Die Wehrmachtjustiz im Zweiten Weltkrieg', ibid., 48. 84. Fennell, 'Courage and cowardice', 100. 85. Jones 'LMF', 448; Brandon, 'LMF in Bomber Command', 120–21. 86. Alan Allport, *Browned Off and Bloody Minded: The British Soldier Goes to War 1939–1945* (New Haven, Conn., 2015), 251, 256. 87. Newlands, *Civilians into Soldiers*, 137–8. 88. Merridale, 'The collective mind', 49–50; Bernd Bonwetsch, 'Stalin, the Red Army, and the "Great Patriotic War"', in Ian Kershaw and Moshe Lewin (eds.), *Stalinism and Nazism: Dictatorships in Comparison* (Cambridge, 1997), 203–6; T. H. Rigby, *Communist Party Membership in the USSR, 1917–1967* (Princeton, NJ, 1968), 246–9. 89. Arne Zoepf, *Wehrmacht zwischen Tradition und Ideologie: Der NS-Führungsoffizier im Zweiten Weltkrieg* (Frankfurt/Main, 1988), 35–9. 90. Jürgen Förster, 'Ludendorff and Hitler in perspective: the battle for the German soldier's mind 1917–1944', *War in History*, 10 (2003), 329–31. 91. Reese, *Why Stalin's Soldiers Fought*, 156–8. 92. Günther Koschorrek, *Blood Red Snow: The Memoirs of a German Soldier on the Eastern Front* (London, 2002), 275–6. 93. *Last Letters from Stalingrad*, 27, letter 12. 94. McManus, *Deadly Brotherhood*, 269–72; Michael Snape, 'War, religion and revival: the United States, British and Canadian armies during the Second World War', in Callum Brown and Michael Snape (eds.), *Secularisation in a Christian World: Essays in Honour of Hugh McLeod* (Farnham, 2010), 146. **95.** Piehler, 'Veterans tell their stories', in Piehler and Pash (eds.), *The United States and the Second World War*, 226. **96.** Moore, *Writing War*, 112–13, 120. **97.** Edward Glover, *The Psychology of Fear and Courage* (London, 1940), 82, 86. **98.** Ahrenfeldt, *Psychiatry in the British Army*, 200–202. **99.** Fennell, 'Courage and cowardice', 110–11. **100.** McManus, *Deadly Brotherhood*, 269–70. **101.** Irving Janis, *Air War and Emotional Stress* (New York, 1951), 129–31. **102.** Helen Fein, *Accounting for Genocide: National Responses and Jewish Victimization during the Holocaust* (New York, 1979). On small emotional communities see too Barbara Rosenwein, 'Problems and methods in the history of emotions', *Passions in Context*, 1 (2010), 10–19. **103.** William Wharton, *Shrapnel* (London, 2012), 155. **104.** Newlands, *Civilians into Soldiers*, 164–7. **105.** McManus, *Deadly Brotherhood*, 323–4. **106.** Simon Wessely, 'Twentieth-century theories on combat motivation and breakdown', *Journal of Contemporary History*, 41 (2006), 277–9. **107.** Thomas Kühne, *The Rise and Fall of Comradeship: Hitler's Soldiers, Male Bonding and Mass Violence in the Twentieth Century* (Cambridge, 2017), 107–11. **108.** Richard Overy, *The Bombing War: Europe 1939–1945* (London, 2013), 351–2. **109.** See for example S. Givens, 'Liberating the Germans: the US Army and looting in Germany during the Second World War', *War in History*, 21 (2014), 33–54. **110.** Newlands, *Civilians into Soldiers*, 63; Merridale, 'The collective mind', 53–4. **111.** Matsumura, 'Combating indiscipline', 92–3; Merridale, *Ivan's War*, 271, 288–9. **112.** Peipei Qiu, Su Zhiliang and Chen Lifei, *Chinese Comfort Women: Testimonies from Imperial Japan's Sex Slaves* (New York, 2013), 21–34; Newlands, *Civilians into Soldiers*, 124–35. **113.** Hester Vaizey, *Surviving Hitler's War: Family Life in Germany 1939–1948* (Basingstoke, 2010), 65; Ann Pfau, 'Allotment Annies and other wayward wives: wartime concerns about female disloyalty and the problem of the returned veteran', in Piehler and Pash (eds.), *The United States and the Second World War*, 100–105. **114.** Michael Snape, *God and Uncle Sam: Religion and America's Armed Forces in World War II* (Woodbridge, Suffolk, 2015), 349, 358–9; Janis, *Air War and Emotional Stress*, 172–4. On airmen see Simon MacKenzie, 'Beating the odds: superstition and human agency in RAF Bomber Command 1942–1945', *War in History*, 22 (2015), 382–400. **115.** Snape, 'War, religion and revival', 138. **116.** Details ibid., 138–49; McManus, *Deadly Brotherhood*, 273–5. **117.** Snape, *God and Uncle Sam*, 327, 332–3, 343. **118.** James Sparrow, *Warfare State: World War II Americans and the Age of Big Government* (New York, 2011), 65–7; Bromberg, *Psychiatry Between the Wars*, 152. **119.** For details of the European bombing war see Overy, *The Bombing War*, passim. For the air war against Japan Kenneth Werrell, *Blankets of Fire: U. S. Bombers over Japan during World War II* (Washington, DC, 1996); Barrett Tillman, *Whirlwind: The Air War against Japan 1942–1945* (New York, 2010). **120.** Edward Glover, *War, Sadism and Pacifism: Further Essays on Group Psychology and War* (London, 1947), 161–6; Edgar Jones et al., 'Civilian morale during the Second World War: responses to air raids re-examined', *Social History of Medicine*, 17 (2004), 463–79; Shephard, *War of Nerves*, 178–9. **121.** Janis, *Air War and Emotional Stress*, 72; Dietmar Süss, *Death from the Skies: How the British and Germans Survived Bombing in World War II* (Oxford, 2014), 344–6. **122.** Gillespie, *Psychological Effects of War*, 107–8; Janis, *Air War and Emotional Stress*, 72. **123.** UEA, Zuckerman Archive, OEMU/57/3, draft report, 'Hull' (n.d. but Nov. 1941). **124.** E. Stengel, 'Air raid phobia', *British Journal of Medical Psychology*, 20 (1944–46), 135–43. **125.** Janis, *Air War and Emotional Stress*, 78–9. **126.** Ibid., 59–60, 73–7. **127.** Shephard, *War of Nerves*, 181–2. **128.** Janis, *Air War and Emotional Stress*, 78; M. I. Dunsdon, 'A psychologist's contribution to air raid problems', *Mental Health (London)*, 2 (1941), 40–41; E. P. Vernon, 'Psychological effects of air raids', *Journal of Abnormal and Social Psychology*, 36 (1941), 457–76. **129.** Janis, *Air War and Emotional Stress*, 103–4, 106–8. **130.** Ibid., 88–91; Gillespie, *Psychological Effects of War*, 126–7. **131.** UEA, Zuckerman Archive, OEMU/57/5, Hull report, Appendix II, Case Histories. **132.** James Stern, *The Hidden Damage* (London, 1990), first published 1947. **133.** Merridale, 'The collective mind', 47–8. **134.** Overy, *The Bombing War*, 462–3. **135.** Yamashita, *Daily Life in Wartime Japan*, 13–14, 17–34. **136.** See for example Mark

Connelly, *We Can Take It! Britain and the Memory of the Second World War* (Harlow, 2004). **137.** On Germany see J. W. Baird, *To Die for Germany: Heroes in the Nazi Pantheon* (Bloomington, Ind., 1990); Neil Gregor, 'A *Schicksalsgemeinschaft*? Allied bombing, civilian morale, and social dissolution in Nuremberg, 1942–1945', *Historical Journal*, 43 (2000), 1051–70; Riedesser and Verderber, '*Maschinengewehre hinter der Front*', 105–6, 163–4; on the Soviet Union, Merridale, 'The collective mind', 43–50. **138.** On Britain see Jalland, *Death in War and Peace*, 132–7; on Japan, Yamashita, *Daily Life in Wartime Japan*, 20–21. **139.** Glover, *Psychology of Fear and Courage*, 62–5. **140.** Cocks, *Psychotherapy in the Third Reich*, 312–14. **141.** Janis, *Air War and Emotional Stress*, 110–11. **142.** George Gallup (ed.), *The Gallup International Public Opinion Polls: Great Britain 1937–1975*, 2 vols. (New York, 1976), i, 37, 43. **143.** Vanessa Chambers, '"Defend us from all perils and dangers of this night": coping with bombing in Britain during the Second World War', in Claudia Baldoli, Andrew Knapp and Richard Overy (eds.), *Bombing, States and Peoples in Western Europe, 1940–1945* (London, 2012), 162–3. **144.** Claudia Baldoli, 'Religion and bombing in Italy, 1940–1945', ibid., 146–8; Claudia Baldoli and Marco Fincardi, 'Italian society under the bombs: propaganda, experience and legend, 1940–1945', *Historical Journal*, 52 (2009), 1030–32; Alan Perry, 'Pippo: an Italian folklore mystery of World War II', *Journal of Folklore Research*, 40 (2003), 115–16, 120–23. **145.** Janis, *Air War and Emotional Stress*, 172–4. **146.** Süss, *Death from the Skies*, 263–6. **147.** Chambers, '"Defend us from all perils"', 156–7. **148.** Baldoli, 'Religion and bombing', 139–49; Süss, *Death from the Skies*, 267–8, 271–2. **149.** Elena Skrjabina, *Siege and Survival: The Odyssey of a Leningrader* (Carbondale, Ill., 1971), 39–41, entries for 15 and 26 Nov. 1941. **150.** Ibid., 24, entry for 5 Sept. 1941. **151.** Olga Kucherenko, *Little Soldiers: How Soviet Children went to War 1941–1945* (Oxford, 2011), 204–6, 226–7. **152.** Details of the reports and cases can be found in Wanke, *Russian/Soviet Military Psychiatry*, 74–8. **153.** Ruth Gay, *Safe Among the Germans: Liberated Jews after World War II* (New Haven, Conn., 2002), 44–5; Dan Stone, *The Liberation of the Camps: The End of the Holocaust and its Aftermath* (New Haven, Conn., 2015), 1–26. **154.** Gay, *Safe Among the Germans*, 74–5. **155.** Joseph Berger, 'Displaced persons: a human tragedy of World War II', *Social Research*, 14 (1947), 49–50; Ralph Segalman, 'The psychology of Jewish displaced persons', *Jewish Social Service Quarterly*, 23/24 (1947), 361, 364–5. **156.** Gay, *Safe Among the Germans*, 67–8. **157.** Daniel Pick, *The Pursuit of the Nazi Mind: Hitler, Hess and the Analysts* (Oxford, 2012). **158.** Tadeusz Grygier, *Oppression: A Study in Social and Criminal Psychology* (London, 1954), xii, 20–23, 27, 42. **159.** David Boder, 'The impact of catastrophe: I: assessment and evaluation', *Journal of Psychology*, 38 (1954), 4–8. **160.** Alan Rosen, *The Wonder of Their Voices: The 1946 Holocaust Interviews of David Boder* (Oxford, 2010), 134–5, 183–6. A full version of the interview has been published in the German translation. See David Boder, *Die Toten habe ich nicht befragt*, ed. Julia Faisst, Alan Rosen and Werner Sollors (Heidelberg, 2011), 125–238. **161.** Rosen, *The Wonder of Their Voices*, 195–8; Boder, *Die Toten habe ich nicht befragt*, 16–17. **162.** Boder, 'The impact of catastrophe', 4, 16, 42–7. **163.** Pfau, 'Allotment Annies', 107–9. **164.** Halliwell, *Therapeutic Revolutions*, 20–22; Erin Redfern, 'The Neurosis of Narrative: American Literature and Psychoanalytic Psychiatry during World War II', doctoral dissertation, Northwestern University, Evanston, Ill., 2003, 16–25. **165.** Halliwell, *Therapeutic Revolutions*, 20, 25. **166.** Axel Schildt, 'Impact of experiences and memories of war on West German society', in Jörg Echternkamp and Stefan Martens (eds.), *Experience and Memory: The Second World War in Europe* (New York, 2010), 200–201. **167.** Lori Watt, *When Empire Comes Home: Repatriation and Reintegration in Postwar Japan* (Cambridge, Mass., 2009), 134–5, 202–3. **168.** Stephen Casey, *When Soldiers Fall: How Americans Have Confronted Combat Losses from World War I to Afghanistan* (New York, 2014), 49–59, 99.

10. Crimes and Atrocities

1. Joshua Rubenstein and Ilya Altman (eds.), *The Unknown Black Book: The Holocaust in the German-Occupied Soviet Territories* (Bloomington, Ind., 2008), 273–4, testimony recorded by M. Grubian. **2.** Anika Walke, *Pioneers and Partisans: An Oral History of Nazi Genocide in Belorussia* (Oxford, 2015), 191, testimony of Leonid Okon. **3.** Rubenstein and Altman (eds.), *The Unknown Black Book*, 274; Walke, *Pioneers and Partisans*, 191. **4.** Howard Ball, *Prosecuting War Crimes and Genocide: The Twentieth-Century Experience* (Lawrence, Kans, 1999), 73–4. **5.** NARA, RG 107, McCloy Papers, Box 1, United Nations War Crimes Commission memorandum, 6 Oct. 1944, Annex A. **6.** Jürgen Matthäus, 'The lessons of Leipzig: punishing German war criminals after the First World War', in Jürgen Matthäus and Patricia Heberer (eds.), *Atrocities on Trial: Historical Perspectives on the Politics of Prosecuting War Crimes* (Lincoln, Nebr., 2008), 4–8; Alfred de Zayas, *The Wehrmacht War Crimes Bureau, 1939–1945* (Lincoln, Nebr., 1989), 5–10. **7.** Joel Hayward, 'Air power, ethics, and civilian immunity during the First World War and its aftermath', *Global War Studies*, 7 (2010), 107–8; Heinz Hanke, *Luftkrieg und Zivilbevölkerung* (Frankfurt/Main, 1991), 71–7. **8.** William Schabas, *Unimaginable Atrocities: Justice, Politics, and Rights at the War Crimes Tribunals* (Oxford, 2012), 25–32. **9.** Peter Schrijvers, *The GI War against Japan: American Soldiers in Asia and the Pacific during World War II* (New York, 2002), 208. **10.** Mary Habeck, 'The modern and the primitive: barbarity and warfare on the Eastern Front', in George Kassimeris (ed.), *The Barbarisation of Warfare* (London, 2006), 91; de Zayas, *Wehrmacht War Crimes Bureau*, 118. **11.** Schrijvers, *The GI War against Japan*, 222. **12.** John McManus, *The Deadly Brotherhood: The American Combat Soldier in World War II* (New York, 1998), 227–30. **13.** De Zayas, *Wehrmacht War Crimes Bureau*, 107–8. **14.** Omer Bartov, *The Eastern Front 1941–45, German Troops and the Barbarisation of Warfare*, 2nd edn (Basingstoke, 2001). See too George Kassimeris, 'The barbarisation of warfare', in *idem* (ed.), *Barbarisation of Warfare*, 1–18. **15.** Yuki Tanaka, *Hidden Horrors: Japanese War Crimes in World War II* (Boulder, Colo., 1996), 195–8. **16.** Aaron Moore, *Writing War: Soldiers Record the Japanese Empire* (Cambridge, Mass., 2013), 90, 111. **17.** Benjamin Uchiyama, *Japan's Carnival War: Mass Culture on the Home Front, 1937–1945* (Cambridge, 2019), 54–64. **18.** Ball, *Prosecuting War Crimes and Genocide*, 67–9. **19.** Moore, *Writing War*, 123. **20.** Meirion Harries and Susie Harries, *Soldiers of the Sun: The Rise and Fall of the Imperial Japanese Army, 1868–1945* (London, 1991), 408–9; Tanaka, *Hidden Horrors*, 21–2. **21.** Moore, *Writing War*, 119. **22.** Gerald Horne, *Race War: White Supremacy and the Japanese Attack on the British Empire* (New York, 2004), 71–2. **23.** Mark Johnston, *Fighting the Enemy: Australian Soldiers and Their Adversaries in World War II* (Cambridge, 2000), 94–9. **24.** Raymond Lamont-Brown, *Ships from Hell: Japanese War Crimes on the High Seas* (Stroud, 2002), 68–9. **25.** Michael Sturma, 'Atrocities, conscience and unrestricted warfare: US submarines during the Second World War', *War in History*, 16 (2009), 450–58. **26.** Ibid., 449–50; John Dower, *War without Mercy: Race and Power in the Pacific War* (New York, 1986), 36. **27.** Johnston, *Fighting the Enemy*, 78–80, 94–5; McManus, *Deadly Brotherhood*, 210–11. **28.** James Weingartner, 'Trophies of war: U. S. troops and the mutilation of Japanese war dead, 1941–1945', *Pacific Historical Review*, 61 (1992), 56–62; Simon Harrison, 'Skull trophies of the Pacific war: transgressive objects of remembrance', *Journal of the Royal Anthropological Institute*, 12 (2006), 818–28. **29.** Schrijvers, *The GI War against Japan*, 207–10; Johnston, *Fighting the Enemy*, 80–82; Craig Cameron, 'Race and identity: the culture of combat in the Pacific war', *International History Review*, 27 (2005), 558–9. **30.** Tarak Barkawi, *Soldiers of Empire: Indian and British Armies in World War II* (Cambridge, 2017), 208–17. **31.** Theo Schulte, *The German Army and Nazi Policies in Occupied Russia* (Oxford, 1989), 317–20. **32.** Jeff Rutherford, *Combat and Genocide on the Eastern Front: The German Infantry's War 1941–1944* (Cambridge, 2014), 69, 81. **33.** Habeck, 'The modern and the primitive', 85; see too Alex Kay, 'A "war in a region beyond state control?" The German–Soviet war 1941–1944', *War in History*, 18 (2011), 111–12. **34.** Felix Römer, 'The Wehrmacht in the war of ideologies', in Alex Kay, Jeff Rutherford and David Stahel (eds.), *Nazi Policy on the Eastern Front, 1941: Total War, Genocide, and Radicalization* (New York, 2012), 74–5, 81. **35.** Sönke Neitzel and Harald Welzer, *Soldaten: Protokolle vom Kämpfen, Töten und Sterben* (Frankfurt/Main, 2011), 135–7; Rutherford, *Combat and Genocide on the Eastern Front*, 86–90; Bartov, *Eastern Front 1941–1945*, 110. **36.** Amaon Sella, *The Value of Human Life in Soviet Warfare* (London, 1992), 100–102. **37.** Günther Koschorrek, *Blood*

Red Snow: The Memoirs of a German Soldier on the Eastern Front (London, 2002), 275. **38.** Catherine Merridale, *Ivan's War: The Red Army 1939–1945* (London, 2005), 110–14. **39.** De Zayas, *Wehrmacht War Crimes Bureau*, 88. **40.** Maria Giusti, *I prigionieri italiani in Russia* (Bologna, 2014), 132. **41.** Felicia Yap, 'Prisoners of war and civilian internees of the Japanese', *Journal of Contemporary History*, 47 (2012), 317; Ball, *Prosecuting War Crimes and Genocide*, 84. **42.** Niall Ferguson, 'Prisoner taking and prisoner killing: the dynamic of defeat, surrender and barbarity in the age of total war', in Kassimeris (ed.), *Barbarisation of Warfare*, 142. **43.** For Soviet figures I am grateful to James Bacque for supplying me with the statistics compiled by the Prison Department of the Soviet Ministry of Foreign Affairs, on 'war prisoners of the former European armies 1941–1945', 28 Apr. 1956. See too *Russkii Arkhiv 13: Nemetskii Voennoplennye v SSSR* (Moscow, 1999), Part 1, 9. On Japanese prisoners see S. I. Kuznetsov, 'The situation of Japanese prisoners of war in Soviet camps', *Journal of Slavic Military Studies*, 8 (1995), 612–29. On Soviet prisoners, Alfred Streim, *Sowjetische Gefangene in Hitlers Vernichtungskrieg: Berichte und Dokumente* (Heidelberg, 1982), 175; Christian Streit, 'Die sowjetische Kriegsgefangenen in den deutschen Lagern', in D. Dahlmann and Gerhard Hirschfeld (eds.), *Lager, Zwangsarbeit, Vertreibung und Deportationen* (Essen, 1999), 403–4. **44.** Giusti, *I prigionieri italiani*, 133 **45.** Eri Hotta, *Japan 1941: Countdown to Infamy* (New York, 2013), 93. **46.** Ball, *Prosecuting War Crimes and Genocide*, 63. **47.** Yap, 'Prisoners of war and civilian internees', 323–4; Tanaka, *Hidden Horrors*, 16–18. **48.** Tanaka, *Hidden Horrors*, 26–7. **49.** Habeck, 'The modern and the primitive', 87. **50.** Christian Hartmann, 'Massensterbung oder Massenvernichtung? Sowjetische Kriegsgefangenen im "Unternehmen Barbarossa"', *Vierteljahreshefte für Zeitgeschichte*, 49 (2001), 105; Merridale, *Ivan's War*, 122–3; Bartov, *Eastern Front 1941–1945*, 111–12. **51.** Christian Streit, *Keine Kameraden: Die Wehrmacht und die sowjetischen Kriegsgefangenen, 1941–1945* (Bonn, 1978), 128. **52.** Stefan Karner, *Im Archipel GUPVI: Kriegsgefangenschaft und Internierung in der Sowjetunion 1941–1956* (Vienna, 1995), 90–94; *Russkii Arkhiv 13*, Part 2, 69, 76, 159–60; Giusti, *I prigionieri italiani*, 127. **53.** Karner, *Im Archipel GUPVI*, 94–104. **54.** Giusti, *I prigionieri italiani*, 100–102, 110–11, 125–9. **55.** Seth Givens, 'Liberating the Germans: the US army and looting in Germany during the Second World War', *War in History*, 21 (2014), 35–6. **56.** Neville Wylie, 'Loot, gold, and tradition in the United Kingdom's financial warfare strategy, 1939–1945', *International History Review*, 31 (2009), 301–2; Ball, *Prosecuting War Crimes and Genocide*, 15–16. **57.** Givens, 'Liberating the Germans', 35–6. **58.** Rutherford, *Combat and Genocide on the Eastern Front*, 107–8. **59.** Zygmunt Klukowski, *Diary of the Years of Occupation 1939–1944* (Urbana, Ill., 1993), 28–30, 47, entries for 20, 23 Sept., 30 Oct. 1939. **60.** Mark Mazower, *Inside Hitler's Greece: The Experience of Occupation, 1941–44* (New Haven, Conn., 1993), 23–4. **61.** Ball, *Prosecuting War Crimes and Genocide*, 64; Harries and Harries, *Soldiers of the Sun*, 411. **62.** Rutherford, *Combat and Genocide on the Eastern Front*, 105–10. **63.** Givens, 'Liberating the Germans', 33, 46–7. **64.** William Wharton, *Shrapnel* (London, 2012), 182–3. **65.** Amir Weiner, '"Something to die for, a lot to kill for": the Soviet system and the barbarisation of warfare', in Kassimeris (ed.), *Barbarisation of Warfare*, 102–5. **66.** Givens, 'Liberating the Germans', 45–6. **67.** Gianluca Fulvetti and Paolo Pezzino (eds.), *Zone di Guerra, Geografie di Sangue: L'atlante delle stragi naziste e fasciste in Italia (1943–1945)* (Bologna, 2016), 96–122. **68.** Massimo Storchi, *Anche contro donne e bambini: Stragi naziste e fasciste nella terra dei fratelli Cervi* (Reggio Emilio, 2016), 11–12. **69.** Peter Lieb, 'Repercussions of Eastern Front experiences on anti-partisan warfare in France 1943–1944', *Journal of Strategic Studies*, 31 (2008), 797–9, 818–19. **70.** Alastair McLauchlan, 'War crimes and crimes against humanity on Okinawa: guilt on both sides', *Journal of Military Ethics*, 13 (2014), 364–77. **71.** Hans van de Ven, *War and Nationalism in China 1925–1945* (London, 2003), 284; Weiner, 'Something to die for', 119–21. **72.** Wendy Lower, *Nazi Empire-Building and the Holocaust in Ukraine* (Chapel Hill, NC, 2005), 19–29 on the colonial character of the German occupation of the East. On the difference between German practice in East and West see Lieb, 'Repercussions of Eastern Front experiences', 797–8, 802–3. **73.** Patrick Bernhard, 'Behind the battle lines: Italian atrocities and the persecution of Arabs, Berbers and Jews in North Africa in World War II', *Holocaust and Genocide Studies*, 26 (2012), 425–32.

74. Patrick Bernhard, 'Die "Kolonialachse". Der NS-Staat und Italienisch-Afrika 1935 bis 1943', in Lutz Klinkhammer and Amedeo Guerrazzi (eds.), *Der 'Achse' im Krieg: Politik, Ideologie und Kriegführung 1939–1945* (Paderborn, 2010), 164–8. For a general study of Italian army atrocities Gianni Oliva, *'Si Ammazza Troppo Poco': I crimini di guerra italiani 1940–43* (Milan, 2006).   75. Alex Kay, 'Transition to genocide, July 1941: Einsatzkommando 9 and the annihilation of Soviet Jewry', *Holocaust and Genocide Studies*, 27 (2013), 411–13; *idem*, 'A "war in a region beyond state control?"', 112–15.   76. Van de Ven, *War and Nationalism in China*, 283–4.   77. Tanaka, *Hidden Horrors*, 186–92; Harries and Harries, *Soldiers of the Sun*, 405.   78. Henning Pieper, 'The German approach to counter-insurgency in the Second World War', *International History Review*, 57 (2015), 631–6; Alexander Prusin, 'A community of violence: structure, participation, and motivation in comparative perspective', *Holocaust and Genocide Studies*, 21 (2007), 5–9.   79. Storchi, *Anche contro donne e bambini*, 29; Ben Shepherd, 'With the Devil in Titoland: a Wehrmacht anti-partisan division in Bosnia-Herzegovina, 1943', *War in History*, 16 (2009), 84; Edward Westermann, '"Ordinary men" or "ideological soldiers"? Police Battalion 310 in Russia, 1942', *German Studies Review*, 21 (1998), 57.   80. Lieb, 'Repercussions of Eastern Front experience', 806; Shepherd, 'With the Devil in Titoland', 84–5.   81. Storchi, *Anche contro donne e bambini*, 23; Lieb, 'Repercussions of Eastern Front experience', 798.   82. Walke, *Pioneers and Partisans*, 191–2; Weiner, 'Something to die for', 117–21.   83. Giovanni Pesce, *And No Quarter: An Italian Partisan in World War II* (Athens, Ohio, 1972), 211.   84. Ibid., 176.   85. Merridale, *Ivan's War*, 269.   86. TNA, AIR 41/5 J. M. Spaight, 'The International Law of the Air 1939–1945', 1946, pp. 1–15.   87. Richard Overy, *The Bombing War: Europe 1939–1945* (London, 2013), 247–9; Peter Gray, 'The gloves will have to come off: a reappraisal of the legitimacy of the RAF bomber offensive against Germany', *Air Power Review*, 13 (2010), 15–16.   88. Ronald Schaffer, 'American military ethics in World War II: the bombing of German civilians', *Journal of American History*, 67 (1980), 321.   89. Charles Webster and Noble Frankland, *The Strategic Air Offensive against Germany*, 4 vols. (London, 1961), iv, 258–60. See too Richard Overy. '"Why we bomb you": liberal war-making and moral relativism in the RAF bomber offensive, 1940–45', in Alan Cromartie (ed.), *Liberal Wars: Anglo-American Strategy, Ideology, and Practice* (London, 2015), 25–9.   90. TNA, AIR 14/1812, Operational Research report, 14 Sept. 1943.   91. TNA, AIR 14/1813, minute from A. G. Dickens for Arthur Harris, 23 Feb. 1945 (Harris marginal notes).   92. Thomas Earle, '"It made a lot of sense to kill skilled workers": the firebombing of Tokyo in March 1945', *Journal of Military History*, 66 (2002), 117–21.   93. Conrad Crane, 'Evolution of U. S. strategic bombing of urban areas', *Historian*, 50 (1987), 37.   94. Cameron, 'Race and identity', 564.   95. Tsuyoshi Hasegawa, 'Were the atomic bombs justified?', in Yuki Tanaka and Marilyn Young (eds.), *Bombing Civilians: A Twentieth-Century History* (New York, 2009), 118–19.   96. Crane, 'Evolution of U. S. strategic bombing', 36.   97. Richard Overy, 'The Nuremberg Trials: international law in the making', in Philippe Sands (ed.), *From Nuremberg to The Hague: The Future of International Criminal Justice* (Cambridge, 2003), 10–11.   98. On colonial violence and genocide see the recent contributions by Michelle Gordon, 'Colonial violence and holocaust studies', *Holocaust Studies*, 21 (2015), 273–6; Tom Lawson, 'Coming to terms with the past: reading and writing colonial genocide in the shadow of the Holocaust', *Holocaust Studies*, 20 (2014), 129–56.   99. Horne, *Race War*, 266, 270.   100. Peter Duus, 'Nagai Ryūtarū and the "White Peril", 1905–1944', *Journal of Asian Studies*, 31 (1971), 41–7.   101. Ronald Takaki, *Double Victory: A Multicultural History of America in World War II* (Boston, Mass., 2001), 148.   102. McManus, *Deadly Brotherhood*, 202; Schrijvers, *The GI War against Japan*, 218–19.   103. Harrison, 'Skull trophies of the Pacific war', 818–21.   104. Johnston, *Fighting the Enemy*, 85–7.   105. Raffael Scheck, '"They are just savages": German massacres of black soldiers from the French army, 1940', *Journal of Modern History*, 77 (2005), 325–40.   106. See for example Mikhail Tyaglyy, 'Were the "Chingené" victims of the Holocaust? Nazi policy toward the Crimean Roma, 1941–1944', *Holocaust and Genocide Studies*, 23 (2009), 26–40. On the fate of the Roma in the East, Johannes Enstad, *Soviet Russians under Nazi Occupation: Fragile Loyalties in World War II* (Cambridge, 2018), 66–70; Brenda Lutz, 'Gypsies as victims of the Holocaust', *Holocaust and Genocide Studies*, 9 (1995), 346–59.   107. Thomas

Kühne, 'Male bonding and shame culture: Hitler's soldiers and the moral basis of genocidal warfare', in Olaf Jensen and Claus-Christian Szejnmann (eds.), *Ordinary People as Mass Murderers: Perpetrators in Comparative Perspective* (Basingstoke, 2008), 69–71. 108. Jürgen Matthäus, 'Controlled escalation: Himmler's men in the summer of 1941 and the Holocaust in the occupied Soviet territories', *Holocaust and Genocide Studies*, 21 (2007), 219–20. 109. Lower, *Nazi Empire-Building*, 75–6; Kay, 'Transition to genocide', 422; Matthäus, 'Controlled escalation', 223. 110. Sara Bender, 'Not only in Jedwabne: accounts of the annihilation of the Jewish shtetlach in north-eastern Poland in the summer of 1941', *Holocaust Studies*, 19 (2013), 2–3, 14, 19–20, 24–5. 111. Leonid Rein 'Local collaboration in the execution of the "final solution" in Nazi-occupied Belorussia', *Holocaust and Genocide Studies*, 20 (2006), 388. 112. Simon Geissbühler, '"He spoke Yiddish like a Jew": neighbours' contribution to the mass killing of Jews in Northern Bukovina and Bessarabia, July 1941', *Holocaust and Genocide Studies*, 28 (2014), 430–36; idem, 'The rape of Jewish women and girls during the first phase of the Romanian offensive in the East, July 1941', *Holocaust Studies*, 19 (2013), 59–65. 113. Rein, 'Local collaboration', 392–4; Eric Haberer, 'The German police and genocide in Belorussia, 1941–1944: part I: police deployment and Nazi genocidal directives', *Journal of Genocide Research*, 3 (2001), 19–20. 114. Rein, 'Local collaboration', 391. 115. Kühne, 'Male bonding and shame culture', 57–8, 70; an interesting case study is Peter Lieb, 'Täter aus Überzeugung? Oberst Carl von Andrian und die Judenmorde der 707 Infanteriedivision 1941/42', *Vierteljahrshefte für Zeitgeschichte*, 50 (2002), 523–4, 536–8. 116. Lower, *Nazi Empire-Building*, 78–81. 117. Andrej Angrick, 'The men of *Einsatzgruppe D*: an inside view of a state-sanctioned killing unit in the "Third Reich"', in Jensen and Szejnmann (eds.), *Ordinary People as Mass Murderers*, 84. 118. Dick de Mildt, *In the Name of the People: Perpetrators of Genocide in the Reflection of Their Post-War Prosecution in West Germany* (The Hague, 1996), 2. 119. Matthäus, 'Controlled escalation', 228–9. 120. Waitman Beorn, 'Negotiating murder: a Panzer signal company and the destruction of the Jews of Peregruznoe 1942', *Holocaust and Genocide Studies*, 23 (2009), 185–95. 121. Christopher Browning, *Ordinary Men: Reserve Police Battalion 101 and the Final Solution in Poland* (London, 1992), 141–2. 122. Jürgen Matthäus, 'Die Beteiligung der Ordnungspolizei am Holocaust', in Wolf Kaiser (ed.), *Täter im Vernichtungskrieg: Der Überfall auf die Sowjetunion und der Völkermord an den Juden* (Berlin, 2002), 168–76. 123. Stephen Fritz, *Ostkrieg: Hitler's War of Extermination in the East* (Lexington, Ky, 2011), 374. 124. See for example Westermann, '"Ordinary men" or "ideological soldiers"?', 43–8. Among the men of Battalion 310 membership in the Party ranged from 38–50 per cent in each police company. 125. There is now an extensive literature on the social psychology of perpetration in the Holocaust. See Richard Overy, '"Ordinary men", extraordinary circumstances: historians, social psychologists and the Holocaust', *Journal of Social Issues*, 70 (2014), 513–38; Arthur Miller, *The Social Psychology of Good and Evil* (New York, 2004), ch. 9. 126. Rein, 'Local collaboration', 394–5. 127. Edward Westermann, 'Stone-cold killers or drunk with murder? Alcohol and atrocity during the Holocaust', *Holocaust and Genocide Studies*, 30 (2016), 4–7. 128. Ilya Ehrenburg and Vasily Grossman, *The Complete Black Book of Russian Jewry*, ed. David Patterson (New Brunswick, NJ, 2002), 382; de Zayas, *Wehrmacht War Crimes Bureau*, 189; Peipei Qiu with Su Zhiliang and Chen Lifei, *Chinese Comfort Women: Testimonies from Imperial Japan's Sex Slaves* (New York, 2013), 22. 129. Gloria Gaggioli, 'Sexual violence in armed conflicts: a violation of international humanitarian law and human rights law', *International Review of the Red Cross*, 96 (2014), 506, 512–13. 130. Nomi Levenkron, 'Death and the maidens: "prostitution", rape, and sexual slavery during World War II', in Sonja Hedgepeth and Rochelle Saidel (eds.), *Sexual Violence against Jewish Women during the Holocaust* (Waltham, Mass., 2010), 15–17. 131. Tanaka, *Hidden Horrors*, 96–7; George Hicks, 'The "comfort women"', in Peter Duus, Ramon Myers and Mark Peattie (eds.), *The Japanese Wartime Empire* (Princeton, NJ, 1996), 310. 132. Nicole Bogue, 'The concentration camp brothel in memory', *Holocaust Studies*, 22 (2016), 208. 133. Annette Timm, 'Sex with a purpose: prostitution, venereal disease, and militarized masculinity in the Third Reich', *Journal of the History of Sexuality*, 11 (2002), 225–7; Janice Matsumura, 'Combating indiscipline in the Imperial Japanese Army: Hayno Torao and psychiatric studies of the crimes of soldiers',

War in History, 23 (2016), 96. **134.** Regina Mühlhäuser, 'The unquestioned crime: sexual violence by German soldiers during the war of annihilation in the Soviet Union 1941–45', in Raphaëlle Branche and Fabrice Virgili (eds.), *Rape in Wartime* (Basingstoke, 2017), 35, 40–42. **135.** Emma Newlands, *Civilians into Soldiers: War, the Body and British Army Recruits 1939–45* (Manchester, 2014), 124–35; Mark Harrison, *Medicine and Victory: British Military Medicine in the Second World War* (Oxford, 2004), 98–104. **136.** Raffaello Pannacci, 'Sex, military brothels and gender violence during the Italian campaign in the USSR, 1941–3', *Journal of Contemporary History*, 55 (2020), 79–86. **137.** Timm, 'Sex with a purpose', 237–50; Levenkron, 'Death and the maidens', 19–20; Helene Sinnreich, 'The rape of Jewish women during the Holocaust', in Hedgepeth and Saidel (eds.), *Sexual Violence against Jewish Women*, 110–15; Jeffrey Burds, 'Sexual violence in Europe during World War II, 1939–1945', *Politics & Society*, 37 (2009), 37–41. **138.** Peipei, *Chinese Comfort Women*, 1, 9–11, 37–8; Hicks, 'The "comfort women"', 311–12. **139.** Hicks, 'The "comfort women"', 312; Tanaka, *Hidden Horrors*, 98–9; Michael Seth, *A Concise History of Modern Korea* (Lanham, Md, 2016), 81–2. **140.** Peipei, *Chinese Comfort Women*, 30–38, 48. The bayoneting story was told by a veteran of the 14th Division, stationed in northern China in the later stages of the war. **141.** Brigitte Halbmayr, 'Sexualised violence against women during Nazi "racial" persecution', in Hedgepeth and Saidel (eds.), *Sexual Violence against Jewish Women*, 33–5; Mühlhäuser, 'The unquestioned crime', 37–8. **142.** Wharton, *Shrapnel*, 189. **143.** David Snyder, *Sex Crimes under the Wehrmacht* (Lincoln, Nebr., 2007), 137. **144.** J. Robert Lilly, *Taken by Force: Rape and American GIs in Europe during World War II* (Basingstoke, 2007), 11; Elisabeth Krimmer, 'Philomena's legacy: rape, the Second World War, and the ethics of reading', *German Quarterly*, 88 (2015), 83–4. **145.** Miriam Gebhardt, *Crimes Unspoken: The Rape of German Women at the End of the Second World War* (Cambridge, 2017), 18–22. **146.** Peipei, *Chinese Comfort Women*, 37–8. **147.** Johnston, *Fighting the Enemy*, 98–9. **148.** Weiner, 'Something to die for', 114–15. **149.** Merridale, *Ivan's War*, 268. **150.** Alexandra Richie, *Warsaw 1944: The Fateful Uprising* (London, 2013), 283, 302. **151.** Elisabeth Wood, 'Conflict-related sexual violence and the policy implications of recent research', *International Review of the Red Cross*, 96 (2014), 472–4. **152.** James Messerschmidt, 'Review symposium: the forgotten victims of World War II: masculinities and rape in Berlin 1945', *Violence Against Women*, 12 (2006), 706–9. **153.** Schrijvers, *The GI War against Japan*, 210–12; McLauchlan, 'War crimes and crimes against humanity', 364–5. **154.** Lilly, *Taken by Force*, 12; Tanaka, *Hidden Horrors*, 101–3; Joanna Bourke, *Rape: A History from 1860 to the Present* (London, 2007), 357–8. **155.** Robert Kramm, 'Haunted by defeat: imperial sexualities, prostitution, and the emergence of postwar Japan', *Journal of World History*, 28 (2017), 606–7. **156.** Lilly, *Taken by Force*, 22–3. **157.** Julie Le Gac, *Vaincre sans gloire: Le corps expéditionnaire français en Italie (novembre 1942–juillet 1944)* (Paris, 2014), 432–46. **158.** Annette Warring, 'Intimate and sexual relations', in Robert Gildea, Olivier Wieviorka and Annette Warring (eds.), *Surviving Hitler and Mussolini: Daily Life in Occupied Europe* (Oxford, 2006), 113. **159.** Snyder, *Sex Crimes under the Wehrmacht*, 149, 157–8. **160.** Birthe Kundrus, 'Forbidden company: domestic relationships between Germans and foreigners 1939 to 1945', *Journal of the History of Sexuality*, 11 (2002), 201–6. **161.** Walke, *Pioneers and Partisans*, 152; Mühlhäuser, 'The unquestioned crime', 38–9. **162.** Snyder, *Sex Crimes under the Wehrmacht*, 138–42; Mühlhäuser, 'The unquestioned crime', 41–2. **163.** Peipei, *Chinese Comfort Women*, 28–9. **164.** Matsumura, 'Combating indiscipline', 91. **165.** Milovan Djilas, *Conversations with Stalin* (New York, 1962), 161. **166.** Gebhardt, *Crimes Unspoken*, 73–5. **167.** Krimmer, 'Philomena's legacy', 90–91. **168.** James Mark, 'Remembering rape: divided social memory of the Red Army in Hungary 1944–1945', *Past & Present*, no. 188 (2005), 133, 140–42. **169.** Svetlana Alexievich, *The Unwomanly Face of War* (London, 2017), xxxvi. **170.** Helene Sinnreich, '"And it was something we didn't talk about": rape of Jewish women during the Holocaust', *Holocaust Studies*, 14 (2008), 10–11. **171.** Anatoly Podolsky, 'The tragic fate of Ukrainian Jewish women under Nazi occupation', in Hedgepeth and Saidel (eds.), *Sexual Violence against Jewish Women*, 99. **172.** Levenkron, 'Death and the maidens', 16–19; Sinnreich, 'The rape of Jewish women', 109–15; Zoë Waxman, 'Rape and sexual abuse in hiding', in Hedgepeth and Saidel (eds.),

Sexual Violence against Jewish Women, 126–31; Westermann, 'Stone-cold killers', 12–13; Burds, 'Sexual violence in Europe', 42–6.   **173.** Podolsky, 'The tragic fate of Ukrainian Jewish women', 102–3; Geissbühler, '"He spoke Yiddish like a Jew"', 430–34.   **174.** Schrijvers, *The GI War against Japan*, 220–21.   **175.** Wharton, *Shrapnel*, 252.   **176.** Moore, *Writing War*, 145.   **177.** Neitzel and Welzer, *Soldaten*, 158–9.   **178.** Ehrenburg and Grossman, *The Complete Black Book*, 388–9.   **179.** Christopher Browning, *Nazi Policy, Jewish Workers, German Killers* (Cambridge, 2000), 155–6. On the psychological significance of order see Harald Welzer, 'On killing and morality: how normal people become mass murderers', in Jensen and Szejnmann (eds.), *Ordinary People as Mass Murderers*, 173–9.   **180.** Theo Schulte, 'The German soldier in occupied Russia', in Paul Addison and Angus Calder (eds.), *Time to Kill: The Soldier's Experience of War in the West, 1939–1945* (London, 1997), 274–6. On the idea of reversing the killing constraint see Dorothea Frank, *Menschen Töten* (Düsseldorf, 2006), 12.   **181.** Sturma, 'Atrocities, conscience and unrestricted warfare', 458.   **182.** Overy, '"Ordinary men," extraordinary circumstances', 518–19, 522–3.   **183.** These were interviews conducted for a BBC documentary on Bomber Command in 1995–6. See Richard Overy, *Bomber Command, 1939–1945* (London, 1997), esp. 198–201 for examples of the interviews.   **184.** McManus, *Deadly Brotherhood*, 206.   **185.** Moore, *Writing War*, 145.   **186.** Hasegawa, 'Were the atomic bombs justified?', 119.   **187.** Andrew Rotter, *Hiroshima: The World's Bomb* (Oxford, 2008), 128, in a letter to Samuel Cavert, 11 Aug. 1945.   **188.** Moore, *Writing War*, 245.   **189.** Andrew Clapham, 'Issues of complexity, complicity and complementarity: from the Nuremberg Trials to the dawn of the International Criminal Court', in Sands, (ed.), *From Nuremberg to The Hague*, 31–3, 40; Ball, *Prosecuting War Crimes and Genocide*, 73.   **190.** Clapham, 'Issues of complexity', 40–41; Ball, *Prosecuting War Crimes and Genocide*, 77; Norbert Ehrenfreund, *The Nuremberg Legacy: How the Nazi War Crimes Trials Changed the Course of History* (New York, 2007), 115–21.   **191.** Beatrice Trefalt, 'Japanese war criminals in Indochina and the French pursuit of justice: local and international constraints', *Journal of Contemporary History*, 49 (2014), 727–9.   **192.** Ball, *Prosecuting War Crimes and Genocide*, 56–7, 74–6; Cameron, 'Race and identity', 564.   **193.** Beorn, 'Negotiating murder', 199.   **194.** Gaggioli, 'Sexual violence in armed conflicts', 512–13, 519–20.   **195.** McManus, *Deadly Brotherhood*, 211.

11. Empires into Nations

1. Amanke Okafor, *Nigeria: Why We Fight for Freedom* (London, 1949), 6.   **2.** TNA, KV2/1853, Colonial Office to Special Branch, 22 Sept. 1950; Security Liaison Office to Director General, MI5, 20 Oct. 1950, 'G. N. A. Okafar'; Director General to Security Liaison Office, West Africa, 12 June. 1950.   **3.** Okafor, *Nigeria*, 5, 30, 39.   **4.** David Roll, *The Hopkins Touch: Harry Hopkins and the Forging of the Alliance to Defeat Hitler* (New York, 2013), 173–4.   **5.** TNA, FO 898/413, Political Warfare Executive, 'Projection of Britain', propaganda to Europe: general policy papers.   **6.** Jean-Christophe Notin, *La campagne d'Italie 1943–1945: Les victoires oubliées de la France* (Paris, 2002), 692–3; Richard Lamb, *War in Italy 1943–1945: A Brutal Story* (London, 1993), 259–60; David Stafford, *Endgame 1945: Victory, Retribution, Liberation* (London, 2007), 354, 469–70.   **7.** Nicola Labanca, *Oltremare: Storia dell'espansione coloniale italiana* (Bologna, 2002), 428–33; Saul Kelly, *Cold War in the Desert: Britain, the United States and the Italian Colonies, 1945–52* (New York, 2000), 164–7.   **8.** Antonio Morone, *L'ultima colonia: Come l'Italia è tornata in Africa 1950–1960* (Rome, 2011), 131–3, 176–7, 383; Kelly, *Cold War in the Desert*, 169–71.   **9.** Ian Connor, *Refugees and Expellees in Post-War Germany* (Manchester, 2007), 8–10 on early German settlements.   **10.** Labanca, *Oltremare*, 438–9; Gerard Cohen, *In War's Wake: Europe's Displaced Persons in the Postwar Order* (New York, 2012), 6.   **11.** Lori Watt, *When Empire Comes Home: Repatriation and Reintegration in Postwar Japan* (Cambridge, Mass., 2009), 1–3, 43–4.   **12.** Louise Young, *Japan's Total Empire: Manchuria and the Culture of Wartime Imperialism* (Berkeley, Calif., 1998), 410–11.   **13.** Watt, *When Empire Comes Home*, 43–7, 97.   **14.** Ibid., 47–50.   **15.** Haruko Cook and Theodore Cook (eds.), *Japan at*

War: An Oral History (New York, 1992), 413–15, testimony of Iitoyo Shōgo, official in the Ministry of Commerce and Industry. **16.** Connor, *Refugees and Expellees*, 13. **17.** Raymond Douglas, *Orderly and Humane: The Expulsion of the Germans after the Second World War* (New Haven, Conn., 2012), 1–2, 93–6. **18.** Ibid., 96. **19.** Ibid., 126, 149. **20.** Ibid., 124–5, 160–11, 309; Ruth Wittlinger, 'Taboo or tradition? The "Germans-as-victims" theme in the Federal Republic until the mid-1990s', in Bill Niven (ed.), *Germans as Victims* (Basingstoke, 2006), 70–73. **21.** Diana Lary, *The Chinese People at War: Human Suffering and Social Transformation, 1937–1945* (Cambridge, 2010), 170. **22.** G. Daniel Cohen, 'Between relief and politics: refugee humanitarianism in occupied Germany', *Journal of Contemporary History*, 43 (2008), 438. **23.** Jessica Reinisch, ' "We shall build anew a powerful nation": UNRRA, internationalism, and national reconstruction in Poland', *Journal of Contemporary History*, 43 (2008), 453–4. **24.** Mark Wyman, *DPs: Europe's Displaced Persons, 1945–1951* (Ithaca, NY, 1998), 39, 46–7. **25.** Ibid., 17–19, 37, 52. There were 844,144 DPs dependent on UNRRA in March 1946, 562,841 in August 1948. **26.** Cohen, 'Between relief and politics', 445, 448–9. **27.** R. Rummell, *Lethal Politics: Soviet Genocide and Mass Murder since 1917* (London, 1996), 194–5; Mark Edele, *Stalin's Defectors: How Red Army Soldiers became Hitler's Collaborators, 1941–1945* (Oxford, 2017), 139–42. **28.** Nicolas Bethell, *The Last Secret: Forcible Repatriation to Russia 1944–1947* (London, 1974), 92–118; Keith Lowe, *Savage Continent: Europe in the Aftermath of World War II* (London, 2012), 252–62. **29.** Cohen, *In War's Wake*, 26. **30.** Wyman, *DPs*, 186–90, 194–5, 202–4. **31.** James Barr, *Lords of the Desert: Britain's Struggle with America to Dominate the Middle East* (London, 2018), 22. **32.** Jessica Pearson, 'Defending the empire at the United Nations: the politics of international colonial oversight in the era of decolonization', *Journal of Imperial and Commonwealth History*, 45 (2017), 528–9. **33.** Jan Eckel, 'Human rights and decolonization: new perspectives and open questions', *Humanity: An International Journal of Human Rights, Humanitarianism and Development*, 1 (2010), 114–16. **34.** Stefanie Wichhart, 'Selling democracy during the second British occupation of Iraq, 1941–5', *Journal of Contemporary History*, 48 (2013), 525–6. **35.** Eckel, 'Human rights and decolonization', 118; Dane Kennedy, *Decolonization: A Very Short Introduction* (Oxford, 2016), 1; W. David McIntyre, *Winding up the British Empire in the Pacific Islands* (Oxford, 2014), 90–91. **36.** Lanxin Xiang, *Recasting the Imperial Far East: Britain and America in China 1945–1950* (Armonk, NY, 1995), 38. **37.** Peter Catterall, 'The plural society: Labour and the Commonwealth idea 1900–1964', *Journal of Imperial and Commonwealth History*, 46 (2018), 830; H. Kumarasingham, 'Liberal ideals and the politics of decolonization', ibid., 818. Montgomery citation from 'Tour of Africa November–December 1947', 10 Dec. 1947. **38.** Kennedy, *Decolonisation*, 34–5. **39.** Geraldien von Frijtag Drabbe Künzel, ' "Germanje": Dutch empire-building in Nazi-occupied Europe', *Journal of Genocide Research*, 19 (2017), 251–3; Bart Luttikhuis and Dirk Moses, 'Mass violence and the end of Dutch colonial empire in Indonesia', *Journal of Genocide Research*, 14 (2012), 260–61; Kennedy, *Decolonization*, 34–5. **40.** Mark Mazower, *No Enchanted Palace: The End of Empire and the Ideological Origins of the United Nations* (Princeton, NJ, 2009), 150–51. **41.** Anne Deighton, 'Entente neo-coloniale? Ernest Bevin and proposals for an Anglo-French Third World Power 1945–1949', *Diplomacy & Statecraft*, 17 (2006), 835–9; Kumarasingham, 'Liberal ideals', 815–16. **42.** Christopher Prior, ' "The community which nobody can define": meanings of the Commonwealth in the late 1940s and 1950s', *Journal of Imperial and Commonwealth History*, 47 (2019), 569–77. **43.** Harry Mace, 'The Eurafrique initiative, Ernest Bevin and Anglo-French relations in the Foreign Office 1945–50', *Diplomacy & Statecraft*, 28 (2017), 601–3. **44.** Deighton, 'Entente neo-coloniale?', 842–5. **45.** Martin Thomas, *Fight or Flight: Britain, France and Their Roads from Empire* (Oxford, 2014), 86–90. **46.** Jason Parker, 'Remapping the Cold War in the tropics: race, communism, and national security in the West Indies', *International History Review*, 24 (2002), 337–9. **47.** Geoffrey Roberts, *Stalin's Wars: From World War to Cold War, 1939–1953* (New Haven, Conn., 2006), 318–19. **48.** Leslie James, 'Playing the Russian game: black radicalism, the press, and Colonial Office attempts to control anti-colonialism in the early Cold War, 1946–50', *Journal of Imperial and Commonwealth History*, 43 (2015), 511–17. **49.** Balázs Szalontai, 'The "sole legal government of Vietnam": the Bao

Dai factor and Soviet attitudes toward Vietnam 1947–1950', *Journal of Cold War Studies*, 20 (2018), 16. **50.** Eckel, 'Human rights and decolonization', 122, 126. **51.** Penny Von Eschen, *Race against Empire: Black Americans and Anticolonialism 1937–1957* (Ithaca, NY, 1997), 45–50; James, 'Playing the Russian game', 509, 512. **52.** Parker, 'Remapping the Cold War in the tropics', 322–3; Von Eschen, *Race against Empire*, 47. **53.** McIntyre, *Winding up the British Empire*, 24–6. **54.** Yasmin Khan, *The Great Partition: The Making of India and Pakistan* (New Haven, Conn., 2007), 25. **55.** Mary Becker, *The All-India Muslim League 1906–1947* (Karachi, 2013), 225–9; Khan, *Great Partition*, 38. **56.** Christopher Bayly and Tim Harper, *Forgotten Wars: The End of Britain's Asian Empire* (London, 2007), 77. **57.** Ranabir Samaddar, 'Policing a riot-torn city: Kolkata, 16–18 August 1946', *Journal of Genocide Research*, 19 (2017), 40–41, 43–5. **58.** Bayly and Harper, *Forgotten Wars*, 253–7. **59.** Thomas, *Fight or Flight*, 108–9. **60.** Bayly and Harper, *Forgotten Wars*, 163–5, 173. **61.** Ibid., 170–71. **62.** William Frederick, 'The killing of Dutch and Eurasians in Indonesia's national revolution (1945–49): a "brief genocide" reconsidered', *Journal of Genocide Research*, 14 (2012), 362–4. **63.** Petra Groen, 'Militant response: the Dutch use of military force and the decolonization of the Dutch East Indies', *Journal of Imperial and Commonwealth History*, 21 (1993), 30–32; Luttikhuis and Moses, 'Mass violence', 257–8. **64.** Jennifer Foray, *Visions of Empire in the Nazi-Occupied Netherlands* (Cambridge, 2012), 296–7, 301–3. **65.** Gert Oostindie, Ireen Hoogenboom and Jonathan Verwey, 'The decolonisation war in Indonesia, 1945–1949: war crimes in Dutch veterans' egodocuments', *War in History*, 25 (2018), 254–5, 265–6; Bart Luttikhuis, 'Generating distrust through intelligence work: psychological terror and the Dutch security services in Indonesia', *War in History*, 25 (2018), 154–7. **66.** Kennedy, *Decolonization*, 53–4; John Darwin, *After Tamerlane: The Global History of Empire since 1405* (London, 2008), 435–6, 450–51. **67.** Vincent Kuitenbrouwer, 'Beyond the "trauma of decolonization": Dutch cultural diplomacy during the West New Guinea question (1950–1962)', *Journal of Imperial and Commonwealth History*, 44 (2016), 306–9, 312–15. **68.** Robert Schulzinger, *A Time for War: The United States and Vietnam 1941–1975* (New York, 1997), 16–17. **69.** Bayly and Harper, *Forgotten Wars*, 148–9. **70.** Ibid., 20; Thomas, *Fight or Flight*, 124–5. **71.** François Guillemot, '"Be men!": fighting and dying for the state of Vietnam (1951–54)', *War & Society*, 31 (2012), 188–95. **72.** Szalontai, 'The "sole legal government of Vietnam"', 3–4, 26–9. **73.** Kennedy, *Decolonization*, 51, 54. **74.** Bayly and Harper, *Forgotten Wars*, 355–6. **75.** Ibid., 428–32; David French, 'Nasty not nice: British counter-insurgency doctrine and practice, 1945–1967', *Small Wars and Insurgencies*, 23 (2012), 747–8. **76.** Bruno Reis, 'The myth of British minimum force in counter-insurgency campaigns during decolonization (1945–1970)', *Journal of Strategic Studies*, 34 (2011), 246–52; French, 'Nasty not nice', 748–9. **77.** Steven Paget, '"A sledgehammer to crack a nut"? Naval gunfire support during the Malayan emergency', *Small Wars and Insurgencies*, 28 (2017), 367–70. **78.** Keith Hack, 'Everyone lived in fear: Malaya and the British way of counter-insurgency', *Small Wars and Insurgencies*, 23 (2012), 671–2; Thomas, *Fight or Flight*, 139–40. **79.** French, 'Nasty not nice', 748. **80.** Hack, 'Everyone lived in fear', 681, 689–92. **81.** Kumarasingham, 'Liberal ideals', 816. **82.** Ian Hall, 'The revolt against the West: decolonisation and its repercussions in British international thought, 1945–75', *International History Review*, 33 (2011), 47. **83.** Pearson, 'Defending the empire', 528–36; Meredith Terretta, '"We had been fooled into thinking that the UN watches over the entire world": human rights, UN Trust Territories, and Africa's decolonisation', *Human Rights Quarterly*, 34 (2012), 332–7. **84.** Terretta, '"We had been fooled into thinking…"', 338–43. **85.** Daniel Branch, 'The enemy within: loyalists and the war against Mau Mau in Kenya', *Journal of African History*, 48 (2007), 298. **86.** Thomas, *Fight or Flight*, 218–19, 223–6. **87.** Branch, 'The enemy within', 293–4, 299. **88.** Timothy Parsons, *The Second British Empire: In the Crucible of the Twentieth Century* (Lanham, Md, 2014), 176–7. **89.** David Anderson, 'British abuse and torture in Kenya's counter-insurgency, 1952–1960', *Small Wars and Insurgencies*, 23 (2012), 701–7; French, 'Nasty not nice', 752–6; Thomas, *Fight or Flight*, 232–3. **90.** Jean-Charles Jauffret, 'The origins of the Algerian war: the reaction of France and its army to the two emergencies of 8 May 1945 and 1 November 1954', *Journal of Imperial and Commonwealth History*, 21 (1993), 19–21. **91.** Thomas, *Fight or Flight*,

288. 92. Kennedy, *Decolonization*, 56–7. 93. Keith Sutton, 'Population resettlement – traumatic upheavals and the Algerian experience', *Journal of Modern African Studies*, 15 (1977), 285–9. 94. Thomas, *Fight or Flight*, 318–28. 95. On France see Frederick Cooper, *Citizenship between Empire and Nation: Remaking France and French Africa* (Princeton, NJ, 2014), 5–9. 96. David Fieldhouse, *Western Imperialism in the Middle East, 1914–1958* (Oxford, 2006), 299–302, 326–7; Aiyaz Husain, *Mapping the End of Empire: American and British Strategic Visions in the Postwar World* (Cambridge, Mass., 2014), 14–15, 135–42; Thomas, *Fight or Flight*, 68–70. 97. Barr, *Lords of the Desert*, 94–6; Fieldhouse, *Western Imperialism*, 232–3. 98. Edward Judge and John Langdon, *The Struggle against Imperialism: Anticolonialism and the Cold War* (Lanham, Md, 2018), 11–12. 99. Alexander Shaw, '"Strong, united, and independent": the British Foreign Office, Anglo-Iranian Oil Company and the internationalization of Iranian politics at the dawn of the Cold War, 1945–46', *Middle Eastern Studies*, 52 (2016), 505–9, 516–17. 100. Barr, *Lords of the Desert*, 126–30, 134–9. 101. Calder Walton, *Empire of Secrets: British Intelligence, the Cold War, and the Twilight of Empire* (London, 2013), 288–92. 102. Fieldhouse, *Western Imperialism*, 107–11. 103. Robert Vitalis, 'The "New Deal" in Egypt: the rise of Anglo-American commercial competition in World War II and the fall of neocolonialism', *Diplomatic History*, 20 (1996), 212–13, 234. 104. Parsons, *The Second British Empire*, 124; John Kent, 'The Egyptian base and the defence of the Middle East 1945–1954', *Journal of Imperial and Commonwealth History*, 21 (1993), 45. 105. Kent, 'Egyptian base', 53–60; Judge and Langdon, *The Struggle against Imperialism*, 78–9. 106. Martin Thomas and Richard Toye, *Arguing about Empire: Imperial Rhetoric in Britain and France 1882–1956* (Oxford, 2017), 207–12, 215–27. 107. Walton, *Empire of Secrets*, 298. 108. Husain, *Mapping the End of Empire*, 29. 109. Barr, *Lords of the Desert*, 24–8, 61; Fieldhouse, *Western Imperialism*, 184–5. 110. Fieldhouse, *Western Imperialism*, 205–6. 111. Stefanie Wichhart, 'The formation of the Arab League and the United Nations, 1944–5', *Journal of Contemporary History*, 54 (2019), 329–31, 336–41. 112. Eliezir Tauber, 'The Arab military force in Palestine prior to the invasion of the Arab armies', *Middle Eastern Studies*, 51 (2016), 951–2, 957–62. 113. Barr, *Lords of the Desert*, 73–4; Fieldhouse, *Western Imperialism*, 187–8. 114. Barr, *Lords of the Desert*, 84–8; Thomas, *Fight or Flight*, 117. 115. Walton, *Empire of Secrets*, 105–6. 116. Wyman, *DPs*, 138–9, 155; Cohen, *In War's Wake*, 131–40. 117. Barr, *Lords of the Desert*, 63–4. 118. Ibid., 88–90. 119. Tauber, 'The Arab military force in Palestine', 966–77; James Bunyan, 'To what extent did the Jewish Brigade contribute to the establishment of Israel?', *Middle Eastern Studies*, 51 (2015), 40–41; Fieldhouse, *Western Imperialism*, 193–5. 120. Wyman, *DPs*, 155. 121. Hans van de Ven, *China at War: Triumph and Tragedy in the Emergence of the New China 1937–1952* (London, 2017), 213–14. 122. Beverley Loke, 'Conceptualizing the role and responsibility of great power: China's participation in negotiations toward a postwar world order', *Diplomacy & Statecraft*, 24 (2013), 213–14. 123. Robert Bickers, *Out of China: How the Chinese Ended the Era of Western Domination* (London, 2017), 230–31; Xiaoyan Liu, *A Partnership for Disorder: China, the United States, and Their Policies for the Postwar Disposition of the Japanese Empire* (Cambridge, 1996), 153. 124. Xiang, *Recasting the Imperial Far East*, 4, 25–6. 125. Ibid., 55. 126. Ibid., 94–5; Sarah Paine, *The Wars for Asia 1911–1949* (Cambridge, 2012), 234. 127. Debi Unger and Irwin Unger, *George Marshall: A Biography* (New York, 2014), 371. 128. Jay Taylor, *The Generalissimo: Chiang Kai-Shek and the Struggle for Modern China* (Cambridge, Mass., 2009), 339–43. 129. Odd Arne Westad, *Decisive Encounters: The Chinese Civil War 1946–1950* (Stanford, Calif., 2003), 35; Taylor, *Generalissimo*, 343; Unger and Unger, *George Marshall*, 375. 130. Liu, *Partnership for Disorder*, 282. 131. Taylor, *Generalissimo*, 350; Paine, *Wars for Asia*, 239–40. 132. Westad, *Decisive Encounters*, 47, 150–53. 133. Diana Lary, *China's Civil War: A Social History, 1945–1949* (Cambridge, 2015), 3; Paine, *Wars for Asia*, 226. 134. Lifeng Li, 'Rural mobilization in the Chinese communist revolution: from the anti-Japanese war to the Chinese civil war', *Journal of Modern Chinese History*, 9 (2015), 103–9. 135. Lary, *China's Civil War*, 89–90. 136. Bickers, *Out of China*, 264–6. 137. Taylor, *Generalissimo*, 381. 138. Unger and Unger, *George Marshall*, 379–81. 139. Paine, *Wars for Asia*, 245, 251. 140. Van de Ven, *China at War*, 244–7. 141. Frank Dikötter, *The Tragedy of*

Liberation: A History of the Chinese Revolution 1945–57 (London, 2013), 4–5. **142.** Ibid., 6–8. **143.** Taylor, *Generalissimo*, 400. **144.** Van de Ven, *China at War*, 251. **145.** Donggil Kim, 'Stalin and the Chinese civil war', *Cold War History*, 10 (2010), 186–91. **146.** Odd Arne Westad, *Restless Empire: China and the World since 1750* (London, 2012), 292. **147.** Dikötter, *Tragedy of Liberation*, 41. **148.** Roland Burke, *Decolonization and the Evolution of International Human Rights* (Philadelphia, Pa, 2010), 27–8. **149.** Dane Kennedy, 'Essay and reflection: on the American empire from a British imperial perspective', *International Historical Review*, 29 (2007), 83–4. A typical example perhaps is Joshua Freeman, *American Empire: The Rise of a Global Power, the Democratic Revolution at Home* (New York, 2012). **150.** Alexander Gogun, 'Conscious movement toward Armageddon: preparation of the Third World War in orders of the USSR War Ministry, 1946–1953', *Journal of Slavic Military Studies*, 32 (2019), 257–79. **151.** McIntyre, *Winding up the British Empire*, 88–9. **152.** Simon Davis, ' "A projected new trusteeship": American internationalism, British imperialism, and the reconstruction of Iran', *Diplomacy & Statecraft*, 17 (2006), 37. **153.** Neil Smith, *American Empire: Roosevelt's Geographer and the Prelude to Globalization* (Stanford, Calif., 2003), 351–5. **154.** Parker, 'Remapping the Cold War in the tropics', 319–22, 328–31. **155.** Daniel Immerwahr, 'The Greater United States: territory and empire in U. S. history', *Diplomatic History*, 40 (2016), 373–4. **156.** A. G. Hopkins, 'Globalisation and decolonisation', *Journal of Imperial and Commonwealth History*, 45 (2017), 738–9. **157.** Alexander Statiev, *The Soviet Counterinsurgency in the Western Borderlands* (Cambridge, 2010), 131. **158.** Ibid., 117, 125, 133. **159.** Ibid., 177, 190. **160.** Commission of the Historians of Latvia, *The Hidden and Forbidden History of Latvia under Soviet and Nazi Occupations 1940–1991* (Riga, 2005), 217–18, 251. **161.** Ibid., 182. **162.** Roberts, *Stalin's Wars*, 247–8. **163.** Mark Kramer, 'Stalin, Soviet policy, and the establishment of a communist bloc in Eastern Europe, 1941–1948', in Timothy Snyder and Ray Brandon (eds.), *Stalin and Europe: Imitation and Domination 1928–1953* (New York, 2014), 270–71. **164.** Ibid., 280–81; Roberts, *Stalin's Wars*, 314–19. **165.** Norman Naimark, *Stalin and the Fate of Europe: The Postwar Struggle for Sovereignty* (Cambridge, Mass., 2019), 18–25. **166.** Walton, *Empire of Secrets*, 224–5. **167.** Kennedy, 'Essay and reflection', 98–9. **168.** Michael Seth, *A Concise History of Modern Korea* (Lanham, Md, 2016), 105; Ronald Spector, 'After Hiroshima: Allied military occupation and the fate of Japan's empire', *Journal of Military History*, 69 (2005), 1132. **169.** Spector, 'After Hiroshima', 1132–4. **170.** Seth, *Concise History of Modern Korea*, 101–5. **171.** *Basic Facts about the United Nations* (New York, 1995), 89–90. **172.** Seth, *Concise History of Modern Korea*, 120–21. **173.** Margery Perham, *The Colonial Reckoning: The Reith Lectures* (London, 1963), 13.

Index

Please note that the military ranks of soldiers, airmen and sailors listed in the index can be found in the main body of the text.

and Norwegian
campaign, 89–90
pacifism in, 646–7, 655,
657–8
and Palestine crisis,
858–61, 862
and Polish crisis, 61–3,
69, 80–82
and post-war
deportations, 830–31,
832, 849
public opinion in, 69–70,
80, 614–15, 637
and resistance
movements, 703–4,
706, 707–8, 711–12
and Soviet–Finnish war,
87–8
and Tehran Conference,
289–91
and war in Burma, 294–5
and war in North Africa,
136–7, 139–41,
239–241, 252–8,
266–70
and war in the West,
85–6, 90–98, 606
weapons output of,
532–3
British Admiralty, 104, 572
British Air Ministry, 72,
486, 571, 578, 581,
582, 790–91, 792
British Army, 85–6, 136–7,
239–41, 291–2, 447–8,
728
and army rations, 398
desertion from, 730
and female recruitment,
392–3
and intervention in
Indonesia, 844
and policy on sex, 806
and psychiatric casualties,
732–3, 735, 738,
739–40
British Army units
Caribbean regiment,
389
Eighth Army, 240, 241,
252, 253, 355, 257,
269, 270, 272, 275,
301–2, 331, 347, 389,
5 512, 730
First Airborne Army, 332
First Armoured Division,
447
First Army, 267
Second Army, 306, 346

Seventh Armoured
Division, 136, 307
Sixth Airborne Division,
306
Twenty-First Army
Group, 298, 333, 335,
345, 514
British Bombing Survey
Unit, 586
British Borneo, 178, 187,
193
British Broadcasting
Corporation (BBC),
487, 626, 639, 704,
747, 751, 878
British Cameroon, 850
British Chiefs of Staff, 76,
77, 86, 87, 103, 112,
117, 141, 181, 246,
289, 325, 331, 338,
347, 512, 578
British Colonial
Development and
Welfare Act (1945), 838
British Colonial Office, 625,
629, 836, 839, 848,
860
British Commonwealth,
656, 750, 811, 837,
843, 856
British Commonwealth Air
Training Scheme, 385
British Emergency Powers
Act (1939), 848
British Empire Exhibition
(1924–5), 19
British Expeditionary Force
(BEF), 84, 92, 93, 95,
97, 549
British Foreign Office, 624,
626, 627, 629, 793,
832, 837, 856
British Guiana, 624
British Home Intelligence,
639
British Home Office, 624
British Information Service,
329
British Joint Planning
Staff, 596
British Labour Party, 615
British League of Nations
Union, 70
British Mental Health
Emergency Committee,
British Ministry of Home
Security, 753
British Ministry of Aircraft
Production, 529

British Ministry of
Economic Warfare 120,
639, 640, 641
British Ministry of Food,
413, 675
British Ministry of
Information,
British Ministry of
Labour, 405
British Naval Staff
College, 379
British Observer Corps, 118
British Pacific Fleet, 354
British Parliamentary Peace
Aims Group, 632
British reverse Lend-Lease,
554
British Solomon Islands,
236, 239, 248, 276,
278, 465, 507, 840
British Somaliland, 50, 132
British Union of Fascists,
629
Brittain, Vera, 650
Brittany, 98, 269, 306, 309,
706
Brive, 713
Brockway, Fenner, 699
Brody, 314
Brokwitz camp, 701
Brooke, Alan, 117, 120,
246, 253, 267, 308,
312, 325, 338, 346
Brown, H. Runham, 647
Browning, Christopher, ix
Broz, Josip see Tito
Brussels, 110, 324, 737, 770
Brut, Michel, 695
Brüx (Most), 60
Bucharest, 316, 814
Buchenwald camp, 111
Buckner, Simon Bolivar,
354, 356
Budapest, 228, 335, 344,
814
Bukovina see Northern
Bukovina
Bulgaria, 134, 138, 200,
228–9, 316, 343, 360,
548, 874
'Bund Report', 626
Burma, 178–80, 187, 193,
195, 196, 197, 289,
290, 292, 328, 357,
389, 416, 475, 555,
561, 588, 621, 683,
705, 727, 731, 748,
771, 777, 808, 840,
842–3, 851